W0230152

Rent-Seeking, Institutions and Reforms In Africa

Theory and Empirical Evidence for Tanzania

Rent-Seeking, Institutions and Reforms In Africa

Theory and Empirical Evidence for Tanzania

by

Pius V. Fischer
NADEL
ETH Zurich
8092 Zurich
Switzerland

Published with support from the Swiss National Science Foundation

Library of Congress Control Number: 2006927374

ISBN-10: 0-387-33772-5 (Printed on acid-free paper) e-ISBN-10: 0-387-33773-3
ISBN-13: 978-0387-33772-2 e-ISBN-13: 978-0387-33773-9

© 2006 Springer Science+Business Media, LLC
All rights reserved. This work may not be translated or copied in whole or in part without the written permission of the publisher (Springer Science+Business Media, Inc., 233 Spring Street, New York, NY 10013, USA), except for brief excerpts in connection with reviews or scholarly analysis. Use in connection with any form of information storage and retrieval, electronic adaptation, computer software, or by similar or dissimilar methodology now known or hereafter developed is forbidden.
The use in this publication of trade names, trademarks, service marks and similar terms, even if they are not identified as such, is not to be taken as an expression of opinion as to whether or not they are subject to proprietary rights.

Printed in the United States of America.

9 8 7 6 5 4 3 2 1

springer.com

Contents

Part II Rent-Seeking: Empirical Evidence for Tanzania

List of Figures

List of Tables

Foreword

This book identifies rent-seeking behaviour as one of the main causes of poor economic performance, observed, among other places, in many countries of Africa. Rent-seeking describes the ability to capture incomes without producing output or making a productive contribution. Since rent-seekers are often an integral part of an ailing economy and resist the adoption of reforms, understanding and anticipating rent-seeking behaviour is crucial for designing more adequate and effective policy reforms.

Following a comprehensive theoretical elaboration of the causes, properties and consequences of rents and rent-seeking strategies in the context of economic reforms and development cooperation, this book presents a detailed case study on rent-seeking within the civil service, parastatal sector and business community. It demonstrates how rent-seekers in Tanzania have systematically delayed or undermined reforms such as tax reforms, trade liberalisation, privatisation or any reforms that aim to restrain corruption and embezzlement. The case study quantifies and evaluates the rent-seeking behaviour of more than 300 parastatal companies, considering their profits and losses, the quality and timeliness of their accounting and the magnitude of support they obtained from 16 different sources.

Though it is often difficult to describe rent-seeking empirically—many aspects are hidden and obscured by all sorts of fake explanations—the study at hand explores the maze of endless, general and disaggregated information and traces as many indications of rent-seeking as possible. This broad and detailed approach makes the study unique not only for Tanzania but also within the literature on rent-seeking and development cooperation.

Preface

This study on rent-seeking is the result of an ETH research project realised in the form of a joint dissertation at the NADEL (ETH Zurich, Switzerland) and the University of Konstanz, Germany. The NADEL (Postgraduate Course on Developing Countries) is one of the few academic institutions in Switzerland where empirical research and teaching on development issues, economics and reform policy, management issues and related topics are focal areas.

The author studied economics at the University of Bern (prize for best degree) and attended a postgraduate programme in international economics at the University of Konstanz. Between 1995 and 2002 he worked as a research assistant at the NADEL. This research project was carried out between 1996 and 2003 and included several field visits to Tanzania (altogether, the author spent 12 months in Tanzania, mostly for the research project, but also for other purposes, such as a consultancy for the World Bank on corruption, and project acquisitions in different regions of the country for field assignments of NADEL students).

The PhD project was supervised by Prof. Dr. Rolf Kappel, head of the NADEL, ETH Zurich, and Prof. Dr. Heinrich W. Ursprung, member of the faculty of economics at the University of Konstanz. The PhD thesis has been awarded the prize 'Förderpreis der Stiftung Wissenschaft und Gesellschaft' of the University of Konstanz for the year 2003/04.

Acknowledgements

A number of people and organisations have contributed directly and indirectly to this study.

Special thanks go to Prof. Dr. Rolf Kappel (ETH, Zurich), who provided many comments and suggestions at various stages of this study, while supervising the PhD project and reading draft manuscripts. I am also very grateful to my brother, Felix Fischer (IMF, Washington, D.C.), who read the manuscript and made numerous valuable comments and suggestions.

I am further indebted to several persons at the ETH Zurich who contributed in one way or the other to this study. I wish to thank the NADEL team, above all Prof. Dr. Ruedi Baumgarter and Dieter Zürcher, who read and commented on some draft sections. Generous support also came from Alfred Schumacher, who spent countless hours scanning hundreds of pages on parastatal data into the computer, as well as several persons at the 'Seminar für Statistik' and Prof. Dr. Awudu Abdulai, who provided statistical support at various stages of this study. Many thanks also go to Lisa Stearns who edited the manuscript (and to David Goldblatt and Shonali Pachauri who edited some earlier sections in Chapters 4 and 5).

The Research Commission and the NADEL of the ETH Zurich provided financial support over several years, and part of the field research included in this study was made possible by a grant (Jeune Chercheur) from SDC (Swiss Agency for Development and Cooperation). I am very grateful to all these organisations for the funding. I would also like to express my sincere thanks to SDC and SECO for making available documents on Tanzania. Furthermore, the local cooperation office of SDC in Dar es Salaam provided me with important logistical support and documentary materials.

People in numerous other organisations and institutions in Tanzania were excellent and helpful hosts and resources, offering me their valuable time for interviews and inquiries and supplying me with numerous reports, documentary materials and specific data on Tanzania. Without their help it would not have been possible to document the Tanzanian reform process in such detail. Many of the interviews also contained sensitive information. In most cases I have therefore chosen not to identify persons by name, to shield them from any repercussions of the publication of this study. The organisations include institutions of the Tanzanian government and related bodies, donor agencies, parastatal companies, research institutes, private organisations and numerous companies in the private sector.[1]

---

1 *Donor institutions* in Dar es Salaam: the Embassy of Sweden, the Royal Netherlands Embassy, the European Union, the British High Commission and DIFID, the World Bank and the IMF Resident Mission.

The Tanzanian Government (including the Zanzibar Revolutionary Government): the Ministry of Finance, the Tanzanian Revenue Authority, the Office of the Controller and Auditor General, the

Needless to say, any errors or omissions that remain are the sole responsibility of the author. Furthermore, the ideas and views expressed in this study on Tanzania are solely my own and do not necessarily, unless quoted directly, represent the views of the above-mentioned donor organisations, the Tanzanian government or other institutions.

Finally, my partner Krista deserves a medal of honour for her gracious patience with me while I was preparing and finalising this manuscript. Her moral support and encouragement, as well as her flexibility in reorganising her own plans during the final year were both caring and extraordinary—thank you.

National Bureau of Statistics, the Ministry of Energy and Minerals and the Ministry of Agriculture & Cooperatives.

Government-related organisations: the Bank of Tanzania, the Parastatal Sector Reform Commission and the Loans and Advances Realisation Trust, as well as parastatal companies, above all Tanzania Audit Corporation, the banks NBC, CRDB, TIB and PBZ, Tanzania Electric Supply Company, Tanzania Telecommunications Company, Parastatal Pensions Fund and National Development Corporation.

The University of Dar es Salaam and other research institutes in Tanzania: Department of Economics, Economic Research Bureau, Department of Political Science and Public Administration, Institute of Development Studies and the Economic And Social Research Foundation (ESRP).

Other institutions and persons: Tanzania Chamber of Commerce, Industry and Agriculture, the Prevention of Corruption Bureau, the National Board of Accountants & Auditors, Members of the Tanzanian Parliament and numerous other interviewees in Tanzania (citizens, expatriates, and above all managers of companies in the private sector).

Abbreviations and Acronyms

ADB	African Development Bank
ADF	African Development Fund
BoS	Bureau of Statistics
BoT	Bank of Tanzania
CAG	Controller and Auditor General
CCM	Chama Cha Mapinduzi
CG	CG meeting: Consultative Group meeting
CIS	Commodity Import Support programme (donor balance of payment support)
CIS-CC	CIS-Cash Cover (payment of the TSh equivalent for the FOREX obtained)
CIS-Sub	CIS-Subsidy component (difference in parallel market rate and official exchange rate)
CRDB	Cooperative and Rural Development Bank
DDC	District Development Corporation
DSM	Dar es Salaam
ERP	Economic Recovery Programme
FOREX	Foreign Exchange (values obtained in a foreign currency)
FY	Financial Year (e.g. FY93 = July 92-June 93
IBRD	International Bank for Reconstruction and Development
ICRG	International Country Risk Guide
IDA	International Development Agency
IMF	International Monetary Fund
LART	Loans and Advances Realisation Trust
LDC	Least Developed Country
TSh m	Millions of TSh
TSh bn	Billions of TSh (1000 million)
MoW	Ministry of Works
NBC	National Bank of Commerce
NESP	National Economic Survival Plan
NGO	Non-Governmental Organisation
NMC	National Milling Corporation
NPA	Non-Performing Assets
NPC	National Price Commission
NUWA	National Urban Water Authority
OCAG	Office of the Controller and Auditor General
ODA	Official Development Assistance
PBZ	Peoples' Bank of Zanzibar
PCB	Prevention of Corruption Bureau
PER	Public Expenditure Review
PFP	Policy Framework Paper
POC	Parastatal Organisation Committee
PPF	Parastatal Pensions Fund
1994 prices	Constant TSh prices of year 1994 (US$1 corresponds to TSh 523)
PSRC	Parastatal Sector Reform Commission
SCOPO	Standing Committee on Parastatal Organisations
SDC	Swiss Agency for Development and Cooperation
SFC	State Fuel Corporation
SGS	Société Générale de Surveillance
SSA	Sub-Saharan Africa
TAC	Tanzania Audit Corporation
TANESCO	Tanzania Electric Supply Co.
TFC	Tanzania Fertilizer Company
THA	Tanzania Harbours Authority
THB	Tanzania Housing Bank
TIB	Tanzania Investment Bank
TIPER	Tanzania and Italian Petroleum Refining Co.
TPDC	Tanzania Petroleum Development Corporation
TR	Treasury
TRA	Tanzania Revenue Authority
TTCL	Tanzania Telecommunications Company
UDA	Shirika la Usafiri Dar es Salaam Ltd (parastatal bus company)
USAID	United States Agency for International Development

Guide for the Quick Reader

This book can be read selectively, depending on the reader's interests and available time. The following comments on Chapters 1 to 9 may be helpful to set priorities.

Chapter 1.1 outlines the reasoning behind this study and the main areas of focus, while Chapter 1.2 provides a detailed overview of Chapters 2 to 9 and an explanation for the approach used in the case study on Tanzania.

In order to be clear about the *definition* of rent-seeking used in this study, Section c) of Chapter 2.1 should not be skipped.

The quick reader interested in the *costs* of rent-seeking addressed in Chapter 3 may look at the concluding Section d) of Chapter 3.2 and read Sections b) and c) of Chapter 3.3 (skimming over the few formal discussions).

The sections in Chapter 4 deal with a large number of topics, which can be read on their own. Especially relevant for the Tanzanian case study is the logic behind engaging in corrupt activities explained in Section a) of Chapter 4.1.

Chapter 5 provides a wealth of background information on *rent-seeking and reforms* and is the direct counterpart of the case study on Tanzania. The quick reader may choose to read just Section b) of Chapter 5.2.

To avoid misinterpretations of the analysis, the reader should not omit Chapter 6.1 (though Chapter 6.2, in particular Sections b) and c) also provides valuable country-specific background information on the rent-seeking environment at the onset of reforms).

The different sections in Chapter 7 can be read individually, depending on the interest of the reader. Sections b) and d) of Chapter 7.1, as well as Section a) and the last part of Section b) of Chapter 7.3 (failure to sanction and prevent embezzling of public funds) make a particularly strong rent-seeking case.

The main results of the rent-seeking analysis on parastatal companies are presented in Section d) of Chapter 8.1 and Sections b) and c) of Chapter 8.2.

Chapter 9 concludes why understanding rent-seeking is relevant for policy-making and development cooperation and is recommended to be read in its entirety.

1 Introduction

1.1 Background, Objectives and Scope of the Study

Sub-Saharan Africa (SSA) remains poor in spite of four decades of intensive development cooperation and concern. According to the Human Development Report (UNDP (2003)), the average annual GDP growth per capita between 1975 and 2001 (measured in purchasing power parities) was –0.9 per cent, and for more than half of the SSA countries the year with the highest per capita GDP fell within the first ten years of that period.[2] The report concludes that for the 1990s (p. 37) 'economies have not grown, half of Africans live in extreme poverty and one third in hunger, and about one-sixth of children die before age five—the same as a decade ago'.

Many reasons have been advanced to explain the generally poor performance in sub-Saharan Africa and other developing countries. The causes can be traced to a combination of events and factors, some of which could not or only to a limited extent be influenced by the countries affected; a major part, however, must be attributed to domestic and cross-border conflicts and wars, and inappropriate policies these countries have been carrying out since the 1970s.

In the past, many governments pursued economic policies that heavily distorted the functioning of markets. Interventions such as over-expansionary fiscal and monetary policy, the administration of prices and the implementation of many ill-advised regulations, contributed to high indebtedness, economic instability, stagnation and decline. The poor management of developing countries' economies has been further exacerbated by a weak rule of law and inappropriate donor support, which allocated substantial aid without sufficiently evaluating the preconditions that make aid work.

Throughout the 1970s, 1980s and 1990s politicians and civil servants in sub-Saharan countries lacked rudimentary checks and balances, leading in many countries to large-scale embezzlement and corruption. This, together with severe economic imbalances, the often poor and erratic public policies, absence of a rule of law and inadequate public service delivery, was reflected in insecure

---

[2] UNDP (2003, p. 278-81). The countries are (in parenthesis year of highest per capita income; asterisk if data do not cover the entire period back to 1975): Dem. Rep of the Congo (1975), Gabon (1976), Mauritania (1976), Senegal (1976), Zambia (1976), Central African Republic (1977), Chad (1977), Nigeria (1977), Côte d'Ivoire (1978), Mali (1979), Niger (1979), Namibia (1980*), Togo (1980), South Africa (1981), Sierra Leone (1982), Ethiopia (1983*), Rwanda (1983), Comoros (1984*), Congo (1984) and Gambia (1984).

Though there are 20 other countries with the highest per capita GDP in the period after 1985, data on seven countries do not cover the entire period back to 1975 (Cap Verde, Angola, Guinea, Mozambique, Tanzania and Uganda). The World Bank (2000c, p. i), for instance, concludes for Tanzania that 'best available estimates suggest that per capita income today is certainly no higher than it was four decades ago'. For the remaining SSA countries (Seychelles, Equatorial Guinea, Liberia and Sao Tome and Principe) there is no information.

property rights, the lack of funding of critical expenditures, above all, spending on maintenance, basic health and education, and a poor and deteriorating infrastructure. The failures created an environment that heavily undermined productive activities and resulted in high costs for society and the poor.

A great number of the problems can be reduced to a very basic phenomenon: *rent-seeking behaviour*, which describes the ability of individuals to capture incomes without producing output or making a productive contribution. Put simply, individuals may decide to produce a specific good, for instance bread, and sell it on the local market. The activity provides them with some income—at the same time it helps others to have more to eat. Alternatively, they may form a gang and roam through town, breaking into houses and stealing whatever they can get hold of. If successful this activity also provides them with some income and, depending on their luck and the weakness of police and judiciary, they may even 'earn' much more than they would if they were only making bread. But this extreme way of earning income is obviously not beneficial to society; it only makes it worse.

The more the rules in a society determine that income can be earned only by making a productive contribution, the more a society will prosper. Unfortunately the real world looks different, in developing as well as industrialised countries. Though the example of stealing was formulated provocatively, poorly performing countries in sub-Saharan Africa (and other areas) have a large number of rent-seekers with key positions in the public and private sector who earn a considerable share of their income without producing output or making a productive contribution.

In its most general form, rent-seeking describes the use of resources to capture a 'transfer' rather than to directly produce a good or service. Rent-seekers are people who steal or appropriate resources, for instance civil servants who embezzle funds and demand bribes from their clients, or smugglers who deprive the government of tax income by investing a lot of time and effort to get their goods across unpatrolled borders.

But rent-seekers are also entrepreneurs who lobby for measures to reduce competition, so that they can sell their goods at much higher prices and earn monopoly profits; or they may be businesspeople who bribe civil servants so that their inefficient company wins a tender. Abstracting from externalities and other distortions, the difference consumers and taxpayers pay for the goods and services of these entrepreneurs, because a market is protected or a tender is not given to the best bidder, reflects the share of income earned non-productively.

This study surveys rent-seeking in general terms and intends to provide additional insights into the causes and consequences of rent-seeking in sub-Saharan Africa.[3] Considering the nature of rent-seeking, its application to Africa and the emphasis on reforms, it is useful to approach an analysis of rent-seeking from three different angles: from the point of view of public choice, New Institutional Economics, and reforms and development cooperation. In particular

---

[3] Note, for better readability, the study will use the terms 'sub-Saharan Africa' and 'Africa' interchangeably, even though the study mainly focuses on countries in sub-Saharan Africa.

the focus on the overlap of the two strands of economic theory and the reform context offers valuable insights to better understand rent-seeking mechanisms and to design more appropriate and effective policy reforms in Africa.

Traditional Theory of Economic Policy, Public Choice and Rent-Seeking

Contrary to the traditional theory of economic policy, which implicitly supposes that the government tries to maximise the society's welfare, public choice theorists describe ruling elites, politicians and bureaucrats as utility-maximising actors who pursue their own interests not only in private activities but also when making public decisions. Furthermore, powerful interest groups are able to exert considerable influence on the formation of government policies, often at the expense of the welfare of the country. In particular because of missing checks and balances, transaction costs, asymmetries in information and free-riding problems, the supply of government policies can deviate considerably from a policy mix that would maximise national welfare. Cynics would therefore suggest that the construction of a society according to a Benthamite vision, i.e. the idea of a benevolent government which aims for the greatest welfare for the largest number of people, is a theoretical construct and can be no more than a goal or artificial reference point.

More realistic is the description of a government where representatives pursue their *own interests* and supply, depending on the constraints (above all the modes of legitimacy building and measures of repression), policies that satisfy the demands of voters, powerful interest groups or the government's own abilities for self-enrichment and power extension. This is the framework of public choice—and it is also the framework in which rent-seeking takes place.

Ironically, though government should be beneficial to society, providing public goods and offsetting externalities and other market failures, it is also government which provides most of the rent-seeking opportunities. These opportunities become manifest in the ability of the state to intervene in the economy and the opportunities for public officials (and collaborating private counterparts) to appropriate or misuse public funds. Tollison (1987, p. 145) concludes that 'basically, rent-seeking is a cost of government activity in general', and Medema (1991, p. 1060) notes, when emphasising that institutions and policies change over time, 'once we allow for the possibility and desirability of change in legal and economic relations, we inevitably introduce rent seeking'.

Efforts to obtain larger slices of the social pie rather than to expand its size can become endemic. Often a single government intervention, if not well designed and implemented carefully, can lead to rent-seeking behaviour on different levels, for instance, rent-seeking when collecting revenues, rent-seeking when spending the revenues and rent-seeking efforts of corrupt individuals to obtain jobs with the government (rent-promising positions involved in revenue collection and spending). Furthermore, as rent-seeking redistributes income, it can change political equilibria, for instance making rent-seekers more influential as they become richer. Even crises can strengthen the rent-seekers' stake in an economy. Rent-seeking systems may therefore have their own dynamics, preventing any desirable change and thereby locking an economy into inefficiency. As Buchanan (1993, p. 1) states, politicians who seek public interest might not be able to survive, but they may be eliminated from the political game in an evolution-like selection process.

Hillman and Swank (2000) introduced the term 'political culture' as an explanatory concept to understand the diversity of government decisions in different societies. They define a *'bad' political culture* as a situation where 'political office or government authority is a licence for private self-enrichment' (p. 3).

A bad political culture obviously describes an extreme form of rent-seeking economy. Africa offers numerous examples where countries have descended to become rent-seeking economies and kleptocracies. Especially ruling elites have managed to divert a large share of resources in the form of non-productive income. Ayittey (1992), for instance, notes that Moi's regime shifted more funds into numbered accounts abroad than Kenya received in the form of aid and foreign investments; the 'Big Man' in Nigeria smuggled into foreign accounts an amount equivalent to Nigeria's large foreign debt, and 60 per cent of the annual budget in the former Zaire is estimated to have been diverted into the personal accounts of Mobutu, his family and cronies—with Mobutu bragging on US television in 1984 he was the second-richest man in the world.[4]

In other countries rent-seeking did not produce extremely rich people, but a large share of the non-productive benefits were eaten up by inefficiencies, again with extremely negative consequences for society. As will be extensively discussed in this study, this has been the case in Tanzania. President Nyerere, who ruled the country from its independence until he voluntarily resigned in 1985, held socialist convictions and pursued a modest lifestyle. Yet his vision to develop an egalitarian and self-reliant society that could enjoy a steady increase in welfare largely failed because he relied too heavily on the assumption that politicians and bureaucrats were benevolent, rejecting a more realistic view of opportunistic behaviour and greed. During more than twenty years of his leadership, Tanzania sadly became a country with a bad political culture, not because Nyerere was a predatory ruler—on the contrary—but because the bureaucracy and affiliated parastatals had become a kleptocracy. Problems continued for a long time after Tanzania became a market economy.

Understanding Rent-Seeking: The Role of Institutions

This study will devote special attention to the role of institutions in explaining rent-seeking. First, it is the complex institutional structure that determines the profitability of rent-seeking activities relative to entrepreneurial and other productive activities (henceforth also called profit-seeking activities). Second, understanding formal and informal institutions is highly relevant for any study that focuses on African economies and governments, as institutional settings usually deviate considerably from what we would find in industrialised

[4] Citations from Rowley (2000, p. 150, 153, 154).

countries. It is a widely held view that many policies and reforms in Africa did not lead to the expected results because they were not sufficiently adapted to the African context, with its specific political, cultural and institutional structures. A deeper understanding of the general institutional 'environment' or 'framework' in African countries promises valuable insights on the modes of rent-seeking and will make it possible to design better policy reforms.

In the early 1990s, attention to the relevance of institutions increased considerably, partly because Douglass North received the Nobel Prize in economics for his influential work *'Institutions, Institutional Change and Economic Performance'* (North (1990)). There are two related branches in economics that focus on the role of institutions: Old and New Institutional Economics. The latter has emerged as a school of thought complementing neo-classical theory. According to Stein (1994, p. 1835), in contrast to the 'old' institutional school, which understood itself as an alternative to neo-classical theory, New Institutional Economics does not fundamentally reject mainstream economics, but criticises neo-classical theory for 'failing to explain the nature of institutions and the role they play in supporting the existence and the functioning of markets'.

Strictly speaking, in an institutional vacuum there is nothing to distinguish between a perfectly competitive market system and a command economy that implements a planning model analogous to the market model (Lal and Myint (1996, p. 324f)). Both approaches lead to the same results. However, as Lal and Myint also emphasise, the situation looks different once monitoring and information requirements, the opportunistic nature of people or specific market failures are taken into consideration. Under these conditions the results depend on the specific institutional setting and the superiority of one system to another can often not be judged in a priori terms and may even depend on practical experience. The same conclusions obviously also hold for less fundamental decisions on policymaking, above all as the rule of law and the character and efficiency of the bureaucracy may vary considerably.

Since Douglass North's institutional framework provides a good summary (and extension) of the institutional approach in economics, it will be briefly outlined below. Essentially, North's framework of institutions is based on a theory of human (economic) behaviour (deviating from neo-classical theory) and on the theory of transaction costs. Figure 1-1 outlines several main aspects of the framework and indicates their link with rent-seeking behaviour. According to North (1990, pp. 4-5) *institutions* are the rules; they define 'the way the game is played' and they determine the opportunities in a society. In other words, they structure incentives in human exchange (political, social and economic), and they reduce uncertainty and limit the set of choices. On the whole they promote productivity-raising and productivity-lowering activities.

Organisations, such as parties, firms, cooperatives and trade unions, as well as political action committees, commercial and non-commercial parastatals, churches, clubs, schools and other lobbying groups in society are the players. They are created to take advantage of opportunities, i.e. they develop strategies and skills to achieve their objectives.

Figure 1-1: Rent-Seeking and North's Institutional Framework

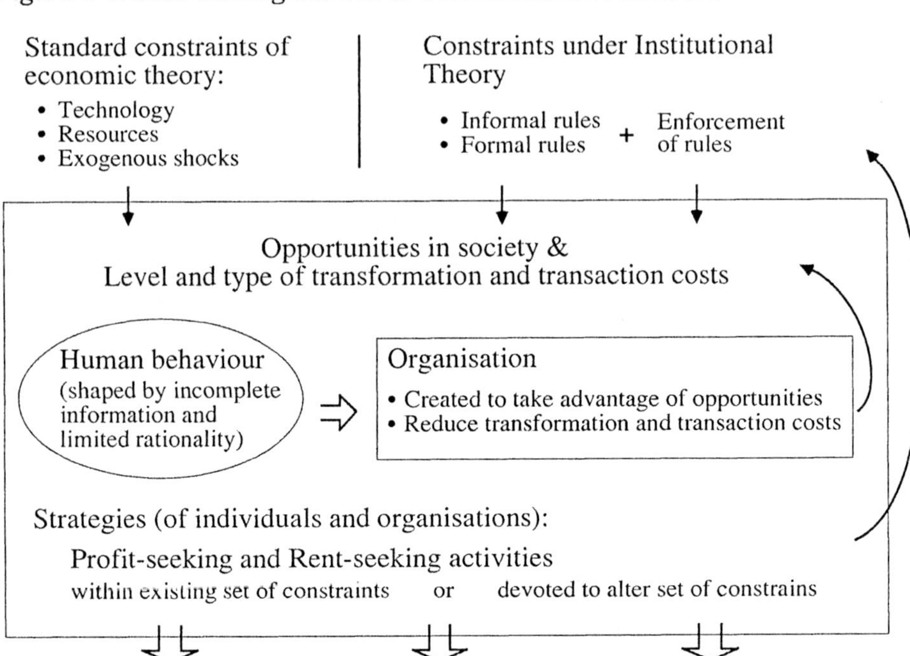

North's framework explicitly differentiates between *formal* and *informal* rules (institutions) and their enforcement characteristics. Informal constraints are part of the inherited culture; formal rules comprise political (and judicial) rules, economic rules and contracts.

Formal and informal institutions can directly or indirectly contribute to the reduction of transaction and transformation costs, so that markets function as flexibly and as efficiently as neo-classical theory assumes. But they can also cause the contrary, by encouraging rent-seeking behaviour and discouraging entrepreneurial and other productive activities and thereby create severe impediments to economic development. Formal and informal rules may also overlap and disagree with each other. Ake (1996, p. 14), for instance, notes on Africa:

> 'The state in Africa has been a maze of antinomies of form and content: the person who holds office may not exercise its powers, ... informal relations often override formal relations... Positions that seem to be held by persons are in fact held by kinship groups; at one point the public is privatised and at another the private is "publicized", and two or more political systems and political cultures in conflict may coexist in the same social formation.'

In fact, one of the main explanations why development in Africa largely failed in the second half of the twentieth century is the *conflict between formal and informal rules* (and relations), which is often manifest in the domination of informal aspects at the expense of a proper implementation of 'modern' formal rules. The lack of enforcement of regulations according to stated objectives largely explains why many countries have become rent-seeking economies and kleptocracies. Absence of the rule of law, non-enforcement of property rights, inadequate policies and the lack of reliable infrastructure have been the main ingredients of the environment so hostile to business, which still characterises most African economies. As North emphasises, an institutional setting that cannot guarantee the enforcement of complex contracts (contracts involving exchange over space and time) explains much of the failure in capturing gains from the division of labour and trade.

All in all, what shapes opportunities in society, and with it rent-seeking incentives, depends on a complex set of institutional features that determine de facto property rights and raise or lower transaction and transformation costs. Institutions influence how people behave. They determine the profitability of rent-seeking relative to profit-seeking activities, the importance of self-interest relative to public interest, the impact of interest groups, the competitive behaviour of rent-seekers, the cost of lobbying for a monopoly or other protection, etc. They are reflected in political systems, structures and organisations of the state. They are shaped by ideologies, traditions and culture and co-determine the configuration and dynamics of social forces.

Organisations, which are embedded in an institutional framework, usually become more efficient over time. However, as North (1990, p. 9) emphasises, organisations that develop in a redistributive rather than productive institutional environment will also become more efficient—but only at making society even more unproductive. In this context the theory of institutions can provide significant insights into the dynamics, extent and type of rent-seeking in a society.

Rent-Seeking, Development Cooperation and Poor Economic Reforms in Africa

In the early 1980s many developing countries found themselves in a desolate economic situation with high indebtedness, high inflation rates, overvalued national currencies, extremely inefficient public companies, shortages and low capacity utilisation, a poor infrastructure, a shrinking tax base and, as a consequence of these problems, negative per capita growth rates. It was during this time that criticism of the development paradigm of the 1960s and 1970s began to develop on a broader front. The large volume of resources pumped into developing countries during the past decades had obviously not achieved expected goals.

Often there were concerns about the well-being of the population, but equally often rent-seeking motives like self-enrichment, power extension or yielding to the demands of powerful interest groups led governments to strongly intervene in their economies. At the same time, many countries received substantial support in the form of international loans and aid. The changed incentive system (on the one hand a direct consequence of inappropriate policies and easy available aid, on the other a result of the poor implementation of many originally well-intended policies) paved the way for a wide range of new rent-seeking activities and made additional interventions necessary. These interventions further increased inefficiencies and enhanced rent-seeking opportunities and finally, partly reinforced by external shocks, destabilised the economies.

What followed in most countries were two decades of economic reforms. In the 1980s policymakers mainly focused on *regaining macro stability*, i.e. implementing stabilisation and liberalisation measures (considered a prerequisite for a return to stable and durable economic development). In the 1990s policymakers, in close collaboration with bilateral and multilateral donors, began to shift their attention to the more complex *institutional reforms*, above all civil service reforms, strengthening of rule of law and privatisation, after it became evident that remedying macroeconomic imbalances was not sufficient in itself to return to growth. An important challenge for reform policies consisted in limiting rent-seeking behaviour and channelling or forcing an ever-larger part of socicty, business community and civil service into productive activities.

However, two decades of reform experience have demonstrated that in many countries reform efforts have been halfhearted and overall reform outcomes poor. Despite urgently needed reforms, essential measures were delayed for years or were not effectively implemented. Furthermore, many countries repeatedly failed to achieve the minimal targets agreed with the donors. Although reforms made great progress from today's perspective compared with fifteen or twenty years ago, the process has been rather slow and costly with many unnecessary setbacks.

The main conclusion of this study is straightforward: it is not primarily a lack of capacity or financial resources which have constrained the efficient implementation of the vast majority of reform measures, but the *resistance and interference of rent-seekers*. Rent-seekers were not only a major impediment to development in the 1970s, they have also constituted a major obstacle to economic reforms and development in the subsequent two decades.

Erroneous economic policies which contributed to economic crises in many LDCs are still profitable for some actors, both in the economy and politics. Most economic reforms aim to remove rents and to increase the profitability of entrepreneurial and other productive activities relative to rent-seeking activities. These reforms directly threaten the economic base of rent-seeking elites, which have either been responsible for the initial rent-creating policy or which have developed as a result of it, mostly because the policies were poorly implemented.

The crucial point advanced in this study is that rent-seekers are often an *integral part of an ailing economy*. When it comes to designing and implementing adequate reforms, they resist and develop strategies to safeguard their easy but unproductive income earning opportunities. Reform measures which ignore this run a great risk of failure.

The seminal World Bank study *'Assessing Aid: What Works, What Doesn't, and Why'* (World Bank (1998a)) demonstrated that reforms and aid can work if designed and implemented appropriately, above all if aid has the right mix of providing ideas and financing projects or the general budget. The study identified the *lack of a good policy environment* and the *weak quality of institutions* (rule of law, efficient civil service, stable macroeconomic environment, open trade regimes and protected property rights) as the main reason a great deal of financial aid did not work.

Since rent-seeking forces can largely explain these missing preconditions, an analysis of rent-seeking can significantly contribute to understanding resistance to the adoption of sound policies. It can guide donors to decide on the appropriate type of aid in poorly performing countries and it can support reform-minded policymakers in designing policies which are not only appropriate but also feasible and sustainable.

There is a large body of literature showing that in the past aid produced rather mixed results. With the rent-seeking problem in mind it is obvious that donors played a twofold role in development cooperation. On the one hand, they *promoted rent-abating policies*. They constituted a powerful interest group and usually tried to represent the interests of the poor and civil society in the recipient country. On the other hand, donors were also *a main target of rent-seeking activities*. Because of inadequate policies, weak institutions (above all lack of accountability and checks and balances in recipient countries), as well as the imprudence of donors, rent-seekers managed to reap a large share of donor support as individuals, interest groups, government bodies and NGOs. Aid originally intended to support a country's development strategy or to finance urgently needed reforms was in many cases grossly misused. This case study on Tanzania will provide numerous examples of halfhearted reforms, setbacks and at times gross embezzlement and misuse of public resources and donor funds in Tanzania during the 1980s and 1990s, particularly prior to President Mkapa's term of office.

Intended Contributions of This Study

The principal aim of this study is to examine rent-seeking patterns and to provide additional *insight into the causes and consequences of rent-seeking* in Africa. Rent-seeking is probably the main impediment to economic development in general and to reforming economic policy in particular. The discussion of rent-seeking will combine explanations of public choice theory and New Institutional Economics, and it will include a detailed assessment of rent-seeking models and rent-seeking costs. Since the majority of rent-seeking models reflect conditions that are typical for industrialised countries, special emphasis will be given to discussing implications of non-rival and insider settings, which better reflect rent-seeking conditions in African economies.

Compared to the state of theoretical research *empirical research* on rent-seeking is still in short supply. One of the main reasons for this is that it is often difficult to observe and measure rent-seeking behaviour directly (and at times it is even risky to investigate the subject). Most empirical studies are therefore limited to approximate descriptions of rent-seeking. Very few attempts have been made to examine rent-seeking in an economy in depth or to asses the trade-offs and social costs associated with it. This study contributes to the empirical research by explaining rent-seeking strategies in more detail in the context of economic reforms and by providing an in-depth empirical analysis and quantification of rents in the parastatal sector in Tanzania. It also compares the resources wasted through rent-seeking with resources allocated for public health and education.

Besides broadening the understanding of rent-seeking in the context of Africa, an important objective of this study is to contribute to *designing better and more effective reforms*. Research in this field is of interest for reform-minded policymakers in developing countries as well as for multilateral and bilateral donors who support reform programmes with financial and technical assistance. Reform programmes can be very clever in terms of (prescriptive) economic policy, but they are useless if they cannot be implemented or politically sustained. Furthermore they become very costly if they suffer setbacks and repeated delays. The modest success of economic reforms in many LDCs and the presumed linkages to rent-seeking and institutional constraints promise high returns on more in-depth analyses in that direction. This study contributes to that field of research by indicating more clearly which institutional reforms in the context of rent-seeking are a necessary precondition for, or should be part of, successful reform programmes.

In general, rent-seeking strategies are complex and appear on different levels. They include direct and indirect resistance on the level of policy formulation and policy implementation, as well as countermeasures if specific unwanted reforms cannot be prevented. The fact that in the 1980s and 1990s many multilateral aid programmes went 'off-track' (i.e. major performance criteria and/or structural benchmarks of the agreement were not achieved) indicates that sufficient consideration was not given to rent-seeking activities and their suppression. Understanding and anticipating rent-seeking strategies therefore contributes importantly to the design of better and more effective policy reforms. As more empirical findings are made available, the policy dialogue between donors and beneficiaries can become more focused and politically more sustainable reform programmes can be implemented. Reforms are ultimately successful if they succeed in diverting scarce and valuable resources from rent-seeking activities into productive use, which in turn is a prerequisite to fight poverty. This is the aim of this study.

1.2 Comments to the Reader and Overview of Chapters

This book aims at linking the theory of rent-seeking (Part I) with empirical research on rent-seeking (Part II). Although the two parts can be read independently, they offer many valuable synergies. The combination of these approaches helps to both reveal and bridge the gap that sometimes exists between abstract rent-seeking theory and the problems surrounding rent-seeking behaviour in the real world.

However, due to the sheer number and diversity of the topics covered, the goal of this book is neither to provide a text for beginners on the theory of rent-seeking nor to discuss individual models in all their details. Where the text reaches a high level of abstraction, non-specialist readers are advised to consult the primary literature quoted or to read the concluding sections, which contain summaries.

With its broad spectrum of themes and topics, and different levels of discourse, the book addresses diverse groups of readers. Those primarily interested in a specific theoretical topic or analysis may want just to skim over the empirical part of the book, whereas readers interested in the case study may prefer to read the first half selectively.

On the one hand, it has been written for people interested in development cooperation and policymaking, especially those working for bilateral and multilateral donors, as well as public officials in government institutions in developing and industrialised countries. It also aims to meet the demands of an academic readership which is primarily interested in formal and non-formal aspects of rent-seeking theory, its application to the African context and empirical research. Finally, since the book includes a detailed case study on Tanzania, it offers people interested in Tanzania a wealth of information on the country's development, its successes and failures. One of the main objectives of the case study is to demonstrate and clarify for Tanzanians the extreme inefficiencies and costs of rent-seeking behaviour for their country.

The book is divided into two main parts. Chapters 2 to 5 (Part I) survey and discuss rent-seeking in general, describing rent-seeking in the context of Africa and rent-seeking problems related to economic and political reforms. The chapters provide a comprehensive overview of different aspects that relate to rents, rent-seeking behaviour, rent-seeking strategies and rent-seeking costs. Depending on the section and topic the discussion moves between a pragmatic and descriptive approach, and a more theoretical and formal focus. Chapters 6 to 8 (Part II) present the case study on Tanzania and Chapter 9 offers conclusions and policy recommendations for Part I and II. The chapters are organised as follows:

Part I: Why Is Rent-Seeking Relevant for Developing Countries and Their Reforms?

Part I begins with a definition and systematic overview of what constitutes rents and rent-seeking activities. Chapter 2.1 outlines aspects important for a *definition of rent-seeking* and explains why the term is more controversial than it may appear at first glance. It examines ambiguous examples, clarifies how the term is used in this study and concludes with a working definition of rent-seeking and an explanation as to why the rent-seeking concept is superior to alternative approaches, such as dealing specifically with corruption, when it comes to addressing issues of development and reforms. Chapter 2.2 expands on the rent-seeking concept, focusing on its nature in developing countries. It provides a systematic overview of the rents themselves, how they are captured and who the major winners and losers are.

Chapter 3 deals with the questions of what determines the *size* of rent-seeking investments to capture a rent (and therefore the individual profitability of rent-seeking activities) and what determines the *costs* of this behaviour for society. Chapters 3.1 and 3.2 address analytical approaches that aim to explain rent-seeking incentives and investments. The discussion starts with an introduction of the most relevant tools in the theoretical analysis of rent-seeking and defines the non-rival rent-seeking case as an important extension and counterpart to the traditional rent-seeking approach—an extension which is indispensable when it comes to analysing developing country settings.

Chapter 3.2 presents a detailed *overview of parameters* and other features of rent-seeking models which determine the value individuals attribute to a given rent and the costs involved in capturing this rent. Having demonstrated that the size of individual rent-seeking investments can vary considerably depending on the specific setting and combination of parameters, Chapter 3.3 explains why the size of *social costs* related to rent-seeking critically depends on many factors, i.e. rents of equal size may imply very different costs in terms of lost development and welfare. This chapter also presents some empirical approaches for measuring rent-seeking costs.

Chapter 4 extends the discussion on rent-seeking beyond the narrow neo-classical approach. It basically explains the rationale, shape and value of the parameters discussed so far in the rent-seeking models. Chapter 4.1 focuses on the individual decision-making situation. Besides relating rent-seeking to profit-seeking, among other things by addressing the individual logic behind engaging in *corrupt activities*, the chapter introduces two main qualifications, borrowing from New Institutional Economics. The first takes up the issue of *transaction costs, limited rationality and opportunism*. Obviously in many instances rent-seekers are unlikely to behave as efficiently as a neo-classical-type model would predict because of transaction costs and limited rationality. However, the argument continues, it is exactly such transaction costs and limited rationality that provide opportunities for rent-seeking. The second qualification places the economic concept of homo oeconomicus in a *sociocultural context*, examining the role of informal constraints such as tradition, habits and family values in explaining rent-seeking.

Since most rent-creating and rent-protecting strategies require some group mobilisation, Chapter 4.2 shifts the focus to a different aggregation level, addressing not the individual but the *group's abilities* to organise for or against rent-seeking transfers. The discussion mainly takes up the theory of collective action.

Chapter 4.3 finally changes the perspective to the highest aggregation level, i.e. the *political setting (and character of states)* in which individuals and interest groups are embedded. Following the treatment of the demand side of rent-seeking in Chapters 4.1 and 4.2, Chapter 4.3 mainly looks at the supply side of the issue. It examines the role of rents as a means to stay in power (in relation to the two alternatives legitimacy-building and repression) and discusses the origin, characteristics and limits of rent consumption by predatory-type governments. Analogously to the presentation of rent-seeking models in Chapter 3, Chapter 4.3 includes a discussion of formal approaches for the academic reader that model rents in a politico-economic framework.

Chapter 5 concludes the first part of the book and discusses various aspects of rent-seeking in the context of economic, political and institutional reforms. Chapter 5.1 addresses the *logic for adopting reforms*, grouping rent-seekers and other interest groups into reform supporters, 'mistaken' opponents and reform antagonists. Since a crisis may also increase rent-seeking opportunities, this chapter also describes the relation between the necessity of reform (i.e. the magnitude of a crisis) and the size of the rents transferred to strategic groups. *Rent-seeking strategies during reforms*, i.e. strategies that finally arise once the decision to adopt reforms has been taken, are the subject of Chapter 5.2, which looks at direct and indirect resistance on the level of policy formulation and implementation (including countervailing measures), and rent-seeking activities that result from the transition phase. It concludes with a summary of hypotheses on reform-related rent-seeking and a brief outline of a *logic model* to anticipate rent-seeking interference.

Part II: Rent-Seeking: Empirical Evidence for Tanzania

Tanzania has been and still is one of the poorest countries in the world in spite of the riches of its land and resources and the country's genuine attraction for tourists, drawn to its friendly people, beautiful beaches, extraordinary wildlife and famous national parks, including Africa's highest peak, Mount Kilimanjaro.

Since its independence in 1961 Tanzania's development strategy has been largely co-financed by donors. However, President Nyerere's vision to develop a prospering, egalitarian and self-reliant society failed mainly because rent-seekers increasingly infiltrated the government's administration as well as strategic positions in the economy. As a consequence, Tanzania manoeuvred itself into a deep crisis at the end of the 1970s and the early 1980s, which was severe even by the standards of sub-Saharan Africa. After several unsuccessful attempts to improve its economy within a socialist framework, Tanzania finally opted for a more liberal market economy in 1986.

Yet the reform process up to 2000 was characterised by many costly *delays and setbacks*. As will be shown, several economic imperatives to balance the economy and improve efficiency were not addressed within a reasonable timeframe; the effective (as opposed to planned or publicly communicated) sequencing of reforms was largely driven by rent-seeking considerations, and there are many clear-cut examples of overt rent appropriation or rent-seeking resistance to reforms. The analysis of the study stands in sharp contrast to the frequent statements about Tanzania's achievements since independence. A striking example of an optimistic view of its history is, for example, Mkapa's speech *'Tanzania Proud of 40-Year Achievement Since Independence'* (see People's Daily, 9 December 2001).

This study elaborates rent-seeking answers to the main problems Tanzania faced in the 1980s and 1990s. From the late 1980s onwards virtually every year donors expressed strong concerns about the slow pace of reforms, in particular the widening gap between Tanzania's intentions and the actual delivery of reforms. In 1994 donors even suspended balance of payments support due to major problems related to tax evasion. Only after 1996 did reform records start to improve.

The discussion in Chapters 6 to 8 will outline in detail how important reform measures have been delayed or undermined by countervailing rent-protecting actions. Many of the problems can be explained by the eagerness of the state bureaucracy, parastatal managers and their employees to appropriate resources. In particular highly inefficient loss-making parastatals, including marketing boards and cooperatives succeeded in capturing a large share of the country's own resources and donor aid many years into the Economic Recovery Programme launched in 1986.

The empirical case study obviously addresses a difficult subject. It is a characteristic feature of a rent-seeking economy that rent-seekers use other arguments than rent-seeking to justify poor performance or delays in policy implementation. Furthermore real flows of resources and the identity of rent-seeking beneficiaries are not evident but rather concealed. The situation makes it difficult to pin down rent-seekers and leaves them in the comfortable position that most unfavourable outcomes can be justified or explained by other arguments than rent-seeking, above all unverifiable explanations, as decisive information is not available.

The approach taken in this study, however, represents an attempt to challenge the rent-seekers' 'argumental' advantage by delving into the maze of endless, general and disaggregated information and tracing as many clues to rent-seeking as possible. Because rent-seeking strategies are numerous, diverse and may relate to different aspects simultaneously, and because individual rent-seekers in Tanzania are embedded in an overall network, the discussion in this study takes a broad approach and covers a large number of reform issues and aspects. Only a broad focus that addresses all relevant aspects in the economy and the government from different angles can provide an adequate picture of the persistence and magnitudes of rent-seeking.

Owing to the poor quality of official statistics, as well as the general problem that many aspects of rent-seeking usually cannot be gleaned from official statistics, it was also necessary to collect primary data (especially to obtain information on parastatal support in a disaggregated form). Because of the difficulties in accessing information and the equally poor quality of primary data, data collection alone (and preparation for the subsequent analyses), demanded two years of work. However, as will be shown, the process of collecting and preparing information in this context is not just an inevitable task related to an empirical investigation but it provides valuable information at the same time on the very rent-seeking behaviour under focus, i.e. information on the strategy to conceal rent-seeking transactions. Struggling with missing data and finding contradictions is therefore not necessarily frustrating—both types of examination, data *collection* and data *evaluation,* enhance the understanding of rent-seeking.

The broad and detailed approach taken in this study, which included, among other things, the calculation of numerous specifications in analysing parastatal data, paid off in the end. Despite remaining uncertainties, all results gave a surprisingly similar picture of rent-seeking—a picture which could not have been drawn with the same accuracy if the analysis had been confined to a few aspects. It is the continued and repeated demonstration of similar problems that finally thwarts the rent-seekers' argumental advantage.

The chapters are organised as follows: Chapter 6 introduces Tanzania; it presents a rent-seeking analysis of the pre-1986 period and lays down the methodology and scope of the subsequent evaluation of reform records.

Chapter 7 is entirely devoted to describing the different reform measures initiated after 1986, including the major delays, setbacks and related costs. Chapter 7.1 illustrates how Tanzania's *poor macroeconomic policy stance* in the 1980s and early 1990s had its origin in the profitable tax evasion business (kept intact by the corrupt but efficient 'parallel' tax administration), in rent-seekers' virtually unlimited access to bank credits and in the rent-seeking allocation of subsidised foreign exchange.

The slow pace in 'unleashing' markets and introducing a 'level playing field' for private actors is the topic of Chapter 7.2. Well into the reform process, policymakers held that markets had to be protected and that parastatal companies needed assistance whenever there was a problem. Chapter 7.2 focuses on the various *price, tariff and quantitative restrictions* in markets and examines the logic of rent-seeking, illustrating among other things, the extremely costly protection in the petroleum refining industry, rent-seeking resistance against the liberalisation of export crop marketing (and processing) and the poor rehabilitation and restructuring of parastatal companies in general.

Chapter 7.3 analyses public service delivery from the perspectives of the *private sector* and *civil service.* After an assessment of the hostile private-sector environment in Tanzania, above all the cumbersome bureaucratic procedures investors have to put up with, the discussion addresses the civil service and highlights the slow progress in improving the overall budget process. It emphasises the failures in the 1990s to implement a speedy reform of public employment, to enforce budget priorities and to prevent the large-scale embezzlement of public funds. This chapter demonstrates that in Tanzania both the individual 'embezzling', as well as interest groups, have institutionalised a rent-seeking distribution of budget funds diverted from society's effective needs. The last section finally concludes with a general assessment of *corruption* and the lack of government commitment.

In contrast to Chapter 7, which is organised according to different reform measures, Chapter 8 analyses indicators of rent-seeking support and embezzlement within the parastatal sector, referring to their *profit and loss statements, quality and timeliness of accounting* and the *amount of support* companies obtained. Chapter 8.1 presents a brief methodological discussion of measuring rent transfers and enterprise performance and groups and characterises the nearly 400 commercial parastatals based on their annual profit and loss statements. The chapter also shows why comparing information can be crucial in a rent-seeking economy and how an evaluation of rent-seeking can greatly benefit if a researcher (or donor) has access to aggregated *and* disaggregated data. The last section of Chapter 8.1 describes the nature of the parastatals' accounting. In particular in the 1980s a large number of the parastatals finalised their annual accounts with many years of delay, and only a small share of the companies received clean audit reports. Understanding the way parastatals report to the government gives an idea of patterns of accountability and adds another telling element to the picture of rent-seeking.

Chapter 8.2 evaluates parastatal support in terms of rent-seeking and soft budget constraints. Section a) describes and quantifies the different *channels of support*, which include information on bank borrowing, Treasury support (loans, investments and guarantees), direct subsidies and the allocation of cheap foreign exchange, as well as arrears on income taxes, dividends and inter-parastatal liabilities (outstanding liabilities on pension fund contributions, electricity, water, and telephone service). Section b) describes the main *beneficiaries, purpose and conditions of support*. Particularly strong evidence of rent-seeking is presented when illustrating two aspects, i.e. parastatals obtained additional support regularly despite unsettled arrears, and major beneficiaries were not good performers but rather were highly inefficient and loss-making. The last section of Chapter 8.2 recapitulates the arguments for evidence of rent-seeking and outlines the costs of rent-seeking, among other things by comparing aggregate support allocated to parastatals with the government's expenditures in health and education.

Chapter 9 finally summarises the main *policy conclusions* for designing and implementing appropriate reforms derived from rent-seeking theory and the Tanzanian case study. Chapter 9.1 explains why understanding rents and anticipating resistance from rent-seekers can offer valuable insights for reform-minded policymakers, and Chapter 9.2 takes up additional aspects relevant for the *donor community*.

Part I

Why Is Rent-Seeking Relevant for Developing Countries and Their Reforms?

2 What Is Rent-Seeking?

The term 'rent-seeking' is more controversial than it may appear at first glance. Even though the term is widely used—or rather, because it is widely used—there is no unanimous consensus on how to define and describe rent-seeking which goes beyond the abstract discussion of transfers. This apparent lack of clarity often becomes a source of confusion or unjustified critique. Having this caveat in mind, this chapter devotes sufficient space to defining and describing rents and rent-seeking activities.[5]

Chapter 2.1 aims to shed light on the term 'rent-seeking'. It outlines aspects important to a rent-seeking definition, discusses various ambiguous examples and clarifies how the term is used in this study. It finally concludes with a working definition and justifies what makes rent-seeking appealing for an analysis of reform. Chapter 2.2 fleshes out the rent-seeking concept, focusing on its content in developing countries. It provides a systematic overview of what the rents are, how they are captured, and who the major winners and losers are. An important conclusion which becomes apparent when looking at the numerous and diverse rent-creating policies is that there is neither a clear-cut nor a static dividing line between rent-seeking and government policies and an assessment strongly depends on the specific context.

2.1 Defining Rent-Seeking—A Matter of Opinion?

> *'Rents and rent-seeking are both ubiquitous and inevitable, and as long as there are rights there will be rent-seeking, both between private and public actors and between private actors themselves. There is no single correct definition of waste and the choice of any definition is selective. The real issue is not minimizing rent-seeking, but how to allocate rents.'*
>
> *Steven M. Medema*[6]

It has been roughly two decades since the term *'rent-seeking'* became an established expression in socioeconomic and political literature. For an early but excellent introduction on rent-seeking see in particular Tollison (1982). In the 1990s the terminology finally entered the vocabulary of donors and policymakers at the operational political stage. As with many widely-used expressions such as 'corruption', 'good governance' or 'bounded rationality', there exists no single valid definition for rent-seeking that specifies in detail the

---

[5] The analytical part of rent-seeking is the subject of Chapter 3. For a description of the most basic rent-seeking model see Tullock (1980).

[6] Quoted from the abstract to the paper Medema (1991).

entire domain of activities it covers. Depending on the author, context and audience, the term may be used differently. In addition, there are other expressions and concepts like *directly unproductive activities, soft budget constraints* or *corruption,* which are either used as a synonym, subset or related but different aspect of rent-seeking.

The most important counterpart to rent-seeking is *profit-seeking.* But even here, the attempt to draw an unambiguous dividing line has turned out to be trickier than it may appear at first glance. The situation is made more difficult if the distribution of property rights is not just taken as given but challenged in a more fundamental way, as for instance argued by Medema in the quote above. The following discussion aims to clarify the most common confusion.

a) The Terms Rents and Rent-Seeking: Why Seeking Rents Is Not Synonymous with Rent-Seeking

The term 'rent-seeking' was introduced by Anne Krueger in 1974 in her famous paper 'The Political Economy of the Rent-Seeking Society', but as Tullock (1994, p. 147) himself notes, the relevant theory had already been developed by Tullock in 1967. His original article 'The Welfare Costs of Tariffs, Monopolies, and Theft' (Tullock (1967)) already specifies many of the important issues rent-seeking theory is dealing with. Strictly speaking, the term 'rent-seeking' is a poor description of what rent-seeking is all about. It should actually contrast with profit-seeking—the more common type of individual maximising behaviour. In either case, however, rents are sought and dissipated.

The difference may be best explained with a simplified example. If a highly efficient company produces cars at a total unit cost of $9000 that can be sold on a free market for $14,000, it earns a rent of $5000 with each car. In a truly competitive environment this rent is of a temporary nature. Over time other companies are likely to become equally efficient and supply similar or even better cars at a lower price. Competition and technical progress may finally drive down the price of the original car (assuming it is still on the market) and the rent will most likely shrink or even disappear. New rents arise with the production of new cars, but these too are only temporary. Abstracting from externalities related to pollution in producing and using cars, the seeking of 'temporary' rents typically improves society's welfare, as the price of cars declines and/or the quality improves. This is the standard story of the welfare-enhancing role of competition usually taught in economic textbooks.

Alternatively, the textbooks may continue, already at an early stage representatives of the company may try to convince the government to ban any car imports as a measure to secure jobs in the domestic car industry. And to be able to realise economies of scale, they may even convince politicians to make the company the sole producer of cars in the country. Incentives to be efficient typically decline. It would not be surprising if the company ends up producing a poor-quality car at the cost of $13,000 and still sells it, given the market monopoly, at a price of $16,000. Assuming that in a non-protected market environment the manufacturer can only charge $6000 for the low-quality car, the difference between $16,000 and $6000 reflects the artificial rent the manufacturer obtains because of the protection. Consumers are paying this additional $10,000, not because they value the car as particularly good, but because they are not given the option to buy better or cheaper cars which already exist outside the protected market. Since in the example the cost of production is even higher than the free-market value of the car, the domestic company would be driven out of business if protection was abolished entirely—a situation, which usually provides policymakers a strong argument to sustain the high level of protection (and inefficiency).

In the above case of protection, the artificial rent of $10,000 has been created by government intervention. As will be outlined later, there are also other reasons for the creation of rents that fall into the category of rent-seeking. All these rents have in common that they indicate unilateral transfers, i.e. they reflect the share of income obtained without generating a productive contribution in exchange. What makes the concept confusing is that economic theory uses the same word for 'good' and 'bad' rents, i.e. as noted above, for the rent earned by the efficient car manufacturer ($5000) and the rent obtained by the inefficient and protected company ($10,000). Since the latter are unilateral transfers, a more suitable expression of rent-seeking distinguishing it from profit-seeking might have been *'transfer-seeking'*. However because the term 'rent-seeking' has long since been adopted into the language, it would be more confusing to use a different designation.

Before looking at the detailed definition of rent-seeking, it may be helpful for the reader to recall how economic theory uses the term 'rent' to describe distinct aspects. Readers not familiar with this aspect of microeconomic theory are adviced to just skim over the following page.

The New Palgrave, a dictionary of economics and law, lists six terms under the heading 'rents' (essay by Alchian (1987, p. 141f)): rents in general, economic rents, quasi-rents (and composite quasi-rents), Ricardian rents, differential rents and monopoly rents. As a general term, a *rent* simply indicates the payment for the use of a resource (land, labour, equipment, idea or even money). An *economic rent* arises to a good whose supply remains constant, irrespective of the price paid for the good, i.e. the price is determined entirely by the demand. Closely related to economic rents are *quasi-rents*, which occur if a resource is unresponsive to price changes during a certain period. In particular industry-specific factors of production cannot shift in the short run (or even long run) to other purposes. Both economic rents and quasi rents have in common that the rent obtained exceeds the amount required to keep the resource in the current use (there is no, or with quasi rents no immediate alternative use).

Ricardian rents characterise differences in rents among units of otherwise homogenous resources. Land of equal fertility or type, for instance, may have a very different value, depending on where it is located (e.g. close to a market place, in the town centre or in a remote area). *Differential rents* (more commonly known as 'producer surpluses' or 'producer rents') arise if different units of resources have a different alternative use. For most goods there are producers who can supply goods more cheaply than others. Their resources invested to produce a good are less costly (they have a lower alternative use, partly because fewer resources are needed as they are utilised more economically). Listing the production costs of each unit from the lowest to the highest provides the traditional upward-sloping supply curve, and the distance from the horizontal price line (equilibrium price of the good) to the production costs indicates the producer rent (in strict economic terms, the extra benefit the factors of production obtain in the current use if compared to what they could earn with the best alternative use).

As Alchian (1987, p. 143) emphasises, it is worth noting that this supply curve should not be confused with an upward rising 'true' supply curve, which reflects increasing marginal costs of production and therefore only variable costs. Earnings that exceed variable costs are partly needed to pay the fixed capital input costs.

Consumer rents (not mentioned in The New Palgrave under the entry 'rents') are, in contrast to 'producer rents', psychological rents. With decreasing marginal benefits of consumption, they arise as the demand of consumers is only expanded to the point where marginal benefits equal the market price of the goods, i.e. consumers pay the same unit price of a good they consume, even though their willingness to pay for the first units is typically higher than what they are willing to pay for the last unit and therefore higher than the market price. Figure 2-1 displays the traditional consumer and producer rents.

Figure 2-1: Consumer and Producer Rents

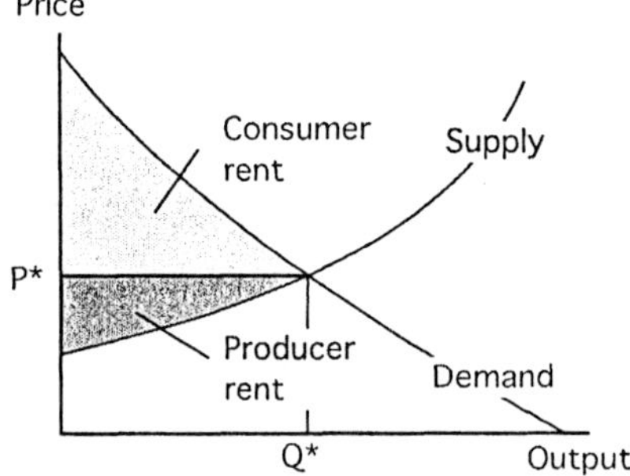

The higher the price P, the higher production, as production also becomes profitable to companies that can only supply at higher costs. Since the equilibrium price P* applies to all producers, more efficient companies earn a producer rent.

On the consumer side, the demand is expanded as long as the willingness to pay for an additional unit does not fall below the market price P. Since P* is the same for all units consumed but the first units provide a higher marginal benefit, consumers also enjoy a rent.

All the above-mentioned rents have in common that they have not been artificially created by restrictions. They may relate to specific skills (as argued with the efficient car company) or they may arise from natural conditions and sheer accident, as is often the case with natural resources (most of them have a market value that exceeds the costs of their extraction and therefore provide a rent to the resource owner or the land owner). Consumer rents simply reflect consumers' preferences.

Created by a combination of valuations, natural restrictions and market forces, rents are an integral part of the market process to capture gains from specialisation and trade. Most important, they motivate economic behaviour. Only with these rents is the link between exceptionally high returns and increased production of the most highly valued goods not distorted (of course, assuming that there are no externalities which reverse this result). Their 'seeking' reflects the normal profit-seeking incentive.

This is not the case with the last type of rents mentioned earlier, the *monopoly rent.* Broadly defined, monopoly rents arise from any kind of artificial restriction on potential competitors that allows an increase of the protected company's wealth. In contrast to rents that attend profit-seeking, artificial rents usually undermine the efficiency-increasing impact of market forces and may even make price incentives irrelevant in the allocation of resources. In addition, as will be outlined later, individuals and interest groups typically spend resources to create and capture these rents—i.e. they engage in rent-seeking activities—often further undermining the efficient use of resources. These rents are discussed in more detail later (similar to the 'natural' rents depicted in Figure 2-1, Figure 2-2 on page 42 outlines a few examples of artificial rents).

Looking at the literature, there is no single definition of rent-seeking and related 'bad' rents. Depending on the focus the latter may be defined narrowly or in a very broad sense. In the narrow context, they relate to the above-mentioned monopoly rents, i.e. they arise from restrictions that prevent a competitive market outcome, such as direct lobbying for a monopoly or lobbying for more or less moderate import protection. In contrast, a broad definition, which is the approach taken in this study (and which has also been addressed in Gordon Tullock's original paper from 1967) proceeds from the more general view of capturing a transfer or, to put it differently, from earning income without being productive.

Even though a broad approach makes it more difficult to delimitate rent-seeking from other types of activities, it permits a more general evaluation of economic behaviour and policies. A broad definition does not contain any of the above-specified profit-seeking rents. It does, however include many different types of transfer-related activities, ranging from companies that lobby to be exempted from paying taxes and interest groups that try to influence budgetary allocations, to smugglers who invest a lot of time and effort to get their goods across unpatrolled borders, civil servants who embezzle funds and demand bribes, as well as the activities of burglars or people who illegally renege on contracts.

Besides the term 'rent-seeking' there are other expressions or concepts which aim to describe similar or related activities. Some economists endeavour to differentiate rent-seeking from *directly unproductive profit-seeking (DUP)* activities, mostly by trying to define one of them as a subset or an inferior variation of the other (e.g. comments or references in Bhagwati (1994, p. 846), Brooks and Heijdra (1988, p. 45), Rowley (1988b, p. 19) or Tollison (1987, p. 143)). Since in principle the two describe the same phenomenon, there is no standard distinction. Sometimes rent-seeking is also distinguished from *corruption*. Such an approach may hold if rent-seeking is defined in the very narrow sense noted above. But even then, there are overlaps. In general, corruption, which is commonly defined as the 'abuse of official power for private financial gain' (Kaufmann (1998a, p. 523)), simply describes an illegal type of rent-seeking activity.

b) Problems with Articulating a Clear Definition and Delimitation

As regards a broad definition of rent-seeking, the dividing line between rent-seeking, profit-seeking and other activities is not as easy to draw as it may first appear. This section addresses three basic questions in defining rent-seeking which refer to specific areas of confusion. First, does rent-seeking always relate to a government activity or responsibility? Second, does it make sense to define rent-seeking from the perspective of inefficiency? Finally and more fundamentally, can rent-seeking be defined at all, given the subjective nature of property rights distribution and society's natural tendency to redistribute income? Many of aspects of the first two questions boil down to the property rights debate.

Anderson, Rowley and Tollison (1988, p. 100) described rent-seeking as 'the pursuit of profits via the use of government coercion' (cited from Brooks and Heijdra (1989, p. 33)); Rowley (2000, p. 141) notes that 'rent-seeking focuses attention on the resources expended by competing interest groups in order to persuade governments to provide returns higher than they could earn in the absence of government protection'. Such definitions give rise to the question whether rent-seeking is always related to *government activity and responsibility*. Evidently, since most artificial rents are created by government interventions, the above definitions are suitable for analysing specific aspects of government policy. For an all-encompassing broad approach however they are less appropriate, in particular as 'bad' rents also arise from market imperfections. Rent-seeking settings cover a continuum from government-related to strictly private settings where the government plays at the most a very passive role.

At the one end is protection effectuated by government policy, which is the most evident case of government involvement in rent creation. If the state is also charged with enforcing a competitive market environment, 'lack of action' can be defined as a passive type of government-induced rent-seeking (e.g. Gelb, Hillman and Ursprung (1995, p. 2)). Tolerating the formation of cartels, allowing entrepreneurs to take advantage of the position of a natural monopoly or not prosecuting burglars and other law-breakers are some examples. Less evident is the role of the government when it tolerates a strike, where mostly unionised workers seek wage increases at the expense of company owners and management (or, depending on pricing policy and elasticities, at the expense of consumers). Whether this is an incidence of rent-seeking and government responsibility evidently depends on the specific circumstances and the definition of property rights. In general, strikes are part of the corporatist model, which reflects an approximation to a functioning labour market.

A typical rent-seeking situation where the state takes neither an active nor a direct passive role is the principal-agent conflict in a company.[7] An employee may not work or may even accept bribes to act against the company's interests, for instance by favouring a more expensive or less reliable supplier. But sometimes authors do not draw an accurate dividing line between rent-seeking and profit-seeking. Medema (1991, p. 1057), for instance, defined a rather odd case of 'vertical' rent-seeking based on an inter-firm relationship:

> '...take the case of inter-firm Christmas gift giving. Be it fruit cake, alcohol, or desk calendars, these gifts are given to cement one's relation with another firm, so that when firm A needs something it runs to firm B rather than firm C. Such activity is rent seeking, plain and simple...'

Medema's position is clearly disputable, in most cases this is a strategy of profit-seeking. The argument hinges on the ability of any actor to freely decide with whom to negotiate and what conditions to accept. As long as free choice is guaranteed, an entrepreneur who provides the best offer—whether or not this includes fruitcake, alcohol or desk calendars—will get the order. This is a free market economy, plain and simple! Only if personal relations outweigh economic criteria as part of a principal-agent conflict, i.e. employees harm the company or the institution they work for by favouring friends or relatives, would this be a case of rent-seeking. A fruitcake might then induce an economic loss of thousands of dollars. The problem occurs as the costs are not borne by the decision-makers but rather by the company or institution they represent.

Ultimately, at the very end of the spectrum rent-seeking takes place in private social life, even though a delimitation critically depends on the society's 'subjective' definition of property rights and duties. It makes sense to define people begging on the street and knocking on doors as rent-seekers, in particular if they have opportunities to work. But it does not make sense to apply the same definition to children who implore their parents to buy ice cream or toys (as for instance mentioned in Laband and Sophocleus (1988, p. 270)), basically because young children are not expected to earn their own income.

The second question addresses the relation of *inefficiency and rent-seeking.* A rent-seeking definition may proceed from the dichotomy between welfare-enhancing and welfare-reducing behaviour. The former would refer to profit-seeking, the latter to rent-seeking. An early definition that includes this type of valuation is for instance given in Buchanan and Tullock (1980, p. 4) (cited from Brooks and Heijdra (1989, p. 32)):

> 'The term rent seeking is designed to describe behaviour in institutional settings where individual efforts to maximise value generate social waste rather than social surplus.'

---

[7] For a brief explanation of the principal-agent concept see Section b) of Chapter 4.1 (page 163f).

Albeit accurate for many rent-seeking situations, the definition is problematic if taken literally, as it classifies any individual maximising behaviour that bears social costs as rent-seeking and labels rent-seeking as always socially wasteful. The crucial point is that even if rent-seeking should be contrasted with profit-seeking, it is more than a negative counterpart.

Earlier it was argued that rents and rent-seeking may result from market imperfections. However, market imperfections can also give rise to welfare-reducing profit-seeking, if externalities, above all negative spillover effects, play a role. And under specific circumstances (it will be discussed in Chapter 3.3) rent-seeking can be beneficial for society. Since these atypical cases have been a source of confusion in differentiating between rent-seeking and profit-seeking, it is worth looking at the matter in more detail and discussing a few examples.

Living in a world where transaction costs matter, where externalities exist and where market participants do not have equal access to information implies an imperfect market situation. More importantly, it entails that competitive markets may not always allocate resources efficiently, as asserted in a general-equilibrium model that abstracts from externalities and incomplete information. It is not far-fetched to assume that some negative externalities may even be so large that certain individual profit-seeking activities will lead to overall social waste, not because individuals are rent-seekers but because the internalisation of the externality has thus far never been addressed by society. *Over-fishing* in the absence of regulations or *polluting activities* whose costs are not paid by the polluter are typical examples where profit-seeking can imply high welfare costs. Clearly, once society has recognised the problem and decides to address it, disregard of efficiency-enhancing regulations or lobbying against their implementation becomes plain rent-seeking.

Some authors describe *advertising*, which is a measure of non-price competition, as an example of wasteful rent-seeking in private sectors (e.g. Tollison (1982, p. 587f) or Yang (1999, p. 432)). Tollison describes the mechanism as follows (p. 587):

> 'Non-colluding firms face a prisoner's dilemma with respect to non-price competition. All could increase their net worth by resisting additional advertising expenditures, but unilateral defections from such an "agreement" appear worthwhile to the individual firm. Yet if all firms defect, "excessive advertising" and lower average profitability appear in the industry.'

Advertising is a necessary task in a world of positive transaction costs. However, it includes externalities that prevent overall advertising from levelling off at an efficient level. Advertising does not just push competitors back along their supply curves, but also induces their supply curves to shift upwards (because of transaction costs the curves not only represent production but also sales costs). To sell the same amount as before competitors will also have to raise their advertising expenditures, again inducing other supply curves to shift. The standard solution to the problem, as suggested in the above quote, is to form a cartel where the members deliberately agree to limit their advertising. Contrary to the negative effects of cartel agreements on common pricing, an agreement to reduce production costs is of course welfare enhancing. Therefore, similar to the externality case of over-fishing or pollution, calling advertising rent-seeking does not seem to be appropriate unless competitors have agreed on limiting advertising and some companies unilaterally defect from it to take advantage of the situation.

Finally, another example of market imperfections that may accompany rents is *trading in financial markets*. There are different motivations to engage in financial trading: people make payments for transactions in real markets or they aim to hedge against the risk of future price changes. Financial transactions, however, are also made by speculators and people who exploit insider information for personal gain. These last two categories have created the perception that financial trading is often a mere rent-seeking activity, in particular as many speculators and traders became very rich without producing any real output. On the other hand, it is accepted that traders can nevertheless exert a positive impact on the functioning of a market system. Murphy, Shleifer and Vishny (1991, p. 506) describe the ambiguous role as follows:

> 'Trading probably raises efficiency since it brings security prices closer to their fundamental values. It might even indirectly contribute to growth if more efficient financial markets reduce the cost of capital. But the main gains from trading come from the transfers of wealth to the smart traders from the less astute who trade with them out of institutional needs or outright stupidity. Even though efficiency improves, transfers are the main source of returns in trading.'

The categorisation of these activities as either rent-seeking or profit-seeking is controversial. A straight answer can only be given for obvious cases that are situated at either end of the spectrum. Speculators in financial markets who have no insider information lose or gain on average with the same probability. They are, in contrast to popular opinion, not rent-seekers but gamblers. On the other hand, there are also financial market participants who deliberately try to maintain an insider constellation, or brokers who deliberately misinform their clients to realise arbitrage gains for themselves. These people are clearly rent-seekers. Treatment of the cases in between, however, depends on the society's definition of property rights, insiders and the rules of exchange. The problem points to the ethical questions whether unresolved asymmetries in information between trading partners, which provide a decisive advantage to one party at the expense of the other party, are legitimate or not.

Hence, even if the pursuit of private gains in trading may contribute to reduce the incompleteness of markets and may promote an efficient allocation of resources in the market system (in fact, sometimes it does the contrary, as overshooting and crashes prove), it is not always legitimate to treat financial trading as a profit-seeking activity. As noted above, the answer hinges on the nature and degree of asymmetry in information that has been exploited and the preferences of the society.

Summing up, the examples of over-fishing, pollution, advertising and financial trading indicate that rent-seeking is not just the opposite of welfare-enhancing profit-seeking. The outcome basically rests on market imperfections (Chapter 4.1 will take up the issue of imperfect markets again, focusing on the role of rent-seeking).

An important aspect of rent-seeking which has also become apparent in the above discussion is that a definition of rents and rent-seeking requires a pre-defined *structure of property rights*. Over-fishing becomes rent-seeking if the society perceives the problem and there are rules to address it; polluters are rent-seekers if they lobby against environmental regulations that aim to implement the society's 'polluter-must-pay' principle, and insider transactions at the stock exchange are only prosecuted if they are defined as illegal insider deals. Ultimately, also the classification of trade union activities as 'rent-seeking' or 'wealth protection' is a matter of defining property rights and evaluating how well labour markets function. This situation points to the third question of *whether the concept of rent-seeking can be useful at all* given the subjective nature of any property rights distribution and society's inherent tendency to redistribute income. The provocative statement in the lead quote 'the real issue is not minimising rent-seeking but how to allocate rents' may suggest the answer is 'no'. Medema (1991, p. 1052), referring to the waste of rent-seeking, notes:

> 'The conception of waste assumes that the status quo structure of rights is correct [Samuels and Mercuro, 1984, pp. 60-63]. Rights change only when there is challenge to / competition for a right. This inevitably involves the expenditure of resources. Hence, to label such expenditure "waste" presumes that rights should not be changed...'

There appears to be a more fundamental misunderstanding of the concept of rent-seeking. What is needed is to differentiate rents from legitimate processes in society which determine primary and secondary income distribution in a market economy. To tackle the problem, two aspects need to be clearly differentiated. On the one hand, there is the goal to *produce output efficiently*, i.e. to use a minimum amount of resources for a given amount of output (or to produce a maximal output with a given amount of input). On the other hand, there is the *society's desire to reallocate income*. A society typically legitimises transfers on two grounds. First, individuals do not have similar chances at the outset (in particular the distribution of property rights is merely coincidental and may even reflect past rent-seeking activities); and second, a perfect market economy does not exist. Market rigidities often do not allow an efficient use of resources and external shocks such as droughts, accidents and disease may lead to economic hardship where affected people cannot be held responsible.

In essence, economists differentiate between three standards of property rights: those which *exist*, those that lead to economic *efficiency* and those that a society finds *legitimate* (e.g. Paul, Miller and Paul (1994)). Rent-seeking theory looks at the link between the first two. Optimally, redistributing income should happen at the link between the second and the third aspect, i.e. output is produced efficiently but redistributed thereafter, given the many inescapable shortcomings in an economy. Seen from this perspective a rent-seeking-free economy can include a large reallocation of income. But this demands that output has been produced efficiently in the first place.

Clearly, the implementation of this first-best approach is often economically difficult to realise or, is politically unfeasible. Resources need to be invested to move from the second to the third standard of property rights. On the one hand, even an optimal solution of reallocating income is unlikely to eliminate all distorting tax effects; on the other, transaction costs and incomplete information also absorb resources since any desired income redistribution has to be communicated, debated and decided upon. It is a characteristic for societal decision-making to be combative, in particular as there is no uniformly accepted view of a just formula for income distribution; societies typically keep the social compact open (Czichowski (1990, p. 185f)).

Nevertheless, what matters is to take the right perspective. The major goal remains to produce output as efficiently as possible. This approach not only guarantees higher welfare and income that can be reallocated, it also makes any redistribution explicit and therefore approved by society. Consequently, the real issue, contrary to Medema's formulation, is indeed to minimise rents and rent-seeking, and only afterwards to reallocate income according to society's vision of a just income distribution.

c) Conclusion: Choosing an Appropriate Approach

As mentioned in Chapter 1, the main motivation of this study is to survey rent-seeking, to provide additional insights into the causes and consequences of rent-seeking in Africa, and to understand how rent-seeking is an impediment to growth and development in general and to broad-based economic, political and institutional reforms in particular. Many developing countries are characterised by poor policies and weak institutional settings, where corruption and embezzlement is rampant and privileged interest groups manage to capture large shares of the nation's income in a decidedly non-productive way. Since the facets of rents and rent appropriation are diverse and there are many links between the different modes of rent appropriation, this study takes a broad approach to rent-seeking.

Before concluding with a working definition of rent-seeking, it is helpful to recall some related approaches to rent-seeking that have been taken to analyse constraints on growth and development. Especially in the 1990s *corruption* was given increasing attention in the literature on developing countries and economic reforms. As noted earlier, corruption reflects a specific type of rent-seeking activity. However, even though important in an analysis of economic efficiency, taken alone it may not suffice to describe important aspects.

For many rent-seekers, it is irrelevant whether they get rents through tax exemptions they have been legally lobbying for, or whether they capture the same benefit through an illegal deal with the customs officer. An analysis of corruption, however, would consider only the latter aspect. Also from an economic point of view, it does not matter whether rents are captured 'legally' or illegally. In both situations rent-seeking would undermine growth and constrain development. Most important in the reform context, however, is the link between different rent-seeking activities. If rent-seekers come under pressure, they are likely to look for other rent-seeking opportunities and not just for a profit-seeking alternative. A one-sided focus on a single type of rent-seeking such as corruption may therefore fail to account for important interactions and possible undesirable consequences. In fact, many countries undergoing reforms experienced an increase in corruption a few years after rent-abolishing reforms were initiated.

Another related approach to rent-seeking is the analysis of *soft budget constraints*—a concept which was originally introduced by János Kornai in 1979 in the context of socialist economies (see Kornai (1979)). Soft budget constraints describe the bailing out of predominantly public companies which receive transfers from the government when revenues do not cover costs. Soft budget constraints are usually not intended ex-ante by a society but are the result of blatant rent-seeking activities. The concept of soft budget constraints is a helpful instrument in a rent-seeking analysis, in particular if it is applied in a broad sense, i.e. if the analysis does not just focus on potential loss-making companies but on any companies that receive additional top-ups.

What about the rent-seeking definition? Clearly, the choice of any particular rent-seeking definition that outlines its domain and distinguishes itself from other concepts is a matter of preference and opinion. There are, however, several aspects that should be considered in any broad definition of rent-seeking. As outlined in this chapter, a critical issue is the line dividing it from profit-seeking. Any behaviour enhancing the welfare of an individual but reducing it for society should not automatically be assigned to rent-seeking (or vice versa). The concept of rent-seeking would then degenerate into a meaningless conglomeration of different, loosely-related activities. Preferably, the definition should also be general and not tie rent-seeking to state activities, even though the state bears a great deal of responsibility by directly creating or passively tolerating artificial rents and 'illegitimate' transfers. For instance, it is important to keep in mind that particularly in developing countries non-governmental organisations (NGOs) can play a very important role in allocating resources, also in a rent-seeking manner. Like government institutions, they provide important services, may receive subsidies and are often supported by donor agencies.

A description of rent-seeking which is not based on a valuation but makes dependence on property rights apparent is mentioned in the article by Brooks, Heijdra and Lowenberg (1990, p. 432):

> 'One possible solution is to define rent seeking as the use of resources to challenge existing property rights, while profit-seeking (or

> entrepreneurship) is viewed as taking place within the status quo framework of property rights.'

And Tollison (1982, p. 578) describes rent-seeking as '*the expenditure of scarce resources to capture an artificially created transfer*'. In principle both approaches are practical definitions. They are simple, refer to transfers in general (emphasising that not just rents in the narrow sense are relevant) and they neither make explicit reference to the state nor tie rent-seeking to welfare-reducing behaviour.

For this study it is preferable to use a definition which distinguishes more explicitly between exogenous and endogenous rents. Depending on the setting rent-seekers expend resources not just to capture rents, but also to create them in the first place. It may also be helpful to use the two terms 'rents' and 'transfers' simultaneously. The former would emphasise rents in the narrow sense, with the latter additionally referring to more direct transfers such as subsidies, theft and embezzlement. What both definitions lack is a reference to society's tendency to reallocate income. As noted earlier, treating any transfer-related activity as rent-seeking does not make sense. Furthermore, sometimes rent-seeking does not include any expenditure of resources, but may reflect a situation where privileged individuals can capture rents without effort, for instance by threats and extortions. The following definition takes account of these considerations. It is the working definition that will be used in this study. Clearly, being only a second-best approach, this definition can be debated (like any other).

> *Rent-seeking is an activity, usually implying the expenditure of scarce resources, to cause and capture artificially-created rents as well as transfers which are not part of society's intended income redistribution.*

It goes without saying that the dividing line is not always clear between transfers that reflect society's vision of a more just income distribution, and transfers which are effected by rent-seeking individuals and interest groups (in contrast to the society's preferences). Nevertheless, looking at economies in the real world, there are typically a far greater number of very clear-cut rent-seeking situations which imply high costs for the majority of the population. Resources are not used efficiently to increase output but rather to carve larger slices out of the little that has been produced. If a large share of the income is 'earned' by privileged groups in a non-productive or even destructive way, it is not surprising that such economies cannot develop and prosper. These are the kind of ailing economies the rent-seeking theory focuses on.

2.2 Rent-Seeking in LDCs

'Political players who might seek to further some conception of an all-encompassing general, or public, interest cannot survive. They tend to be eliminated from the political game in the evolution-like selection process.'

James M. Buchanan (1993, p. 1)

A lot of rent-seeking is closely related to government activities; however, the discussion on defining rent-seeking emphasised that governments are more than just 'organised and legitimised theft' (Tollison (1987, p. 155)), as cynics may claim. They are instruments of any society to *correct for market imperfections*, in particular to address externalities, to provide public goods (national security, rule of law, environmental protection, etc.) and to redistribute income according to the society's vision of a more just income distribution. To truly understand the duality between rents and well-intended economic policies it is essential to be aware of both motivations.

A specific government activity may be associated with *three different situations*. First, the state intervenes because of an externality or desired reallocation of income. Measures are efficiently undertaken, have the expected outcome and are not related to rent-seeking. This situation reflects an optimal outcome and is also the neo-classical or 'textbook' benchmark. Second, the state intervenes with the same intention, but the measures provoke rent-seeking activities as an unwanted by-product. Depending on the constellation, the society might still be willing to accept these secondary effects in favour of the economic policy intended in the first place. And third, measures may be implemented for the sole motivation of creating and capturing rents, i.e. these measures reflect the victory of powerful interest groups over society's benevolent interests.

Over time the characterisation of a state activity may shift from the first to the second type and then, as rent-seekers increasingly mobilise and influence economic rules to their advantage, to the third. The opening quotation—it referred to democratic countries but can easily be applied to any other setting—also makes a rather pessimistic assessment and raises the legitimate question as to whether a society that proceeds from a Benthamite vision (achieving the greatest welfare for the largest number of people) can ever be protected against the harmful consequences of rent-seeking forces. Clearly, a satisfactory assessment will require examining the character of the society and focusing on the different types of interest groups; it also depends on its government. Chapter 4 will examine these aspects in more detail. The following discussion, in contrast, does not aim to address fundamentals of rent-seeking but will describe the phenomenon of rent-seeking and its outcome in a general way. Section a) focuses on the link between economic policy and rent creation, starting with a brief reference to development policies. Section b) outlines a typology of rent-seeking activities and Section c) finally concludes with an assessment of common winners and losers in rent-seeking.

a) Economic Policy and Rent Creation in LDCs

At independence, most developing countries found themselves in a situation where their economy was fragile, not well developed and with substantial market imperfections. Some countries had a fairly good infrastructure but no management and government skills, and in many countries development was largely confined to expatriate elites.

Since market imperfections negatively affect the allocation and use of resources and constrain a country's future potential for rapid and sustainable development, governments usually try to address the problem with an active development policy. In LDCs such policies typically focus on guiding and accelerating structural changes that move a country from a volatile agrarian economy to a well-diversified industrial nation. As widely discussed in the economic literature, two distinct strategies (or a sequential combination thereof) have been pursued: an *inward-looking import-substitution strategy* and an *outward-looking, export-led approach* (see, for instance, Perkins, et al. (2001, p. 677f)). Most developing countries (as well as many European countries in earlier days) heavily relied on the import-substitution strategy.

The rationale for government support and intervention rests on two lines of reasoning, the *infant industry argument* and the *externality problem*. To develop an industry takes time and a new industry is unlikely to compete successfully against well-established companies abroad that have already had plenty opportunities to accumulate know-how, experience and capital reserves. At least during the first years, major losses are likely to occur even though future benefits are supposed to compensate past losses. The problem is, the argument continues, that capital markets in developing countries often were not able to pre-finance these losses, because capital markets were inexistent or under-developed. Some kind of government support, for instance in the form of protection, is therefore required. This protection would then be reduced and eliminated after a few years.

More important from a dynamic development perspective is the externality argument. A project may not be economically viable in the short and longer run, but it may exert positive externalities for the development of upstream, similar and downstream industries; even if the company's private return on the investment is negative the social return can nonetheless be positive. Optimally, a government chooses the level of support or protection that makes socially desirable projects also economically viable for private investors.

Out of the two development strategies, import substitution has been particularly appealing to policymakers since the replacement of imports with own goods promises to reduce the country's shortage of foreign exchange and the policy immediately generates jobs. Of course an export-led growth strategy, which primarily relies on supporting industries that are competitive internationally, has the same impact but the preconditions are harder to meet. In contrast to a strict import-substitution policy, where domestic consumers can be prohibited from buying imported goods (they are virtually forced to use the domestic products), an export strategy cannot pressure anybody abroad to buy the country's goods, it can only try to make these goods sufficiently attractive. This apparently small difference in incentives has had substantial consequences for the success of the two strategies.

Three decades after the vast majority of the developing countries had become independent, Findlay (1990, p. 194) described the major features of third world economies as follows:

> 'These are the extensive growth of government relative to the private sector, the pervasiveness of "corruption" in varied forms, the intensity of trade restrictions and the associated phenomenon of the "import substitution syndrome", the "urban bias" of economic policy and resource allocation and the degree of dependence on foreign capital.'

Other characteristics include the lack of diversity of export products, the state's limited administrative capacity, the poor quality of basic infrastructure or the very unequal distribution of income and wealth. The combination of these factors has further made developing countries especially vulnerable to internal and external shocks. The consequences are felt strongest in the poorest countries. Because income, living standards and social services are often far beyond any acceptable minimum level, internal and external shocks can seriously threaten the lives of many people.

What has happened? Without going into details, many of the intended measures obviously did not have the expected impact, partly because of external shocks and partly because measures were not properly designed or implemented. The *rent-seeking perspective*, however, offers a clear-cut answer. In spite of originally good intentions, the developing strategy pursued often failed to guide individual activities into productive spheres; instead, many of the state interventions offered privileged people opportunities to gain income in a non-productive or even destructive way. It is therefore not surprising that, for instance, protectionism granted to support infant industries has never been reduced. The rent-seeking outcome is in contrast to the traditional Benthamite vision, which assumes that the state is concerned to guarantee an efficient allocation of resources within the country.

Table 2-1 (p. 38f) gives a general overview of state activities that potentially relate to rent-seeking behaviour. As noted earlier, almost any government activity may induce rent-seeking activities to some extent. This is not surprising but is entirely in line with Tollison's statement mentioned in Chapter 1, 'basically rent-seeking is a cost of government activity in general' (Tollison (1987, p. 145)). The table has to be interpreted accordingly. It outlines possible areas of rent creation and rent-seeking but does not claim that the policies are necessarily related to rents and rent-seeking.

The table groups state activities into three broad categories. Besides traditional market interventions, the government may create rents *actively* as a market participant and it typically creates rents *passively* when it fails to set up an institutional setting that guarantees secure property rights and a competitive market environment. In general, interventions may range from small price interventions in the form of moderate taxes and subsidies, to rigid quantity and other non-price regulations up to the complex situation where the state nationalises entire industries. And, as will be further explained below, rents are associated with a failure to intervene. For both cases, a crucial determinant of rent-seeking is often the amount of discretion, i.e. the more freedom of choice state activities involve (either related to an intervention or to the lack of it) the more they are prone to rent-seeking activities.

Although the table provides a systematic overview of government activities, the categorisation remains an approximate solution. One problem is that some policy measures overlap and their distinction is partly artificial. Measures may imply other interventions or they may directly affect other markets. A case in point is the dividing line between price, quantity and other interventions. Price ceilings and multiple exchange rates, for instance, typically demand additional measures to allocate the scarce goods and foreign exchange. Another shortcoming from the rent perspective is that a rent does not necessarily result from one policy measure alone, but may reflect a combination of several interventions. An import quota, for instance, is not of much value and has no impact on the level of imports if taxes and other cumbersome regulations reduce the imported amount below the quota level. Or reducing import taxes from 500% to 120% only may not affect rents if there are still no goods officially imported.

Depending on the rent-specific focus alternative classifications are therefore preferable. One approach is to differentiate between selected markets in agriculture, manufacturing and trade, or to differentiate between reform efforts that intend to abolish rents (macroeconomic reforms, liberalisation, deregulation, privatisation and institutional reforms). Alternatively, one may concentrate on the impact of rent-seeking on the government budget and distinguish on the one hand, rents that are distributed directly from the budget, such as subsidies, cheap treasury loans, overpaid jobs in the civil service and overpriced contracts, and on the other hand rents which are created by the government's power to restrict market forces from operating freely (price ceiling, licensing, permits, etc.). Finally, when focusing on the source of the rent, state activities may be grouped according to McChesney's differentiation between public rent creation and private rent extraction (McChesney (1987)). This study will refer to some of these alternative classifications later.

The first part of Table 2-1 summarises the traditional state interventions in different input and output markets. *Taxation* typically provokes legal and illegal tax-evading activities as well as lobbying by interest groups to be exempted from taxation. The different treatment of individuals, companies or entire sectors with other than the usual tax progression is characteristic of many developing countries. Combined with poor capacity and frequent corruption in the tax and customs administration, both smuggling and false declarations mutually agreed between businesspeople and tax enforcers are often the rule rather than the exception.

Table 2-1 (a-c): State Activities—Potential Cause and Outcome of Rent-Seeking

a) Selective Market Interventions

		Price *Increase or reduction in price, adopting price ceilings*	*Quantity* *Limitations on output, transactions or number of companies*	*Other* *Bureaucratic regulation interfering in market activities*
Goods and service markets	*Within country*	Taxes and subsidies (sector-wide, diverse or discretionary) Floor and maximum prices	Industrial licensing Restrictions on the number of companies (e.g. monopolies)	Regulations to establish and run business, standard & minimum quality requirements
	In relation to world economy	Import and export tariffs, overvalued (dual or multiple) exchange rates Adjustment of import prices to national level	Import & export quota, foreign exchange controls, ban of goods to be imported or exported Restricting the number of trading companies	Regulations on customs and border crossing documentation
Credit markets	*Within country*	Subsidised credits Regulated spread Fixing lower than market clearing interest rates	Assigning monopoly rights for selected financial transactions Restricting number of financial institutions	Regulations to carry out financial transactions (e.g. provisioning) and to establish and run financial institutions
	In relation to world economy	Interest equalisation taxes Dual or multiple exchange rates on capital transactions	Foreign exchange controls, quantitative restrictions on capital movements	As above
Labour markets		Prescribed minimum wages or wage indexation	Oblige company or institutions to employ university graduates	Regulations to employ, promote or dismiss workers
Land markets		Fixed or maximum prices	Regulate size of attainable land, real estate allocation	Regulations on land use and scope of property

b) State as Entrepreneur or Client

Nationalising activities or entire industries Public enterprises mostly with soft budget constraints and priority treatment with regard to price, quantity and financing; marketing boards taking over purchase and/or sale, state bailing out the banks' accumulated bad debts

Awarding public procurement contracts and jobs: Preferential treatment of less qualified applicants

Providing public services: Passports, identity cards, social and infrastructure services, statistical data, etc.

c) Failure in Providing Institutions Which Adequately Restrain Rent-Seeking (Passive Rent Creation)

Rule of law (weak jurisdiction)	Property rights not secure because of discretionary application of regulations and failure of the state to prosecute corruption, blackmail, expropriation, breaking of contracts, externalisation of costs, burglary, etc.
Uncompetitive market environment	Allowing for cartel agreements Tolerating rent extraction by natural monopolies

Implicit taxation also takes the form of foreign exchange regulations. Substantial and long-lasting *exchange rate overvaluations* have been (and still are in some countries) the most consequential price intervention and often reflect successful pressures from privileged interest groups. The policy-induced shortage of foreign exchange at the official rate typically requires additional quantitative interventions, which further widen the scope of rent-seeking activities. Over-invoicing of imports, illegal arbitrage deals between parallel and official foreign exchange markets or 'mistaken' applications of wrong exchange rates at the treasury or the country's national bank are typical rent-seeking-related outcomes. As widely perceived, the agriculture sector has been suffering most from exchange-rate overvaluation. The one-sided extraction of agricultural surplus at the official exchange rate has not just negatively affected the growth potential of many countries but has equally been a major source of macro imbalances, in particular if the government relied on financing a large part of the budget with the volatile agriculture surplus.

Similar to shortages in the foreign exchange market, shortages caused by *maximum price regulations* on goods and services, as well as capital (interest rates below market clearing rates) require an additional allocation mechanism, which in most cases involves sizeable rent-seeking activities. In particular the allocation of cheap credits has created major rent-seeking opportunities. Since privileged interest groups may receive credits also at higher interest rates but subsequently default on the loan, a meaningful evaluation needs to be made ex-post.

In contrast to maximum price regulations, the setting of *prices above market-clearing rates* often reflects producers' lobbying efforts and is undertaken in a protected environment. National price commissions typically set these prices according to a cost-plus pricing system, where costs are to a considerable extent negotiable, i.e. the final output price reflects the sum of stated costs including a certain mark-up.

An evaluation of *minimum wage regulations* may require a careful analysis. Regulations either refer to the entire formal labour market or are limited to the public or civil service only. Even though regulations in labour markets can be the outcome of rent-seeking activities of well-organised trade unions, they may equally represent a measure to restrict entrepreneurs from taking advantage of general market failures. Likewise, an assessment of wage indexation may not be obvious from the outset. In the majority of the cases wage indexation protects wage earners from being gradually 'expropriated' by inflation. However, the measure may also prevent a fall in real wages when they are suggested by economic indicators and therefore create similar rents as with unjustified minimum wages. Finally, an aspect related to wage policies is the treatment of pensions (minimum pension, adjustment to inflation, etc.).

Higher wages officially approved or unofficially earned by corruption can raise unemployment rates when individuals give up low-paid jobs in search of the rents available in public employment. For a formal discussion see, for instance, World Bank (1990b, p. 25f), Demery and Addison (1993) or Fischer (1994, p. 26f). Furthermore, it has often been argued that scholars will invest significant time in accumulating special educational qualifications that enhance their chances to get an overpaid job (e.g. Mohammad and Whalley (1984, p. 400)).

As noted earlier, *quantitative and other interventions* often accompany price interventions. The assignment of monopoly rights or quotas reflects the most standard rent-seeking case. In LDCs monopolistic restrictions have typically affected all sectors, i.e. trading and processing in agriculture, mining, manufacturing, as well as services such as utility, transport, tourism and banking. In the majority of cases, the rent-creating intervention is not directed at private companies but public companies. Other regulations include obtaining permits for various activities, restrictions on labour and land (hiring and firing workers, administrative allocation of land, etc.) or quality requirements. Regulations often demand the periodic filing of a large number of forms. Regulations may also involve more than a hundred bureaucratic steps before a company can start a business and operate. They therefore effectively protect incumbents against new entrants, for instance foreign investors. Especially in a highly corrupt environment cumbersome bureaucratic regulations are accompanied by major delays and high levels of bribery.

This last aspect points to an important feature of rents and rent-seeking. Rents are not just created for private-sector people and companies but also for individuals who are part of the rent-producing apparatus, i.e. civil servants within the government. McChesney (1987) has introduced a useful differentiation between public rent creation and private rent extraction (the latter referring to 'good' rents, i.e. consumer and producer rents of profit-seeking activities).[8] In both cases government officials can reap rents from society. In the former, they may get a share of the benefits they create for individuals and companies (e.g. retain some of the subsidies they grant to a company); in the latter they cause losses to others, for instance, as McChesney (1997, p. 25) notes, by extorting payments for 'withholding action that would destroy existing private rents'.

---

8 As explained earlier and outlined in Figure 2-1, producer and consumer rents are not artificial rents and should not be confused with the concept of rent-seeking. They motivate economic behaviour and are an integral part of the market process to obtain gains from specialisation and trade. Their 'seeking' reflects the normal profit-seeking incentive.

Figure 2-2 outlines for a few selected examples additional rents that arise for *producers* from limiting competition and rents that *government officials* may obtain.[9] Both aspects are indicated with grey areas; the dark grey areas, however, refer to private rent extraction only, i.e. they signify the possible extraction of private consumer and producer rents by government officials. In addition, the diagrams indicate the traditional *welfare losses* involved (dotted areas), which are also called 'Harberger triangles' (according to Arnold Harberger's seminal contribution to measure welfare losses empirically; for a discussion see, for instance, Hines (1999)). The size of the rents and welfare losses depends on the elasticities of demand and supply, as well as the level of market intervention. Assuming that the country is not large enough to affect the prices on the world market, world demand and supply are drawn as horizontal lines.

The import tariff in a), the export subsidy in b) as well as the subsidy on non-tradeables in c)[10] allow domestic producers to earn more for each unit they sell. Given the higher revenue, producers typically expand their production, even though the additionally produced units imply higher costs than benefits for society (and therefore a net loss). The extra benefit in diagram a) or b) for producers is the output level B times τ respectively s, minus increased unit production costs associated with the additional units sold (dotted rectangle ABC). In diagram c) with a downward sloping demand curve the market price falls as the output level increases, dampening the benefit to producers (part of the subsidy is captured by the consumers).

Unlike diagrams a) to c), in diagrams d) to f) production is not expanded but reduced (or threatened to be reduced). Diagram d) indicates the optimal output level of a monopolist who limits output to sell remaining goods at a higher price.[11] Reducing output from the competitive level (A) to the level that maximises net revenue (B) increases the monopoly rent from zero to the rectangle $P^* P_M BC$. The diagrams e) and f) address cases of private *rent extraction*, an aspect which has been described in detail by McChesney (1997). For a brief reference in the context of African countries see also Rowley (2000, p. 142-44) who even concludes 'rent extraction is the raison d'être of African dictatorships' (p. 143).

---

9 The selection is arbitrary. Figure 2-2 may be extended by other LDC-relevant examples such as the case of import quota restrictions, an example that indicates the interaction between formal wage policies and informal labour markets, an assessment of overvaluation in a specific sector or a more sophisticated outline of different overlapping policies. All these interventions (or combinations thereof) are characterised by some kind of direct and indirect rent creation.

10 *Non-tradeables* are goods and services, which are—because of their nature and related transaction costs— always consumed in the country they origin; they therefore do not face direct competition from abroad. The categorisation in tradeables and non-tradeables and its dependence on transaction costs q is determined by the price relation: $P_{exportable} \leq P_{\text{world market}} /(1+q_{exp.}) \leq P_{non\text{-}tradeable} \leq P_{\text{world market}} (1+q_{imp.}) \leq P_{importables}$, whereas exportables are domestic goods which are consumed in the country and can also be exported; importables are domestic goods consumed in the country which also face import competition from abroad.

11 For simplicity, the diagram is drawn with the usual horizontal cost curve since a reduction in output with an upward-sloping curve additionally implies that some producer rents are lost, making the graphical depiction of the monopoly case unnecessarily complex.

Figure 2-2 (a-f): A Schematic Depiction of Policy-Related Rents

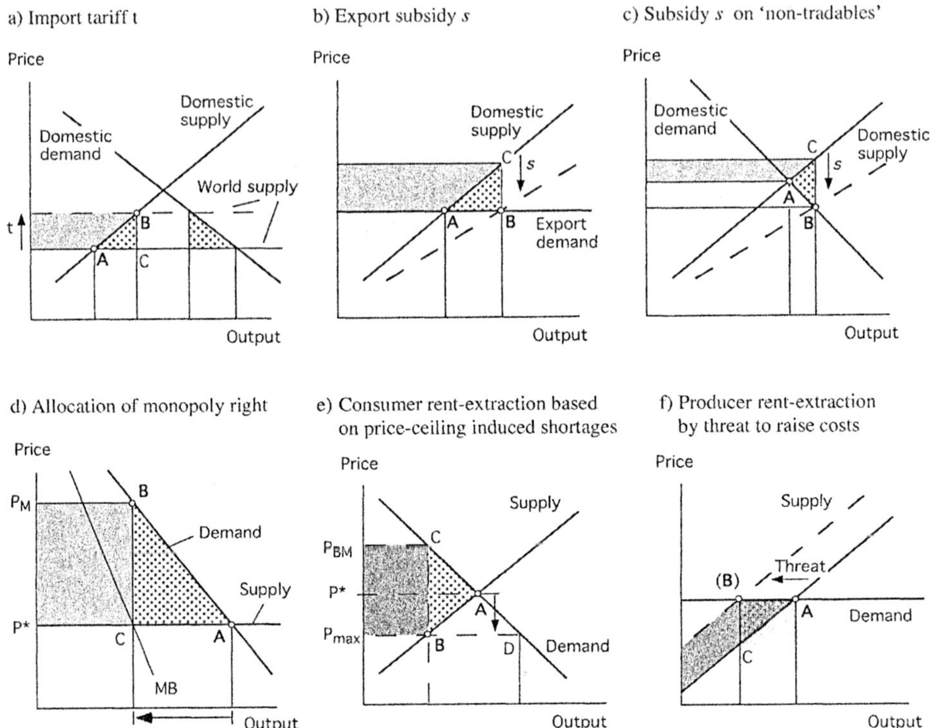

The diagrams delineate six cases of market interventions with their resulting rents and opportunities of rent extraction. Indicated are the policy's effect on *inland price* and *output* (move from A to B), *producer rents* (grey areas in a-d), areas of potential *private rent extraction* (dark area in e and f) and traditional *welfare loss* (dotted triangles). At the core of rent-seeking theory is the insight that rent-seekers use resources to create and capture these rents; rents and rent-seeking activities may thereby cause substantial welfare-reducing distortions.

Diagram e) displays how price controls can provide opportunities for rent extraction. Keeping prices below the market-clearing level generates the situation where demand exceeds supply ($P_{max}D > P_{max}B$) and where the willingness to pay for the reduced amount of goods and services available (P_{BM}) exceeds both the government-dictated maximum price P_{max}, as well as the original, free market equilibrium price P*. Corrupt officials typically distribute a share of the goods and services in short supply to friends and relatives or they charge an illegal higher parallel market rate (black market rate) P_{BM}. In a corrupt environment the policy therefore effects the contrary of what is usually intended with socially-motivated minimum price regulations (i.e. providing inexpensive goods and services to people in need).

Diagram f) finally shows a situation where politicians threaten producers to impose additional costs that shift the producers' supply curves upwards (and to the left). To prevent such a negative outcome producers are willing to pay politicians at the most the potential loss in producer rents, i.e. the grey area.[12]

Besides selective market interventions, a state can create rents by participating as an *entrepreneur or client*. This aspect is summarised in the second part of Table 2-1 (p. 38) and includes three aspects.

The potentially most comprehensive intervention is the situation where the government takes over a company or an entire industry. *State-owned companies*—also called *parastatals or public companies*—are not directly integrated into the government budget but have a budget and accounting system of their own (Eriksson (1993, p. 1)). Sometimes they are just a measure to carry out the market interventions described above.

State-owned enterprises generally face a mixture of different non-free-market conditions, which can make an analysis of rents and rent-seeking quite complex. Many state-owned enterprises are given monopoly powers, which they also exert. Public enterprises, however, may equally be obliged to sell their products at very low prices. This may cause shortages and again create scope for rent-promising black market activities.

Most public enterprises are not subject to a binding budget constraint. Even though officially stipulated, they are not forced to operate according to commercial criteria, and because of frequent government interference in many cases they are even not allowed to do so. In particular soft budget constraints in the financial sector have been costly and explain a great deal of soft budget constraints in the economy (credits have been largely allocated to uncredit-worthy clients and politically-controlled central banks, and commercial banks offer much more leeway for money creation). Governments support parastatals in industrialised countries as well, but political opportunities to cover deficits of state-owned enterprises are, apart from a few exceptions, much more limited, especially as the allocation of support is under parliamentary scrutiny.

Besides running own companies, *awarding public contracts* is a second way a government can directly participate in a market and may create and allocate rents. Treasuries and ministries of works, which are both in charge of allocating substantial amounts of own government funds as well as donor funds, approve projects and contracts worth millions of dollars. Demanding services from private and public companies per se does not create rents; it does, however, if the procurement is not carried out according to commercial criteria but favours certain individuals and companies, and if the contracts are overpriced and only partly enforced. Under such conditions the government's acting as a client also undermines a competitive market outcome, as is the case when the government directly intervenes in markets.

Finally, any government typically provides *direct services* that are important in a society. These services are either of an administrative-legal nature such as issuing identity cards and passports or allocating specific certificates and permits

12 Again the example is kept simple, this time with the choice of a horizontal demand curve (with a downward sloping curve, the reduction in output has an additional beneficial impact on producers as it increases the market price).

related to free healthcare and education. A government may also produce a service itself, for instance, collecting and categorising statistical information. If not directly integrated in the main budget, such activities are often undertaken as non-commercial parastatals, or in more recent years (in the course of reforms that aim to improve the efficiency of the civil service) as executive agencies which function as semi-autonomous government bodies. The higher the difference between the value of the service and the official price, the higher potential benefits of public officials from extorting or accepting bribes.

The last section of Table 2-1 summarises incidences where the state *creates rents passively* when it fails to provide a favourable institutional setting characterised by secure property rights and a competitive market environment. *Weak rule of law* partly overlaps with the rent creation mentioned in Sections a) and b) of Table 2-1, as it does not just cover private rent-seeking settings but equally subsumes the non-prosecution of any illegal government-related rent-seeking activity that may arise with the poor implementation of the policies outlined in the table.[13]

In many LDCs, as well as economies in transition in eastern Europe and the former Soviet Union, contract violation, corruption, blackmail or burglary are poorly prosecuted by the state. Although the situation is not perfect in other countries, there is still a major difference in the degree one can rely on secure property rights and contract enforcement (e.g. North (1990, p. 59)). North even sees the inability of societies to develop effective, low-cost enforcement of contracts as the 'most important source of stagnation to be observed in the history of nations and of contemporary underdevelopment in the Third World' (North (1990, p. 54)).

Weak rule of law has several patterns. A situation may not be regulated at all or institutions to enforce a regulation are lacking. A country may not have formulated appropriate bankruptcy laws or may lack regulations that effectively address new forms of crime such as computer fraud. However, far more common is the deliberate non-implementation of established rules, norms and regulations. In most incidences the situation reflects a lack of commitment from the top leadership and is therefore neither a problem of capacity or a principal-agent conflict between rulers and their implementing subordinates, but a calculated measure of the ruling elite and its entourage to enrich themselves.

In settings where corruption is institutionalised, regulations are typically not clear and include a large scope of discretion and interpretation. They may change frequently so that individuals cannot rely on their property rights, and they may be formulated in a way to offer indirect but obvious opportunities of personal enrichment. Pritzl (1997, p. 192), for instance, notes that Brazil's insolvency regulation included up to two years' prolongation of debts at zero-

[13] The term 'rule of law' has been used in a narrow and in a broad sense. The International Country Risk Guide (ICRG (2003)), for instance, applies a broad definition for their variable 'rule of law'. They describe the term as the 'degree to which the citizens of a country are willing to accept the established institutions to make and implement laws and adjudicate disputes'. With their definition, high scores not only indicate a strong court system, but also sound political institutions and provisions for an orderly succession of power.

interest rates even when monthly inflation rates were running at two digits. Clearly, under conditions of ambiguous and rent-seeking-type regulations many beneficial activities which would enhance welfare by realising gains from production and trade are simply not undertaken.

Finally, as noted above, besides the failure of the state to provide an institutional setting with secure property rights, the state can create rents passively when it *fails to guarantee a competitive market environment.* Even though the state plays only an indirect role, this is another example of a more traditional type of rent-seeking. Cases in point are tolerating cartel agreements or allowing private companies in the position of a natural monopoly to extract monopoly rents.

All in all, government activities may or may not relate to rents and rent-seeking. Rent-seeking behaviour is not only an outcome of rent-creating policies, but also to a considerable extent the consequence of a poor implementation of government policies. Institutionally weak states are often not able to cope with self-imposed interventions or, more frequently, ruling elites deliberately abuse the power of the state to enrich themselves and to allocate rents to cronies. Therefore, given the differing character of states and institutional capacities similar policy measures, whether or not socially motivated, may have very different implications if adopted in a setting of secure property rights or in a setting where bribery is neither investigated nor prosecuted.

b) Rent-Seeking Activities in LDCs

Since on the one hand a *single state intervention or activity* may induce rent-seeking on different levels, and on the other hand *rent-seeking activities* of different interventions may be quite similar, it is helpful to distinguish the two aspects in an overview. The same holds for the identity of rent-seekers and those who lose out. Economic policies typically overlap; they only jointly determine the value of the rents. Rent-seeking winners and losers may therefore be associated with different policies and rent-seeking activities. This section will outline a typology of rent-seeking activities.

Depending on the character of the state, individual opportunities to create and capture rents may be considerably enhanced if individuals are not outside the government but work in government institutions (and related organisations). This is especially true for countries with a weak rule of law and no or ineffective democratic checks and balances. In most poorly-managed developing countries a major part of rent-seeking is done from a position inside the government. Government officials, here defined in a broad way, comprise legislators and executing and enforcing agencies, i.e. parliamentarians and bureaucrats in the narrow sense (people working in ministries and departments of central and local governments), as well as people in the army and police force, judges and parastatal managers and employees.

Table 2-2 surveys rent-seeking activities from a position outside the government and Table 2-3 (p. 50) outlines rent-seeking activities of people inside government institutions and related organisations.[14] Even though the tables include an overlap in two-sided rent-seeking situations (e.g. cases of cost-reducing and benefit-enhancing corruption), they offer a practical introduction and overview.

In developing countries, some of the functions of the government are carried out by another important group of actors, i.e. *the donor community*. Donors either operate directly in the country or they channel funds indirectly through government institutions and non-government organisations (NGOs). Since donors typically allocate large amounts of funds, they are also targets of rent-seeking activities. The tables therefore not only apply to government institutions in the narrow sense as rent-creating and distributing institutions, but hold for donor organisations and local NGOs that carry out similar functions.

The first part of Table 2-2 outlines rent-seeking investments to *change rules, laws and regulations* in one's favour and rent-seeking investments to *protect already secured rents*. In most societies a considerable number of individuals and interest groups succeed in influencing regulations to their own advantage at the expense of public welfare. Efforts to maintain a high level of protection in the agriculture sector or successful lobbying against the introduction of cost-internalising measures are common examples in industrialised countries.[15]

Depending on the rent-creating (or rent-protecting) policy as well as the political and institutional setting in the country, rent-seekers need to influence legal, political or economic rules and have to address different key groups and institutions. These include members of the cabinet, parliamentary committees and supervisory boards, principal secretaries and other senior civil servants, as well as public officials in the broad sense, i.e. judges to influence legal proceedings and court judgements, police and military colonels who are important in the decision-making process, or board members of parastatal companies who have a say on price regulations and other market interventions. Rent-seekers may equally have to address public opinion in general (voters) or specific interest groups such as opposition parties, ethnic and religious groups, unions and business associations.

The related rent-seeking activities include lobbying (e.g. ensuring constant presence on a specific matter) or public information campaigns in the media, bribery and cultivating patronage relations, also food riots, violent strikes and other militant demonstrations. Especially when it comes to implementing unpopular stabilisation measures potential violent reactions can constitute a real threat to policymakers.

---

[14] The structuring of the tables partly draws on Mbaku (1992) who analysed bureaucratic corruption as a rent-seeking behaviour. For an alternative typology and listing of corrupt activities, see, among others, Kaufmann (1998b, p. 167-171)), who differentiates between the categories bribes, theft, patronage and influence peddling.

[15] For an early example of the environmental debate, for instance, see Buser (1984), who addresses legislation in Switzerland.

Table 2-2 (a-c): Rent-Seeking Activities from a Position Outside Government and Government-Related Institutions

a) Rent-creating and protecting activities

Influence key persons, groups and institutions within society to create or defend a rent-bearing regulation or procedure

Measures: Lobbying, sponsoring, (dis)information campaigns; bribery and exploiting patronage relations; demonstrations, strikes and riots

b) Rent-capturing activities

I. Public official supplies rent

- Comply with criteria (laws and rules): 'factual' approach
  Distribution according to application arguments and intensity (paperwork), installed capacity, type of goods produced, number of applicants, queuing, etc.
- Influence rent-distributing agency: 'personal' approach
  Distribution based on bribery and patronage. Effected influence or transaction is often illegal (benefit enhancing and cost reducing corruption)

II. Public official does not directly supply the rent

- Bypass bureaucrat by smuggling, capital flight or cheating.
- Force transfers in private sector (expropriation, robbery, blackmail, threat, etc.)

c) Efforts to become part of the rent-producing government

I. Entry by non-violent means

- Choose a higher or specific education to enhance chances to get a job in the rent-distributing bureaucracy
- Influence key persons, groups and institutions in society (bribery and patronage, campaigns, etc.) to enhance the chances of being elected or appointed to a rent-promising position

II. Capturing the rent-creating government

- Come to power by coup d'état or military revolt

Most bribes are in the form of cash payments. Bribery may also take the form of in-kind transfers, which include all sorts of benefits, such as free dinners, shares in a company, the promise to organise a job for a relative of the rent-distributing official, or, most typically in shortage-ridden and corrupt economies, making available goods or services which are difficult to obtain. Personal and patronage relations include godparenthood and marriages (among relatives of beneficiaries and the families of the rent-creating officials) or taking advantage of membership in the same tribe, political party or religious group. The relevance of campaigns and campaign contributions obviously rises with the level of democratisation, and bribery and cultivating patronage relations are far more prevalent in LDCs than industrialised countries.

Rents are frequently created without specifying the exact beneficiaries in advance. In addition, some policies (or the weak implementation of policies) generate situations where rents are not offered but can nevertheless be seized illegally (explained below). Both situations typically induce *rent-seeking investments to capture rents*. The activities are summarised in the second part of Table 2-2.

As noted earlier, price interventions, which lead to a situation where demand exceeds supply, require an additional allocation mechanism. Price interventions may apply to goods or services, bank loans (interest rates) or foreign exchange. The more an economy becomes unbalanced the larger the shortages are and the more valuable implicit rents become. Rents may also take the form of preferential access to subsidies, cheap loans and investments from the treasury; or they may come from donor aid (donor funds are often channelled through the treasury and redistributed as loans or grants to the recipients).

In general, the rent-seeking investments necessary to obtain rents depend on the rules of distribution, above all the freedom of choice (discretion) of public officials. Depending on the setting, complying with strict criteria (factual approach) or relying on bribery and patronage relations (personal approach) may become the dominant rent-seeking strategy. The latter are in most cases illegal and describe two-sided rent-seeking situations where regulations are bent and the public official captures a share of the rent. However 'factual' approaches may also include illegal activities, for instance when applicants falsify information (e.g. accounting figures) to obtain benefits.

Rents which are not supplied by a public official or authority but which are illegally acquired include both public and private settings. A smuggler may not bribe the customs officer but choose a hidden route to get goods across the border. Burglars or citizens who renege on contracts obtain rents that are not voluntarily given. As outlined earlier, these rent-seeking opportunities arise from the failure of the state to secure property rights. As long as it pays to smuggle goods or to force transfers from others by blackmail, expropriation or robbery, this kind of rent-seeking activity will endur. Clearly, in many countries the distinction between rents which are offered and those which are not is blurred. For example, burglars or criminals who are caught may easily bribe their way out before, during or even after legal proceedings.

Because rent-seeking opportunities for individuals are usually enhanced if they belong to the government and government-related institutions—in many non-democratic settings rents are simply not available for those who are outside the politically dominant groups (Mbaku (1992, p. 250))—the last section in Table 2-2 shows the *efforts of rent-seekers to become part of the rent-producing apparatus*.

There are undoubtedly many valuable reasons for individuals and parties to participate in government or even to get into a ruling position. However, many African countries saw predatory rulers come to power with virtually no other motivation than enriching themselves and their entourage (in particular, the discussion in Chapter 4.3 will look at this aspect). Mbaku (1992, p. 250) even identifies violence (besides bureaucratic corruption) as the most important kind of rent-seeking behaviour in developing countries. Moreover, people who try to acquire jobs in the middle and lower level bureaucracy often use pseudo-legal and illegal means to get their positions.

At this stage, as several economists have argued, transfers like bribes to public officials can become wasteful to society indirectly. Time and resources dedicated to higher education are often 'wasted', for instance when university graduates become corrupt customs officers whose main motivation is to divert funds into their own pockets. Furthermore, individuals may accept a long period of unemployment while endeavouring to get into a rent-promising position, even though their skills would enable them to pursue productive activities in the private sector. The sizeable rents customs officers, tax enforcers, judges and people issuing import and export licences can obtain become apparent from the bribes candidates are prepared to pay to be appointed to such positions. The amount may even exceed the official annual wage by a multiple. Finally, substantial costs for the society are incurred with the most violent form of penetrating the state apparatus, i.e. the destruction and murder involved in a coup d'état.

Once individuals have obtained a position inside government and government-related institutions, rent-seeking opportunities are typically enhanced. In contrast to industrialised countries, public officials in developing countries have much more leeway to create rents themselves or to capture a share of the rents they ought to distribute. This is partly due to the weak capacity of state institutions to enforce property rights and to control public officials, and partly a calculated measure of the ruler to benefit supporters. Most of the rent-seeking activities therefore take the form of bureaucratic corruption. Table 2-3 summarises rent-seeking activities from a position inside the government (and related institutions).

Similar to the description in Table 2-2, public officials may either engage in rent-seeking activities to *create and protect* rents or to *capture* rents. Table 2-3 is grouped accordingly. Although many of the rent-creating and rent-protecting activities are legal in nature, most of them directly relate to bureaucratic corruption, as they aim to create or maintain an environment where illegal rent-seeking activities are feasible and highly rewarded. Critical factors are the cost components of corruption, which include the probabilities of being discovered, caught, sentenced and punished, as well as different aspects that relate to the size of rents.[16] The larger the responsibilities, power and discretion of public officials, and the more monopolistic the structure of the 'rent-distributing' agency, the larger are the potential rents.

Making sure that procedures, laws and regulations are formulated in an ambiguous and ill-defined way increases discretion, as the room for interpretation and subjective decision-making is enhanced. Making processes more complex and choosing projects that are capital-intensive and unique increase

---

16 This aspect will be discussed in Chapter 4 (see, among others, Tables 4-1 and 4-5 on the pages 153 and 217).

Table 2-3 (a-b): Rent-Seeking Activities from a Position Inside Government and Government-Related Institutions

a) Rent-creating and rent-protecting activities by public officials

Set regulations, make decisions and conduct operational work in a way that maximises the level of rents that can be extracted

Oppose any structural and operational reforms that reduce opportunities to capture rents

b) Rent-capturing activities by public officials

I. Private rent extraction (basis: extorting payments)
Cost-enhancing and benefit-reducing corruption

- When distributing goods which are in shortage due to price ceilings, charge buyers what approximates a competitive price for the product
- Appropriate a portion of the monopoly profit associated with the licence by charging buyers a price higher than the one set by government regulation
- Abuse the state's coercive power to extort side payments from the private sector by first threatening and then by forbearing to impose harmful regulations
- Directly appropriate benefits of individuals, e.g. delay payments and appropriate the interest generated

II. Private rent creation (basis: accepting bribes and cultivating patronage)
Cost-reducing and benefit-enhancing corruption

- Offer exemptions from compliance with certain regulations (such as tax regulations) on condition that the savings generated are shared
- Offer transfer benefits to individuals or groups in excess of the amounts they are legally due on the condition of sharing the gains

III. Theft (basis: theft of public property)

Losses of cash, stores and other public assets. Embezzling funds through fake transactions (unvouched and improperly vouched expenditures, unjustified allowances, employing ghost workers, etc.)

Source: Examples of cost and benefit enhancing/reducing corruption from Mbaku (1992, p. 254), reference to threat from McChesney (1997, p. 19)

opportunities for rent extraction. Reducing the probability or costs of being caught in a corrupt transaction again increases the relative profitability of bureaucratic corruption.

In many developing countries ruling elites deliberately grant discretion and keep cost components of corruption low. This enables them to benefit subordinate bureaucrats, to channel resources to selective regime supporters outside the government and to punish individuals and groups hostile to the regime. Because reforms typically aim to reduce these opportunities, they generate direct and indirect rent-seeking resistance.

The second part of Table 2-3 differentiates between the three rent-capturing activities *private rent extraction, private rent creation* and *theft*. It partly incorporates McChesney's division between private rent extraction and public rent creation, as well as Mbaku's distinction of four classes of corrupt activities which either increase or reduce cost and benefits to private clients. As noted earlier, the case of private rent creation overlaps with the rent-seeking situation described in Section b) of Table 2-2 ('personal approach'); it takes, however, the counterpart's perspective. Finally, in the third case (theft) the public official is not necessary in contact with a private counterpart but may steal public property from the government or from a government-related institution.

Private rent extraction is based on extortion, here understood in a broad sense, i.e. extortion may equally relate to the distribution of public benefits, for instance demanding a higher price for subsidised goods an individual is legally due (this approach contrasts McChesney's more strict delimitation of private rent extraction from 'public rent creation'). There are many ways public officials can extract payments from individuals or directly withhold some of the benefits individuals should obtain. The high potential of rent extraction from shortages caused by price ceilings has already been outlined in Figure 2-2. Another even more harmful activity for economic development is the deliberate creation of bureaucratic impediments.

Futile layers of bureaucracy and ridiculously cumbersome procedures, in particular the deliberate delay or selective denial of services, provide public officials ample opportunities to extort payments in exchange for expediting and shortening processes or approving permits. Even though private companies typically react to harassments by escaping into the informal sector, this option is usually only available for very small companies (one-man undertakings or family businesses with only few workers) or for specific activities. Similar to goods in short supply, the monopolistic supply of permits and services, which often are not costly but indispensable to private clients, permit much higher prices to be charged than the ones officially approved. Many of these permits and services do not include a transfer of rents to private clients. As McChesney (1997, p. 27) notes, occupational licence, corporate charter and building permits, for instance, are privileges, which are easily obtained and do not prevent entry in any effective way, however, the 'selective denial of these privileges unless certain wealth is surrendered provides a fertile source of rent extraction'.

Finally, politicians and civil servants may even directly approach private companies or individuals by threatening to introduce a policy that would diminish part of their welfare, as for instance outlined in diagram f) in Figure 2-2 (p. 42). In general, the policy may include a threat to introduce price controls, to withdraw a privilege or to raise costs (see McChesney (1997, p. 26f) for a more detailed discussion).

The second group of rent-capturing activities outlined in Table 2-3 is *private rent creation*, which describes a situation where both parties illegitimately benefit from a cost-reducing or benefit-enhancing transaction. In contrast to the case of extortion, where private companies or individuals pay the official for not reducing their welfare, here they compensate public officials for an illegitimate increase in their welfare.

Cost-reducing corruption includes illegitimate tax reductions, the evasion of regulations such as security prescriptions or environmental laws or a public official not prosecuting obvious illegal activities such as drug trafficking, smuggling and money laundering. Tax enforcers and customs officials, for instance, may misclassify or underreport taxable items, issue certificates of exemptions for individuals and companies who do not qualify, remove or falsify taxpayers' records, cheat on tax refund claims or write off tax-related debts.

An area particularly prone to abuse is bonded warehousing. Bonded warehouses are special compounds for the storage of untaxed goods in transit, i.e. they store goods from abroad to be transferred to other countries. However, because of leakages these goods often find their way untaxed into domestic markets. Leakages mostly result from poor record keeping. Officials, in collaboration with private clients, may even set fires to destroy transit documents.

Cost-reducing corruption is also prevalent in law-enforcement institutions. As noted in World Bank (2001b, p. 7) 'the goal is to "pin" someone in a violation of the law and then to allow them to negotiate their way out, at a price'.

Benefit-enhancing corruption includes among other things the distribution of subsidised goods and services to individuals who do not qualify for such, the preferential treatment of companies in procurement contracts, the provision of monopoly rights or the selling of state property at far too low prices. In particular procurement and the related tendering processes have been a major area of corruption.

A company may not be able to tender unless it pays a hidden 10%. A senior public official will then provide the necessary insider information to win the tender or the official can influence the result by altering the weighting of the criteria. In highly corrupt settings, the tendering parties themselves may agree in advance who is going to submit tenders and whose turn it is to win. After the winner of the tender is determined, additional kickbacks typically flow to the ministry. The government itself provides the extra money needed by substantially inflating the project budget. Not infrequently the list of possible contractors consists of companies of people in the government and close friends only, i.e. though the books show private companies these belong to people in the ministry and affiliated friends. Finally, if bribery and personal enrichment do not leave sufficient funds to execute the project properly, quality suffers badly or the government can provide additional funds to compensate for 'unforeseen' cost overruns.

Theft constitutes the last category of rent-capturing activities outlined in Table 2-3, here defined as a situation where an official directly appropriates public funds. In an environment where theft is prevalent, corrupt public officials will typically conceal balances and transactions. Accounting standards are generally poor and accountants may fail to produce financial statements, such as bank reconciliation statements. Furthermore, complaints and recommendations from the Office of the Controller and Auditor General (OCAG) (an institution charged with producing independent audit reviews of public accounts) are persistently disregarded. The empirical section on Tanzania will quote many examples related to large-scale embezzlement and ignoring OCAG complaints.

Tables 2-2 and 2-3 showed one possible way to structure rent-seeking activities, even though the classification of cases is not always clear-cut, as the following two examples demonstrate. If public officials are empowered to determine quality grades of commodities corruption may either relate to benefit-enhancing or benefit-reducing corruption, depending on the final assessment. Likewise the dividing line between private rent extraction by extortion and public rent creation is at times blurred. McChesney (1997, p. 68), referring to Brook, notes that Fernando Collor de Mello, Brazil's president from 1990 to 1992, was a master in 'creating rents for a price with one hand while extracting existing private rents with the other', by introducing high taxes and then selling the relief worth hundreds of million dollars for a fifth in payments to him.

c) Who Wins and Loses from Rent-Seeking in LDCs?

Having discussed rent-related policies and rent-seeking activities, this last section rounds off the survey with an assessment of rent-seeking winners and losers. Two characteristics determined the dividing line between the groups that have been more successful in obtaining benefits in a poor policy environment, and other groups that have immediately lost. The first aspect is the unequal distribution of legal and illegal *financial support, social services and infrastructure facilities*; the second is the substantial *exchange rate overvaluation*, partly combined with *import restrictions*, which persisted in many countries over long periods of time.

In most countries policies and distortions put the *rural population* at a clear disadvantage relative to citizens in *urban areas*. Though a considerable share of the population lives in rural areas, they have not obtained the attention and resources they deserve. Usually shortages of goods first appear outside urban centres; rural hospitals obtain fewer medicines, and rural teachers sometimes have to wait for months before they get paid. Rural roads are often not passable in the rainy seasons and it may be decades before the central government allocates funds to fix the problem permanently. A large body of literature supports the general perception that a major part of the subsidies, treasury investments and other types of government support have not benefited the rural poor.[17]

Farmers are generally seen as net losers affected by the poor policies in developing countries, though rents and rent extraction have sometimes varied considerably in the agricultural sector depending on the country, the period of

[17] E.g. IMF (1986, p. 39), Bourguignon and Morrisson (1992, p. 42) or Krueger (1996, p. 167f).

time and the crop or livestock. In addition, policies can affect sub-groups like subsistence farmers, medium-sized farmers, big landowners and landless farm labourers differently.

Krueger (1996) provides a good overview of the bias against the agricultural sector. Evaluating the findings of a comprehensive study of eighteen developing countries, she notes (p. 174), 'the share of investment expenditures allocated to increasing agricultural infrastructure (including such diverse items as rural roads, irrigation, storage capacity, and rural education) was far smaller than the share of taxes (explicit plus implicit) that agriculture paid'. Furthermore, agricultural pricing policies (basically the suppression of producer prices) increased income inequality, as a significant part of the costs was borne by landless rural labourers and poor farmers. Beneficiaries, by contrast, were in most cases in the middle and upper income groups (p. 168). Finally, farmers also suffered losses in purchasing power because of the high prices of protected manufactured goods (p. 168).

The bias against agriculture has been particularly pronounced in Africa. According to another study from Krueger (cited in Rodrik (1997, p. 58)), taxation of agriculture through marketing boards and low producer prices averaged 23% in Africa, while it was only 2.5% in Asia and 6.4% in Latin America. Including the effects of exchange rate overvaluation and import restrictions, the study even concludes that taxation in Africa more than doubled to 51.6%.

The extraction of agriculture surplus is commonly justified with the need to finance an industry development strategy. However, besides the fact that a lot of resources were embezzled within government institutions, much taxation was 'dissipated', as also argued in Krueger (1996, p. 167), by the inefficiency of marketing boards, transfers to urban consumers and large-scale embezzlement and inefficient investments in public enterprises.

Consumers are usually mentioned as a group with interests that are difficult to organise. For LDCs, this argument has to be differentiated since urban consumers can also become unruly if key prices rise. Nevertheless, though a change in the subsidisation of a basic foodstuff can provoke immediate protest and food riots, policies limiting competition, which indirectly lead to higher prices and lower quality, are not an issue to make consumers take to the streets. Furthermore, in developing countries a considerable share of revenue is raised by indirect taxes which are typically regressive in nature, and middle and upper-income families often enjoy privileged access to subsidised goods. Poorer consumers therefore appear to be on the losing side, while rich people can secure substantial benefits.

Students organise for different reasons, many of them not related to rent-seeking. Being well-educated and organised at university, they can constitute a powerful and volatile interest group and even revolt in highly repressed countries. They can sometimes successfully promote their personal interests if the government threatens to curtail benefits at the university.

However, much more relevant for the analysis here is that in most developing countries university places are often only available for children of privileged families. These families, usually part of the ruling elites, have been successful in lobbying against a reduction in government expenditures on university education. In most cases government support not only includes payment for classrooms, research expenses and teaching but also boarding costs, which relatively wealthy families could easily pay. Obviously, the allocation of benefits mostly to wealthy families is unlikely to reflect the preferences of society in a poor country. The rent-seeking allocation becomes even more apparent, considering the limited budget for education, and the high trade-offs between financing a student at university and financing pupils in primary schools. In Tanzania, for instance, the cost of a university education is equivalent to that for 238 primary school students (see page 403).

Private companies constitute a particularly heterogeneous group, i.e. there are many factors which determine whether an individual company benefits or loses from rent-seeking policies and rent-seeking activities. Companies which are situated in or near the capital generally find it easier to influence public officials in the policymaking process than their rural counterparts, and they can more easily access various types of government and donor support (e.g. grants, subsidised credits or underpriced foreign exchange). The size of benefits and costs, however, further depends on whether a company produces in the import-substituting or exporting sector, whether production has to rely on access to scarce goods or imported goods. It further depends on the size of the companies and more generally on the government's public service delivery, above all the creation of an enabling and supportive private sector environment. In a corrupt environment, for instance, small and medium-sized enterprises usually suffer more than large companies. Tanzi and Davoodi (2000, p. 8) elaborated on this aspect:

> 'Large enterprises ... have specialized departments; they can use "facilitators"-individuals with skills to bypass the regulations and tax laws; their size protects them from petty bureaucrats; and they can use political power to further their rent-seeking corruption to their advantage. For large enterprises corruption is often of a cost-reducing kind as it allows them to enjoy monopoly rents and scale economies; whereas for small and medium size enterprises it is often of a cost-increasing kind because they have to make payments which do not contribute to the productivity or profitability of the firm but that are necessary for their survivability.'

Private-sector labour has rarely been organised in developing countries (in contrast to industrialised countries). Nabli and Nugent (1989, p. 98) mention mining and other extractive industries as examples, as well as situations where unions appeared at an early stage because they were formed for political reasons (clientelism) or because they emerged as countervailing forces against the management of multinational enterprises.

Besides the extent of unionism, the interaction of the formal with the informal sector is a crucial aspect which codetermines possible rent distributions between capital owners, managers and workers. Informal workers usually cannot exert power as an interest group. This explains, as Bourguignon and Morrisson observed, the adverse effect in many developing countries that during a recession wages usually fall more than profits. They argue 'the informal sector represents a labour reserve which makes it easier to cut real wages during a recession' (Bourguignon and Morrisson (1992, p. 36)).

Bureaucrats and politicians are an interest group that includes major rent-seeking profiteers in most developing countries. As employees in the state administration or nominated representatives in leading or controlling committees, many of them attained high privileges and exploited a wide range of rent-creating and rent-capturing activities. In particular public officials in the treasury (including the tax and customs departments) and other government institutions that allocate permits, benefits, and contracts (ministries of works, local housing, health, or natural resource and tourism, etc.), as well as official prosecutors and judges or members of parliaments and parliamentary committees have been in a position of receiving or extorting substantial extra benefits. The same argument applies to local governments and provincial authorities, which have frequently been accused of being involved in corrupt activities. In general, depending on the character of the state, the policies in the centre and the level of decentralisation, a larger distance from the centre may enhance or reduce rent-seeking opportunities.[18]

The *parastatal sector* is an area where substantial rents have been created. Living on soft budget constraints, many of the parastatal companies turned into bastions of inefficiency and embezzlement. A combination of government support, monopoly protection and patronage permitted companies to survive for decades despite persisting losses, lack of accountability, poor services and, because of the low quality, excessive prices for manufactured goods (in many cases these prices are determined by simple cost-plus calculations, which imply that there is no incentive for saving costs as additional costs can always be added to the final output price).

Inefficiencies are particularly costly if parastatals fail to provide essential goods and services and there is no private sector alternative (e.g. monopoly parastatals in charge of public transport, the supply of electricity or telecommunication services). Top managers as well as select middle and low-level employees are often the main beneficiaries of the rents in parastatal companies. However, members of supervising boards, civil servants in certain ministries, as well as customers with preferential access to goods and services in short supply may also appropriate a considerable share of the benefits.

Finally, *military and police forces*, as well as individuals of *tribal or religious groups* that are represented by the ruling elites often belong to the main rent-seeking winners, particularly in non-democratic settings. As Kimenyi

[18] For a formal discussion on some related aspects, see, for instance, Epstein, Hillman and Ursprung (1998).

and Mbaku (1995, p. 701) note, in non-democratic systems (which still characterise many developing countries) groups with greater potential to impose force dominate competition for rents, i.e. a regime may for instance not be able to reduce allocations to the military as it would create discontent and destabilise the government. Often the army receives benefits without having lobbied much for them. In this case, the mere threat of violence can generate substantial rent allocations.

All in all, this brief assessment of rent-seeking beneficiaries and losers gives an idea of general patterns of support in LDCs; it cannot replace a detailed, country-specific analysis, however. Furthermore, an interest group analysis is not without limitations. As Haggard and Webb (1993, p. 144), referring to Nelson, note, individuals simultaneously occupy several positions—as consumers, producers, savers, members of a family, religion or tribe—which may not coincide. The discussion therefore mainly provides a general idea and may have to be extended by a more detailed country-specific typology which takes into consideration the overlap of different roles, policies and regulations.

Ultimately, evaluating the costs and benefits of rent-seeking from a *dynamic and long-term* perspective will most likely reveal that a vast majority of citizens are net losers. Though individuals or specific interest groups may benefit from a single rent-creating policy, other rent-seekers benefit from other rent-creating policies and thereby impose high costs on society. (Frequently the cost of a specific rent-seeking activity comprises a multitude of benefits reaped by rent-seekers.) As long as the individual benefits are not very high, overall rent-seeking costs are likely to dominate for all groups. Chapter 3 (in particular Chapter 3.3) discusses numerous aspects which determine the rent-seeking costs imposed on society, and the case study on Tanzania offers many examples which demonstrate the high costs and overt inefficiency of rent-seeking policies and activities.

This chapter has repeatedly emphasised the *twofold role* of governments, i.e. although a government has to undertake important and indispensable functions in a society, it is also the government that can create most of the rent-seeking opportunities. This duality is also illustrated in Table 2-1 (p. 38f), which lists many traditional government policies and interventions that may or may not create rent-seeking activities. Particularly relevant is the insight that a great deal of rent-seeking cannot be explained by a specific government policy or regulation alone; what often matters much more is the implementation and enforcement of the policy or regulation.

Whether policymakers undertake activities and regulations that benefit a society largely depends on the quality of *checks and balances*. In a country with strong rent-seeking forces and a lack of checks and balances, interventions and other activities of the state have to be reconsidered, as the state cannot be sufficiently protected against rent-seeking by civil servants and powerful interest groups. Checks and balances ultimately determine the type and appropriate size of a government in a society and the optimal level of flexibility and discretion built into the bureaucratic apparatus. The higher the risk that the government's power can be misused, the smaller is the optimal size for the government, and it becomes more relevant to implement rigid systems which allow only little freedom of choice.

But since policymakers are frequently rent-seekers themselves and impede the implementation of checks and balances, conclusions on the optimal size of governments are not of much policy relevance in a country with an adverse political culture. Suggestions can however guide the subset of truly benevolent-minded policymakers as well as bilateral and multilateral donors that may have an influence on the government's policymaking.

In Africa many countries have become rent-seeking economies, where a great number of civil servants, lawyers and parastatal managers only marginally act in society's interest, focusing instead on earning income in a non-productive (and even destructive) way. As demonstrated in this chapter, there are many possible rent-seeking opportunities and even the definition of rents is not necessarily clear-cut. Societies in developing countries obviously face much larger principal-agent conflicts between citizens and the state than industrialised countries. Rent-creating policies may still be officially justified with arguments concerning market failure; a closer look, however, reveals that in countries with a weak rule of law and no checks and balances many of these arguments are used to hide rent-seeking avarice. Actions taken are then not properly designed; they do not reach their originally intended targets and largely serve as a vehicle to appropriate rents.

It goes without saying that industrialised countries are not free from rent-seeking activities and related inefficiencies either. In fact, no society is free of rent-seeking, and costs generated by rent-seeking in industrialised countries are probably also substantial. However, the picture of rent-seeking in developing countries, above all in sub-Saharan Africa, is different. What distinguishes many of these countries from industrialised countries is the much higher degree of such rent-seeking activities. And since average incomes in these countries are very low, rent-creating and rent-protecting activities exert a particularly negative impact both on the poor and on the countries' development prospects. Unlike most industrialised countries, LDCs can simply less afford to be inefficient.

The need for major reforms in countries which have become rent-seeking economies is clear. The challenge of reform policies mainly consists in limiting rent-seeking and reversing the negative trends in many of these countries by guiding or forcing an ever-larger part of the society, business community, and civil servants into productive activities. Rent-seekers will, however, not give up their privileges without resistance. Above all, the lack of checks and balances and transparency, and the ease of hiding rent-seeking activities gives them a competitive edge. The half-hearted reforms, delays and setbacks experienced in many countries in sub-Saharan Africa in the 1980s and 1990s clearly demonstrated rent-seekers' endurance and success to date.

To address problems more permanently, it is vital to understand rent-seeking behaviour and its underlying mechanisms. Chapters 3 to 5 will elaborate on these insights. A deeper understanding of rent-seeking can contribute to addressing the fundamental problem cited in the opening quotation on page 34, cutting the Gordian knot so that political players who seek to further the public interest are not eliminated in a selection process motivated by rent-seeking, but can instead survive and guide society into productive spheres.

3 Evaluating Rents, Rent-Seeking Investments and Rent-Seeking Costs

Focusing on rents, rent-seeking investments, dissipation and efficiency, this chapter addresses analytical approaches that aim to explain rent-seeking incentives and investments in general and costs of rent-seeking in particular. The third part of the chapter also evaluates costs from a broader welfare perspective and surveys several empirical studies. The analytical literature on rent-seeking has grown to a very large number of books and papers which address the question of what determines rent-seeking investments and related costs. This body of literature has come up with numerous formal models that predict the level of rent-seeking investments. Since a broad-based overview of these models is a complex and extended undertaking, it is tempting to confine an analysis to a few examples and generalise thereafter. Such a simplification can, however, be misleading. Models can point out very interesting aspects of an issue, but without a closer consideration of alternative specifications a model should never be taken on its own to derive policy recommendations. Each model is based on a set of assumptions. The real world is much more complex and has many facets which reflect a wide range of possible assumptions. Given this qualification, this chapter devotes considerable space to describing the many alternative specifications and settings of models.

Apart from providing a general survey, the discussion of models contributes to a more thorough understanding of rent-seeking incentives and costs; it helps reveal why rent-seeking is a bargain in many situations and why it has spread so widely. A broad perspective also contributes to a better understanding of rent-seekers' opposition to reforms which aim to reduce or eliminate rent-seeking. Opposition is likely to depend on the level, timing and type of past and ongoing rent-seeking activities—an aspect which will be taken up again in Chapter 5. Clearly, changes in policies can affect rent-seeking behaviour very differently, depending on the features of the rent-seeking mechanisms. If policy alternatives are not evaluated carefully, rent-abating policies can easily lead to an unintended increase in rent-seeking.

To demonstrate possible interactions and complications it is necessary to refer to many different rent-seeking models. Given the limits of this book, it is not possible to describe these models in full detail. Therefore the following discussion frequently describes only selected but important aspects and results of the models. As a consequence it may happen that readers who are not familiar with the models may have difficulties fully understanding the discussion. In such cases, interested readers are referred to the original sources.

The emphasis of Chapters 3.1 and 3.2 is put on the *individual* rent-seeking perspective (how much does a rent-seeker invest to get a transfer?). In particular Chapter 3.2 will survey many aspects which determine and characterise the individual incentive to engage in rent-seeking activities. Since this overview is quite comprehensive, Chapter 3.2 may also be read selectively, i.e. the reader may skip a few paragraphs or even go directly from the introduction to the concluding Section d). Having explained the behaviour and incentives of rent-seekers, Chapter 3.3 finally focuses on an overall assessment of rent-seeking costs that arise to *society*. The different aspects addressed are an important extension of the preceding discussion on rent-seeking models and make the limited scope of these models in assessing overall rent-seeking costs apparent. Chapter 3.3 also includes an overview of empirical approaches which aim to measure rent-seeking costs, and concludes with an assessment of what characterises LDC-relevant rent-seeking settings.

3.1 Rents, Competition, Non-Rival Settings and the Concept of Dissipation

'I can suggest no way of measuring these expenditures, but the potential returns are large, and it would be quite surprising if the investment was not also sizeable.'

Gordon Tullock 1967, on rent-seeking investments

How much do rent-seekers invest to capture a transfer? This is undoubtedly the most frequently asked question in the literature on rent-seeking. Theoretical model approaches have attracted much of the debate and have drawn attention away from other, no less important aspects. Nevertheless, the matter of dissipation—here understood as the ratio of total rent-seeking investments undertaken to rents sought—remains an important element of any rent-seeking evaluation and determines, among other things, the amount of individual gains involved.

Section a) sets off with the concept of 'perfect competition' for rents and goes on to summarise the basic Tullock game, which has become 'a standard tool in the theoretical analysis of rent-seeking'(Baye, Kovenock and De Vries (1999, p. 439)). As an important extension to an analysis in developing countries, this section also points to another type of rent-seeking situation: the non-rival setting—a case which has not been adequately addressed in the standard rent-seeking literature. Finally, given the relevance of dissipation in an analysis of rent-seeking incentives and related costs, Section b) is devoted to a broader discussion of this term. Outlining various definitions, it also specifies sources of potential misunderstanding.

a) Rent-Seekers Seeking Rents: Bargain or Flop?

The Crux of Measuring Rent-Seeking Investments

To analyse rents, rent-seeking investments and related costs it is helpful to recall the schematic depiction of typical rent-creating situations displayed in Figure 2-2 on page 42 (Figure 3-1 reiterates one example, the standard monopoly case.) The interventions described in Figure 2-2 all reflect some type of rent transfer and losses, effected by implicit or clearly visible taxes and subsidies. In Figure 3-1 the monopoly rent P_mP_cCB (grey rectangle) indicates the transfer and the triangle ABC (dotted area) the traditional welfare loss. The pioneering contribution of Tullock's original paper on rent-seeking was the insight that when measuring welfare cost, one cannot only calculate the usual 'Harberger triangles' (dotted areas) but must include other costs:

> 'Generally governments do not impose protective tariffs on their own. They have to be lobbied or pressured into doing so by the expenditure of resources in political activity. One would anticipate that the domestic producers would invest resources in lobbying for the tariff until the marginal return on the last dollar so spent was equal to its likely return producing the transfer. There might also be other interests trying to prevent the transfer and putting resources into influencing the government in the other direction. These expenditures, which may simply offset each other to some extent, are purely wasteful from the standpoint of society as a whole…' (Tullock (1967, p. 228))

These expenditures or investments are, of course, what Anne Krueger seven years later was going to call *rent-seeking*.

As a first approach to the problem of measuring rent-seeking investments, economists applied the concept of *perfect competition* to rent-seeking theory. It is reasonable to think that a rent-seeker is willing to spend at the most the present value of the expected rent to be transferred; and because perfect competition, in particular free entry, is assumed, investment may indeed reach this maximum (assuming that other rent-seekers will enter, as long extra profits are not driven down to zero). Under this premise, the grey areas in Figure 2-2 and Figure 3-1 will not only represent the rents transferred, but also aggregated rent-seeking investments undertaken to get these rents. These investments have become known as the Tullock costs.

The implications of perfect competition are straightforward. Under such conditions, the size of rent-seeking investments is indirectly measurable. Moreover, in aggregate, rent-seekers cannot enrich themselves; rents are fully dissipated in the attempt to capture them. This postulate of *full dissipation* goes back to Posner (1975) and has been illustrated in the context of allocating a monopoly right (Figure 3-1).

Figure 3-1: Rent-Seeking and the Allocation of a Monopoly Right

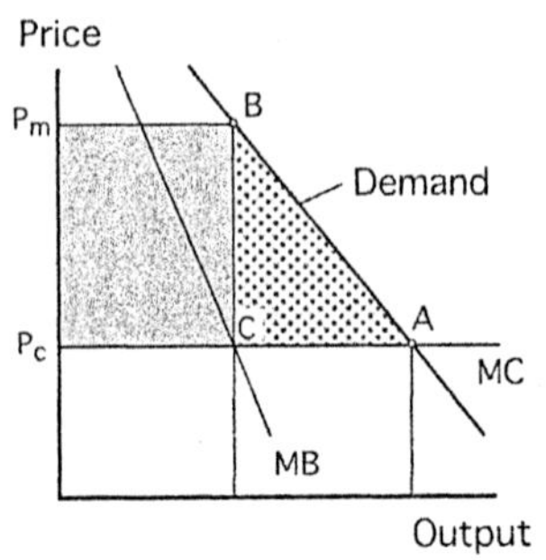

At the core of rent-seeking theory is the insight that rent-seekers use resources to create and capture rents. The monopoly case has been usually taken to discuss the welfare implications. The producer rent is indicated with the grey area and the traditional welfare loss, i.e. the Harberger triangle, with the dotted area.

In a perfect competitive setting where different applicants compete to get the monopoly right, it is argued that they may invest together as much as P_mP_cCB (e.g. Tullock (1994, p. 148)). As this investment is not productive, it is part of the welfare losses induced by market intervention (the exact impact depends on different factors, which will be taken up in Chapter 3.3). The area P_mP_cCB has also become known as the Tullock rectangle, to contrast it with the traditional Harberger loss (ABC).

Several researchers have taken the approach of measuring rents as an approximation to empirically assess the costs of rent-seeking. For developing countries see for instance Mohammad and Whalley (1984) on India, or Ampofu-Tuffuor, DeLorme and Kamerschen (1991) on Ghana. In the former paper the authors conclude (p. 410) that rent-seeking costs amounted to approximately 30-45% of GNP in 1980-81. In the case of Ghana, Ampofu-Tuffuor, DeLorme and Kamerschen (1991, p. 555) find, using the same methodology, values between 18% and 25% (years 1981 and 1984). Although these results are striking, they remain speculative. The investigation neither differentiates social costs related to rent-seeking activities, nor does it sufficiently address the possibility of different levels of dissipation.

Most economists will agree that the package of assumptions required for full dissipation is exceptional and not given in most real rent-seeking situations. On the one hand, many rent-seeking settings are not perfectly competitive (or not competitive at all); they may involve barriers to entry, substantial asymmetries among rent-seekers, cooperative strategies or just consist of a single rent-seeker lobbying for some kind of protection or a bureaucrat extracting private rents from an individual or private company. On the other hand, most competitive rent-seeking settings bear the characteristic that average costs and marginal costs are not identical, which implies that the sum of optimal individual rent-seeking investments does not match the value of the rents at stake (Tullock (1980, p. 97f)). These qualifications therefore require another approach than just adding rents. An alternative solution is given when there is information about the *specific level of dissipation.* It allows rent-seeking activities to be estimated by multiplying rents with a calculated factor for dissipation.

In the 1980s and 1990s, there were a large number of rent-seeking models focusing on this problem, discussing parameters that determine the level of dissipation. Their usefulness for empirical estimates of rent-seeking has nevertheless remained limited, as the information needed to choose or design an appropriate model structure and to estimate the values of the parameters involved seems to be at least as difficult as directly measuring rent-seeking activities.

Still, the literature on dissipation has provided many important insights for understanding, elaborating and addressing rent-seeking incentives and rent-seeking costs in general. If policymakers aim to reduce rent-seeking activities, it is sufficient that they know the structure of the rent-seeking setting (including the parameters, which determine the extent of rent-seeking in the specific situation) and, much less relevant, that they have an exact idea about the actual magnitude of rent-seeking activities. In addition, even though many conclusions cannot be drawn directly from Tullock-like rent-seeking models, the literature provides fertile ground for working on extensions.

Modelling Rent-Seeking: Standard Tullock Approach and Non-Rival Settings

In contrast to profit-seeking activities where expenditures constitute outlays to cover the costs of production, rent-seeking investments are not directly made to produce a good or service but to *influence the probability* of getting a rent (Corcoran (1984, p. 89)). A rent-seeking model therefore specifies the relation between rent-seeking investments and an expected 'prize'. These investments usually do not guarantee the prize but only a certain probability of 'winning' it, which can be formally written as the function $\pi_i(x_i, \ldots)$, where x_i represents the individual i's rent-seeking (in the literature on rent-seeking the function is often more abstractly referred to as 'contest-success function'). The probability π_i of individual i to win the prize depends on different factors, in most rent-seeking settings also on investments of other rent-seekers. This interdependence on others made game theory—a discipline which focuses on the 'behaviour of decision-makers (players) whose decisions affect each other' (Aumann (1987, p. 460))—an important tool for analysing many rent-seeking problems. Common descriptions of the dependence on other rent-seekers usually match the following general structure:

$$\pi_i(x_1,..,x_n)=\frac{f_i(x_i)}{\sum_{i=1}^{n} f_i(x_i)}, \text{ where}$$

n Number of rent-seekers
x_i Rent-seeking investment of individual i
$f_i(\,)$ Individual function of influence of rent-seeking outlays

With identical rent-seekers, $f_i(x_i)$ simplifies to $f(x_i)$. Another, less common approach is the difference form, where the relative success of rent-seekers is not determined by the ratio of their outlays but by the differences (for a brief reference see page 99f).

In 1980 Gordon Tullock presented a *basic model of efficient rent-seeking*, using a probability of winning function similar to the structure given in the above formula. Already five years earlier, he had introduced a two-player-version of this model as a tool to analyse investments in court procedures where two conflicting parties attempt to win (see Tullock (1975)).

Tullock's model marked the main starting point of the formal literature on rent-seeking and provoked a large series of articles, in particular as it included the apparently counterintuitive outcome of overdissipation, i.e. the possibility that rent-seekers spend more than the value of the rent. As the model has been widely discussed and constitutes the basis of many rent-seeking games, it will be summarised below.[19]

Tullock was the first to formalise the rent-seeking situation as a lottery. He assumed that rent-seekers can buy tickets, as many as they want to. These tickets are then combined and the winner is determined by drawing one ticket out of the lot sold. The problem rent-seekers face is to purchase the appropriate number of tickets to maximise the net present value of their investment. Unfortunately, this investment also depends on the number of tickets sold to all others. To find a solution, the model concludes that if there is a correct strategy, everybody will follow it and all participants will thus invest exactly the same amount of money. (Using game-theoretic notations, the model specifies a solution in 'pure' strategies.)

Tullock constructed the probability of winning function in a simple way, assuming that all individuals were identical. He defined $f(x_i) = x^r$ as the individual player's production function for influence in lobbying. The parameter r ($r>0$) was introduced to examine the impact of different marginal costs of influencing the probability of winning (the discussion in Chapter 3.2 will often refer to it as the 'parameter r'). In the simplest version where $r=1$, the probability of winning is given by the ratio between 'own investment' and 'total investments' and the expected pay-out becomes this ratio times the prize, minus individual rent-seeking outlays undertaken. The rent-seekers maximising function, as well as originally stated equilibrium investments for specific numbers of rent-seekers and specific values in the production function ($r=1$: linear relation, $r>1$: economies of scale, $r<1$: diseconomies of scale) are displayed in Table 3-1.

The two grey areas indicate situations with *overdissipation*, where total rent-seeking payments are larger than the prize. However, as Tullock himself notes, they do not constitute a Nash equilibrium, i.e. a situation where no player can be better off by choosing a different strategy (investment level), given the choice of all other players.[20] Such exceptional high rent-seeking investments can only arise if the game procedure is modified and includes sunk costs (if investments can no longer be withdrawn, the equilibrium characterises the point where neither player can gain by further increasing investments). However, as many authors emphasise, these outcomes constitute a negative-sum game and would never be played if anticipated and, of course, if the zero option is still feasible, i.e. if sunk costs are absent. (For a graphical explanation of the problem see Allard (1988, p. 5f).)

---

[19] For a more complete description see Tullock's original article (1980) (the following description of the Tullock model will draw on it) or the articles in Rowley, Tollison and Tullock (1988, p. 91-126).

[20] Tullock (1980, p. 105, 107), (1988a, p. 94). Baye, Kovenock and De Vries (1994) showed that the original Tullock game (which rests on simultaneous moves), does not contain a Nash equilibrium in pure strategies for $r>2n/(n-1)$. The problem was that 'the symmetric solution to the players' first-order conditions for expected payoff maximization does not yield a global maximum; at this solution players have a negative expected payoff, which is dominated by bidding zero' (Baye, Kovenock and De Vries (1999, p. 440f)). However, they provided a solution in mixed strategies, which indicates underdissipation (Baye, Kovenock and De Vries (1994)).

Table 3-1: Efficient Rent-Seeking in the Original Tullock Game (for $x_i>0$)[21]

$$\text{Max} \frac{x_1^r}{x_1^r + \sum_{i=2}^{n} x_i^r} \bullet 100 - x_1,$$

where

x_i: Investment of individual i

n: Total number of players

r: Productivity parameter of rent-seeking investment

100: Prize

Individual and total rent-seeking investments
as a function of r (marginal costs) and n (total number of players)

r	n=2	n=4	n=10	n→∞
1/3	8.3 / 16.6	6.2 / 25.0	3.0 / 30.0	- / 33.3
1/2	12.5 / 25.0	9.3 / 37.4	4.5 / 45.0	- / 50.0
1	25.0 / 50.0	18.7 / 75.0	9.0 / 90.0	- / 100.0
2	50.0 / 100.0	37.5 / 150.0	18.0 / 80.0	- / 200.0
3	75.0 / 150.0	56.2 / 225.0	27.0 / 270.0	- / 300.0
5	125.0 / 250.0	93.7 / 375.0	45.0 / 450.0	- / 500.0
8	200.0 / 400.0	150.0 / 600.0	72.0 / 720.0	- / 800.0

The table indicates 'optimal' rent-seeking investments for individual players and the corresponding total of all players, as they were originally assumed ($x^* = \text{Prize} \cdot r(n-1)/n^2$, see Higgins, Shughart and Tollison (1985, p. 249)). Surprisingly, full dissipation arises only in one case (marked by the dotted frame). Underdissipation is given in the white area and overdissipation in the grey areas (in the darker grey area, individual investment is even higher than the prize to be won). However, as mathematically shown by Baye, Kovenock and De Vries (1994), overdissipation does not constitute a Nash equilibrium in pure strategies (see Footnote 20).

Source: Data according to Tables 6.1 and 6.2 in Tullock (1980, p. 102)

What basically caused the confusion in the Tullock game is the problem that 'the simple rule—do not play such games—is not correct, because if it were the correct rule, then anyone who violated it could make large profits' (Tullock (1980, p. 108)). As has been argued later (e.g. Bartsch and Thomas (1995, p. 175)), this problem can only be solved by randomising the strategies, i.e. individuals may sometimes play, and sometimes they do not.

Disregarding the fact that the case of overdissipation requires further assumptions to materialise, Tullock's model set off a large discussion in the formal literature on rent-seeking, as it clearly demonstrated that *full dissipation* may not be a likely outcome in many competitive rent-seeking settings. The maximising function used by Tullock has been adopted, modified and extended in numerous rent-seeking models. Most solutions in these models indicate underdissipation. Overdissipation may arise in some cases, however not ex-ante, but as a particular outcome ex-post if there are random strategies (see, for instance, Baye, Kovenock and De Vries (1999)) or in a 'myopic' setting where sunk costs are included and overdissipation is not anticipated.

Competitive rent-seeking models with probability of winning functions that reflect the game-theoretic structure of the function displayed on page 65 can be seen as an extension of the original Tullock approach. They cover important rent-seeking situations and have been thoroughly discussed in the rent-seeking literature. In the following discussion, they will be referred to as the *'traditional' rent-seeking approaches*.

[21] Simplified, if $x_i=0$ $\forall$ i=1...n, the probability of winning is 1/n, which would be part of the maximising function and thus avoid any expected dissipation.

That rent-seeking settings are of a competitive nature is a strong assumption; it does, however, not reflect many important rent-seeking settings in developing countries. Having the overview on rent-seeking activities in Chapter 2.2 in mind, rent-seeking is often much closer to a non-rival type, for instance, when state officials extract private rents from individuals and companies or businessmen collude with civil servants to engage in cost-reducing and benefit-enhancing corruption. Confining an analysis to a discussion of the basic Tullock model and related approaches would therefore miss many important features of rent-seeking in LDCs. To emphasise this point, this chapter defines the *non-rival setting* as an explicit counterpart to the traditional rent-seeking approach.

In a non-competitive setting, optimal rent-seeking decisions are not much affected by the behaviour of other rent-seekers (except the rent-seeking counterpart who may be involved in the deal and get a share of the rent), and the rent-seeking equilibrium is typically constrained by other factors than rent-seeking competition. If the interaction with other (non-colluding) rent-seekers is less relevant, non-existent or part of a past 'sunk' rent-seeking stage, formally, the rent-seeking contest does not reflect a situation where several rent-seekers compete for one prize. Each rent-seeker may invest in rent-seeking, without significantly affecting opportunities of other rent-seekers.

Figure 3-2 provides a schematic depiction of the two contrasting rent-seeking situations: the *competitive traditional approach* and the *strictly non-rival setting*. They can be regarded as two polar cases of a continuum of different rent-seeking settings, which are relevant in LDCs. Rent-seekers in a non-rival situation usually make outlays to capture easy attainable rents. They may be in a strong privileged position, operate in an area with natural barriers or enjoy insider status. For instance an importer who does not face competition from other importers may bribe tax authorities to bring goods free of tax into the country. The maximum amount of goods imported, and therefore the maximum rents attainable, may not just depend on the direct costs of influencing tax authorities, but on the country's demand for imported goods, the rent-seeker's capacity to use or distribute the goods and/or the capability to keep the illegal tax-evasion activity sufficiently concealed.

The less competitive a rent-seeking situation is the more will the supply of rents be constrained by other factors than direct rent-seeking outlays. As will be argued later, this may have decisive implications when it comes to evaluating the impact of parameter variations. Traditional rent-seeking models have largely ignored this possibility of non-rivalry when discussing the impact of parameter variations on rent-seeking, partially because the bulk of the analytical rent-seeking literature simply focused on the institutional framework most prevalent in industrialised countries, where, for instance, sustained market frictions are less relevant. Only the literature on corruption has devoted considerable attention to the 'single rent-seeker lobbying'-type of rent-seeking, however, from another perspective.[22]

---

[22] This aspect will be taken up in Chapter 4; see, among others, the logic of engaging in corrupt activities displayed in Table 4-1 on page 153.

Figure 3-2: Competitive Versus Non-Rival Setting

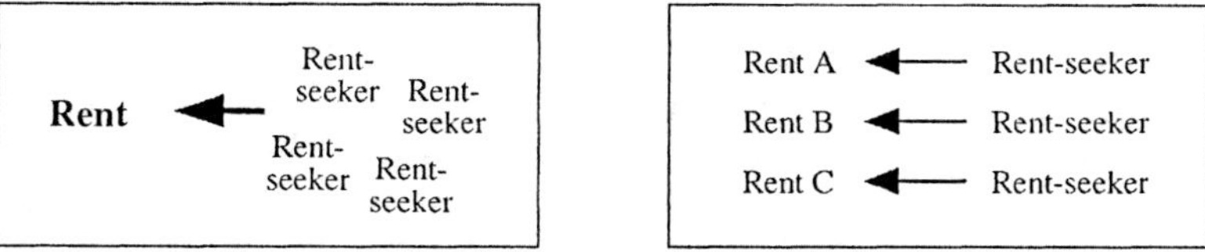

In contrast to a traditional competitive rent-seeking contest (left), a non-rival setting (right) characterises a situation where rent-seekers spend a specific amount of resources to capture a rent, mostly with near-certainty. This high level of certainty is attainable as the equilibrium is constrained by other factors than competing rent-seeking outlays. Unlike in competitive settings, where both winners and losers make irretrievable rent-seeking outlays, the focus in a non-rival setting is on 'how much is necessary to get the rent'.

Unlike in traditional contests, having spent the optimal level of rent-seeking investments, the rent is often allocated with near certainty, i.e. these rent-seekers make a specific investment to get an almost 100% probability to capture the rent. Most of these settings therefore involve no or little sunk costs (which is in particular evident in the case where outlays are contingent on a successful outcome). Furthermore, in many such settings it can be expected that dissipation tends to be low (compared to a competitive situation).

An argument often taken up is that there has been a preceding rent-seeking contest where rent-seekers made outlays to get into the favoured position. A businessman may have bribed civil servants to get a business licence in the first place. At least in theory, in a 'perfect' rent-extracting situation, where the corrupt civil servant extorts payments for a licence or where licences are limited and several companies compete, the price for a licence may come close to the net present value of the profits that will accrue in the business (including the rents from future tax evasion). The public officials, on the other hand, may have spent a large share of their benefits to get into the privileged position. Outlays predicted with the traditional rent-seeking approach have then simply taken place in the previous contest and the non-rival setting of low rent-seeking investments simply reflects a *partial consideration*. In many cases this is true; there are however also many other situations.

A large number of civil servants have become considerably rich and so have smugglers and other rent-seekers. One reason is that there are many rent-seeking settings where a privileged position is attained without, or hardly any, effort. An individual may just 'by chance' belong to the same tribe, party or family as the rent-distributor who gained power. Or a person simply has the luck to be in the right business, or have the specific infrastructure or connections that allows him to take advantage of a new rent-seeking opportunity. Given incomplete information and limited rationality it is evident that not every future opportunity is foreseen and contested for (on this, see also Allard (1988, p. 10f)). In effect, many preceding rent-seeking contests are of a non-rival nature, too.

More important, however, is the second qualification. Even if there has been a preceding rent-seeking contest which determined the privileged individuals, a partial analysis of subsequent non-rival rent-seeking situations can still provide valuable insights to derive policy conclusions or to formulate priorities when it comes to *implementing policy reforms*.

As noted earlier, many developing countries have become rent-seeking economies. These economies are characterised by a poor policy environment, a weak rule of law, and most importantly, these economies include a large number of established rent-seekers. Reforms initiated by a few reform-minded policymakers directly threaten the economic base of rent-seeking elites, which either have been responsible for the initial rent-creating policy or have developed as a result of it. Since rent-seekers are likely to resist, it is important to understand their potential reactions when designing and implementing rent-abating policy reforms.

What matters for the discussion here is that policy measures will affect rent-seeking settings at different stages. If individuals have already gained a privileged position, which is the standard situation in rent-seeking economies, the non-rival setting has to be explicitly taken into account when formulating reform policies. For instance, as will be argued in Section c) of Chapter 3.2, reducing the marginal productivity of rent-seeking will decrease rent-seeking efforts and therefore dissipation in a competitive setting, but may have the opposite effect in a non-rival environment (rent-seekers may simply increase their efforts to retain their near 100% access). It can be expected that the bulk of resistance against rent-abating policy measures will come from these groups.

With the non-rival rent-seeking situation as well as the results of the traditional rent-seeking literature in mind, it is reasonable to assume that underdissipation is a likely outcome of many institutional settings that can be found in reality. Hence, rent-seeking indeed seems to be a bargain for rent-seekers—a finding which supports (or at least does not contradict) the assumption that rent-seeking is a widespread phenomenon. The concept of rent-seekers' full dissipation may be thus seen, at most, as a theoretical construct; a benchmark or starting point for investigating the level of rent-seeking investment (Tollison (1987, p. 148f)).

b) How to Define Dissipation: Taking Different Perspectives

As noted above, information on dissipation not only helps to assess rent-seeking costs, understanding factors which determine dissipation also explains why rent-seeking is a bargain and why it spreads in a society. Because the term dissipation is used differently and is a main subject of this chapter, sufficient space will be devoted to clarify this concept.

It appears that the rent-seeking literature has not provided a systematic approach to define dissipation. This shortcoming contributed to misunderstandings about the impact of rent-seeking parameters as well as misunderstandings related to the possibility of overdissipation. In general, the term 'dissipation' is used to characterise two different aspects. In most papers on formal models the term refers to the *ratio of rent-seeking investments undertaken to rents sought*, irrespectively of the type of investment. This will be the definition used in Chapter 3.2.

A different definition is usually applied in the context of analysing social costs. Dissipation then characterises *rent-seeking investments which do not take the form of mere transfers*, but investments where resources are 'dissipated', i.e. 'used up' or 'wasted' in the rent-seeking process. A single rent-seeker may not care whether his or her investment takes the form of a bribe or time-consuming paperwork, but society will. In the former case, society seems to be better off. This differentiation between 'dissipation' and 'transfer' will be a focus of Chapter 3.3. The issue is further complicated as transfers may be dissipated at other stages and rent-seeking can imply substantial indirect costs which have to be taken in consideration when relating rents to social cost.

In the remaining discussion in this section, problems and potential misinterpretations related to the first definition (ratio of rent-seeking investments undertaken to rents sought) are explained, including additional considerations as regards social costs. The discussion is relevant for the reader who is interested in the detailed evaluation of the analysis on the impact of parameter variations in Chapters 3.2 and 3.3. As will be demonstrated, the concept of dissipation turns out to be less clear than it may appear at first glance. It is simple and straightforward in an abstract setting where rent-seeking investments are related to exogenously defined rents, but becomes confusing if the rent is endogenous and if the contest includes opposition.

Figure 3-3 shows four different rent-seeking settings with increasing complexity. The rent transferred is always indicated with the bold rectangle 'abcd'. Black areas represent rent-seeking investments and grey areas rent-protecting outlays, i.e. outlays of individuals who try to prevent the rent transfer. Finally, the transfer may involve dead-weight losses (Harberger triangles). Potential and actual dead-weight losses are marked as dotted areas.

Diagram i) represents the simplest rent-seeking setting. As the rent is exogenous and fixed, dissipation is unambiguously defined by the black area divided by the rectangle 'abcd'. Partly confusing is the situation where the rent is endogenous (diagrams ii to iv). This time the size of the rent also depends on rent-seeking outlays. It implies that the impact of a variation in the value of a parameter on dissipation needs to be evaluated more carefully, as both basis and outlays change, i.e. the size of the rectangle 'abcd' is a function of rent-seeking outlays and may vary in the diagrams ii) and iii) between zero and 'abef' and in diagram iv) between zero and 'agei'.[23]

[23] As an alternative approach to circumvent this problem, the change in rent-seeking outlays may be evaluated against a theoretical maximum rent contestable (i.e. rectangle 'abef'). Such a perspective may be taken in a setting where outlays of rent-seekers are more directly related to the maximum rent (they may have no specific idea about how much will be transferred and what share they can get from it). This approach is unusual, however.

Figure 3-3: Dissipation: Different Settings and Approaches

a) Rents, outlays & Harberger losses

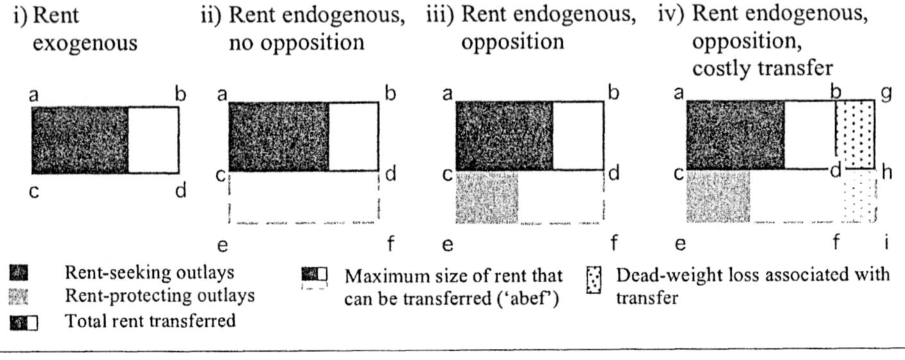

b) Alternative definitions of dissipation $\left(\frac{\text{Outlays (\& loss)}}{\text{Rents}}\right)$

Partial consideration:

- Dissipation by rent-seeker
- Dissipation by rent-protector

Overall consideration (with/without dead-weight loss):

Rents	Outlays (& loss): (+) or (+ +)
	Overall dissipation relative to rents at stake
	Overall dissipation relative to rents transferred

Whereas in diagrams i) and ii) dissipation is generally defined in the same manner, in (iii) confusion may arise over whether or not to include opposition against rent-seeking. In the usual narrow definition of dissipation, the focus is on how much rent-seekers invest to capture a transfer. Then outlays of opposing forces, which aim to prevent the transfer, are not part of dissipation. There are, however, good arguments for including these outlays as they indirectly relate to rent-seeking activities and are an important component of social costs.

Including opposition makes the situation more complex. Strictly speaking, there are two different dissipations: The rent-seekers' dissipation, which is related to the rent transferred, and the opponents' dissipation, which should be related to the amount they managed to keep (rectangle 'cdef'). Within such a framework it can be argued that no rational rent-seeker would spend more than 'abcd' to obtain 'abcd' and no rational opponent would spend more than 'cdef' to keep 'cdef'. Of course, this is an ex-post consideration. The position of the line 'cd' depends on the relative outlays of the two groups and would be at 'ef' with no opposition and at 'ab' with no rent-seeking activities. With an overall calculation of dissipation, in contrast, the exact position of the line does not matter. Total outlays (black and grey areas) are related to the sum of the rectangles, which is always 'abef'.

Finally, diagram iv) introduces asymmetry in the stakes. Asymmetries arise if there are leakages in the transfer as producers move away from the social production optimum (i.e. the transfer received by the rent-seeking group is smaller than what the other side loses). The difference (dotted area) between the maximum amount, rent-seekers can capture ('abef') and the maximum loss of the counterpart suffers ('agei') reflects dead-weight losses (Harberger triangles, see also dotted areas in Figure 3-1).

The question emerges as to the appropriate definition of overall dissipation in a setting which includes opposition. If the focus is on individual rent-seekers, the narrow definition, which only captures their rents and outlays, is appropriate (in fact, such an approach would be in line with the title given to Section a) 'Rent-seekers Seeking Rents: Bargain or Flop?'). If, however, social costs of rent transfers are of interest (the focus of Chapter 3.3), total outlays (black and grey areas), as well as additional costs related with the dead-weight loss ('bgdh'), need to be included. Total outlays (with or without dead-weight loss) can then be compared with either the total rents at stake (rectangle 'agei') or the actual rent transferred ('abcd'). Evidently, in the latter case, overdissipation can easily arise.

In a similar manner overdissipation can arise in a transfer-seeking contest, which characterises a rent-seeking situation where rent-seeking losers pay the prize to the rent-seeking winners.[24] Strictly speaking, any contest with opposition (where opponents pay for the rent if they lose) can be regarded as a transfer-seeking contest. Transfer-seeking contests are part of the broader category of models of conflict (for a comparison with 'standard' rent-seeking approaches see Neary (1997)). Models of conflict emphasise the impossibility to withdraw own resources from the 'rent-seeking' game. The most common example is military invasion. Overdissipation easily occurs if outlays are compared with the wealth transfer that has been realised.

So far, the discussion has presented, in a schematic way, different reasons for potential misunderstandings of the term 'dissipation'. The reasons either referred to the problem of which rent-seeking outlays count or what the basis is for relating these outlays. Five additional aspects are taken up below, which are relevant for the subsequent discussion on rent-seeking parameters.

First, most rent-seeking settings are characterised by *differences in valuation* of the rent. The question then becomes whether rent-seeking outlays are related to some 'objective' valuation (which somehow reflect costs), to an average valuation or to a valuation of a specific rent-seeker. This aspect is not as trivial as it may appear at first glance, especially if one focuses on comparative static analysis. For instance, what is the impact on dissipation if a monopoly right is granted to one of several applicants and the valuation of a monopoly right increases for one rent-seeker, after having invested in a new technology, which allows him to get the most out of a monopoly situation? Evidently, the choice of a basis depends on the focus of the question, which may itself depend on the nature of the specific setting.

---

[24] Though some authors differentiate between rent-seeking contests in the narrow sense and transfer-seeking contests, this differentiation is not established in the literature.

Second, a similar problem arises if the rent is a *public good*. The costs to supply a public good and the aggregated value individuals place on it may diverge widely. Again, whether rent-seeking outlays are related to the costs, for instance the costs of supplying another road, or whether they are compared with the aggregate value individuals give to this road, is a matter of perspective and depends on the context.

Third, there are many instances where rent-seeking activities do not relate to the overall transfer achieved, but to a share of the transfer, i.e. a rent-seeking setting may be characterised by some *pre-specified income-distribution* in the absence of rent-seeking activities. For instance, there is always scope to influence a government budget allocation and many budget items are in fact a pure outcome of rent-seeking activities—however not all. If a government undertakes sound policies and is accountable to its citizens, a large share of the funds will be allocated according to the society's preferences on how to use budget resources. The measurement of dissipation therefore depends on whether rent-seeking outlays are divided by the entire rent that has been transferred or, more accurately, whether rent-seeking outlays are divided by the share of the rent that has been contested. Yet this distinction between rents and 'socially justified' transfers is often not obvious and therefore disputable. The problem points to the more general difficulty of defining rents and rent-seeking discussed in Chapter 2.1. What matters is to make the chosen approach sufficiently transparent.

Fourth, there are situations where rent-seekers do *not invest their own resources* to obtain a personal benefit. Opportunities to misallocate state resources and donor funds for rent-seeking purposes are numerous and diverse in governments with poorly implemented guidelines and missing checks and balances. For instance, a parastatal manager may decide to undertake an entirely unnecessary business trip, which costs the company $2000, but offers the manager the opportunity to appropriate $200 in travel allowances. Not gambling with own resources, rent-seekers may therefore not be constrained in their outlays by the expected size of the rent they get. Overdissipation can easily arise if the personal rent appropriated ($200) is related to the costs it caused ($2000).

Finally, misunderstanding may arise as the concept of dissipation can also be applied to a partial, rather than overall consideration. Clark and Riis (1998, p. 617f), for instance, introduced an interesting case of overdissipation. They asked whether *increases* in the value of a rent can be overdissipated. In fact, within their specific multi-prize rent-seeking model, this type of 'partial' overdissipation turns out to be a feasible outcome (see the discussion following on page 102). Similarly, one may consider an exogenous increase in the value of the rent-seeking productivity parameter, in a setting where the total size of the rent depends on aggregate rent-seeking efforts (e.g. Chung (1996)). Depending on the values of the parameters, the increase in total rent-seeking efforts may be larger than the increase in the size of the rent, thereby making rent-seekers worse off.

3.2 Factors that Determine Dissipation

a) Overview and Preliminary Comments

Table 3-2 lists parameters and features which have to a greater or lesser extent been addressed in the literature on rent-seeking. They determine in direct or indirect ways the level of rent dissipation. Incentives to engage in rent-seeking activities come from two sources: the *value* an individual attributes to a given rent and the *costs* involved to capture this rent. The items presented in the table and the discussion in the following Sections b) and c) are grouped accordingly.

Table 3-2: Characteristics of Rent-Seeking Settings

Factors which determine the value attributed to the rent (objective and subjective valuation)	
• Rent characteristics	Size and certainty of rent Public good character of rent or regulation
• Personal valuation	Valuation, alternative income and attitudes towards rent-seeking Attitude towards risk Asymmetries in valuation
Factors which determine the costs to capture the rent (contest-success-situation)	
• Rent-seeking costs in general	Autonomy of rent-producing and rent-distributing institutions Structure of authority (committee, multiple source) Starting point Rent-seeking opposition Means of exerting influence (threat and conditional outlays)
• Allocation among rent-seekers	Number of rent-seekers involved Winning rule (degree of discrimination, lobbying for share or all) Winning procedure (single-stage versus multiple-stage contests) Group contests Asymmetries in power; insider settings and barriers to entry
• Strategies of rent-seekers	Assumptions on perception, rationality and equilibrium Dynamic interaction (timing/sequencing) Cooperation

Dissipation typically increases with the intensity of competition. As many aspects of the table directly relate to this intensity, the 'level of competition' has not been listed as a separate item. Competition-reducing effects may either arise as the value of a parameter increases or falls for all rent-seekers involved; or they result from differences among rent-seekers, i.e. the value of a parameter varies among rent-seekers. Most settings in the real world are characterised by such asymmetries, in particular asymmetries in power and valuation are common.

Clearly, many of the items presented in Table 3-2 are closely *interlinked* and relate to each other. This implies that subdivisions in the table are artificial and basically serve a 'didactical' purpose.[25] Furthermore, classifying and separating parameters and other features inevitably involves a compromise and depends on the chosen perspective and emphasis.

An important conclusion that arises from this is that *insights* on dissipation have to be *interpreted and applied carefully*. In many instances it is not possible to make a single, generally valid statement on how a parameter affects dissipation. This becomes evident if one compares the different models discussed in the literature on rent-seeking or focuses on other settings which are much closer to the non-rival rent-seeking type. Properties of parameters with regard to dissipation may strongly depend on other features of the model, in particular, assumptions about its structure, equilibrium strategies and the values of the remaining parameters involved. Alterations therein may not only increase or lessen the impact of the parameter under focus, but even, as will be shown, reverse the sign. Dissipation is always a function of the *overall* picture and more detailed statements about the impact of one parameter often require a simultaneous specification of all others, including the model structure.

Because this chapter finally aims to make conclusions on rent-seeking in developing-country settings in general, and on rent-seeking strategies in the reform process in particular, the discussion will take a broad approach. Besides the equal emphasis on *traditional* Tullock-type rent-seeking contests and related approaches as well as *non-rival* settings, the discussion also considers possible implications that result from the *interaction between different settings*, and explicitly includes, where relevant, the profit-seeking alternative. A simultaneous evaluation of several rent-seeking situations is particularly relevant in a situation where the country has a bad political culture and has become a rent-seeking economy. Being under pressure, rent-seekers are likely to apply 'evading' strategies, which alter rent-seeking outcomes in other settings not directly addressed. If parameter variations relate to an overall multi-rent-seeking environment, concentrating on a single rent-seeking incidence can therefore be misleading.

In Chapter 2.2 three different types of relations among rent-seekers were outlined: settings where rent-seekers are outside rent-producing institutions,

[25] A differentiation between the value attributed to a rent and the cost of capturing this rent becomes blurred if the size of the rent (and therefore the value) is endogenous and depends on rent-seeking outlays. Group formation (included under 'allocation among rent-seekers') is highly relevant when discussing public goods and cooperation. The 'structure of the authority' is considered separately, even though it co-determines the level of autonomy of the rent-distributing authority, i.e. how costly it is to influence this authority. The parameters 'number of rent-seekers' and 'extent of insider/outsider asymmetry' relate to each other in the sense that a fixed number of rent-seekers can be seen as an extreme case of insider/outsider asymmetry. Finally, an aspect which is usually included in the structure of the rent-seeking model and the equilibrium solution (and not discussed in isolation) is the rationality assumption inherent in Cournot-Nash behaviour.

two-sided rent-seeking situations, such as cases of cost-reducing and benefit-enhancing corruption and situations where only state officials act as rent-seekers (e.g. private rent extraction by means of cost-enhancing and benefit-reducing corruption). For the discussion of many parameters, this differentiation is not relevant, although an explicit distinction will be made if necessary.

As noted earlier, the following Sections b) and c) can be read selectively, depending on the interest of the reader. The main goal of the discussion is to demonstrate (as summarised in Section d) that the impact of parameter variations (and therefore the relation between rents and rent-seeking investments) varies widely depending on the setting.

The formal description of the items indicated in Table 3-2 will sometimes be brief. Furthermore, the primary focus is on dissipation and not on the qualitative structure of the equilibrium specified in the models (such as an identification of pure or mixed strategies). For more information, the reader is advised to consult the quoted papers. For an earlier discussion and survey of the traditional literature on dissipation, in particular the Tullock-type rent-seeking games, see Nitzan (1994a) and Bartsch and Thomas (1993) or the compact, less formal overview in Gelb, Hillman and Ursprung (1995).

b) What Determines the Value of the Rent?

Incentives to engage in rent-seeking activities come from two sources, the *value* an individual attributes to a given rent and the *costs* involved in capturing this rent. This section will focus on the value aspect. *Rent characteristics*, like size, certainty and public good character, as well as differences in *personal valuations* (subjective valuation of a rent-seeking situation, alternative income earning opportunities and attitudes towards risk) critically determine rent-seeking investments.

Characteristics of the Rent

This first topic in Table 3-2 summarises 'objective' attributes of a rent. Obviously, the *size of a rent* is likely to increase the rent-seekers' willingness to make rent-seeking outlays. Assuming that income has a constant marginal utility implies that the relative changes of rents and outlays are the same, i.e. dissipation is not affected, even though social costs may increase due to the quantity effect.[26] With *decreasing marginal utility*, the increase in rent-seeking investment falls short of the relative increase in the size of the rent and dissipation falls. More interesting and less trivial are situations where rent-seeking outlays do not change at all or even fall once the rent is increased.

---

[26] For instance, if rent-seekers invest 20 to obtain 50, they will invest 40 to obtain 100. In both cases the rate of dissipation is the same.

Rent-seeking outlays may not change in a *non-rival* rent-seeking setting, where rent-seekers make specific outlays to obtain a rent with near certainty. The crucial point is that a larger rent does not necessarily affect the level of rent-seeking investments required to obtain the rent if the rent-seeking situation is not competitive. If rent-seeking investments remain constant, dissipation clearly falls, as the basis (the size of the rent) becomes larger.

Under specific assumptions, rent-seeking outlays may even fall if the size of the rent increases. This may be the case in a situation where the rent is split into several prizes and an increase in the rent does not refer to the size of the individual prize, but to the *number of prizes* that can be contested. If fifty rent-seekers originally compete for twenty prizes of equal size, and each rent-seeker is unlikely to get more than one prize (this assumption is crucial), investments will fall if the number of prizes is increased to forty. Competition is simply less severe. This aspect has been addressed by Clark and Riis (1998), who developed a multi-prize rent-seeking model (the results of the model are discussed in more detail on page 102).

Closely related to the size of the rent is the *certainty* that the rent is supplied. Strictly speaking, economists differentiate between 'uncertainty' (unknown probabilities) and 'risk' (known probabilities). Here 'uncertainty' is used for both situations.

In simple Tullock-type rent-seeking settings, the general result holds that the less certain a rent is, the lower its value and the less resources will be invested to obtain the rent. Uncertainty may not only characterise a situation where it is uncertain that a rent is supplied at all, but also a situation where the size (or durability) of a rent is uncertain. In the real world, many rents are far from certain and may, once obtained, be eroded over time by political and market forces. Tullock (1988c, p. 56), for instance, concludes that 'monopolies are probably among the least secure type of investment'.

In countries with unstable and rapidly changing political constellations, future rents are not of much value. In a corrupt environment, for instance, new bureaucrats in key positions are unlikely to accept an original agreement unless they are also compensated. Uncertainty also arises in politically stable situations, for instance, in settings where corruption remains unpredictable, even though public officials are the same. Rents also erode in other ways. Import licences may bear a high risk that domestic demand for imported goods will drastically fall or that authorities will substantially raise quantities to reward other groups. An erratic state policy in particular is an important source of considerable uncertainties but also of additional rent-seeking opportunities. Another source of uncertainty is opposition to rent extraction. Finally, uncertainty may increase for bureaucrats in situations of private rent extraction, if the country has strengthened legal institutions. A case in point is the introduction of telephone hotlines, where extorted businesspeople are given opportunities to report their case.

Thus far it has been implicitly assumed that the level of uncertainty is exogenously given. If *certainty* depends on *total rent-seeking outlays*, the opposite relation may hold, i.e. exogenously increasing uncertainty that a rent is supplied may induce rent-seekers to spend additional resources to counter this effect. The outcome does however depend on how the change in certainty affects the marginal productivity of rent-seeking investments. Particularly in non-rival rent-seeking settings where rent-seeking profits are not fully dissipated, an adverse outcome is very likely. As this aspect more closely relates to the costs needed to capture a rent, it will be taken up later on.[27]

The second aspect outlined in the overview in Table 3-2 is the *public good* character of a rent or regulation. For instance, individuals may lobby for a better road which is not a priority in the country as it benefits only a few people, or they may lobby for a subsidy regulation that reduces the price of a specific input. Analysing public good aspects inevitably relates to questions of group formation, as a public good by definition always benefits more than one individual (in the above example, beneficiaries are the users of the road and those who depend on the subsidised input, respectively). Since 'group formation' will be considered separately at the end of Section c) the discussion here will be kept short. Focusing on dissipation, two implications of public goods stand out. First, free-riding incentives may arise and reduce rent-seeking investments. Some people may anticipate that others are already successfully lobbying for the rent and may therefore not make any contributions, even though they benefit from the rent or regulation. Secondly, rent transferred may diverge widely from the individual value attributed to the rent, and with it rent-seeking investments.

Katz, Nitzan and Rosenberg (1990) elaborated the pure public good situation within the stylised Tullock rent-seeking contest. They showed that in a setting where *m groups* of individuals compete for a *public good*, overall dissipation is similar to the result derived from the basic Tullock game, with only *m individuals* competing for a *single prize* whose size equals the benefit one individual can obtain in the public good case. As they note, in the pure public good case with two groups, total rent-seeking done for the public good is equal to only one half of the benefit to one individual (Katz, Nitzan and Rosenberg (1990, p. 52)). This outcome reflects the free-riding behaviour that arises with individual non-cooperative decision-making. If rent-seeking investments are related to the aggregated value the winning group assigns to the public good (and not to the costs to supply the public good), dissipation may be very small. Clearly, members of groups in public good contests have a strong incentive to coordinate their rent-seeking efforts. If they manage to *cooperate*, rent-seeking investments will increase again (see reference to this model on page 115f).

The situation is different if individuals within one group value the public good differently. This has been addressed by Baik (1993). He argues that what matters is the highest valuation within each group, as only the 'hungriest' rent-

[27] The most relevant aspects are described in Figure 3-6 on page 88.

seekers of each group will make any rent-seeking outlays. The contest is then reduced to a private good contest, where the *m* hungriest individuals compete against each other. Their valuation does not have to be equal, which again would reduce rent-seeking outlays as compared with a situation of equal valuation (see discussion on asymmetries later in this section).

For contributions on rent-seeking which deal with different aspects of public goods, see, among others, Ursprung (1990), Nitzan (1994b), or Loehman, Quesnel and Babb (1996). Ursprung (1990) puts the public good aspects into a candidate-election-framework where candidates promise a specific allocation of the budget. The rent that is at stake for the members of a group equals the difference between the transfer they receive if their candidate wins and the transfer they receive with an alternative candidate taking office. Nitzan (1994b) presents a model where authorities decide between dividing the budget into several components and making each component a private or public good. And Loehman, Quesnel and Babb (1996) finally address the impact of risk aversion on free-riding (see reference on page 84).

How relevant is the public good aspect in the rent-seeking context? The standard case, where the rent itself has public good character (and not the regulation that creates the rent), does not reflect a typical rent-seeking problem. It mostly refers to an application of the rent-seeking concept to a special area, where the focus lies on providing state duties rather than rents. It basically deals with questions such as: Which public goods arc produced? Which interest groups will be considered first or best? Allocating streetlights, building roads, digging wells and making decisions about which village will get a telephone line first are examples (see, for instance, the model presented in Linster (1993)). This type of rent-seeking for public goods is likely to be widespread in developing countries with a large share of donor-financed development projects. Clearly, the differentiation between rent-seeking and justified support depends on whether support is allocated according to the preferences and needs of a society. In particular in highly corrupt countries support is often misused and allocated according to other criteria.

More relevant to a rent-seeking analysis is an application of the public good aspect (in particular the problem of free-riding) to the process of introducing and altering laws and regulations. The situation describes endogenous rent-seeking where rent-seekers try to exert influence on formal rules. The rent itself remains a private good, but the regulation rent-seekers are lobbying for has public good character. If a specific group of import-dependent companies successfully lobbies against a devaluation of the country's overvalued currency, rents do not only accrue to them, but to anybody who has access to foreign currency at this favourable rate, regardless of the original lobbying contribution. This simpler problem of free-riding has not gained the attention it deserves in the rent-seeking literature. While in the above 'standard' public-good-setting different groups of rent-seekers compete to get a group-specific public good, here a few cooperating individuals lobby for a rent-creating regulation which finally benefits them and many other passive members of the interest group. If the group succeeds despite vast free-riding behaviour among the people who benefit, a low level of dissipation will result.

In both situations, the standard public good case or regulation, the model may include rent-seeking opposition (actions of those who lose if rent-seekers win) and the public good aspect becomes a problem for them too. Consumers often face severe problems to overcome free-riding incentives as they are usually much more difficult to organise (given their large number and dispersion). The public-good aspect of opposition is also relevant in the case of private rent extraction, where state officials extort individuals to make additional payments for services they are supposed to obtain. The build-up or strengthening of effective legal institutions, which guarantee secure property rights and detect and prosecute the violation of laws and regulations, is a public good. All in all, rent-seeking contests tend to be characterised by a fairly low level of dissipation, if public good aspects matter and cooperation among members of a group does not arise or is incomplete.

Personal Valuation

The second part of Table 3-2 summarises features which are partly of a subjective nature and are usually included as parameters within the individual utility function. They influence the relevance and subjective valuation of the rent and thereby affect dissipation.

The *specific valuation* of a rent may be quite different from its market-based ('objective') value. Depending on the capabilities and opportunities of the rent-seekers, their transaction costs, sunk cost considerations, etc., this valuation may vary considerably. It may be especially high if it includes non-monetary components, which are not rewarded by the market. For instance, holding off competition from abroad by state protectionism may be the only short-term and medium-term measure to keep a whole industry in business. People who lobby for this protection may determine their efforts not so much on the rent they get but on the value they attribute to stay in business. Power, responsibility, prestige, reputation (e.g. not losing face) or security can be important non-monetary components. The crucial point is that from a strict market perspective staying in business has no value per se. The problem is particularly relevant in situations where broad-based reforms (measures of stabilisation and structural adjustment) reveal that a large number of companies cannot survive without having access to continued support and protection. Hence if rents bear non-market values or the individual value is higher than the value determined by the implicit monetary rent transfer, dissipation, which is measured in relation to the latter, tends to be higher. Altruism and other externalities which lead to a positive valuation if somebody else wins the rent would work in the other direction (for a generalised model see Linster (1993)).

An important aspect of the individual utility attributed to a rent is *alternative income earning opportunities*. Better profit-seeking opportunities may not only reduce the number of rent-seeking cases, but also the level of dissipation (assuming that the marginal benefit of an additional effort in rent-seeking or profit-seeking will be equal, but positive). Unfortunately, in LDCs income earning opportunities are usually small (at least for the major part of the population), a feature which points to a generally higher level of rent-seeking and dissipation. The positive impact of alternative income earning opportunities to reduce rent-seeking is reinforced if there are *negative attitudes towards rent-seeking*. They may arise if the activity is illegal and/or involves social sanctions. The relation between the profitability of rent-seeking, alternative income earning opportunities and negative attitudes towards rent-seeking will be considered again from a broader perspective in Section a) of Chapter 4.1.

The personal valuation of the rent further depends on *attitudes towards risk*. This aspect will be discussed in more detail to demonstrate how assumptions on the scope and structure of a rent-seeking model critically determine the impact of a parameter. In various papers which describe formal rent-seeking models, it has been argued that introducing risk aversion into the model lowers rent-seeking investments and thus dissipation (see, for instance, the overview in Bartsch and Thomas (1993, p. 12f) or Nitzan (1994a, p. 45f)). For rent-seeking situations which have the structure of a Tullock-like game-theoretic setting, this conclusion is correct. There are however many rent-seeking situations where an increase in risk aversion may have the contrary effect, i.e. increase rent-seeking activities and dissipation. Two examples are presented here. The first argument relates to the profit-seeking alternative, the second partly qualifies the standard game-theoretic assumption applied to rent-seeking models.

To reduce complexity, most rent-seeking models narrowly focus on a single rent-seeking contest and abstract from the more complex environment in which the rent-seeking case is embedded. This simplified approach may be misleading when results of the model (derived from a comparative static analysis) become the basis of policy recommendations. As the example of risk aversion will demonstrate, it is sometimes necessary to broaden the framework and to explicitly take into account *interactions between rent-seeking and profit-seeking*.

If individuals allocate resources between profit-seeking and rent-seeking strategies, and all activities bear risks, for certain people and periods of time, profit-seeking activities may be even riskier than rent-seeking alternatives. In such a situation obviously the opposite relation of risk and rent-seeking holds, i.e. the more risk-averse individuals are, the more they will invest in rent-seeking. Or taking the comparative-static perspective, if profit-seeking activities are riskier than rent-seeking activities, an individual who becomes more risk-averse will increase the share of resources allocated to rent-seeking. In the 1980s and 1990s many developing countries were characterised by an environment that was clearly hostile to business, which encouraged rent-seeking rather than profit-seeking activities. It appears that many privileged rent-seekers did not face much risk in their activities. On the contrary, as public policies have often been erratic and property rights poorly enforced, it would have been much riskier for them to engage in proper profit-seeking activities. Risk-averse individuals thus tended to favour rent-seeking activities.

The same argument of deciding between different alternatives holds if rent-seekers face several rent-seeking opportunities. Narrowly focusing on one rent-seeking contest may not permit an adequate description of the impact of risk aversion if resources can be shifted between rent-seeking contests that bear different levels of risk.

The second argument why risk aversion may increase rent-seeking activities addresses the appropriateness of the game-theoretic approach taken in the literature on rent-seeking. One may easily get the impression that this approach is the only valid method for analysing rent-seeking situations. As noted earlier, game theory focuses on the individual decision-making situation where the optimal strategy depends on the other players' behaviour and vice versa. In a world of incomplete information rent-seekers may not always fully take into account these interactions. In addition, there are many rent-seeking settings which are closer to a 'single rent-seeker-lobbying' contest, i.e. a non-rival situation. If the model structure includes such features, risk aversion may affect dissipation quite differently.

Risk-averse individuals typically *hedge* against unfavourable outcomes. There is no reason to assume why they should not do the same in many rent-seeking situations. Risk-averse students, for instance, are likely to invest more time and effort in trying to get a scholarship than their risk-neutral fellow competitors. They will ask more people to write a letter of recommendation that can be included in the application and they may even try to personally contact the authorities who decide on the scholarship.

In non-rival rent-seeking settings hedging against unfavourable outcomes happens, for instance, when an entrepreneur engages in cost-reducing or benefit-enhancing corruption. The rent-seeker may not know which 'state of the world' is relevant to him or her. Insecurity about the probabilities to win (i.e. uncertainty), which translates into insecurity about the level of investments needed to obtain a rent, can explain a dissipation-increasing outcome of risk aversion. Risk aversion may also lead to an increase in rent-seeking investments in a setting of known probabilities, if risk aversion implies a non-linear valuation of these probabilities. Figure 3-4 displays two stylised examples.

As argued, what distinguishes these examples from the 'standard' rent-seeking settings is the basic structure of the rent-seeking situation, in particular how risk aversion and the interaction between different rent-seekers is included. Tullock's original efficient-rent-seeking model focuses on an equilibrium in pure strategies of identical, rational rent-seekers who lobby for a single, indivisible rent. This model cannot sufficiently describe the trade-off between higher expected returns and lower risk, which would be relevant in settings where hedging against unfavourable outcomes is common, for instance, because the setting is of a non-rival nature. Of course, unilaterally increasing rent-seeking investment in the Tullock game would increase the probability to win and thus reduce risk while simultaneously reduce the expected payoff, but the literature suggests the contrary, that risk averse rent-seekers would reduce their investments. What finally matters when it comes to drawing policy conclusions is to differentiate between rent-seeking settings where a change in risk increases or decreases rent-seeking activities.

Figure 3-4: Rent-Seeking Investments and Risk Aversion

a) Uncertainty and risk aversion

Situation: Prize = \$100, probabilities unknown
Depending on unknown lobbying activities of other competitors, \$60, \$20 or nothing may be needed to win the prize.

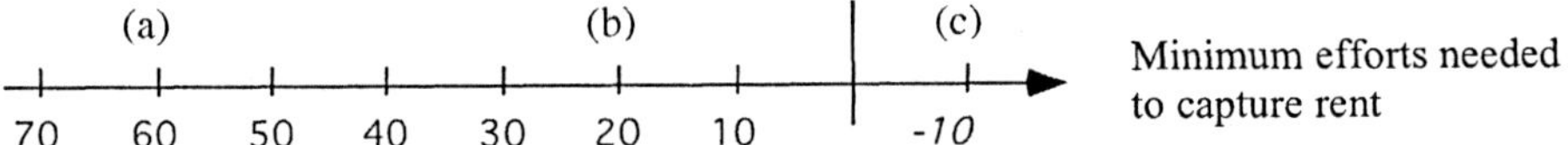

Rent-seekers have no idea whether they face state a, b or c. A risk-averse rent-seeker may not invest at all (which would be in line with the standard result where risk aversion reduces rent-seeking). If the risk-averse rent-seeker decides to invest, the rent-seeker is likely to hedge against state (a) and spend \$60. A less risk-averse rent-seeker may only hedge against (b) and spend \$20.

b) Risk and risk aversion

Situation: Prize = \$1000, all probabilities are known
Rent-seekers have to decide between investing \$50, where the probability to win is 90%, and \$200, which increases this probability to 99%.

A possible approach to including attitudes towards risk is to adjust the probabilities (pr) with an exponent x (pr^X); whereas x>1 indicates risk aversion, x=1 risk neutrality and 0<x<1 risk liking. In the example given below, the exponent 2 has been chosen for the risk-averse rent-seeker. The lower the probability (i.e. the higher the risk), the larger becomes the downward correction of the subjective valuation of a risky situation. (Probability 1.0→ 1.0, 0.9→ 0.81, 0.8→ 0.64, ...).

b1) Perception and choice of the risk-neutral rent-seeker

$$-50 + \begin{cases} 0.9 & 1000 \\ 0.1 & 0 \end{cases} = \underline{\underline{850}} \longleftarrow$$

$$-200 + \begin{cases} 0.99 & 1000 \\ 0.01 & 0 \end{cases} = \underline{\underline{790}}$$

b2) Perception and choice of the risk-averse rent-seeker (valuation of probabilities adjusted to account for risk aversion: pr^2)

$$-50 + \begin{cases} 0.81 & 1000 \\ 0.01 & 0 \end{cases} = \underline{\underline{760}}$$

$$-200 + \begin{cases} 0.98 & 1000 \\ 0.00 & 0 \end{cases} = \underline{\underline{780}} \longleftarrow$$

The calculations indicate optimal rent-seeking decisions of a risk-neutral and a risk-averse rent-seeker. In contrast to the standard outcome, here risk aversion increases rent-seeking investments and therefore dissipation. Using the above specification of risk aversion, the subjectively adjusted net present value is higher to the risk averse rent-seeker, with an investment of \$200 rather than \$50.

Loehman, Quesnel and Babb (1996) seem to have been the first to consider the possibility of an increase in rent-seeking due to risk aversion. Focusing on a public good situation, where rent-seekers cannot be sure about the contributions of others, they argued that risk aversion may counter the traditional free-rider effect and increase contribution. It is surprising that this deviating effect of risk aversion, which indeed characterises human behaviour in many situations, has received hardly any attention in the literature on rent-seeking. Most of the literature on rent-seeking focuses narrowly on the Tullock-type rent-seeking game. If analytical rent-seeking models aim at capturing other realistic settings, the above examples indicate that there is large area for further work.

Another important aspect concerning the valuation of rents is *asymmetries in valuation*. Under 'normal' conditions, as given in traditional rent-seeking approaches, it can be assumed that the higher the valuation rent-seekers place on a rent, the more they are prepared to invest to obtain this rent. In settings in the real world, valuations are likely to differ among rent-seekers and therefore also the incentives to engage in rent-seeking activities. However, to derive the impact of asymmetries in valuation one has to go beyond calculating average values.

Many authors have explicitly addressed asymmetries in valuations in rent-seeking models, as it is an important determinant of dissipation. If rent-seekers place different valuations on a rent, overall dissipation usually falls as compared to a situation where all rent-seekers place the average valuation. This phenomenon has become known as the *'preemption' effect*. It also arises with asymmetries in power. The logic is simple: competition will be stronger the smaller the differences among rent-seekers are. However, these differences have to be *perceived* by all.

The magnitude of the fall in dissipation depends on the specific probability-to-win function. Hillman and Riley (1989) were among the first to elaborate the impact of asymmetries in valuation. They differentiated between two probability of winning functions: the Tullock lottery setting and a second, perfectly discriminating version where the rent-seeker with the highest outlays wins. Based on their results they conclude that 'a larger value assigned to the political prize by a rival is a barrier to entry for lower-valuation contenders' (Hillman and Riley (1989, p. 19)). In addition, they focus on the problem of uncertainty about the other rent-seekers' valuations, showing that this uncertainty will erode the above-mentioned 'barrier of entry'. For a more recent paper on asymmetry in valuation which also addresses different values of the productivity parameter r in the Tullock game, see Nti (1999). Other authors discuss and extend the above-mentioned perfectly discriminating version (e.g. Riley (1999) or Che and Gale (2000)). Results of the different models are in general in line with what has been noted in this section, i.e. 'the more skewed the valuations, the smaller the fraction of the value dissipated in rent-seeking' (Nti (1999, p. 421)). Additional information on the impact of asymmetries in valuation follow in Section c) when addressing winning rules (page 100f, in particular Table 3-3) and asymmetries in power (page 109).

c) What Are the Costs to Capture the Rent?

Having discussed the factors that determine the *value* attributed to a rent, this section turns its attention to the *rent-seeking process*. Besides the general costs of influencing rent-setters or rent-distributing authorities (politicians, bureaucrats and donors), costs depend on the rent-seekers' interaction, the division of the prize and the strategies rent-seekers pursue. The costs of rent-seeking addressed here and the benefits discussed in Section b) together determine the incentive to engage in rent-seeking activities and the level of total and individual dissipation.

As rent-seeking contests and related costs are complex, it is helpful to start with a brief outline which describes the *structure and possible competing elements* of rent-seeking settings. Figure 3-5 summarises these aspects and can be applied to situations where rent-seekers act from a position outside or inside the rent-creating government and government-related institutions.[28]

Figure 3-5: Structure and Competing Elements in Rent-Seeking Settings

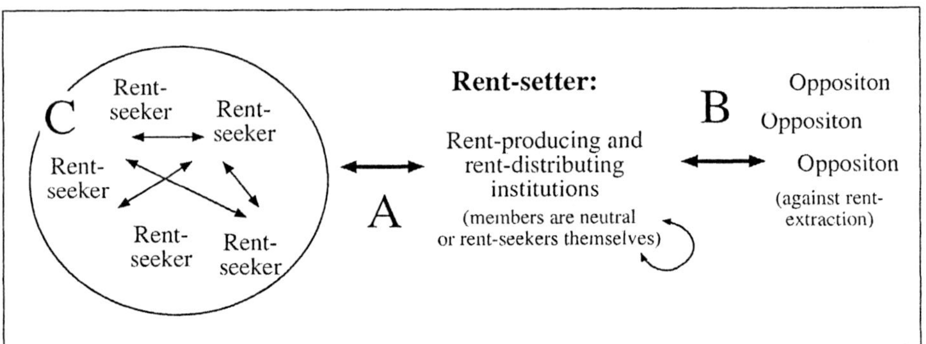

Depending on the setting, rent-seeking activities involve different cost components. At the core are the efforts to influence policymakers, superior officials or other rent-creating and rent-distributing authorities. Costs in A, however, do not only relate to the rent-setters' preferences (which may include rent-seeking intentions and reflect the competitive structure rent-setters are embedded in); they may also depend on the impact of groups lobbying against the transfer B and/or the competitive structure of the rent-seeking group in C.

It makes a difference if rent-seekers have to make efforts to get an already existing rent (e.g. underpriced resources or foreign exchange at below market prices) or if they also need to make sure that the rent is created in the first place. Depending on whether rent-seekers act from a position inside or outside the rent-producing institutions, they will have to influence policymakers, superior officials or other rent-distributing authorities. The rent-seeking setting may be

[28] As noted in Section a), in most cases the discussion will not explicitly differentiate between the two rent-seeking positions. What matters for dissipation are the characteristics of the setting, in particular whether the setting is of a non-rival or rival nature.

additionally characterised by strong opposition against the rent transfer, or it may involve severe rent-seeking competition among rent-seekers. The simple structure of the probability of winning function displayed on page 65 ($\pi_i = f(x_i)/\sum f(x_i)$) expresses A with f(x) and competition in C by the ratio $f(x_i)/\sum f(x_i)$. With a single rent-seeker or a perfectly cooperating group, rent-seeking outlays are determined by A (and may include costs related with B).

To avoid confusion in two-sided rent-seeking situations, a partial focus will be taken. It either refers to the perspective of the corrupt bureaucrat or the perspective of the corrupting private counterpart. In both cases, the rent-seeker is seen from the position C in Figure 3-5 (i.e. in the case of the rent-seeking bureaucrat, the rent-setter is, for instance, the superior official). A one-sided perspective still permits an analysis of rent-seeking incentives, but nevertheless remains partial as the final outcome, i.e. the intersection of the 'supply' and 'demand' for rents (which even gets blurred in a two-sided rent-seeking situation) is determined by the interaction of the two rent-seeking parties.

Rent-Seeking Costs in General

The general feature of how costly it is to influence policymakers, superior officials or rent-distributing authorities is summarised with the term *'autonomy'* of the rent-setter, i.e. the less decisions of rent-setters are influenced by activities of rent-seekers, the more autonomous are the rent-setters. In many competitive rent-seeking settings, rent-seeking expenditures and dissipation tend to fall once autonomy increases. It simply pays less to invest in rent-seeking. However, as will be argued below, depending on the setting this intuitive result does not necessarily hold. What matters are the marginal cost and benefits of influence.

In the simplest Tullock rent-seeking situation, where the rent is exogenous and competitive, higher autonomy reduces rent-seeking activities. In such a setting rent-seeking efforts determine only the relative distribution among rent-seekers (contest C in Figure 3-5) and not the total amount of rents or the probability that the rent is allocated at all. For instance, assuming in the original Tullock game a low value for r to represent autonomy of the rent-distributing authority, e.g. $r = 0.33$ instead of 1, total rent-seeking investments also decline to one third of the original value (see results in Table 3-1 on page 67).

The situation becomes more complex if the rent-seeking setting is constrained by other than competitive rent-seeking forces or if the rent is of endogenous nature (endogenous size or endogenous certainty of supply). Higher autonomy, i.e. making it harder to influence authorities, may then not just influence the distribution of rents but also size and certainty. This may result in an increase in dissipation or even an increase in rent-seeking investments.

If the *size of the rent is endogenous*, i.e. if the size depends on the level of rent-seeking activities, higher autonomy not only implies smaller rent-seeking investments but also smaller rents. Dissipation, measured by the ratio of total rent-seeking investments to effective transfers realised, may thus fall, remain constant or rise, depending on the properties of the rent-seeking cost curve. Of course, from an efficiency perspective a rise in dissipation is not necessarily negative, if it only results from a less than proportional fall in rent-seeking investments relative to the rents sought. To analyse the impact in a Tullock rent-seeking model, where the total size of the rent depends on aggregate rent-seeking efforts see, for instance, Chung (1996). Only if the size of the endogenous rent has an upper limit (e.g. as assumed in Long and Vousden (1987)) and outlays are related to this fixed maximum possible transfer, will higher autonomy in a Tullock-like setting always imply a lower ratio.

In a *non-rival setting*, in contrast, higher autonomy can easily increase rent-seeking outlays and dissipation. This may happen if the costs needed to obtain a rent do not become prohibitive but remain below a critical level. In Tanzania, for instance, the new Tanzanian Revenue Authority (TRA) replaced the highly corrupt Tax and Customs Department. Salaries were substantially increased to make tax-collectors more immune against bribery. This measure apparently increased the autonomy of rent-distributors (tax enforcers) in the sense that the previous level of bribes was no longer sufficient to obtain illegal tax exemptions. Rent-seeking seen from the perspective of corrupt businesspeople has become less profitable. However, not having reached the critical level—the minimum bribe demanded is still smaller than the maximum bribe offered (Table 4-1 on page 153 addresses this aspect in detail)—the measure did not reduce rent-seeking activities. It simply increased the bribes necessary to bring in the goods free of tax, and many dishonest businesspeople were prepared to pay.

An increase in autonomy may also translate into a reduction of the *certainty* that the rent is supplied. As noted earlier (page 78), if there is a link between rent-seeking outlays and the certainty of supply, a reduction in the probability may then be reversed by an increase in rent-seeking investments. Figure 3-6 outlines this aspect.

Figure 3-6: Optimal Rent-Seeking Investments and Endogenous Insecurity

The rectangles indicate the size of the rent (broken line where insecure) and the share of rent-seeking investments (black areas). In equilibrium marginal costs of rent-seeking usually equal marginal benefits. With an exogenous increase in uncertainty, this equality will no longer hold. The net present value of the investment drops, but the rent-seeker may be able to partly counter this effect by raising investments. Depending on the properties of the cost function, the increase may fully or only partly reverse the exogenous fall in 'security'; the rent-seeking opportunity, however, has become less profitable as dissipation is clearly higher.

For non-rival settings, the impact is similar to the one described in the tax collector's example above. In other than non-rival situations, where several rent-seekers compete for a rent, the outcome depends among other things on how the equilibrium is constrained, and whether the increase in autonomy affects the certainty of supply alone or also alters the ability to influence the choice of the rent-seeking winner. For either situation, competitive or non-competitive, the example shown in Figure 3-6 represents one possible solution. If, alternatively, the reduction in certainty is sufficiently large, rent-seeking outlays may also drop to zero. This outcome is, however, less likely if rent-seeking investments are done sequentially and therefore involve a large share of sunk costs.

Finally, important insights can be derived from a *multiple rent-seeking-contest perspective*. Rent-seeking economies are usually characterised by situations where rent-seekers simultaneously engage in several rent-seeking activities or they are in a position to make use of different rent-seeking alternatives. Attempts to reduce rent-seeking by an overall increase in the autonomy of policymakers, superior officials or rent-distributing authorities may induce rent-seekers to reallocate investments from contests which entirely lost their profitability to other contests. Under such conditions, higher autonomy would imply fewer rent-seeking contests but higher investment and dissipation related within the ones that remain. Or alternatively, rent-seekers can even create new opportunities. Higher autonomy would then imply an increasing or decreasing number of rent-seeking contests but higher dissipation. Such rent-seeking strategies are in particular relevant in a situation where a country undertakes broad-based measures of stabilisation and structural adjustment. Rent-seekers then come under pressure from different sides, but often find new opportunities to compensate part of their 'losses'.

All in all, making it more difficult to influence policymakers, superior officials or rent-distributing authorities may reduce rent-seeking activities in traditional rent-seeking contests, in particular, if there are no relations to other rent-seeking settings. If the rents are endogenous or if they reflect non-rival settings, higher autonomy may lead to a sharp increase in rent-seeking activities and dissipation. A similar outcome is possible if different rent-seeking settings are linked. Closing down a rent-seeking opportunity in the reform process tends to increase pressure on other sources of rent extraction. The impact on dissipation depends on the overall setting. Unfortunately, such inter-linked phenomena appear not to have been addressed in the formal literature on rent-seeking.

So far, autonomy has been treated in a general, abstract way. The extent of the autonomy of rent-creating and distributing institutions, in particular their sensitivity to rent-seeking investments, depends on a variety of factors. The discussion here, however, will be confined to the narrow perspective on dissipation and leave equally relevant aspects, such as the question whether authorities depend on being reelected or need to strategically allocate rents, to the discussion in Chapter 4.3.

The *structure of an authority* may decisively co-determine autonomy and the level of dissipation. A rent-seeking situation may look very different if a committee rather than a single person takes decisions or if several independent authorities can decide and allocate a specific rent. The situation is also different if allocations of rents have to be scrutinised by the parliament or if a senior bureaucrat can take the decision alone.

Abstracting from differences between individuals, i.e. assuming that individuals are identical, it is less costly to influence one person than a group of people. Allocating rents based on the *decision of a committee* instead of a decision made by one person may thus have a similar impact on rent-seeking efforts as would raising autonomy. Rent-seeking situations where committees play a role are usually characterised by asymmetries among committee members, i.e. not all committee members can be influenced in the same way. The level of rent-seeking investments and dissipation then depends on explicit assumptions about the committee, in particular the number of committee members, their relative sensitivities to rent-seeking expenditures, as well as the decision rule they apply (for specific applications, see, among others, Congleton (1984) or Amegashie (1999a)). Possible decision rules of a committee range from simple majority votes to a strict unanimity requirement; furthermore, committee members may decide simultaneously or in a sequenced manner. Another option is that each member of a committee (or a subset of members) is entitled to allocate rents.

If rent-seekers are able to choose between *several rent suppliers*, i.e. rents are not just allocated by one person (or an office where decisions are made together), rent-seeking opportunities generally improve and dissipation falls. Many non-rival rent-seeking settings are characterised by this situation. Smugglers, for instance, may have the opportunity to collude with various customs officers to evade customs duties. The example equally demonstrates another aspect, i.e. the outcome may critically depend on whether authorities are rent-seekers themselves.

Shleifer and Vishny (1993) present an interesting differentiation of the competitive structure of corrupt agencies. Even though they focus on the bureaucrats' rent-seeking behaviour and do not simultaneously specify possible rent-seeking competition among individuals who try to influence these authorities, their model can be used to give an example of the two aspects mentioned above (committee decision and several suppliers).

As discussed in Chapter 2.2, bureaucrats may extort private rents from companies and individuals, for instance when the latter depend on work permits, passports or business licences. These activities have been referred to as cost-enhancing and benefit-reducing corruption. Bureaucrats may equally benefit individuals by allocating specific rents such as subsidised foreign exchange, underpriced inputs or unjustified tax exemptions and permits. The bureaucrat then colludes with the counterpart and seizes a share of the rent. Following Shleifer and Vishny's framework, the rents or permits that individuals and companies get may depend on a combination of different rights; in addition, rights may be supplied by different agencies.

Shleifer and Vishny compare the three different situations of one agency supplying all rights, competing agencies supplying complementary rights and competing agencies each supplying all rights (see also the summary in Khan (1996, p. 17)). In the third case, competition between bureaucrats will drive down the price for the rights and thus dissipation of the rent-seeking applicant. Where agencies supply complementary rights, dissipation of rent-seeking applicants is likely to be highest. As Shleifer and Vishny (1993, p. 605f) note, these agencies behave like independent monopolists and maximise their bribe income without taking their negative impact on other agencies into account, with the effect that bribes will be too high and output low. Finally, they show that an agency which supplies all rights will behave like a monopolist and set an intermediate price that maximises the total collection of bribes.

All in all, the reference to Shleifer and Vishny emphasises that the cost to influence bureaucrats can critically depend on the specific structure of the agency. Similarly, taking the perspective of the rent-seeking bureaucrat, Shleifer and Vishny's approach indicates how bureaucrats may be constrained in extracting rents for themselves. The situation becomes in particular complex in a two-sided competitive setting where the final outcome depends on whether the equilibrium is more constrained by competition among applicants or competition among bureaucrats. In addition, in such a rent-seeking situation it is necessary to clarify the focus and the range dissipation refers to. The problem is that rent-seeking investments of individuals and companies mostly take the form of bribes, which constitute the rents taken by the other side. If these transfers are not defined to constitute part of dissipation, a more specific approach is necessary, which differentiates between different types of rent-seeking investments.

Besides the two aspects autonomy and structure of the authority, dissipation may also depend on the *starting point*, i.e. rent-seeking outlays necessary to capture a rent do not only reflect the costs needed to influence policymakers, superior officials or rent-distributing authorities, they also depend on the specification of a possible rent distribution in the absence of rent-seeking activities. In some instances preceding rent-seeking activities only lead to the introduction of a rent-creating policy, without simultaneously specifying the effective distribution of the rent, which may then become subject to an additional contest. Furthermore, rent-distributing authorities obviously have preferences themselves. In an imperfect political market, politicians may create rents or decide against the abolition of rents, not because the decision reflects the preferences of the society but because the prevailing ideology, personal interests and the rules to remain in office make this decision the most favourable strategy. The argument holds even if politicians only benefit little (as compared to the rents created and the costs to the society).[29]

---

[29] For instance, in a one-party system, it may not be opportune to argue for the privatisation of highly inefficient parastatal companies. The benefit of the politicians voting against privatisation may be an increase in reputation or slightly higher chances to get into a higher position within the party.

Most rent-seeking models assume a situation where there is either no pre-suggested rent allocation or, in an exogenous rent-seeking contest, where there is an equal distribution of rents as long as no competitor makes positive outlays (the allocation to non-contributing rent-seekers then usually drops to zero as soon as the first rent-seeker makes a positive investment). These assumptions are not appropriate for many of the settings in the real world.

If there is a predetermined rent allocation, rent-seeking efforts may not correlate highly with the achieved ex-post allocation of rents. In such a setting, dissipation is again a matter of definition and focus, as it depends on whether rent-seeking outlays are defined as a ratio of the entire rent, a ratio of the change in the size of the rent rent-seekers aimed to obtain or whether outlays are defined as a ratio of the change rent-seekers actually realised. This caveat has already been mentioned when defining dissipation. Most settings with pre-specified rent allocations imply a low level of dissipation, if dissipation includes the entire rent as a basis.

A specific starting point may either refer to the contest between rent-seekers and losing counterparts or to the allocation of rents among the rent-seekers. The sections on opposition and asymmetries in power will take up this aspect again. One way to include a specific rent allocation is to use a difference-form contest-success function (see reference on page 99f). This function can include rent allocations to individuals who do not engage in rent-seeking activities.

Looking at the structure and competing elements of rent-seeking settings presented in Figure 3-5, so far, the discourse basically focused on rent-seeking costs which can be explained by the specific structure in A. Equally important for dissipation is an assessment of possible *opposition against the rent transfer* (indicated with B in Figure 3-5).

In essence, introducing opposition to a rent-seeking setting has a similar effect as raising the rent-setter's autonomy. An assessment of opposition does however bring in additional aspects. First, opposition affects the behaviour of rent-setters; in the extreme, rent-setters only act as intermediaries between competing forces. The intensity of opposition depends on the size of the transfer at stake, as well as on the specific features of the opposition group, among others, their abilities to solve free-riding problems. And second, unlike situations of exogenous decisions by rent-setters, which do not include opposition, activities of opposing forces add to the level of dissipation. The discussion here therefore explicitly considers two definitions of dissipation, the standard rent-seekers' focus and the broader approach, which includes outlays of opponents, denominated as *'overall dissipation'*.

In the literature, the terms 'rent avoidance', 'rent protection' and 'rent defending' have been used interchangeably to indicate resistance. Some authors, however, suggest a differentiation, for instance applying rent avoidance for opposition against the creation of rents (see Fleming (1998, p. 279)). Strictly speaking, none of the terms is satisfactory. On the one hand, consumers who lobby against a creation of a monopoly aim to protect their wealth (or surplus) and not rents in the rent-seeking sense. On the other hand, there are also rent-protecting activities of rent-seekers if their rents are in danger of being taken away, which is plain rent-seeking behaviour. The poor reform records of many developing countries in the 1980s and 1990s are to a large extent a reflection of these latter activities.

If opposition can overcome the *free-riding* problem (or at least credibly threaten to do so), rent-seeking becomes less attractive and rent transfers are likely to be less frequent or smaller in size. As mentioned above, the situation may be compared with raising autonomy in an endogenous rent-seeking contest. The specific impact on dissipation, however, depends on its *definition* as well as on assumptions about the *anticipation* of resistance, the *relative costs* of lobbying, the *relevance of rent-setters preferences* and other features such as the possibility that the relation between rent-seeking and opposition is *non-linear* (explained below).

Taking opposition into account implies, among other things, concentrating more directly on the link between the size of the rent and potential resistance. It is therefore helpful to use a schematic depiction of the rent. Following the frequently applied approach in the literature, the impact of introducing opposition may be best demonstrated with the stylised monopoly case. Figure 3-7 reiterates the diagram presented in Figure 3-1 and adds another diagram to indicate the effect of insecurity, which results from opposition.

Abstracting from sunk costs, insecurity about the rent and marginal cost considerations, rent-seekers will at the most spend the value of the rent, which is the Tullock rectangle P_mP_cCB (grey area in diagram a) of Figure 3-7). If the monopoly is created, consumers not only lose this rectangle, but also the Harberger-triangle (dotted area ABC). Applying the same logic, they may at the most be willing to spend P_mP_cAB to prevent this transfer. Hence, in extreme, i.e. if there is *myopia* and full dissipation on the side of rent-seekers and opposition, the situation may indicate a case of very high 'overall' overdissipation, where total outlays are more than twice as large as the monopoly rent at stake. This result reflects the provocative and criticised outcome presented by Wenders (1987), even though he does not assume myopic behaviour. He justifies the possible result with a prisoner's dilemma situation, arguing that both parties, 'neither buyers nor sellers may refrain from spending the maximum amount they each have at stake; [if] either voluntarily spends less, they will be taken advantage of by the other side' (Wenders (1987, p. 458)).

Clearly, there is a flaw in Wenders's analysis. To assess how much rent-seekers and consumers actually spend and to determine the joint maximum outlay requires a clearer definition of the rent-seeking setting. In a situation where opposition is somehow *anticipated*, it can be assumed that the rent is not taken for granted. If rent-seekers perceive a less than 100% chance that the monopoly is created (or sustained), the expected value of the transfer and rent-seeking outlays to capture this rent decline. The reduced expected value of the monopoly rent is indicated with the smaller grey area in diagram b) of

Figure 3-7: Monopoly, Rent-Seeking and Consumer Opposition

a) Producer rent and consumer loss arising from a monopoly

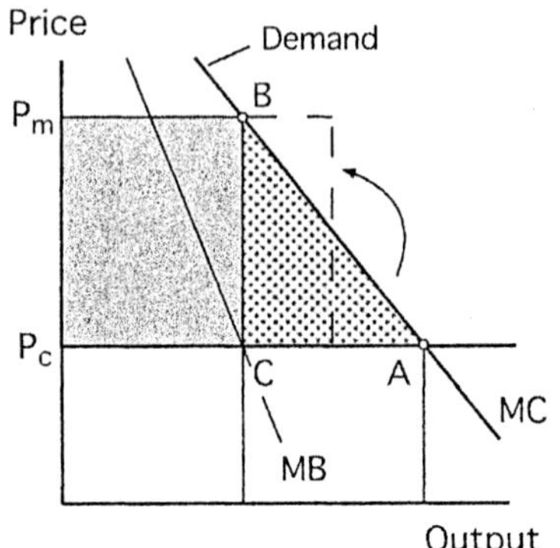

b) Schematic depiction of expected transfer and maximum efforts

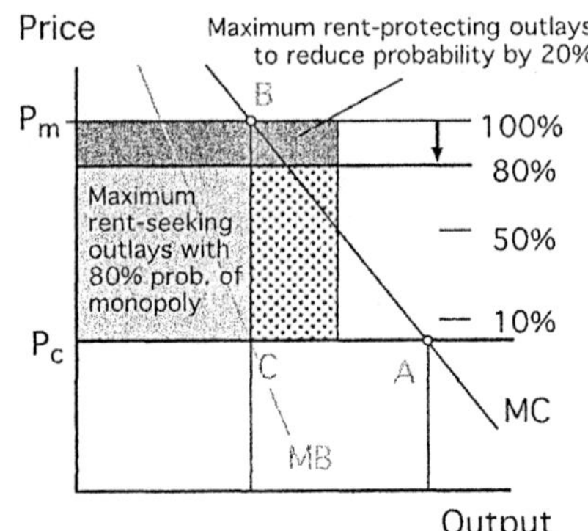

The announcement of a monopoly regulation may provoke resistance among consumers. To gain a 20% probability that the monopoly is not implemented or sustained, consumers will spend at the most the reduction in the expected loss, which is the dark grey rectangle. Rent-seeking companies may perceive the reduced chance that a monopoly is sustained. The expected value of the rent (grey area) declines and therefore maximum rent-seeking outlays to compete for the monopoly right.

Figure 3-7.[30] The impact of introducing opposition on the rent-seekers' dissipation is therefore similar to raising the rent-distributor's autonomy in an exogenous rent-seeking setting.

The situation changes if the definition of dissipation includes consumer outlays. How much will risk-neutral consumers spend to convince policymakers not to introduce the monopoly (or in the above case to reduce the chances from 100% down to e.g. 80%)? The answer is at the most the reduction of their expected loss. This reduction is derived by the dark grey rectangle. In contrast to the above case of myopia, extreme 'overall' overdissipation will not arise any more, even though some overdissipation is still possible, as the sum of the grey and dark grey areas in b) is larger than the monopoly rent in a). The more the consumers manage to reduce the probability that the monopoly is introduced or sustained, the larger their maximum feasible outlays (dark grey rectangle), the larger the possible difference between the case with and without opposition.

The description of the rent at stake provides some insights on maximum rent-seeking outlays. However, direct conclusions on dissipation are limited to the stylised cases mentioned earlier. Figure 3-7 cannot capture the dynamics

30 Already in 1980, Baysinger and Tollison (1980) presented a similar approach to analyse the impact of opposition under uncertainty. Under the assumption that the monopoly and the competitive outcome is equally likely, they defined the value of the expected rent as the value that corresponds to the price $P_{exp.} = (P_m+P_c)/2$, rather than using 50% of the rent at $P=P_m$ (see also Brooks and Heijdra (1989, p. 36f)). If expected producer and consumer rents are then added together, their specification leads to an area larger than the original Tullock and Harberger triangle at $P=P_m$, an outcome, which for instance Ellingsen (1991, p. 655) criticises as being impossible.

between rent-seekers, rent-setters and opposition but only provides a static picture of maximum rent-seeking and rent-protecting outlays. To describe the actual rent-seeking contest, other aspects need to be included.

Free-riding incentives, as well as the ability to overcome such incentives, explain whether and to what extent opposition will form. Most settings in the real world are characterised by severe free-riding problems on the rent-protecting side. Effective rent protection may require organising a large number of consumers with very low individual stakes. Rent-seekers are likely to anticipate these difficulties. As opposition becomes less probable, the expected value of the rent is accordingly higher. In contrast to this situation, in cases where free-riding is not an issue, rent-seekers may be aware of the larger stake of the losing counterpart and thus anticipate their higher probability to react. This will affect the rent-seekers' perception about the expected value of the rent and would reduce dissipation as opposed to a setting where they do not foresee this asymmetry (note the similarity to the competition-reducing effect of differences in valuation mentioned earlier).

What may also be observed is a *non-linear reaction* of opposition, i.e. opposition is mute while the rent remains below a critical level, for instance as free-riding incentives dominate, but it becomes vociferous once this level is exceeded. Consumers usually tolerate a certain level of rent extraction without opposition (see, for instance, Cairns and Long (1991)). The same may be true for individuals and companies in the case of private rent extraction, where bureaucrats extort side payments. If rent-seekers perceive a non-linear reaction, they are likely to adjust their strategies and keep their demands for rents on the lower side. A 'critical mass model' would capture this feature. As long as opposition does not become active, dissipation will be determined by the costs and competitive situation of the rent-seekers' side.

Similar to what has been discussed in the context of the rent-seeking setting in A of Figure 3-5, the *autonomy of the rent-setter* and the *starting point* also affect the costs of rent-seeking opposition. The impact of opposition depends on whether and to what extent preferences of the rent-setter count and what these preferences look like. What finally matters for dissipation are the rent-seekers' and opponents' relative costs for influencing policymakers (i.e. their relative power). If consumers are powerful, in the sense that they only need moderate outlays to reduce the chance that the monopoly is created (e.g. only a third of the dark grey area to get a reduction from 100% to 80%) but rent-seekers' outlays are characterised by nearly full dissipation of their expected rent (grey area), dissipation will fall with the introduction of opposition, regardless of whether the definition of dissipation includes consumer outlays or not. Of course, the situation may also be the other way round and therefore lead to an increase in dissipation.

Similarly, if the starting point without consumer resistance is not at 100% probability that the monopoly is created, but lower, for instance at 50% or even at 10% (which reflects more secure property rights on the consumer side), maximum rent-seeking outlays of consumers and rent-seekers are lower, correspondingly. The impact of opposition on dissipation, as compared to a situation with no opposition, will again depend on the above-mentioned relative costs of influencing policymakers.

Summing up, an assessment of rent-seeking settings that include opposition is complex. Opposition makes rent-seeking behaviour more costly and may prevent some rent transfers and the dead-weight losses associated with these transfers. The impact on rent-seekers' dissipation depends on the specific setting. What matters is whether (and to what extent) opposition is anticipated, how powerful opposing forces are, and what position and influence the rent-setter takes between the two competing groups. For some stylised models which explicitly address the impact of anticipated opposition see Ellingsen (1991), Fabella (1995) or Baik (1999). With most model specifications, opposition reduces total social costs. Clearly, the question of how rent-seekers and opposing groups organise has many more facets. Given its importance in determining the success or failure of rent-seeking activities, Chapter 4.2 will be devoted to an interest group analysis, summarising factors which determine the abilities and incentives of interest groups to organise and provoke conflict.

So far not much has been said about the question of *how* rent-seekers and opposing groups can exert influence. Allowing for different *'means of exerting influence'* qualifies the most frequently used assumption in the literature on rent-seeking, i.e. rent-seeking outlays are always sunk and not conditional to a rent-seeking outcome. There are in particular two alternative ways of exerting influence, which may affect rent-seeking costs: threat and conditional outlays.

McChesney (1987) explicitly points to the situation of extracting rents by *threat*, when discussing the case of private rent extraction by state officials (recall reference to McChesney in Chapter 2.2). The use of threat may also matter in rent-seeking situations, where the state creates and distributes rents. If companies supply a good or service which is indispensable for a smooth functioning of the economy, they may threaten to cease the production or to stop the service, unless the government guarantees the support they are lobbying for. Dependencies between the government and the parastatal sector have been common. As will be demonstrated in the case study on Tanzania, several of the monopoly companies, above all utility parastatals, were in a powerful position since the government depended on their functioning and could not risk their collapse by reducing rent-seeking support. The companies therefore did not have to invest a lot in rent-seeking activities.

Similarly, military leaders may demand high wages and other fringe benefits for supporting the current government, simply by threatening to withdraw their support. As long as the threat does not materialise, rent-seeking outlays may be very small. Threat can therefore be a powerful instrument to receive rents and it can explain a low level of dissipation.[31] The literature on rent-seeking models

[31] Of course, to be powerful threat has to be credible. For a discussion on this aspect, see McChesney (1997, p. 38f).

seems to have only indirectly addressed the possibility of threat in rent-seeking contests, for instance by allowing for asymmetries in power among rent-seekers.

Another type of influence is *conditional outlays*. Instead of making substantial rent-seeking investments in advance, the bulk of rent-seeking costs may occur ex-post. Ex-ante, rent-seekers may promise favours in return for the rent and only provide them once they are assured of getting the rent. This type of rent-seeking investment characterises many rent-seeking situations in developing countries. It is prevalent with cost-reducing and benefit-enhancing corruption, but also where different rent-seekers compete for a single prize, for instance in the allocating of an overpriced public contract. A considerable share of the rent is then shared between the bureaucrats and the most 'deserving' rent-seeker, ex-post.

In contrast to a situation involving threat, outlays for the 'winning' rent-seeker may be substantial. Rent-seeking outlays do however mostly take the form of transfers. Theoretically, if the rent allocation reflects the situation of an auction, the rent would be always awarded to the rent-seeker who values the prize most (see for instance, Riley (1999, p. 205), who mentions in his model a case of 'no fixed costs', where the contest is over as soon as it starts, and the rent-seeker with the highest valuation is the winner).[32] However, in many rent-seeking situations in developing countries other criteria, such as patronage, are equally relevant and may determine the winner.

Allocation Between Rent-Seekers

So far not so much has been said about how the rules on the *allocation of rents among rent-seekers* explain the level of rent-seeking activity and dissipation (contest C in Figure 3-5 on page 86). Relevant aspects are the number of rent-seekers, the winning rule (how to win and whether there are several winners or only one), the character of winning procedures, active or implicit group formation and the distribution of power among rent-seekers. These factors directly translate into the level of competition and thereby co-determine rent-seekers' dissipation.[33]

The *number of rent-seekers* is important to determine the extent of competition for rents. Within Tullock-type models, the general result holds that the larger the number of rent-seekers competing for a given rent, the higher is the level of dissipation (see for instance the results of the original Tullock model in Table 3-1 on page 64). With *free entry*, which usually refers to the long run perspective, and constant marginal returns to rent-seeking ($r=1$), these models

[32] He mentions this aspect in his concluding remarks, but the section, where this specification should have been discussed, is apparently missing in the publication.

[33] Because of the complexity of the interactions, the discussion in this section reaches at times a high level of abstraction. This explains why there are fewer links to LDC specific settings. The reader not familiar with these models may skim over the pages or go directly to the next subsection on page 111.

suggest dissipation to be complete, as they assume that entry will only cease once expected profits have been driven down to zero.[34]

There are however many instances where the general result of higher dissipation in the long-run will not hold. Two lines of argumentation are considered below. First, the number of rent-seekers may remain limited, and second, under specific conditions a higher number of rent-seekers may even reduce dissipation.

The literature on rent-seeking has presented many models which analyse limitations in the number of rent-seekers.[35] Only a few individuals may enter a rent-seeking contest if *information* on rent-seeking opportunities *spreads too slowly* or if the setting is characterised by explicit and implicit *barriers to entry*.

The rent may only be available for a subset of individuals that complies with some specified criteria, such as living in a particular area, having a certain age or income, being a manager of a parastatal company, an exporter of certain goods or being a member of a specific profession, tribe or clan. The number of potential rent-seekers in such a subset may then be smaller than the number that participates in a model with free entry.

High barriers to entry also arise with insider/outsider asymmetries and high entry fees. Or they result from a combination of features where only a small number of rent-seekers have an incentive to participate. This is for instance the case if a perfectly discriminating winning rule (where the rent-seeker with the highest outlays always wins) coincides with asymmetries in valuation among potential participants. Hillman and Riley (1989, p. 35) demonstrate with such a model that 'only the two agents with the highest valuations have an incentive to actively contest the prize' and dissipation will be lower the larger these asymmetries are. A similar effect, however with no impact on dissipation, is given in a situation where members within a group place different valuations on a public good that is contested. As noted before, when addressing public goods, only the member of each group with the highest valuation will participate in the contest (Baik (1993)).

The second argument directly qualifies the impact of the number of rent-seekers. Under specific conditions an increase in the number of rent-seekers may result in a reduction of overall dissipation. Most evident is this aspect in a *rent-seeking situation with competing groups* that includes strong free-riding incentives. Individuals may be rewarded only according to membership in the group and not according to their effort. This example will be taken up later when discussing the issue of group formation.

A less trivial case has been demonstrated by Amegashie (1999b) who developed a model where the rent has a fixed and a variable component. Within his framework the rent-seeking winner gets a minimum rent along with an additional rent where the size depends on the individual rent-seeking outlays

---

34 For a collection of articles which address free entry or large number of rent-seekers in the Tullock-type model, see Rowley, Tollison and Tullock (1988), Chapters 8-11.

35 See for instance the summary on endogenising the number of rent-seekers in Nitzan (1994a, p. 53f).

(and not on the total outlays of all rent-seekers). This *personal size effect* may be relevant where rent-seekers lobby for a monopoly with a variable duration (Amegashie (1999b, p. 58)), or where the monopoly prize finally tolerated by the authorities varies between a minimum level, which is larger than the competitive price, and the optimal monopoly price that maximises the rent ($P_M > P_{min} > P_C$). Under such conditions, a larger number of rent-seekers may imply a more than proportional decrease in individual rent-seeking outlays, as individuals not only perceive a smaller chance to win the rent, but also a smaller prize (variable component) once their outlays decrease. Amegashie (1999b, p. 61) concludes that 'a priori, there is no reason why individual lobbying expenditures should always be inelastic with respect to changes in the number of lobbyists'.

Much of the impact on dissipation and the competitive structure among rent-seekers is determined by the type of *winning rule* applied in the rent-seeking contest. It addresses the question of how rent-seeking investments affect the probability of winning and the size of the expected prize. A practicable approach to discuss this topic is to differentiate between two dimensions: *the degree of discrimination* and the possibility of *rent-sharing*. Two polar cases of probability of winning functions which cover the spectrum of discrimination and non-discrimination have been widely discussed and applied in the rent-seeking literature: Tullock's original *non-discriminating lottery case* (as summarised in Table 3-1) and the *perfectly discriminating all-pay auction* (which has been introduced in particular by Hillman and Samet (1987)).

In a perfectly discriminating contest the rent-seeker with the highest outlays always wins (if there are *m* rent-seekers placing the same highest outlays, the probability to win becomes *1/m* or the prize is shared). This winning rule resembles an auction, but differs in one principal respect: both winners and losers have to pay the price they offer. A variant from this is the *war of attrition* formulation (or 'second prize all-pay auction'), where the winner does not pay the highest but the second highest bid. The rule reflects the idea that competition continues till the second last rent-seeker withdraws and the last one becomes the winner (for an application see Riley (1999)). In contrast to perfect discrimination, a non-discriminating winning rule gives all rent-seekers who participate a chance of winning, with the probability of winning being higher the larger own rent-seeking investments are and the smaller the total investments of all others are.

Another family of contest-success functions has been suggested by Hirshleifer (1989), where the relative success of rent-seekers is not determined by the ratio of their outlays but by the differences between outlays. This *difference-form* version, as well as the Tullock case, coincides with the winning rule of the all-pay auction, if they apply infinite sensitivities (i.e., for instance in the Tullock case, $r=\infty$).[36]

[36] Che and Gale (2000) offer an interesting generalisation to characterise the equilibrium properties in the above-mentioned success functions. They define a *'piecewise linear success function'* as

Each probability of winning function has its area of application where it best reflects patterns of rent-seeking competition. Hirshleifer (1989, p. 103), for instance, argues that an important advantage of the difference form is that 'a player can have some chance...even without committing resources to the contest'. In addition, as he notes (p. 106), peace in the sense of zero outlays (and thus zero dissipation) may easily hold as a stable Cournot-Nash solution, as the marginal impact from defecting is not a huge discrete jump in success. By the same logic, a one-sided rent-seeking investment is also a possible equilibrium outcome. Hence, like with the all-pay auction, the emphasis in his model is on the difference and not on the relative size.[37] A perfectly discriminating winning rule, in contrast, may apply to a rent-seeking situation of corrupt bureaucrats that allocate a prize, such as an overpaid public contract, to one out of several applicants, who are not personally affiliated. What matters for these bureaucrats is the highest bribe offered to them.

The choice of a specific probability to win function also determines the impact of other parameters on dissipation. This aspect will be taken up below.[38] The examples corroborate the main contention of this chapter that it is important to include the entire structure of the rent-seeking situation before deriving policy conclusions on specific parameters.

Hillman and Samet (1987) demonstrate with the all-pay auction winning rule that full dissipation does not necessarily require a competitive environment. They show that with an equal valuation of the rent 'dissipation remains exceptionally complete without regard for the number of contenders' (p. 66). This contrasts the incomplete dissipation derived from the Tullock-lottery winning rule or the above mentioned difference-form function where even zero outlays may occur as an equilibrium.[39]

That the impact of a parameter on dissipation varies with the specific winning rule can also be demonstrated with *asymmetries in valuation*. Table 3-3 summarises dissipation in two-player rent-seeking situations and distinguishes between five different probability-to-win-functions. As indicated in the table, the impact of asymmetries in valuation is weakest in the lottery case, and

---

follows: $f(x_i\text{-}x_j) = max\ \{min\{0.5 + s\ (x_i\text{-}x_j),1\},\ 0\}$; s represents the sensitivity to effort and x_i-x_j the difference between rent-seeking outlays in the two-person case. Within a specified range, which depends on the value of the parameter s, the rent-seeker's success varies according to a difference-form function (with the probabilities one (above) and zero (below)). The value of the parameter s can be chosen to apply different sensitivities. As they note, 'at one extreme, when s=0, the outcome is completely insensitive to effort' (which characterises the symmetric Tullock equilibrium, where everybody invests the same amount and the winner is determined by a simple lottery, irrespective of the total level of rent-seeking investments); 'at the other extreme, when s=∞, the contest coincides with the all-pay auction, which is infinitely sensitive at the margin' (Che and Gale (2000, p. 25)).

[37] For a general approach to difference-form functions see, for instance, Baik (1998).

[38] Note already the discussion on the 'valuation' of the rent or the 'number of players' demonstrated this aspect.

[39] For an experimental examination of dissipation where the lottery case and the all-pay auction are compared, see Potters, De Vries and Van Winden (1998) or Davis and Reilly (1998). They provide some evidence of the different impact of the two winning rules, at least with regard to their qualitative predictions.

strongest in a war of attrition setting. The different impacts also explain why dissipation does not remain highest or lowest with a specific winning rule. The recommendation to change the winning rule, e.g. from all-pay auction to lottery (as a measure to reduce dissipation) depends, at least in this stylised two-player setting, on the extent of asymmetries in valuation. In the example, the change in the winning rule would only produce the desired effect, if asymmetries are sufficiently small (v being larger than 0.4).

Table 3-3: Dissipation and Asymmetry with Different Stylised Probability-to-Win Functions

Asymmetry in valuation of rent-seekers x and y: v = V_y/V_x	0.1	0.2	0.3	0.4	0.5	0.6	0.7	0.8	0.9	1.0
Tullock Lottery, r=1	17	28	36	41	44	47	48	49	50	50
All-Pay Auction	10	20	30	40	50	60	70	80	90	100
All-Pay Auction 90% [a]	9	19	28	38	48	58	68	79	89	100
War of Attrition 90% [a]	2	4	8	13	19	29	38	53	73	100
War of Attrition	0	0	0	0	0	0	0	0	0	100

Values of dissipation: Percentage values (total rent-seeking outlays relative to average valuation).

a: The price the winner has to pay is determined by a linear combination of the highest price (all-pay auction) and the second highest price (war of attrition).

Source: Tullock lottery: Data calculated according to formula given in Leininger (1993, p. 48) [40]
All-pay auction and war of attrition: Data transformed from Table 10.2 in Riley (1999, p. 102) [41]

Having discussed the degree of discrimination, the second dimension of the winning rule, which affects rent-seeking costs and dissipation, addresses characteristics of rent distribution. Individuals may try to get a *share of a rent* (for instance when they apply for underpriced resources or some support financed by a special fund) or they may lobby for an *indivisible single rent* that comes along with a certain job position, a government contract, a monopoly right or a parastatal divestiture.

The analytically simplest way to include rent-sharing in a lottery-like situation is to assume that the share of the rent allocated to the rent-seeker is described by the rent-seeker's probability of winning functions. This specification does not change the results on dissipation derived from the

[40] Rent-seeking expenditure are given by $x^* + y^* = \frac{a \cdot v}{(a+v)^2}(V_x + V_y)$. Assuming a=1 (equal power) and dividing the term by $(V_x+V_y)/2$ yields dissipation relative to the average value, which is $\frac{x^* + y^*}{(V_x + V_y)/2} = \frac{v}{(1+v)^2} \cdot 2$

[41] Table 10.1 and 10.2 in Riley (1999, p. 102) display dissipation rates relative to high and low valuation (V_x, V_y). Dissipation relative to the average can be calculated by multiplying the values in 10.2 with the term $\left(\frac{2v}{1+v}\right)$, since substituting $V_x = \frac{V_y}{v}$ into $\frac{x^* + y^*}{(V_x + V_y)/2} = \frac{x^* + y^*}{(V_y/v) + V_y} \cdot 2 = \frac{x^* + y^*}{V_y(1/v + 1)} \cdot 2 = \frac{x^* + y^*}{V_y} \cdot \left(\frac{2v}{1+v}\right)$.

standard rent-seeking models. It can, however, not describe the dynamics which may be inherent in multi-prize rent-seeking contests. If the rent-seekers know the competitors' level of investments, the rent-seeking situation simply reduces to an investment where rent-seekers receive a well-defined share with certainty.

Slightly more demanding are models that include several prizes allocated to an even larger group of rent-seekers or where there is explicit uncertainty introduced in the shares. Stylised models suggest that with free entry dissipation will be complete, irrespective of whether rent-seekers lobby for a share of the rent or the entire rent.[42] However, in many instances free entry is not given or cannot develop its full impact, as the pool of candidates remains limited. Under such conditions, rent-sharing is likely to affect dissipation. A fixed-number case has been addressed by Clark and Riis (1998). They describe an interesting model that includes different features of rent-seekers lobbying for one out of several prizes. The model is of the Tullock-lottery type and assumes an exogenous number of rent-seekers. The main results on dissipation can be summarised as follows:

First, if a *single prize is divided into several smaller units*, assuming constant marginal utility, total rent-seeking outlays (and thus dissipation) fall. In contrast, if the rent-seekers' marginal utility is *decreasing*, dividing rents into several prizes may increase total rent-seeking. (Decreasing marginal utility implies that the total value of several small units distributed to different individuals is higher than a single large unit assigned to one rent-seeker.)

Second, the authors show that increasing total rents by *awarding an extra prize* may reduce total rent-seeking outlays and thus dissipation. The result depends on the assumption that a rent-seeker is only allowed to obtain one prize. As the authors emphasise, this at first glance surprising result contrasts traditional single-prize rent-seeking settings where an increase in the prize will unambiguously raise rent-seeking.

Third, Clark and Riis address the possibility that the *prizes differ* in size and show that *ordering* may affect total rent-seeking outlays and therefore dissipation. Larger rent-seeking investments not only raise the probability to win one out of several prizes, higher investments also increase the likelihood to be among the first winners. If prizes differ in value and rent-seekers cannot lobby for one specific prize, it matters whether a rent-seeker is the first or the last winner. As Clark and Riis argue, within such a setting rent-seeking investment and thus dissipation can be reduced if prizes are drawn for in ascending rather than descending order of value (rent-seekers want to win but they prefer to be a late rather than an early winner, which gives them an incentive to invest less).

Fourth, the authors point to an interesting possibility of *partial overdissipation*. Within their framework, an increase in the value of one or several prizes may raise rent-seeking investments by more than the increase of the prize. This aspect can be best demonstrated with a fictive numeric example.

---

[42] See for instance Clark and Riis (1996) for the original Tullock rent-seeking game or an early but more specific model in Long and Vousden (1987); the latter treats endogenous rents and includes the 'traditional' dissipation-reducing impact of risk aversion.

The prizes of a rent-seeking situation may be ordered in the following manner: 1, 1, 1, 1, 100. As it is not lucrative to be among the first four winners, overall rent-seeking investments are low. However, increasing the first prize to 100 breaks this disincentive. Rent-seeking investment not only increase because of the larger value of the total prize sum (203 instead of 104), but also because the disincentive to be the first winner is removed. The increase in rent-seeking investment may therefore be larger than the increase in the prize.

Finally, Clark and Riis elaborate a variation of the multi-winner contest, where prizes are allocated on the basis of *different contests*. In each contest the winner is eliminated and the remaining rent-seekers compete again in the contests that follow. This formulation leads to a higher level of rent-seeking investments.

The results derived from the model of Clark and Riis (1998) reflect only one possible impact rent-sharing has on dissipation. Barut and Kovenock (1998), for instance, show that the common result of full dissipation with an all-pay auction winning rule also holds in the multiple prize setting where a fixed number of players, complete information and symmetric valuations are assumed. There are many other settings where the impact of rent-sharing on dissipation may differ considerably.

In general terms, it can be emphasised that rent-seeking situations that include some kind of rent-sharing (e.g. several prizes) are frequent. Moreover, conflicts are often solved by a compromise. In many settings rent-setters have a tendency to try to be 'fair' (at least a little) and consider several rent-seekers, even though some rent-seekers may nevertheless be able to capture sizeable shares. With divisible rents and relatively equal power, the function that defines the relation between rent-seeking investments and expected prize will often have a concave shape *(decreasing marginal productivity)* where moderate lobbying activities may suffice to secure a portion of a rent, but very high investments are required to seize a large share.

With single, indivisible rents the relation between rent-seeking investment and expected output is likely to differ from this. Unless there is a strong asymmetry in power or valuation between rent-seekers or there is just a single rent-seeker lobbying, substantial rent-seeking investments may be needed to raise the chances of winning to noticeable levels. Furthermore, an indivisible rent may imply severe competition if involved parties are all committed to win and invest correspondingly. In particular, if there are sunk costs involved, even overdissipation may be a feasible outcome. If these rent-seekers had been given the possibility to lobby for shares, it certainly would have defused the situation and overall rent-seeking investment would have turned out to be lower.

The impact of rent-sharing on dissipation nevertheless depends on further assumptions. In the case of divisible rents, where moderate lobbying is sufficient to secure a share of the rent and where marginal costs to obtain further rents steadily rise, a lower equilibrium level of dissipation might be expected, in particular if the number of rent-seekers is limited. But the emphasis is on 'might', as the problem cannot be satisfactory analysed in isolation. For instance, the answer is likely to vary if the setting includes risk aversion in contrast to a setting with myopia and sunk costs. Highly risk-averse rent-seekers are inclined to invest more where they can lobby for a share, than in a 'one-winner-takes-all' situation, which is more risky and may therefore be avoided.

Closely related to the winning rule is the specific *winning procedure*. Many rent-seeking situations are not of a one-shot nature but depend on several contests, which include some kind of subsequent short-listing or other limitation. Some multi-stage contests likewise include aspects of *group formation*, in the sense that the procedure defines intermediate winners, which are not selected individually, but are determined as a group. An allocation of donor funds (assuming funds are partly appropriated by rent-seekers) may follow a multi-stage rent-seeking contest and, depending on the situation, include implications of group formation. Fleming (1998), for instance, describes this situation in the context of rural development projects. He notes (p. 281) that in the first round rent-seekers may try to influence the initial selection of projects and their targeted beneficiaries; in the second round, if they have been successful, they finally compete to influence the distribution of funds within the project.

There are many formal rent-seeking models which include, by one way or the other, different stages in the rent-seeking contests. Of interest here is the question, first, whether the introduction of several stages will affect total rent-seeking outlays and dissipation, and second, whether the outcome depends on the relative characteristics in the different stages. The answer to both questions depends on the specific design of the contest.

A multi-stage case of full dissipation can be constructed fairly easy, by assuming, among other things, complete information and free entry into the first rent-seeking contest. See, for instance, Higgins, Shughart and Tollison (1985) who formulated a two-stage version of the Tullock game, where individuals in the first stage have to make outlays to be able to compete in the second stage. They defined the expected number of active rent-seekers by a zero-profit condition, which implies full dissipation. More interesting for the discussion are therefore settings where dissipation is not complete.

An attempt to characterise the impact of different stages, in particular *different sensitivities* between the stages, has been presented by Amegashie (1999a). He defines a two-tier Tullock game with a fixed number of rent-seekers, where a few rent-seekers are selected in the first stage (based on competing rent-seeking outlays) to be able to compete for a prize in the second stage. The winning procedure is similar to the one applied in the Olympic games, i.e. there are preliminary competitions in different groups, whose winners finally compete against each other. His basic result is that rent-seeking expenditure in any single-stage setting can be reduced by introducing a preliminary stage, with a sufficiently low-sensitive administrator (Amegashie (1999a, p. 71)). In the standard Tullock contest low-sensitivity is represented with a low value of the parameter r. As in Amegashie's framework total rent-seeking outlays fall with a smaller value of r in the preliminary contest and a higher value of r in the final contest, simply swapping the two administrators would imply lower total rent-seeking outlays (granted that the values of r differ). Amegashie (1999a, p. 69) even derives the following paradoxical result:

> 'If the administrator in charge of the preliminary contest is sensitive to (socially wasteful) rent-seeking expenditures (...), then it may be welfare-improving for the administrator in charge of the final contest to have some sensitivity to rent-seeking expenditures (...), rather than no sensitivity'.

Amegashie's results of the possible positive impact of introducing a preliminary stage or increasing the sensitivity of the administrator in the final contest are striking but nevertheless dependent on the overall structure of the rent-seeking setting. If the setting is different, his results may no longer hold. For instance, introducing a preliminary stage in a *non-rival* setting will most likely increase total rent-seeking outlays. Such a situation may occur as a result of economic and political reforms, if measures are poorly implemented or if measures are sequenced in an inappropriate way. Allowing a wider group of people to participate in the government may increase competition for rent-promising jobs, if rents are not abolished simultaneously. Another case with a different structure is the multi-prize model of Clark and Riis (1996), which has been discussed in the previous section on sharing rules. It implies higher rent-seeking investments, if the prizes were allocated on the basis of different contests and not in a one-stage allocation. Finally, rent-seeking contests with several stages may include aspects of *group formation*, which again can imply different outcomes, depending on the structure and specific group-sharing rules. The discussion below takes up this aspect.

Many rent-seeking contests include some kind of implicit or explicit *group formation*. Group formation is defined here as implicit if rent-seekers do not actively create a group to lobby for a rent, but individual rent-seekers benefit at least at some stages of the contest from the effort of others. The most apparent example is the situation where rent-seekers lobby for a public good (or a regulation that includes public good aspects). In other instances, rent-seekers actively join together to capture a rent. The rent, which may reflect underpriced foreign currency, scarce resources or direct subsidies from the budget, will then be shared according to a defined group-sharing rule.

Standard models of group formation suggest that dissipation tends to fall. As Nitzan (1994a, p. 49) concludes, this is due to an expected reduction in the intensity of competition (there are only a few competing groups instead of numerous individuals competing against each other), and to free-riding incentives that may arise within groups. The results are, however, sensitive to the group-sharing rules applied in the rent-seeking contest.

A common approach to describing decision-making in a group contest is to split the decision problem into two stages, where in the first stage the rent-seeking group tries to obtain the rent, and in the second stage the rent is somehow allocated among the members. Group-sharing rules may either specify a division which is based on *relative effort* (it would minimise free-riding incentives), an *equal-division rule* or a combination of the two rules.[43] The decision may however also be completely independent of the preceding group contest. Whatever rule is chosen, it is convenient to assume that sharing rules are known in advance and therefore taken into account by individuals when they decide on their contribution to the group.

Nitzan (1991) investigates the impact of group-sharing rules (relative effort and equal distribution) in the simple Tullock rent-seeking setting with r=1. If the rents are distributed according to relative efforts, the outcome is identical to a setting without group formation. Dissipation therefore only increases with the total number of rent-seekers and is independent of the number of groups and the distribution of individuals among the groups. In contrast, if the group applies an equal sharing rule, a strong free-rider incentive is introduced, which is the larger the more members are included in the group. Dissipation becomes positively related to the total number of competing groups and negatively to the total number of rent-seekers. Finally, as can be expected, with a linear combination of the two sharing rules, dissipation still increases with the number of groups but is ambiguous with regard to the number of rent-seekers (as the impact depends on the relative size of the different parameters). In all three cases, however, changing the distribution of individuals across the groups would not affect the extent of dissipation (Nitzan (1991, p. 1532)).

As the individual incentive to engage in rent-seeking activities depends on the group size and group-sharing rule, Baik and Lee (1997, p. 129) addressed an endogenisation of these two aspects. Given inter-group mobility of members, they conclude (p. 129) that 'groups tend to be of equal size, and that the optimal sharing rule places great emphasis on relative outlays'.[44] The latter aspect therefore implies that dissipation is not much smaller than in the simpler case of no group formation.

A model with a different two-stage structure has been developed by Katz and Tokatlidu (1996). They partly cut the link between group contest and individual reward, focusing on a rent-seeking situation where groups first compete to win a rent, and only afterwards, once the rent is obtained, members of the winning group compete again to determine the relative share among them (respectively the final winner). As they note (p. 600), with their framework the first contest has a *pure public good character*. Unlike the above-mentioned settings, this time the distribution of individuals among groups matters and affects the level of dissipation. The mechanism rests on the outcome that asymmetries in group size imply a different valuation of the rent (p. 600). The value of the rent is lower for a member of the larger group, 'first, because the prize is diluted by the number of members, and second, because large groups are more wasteful in the second round' (Katz and Tokatlidu (1996, p. 602)).

In their framework dissipation tends to be lower as compared to a one stage rent-seeking contest with no group formation. This follows from the fact that in

---

[43] For a formal discussion of the properties, see Davis and Reilly (1999).

[44] On the impact of different group size on the sharing rule, see also Lee (1995).

the first 'public-good' stage, rent-seeking outlays are minimal (see the discussion of a model from Katz, Nitzan and Rosenberg (1990) on page 79); in the second stage only the members of the winning group compete, which implies a smaller number of rent-seekers in the second, 'private-good' stage. In addition, it is the smallest group which has the highest probability to enter the second stage, as their members value the 'public good' highest and are therefore most likely to win (Katz and Tokatlidu (1996, p. 604)).

Summing up, the above-mentioned models of group formation address the independent individual decision-making situation in group contests. They indicate that dissipation tends to be lower as compared to a setting with no group formation. Depending on the setting, dissipation may positively or negatively relate to the number of rent-seekers, it may increase with the number of competing groups or fall with larger asymmetries among groups.

The major shortcoming of the literature on group formation is that in most cases they treat the group setting as exogenously given. In their evaluation of dissipation the above mentioned papers do not address a more differentiated analysis of the *benchmark of 'no group formation'*, which is relevant if the group has been created actively (i.e. the group is not just a reflection of the specific rent-seeking structure). Not accounting for the active role of group formation, these papers ignore the possible incentives that group formation may have on rent-seeking behaviour. If the focus is extended, more relevant results may be derived. There are arguments which point to either an increase or reduction of dissipation. What finally matters depends on the specific setting.

On the one hand, it can be assumed that group formation is often associated with *decreasing costs in lobbying* (as compared to a situation where rent-seekers compete on their own). The different impacts of the number of rent-seekers, the number of groups and the distribution of individuals among the groups would have to be reassessed. If group formation decreases the cost of lobbying, a reduction in the overall level of dissipation can be expected. Another dissipation reducing impact results from the fact that the probability of *cooperation* between different groups is enhanced if rent-seekers are organised in groups. Surprisingly, rent-seeking models that focus on group formation have neglected the aspect of cooperation. They mostly just consider the 'independent' individual decision-making situation in the group contest. As will be discussed further below, if cooperation between different groups occurs, rent-seeking costs and dissipation are likely to decline.

On the other hand, there are also situations which point to a possible increase of rent-seeking activities due to group formation. In some instances, people do not engage in rent-seeking activities on their own because they judge their chances of winning as too low. But they may *become active* once they are given the opportunity to join a group. The positive incentive may either reflect the above-mentioned reduction in the costs of lobbying, or be a consequence of the possibility of rent-sharing. If group formation enables rent-sharing, it may reduce the risk of getting nothing and therefore provide an additional incentive to make rent-seeking outlays. Hence, in a situation where rent-seekers only become active because they manage to form a group, total rent-seeking outlays and dissipation increase.

Finally, if group formation alters the *distribution of power* in the rent-seeking setting, the level of dissipation may raise or fall depending on the new structure of the relative power between the groups. The aspect of asymmetries in power is the subject of the following discussion.

So far it has been argued that the allocation of rents among rent-seekers depends on the number of rent-seekers, the winning rule, the winning procedure and group formation. Probably the most relevant parameters for dissipation are *asymmetries in power* among rent-seekers, i.e. not all rent-seekers exert the same influence with a given level of rent-seeking investments. Many aspects have already been addressed in the previous subsection on rent-seeking costs in general. Asymmetries in power determine the relative capabilities of securing rents and therefore the incentives to make rent-seeking outlays. Using Tullock's simple lottery notation, asymmetries in power imply that not every rent-seeker will get the same amount of tickets for each dollar invested. Tullock included this aspect already in his original articles (see Tullock (1975, p. 752f), or Tullock (1980, p. 109f)). In the most extreme form of asymmetry, rent-seeking resembles a non-rival setting where all competitors are excluded. Particularly in developing countries asymmetries in power are large. They are likely to matter when it comes to reallocating and reducing rents in the reform process.

Differences in power can occur and affect rent-seeking effectiveness in many ways. Formally this may be demonstrated with the individual player's production function for influence in lobbying $f_i(x_i)$ introduced on page 65. Allowing for differences in fixed costs and/or differences with regard to rent-seeking productivities, the term $f_i(x_i)$ can be extended to the general form: $\gamma_i f_i(\alpha_i x_i + \beta_i) + \delta_i$ where α_i, $\gamma_i \geq 0$ and β_i, $\delta_i \in [-\infty,+\infty]$. The same (with different parameter values) would apply to all other rent-seekers.

The parameters α, β, γ, δ represent alternative ways to include the qualitative implication of asymmetries and would therefore not all be applied together. δ or β may represent a predefined skewed probability of rent allocation in the absence of rent-seeking efforts, as discussed on page 91f, while the parameters α and γ would directly alter the productivity of rent-seeking investments. Most models which focus on asymmetries in power set $f_i(x_i)=x$ (e.g. the Tullock r=1 case) and multiply rent-seeking efforts of one rent-seeker by a parameter 'a' (which is in the above formula α respectively γ). The Tullock probability of winning function, given on page 67 then becomes for the asymmetric player $\pi(x_1)= ax_1 / (ax_1 + \sum_{i=2}^{n} x_i)$.

As already noted in discussing the properties of the valuation of the rents, asymmetries in valuation and power have much in common. The main result derived from rent-seeking models is the *preemption effect*, which implies a reduction in dissipation and shows that rent-seekers reduce their investments if they perceive unequal power (or unequal stakes). With asymmetries competition is less severe and would finally disappear if winners and losers were determined in advance.

Che and Gale (2000) investigated the preemption effect with a general probability of winning function that allows for different specifications (for a brief description recall Footnote 36). They conclude (Che and Gale (2000, p. 46)) that underdissipation induced by preemption is a general feature and helps in understanding the paradox noted by Tullock, i.e. rent-seeking settings in the real world are often characterised by significant underdissipation. The conclusion can be formulated even more strongly. It appears that asymmetries, either related to power or valuation, are the most important reason that makes rent-seeking a bargain. In fact, the profitability-enhancing role of asymmetries has already been emphasised by Hillman and Riley (1989, p. 36) in the context of transfer-seeking contests that include dead-weight losses. They argue that such contests could only exist because of asymmetries, as the expected value of engaging in the transfer-seeking contest would be negative otherwise.

The relation between asymmetries in power and asymmetries in valuation is given as follows. A bias in power (a_i) that increases the chances of winning can be neutralised by some opposite bias in valuation (V_i), as a rent-seeker who does not much value a rent spends less to seize it. In the simple two-player Tullock lottery case with r=1, equal probability to win holds as long as $a_x/a_y=V_y/V_x$ (see, for instance, Leininger (1993, p. 49)).

There are however also significant differences which are evident when it comes to evaluating *costs*. With respect to rent-seeking outlays it matters whether an increase in valuation rather than an increase in power causes the asymmetry. The following example demonstrates this aspect in a simple way. If the valuation of a rent increases from 100 to 1000, a rent-seeker may be willing to spend at the most 1000. If, alternatively, the power increases by the factor ten, the rent-seeker who is stronger but still values the rent at 100 will not spend more than 100 (the probability to win, however, will be much higher).

Another point is the proper assessment of the *interaction* between the two types of asymmetries. For instance, the perfectly discriminating all-pay auction model with different valuation predicts that only the two rent-seekers with the highest valuations will compete and total rent-seeking outlays will be, on average, equal to the lower valuation (see Hillman and Riley (1989, p. 24)). This outcome will no longer hold if there is another rent-seeker with a lower valuation but a much higher rent-seeking power.

The failure to account for interactions between power and valuation may also lead to mistaken policy conclusions, as asymmetries therein may cancel out each other, thereby intensifying competition and rent-seeking outlays. This aspect has for instance been taken up by Baik (1994, p. 376):

> 'Tullock argues that social costs can be lowered by introducing a bias into the selection process. However, this argument is based on a model in which two players value the prize equally. ... If bias is introduced in favour of the player who values the prize lower, then social costs may increase.'

Such a cost-increasing constellation may materialise in the reform process. A government may decide to withdraw support from inefficient parastatal companies and make it available to more viable companies. The former, being on the verge of bankruptcy, would value support much more high, but given the new policy, would find it more difficult to argue for support. Asymmetries in valuation and power then pull in opposite directions. Differences may cancel each other out and the rent-seeking situation would become more balanced, implying an increase in total rent-seeking efforts.

Rent-seekers have an incentive to increase their power relative to others. In two-sided rent-seeking contests, this incentive may be neutralised by actions of the rent-seeking authority. Like honest bureaucrats, corrupt bureaucrats have an interest in making the playing field 'level', although for another reason: it simply allows them to maximise income from potential bribes.[45]

How relevant are asymmetries in power in developing countries? In many cases, patronage relations are important and there is little or no competition. In other cases, for instance when civil servants provide services and permits for a large number of mostly 'anonymous' clients and bribery is common, the playing field is more level. Sometimes the access to rents depends on whether an individual belongs to a non-competitive privileged group ('inner circle') or a highly competitive 'outer circle'. Finally, large differences in power can imply that a rent-seeking situation is characterised by a 'fixed number of rent-seekers' (i.e. *entry barriers* are sufficiently high to keep outsiders away). Rent-seeking may then even degenerate to a non-rival situation with almost predetermined rent allocation among insiders. In general it can be assumed that non-rival situations are a common feature in many rent-seeking settings in LDCs.

The aspect of *insider/outsider asymmetries* has been treated in different rent-seeking models. In a strong formulation the two groups no longer compete, but outsiders first have to make outlays to become insiders, before they can finally join the rent-seeking contest. If such preliminary outlays exist and are taken into account, dissipation is higher (compared to the situation where only the second stage is considered). The overall impact nevertheless depends on the specific characterisation of the two (or more) rent-seeking situations.

Two-stage rent-seeking contests (as described in the previous section under 'winning procedure') can be used as a tool to analyse the dissipation-increasing relation of outsiders who try to become insiders. In many realistic settings, the second stage would, however, be of a non-rival type. For an extended model which includes a specification of the relation between insider and outsider see Hillman and Ursprung (2000). With their framework, which focuses on subsequent stages of political liberalisation in countries with an adverse political culture, they show how releasing asymmetries increases rent-seeking outlays and dissipation. The model nicely demonstrates that increasing competition for rents without simultaneously addressing rent-seeking opportunities can initiate a further economic decline.

---

[45] See Baye, Kovenock and De Vries (1993) who introduced the term *'exclusion principle'* and thereby provided a logic for such outcomes.

Strategies of Rent-Seekers

Some of the rent-seeking costs are not explained by the rent-seeking setting but depend on the strategies and capabilities of the rent-seekers themselves. Three extensions to the previous discussion are considered below. The first is a general critique on the rationality assumptions and the smooth functioning of markets. The second and third extensions address alternative behavioural patterns which differ from the one stipulated in the simultaneous one-shot, non-cooperative rent-seeking games. The behavioural patterns describe dynamic or sequential solutions, as well as cooperative strategies.

Conclusions on the level of dissipation derived from rent-seeking models depend on assumptions about *human perception, rationality and equilibrium.* Decision-making in the real world is characterised by incomplete information and limited rationality. Rent-seekers may find themselves in situations where they do not know much about the marginal impact of their efforts and where they can only approximately take the behaviour of all others into account. Given the rapidly changing environments and information constraints, rent-seekers may fail to anticipate important aspects; they may be manipulated by others and simply conduct satisfying strategies. Under such conditions, dissipation may deviate considerably from what stylised rent-seeking models predict.

Sometimes profitable 'insider situations' can continue for a long time without being eroded by potential entrants. Hazlett and Michaels (1993), for instance, investigated rent-seeking in the context of 'cellular telephone licence lotteries', where geographically separated markets were sequentially opened. Based on their empirical findings they conclude:

> 'Dissipation was far from total, despite the theoretical expectation that open entry and unbiasedness would lead to full dissipation. It appears that a marginal rent-seeker could have purchased a ticket with positive expected profits, even without possessing specific capital or inside information as traditionally defined. The length of time during which such positive profit opportunities remained available is striking.' (Hazlett and Michaels (1993, p. 432))

Transaction costs partly explain this outcome. Equally important are assumptions regarding individual behaviour. Game theory, the main approach applied in rent-seeking models, helps in an understanding of intuition; it can show the dynamics of many interactions and make forces that are at work apparent (Baird (1998, 193f)). However, in their simplification, game-theoretical models often apply assumptions which are too demanding to describe individual behaviour in a specific situation, and the game-theoretical concept may make the solution trivial. Already Tullock's original model depended on a disputable assumption:

> 'I am going to assume that if there is a correct solution for individual strategy, then each player will assume that the other parties can also figure out what that correct solution is.' (Tullock (1980, p. 99))

For many questions and applications this assumption is not a shortcoming but a real advantage for simplifying the mathematical problem and describing the rent-seeking situation in an appropriate way. However, there are other situations where results are sensitive to variations in assumptions about people's beliefs as to how the world functions and how they interact. It may then not be possible to represent decision-making by an interactive model of efficient rent-seeking that takes account of the behaviour of all participants. What is needed are models which apply simpler strategies, such as trial and error. Tullock's optimal level of investment, for instance, is highly sensitive to what all other rent-seekers do. If only one of them behaves differently, the result will change. Equally important is that decision-making may be influenced by considerations other than profit-maximising and may include emotions and predefined behaviour reflecting tradition and cultural values. (Some of the limitations on the profit-maximising 'homo oeconomicus' will be discussed in more detail in Chapter 4.1).

In an empirical investigation of 'rational' rent-seeking, Potters, De Vries and Van Winden (1998, p. 793) identified three categories of subjects: *gamesmen*, who understand the strategic nature of the rent-seeking situation, *confused people*, who simply randomise their bids, and *backward-looking individuals* who base their decision on outcomes of earlier rounds. Even though their results do not question the qualitative predictive power of rent-seeking models in simple rent-seeking situations, they emphasise (p. 793f) that further research should account for these differences, in particular for the behaviour of backward-looking individuals, who constitute a large group.

Clearly, it would not be true to maintain that the literature on formal rent-seeking models has not addressed features which describe situations of incomplete information or limited rationality. Some of them include these aspects by their limited or simplified approach, and other models more explicitly tackle problems of limited rationality or incomplete information.[46] The crucial point is however that the majority of rent-seeking models do not include such aspects, and may therefore suggest mistaken conclusions. Further work is necessary—not to incorporate each and every aspect into the models—but to offer a larger selection of models which include different situations where the above-mentioned constraints matter. Given the limited availability of information when making rent-seeking decisions, it is sometimes also helpful to elaborate partial considerations which do not focus on the interaction of rent-seekers (e.g. the case of uncertainty presented in Figure 3-4 on page 84).

Another qualification is the focus on *equilibrium*. In many situations the environment is changing rapidly or information does not spread fast enough. It can imply that an optimal rent-seeking equilibrium is never reached. The telephone lottery case mentioned earlier may be a case in point. The crucial point is that paths towards equilibria can be characterised by substantial over- and under-shooting. Static models cannot describe these features. Similarly, if a

[46] See, for instance, Clark (1997) on a model which includes learning, or Baik and Shogren (1995) who demonstrate in their model of 'unknown relative abilities' that efforts may be higher compared to a situation of known abilities.

'system' has not yet reached the equilibrium, deviating results may likewise arise in an analysis of comparative statics. In the reform context, where conditions change rapidly and information does not flow sufficiently quickly and smoothly, this qualification is particularly relevant.

With the exception of the note in the paragraph above, attention has so far been directed to static rent-seeking situations. Many interactions between individuals are, however, inherently *dynamic*. Rent-seekers may interact over time and make decisions in response to what others have been doing. Rent-seeking games that model simultaneous decision-making may therefore not always be appropriate to capture the essence of these situations. Indeed, various papers suggest that the level of dissipation depends on whether rent-seeking investments are undertaken in a *sequential order* rather than simultaneously. The simplest cases of dynamic interactions are rent-seeking contests with sequential moves where each rent-seeker only makes an investment once. In these models some rent-seekers perceive the investment of others before they themselves make their outlays. The situation can be further complicated if a few individuals have several chances to increase their outlays, after having become aware of the rent-seeking investments of others. This type of dynamic asymmetry, however, has apparently not been investigated in the literature on rent-seeking.

The change in dissipation from introducing sequential moves (as compared to a situation where rent-seekers move simultaneously) depends again on the specific setting. The rationality assumption usually applied in settings where each rent-seeker makes rent-seeking outlays once (but in a sequential order), draws from the Stackelberg leadership in oligopoly theory, i.e. the first rent-seeker makes his or her optimal outlay by taking into account the reaction of the other rent-seekers who make their outlays thereafter. Glazer and Hassin (2000) have discussed this aspect for the standard Tullock lottery case with $r=1$. They show that if the game is played in a Stackelberg manner, the first mover makes a much larger outlay than the later movers (except for the case of two players, where the Stackelberg version is identical to the standard Cournot-Nash solution). In addition, all players make smaller profits and overall dissipation is therefore higher than in the original Tullock setting. Glazer and Hassin (2000, p. 227) also show that profits of the first mover can be higher than in the Tullock setting if the remaining rent-seekers play simultaneously after the first rent-seeker has made the outlay. This type of contest has become known as the Dixit-game.

Again a different result may hold if rent-seekers are not identical. Leininger (1993) demonstrates for the $n=2$ Tullock case that if there are asymmetries between rent-seekers, playing a rent-seeking game sequentially can reduce dissipation if the rent-seeker with the *lower valuation moves first* (the same result is given in Baik (1994)). He concludes that the first-mover incentive does not necessary hold for all players. Whether the results also apply to situations with more than two rent-seekers would have to be analysed. The framework however becomes complex so that it may be questionable whether limited rational individuals behave according to the game-theoretical solution.

An analysis of sequential moves is particularly interesting since some rent-seeking settings, such as the original Tullock lottery with r>1, include a strong first mover advantage. It allows the first rent-seeker (or the first few rent-seekers) to make sufficiently large investments that the payoff for any subsequent rent-seeker would become negative. This strategy has become known as the *preemptive bet.* Already Corcoran and Karels (1985) discussed this strategic investment in the context of limiting the number of rent-seekers in the long run. They calculated the range of pre-emptory investments in the Tullock lottery case. For instance if r=3, it would be sufficient for the first rent-seeker to bet 53% of the prize, so that the net present value for any other potential rent-seeker becomes negative (Table 3 in Corcoran and Karels (1985, p. 335f)).

Even though playing preemptive strategies is preferable, empirical studies indicate that individuals may behave much differently. Weimann, Yang and Vogt (2000), for instance, conclude from their laboratory experiments that 'the theoretically predicted first-mover advantage does not exist empirically' (p. 405). They criticise theoretical work for not describing the relevant interactions:

> 'The game theorists sees only one kind of asymmetry in the game, namely that caused by the fact that the first mover can make preemptive bids and the second mover rationally is to yield. But there is a second asymmetry: The second mover has the option to punish, however "irrational" this may appear, and in such cases their costs are far lower than the loss the first mover has to suffer.' (Weimann, Yang and Vogt (2000, p. 420))

Since second movers were punishing preemptive bids by the first mover, 'rational' first movers kept playing *cooperatively*. The authors conclude that the 'punishment by the second movers, consequently, turns out to be a very profitable way of being 'non-rational' in a game theoretical sense' (p. 420). The example is a good illustration of the qualification made earlier that emotions can exert an important influence in making decisions. This has become particularly evident in the last round in the experiment analysed by Weimann, Yang and Vogt. As the authors note (p. 419), some second movers still continued to punish a preemptive opening, even though it did not make sense from an economic profit-maximising perspective.

Other studies also question the first-mover strategy. Emphasising cognitive limits, Shogren and Baik (1992, p. 198), for instance, observed that first movers 'ignored the advantage that the strategic precommitment gave them and instead selected the expenditure to maximise returns given a simultaneous move game'.

These examples demonstrate that rationality assumptions often used in game theory which narrowly focus on profits do not necessarily hold. As noted before, this aspect will be considered again in Chapter 4.1. Section b) will emphasise how limited rationality and incomplete information play a twofold role (qualifying results derived from simplistic rent-seeking models on the one hand, and showing why rent-seeking can be profitable at all, on the other) and Section

c) will address the specific role of culture, values and norms in shaping individual decision-making.

The last element in the overview of rent-seeking aspects on page 75 is *cooperation.* Above it was argued that choosing specific strategies may reduce individual rent-seeking costs and thereby increase the profitability of rent-seeking for a strategically-acting rent-seeker. The same conclusion holds for cooperation, i.e. in many settings rent-seeking costs and dissipation can be reduced substantially if rent-seekers cooperate. In the extreme case the rent-seeking contest characterised as C in Figure 3-5 on page 86 'collapses' so that dissipation is entirely determined by the contest in A (and B).

Patterns of cooperation typically emerge in situations which are repetitive. Repetition helps to overcome part of the problem of incomplete information, above all information about the behaviour of other players. Linster (1994) discusses rent-seeking models where symmetric or asymmetric players cooperate to their joint advantage in a repeated Tullock game. With symmetric players the solution is obvious: nobody would make any efforts. With asymmetric players minimal outlays are undertaken, 'primarily to close the bargaining set' (Linster (1994, p. 33)).

Cooperation may however also lead to an increase in rent-seeking outlays and dissipation. Two examples are presented below. The first is based on Chung (1996), who examines a rent-seeking model of the Tullock type, where the size of the rent is a positive function of aggregate rent-seeking efforts. The second example introduces partial cooperation into a rent-seeking contest for a public good.

In Chung's endogenous rent-seeking framework, rent-seeking outlays of an individual are not just negative for other rent-seekers (reducing their probability to win). Rent-seeking investments also include a *positive externality,* as outlays of rent-seekers increase the size of the rent. Under perfect cooperation, rent-seeking profits are highest if the level of total rent-seeking investment is chosen so that it maximises the difference between the endogenous rent (which depends on the level of investment) and the investment itself (see Chung (1996, p. 58)). As Chung notes (p. 61), within his framework total non-cooperative rent-seeking investments fall below the profit-maximising level if the value of r is sufficiently small. In such a constellation, introducing cooperation would increase rent-seeking investments.

The second example, which presents a case of *partial cooperation,* builds on the results of the public-good model from Katz, Nitzan and Rosenberg (1990), mentioned on page 79. To demonstrate the case, a numerical calculation is presented below, using a Tullock-type model with $r=1$. Assuming that there are *two groups* of *ten* individuals competing for a public good, and each individual values the public good as \$100, Katz, Nitzan and Rosenberg (1990, p. 52) show that each group would only invest a fourth of the benefit to one individual. This result occurs because of free-riding incentives among members of a group. In the numerical example the investment equals \$25 and sharply contrasts with the aggregated value a group places on the public good, i.e. 10·\$100= \$1000.

If the members of one group manage to cooperate, the group has a strong incentive to increase rent-seeking investments and thereby raise their expected net benefit. If one group sticks to only \$25, the optimal investment of the other (cooperating) group would become \$133.[47] Surely the solution cannot be an anticipated equilibrium of all parties. The optimal investment level of the members of the non-cooperating group changes if they foresee the high rent-seeking investment of the cooperating group. In fact, none of the members of the non-cooperating group would invest any more, as the net present value becomes negative.[48] This again would allow the cooperating group to reduce their investments, at least down to the preemptive bet, which equals \$100.[49]

What happens if the second group also cooperates? Then the two groups would both end up investing \$250, as can be derived from the standard Tullock model with two players (see Table 3-1). In fact, total rent-seeking outlays may even be higher if costs of cooperation are included.

All in all, the two examples demonstrate that, depending on the type of externality and the scope of cooperation, cooperation can increase rent-seeking investment. The example of the model from Chung (1996) includes two types of rent-seeking externalities associated with individual rent-seeking investment (the negative impact on the winning probability of other rent-seekers and the positive impact on the size of the rent). In this model, cooperation does not a priori reduce rent-seeking activities. The impact on dissipation depends on the specific parameter values. In the second example (pure public good case), cooperation remained partial. Such a situation leads to a reduction in free-riding, but not to a reduction in the costly competition between rent-seeking groups. Only if cooperation is perfect, i.e. if the two groups are mutually working together to their joint benefit, do rent-seeking investments decline to near zero.

---

47 This result draws on the standard two-player Tullock model: Max $\frac{x}{x+25}\cdot 1000 - x$ $\rightarrow x^* = \sqrt{1000\cdot 25} - 25 = 133.11$

48 Given \$133 total investments of the cooperating group, the optimal investment of a member of the non-cooperating group is:

$$x^* = \frac{\sqrt{mY\cdot\alpha R} - mY}{n} = \frac{\sqrt{133\cdot 100} - 133}{10} = -1.77\ .$$

m, n	members of group
Y	individual rent-seeking investments
αR	individual valuation of public good

Source: rearranged formula (7) in Katz, Nitzan and Rosenberg (1990, p. 51)

49 The preemptive bet can be determined by setting $x^*=0$ in the above formula (Footnote 48) and solving for mY. It follows mY=αR=\$100.

d) Dissipation: Summary and Conclusion

Table 3-4 summarises the main results of the discussion. Head entries describe characteristic parameters and other features of rent-seeking models together with their expected 'normal' impact on dissipation. Attached to head entries are selected alternative specifications of the rent-seeking setting, which can explain a different impact on dissipation. Because changes of total rent-seeking investments and dissipation do not necessarily point in the same direction in endogenous rents-seeking situations, information on rent-seeking outlays are explicitly given in parentheses if the direction differs from what has been denoted with dissipation. Furthermore, a few comments have been added, in particular if the outcome depends on the definition of dissipation.

What finally emerges is a very heterogeneous picture of results—a picture that seems to be, at least at first glance, more confusing than helpful in understanding how much rent-seekers invest to capture a transfer and how policymakers should interfere in the rent-seeking situation. Despite this complexity, or rather *because* of this complexity, many valuable insights and policy recommendations can be derived. The remaining section of this chapter will start with a summary of general conclusions on rent-seeking and dissipation, and then mention a few policy aspects relevant for LDCs and the reform process, based on the summary in Table 3-4.

General Conclusions on Rent-Seeking and Dissipation

Four major conclusions stand out. First, the scope of the results from rent-seeking models is in a large majority of cases limited to the specific structure addressed in the model. This insight is particularly important for deriving conclusions from policy-induced parameter variations. What matters and determines dissipation and the profitability of rent-seeking is the *entire set of parameters* that shape rent-seeking settings. One solution to address this problem is to elaborate an overview which is not based on a simple list of parameters, but which describes a typology of rent-seeking settings that are based on the most characteristic features and parameter constellations. It would be desirable if the literature on formal rent-seeking models extended the discussion and shifted the emphasis away from the more narrow focus on parameters to a broader description of empirically-relevant rent-seeking settings. This approach would include, where necessary, assumptions on specific parameter values (which are in fact implicit whenever a parameter is not explicitly included in the model). It can be expected that this broader, empirically-driven approach allows for more clear-cut policy conclusions, for instance when comparing different winning procedures, like the Tullock-lottery winning rule with an all-pay auction.

Table 3-4: Indicative Impact of Parameter Variations on Dissipation

Parameter	Impact
Size of rent	o (+)
Decreasing marginal utility	– (+)
Non–rival setting	– (o)
Increasing number of prizes	–[a]
Certainty of rent	+[b]
Certainty depending on outlays	–
Public good	–
Including cooperation within group	o
Valuation in general	+[b]
Attitudes towards risk	–
Interaction with profit-seeking	+[c]
Hedging and absence of interaction	+
Asymmetries in valuation	–
Asymmetry not perceived	o
Autonomy of rent-setter	–
Size of rent is endogenous	+/– (–)
Non-rival setting	+[d]
Certainty of rent is endogenous	+[d, e]
Including interaction with other settings	+[f] (–)
Structure of authority	
Committee decisions[g]	+/–
Several suppliers	–
Starting point	–[h]
Opposition	–[i]
No anticipation (myopia)[i]	+[j] (o)
Free-riding, non-linear reaction	+/–
Relative power, starting point	+/–
Means of exerting influence	
Threat	–
Conditional outlays	–
Number of rent-seekers	+
Participating number remains limited	–[k]
Group contest with free-riding	–
Personal size effect	–[l]
Winning rule (other than lottery)	+/–
Including asymmetries	+/–
Winning rule (introducing rent-sharing)	o
Declining marginal utility, several contests	+
Declining marginal productivity	–
Active because of less risk[m]	+
Less severe competition	–
Winning procedure (multi-stage case)	o
Different sensitivities	+/–
Non-rival contest	+
Group contest	o[n]
Equal sharing rule	–
First stage is pure public good	–[o]
Decreasing costs with group, cooperation	–
Active because of group formation	+
Group changes asymmetries in power	+/–
Asymmetries in power	–
Interaction with other asymmetries	+/–
Perception and rationality	+/–
Dynamic interaction	
Stackelberg behaviour	+
First mover with lower valuation	–
Preemptive bet	+/–
Cooperation of first mover	–
Cooperation	–
Positive externality	+[l]
Partial cooperation with public good	+

(..) Change in rent-seeking outlays different from change in dissipation
a Rent-seekers allowed to obtain one prize only
b Relative to fixed size of rent
c If profit-seeking is riskier
d Rise in autonomy not above critical level
e Catching up 'certainty' dominates
f Relative to aggregated total
g May increase or decrease autonomy
h If basis refers to entire transfer
i Rent-seekers' outlays only
j If transfer becomes smaller due to opposition
k In comparison with unlimited access
l Possible outcome, if externality dominates
m Assuming risk-averse individuals
n Distribution according to relative effort
o Assuming unequal distribution of individuals

Second, the previous discussion clearly indicates that there is only a weak relation between rents and rent-seeking investments. In the vast majority of rent-seeking settings in the real world, stylised perfect market conditions do not prevail. Many rent-seeking settings include barriers of entry, information may not flow quickly enough, asymmetries in power and valuation exist, rent-seekers have different means of exerting influence and they may join groups and cooperate. The hypothesis of *full dissipation* is therefore no more than a theoretical construct or benchmark. Having this in mind, any study that takes *rents as an estimate for rent-seeking* activities is highly speculative and most likely misleading.

Third, whether *overdissipation* is feasible or not is to a large extent a matter of definition and focus. Clearly, no individual is prepared to spend more for a rent than the value attributed to it. Within such a narrow perspective (i.e. only focusing on what rent-seekers have to pay from their own pockets), overdissipation can only arise in a setting of myopia and sunk costs. With a broader definition of dissipation that also takes other costs into consideration the situation looks different, and overdissipation can easily happen. This is for instance the case in many settings that include opposition. The outcome is however dependent on a 'skewed' definition of dissipation, i.e. countervailing rent-protecting activities are defined as part of rent-seeking related outlays; the sum of outlays, however, is not compared with the potential amount that is at stake but only with the transfer effected from the contest. In contrast to that, a clear-cut case of overdissipation (it does not depend on including opposition) is possible if rent-seekers make their investments out of other than personal resources. This is for instance the case when parastatal managers misallocate state resources to capture a small share of it—clearly a high-cost rent-seeking example, which is most relevant in many LDCs.

Fourth, rent-seeking is indeed a *bargain*, but only for rent-seekers. Many points discussed and listed in Table 3-4 explain why the level of dissipation may be rather low. Asymmetries in power and valuation, largely pre-defined rent allocations and non-rival settings, as well as less costly means of exerting influence (threat and conditional outlays) can make rent-seeking an extremely profitable undertaking. It is therefore important that reform measures directly address and reduce rent-seeking opportunities, that they increase their costs and offer better profit-seeking alternatives.

What Policy Recommendation Can Be Derived from the Entries Listed in Table 3-4?

Recommendations which aim at reducing or eliminating rent-seeking opportunities will be ignored if they negatively affect the rent-seeking opportunities of policymakers. There is however always a coalition of international donors and some reform-minded politicians from the administration, who can get important insights from a rent-seeking analysis. The following suggestions are aimed at them.

On the whole, considering the variety and diversity of rent-seeking models, policymakers who intend to address rent-seeking cannot rely on generalisations from a single rent-seeking model but have to analyse rent-seeking situations on a case-by-case basis. Table 3-4 can give some clues on which parameters matter, and it can help to assess the impact of variations in parameters in an indicative way. But it has to be kept in mind that these parameters can only provide limited insights. To fully understand rent-seeking problems, one needs to examine the entire political economy, an aspect that will be further elaborated in Chapter 4.

The *size* and *certainty* of rents are important aspects which determine rent-seeking activities. They typically change in the reform process and, as will be argued in Chapter 5.1, they also directly relate to the intensity of economic crises, for example if the rent depends on the level of inflation or shortages caused by the crises. An anticipation of rent-seeking reactions to policy-induced and crises-related changes in rents, in particular an assessment of reactions in non-rival settings, can help in formulating more appropriate reform measures.

Another issue is the *public good* character of a rent. Allocations of donor projects, if not monitored carefully, may degenerate to a rent-seeking situation where the rent itself is a public good. Though in this case rent-seeking investments may not be high, it can be expected that projects will have a higher chance of failure if the allocation has been based on rent-seeking motives. Particularly relevant when it comes to implementing broad-based measures of stabilisation and structural adjustment are considerations as to what determines the public good character of regulations and the level of free-riding involved (on both sides, rent-seeking and opposition). Both aspects critically determine the probability or sustainability of rent-distributing policies and associated rent-seeking and rent-protecting outlays. The extent of the public good character of regulations partly depends on the competitive structure of the economy. The more monopolistic the structure in the economy is, the more will specific rent-seeking regulations only benefit one or few companies. This implies that free-riding on the rent-seeking side will be minimal. Rent-seeking investments are higher, increasing the chances that rent-seeking regulations are implemented.

The second group of entries summarised in Table 3-4 outlines aspects which determine, together with the above-mentioned rent characteristics, the value attributed to the rent. The individual *valuation* of a rent may deviate from its 'objective', market based value, in particular if the rent includes 'non-monetary' components. A high subjective valuation of a rent may explain severe rent-seeking resistance in the reform process, for instance in the case of large-scale retrenchments of parastatal employees or civil servants. An assessment of what determines the value of the rent that goes beyond a simple monetary calculation may provide useful insights to overcome rent-seeking resistance. Making profit-seeking activities less *risky* is another promising avenue to address rent-seeking behaviour in an indirect way. Knowledge about *differences in valuation* can contribute to understanding and anticipating the changes in rent-seeking contests that may occur if reform measures selectively affect the valuation of rents among competing rent-seekers.

On the cost side of rent-seeking, a clearer differentiation is necessary for policy measures that increase *autonomy* of rent-setters. Even though it is generally desirable to increase the costs to influence policymakers and civil servants, mechanisms that make them less sensitive to rent-seeking investments have to be understood in full. In particular a non-rival setting requires a more detailed evaluation, for instance, making sure that the critical level is reached from where on rent-seeking activities fall as autonomy further increases. Equally relevant is an assessment of the interactions with other rent-seeking opportunities. Defining a rent-seeking immune *structure of authority* could be more explicitly considered in civil service reforms. Optimally, these reforms would include a preceding analysis of the different rent-seeking patterns in the civil service.

The *starting point* can be influenced by a public debate on rent-seeking costs, which is further eased if there are free and independent media. *Opposition* matters in rent-seeking contests. Their contribution to reduce rent-seeking is highest if opposition can form and act in a non-costly way. Actively strengthening anti-rent-seeking forces by reducing their organisation costs and enlarging their influence on rent-setters offer promising avenues. Finally, a better assessment of the *means of exerting influence* helps in understanding rent-seeking strategies and related costs; it helps in setting priorities in the reform process and provides knowledge on how to address rent-seeking settings.

The second column in Table 3-4 summarises the last two groups of rent-seeking features (cost aspects related with the allocation of rents between rent-seekers and costs related with the strategies they undertake). The *number of rent-seekers, winning rules and winning procedures*, as well as the level of *asymmetries in power* (either among rent-seekers or between rent-seekers and rent-protecting forces) are likely to be affected by economic, political and institutional reforms. Rent-seeking costs may increase during reforms, for instance as entry barriers fall and insider settings become more competitive, as shown in the model of Hillman and Ursprung (2000). Or additional stages may be built in the rent-seeking process, which either imply an increase or decrease of rent-seeking costs. The changing environment may also offer many new rent-seeking opportunities. A detailed assessment of the character of rent-seeking contests that exist before, during and after measures of stabilisation and structural adjustment are implemented, contributes to a more adequate policy formulation and sequencing.

To be able to anticipate the reaction of rent-seekers in the reform process, two conclusions are especially worth mentioning. First, as noted earlier, reforms may affect rent-seeking contests at *different stages*. A multi-stage contest may describe a situation where rent-seekers first try to become insiders and then, having become insiders, compete (or cooperate) to seize the rents. Non-rival rent-seeking settings often reflect a partial consideration (e.g. the second stage) of an overall contest. Since policy measures can affect rent-seeking settings on different levels in different ways, both perspectives matter when defining policy recommendations, i.e. partial considerations, which focus on the behaviour of rent-seekers on a single stage, as well as an overall assessment of the rent-seeking setting (which captures the interaction between the stages).

Second, rent-seekers are likely to react in different ways to reform measures that threaten their rents. This requires taking a sufficiently broad focus that considers *all relevant rent-seeking opportunities simultaneously* and also includes an assessment of profit-seeking alternatives. During the reform process, rent-seekers will adjust their behaviour, however not necessarily in the desired direction. They may take advantage of other rent-seeking opportunities which have not yet been exploited or which either have been purposely created or become available from the transition phase. Depending on the setting, the new rent-seeking opportunities may be very different. Rent-seeking may shift from legal to illegal activities, or the rent-seeking situation may change from a non-rival setting to a competitive setting. A one-sided focus on one rent-seeking situation or a limitation to one type of rent-seeking behaviour (e.g. corruption) can therefore fail to include all relevant interactions and alternatives.

3.3 Rent-Seeking and the Costs for Society

> *'If the basic institutional framework makes income redistribution (piracy) the preferred (most profitable) economic opportunity, we can expect a very different development of knowledge and skills than a productivity-increasing [ ] economic opportunity would entail.'*
>
> *Douglass C. North (1990, p. 78)*

Rent-seeking behaviour is present in any society and it may exert, depending on its character and prevalence, a large impact on the country's level and distribution of welfare. Institutional economists, such as Douglass North, emphasise that long-term development of a country may vary considerably, depending on whether political and economic institutions favour redistributive or productive activities. Particularly in the long run the costs of rent-seeking can be substantial.

So far Chapter 3 has presented a detailed overview of what determines the level of rent-seeking investments and related dissipation. The analysis aimed not only at a better understanding of rent-seeking incentives, but also of the costs of rent-seeking. Certainly, the discussion considered many features relevant for such an analysis, but insights based on the behaviour and incentives of rent-seekers are by no means sufficient to assess the impact of rent-seeking on the *welfare of a society*. Chapter 3.3 extends the overall discussion on rent-seeking, treating additional aspects which are crucial for a comprehensive and more differentiated evaluation of rent-seeking costs.

Section a) explains welfare effects in general terms and briefly surveys empirical approaches which measure rent-seeking costs. Section b) then addresses four aspects essential in a cost evaluation. They provide valuable insights for policymakers to set priorities when it comes to tackling rent-seeking problems. Section c) finally shifts the focus to Chapter 3 as a whole, concluding with an assessment of the relevance of rent-seeking theory and an appraisal of rent-seeking costs in LDC relevant settings.

a) Necessity Versus Empirical Practicability

Why a Differentiated Approach Matters

From a theoretical point of view, studies that attempt to measure rent-seeking costs may include three different levels of scope and 'complexity'. Approaches which only include the first, most basic level largely confine themselves to what has been addressed in Section a) of Chapter 3.1, i.e. they measure rents as an *approximation for rent-seeking activities* and rent-seeking costs. These studies typically take a macro perspective. More demanding is an investigation of rent-seeking costs which likewise *addresses the level of dissipation*, as discussed in detail in Chapter 3.2. Such approaches would not just focus on rents but include a more differentiated method to estimate the level of rent-seeking activities associated with the rents identified in the economy. Having the overall welfare perspective in mind, the present section finally points to a third level of 'complexity' or 'perfection' that may be included in a rent-seeking cost analysis. The focus shifts from the partial perspective of Chapter 3.2 to take a closer *dynamic and general equilibrium position.*

The impact rent-seeking exerts on the welfare of a society may be best visualised with a simplified diagram. Broadly speaking, welfare effects that come along with rent-seeking either are a consequence of the rent-seeking activity itself or derive from the change in incentives rent-seeking implies and the redistribution of income associated with the rent-seeking process. Figure 3-8 shows in a stylised way the social costs related with these aspects. It outlines the production frontier of an economy, which consists of two goods only and a rent-seeking alternative. Furthermore, to keep the diagram simple, the country is assumed not to trade with other countries, i.e. production and consumption points coincide (for an example including foreign trade see Figure 3-9 on page 136).

If there is no rent-seeking, the country faces the standard trade-off between producing the goods x and y, i.e. the more resources it devotes to produce good x, the less is available for the production of good y and vice versa. The maximum output the country can achieve is indicated with the transformation curve going through x, A and y. Since there is no foreign trade, the country will choose the output level where the highest indifference curve is tangential to the transformation curve, i.e. point A.[50]

In a rent-seeking economy, in contrast, some of the resources are wasted when individuals try to attain a transfer. Individuals invest resources to influence politicians to provide rent-creating policies and they compete for the rents allocated by the authorities. However, only resources directly invested in rent-seeking that do not take the form of mere transfers are no longer available for the production of the goods x and y. They reduce the maximum production possibility of the country; point A in Figure 3-8 is no longer feasible. In addition, the limitation of efficient production (a consequence of distorted incentives) prevents the country from making the best of the remaining resources. Instead of realising B, output falls below the production potential down to C.

Obviously, a partial rent-seeking analysis which only focuses on rents and rent-seeking investments, as discussed in Chapter 3.2, cannot describe these aspects, and constructing an all-encompassing rent-seeking model would be far too complex. However, with an empirical study it is possible to measure or isolate some aspects related to these costs. Yet given the difficulty in obtaining information and measuring rent-seeking activities, empirical analyses are

[50] Indifference curves specify preferences, here the preferences of the country. All points along an indifference curve represent the same level of utility and a higher indifference curve denotes a higher level of utility.

Figure 3-8: Schematic Depiction of Social Costs Related to Rent-Seeking

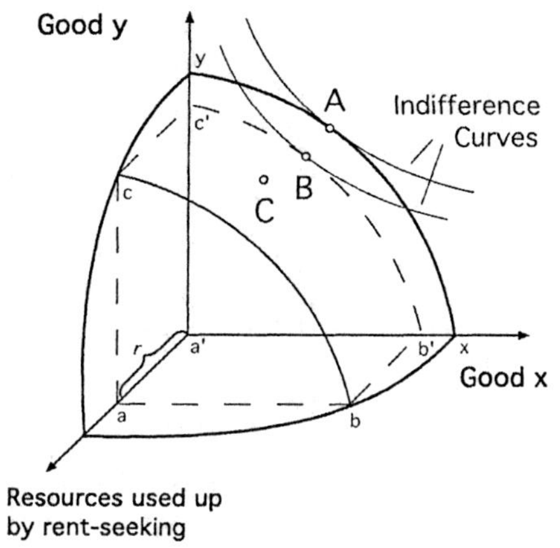

The diagram represents a three-dimensional production frontier. The country uses its resources for productive activities (production of goods x and y) as well as for rent-seeking. If no resources are invested in rent-seeking, the country will realise output level A. With rent-seeking, however, this level is no longer feasible.

First, resources invested in rent-seeking which do not take the form of transfers are lost to society. The corresponding production possibility curve of the remaining two goods shrinks. In the case of *r* resources invested in such a way, the remaining segment will be abc (or a'b'c' on a two-dimensional schedule with no explicit axis for rent-seeking).

Second, since rent-seeking not only absorbs resources directly but prevents the country from producing goods in the most efficient way (regardless whether rent-seeking takes the form of transfers), the country finally realises an output level which is even below its reduced production possibility curve (point C instead of B).

Source: Three-dimensional production frontier and respective inward shift in the two-dimensional space according to Figure 3.2 in Brooks and Heijdra (1988, p. 30)

typically based on hypothetical and sometimes arbitrary assumptions which mirror the compromise between theory, the availability of data and the researcher's time and resource constraints. In addition, most studies only focus on a very limited number of rent-seeking relevant aspects. The following overview of empirical work makes these qualifications apparent.

Empirical Approaches to Determine Rent-Seeking Costs

Studies that attempt to measure rent-seeking costs may be grouped according to the three different levels of focus, scope and complexity specified above. The first group comprises studies which measure rents, the second group covers approaches which effectively observe rent-seeking outlays, and the third group summarises empirical work which relates estimates of rent-seeking to parameters such as income or growth. The latter group also measures some indirect costs to society.

Studies that measure rents as an *approximation for rent-seeking activities* and rent-seeking costs are rare. The studies of Mohammad and Whalley (1984) and Ampofu-Tuffuor, DeLorme and Kamerschen (1991) referred to in Chapter 3.1 (page 64) are examples of this category. Both directly add up rents to draw conclusions on rent-seeking costs, without effectively measuring the level of dissipation. According to their estimates, in highly regulated economies annual rent-seeking costs may approach one third to almost one half of GNP. The authors however acknowledge that results are likely to differ if evaluated from a general equilibrium perspective. A second study by Mohammad (Blomqvist and

Mohammad (1986)) also provides information on calculating rents; the authors however do not equate rents with costs but use the data as input in a computable general equilibrium model (CGE-model).

Dougan (1991) presents a paper with the questionable suggestion of adding up aggregate current income and the net deficit of the public sector as an estimate for rent-seeking costs (p. 661). The approach rests on two extreme and inappropriate assumptions. First, all government expenditure relates to rent-seeking and is therefore wasteful; and second, any income that is left untaxed is untaxed because of rent-seeking. (Apparently he assumes that only a 100% tax-rate on all income is not associated with any tax-avoiding rent-seeking activities.)

Finally, another example of the first category (measuring rents as an approximation for rent-seeking costs) is the series of articles initiated by Katz and Rosenberg (1989) on the measurability of budget-related rent-seeking.[51] Unlike Dougan's oversimplified approach, Katz and Rosenberg do not use overall government expenditures but changes in budget allocation as an estimate for rent-seeking outlays (assuming full dissipation when concluding on rent-seeking costs). The approach is again open to a variety of criticism, in particular since budget allocations also change without rent-seeking efforts. As Schnytzer (1994, p. 358f) notes, changes may reflect government, social or development policy, they may depend on the system or relate to fluctuations in prices of budget inputs such as oil revenues. In addition, he emphasises (p. 360) with 'the presence of rent protecting behaviour, there may be no correlation between the Katz-Rosenberg measure of resources allocated to rent-seeking and the value of rents achieved'. Taking up the argument presented in the discussion on opposition (p. 92f), the basis for determining dissipation is neither the change in budget allocation that can be observed, nor the realised total allocation but the share of rents that has been at stake for reallocation.

Empirically more demanding are studies that belong to the second category, i.e. studies on rent-seeking costs, which directly *address the level of dissipation* by observing rent-seeking outlays. Given the complexity and the need to include micro-level data, it is not surprising that empirical approaches of this type are virtually non-existent. There are only a few studies that directly observe and measure rent-seeking activities within a specific limited setting and relate these outlays to the rents that have been transferred. In most cases, such approaches refer to laboratory experiments, i.e. experimental work which aims at providing evidence of stylised rent-seeking models.[52]

Actual rent-seeking (or rent-protecting) outlays can also be measured indirectly. McChesney (1997, p. 73f), for instance, who refers to a study from Beck, Hoskins and Connolly (1992), suggests looking at movements of the

---

[51] See also Scully (1991) and comments by Katz and Rosenberg (1994), as well as Schnytzer (1994) and Allard (1995).

[52] See, among others, Millner and Pratt (1989), Millner and Pratt (1991), Shogren and Baik (1991), Potters, De Vries and Van Winden (1998) and Weimann, Yang and Vogt (2000). A non-laboratory case, as mentioned earlier on page 111, is the case study by Hazlett and Michaels (1993) of the telephone licence lottery.

firms' stock prices. In short, if politicians announce a policy that reduces private gains, stock prices of the threatened firms decline. If there is no lobbying and side payments a subsequent withdrawal of the proposal should increase the stock prices again by the same amount.[53] However, if stock prices rise less or even remain unaffected by removal of the threat, the firms are left poorer although the legislation was not passed. The difference can be used as a measure to indicate rent-seeking investments undertaken by the firms to prevent the policy (however only if stock markets are reasonably efficient).[54]

Even though empirical studies of the two categories may be very sophisticated, they ignore costs related to the limitation of efficiency (i.e., as noted above, the move from point B to C in Figure 3-8) and they fail to differentiate between 'wasteful' rent-seeking investments and mere transfers. In particular in a dynamic and long-term perspective indirect costs from rent-seeking may be substantial. Total rent-seeking costs may therefore depend more on the nature of the rent-seeking setting than on the initial size of rents and rent-seeking outlays.

Unfortunately it is extremely difficult, if not impossible, to address all relevant rent-seeking forces that move an economy from a point A to the inefficient position in C. Empirical studies that try to capture these effects have therefore taken indirect and 'general' approaches. They do not provide a detailed breakdown of rent-seeking forces and related costs but simply run regression analyses with *estimates of rent-seeking that indicate costs to society*. If the rent-seeking coefficient is significant and has the expected sign it is assumed to adequately represent rent-seeking and the parameter value is used to conclude on rent-seeking costs. This group of approaches comprises the third category.

Besides measuring rents directly (e.g. Gallagher (1991)), the following *indicators of rent-seeking* have been applied or suggested: the ratio of total government expenditures to total economic output (Grossman (1988)), the percentage of workers employed in federal and state government jobs (Durden (1990)), the number of practising lawyers (Laband and Sophocleus (1988), Magee, Brock and Young (1989)) or the level of college enrolment in law relative to enrolment in engineering (Murphy, Shleifer and Vishny (1991)). Some papers present similar analyses but do not explicitly mention rent-seeking. Barro (1991, p. 430f), for instance, measures the negative impact of government consumption on growth (consumption defined as government consumption less government spending on education and defence). Finally, there is a broad literature on corruption and soft budget constraints which addresses specific aspects of rent-seeking and provides empirical evidence on related costs. Mauro

---

53 Strictly speaking, it only happens if the companies expect a future introduction of the harmful policy with the same probability as they did before the first threat had been announced.

54 Note the difference may represent true rent-seeking investments, i.e. a firm tries to prevent a cost-internalising policy or a legitimate tax claim. The difference may also indicate the size of private rent extraction, i.e. the firm is a victim of public officials who threaten to implement unwanted measures so as to extort side payments. In the latter situation, which is the case discussed in McChesney (1997), the perspective changes and the method effectively measures the size of the rent transferred.

(1995, 1996, 1998) or Tanzi and Davoodi (1997, 2000), for instance, regress indexes on corruption on growth, investment and government expenditures. And Raiser (1996, p. 76f) estimates the relation of soft budget constraints to growth and inflation.

In addition to different indicators of rent-seeking, the choice of the *dependent variable* also varies among the studies. The impact of rent-seeking has been evaluated on variables such as family income (Durden (1990)) or real GNP (Laband and Sophocleus (1988)), the growth of total economic output (Grossman (1988)) or the growth of real GDP per capita (Murphy, Shleifer and Vishny (1991)), the performance of parastatal and private companies (e.g. soft budget analysis in Majumdar (1998)), the saving and investment ratio (Courbois (1991)), the level of foreign direct investment (Wei (1997b)), the gross social rate of return on investment and the investment rate (Gallagher (1991)), or the quality and composition of public investments (Mauro (1996, 1998) and Tanzi and Davoodi (1997, 2000)). The latter studies use performance indicators of infrastructure (the percentage of paved roads and railway diesel engines in good condition, the percentage of water and electric power losses as well as faults in telecommunication) as an estimate for the quality of public investments.

It is not possible to generalise or to directly compare all the results on rent-seeking costs obtained in these papers. Estimates and conclusions differ, depending on the choice of the data set (country and period), the specific combination of the indicators of rent-seeking and the measurement of costs, as well as the general methods and corrections applied, in particular the number and type of other parameters involved in the regression analysis.

A lot of empirical rent-seeking work has been done for the United States. For instance, addressing the US economy, Laband and Sophocleus (1988) find rent-seeking costs to amount to 22.6% of GNP, Grossman (1988) estimates the impact of the relative size of government expenditures on growth to be - 0.416, and Durden (1990) concludes that average income per family decreases from federal and state government employment outside the South by US$217.57 (146.72 + 70.80), but increases in the South by US$84.28 (-170.90 + 86.92), amounting to overall net losses of roughly $30 billion.[55, 56]

Murphy, Shleifer and Vishny (1991, p. 524) make a cross-country analysis of 91 countries. They find (p. 524) if an extra 10% of enrolment were in law (this roughly corresponds to doubling enrolments) growth would fall 0.3% per year. From their analysis they conclude (p. 529) that 'the most important effect

---

55 As Durden (1990, p. 287f) notes, government employment not only affects the level of family income in negative ways (government employment as a measure for wasteful rent-seeking). It can also substitute for unemployment or for lower-paying jobs in the private sector and thereby increase income. According to his study, the positive effect dominates in the southern US (one explanation being that that region draws money and resources away from other regions).

56 The *state government* effect on employment (86.92) is not significant at the 5% confidence level. Durden estimates the overall loss to non-South regions to be $39.8 billion (13.6 + 22.2). The benefit to the South from the positive *federal government* effect is $12.8 billion. As he notes, the benefit would halve if the not quite significant effect of *state government* employment is added.

of lawyers on growth is the opportunity cost of not having talented people as innovators'.

And Mauro (1997, p. 9f) notes, drawing from his earlier study (Mauro (1996)), if the corruption index improves by one standard deviation investment rates increase by more than 4%, spending on education rises around 0.5% and the annual growth rate of per capita GDP goes up by over half a percentage point.

The examples quoted provide information on rent-seeking costs in a very general way. However, as the focus is mostly on the highest aggregation level, the studies typically fail to describe rent-seeking processes as well as the different types and patterns of rent-seeking costs. Optimally, an empirical rent-seeking analysis would include aspects of all the three 'levels' specified above, i.e. the study would include selective information on rents, rent-seeking investments and information on the different types of rent-seeking costs. Even though it is virtually impossible to evaluate all relevant costs that are associated with a rent-seeking situation, this caveat does not justify taking an over-simplistic approach. Often moderate efforts can provide some useful additional information.

b) Tools to Evaluate Rent-Seeking Costs

At least when it comes to interpreting social costs and to make policy recommendations and setting priorities, a rent-seeking analysis should go beyond measuring rents and rent-seeking investments and take a more differentiated perspective. This section suggests that an assessment of rent-seeking costs should consider at least four additional aspects: the *type* of rent-seeking investments, the rent-seeking *allocation* process, the *setting* surrounding rent-seeking and the impact of choosing a specific *benchmark*.[57]

What Do Rent-Seeking Investments Look Like?

Rent-seeking activities may take very different forms, ranging from mere *threats* to money and in-kind *transfers* (e.g. dinners or scarce goods) to *investments* where real resources are used up and no longer available for other purposes. In an analysis of the impact of rent-seeking on welfare, such a differentiation matters. From society's perspective, dissipation can therefore be defined to characterise a situation where rent-seeking investments do not take the form of transfers but where resources are 'dissipated', i.e. 'wasted' in the rent-seeking process (recall the definition in Chapter 3.1).

Economically it makes a difference whether smugglers use the main road and simply bribe customs officials to move 'hot' goods across the border, or

[57] The discussion partly draws on an early but comprehensive survey of rent-seeking from Brooks and Heijdra (1989), who emphasise the relevance of general equilibrium and dynamic approaches, as well as the significance of transaction costs and property rights.

whether they decide to move the goods along a hidden and cumbersome path which takes them four days instead of two hours to reach the same destination. In the latter situation, human resources are effectively wasted from the society's point of view, as it does not make sense to use the path if there is already a much faster road.

A striking example of pure resource waste is the case of export fraud mentioned in Krueger (1993, p. 21). Peruvian authorities discovered that large amounts of rocks were officially exported and then dumped into the sea. The only purpose of this activity was to collect export subsidies. Dumping rocks into the sea is not beneficial to anybody, but for the specific dealers rent-seeking rewards offered higher individual benefits than did other activities such as maintaining roads or repairing telephone installations. Since in Krueger's example the resources spent on rent-seeking neither represent a transfer nor the production of a good or service, from society's perspective these resources are entirely wasted. They may be interpreted as transaction costs of the rent-seeking process.

Yet what makes an assessment of rent-seeking costs complex is that there is no simple dividing line between transfer and waste and most rent-seeking situations involve both. Recipients of in-kind transfers, for instance, usually place a lower value on the transfer they receive than the cash equivalent. In addition, as many authors have emphasised, transfers may be 'dissipated' on other levels when recipients of bribes spend resources to obtain rent-bearing positions.

Hillman and Katz (1987) formulate a general multi-tier rent-seeking model where the share of rent-seeking investments that takes the form of transfers becomes a prize in another contest. As they note (p. 129f) 'the sequencing of contests continues until transfers finally accrue to positions which are not contestable, or a stage is reached where contenders pay no bribes and employ only real resources in contesting a position'. Under such competitive conditions all transfers are bound to become wasteful. In reality, however, settings are usually less competitive and correspondingly the transmission process from transfer to waste is less complete. In addition, people who are in a position to receive bribes from other rent-seekers have a strong incentive to make sure that rent-seeking investments take the form of transfers (e.g. Rowley and Tollison (1988, p. 222f)).

The type of rent-seeking investments also matters in a broader context. If rent-seeking investments require frequent trips to the capital or organising banquets (inviting politicians and senior civil servants), companies from sectors such as public transport or catering benefit indirectly. In general, the additional demand of the goods and services that are needed in the rent-seeking process increases the gains of these producers, and it may negatively affect 'traditional' consumer rents if prices rise due to the rent-seeking demand. For an example of a simplified general equilibrium setting, which outlines these interactions and cost implications, see the models discussed in Brooks and Heijdra (1988, p. 32f, and 1989, p. 39f).

Obviously it is not possible to trace all secondary and subsequent effects of a rent-seeking investment. Nevertheless, considering the most important effects allows a more differentiated evaluation to be made concerning the waste associated with dissipation.

How Efficient Is the Rent-Seeking Allocation Mechanism?

That rent-seeking costs do not just emanate from the investments to create and capture rents, but also originate from allocative inefficiencies has been discussed in the previous chapters and outlined in various figures (e.g. Figures 2-2 and 3-1 on pages 42 and 64). The Harberger triangles in the diagrams, however, only reflect a *partial* and *static* picture of the rent-seeking situation and therefore fail to describe other relevant distortions and externalities.

The majority of rent-seeking settings in the real world consist of more than rent-seeking investments and the rents individuals are fighting for. They also imply some kind of economic activity undertaken by the rent-seeking winner in a more or less efficient way. Contrary to the common assumption in rent-seeking models, individuals are not identical with regard to this aspect, i.e. *the size of inefficiencies depends on who wins the rent-seeking game.* Or to put it differently, if inefficiencies are treated as part of the rents transferred, there are many rent-seeking settings where the size of the rent depends on the rent-seeking winner.

A case in point is tendering for construction contracts. In a corrupt environment, tendering processes involve a lot of bribery and the winner usually gets a sizeable rent, as construction projects are often overpriced and offer additional leeway to save costs, ex-post, by illegitimately reducing the quality. From an economic point of view, what often matters most is the simple question whether or not the project has been finally realised in a satisfactory way. A Tanzanian citizen, for instance, once noted:

> 'Tanzanians of Indian origin take "commission" and the road is done. Indigenous Tanzanians also take "commission", but in the end, the road is not done' (personal communication, Dar es Salaam, November 1996).

Although the statement is not meant to be racist (in fact it comes from an indigenous Tanzanian), it does not hold in this absolute form. Many Tanzanian of Indian origin have been involved in project failures and there are also reliable indigenous Tanzanians. What the quote does emphasise is the potential ex-post-nature of extracting rents, which may vary considerably depending on the setting and participants. Besides reducing quality the initial low bid may also be adjusted upwards (to compensate for 'unforeseen' cost-overruns). Both the poor quality and the high costs of government and donor-related projects often observed in developing countries are to a large extent the result of such rent-seeking processes.

In situations where the level of bribery determines the contest and where rent-seekers anticipate the possibility of extracting additional rents, the rent-seeker with the least scruples about reducing quality can offer the highest bribe and therefore will most likely win. Ultimately, in a thoroughly corrupt environment, the total project budget becomes the price and everybody involved gets rich, but hardly any money is left to do the job and the project may even not be implemented at all. Especially if the social return of a project would have been very high, the costs of not adequately implementing it are considerable. Cynical references to the possibly high level of embezzlement connected with public funds are frequent. Winiecki (1991, p. 29), for instance, notes with regard to Soviet-type economies that 'it is the ruler's aggregate product rather than the ruler's rent that tends to get dissipated'.[58]

Fortunately there are also settings where the direct relation between bribery and quality reduction does not hold, i.e. the most corrupt rent-seeker may not win and costs to society vary. The outcome of a rent-seeking contest may depend on the extent of patronage relations, reputation and efficiency. In addition, in some situations the possibility of extracting rents ex-post is not anticipated or it is considered very low and therefore not taken into account. In cases where rent-seeking opportunities from cheating arise ex-post, the reduction in quality of the project (and the level of bribery that quality requirements are not enforced) depends on the identity of the winner in the first contest.

The dependence of inefficiencies on the rent-seeking winner equally matters in other settings, such as procurement in general, the assignment of monopoly rights or the distribution of limited permits. Unfortunately it appears that situations where rent-seekers do not just bribe to get a permit or contract but also have to be very good are much less frequent.

So far it has been emphasised that a rent-seeking situation is not an isolated contest but typically involves some kind of economic activity. It is the rent-seeking winner who carries out this activity, which may be done in a more or less efficient way. However, rent-seeking does not just affect the *efficiency* of a specific economic activity underlying a rent-seeking contest. Rent-seeking may equally interfere in the preceding decision-making situation on resource allocation, i.e. it may directly distort the more fundamental decision *what activities* are undertaken at all. The literature on corruption addresses this aspect in detail for public resources.[59] A rent-seeking-induced misallocation of resources occurs if public officials do not allocate funds to projects with the highest social returns, but to activities that offer the best opportunities to collect extra rent-seeking income.

There are basically three different types of resource misallocation related to the composition of government expenditures discussed in the literature.

First, projects tend to be too large in size. The extraction of corrupt income is easier with capital goods—goods which are more extensively used in large

[58] This is basically saying that the ruler's aggregate product becomes the rent. For instance, the government may not just allocate scarce goods at low prices; bureaucrats often allocate goods to friends without even charging the subsidised price or goods are simply stolen.

[59] See, among others, Mauro (1995, 1996, 1997, 1998), Tanzi and Davoodi (1997, 1998, 2000) or Gupta, de Mello and Sharan (2000).

projects. Furthermore, as for instance noted in Tanzi and Davoodi (1997, p. 6), 'when commissions are calculated as a percentage of projects' costs, the public officials... have a vested interest in increasing the scope or the size of the projects'.

Second, maintenance is neglected in favour of new projects since the latter offer better opportunities to extract bribes. Tanzi and Davoodi even assert that in cases of extreme corruption operation and maintenance of infrastructure are not just reduced as funds are preferably allocated to new projects. The reduction of maintenance may be done purposely, so that the infrastructure deteriorates quickly to the point where it needs to be rebuilt (Tanzi and Davoodi (1997, p. 9)).

Third, besides the misallocation of resources within a sector, corruption and other rent-seeking activities may also imply a misallocation of resources between sectors. For instance, different authors argue that road construction or military spending offers better rent-seeking opportunities than expenditures on health and education.[60] The large stock of military assets, the general secrecy surrounding defence outlays, the reduced transparency in the procurement of military equipment and the relatively high capital-intensity of defence projects (Gupta, de Mello and Sharan (2000, p. 6)) make the military sector a particularly prone area for corruption.

The distortion of resource allocation caused by rent-seeking is not confined to the public sector but affects the entire economy. Rent-seeking has complex income, substitution and tax effects. For instance, in an environment of insecure property rights economic activities will be lower. Already in 1967 Tullock noted, 'one way of minimising loss by theft is to have little or nothing to steal' (Tullock (1967, p. 229)). Furthermore, as discussed in Chapter 3.2, resources are invested to protect against rent extraction.

In particular corruption has negatively affected the private sector. Distorting tax effects of corruption are highest in settings where bribery does not guarantee performance. The 1997 World Development Report, for instance, presents a study of 39 industrialised and developing countries showing that countries with high corruption have a smaller gross investment to GDP ratio (World Bank (1997c, p. 103)) and the negative effect is highest if corruption is also less predictable.[61] Tanzi and Davoodi (2000, p. 5f) emphasise the positive role of small and medium-sized enterprises (they are more innovative, less capital-intensive and contribute to growth in normal and recession times), but they also emphasise that corruption harms these companies most:

> 'Bribe payments may amount to a substantial portion of small and medium size enterprises' operating costs which can drive them out of

[60] See, among others, Mauro (1995, 1996, 1998), Gupta, Davoodi and Alonso-Terme (1998)) and Gupta, de Mello and Sharan (2000).

[61] Gross investments as a percentage of GDP are 12.3% if corruption is high and the predictability is low, 19.5% if corruption is high but predictable, 21.3% if corruption is low but unpredictable and 28.5% if corruption is both low and predictable.

business since they tend to operate in more competitive environments than large enterprises.' (Tanzi and Davoodi (2000, p. 8))[62]

Finally, also the effects on income distribution from non-petty corruption appears to negatively affect the economies of developing counties. In particular funds appropriated by large-scale corruption benefit the domestic economy only marginally. If not transferred into numbered accounts abroad, these funds are generally spent on expensive private houses or imported luxury goods.

Of course there are rent-seeking settings where at least some of the effects of income distribution benefit a poorer segment of the population. Rent-seekers may not be able to keep the rents themselves but may be forced to pass them on. A case in point is smuggling and tax evasion in a highly competitive environment where benefits originally reaped by the smugglers may finally accrue to consumers in the form of cheaper goods. However, these rent-seeking activities may nonetheless exert a negative impact on the economy, for instance, when smuggling destroys the tax-paying domestic industry. In addition, a considerable share of the benefits may flow into the pockets of corrupt but wealthy customs officials.

Costs from a misallocation of resources caused by rent-seeking are particularly high *in the long run*. Widespread and persistent rent-seeking is likely to constrain development and to force the country onto a lower or even negative growth path. As argued in Chapter 1, the average annual GDP growth per capita in sub-Saharan Africa between 1975 and 2001 (measured in purchasing power parities) was –0.9%, and for more than half of the countries the year with the highest per capita GDP occurred within the first ten years of that period. Though there are also other reasons for this development, rent-seeking is a major cause.

In a thoroughly corrupt environment, which typically involves a corrupt leadership, honest officials and businesspeople often cannot survive. In the above-mentioned case of tax evasion, for instance, competition is likely to drive honest traders and domestic producers out of business. Long-run costs also arise from the distortion of human capital formation. Several authors point to this, including Murphy, Shleifer and Vishny (1991, p. 505) who emphasise that 'talented people do not become entrepreneurs, but join the government bureaucracy, army, organized religion, and other rent-seeking ... activities because these sectors offer the highest prizes'.

Finally, long-run costs are high because the share of waste associated with mere transfer usually increases. On the one hand, as noted earlier, transfers such as bribes are often dissipated on other levels when officials try to get into rent-promising positions. On the other hand, inefficiencies are not static but typically increase over time. This happens for instance when parastatal companies face soft budget constraints, i.e. they may benefit from government support whenever revenues do not cover costs. As will be argued in Chapter 5 and outlined in the case study on Tanzania, once a great deal of the rents have been dissipated by

[62] Recall also the reference to Tanzi and Davoodi in Chapter 2.2 (p. 55).

inefficiencies, it becomes difficult, if not impossible, to remove rents without driving entire industries into bankruptcy. Rent-seeking resistance then changes its quality and becomes a matter of plain survival.

All in all, the efficiency of the rent-seeking-related allocation of resources is a critical determinant of rent-seeking costs. Depending on the contest and the time horizon, these costs can vary considerably. The magnitude of costs, however, equally depends on the presence of other distortions in the economy. This aspect, which will be treated below, is especially relevant in developing-country settings, where distortions tend to be much higher and more complex.

In What Setting Is Rent-Seeking Imbedded?

More than two decades ago, Bhagwati and Srinivasan presented an interesting analysis (Bhagwati and Srinivasan (1980), Bhagwati (1980)), arguing that in the presence of distortions, lobbying activities for revenues or tariffs may even improve welfare, as compared to a situation, where the policy is carried out without lobbying. In such settings, the shadow price of a productive factor may become negative, implying among other things that throwing away or wasting specific resources can even be beneficial (Bhagwati (1994, p. 846)).

That rent-seeking may exert a positive impact on the country's output is intuitively understandable. In a distorted environment, changes in factor prices induced by rent-seeking may act as a countervailing force to existing distortions and indirectly contribute to an increase in output. However, since the result is of an arbitrary nature—rent-seeking forces may equally pull in the other direction, i.e. reinforce existing distortions—a case-by-case analysis becomes inevitable.

To demonstrate the relevance of distortions in affecting rent-seeking costs, an example will be briefly discussed. Figure 3-9 reiterates the basic diagram presented in Bhagwati (1980, p. 358). It shows the production frontier and production points of a small, open economy, i.e. an economy which trades on international markets but is not large enough to affect world market prices. The figure has been slightly modified and extended to explicitly include both cases, a welfare-increasing and a welfare-reducing rent-seeking situation.

In the absence of rent-seeking and other distortions, the country chooses the production point, where the world price ratio p* is tangential to the production frontier (point P*) and consumption, where the highest indifference curve is tangent to the world price ratio (point C, henceforth not explicitly shown with other production points). To compare different levels of output in the diagram, output can be measured in terms of a specific good, i.e. if the country produces at P*, the value of the output in terms of good x is X*. Exogenously introducing a tariff changes the domestic price ratio and the new production point becomes P_t or P_{tt}, depending on the size of the tariff (or in terms of good x, output drops from X* to X_t or from X* to X_{tt}, respectively).

Bhagwati contrasts this non-rent-seeking situation with a second setting which additionally includes rent-seeking outlays, i.e. it is assumed that resources are spent in lobbying to achieve the tariff policy. As already discussed in Figure

3-8, the production possibility curve of goods x and y shrinks. The crucial point is that the inward shift does not need to be proportional but depends on whether rent-seeking 'consumes' resources which are more intensively used in the production of good x or y. The new production points become P_t^r or P_{tt}^r and the corresponding output level in terms of good x are X_t^r and X_{tt}^r. As can be seen from the diagram, in the case of the high tax rate, rent-seeking outlays effectively increased welfare as compared to the situation where the same policy was introduced without rent-seeking outlays ($X_{tt}^r > X_{tt}$). This result is arbitrary and results from the way the new production frontier has been drawn. A necessary condition for the result to occur is, as Bhagwati (1980, p. 360) notes, that the output of the non-lobbying sector (good x), which has been negatively affected by the tariff policy, increases again.

Figure 3-9: Costs and Rent-Seeking in a Distorted Environment

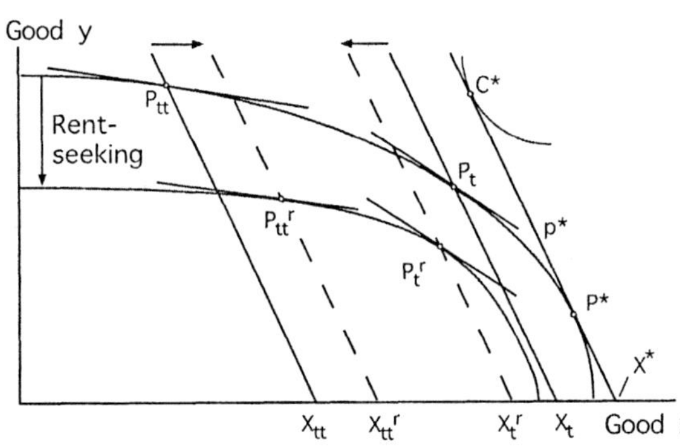

The diagram outlines the production points (P) of a small open economy, which introduces a distorting tariff of medium or large size (indices t and tt). Costs measured as 'output lost in terms of good x' are then compared with a second setting, which assumes that resources are additionally 'wasted' by rent-seeking activities.

Comparing the different outputs reveals that rent-seeking outlays do not necessarily reduce welfare if rent-seeking happens in a distorted environment. In the diagram, welfare declines with the medium tax rate ($X_t^r < X_t$), but increases in the more distorting high-tax case ($X_{tt}^r > X_{tt}$).

Source: Drawing in extension to Figure 1 in Bhagwati (1980, p. 358)

Figure 3-9 can also be interpreted in a general way, i.e. the rent-seeking activity may not necessarily relate to the tariff policy specified above but may represent any other lobbying for income redistribution. However, even though Bhagwati and Srinivasan's analysis is striking, it largely remains an empirical matter to investigate in which settings rent-seeking forces pull in the direction where they offset other distortions. To be realistic, these situations appear to be rare. Most rent-seeking activities in LDCs have been responsible for the introduction of highly distorting and therefore costly policies. In terms of Figure 3-9, these policies do not represent a change from X_{tt} to X_{tt}^r or X_t to X_t^r, but simply a change from X* down to either X_t^r or X_{tt}^r.

Bhagwati and Srinivasan have provoked a series of articles which address the issue of rent-seeking costs in second-best economies. As noted in Chapter 2.1, Bhagwati even introduced an alternative term for rent-seeking, i.e. *directly unproductive, profit-seeking (DUP) activities* (Bhagwati (1982)), a term which suggests that the indirect impact of rent-seeking may well be productive.

The theory of second-best economies relates to rent-seeking in two ways. On the one hand, it provides insights into the *size of rent-seeking costs* in distorted or constrained economies, i.e. cost may be higher or lower than in a simplified neo-classical setting. Blomqvist and Mohammad (1986), for instance, compare within a general equilibrium framework different assumptions concerning the way rent-yielding licences are allocated (e.g. based on education or according to lobbying activities). In the model they emphasise that other distortions such as taxes or subsidies critically affect the magnitude of rent-seeking costs. Mitchell (1993) specifies a 'positive' rent-seeking case, which is based on capital accumulation (import licences of intermediate goods are not distributed evenly but allocated according to the firms' capacity, which in the specific model leads to an increase in the capital stock and improved welfare). On the other hand, the theory treats rent-seeking as given and derives *second-best rules* for the formulation of economic policies. Lee and Tollison (1988), for instance, reconsider optimal taxation in a rent-seeking environment, and Anam and Katz (1988) and Anam (1989) outline the role of dissipation in determining second-best rules.

Besides the possible beneficial effect of rent-seeking in reducing price distortions, there are many other ways to link rent-seeking to an environment where it exerts positive externalities. The favourable impact may be of a systematic nature (e.g. linking rent-seeking to knowledge accumulation, stability or a reduction of information deficits) or it may happen by simple coincidence as many features occur simultaneously. Below a few examples of less detrimental or even beneficial rent-seeking settings are discussed and critically evaluated.

As noted above, rent-seeking may turn out to be beneficial if *several factors coincide*. An example is smuggling. Given widespread unemployment in developing countries, smuggling may not always tie resources that have an immediate alternative use. For instance, avoiding the main road and hiring otherwise unemployed people to carry smuggled goods across unguarded borders may not imply direct economic costs. If there is no domestic import-competing industry, if the state is thoroughly corrupt and misuses any tax funds it gets hold of, and if smugglers pass on a large share of their benefits to consumers, the rent-seeking case may become very beneficial.

The literature on corruption has raised similar arguments, describing second-best situations where corruption exerts a beneficial impact, i.e. corruption may release constraints or solve allocation problems:

> 'In terms of economic growth the only thing worse than a society with a rigid, overcentralized, dishonest bureaucracy is one with a rigid, overcentralized honest bureaucracy.' (Samuel Huntington, cited from Klitgaard (2000, p. 2))

This frequently-quoted statement is certainly appealing in a static second-best world. But it misses the much more important dynamic perspective. It has long been demonstrated that the 'grease the wheels' argument, as well as others that assign a positive role to corruption, has major flaws. For arguments and counterarguments of the revisionist view, see for instance Kaufmann (1997) or Rose-Ackermann (1998). The three main counterarguments are summarised below.

First, counterproductive regulations which make the grease necessary have usually been created deliberately as a measure to extract bribes, i.e. if there had been no opportunity to extract bribes, these regulations would not have been implemented in the first place. Furthermore, payments will not be limited to avoid inefficient regulation only. They are likely to circumvent any government regulation that affects individual profits, i.e. also regulation which would have been beneficial to society.

Secondly, bribery is unlikely to imitate an efficient market, which equates supply and demand. As argued earlier, it is not necessarily the most efficient firm with the lowest costs which can afford the highest bribe, but often the rent-seeker with the least scruples to offer sub-standard quality. In addition, there are many situations, where public goods and other benefits are not meant to be allocated to the highest bidder but according to the needs of a targeted group, i.e. the recipient has to be qualified to receive the benefit.

Thirdly, a corrupt market may not provide equal access to potential participants, information may flow less smoothly and a corrupt market may be more uncertain and include additional costs, such as hiding activities.

Another case where rent-seeking may exert a positive impact is a situation where it contributes to *reducing conflicts* or to *increasing stability*. Lewis (1994, p. 424), for instance, acknowledges rent-seeking to be 'in tension with more efficient resource allocations', but emphasises that 'the strategic allocation of rents may also stabilize developmental regimes and foster acceptance of growth-oriented policies'. Obviously political stability is an important determinant of growth. This aspect is hardly disputed and has been empirically shown (e.g. Barro (1991, p. 432)). However, rent-seeking can also be a major source of political instability, as the history of many African countries demonstrates. Between 1958 and 1984, there were more than a hundred successful or attempted military coups and more than a hundred reported plots (McGowan and Johnson (1984, p. 638)). UNDP (2003, p. 45) notes for the period 1990-2001 that there were 57 major armed conflicts in 45 locations, sub-Saharan Africa being the hardest-hit region. It can be assumed that a large number of the conflicts, coups and plots were primarily motivated by rent-seeking interests aiming to capture the state apparatus.

Finally, several authors attribute to rent-seeking a possible beneficial *information-enhancing role* in settings characterised by incomplete information and high transaction costs. Tullock, for instance, points out 'rent-seeking may not be 100 percent wasteful since it may reveal valuable information to the holder of the sought-after property rights' (comment in Laband and Sophocleus (1988, p. 274)). Brooks and Heijdra (1989, p. 45f), drawing on Barzel (1985) note as regards occupational licensing:

> 'In a world of zero transaction costs, which is the model implicitly used by rent-seeking theorists, occupational licensing can only be understood as an attempt to capture monopoly rents. In the world of costly information, however, occupational licensing can be interpreted as a device which economizes on the cost of search and information; imperfectly informed consumers are assured of at least a minimum quality standard.'

For other examples that outline an information-enhancing role of rent-seeking see for instance the case of competition for a monopoly addressed in Medema (1991, p. 1055f), or Bellin's discussion of cronyism in Tunisia (Bellin (1994, p. 432)). However, even though the information argument holds under specific conditions, its relevance should not be overstated. Most of these examples do not address typical rent-seeking situations and, as will be outlined in Section b) of Chapter 4.1, it is exactly incomplete information and transaction costs which create the most rent-seeking opportunities.

Summing up, Bhagwati and Srinivasan's emphasis on the possible second-best nature of rent-seeking settings, the revisionist view of corruption, as well as all other examples where rent-seeking is accompanied by some kind of positive externality point to important aspects in a rent-seeking evaluation. However, finding incidences where rent-seeking exerts a net positive impact on welfare does not imply an uncritical tolerance or acceptance of rent-seeking as a welfare-enhancing device. This may be short-sighted, and seen from a dynamic perspective even wrong. To assess rent-seeking costs and to derive policy conclusions requires an evaluation of all other feasible alternatives. In many incidences, it is possible and more beneficial to directly address externalities that accompany rent-seeking without tolerating the underlying rent-creating policy.

What Is the Appropriate Benchmark for Evaluating Rent-Seeking Costs?

Since rent-seeking never takes place in an institutional vacuum, institutional economists in particular have emphasised that the choice of a benchmark for evaluating rent-seeking costs is not evident from the outset. The qualification is important as any reference point decisively determines the costs of rent-seeking identified. For instance, it makes a difference if the rent-seeking outcome X_t^r in Figure 3-9 is compared with X_t or with X^*. Even though benchmarks may be clear-cut for some specific questions, the problem can be fundamental in nature and take the evaluation of rent-seeking back to the crucial definition of rents and rent-seeking.

Below two aspects affecting the assessment of rent-seeking costs are considered: the definition of the first best alternative, and, the treatment of an income redistribution induced by rent-seeking. These aspects closely relate to the basic objectives of society mentioned earlier in Chapter 2.1, i.e. the goal of producing output efficiently and the goal of reallocating income according to society's vision of a just distribution.

In many instances there is *no first best alternative available* to produce output in an efficient way. Williamson (1994, p. 188), for instance, notes on governments in general, 'if all feasible forms of organization are flawed, references to benign government, costless regulation, omniscient courts, and the like are operationally irrelevant'. Brooks and Heijdra (1989, p. 46)), who refer to Barzel (1985), emphasise:

> 'Our world is not the Walrasian one in which all "property rights are complete and costlessly enforced" (Barzel, 1985, p. 7) and where by implication all protective activity is wasteful. To argue that all resource expenditures on locks, close circuit cameras, and safe-cracking devices represent waste, is only interesting if there exists a feasible institutional form in which theft would not exist. Rent-seeking activities should be analysed by means of a comparative institutional perspective.' (Brooks and Heijdra (1989, p. 46))

This latter aspect is also suggested by Williamson (1994, p. 185), who specifies an alternative definition of efficiency, i.e. efficient is 'an outcome for which no feasible superior alternative can be described and implemented with net gains'. Clearly the suggestion does not eliminate the problem of finding the most efficient benchmark, i.e. defining which of the theoretical outcomes are feasible and which are not. Yet the quality of any rent-seeking analysis can be greatly improved by taking a broader perspective and differentiating in assessments of rent-seeking costs between several benchmarks and their likely feasibility.

Looking at the literature on rent-seeking, there are papers which explicitly point in this direction or take a comparative institutional perspective. Gradstein (1993), for instance, presents a welfare comparison of two imperfect allocation systems, the private provision of a public good with its free-riding incentives or the public provision with its rent-seeking incentives. Cullis and Jones (1992) and Medema (1991, p. 1056f) emphasise rent-seeking costs depend on the level and type of X-inefficiencies. X-inefficiencies arise if producers do not maximise profits but pursue, for instance, a minimum profit constraint. Especially in monopolistic situations producers do not drive costs to the least-cost position. The critical question is whether or not to count X-inefficiencies as part of rent-seeking costs. At least in a setting where rent-seekers lobby for a natural monopoly—in this situation X-inefficiencies most likely arise with or without rent-seeking—the benchmark cannot just be a least-cost situation.

The second aspect of choosing an appropriate benchmark relates to the proper evaluation of *income redistribution*. Since rent-seeking distributes income differently from what market forces would do, it indirectly undermines or supports society's preferences. The question emerges, whether an evaluation of rent-seeking costs has to take these 'secondary' effects into account. An example of possible positive income distribution effects is for instance noted in the 1996-98 OECD research programme on the sustainability of growth in poorer countries:

> 'There are signs that the reduction of distortions and renewed growth in Ghana over the last ten years have not improved the population's sense of well-being. This paradox could stem from the fact that the rents associated with these distortions were widely distributed among the population to begin with.' (OECD (1995, pp. 38f))

Being aware that 'in a world of positive transaction costs, resources are inevitably used in redistribute activities' (Brooks and Heijdra (1989, p. 45), referring to Barzel (1985)), rent-seeking may need an alternative benchmark. The reference to the OECD programme suggests not to treat all rent-seeking costs as costs if rent-seeking contributes to a more favourable income redistribution. Or to put it differently, the relevant benchmark for rent-seeking is a setting that includes the costs of redistributing income where society achieves the same level of utility. Such an approach would however require defining a social welfare function.

The matter of income distribution relates to the discussion on externalities addressed earlier. Besides the fact that rent-seeking is usually a very inefficient way of redistributing income—as already emphasised in Chapter 2.1, the goal is to produce output efficiently and only afterwards to reallocate income according to society's vision of a just distribution—in most incidences rent-seeking also leads to a distribution of income which is less in line with what a society perceives as just and desirable (different members of a society have a very unequal ability to rent-seek and it appears that wealthier people are better at it). Therefore in most settings taking income redistribution into account makes rent-seeking an even more costly endeavour.

c) Conclusion: Rent-Seeking Costs and LDC Settings

Depending on its character and prevalence rent-seeking may indeed have a strong negative impact on the efficiency of output and the allocation of income. Broadly speaking, rent-seeking causes *'pecuniary' transfers*, which are the difference between distorted factor payments and the payments valued at competitive factor prices. And rent-seeking is responsible for *technical and allocative inefficiencies*, implying that less resources would have been needed to produce an output that guarantees the same level of utility.

The fundamental novelty introduced with the rent-seeking concept, i.e. costs of inappropriate policies may not just arise from losses associated with 'classical' inefficiencies (Harberger triangles) but may also come from investments to create and capture the policy-induced transfers (Tullock rectangles), opened a new and important perspective in welfare theory. Chapter 3.2 demonstrated that the size of investments to capture rents can vary considerably and Chapter 3.3 emphasised that also the costs related to the type of investments, as well as the size of Harberger triangles, vary and depend on the specific setting. It can make a big difference if costs are not just evaluated from a static but dynamic and long-term perspective and costs again differ if rent-seeking takes place in a distorted environment.

Evidently rent-seeking is not a simple and uniform phenomenon, and assessing its impact and deriving more differentiated recommendations may require a complex context-specific evaluation on a case-by-case basis. The four questions posed in Section b) provide an important extension to the specific rent-seeking analysis on dissipation outlined in Chapter 3.2.

Having discussed rent-seeking incentives and related costs, what is of interest for policymakers is whether LDC settings are characterised by some specific patterns that allow general conclusions. Looking at highly-regulated economies in LDCs, rent-seekers typically compete for scarce goods, import licences and undervalued foreign exchange, cheap credits and subsidies, special treatments in public procurement including the illegitimate winning of overpriced tender contracts. They lobby for general budget support, higher monopoly protection, favourable price interventions such as a reduction in input prices and an increase in output prices. Finally, rent-seekers may compete to get into a promising position in the government bureaucracy, NGOs or local donor agencies and they may try to place their children into one of the limited but highly subsidised university places.

Chapter 3.2 identified competition to be the most important factor that determines the level of rent-seeking investments. However, as emphasised, it appears that true competition for rents is only relevant for a limited number of settings in LDCs. Even though it is not possible to generalise for all situations, three characteristic features stand out. First, the majority of rent-seeking settings in LDCs are of a pronounced *non-rival* nature or they include considerable asymmetries. Second, and partly in consequence of the first aspect, most direct *rent-seeking investments* do not appear to be costly. Third, in contrast, *inefficiencies* related to rent-seeking policies appear to be very high.

The *non-rival nature* of rent-seeking settings or the pronounced asymmetries largely reflect the limited and unequal access of individuals and groups in LDCs to public resources. Many of the rent-seeking opportunities only apply to members of the ruling elites and their entourage. In particular patronage relations are important and predetermine rent-seeking outcomes, for instance when it comes to employing bureaucrats and parastatal managers or deciding on procurement contracts.

The standard Tullock rent-seeking setting, i.e. a winner-takes-all situation where several rent-seekers compete for one prize, is therefore not of much relevance to LDCs. Only in countries where violent groups compete to capture the state apparatus can rent-seeking games resemble a Tullock situation. However, once the group has obtained power the distribution of rents to extended families and cronies largely takes the form of non-rival allocations.

Even public procurement is often an insider deal and tendering frequently includes illegal arrangements that eliminate competition among participants, partly facilitated by the repetitive nature of government procurement. In such a situation companies may simply share the prize sequentially, i.e. having colluded, only one company submits a competitive (however overpriced) bid, while all other companies either do not participate or submit proposals which are bound to lose. In a subsequent tender it will be the turn of another company to place the 'best' offer and so forth.

Likewise, large-scale corruption typically involves members of a limited circle. Besides the objective of not sharing the 'loot' with too many people, a limited circle also minimises risk. As for instance noted in Cremer (2000, p. 42f) corrupt officials often prefer contracts with the same partners and they are likely to favour politically influential people.

In many endogenous rent-seeking situations non-rivalry results when opposition is absent, either because it is weak (it cannot overcome the difficulties of getting organised) or because there are other means to compensate affected parties. Government-administered maximum prices, for instance, may not bother an affected parastatal if the company lives on soft budget constraints anyway.

Given the limitation in access, some rent-seeking settings are more like situations where prizes match or exceed the number of competing applicants. There may be very little 'competition' if only a limited number of employees in a marketing board are in a position to steal and resell part of the crop (leaving enough to be sold officially). Other prizes, such as cheap bank credits or treasury loans can even be expanded by running deficits and printing money to be able to satisfy all members of an inner circle. What appears to constrain the size of individual 'allocations' in these settings is an understanding of what can be stolen without making theft too obvious or without provoking excessively negative consequences, for instance from the donor side.

The second characteristic feature of rent-seeking settings relates to dissipation. Apart from a few exceptions *direct investments to capture rents* are either very *small* or of a *transfer* type and therefore not costly in terms of resource waste. Or to put it differently, from a partial and static perspective it appears that resources spent on Tullock rectangles are insignificant. On the one hand, an outcome from the above conclusion is that many rent-seeking settings are of a non-rival type or include pronounced asymmetries. On the other hand, a major part of rent-seeking investments in LDCs takes the form of bribes, conditional outlays or threat.

In a highly-regulated and corrupt economy bribery typically becomes the most frequent type of rent-seeking activity. Part of bribery takes the form of conditional outlays. The latter are often embedded in tendering processes with an institutionalised kickback system, i.e. project budgets include the bribe to be paid to the 'rent'-allocating official. In a competitive setting the rent-seeker who promises to give up the largest share becomes the winner. Credibility is assured, as many of these rent-seeking situations are repetitive. Seen from this perspective, a major part of rent-seeking outlays is carried out ex-post, after the winner has been determined (the rent is basically shared with the official).

Also military forces may not need to make major rent-seeking investments. As part of the ruling elites, they can rely on threats to get special treatment such as higher wages, new vehicles or generous food and other allowances. Often they also enjoy preferential access to the state budget, which allows them to secure allocations even when major budget cuts are undertaken. Good relations with the armed forces is an important cornerstone for many LDC governments to remain at power.

In contrast, using violent means to get inside the rent-producing apparatus often results in high and costly dissipation. Especially long-lasting armed conflicts can imply very high rates of dissipation, i.e. there is only little of the loot left to be shared among the winners. What makes these rent-seeking settings particularly costly is the fact that they include a large amount of externalised costs.

Finally, from an intermediate and dynamic perspective, economic reforms appear to have increased the size of direct rent-seeking investments in the short and medium term. Hardening budget constraints on parastatal companies, for instance, exerted more and more pressure, transforming some of the originally non-rival situations into competitive settings. Of course, once reforms are implemented effectively, in particular if the sequencing and fine-tuning has been well designed and realised, reforms can also reduce many policy-related inefficiencies and the net effect is most likely to be positive. Unfortunately, as will be outlined in detail in Chapter 5, rent-seekers again often prevent such favourable outcomes, as they find many ways to interfere into this process.

The very *high level of inefficiencies* associated with rent-seeking policies is the third characteristic feature of LDC settings. Most of the distorting policies adopted in developing countries either are an outcome of rent-seeking forces or they have been implemented for other reasons, but rent-seeking forces prevented their effective functioning and disallowed a later reversal when policies became too costly. Considering the numerous and varied rent-seeking forces, it is not far-fetched to conclude that government interference in the form of cumbersome and unpredictable bureaucracies, unreasonable economic policies and non-adherence to budget priorities has turned out to be the major cause of a reduction in growth and welfare in LDCs, as well as the major cause of an undesirable income distribution.

Although in a distorted environment rent-seeking may increase efficiency, such situations appear to be rare exceptions. As noted above, distortions are more likely to cause additional and costly rent-seeking activities. The question arises whether there are any realistic settings where rent-seeking systematically exerts a beneficial impact on the welfare of a country. A case may be made for rent-seeking that is directed to increase foreign aid. Since the country does not pay for the transfer, at least in theory, the country can be better off.

However, even foreign aid in the form of grants can reduce welfare, if it increases distortions, for instance by facilitating the build-up and expansion of a protected and capital-intensive import-substituting sector. Collier has brought up this point; for an illustration, see for instance Adam, et al. (1994, p. 102). The diagram shows the expansion of a production frontier in a distorted environment, where a one-sided outward shift induced by foreign aid diminishes production in the already suppressed labour-intensive export sector. Similar to the method applied in Figure 3-9, output declines if valued at non-distorted prices.

What makes rent-seeking particularly costly in LDCs is the apparent increase in inefficiencies over time; or to put it differently, it appears that technical and allocative inefficiencies have increased at the expense of 'pecuniary' transfers, i.e. in the long run, many successful rent-seekers do not get rich (or they could be much richer), but underlying economic activities become increasingly inefficient. This is evident in the parastatal sector, which in most developing countries depended on an ever-increasing amount of direct and indirect support. Enjoying monopoly protection, parastatals typically dissipate a large share of their rents with inefficiencies and much less through rent-seeking competition.

A main problem with inefficiencies associated with rent-seeking policies is that they do not just provide a strong argument for reforms, but may also become a major impediment to reforms, i.e. inefficiencies can provoke severe opposition and therefore make economic reforms difficult to implement. As noted earlier, discontinuation of a rent-seeking related policy may not just eliminate excess profits, but drive an entire economic sector to ruin. It is a major task of policymakers in reforming countries to overcome this.

Applying a broad definition of dissipation, which relates all rent-seeking costs (outlays and inefficiencies) to the rents transferred, suggests a high rate of overdissipation in LDCs. This is of course an extremely inefficient way of transferring income. It appears that in developing countries an externalisation of costs is possible on a much larger scale than in other countries. The availability of easy-obtainable donor support has certainly contributed to this outcome, also the situation that many rent-seekers do not gamble with own funds but public resources and can therefore afford very high inefficiencies to capture small transfers.

The conclusion that rent-seeking settings in LDCs are characterised by generally low rent-seeking investments but very high inefficiencies may provoke the question whether rent-seeking theory is at all relevant for LDCs, if costs are basically associated with Harberger triangles and not Tullock rectangles. Cynics may argue that it is more appropriate to bring the emphasis of research entirely back to the classical welfare analysis. Such a conclusion would be wrong. Rent-seeking theory provides insights which go beyond measuring Tullock rectangles and related investments, basically for two reasons.

First, in endogenous rent-seeking settings rent-seeking theory can explain why distorting policies are implemented in the first place. Even if the major part of costs was related to Harberger triangles, understanding rent-seeking incentives helps to address the problem at its source. An institutional environment with less or unattractive rent-seeking opportunities will prevent the implementation of many distorting and costly policies. Or to put it differently, if in an endogenous setting incentives to create and capture transfers disappear, welfare losses in the form of Harberger costs will equally vanish. As discussed earlier, rent-seeking incentives do not just depend on the size of the rent but also on how costly it is to access them.

In particular donors, which allocate large amounts of funds to developing countries, are principal targets of rent-seeking forces. If donors understand the factors that determine rent-seeking incentives and behaviour, and if they apply these insights to design, monitor and evaluate projects, programmes and budget support, performance will certainly improve. The major challenge is to provide support in a form that restrains rent-seeking and increases the profitability of profit-seeking, i.e. to guide or force an ever larger part of the society, business community, and population of civil servants into productive activities.

Second, the knowledge that there is no uniform relationship between the amount of rents transferred and welfare costs, i.e. transfers of equal size can imply very different welfare costs, enables differentiated policy conclusions to be formulated. To the extent that it is possible to detach efficiency from rent-seeking transfers, policies may be formulated to address costs without interfering too much in the rent-allocating process. A case in point, which will be addressed in Chapter 4.3, is political stability. In a setting where it is not possible to abolish rent-related transfers since these transfers constitute an important component that guarantees stability, it may at least be possible to reduce some rent-related costs. Especially in a donor-driven reform context, it can be crucial to choose this second-best approach, instead of urging a government to abolish rent-distributing policies and thereby risk rejection of the entire reform package. In the parastatal sector for instance, a second-best approach may demand closing down all non-viable companies, while simultaneously guaranteeing dismissed managers and employees a 'golden handshake'.

This chapter has reviewed many important aspects of rent-seeking settings, focusing on rents, rent-seeking incentives and related costs. But to truly understand the dynamics of rent-seeking and rent-seeking opposition, more background information is necessary. Chapter 4 will broaden the perspective and discuss several topics which will contribute to an understanding of why rent-seeking situations are created in the first place.

4 Addressing Fundamentals: Explaining the Motivation for and Success of Rent-Seeking Behaviour and Policies

'In a world of zero transaction and information costs only welfare-enhancing transfers will be passed by political representatives. When information and transaction costs are possible, some groups will be able to organise and acquire information more cheaply than others, and these differences among groups will give rise to a demand and supply of wealth transfers.'

Robert D. Tollison (1982, p. 589)

Having discussed different factors that determine rent-seeking investments and rent-seeking costs in Chapter 3, this chapter extends the discussion, focusing on why rents are created in the first place and why individuals and groups engage in rent-seeking rather than profit-seeking activities. It will look at rent-seeking from a broader individual, social, interest group and political perspective. It also explains the specific shape or value of the parameters and model structures presented in Chapter 3, and will provide an answer to the crucial question as to why society allows rent-seeking despite its detrimental effects.

The discussion is organised as follows. Chapter 4.1 discusses additional aspects of the individual decision-making situation. The first section explicitly relates rent-seeking to profit-seeking. Sections b) and c) discuss transaction costs, limited rationality and opportunism, as well as informal constraints such as tradition, habits and family values. These question and augment the narrow neo-classical approach and contribute to a better understanding of rent-seeking behaviour.

However, since most rent-creating and rent-protecting strategies also require some group mobilisation, Chapter 4.2 shifts the focus to a different aggregation level, addressing not the individual but the group's abilities to organise for or against rent-seeking transfers. In Chapter 4.3 the perspective again changes to a higher level. Looking at the political, institutional and economic setting in which rent-seeking individuals and groups are embedded, it reaches the most encompassing aggregation level. Conclusions that can be drawn from this perspective are essential to understanding rent-seeking in a broader context. While Chapters 4.1 and 4.2 concentrate on the demand side of rent-seeking, Chapter 4.3 mainly treats the supply side.

4.1 Individual Decision-Making: Utility-Maximising, Incomplete Markets and Informal Constraints

Interesting insights into rent-seeking behaviour can be gained by looking at the individual decision-making situation of choosing between profit-seeking and rent-seeking, including the widely discussed *limitations of neo-classical economics* and criticism of the concept of *homo oeconomicus*. The discussion in Chapter 3.2 emphasised that the profit-seeking alternative is an important determinant of rent-seeking behaviour and that rent-seeking settings are also constrained by asymmetries in information or limited rationality. Preconditions for efficient markets are missing not only in the sophisticated economies of industrialised countries but also—and obviously to a much larger extent—in developing countries. As will be outlined in this and later chapters, it is essentially the *incompleteness of economic and political markets* that provides valuable insights into rent-seeking behaviour and its limitations.

Section a) starts with a neo-classical model of utility maximisation. It looks at the link between profit-seeking and rent-seeking, discussing the issue with a simplified utility function that considers rent-seeking as an explicit alternative. This section also addresses the logic behind engaging in corrupt activities—the most important illegal type of rent-seeking.

The treatment of limited rationality and transaction costs in Section b) criticises and augments the narrow neo-classical model, arguing that in many instances rent-seekers are unlikely to behave as efficiently as such a model would predict. However, as the argument continues, transaction costs and limited rationality actually provide opportunities for rent-seeking. Section c) again extends the critique, this time from a sociocultural perspective. Introducing a number of informal constraints, it places the economic concept of the homo oeconomicus in a sociocultural context.

a) The Choice Between Rent-Seeking and Profit-Seeking

From the perspective of the individual decision-making situation, rent-seeking simply represents an alternative source of income to profit-seeking (entrepreneurial and other productive activities). At least for the purposes of distinguishing rent-seeking from profit-seeking, there is no need to invent a 'cousin' to the homo oeconomicus, i.e. individuals are mainly concerned with earning income and, depending on their abilities and the prevailing formal and informal institutions in a country, they will make use of rent-seeking and profit-seeking opportunities whenever they turn out to be profitable.

Below, a simplified utility function is presented that explicitly treats rent-seeking behaviour as an alternative to profit-seeking. In the real world rent-seeking is apparently not so isolated an issue as the function may suggest, i.e. many economic activities include income from both sources. But the goal of introducing this formal description is to structure the discussion in this and later sections, which provide further insights on the value of parameters and reconsider some critical assumptions on rent-seeking models and rent-seeking theory in general. Formally, the maximisation of the individual utility may look as follows:

$$\text{Max } U = \alpha Y_P + \beta Y_R$$
$$= \alpha f_P(r_P) + \beta f_R(r_R) \quad , \text{ subject to } r_P + r_R \leq R$$

Abstracting from consumption, utility is derived from income Y earned by profit-seeking activities and rent-seeking activities (indices P and R respectively). Parameters α and β are introduced to allow for different valuations. The two income-generating functions $f_P(r_P)$ and $f_R(r_R)$ indicate the relationship between resources invested and income earned. They determine the individual profitability of profit-seeking and rent-seeking activities. Resources available are limited by R.[63]

The utility function has been kept as simple as possible. A decline in the relative importance of rent-seeking compared to profit-seeking activities may originate from *three different sources:* improved opportunities to earn alternative incomes (i.e. a rise in the profitability of r_P due to a change in f_P), a reduction in the profitability of rent-seeking (change in f_R) and a relative decrease in the valuation of rent-seeking benefits ($\Delta\, \beta/\alpha < 0$). These three aspects are discussed below.

In the case of developing countries it is often argued that the lack of private-sector opportunities to obtain income via productive activities explains a great deal of rent-seeking behaviour. Another argument of the *'no better alternative'* type focuses on conditions within the public sector in which salaries paid to civil servants are often very small;[64] low and declining wages may then contribute to a rise in rent-seeking behaviour.

Poor economic policy and market failures largely explain the scarcity of profitable, non-rent-seeking activities. There is not much room for potential entrepreneurs to carry out productive undertakings if basic property rights cannot be guaranteed, if the infrastructure is poor and functioning credit markets are absent. Innovative people may prefer to join government bureaucracies where official payoffs *and* unofficial opportunities seem to be more promising. In LDCs a considerable part of market failures originate from insurmountable institutional difficulties. Much of these difficulties however are directly or indirectly related to successful rent-seeking activities and are mirrored in the

---

63 Two aspects are worth mentioning. First, formally, one may monetise the valuations (α, β) and incorporate them in Y_P and Y_R, like any other cost or benefit related to the income earning strategy. The notation used here has been chosen for simplicity and to make more explicit the contention that the same quantity of earned income may have different values. Second, R is not necessarily fixed, i.e. in an intertemporal analysis R would become a function of previous incomes and consumption.

64 Of course, depending on the country, time-period and specific job position in the bureaucracy, the contrary may also hold.

failure of the government to undertake sound economic policies, guarantee property rights and develop an infrastructure supportive of the private-sector.

The *negative relationship* between the two sets of income earning opportunities has been a widely observed feature of both contemporary and historical economies.[65] Figure 4-1 depicts a few stylised paths. The area around the diagonal I - III symbolises the negative correlation between profit-seeking and rent-seeking, while the corners II and IV stand for other, more unusual or extreme constellations. The corners I to IV are theoretical benchmarks. 'Top left' may represent an economy described in a standard neo-classical general equilibrium model that does not take rent-seeking and market failures into account.

Figure 4-1: Schematic Relation of Rent-Seeking and Profit-Seeking

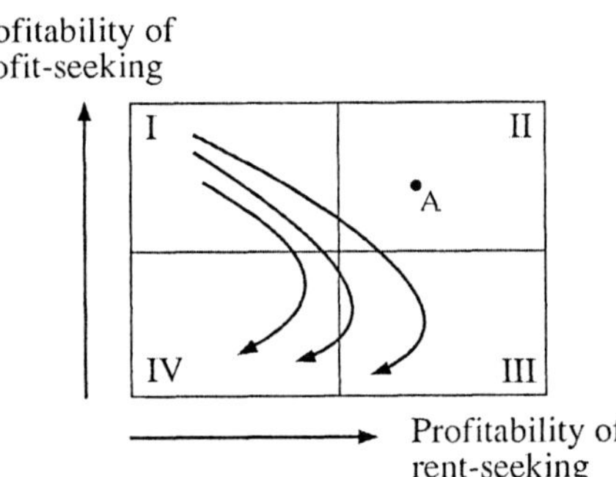

The four sections indicate possible combinations of profitability in rent-seeking and profit-seeking. The majority of the economies are likely to be placed along the stylised paths. Point A denotes an unusual situation where both types of activities are highly profitable.

As outlined earlier, it is the institutional setting, largely reflected by government policies, which determines the individual profitability of rent-seeking activities and hence their relative importance. Changing the setting to favour rent-seeking activities moves the economy towards III. Not only does the profitability of rent-seeking rise, the profitability of non-rent-seeking activities also declines due to the 'tax effect' of rent-seeking (rent-seekers directly or indirectly appropriate income from profit-seekers). In the extreme, this may reach a state where true opportunities to earn income with 'productive activities' almost entirely vanish and rent-seeking becomes pervasive. Many pre-reform developing countries with severe economic imbalances have found themselves in this situation. There are however limits in such a development.

The profitability of rent-seeking also depends on the resources and the output of the country that can be appropriated. As discussed in Chapter 3, rent-seeking can be accompanied by high 'dead-weight losses' as well as other distortions and negative incentives that reduce the level of output. These aspects explain why rent-seekers can only reap a share of the output and why the benefits to them are smaller than the losses incurred to society. Once an economy arrives at a stage where a large part of production ceases or shifts to a parallel economy, opportunities to extract rents disappear. This tendency is

[65] For a discourse about the Industrial Revolution, see for instance Tullock (1988d).

included in Figure 4-1, specifically where the stylised paths turn towards the lower left.

Mancur Olson has introduced the metaphor distinguishing between 'stationary' and 'roving' bandits as a concept to describe the costs and consequences of theft and other means of rent extraction.[66] Stationary bandits can seize and hold a given territory from where they extract rents; they therefore have an encompassing interest in the well-being of their victims, i.e. they care about the economic base from which they extract the rents. Roving bandits in contrast would kill the goose that lays the golden egg.

The more the setting is characterised by roving rather than stationary bandits, the faster will be the move towards III and IV. Competition among rent-seekers can explain why rent-seekers end up in a prisoner's dilemma situation and behave like roving bandits. It is worth noting however that in many LDCs the speed of moving towards IV has been slowed down by substantial aid from donors that, intentionally or not, was based on soft conditions and has been appropriated by rent-seekers.

In our world of market interventions and market failures, in many countries rent-seeking has also become an integral part of entrepreneurship. Above all in countries with poor institutions, a bad political culture and a weak rule of law, rent-seeking is even a precondition for entering into business. It may therefore be argued that enterprise success is not only a function of the capability to introduce new goods, technologies or organisations, or to open a new market. It is also a function of how clever enterprise managers are in finding legal, quasi-legal or even illegal rent-seeking avenues, either to achieve the above-mentioned goals or to increase their income. In many countries which have become entirely rent-seeking economies, honest people are simply driven out of business. Baumol (1990, p. 897) even argues that the list of Schumpeterian innovations should be expanded to include innovations in rent-seeking procedures.

Obviously, although these activities are profitable for the successful rent-seeking enterprise, they impose high costs on others and are not profitable for society as a whole. In effect they reduce the profitability of profit-seeking activities (formally incorporated in $f_P(r_P)$). Taking into account the negative impact other rent-seekers impose on them, above all the long-term dynamics that reduce growth, rent-seekers would prefer a world without rent-seeking.

In Chapter 3.3 it was noted that under very specific conditions rent-seeking may include positive externalities. Point A in Figure 4-1 indicates a situation where the attractiveness of productive activities is kept intact despite profitable rent-seeking opportunities. Similar to a tax that is levied to finance public expenditures, rent-seeking has incentive and redistribution effects. At least theoretically, rent-seeking 'rules' may be set up such that they minimise negative incentives (or even cancel out other distortions); at the same time they may exploit the possibility of productivity-enhancing income redistribution. Limited access to rents combined with rent extraction from large groups such as

---

[66] See for instance McGuire and Olson (1996) or Olson (2000).

consumers or taxpayers minimises the former negative effect. If rents are then used to overcome market failures and are invested efficiently in the development of other markets, positive effects may dominate.

Unfortunately, such a favourable rent-seeking picture is rather the exception than the rule. An example is Korea in the 1960s, which provided protection based on the infant industry argument, but with the condition that efficiency criteria be adhered to. As for instance noted in Perkins, et al. (2001, p. 714), Korea's trade strategies were highly interventionist; they included high protective barriers against specific imports and controlled interest rates at below-market levels to direct cheap credit to favoured companies. In contrast to many other countries, however, privileged companies could only take advantage of protection and other distortions if they met stringent export targets.

Having discussed the relation between profit-seeking and rent-seeking, a means of combating rent-seeking activities is to directly raise rent-seeking costs or lower the benefits (formally $f_R^{new}(r_R) < f_R(r_R)$). The *profitability of rent-seeking* depends on the ease with which transfers are 'created' as well as on the costs involved in capturing them. Chapter 3 described many parameters which determine the level of dissipation and thereby the individual profitability of rent-seeking. In LDCs insecure property rights, high costs of implementing and monitoring market interventions and the lack of checks and balances, above all transparency and accountability in raising and spending public funds, largely explain the low costs of 'illegal' rent-seeking activities such as fraud, embezzlement and tax evasion. On the other hand, the ease with which some privileged interest groups have influenced economic policies accounts for the high level of 'legal' (policy-determined) rent transfers.

A very good and simple model which can explain the profitability of corruption (and rent-seeking in general) is the framework of corruption from Neugebauer (1978). It outlines the conditions under which corruption remains profitable and can explain why many reform measures intended to address rent-seeking and corruption turned out to be ineffective. The model does not focus on the interaction between different competing rent-seekers who approach a public official, but it is an excellent model to describe a situation of partial non-rivalry and bribing. As argued in Chapter 3, many corrupt rent-seeking activities comprise non-rival rent-seeking settings, where rent-seekers do not compete for one price but make specific outlays to obtain a rent.

The model is presented in Table 4-1.[67] It has been slightly adjusted so that it can be applied to a broader range of activities, including situations where individuals do not collude with but circumvent state officials (e.g. certain smuggling and other tax-evading activities) or incidences of corruption which do not occur within government institutions but within donor agencies and NGOs.[68]

---

[67] The description partly draws on Pritzl (1997, p. 81-160), who refers to Neugebauer and provides a good outline of costs and benefits of corruption.

[68] For an overview of corruption in development cooperation, see Cremer (2000).

Table 4-1: A Generic Model for Corrupt Activities

a) Necessary conditions for activities involving bribery

Briber *i*:

Probability of success *(r)* • Value of benefit *(V)*	≥	Transaction costs (T_i) + Opportunity costs (O_i) + Moral costs (M_i) + Bribe offered (B_i) + Probability of failure *(1-r)* • Punishment (P_i)

Receiver of bribe *j*:

Probability of success *(r)* • Bribe demanded (B_j)	≥	Transaction costs (T_j) + Opportunity costs (O_j) + Moral costs (M_j) + Probability of failure *(1-r)* • Punishment (P_j)

Successful deal (Maximum bribe offered ≥ Minimum bribe demanded):

$$B_i^{max} = rV - [T_i+O_i+M_i+(1-r)\,P_i] \quad \geq \quad B_j^{min} = 1/r \cdot [T_j+O_j+M_j+(1-r)\,P_j]$$

b) Necessary conditions for activities that do not involve bribes

Probability of success (r) • Value of benefit (V)	≥	Transaction costs (T*)* + Opportunity costs *(O)* + Moral costs *(M)* + Probability of failure *(1-r)* • Punishment *(P)*

Factors that determine the size of the parameters and the prevalence of corruption

Value of benefit *(V, B)*: May increase with shortages caused by interventions and regulations and depends on the bureaucrat's discretionary power, the ease of producing benefit (for instance with non-standardised contracts) or the possibilities of extortion.

Transaction costs of corrupt activity *(T):* Costs to hide transaction, information costs, costs of negotiation and enforcement, cost of kickbacks to other officials.

Opportunity costs *(O)*: Foregone profit-seeking activities. Deal may also damage own situation (salary related to performance, prospects for promotion, prospects of future rent extraction).

Moral costs *(M)*: Feelings of guilt and moral scruples.

Probability of success *(r)* = (1- Probability of failure): Risks of making contacts, risks of discovering the transaction (at exchange or when using the benefits).

Level and probability of punishment *(P)*: Costs of punishment (the imposition of fines, job loss, and imprisonment), probabilities of investigation, sentence, and sentence execution.

Frequency: Number of profitable interactions, i.e. the number of cases where the necessary conditions hold.

Source: Basic framework of bribery based on Neugebauer (1978, p. 15f). The distinction between 'active' and 'passive' parties to the 'agreement' (i.e. private individual versus bureaucrat or NGO office holder) has not been specified since both parties can take an active or passive position.

As shown in the overview in Chapter 2.2, *illegal benefits* to government officials include theft and diversion of state assets as well as bribes and kickbacks extracted from individuals and companies. Private companies and individuals, on the other hand, may profit from allocation of scarce resources, better conditions for private business (in terms of prices, quantities or quality), speeding up administrative processes, and support for illegal activities. In addition, benefits may also be of an indirect sort, i.e. individuals may pay bribes to avoid artificially imposed difficulties.

The costs of corrupt activities depend on many factors and the size and relevance of each component typically varies among 'contracting' parties. Since corrupt deals need to be undertaken in secrecy and cannot be legally enforced, *transaction costs* are often higher in corrupt markets than in legal markets. Also the higher the profit-seeking *opportunities* in an economy, the more costly are the time and resources diverted to corrupt activities (e.g. the maintenance of strategic connections). *Moral costs* are non-material and include feelings of guilt from the transgression of moral scruples when undertaking the corrupt activity. However as Pritzl (1997, p. 128f) notes, to the extent that solidarity with the family and tribe is valued higher than loyalty to the state, the moral costs of corruption will be low or may even become benefits.

Bribery is usually not a cost component for public officials but for their private counterpart. Only when public officials depend on the support of collaborators (for instance when they require backing from higher levels), the costs of bribery can account for a large share of the rent seized. To keep the equations simple, these additional bribery expenses are subsumed within transaction costs. Finally, the *costs of failure* depend on the probability of being discovered and the costs and probabilities of subsequent levels of prosecution (not explicitly indicated in the figure). Discovery, criminal investigation, conviction and punishment may include further opportunity costs and moral costs (especially losses in reputation and standing).

Depending on the type, a corrupt transaction may either involve single or multiple parties. Bribery always involves at least two parties per definition; this would also apply to embezzlement if it involved benefit-enhancing corruption where public officials illegitimately transfer state or project funds to another person. Nepotism also may depend on a bribe. Probably more frequently nepotism represents a favour to a relative or friend without direct remuneration. In this case the bureaucrat's calculation can be shown with the equation in part b), and the value of the benefit is non-monetary. Finally, bribery that is based on extortion can be derived from the equations in part a). Abstracting from cost-components, the maximum bribe offered by individuals who have been extorted is the value of the service or benefit they should legitimately receive from the bureaucrat.

The crucial message of the model is that addressing the value of one or several parameters may have no impact on the final outcome, which only depends on whether the inequalities continue to hold. These inequalities, i.e. the necessary conditions for the profitability of corrupt transactions, are determined by the interaction of different parameters. The larger the difference between the two sides of the inequalities and the more numerous the situations where the inequalities hold, the more prevalent is corruption in the economy.

In most instances significantly reducing corruption therefore requires that several parameters be addressed simultaneously. Especially if the difference between the two sides of the inequality is large, changes must exceed a *minimum threshold* to become effective. This aspect has been emphasised in Chapter 3, in discussing the possible adverse reaction of measures that raise the cost of rent-seeking. For instance, if income from bribery is very high, higher wages, which increase the cost of job loss, will have no influence on corruption. The result reflects a 'shirking model', which contrasts with the 'fair wage hypothesis' where higher wages reduce corruption (Jain (1998, p. 75)). In a setting where the probability of failure remains virtually zero, wages can even overtake the level of bribery income and still have no impact on reducing corruption.

The inequalities displayed in Table 4-1 are also helpful to indicate why corruption increases as economic and political *conditions change*. For instance, maximising utility may translate into more frequent and economically detrimental rent-seeking activities because of the short-term character of a specific political or economic situation. A bureaucratic position may be far from secure if state interventions are changing rapidly or the political balance of power is not stable. Responding to this insecurity, a bureaucrat might then act according to the maxim 'as long as you have the job, get the most out of it; it won't last'.

Similar situations are found in the reform context once retrenchment or privatisation is announced. If bureaucrats and parastatal employees have little to lose from being fired, corruption is likely to increase. The same rationale where short-term considerations dominate also applies at the governmental level. If a dictatorship becomes less stable, 'stationary' bandits are likely to become 'roving' bandits with negative consequences for economic development (e.g. Rowley (2000, p. 142)). The change in the environment may be reflected in a decline in opportunity costs and costs of punishment (costs related to losing rent-seeking privileges).[69]

The generic model for corrupt activities presented in Table 4-1 has been kept simple. Depending on the source, characteristics and prevalence of corruption, the content of the variables vary considerably in different settings, also implying different incentives and opportunities for profit-seeking activities. Following the overview in Kaufmann (1998b, p. 135-37) corrupt settings may be characterised by a high versus low incidence of bribery or corruption, grand versus petty corruption, and individualised versus systemic (and endemic) corruption. Corruption may be predicable or it may assure nothing, i.e. a bribe may not guarantee performance but only increase the chances of success.

[69] An increase in rent extraction may also come about in a more subtle way. In Congo, for instance, when the new leaders came to power in 1992, they discovered that the previous government 'had sold forward several years' worth of the country's oil production to avoid restoring budgetary austerity during its waning days in office' (Van de Walle (1994, p. 486f)).

Corruption can be well-organised (centralised) or anarchic (decentralised); it may derive from a steady-state situation, or it may be external-shock induced. The reputation of corruption may be history-dependent or emerge from the high incidence of corruption in neighbouring countries.

Finally, corruption is usually characterised by asymmetries in rise and decline, i.e. significant improvements may demand very bold reforms which also need to be thoroughly implemented. Rose-Ackermann (1998, p. 520) for instance, referring to other authors, notes that corruption may quickly increase if the probability of a regime change increases; however when the uncertainty is resolved the country may be trapped in the new high corruption equilibrium.

Chapter 4.3 and the empirical part on Tanzania will provide further insights on corruption, including insights on what determines the shape and value of the different parameters in Table 4-1.

Looking at the utility function introduced at the beginning of this section, one last feature remains to be clarified: the possibility of influencing the *valuation of income* stemming from rent-seeking in contrast to income from other sources ($\Delta\ \beta/\alpha$). Table 4-1 partly includes this feature with the moral cost component. The argument is as follows: In a manner similar to consumer goods, different sources of income represent different levels of status within society. It is thus not irrelevant whether a dollar is earned by teaching at a university, attending a meeting, constructing a house, or by stealing from or cheating the state, even when the same level of effort is involved in each case. The argument also relates to expenditures. Jain (1998, p. 25f) notes that anthropologists have long recognised that 'source of income is an important determinant of consumption pattern—contradicting economists' notation that one dollar is as good as any other dollar'.

In Tanzania, for instance, the valuation of income earned by corruption has changed over time. Before corruption became part of the country's principal reform agenda, anyone who was rich was admired by society. They were viewed as clever and lucky people who knew how to make money. The question of 'how' the money was earned was of negligible concern. This has changed in the meantime and rich people are losing some of their status. Earning income through corruption has not only become a riskier undertaking, it has also become socially sanctioned—more negative value is attached to it.

Can corrupt and other rent-seeking activities be notably reduced by moralising the issue? There have been many historical cases of such moralising without addressing economic fundamentals—nearly all of them failures. Such attempts are doomed to fail from the outset. In Tanzania as well, President Nyerere tried to fight the growth of the parallel economy by calling its participants smugglers, saboteurs, hoarders and racketeers (e.g. Maliyamkono and Bagachwa (1990, p. xii ff)), but it was in vain. This raises the question whether moral appeals can ever be considered a legitimate policy measure. The answer is yes, but only if they are introduced as a concomitant tool. They are only plausible where economic fundamentals are simultaneously addressed so that the signals do not contradict. In such a setting moralising is likely to have the greatest impact when for instance it is used to bridge certain institutional deficiencies. It can however never replace appropriate economic policies.

Summing up, the basic message derived from the 'homo oeconomicus' line of thinking is straightforward: an individual will make use of rent-seeking opportunities whenever they turn out to be profitable. Emphasising the interaction between profit-seeking and rent-seeking, the discussion pointed out several means to reduce the relative profitability of rent-seeking. Political measures that try to influence the relative valuation of rent-seeking (β/α) will only have an impact if economic fundamentals have also been addressed. Fundamentals are addressed by a change in f_R, for instance, by altering different variables in the equations displayed in Table 4-1 or the parameters on dissipation summarised in Table 3-4. However, the equations in Table 4-1 also demonstrate that a reduction in corruption may depend on addressing different variables simultaneously. As will be argued in Chapter 5, where corruption and other rent-seeking activities are part of the political culture strategies of rent-seekers are numerous and diverse and may effectively undermine this process, in particular by preventing the abolition of binding constraints.

Political measures that try to address fundamentals can be especially effective if they work from both sides, i.e. reducing the profitability of rent-seeking and increasing that of other activities (f_P), for instance by making profit-seeking activities less risky. Given the negative relationship, for many years the contrary situation has obtained in developing countries; people have suffered from declining real wages and seen increasing rewards from illegal activities. In particular insecure property rights and instability increased transaction costs for profit-seeking activities and reduced those for rent-seeking, making the latter more advantageous (e.g. Pritzl (1997, p. 123)).

A third approach to reduce rent-seeking is given by directly changing f_P. This is an appropriate measure if reasons other than rent-seeking, such as certain market failures, account for the lack of profitable undertakings. In an environment where market-supporting institutions fail or are absent, a great deal of improvement is usually possible just by correcting the institutional gap. Unfortunately, many policymakers still equate social policy with distributing rents and other favours, without being aware that much of social policy simply consists in making welfare-enhancing profit-seeking activities profitable. For instance, in many LDCs efficient credit markets have been lacking for years and micro credits could only be obtained at extortionate interest rates. The appropriate policy in such a setting is not that of primarily distributing subsidised credits—if the government is weak and civil servants corrupt, the benefits will be appropriate by others than those who deserve them—what is needed is simply closing the institutional gap, i.e. creating an efficient financial intermediation.

The following sections and chapters further elaborate on elements that explain the shape of f_R and f_P in the utility function, i.e. the conditions, problems and perception of individuals who try to achieve this maximising task.

b) Limited Rationality, Opportunism and Transaction Costs: Boundary, Cause and Catalyst for Rent-Seeking?

> *'Imperfect information opens up a Pandora's box of possibilities! To be sure, when we walk into these new territories, our ground may not be as firm; we may not be as confident that we are making the right assumptions; but surely that must be better than making assumptions that we know are wrong.'*
>
> *Joseph E. Stiglitz (1992, p. 60)*

This section resumes and deepens the discussion on limited rationality addressed in Chapter 3.2, but with a broad focus. On the one hand, being aware of issues related to limited rationality, opportunism and transaction costs questions the behaviour described in standard rent-seeking models. On the other hand, this strand of economic theory also contributes to explaining why rent-seeking occurs in the first place. To outline this aspect, the discussion starts with a more general reference to the economic theory of incomplete markets and efficient decision-making.

Neo-Classical Settings Versus Incomplete Markets

More than two hundred years ago Adam Smith's famous story about the butcher, the brewer and the baker laid the foundations of classical economics. The much-quoted concept of the 'invisible hand'—that actions chosen on the basis of self-interest lead to a social optimum—unambiguously holds in a setting with perfect and complete markets. This has been elaborated in detail within the general equilibrium framework. The theory states that under certain conditions (which are unfortunately quite restrictive and therefore sometimes far from typical settings in the real world) competitive markets allocate resources efficiently. The problem of uncertainty about the future is by-passed by introducing a complete set of contingent markets. However, as has been frequently demonstrated, once transaction costs and limited rationality are introduced issues of uncertainty inevitably become relevant, and self-interest may translate into opportunistic behaviour, destroying the desirable outcome of the social optimum. Many rent-seeking situations closely relate to such market failures. The following discussion attempts to pursue this line of argument.[70]

In theory, to be able to *maximise utility* an individual needs not only information on all relevant alternatives but also the capability of determining the optimal solution. Furthermore all relevant markets must exist and property rights must be enforced. Standard neo-classical models typically operate in frameworks that assume these preconditions hold. It is common knowledge that the real world is quite different. As has been widely debated (especially within

[70] The overview of the incompleteness of markets, where not otherwise indicated, is based on Magill and Quinzii (1996), Bonus and Maselli (1997) and Laffont (1989). For a critical reflection on neo-classical behavioural assumptions see also North (1990, p. 17-26).

institutional economics), collecting information is not only costly, individuals also fail to process all relevant information and are often unable to determine the optimal strategy. In addition, important markets are absent and property rights insufficiently enforced. Individual decision-making hence does not take place in an optimal setting, as described in standard neo-classical models, but in a setting with deficiencies and uncertainties. Three central aspects of institutional economics (summarised in Table 4-2) address this issue: limited rationality, opportunism, and transaction costs. They are closely linked.

There are several channels through which limited rationality affects a decision-making situation. The first concerns one's ability to obtain *information about the present and future state of the world.* A particular problem stems from one's inability to select the relevant data from the abundant information available, while the second problem stems from the opposite effect, i.e. the lack of information on aspects important for decision-making. Making assumptions becomes inevitable. Particularly decisions based on assumptions about future developments may involve significant uncertainties. Even though for a variety of events it is not difficult to estimate probabilities and to secure against unfavourable outcomes, there are important cases where security markets are absent or too expensive to make use of. The problem is especially pronounced in developing countries with unstable and unpredictable governments. Since collecting information is costly, it is rational to curtail the search and make decisions under uncertainties. One consequence is that contracts are incomplete, sometimes generating conflicts when important outcomes are not considered and included.

The second channel of limited rationality relates to *insecurity about the behaviour of other agents*. People are opportunistic. In contrast to the neo-classical egoist, who acts within the framework of legislation and never violates contracts, an opportunist also engages in illegal activities and tries to hide essential information. Even though opportunism represents an important type of rent-seeking, it is primarily the principal-agent-theory that deals with it. Asymmetry in information (which is an outcome of different incentives and costs to access information) and flaws in enforcement explain most opportunistic behaviour. They raise transaction costs involved in contracts, both costs that occur ex-ante as well as monitoring and enforcement costs. It is especially here through this second channel of limited rationality that institutions play a crucial role in reducing transaction costs.

The third channel through which limited rationality affects decision-making situations does not concern an information problem but the limited capacity of individuals to determine an optimal strategy once information is available. The problem is known as bounded rationality. The human mind is not only unable to process large quantities of data, it is also limited in its ability to carry out complex mathematical tasks. This is however only part of the story since individuals sometimes even fail to make quite simple calculations. Simon (1987a, p. 224), for instance, mentions in the context of flood insurance that 'people tend to ignore low-probability, high-consequence events, unless they

Table 4-2: Features Commonly Absent in Standard Neo-Classical Settings

Limited rationality — Types of limitation:		Transaction costs (Costs to overcome or reduce deficiencies)
• **Uncertainty about the present and future state of the world** Limited ability to collect information on all relevant alternatives	→ **Incomplete contracts**	• Information costs to generate alternatives • Costs to resolve disputes (due to unforeseen events)
• **Uncertainty about the behaviour of other agents** Agents are opportunistic: They may hide important information, violate contracts and disregard laws	→ **Principal-agent conflict** (Asymmetry in information: moral hazard and adverse selection)	• Information costs • Monitoring costs • Enforcement costs
• **Limited capacity to calculate optimal strategy** ('bounded rationality')	→ **Suboptimal decisions**	• Costs to calculate optimal strategy

Source: Overview based on descriptions in Magill and Quinzii (1996), Bonus and Maselli (1997) and Laffont (1989)

have had rather direct past personal experience of them'. He even stresses that such behaviour cannot be reconciled with any model of utility maximisation. Selten seems to provide part of the answer. He emphasises that there are motivational as well as cognitive limits on rationality:

> 'The motivational limits of rationality are due to a separation of cognition and decision. ... A person may know very well what action is best for him and yet he may find himself unable to take it.' (Selten (1990, p. 651))

Selten concludes that decisions are not only made by the conscious mind, but emerge from inaccessible parts of the brain. In addition, emotions influence the conscious mind:

> 'Emotions like anger or hunger focus the attention on a narrow set of activities related to temporary goals and fears and thereby control the direction of thinking and imagination.' (Selten (1990, p. 652)).

Similarly, Schlicht (1990, p. 712) admits a possible strategic role for emotions, stating that 'honesty, guilt, pride, love are not simply constraints but quite active determinants of action'. Emotions may for instance partly explain the paradox of voting: An individual votes to express his or her emotions, not just because he or she wants to alter the outcome (Tullock (1989, p. 21)). From a strictly economic point of view, emotions are a problem if they do not just influence components of the utility function but provoke behaviour that largely ignores it.

Economic experiments in 'laboratories' have revealed various patterns of human behaviour that differ from rational behaviour described in standard neo-classical settings. They show, among other things, that individuals make different choices among settings that are equivalent in terms of wealth. Asymmetric weighting of gains and losses, endowment effects, not knowing one's own utility function, and short-term myopia as described in Kahneman (1994) are a few of the relevant catchwords. Also the laboratory experiment by Weimann, Yang and Vogt (2000) discussed in Chapter 3.2 provided an example where emotions lead to economically irrational behaviour. As noted on page 114, second movers continued to punish a preemptive opening in the very last round, even though it did not make sense from the perspective of economic profit-maximising.

All in all, the individual decision making situation, compared to a standard neo-classical setting, is characterised by *deficiencies and uncertainties.* Costs and limits to generate the relevant information call for suboptimal strategies, however rational, if transaction costs are taken into account. Individuals use different methods to generate alternatives; they have to apply estimating procedures and strategies to deal with uncertainties. One consequence is, as Simon emphasised, that when building a theory one needs to distinguish between the real world and the actor's perception of it and reasoning about it (cited in North (1990, p. 23)). Furthermore Heiner argues that the greater the gap between the agents' competence in deciphering problems and their difficulty in selecting the most preferred alternatives, the more likely they will impose regularised and very limited patterns of response (North (1990, p. 23)). Hence instead of strictly maximising utility individuals will adopt simpler procedures in many situations. That is, they will rely on habits, routines and rules of thumb, and follow satisfying strategies that aim to reach a certain utility level or to cover certain costs. As a result their decisions may sometimes be quite far from what neo-classical models predict.

What Are the Conclusions for Rent-Seeking?

Obviously transaction costs and limited rationality will also call into question the behaviour of the 'extended' homo oeconomicus, i.e. the homo oeconomicus who is pursuing not only profit-seeking but also rent-seeking strategies. Many rent-seeking models, especially those that focus on dissipation, are based on rationality assumptions similar to the ones criticised in the above discussion. It will be a major task of empirical research to find out in which situations these qualifications are relevant. For situations where transaction costs and limited rationality are identified as an important constraint, models should be adjusted, for instance to take satisfying strategies into account or to allow for varying degrees of available information or non-rational interference. Given the difficulty in observing individual behaviour, these models would not necessarily have to include very clear-cut and empirically validated assumptions on a specific behaviour. As emphasised in the quote from Stigliz in the introduction to Section b) (he refers to imperfect information in economic models in general), making only vague assumptions is sometimes better than making assumptions that are known to be wrong.

There are two lines of reasoning that counter the criticism of rationality assumptions. One of them refers to the *'as if construct'* from Friedman and Savage. A billiard player makes his shots as if he knows the complicated mathematical formulas (Schlicht (1990, p. 707)). The concept of abstract rationality then only serves as an approach to describe this behaviour. Another example, which is mathematically even more complex to grasp, would be a mathematical formulation of the choice of which painting to favour. Certainly the 'as if construct'-argument is legitimate for problems that are easily solved through intuition but complex to describe mathematically.

However there are many other problems that run counter to intuition. Mathematically they may even be very simple. The original Tullock game discussed in Chapter 3.1 is a good example. Tullock describes the decision-making problem of rational players as follows:

> 'With two players and constant marginal costs, for example, each will invest \$25 for a 50-50 chance of \$100. This seems absurd, but if the reader will experiment with his pocket calculator he will quickly discover that if he invests more, he increases the likelihood that he will win but with the winnings less than the value of the investment.' (Tullock (1988a, p. 93))

The crucial question is to find out in which situation individuals are more inclined to make use of the calculator rather than simply rely on their intuition. Tullock's case looks even more 'absurd' once we allow for rising marginal costs of influencing the probability of winning.

The above example of the billiard player points to another problem: playing billiards is a highly repetitive game, in contrast to some rent-seeking situations that are not. To become expert one may have to practice a shot a thousand times. Using a model that stresses the physical results of motion theory to analyse the very first shots of a player who has never played billiards before is likely to yield misleading results. Therefore, in particular in new and non-repetitive rent-seeking situations, insights from rational rent-seeking models may have to be applied with caution.

A non-repetitive rent-seeking situation may also lead to a different outcome, as risk aversion matters: In a television quiz, a player was offered either \$40,000 for certain or \$1 million with a probability of 25%. The net present value of the latter option is clearly higher for a risk-neutral person (0.25·\$1 million = 250,000 is more than six times higher than \$40,000). A repetitive situation for the player would reduce risk. Nevertheless, when not in a repetitive situation, players often opt for the risk-free \$40,000. Similar behaviour that appears at first glance economically irrational may also explain overinvestment in traditional rent-seeking situations.

The second argument that tries to defend rationality assumptions claims that in some situations it is *sufficient to have only a few people who act* in a *rational* way. Scott (1994, p. 317) notes that markets are quite a powerful form of institutional response to bounded rationality; they 'can turn cognitive defects into money machines, and in the process establish prices that tend to correct this type of bounded rationality'. Like the first defence, this statement is legitimate in several situations. Many rent-seeking contests however involve just a small number of participants. The smaller the settings, the less likely they will include clever arbitrageurs. In addition, most decisions on optimal rent-seeking investments require ideas about the behaviour of all other participants. Introducing just one rational player cannot solve the problem.

This aspect can be demonstrated with the Tullock puzzle mentioned above. With two players and constant marginal costs it is only rational to invest \$25 for a 50-50 chance of \$100 if the other player does the same. If the other player behaves irrationally and invests \$50, the optimal choice of the first player would become \$20.7[71]. Hence results concerning the level of dissipation will strongly depend on the behaviour of all participants.

In the introduction it was emphasised that transaction costs and limited rationality do not just point to *limits of rent-seeking models* of the rational, 'neo-classical' type. The two concepts also provide explanations for the *prevalence of rent-seeking* in society. This aspect can be explained by looking at the circumstances under which decision-making at different levels takes place. Following North (1990, p. 47), decision-making situations may be categorised hierarchically as decisions about contracts, economic rules or political rules. Table 4-3 describes each briefly and indicates the type of rent-seeking activity typically associated with each.

Table 4-3: Level of Decision-Making and Rent-Seeking Opportunities

Level	Rent-seeking
I. Conclusion of contracts, enforcement of property rights ('ordinary' economic activity, which is based on prevailing rules)	Capture rents
II. Change of 'economic' rules (they alter property rights)	Create rents
III. Change in the political system that determines how rules can be altered (meta-level: type of state and society)	Influence or capture apparatus that creates rents

Source: First column (distinction between the three levels of contracts) according to North (1990, p. 47)

On the contract level, much successful rent-seeking reflects a lack of secure property rights. As described in Chapter 2.2, property rights are weak because of the discretionary application of regulations, as well as the non-interest or failure of the state to prosecute offences such as embezzlement, blackmail, breaching contracts or burglary. In a world of complete information most of these activities would obviously not happen.

To analyse situations of asymmetries in information and transaction costs, institutional economics introduced the concept of the *principal-agent conflict.* At its core is a certain representation (in legal terms: agency), either well-specified (e.g. in an employment contract or mandate) or implicit in another

71 Max $\frac{x}{x+50}\cdot 100 - x \Rightarrow x = \sqrt{5000} - 50 = \underline{\underline{20.7}}$

economic relation (e.g. a simple exchange contract). The principal-agent conflict occurs because the principal cannot fully observe the action of the agent (or contracting party). An agent may conceal important information (which may lead to adverse selection) or part of the activity (moral hazard). Both result in rent transfers and undermine the wealth of the principal.

The principal-agent model has been applied to problems in very different settings. It refers to contracts in the narrow sense as well as to other relations such as unlawful acts, environmental pollution, or the relation between the state and its citizens (the citizens being the principal and the government the agent).[72]

Transaction costs (and the related limited rationality) together with opportunism explain the principal-agent conflict. In a simple exchange contract for instance, rents may be extracted by selling a product of much lower quality than agreed. Since the measurement of the quality attributes is costly, the buyer will not invest many resources to assess them. The rent obtained is equal to the difference between the 'real' value of the good or service (market value if all the attributes are known to the contract partners) and the value agreed to in the contract on the grounds of incomplete or asymmetric information. A contract partner may also unilaterally cancel a deal or even refuse to deliver even though the other partner met the obligation.

In all the cases cited, complete anticipation of the behaviour of the agent would make rent transfers impossible. In the real world, however, transaction costs prevent contracting parties from getting all necessary information and force them to make decisions under uncertainty. Even though a principal is rational in reducing information costs and not becoming fully informed, the contract decision is a 'limited' rational one, i.e. rational given available information (and mental capacity).

A more typical area in which the principal-agent concept is often applied refers to the relation between employer and employee. Since an employer (principal) cannot fully supervise the activities of employees (agents), a labourer can cite factors other than shirking or embezzlement to explain any low output. This is a rent-seeking situation where the state has neither an active nor a passive role in creating the rent (recall the definition of rent-seeking in Chapter 2.1).

Obviously, when the state acts as an employer it faces the same conflict that private enterprises do. In parastatals and state bureaucracies stealing, shirking and corruption caused by a lack of supervision (and not deliberately intended as part of the political rent-distributing mechanism) are examples of such cases. Again, the combination of transaction costs (costly supervision) and opportunism permits these rent transfers and makes rent-seeking a profitable undertaking.

Finally, particularly relevant for the discussion in this study is the principal-agent conflict between citizens and the government. In a stylised and perfect model of government (which is implicitly assumed in the traditional theory of economic policy), a government tries to maximise the citizens' welfare, and

---

[72] For a general introduction to the principal-agent conflict see for instance Richter (1994, p. 16-22).

politicians and bureaucrats are accountable to the citizens. The real world however is not characterised by complete information. Citizens are only limited rational and important checks and balances are often either not implemented or enforced. This situation explains the principal-agent conflict between citizens and government, i.e. citizens know relatively little about the activities of government, while the government has a lot of information and knows best how to manipulate the public sector.

The mechanisms by which information deficits open up rent-seeking opportunities can also work through other channels than the principal-agent conflict. Chapter 3.3 mentioned a possible information-enhancing role of rent-seeking. Bellin (1994), for instance, describes the situation in Tunisia where both the state elite and industrialists depend on each other. According to Bellin, preferential treatment (she calls it *cronyism*) is seen as a rational response to an information problem:

> 'Businessmen need contacts on the inside just to get through the system and get the information necessary to play by the government's rules. On the state side there is the fact that state elites often don't have the technical data and/or training necessary to assess the projects they are called upon to approve. Under these conditions bureaucrats are often forced to fall back on the advice of friends in the business to decide whether a project is viable or a borrower trustworthy.' (Bellin (1994, p. 432))

She then attributes a positive role to rent-seeking, concluding that cronyism should not necessarily be seen as subverting economic rationality. She argues that 'where dependable information is scarce, reliance on personal contacts may actually abet the rational allocation of economic resources rather than subvert it' (Bellin (1994, p. 432)). Although true in principle, this appears to be short-sighted since many of these information problems, especially those related to government rules, are homemade (and hence likely part of the game to mediate rents politically).

The example still illustrates an important point. Information problems can lead to *collusion*, which then enhances rent-seeking opportunities. Over time such relations become stronger. They help to reduce transaction costs and turn rent-seeking activities into insider games. Tietz (1990, p. 665) describes this aspect, not in the context of rent-seeking but in general terms:

> 'A relational equilibrium may be self-stabilizing: it decreases the transaction costs within the relation, while increasing search costs outside the relation, since the frequency of contracts with and the information about other potential partners are reduced'.

Appropriate government institutions, such as a more efficient state bureaucracy sound economic policies including open markets will reduce some of these information problems and make 'insider' relations less important.[73]

[73] Nevertheless, it cannot be expected that rent-seeking activities will disappear afterwards. Vested interests originally created by collusion due to the lack of information are likely to endure. The alleviation of the information problem is thus more likely a necessary but not sufficient condition.

So far, most of the rent-seeking examples discussed referred to the first level of decision-making and involved, to a greater or lesser extent, some type of illegality. On the contract level rents are also captured legally according to well-defined economic rules, as outlined in detail in the overview in Chapter 2.2. The creation of rents by market interventions reflects the second level of decision-making indicated in Table 4-3. Again, limited rationality and transaction costs can explain a great deal of rent-seeking activities on this level, i.e. people do not oppose policies that actually harm them. Much of it relates to interest group theory, which will be the subject of Chapter 4.2. The following discussion is therefore kept short and will concentrate on incomplete information.

Three interrelated aspects referring to the costliness of information discussed in institutional economics and interest group theory explain the success of rent-seeking activities. First, the *same information is often of different value* to individuals; their willingness to pay for it thus also varies. Economic policies regularly transfer rents from large groups to much smaller groups. Abstracting from inefficiencies involved in the transfer, costs and benefits per individual will differ and so will incentives to become informed. Second, costs of *accessing* information differ. People who have easier access to information are generally better informed and can make use of their advantage. Interest groups, for instance, who lobby for some type of protection know their true economic situation much better than outsiders do. Many rent-seeking contests are characterised by some insider advantage to the access of information. Third, costs (and related limits) of *processing* information can lead to asymmetries in information that favour rent transfers. People often lack incentives to oppose certain changes in economic policy because they are not able to assess the true costs of the policy. Tullock provides a good example:

> 'The arguments for a protective tariff are simple and superficially obvious, while the arguments against it are unfortunately complicated and indirect. Granted that the voter has no motive for becoming well informed, he or she will buy the simpler of the two explanations. Under these circumstances, a rent-seeker seeking protective tariffs does not actually have to engage in too much lobbying.' (Tullock (1988b, p. 476))

Unequal access and interpretation of information not only explain why rent-seekers are successful, they also explain a point emphasised in Chapter 3.3, i.e. that rent transfers are a very inefficient form of income redistribution. It has long been shown that special privileges to interest groups are much less costly if they are provided through direct cash payments and not through indirect policy interventions which distort prices and quantities. Living in a world of limited rationality, interest groups, however, choose the second, much more socially costly strategy, knowing that voters would not agree to cash transfers since these would make the true costs involved in the policy measure too obvious (see, for instance, the article quoted above, or Tullock (1989, 19f) on this).

This brief account of information costs has shown that also on the second level of decision making, rent-seeking strategies can be successful due to a lack of information or basic informational asymmetries. Many decisions are made by third parties, and individuals who are thereby made worse off are not much aware of it. In direct democracies people often vote on issues with very limited information about them. Many people do not even bother to vote at all, which again favours rent transfers. In authoritarian regimes as well there are many policy issues whose consequences are more difficult to grasp and thus only moderately opposed. Furthermore, as already emphasised in Chapter 2.2, many policies are officially communicated as social interventions. A closer lock, however, reveals that policy measures often do not reach targeted groups and their intended purposes but directly benefit privileged rent-seeking groups.

Finally, at the third level of decision-making, problems can be similar to those described on the second level, i.e. the transaction costs and limited rationality of affected people explain rent-seeking outcomes. Political systems can take very different forms. Depending on the specifications, special interest groups can have considerable influence, as noted earlier, even in established democracies. And an outcome where a group captures the state by violence alone represents an obvious situation of limited rationality and transaction costs.[74]

Summing up, limited rationality and transaction costs are indeed 'boundary, cause and catalyst to rent-seeking'. A closer look at these issues contributes to a better understanding of the success of rent-seeking activities and allows specification of policy measures that can reduce their relative importance. The crucial role of incomplete information is striking. In fact, information problems are not just a temporary element of friction but a constitutional component of economic processes (Picot and Wolff (1997, p. 1870)). Much rent-seeking directly relates to limited rationality and transaction costs.

Rationality assumptions are a complex matter. They refer to different aspects and can be implemented to a different degree. What makes economic modelling and its interpretation delicate is that in real settings it is not always evident from the outset how much rationality can be expected from humans when they make their decisions, in particular what kind of information they consider. Uncritically applying rationality assumptions related to specific information can easily lead to wrong conclusions. Olson's provocative statement on pricing strategies in competitive markets brings this aspect to the fore:

> 'For it would be quite as reasonable to argue that prices will never fall below the levels a monopoly would have charged in a perfectly competitive market, because if one firm increased its output, other firms would also, and the price would fall; but each firm could foresee this, so it would not start a chain of price-destroying increases in output.' (Olson (1965, p. 12))

As noted earlier, the concept of perfect rationality is helpful in 'situations so transparent that the optimum can be reasonably approximated by an ordinary

[74] With perfect foresight a war would never happen but a negotiated solution would be found which was in the interest of all affected parties.

human mind' (Simon (1987b, p. 267)) and where individuals are not trapped in a prisoner's dilemma situation. However with many problems these situations are rather the exception than the rule. Economic modelling demonstrates that optimal solutions can be very complex and difficult to find. Such tasks can exceed most people's mental capacity. Predicting their behaviour may require alternative concepts, especially when solutions run counter to intuition.

This contrasts with the general situation of many rent-seeking models whose conclusions are usually derived from the same rationality assumption as applied in other neo-classical models. Granted that some rent transfers happen because people do not act rationally, in these cases the implicit inconsistency in neo-classical rent-seeking approaches cannot be denied: Rent-seekers are expected to be *fully rational* in many respects; rents, however, are transferred as a result of *limited rationality* on the part of the losing groups. It can be expected that in many real situations information problems and limited rationality relate to both groups.

Though many insights of parameter variations derived from these models still remain applicable to real settings, as long as the correct structure of the model has been chosen, one has to be careful when interpreting the models. As the discussion in Chapter 3 also demonstrated, in some cases behavioural assumptions directly determine the direction how parameter variations affect rent-seeking behaviour. Choosing a rent-seeking model then requires making decisions on which rationality assumption applies. In the extreme, the choice determines whether the behaviour of rent-seekers reflects a rival or non-rival setting or whether it includes one or several anticipated rent-seeking stages.

Another important aspect discussed in this section is *transaction costs*. In developing countries transaction costs are typically high and insecurity part of everyday life. Transaction costs are partly responsible for market rigidities; they may determine whether rent-seeking settings remain insider settings or why some arbitrage relations are not fully exploited. It appears that unexploited rents in developing countries are much more common and frequently persist for a longer time.

Nobody would dispute that in LDCs broad-based reductions in transaction costs (especially information and enforcement costs) are crucial for future growth and development. In addition, as emphasised in this section, not understanding the true costs of a policy measure accounts for a great deal of weak rent protection in LDCs (as well as in industrialised countries), though violence also plays an important part. Improving education and making it accessible to a larger part of the population will help people become more critical when evaluating government policies. Most important is however the implementation of a rule of law, above all checks and balances, which includes transparent rules and publicly available information as well as secure property rights in general. Together these measures contribute much to reducing the relative attractiveness of rent-seeking behaviour. Yet implementing them may take a long time. To do so society must find a way to overcome the resistance of rent-seeking elites, who are obviously not interested to have such measures implemented.

Following the examination in Section a) of the relative importance of rent-seeking and profit-seeking activities from the perspective of individuals who need to maximise a 'rent-seeking adjusted' utility function, this section criticised and augmented the simplified neo-classical model, stressing that many realistic settings are characterised by incomplete markets due to transaction costs, limited rationality and opportunism. The following Section c) places the economic concept into a sociocultural context, addressing different values and rationales for interaction. As will be argued, broadening the focus to account for both formal and informal constraints contributes to an understanding of rent-seeking behaviour and incentives.

c) Shaping Behaviour Through Informal Constraints: How Culture, Values and Norms Matter

> *'One day a Hausaman, a Yourubaman and an Igbo set off on a trip and came across a wild mango tree laden with fruit. The Hausaman said, "These fruits look lovely, let us pray that Allah makes them fall for us." And the Yourubaman said, "I will go home and seek the help of my kinsmen to help me climb up and pick some."...But the Igbo said nothing, he was busy working out how much money he could make if he picked the whole tree and took the crop to market...[He] simply rolled up his sleeves, climbed the tree and after much sweat and toil picked the lot, but when he climbed back onto the ground he found his two friends were already arguing and politicking about sharing the harvest.'*
>
> *Nigerian anecdote, told in New Africa, August 1988*

The Nigerian anecdote (cited from Ayittey (1991, p. 37)) is a good example of how individual behaviour may vary considerably between different societies. To fully understand the impact of culture, values and norms requires a broad perspective. Sjöstrand (1992) has provided an interesting overview of human interactions that embeds the rational economic transaction in a broader social setting. As it contributes to an understanding of rent-seeking, the concept is briefly summarised below.[75]

Sjöstrand argues that two perspectives dominated institutional approaches in the 1990s, one of them focusing on *legal foundations* and the other on *human (inter)actions and their rationale*. The latter uses 'a more complex view of people as cultural and social people' and includes so-called 'irrational' behaviour in its analysis. Understanding individual behaviour requires looking at

[75] For improved readability, detailed page references for the description of the six institutions are largely omitted here. The description is based on Sjöstrand (1992, p. 1007-40).

the multiple reasons and facets of interpersonal relations and nearly continuous exchange:

> 'Individual actions have a meaning that extends beyond the actual exchange of something. Many institutionalists refuse to reduce people to something like the classical notion of *homo oeconomicus*. People are also characterized by other crucial qualities and rationales, therefore making exchange process complex.' (Sjöstrand (1992, p. 1018f))

At the centre of this perspective is the insight that 'individuals try to find (or create) a meaning for their lives through human interactions and communication (including religious activities)'. Calculation (the basic principle of the homo oeconomicus) is therefore only one aspect. Other authors have also pointed to the central role of human interaction. Bénézet Bujo, for instance, even puts it more strongly, emphasising that in many cultures in Africa a person only becomes a human by interaction.[76]

Many of values, habits and traditions are not codified in formal rules; they largely influence individual choice through informal constraints. Table 4-4 shows the six institutions comprising the infrastructure of human interaction and exchange described in Sjöstrand's article. As a whole, they 'express normative systems that are sometimes matched by legal constructions and sometimes rely on custom or shared ideals and beliefs'. The six institutions 'simultaneously function as rationality context for individual (inter)actions'.

Table 4-4: The Institutional Repertoire for Human Interaction and Exchanges in Society

Forms of interaction:	Interaction rationale: Calculative	Ideational	Genuine
Hierarchic	*Corporation*	*Association*	*Clan*
Network type	*Market*	*(Social) Movement*	*Circle*
Reproduced basis for existence:	Capital	Membership	Trust

Source: According to Tables 4 and 5 in Sjöstrand (1992, p. 1028, 1034)

Interactions are either of a hierarchic or a network type (symmetric), and they reduce uncertainty. Sjöstrand argues that only two of them *(corporation and market)* are characterised as rational by neo-classical economists. *Social movement and association,* which provide social or cultural identity, (re)distribute wealth and other qualities of life based on ideals (manifested as rules and norms). The sharing of ideals, beliefs, and values creates a 'common understanding that contributes to trusting relationships and prevents opportunistic behaviour'. *Circle and clan*, finally, are based on genuine relations

76 Interview on his book Bujo (2000) on Swiss Radio DRS 2, 19.11.2000, 8.30-9.00.

and are manifested in friendship or love relationships. 'These institutions provide a kind of "biological" or "personal" identity to people' through relations such as kinship, family ties, friendship and closeness.

The overview given in Table 4-4 is an interesting approach to structuring human interaction. Nevertheless, many economists would argue that ideational and genuine rationales are meant to be included in the concept of homo oeconomicus, basically as non-monetary values in the utility function. In theory this justification is certainly true. The crucial point however is that traditional economists tend to ignore such specifications when it finally comes to modelling and interpreting economic relations and deriving policy recommendations.

To the extent that religion, traditions and ideologies (as well as specific values and norms such as self-sacrifice, altruism and issues of fairness) are important rationales that shape human behaviour, they need to be more explicitly accounted for—if not directly in the model, then at least when it comes to interpreting the results. As North (1990, p. 36) states, 'that informal constraints are important in themselves ... can be observed from the evidence that the same formal rules and/or constitutions imposed on different societies produce different outcomes' (see also Van Arkadie (1989, p. 155)). These constraints also explain why people may react very differently to the same economic signals.

The anecdote in this section which exaggerates the differences Nigerians see among themselves, illustrates this point. Obviously, to account for differences in the behaviour of Hausa, Yoruba and Igbo, the concept of homo oeconomicus would have to be extended and fleshed out. Although wealth-maximising behaviour may be a very important aspect of life, it does not cover the entire domain of social interaction. As many authors emphasise, depending on the specific setting behaviour may deviate considerably from what we would expect from the pure pursuit of *economic* self-interest. These deviations stem from other values and from a complex set of further informal constraints.

Non-market decision-making takes place in families, clans and tribes as well as local cooperatives and corporations. It may involve different voting procedures and/or it may be based on hierarchical lines of authority as indicated in Table 4-4. Furthermore, culturally defined means of attaining goals, which reflect the values of a given society, do not need to be economically efficient (Smedley (1994, p. 100)). And making the connection to Section b), even though an individual tries to maximise wealth, shared values such as ideologies and culture also largely influence the perception and thereby the outcome of maximising (and satisfying) behaviour that takes place under conditions of incomplete information. In the words of Douglass North (1990, p. 37), 'culture provides a language-based conceptual framework for encoding and interpreting the information'.

All in all, societies characterised by strong communal values and structures, where people identify themselves far more with the interest of the group or community than with their personal interests and where possible means of attaining goals are culturally circumscribed and narrowed, may generate outcomes that deviate from what simple economic models of the modern world would predict. Similar to the discussion in Section b), informal constraints which qualify some of the results deduced from standard economic theory may also explain variations in expected rent-seeking behaviour. In the following some aspects will be briefly treated and related to rent-seeking and adjustment in Africa.

Do Informal Constraints Require a Different Rent-Seeking Perspective?

The different rationales of human interaction in Table 4-4 may suggest taking a modified rent-seeking perspective when it comes to assessing developing-country economies. On the one hand, it can be argued that ideational and genuine rationales inform many non-materialistic values which are difficult to reconcile with a *wealth-maximising rent-seeking framework*. On the other hand, these values may equally question the 'western' concept, idea or definition of *property rights*.

For instance, an often raised argument relating to the first point is that 'non-western colleagues who seek pay-offs may have concerns beyond their personal enrichment' (The Economist (1999, p. 23)). As emphasised above, other values may be equally important to African people. An example that also emphasises the second point is the case of nepotism. In many African societies, nepotism is perceived as a right, not just a favour. The higher the position of an African bureaucrat, the larger the expectations of family members and the greater the pressure to mediate jobs.

Outcomes that look like rent-seeking may therefore derive from other rationales according to which maximising wealth is only a minor side issue and people are not so concerned about the economic inefficiencies involved. Or activities may simply not be perceived as rent-seeking since they depend on a different definition of property rights. Bujo (Footnote 76), for instance, emphasises that in many African culture people only own property with respect to society and society has a right to what an individual possesses. Jackson and Rosberg (1985) characterise the behaviour of the African bureaucrats as largely community determined:

> 'Their moral conduct may well be shaped by the indigenous communities to which they belong—kinship, clan, sectarian, patron-client, or ethno-regional groups—which are still firmly rooted in most countries. When most Africans think of their obligations, they are likely to think first of their communal obligations and only belatedly, if at all, of their civic duties.' (quoted in Gulhati (1988, p. 13))

This statement contrasts sharply with the characterisation of East Asians by Ranis (1989, p. 1445). He argues that 'East Asian citizens think of themselves as having certain obligations to the state, feel the need to reach a consensus and not to make too many unreasonable demands on the government'. He himself emphasises that in other LDCs 'citizens think more of their rights in a struggle with other interest groups'.

Besides Africans' obligations to share benefits with kinfolk or extended family, other important rent-seeking drivers are the traditional role of gifts (which in some African cultures can constitute an important source of income) and traditional respect for elders (Mbaku (1992, p. 261), referring to other authors). Finally, other values may be decisive in some African societies, such as a low 'moral resistance to debt creation' (Rowley (1988a, p. 456)), which evidently has prevailed in most developing countries, or more blatant rationales like a 'culture of winner takes all' (Gibbon (1992, p. 77) cites this to explain the lack of African democratisation).

Keeping these distinct values and motivations in mind, what different perspective on rent-seeking should be taken? Three aspects are worth mentioning.

First, a possible conclusion is to *defend and morally justify* rent-seeking behaviour as an integral component of non-western values. In fact many people in LDCs do not perceive corruption as illegal behaviour but as a legitimate means to make a living. This approach is quite problematic, however, as 'rent-seekers' typically do not gamble with their own resources. Rent-seekers in Africa have exploited not just the wealth of their countries, but also donor resources—resources which became necessary partly because of rent-seeking related mismanagement. Only from an economically self-reliant position (i.e. independent of donor support) can a nation be left to decide between 'culturally-rooted' rent-seeking policies and wealth-maximising strategies based on western values. However, as LDCs are by definition very poor and largely depend on considerable external support this rule is highly rhetorical. In addition, making the costs and redistributive consequences of these rent-seeking policies transparent is likely to provoke strong resistance within the country.

Second, to the extent that African values support rent-seeking behaviour, safeguards against a misuse of donor resources need to be much *more stringent*, maybe even overemphasising the need for accountability and far-reaching checks and balances. This requires that a larger share of donor money be used to build up an institutional framework that restrains rent-seeking. In particular, requirements for closer monitoring of bureaucrats should not be underestimated. In general, the fewer safeguards a government can guarantee, the more the emphasis of support needs to shift from financial contributions to providing exclusively ideas and technical advice, above all explaining and making transparent the cost of rent-seeking policies.

Third, on the theoretical side, *rent-seeking models* that are used to make policy conclusions may need to be selected or interpreted carefully; in the extreme they may also have to be adjusted. Many rent-seeking models on dissipation do not include informal constraints. At most, an exogenous parameter for the valuation of the rent or a parameter that allows for modelling insider advantage is introduced. Since the rationale for engaging in rent-seeking (as well as the resulting dissipation) crucially depends on the value of such parameters, it would be preferable to specify and explain them further.

Simplifications are less of a problem when they lead to outcomes that parallel economic logic, but rent-seeking behaviour not driven by wealth-maximising concerns but which is a side product of the pursuit of other, non-monetary values and constraints, would need an extended approach to be understood in full. Granted that bureaucrats or top leaders mediate rents as part of a gift with symbolic, non-monetary meaning, a pure model of 'efficient' rent-seeking is unlikely to describe their behaviour or the behaviour of the recipient. Such a model may overstate or understate true rent-seeking investments and fail to explain the amount of rents transferred.

An important insight then that should find its way into policy formulation is that economic signals may not always suffice to restrain rent-seeking behaviour. Although they are a necessary condition, economic incentives need to be backed by specific measures that address informal constraints. Or alternatively, as argued above, economic signals have to be much more radical to compensate for these culture-based values that are not directly rent-related.

Interaction of Formal and Informal Constraints

The discussion so far demonstrated that informal constraints or institutions which usually coexist with formal institutions, may be important influences on economic outcomes. As debated in the institutional literature, formal and informal institutions may both supplement and substitute for one another. Together they determine and shape the type of exchange in society. Since rent-seeking behaviour is also determined by both types of institutions and since economic reforms typically address only formal institutions, a closer look at the interaction of formal and informal institutions and their relative importance can add to insights into rent-seeking behaviour and help in understanding the effectiveness of policy changes.

What causes tensions between formal and informal constraints is that shifts in institutions may not be smooth, and they may yield contradictory signals. The following discussion takes up this aspect in a general way, specifying four possible situations for interactions. Formal institutions may be *newly created;* they may turn out to be *weak*, they may *break down*; and they may be *kept unchanged.* In all situations, the interaction with the informal environment may determine a specific rent-seeking outcome.

First, when *new legal institutions* are introduced, traditional informal institutions may remain in place, thereby interfering with the intended impact of formal institutions. Nepotism is a case in point; it was economically justified in primitive society but lost this once new formal institutions were implemented. North (1990, p. 34f) summarises three patterns of exchange reflecting different levels of economic development and increasing backing by formal constraints. The first type, personal exchange, is dominant in primitive societies. Transactions are characterised by repetitive dealings, cultural homogeneity and a lack of third party enforcement. Transaction costs are typically low and transformation costs, due to rudimentary specialisation, are very high. The second pattern of exchange involves more complex impersonal exchange, guided and constrained however, as North notes, through kinship ties, bonding, exchanging hostages or merchant codes of conduct. The third is characterised by impersonal exchange with third party enforcement, and is according to North 'the critical underpinning of successful modern economies' (p. 35).

In archaic societies it is economically rational to restrict exchange to family members and close friends, even though benefits from greater specialisation are foregone. This is because there are no institutions to prevent opportunism and enforcement of contracts is difficult to guarantee. Within the family opportunism is not a concern because it is possible to impose social sanctions. With the development of the modern state the situation changed greatly. Formal institutions were created to guarantee the enforcement of impersonal contracts. Even though they replaced informal institutions, some still survived.

Nepotism—having become part of the culture, i.e. part of the system of shared values and norms—did not disappear but still coexists with the new institutions. But within the new formal setting and property rights, nepotism is perceived as rent-seeking; it undermines a more efficient allocation of resources. Another argument which explains why nepotism survived the introduction of new institutions is that it has a genuine interaction rationale, i.e., as noted earlier, it reflects a strong desire to help loved ones (see Table 4-4). Both explanations are likely to hold, even though their relative importance may vary among societies.

Theoretically, any introduction of formal institutions may conflict with existing informal institutions. The problem is more likely if changes are very complex and imposed from outside. A change in the political and economic system, for instance through colonialisation and decolonialisation or more specifically in the course of broad-based political and economic reforms, is likely to provide many potential causes of friction. This line of reasoning partly explains why many social policies of modern states adopted in LDCs have degenerated to become mere rent-seeking instruments. This argument, which also reflects a case of neo-patrimonialism, will be taken up again in Chapter 4.3.

The second argument concerning the interaction of formal and informal constraints is related to the first and addresses the *strength of formal institutions*. To the extent that institutions are weak, informal constraints are likely to become more important. North (1990, p. 35) emphasises that in complex societies returns on opportunism, cheating, and shirking rise, and coercive third party enforcement becomes essential. It now appears that LDCs are in something of an intermediate state. Many of these countries are characterised by weak formal institutions, even though very complex exchanges are already taking place (nationwide and international transactions and, more importantly, large-scale redistribution within the state apparatus). In such a setting, where formal institutions are not sufficiently developed or enforced, informal institutions remain important and may reinforce rent-seeking activities, as indeed seems to have happened in developing countries. Rent-seeking is then prevalent not only because formal institutions are weak but also because values such as nepotism further encourage it. Of course, there is also a direct link between the two aspects, i.e. formal institutions remain weak because informal institutions prevent them from being properly implemented.

The impact of informal institutions becomes even stronger when formal institutions *break down*, for instance as a result of a war. Previously restrained informal institutions may then become relevant again and, as argued above, increase rent-seeking activities. The reversion to traditional relations such as ethnic ties is especially likely to promote rent-seeking politics through tribalism and nepotism—a hazard that remains acute in most African LDCs.

Finally, shifts in informal institutions may explain an increase in rent-seeking activities, even though *formal institutions remain unchanged.* A good example is the rise in theft related to unattended property that has marked the development in industrialised as well as developing countries during the last three decades. Walking along African beaches was much safer in the mid-1970s than it is now. In many regions people routinely left belongings in the sand, sure of finding them when they returned. In China locking one's hotel room was even perceived as an insult, casting aspersions on the honesty of the owner. Middle-aged people in industrialised countries remember when they could leave their bicycles unlocked, even in cities. All of this has dramatically changed.

The development is not the result of a weakening in formal rules but of a dilution of more efficient informal institutions and the weakening of individuals' communal integration. The literature on social cohesion and anomie discusses this development. Murell (1994, p. 203), drawing on Ellickson (1991), even argues that 'social arrangements might be more powerful than the government in establishing the rules that provide the background conditions for economic interactions'. This statement is certainly plausible for many instances of opportunistic behaviour but unfortunately of limited help when it comes to deriving policy recommendations, essentially because social arrangements (understood here as informal constraints) cannot be simply planned, changed and implemented. They develop slowly over time as people interact and general economic conditions alter.

Nevertheless, even though it is not possible to prescribe basic social structures such as household size or integration into communities (except in a totalitarian regime), there is scope for indirect action. Policies that aim to promote certain values such as a 'culture of fairness', or policies that prevent the social marginalisation of certain groups through education and a social network are promising approaches and have a long history in the field of social work and communal politics.

Informal Constraints, Development Cooperation and Economic Reforms

In Chapter 1.1 it was noted that in the past many governments followed economic policies that seriously distorted the functioning of markets, causing high indebtedness, economic instability, stagnation and decline. The failures created an environment that heavily undermined productive activities and resulted in high costs to society and the poor. What followed were economic reforms, often halfhearted and weak, i.e. essential measures were delayed for years or were not effectively implemented. Many countries also repeatedly failed to achieve the minimal targets agreed with donors.

If some of the reasons for ill-guided development and subsequent poor reform records can be found within African traditions, cultures and norms, e.g. situations where informal rules contradict modern formal rules, the question arises as to what has gone wrong. Have modern economic policies (and reforms) not been adapted to the African context or are there even some African norms and rules that are not compatible with a modern state and development, provocatively implying that Africa is not ready or capable of implementing well-designed policy prescriptions? A differentiated answer is called for.

Sound economic policies are obviously a prerequisite for a country to achieve growth and sustainable development and to reduce poverty. The main question is *how to get there*, i.e. how to formulate policies and reforms that can be implemented, even in a political and cultural context where the implementation of such policy may be difficult. However in most cases African culture is not in conflict with modern rules; the problem is mainly the *misuse* of this culture for personal benefit. These two aspects are briefly addressed below.

Many donor-imposed projects and reform programmes in the past appear not to have explicitly taken informal constraints into account. Projects and reform packages that ignore the different values and constraints of African people can fail, either because implementation is opposed or because they do not produce expected outcomes as individuals react differently to economic signals. Ake (1996, p. 15), for instance, notes as regards development strategies:

> 'Culture, like the institutional framework, has been largely ignored as if it, too, had no serious implications for the success of development strategies. It is easy enough theoretically to discount the cultural factor in the development paradigm. But that has been a costly error. African culture has fiercely resisted and threatened every project that fails to come to terms with it, even as it is acted upon and changed.'

An explicit inclusion of informal constraints helps in better adapting reform packages to country-specific settings, permits anticipation of possible evading strategies, and points to areas where strong formal institutional backing of economic policies is required. For instance, if culturally-based rent-seeking forces are important, the distinction between legal and illegal rent-seeking may not be so relevant to rent-seekers. Reducing opportunities at one end will simply induce them to shift their efforts to the other end.

In general, informal constraints may help in making decisions with regard to the speed, sequencing and fine-tuning of reform measures. More closely integrating a broader group of country politicians, bureaucrats, and members of the civil society with their local and country-specific knowledge into the process of design, decision-making, implementation and monitoring may be one possible strategy to better account for informal constraints. This aspect (avoiding the external imposition of adjustment programmes by donors or by a narrowly-defined group of reform-minded technocrats in the recipient country) was much debated in the 1990s under the rubric of *'ownership'*. Although very useful on the whole, it has greater limitations for countries with a pronounced 'culture of rent-seeking' and where rent-seeking interest groups are strong. Clearly governments are not homogenous. Finding the right mix between ownership and conditionality—the latter may more closely reflect ownership of reform-minded people within the government and civil society—is a difficult process and may not be clear from the outset. The relative importance of the two aspects will also depend on the specific policy or sector under focus.

Institutionalists emphasise that informal constraints usually change slowly (see, for instance North (1990, p. 83f)). This is especially true with habits. As the saying *'old habits die hard'* suggests, habits are likely to be adapted to new situations. Reform measures that radically alter formal institutions need to anticipate such behaviour. Habits may relate to specific activities as well as to how people reason and make decisions. The weaker tradition of competition in contrast to cooperation has been mentioned as a possible reason for corruption or rent-seeking in general. Mbaku (1992, p. 261) cites this aspect with regard to developing countries, stating that 'in many developing societies, it is argued that individuals are expected to achieve success through cooperation and not through individualism'. Gelb, Hillman and Ursprung (1995, p. 3) refer to it from a more organisational viewpoint in the context of communist economies in transition:

> 'The socialist economies were ... monopolistically structured. Each enterprise had an assigned task of production or distribution. Duplication of assignment of tasks was avoided as wasteful, and as making central control of the economy more difficult. The end of planned central control consequently released monopolies in a market environment. Managers of the firms had no tradition or knowledge of competition, but did have a tradition of cooperation.'

There are also many African countries where entrepreneurs within both the private and public sectors have been protected against competition for decades. If habits (and related skills) are not directly addressed with suitable measures and institutions, they may become a strong impediment in the reform process and partly explain why individuals fail to react to economic incentives.

The final argument brings the discussion back to the *economic logic* emphasised in Section a). Most of the discussion here in Section c) has focused on a criticism of the over-simplified concept of the homo oeconomicus, pointing to possible informal constraints. But it would be wrong to conclude that economic incentives are not important. On the contrary, as noted earlier, economic incentives are the most important determinant of corruption, as well as rent-seeking in general. In settings where detrimental but culturally-rooted behaviour matters, thorough economic incentives become even more important.

For instance, many anthropologists would agree that ancient African gift-giving traditions are not closely related to the extremely high level of bribery, embezzlement and nepotism seen in many African countries. In many countries where theft and other rent-seeking activities are prevalent, original traditions still matter but they have 'mutated', i.e. they are used selectively and opportunistically as a pretext for personal enrichment.

This adverse development appears to have happened in many cultures, not only in Africa. Critics of the 'cultural hypothesis' therefore correctly argue that detrimental rent-seeking behaviour is also widespread in countries with different cultures but similar economic policies (e.g. Cremer (2000, p. 32)). In such situations, what is most important is to reduce the discretion of bureaucrats and to get economic policies right. Mbaku (1992, p. 262) argues since bureaucratic corruption is 'primarily a rent-seeking behaviour which is associated with government intervention in the economy ... clean up must start with efforts to eliminate the opportunities for rent-seeking'. The major problem however is that the beneficiaries of corruption are usually also the ones who implement the policies and clean-ups are therefore difficult.

This discourse on informal constraints has provided additional explanations for rent-seeking behaviour and possible rent-seeking resistance to policy reforms, but it was not meant to question the economic framework or to de-emphasise the need for thorough economic reforms. If anything, it questioned the ability of a society to introduce reforms or, as argued earlier, the ability to determine the level of rent-seeking investments in a simple rent-seeking model.

The most fundamental problem related to evaluating rent-seeking policies in a sociocultural context is that rent-seeking is a *concept of economic theory*. It describes a mode how economists analyse the consequences of economic policies in a society. Although economic concepts can be highly effective in demonstrating the costs and benefits of a specific policy, they are not an accurate picture of how humans think and act, i.e. it cannot be expected that other people understand and solve problems in the same way. A principal goal of development cooperation should therefore be to make the costs of rent-seeking policies as transparent and understandable as possible and to promote projects that contribute to the general knowledge of economics. There is definitely a strong economic link to 'cultural' values; i.e. social norms and values are not without opportunity costs. To the extent that values become too expensive they are likely to lose their binding impact.[77]

Chapter 4.1 aimed to enhance the understanding of rent-seeking behaviour from the perspective of individual decision-making. Although important, these insights are incomplete contributions towards understanding the prevalence of rent-seeking in societies. The following chapters will approach an analysis of rent-seeking from other angles. The discussion of interest group behaviour (Chapter 4.2) and the analysis of political markets (Chapter 4.3) will provide

---

[77] See for instance Schubert (1992, p. 7), who refers to Olson.

important insights essential for a deeper understanding of why rents are created and successfully captured.

4.2 Interest Groups, Collective Action and Rent-Seeking

'In small groups with common interests there is...a surprising tendency for the "exploitation" of the great by the small.'

Mancur Olson (1965, p. 35)

The crucial role of interest groups in rent-seeking has been addressed several times, for instance when discussing winners and their losing counterparts in Chapter 2 or in presenting rent-seeking models in Chapter 3.[78] What makes interest group theory interesting for rent-seeking is that it provides many clear explanations as to why rent-seeking is a bargain. Most changes in economic policy that reallocate property rights and distribute rents involve a great deal of interest group activity.

If all interests in society could be organised and have equal voices, opposition to rent transfers would in general be strong and make rent-seeking unattractive in many situations. A symmetric representation of individuals is however far from realistic, essentially because of transaction costs (and related limited rationality) inherent in political markets. In fact, differences in the ability to organise and to provoke conflict are such important determinants of power and success that the simple case where a majority wins over a minority appears to be an exception in the political economy of rent-seeking. As the above quote shows, as far back as 1965 Mancur Olson emphasised this 'surprising tendency' towards the exploitation of large groups by smaller groups.

Interest group theory in general and the *theory of collective action* in particular provide crucial insights into why certain groups successfully organise and advance their interests while other groups fail to do so. In Chapter 4.1 the discussion focused on the individual decision-making situation. Even though the focus will now shift to group-related aspects, the individual calculus will remain important, as collective action can also be explained by individual, self-interested motivation.

Of course not all collective action and interest group theory necessarily relates to rent-seeking contests. Olson (1982, p. 42) makes this distinction clear, stating that an 'organization can in principle serve its members either by making the pie the society produces larger, so that its members would get larger slices even with the same shares as before, or alternatively by obtaining larger shares or slices of the social pie for its members'. But he also admits that the latter—he calls them distributional coalitions (Olson (1982, p. 44))—are much more common.

The following sections recapitulate and examine generally, and with regard to LDCs, those factors that explain the rent-seeking success of different groups

[78] Chapter 3 has considered interest groups in several ways, for instance in describing models where rent-seekers act in groups, outlining the public good character of rents and rent-related regulations or emphasising that the strength of opposition to rent-seeking is to a large extent a matter of organising resistance and overcoming free-riding problems.

and their counterparts' corresponding failure in wealth protection. The abilities and incentives of a group to organise for collective action are addressed in Section a). The outcome depends greatly on perceptions, transaction costs and overcoming free-rider problems. Section b) discusses the ability of a group to provoke conflict, which manifests itself in political blackmail and violence and focuses on the interaction of different interest groups and their environment. Section c) finally summarises and draws conclusions for rent-seeking and reforms.

a) Abilities and Incentives to Organise for Collective Action

In 1965 Mancur Olson published his seminal work *'The Logic of Collective Action'.* He argued that small groups in particular enjoyed an advantage in pursuing their collective goals. He provided a variety of arguments as to why large groups such as consumers, taxpayers and the unemployed cannot organise themselves for collective action. Many of his arguments have since been further elaborated, others have been added and the discussion has become quite sophisticated. The most relevant arguments are presented below. Whether individuals organise to engage in rent-seeking activities or whether they organise to prevent an expropriation by other rent-seeking groups depends on several conditions: individuals have to be aware of the issue, they have to be able to identify and communicate a common goal within the group, individual benefits need to be sufficiently large, and the group must be able to address free-riding incentives.

Do Individuals Perceive Problems That Require Collective Action?

The question raised here continues the issue of limited rationality discussed in Chapter 4.1. *Access to information* about the costs or benefits of a certain policy can vary substantially between interest groups and thus explain success or failure in rent-seeking. An example which illustrates how access to information shapes rent-seeking strategies is the way income tax structures are designed. Even though they are often progressive they are typically rife with loopholes to favour certain wealthier taxpayers. Olson (1982, p. 27) makes this point, stating that while populist considerations dictate a considerable degree of progression (this can be easily observed), details of tax laws are far less widely known. Therefore lobbies for special interests are much more likely to succeed when 'matters are detailed or complex but not when they are general and simple' (Olson (1982, p. 69f)). This argument also applies to LDCs, considering the extreme complexity of regulations that have been prevalent in these countries.

Discrepancies in assessing true costs or benefits also arise in other ways. Even when information is available the *competence to interpret* this information may vary among interest groups to such an extent that rent transfers become an easy undertaking. People with only rudimentary knowledge of economics are usually less aware of implicit transfers involved in certain policies and hence do not organise against them. In the extreme they might even support their own exploitation, as argued in Tullock's voter example of protection quoted earlier on page 166.

Looking at economic policies in LDCs and the reactions of negatively affected individuals suggests that distorted perceptions matter. Consumers will generally oppose a reduction in subsidies that raises consumer prises, but the poor quality and high prices that result from excessive protectionism will not induce them to take to the streets. The same is true for agricultural policy. Krueger (1996, p. 170), for instance, states:

> 'Although farmers' groups lobbied for better treatment with respect to process of their outputs and inputs, they were silent when it came to issues of macroeconomic policy, including protection and the exchange rate, which arguably affected them as much as did decisions with respect to producer prices.'

Distorted perceptions have also opened avenues to the ruling elites to gain support from groups they actually exploited. Providing a few strategic incentives such as agricultural inputs for farmers sometimes appears to be sufficient to give the group a feeling of being supported.

All in all, one important precondition to prevent rent-seeking transfers is that individuals who are negatively affected by a policy *perceive* the wealth transfer it involves. The problem seems to be especially pronounced in the poorest countries where not only the general distribution of information is a handicap, but economic knowledge of the consequences of specific rent-seeking policies may also be poor.

Are Costs to Communicate a Common Goal Sufficiently Low?

Above, it was essentially *limited rationality*, caused by a lack of information or by a failure in its interpretation, that explained why individuals failed to organise for or against rent transfers. However, for collective action to mobilise it is not sufficient that individuals are able to access and interpret all relevant information so that they understand the rents at stake. It is equally important that organisation costs are sufficiently low. This aspect refers to *transaction costs* understood in a *narrow* sense.

The more *geographically dispersed* members of an interest group are, the more difficult and costly communication between them becomes. The problem is compounded in most LDCs, where efficient, nationwide *communication infrastructures* (mass media, including broad-based internet access, as well as private communication means) are not sufficiently developed. This further raises potential organisation costs of well-dispersed interest groups.

In particular rural interest groups, like small farmers, find it difficult jointly to express and advance their interests. Millner pointed to an interesting incongruity that 'the number of farmers has a positive impact on its influence in developed countries but a negative … in less developed countries' (Potters and Sloof (1996, p. 418)), or to put it differently, rich countries subsidise agriculture even though farmers are a small minority while poor countries, where farmers constitute the majority, levy heavy taxes on agriculture (e.g. Krueger (1996, p. 163)). Potters and Sloof suggest lower democratic quality in LDCs and low welfare as a possible explanation for this outcome; an equally important reason, besides many others, is the more poorly developed communication infrastructure mentioned above.[79]

In addition to geographic considerations, the question of how dispersed potential interest groups are also applies at the *intermediate level*. As has been argued, a multitude of small entities is usually more difficult to organise than a few large ones. According to this logic, Zouari (1989, p. 327) notes for Tunisia that it is not a surprise to find trade unionism well established in the public sector, where worker concentration is ten times greater than in the private sector. In most LDCs public workers have been in privileged positions. Even though there are many other factors responsible for this outcome, the influence of higher worker concentration cannot be neglected.

Social proximity among group members is another factor that determines costs involved in collective action. Social proximity often overlaps with Olson's distinction between narrow and encompassing interest groups. Encompassing interest groups are usually much more heterogeneous and hence more difficult to organise, although larger economies of scale may partly neutralise the organisational disadvantage.

Interest groups' prospects for collective action are enhanced if an *established organisation* already exists that to some extent represents their interests. While such an organisation may be left over from previous similar interest constellations, it might also have come into existence as an instrument to manage and carry out a specific regulation. If marketing boards—which in many LDCs have degenerated into an instrument of rent extraction—become privatised and the property of the farmers themselves, these farmers may well use the boards' organisational infrastructure as a mouthpiece to coordinate and express their future demands. The cost aspect of organisation may be summarised as follows:

> '[Organisation costs] are like start-up costs. Once they are borne, they do not affect marginal costs. Groups that have already incurred start-up costs, for reasons unrelated to lobbying, will have a comparative advantage in seeking transfers.' (Tollison (1982, p. 590))

---

[79] To fully understand the paradox, obviously also other factors have to be taken into consideration. For instance, Nabli and Nugent (1989, p. 101), referring to various authors, explain the paradox by emphasising the change in the interest group constellation at higher levels of development as follows: 'As development proceeds and massive rural-urban migration takes place…the industrial sector becomes larger, less geographically concentrated, more heterogeneous and thus more difficult to organize. At the same time, as agriculturalists become fewer in number, more concentrated in specific commercial crops, more dependent on the ability to market their agricultural surplus, and better endowed with capital, transport and communications, and for whom exit is a less viable possibility, both their need for collective action and their ability to bring it about are greatly enhanced. Also, because of the smaller size of the agricultural sector, the cost burden of agricultural subsidies is not likely to be as threatening to other potential coalition partners as they would have been before.'

Whether an organisation makes collective action easier also depends on its nature. In many countries farmers have been organised in cooperatives for years, but these structures have exploited rather than strengthened them. On the other hand (drawing from the overview in Nabli and Nugent (1989, p. 118-21)), strong *collective action* may also appear *without an organisation*, as consumer revolts in LDCs demonstrate. In such cases interest groups form rapidly just to achieve a specific objective and then disappear again. Critical mass models explain their creation:

> 'A collective action will obtain only if individuals expect that a "critical mass" of individuals will engage in it. In that case, when the process is started, it feeds on itself, and other individuals increasingly join the action.' (Nabli and Nugent (1989, p. 119))

The success of this type of collective action depends strongly on the reaction of the government, which might crush the action immediately, suppress all information about the action, or deliberately falsely underreport the extent of participation in it.

So far it has been argued that physical and social proximity as well as the existence of already established organisations may help to reduce transaction costs of interest group formation. Another aspect is *political entrepreneurship.* According to Hardin (1982), political entrepreneurs are 'people who, for their own career reasons, find it in their private interest to work to provide collective benefits to relevant groups' (cited from Nabli and Nugent (1989, p. 93)). Senator D'Amato, who attacked Swiss Banks for the sake of a Jewish constituency, provides a textbook example. Political entrepreneurs, however, seem to be more prominent in well-established democracies than in LDCs, mostly because of different patterns of interest group representation and interest group action.

Are the Benefits of Collective Action Sufficiently Large?

Even when individuals are aware of policy-induced rent transfers (and transaction costs related to communication and identifying a common goal are not prohibitive) the benefits of collective action need to be sufficiently large. In general the smaller, more uncertain and less visible the individual benefits from organising are, the lower is the incentive to do so. Olson (1982, p. 34) explains this with a simple numerical example. He argued that even when the aggregate demand for a collective good is the same, it makes quite a difference whether twenty-five individuals lobby for a collective good worth \$1000 or five thousand lobby for a collective good worth \$5. Rent-seeking contests that address policy changes regularly combine the two patterns; rent transfers, which are appropriated by a few individuals, are usually financed by a much larger community. Hence costs borne by a single member of the losing group are, due to division by a larger number, much smaller (and often less directly visible), with the effect that individual costs become too small to bother about. Rent-seekers' individual benefits, in contrast, remain sufficiently large, which explains their strong incentives for collective action. This difference in the size of the individual slice explains to a large extent the prevalence of insufficient rent protection. The losing group not only faces smaller benefits from collective action; since its members are more numerous collective action is likely to be more costly to organise. Situations where small organised groups transfer benefits from large, diffuse, unorganised communities of interest are thus very common in industrialised as well as developing countries.

There are two qualifications to note, even though they do not usually change the result. First, *'transfers'* should not be confused with *'costs'* or *'benefits'*. As outlined in particular in Chapter 3, total costs borne by the losing group are also ex-ante larger than total benefits received by the winning coalition, if there are inefficiencies related with the transfer. Second, there are also other aspects that determine individual costs and benefits and thus incentives for collective action. For instance, as often argued, farmers' access to alternative *exit solutions* has been an important feature explaining their absence in 'voice' and collective action against a specific policy. Also, the level of transfers at stake and therefore the extent of potential benefits of collective action may depend on the group's ability to address *free-riding* problems. The next section focuses on this topic.

Can the Group Raise the Critical Minimum Support for Collective Action?

The ability of the group to handle free-riding incentives is one of the most decisive determinants of successful group formation and has been widely discussed within collective action theory. Formally the free-riding problem represents an n-player prisoner dilemma situation. As noted earlier, most rent-seeking endeavours that aim to influence economic policy include aspects of group formation and therefore face free-riding problems related to participation in collective action. The negative incentive can be summarised as follows:

> 'A person will realise that if others organise, the value added to the group by their membership will be insignificant. Also, since the good in question is collective (since policy choices rectified by public bodies are collective), people will benefit from an organised group's acquisition of the good regardless of whether they participated in the process by which it was obtained' (Zeigler (1992, p. 379))

Olson demonstrates that the larger the group whose interests have to be voiced and advanced, the higher will be the incentive for an individual to free-ride and the less likely that the group will organise. He categorises the groups into privileged, intermediate, and latent groups. Only in the first are individual benefits of collective action larger than the costs of providing the collective good alone. He argues however that even in such a situation the collective good may not be provided since each individual may wait for someone else to take the initiative. (Olson (1965, p. 50f))

Depending on the character of the public good at stake, free-riding may not only refer to *participation* in collective action but also to the *adherence to group decisions*. This differentiation coincides with Olson's distinction between exclusive and inclusive collective goods (Olson (1965, p. 36ff)). A group may for example try to form a price cartel. In contrast to the free-riding problem mentioned above, free-riding here undermines and eventually destroys the rent the group attempts to organise for. Individual benefits of group formation will thus critically depend on the group's ability to prevent free-riding incentives mostly or entirely.

In LDCs most sectors within the *industry* have been protected against foreign competition, and competition among domestic enterprises has been very low or, when a single company remains, even absent. For these companies free-riding based on exclusive collective goods has usually not been a problem. The situation differs with formal *commercial* enterprises. They often face severe competition from the informal sector, either through their own supply (as with construction, food and many services such as taxi driving or retail trade), or through smuggling. Likewise, the informal sector has also undermined the strength of unions. All in all, where competition from the unorganisable informal sector has been strong, organising for an exclusive collective good has been much more difficult and therefore has in most cases not taken place.

In the literature different measures to overcome free-riding problems have been proposed. The examples presented below mostly draw from Nugent (1989, p. 317f). The most common strategy is to offer a *private good* for participation (e.g. providing members with up-to-date information on relevant laws, foreign market opportunities and technological developments; providing members a list of customers who have in the past proved themselves unreliable; simplifying and unifying accounting procedures; giving members the right to participate in international meetings with expenses paid by the organisation). A group may also try to make contributions *look fair* (varying payments by size of firm, linking payments to voting rights or services rendered). Another strategy is to increase *social pressure* (e.g. by circulating a list of members delinquent in their payments) or simply make participation *compulsory* (automatically including contributions to student associations in student fees, directly deducting union contributions from public wages). Finally, a further successful strategy has been to *convert* a public good *into a private good.* A group may, for instance, decide to lobby for quotas instead of lower tariffs. Drawing from Rowley and Tollison (1988, p. 229), they note that since import quota licences are often unavailable to new entrants, 'this limits the free rider problem associated with rent-seeking into tariff revenues'.

The different strategies mentioned in this section contribute to lowering free-riding incentives. Nevertheless the challenges confronting interest groups vary substantially. Not only do interest groups have different minimum levels of support required for successful collective action but depending on the groups' composition and goals, the prospects of implementing strategies to reduce free-riding will also vary (e.g. in the above example, the option of turning a public good into a private good is not available to the losing consumer side).

b) The Ability to Provoke Conflict, Interest Group Interaction and the Surrounding Setting

The ability to organise for collective action is only one aspect that accounts for differences in power between interest groups and hence rent-seeking success. Equally important is the ability to provoke conflict. In addition, success or failure of collective action hinges not just on the activities of a single group but also on the strategies chosen by other interest groups and the specific environment.

The ability to provoke conflict manifests itself through forms of political blackmail and violence. An interest group may be in the position to *refuse* or seriously threaten to refuse *a service that is indispensable* for the smooth functioning of a society (Massing (1987, p. 388)). Powerful interest groups usually mentioned in this context are employees of monopoly industries such as public transport, telecommunication and telephone services, or utilities. Strikes in these sectors can cause a sudden breakdown in economic activity, mostly in urban areas. Strikes are especially powerful since they are often much more costly to society than the pay rise at stake.

A related aspect, even though it does not depend on group formation, is private rent extraction, i.e. individuals may *exert power* and extract rents *owing to their job positions*. Corrupt bureaucrats in the narrow sense, but also soldiers and lawyers fall into this classification. Even though they do not need to act explicitly as a group, they represent very powerful interest groups that may successfully undermine any reform efforts aiming to remove their 'extra' benefits.

Obviously, groups may also be in a *position to initiate or carry out armed conflicts*. The ruling elite, military sub-units, as well as tribal and religious groups belong to this category. Many rent-seekers have simply captured the state apparatus with coup d'états or military revolts. The numerous revolts and civil wars in African countries clearly indicate this aspect. Rent-seeking success related to the power to carry out armed conflicts, however, also becomes manifest in other ways, i.e. armed conflicts only represent the tip of the iceberg; transfers achieved by the mere threat of violence are much more frequent.

A soft version of armed conflict is *violent demonstrations*, which may apply to very different interest groups. Students are said to have become violent in many countries (even though the behaviour of police and the army has certainly contributed much to the violent escalation observed). Not only do increases in university fees or reductions in enrolment draw them to the streets but also many general concerns. Chazan, et al. (1988, p. 90), for instance, describe the latter aspect as follows:

> 'Students have ... emerged as a vital barometer of the status of particular regimes, being among the first groups to voice discontent and to indicate levels of dissatisfaction with government policies. Although not an economic force, students groups have played an important role in molding popular attitudes.'

Apart from strikes, most of the above-mentioned manifestations are more prevalent in developing countries than in industrialised countries, an outcome which is to some extent attributable to the lack of democratic checks and balances and the (deliberately) weak legal and administrative capacity of the state often found in developing countries. Strikes however have been less frequent in these countries. This is especially true in Africa, where social classes have been less highly developed (e.g. Bienen (1993, p. 273)).

As mentioned before, the success of collective action also depends on the strategies of other interest groups. There are three basic types of relationships between interest groups.

First and most obvious, *strategies of other groups* may be *in competition* with the primary group's objectives. This is for instance the case with most budget-related rent-seeking. Several interest groups may lobby for a higher share of limited funds such as foreign exchange at preferential rates, or for cheap treasury loans and other subsidies.

Second, strategies can also be *neutral* with respect to one another. A group seeking support may for instance lobby for preferential access to credits; another may exert pressure for direct subsidies. This aspect is important when it comes to interpreting certain policy outcomes. As has been discussed in the literature, a better ability of an interest group to organise and to provoke conflict does not necessarily imply a greater role in influencing certain policy decisions. Groups may favour very different instruments. This is illustrated by Becheri (1989)'s study on interest rate determination in Tunisia. Farmers rather than public enterprises and industrialists enjoyed essentially preferential conditions, even though the enterprises and industrialists were very influential interest groups in Tunisia and the main borrowers. The latter had simply lobbied for other policy options. For public enterprises, Becheri (1989, p. 388) argued:

> 'Since public entreprises are generally underfinanced to begin with and then quite frequently continue to run deficits in their operating budgets, obtaining credit is their top priority. Hence, preferential interest rates are of only secondary importance to public enterprises.'

Industrialists, on the other hand, enjoyed high prices for finished goods, protection from foreign competition, tax exemptions and also large amounts of credit (Becheri (1989, p. 387)).

Third, besides neutral and competing relations, strategies of interest groups may also be *complementary*, i.e. supporting objectives of other groups. Hirschman's *'tunnel effect'*, where the success of a group anticipates subsequent improvements for other groups (Nabli and Nugent (1989, p. 94)), is an example. If a group, for instance, succeeds in lobbying for a lower group-specific VAT rate, the probability increases that other groups will succeed in their future requests. A very specific interpretation of the 'tunnel effect' may be, as Grissa sees it, the close relation between public enterprises and bureaucrats, where any loyal bureaucrat or legislator can count on once having a leading position in a parastatal. Hence, as Grissa remarks, it is 'not in the interest of any member of the group to "blow the whistle" ' (Grissa (1989, p. 415f)). Closely related to

Hirschman's tunnel effect is the *'foot in the door strategy'*, even though this usually refers to a single interest group. The group's strategy is first to focus on the acceptance of a certain policy intervention (limiting the amount of rents sought to a small level or for a temporary period) and then to use it as a basis for subsequent expansion in both scope and duration (Nugent (1989, p. 317, 318)). Still within the context of the last category of complementary strategies, one may also subsume very direct forms of collaboration, such as vote trading and other arrangements.

Besides the interaction of different interest groups, another important consideration, which also influences interest group success is the specific *economic, political, institutional and sociocultural setting* interest groups are embedded in. Balance of power, coalition building, fragmentation and party-structure, as well as ideology and the general agenda are a few catchwords from the interest group literature. In Africa, tribalism may also thoroughly influence the political arena. Since many of these aspects will be considered in Chapter 4.3, which also addresses the political setting in a broader socioeconomic context, the discussion here will be brief.

A critical determinant for an interest group is the *composition of the ruling coalition* (often shaped by tribal considerations). This explains why interest groups with very weak power characteristics may still be successful. The matter may be illustrated by comparing the situation of the agriculture sector in different countries. In general, as Krueger (1996, p. 171) notes in her survey article on agricultural policies, 'countries in which agricultural representatives were in the ruling coalition turned out to discriminate less'. Ghana and Kenya provide good examples:

> 'In Ghana, Kwame Nkrumah's coalition excluded all significant rural interests and governed with little regard to their well-being. By contrast, in Kenya, the ruling coalition had strong ties with rural interests, and agriculture fared much better' (Krueger (1993, p. 65), drawing from Bates).

The situation in formerly socialist Tanzania might be taken as another example where peasants have been constantly exploited. Looking at the structure of the agricultural sector (strong cooperatives and an organisation in Ujama villages), one might expect peasants to be more powerful. Over the years, however, farmers never managed to successfully oppose large rent extractions. The power was not with farmers but the government, marketing boards and the newly imposed cooperatives (which had been abolished in the 1970s). The examples indicate that depending on the political constellation 'peasant success' may be very different from 'peasant organisation'.

Another decisive factor obviously related to the strategies of the ruling coalition is the prevailing *ideology*. To a great degree it explains the extent of policy interventions 'allowed' in an economy. As interest groups often use ideological concerns as a pretext for their true rent-related ambitions, they are much more likely to be successful in 'interventionist-socialist' than 'nightwatchman-liberal' economies.

Finally, success or failure in lobbying for a policy outcome may be explained by the *general environment*, i.e. external shocks, developments in the economy, whether a country has taken up negotiations with the IMF and World Bank, and events and problems in other countries. These factors influence the political debate and with it the chances of interest groups to advance their cause.

Political and sociocultural factors not only influence the power of interest groups; they may have a much deeper impact by directly shaping *patterns of interest group representation* in a country (horizontal versus vertical, corporatist versus partisan). The specific vertical structure in many African countries has been widely noticed. Following Gaillard and Rüegg (1987, p. 9, they refer to various authors), because of the large economic differences in developing countries, one might expect a political organisation on the basis of social classes; however, what is often observed are vertical relations that cut through classes. Different parties, they continue, then do not represent different well-defined social classes but have a similar member and voter structure as well as diffuse party programmes. Both patronage relations and tribalism in general have accounted for Africa's specific interest group pattern:

> 'Social classes have been more weakly developed in Africa than in Asia or Latin America or the Middle East. Leaders have been less tied to social constituencies other than ethnic ones and thus have spoken less for classes or representatives of class interest.' (Bienen (1993, p. 273))

Kenya provides a striking example where government policy has largely degenerated to tribal politics and patron-client relations. In neighbouring Tanzania, as a very different case, tribalism has been virtually absent in politics. There it was the socialist one-party history that greatly shaped patterns of interest group representation. In this setting, where almost everything was regulated through the one-party-system, only church groups managed to develop a stronger influence. By contrast, professional economic interests (other than party-bureaucrat-parastatal relations) have been practically non-existent. Only several years after liberalisation was initiated, have professional interest groups now begun to gain momentum.

All in all, each matter has its own community of interest behind it. However, of the many stakes in society, only a few lead to strong interest group formations, to some extent depending on political and sociocultural factors. Tribalism and patron-client-relations are not the only factors that make Africa a special interest group case. Since in Africa cultural homogeneity, the composition of civil society and the shape of social structures have varied substantially within countries (Chazan, et al. (1988, p. 94)), different patterns of interest group representations are likely to be observed, an aspect that should be taken into account when addressing policy reforms.

c) Summary and Conclusion: Addressing Rent-Seeking Power

Interest group theory is relevant and explains several of the parameters outlined in Chapter 3. Two years before Tullock's original paper on rent-seeking in 1967, Olson had already presented, albeit with a different focus, many of the important tools for understanding group related rent-seeking behaviour. This strand of economic theory has been considerably extended since. As widely debated in the literature, the power of interest groups is largely determined by their ability to organise and to provoke conflict. It also depends on factors which shape the overall setting in which interest groups are embedded. Together these explain why different groups in society face very different conditions for expressing and promoting their interests (and rights) and why there are so many opportunities in societies to earn income without being productive.

In contrast to many rent-capturing activities, rent-creating strategies usually require a fair amount of group mobilisation. As has been shown, important exogenous factors that affect the interest group's ability to mobilise for collective action include group size, physical and social proximity, the pre-existence of an organisation, level and type of individual costs and benefits at stake, as well as the type of free-riding problems the group is confronted with. Most critical becomes the question whether the group can solve or sufficiently reduce free-riding problems.

Endogenous rent-seeking contests are frequently characterised by the situation where small groups try to extract rents financed by much larger communities. The larger group then not only finds it more difficult to mobilise against the rent transfer as free-riding problems are expected to be greater but the unfavourable group structure also accounts for the smaller individual level of benefits at stake. The difficulties of the larger group are further aggravated by generally greater communication problems (which are especially severe in LDCs). Last but not least, the awareness of the rent-extracting situation is usually lower. Taken together, these features provide a very strong argument for successful rent-creating strategies of small groups, or, to quote Olson (1965, p. 35) again, 'a surprising tendency for the "exploitation" of the great by the small'. Evidently this interest group outcome is one of the most important reasons why rent-seeking is profitable and why it has spread so much. Assuming the contrary (i.e. majorities generally win over minorities) would leave much less rent to be distributed to each winning individual; in addition to the losses associated with transferring rents, rents (extracted from minorities) also have to be shared by larger numbers.

Olson grouped the factors that make collective action possible in terms of two conditions (one of which is sufficient for collective action): the number of individuals has to be sufficiently small and/or the group has to have access to 'selective incentives' (Olson (1987, p. 474)). The former relates to the problems that have been covered in the discussion of the first four questions raised in Section a), and the latter obviously coincides with the solutions given in the last one.

The group's success is not only a matter of group mobilisation but also depends on the group leaders' skills. The right decision on how to design, voice and sequence collective objectives (e.g. choosing an appropriate 'foot-in-the-door strategy') may decide between success and failure. Likewise in settings where transaction costs and limited rationality are high, opportunities to conceal the true costs and exaggerate the benefits are crucial in negotiations. As North (1990, p. 16) and many others have argued, 'in a zero-transaction-cost world, bargaining strength does not affect the efficiency of outcomes, but in a world of positive transaction costs it does'. Finally, the success of strategies is also highly influenced by many exogenous factors determined by the sociocultural, political, economic and institutional setting.

All in all, the dissimilarity of problems interest groups are confronted with (especially with mobilising for collective action), together with the differences in their ability to formulate and carry out strategies have significantly contributed to the profitability of rent-seeking activities. These differences seem to be much larger in developing countries than in the rest of the world. Transaction costs especially appear to be less equally 'distributed' among winning and losing groups.

Interest group theory also contributes to an understanding of the contention made in Chapter 3 why many rent-seeking settings in LDCs are insider settings and why they can include very high levels of inefficiencies. On the one hand, and most obviously, different interest groups in LDCs have very dissimilar access to public resources. Abstracting from party and tribe affiliation, which are the most dominant factors in many LDCs, limited rent-seeking chances also correspond to the factors specified in interest group theory. On the other hand, the high level of inefficiencies 'tolerated' by the ruling elites is a reflection of severe inequalities among affected interest groups. As emphasised by Tollison (see quote at the introduction to Chapter 4), 'in a world of zero transaction and information costs only welfare-enhancing transfers will be passed by political representatives'. But the reality, in particular in developing countries, looks different. All over the world, small privileged groups have easily obtained favours at the expense of high social costs.

Interest Group Theory and Policy Reforms

What conclusions can be drawn to assess, design and implement policy reforms in developing countries? Basically there are two partly-related lines of recommendations: those that aim to reduce the profitability of rent-seeking in general and those that address rent-seeking opposition within the reform process in particular.

If society wants to *reduce the profitability* of rent-creating strategies, the most obvious approach from the interest group perspective is to address the chain of unfavourable patterns that determine unequal collective action. In LDCs probably the most important measure would be to raise the level of awareness in the general public about the consequences of specific policies, not only through better education in basic economics in schools and guaranteeing a free press, but also through a closer cooperation between media and scientific institutes such as universities and other research institutions. A series of understandable articles in the local newspaper or discussions on the radio may turn out to be 'low budget, high impact' measures. Another promising avenue is to strengthen the position of consumers. In many countries consumer programmes on TV have become powerful and are among the most highly watched regular programmes. Even though such an arrangement seems to be more difficult to adapt to developing countries and would mainly reach people living in towns, it might still be worth attempting it. Other measures could address the ability to generate conflict. A possible strategy would be privatising and introducing competition for services indispensable to society.

The second line of argument addresses opposition to *reform implementation.* As noted earlier, implementation of reforms was poor in many countries throughout the 1980s and even 1990s. Powerful rent-seeking interest groups within and outside the ruling elites have largely accounted for this disappointing record. Even though it is naïve to expect that all opposition can be handled, a better assessment of the interest group constellation at the outset, together with a well-targeted strategy that addresses possible interest group reactions to reform measures, would certainly improve performance. Addressing opposition at its root, accounting for possible critical mass developments, considering interest group arithmetic and networks, as well as strengthening perceptions and the voice of reform beneficiaries are a few relevant catchwords.

Chapter 3 stressed that addressing rents in the reform process requires taking a sufficiently broad perspective which considers all relevant rent-seeking opportunities simultaneously and includes an assessment of profit-seeking alternatives. This aspect particularly applies to shifts in interest group strategies and interactions. When reforms are implemented, certain channels of support are no longer available and interest group strategies change. The case study on Tanzania in Part II will illustrate this in detail.

With reform beneficiaries, strengthening of the group, information and communication are a large part of the task. Helping reform-friendly producer and consumer organisations to get started and including them in the policymaking process may have a high impact, especially when patterns of interest group representation have been unfavourable to reforms in the past. Bates and Krueger (1993, p. 460), for example, summarise other authors in stating that 'corporatist forms of interest group representation [in contrast to partisan] help to sustain openness in international trade, facilitating the policy adjustments needed for liberal trade regimes'. They argue that in such a system these interest groups bargain at the national level and their leaders are often themselves brought into the government.

Finally, the donors' community could play an important role in counterbalancing the inequality between powerful rent-seekers and the exploited poor through various types of conditionality when deciding on project support, programme support, or general balance of payments and budget support (donors being one form of interest groups that defend the interests of the poor).

Conditionalities need however to be well specified and take a broad perspective. Many of those applied in the 1980s and 1990s have proved to be ineffective. A main problem is that the implementation of many recommendations derived from an interest group analysis requires a considerable amount of commitment from the top leadership, which is often not given. If they are the rent-seekers themselves or depend on the support of specific groups they may not implement these suggestions. But even in the worst case where all recommendations from interest group theory are ignored by the ruling elites, there is always a coalition of international donors and some reform-minded politicians from the administration who can take up and implement important aspects and may thereby move the economy towards a more efficient equilibrium.

4.3 Rent-Seeking and Political Markets

Having focused on individual and group-related aspects in 4.1 and 4.2, this chapter presents the last major extension of the rent-seeking discussion. That the state takes a crucial role in actively and passively creating rents has already been extensively discussed in earlier chapters. Here this aspect is treated in more detail. An analysis of the internal structure of the state will shed light on the power characteristics of different entities within the system; it complements the results and explanations obtained from the interest group analysis and thereby provides valuable insight into why rents are created and supplied.

a) Introduction: Typology of States

To understand the government's stake in shaping rent-seeking behaviour, it is helpful to start with a brief outline of different regimes. Governments vary with regard to their role they take in a society, i.e. the size and type of interventions the scope of preferences they represent, including the kind of interest group mobilisation they tolerate.

Following the literature of political science (Jesse (1998, p. 591f)), states are most commonly grouped according to their power sharing characteristics. On the one side there are *constitutional systems* such as parliamentarian and presidential governments. They are characterised by a division, distribution and competition of power. The other group comprises *autocratic governments*. Unlike constitutional systems their power usually resides undivided in the hands of a single person, clique or party. This division however only serves as a crude classification. (Different types of power accumulation are also found within constitutional systems, and most autocratic systems contain various mechanisms of power limitation.)

More practical is a categorisation along a *continuum* ranging from liberal democracies to totalitarian regimes (Lauth (1998, p. 31)). An all-embracing ideology, a system of terror and complete control of the economy and society are typical features of the latter. Authoritarian systems fall somewhere in the middle of the continuum, depending on the extent of political participation and pluralism they allow.

Freedom House—a non-profit organisation based in New York—has been monitoring political rights and civil liberties for over forty years and now covers every country in the world. They define political rights as rights that 'enable people to participate freely in the political process' (giving the people the choice of determining the nature of the system and its leaders) and civil liberties as 'freedoms to develop views, institutions and personal autonomy apart from the state' (Finn (1994, p. 671)).

According to the Freedom House annual report (e.g. Finn (1994, p. 672f)), the *civil liberties* index describes features such as free and independent media, freedom of assembly and demonstration, equal treatment of citizens under law, and freedom from political terror, torture and unjustified imprisonment. It furthermore values the presence of free professional organisations, businesses, cooperatives and religious institutions; personal social freedoms (gender equality, property rights, freedom of movement, choice of marriage and size of family), equality of opportunities (freedom from exploitation by landlords, employers, unions and bureaucrats) and the freedom from government corruption. The *political rights* category, in contrast, addresses questions such as whether the head of the state and the legislative are elected through free and fair elections, whether people have a right to organise in different political parties, whether 'true' opposition groups are tolerated, whether minority groups have a reasonable autonomy or participation, and whether political power is decentralised.

The Freedom House country-rating index, also known as the *Gastil-index*, serves as a good indicator for locating states along the continuum of liberal democracies and totalitarian regimes. Figure 4-2, which is based on the Freedom House ratings, gives a rough picture of the political landscape of Sub- Saharan-Africa for the years 1976/77 and 2001/02 and compares it with that of the group of high income countries in 2001/02. The extent of political rights is measured along the horizontal axes, civil liberties along the vertical (on each scale, 1 represents the freest, 7 the least free).

Figure 4-2: Political Rights and Civil Liberties

Sub-Saharan Africa 1976/77

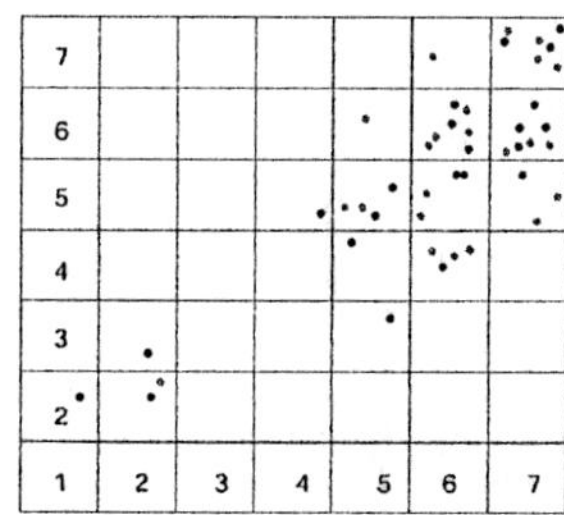

Sub-Saharan Africa 2001/02

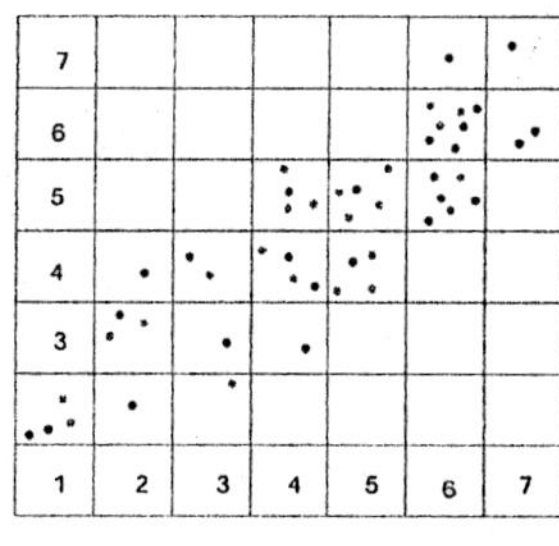

High-income countries 2001/02

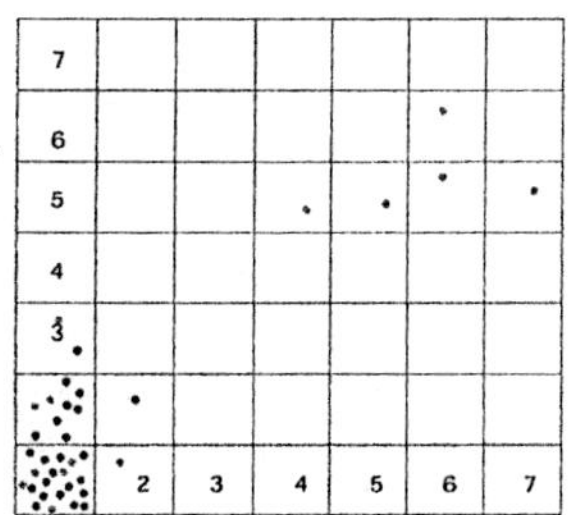

The XY-scatters depict the Freedom House classification of political rights (horizontal axes) and civil liberties (vertical axes) for different country samples. In the first two diagrams grey dots refer to the sub-sample West Africa, in the third diagram to the non-OECD country group. On each scale, 1 represents the freest, 7 the least free. Within the square, however, the distribution of dots is random. While Freedom House makes available the rating scores (1-7) for each country, they have a policy of not disclosing the raw points for these countries (0-36 for political rights and 0-52 for civil liberties). To depict an XY-scatter, the dots therefore had to be randomly distributed within a category, i.e. there is no additional information available other than the number of countries that fall into one square.

Source: Figures of country ratings from Freedom House (2002), country classification according to World Development Report (World Bank (1998c))

In the figure three well-known features are clearly visible: the positive correlation between political rights and civil liberties, the distinct not-free classification of African states and the partial dilution of this pattern as a result of the democratic wave at the beginning of the 1990s (for a diagram which indicates the change over time see Figure 4-5 on page 209). For 1976/77, only Seychelles, The Gambia, Mauritius and Botswana are rated as countries with far reaching political rights and civil liberties (13 countries are rated as partially free, and 28 as not free).[80] However the country classified as freest, Seychelles, kept this rating for one year only, and The Gambia drops out of the group at the beginning of the 1980s. Only Mauritius and Botswana keep their free rating, accompanied by up to three other countries that come and go during the following years (Djibouti, Burkina Faso, Nigeria and Namibia). In 1992 the number of free countries reaches eight and increases to nine after the millennium. For 2001/02 (values in parentheses refer to 1976/77) 19% (9%) of the countries are rated as free, 50% (29%) as partly free and 31% (62%) as not free.

The picture of Africa sharply contrasts the group of high-income countries, which can be divided into the sub-groups OECD and non-OECD countries. In 2000/01, with the exception of Singapore, all high-income countries not rated as free were oil-exporting states (Brunei, Kuwait, Qatar and United Arab Emirates). Also not surprisingly, OECD countries are considered the freest. In 2001/02 political rights of the OECD group are all rated as 1 except for Korea's 2. Ratings of civil liberties are slightly less free but still very favourable: 15 OECD countries are rated as 1, eight as 2 and only one (Greece) as 3.[81] This picture has not differed much in the past. Evaluating all OECD members during the last twenty-five years shows that political rights have been rated as 1 in 87% of the cases and as 2 in 9%, (civil liberties as 1 in 65%, and 2 in 28%). Turkey and Mexico account for 96% of the political rights ratings other than 1 and 2 (and 71% of those for civil liberties).

The Freedom House data clearly support the general perception that the countries in sub-Saharan-Africa have had much less liberal systems than those in high-income countries. A worldwide comparison also suggests that sub-Saharan Africa still contains many countries rated 'not free'. Figure 4-3 depicts the situation that obtained shortly after the democratic spring. Scattered along a continuum running from liberal democracies to totalitarian regimes several African states still find themselves quite far from democracy. This has implications for the type of rent-seeking behaviour and explains why 'non-rival' rent-seeking situations are common in developing countries (once a group has obtained power). Rulers in these countries generally face few constraints in creating and allocating rents and the power among interest groups varies decisively between different groups. Mbaku (1992, p. 249f) describes the strong position a ruler holds as follows:

---

80 Freedom House rates countries whose combined averages for political rights and for civil liberties fall between 1.0 and 2.5 as 'free' between 3.0 and 5.5 'partly free' and between 5.5 and 7.0 'not free'.

81 Not included in the figure are the five middle-income OECD countries: Czech Rep. (1/2), Hungary (1/2), Poland (1/2), Turkey (4/5) and Mexico (2/3).

Figure 4-3: The Map of Freedom, January 1994

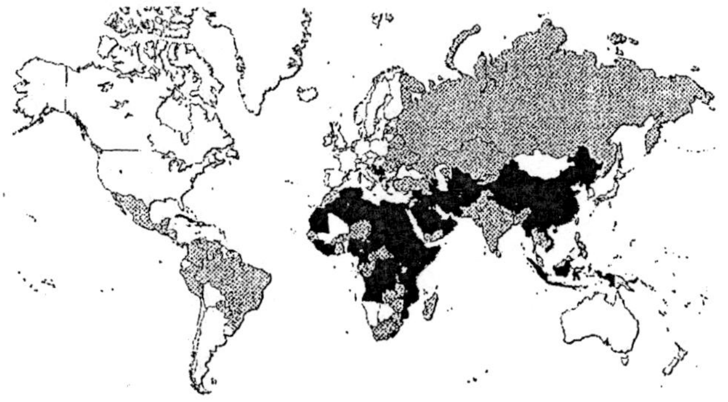

The map displays the Freedom House classification of countries according to the three basic categories. White areas indicate free countries; grey areas partly free countries and black areas not free countries. The ranking combines both political rights and civil liberties (see definition in Footnote 80).

Source: Freedom House (Finn (1994, p. 92f))

> 'Many developing countries have governments in which legislatures do not exist or if they do, do not function properly. Many of these countries are ruled by decree, with legislators serving at the pleasure of the ruler, who usually is either a militarian or civilian dictator. The ruler has a monopoly on the supply of legislation, creates rents by decree, and has significant input into their allocation.'

Even though Mbaku is referring to developing countries in general, the description closely reflects the situation in African countries. Undoubtedly a rent-seeking free society is also not realistic in systems with more favourable checks and balances. On the one hand, it is not entirely possible to stop those who run the government from acting in their own (rent-seeking) interest. On the other hand, government policy is not immune to unbalanced interest group influence from outside the government.

Rents are thus likely to have a place in all political systems, although the extent and type of rent appropriation may vary considerably. To assess their importance, answers to the following three questions are essential: First, what role do rents have within a system to secure stability and keep incumbents in power? Second, to what extent are rents an instrument of exploitation and self-enrichment? And third, what politico-institutional mechanisms facilitate rent-seeking activities of interest groups? All these aspects (power preservation, exploitation and interest group strength) are closely related.

Lal and Myint (1996, p. 260-64) provide a *typology of states* that accounts for many of the questions posed and may thus serve as a starting point. The typology is briefly described in Figure 4-4. Lal and Myint distinguish between autonomous and factional states. The former are much less constrained and therefore more able to pursue objectives of their own, while the behaviour of the latter is an outcome of collective decision-making subject to different constraints and may, in the extreme, simply reflect a pressure group equilibrium. The opportunistic nature of self-interested individuals running the government, on the other hand, reveals itself in its most extreme form in the predatory type of states. As Lal and Myint (1996, p. 261) argue, in these governments citizens' welfare 'may at best be only a very minor direct component of the state's objective function' and choices between social objectives are likely to be erratic.

Figure 4-4: Typology of States According to Lal and Myint

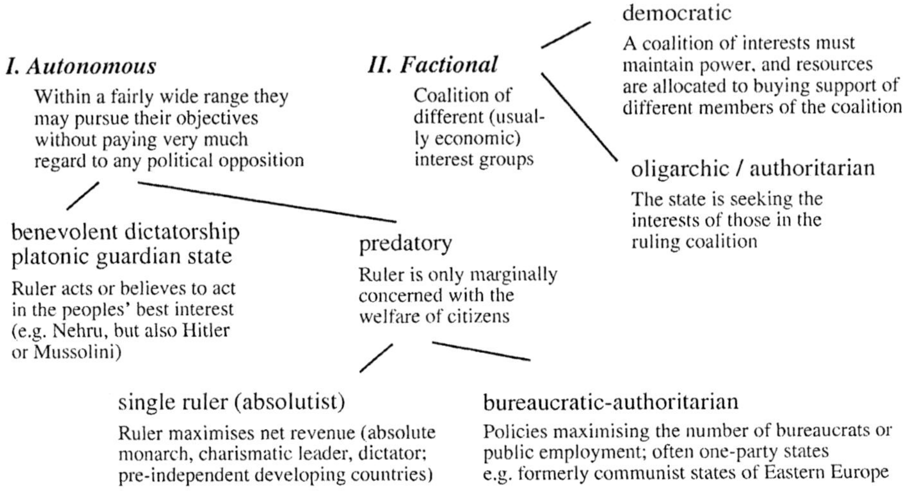

Source: Summarised from Lal and Myint (1996, p. 260-64), and Krueger (1993, pp. 59-66) who herself refers to a World Bank Comparative Study of Lal and Myint from 1990

Depending on the focus other authors have developed alternative typologies. Findlay (1990, p. 199f), for instance, differentiates between traditional monarchies, traditional dictatorships, right-wing authoritarian states, left-wing authoritarian states and democratic states. Or Chazan, et al. (1988, p. 133f) provide a classification of African states, grouping the countries into administrative-hegemonial, pluralist, party-mobilising, party-centralist, personal-coercive, populist and ambiguous regimes.

In the following sections the different subjects presented here are addressed in more detail. Besides the general assessment of rents within political systems, the discussion will mainly focus on African countries. Section b) describes the role of rents as a means to stay in power, addressing the possible alternatives of legitimacy and repression; Section c) analyses rents in the context of a government's own consumption. Neo-patrimonialism and decolonialisation provide some insights into predatory behaviour. The discussion will also briefly recall different modes of rent extraction, among others making reference to systemic corruption, which is a characteristic system component in predatory states. Having shown the different stakes of rents in political systems, in Section d) the matter is summarised in a brief discussion of formal approaches that model rents in a politico-economic framework. Section e) finally draws conclusions.

b) Government's Struggle to Stay in Power

> *'Stability observed in many developing countries is a result of a rent-seeking equilibrium between well organised interest groups...'*
>
> *Kimenyi and Mbaku (1993, p. 385)*

It has been emphasised several times that stability is an important aspect of an institutional environment that supports profit-seeking activities. However, assuming that profit-seeking requires stability, the above quote from Kimenyi and Mbaku may even suggest an incompatibility, i.e. in many developing countries there is no stability without successful rent-seeking.[82] Obviously, in order to understand or even solve this catch-22 situation it is necessary to look at the different alternatives a government has to stay in power.

In the politico-economic literature it is widely recognised that a government's ability to stay in power rests on three basic building blocks: legitimacy, the supply of rents (carrots), and repression and violence (sticks).[83] Depending on the setting and magnitudes, a single instrument may or may not be sufficient to secure the government's hold on power. Consequently, to understand the function of rents as a 'carrot' (or to address the catch-22 problem cited) it is also important to assess the two alternative instruments. The three instruments are discussed below. Often closely related, they provide a number of insights helpful to understanding and addressing rent-seeking supply.

Legitimacy: A Conflict Between Traditions, Charisma and Modern Values?

Max Weber's well-known distinction between traditional, charismatic and legal legitimacy is a practical tool when it comes to analysing African states. Over the years most African governments' hold on power has depended, directly or indirectly, on one or another of these forms of legitimacy. These forms overlap and coexist, but they also sometimes sequentially replace one another.

Appointing a country's ruler *by tradition* (as in kingship, where the ruler comes from a certain clan or tribe) has lost significance over the years. This form of traditional legitimacy however has not disappeared entirely; in some situations it has simply shifted from a direct nomination of the ruler to a more indirect influence taking the form of a strong interest group influence. Such two-tiered settings may imply considerable rent transfers. Especially where modern democratic forms of legitimacy have remained weak (addressed below), the ruling coalition may still depend heavily on traditional sources of legitimisation. Not having come to power by heritage or other forms of cultural enactment, such rulers have to gain support from former traditional rulers through rent-transferring interest group policies.

---

82 Recall also the reference to stability in Chapter 3.3 on page 138.

83 For methodological reasons, the first two are separate, although supplying rents is a way of buying legitimacy.

Another indirect form of the relation of traditional legitimacy to rents involves autonomous areas. There are still many partly autonomous areas in African countries based on historical patterns of legitimacy (remnants of previous kingdoms or autonomous areas with a dominant tribe or clan). This autonomy may make the central government's policies more difficult, especially when it comes to addressing rents. In Tanzania for instance, the government in Zanzibar which is fairly independent from the mainland Tanganyika, has considerably thwarted the central government's attempts to reduce smuggling. Long after economic reforms commenced in 1986, the 'Zanzibar route' remained an impressive rent-capturing device, undermining Tanzania's ability to balance its budget (this will be treated in more detail in Section b) of Chapter 7.1).

The second way to gain legitimacy is through *charismatic leadership*. In Africa, as Chazan, et al. (1988, p. 157) note, especially socialist leaders belonging to the first generation after independence have been of the charismatic sort (e.g. Kwame Kkrumah, Julius Nyerere, Sekou Touré, Houari Boumediennne and Ahmed Ben Bella). They further observe that in Africa charismatic leadership has been tied to a commitment to implement ideological concepts. The most characteristic feature of 'charismatic' legitimisation, however, is its very strong emphasis on the ruler's personality:

> 'With the exception of Nyerere, who subordinated personal ambitions ... to the political vision he sought to bring about, charismatic leaders nurtured an image of themselves as the embodiment of the nation, the state, power, and the future.' (Chazan, et al. (1988, p. 157))

Charismatic rulers are generally very powerful. Even though such a ruler is likely to use some force to strengthen his position, he does not usually depend on distributing rents further to enhance his legitimacy. With a non-charismatic successor however the situation may dramatically change and supplying rents may become very important.

The third Weberian type of legitimacy refers to that which characterises all modern economies: a *democratic legitimation* of the state. Although it has been formally implemented in many African countries, this type of legitimisation still has a very weak standing there. In many African countries, elections still play a minor role, they are often rigged and have rarely been a mechanism for replacing leaders or regimes. More commonly, as political scientists have argued, they are of symbolic value: internally to demonstrate clientelistic relations, externally to ensure that the state is recognised by other countries.

The smaller legitimating effect of elections is partly understandable when one considers that the process of democratisation in Africa has been fairly weak and limited. Young democracies are not only characterised by authoritarian political enclaves; in addition, democratically organised institutions contrast with authoritarian entities of civil society such as family, religious groups, enterprises and unions (Lauth (1998, p. 31f)). The neglect of democratic elements under colonialism combined with hasty democratisation afterwards largely accounts for this situation. Mbaku (1992, p. 251f), citing Fatton (1990, p. 457) summarises this as follows:

> 'Most European colonial institutional frameworks were primarily "structures of exploitation, despotism, and degradation"... Shortly after World War II, when it became clear that many of their colonies would soon be granted independence, the European countries hurriedly put into effect a program of democratisation... Many of the new constitutions designed for the emerging states were not structured to reflect domestic realities, needs, customs, or political and economic aspirations. As a result, the instruments were never able to acquire legitimacy...
>
> Shortly after independence, many of the parliamentary models left by the Europeans collapsed and from them emerged different forms of military and civilian dictatorships.'

This reference to the colonial and postcolonial area not only helps explain the lack of democratic legitimisation (which might then be responsible for the government's supply of rents to buy legitimacy), it also explains rents as a result of copying the leadership style of the colonial rule. Section c), which addresses governments' predatory consumption, will examine the second aspect.

The preceding comments on democratic legitimisation as a substitute for rents, however, require an important qualification. Political scientists have long noted that votes and elections may also activate the supply of rents. The literature on election cycles focuses on the latter aspect in particular. It can be expected that, ceteris paribus, the weaker a government, the more likely its re-election will depend on rents. The issue of election cycles appears to be particularly relevant in African countries. Block (2002, p. 206) for instance notes:

> 'In contrast to other developed and developing regions, Africa's nascent democracies often have weaker institutions, impose fewer restrictions on government actions and accountability, and rarely have independent central banks (at least among the non-CFA countries). This latter institutional distinction makes Africa uniquely relevant to the study of political business cycles...'

Besides the three Weberian forms of legitimacy—traditional, charismatic and legal—another way to examine legitimacy is to distinguish between the government's (the ruler's) *nomination or seizure of power* and the government's *service delivery*. The former refers to acquiring legitimacy by tradition. Charismatic leadership, by contrast, is more closely related with the latter. Legitimacy by democratic procedures falls somewhere in between, depending on the length of the re-election cycle.

The better a government can positively influence the economic situation of the population, the stronger will be its standing. Its reputation however will not only depend on positive growth, sound policies and macroeconomic stability; equally important is the extent to which the economic situation is attributed to the ruling coalition, as for instance argued in Frey and Eichenberger (1994, p.

179f). They emphasise that a government will be less accountable for a worsening situation if it can successfully blame a former government or foreign forces (boycotts, changes in oil prices and terms of trade), if expectations of the population have been low or if affected interest groups relate the crisis to their own behaviour and bad luck.

Ideology strongly influences perception of the ruler's capabilities. Afro-Marxism for instance has—in the words of Chazan, et al. (1988, p. 153)—'uniformly attribute[d] the maladies of the African experience to the lingering effects of imperialism and the ongoing perniciousness of neocolonial influences both within and outside Africa'. Especially in totalitarian regimes, ideology has been a decisive factor. Although ideology may strengthen the position of a ruler and thereby reduce rent requirements, its net effect on rent transfers will also largely depend on the ideology's content and interpretation.

As emphasised in Chapter 2, defining rents is to some extent a matter of defining property rights, especially as all societies reallocate income and pursue a specific development strategy. From the perspective of a liberal-minded free-market economy, some ideologically-motivated transfers may therefore be regarded as rents. More common howcvcr is the misuse of ideology as a pretext for rent appropriation, which happened in both African-socialist as well as Soviet-type economies (e.g. Winiecki (1991, p. 6f)). In general, ideology will increase or lower the political weight of different interest groups and thereby influence their rent-seeking prospects.

This brief account of legitimacy has pointed to several ways that legitimacy may influence the supply of rents of a government or a single ruler. Especially in African countries, legitimacy building is multi-layered and thus complex. Modern forms have only partly replaced traditional forms of legitimation, mostly because democratic values have never been sufficiently supported in society. Economic development in general as well as economic reforms in particular influence or transform opportunities of legitimation. They may even provoke a legitimacy crisis that questions both the abilities of the ruler in power and the legitimising system as a whole. For instance this may be the case when a reform agenda also includes political liberalisation. More frequent however are moderate shifts in legitimation that affect the government's standing and perhaps also its rent-supplying behaviour. The role of rents in strengthening the hold on power will now be addressed in more detail.

Buying Legitimacy: Carrots—Supplement, Bridging Device or Main Cornerstone?

The previous discussion outlined different ways a government may legitimate itself, other than directly supplying rents. Traditional, charismatic and legal legitimacy were raised, as well as the ability to run an economy. Nevertheless it was not possible to refrain from discussing rent aspects, as different forms of legitimisation commonly relate to them. Rents may be important as an indirect vehicle of traditional legitimacy-building; they have their stake in democratic elections and votes, and not infrequently they appear well covered under ideological pretexts. However rents may also have a very direct legitimising function and not relate to other modes of legitimisation. This is typically the case when all other forms are insignificant or simply lacking. In such cases, rents do not just consolidate an already comfortable position (supplement) or function as a bridging instrument to overcome temporary legitimisation problems: they are the cornerstones for building legitimacy.

In general, the better a government can positively influence the economic situation of its 'constituency', the stronger is its standing. Supplying an institutional framework favourable to economic growth and development is an option. But it is more direct, quicker and easier to establish a straight supply of rents to different key interest groups. It is therefore not surprising that political systems that lack other forms of legitimisation often do not allow for an impersonal market mechanism. As emphasised in Pritzl (1997, p. 171f) rulers usually try to personalise and politicise as many activities as possible to be able to claim them as personal achievements. A related aspect is that in many countries only personal and not institutional loyalties exist (Pritzl (1997, p. 170))—an observation that points to the overlap of traditional and modern (democratic) systems of legitimisation mentioned above.

In Africa an important element of political network and stability has been the development of different *patronage ties*. These also reflect the strong emphasis on personal networks. A categorisation is mentioned in Chazan, et al. (1988, p. 172-77), who distinguish between national-local patronage, patronage according to the position in the decision-making apparatus, patronage on the basis of solidarity ties, associational patronage and individual patronage. Primarily *patronage based on solidarity ties*, where the political weight is reversed, but also to some extent *national-local patronage* directly applies rents as an instrument of power maintenance. The other patronage types partly explain rents as a means of government enrichment, which will be addressed in Section c).

Following Chazan, et al. (1988, p. 173f), patronage relations based on solidarity ties are prevalent in countries where cultural forms of social organisation and differentiation are particularly pronounced such as Rwanda, Burundi, Sudan, and South Africa; national-local patronage is found in countries where elections still take place or where parties have survived (Tanzania, Zambia, Algeria, Senegal and Kenya). Public employment especially has been used as an important vehicle of power maintenance (and rent appropriation). Bigsten and Moene (1996, p. 185), for instance, describe this situation in Kenya as follows:

> 'The ruling group in Kenya tries to build and maintain a sufficient power base to remain in office. This is partly done by hiring a large number of civil servants who are dependent on and therefore loyal to the regime. Expanding the public bureaucracy is thus an important part of the coalition-building efforts of the ruling elite in Kenya.'

Even though public employment per se does not qualify as a rent transfer, the rent aspect becomes evident when one considers that public employment has been excessive and highly inefficient in practically all African LDCs and has provided civil servants an important opportunity to appropriate a share of public funds.

Maintaining power also strongly relates to the ability of a government to solve *conflicts*. Depending on the type of conflict the government is confronted with, rents may then act as an important conflict-resolving factor. A careful distinction between different types of conflicts can thus reveal further insights into the role of rents in a political setting and delineate other alternatives such as the use of power and violence.

Chazan, et al. (1988, p. 183f) describe five different types of conflicts.[84] *Elite conflicts* are the most common form because they relate to everyday activities of the political leadership (bureaucratic appointments, policy directions, governmental allocations, etc.). *Factional conflicts* are wider in scope: they refer to disputes over access and control of the government and have been most noticeable in regimes with elaborate patronage networks. They are important in consolidating national identities and norms. Factional conflicts include demands such as access to jobs for supporters, expanded educational opportunities, salary hikes, higher producer prices, as well as funds for local development and improved infrastructure.

Communal conflicts (mostly strong ethnic conflicts) are a more direct threat to the state. In contrast to elite and factional disputes, they question not just the legitimacy of specific regimes but also the state power. They often lead to successional demands and provoke direct military confrontation and civil wars. The fourth type, *mass conflicts*, concerns political movements which aim to induce a rapid, complete and permanent change of the power structure. They are less common in independent Africa (e.g. the Ethiopian revolution of 1974). Finally, *popular conflicts* refer to conflicts from below. They are a quiet rebellion against the authority of the state. The proliferation of the informal economy in particular is an important feature. Popular conflicts emerged in most parts of Africa in the third decade of independence.

Bearing in mind these five types of conflicts, rents are an important instrument of power maintenance when it comes to addressing factional conflicts. Chazan, et al. (1988, p. 189) themselves note that with factional conflicts, 'allocations are the main instrument of conflict management'. Non-violent strategies related to communal conflicts are more diverse and refer to balancing representation, implanting national identities (as successfully conducted in Tanzania), and granting some administrative autonomy. Nevertheless, depending on the specific power constellation, paying off opposition groups with rents can become an important strategy.

Such an approach however is not feasible for mass or popular conflicts. Mass conflicts are usually addressed with long-lasting and intense violence (e.g.

---

[84] The following summary draws from Chazan, et al. (1988, p. 183-203).

against Unita or Renamo). The shift of economic activities to the informal sector in the case of popular conflicts is a direct rent-protecting response to a predatory state. Resolving popular conflicts may require far-reaching economic and political reforms that undermine the government's interests. More commonly observed is thus a muddling-through policy by which the ruling coalition tries to keep this type of conflict at a bearable level. Finally, to complete the discussion, elite conflicts are closely linked with rent allocations. These allocations however refer to the ruling coalition's own rent appropriation strategies (addressed in Section c) and are thus not so much an issue of power maintenance.

So far it has been argued that rents are (in contrast to the general provision of economic development) a direct and comparably easy way to buy legitimacy. Rent transfers are often embedded in patronage ties and may be an important conflict-resolving instrument. But rents do not necessarily have to be transferred explicitly. The supply of rents may also take indirect forms such as not intervening against smugglers or Mafia-like organisations. In Paraguay for instance, Alfredo Stroessner ruled for decades with a coalition of the military, smugglers and drug traffickers (Pritzl (1997, p. 230)).

The question of how important rents finally are and how much they constrain the action of a government rests on a combination of many factors and can only be addressed empirically. In particular weak governments may have no other choice than supplying rents. An example of this type is the electricity pay rate policy in Zanzibar largely motivated by the local government's concern to remain in office. Employees of the State Fuel Corporation and donors described the situation in 1998 as follows (personal communication in Zanzibar, March 1998).

Political Zanzibar consists of the two islands Zanzibar (locally known as Unguja) and Pemba. The electricity supply run by the State Fuel Corporation is in a desperate state and is in fact on the brink of completely breaking down due to lack of maintenance. Especially when it becomes necessary to replace the central unit and the maritime cable that connects Unguja with the mainland of Tanzania, the power failure is likely to last for months as no backup system is available. In spite of this threat and the desperate need for funds, the State Fuel Corporation has adopted a pricing policy that lacks the most basic economic logic and is based entirely on political considerations. Costs of generating power for Pemba are TSh 80 per kWh; the power is however sold for TSh 30. The missing funds are drawn from the gross profits in Unguja, which gets its electricity for TSh 16 by a maritime cable from the mainland (and sells it for TSh 30). This cross-subvention leaves the company with no money for maintenance.

On the political side, the Zanzibar government has been struggling to stay in power for many years. Only with the manipulation of the elections in 1995 did it manage to remain in office. Raising electricity prices in Pemba would obviously seal its fate. The issue is especially sensitive, as the share of household consumption (in contrast to industrial use) is very high in Zanzibar (65%). Any rise in tariffs will thus directly affect household income.

In the example of the State Fuel Corporation rents have been provided to a broader community (although they bypass the very poor, who have no electricity). Considering the already weak standing of the local government, these rents appear to maintain the balance of power. Depending on the political constellation, rents may also have to be supplied to a few or several narrowly-defined interest groups. Such groups may be very powerful and shape government policy considerably. Kimenyi and Mbaku (1993, p. 385) even go so far as to argue, as noted above that 'stability observed in many developing countries is a result of a rent-seeking equilibrium between well organised interest groups'. If this is true, 'carrots' are indeed not just a 'supplement' but a 'cornerstone' of legitimacy-building, and economic reforms, which typically address rents, are bound to be very fragile and difficult to sustain.

Repression and Violence: Protecting Values, Replacing Legitimacy or Simply Avarice?

Africa is known for its warlike internal conflicts. Many reasons account for this, the most frequently mentioned being the lack of social or cultural homogeneity. Another way to look at the problem is to address the institutional side of African states. Bienen (1993, p. 271), for instance, makes a clear-cut statement, arguing that 'violence in Africa is a function of leaders trying to stay in power in systems where institutions are weak'. Seen from this perspective, violence—or rather repression as a more encompassing term—certainly has a legitimacy-replacing function and may directly contribute to a ruler's ability to maintain power. Nevertheless, without further analysis it is not possible to draw conclusions about the rent-supplying behaviour of a government, as repression may not only *replace* but also *facilitate* rent transfers.

Repression usually reduces both political and societal pluralism. The Freedom House indices of political rights and civil liberties introduced in Section a) may serve as a good measure of the degree of repression, even though the index on civil liberties also includes items which do not directly relate to power maintenance but to tradition and ideological concerns (recall the description on page 196f).

Figure 4-5 displays an overview of the development of political rights and civil liberties in sub-Saharan Africa during the last twenty-five years. It indicates for each year the percentage of countries rated between 1 (freest) and 7 (least free). Most striking is the very high percentage of countries rated as 6 or 7 until the end of the 1980s and the sharp decline afterwards. The reduction reflects the democratic 'spring' and is partly a result of rising political conditionality from donors in the 1990s. Even though the situation has greatly improved during the last decade, repression remains a decisive factor in almost 40% of sub-Saharan-countries. The change in the level of political and civil repression is likely to have affected the government's behaviour in creating and supplying rents and should thus be accounted for in a rent-seeking evaluation. However, a case-by-case analysis is necessary as not all repression relates to the supply of rents.

Figure 4-5: The Development of Political Rights and Civil Liberties in Sub-Saharan Africa

Political rights 1976/77-2001/02

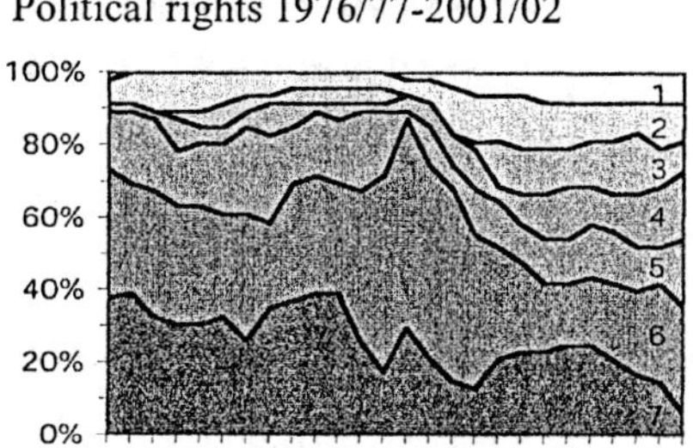

Civil liberties 1976/77-2001/02

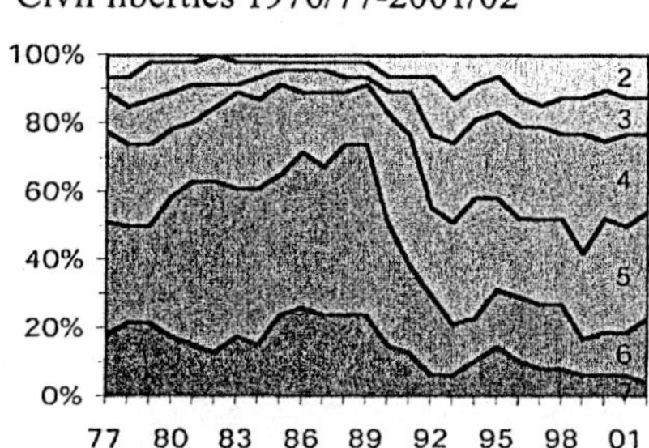

Each shade represents one of the seven Freedom House categories (1 most free, 7 least free) and displays the percentage share of countries assigned to the category. For instance in 1977 approximately 15% (i.e. 89-73%) of the countries were rated as 5 with regard to political rights and 25% (i.e. 77-52%) with regard to civil liberties. Most striking is the development of the combined ratings 6 and 7, which show an upward trend towards the end of the 1980s and a sharp decline thereafter. The sample begins with 45 countries and ends with 48. The new entries are (in parentheses rating of first year): Djibouti 1977/78 (2/2), Namibia 1989/90 (4/3) and Eritrea 1993/94 (6/5).

Source: Figures of country ratings from Freedom House (2002), country classification according to World Development Report (World Bank (1998c))

Repression and violence may be applied for essentially three related reasons: to implement an ideology, to suppress any opposition and/or to appropriate rents. The first aspect, the *implementation of ideological concepts* only relates to the supply of rents inasmuch as the rent is part of the ideology. In contrast to regimes in Latin America that tortured and killed to fight communism or those in the Middle East that repressed their populations in the name of Allah, most sub-Saharan African countries lack such ideological agendas (Bienen (1993, p. 273)). The other two motivations have been much more important.

Repression in pursuit of *power maintenance* aims to prevent other groups from voicing discontent and becoming a threat to the ruling coalition. The problem is less severe if the costs of losing power are not so high. Frey and Eichenberger (1994, p. 177) call this the 'Duvalier-Marcos' effect: 'both did not fight to the end ...because they had the means to live well in another country'. Evidently the situation dramatically changes when rulers, once they lose power, are deprived of their property or fear for their lives.

The most relevant tools of repression are economic repression and violence. Cohen (1993, p. 473), for instance, notes about President Moi that he 'encouraged his supporters in the ministries and parastatals to hamper businessmen...who criticised his administration or declined to pay "rents" ', among other things by refusing to allocate import licences and foreign exchange, denying land transfers or bank loans, failing to extend public financial support to troubled banks, not issuing waivers on customs duties and government taxes, terminating public power, water, and telephone services, not allocating port facility berths or air cargo space, and using tax departments to aggressively investigate opponents (see also Mair (1996, p. 16) on a reference to Cohen).

Sub-Saharan-African leaders who have been associated with large scale violence against opponents are (quoting from Bienen (1993, p. 275)) Amin (Uganda), Banda (Malawi), Bokassa (Central African Republic), Gaffer Nimeiri (Sudan), Macias (Equatorial Guinea), Mengistu (Ethiopia), Mobutu (Zaire), Ngouabi (Congo), Obote (Uganda), Samuel Doe (Liberia) and Sekou Touré (Guinea).

The better the ability of rulers to repress, the less they depend on alternative means of power maintenance such as democratic legitimation or the supply of rents. For an empirical study that investigates the former relationship (repression versus legitimation), see for instance Kimenyi and Mbaku (1995) (their article focuses on developing countries and addresses the negative relation between military expenditure and political democracy). The choice along the second trade-off (repression versus rents) is likely to correlate (as does the first one) with the basic type of state. Totalitarian states are usually characterised as highly repressive states. It is thus not far-fetched to expect that in such systems the supply of rents is less important as a legitimising device than for instance in authoritarian states. This view is also found in Pritzl (1997, p. 166), who contrasts the two systems, arguing that in authoritarian states opposition groups are usually less repressed than paid off with material incentives. But ruling by mere repression has its limits. As Chazan, et al. (1988, p. 211) argue, since military governments are confronted with continuous problems of legitimation (more directly than civilian regimes), they are inherently transitory, if they do not reform themselves (for instance undergoing a process of civilianisation), they will be replaced.

The third aspect directly relates to rents, but with the opposite effect. Ruling elites have often abused their power to *secure massive rent appropriation* for their own consumption, as well as to finance the army. Idi Amin and Sese Seko Mobutu, for instance, used the state as if it were their own private domain. With their repression and violence they managed to secure a large flow of rents into their families' pockets. Kimenyi and Mbaku (1995, p. 2) even argue that in autocratic governments 'political violence usually emerges as the most important rent-seeking behaviour'. Violence then not only spreads from the ruling elite but also, as noted earlier, from oppositional groups who try to get direct access to the rent-creating apparatus by simply taking over the state. The role rents play as an instrument of exploitation and self-enrichment is the subject of the following Section c).

c) Government's Rent Consumption

> *'If you want to steal, steal a little and do so intelligently, in a nice way. If you steal so that you become rich overnight, you'll be caught.'*
>
> *Sese Seko Mobutu, Dictator of Zaire, May 1976.*[85]

Following the discussion of the role of rents in maintaining stability and power, this section addresses in more detail the second question raised in the introduction: To what extent are rents an instrument of self-enrichment of individual politicians? The focus will be on factors that give rise to the most extreme form (predatory type) of state and point to the limits of such behaviour. In contrast to Section b), which emphasised the share of rents interest groups manage to appropriate, this discussion will emphasise rents that remain within the ruling coalition and its entourage.[86]

In general, the amount of rents that are appropriated by the ruling coalition depends on the characteristics of the state. It will be lower in states with a weak control of the economy and those with far-reaching checks and balances. In Lal and Myint's typology (Figure 4-4 on page 200) government rent appropriation is highest in the autonomous-predatory type of state. In its most extreme form, rulers are not concerned with the well-being of the population outside the narrow 'presidential clique' and their families. This behaviour of predatory rulers sharply contrasts with the traditional functions assigned to government. Unfortunately sub-Saharan Africa provides many examples that come close to this pure predatory type.

Bienen (1993, p. 273), for instance, argues that Idi Amin, Jean-Bedel Bokassa and Macias Nguemas 'seemed to have no social or political agenda other than maintaining themselves in power and perhaps bolstering an ethnic group'. Pointing to the lack of 'superior' goals Bienen then even generalises that 'most African despots seem to be aberrant personalities with few social and economic goals other than self-enrichment'.

Mobutu also provides a textbook example of a predatory ruler. His fraudulent attitudes towards public property were already apparent in the 1970s, for instance in the speech to the members of the government and administration quoted above. Mobutu used the treasury as if it was his own purse; he was even known to 'hire a concord to travel from his capital to France for appointments with his dentist' (Jain (1998, p. 2f)). According to Ayittey (1992, p. 233, 252),[87] in 1984 Mobutu even bragged on US national television that he was the second richest man in the world, with more than 8 billion dollars, and throughout his

---

[85] LeVine (1993, p. 277) quoting from Péan (1988): 'Si Vous désirez voler, volez un peu et intelligement, d'une jolie manière. Si vous volez tant que vous deveniez riche en une seule nuit, on vous attrapera...'

[86] Clearly this distinction may not always be clear-cut—whether or not individuals and interest groups belong to this group is to some extent a matter of definition—but the different focus better contributes to an understanding of rent-seeking.

[87] Cited from Rowley (2000, p. 154).

rule 60% of the annual budget of Zaire is estimated to have been diverted into his personal accounts, the accounts of his families and his cronies. Other sources estimate the amount of money appropriated by Mobutu to equal half of the country's external debt (Bjorvatn (1995, p. 149)).

Even though in many African countries self-enrichment has by far not reached such extreme levels, it has been relevant in most African states (and of course, in other countries). The Ghanaian ruler Ignatius Kutu Acheampong or the Nigerian finance minister Omaru Dikko may be cited as other extreme examples who managed to systematically plunder the state (Chazan, et al. (1988, p. 175)). Also Daniel arap Moi shifted billions of dollars into numbered accounts abroad.

What are the reasons for the predatory behaviour of these African rulers? Possible answers may not only shed light on the sources of rent-seeking but also allow policymakers to address the problem in a more fundamental way. At least at independence, the political rights and civil liberties of most African states looked fairly promising and rulers' self-enrichment had not been perceived as a real problem. The subsequent years however reversed most of the hastily established democratic achievements. Findlay (1990, p. 196f), referring to other authors, provides a noteworthy description of this aspect:

> 'The "modern state" evolved in the West during the course of a millennium from feudalism, through the "ständestaat" and the absolutist state to the constitutional state of the nineteenth century, culminating in the universal suffrage and the welfare state today.'
>
> '...Third World states have sadly given the impression, in many cases, of running the film backwards, at an accelerated rate that covers the same distance in less than half a century.'

There are two main concepts that try to explain the origins of predatory behaviour, which go beyond a simple reference to weak institutions. The first emphasises the different values in developing countries, referring to disconnection and neo-patrimonialism, while the second approach identifies mistakes of colonisation as the main evil. The two lines of reasoning need not be mutually exclusive. They provide examples of frictions between formal and informal institutions, as explained in Section c) of Chapter 4.1.

Neo-Patrimonialism and Colonial Rule: An Excuse for Predatory Behaviour?

Following Gaillard and Rüegg (1987, p. 15, who refer to other authors), *neo-patrimonialism* is the product of the historical contact of the patrimonial system with modern bureaucracy: Behind the state façade, resources are distributed according to ancient patterns of thought and behaviour. The neo-patrimonial concept may be best described as follows:

> 'A patrimonial ruler of the pure type would give gifts to his followers and kinsmen to cement their loyalty..., these gifts coming out of his own personal resources, since such a system would lack any distinction

between the private and public purse. A modern Third World leader, however, who wanted to perform essentially the same activity of rewarding followers and kinsmen would do so typically by assigning them jobs or import licenses or contracts…' (Findlay (1990, p. 198))

Neo-patrimonialism can be regarded as a common feature in the culture of developing-country politics which originates from a disconnection in development between civil society and state institutions. Neo-patrimonialism clearly applies to African countries and many others as well.

Chazan, et al. (1988, p. 172-77) summarise five political modes of patronage organised along several quite distinct lines. As already outlined in Section b), rents are used as an instrument to maintain power whereas patronage is based on *solidarity ties* (resources are provided in return for support, and the political weight is reversed), and to a lesser extent with *national-local patronage* (prevalent in countries with elections or surviving parties). In contrast, with individual patronage, patronage according to the position in the decision-making apparatus and associational patronage, rents are basically created for the ruling elites' own consumption.

According to the description in Chazan, et al. (1988, p. 172f) *individual patronage* is a highly personal form where people align themselves with personal strongmen or warlords who are capable of providing security. It applies to situations where formal and encompassing clientelistic networks have broken down such as in Chad and Uganda in the 1960s and 1970s. *Patronage according to the position in the decision-making apparatus* strongly resembles national-local patronage. It is however more administrative and centrally controlled than its electorally-rooted counterpart. There is an entire series of patrons and clients along the length of the administrative ladder. Lastly, *associational patronage*, more haphazard than the bureaucratic type described above, is mostly found in populist regimes, which officially denounce patronage but allow such relations to survive in other forms. Popular organisations are usually a key vehicle for the disbursement of benefits, as is membership in government-approved worker or village cooperatives.

Even though this analysis provides some insights into the sources of the rent-seeking problem, the value of direct policy recommendations derived from this analysis is limited since the government itself will try to prevent any effective reforms. In cases of individual patronage a change in leadership is obviously indispensable. Democratisation, as another measure, is most helpful in countries where patronage relations are not electorally rooted. Thorough reforms of the civil service, which introduce accountability and transparency, are important in any setting; however the chances that the reforms will be effectively implemented and sustained vary and depend on the specific situation, and to some extent on the policies of the donors. The chances may for instance be higher in some settings of associational patronage. In a situation where patronage is associated with a position in the decision-making apparatus, high commitment and uncompromising endurance is necessary from the top leadership.

The second concept that tries to explain the origins of predatory behaviour draws on *colonialism*, comprising three aspects: colonial behaviour and leadership style, hasty democratisation, and the colonial institutions inherited by the new governments. Szeftel (1998, p. 236) argues that the colonial way of accumulating capital produced underdevelopment, deprivation and racial exclusion, making 'power and access to the state's resources the primary focus of material expectations'. The continuation of policy on these foundations, which also implies copying the behaviour and leadership style of the colonial rulers, would then provide an explanation for the predatory behaviour to be found in many LDCs. Referring to Sierra Leone, where a colonial export economy, patronage structures of electoral mobilisation and a powerful central authority coincide, Szeftel (1998, p. 237) describes the problem succinctly:

> 'In such circumstances, access is everything and its absence means exclusion from the resources provided by office. Politics becomes a winner-takes-all game in which power allows private appropriation of state resources...The process becomes self-defeating, increasing social divisions and corruption and finally culminating in "a crisis of clientelism" (Allen, 1995:305). The result is increasing authoritarianism as leaders cling to power.'

Allen (1995) even makes a connection between weak democratisation and the preferential treatment of specific ethnic groups, arguing that 'hastily organized elections encouraged the development of support through ethnic and regional networks'(Szeftel (1998, p. 236)). This statement points to the problem that a rash implementation of democratic rules may be difficult to sustain, and under certain conditions may even enhance the problem of ethnic conflicts and encourage rent-transferring policies.

Finally, not only the leadership style but a closely related factor noted above is that many of the institutions transferred to African hands encouraged the predatory behaviour of the rulers in power. Chazan, et al. (1988, p. 41), for instance, describe these institutions as 'bureaucratically designed, authoritarian in nature, and primarily concerned with issues of domination rather than legitimacy'. Besides administrative units, many monopolies (especially export marketing boards) are a legacy of the colonial period.

Here too, it is not possible to derive direct recommendations that can change the behaviour of predatory rulers. It is obviously irrelevant whether or not the ruler's behaviour can be explained by reference to the adaptation of colonialist policy, a lack of democratisation or by institutions inherited from the colonial period. In any case, predatory rulers are unlikely to give up their rents. What is needed are radical or long-term approaches based on the promotion and strengthening of democratic values and a change in power. Particularly difficult is the situation where neo-patrimonial motivation also predominates. If the argument holds, a cultural conflict is irrefutable and the problem has a strong ethnological dimension. The most important strategy is to try to make the costs of their behaviour more transparent.

All in all, it may be impossible, at least in the short- and mid-term, to control rent-seeking. Both arguments, namely neo-patrimonialism and colonial rule, provide insights into predatory rent-seeking behaviour but no clear solutions to address the problem. At most they indicate that the issue is not just a matter of getting institutions right, basically because policy recommendations cannot be implemented. Depending on the context, more encompassing approaches have to be addressed and donors have to be particularly careful in the type of support they provide. As emphasised in Chapter 3.3, where rent-seeking cannot be eliminated a second-best solution must be sought. Donor support, for instance, could be confined to providing ideas only. Some efforts may also be directed to limiting the detrimental impact of rent-seeking, essentially by shifting it to areas where the social costs are lowest.

What Characterises Modes and Limits of Rent Extraction?

As outlined in detail in Chapter 2.2, once in control of the state apparatus the possibilities to extract rents from an economy are numerous and diverse. Countries may be grouped according to the relative emphasis rent-seekers assign to two modes of rent extraction: rent extraction through the *public sector* (mainly parastatals, state bureaucracy and the army) or rent extraction in the well-protected *private* economy. For instance, in East Africa the state bourgeoisie of Tanzania and Mozambique is 'based rather narrowly on the state machine itself', while the state bourgeoisie in Kenya and Malawi 'used their positions in the state to accumulate in formally "private" spheres' (Gibbon (1992, p. 165)). Bigsten and Moene (1996, p. 182) point to the large private stakes in agriculture and urban activities that Kenya's top politicians (and associated groups within the bureaucracy) hold. This is basically a result of their insider positions and a strategy of forcing the government to buy from their businesses.

Extracting rents in public spheres has been widespread in developing countries. This is also true in many countries that allowed large private sectors. Parastatals offer a variety of opportunities to strengthen the ruler's position and to create and appropriate rents. Parastatal output as well as well-paid managerial positions can be allocated according to political considerations, nepotism and motives of self-enrichment. In particular in predatory-type states employment, promotion and increases in salary hardly depend on qualifications and work performance but on the loyalty to higher officials and top leaders. The room for manoeuvre in making decisions on the flow of support given to parastatals strengthens the standing of top leaders. Moreover monitoring parastatals becomes an extra avenue of rent extraction.

A strategic position in a public enterprise, but also a position in higher rankings of state bureaucracy, can turn out to be ideal for family members and friends. On-the-job leisure, embezzlement, theft, delegation of workers to do private jobs and so on, are not a threat to state enterprises as long as soft budget constraints and monopoly power hold, nor need they threaten the position of the bureaucrat inasmuch as backing from higher levels is assured. As noted earlier, blackmail and bribery offer particular lucrative sources of income.

Under these conditions, it is not surprising to find individuals bribing a multiple of the official annual wage for a specific position they are trying to get. Pritzl (1997, p. 98), referring to Klitgaard (1991), for instance, mentions that US$75,000 had been paid for a job with an annual wage of US$10,000 (Philippines, mid-1970s, for a job in the Bureau of Internal Revenue). In many instances, these jobs are also allocated according to other considerations (nepotism and patronage in general).

Modes of rent appropriation in *private spheres* are also numerous and diverse, and opportunities may increase if a government privatises its public companies. There is a multitude of specific favours that can be granted to private companies. Parliamentarians, ministers and other public office holders may even establish own banks and other financial institutions to personally appropriate rents. Bigsten and Moene (1996, p. 191f) describe this type of activity for Kenya:

> 'A minister with one of the 255 parastatals under his control is for instance allowed to set up a bank or financial institution and order the parastatal to deposit its money there. The bank can then lend money to the minister, his firms or his associates who later default on the loans while the insolvent bank is bailed out by the government.'

Another procedure is to set up charitable foundations and other NGO-like bodies to which large amounts of public money are 'donated'. Pritzl (1997, p. 192) cites a striking example from Pinheiro (1994), who reports that the Brazilian government decided, after large-scale embezzlement had been discovered in 1994, to exclude 3200 non-profit foundations from future public money!

The more a government is of a predatory type, the more legal and illegal modes of rent extraction are of a *systemic nature,* reaching a high level of institutionalisation. Rent extraction becomes a crucial and deliberate element of the government apparatus. In particular the literature on corruption has described the phenomenon of 'systemic corruption' in detail—a situation where corruption is not primarily a principal-agent problem between state officials and top leaders, but a calculated measure of the ruler to benefit (and control) its supporters. As frequently emphasised, in contrast to other means of rent transfers corruption has the advantage of strengthening the dependency of corrupt officials on those at higher levels, as leaders may initiate legal proceedings against their subordinates any time they wish (e.g. Rose-Ackermann (1998, p. 520)).

The most extreme and blatant example of a blessing from the top is probably Mobutu's much-quoted speech to the members of the Zairian government and administration cited at the beginning of this section. With institutionalised corruption, rents under public official control will be high and cost components of corruption deliberately kept low. This aspect has been addressed in Chapter 4.1 (recall the parameters on corruption, displayed in Table 4-1 on page 153). As emphasised there, the lower the probability of failure and the lower punishment, transaction costs and opportunity costs and the higher the benefits of corrupt activities, the more frequently will the inequalities hold and the more corruption will spread in an economy.

Table 4-5 outlines the different components related to the costs of failure. The probability that a corrupt deal will be discovered declines with the prevalence of corruption in the country. A lack of transparency in the judicial system, the ease with which legal proceedings can be delayed, impeded or dropped, the appointment of corrupt lawyers by rulers and the absence of punishment and confiscation of assets upon conviction are only a few characteristics of settings where corruption is systemic. Taken together, these make the potential costs of failure approach zero.

Table 4-5: Costs of Failure from Corruption

=	*Probability of being discovered*	•	**Cost of being discovered**					
+	"	•	*Probability of investigation*	•	**Cost of being investigated**			
+	"	•	"	•	*Probability of being sentenced*	•	**Cost of being sentenced**	
+	"	•	"	•	"	•	*Probability of sentence execution*	• **Cost of punishment**

Probabilities of failure indicate the likelihood of action once the previous level has been reached. Terms used are based on broad definitions, and actions do not necessarily comprise formal procedures (e.g. imprisonment without a legal sentence would imply an informal conviction).

Source: According to descriptions in Pritzl (1997, p. 134f) but with minor adjustments (slightly different notations for probabilities and related interpretation; correction for apparent misprint: the four costs of failure are additive and not multiplicative)

Officials are then expected to be corrupt. Their officially low wages do not need to be adjusted over time, as their side incomes (entirely tax-free) represent a much larger contribution to living expenses. Especially within the parastatal sector, tax and customs administration, ministry of works, land and resource departments, as well as the police, military and justice, corruption will flourish. Mufuruki and Rugemalira (1996), for instance, described the low-cost, high-benefit situation of tax evasion in Tanzania under Mwinyi's presidency as follows:

> 'Another window of opportunity for tax evasion is created by the eagerness of the tax enforcers to co-operate, assist or even offer guidance on how to beat the system, at a fee of course.'
>
> 'The prospect of cheating is made doubly attractive by the high rewards in the event of successful evasion and the low risk of conviction if the cheating bid fails.'

Even though Tanzania to some extent is also a case where the bureaucracy has assumed great power and become a strong interest group detached from ideologues and top leaders, corruption under Mwinyi did not bypass the president's office.

So far it has been emphasised that a predatory government has many possibilities for extracting and mediating rents through the public as well as the private sector. Most of these actions are corrupt; but strategically lowering the costs of corruption makes it a very effective tool of rent appropriation. An important question that arises refers to the *limits* of such behaviour.

The amount of resources that ruling elites and their entourage can extract from an economy depends on economic limits (size and structure of the economy) and related institutional limits (the rent-extracting apparatus), as well as on political limits inside and outside the ruling coalition. Below, these limits will be briefly surveyed in general terms. The subsequent Section d), which focuses on politico-economic models, elaborates the different aspects again in more detail.

Limits may be exogenous to the ruler at any period of time, to some extent, however, they equally reflect intertemporal trade-offs between present and future rent consumption. Depending on the time horizon the ruler focuses on, limiting rent extraction is also in the interest of a predatory ruler and therefore self-imposed.

Drawing on Frey and Eichenberger (1994, p. 181f), the ability of a government to raise resources (*economic limits*) will be higher the more closed an economy is, the more immovable natural resources there are (e.g. oil), the fewer the possibilities to switch to the shadow economy, and the larger the share of the economy controlled by the government. As the authors note, this ability is further enhanced the better developed the system of taxation and the more efficient the tax bureaucracy is.

Limits also depend on the manner of rent extraction, as for instance outlined in Chapter 4.1 with reference to stationary and roving bandits or more generally with the relation between the profitabilities of rent-seeking and profit-seeking. These limits may arise from a constellation where rent-seeking activities exceed the revenue-maximising level. Extreme rent extraction typically destroys the economic basis and leads to a growing informal sector. Especially in sub-Saharan Africa the informal sector has accounted for a large amount of economic activity.

Finally, donors can enhance the ability to appropriate resources, either directly, if funds from donors are embezzled, or indirectly, as projects from donors strengthen a corrupt government administration, i.e. by increasing its power to extract rents from the economy.

Political limits of rent extraction, as noted in Section b), are a function of the legitimacy of the ruling coalition (which is shaped by the country's ideology), as well as of the possibilities for repressing opponents (people from whom rents are extracted, but also challengers who attempt to take control of the state). Findlay (1990, p. 199) describes the relation as follows:

> 'The more successful the neo-patrimonial state is in its predatory exactions on society, however, the less the "legitimacy" of the regime in the eyes of the people, since the more blatant will be the violation of the

> publicly proclaimed rational-legal norms. The response to this is typically political repression of varying degrees of severity, depending upon the magnitude of the perceived threat. Also, the more valuable the "prize" of the control of the state, the more intense will be the pressure of rival claimants, and the regime will have to face the problem of how wide or narrow to make the coalition that enjoys the benefits of rule.'

Examples where the gap between the standard of living of the rulers and the population has gone beyond 'acceptable' limits and has provoked popular resentment are for instance Nigeria, Zaire and Gabon (Chazan, et al. (1988, p. 176)). A critical problem is certainly the high dependence on rent extraction by 'illegal' means, i.e. corruption. Lafay and Lecaillon (1993, p. 29) note that accusing the regime of corruption has been a favourite propaganda weapon of opposition groups in developing countries, and they conclude, 'corruption is certainly the form of rent-seeking that leads to the greatest political destabilization'. The following quote from Kimenyi supports this view:

> 'Between 1958 and 1984, there were 56 successful military coups in sub-Saharan African countries, 65 attempted coups, and 109 reported plots (McGowan and Johnson, 1984). In most of the successful coups, the new leaders almost have always claimed that the former leader was removed because of corruption and tribalism.' (Kimenyi (1989, p. 343))

Furthermore, as noted earlier, how rent appropriation affects the legitimacy of a government is also a function of the prevalent ideology and the government's development strategy. In an interventionist-socialistic setting it is easier to hide the appropriation of rents than in a more liberal economy.

Finally, under specific conditions the opportunity for rent extraction itself may cause instability and thereby limit rent extraction by a member of the ruling elite to a short period. According to Chazan, et al. (1988, p. 184), 'conflicts within the political centre are the most common form of political strife in Africa'. The scope of stable rent extraction will thus also depend on the ability of the regime to handle these problems. Chazan, et al. (1988, p. 185) mention Jomo Kenyatta and Felix Houphouët (Cote d'Ivoire) as very successful leaders in this regard: Using a mixture of cooptation and repression they proved to be masters in managing elite discontent.

The crucial point is that patronage systems do not need to be stable. As Chazan, et al. (1988, p. 177) emphasise and conclude, although they help to engender political support (and therefore establish a rent-seeking equilibrium) they also increase competition within the elite: 'It appears as if with clientelism no stability, without it no support'.[88]

Since the behaviour of the ruler depends on the different types of limits and limits may also relate to one another, politico-economic models are particularly

---

[88] This statement does not necessarily contradict the contention cited in the introduction to Section b) that the stability observed in many developing countries is a result of a rent-seeking equilibrium. It brings in another dimension, basically that rent-bearing positions may fluctuate rather frequently and therefore equally explain why many office holders behave like roving bandits.

appealing in examining the relevance and interaction of different constraints. Section d), which summarises the role of rents in a political system from a formal perspective, will therefore describe economic and political constraints on rent extraction in more detail.

d) Approaches to Model Rents in a Politico-Economic Framework

Chapter 3 surveyed a large number of rent-seeking models, but only marginally addressed political systems and the supply of rents. In particular factors that explain the preferences and constraints of rent-setters and the activities of interest groups have not yet been examined. Chapter 4 aimed to close this gap. This section describes some simple politico-economic models. There are no unexpected results; some of the models are trivial and most do not include all aspects important for describing a real political and economic situation in a specific country, as the real world is obviously much more complex. Nevertheless they can be helpful in clarifying the consequences of specific preferences (incorporated in the ruler's maximising functions) and the interaction of different political and economic constraints. Models that describe how rents are created and distributed within a more or less elaborated politico-economic framework may also be combined with features of rent-seeking models outlined in Chapter 3.[89]

The questions of what determines government policies has been extensively addressed by *public choice* theorists. Lal and Myint (1996, p. 11f) classify their approaches into five areas. The first addresses voting behaviour in different institutional settings and provides insights into the outcome of competitive elections (such as the median voter theorem). The second area also explains policy as the outcome of preferences of political parties, however from a dynamic perspective. As Lal and Myint state, it focuses on how governments time their policies (such as decisions on spending and taxation) with an eye on the election date—an aspect which has become known as the political business cycle. The third area combines competing pressure-group models and reflects the most direct elaboration of rent-seeking. It covers models that describe the success of interest groups, rent-seeking models which are concerned with the resource costs of lobbying activities (outlined in Chapter 3.2), and pressure group models that endogenously determine policy variables such as tariffs and subsidies. The fourth area addresses the behaviour of bureaucrats, and the fifth refers to the theory of constitutions.

The following discussion will consider several aspects of the issues outlined above. The first part focuses on the basic structure of the government's maximising function, while the second part elaborates on the government's constraints.

---

[89] Like the discussion in Chapter 3, the description of models in this section will be brief and only outline the general structure. For more information the reader is referred to the literature cited.

Defining the Government's Maximising Behaviour in Democratic and Autocratic Settings

At the heart of any politico-economic model is a maximising function, which indicates the self-interest of the ruler or ruling coalition in power (in contrast to the pure benevolent behaviour subsumed in traditional welfare economics). Preferably the function incorporates the two aspects of staying in power and rent consumption. The former not only relates the maximising task to future rents but also allows additional negative consequences to be introduced if power is lost. The model is then 'kept together' by some type of economic or political constraints. Economic constraints usually refer to limits in taxing the economy, political constraints to the negative link between rent extraction and maintaining power. A decisive characteristic in politico-economic models which demarcates democratic from autocratic settings is how the model specifies the way the ruler appropriates rents.

Figure 4-6 depicts a maximising function in a very general form. It may serve as a starting point to model the behaviour of state leaders within different type of governments, from democratically elected parliamentarians to self-centred predatory rulers. *Y* (salary) and αR (net rent income) indicate the benefits from being in office, while possible losses from transferring rents are given by $1-\alpha$ ($0 \leq \alpha \leq 1$). Being out of office leaves the ruler or ruling coalition with an income (or wealth) of *V*. The probability of remaining in office is represented with the function $\beta(w)$.

Figure 4-6: A General Maximising Function

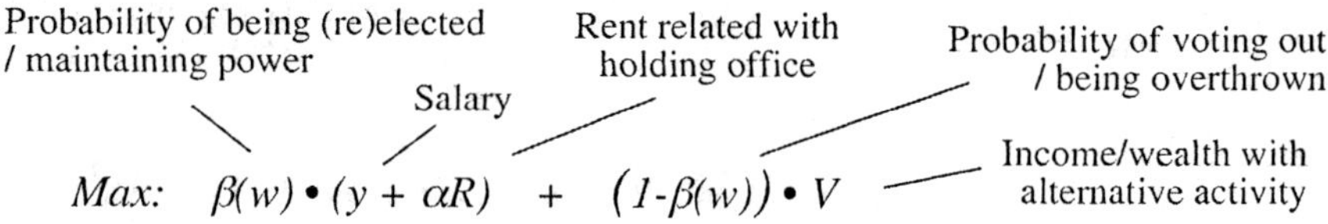

Source: Formal utility function according to Applebaum and Katz (1987, p. 689)

The function is originally taken from Applebaum and Katz (1987) who developed an endogenous rent-seeking model within a democratic framework. In the following, their model will be briefly outlined and compared with specifications necessary to capture the behaviour of an autocratic predatory state.

To fully understand the government's maximising behaviour, it is equally relevant to elaborate the interaction of different constraints. Besides the above *regulator's* maximising function, Applebaum and Katz specify two other groups in their model: rent-seeking *firms* who lobby and compete for regulations that provide them with a rent *S* and *consumers* who bear the cost of this regulation. The mechanism that holds the model together works as follows: Lobbying activities of firms benefit the ruler. These benefits *(αR)* are higher the larger the rent S created by the regulation is (firms increase their rent-seeking investments R with larger S). However, the regulation negatively affects consumers (as they bear the costs). As the largest voting block, they may threaten the position of the regulator by reducing their political support. The ruler thus has a trade-off between own rent consumption αR and political support to remain in office (represented by $\beta(w)$). Formally, Applebaum and Katz specified the firm i's profit-maximising function (there are n firms) using the standard Tullock approach outlined in Chapter 3.1:

$$\text{Max } [\pi_i \equiv P_i(S - x_i) + (1 - P_i)(-x_i)], \text{ whereas } P_i = \frac{\alpha x_i}{other + \alpha x_i}.$$

The firm i's probability of success from lobbying *(P_i)* depends positively on its own rent-seeking investments x_i and is negatively correlated with the investment of all other competing firms *('other'* $= (n-1)\alpha\bar{x}$*)*. The amount of rents captured by the regulator *(αR)* and the change in welfare of consumer *(w)* are given by

$$\alpha R = \sum_{i=1}^{n} \alpha x_i \quad \text{and} \quad w = -S .$$

The change in welfare of consumer directly affects the probability of the regulator to remain in office $\beta(w)$. As can be easily derived from the model, the smaller y is, the larger V is and the less sensitively β reacts to changes in w (for instance as a result of limited rationality), the more rents and rent-seeking will spread. The regulator further profits from a low 'leakage' *($1-\alpha$)* and—according to the Tullock rent-seeking specification—from a high number of firms n (recall total rent-seeking investment shown in Table 3-1 on page 67).

Obviously, the model presented here is a simple construction and the results with regard to y, V, β *and* α are not spectacular, but they nevertheless indicate possible interactions of the parameters. Depending on the questions and the setting in focus the model can be further refined and extended to include additional parameters specified in this and earlier chapters. Applebaum and Katz, for instance, also differentiate between a short and long run (in the long run, firms are free to exit and enter). They also discuss the case where firms form a coalition to confront the regulator and thereby reduce rent-seeking outlays.

Another extension of the Applebaum-Katz-Model would be a more detailed specification of β that allows for different interest groups and the possible legitimacy-buying role of rents. This is the approach of Wise and Sandler (1994), who provide an application of the Applebaum and Katz model for investigating pesticide legislation in the United States. A model may also include more complex and dynamic features such as the impact of political business cycles on the ruler's rent-seeking behaviour. Rent-seeking variations over time would depend on the extent of the short-sightedness of voters and the role of rents (the share of rents for own consumption versus rents as a mean to buy legitimacy). Or the model may explicitly take into account aspects like limited rationality, incomplete information and ideology.[90]

So far the examples have referred to democratic settings. The maximising function depicted in Figure 4-6 may also be applied to an *autocratic framework*, however with different specifications for *R*, *β(w) and V.*

First of all, strategies to appropriate rents (R) are likely to differ. Being less constrained, the ruling coalition, including privileged subordinates, will not just benefit from transfers that are 'offered' by interest groups in exchange for policy favours. They will also directly appropriate rents from the state budget (through embezzlement of funds in the administration and public enterprises). The maximum of resources a state can directly extract from an economy may thus become an important constraint and needs to be further defined. Comparing different regimes, the share of income from *R* (and not *y*), is typically higher in authoritarian and totalitarian regimes. This assessment does not imply however that rents are less important in a democratic setting, as the sum of *R* and *S* matters, i.e. the rents appropriated from inside and outside the state apparatus.

Basic models that only elaborate the government's direct rent consumption typically describe rulers as budget maximisers; or they apply a more sophisticated variation thereof which does not focus on the budget output but the surplus (the difference between revenue and costs). Government consumption is then not further specified, but approximated by the budget or the surplus.[91]

The second adjustment of the maximising function refers to the component *β(w)*. In an autocratic setting, the probability to maintain power will not just depend on the voters' welfare (or interest group's welfare in general, as demands are also expressed by other means than votes). It also depends on the ability of the ruling coalition to suppress opponents. Most preferably, *β(w)* is disaggregated into the components legitimacy, carrots (rents) and stick (repression), as discussed in Section b). The level of legitimacy (traditional, charismatic and democratic) will codetermine the amount of net resources the ruling coalition can extract from the economy and use for its own rent consumption, sticks and carrots. The proportion of 'stick' is typically highest in totalitarian regimes.

Finally, the last item of the maximising function *(V)* will not just incorporate alternative employment, but also negative sanctions related to losing power (incarceration, deprivation of property or even loss of life).

Frey and Eichenberger (1994) outline in a non-formal way how the different parameters may interact. Their model includes the specifications discussed above and the trade-off between support *(β)* and own rent consumption *(R)*

90 For a model of investment in the manipulation of voter information in a world of uncertainty see Congleton (1991). Even though his approach does not account for the ruler's rent-seeking behaviour (policy is simply determined by the median voter decision), several elements can be used in the above setting.

91 For a brief description of the Parkinson-Niskanen budget-maximising function and the Migue-Balanger surplus-maximising function see Duncombe, Miner and Ruggiero (1997) or Rowley and Elgin (1988).

within a 'demand and supply of support' framework (see Figure 4-7). The probability of the government staying in power depends on the population's support and opposition. The government's instruments to muster support and control opposition include the three aspects discussed in Section b): economic policy (legitimacy), bribery (carrots) and suppression (stick). Frey and Eichenberger assume that the marginal impact of these instruments is decreasing. The supply curve therefore has a positive slope, indicating increasing marginal costs of generating 'support'. The government's demand for support, on the other hand, is larger the smaller the price is. It reflects the trade-off that resources invested in support cannot be appropriated for own consumption. The intersection of the demand and supply curves indicates the equilibrium level of support and the amount of resources invested therein. As in the democratic setting, the model can be further extended to specify the amount of rents appropriated by the ruler and the rents distributed in the economy.

Figure 4-7: Demand and Supply of Support

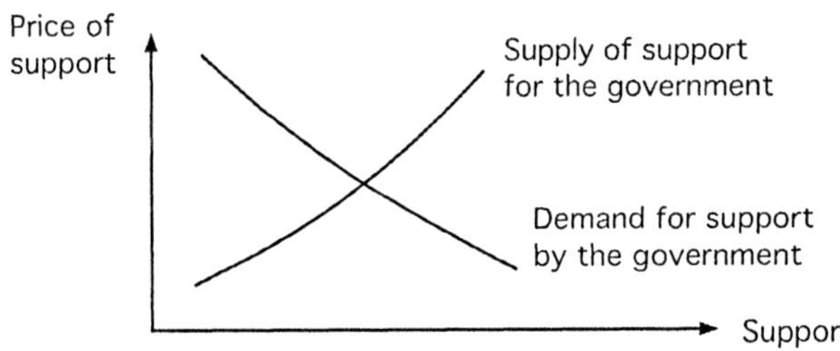

The government's economic policy, bribery and force generate support (in the last case involuntary). Its demand for support typically falls the higher the price for support. The position of the curves depends among other things on the institutional setting in the country.

Source: Drawn according to Figure 2 in Frey and Eichenberger (1994, p. 175)

Frey and Eichenberger (1994, p. 176-78) outline institutional conditions that determine the position of the curves. As they note, a rise in resources that can be extracted from the economy (appropriability), an increase in the costs of losing power or a change in political institutions that lead to more severe competition between the government and opposition will shift the demand curve to the right. The position of the supply curve depends among other things on the government's ability, with given resources, to impose sanctions on the population or improve their economic conditions, and on the extent to which economic conditions are attributed to the government's policy (see also references to Frey and Eichenberger earlier in this chapter).

The authors finally apply their model to a setting where a country needs to undertake unpopular reforms. They discuss factors that determine the appropriability of credits and the attributability of recession (recession which is a result of conditionalities and price reforms). Emphasising the central role of attributability in their model, they conclude that 'objectively equivalent change in economic conditions may thus have a quite different impact on the government's survival chance and therewith on its behaviour' (Frey and Eichenberger (1994, p. 188)).

Alternative Ways of Elaborating Economic and Political Constraints in Predatory Settings

Having discussed the government's maximising function in a democratic and autocratic framework, this section goes on to elaborate on elements that shape and constrain mainly predatory rulers in maximising rent consumption, staying in power or both. In the politico-economic literature there are numerous models which describe the behaviour of a predatory government or the behaviour of a weak government surrounded by powerful predatory-type interest groups. A few models only specify the rent-consumption side, other models focus entirely on power maintenance, and a third group, like the above-mentioned approach of Applebaum and Katz (1987) or the model of Frey and Eichenberger (1994), addresses both aspects.

The following discussion starts with a simple general equilibrium model, which focuses on economic constraints and indicates the predatory ruler's own interest in investing in the economy. Other models are then surveyed which include alternative economic constraints or which build on the first model but likewise specify power maintenance. The survey concludes with a brief outline of further extensions.

Findlay and Wilson (1987) introduced a Leviathan model, which explains the predatory aspect of a state but without neglecting the state's productive side. Later, Findlay (1990) presented an extension to the model, endogenising tax rate and labour supply.[92]

Findlay differentiates between three types of government behaviour: a surplus and a budget (employment) maximising version and a counterfactual type where the ruler maximises social welfare (defined as maximising private sector output). To include the possible productivity-increasing impact of the government on the private sector, the model specifies two sectors, a *private* and a *public sector*. The latter however only serves as an intermediate input to raise productivity in the private sector. As Findlay (1990, p. 201) notes, 'public expenditure on administration, law and order, roads, justice and so on acts as an "externality" to private economic activities, enhancing the private output from private inputs'.

Public expenditures are not only beneficial to the private sector, enlarging the public sector also bears costs. On the one hand, the work force is diverted from the private sector; on the other, public expenditures have to be financed by taxes. The larger these taxes and the more workers are taken away from the private sector, the larger is the negative impact on private output. With a small public sector benefits still outweigh costs. However, as the marginal benefits of

[92] Several authors have treated this model; see, for instance, Eggertsson (1990, p. 319-26), Lal (1988, p. 297-301) or Lal and Myint (1996, p. 264-69). The following description of the model is based on Findlay (1990) (the terms 'Findlay's model' or 'Findlay-Wilson-model' are used interchangeably).

enlarging the public sector decrease and marginal cost rise, there comes a point where the public sector has an optimal size and a further extension then reduces social welfare. Findlay shows that a predatory government that maximises budget (public employment) or surplus (difference of government revenue and expenditures) will not choose the socially optimal level of government size.

Figure 4-8 depicts the results with an exogenous tax rate. Not shown in the figure is the private sector's output, which first rises with an increase in public employment and then, as additional costs outweigh further benefits, falls again. The employment level that maximises private sector output, however, can be easily derived from the state's revenue function. As it represents a fixed portion of the country's output (the tax rate is exogenous), both maximums coincide at the same public employment level.

Figure 4-8: Maximising Output, Surplus or Public Employment with an Exogenous Tax Rate t

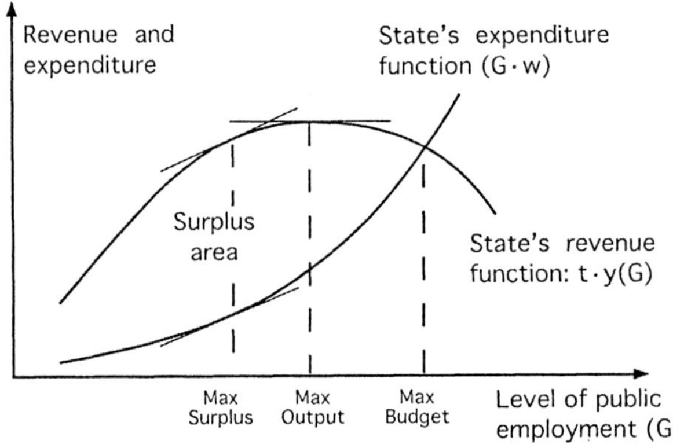

Given the exogenous tax rate t, state revenues are a fixed portion of national income y, which first increases with higher public employment and then falls again. State expenditures include wage costs $(G{\cdot}w)$. The government's decision on the preferred public employment level depends on whether it maximises surplus, national income y or public employment G (not violating the budget constraint).

Source: Drawn according to Figure 1 in Findlay (1990, p. 203)

State expenditures include wage costs. According to the general-equilibrium specification, public wages are determined by the marginal productivity of labour in the private sector. The more labour the government wants to employ, the higher is the wage it has to pay for. Findlay concludes, as shown in the figure, that public employment will be under-supplied in the surplus-maximising case and over-supplied with a budget-maximising ruler. He finally endogenises the tax rate and the country's labour supply (the latter becoming an increasing function of the after-tax wage rate). Each tax rate t would give a different diagram (expenditure and revenue function depicted in Figure 4-8 change). A rational predatory government then chooses the tax rate that contains the largest maximum surplus or the largest maximum public employment.

As Findlay himself notes, the model is constructed in a very simple way. Results with regard to the *surplus-maximising hypothesis* are not spectacular and reflect intuitive expectations. The model demonstrates that even a predatory government will invest in the economy, as it depends on its output. Being concerned with maximising surplus, these investments will be smaller than the social optimum. The model also indicates the maximum rent that can be extracted from the economy.

Not specified in the model are political constraints. Constraints to appropriate rents may be exogenously introduced, fixing the tax rate t below the level which provides the government the largest maximum surplus.[93] Another way to include political constraints is to introduce a minimum public employment level (to the right of the surplus-maximising case). It would reflect an interest group setting where the government position is not strong enough to reduce the level of public employment without a risk of losing power.

The second hypothesis, the *budget-maximising bureaucratic version*, is somewhat strangely formulated in the Findlay-Wilson model. Part of the confusion is due to Findlay's description of the maximising task treating public employment the same as public expenditure or budget (see Findlay (1990, p. 204, 205, 207)). Looking at Figure 4-8, evidently budget is not maximised where state expenditure and revenue meet (as Findlay puts it, focusing on employment), but simply at the peak of the state's revenue function. The reason for Findlay's different solution is that he treats the surplus not as part of the budget—a specification which does not make much sense.

The situation even gets trickier when it comes to interpreting and comparing the results. The major impediment is the implicit assumption on *public employment productivity* and the related *definition of rents,* which gets blurred. In the model it is not clear where to place inefficiencies related to public employment. Inefficiencies arise either because public employees do not work hard enough or they supply a public good with minor or no benefit to the private sector.

If public sector workers engage in phantom tasks or build cathedrals in the jungle to cream off bribes, even at zero costs they would not raise private sector productivity. The reason is not an oversupply of the public good (where the provision of public goods has reached such a high level that the marginal costs of further 'units' outweigh marginal benefits), but simply a poor (and often rent-seeking) decision on what public good to supply.

In many LDCs public employment is high because it is a major vehicle to extract and mediate rents. As argued earlier, these rents are partly consumed by inefficiencies and partly appropriated by money and in-kind transfers. Embezzling funds, stealing state property, on-the-job leisure, extracting rents by extortion are a few examples. In particular the last example explains the frequently observed phenomenon that additional layers of bureaucracy are introduced which do not support the private sector but are a major impediment to private sector activity. The budget (employment) maximising solution given in Figure 4-8 does not account for these aspects. As inefficiency related to

[93] This interpretation is also given in Findlay (1990, p. 202) when he justifies the exogenous treatment of the tax rate, arguing that the ruler may not be able to raise the rate above a specified level.

public employment is indeed an important constraint in LDCs, two interpretations of the Findlay-Wilson-model are briefly discussed. They both include major reservations.

First, the horizontal axis in Figure 4-8 indicates efficient public employment. Findlay's budget-maximising case then effectively describes a situation where public goods are oversupplied (the country has too much of them). But it also implies that maximising budget does not involve rents other than misallocations of the workforce, i.e. employing too many people in the public sector (who still do their best). With this interpretation the budget maximisation outcome depicted in Figure 4-8 is simply a theoretical construct and far from what characterises any LDC. Obviously, if rents were included the model would have a twofold rent-specification: the surplus and some undefined share in the state expenditure function, which would have to be explained and defined in relation to the private sector and public sector output. This aspect is addressed below.

Alternatively to the first interpretation one may assume that public employment in Findlay's model includes inefficiencies. Since these are not specified they are exogenous to the model. This approach makes the budget-maximising variant more realistic, but is burdened with a twofold rent-specification (exogenous rents and rents defined as public employment). In addition a comparison of the three cases is problematic. The argument hinges on the exogenously assumed inefficiencies. To be realistic they need to be different in the three maximising hypotheses.

A ruler who is concerned with maximising output is likely to have the least inefficiencies related with public employment, followed by the ruler who aims to create the largest surplus possible. Public employment maximisers are usually not so much worried about employment inefficiencies and jobs are often supplied as a means of distributing additional rents which are attainable from the job position (on-the-job leisure, income from bribes, embezzling funds through allowances, etc.). Hence, as inefficiencies differ, each case has its own revenue function with its own surplus, output and employment maximums (smaller revenue functions are related to higher inefficiencies). This may have implications for Findlay's original result.

Figure 4-9 shows a specific outcome which changes the result. As can be deduced, shifting the revenue function of the surplus-maximising case inwards will not change its relative position with regard to the output-maximising case. The relative location of the budget (employment) maximising case, by contrast, now depends on the level of inefficiencies involved. In the extreme, as shown in Figure 4-9, the intersection may even be left to the surplus-maximising solution, implying the paradoxical outcome that because of much higher inefficiencies fewer workers are employed in the public employment-maximising case.

Many developing countries have been or still are characterised by large and often unaffordable public sectors. This aspect is, however, not well specified in the Findlay-Wilson model, basically as the link between public employment efficiency, rent appropriation and private sector output is not sufficiently

Figure 4-9: Maximising Output, Surplus and Public Employment with Different Efficiency Assumptions

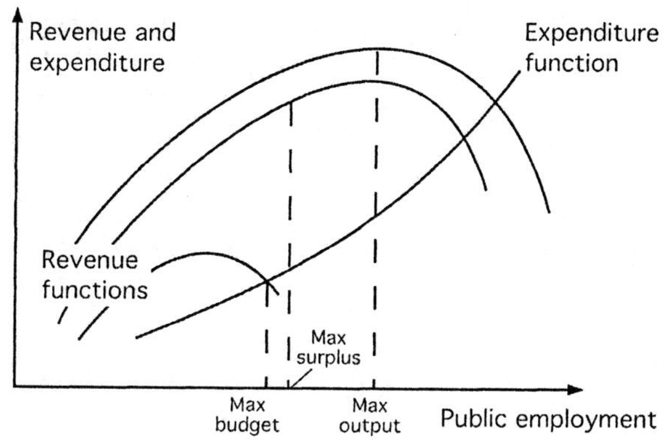

The shape of the revenue function depends, among other things, on public employment efficiency. The higher the efficiency, the larger are private sector output and tax income. Depending on the maximising strategy pursued, efficiency may vary considerably. The diagram depicts an extreme situation where public employment efficiency is very low in the budget-maximising model variant, and relatively high in the other two, leading to a different outcome than that described in Findlay (1990) (see Figure 4-8).

Source: Own drawing based on alternative efficiency assumptions in the Findlay-Wilson model

elaborated. Despite large public sectors, many developing countries typically fail to allocate sufficient resources to core activities, such as supplying and maintaining a basic infrastructure, providing social services or developing an institutional framework that guarantees secure property rights. Since public employment is typically related to appropriating 'surplus', the differentiation between maximising surplus and maximising budget is difficult to delineate. At the most, the employment-maximising variant additionally suggests, though not in a straightforward way, why overemployment may occur in specific government departments.

Focusing on economic constraints and the reasons a predatory ruler might invest in an economy, there are two important aspects not addressed in the model. The first relates to the behaviour of the 'roving bandit' (as explained on page 151), the second to the efficiency of the tax administration.

Obviously, the Findlay-Wilson model describes the behaviour of a *'stationary bandit'* but not predatory rent extraction by *'roving bandits'*. That Idi Amin managed to destroy the Ugandan economy in a short time is difficult to explain with one of Findlay's maximising frameworks. Amin not only failed to invest into the economy; he actually did the contrary, destroying the economic basis from which rents were extracted.

There are several arguments which explain the behaviour of roving bandits. As noted in Chapter 4.1, most important is the time horizon of a ruler. There is no incentive to invest in an economy if the benefits cannot be reaped afterwards. Idi Amin, however, did not appear to have been constrained by time. Another way of looking at the problem is to argue that this was an example of severe limited rationality.[94] Amin was therefore probably not aware of the damage he

[94] In fact, Amin was not well educated and did not fundamentally understand how an economy works.

was causing when he chased away the Asian minority. It can also be argued that taxing income from the Asian minority was not a feasible opportunity for him, but there were others. In the Findlay-Wilson model a functioning economy is a precondition for any rent extraction. However Idi Amin was plundering the economy basically by expropriating assets from the Asian minority. Under specific conditions a predatory ruler may therefore focus on wealth (assets) and not income (flows). The relative importance of flow and asset considerations will be a function of the ruler's limited rationality in general and short-sightedness in particular, the ease of appropriating wealth relative to income, as well as time preferences and the period the ruling coalition expects to remain in office.

Partly related to the logic of the roving bandit is the second aspect not included in the Findlay-Wilson model, i.e. a more detailed specification *of how the ruler can appropriate rents*. A tax administration is usually not able to tax all economic sectors with equal success. From the predatory ruler's perspective it does not make sense to invest in economic sectors where no or only few rents can be appropriated directly or indirectly (indirectly in the sense that the sector exerts sufficient positive externalities on other taxable sectors). Considering this, it is understandable why a predatory government may fail to finance even the most important welfare-enhancing projects that would substantially increase the country's non-taxable output.

The type and efficiency of the ruler's tax administration are critical determinants of the amount of rents that can be appropriated from an economy. Several models have considered this type of economic constraint, elaborating the relation between taxable and non-taxable sectors. Two basic models are presented in Findlay (1990). They focus on the ruler's limited ability to tax the economy and include two different private sectors, but omit productive public expenditures.

The first model (Findlay (1990, p. 207f)) describes a revenue-maximising marketing board which acts like a monopolist. Unlike the Findlay-Wilson-model, economic constraints to extract surplus are not just determined by limited factors of production but by the people's ability to escape taxation by shifting production. The model is of a *Ricardo-Viner type* with land and capital as sector specific inputs in agriculture and manufacturing respectively.[95] The higher the taxes on agriculture, the more people will look for employment in the non-taxed manufacturing sector. Findlay concludes that as workers are released to the manufacturing sector, additional foreign capital flows in to employ them with the effect that the economy becomes more industrialised, less well off (due to the dead-weight loss in the agricultural sector) and dependent on foreign capital. The model has been subject to further extensions.[96]

Findlay (1990, p. 211f) also outlines a *Heckscher-Ohlin approach* where state revenues are not derived from taxes but from tariffs on imports. The higher

---

[95] The model assumes that in the manufacturing sector there is always a fixed amount of capital per worker earning a fixed return r, which implies that the marginal productivity of labour and thus the wage rate also remains constant. Assuming perfect capital mobility and fixed world market prices, the wage rate is determined by the exogenous interest rate r.

[96] See, for instance, Bjorvatn (1995); the model will be taken up later in this section.

the tariff, the smaller the tax base, as the country replaces imports by expanding its own, non-taxed production of importables. Economic constraints of this Leviathan model are thus similar to the ones specified above where economic limits are determined by shifts in production.

A ruler who aims at maximising revenues would try to tax all formal sectors. Part of the production then typically shifts to the informal sector, where output cannot be taxed directly. Since tax administrations in many developing countries have been weak, a large share of economic activities, especially related to construction, food (e.g. subsistence production), and services such as retail trade or taxi driving, remain out of reach for the government.[97]

Summing up, economic constraints of the Leviathan typically arise from four sources. The countries' maximum output is constrained by limited factors of production, the countries' tax administration is constrained by the way it can extract taxes and its ability to reach the entire output, and finally, related to this, the Leviathan is further constrained as individuals engage in tax-avoiding strategies, shifting their activities to areas with low or no taxation. A predatory ruler may influence taxable output by supplying public goods which enhance private productivity and may increase revenues by setting up a more effective tax administration.

So far the focus has been directed towards a further elaboration of economic constraints. That *political constraints* are an important determinant of rents was emphasised earlier. As indicated with the models from Applebaum and Katz (1987) and Frey and Eichenberger (1994), simple models can also illustrate how rent consumption of governments and interest groups can depend on the combination of different economic and political constraints. In the remaining section a few additional models will be reviewed which explicitly elaborate political constraints. The discussion starts with an extension of two models presented above and goes on to describe a detailed model of a state with several interest groups.

Lal (1988, p. 297f) has extend the *Findlay-Wilson approach* by introducing a formal explanation of the maximum tax rate.[98] In addition to wage costs related with public employment, he assumes that there are also fixed capital costs which are needed to capture and maintain the state. The crucial assumption is that some of these costs are sunk and would only occur for a new entrant. Lal mentions as entry costs physical barriers (geographical), military costs and ideological costs (for instance related with religion).

A ruler may secure his position by choosing a tax rate that leaves him a surplus which is smaller than the *challenger's entry costs*. A challenger who tries to capture the state would then not be able to choose a lower tax rate and

[97] For a model of a Leviathan, which attempts to elaborate the relation between the formal and informal sector, see also Marcouiller and Young (1995). Their model, which is formally demanding, also elaborates the positive impact of public employment on private sector output—an aspect not addressed in the Ricardo-Viner and Heckscher-Ohlin approaches.

[98] See also Lal and Myint (1996, p. 264f).

still earn a surplus or break even. With this specification Lal implicitly assumes that a new entrant needs to charge a lower tax rate than the incumbent. Even though this is an interesting formulation, it seems to be rather alien to most LDC settings. This type of political constraint may at best apply to a situation with very strong interest groups that can always successfully prevent high tax rates. Or it may represent a setting where the prospects for raising tax income are severely constrained by economic limits or by a weak tax administration (implying that economic rather than political constraints are binding).

A more sophisticated elaboration of the political constraint is presented in Bjorvatn (1995). His model is an extension of *Findlay's Ricardo-Viner approach* mentioned earlier. Similar to the Findlay marketing board specification, the government raises revenues by taxing the agricultural sector. The urban sector however is not only strong enough to resist taxation, it is also able to *seize a share* of government revenues. To stay in power, the government has to offer part of its revenues to the 'politically influential urban population in the form of low productive but well paid public sector employment', i.e. jobs in the bureaucracy, police, military and state enterprises (Bjorvatn (1995, p. 137)). For simplicity's sake, Bjorvatn also assumes that the public sector is completely unproductive. The share of income that remains in the hands of the government is a positive function of the government's charisma and depends negatively on the size of the pressure group (urban sector). The government maximises its revenue by choosing the optimal tax rate. Raising the tax rate increases migration from the rural to the urban sector and thus lowers the tax base (economic limits); it also increases political pressures as the urban population grows.

Bjorvatn's model is interesting as it also elaborates on the impact of pre-existing distortions and specifies rent dissipation in the urban sector. Distortions are introduced with the assumption that labour communities in the rural sector share income—a feature common in Africa. He notes (p. 49) 'peasants own the land they work on and share the land rent evenly between members of the group' with the effect that 'labour is remunerated according to after tax average rather than marginal product'. In the absence of any taxation this construction implies an oversupply of labour in the agriculture sector; rent-seeking, by contrast, leads to a shift of employment away from agriculture. The beneficial correction however should not be overstated. On the one hand, the negative impact of a Leviathan (using surplus for own consumption) is most likely to outweigh benefits; on the other hand, the 'correction' is likely to 'overshoot', i.e. it is likely to lead to inefficient low employment in agriculture.

Chapter 2.2 mentioned that higher wages officially approved or unofficially earned by corruption can raise unemployment rates when individuals give up low-paid jobs to pursue the rents available in public employment. Bjorvatn also specifies this type of rent dissipation in his model. People either work in the agriculture or manufacturing sector, or they decide to lobby for public employment. Those who lobby but fail to get a public job suffer from unemployment. In the equilibrium, the expected wage from lobbying (probability of receiving a public employment job times public employment wage) will equal the wage rate in agriculture or manufacturing. Higher wage differentials between private and public employment are thus accompanied by higher rates of urban unemployment.[99]

Rent-seeking activities of the urban population pursuing employment in the public sector and the resources wasted in the public sector both make the country less well off. Bjorvatn (1995, p. 145) concludes that in contrast to Findlay's Ricardo-Viner version, industrialisation is not a necessary outcome but depends on the autonomy of the state vis-à-vis influential groups. Furthermore, but not specified in the model, it also depends on how the state spends its share of the surplus.

An even more *complex interest group approach* has been presented by Pedersen (1997). As in the previous model, political constraints are introduced by assigning power to interest groups. The model treats five different social groups: farmers (supplying agricultural goods), an urban group of marginalised unproductive people, two influential urban groups (workers and capitalist who together produce industrial goods) and urban public employees.

Unlike Bjorvatn's formulation, the state explicitly invests in the economy by supplying an infrastructure good, which raises private productivity. In addition the state also provides general and group-specific public goods free of charge. Public revenues and expenditures are determined according to the interest group's relative power and influence.

In Pedersen's model, farmers and marginalised urban groups are the least powerful; they are thus only left with a minimum level of income and receive no group-specific public goods. The minimum-income specification may be interpreted as a political or economic (institutional) constraint in taxing these groups. With regard to the distribution of the remaining income, Pedersen discusses two formulations, which cover the opposite cases of a weak and an autonomous predatory state.

In the first version, public employees only take a passive rent-seeking role. This version may be called a 'predatory interest group model' ('interest group' because different groups and not state leaders try to seize public revenues and 'predatory' as they leave farmers and marginalised urban groups with hardly any income). The public employees decide how much to supply of the general and group-specific public goods and how heavily to tax the two powerful urban groups. Taking a passive role, they simply maximise the welfare of the powerful groups, weighted according to their relative political influence. Public employees however do not come away empty-handed, as the model also includes bribery (interest groups can increase their influence by bribing public employees). The rent appropriation mechanism of the state given here is thus similar to the one discussed in the democratic approach of Applebaum and Katz (1987), where the state only captured rents offered by interest groups in exchange for policy favours.

---

[99] This formulation derives from Harris and Todaro (1970), who analysed migration models (Demery and Addison (1993, p. 336)).

The situation changes in Pedersen's second model formulation of a strong state, where public employees maximise their wealth in a Leviathan fashion and also appropriate rents directly from the state budget. Within this alternative approach public employees determine their own income after taxes and supply public goods which basically satisfy their own needs. Furthermore parameters are set such that aggregated rent-seeking investments of interest groups for remaining benefits, and thus bribes obtained by public employees are maximal.

Pederson's model contains various interesting LDC features, especially if one takes a middle course between the two versions described above. He accounts for five different social groups, rent-seeking competition between strong private groups, a state bureaucracy, which, depending on the model specification, partly acts according to the preferences of powerful interest groups and partly extracts rents itself, and different group-specific public goods, which reflect the reality that some social groups will not profit from their supply.

The model also allows different policy issues to be addressed, for instance the problem of fungibility. Within his framework, because of the minimum income level specification, unconditional aid would not reach the poor. As Pedersen (1997, p. 366) notes, one strategy to address this problem is to convince the political decision-maker to raise the minimum-income level; another strategy is to make the poor able to participate in political competition. The latter may include donor conditionality to introduce specific steps toward democratisation; the former, the claim that a minimum share of the state budget is used for low-budget, high-impact expenditures such as primary education and rural vaccination.

The model however also has its weaknesses. Unfortunately in the second version Pedersen does not elaborate political and economic constraints of the Leviathan in a satisfactory way, using formulations such as 'in this particular set-up the only reason for the political decision-maker to leave the competing private groups with positive amounts of income at all is their dependence on the private groups' demand for the genuine public good' (Pedersen (1997, p. 368)). It would however not be too difficult to define more realistic constraints. The model may include a combination of political constraints according to Bjorvatn's approach and a more specific formulation of increasing marginal costs in appropriating resources (both reflecting the trade-off between rent consumption and power maintenance).

Another weakness of the model, as criticised in an extended way in Findlay's framework, is that the model does not sufficiently account for inefficiencies related to public investments and does not link these inefficiencies to the rent-seeking strategies of the different interest groups. According to Pedersen's model specification, the state first chooses an optimal level of public investment to maximise private output in industry and agriculture, secures a minimum level of income of the two non-influential interest groups and redistributes the rest of national income according to the relative power and rent-seeking competition of the remaining groups. A solution which would come closer to an LDC setting and which would be more powerful in reflecting economic constraints is to specify a simultaneous distribution of state revenues between competing interest groups, bureaucrats and public investment. The use of resources for public investment may itself involve rent-seeking activities that reduce efficiency. The model would then describe a situation where the rent-seeking equilibrium of different interest groups is attended by an inefficient public sector. Highly productive investments cannot be undertaken, not only due to a lack of funds but also because the investments themselves are subject to a rent-seeking process.

Summing up, the three models presented above provided further examples of how to specify political constraints. In Lal's approach benefits need to be smaller than the challengers' entry costs; Bjorvatn defines public employees, who capture a share of the ruler's revenues; and Pedersen's analysis includes five groups with different economic and political stakes. The ruler's ability to remain in office, which depends on *legitimacy, repression and rents*, has not been elaborated in detail but can be partly represented with the parameters specified in the models. Lal's extension of the Findlay-Wilson model does not account for rents to remain in office but it can easily explain legitimacy and repression. Legitimacy and repression shape the level of entry costs and thereby codetermine the ruler's maximum surplus. Unlike Lal's approach, Bjorvatn explicitly includes rents which are supplied as carrots to remain in office. Within his framework, legitimacy and repression enter the parameter which determines the share of rents seized by the influential urban population. And finally, the more complex approach of Pedersen offers many ways to include the three aspects of staying in office.

Though limited in describing all the important aspects of a real setting, politico-economic models can be helpful tools for explaining and elaborating particular relations and interactions, such as the possible divergence between rulers and the public administration (civil servants implementing decisions), the dichotomy between the 'productive' and 'predatory' aspects of states, the link between rent consumption and power maintenance, the impact of extreme rent extraction on the health of the economy, the consequences of foreign borrowing and aid or the impact of political and economic constraints on pre-existing distortions. Depending on the questions and the real setting in focus, the behaviour of different interest groups, as well as political, economic and related institutional constraints, can be modified or extended, for instance to more explicitly evaluate the ruler's conduct in the reform context.

Dessus, Lafay and Morrisson (1998) propose an interesting model which is not of a predatory type but which focuses on the *interaction between the political and economic sphere*. They operate with the hypothesis that the government minimises its probability of collapse by choosing among the trade-offs of stabilisation versus expansion (economic measure) and repression versus liberalisation (political measure). The decision to stabilise is estimated as a function of the economic situation (level of foreign reserves, indebtedness, GDP growth) and political pressures (external pressures and demonstrations). The model reflects the realistic situation that domestic unpopularity (which includes coups d'état) rises with stabilisation measures and can be controlled by higher repression; higher repression and a less consequent stabilisation however increase unpopularity abroad and may thus undermine donor support. Similar to the approach taken by Frey and Eichenberger (1994), these different relations may be explicitly elaborated in a model of a predatory ruler (or predatory interest groups), for instance by including formal features of critical mass models to describe the effects of demonstrations and coups. Insights from such models may equally help to answer questions with regard to design, timing and sequencing of rent-abating reform measures and democratisation. There may well be a conflict between political and economic reforms.[100]

Taking a longer-term focus, another fruitful extension is to elaborate on *growth effects* in Leviathan models. Bigsten and Moene (1996), for instance, have presented a rent-seeking model for Kenya that focuses on expenditures, investments and savings and shows the different growth implications of surplus labour, bribes and rent-seeking investments.

Finally, the behaviour of a Leviathan may also be investigated with regard to *different economic regimes*. Such an approach has been taken by Yeldan and Roe (1991) who describe a computable general equilibrium model (CGE model) with an endogenous rent-seeking specification of pressure. With their framework they evaluate the impact of alternative trade regimes (adjustment with flexible exchange rate, premium rationing, external government borrowing). The model is of the weak-state type similar to the one described by Pedersen (1997) (where the state maximises the welfare of some interest groups, weighted according to their political influence) and indicates, as Yeldan and Roe (1991, p. 579) note, that rent-seeking behaviour will not just be directed to a partial set of instruments but to different structural parameters of the system.

All in all, rent-seeking relations in the real world are complex; they may be hierarchical and reflect patronage relations, they may be based on extortion and principal-agent conflicts, or they may simply constitute rent-seeking contests between competing individuals or groups. Models, even though limited in scope, can be an effective tool for explaining these relations and the interaction between different rent-seeking related parameters. They also make it possible to evaluate the impact of specific distortions and constraints—an aspect which is highly relevant in developing-country settings.

There are indeed many factors which determine the *supply of* and *demand for rents* in an economy. The models presented contribute to explain the level of dissipation, the behaviour of specific interest groups and the role of governments in supplying and consuming rents. Depending on the focus, simple rent-seeking models and models that outline a politico-economic framework can be brought together.[101] Yet, the overview in this section also showed that the models are limited in describing real settings. Many of them are basically 'implication

[100] See for instance Block (2002) for an empirical investigation of this problem in the context of Africa.

[101] This approach has for instance been applied by Applebaum and Katz (1987) and Bjorvatn (1995).

games' or 'thought experiments' (i.e. they demonstrate if a, b and c holds then d, e and f follows). In many cases they are therefore of limited value for deriving policy recommendations, above all in situations where models provide trivial or irrelevant results as the setting in the real world is much more complex and includes many more constraints.

e) Conclusion: Why Taking an Overall Perspective Is Important

Chapter 3 presented a large number of parameters which determine rent-seeking behaviour. But it also emphasised that evaluating rent-seeking and making policy recommendations entails choosing an appropriate rent-seeking model and this requires assumptions about specific parameter values. Chapter 4 elaborated some of these aspects. A broader analysis of the individual decision-making situation, discussion of what determines the power of interest groups, and the subsequent assessment of what characterises different governments explain why rent-seeking is often a bargain, why many rent-seeking settings in developing countries are of a non-rival nature, why rent-seeking opportunities may include preceding rent-seeking contests and what they look like. Especially the discussion on the government's behaviour in supplying rents indicated that rents are not an isolated issue but have to be evaluated within the overall politico-economic context. This is crucial when it comes to assessing economic reforms and drawing policy conclusions. The concluding discussion below reexamines the distinct role rents hold within a state and addresses some policy recommendations that focus on rent-seeking in general and inefficient political markets in particular.

Rents Cannot Be Treated as an Isolated Issue

As outlined in this chapter, understanding rents in an economy requires evaluating the government's means of holding onto power and its attitudes towards own rent consumption, and elaborating constraints that limit rent extraction. Since the three basic cornerstones legitimacy, carrots (rents) and sticks (repression and violence) are closely *linked*—they may either substitute or complement one other—a deeper understanding of the government's behaviour in supplying rents also requires an analysis of the other two aspects. For instance it may be argued that many African governments lack moral legitimacy; they therefore have to rely much more on the use of force and material incentives to maintain power.

Rents can become a crucial *system-stabilising element*, especially in weak states. More generally, in countries with an adverse political culture where sizeable rents are appropriated by ruling elites or by powerful predatory-type interest groups, rents are typically a central component of the state, i.e. they constitute the raison d'être of a predatory system. This feature is partly mirrored in the 'multifunctional' character of public positions. In most developing countries a public job not only serves to carry out administrative duties or to run a public company, but also includes other political, economic and social functions—an aspect which has been widely noted in the African context and which has important policy implications.[102]

Depending on the setting, *channels of mediating rents* vary. If the ruling elites mainly use the assignment of jobs in the civil service as a reward for political support, they are likely to allow and promote significant budgetary discretion (e.g. Mbaku (1992, p. 251)). On the other hand, if the ruler depends on the support of certain economic groups, transferring rents by economic policy will become a critical measure and rents will predominantly take the form of specific economic interventions and subsidies. Furthermore, leakage on the level of bureaucracy might be less desirable. Finally, a powerful predatory ruler may distribute rents according to very narrow criteria (e.g. beneficiaries being a member of the ruling clan or belonging to the inner circle of the ruling party). Beneficiaries then typically obtain strategic rent-bearing public positions within the customs department, treasury or ministry of works, or they are entrepreneurs in the private sector benefiting from selective protection and direct government support.

Obviously rents are not only important for the central government. The role of rents as a vehicle for maintaining power also applies to the behaviour of *district and communal* leaders (they may not have been appointed by the top leadership). An interesting development is the change in the qualities needed to be elected as a village leader (and therefore likewise the qualities needed to remain in office). These have changed over the last fifty years, basically as a result of the growing redistributional role of the state.[103]

As for instance explained in Baumgartner, et al. (2002), in India in earlier times a village leader was expected to be able to ensure sustainable use of common pool resources of the community such as pasture grounds, village forests and irrigation water. Nowadays an elected leader has to ensure access by the community to external resources in the form of subsidies, development programmes and the like. The skills thus required to remain in office (or to become a village leader) have shifted from competence in mobilising internal resources to rent-seeking skills (or in the words of Baumgartner, et al. (2002, p. 264) 'In the pattern of leadership emerging today, the sustainable management of natural resources has lost priority in favour of efficient tapping of external resources from government and non-government sources.').

Whether a government has comfortable backing within a country or faces a daily struggle to maintain power and has to rely on instruments such as repression and the supply of rents, may be partly determined *exogenously*. Rulers may face an unfavourable power constellation that has institutional origins (e.g. constitutional blockades that prevent sound policymaking or election rules that lead to different majorities within government and parliament). Particularly relevant in many African countries are unfavourable

---

[102] See for instance Pritzl (1997, p. 199f, 231).

[103] This argument applies to developing as well as industrialised countries.

ethnic constellations, for instance situations where several large and economically different ethnic groups compete for power (e.g. Rwanda, Burundi, Uganda or Kenya). A great deal of the *relative importance* of legitimacy, carrots and sticks is however homemade and results from ill-conceived and poorly implemented policies. Idi Amin, for instance, had to use more and more force to stay in power, increasingly relying on ethnic relations within the army (Bienen (1993, p. 272)).

The discussion in this chapter also showed that it is not possible to order the relative importance of rents along a continuum from democratic to totalitarian states, nor is it possible to argue from the outset that a specific system (democratic, authoritarian or totalitarian) is accompanied by many or few rent-seeking activities. Under 'optimal' conditions, *democratisation* reduces the amount of rents supplied in an economy, for instance, when it strengthens the political participation of hitherto rent-seeking victims or when it increases institutional costs related to rent-seeking activities above a critical level. Gallagher (1991, p. 62), drawing on Ekelund and Tollison (1981), notes:

> 'Institutional costs are related to the degree of power centralisation of the state ... Under a democratic system of great institutional competition, where the legislative and executive branches of government must be lobbied and influenced, where public opinion and public accountability must be factored into decisions, and where the certainty of judicial enforcement is in question, institutional cost [i.e. the cost of rent-seeking] will be great.'

He concludes that 'competing components of government in modern day Africa will raise the costs facing rent-seeking' (Gallagher (1991, p. 63)).

However, as widely argued in the literature on public choice, neither free elections nor decisions based on votes can entirely safeguard against rent-seeking policies. In a democratic setting interest groups may influence and shape politics through various formal and informal channels, sometimes to promote profit-seeking activities, sometimes however to promote their rent-seeking interests. Election cycles, logrolling and selective vote-trading, the strategic design of constituencies, as well as formal and informal influences on the pre-parliamentarian process are relevant in this respect.[104]

Institutional costs of influence also vary among *autocratic* settings. Costs do not just depend on the number of people or institutions to influence (which increases with democratisation); equally relevant is the question of how costly it is to influence a ruler, committee or a specific office. At least theoretically, a powerful autocratic regime could prevent any rent-seeking policies and maximise social welfare.

Considering the range of political systems, from free democracies and authoritarian governments to totalitarian regimes, it is thus evident that at one end democratic legitimisation and on the other repression will be important.

[104] For a valuable contribution to this subject see Olson's famous book *'The Rise and Decline of Nations'* (Olson (1982)).

Both however may still involve large amounts of rents: in weak populist democracies as carrots to win elections, in strong totalitarian states as the loot of the predatory regime. This has implications for the feasibility of rent-abating economic reforms, if reforms simultaneously include political liberalisation. The subject will be taken up again in Chapter 5.[105]

Having in mind the typology of states, a differentiated perspective is also necessary to assess the *size and type of rent-related costs* explained in Chapter 3. Rent-seeking investments (dissipation) and the inefficiencies arising from the rent-seeking policy may vary considerably between different states. A totalitarian regime may be characterised by large rent transfers but low rent-seeking activities, as 'rent-seeking' property rights are well specified. Inefficiencies mainly arise from Harberger triangles, i.e. dead-weight losses, and not Tullock rectangles (recall the description outlined in Figure 3-1 on page 64). By contrast, a democratic setting may include only little rent transfers but high rent-seeking investments. The society may be trapped in a prisoner's dilemma, similar to the case of over-advertising described in Chapter 2.1 (p. 28). Every group would engage in ongoing rent-seeking or rent-protecting activities; if one group desisted, it would immediately be exploited by others. Inefficiencies are then less a result of economic policy but rather of rent-seeking outlays (Tullock rectangles).[106]

Finally, rents may not only have a very specific role within a politico-economic framework, changes in the political setting also affect the rent-seeking contest, i.e. the parameters outlined in Chapter 3. A change in the political setting may influence the size and certainty of rents, the value of supplying rents, the number of participating rent-seekers, winning rules and procedures as well as asymmetries among rent-seekers—all with implications on rent-seeking costs.

All in all, the conclusions drawn in Chapter 3 are again supported by the insights derived from Chapter 4. To determine rent-seeking or the impact of certain parameter variations one must be aware of the *entire setting*, i.e. focus on all relevant parameters simultaneously. The parameters determine, among other things, the profitability of profit-seeking, the strength of interest groups or the government's hold on power in a specific political system; they reflect assumptions about rationality, transaction costs and information costs, as well as specific cultural values and habits.

The discussion in Chapter 4 in particular provides insights as to why there is only a *weak relation* between rents and the level of rent-seeking activities. In LDCs many groups in powerful positions obtain rents with little effort. For them rent-seeking is a bargain, but at the cost of a large majority that loses out. Many predatory rulers and predatory-type interest groups have not hesitated to

---

[105] For a discussion whether democratic or authoritarian governments are better reformers, see also Haggard and Webb (1993).

[106] Tommasi and Velasco (1996, p. 194f) include a brief reference to rent-seeking models where participants are trapped in Pareto-inefficient Nash equilibria, i.e. situations where all participants would be better off if they reduced their demands, but unilaterally demanding less is not rational for each individual player.

severely constrain the development of their country's economy. High costs partly occur because rents are often not extracted from sectors where the economic damage would be relatively small but from sectors where rents can be extracted most easily (economically and politically). Destroying an economy so that narrowly defined ruling elites can personally enrich themselves indeed describes a case of severe overdissipation.

Why a Modern Democratic System Is Still the First-Best Solution

The fundamental insight of political economy, which states that *'political rationality'* often dominates *'economic rationality'*, has been central to explaining rent-seeking behaviour. The domination of political rationality is not a source of concern if political markets are efficient; this is however not the case, basically because of transaction costs and incomplete information. Transaction costs and incomplete information ultimately explain why powerful interest groups undertake activities which incur very high costs to society, for instance when they capture the state by violence and succeed because of military superiority.

As emphasised with the opening quotes of Chapter 2.2 and this chapter, different interests in a society cannot organise themselves equally well and politicians who might serve the public interest are frequently eliminated from the political stage. Olson (1987, p. 476) even concludes that the logic of collective action is in fact *'a general statement of the logic of market failure'*. The inefficiency of political markets, which translates into inefficient economic policies, has to be kept in mind when addressing policy recommendations on rent-seeking, i.e. first-best solutions on sound policymaking often cannot be implemented in both authoritarian states and modern democracies.

There is a large body of literature which explains that also in democracies there is not necessarily a direct relation between the policymakers' chances of being elected and their effective supply of welfare-enhancing policies. As noted earlier, if transaction costs and information costs are a real constraint, special interest groups can decisively influence democratic outcomes at their own personal benefit. They may have the financial means to restrain the spread of objective and balanced information. As long as a great deal of information on interpreting policy outcomes is supplied by financially powerful interest groups, incomplete information may remain a serious obstacle, and welfare-reducing rent-seeking policies can also spread in democratic settings especially if matters are too complex to be understood. Under these conditions the following statement from Fessler (1986, p. 798) is a provocative contention:

> 'a U.S. Senator is primarily interested in two things—one, to be elected, and the other, to be reelected' (cited from McChesney (1997, p. 47)).

After considering several arguments which point to the possible failure of democratic systems, the question may emerge whether it makes any sense to promote the creation of modern democratic systems. The answer is obviously yes. Under optimal conditions Fessler's statement is not a concern but guarantees that politicians act in the interest of the citizens they represent. Despite these qualifications, the main question is therefore not whether to establish democratic rules but *how* to establish them so that any negative consequences of unbalanced representation can be avoided. Democracies with functioning checks and balances can be very efficient in restraining rent-seeking behaviour. The reduction or elimination of rent-seeking policies critically depends on whether democratic rules can effectively strengthen victims of rent-seeking.

North (1990, p. 109) cites the following as conditions necessary for a political market to approximate the zero transaction cost model for efficient economic exchange: Actors need to be fully informed, apply correct models, and must be able to communicate the results with low enough transaction costs. Furthermore, in a perfect political market, 'votes' would be weighted according to the aggregate net gains or losses. As North concludes, a *modern democratic society with secure property rights* (and universal suffrage) provides the closest approximation to such conditions.

Sound political institutions, a strong court system and provisions for an orderly succession of power (also defined as *rule of law* in the broad sense), as well as a free and critical media, can be very effective in preventing rent-seeking policies if the problem of transaction costs and incomplete information is sufficiently controlled. In particular because of the need to reduce information costs and transaction costs, a modern democratic society not only demands the introduction of political liberties, but civil liberties as well. The main goal is to come as close as possible to an optimum situation that guarantees a free flow and appropriate interpretation of information. This prevents the implementation of weak and 'inefficient' democratic systems that are driven by populist decision-making, i.e. decision-making which aims to maximise votes not on the basis of sound and consistent policies but on the basis of citizens hampered by incomplete information and ignorant of economic fundamentals.

How to Get There and What Is the Role of Donors?

Though these suggestions are valuable, they do not address the problem of how to implement secure property rights, checks and balances, or political reforms in general. If rulers are rent-seekers themselves, they will have no interest in implementing such measures. Not only may own initiatives be very limited or absent, ruling elites may forcefully oppose and suppress any initiative introduced from civil society. At the most, rulers may implement policies in selected areas where they are not affected or where they can personally benefit. For instance they may increase the security of property rights by establishing effective land legislation, if they are themselves major landowners (e.g. Bates (1988, p. 243f)). In a country with an adverse political culture one cannot rely on far-reaching and effective reforms from the ruling elites, even if some of them are stated publicly.

In such situations the abilities of donors to influence a political transition are limited. Donors may try to identify selective areas where some reforms are feasible. In the worst case, donors may limit themselves to communicating the benchmark needed to obtain support. There are usually more options however. Donors can promote and support activities that are suitable to develop or increase checks and balances in the society. Depending on the extent of reform-minded forces in the country (and government repression), activities range from increasing public awareness, strengthening the media, creating watchdog organisations, and helping other organisations to develop and increase their capacity, to effectively providing advice and financial support in implementing effective systems of control, accountability and transparency, adopting constitutional provisions such as requirements of balanced budgets, strengthening the parliament's role in controlling the budget or establishing an independent central bank.

But looking at past reform records, the reality looks different. Donors have often pressured governments to undertake reforms and in doing so were not sufficiently critical with their aid. Many recipient governments, by contrast, pretended to cooperate or to have the power and means to sustain reforms. In effect many reform programmes experienced setbacks, as rent-seeking problems were not anticipated. Even though some reform efforts occurred as a by-product of economic and political constraints, many were only agreed on paper, others were implemented but undermined by countervailing forces, and a few failed as the general public did not sufficiently understand the economic imperatives. Often there was no effective commitment from the top leadership, or rulers lost legitimacy and had to buy it back with interest group and populist policies. Depending on the probability of survival and the instruments available, the introduction of sound economic policies and political reforms was not relevant for the survival of the ruling elites.

To be able to design more adequate reform programmes which can also be implemented and sustained, it is decisive to understand rent-seeking strategies in full. Insights into resistance from rent-seekers are important for a reform-minded government as well as for donors, which have to decide on the type of aid, and above all whether or not to support a government reform programme. Chapter 5 addresses rent-seeking problems related to broad-based economic, political and institutional reforms. It will examine on what determines reform support and opposition and elaborate on the problems associated with designing and implementing rent-abating polices.

5 Reforms, Rent-Seeking and Rent-Seeking Opposition

What matters is anticipating the behaviour of the powerful

An old saying that still holds true

In Chapters 1 and 2 it was explained that in the past many governments followed economic policies that heavily distorted the functioning of markets. Interventions such as over-expansionary fiscal and monetary policy, the administration of prices and the implementation of many ill-advised regulations, contributed to high indebtedness, economic instability, stagnation and decline. These failures created an environment that heavily undermined productive activities and resulted in high costs for society and the poor.

Towards the end of the 1970s and the beginning of the 1980s, a great number of developing countries faced severe economic problems, which brought their growth rates down and constrained their future development. The situations called for immediate action, in particular economic reforms in the form of short and medium-term stabilisation, as well as more fundamental and longer-lasting structural adjustments. Since most of the necessary reforms also demanded substantial reductions in rents, reforms interfered with well-established rent-seeking settings and critically threatened the wealth of hitherto successful rent-seekers.

What followed in most countries were decades of economic reforms, which often have been half-hearted and poor. Despite urgently needed reforms, essential measures were delayed for years or were not effectively implemented. Furthermore many countries repeatedly failed to achieve the minimal targets agreed with donors.

Though the reasons for these problems are numerous, the main argument advanced here is the strong resistance of rent-seeking groups which had benefited from the inefficient system. Reforms did not produce expected results because reform-minded governments underestimated the power of rent-seeking resistance or because donors had been too naïve in believing that governments in predatory-type regimes had an interest in adopting true reforms. In many cases the governments were primarily interested in sustaining a high level of donor support, which allowed them to continue their rent-seeking policies.

For donors and reform technocrats within the country it is crucial to understand the forces that lead to the reform decision and to anticipate possible strategies of rent-seekers, who may counteract and undermine suggested reforms. Only a detailed approach allows evaluation of whether suggested reform measures are appropriate and can be implemented and sustained. Furthermore insights into what affects the adoption of reforms will provide ideas as to how to approach predatory-type settings, i.e. such insights may help reform-minded forces within the country and donors to identify critical measures and conditions that could increase the probability that efficient reforms would be adopted in the near or later future.

In the previous chapters the discussion referred to many issues of introducing reforms directly and indirectly when addressing the origin, role, extent and impact of rents and rent-seeking activities, without however addressing in detail the feasibility of reforms. This chapter examines more systematically the role of rents and rent-seeking in the context of the broad-based economic, institutional and political reforms. Applying many of the insights and conclusions elaborated thus far, this chapter also concludes Part I and represents the main theoretical counterpart (and introduction) to the case study on Tanzania in Part II.

Chapter 5.1 is devoted to elaborating on the logic behind adopting reforms. Section a) addresses the question: who is going to resist, and why? It groups rent-seekers and other interest groups into reform supporters, 'mistaken' opponents and reform antagonists, and surveys some possible strategies for building a sufficiently strong coalition of reform support. Since in predatory-type governments policymakers are themselves rent-seekers or simply function as mediators between powerful predatory-type interest groups, Section b) outlines the critical relationship between the necessity for reform (i.e. the magnitude of a crisis) and the size of the rents transferred to strategic groups.

Chapter 5.2 directly focuses on the reform process, examining different rent-seeking strategies during reforms, which comprise direct and indirect resistance on the level of policy formulation and implementation (including countervailing measures), and rent-seeking activities that result from the transition. It concludes with a summary of hypotheses on rent-seeking in the context of broad-based economic, institutional and political reforms and a brief outline of a logic model to anticipate rent-seeking interference.

5.1 Rent-Seeking in the Run-up to Reforms

Many reforms have become necessary because powerful rent-seeking interests pressed for the implementation of poor policies. These policies hampered economic development and threw the economy out of balance. Often a fatal relationship between economic imbalance, the need for further interventions and the growing size of rents accelerated the economic decline. All over the world, examples can be found which impressively demonstrate the link between rent-seeking, economic imbalance and the need for reforms. Åslund (1994, p. 26), for instance, notes that in Russia the main reason for the strong inflationary pressures experienced there, which finally ended in hyperinflation, was the 'extreme rent-seeking by a narrow stratum of society'. The case study on Tanzania will also provide an example where rent-seeking forces within the bureaucracy and the parastatal sector drove the economy to near collapse in the 1980s.

Although in many cases rent-seekers lobby for the adoption of a rent-creating policy or simply take over the rent-creating state apparatus, the causality between policy and rent-seeking has also gone the other way. As noted in the introduction to Chapter 2.2, in many countries policy interventions were originally driven by social, ideological and other non-rent-seeking considerations, but subsequently created rent-seeking forces as an unwanted side product. These forces then steadily undermined the goals originally intended with the policy. Furthermore rent-seekers took a strong stake in maintaining the policies, even in times when conditions, perceptions and views had changed and policies were no longer affordable. They thereby contributed to the growing and costly imbalances.

What follows from this dual perspective is that reform countries, ex-ante, typically find themselves entrapped in a pronounced rent-seeking environment. Rent-seekers (whether responsible for the initial rent-creating policy or having developed as a result of it) are thus often an *integral part of the ailing economy.* Considering that rent-seeking has indeed been a bargain, rent-seekers are likely to resist and develop strategies to safeguard their easier but unproductive income earning opportunities when it finally comes to designing and implementing adequate reform measures. Reform agendas which ignore this run a great risk of failing.

Hardly anyone would dispute that it makes a big difference whether reforms are implemented in an environment with or without deep-rooted rent-seeking forces. Since the latter has often been the implicit assumption in the programmes designed and promoted by the donor community, it is not surprising that many reform measures have not shown the expected results, either because rent-seekers opposed specific reform components or because they managed to successfully adjust their strategies.

a) What Distinguishes Reform Advocates from Opponents?

There exists a broad literature on the political economy of reforms, which addresses the question of who will support or oppose reforms.[107] This section extends the review on interest groups presented in Chapter 4.2 by discussing interest group characteristics which are relevant in the reform context. The discussion provides an overview of different arguments which explain why a government finally adopts reforms.

As outlined earlier, on the one hand, interest groups outside the state apparatus may be very powerful and constrain activities of the state; on the other hand, the state leaders themselves (and their entourage) are frequently the largest obstacle to reforms or important sections thereof. In their privileged position,

[107] The following articles provide a good overview, where the interested reader will find plenty of information (this section partly draws from them): Gulhati (1988), Haggard and Webb (1993), Bates and Krueger (1993), Morrisson, Haggard and Lafay (1995), Tommasi and Velasco (1996) and Rodrik (1997).

they may enrich themselves through government institutions and public enterprises, or they may benefit from measures which illegitimately support their own economic activities in the private sector. In Kenya and Malawi for instance, it was the president himself, who was a large maize farmer and thus blocked the liberalisation of maize marketing for a long time (Betz (1995, p. 37), Toye (1992, p. 190f)).

In a country with a bad political culture the final decision to give into reforms may simply emanate from an egoistic act of 'self-preservation or legitimacy enhancement' (Gulhati (1988, p. 34)), and not from concern about the well-being of the population. Reforms then occur as a by-product of a more complex struggle for power, status and self-enrichment. Given the rent-seeking motivations these reforms are often poorly designed or are not sustainable.

Still, there is no clear dividing line between reform support and opposition that matches the theoretical distinction between profit-seeker and rent-seeker. As will be argued, many reasons other than rent-seeking explain why reforms are slowed down or postponed, and why particular measures from the reform agenda are excluded. A strict rent-seeking approach cannot describe all reform problems. This gives rent-seekers an advantage in their argumentation, i.e. they can cite reasons other than earning rent income to explain poor reform records or resistance to reforms.

Most reforms mean there will be costs for certain interest groups, i.e. reforms will not compensate losers which have been benefiting from embezzlement or from a previous bonanza period. Unless there is an inexhaustible source of insufficiently monitored and evaluated donor support, which renders adjustment superfluous, the relevant question is not *whether to adjust or not, but how*. It includes the option 'to do nothing', which is the most costly and extreme form of 'adjustment'. Compared to this alternative, reforms are a 'positive sum game', i.e. the benefits are higher than the additional cost. From a welfare-theoretical point of view, such reforms should therefore always be adopted. Unfortunately the real world is not that simple.

At the core of the problem is the 'nonneutrality in the way that the gains and losses from the reform are distributed within society' (Fernandez and Rodrik (1991, p. 1146)). As emphasised in the previous chapter, political markets are not perfect and limited rationality and transaction costs matter. Not all interest groups can organise themselves equally well, and many countries are still a long way from efficient democratic checks and balances. Interests of individuals thus have different weights, and reforms only become attractive to the people in power and influential interest groups if they can assure compensation for the rents they will lose with the reform. However this is hardly feasible as, among other reasons, it would make the huge and mostly unfair income transfers far too transparent.

Besides purely rent considerations, an important impediment to the adoption of reforms is *rigidities in the economy*, which may imply very high short and medium-term adjustment costs. If the change in policies is not accompanied by a sufficiently speedy reallocation of resources, intermediate adjustment costs can become substantial and affect a broad community of interests. Also short-term stabilisation measures entail that average incomes commonly decline during the initial period of the reform. This development is often referred to as the *J-curve effect*. Figure 5-1, which describes different possible costs and benefits associated with reforms, captures this feature with the curves A to D. Besides indicating different reform strategies, the curves may also show changes in income of different individuals during reforms or they may indicate different possible scenarios as to how a specific reform measure affects national income in a country (explained below).

Figure 5-1: Adjustment Costs and Benefits from the Reform

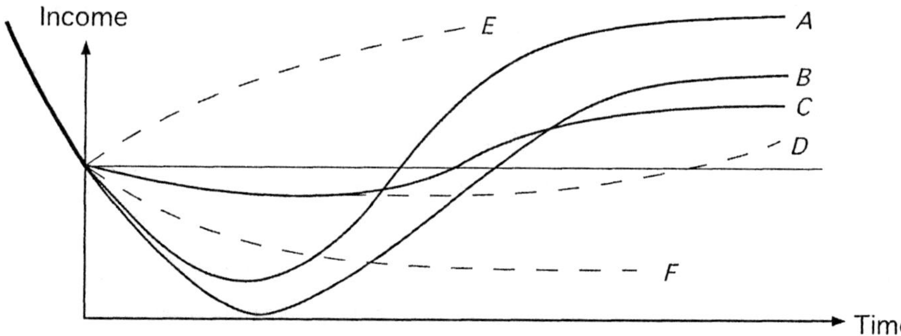

The diagram indicates possible developments in income from reforms and may be used to demonstrate different aspects.

First, the curves *A-D* may reflect costs and benefits of *different reform strategies*, *E* a theoretical benchmark without rigidities and *F* the situation of 'doing nothing'. According to the curves, strategy *B* is inferior to *A*; *A* includes higher adjustment costs than *C*, but has a higher expected income in the future.

Second, the curves may represent the development of income of *different individuals*. On average, income declines at the beginning and rises thereafter to higher levels. Some individuals however may have to wait considerably longer *(D)*, others win from the outset *(E)* or lose *(F)*. The last may represent income of rent-seeking elites who lose from uncompensated reforms.

Third, the curves may reflect insecurity related to the reform and present *different possible scenarios* of cost and benefits from a single strategy.

Trying to understand the adoption (and sustainability) of reforms, two questions are particularly relevant: how to mobilise reform beneficiaries to form a sufficiently strong coalition of reform support, and how rent-seeking behaviour affects the balance between reform supporters and opponents.

Reform Beneficiaries: Active Versus Passive Support and 'Mistaken' Opponents

For most reform packages it is not difficult to ascertain immediate winners and losers. Beneficiaries are typically found within groups who could not benefit from the pre-reform patronage systems, groups which have been overtaxed or severely constrained by specific regulations or the unavailability of important goods and services. Depending on the setting, beneficiaries of certain reform measures also coincide with specific ethnic groups. In Kenya for instance, Kikuyu and Luo largely supported reforms, while politicians from Kalenjin and Maasai opposed them, as they feared losing their patronage opportunities (Mair (1996, p. 30, 57f)). Potential winners and losers may also be identified according to economic models or theorems, which can be a useful tool for policymakers if policy changes are more complex or affect specific groups indirectly.[108]

Obviously the larger the number and the more powerful reform supporters, the easier it is, ceteris paribus, to implement a reform programme. Being a reform beneficiary however does not necessarily explain active reform support. Chapter 4 surveyed a great number of aspects which determine whether or not specific interest groups will voice their demands. What makes reforms difficult is that a large number of reform beneficiaries live in rural areas. Their unfavourable power characteristics explain why reform advocates are often entirely *passive* and fail to express their pro-reform opinions. Their contribution is then reduced to merely not opposing reform, which may not be sufficient if other groups actively speak out against reforms.

Some potentially winning groups may even oppose reforms. The complex set of different costs and benefits that adjustment creates, together with incomplete information and limited rationality, explains this outcome and typically affects groups that are not direct or immediate beneficiaries of reforms.

At the core of the problem is the limited ability of many citizens *to assess the potential benefits and costs of policy change.* The problem partly arises as costs must be borne immediately, whereas benefits are uncertain and in the future. Benefits are therefore to a much lesser extent perceived and included in the calculation of potential winners. Of course the problem acquires another dimension in some LDCs where poverty really is extensive and welfare systems to cushion these costs are non-existent or inadequate. Haggard and Webb (1993, p. 149) note, that 'under such conditions they [voters] might support governments that deliver short-term material benefits, even at the expense of long-run welfare' (in Figure 5-1, this strategy implies choosing *C* instead of *A*). Nevertheless, most opposition cannot be reduced to mere time preference. If people perceived future benefits more clearly and took them for granted, they would be much more inclined to accept high short-term and medium-term costs.

Often insecurity related to the impact of suggested reforms means uncertainty, not calculable risk. Citizens may not know their costs and benefits, i.e. the shape of the curves drawn in Figure 5-1 (third interpretation). As Bates and Krueger (1993, p. 456) emphasise, even economists are unable to determine the precise impact of macroeconomic policies on specific interests. They conclude that other people—such as workers in a given industry or firms that

[108] The Ricardo-Viner model for instance permits investigation of the different impact of policy changes on mobile and immobile factors of production, and the Stolper-Samuelson theorem explains the favourable effect of trade restrictions for owners of the relatively scarce factor of production.

use specific technologies and produce for particular markets or people who live in certain regions—may also not know whether they will benefit or lose from reform.

Related to this is the general limitation of interest group theory noted earlier in Chapter 2.2, i.e. the situation that 'individuals, households, and firms occupy several positions in the economic structure simultaneously' (Haggard and Webb (1993, p. 144)). Haggard and Webb conclude that in times of rapid economic change people may therefore not know in advance whether their interests will be affected. In fact even within a sector that is generally favoured by the reform, it is not possible to know, ex-ante, who exactly is going to succeed under the new conditions.

What follows is, as many authors point out, a bias in favour of the status quo, which is usually better known and thus less risky. Rodrik (1997, p. 65) illustrates a numerical example which addresses the essence of the problem.[109] He argues that a majority of people may work for the import-competing sector where individuals are losers in expected-value terms and therefore vote against reforms. Ex-post however there may well be a pro-reform majority as some individuals of the import-competing sector will nevertheless win (for instance, as they move to another sector or just become more competitive). He concludes that 'this is a case where incomplete information blocks a reform from being adopted even though the reform would be politically popular if imposed dictatorially'.

Mistaken opposition to reforms not only originates from the limited ability to assess future benefits and costs of a policy change. The problem may be more fundamental. A considerable part of the population may *not sufficiently understand important aspects of economics*. Situations where people behaved in a contradictory way occurred in many reforming countries. Tommasi and Velasco (1996, p. 224f), for instance, note:

> 'In the early 1990s, close to three-quarters of Chileans polled systematically opposed "measures that would restrict the availability or increase the price of imported goods". In the same set of polls, roughly the same proportion strongly endorsed the notion "government should take the appropriate measures to protect national producers from foreign competition". Results of this sort emerge with even greater absurdity in Eastern Europe, where the population has no previous experience of market economy and the politics necessary to administer it. This has led Jeffrey Sachs to argue that in such countries it is pointless to seek consensus in the early stages of reform; people are simply too confused.'

Finally, *strategic behaviour* can explain why groups oppose economic reforms even though they benefit from them. The argument may apply to a set of reform measures and may also relate to 'moderate' rent-seekers. (Even though they do not profit from the reform measures that abolish their rents, some of them are

---

[109] The framework was first advanced by Fernandez and Rodrik (1991).

likely to profit from the reform as a whole.) An example is the adoption of austerity policies. Though it is generally not disputed that in a situation of severe internal imbalances some expenditure-reducing policies are necessary, with the announcement of such reforms interest group competition typically becomes 'competition for avoiding the consequences of austerity' (Grissa (1989, p. 424) on Tunisia). Each group may block reforms as it expects other groups to bear the costs. The constellation characterises a prisoner's dilemma situation.[110]

Rent-Seekers: A Clear or Ambiguous Picture?

That rent-seekers are not likely to support reforms which threaten their wealth does not need further explanation. However there is not necessarily a simple relationship between the size of the rents and reform resistance. Furthermore rent-seeking forces in an economy also worsen the picture of 'mistaken' opponents described above. Three aspects are considered below: what constitutes the rent and determines its value; the character of dissipation; and the alternative income earning opportunities.

It may seem trivial to point out that the *size or value of the rent* matters. However, depending on the situation, it is not always easy to identify what exactly constitutes the rent and who benefits from it. The removal of a rent-creating policy may affect several parties and therefore generate resistance from different angles. Winiecki (1991, pp. 4f), for instance, emphasises that in the Soviet economic system resistance to reform of economic administration and enterprises was not just a matter of employment, salary and perks of the bureaucrats engaged; other aspects were equally important. They included the 'nomenklatura', i.e. the right of the Communist Party apparatus to recommend and approve appointments for all managerial positions (they could also designate themselves), and the kickbacks to those who appointed the bureaucrats and to other superiors and colleagues who helped bureaucrats in their careers. He thus concludes (p. 6) that partial liquidation of the bureaucracy not only affects the bureaucrats employed there, but also 'reduces the pool of available well-paid jobs to which party apparatchiks may be appointed through nomenklatura' and the kickbacks to other privileged people.

In many African economies with distinct patronage relations, similar relations have been relevant. 'Nomenklatura' may be firmly in the hands of a specific ethnic group or the inner circle of the ruling party and explain why both bureaucrats as well as the latter groups oppose reforms. In general, if reforms affect several powerful groups simultaneously they are unlikely to be adopted.

Evaluation of a rent-seeking situation may also be complex as the value an individual attributes to rent-seeking situations may not be obvious from the outset. Privatisation or the closure of inefficient parastatal companies, for instance, may also imply a revaluation of skills, which negatively affects rent-seekers. Managers who have been previously employed on the basis of loyalty

---

[110] For a formal model which takes up this aspect and explains the delay of reforms, see also Drazen (1996).

rather than merit would not just lose the rents associated with their position (embezzling funds and stealing state property), but would also find it difficult to get a new job. Winiecki describes the problem parastatal managers face in Soviet economies as follows:

> 'In any merit-based competition they would be at a strong disadvantage. Entrepreneurship, risk-taking and flexibility are not their forte. What they do know—for example, how to cultivate political links, bargain for plan change, apply for larger and earlier input supplies, manipulate output structure and doctor reports sent to their superiors—is useless in the market-type environment.' (Winiecki (1991, p. 44f))

Furthermore, as outlined in Chapter 4, rents may have non-monetary components and derive from other rationales according to which maximising wealth is only a minor side issue, or rents play a crucial role in guaranteeing the stability of a political system.

The second aspect is the *type and level of dissipation*. As extensively discussed in Chapter 3, dissipation determines the profitability of rent-seeking and takes two distinct forms, i.e. it is not only caused by rent-seeking investments but also occurs through technical and allocative inefficiencies (dead-weight losses or Harberger costs). This differentiation, as well as the specific 'timing' of dissipation, may contribute to a better understanding of the degree of resistance from rent-seekers.

In a situation where all rents are constantly dissipated by rent-seeking outlays, rent-seeking is not a bargain and abolishing a rent-seeking situation may not provoke much resistance. More critical is a situation where rents have been dissipated through inefficiencies. If adjustment was only a matter of removing rents from previous 'profiteers' and distributing them back to the groups on the losing side, it would be much less difficult to carry out. A thoroughly protected industry, however, will typically have 'consumed' most of its rents by its inefficient manner of conducting business. These inefficiencies, which have been created by access to artificial rents, do not simply disappear once the rents have been removed. In many instances rent-seekers are not innovative, talented or flexible enough to adapt to new profit-seeking conditions. Abolishment of the rents reduces their income beyond 'normal levels', i.e. it drives them into loss and ruin.

Under certain conditions the timing of dissipation may determine how forceful rent-seekers react to rent-abolishing policies. If all rent-seeking investments have been made up front but are not yet amortised, the consequences of abolishing the rent-creating policy may be felt more acutely and therefore provoke stronger resistance. In the same way, a group which has just obtained power after a long period of war is unlikely to implement rent-abating policies but will redirect the rents to themselves and share the loot among their families, allies and friends. By contrast, in a setting with ongoing rent-seeking investments, abolishing the rent-creating policy would at least not imply that rent-seekers' earlier efforts had been in vain.

The distinction between up-front and ongoing rent-seeking expenditures is also relevant in assessing the welfare implications associated with a change in policy. Using the notation of Chapter 3, if all rent-seeking outlays are made up front, only Harberger costs and not costs related to Tullock rectangles can be retrieved.[111]

All in all, depending on the specific characteristics of dissipation, the removal of the same volume of artificial rents may provoke opposition to a very different degree, either because there are large net benefits from rent-seeking or because there are substantial rent-related costs that continue after the removal of the rent. Unfortunately particularly in developing countries favourable constellations are more the exception than the rule. A great deal of rent-seeking investments are made up front, for instance when a specific group captures the rent-producing apparatus. In addition, as noted in Chapter 3, technical and allocative inefficiencies will have increased over time at the expense of 'pecuniary' transfers.

The third aspect which affects the value of a rent-seeking situation is *alternative income earning opportunities*. Rent-seekers may support rent-abolishing reforms for several reasons. Most obvious is the situation where rent-seeking is not a bargain and rent-seekers expect to make a better living under the new post-reform 'profit-seeking' conditions. The case can be put even more strongly. Even if rent-seeking is a bargain people may still favour reforms as long as alternative income earning opportunities will be sufficiently high. In a rent-seeking economy there are typically many 'petty' rent-seekers who make their way through the bureaucracy, obtaining undue benefits and favours. Under the prevailing system they may derive a considerable part of their income from rent-seeking sources. Some of them may however also have great potential to develop and prosper in a new profit-seeking environment. In particular, if all other rent-seekers are losing their privileges they may not object to giving them up too.

A similar drive for reform support may arise among those low-level civil servants with low official salaries. As often argued, not being able to make a living from their salaries they depend on top-ups such as receiving bribes or misappropriating state property. If the state can offer them a salary competitive with the private sector or if the probability for reemployment in the private sector (once reforms are initiated) is sufficiently high, some civil servants may not oppose reforms.

Rodrik (1995) elaborated the feature in a formal model which addresses the dynamics of political support for reform. The more civil servants expect to find a job in the private sector, the more they will support reforms (and, as argued in Rodrik's paper, even vote against their own subsidies). Clearly, in most developing countries increasing salaries is only a feasible option once the size of the government has been reduced substantially. Civil service reforms as well as

---

[111] For an early discussion of this aspect, see also Crew (1987) and Crew and Rowley (1988), who examine the welfare impact of deregulation.

the creation of a business-friendly environment, however, usually take a long time.

The last group of arguments again addresses the problem of mistaken reform opponents. Three arguments are considered here which are based on incomplete information, limited rationality and emotions. First, petty rent-seeking may contribute to an *inaccurate evaluation of ongoing benefits and costs*. It may be hypothesised that the extent to which people are successfully engaged in numerous little rent-seeking activities like smuggling and bribery, or are favoured because they can jump some queues, may reduce their perception of the total costs incurred to them by the big rent-seekers. Even though they are net losers they may not be aware of this.

Second, as outlined in Chapter 4.1, incomplete information and limited rationality create fertile ground for rent-seeking activities. It can be assumed that rent-seekers find it *easier to influence* citizens if they are uncertain and do not understand the impact of reform policies. Bates and Krueger (1993, p. 456) for instance note:

> 'Under conditions of uncertainty, people's beliefs of where their economic interests lie can be created and organised by political activists; rather than shaping events, notions of self-interest are instead themselves shaped and formed. In pursuing their economic interests, people act in response to ideology.'

Ideology itself is not the matter of concern, but the misuse of ideological arguments as a pretext for rent appropriation.

Third, Krueger (1989) also emphasises that uncertainty related to reforms has an *'identity bias'*. The identity of losers in contrast to that of potential winners, is better known and thus creates stronger sympathy among the population. Living in a world of incomplete information and limited rationality, powerful rent-seeking groups may even find strong support among members of social classes exploited by them.

This brief account of the role of rent-seekers in affecting the balance between reform supporters and opponents demonstrates that rent-seeking may not offer a simple, straightforward picture. Rent-seeking opposition is not just a function of the size of the rent. Among other things, it depends on the composition of the rent, on the type, level and timing of dissipation, as well as on alternative income earning opportunities. Petty rent-seekers (if not too constrained by limited rationality) may also favour economic reforms. From this it follows that there is no exact dividing line between reform opposition and support that matches the theoretical distinction between rent-seeker and profit-seeker. On aggregate, however, rent-seekers exert a clearly negative influence. Living in a world of uncertainty, they may also find it relatively easy to convince other groups to oppose reforms. Taken together, the arguments—inefficient political markets, strong rent-seekers and the prevalence of 'mistaken' opponents—explain why it can take considerable time before reforms are finally undertaken.

Breaking Opposition: Designing Appropriate Strategies

Different strategies have been suggested to address this picture of strong rent-seeking resistance to reforms and mistaken opponents. At their centre is the challenge of building a sufficiently strong coalition of reform support without greatly undermining reform goals. The strategies address the *contents, sequence and speed* of economic reforms, as well as selective steps for enhancing political and civil liberties.

Obviously, a common and 'cheap' solution for coming to terms with opposition is to *exclude* certain critical measures from the reform agenda, at least for a specific period of time. Most reforming countries have followed this path and implemented reform packages which at the outset were half-hearted and hesitant. Although they were welfare-enhancing compared to doing nothing, the strategy implied further inefficiency and sometimes tolerated for years considerable rent transfers to potentially destabilising groups.

More demanding than just excluding or postponing specific reform measures is to tackle them and offer (if it cannot be avoided) some *compensation* to losers. The critical question then becomes how and how much. At least in theory, welfare-enhancing reforms should have plenty of gains left over to pay off losers. However, as noted earlier, most of the benefits arise with a considerable lag; furthermore they would have to be extracted from other groups and may imply unwanted distributional consequences. Finally, if not well targeted compensation may undermine reform objectives, especially those of increasing competition and abolishing rents. Ideally, as Haggard and Webb (1993, p. 161) note, compensation should aim to 'ease rather than reduce the reallocation of labour and capital in line with movements in relative prices'. Unfortunately such requirements are not easy to accomplish and are especially difficult in a strong rent-seeking environment.

The need to compensate losers may be circumvented with a *'root and branch'* reform. As Rowley (1988a, p. 460) notes, 'whereas no single set of winners will agree to uncompensated rent releases, many groups simultaneously may agree to eliminate all rent-seeking opportunities, in return for some share of the wealth enhancement that must result'. Rowley uses this argument to point to an interesting paradox, that under certain conditions a resolution of rent-seeking becomes easier if rent-seeking is 'more generalised'.

The pro and cons of bundling reforms are widely debated in the literature. Especially in economies with many rent-seekers or 'veto' players, a 'bundling' strategy, where several measures are taken simultaneously, can prove to be the only way to override opposition. It offers 'something to everyone' and may avoid time inconsistency (Tommasi and Velasco (1996, p. 209)).

The literature however also presents politico-economic arguments where *unbundling* cuts the Gordian knot.[112] The argument is similar to the one advanced by Fernandez and Rodrik (1991) mentioned earlier: In a situation

[112] See Wei (1997a), or an earlier discussion in Tommasi and Velasco (1996, p. 206f), who refer to Wei.

where the entire import-competing sector blocks trade liberalisation, removing barriers on imports only in selected sectors may leave a sufficiently strong coalition of reform support. If the subsequent change in policy induces a sufficient reallocation of labour from adversely affected sectors to the booming export industry later on, there will also be a majority to remove the barriers in the remaining import sectors.

Depending on the constellation, the sequence may be determined according to welfare consideration (reform sectors first where costs of rent-seeking are highest) or by interest group considerations (reform sectors first where resistance is lowest). The latter may imply starting with sectors where rent-seeking is not so much a bargain, for instance, as rent-seeking investments are high and ongoing. In fact measures which reduce the profitability of rent-seeking may pave the way for future rent-abolishing reforms. But there are also other arguments, in particular technical reasons, which determine whether or not and how to bundle reforms. Furthermore, as will be outlined in Chapter 5.2, an inappropriate sequence or speed of reform measures can offer other rent-seeking opportunities which undermine reform success.

Finally, Chapter 4 included many suggestions for mobilising reform advocates and disillusioning 'mistaken' opponents, for instance by addressing the unfavourable patterns that determine weak collective action of interest groups receptive to reform. An important aspect is to secure sufficient resources to *communicate the cost and benefits of reforms*. As indicated with the J-curve in Figure 5-1, if a majority loses at the outset they need to be well informed to support reforms. Communicating reforms shapes public opinion, educates people and contributes to reducing the problem of incomplete information.

Under certain conditions, *political liberalisation* may positively affect the balance between reform support and opposition. However, as noted earlier, there is no straight answer as to whether authoritarian or democratic countries are better reformers, and results critically depend on the preferences and behaviour of the rulers, as well as the extent of limited rationality and incomplete information within the society.[113] Especially during the difficult stabilisation period, political liberalisation may cut both ways.

Block (2002, p. 224), for instance, finds that electorally motivated macroeconomic interventions in Africa directly undermined ongoing economic reform programmes (to reduce deficits, restrain money growth and inflation, and liberalise foreign exchange regimes and capital markets) and he concludes: 'democratisation, however desirable in its own right, represents a challenge to the sustainability of economic reform'. The main question is obviously the counterfactual one, i.e. whether an authoritarian government in the same country would have used its 'freedom' in decision-making to perform better. The World Bank (1998a, p. 18), for instance, cites empirical evidence that the probability of success has been higher for newly-elected reform governments than for authoritarian governments in power for a long time.

[113] For a brief overview of the debate see Haggard and Webb (1993, pp. 144-48).

b) Crisis for Whom? Rents, Crises and Political Relevance

Thus far not much has been said about the magnitude of the 'necessity' of reform and its relation to rent-seekers. That crises positively influence a country's willingness to introduce reforms seems to be comprehensible, at least from an intuitive point of view. Surprisingly, however, empirical evidence does not show such a clear link. A workshop report by Gulhati (1988, p. 9) concludes for sub-Saharan Africa that there is 'hardly any relation between the magnitude of policy distortions and the intensity of reforms'.[114]

One answer to this puzzle is, as frequently noted, the different perceptions of what constitutes a crisis. For instance, the same rates of inflation can provoke an immediate policy response in one country, whereas in another they would not even be criticised (Krueger (1993, p. 124)). However, more relevant for understanding how large a crisis has to be before a government implements effective economic reforms is the political economy of a country, in particular, an assessment of how ruling elites and powerful interest groups are affected by the crisis. As will be argued below, crises affect rents through various channels and rent-seekers can even benefit.

Most economic crises in developing countries have been characterised by the combination of a large internal and external imbalance. High inflation, negative real interest rates, an unsustainable debt position and, depending on the exchange rate regime, a strongly overvalued exchange rate and severe import rationing are typical features of these economies. Furthermore growth rates are usually low or negative, the country lacks important inputs, goods or services, and unemployment rates are very high.

To better understand how a crisis can affect rents and rent-seeking opposition to reforms, it is helpful to group rents into *budget-related*, *scarcity-related* and *inflation-related* rents. Open and direct transfers (subsidies) to selected companies, unjustified high allowances paid to civil servants, civil servants' embezzling of funds, misappropriation of tender-based funds, or a moderate settlement of outstanding parastatals' debt by the government are examples of *budget-related* rents. These funds depend more directly on the size of the available budget, at least in the medium and longer term.

The second group comprises rents which directly relate to *scarcities*. They have their origin in price and quantity interventions in markets where demand exceeds available supply and rationing becomes necessary. Scarcities typically allow bureaucrats to extort payments from people who are supposed to receive the funds, goods or services. Foreign exchange rationing has probably been the most significant rent-creating scarcity in LDCs. Similar scarcity rents derive from state-controlled consumer goods and inputs. Sometimes only a few public companies (and selected private companies) enjoy access to scarce inputs and

---

[114] The report lists a World Bank classification of 29 sub-Saharan countries according to their 'magnitude of distortions' at the end of the 1970s and compares it with the intensity and duration of reforms between 1980 and 1986.

thereby become the sole producer of specific goods, which allows them to further exploit monopoly rents.

Closely linked to the second group are *inflation-related* rents. They derive from prices that are not, or are with a considerable lag, adjusted to inflation. Common examples are fixed nominal interest rates or fixed prices of energy and utility services. Åslund (1994, p. 26f), for instance, mentions that in Russia:

> 'Until September 1993, subsidized credits were issued by the state at an interest rate of 10 to 25% per annum, while inflation in 1992 amounted to 2500%...'
>
> 'Several of the internal Russian energy prices; coal, gas, and electricity, have fallen to a few percent of world prices. As the domestic oil price has tended to be about one-fifth of the world price, the possession of a license and quota for oil exports has been worth a great deal...'

Obviously the higher the imbalances are, the larger is the size of these rents. Even though hyperinflation has not been prevalent in sub-Saharan economies, inflation-related rents have nevertheless substantially benefited many privileged groups, above all groups that enjoyed access to cheap credits.

Differentiation between these three sources of rents aids an understanding of the distinct evolution of rents in an economy, as a crisis intensifies, and therefore allows conclusions to be drawn regarding possible opposition from rent-seekers. However, many rents are simultaneously linked to budgets, scarcity and inflation. The grouping is a matter of degree and depends on the driving force of the rent. For instance a subsidy which reduces prices of imports to a fixed price in domestic currency (by paying the difference) will increase with higher domestic inflation, but will nevertheless have to be financed through the budget. What matters for the grouping is whether the size of the budget or the level of inflation determines the rent transferred to rent-seekers. As the crisis intensifies, relevant constraints typically change.

The Impact of a Moderate Crisis

A crisis affects an economy in different ways. Most evident is the negative influence it exerts on the productive side. Output will decline and sooner or later also diminish rents that can be extracted from the economy. However, because of the distinct sequence of size and allocation of rents, the net effect is usually quite different for selective rent-seeking beneficiaries than for the general population, basically because scarcity-related and inflation-related rents grow as the economy becomes increasingly imbalanced.

A decline in output especially affects budget-related rents, which depend more directly on taxing the economy. The impact is likely to be negative for most rent-seekers. Having already appropriated a large share of the budget—a typical feature of predatory-type rent-seeking economies—there may not be much leeway to pass on the costs of a budget reduction to other groups. In addition, inflationary financing of the budget only provides short-term relief, as it eats into the real value of the state budget. By contrast, as long as the crisis is not too large specific rent-seeking groups will gain from the impact of the crisis on scarcity and inflation-related rents. These rents are by definition not so closely linked to the size of the budget. Their per-unit extraction, which is partly captured from 'forced' suppliers, rises with larger imbalances.

The crisis-induced decline in output increases the number of goods which are in short supply and reduces the amount of rationed goods available. What makes this development beneficial to powerful rent-seekers is that most of them enjoy privileged access to rationed goods. Even though goods become scarcer, these rent-seekers may not suffer much from such a decline, as they can rely on priority treatment. More importantly, as implicit rents of rationed goods are valuable, some powerful rent-seekers are likely to capture even larger quantities, and profit as intermediaries from selling the surplus. Unlike budget-related rents, it is usually easier to pass on the costs from rationing to other groups.

Finally, inflation-related rents have the largest potential for an increase in value. Rent-seeking pressure on the budget typically causes excessive spending, which is usually financed in an inflationary manner. Also the decline in output reduces government revenues and increases the pressure for inflationary financing. Crises are thus often accompanied by considerable monetary imbalances. Once inflation reaches very high levels and persists for a few years, the grant component of credits with low regulated nominal interest rates easily approaches 100%. The benefit to rent-seekers likewise depends on the quantities they obtain. Goods and funds that include inflation-related rents may increase or decline, depending on the country's policy. Often, inflation-related rents are already fully captured by rent-seekers, with the effect that there is not much scope to further enlarge their relative share. Table 5-1 summarises the likely impact of a 'moderate' crisis on rents and the relative share taken by powerful rent-seekers.

In the earlier stages of a crisis, budget losses to rent-seekers may still be relatively small compared to the increasing benefits from scarcity and inflation-related rents (some budget-related rents may even be financed by additional outside borrowing). This positive net impact may last quite a long time. For a certain interval, as long as the crisis does not reach a critical level, a clear negative relation between the intensity of a crisis and the desirability of reforms may be observed, i.e. the larger the crisis, the larger the net rents received by the 'powerful' and the less attractive reforms for the ruling elites. The extent of such a relation will critically depend on the relative size and strength of the different rent-seeking groups in the economy.

Intensifying Crises and Turnaround

As the crisis worsens and the economy dwindles further, budget-related sources shrink at an even faster speed. Government revenues, which are the basis of budget-related rents, are not only small because the country produces less, but also because the state typically loses control over the economy. Bates and Krueger (1993, p. 452) describe this phenomenon as the *'withering away of the*

Table 5-1: Possible Impact of a 'Moderate' Crisis on Rents and Rent-Seekers

Rents related to	Total supply of rent-related funds or goods in the economy	Supply to powerful rent-seekers	Change in real value of rent (per unit of supplied funds or goods)	Change in relative share captured by powerful rent-seekers	Net impact on rent-seekers
Budget	↓↓↓	↓↓	o / -	+	**neg**
Scarcity	↗→↘	↗→↘	+ +	+ + +	**pos**
Inflation	↗→↘	↗→↘	+ + +	o / + / + +	**pos**

Crises exert a negative impact on the economy's output. This affects rent-related funds and goods in different ways. Government revenues, which depend on taxing the economy, decline. Rent-bearing rationed goods increase in number (more goods are rationed) and decrease in quantity (rationed goods become scarcer). The supply of goods and funds that include inflation-related rents will vary according to the country's policy reaction to the crisis.

The impact of a moderate crisis on budget-related rents is usually negative for rent-seekers, even though they are likely to capture larger shares. Inflation may further reduce the real value of the budget. In contrast to that, powerful rent-seekers often gain with rationed goods. They not only manage to significantly increase their shares; implicit rents, in addition, rise in value. Inflation-related rents have an even larger potential for an increase in value, i.e. the grant component of goods and credits acquired can come close to 100%.

state'. As they note, the growing size of the informal sector, the emergence of widespread smuggling and other evasions of regulations, together with the loss of revenue from the inflation tax can dramatically reduce government income.

In addition, an ever-tightening state budget will sooner or later constrain the availability of some other, scarcity and inflation-related rents. Inflation-related rents can often rely on a preferential or even automatic access to the budget (contingent liabilities commonly lead to budget overruns and are financed in an inflationary manner). As the crisis intensifies, this easy way of financing may not be possible any more or it may be deliberately limited as it turns out to be too costly. A binding budget for inflation-related rents nevertheless does not have to affect powerful rent-seekers, if there are still other groups benefiting from the rent policy. Budget constraints are then likely to first reduce their access and inflation will continue, at least for some time, to determine the size of inflation-related rents transferred to the powerful.

A severe crisis likewise affects scarcity-related rents. Although implicit rents of rationed goods, soft credits and official foreign exchange allocations increase, these rent-bearing funds and goods are less and less available. Once their allocation to 'average' citizens has been reduced to a minimum, a further decrease in scarce funds and resources inevitably affects major rent-seekers.

The development of rents has been summarised in Figure 5-2. Despite initial 'benefits' as described in Table 5-1, a crisis may finally reach a point where it exerts an overall negative impact on powerful rent-seekers. The loss in rent income may become so substantial that rent-seekers finally favour efficiency-enhancing reforms, even though such reforms may threaten some of their remaining rents. Furthermore dissipation typically rises as competition for remaining rents becomes more severe. This again reduces rent-seeking resistance towards reforms.

Figure 5-2: Rents and the Crisis

A rent-seeking economy usually distributes different budget, scarcity and inflation-related rents, which all depend on the intensity of the crisis. The diagram outlines a possible evolution of these rents, as the crisis develops and intensifies. Causality between rents and crisis typically runs both ways.

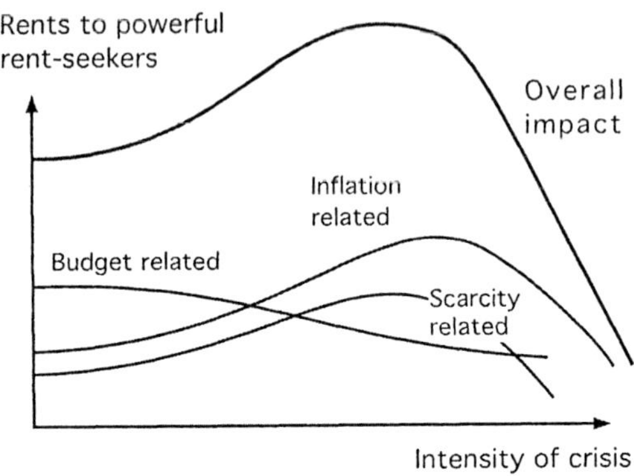

All in all, crises may reach a stage where major rent-seekers find *themselves* in a crisis and therefore become reform advocates. Their expected pay-off from reforming is then larger than the pay-off from keeping the status quo. The initially positive effect of a crisis on selective rent-seekers may nevertheless last sufficiently long to bring about the collapse of an entire economy. The Tanzanian situation during the first half of the 1980s comes close to such a scenario, even though other aspects than rent-seeking have been relevant in determining crisis and reform resistance there.

How severe a crisis has to be and what shapes the interval during which the crisis benefits rent-seekers critically depends on the politico-economic setting, in particular the size and political strength of the rent-seeking groups in power. The smaller in number ruling elites and their benefiting rent-seeking clienteles are, the easier it is to pass on the costs of the crisis to other groups and the longer it will be possible to benefit from scarcity and inflation-related rents while others are losing out.

Additional Considerations in Evaluating Crises

The picture of the relevance of a crisis drawn so far has been purposely kept simple. The goal was to demonstrate the main driving forces that influence rents during a crisis. For an adequate interpretation of a specific situation many more aspects have to be taken into consideration. Three in particular are worth mentioning.

First, the decision to reform is not only a matter of rents. Equally important, is *political pressure* from other groups who push the government to introduce reforms. Under 'normal' conditions such pressure increases as a crisis intensifies and adds a growing negative component to the overall rent-seekers' impact outlined in Table 5-1. In effect, a country may finally introduce reforms not because powerful rent-seekers have decided to do so, but because a sufficiently pro-reform majority has been mobilised against the ruling elites.

Second, the differentiation between powerful rent-seekers and the remaining population is not necessarily static, nor immediate. Rent-seekers may be ordered along a *continuum* from less to more powerful groups and individuals. Following the description of Table 5-1, as the crisis intensifies individual rent-seekers will increase the relative share of rents they capture. The benefiting group however becomes smaller, as marginal (less powerful) rent-seekers drop out. This of course will affect the political balance of reform support and opposition.

Third, the ruling elite's option is not just to reform or not. Between the two extreme positions of implementing thorough reforms and doing nothing exists a broad range of *intermediate alternatives* to react to the crisis. It has often been observed that the pressure for further reforms lessens once the first few reform steps have been taken. Selected and half-hearted reforms can keep an economy in a state where benefits to rent-seekers are high or even maximised. The stop-and-go policies observed in many developing countries may reflect such a situation. Haggard and Webb (1993, p. 153) describe this relationship as follows:

> 'As the crisis winds down, the urgency of reform lessens and the political forces resistant to reform typically revive. The outcome can be a cycle of policy deterioration, economic crises, temporary or partial policy reform, recovery, and relapse.'

Nevertheless, there have also been more successful developments where a crisis has led to a thorough and lasting change in the power constellation. For instance, once inefficiencies are widely perceived and ideology uncovered as a rent-seeking instrument, groups who support reform may become sufficiently strong to make the process irreversible. They may press for a new government, which will enjoy the usual benefits of a 'honeymoon' period to start off with the difficult stabilisation of the economy.

All in all, the stylised rent-determining channels of a crisis help in understanding and analysing resistance to reforms as a crisis develops and intensifies. Even though the perspective does not include the essence of a reform decision in its entirety, it describes an important part.[115] As noted above, rent-seekers may finally accept to reforms once they are under sufficient pressure (or they may be overruled by a pro-reform majority). What usually happens then is that rent-seekers develop other strategies to secure their unproductive income earning

---

[115] For an interesting paper which elaborates several aspects of the demand and supply for reforms, see also Beez and Mäder (1997).

opportunities. The strategies relate to both direct and indirect resistance to specific measures as well as selected support to take advantage of rent-seeking opportunities that arise as a side product of not-well-targeted reform measures. These issues are addressed in the following chapter.

5.2 Adopting and Implementing Reforms

a) Rent-Seeking Strategies During Reforms

> *'While the ongoing reforms had resulted in many of the prevailing regulations being eliminated, the problem was that they had not eliminated the regulators.'*
>
> *Senior official in India, cited from Kaufmann (1998b, p. 139f)*

Having surveyed arguments that explain why a government finally decides to adopt reforms, this chapter focuses on the reform process and reviews problems which are highly relevant for reform-minded politicians within the country, as well as for donors who provide aid in the form of project and programme support, balance of payments support and budget support (usually conditional on sound economic policies or some promised reform steps).

From the earlier discussion however it follows that a government's decision to introduce reforms may be based on a weak coalition of support. It hardly ever rests on the unanimous agreement of all affected parties. On the contrary, the political environment may have just changed slightly and tipped the balance in favour of support for reform. Even more important, since some reform steps are the result of donor conditionalities, the interest of the government may lie in *obtaining promised resources* offered in exchange for some economic reforms and not necessarily on the conditionalities accepted. Whatever the background may be, reforms are typically carried out in a more or less intense environment of opposition, where direct or indirect rent-seeking resistance is likely to occur either from the government itself or from groups which have been overruled by the government's decision.[116] Additionally, the sequence and speed of reform implementation also offers new opportunities to rent-seekers to enrich themselves. Rent-seeking strategies are thus not just a question of reform resistance.

Looking at the reform records of developing countries in the 1980s and 1990s, the performance of a vast majority of reform programmes has been rather poor or at best moderate. Shortcomings and complications have been numerous and typically appeared at different stages. Table 5-2 groups the reform process into the three sequential steps *policy formulation, policy implementation* and *policy outcome*. As will be argued below, it appears that many problems in the reform process are directly and indirectly related to rent-seeking activities.

Deficiencies and complications on the level of *policy formulation* arise if the measures planned are not suitable or sufficient to address a specific problem, for instance a severe economic imbalance or an allocative inefficiency in a specific market. Often fairly open rent-seeking resistance accounts for the lack of

[116] As noted earlier, there are many intermediate alternatives between the extreme positions of implementing thorough reforms and doing nothing.

planning of appropriate policies. The ruling elites may severely resist reform in strategic areas with high rents, for instance by not adjusting overvalued exchange rates, by opposing the closure or privatisation of hopelessly inefficient parastatals, or by not liberalising an inefficient marketing system. As noted earlier, they may be the principal direct profiteers in an inefficient system or they may depend on the distribution of rents to other powerful groups. Policymakers then typically bring up other reasons than rent-seeking for not adopting the policy. Supposed concerns about quality or, more fundamentally, a disbelief in market forces, are frequently raised arguments.

Table 5-2: Uncertainty, Complications and Rent-Seeking Resistance in the Reform Process

Policy Formulation	I. What should have been planned? ('best case')	↔	What has been planned?			
Policy Implementation			II. What has been planned?	↔	What has been implemented?		
Policy Outcome					III. What has been the result of implementation?	↔	What has been expected?

It goes without saying that the question 'What should have been planned?' is provocative. It requires an idea of the 'right policy', including timing and sequencing. However, as indicated earlier, the detailed design and choice of specific measures is partly normative, i.e. different strategies include different levels and distributions of adjustment costs (recall the curves drawn in Figure 5-1). Furthermore, given the problem of uncertainty, a final choice is in some cases not possible ex-ante, but results from a process of trial and error. The neo-classical benchmark—which is to 'do all reforms simultaneously' (Tommasi and Velasco (1996, p. 204))—is simply not helpful when it comes to addressing a real situation where the development of efficiency-enhancing institutions takes time, where rigidities prevent a smooth adjustment and where the capacity of a country to carry out reforms may be considerably limited. For a specific situation, and given the general uncertainty surrounding reforms, there are therefore arguments and reasons to slow down, postpone or even to exclude particular measures from the reform agenda. This ambiguity helps the position of rent-seekers and makes identification of rent-seeking resistance on the level of policy formulation especially difficult.

Even so, there are also many economic imperatives where there is widespread agreement among policy advisers and technocrats on what to do. To limit the deficit to an affordable level and to abstain from excessive inflationary financing, to devalue a severely overvalued exchange rate, and to introduce checks and balances, in particular accountability within bureaucracy and parastatal companies, are a few examples.

If the opposition of rent-seekers to the formulation of reform measures is not possible or if it becomes too apparent, resistance is likely to shift. As widely perceived, it will be on the level of *policy implementation*, where rent-seeking groups enjoy a strategic advantage in resisting reforms which have been determined by government technocrats or pressured by donor conditionality. Especially government bureaucracy is difficult to monitor.

Sometimes the announcement of a reform measure is highly welcomed among the donor community, in particular if a government had been unwilling to address a specific problem for years. However, government position papers, budget speeches and other strategic documents on reforming the economy include a large number of announcements which have not been followed by effective implementation. The Tanzanian case study will provide many such examples.

As with the level of policy formulation, on the implementation level too it may be difficult to uncover rent-seeking resistance, basically because there are always other explanations, such as technical and capacity-related problems, to justify delays or even to argue that certain measures cannot be implemented at all. In addition, some implementation targets, such as a strengthening of supervisory agencies, are not as easy to observe and quantify.

Yet even though demands and problems related to policy formulation and implementation can be substantial and should not be underestimated, explanations that persistently cite other reasons than rent-seeking for major delays and setbacks are usually flawed. Lafay and Lecaillon (1993, p. 19) have formulated this in a diplomatic way:

> 'Actual public decisions, however, depart too often and too systematically from the technical optimum ... There is every reason to believe that governments are less naïve and less inexperienced than economists suppose, and that their "errors" are to a large extent deliberate and simply demonstrate the lack of correlation between the functions of the public decision-makers' real objectives and the function of "collective well-being".'

Finally, some reform measures may not show the *expected outcome*, even though they have been fairly well planned and implemented. This aspect reflects the third level outlined in Table 5-2. It is partly a result of the above-mentioned problem of incomplete information and limited rationality, which implies that reforms are sometimes an iterative planning and implementation process. In particular adverse developments in world markets, unfavourable weather conditions, negative side effects of other policies or overenthusiastic expectations of supply responses may explain an unsatisfactory outcome to implemented measures. However, again on this third level, rent-seeking strategies may contribute a great deal to explaining the unsatisfactory outcome.

First, policy measures may not show expected results as they are implemented in an *existing rent-seeking environment* which has not been taken into consideration. For instance, devaluation may not eliminate the parallel market if transactions on the parallel market are necessary to cover illegal activities, such as widespread smuggling. Or raising prices of medicines to introduce 'true costs' may overshoot, if bribery is still necessary to obtain the now correctly-priced drugs. These complications arise from rent-seeking activities which are already present at the outset of reform.

More closely related to the reform are complications where rent-seeking strategies *arise as a result of the reform process*. Table 5-3 surveys these strategies. They are grouped into two broad categories: direct and indirect rent-seeking resistance against reform measures, and rent-seeking activities which take advantage of reform steps and the transition.

Table 5-3: Rent-Seeking Strategies and the Reform Process

		direct	indirect
Rent-seeking resistance against reform measure:	• Policy formulation	x	x
	• Policy implementation	x	x
	• Countervailing action		x
Reforms and the transition phase: (Taking advantage of new rent-seeking opportunities)	• Rent-seeking reformer		
	• Economic, political and related institutional transition		

Direct resistance applies to a narrow definition of rent-seeking opposition to a reform measure and refers to what has been subsumed in Table 5-2 (p. 266) within the first two levels (a measure is either excluded from the agenda or not implemented). *Indirect resistance* and rent-seeking related with *reform and transition* summarise rent-seeking arguments which explain why the outcome of a policy may deviate from what has been expected, either entirely or at least related to some important aspects (third level in Table 5-2). It is clear that any reform which does not show satisfactory results will need more appropriate policies to be planned and implemented. Not dealt with at the outset, these problems feed into the next planning and implementation stage. In the following two sections the different indirect strategies, as well as rent-seeking from the transition phase, will be addressed in more detail.

Indirect Rent-Seeking Resistance

In contrast to direct resistance against a reform measure, indirect resistance comprises rent-seeking strategies which are more diverse and therefore more difficult to control and anticipate. They range from straight countervailing actions to more complex and less apparent strategies and have in common that, at least at a quick glance, the reform measure is not directly opposed and 'fairly' implemented. A great deal of the rents related to the original rent-creating policy may however not disappear, or they may be compensated by additional rent-capturing strategies. As indicated in Table 5-3, indirect strategies refer to policy formulation and policy implementation, and they include countervailing actions.

On the level of *policy formulation,* indirect resistance describes a situation where policymakers formulate measures that predominantly address *non-binding constraints*. Reform steps are then not sequenced according to economic and institutional logic (e.g. eliminate the worst distortions and give priority to capacity-relieving reforms), but according to rent-protecting considerations, i.e. the first few measures taken will not or only marginally affect rents in the economy. What makes it an indirect strategy on the level of planning is that without looking into details the reform agenda may give the impression that the government is already doing a lot to address a specific problem.

As mentioned earlier, there is usually much room to justify why some measures have not yet been planned or are still limited in scope. The government may emphasise its limited capacity to carry out several reform steps simultaneously and, being unsure of the results, it may reason that it is best to start with few measures and wait for their results to materialise (of course not unhappy that the measures undertaken so far did not abolish rents of the major rent-seekers). The argument of addressing non-binding constraints applies either to the scope of a single measure or to the interaction of a group of measures.

The OGL facility (Open General Licence), a scheme to gradually liberalise imports in an economy, serves as a good example to demonstrate the case of a single measure. At the onset, an OGL list specifies an increasing number of goods that can be freely imported. Once the list has become large, it is usually converted into a negative list (indicating goods that are not free), and the list then becomes shorter with further liberalisation.

Two arguments explain why in earlier stages, or even after quite a while, the OGL facility may not reach its underlying targets. On the one hand, a country may liberalise 95% of its protected goods but if the remaining 5% make up 80% in volume not much will have changed (see also World Bank (1994a, p. 73)). On the other hand, in the early stages the sequence of goods listed may even increase effective protection. As noted by the World Bank (1994a, p. 72) 'the first goods placed on an OGL list are those that are not produced domestically (so no one lobbies against them), but that are required as inputs for domestic production (so producers who use them lobby for them)'. The World Bank concludes that placing the input rather than the final product on the list will lower input costs without altering the prices of the final product and therefore raise effective protection.

Similarly, in the export sector measures are often sequenced so as to protect rents for the longest possible period. Tanzania for instance addressed its non-traditional export sector in the mid-1980s, almost a decade before it finally liberalised its considerably more voluminous traditional exports (see discussion in Chapter 7.2).

The strategy to address non-binding constraints also applies to the situation where the success of a reform goal depends on a set of policy measures. The most prevalent example is the problem of fighting corruption. As outlined in Table 4-1 on page 153, the necessary conditions for the profitability of corrupt transactions reflect an interaction between many different parameters, and significantly reducing corruption requires that these parameters be addressed simultaneously. Many of the developing countries, which had anti-corruption measures on their agendas for years, did not reduce the level of corruption, mostly as the probability of failure of corrupt transactions remained virtually zero. The case of Tanzania also provides striking examples (see, above all, the discussion in Chapter 7.3).

Another example where reform success may depend on addressing several measures simultaneously is the case of trade protection. As emphasised by the World Bank (1994a, p. 64f) trade protection has often been complex so that different protective measures overlapped. If licence procedures are cumbersome, pseudo-quality requirements prohibitive, and foreign exchange rationing still present, reforming tariffs alone may not reduce effective protection. In addition, formal liberalisation of a market will not increase the efficiency of parastatal companies therein if they continue to operate under a soft budget constraint (parastatals may even undercut efficient competitors). They may for instance be shielded from the effects of competition as they continue to benefit from preferential credits (on which they later default). Or devaluation may not benefit farmers who produce export crops if the monopoly of marketing boards has not been abolished and marketing boards do not pass on the gains from the devaluation to the farmers.

Besides policy formulation, also on the level of *policy implementation* there are many ways to resist reforms. A critical measure may be much delayed (direct resistance) or important subordinated and complementary steps deliberately not carried out (indirect resistance within a single measure respectively within a group of measures). A government may introduce a new regulation, but if the regulation is unwanted it may not enforce it, for instance by not implementing or strengthening the necessary supervisory agencies.

Strategies are sometimes even more basic. A frequent complaint is that policymakers are quick to support the idea of conducting studies on a specific problem, in particular if the studies are financed by the donor community. What then happens however is that one study follows the next, without the country ever reaching the stage of effectively addressing reforms. The studies basically serve as a pretext to demonstrate that the government is doing something. Time-consuming and unimplemented, they effectively hold off and delay reforms.

Direct and indirect opposition on the level of policy formulation and policy implementation are usually substitutes and depend on the relative costs.[117] As costs change over time, opposition likewise shifts from one level to the other. For instance, for almost ten years the local government in Zanzibar (Tanzania)

[117] To some extent the differentiation is a matter of perspective and definition.

resisted harmonising its low tariff rates with the mainland. The tax differential was the cause of major tax-evading transactions, known as the 'Zanzibar route'. As will be explained in Chapter 7.1 goods were brought in through Zanzibar and then sold on the mainland. After a lot of pressure Zanzibar finally agreed to adjust its rates; the Zanzibar route however did not disappear. Even though official tariffs were the same on the mainland as in Zanzibar, incentives to import through Zanzibar remained. Opposition simply shifted to the implementation level. Importers did pay higher tariffs, but apparently they colluded with Zanzibar officials, making sure that they only paid taxes for a share of goods they imported (personal communication in Dar es Salaam, March 2000).

Countervailing actions against specific reform measures are the third indirect way of reform resistance indicated in Table 5-3. Unlike the indirect rent-protecting strategy discussed above, with countervailing actions a new binding policy is deliberately created to replace another (and not already present at the outset). The strategy may become especially relevant if the effective implementation of an unwanted policy measure cannot be prevented. As Toye (1992, p. 196) notes, referring to the findings of a case study on policy-based lending (Mosley, Harrigan and Toye (1991)) 'a government could comply with a loan condition, but at the same time take other actions not specifically prohibited which had the effect of neutralising that compliance'.

The government may give in to demands to liberalise a sector while introducing high bureaucratic barriers to benefit remaining parastatal companies. Or it may introduce important regulatory and fiscal measures together with an increase of opportunities for 'cronies' to evade them. In many instances governments reduce exemptions on taxation while simultaneously creating new loopholes. Lewis and Stein (1997, p. 10), for instance, described the regulatory environment in the financial sector of Nigeria as being schizophrenic, 'embodying both a mandate for control [in adherence with IFI conditions] and widening room for evasion'. The case study on Tanzania will also reveal many examples.

Countervailing actions may be implemented immediately, or reflect a gradual process. Mair (1996, p. 45f), for instance, notes that in Kenya Moi used to take one big step forward and several small steps back, in effect leaving the country not far from the initial pre-reform position. He illustrates the case of formally introducing but never accepting multipartyism. As he notes, despite the implementation of the multi-party system, Moi refused to have formal contacts with the opposition, refused to transfer public investments into constituencies which had been won by the opposition, and severely violated the freedom of press and assembly to restrain opposing forces.

Opportunities for countervailing actions are especially numerous and diverse within the parastatal sector. Table 5-4 illustrates the case of African Gourmet Coffee, an efficient private company which was set up after Malawi liberalised its coffee market. Even though the company effectively tripled the prices paid to farmers, it was never given a 'level playing field'. Not being able to compete against a highly inefficient and still-protected government marketing system, it finally had to close down.

Table 5-4: Coffee Market Liberalisation and Effective Resistance in Malawi—The Case of African Gourmet Coffee (AGC)

The pre-reform situation, investment decision and competitive offer:
Between 1991 and 1994 the Coffee Authority's marketing expenses in Malawi averaged 80% of revenues, excluding depreciation, cost of farmer loan defaults and debt interests. Thus total processing and handling cost could not have averaged much less than 90% of revenue. It is no surprise that little was left to pay farmers. The decision to enter the market with the new firm, African Gourmet Coffee (AGC), began with some simple arithmetic. In August 1994, the New York spot market for green coffee was $4.49/Kg, shipping costs were estimated to be $0.25/Kg and the price paid to farmers in Malawi was only $0.43/Kg (green equivalent).

By the middle of the 1995 season, AGC had developed the logistics to buy coffee in villages. New York prices meanwhile had dropped to near 3.30/kg. AGC announced a cash farm price of $1.88/kg, more than four times as large than the Coffee Authority's 1994 price. The Authority responded immediately by raising its price to 1.10/Kg. The latter would be paid at end of season when inflation would reduce its present value to around $0.94/Kg, so it represented barely one-half the AGC offer. Nevertheless, the Authority captured 90% of the 1995 smallholder crop.

The first countervailing action: The key to its success was control of the twenty-seven village-level pulperies. Soon after AGC's appearance, the Authority declared that farmers intending to sell to non-Authority entities would be barred from pulpery use. The level playing field had developed a pronounced tilt. After extensive negotiations, AGC had obtained an agreement with the minister of agriculture that the new farm cooperatives would be permitted 'equal access' to village pulping facilities.

The second countervailing action: Just as harvest was beginning, the Coffee Authority made the following catch-22 statement: farmers wishing to sell cherry (= ripe coffee on the tree) to a cooperative would first have to pay a pulpery user fee, while those selling to the Authority would be exempt. Few growers could pay such a fee even if they wished to, since little money is available in mountain villages until the cherry has been processed and payment for it received. AGC petitioned the Ministry—which, it transpired, had never authorised the fee—to intervene. The user fee controversy dragged on for two months, into the middle of the 1996 harvest season. The Minister announced that it would cut the fees in half and require payment only at the end of the year. Meanwhile, however, the Authority had captured most of the early harvest through its user fee pronouncement.

The third countervailing action and AGC's bankruptcy: As the teeth in its user fee threat solved, the Authority showed it had other weapons in its market share arsenal: it began simply to renege on its earlier agreement to share pulpery time on a volume-proportionate basis with farmer cooperatives. This move was illegal but forced members to sell to the Authority. By year-end the Coffee Authority had, despite farm prices effectively 34% lower than its competitor's, purchased 75% of the smallholder crop. In the face of substantial size economies and lobbying costs, AGC lost US$83,000, bringing its total two-year loss to US$104,000. In mid-1997, African Gourmet Coffee informed the Agriculture Ministry that it was withdrawing its investments. The competition that had tripled farm incomes had evaporated.

Source: Buccola and McCandlish (1999, p. 360-65), quotation marks omitted

---

The case of coffee market liberalisation clearly demonstrates that if an activity in a market depends on several steps (collection, transport, processing, etc.) the implementation of countermeasures is particularly easy.

Many of the parastatal companies in Africa managed for years to enjoy undue protection and to live on soft budget constraints, partly by compensating the removal of a specific type of support with an increase or creation of another. Furthermore, as will be discussed below, once privatisation has become inevitable some of the ruling elites and their cronies may again benefit from insider sales or the simultaneous creation of protection in the privatised market, with the effect that rent extraction simply changes its mode from extraction through the state apparatus to extraction in protected private spheres.

Reforms and the Transition Phase: Taking Advantage of New Rent-Seeking Opportunities

As noted earlier, rent-seeking is not only a matter of reform resistance. The reform process also offers additional rent-seeking opportunities, which are not linked to reform opposition (at least not at the outset), but which depend on single reform measures and closely relate to the transition phase.

The economic transition typically involves a move towards a system with a larger role for market forces and private sector activities. It either sets off from an entirely planned economy, from an interventionist market system dominated by a large parastatal sector or from an economy with a large but highly protected private sector. Political transitions accompanying economic reforms have usually been characterised by a move towards a more democratic order. Democratisation may range from an introduction of selected democratic principles, such as free elections or an explicit abstention of repressive measures, to a more fundamental change which comprises a transition from an authoritarian (or even totalitarian) regime to a liberal democracy. Finally, economic and political transitions are always accompanied by a change of the institutional framework that underlies the economic and political system. Many complications in the transition arise as changes within the institutional framework lag behind developments in other areas.

Rent-seeking opportunities from the transition have been widely discussed in the context of system transformation in Soviet-type economies, on which the following discussion will partly draw (for an overview of rents in the transition phase, see for instance, Gelb, Hillman and Ursprung (1995)). Even though the transition literature confines itself to describing countries of the former communist bloc, many problems are equally relevant in other adjusting countries. This is also emphasised in the 1996 World Development Report 'From Plan to Market':

> 'What distinguishes transition from reforms in other countries is the systemic change involved: reform must penetrate to the fundamental rules of the game, to the institutions that shape behaviour and guide organisations. This makes it a profound social transition as well as an

economic one. Similar changes have been needed in many other countries, and the transition experience is therefore of interest to them as well.' (World Bank (1996b, p. 1))

Countries like Tanzania, Mozambique, Ghana or Nigeria, for instance—where the parastatal sector has been large and dominated the formal economy, and where price interventions have been pervasive—faced many similar tasks of system transformation as did economies in transition of the former communist bloc. What distinguishes them from economies in transition are mainly the starting conditions, i.e. their different sectoral structure, and the weight given to different issues related to development and transitions.

Economies of LDCs are typically characterised by a high share of agriculture and small businesses. In many of these countries industry is barely developed. This contrasts with most of the countries of the former communist bloc, where a large well-established industrial sector already existed. There, privatisation became a more complicated and larger task. In addition, the CMEA (Council of Mutual Economic Assistance) had contributed to the development of a poorly diversified and highly interdependent economy different in structure to that in LDCs.

Rent-seeking which is not directed against reforms but results from transition and takes advantage of certain reform measures, arises from two sources (recall the list in Table 5-3). On the one hand, many of the politicians and bureaucrats who plan and carry out reforms are *themselves rent-seekers*. On the other hand, the transition takes time and may be characterised by *intermediate frictions*, such as contradictions and inefficiencies, which offer rent-seeking opportunities.

In countries with an adverse political culture, implementing specific reform measures (usually supported by donors) can even increase the share of rents a predatory government extracts from the economy. The problems occur if reforms *empower* a government without simultaneously constraining the bureaucrats in their corrupt rent-seeking behaviour. Many essential reform measures require strengthening government institutions, for instance to improve the administration in collecting tax revenues or to strengthen bodies which enforce rules and regulations. However, if not well targeted empowerment reduces the institutional limits to rent extraction, making governments more efficient in what they have been doing before, i.e. appropriating rents and embezzling funds through corruption.

For instance, unless there is strong interest group resistance, a government is unlikely to oppose donor-supported reforms which broaden the tax base and increase the government's ability to levy taxes. These measures are usually part of a stabilisation package which, among other things, aims to get the budget deficit closer to a sustainable level. However, introducing tax identification numbers, supplying customs officials with better means of communication between transit points, or equipping customs police with expensive jeeps to control the border and catch smugglers may strengthen their ability to extort additional bribes. The problem in Côte d'Ivoire at the end of the 1980s, where the widening of the tax base did not increase government receipts, partly reflects this situation:

> 'A new tax collecting mechanism was introduced in an attempt to capture "the informal sector"...This innovation made small-scale traders vulnerable to extortion practised by the state's tax enforcers. It also intensified pressure on importers and wholesalers to avoid the internal tax burden altogether. The cumulative result was more fraud and contraband.' (Boone (1994, p. 459))

As will be illustrated in Chapter 7.1, to some extent Tanzania also presented an ambiguous picture after their tax administration had been strengthened. Though donors may be pleased if government revenues increase—improving revenue collection is in fact a very important goal in most LDCs—in a corrupt environment side payments into unofficial pockets may even be boosted more. If the informal economy, which successfully evades taxes and other regulations, uses resources more efficiently than a corrupt government administration, 'inadequately' strengthening the government would even have a negative impact on private sector activity and thereby hamper the future development of the country. Obviously, a better design or sequence of reform measures can solve the problem (or at least minimise unwanted negative side effects). This may however not be in the interest of the ruling elites. Correspondingly, like strengthening the tax administration, empowering the police force can make police officers more efficient in harassing people and extorting side payments—this time to a considerable extent from innocent victims as well.

Both empowerment as well as the strategy mentioned earlier of addressing non-binding constraints create, reallocate or sustain rents because important complementary measures are not implemented. Reforms also provide rent-seeking opportunities as some reform steps are implemented in a 'rent-seeking' manner. *Privatisation or land reforms* are particularly susceptible areas that allow, if not well targeted, massive enrichment by ruling elites and their entourage. As widely noted, without well-specified and closely monitored procedures which restrict a state apparatus driven by rent-seeking from being corrupt, privatisation is unlikely to be a fair and open process, but rather characterised by insider deals, bribery and patronage considerations. The problem has been well documented for countries in eastern Europe and the former Soviet Union. The Economist (1999, p. 25), referring to Russia, puts it strikingly in stating that privatisation has become 'an orgy of sweetheart deals'.

Following the survey in Gelb, Hillman and Ursprung (1995, p. 6), the purchase of companies (or some assets thereof) at far below market prices provides much-favoured rents. In particular parastatal managers enjoy a strategic position. They and other insiders may withhold or distort information (e.g. report figures for lower than actual profitability) to reduce the valuation of the company, which is then sold at less than the market value. The new owners may be the managers themselves, members of supervising agencies, such as civil servants in parent ministries and supervisory boards, other stakeholders in the privatisation process, and obviously relatives and friends. It is not far-fetched to hypothesise that in an economy driven by rent-seeking, expected rents from privatisation may be a key element in overcoming resistance against privatisation. Some of the previous gains related to the parastatal or bureaucratic position are then simply transformed into gains from the 'insider' sale.

Besides the problem of corrupt state administration, rent-seeking opportunities are created and rent transfers facilitated because the *economic, political* and related *institutional transition* takes time and involves intermediate frictions. Markets may develop and adjust only slowly to a new situation. The shift from 'plan' and 'intervention' to a more liberal market system has therefore often been accompanied by rigidities and imperfections, which sustained and even increased intermediate scarcity-related and monopoly-related rents.

Furthermore, especially the transition in eastern Europe and the former Soviet Union, which also included a major political transition, required a thorough reorganisation of state institutions. As many authors have emphasised, the redefinition of core state activities, as well as the change to a new legal apparatus included a weakening (or breakdown) of an old system without providing an immediate new alternative. It thereby created vast rent-seeking opportunities, in particular corrupt activities, which partly undermined reform success. Åslund (1994, p. 28f), for instance, notes on the weak state in eastern Europe:

> 'In a Communist society, the legal apparatus in a Western sense was rudimentary, while the previous abundant arbitrary repression is not permissible in a democratic society. The control functions of the Communist Party are gone.'
>
> 'Criminality has flourished in the wake of Communism, and law enforcement is miserable because the old dictatorial repressive system no longer functions and, as yet, little rule of law has been established because it takes time to evolve an appropriate legal apparatus.'

A functioning legal system not only requires laws which address crime and violence, but appropriate laws and regulations to ease and support transactions in a market economy.

In many African countries as well, intermediate weaknesses have increased rent-seeking opportunities leading among other things to an increase in corruption. Rent-seeking opportunities frequently arise from weaknesses and loopholes with rules and regulations and their selective non-enforcement. They may also result from a combination of intermediate institutional weaknesses and frictions from slow adjustment and markets characterised by shortages. Sometimes weaknesses coincide with a coup d'état or military revolts. Rent-capturing opportunities which occur in both the public sector and the growing private sector include *profit shifting*, *asset stripping*, *insider privatisation* and rents obtained through a system of *crony capitalism*.

Profit shifting resembles transfer-pricing methods of multinational companies; funds are however not necessarily transferred abroad and they are shifted to an independent company or contract partner (e.g. fixing 'artificially' high prices for inputs and assets bought or low prices for the goods and assets sold). In countries with a weak legal framework profit shifting is common (mostly shifting profits from a parastatal to private companies), and the 'price' is shared between involved parties. Similar practices of profit shifting can also take place in strictly private spheres, where a private company shifts funds to another, before it files for bankruptcy and defaults on its loans.

Profit shifting can mushroom during the reform process as a result of a weakened parastatal control and an increase in private sector activity which is not backed by an institutional setting that sufficiently guarantees secure property rights. Again, the problem has been particularly prevalent in eastern Europe and the former Soviet Union. The Economist (1999, p. 23), for instance, remarks regarding Bulgaria:

> 'As in many other ex-communist countries, Bulgaria's factory bosses saw the advent of the free market as an opportunity for plunder. They paid too much for raw materials, and charged too little for finished goods. To cover their losses, they borrowed from the banks. The government of barely reformed communists, itself up to its neck in shady business dealings, winked at the stripping of the banks.'

In many African countries, where private sector activity has always played a larger role, profit shifting was common practice before, although it most likely increased during the reform process.

A related form of rent appropriation is *asset stripping*, usually associated with a pre-announced (or expected) closure or privatisation of a parastatal company. As mentioned in Chapter 4.1, if parastatal employees know in advance that the company is going to close or that they will lose their jobs because of the announced retrenchment, the incentive structure changes to favour rent-seeking. Having little to lose from being fired, asset stripping and other risky corrupt transactions are likely to increase. A more appropriate formulation of the reform policy, such as avoiding pre-announced but not implemented retrenchments or making retrenchment dependent on merit, can overcome some of these problems (Adam, et al. (1994, p. 143)).

Closely related to insider privatisation is the syndrome of *crony capitalism*. It describes the situation where 'market opportunities and scarcity rents are preferentially available to political insiders and associates of senior officials' (Lewis and Stein (1997, p. 18)). These companies can be extremely inefficient, but nevertheless make huge profits, as for instance outlined in Winiecki (1991, p. 10f):

> 'New groups of pseudo-entrepreneurs are emerging in the private sector...They compete with other private firms and state enterprises not by lower production costs and better product or faster reaction to the requirements of the market, but by their political connections with the state sector that ensure them a steady flow of material inputs in short supply, as well as productive equipment, building permits, bank credits, etc.'

> 'Firms set up, for example by a party secretary's wife, a minister's son and a security police colonel's brother, can be even less efficient than state enterprises. Their cost may be higher but they still make hefty profits just for supplying their costly goods to the shortage ridden markets.'

Even though Winiecki refers to eastern Europe and the former Soviet Union, the description clearly reflects the situation in many African countries as well.[118]

What follows from the above consideration of profit shifting, asset stripping, insider privatisation and crony capitalism is that rent-seekers may have very different stakes during the reform process and therefore different (and varying) interests in speeding up, slowing down, altering or preventing certain reform measures. Insider privatisation may simply represent an alternative to other modes of rent appropriation, such as profit shifting and asset stripping.[119] In contrast to the economies of eastern Europe and the former Soviet Union, which rushed into privatisation, rent-seeking pay-offs in Africa greatly favoured the delay of privatisation.

b) Summary and Conclusion: Policy Recommendations on Designing Adequate Reforms

Broad-based reforms have been urgent in most developing countries in the past decades. In sub-Saharan Africa the consequences of poor policies, which included higher rates of malnutrition and failures in curbing the spread of diseases, even directly and indirectly threatened the lives of many people, above all the poor. Despite the urgent need for economic reforms, a large number of essential measures were not or only poorly implemented. The main conclusion of this study is straightforward: it is often not a lack of capacity or financial resources which have constrained the efficient implementation of reform measures, but rent-seekers' resistance and interference.

Not accounting for rent-seeking in the reform process is a common problem, which applies to many regions in the world. It has proved to be costly in particular for two reasons. On the one hand, rent-seeking interference prevented and undermined important *welfare-enhancing reforms*; on the other hand, it also made *income distribution* more unequal as state elites preserved and reallocated rents to favour themselves and their already privileged cronies.[120]

---

[118] See for instance Lewis and Stein (1997) and their reference to the case studies Senegal, Cote d'Ivoire, Cameroon, Nigeria and Kenya (Footnote 2 in their article).

[119] For a model which describes the manager or bureaucrat's self-interest in supporting privatisation, see for instance Schnytzer (1995), who argues that rational communists will support privatisation and take a share thereof once they perceive that privatisation is inevitable and insider privatisation only feasible while the state is still weak.

[120] Alexeev (1999), for instance, elaborates the latter aspect with a rent-seeking model on privatisation in Russia, demonstrating that the incumbency advantage of enterprise managers strongly magnifies the pre-reform wealth inequality.

Inefficiencies occurred especially as many of the adopted reforms continued to protect and favour hitherto privileged elites. Lewis and Stein (1997), referring to the financial liberalisation in Nigeria, conclude that nominal reforms had unintended and highly detrimental effects. In their paper they describe how liberalisation in the financial sector 'was quickly captured by a clientalist state as a means of reallocating rents to strategic constituents' (Lewis and Stein (1997, p. 5)). Winiecki's passage on pseudo-entrepreneurs cited above provides another example of rent-seeking related inefficiencies in reform.

Additionally, Robert Leiken notes on the problem of corruption (citation taken from Kaufmann (1997, p. 5)):

> 'Where corruption is systemic, market and administrative reforms... may even become counterproductive... Loosening government controls can facilitate illicit... economic activity. Moreover, bureaucrats have been known to compensate for lost revenues by extracting new "fees" in other areas.'

As already emphasised in Chapter 1.1, reforms can work if they are designed in a consistent way and vigorously implemented. This is also the response of Kaufmann to Leiken and the main conclusion of the well-known study *'Assessing Aid: What Works, What Doesn't, and Why'* (World Bank (1998a)). Yet the main challenge for reform-minded politicians and technocrats as well as donors still remains to find out how to design efficient reforms that can be implemented and sustained. Reforms demand commitment, and the implementation of adequate reforms requires a great deal of information and is often not politically feasible. It is here that the rent-seeking perspective comes in and provides crucial insights, as regards both designing and monitoring reforms, and offering suggestions on what to do if a government is of a predatory type and has no interest in adopting reforms. Insights from a comprehensive analysis of rent-seeking can indicate in more detail which preconditions and aspects matter. Four major conclusions on rent-seeking and reforms are summarised below, followed by an assessment of the role of donors and a brief description of a tool for anticipating interference from rent-seekers.

Understanding Rent-Seeking: Four Major Conclusions

First, it is important to understand *why reforms are postponed and why they are finally implemented.* This and earlier chapters outlined a great number of aspects which determine the size of rents, the profitability of rent-seeking and the stake of different individuals and interest groups in a society. As long as rent-seeking is profitable to the ruling elites and powerful interest groups, resistance against rent-abolishing policies will be high. The profitability of rent-seeking however does not remain unchanged. In particular the political and economic limits of rent extractions change over time, reflecting changes in power constellations and the ability of interest groups to organise and voice conflict, changes in shared values and ideological interpretations, as well as economic factors and consequences of protracted negligence, mismanagement and abuse.

To evaluate the circumstances relevant for the adoption of reforms, the following questions are important: Which interest groups are in a crisis? Why are they in a crisis? What are the possible rent-seeking and profit-seeking strategies to solve the problem? And what stake do individuals and groups have in the politico-economic process, in particular in promoting, deciding and implementing reforms? An assessment also needs to include a detailed consideration of the different options in obtaining donor support in exchange for reforms. Table 5-5 summarises the rent-seeking hypotheses reviewed in this chapter which affect the decision to adopt reforms.

Table 5-5: Rent-Seeking-Related Hypotheses and Conclusions on Adopting Reforms

(Hypotheses and Conclusions to be continued in Table 5-7)

Rulers' self-interest

H1 Ruling elites are frequently the largest obstacle to reforms.

H2 Reforms are adopted as an egoistic act of self-preservation and legitimacy enhancement.

H3 Reforms occur as a by-product of a more complex struggle for power, status and self-enrichment.

H4 Reforms may only become attractive to the people in power and influential interest groups if they can assure compensation for the rents they lose with the reform.

H5 Partial reforms may be possible if specific rents are not affected.

H6 Depending on the political constellation and distribution of rents, reforms are only feasible if either bundled or unbundled.

Character of rent

H7 Reforms are difficult if they affect several powerful rent-seeking groups simultaneously.

H8 If rent dissipation is high and takes the form of ongoing investment, resistance is low.

H9 A high share of rent dissipation through inefficiencies combined with a limited ability to adapt to new profit-seeking conditions causes strong resistance.

H10 Up-front rent-seeking investments that have not been amortised may provoke strong resistance.

H11 The better alternative income earning opportunities are, the smaller rent-seeking resistance is.

H12 The more time passes, the larger the share of dissipation wasted through inefficiencies, and the more difficult it is to adopt reforms.

H13 Measures which reduce the profitability of rent-seeking pave the way for future rent-abolishing policies.

Crises

H14 Many of the beneficiaries of early reforms face unfavourable conditions for organising and expressing conflict.

H15 A moderate crisis may not affect rent-seekers, as they do not bear the costs of the crisis.

H16 A moderate crisis increases scarcity-related and inflation-related rents, and reduces budget-related rents. As long as a crisis has not reached a critical level, the interest of rent-seekers to adopt reforms may even decline.

H17 As a crisis becomes severe rents of powerful rent-seekers also shrink.

H18 As a crisis becomes severe competition (and with it dissipation) for remaining rents increases, which again reduces the profitability of rent-seeking.

Incomplete information

H19 Incomplete information leads to a bias in favour of the status quo and therefore helps the rent-seekers' stake.

H20 Knowing the identity of losers but not necessarily the identity of future winners helps the position of rent-seekers.

H21 With incomplete information and limited rationality (e.g. citizens who do not sufficiently understand economics) rent-seekers find it easier to influence potential beneficiaries of reforms to vote against reforms.

H22 Petty rent-seekers, who benefit from numerous little rent-seeking opportunities, may fail to accurately assess how they can benefit from reforms.

A real understanding of the motivation for reforms enables conclusions to be made regarding the extent and type of *commitment* towards reforms, not just in general terms but for each reform step and with regard to each affected interest group. It therefore permits rent-seeking resistance or interference to be anticipated and makes it possible to estimate the probability of success of specific reform components. In an adverse political setting, where reforms depend on a sufficiently strong coalition of support, it will be difficult, if not impossible, to address major rents, at least in the short and medium term. Reform-minded forces within the country and donors in particular have to be realistic as regards this constraint and adjust their policies and approaches correspondingly, for instance, as mentioned in Chapter 4, by promoting and supporting activities that can help develop or increase checks and balances in society. In the worst case, donors may limit themselves to communicating the benchmark needed to obtain support.

Second, as discussed in this chapter, rent-seeking is *not only a matter of resistance to reform*. Measures to address opposition to reforms are important but not sufficient to guarantee the success of reforms. Many rent-seeking opportunities arise during the transition phase because reformers are themselves rent-seekers and may even be empowered by the adoption of certain donor-supported projects. Reforms also include measures which involve large reallocations of property rights and may thus encourage illegitimate manipulations by rent-seeking policymakers, civil servants or managers of parastatal companies. Furthermore, rent-seeking opportunities arise as components in the economic, political and related institutional transition may not adjust sufficiently quickly (or proceed at a different speed), causing intermediate rent-creating frictions, for instance hybrid systems where old and new institutions overlap. If rent-seekers within the ruling elites and civil service perceive these opportunities, they are likely to undertake actions aimed at extending the transition phase and thus again undermine reform goals.

All these problems have indeed constrained reforms, and assessments such as 'reforms institutionalized outright theft and other forms of corruption by government officials' (Kaufmann (1998a, p. 524)) or 'in the short run it is essential to realise that a decision by the state tends to be oriented towards the enrichment of certain individual bureaucrats' (Åslund (1994, p. 29)) not only hold for countries in eastern Europe and the former Soviet Union. They are equally relevant for many sub-Saharan countries with entrenched rent-seeking forces within ruling elites and bureaucracy.

The problems indicate that above all the sequencing and implementation of reforms has to be carefully designed and monitored, preferably supported by checks and balances from inside the reforming society. However, here too it has to be admitted that with regard to many political constellations in LDCs an unfair distribution of rents in the transition cannot be excluded entirely or may even be a precondition for certain reforms to be carried out. If this is the case and these reforms pave the way for greater efficiency, reformers may have to put up with this unwanted complication. Most important is to thoroughly understand the conflict between the goals of efficiency and equity, and to evaluate all feasible alternatives carefully (including an adoption of all measures that can lessen unwanted negative side effects).

Third, *the intentions of rent-seekers* are particularly *easy to hide* in the context of reforms. Reforms are an extended process; they depend on the government's capacity to carry out reforms, and they may be characterised by uncertainties related to the reform environment as well as to the impact of specific policies. Rent-seekers will take advantage of this ambiguity. They will raise other arguments to hide their true intentions. Delaying the implementation of reform measures or predominantly addressing non-binding constraints is effective, as reforms are not a single immediate event, but an extended, sequenced process.

Unless rent-seeking takes very obvious forms, it may be difficult to distinguish rent-seeking considerations from other motives. A poor sequence or timing of reform measures, or a delay in their implementation may or may not be motivated by rent-seekers; to some extent the differentiation is a matter of degree. Furthermore, even though commitment from the top leadership is crucial to the success of reforms, ruling elites can also blame other groups for the failure of specific reforms, for instance the lack of cooperation of middle and lower-level bureaucrats. The rent-seeking problem then acquired a strong capacity-related dimension.

Nevertheless, as emphasised earlier, it would be naïve to believe that all frictions which finally lead to substantial rents are simply a result of 'accident' and incapability. More frequently problems are not a principal-agent conflict between reform-minded leaders and predatory-like bureaucrats but result from a lack of commitment among the top leadership, who are not accountable to their citizens, i.e. there is a principal-agent conflict between the citizens and the government. A weak reform-minded president may also have to appoint powerful rent-seeking elites to strategic positions, in effect largely diminishing the prospects of implementing true reforms.

Fourth, *rent-seeking strategies in the reform process are numerous and diverse* and thus not easy to control and anticipate. Strategies to prevent or compensate the loss of rents range from outright opposition and countervailing measures to more complex and less apparent actions. Table 5-6 gives three dimensions which summarise this variation.

Table 5-6: Three Dimensions on Rents and Rent-Seeking Strategies During Reforms

deliberately created	clearly formulated	relates to reforming policy
or	or	or
a result of transition only	institutional friction	relates to other area

Rents may be based on actions which are *deliberately* taken to undermine or prevent the rent-abating effect of a reform measure; or they may simply result from the sub-optimal timing and sequencing of different measures during the reform process (i.e. the policymakers did not intend to create these rents). Intended or not, rents may be based on *clearly-formulated* policies or can be the result of *institutional frictions* (for instance, because measures are not well implemented). The last dimension finally deals with the aspect that rents may either refer to the *policy domain under reform* or arise in a *different area* (i.e. rent-seekers compensate losses in one area with additional rents from another).

The different dimensions again reinforce the contention in Chapter 3 that a sufficiently broad focus is necessary that considers all relevant rent-seeking opportunities simultaneously. Furthermore, a one-sided focus on a single type of rent-seeking activity, such as corruption, can be misleading, as it may not show important interactions with other modes of rent appropriation, such as benefiting from rigidities in the transition. Table 5-7 summarises, in addition to Table 5-5, the hypothesis and conclusions regarding interference from rent-seekers when implementing reforms.

Table 5-7: Rent-Seeking Hypotheses and Conclusions on Implementing Reforms

(continued from Table 5-5)

General

H23 The impact of a reform measure varies if adopted in a setting with or without rent-seeking.

H24 Rent-seekers are often an integral part of an ailing economy.

H25 During the transition phase of implementing reforms the incentive structure may adversely change to favour certain rent-seeking activities.

H26 Rent-seekers have different stakes during the reform process and therefore different (and varying) interests to speed up, slow down, alter or prevent certain reform measures.

H27 Expected rents from the transition may constitute a key element to overcome resistance against reforms.

H28 With specific reforms, such as privatisation, all three strategies of opposing, delaying and speeding up reforms offer opportunities to sustain rent income.

H29 Resistance on the level of policy formulation, policy implementation and countervailing action are substitutes and depend on the relative costs.

H30 If rent-seeking opposition against the formulation of reform measures is not possible or if it becomes too apparent, resistance shifts to the level of implementation or it appears as countervailing actions.

H31 Rent-seeking policymakers reform sectors first which benefit them or which are not very relevant.

H32 Rent-seekers may allow only selected reforms which restore their lost rents.

H33 Rent-seekers may not pass on benefits from selected steps of liberalisation.

H34 Rent-seekers transform rents from protection into rents from the transition phase.

H35 Rent-seeking strategies are particularly easy if an activity depends on several preceding and subsequent steps.

Hiding

H36 Rent-seekers hide behind arguments of uncertainty and limited capacity, which allows them to slow down, postpone or exclude reform measures.

H37 Rent-seekers enjoy a strategic position to withhold or distort information.

H38 In particular on the level of reform implementation rent-seekers enjoy a strategic advantage.

H39 Rent-seeking strategies (not planning or implementing specific measures, countervailing actions) are easier in an environment of market imperfections.

Addressing non-binding constraints

H40 Policymakers formulate measures that predominantly address non-binding constraints.

H41 Important necessary measures are often delayed, not implemented or not enforced.

H42 If a measure requires several complementary actions to be effective, only a few may be implemented.

H43 If different rent-creating policies overlap, only a few may be addressed.

H44 Announcing but not implementing reforms can be a strategy of resistance.

H45 The longer time is wasted with ongoing studies, the more can effective implementation be postponed.

H46 A way to conceal rent-seeking strategies is to implement resistance gradually, in small steps.

Countervailing actions

H47 Countervailing actions are important if the implementation of an unwanted policy cannot be prevented.

H48 Countervailing actions replace the loss of rent-sustaining constraints.

H49 Countervailing actions offset new rent-abating regulations.

Empowerment / Reform-related resource allocation

H50 Empowerment can reduce the institutional limits of rent extraction.

H51 Rent-seeking benefits from empowerment arise as other important reform measures are not implemented.

H52 If reforms imply reallocating resources, this reallocation can be implemented in a rent-seeking manner, i.e. it may predominately benefit previous rent-seekers (rent-seekers obtain assets and rights from the reform at below-market prices).

Frictions

H53 Frictions involved in the economic, political and institutional transition sustain or increase rent-seeking opportunities.

H54 The weakening of an old system without providing an immediate new and efficient alternative offers many rent-seeking opportunities.

H55 In particular the non-enforcement of regulation offers rent-seeking opportunities.

H56 Rents created by frictions are preferentially available to powerful rent-seeking elites.

H57 Frictions allow huge profits to be made despite extreme inefficiencies.

Clearly, rent-seeking strategies are especially numerous since reforms often address situations where rent-seeking elites have already captured the state apparatus and where rent-seekers have 'settled' into their privileged positions, i.e. reforms not only threaten rents in general but also predominantly address the second, *non-rival* stage of rent-seeking. This implies that rent-seekers have much more room to fight back. They can afford to invest substantial resources without losing too much of their net profits. In effect, what often changes with an inappropriate adoption of reforms is the level of rent-seeking investments and with it dissipation, but not necessarily the volume of profit-seeking activities. Given the large number and variety of possible strategies, the negative consequences of rent-seeking are particularly difficult to avoid in countries with an adverse political culture.

In Chapter 3 it was argued that reducing rent-seeking in a non-rival situation requires that a critical level be reached. This insight is crucial. Looking at the poor reform records of the past and the fact that many of the powerful rent-seekers managed to retain their rents (or at least considerable shares thereof) despite ongoing reforms, it can be assumed that in many cases this critical level was not reached. It also implies that resources which were invested or granted by donors as part of a reform package have to a considerable extent been ineffective and wasted, i.e. dissipated through the rent-seekers' countervailing actions. Especially in countries where rents play a crucial system-stabilising role, pressures to maintain rents are substantial and therefore represent, if not anticipated, a very high risk of undermining donor-supported reform programmes.

Designing and Monitoring Adequate Reforms: Concluding Thoughts on How to Deal with the Rent-Seeking Problem

This chapter elaborated many arguments explaining how reforms can be successfully undermined by entrenched rent-seeking forces. The warnings and suggestions made are relevant for both reform-minded policymakers within and outside the government, as well as members of the donor community, who have been supporting and assisting the design and implementation of economic, political and institutional reforms in LDCs.

Reforms work if formulated and designed appropriately. The direct involvement and interference of rent-seeking forces on the level of policymaking, policy implementation and policy outcome (recall Tables 5-2 and 5-3), however, have implications for both the sequencing of reform measures as well as the type of donor involvement. As noted earlier, in a country with an adverse political culture where the government's primary motivation is self-enrichment and strategically allocating rents to selective interest groups, donors cannot do much more than communicate better policies. In such a situation reforms are first needed from inside the country, which often implies that a change in leadership is also necessary.

In predatory-type systems, the main goal is basically to identify support that can increase the probability that sound policies are implemented in future. This support would be limited to providing ideas and supporting activities that are suitable to strengthen democratic elements, above all checks and balances. Once forces that restrain rent-seeking have gained sufficient weight and influence government policymaking, more and more reforms become feasible. The emphasis of donor support would then shift from providing ideas and selectively strengthening reform-minded elements, to supporting specific areas of reform (such as limiting government interventions in the economy, implementing checks and balances and strengthening the civil society), to broader programme and budget support.

As emphasised in the World Bank's 'Assessing Aid' study (World Bank (1998a)) aid works if it is designed appropriately and if it achieves the right balance between providing ideas and financing projects or general budgets. The latter demands sound economic management, i.e. it is only feasible for countries with a favourable policy environment and good institutions (rule of law, efficient civil service, stable macroeconomic environment, open trade regimes and protected property rights). At all stages of support, however, an appropriate assessment of the rent-seeking environment is crucial. The more pronounced rent-seeking forces are in a country, the more careful reform technocrats and donors will have to be.

A practicable way to evaluate alternative reform measures and to assess whether these measures are efficiently coordinated with other reform steps is to specify in detail how a measure is assumed to work, i.e. to explicitly list the chain of assumptions which are expected to lead to the intended outcome (this approach is also referred to as *'theory-based' evaluation* or developing a *'logic model'*).[121] Knowing all the assumptions underlying a suggested reform measure helps reform-minded policymakers and donors to sequence and fine-tune the reform, above all to safeguard against different kinds of complications.

Once the detailed line of assumptions on how a measure is expected to work has been made explicit, possible interferences from rent-seekers can be analysed according to the hypotheses and conclusions outlined in the tables above. Table

[121] The Operations Evaluation Department (OED) of the World Bank, for instance, has included such an approach in its evaluation of country programmes with respect to the Bank's anti-corruption strategy (e.g. applied in World Bank (2001b)). Most donors include related approaches in their project and programme cycle management (logical framework analysis). For a discussion of the concept of theory-based evaluation, see Weiss (1995).

5-8 gives an example of a logic model which addresses rent-seeking interferences in general terms. It specifies the assumptions underlying *assistance and training to improve the tax administration*, including the conditions necessary to justify donor involvement (A1-A3), as well as the final goals to improve government services and welfare or to reduce poverty (A7-A8). The case serves as a good example for demonstrating interference from rent-seekers on different levels and will be briefly discussed below.

Table 5-8: A Logic Model for Improving Tax Administration by Assistance and Training

A1 Improving tax administration and tax laws is complex and costly.

A2 The government lacks experience and resources to implement reforms.

A3 The government has a clear commitment to implement reforms.

	Donors' assistance & training		**Rent-seeking interference** **Reasons for failure:**
	↓		
A4	Tax legislation improves and officials have better knowledge and equipment to combat corruption.	⇔	Government is not committed. Design or implementation is not appropriate. Officials cannot do a better job.
	↓		
A5	Officials use knowledge and equipment to do a better job.	⇔	Officials have little or no incentive to use acquired knowledge and better equipment. → Measures are not effective; loopholes remain and corruption remains rampant.
	↓		
A6	Less petty corruption (illegal tax exemptions, wrong tax assessments). Government increases tax revenues.	⇔	Rent-seekers shift their activities to other areas (e.g. more smuggling instead of wrong tax assessments). → Government revenues do not increase.
	↓		
A7	Budget deficit reduces; spending in core activities increases; government service improves.	⇔	Additional funds are captured by rent-seekers. They are not used for core activities or to reduce the budget deficit. → Government service does not improve.
	↓		
A8	Welfare improves and poverty declines.	⇔	Measures taken are not sufficient. → The situation of the poor does not improve.

Depending on the objectives in focus, an analysis may be confined to addressing only a few steps, for instance assumptions which are narrowly related to a specific project (A4 to A6). However, as emphasised above, in particular in environments with strong rent-seeking forces, rent-seeking strategies are diverse and may not just undermine the implementation of a specific measure, but negatively affect the expected beneficial impact on subsequent steps. Taking a broad perspective, which includes the entire range of assumptions to reach a final goal, helps to identify rent-seeking strategies and provides crucial information on sequencing, fine-tuning and bundling reforms.

Table 5-8 demonstrates that there are many possible ways in which the chain of assumptions which leads to the final goal may break. Even the preceding question whether donors should be involved in supporting a specific reform measure is not simple. The decision does not just depend on assessing the desirability of a reform measure but also concerns the more fundamental problem of *aid fungibility*, i.e. whether additional efforts of donors may be offset by a reduction in efforts made by the government.

Aid fungibility, which has been widely debated in development cooperation, is a real constraint in a strong rent-seeking environment. In predatory-type governments reforms may have been adopted as powerful rent-seekers lost easier but unproductive rent-seeking opportunities. If this assumption holds, their major concern is not to undertake reforms that benefit their citizens but to recoup lost rent-seeking income, preferably with donor support. If assumption A2 in Table 5-8 does not hold, in the extreme the net impact of aid is that of feeding a rent-seeking economy, i.e. additional donor support does not increase the share of resources benefiting efficient reforms and the poor but simply relieves the pressure on rent-seekers.

With many reform measures, LDC governments indeed lack experience and resources, and the main question is whether a government is committed to implementing a specific measure. The problem of commitment applies to the top leadership as well as to the middle-level and lower-level bureaucracy. In the example for improving the tax administration, the design or implementation of donor assistance and training may fail if important stakeholders within the tax administration are not committed. Assumption A4 breaks down if rent-seeking strategies prevent effective implementation of donor support, and A5 breaks down if officials in the tax administration do not use the acquired knowledge or equipment to increase government revenues. Furthermore, as explained earlier, to reduce corruption several measures must be addressed simultaneously (recall the equations presented in Figure 4-1 on page 150), and in the case of empowerment donor support may even increase the rent-seeking opportunities of corrupt officials, especially if the costs and probabilities of punishment have not been affected.

If private tax evaders rather than public officials are the driving force in a rent-secking setting, rent-seeking may remain rampant even with a less corrupt tax administration (revenue does not increase, assumptions A6 breaks down). More critical is assumption A7, i.e. the question of what happens with additional government revenues. In predatory-type governments, rent-seeking pressures may be high enough to absorb any increase in government revenues (assumption A7 breaks down). Finally, the adopted measure may fail to improve the situation of the poor, as other binding rent-seeking constraints which negatively affect the poor have not been addressed yet.

All in all, the example given above demonstrates that there is usually a long chain of assumptions which have to hold before a measure can be effectively implemented and the final objective achieved. As emphasised in the introduction to Chapter 5, it makes a big difference whether reforms are to be implemented in an environment with or without deep-rooted rent-seeking forces. What matters for reform-minded policymakers and donors is to anticipate the behaviour of rent-seekers and adjust the design and sequencing of reform measures correspondingly. Donors especially have to be much more careful in assessing whether reforms are effectively wanted by the ruling elites and citizens. If a government can credibly demonstrate that it wants to undertake specific reforms and if it also has the power to implement these, then donors can support a reform programme.

These requirements have not been sufficiently addressed in the past. Though donors have invested considerable resources in developing countries in the last four decades, too many projects have failed and entire reform programmes have gone 'off-track' as major performance criteria and/or structural benchmarks of the agreement were not achieved. Furthermore, even in areas where encouraging and positive results have been realised, the same targets could have been achieved more efficiently if interference from rent-seekers had been better anticipated.

The highest costs, finally, have occurred in cases where inadequate donor support even strengthened the position of rent-seekers. In the worst case, efforts originally targeted to alleviate poverty and to increase the country's development potential have only helped sustain the rent-seeking economy. In fact in many countries ongoing reforms have taken so many years that it provokes the question whether policymakers are dealing with a *transitional phenomenon* or an *intrinsic characteristic* of a developing country, i.e. the transition phase will never end.

The Tanzanian case, which will be extensively addressed in the remaining chapters, provides an example of a predatory-type bureaucracy which for many years misused ideology as a pretext for large-scale rent appropriation. The case study shows in detail how rent-seeking strategies undermined originally benevolent goals and how powerful rent-seekers 'efficiently' interfered in the reform process, further limiting growth and development. The Tanzanian case is therefore also an example where a large amount of donor support has been dissipated through the interference of rent-seekers, both in the run-up to reforms as well as throughout the reform process.

Part II

Rent-Seeking: Empirical Evidence for Tanzania

6 From Socialist Ideology to Rent-Seeking Reality

This chapter presents a rent-seeking analysis of the pre-1986 period and lays down the methodology and scope of the subsequent discussion on the major delays, setbacks and costs of the reform process starting in 1986. In particular Sections b) to d) of Chapter 6.2 provide important background information to the analysis of rent-seeking and economic reforms in Chapters 7 and 8. As will be argued, rent-seekers have greatly (even predominantly) contributed to the poor reform records in Tanzania in the 1980s and 1990s.

6.1 Preliminary Comments on How to Define and Observe Rents in Tanzania

A rent-seeking analysis of reform efforts is not as simple as it may appear at first glance. The following preliminary comments raise two aspects which link the discussion of the previous chapters with the methodological approach taken here.

The General Conceptual Problem of Defining Rents in Tanzania

Critics may argue that there can be no final agreement on what constitutes rents in Tanzania and an analysis of rent-seeking would therefore be highly subjective. Chapter 2 showed that an analysis of rents and rent-seeking requires an agreement on the *structure of property rights* against which to evaluate rent-seeking. Because a society also redistributes income it can be sometimes difficult to clearly differentiate between transfers that reflect the society's vision of a more just and efficient income distribution and transfers which do not correspond to the society's preferences but are effected by successful rent-seeking activities.

Tanzania's development strategy since independence has been largely co-financed by donors, and it has not been uncontroversial. Especially after the late 1970s disagreements between the donors and the country's leadership on necessary policy changes increased substantially. Even in 1986 when the Tanzanian leadership fundamentally changed the direction of its official policy, some discrepancies remained and additional differences arose between the party and reform-minded technocrats. All these aspects also make a definition of rents difficult.

Strictly speaking, rent-seeking behaviour can be explained according to the *system of property rights* within which the economy operates (socialist or free market). The allocation of substantial support to parastatal companies for instance, may then only be seen as rent-seeking if the benchmark was a free market economy, but not if it was a socialist economy. As a third alternative, rent-seeking can also be evaluated using the benchmark of a desired *change in the system*, i.e. in the case of the Tanzanian reform process the transition from a directive-socialist to an open market economy. The possibility to refer to different benchmarks may therefore question a rent-seeking analysis.

However, because of Tanzania's poor performance since independence, a rent-seeking analysis would not look much different if the benchmark was the socialist economy Nyerere wanted to create or if it was the liberal market economy donors were finally pressing for. Both systems (assuming they work) aim for an efficient allocation of resources (efficient in the sense of reaching their development goals). Regardless whether the benchmark is a socialist-dirigiste or free-market economy, the degree of embezzlement and indifference in the bureaucracy and parastatal companies represents pure rent-seeking behaviour. This insight is crucial; it implies that Tanzania has also become a rent-seeking economy if evaluated against the socialist benchmark.

After several unsuccessful attempts to improve the economy within the socialist framework, Tanzania finally opted in 1986 for a more liberal market economy. Undoubtedly this decision did not reflect an unanimous agreement among policymakers and other stakeholders and it was also driven by rent-seeking considerations (some of the rents simply depended on the high level of donor support).

The following analysis however will evaluate rent-seeking against the free-market reform benchmark, i.e. the goal of creating a liberal market economy. On the one hand, it represents the official position of the country's leadership; on the other hand, there were no feasible socialist policy recommendations within the old development strategy which could have addressed the high imbalances in the economy or could have solved the burdensome rent-seeking problem.

Overcoming Practical Problems: How to Identify and Measure Rent-Seeking in the Tanzanian Reform Process?

Chapter 5.2 grouped the reform process into three sequential steps: policy formulation, policy implementation and policy outcome. Several arguments have been raised to explain why a rent-seeking analysis of reform efforts is difficult or sometimes even impossible. Besides the problem that policy performance depends on many different factors and rent-seeking may only be one cause of failure, the specific design, timing and sequencing of reform measures is not necessarily clear.

As argued, decisions connected with the reform include the choice on different levels and distributions of adjustment costs; institutions take time to develop and market rigidities may prevent a smooth transition. In addition, the capacity of a government to undertake reforms can be so limited that measures may need to be postponed and targets cannot be met within the specified time horizon. Furthermore adverse developments in world markets, unfavourable weather conditions or unintended negative side effects of other policies can make an evaluation of targets based on output indicators impracticable.

Even though these qualifications are justified in general and have to be taken seriously, the situation in Tanzania was often not so ambiguous. As will be explained, during the ten year reform period starting in 1986 several economic imperatives to balance the economy and to improve efficiency were not addressed in a timely way, the sequencing of reforms was partly driven by rent-seeking considerations and there were many clear-cut examples of overt rent appropriation or rent-seeking resistance to reforms.

Partly related to this qualification is the problem of *quantifying* rents and rent-seeking activities. Since rent-seekers typically use other than rent-seeking arguments to justify poor performance or delays in policy implementation it can be expected that data on rent-seeking flows will also be distorted or concealed. Besides the general problem that many aspects of rent-seeking are not visible from statistics, in Tanzania statistical information has been poor, particularly in the 1980s. Much of the information needed to measure rents and rent-seeking activities was therefore not directly available.

Both the comparison of official statistics as well as primary data collection revealed several inconsistencies and problems of missing data. Quite often collecting the same information from two sources meant trouble, as the information deviated substantially. Evaluating individual data instead of aggregates could even make the situation worse as it makes discrepancies more evident. Do these concerns imply that it is not possible to evaluate the data properly in terms of rent-seeking? There are good arguments to claim the contrary.

On the one hand, the process of collecting information provides valuable *ancillary information* on the very rent-seeking case in focus, i.e. information on the strategy of obscuring rent-seeking transactions. Chapter 8 in particular will devote considerable space to describing the process of collecting and scrutinising data. On the other hand, lack of data or distortions only impede an analysis if the magnitudes are very large. In most cases it was possible to adjust data and to correct obvious misprints or evaluate different specifications (reflecting different assumptions regarding distortions or missing information). Therefore most of the information collected could be used as a reliable indicator or estimate for rents or rent-seeking.

6.2 Economic Policies Prior to 1986 and the Country's Development up to 2000

There is a broad literature on Tanzania, which describes the country's development since independence, its early struggle with imbalances, the lack of policy response to crises and the subsequent economic collapse at the beginning of the 1980s. Berg-Schlosser and Siegler (1990), Henley (1993), Hofmeier (1993) and World Bank (1990a), as well as Campbell and Loxley (1989), Campbell and Stein (1992), Hyden and Karlstrom (1993), Rösch (1995) and Wagao (1992) provide general information on Tanzania's development since independence. The latter group of articles and books includes comprehensive information on economic problems and resistance to reforms starting at the end of the 1970s. Finally, a political and interest group analysis and comparison with the neighbouring countries Kenya and Uganda is elaborated in Berg-Schlosser and Siegler (1990) and Mair (1996).

The sections in this chapter will draw on this literature. General information on Tanzania will not be quoted explicitly. Since the introduction is kept brief, it may not sufficiently reflect all important aspects and intentions of Tanzania's development strategy or the facets of its resistance towards the recommended policy reforms. The interested reader is referred to the literature cited.

a) Country Data

Tanzania is located at the East African coast and shares frontiers with Kenya and Uganda to the north, Rwanda, Burundi and Democratic Republic of Congo (former Zaire) to the west, and Zambia, Malawi and Mozambique to the south. It is still a predominantly agricultural economy whose major exports are coffee and cotton. Seen from the tourist's perspective, Tanzania is a promising country, with beautiful beaches, extraordinarily rich wildlife and famous national parks, including Africa's highest mountain, Mount Kilimanjaro.

Like most African countries, Tanzania has its origins in the colonial period. In 1891 the mainland Tanganyika became a colony of the German Reich and was taken over by the British in 1920. Three years after its independence in 1961, Tanganyika formed a union with the islands of Zanzibar (Unguja and Pemba) and became the United Republic of Tanzania.

In contrast to the situation in neighbouring countries, Tanzania has a favourable ethnic composition. There are 120 different ethnic groups; the five largest groups only make up one quarter of the population (Berg-Schlosser and Siegler (1990, p. 136)). As many authors point out, this explains why Tanzania has thus far escaped major tribal conflicts (no single group is sufficiently large to dominate the others).

Julius Nyerere became the first president of Tanzania after independence. He transformed the republic into a one-party system and remained president till he voluntarily resigned in 1985 (remaining chairman of the party until 1990). Already soon after taking office, he proved to be a real master in controlling and eliminating any type of opposition. He merged virtually all important groups such as trade unions, cooperatives or social organisations into the one-party structure. His party, the Tanganyika African National Union (TANU) was later transformed into the *Chama Cha Mapinduzi* (CCM or the Party of the Revolution). Freedom House (see Chapter 4.3, p. 196f) has been rating the country's civil liberties and political rights as 'not free' from 1972/73 (where the first data was available) until the mid-1990s (with the only exception of 'partly free' in 1992/93). Only from 1995/96 onward was the country rated as partly free. Nyerere was very successful in unifying the multilingual nation. He established Swahili (besides the colonial language English) as a national language.

On the economic front, he can be seen as the founder of African socialism. Based on the *Arusha Declaration*, the *Ujamaa ideology* and the *Basic Industry Strategy*, Tanzania's income remained low but was much more equally distributed than in other countries.[122] A success of the socialist approach was reflected in the situation that Tanzania always had a large positive deviation in the cross-country ranking of many social indicators compared to the ranking according to per-capita income (see for instance Hofmeier (1993, p. 195)). Unfortunately after the early 1980s social indicators deteriorated again.

Tables 6-1 and 6-2 summarise selected data, on how the country has developed since independence and how it compares to other parts of the world.[123] The low figure of the GDP per capita expressed in purchasing power parity (PPP US$523) is striking compared to the average for sub-Saharan Africa ($1690) or neighbouring countries such as Kenya ($1022), Uganda ($1208) and Mozambique ($854).[124] Out of 173 countries listed in the Human Development Report 2002, only Sierra Leone has a smaller GDP per capita value ($490). Equally striking are differences if the GDP of Tanzania is compared with the GDP of Asian Tigers. Malaysia, for instance, whose per capita GDP was similar to Tanzania's GDP at independence in 1961, shows in 2000 a purchasing power parity more than 17 times as high ($9068). The World Bank even concludes that the 'best available estimates suggest that per capita income today is certainly no higher than it was four decades ago' (World Bank (2000c, p. i)) and World Bank assistance to Tanzania has therefore had only a limited impact on growth and poverty reduction. This judgement most likely also holds for many other donors if they would critically evaluate their engagement.

---

[122] As will be explained later, 'ujamaa' means 'family' and points to the strong family solidarity within traditional African societies.

[123] As the data cover a long period and are taken from different sources, some minor inconsistencies in the definition and compilation of the aggregates may be included.

[124] 'At the PPP rate, one dollar has the same purchasing power over domestic GDP as the US dollar has over US GDP. PPP could also be expressed in other national currencies or in special drawing rights (SDRs). PPP rates allow a standard comparison of real price levels between countries, just as conventional price indices allow comparison of real values over time; nominal exchange rates may over- or undervalue purchasing power.' (UNDP (2000, p. 281))

Table 6-1: United Republic of Tanzania: Development after Independence

Area: 945,200 km^2 (the area of Germany, France and Switzerland combined)
Capital: Dodoma (200,000 inhabitants), unofficial political and economic capital: Dar es Salaam (more than 2 million inhabitants)
Currency: Tanzania Shilling (TSh)

Social and Demographic Indicators	1965	1975	1980	1985	1990	1995	2000
Population Characteristics							
Total population (million)	11.8	15.9	18.6	21.8	24.7	29.6	33.7
Urban population (% of total)	5%	10%	15%	18%	21%	27%	32%
Life expectancy	44	48	50	51	50	48	44
Health and Education							
Infant mortality (per thousand live births)	135 [c]	113 [d]	108	102	99	87	104
Adult illiteracy rate	63% [e]	57%	50%	43%	36%	30%	25%
Primary enrolment (% of 6-11 yr. olds) [a]	32%	53%	93%	75%	70%	67%	47%
Secondary enrolment (% of 12-17 yr. olds) [a]	2%	3%	3%	3%	4%	5%	5%

Economic and Financial Indicators	1965	1975	1980	1985	1990	1995	2000
Money and Prices							
TSh per US$ (official rates, annual average)	7.1	7.4	8.2	17.5	195	575	800
TSh per US$ (parallel market rates)			21	66.5	292	587	
Consumer Price Index (CPI)	0.34	1.11	2.07	7.72	29.8	100	181
Gross Domestic Product (GDP)							
GDP production based (TSh bn)	6	19	42	112	831	3021	7226
GDP per capita (at constant prices of 1995, in TSh 1000 and US$) [b]	*155* *$269*	*112* *$195*	*110* *$191*	*67* *$116*	*113* *$197*	*107* *$185*	*114* *$198*
Share of agriculture	46%	45% [f]	54%	58%	59%	58%	45%
Share of industry	14%	16% [f]	13%	8%	12%	17%	15%
Share of services	40%	39% [f]	33%	33%	29%	24%	40%
Debt and Aid (constant US$ of 1995)							
Total external debt (US$ million)	45 [e]	1,168	4,064	6,342	5,867	7,406	5,746 [g]
Aid: Net Disbursements of ODA (total in US$ million, and per capita in US$)	189 [h] -	605 9	889 28	695 15	1,290 42	877 30	1,117 [g] 27 [i]

a: Since enrolments include pupils above the school age values can exceed 100%.
b: Indicative only. There are no comparable time series of GDP since 1965. The data show the production based GDP per capita, deflated by the consumer price index and converted into US$ for the year 1995 (using the GDP deflator instead of CPI would have distorted the series even more).
c: 1967; d: 1977; e: 1970; f: 1976; g: 1998; h: 1969

Source: IMF (2001), UNDP (2002), World Bank (2001a)

The conclusion on the low impact of aid may be surprising considering that Tanzania has traditionally been a country with a large share of aid. Evaluated at constant prices of 1995, annual disbursements of aid averaged US$320 million between 1969 and 1975, jumped to almost US$800 million between 1976 and 1985 and levelled off at more than US$1 billion between 1986 and 2000.

Table 6-2: Tanzania in Comparison with the Rest of the World

GDP, Health and Education	GDP per Capita (PPP US$ 2000) [a]	Human Development Index (2000) [b]	Life expectancy (years) at birth (2000)	People not expected to survive to age 40 (1998)	Combined gross enrolment ratio (1999) [c]	Adult literacy rate (% age 15 and above) (1998)
Tanzania	523	0.44	51.1	35.4%	32%	73.6
Sub-Saharan Africa	1,690	0.47	48.7	34.6%	42%	58.5
All Dev. Countries	3,783	0.65	64.7	14.3%	61%	72.3
High income	27,639	0.94	78.2	3.0%	93%	98.6
OECD	23,569	0.91	76.8	3.9%	87%	97.4
World	7,446	0.72	66.9	12.3%	65%	78.8

Health, Energy and Communication	% Undernourished people (1997/99)	% Using improved water sources (2000)	% Adults (age 15-49) with HIV / AIDS (2001)	% Traditional fuel consumption (1997) [d]	Electricity consumption per capita (1999) [e]	Telephone connections per 1000 people (2000) [f]
Tanzania	46%	54%	7.8%	91.4%	55	10
Sub-Saharan Africa	34%	54%	8.0%	62.9%	469	34
All Dev. Countries	17%	78%	1.3%	16.7%	745	130
High income	-	-	0.3%	3.4%	8,431	1,132
OECD	-	-	0.3%	3.3%	7,001	983
World	-	81%	1.2%	8.2%	2,066	284

Demographic Trends	Population in millions (in parentheses: share Tanzania)			
	1960	1975	2000	2015
Tanzania	10.2	15.9	35.1	49.3
Sub-Saharan Africa	211 (4.80%)	303 (5.25%)	606 (5.79%)	866 (5.69%)
All Dev. Countries	2054 (0.50%)	2928 (0.54%)	4695 (0.75%)	5773 (0.85%)
World	2994 (0.34%)	4017 (0.40%)	6087 (0.58%)	7207 (0.68%)

a: PPP: Purchasing Power Parity (see Footnote 124 on page 297); b: Composite of life expectancy, adult literacy, school enrolment and GDP; c: Primary, secondary and tertiary; d: Per cent of total energy use; e: Kilowatt hours; f: Sum of telephone mainlines and cellular mobile subscribers

Source: UNDP (1997, 2000, 2003)

Part of Tanzania's poor performance can be explained by adverse external shocks it suffered in the 1970s (oil price crises, droughts, the general decline of world prices for agricultural products, the break-up of the East African Community and the war against Idi Amin). The major part however is primarily a result of the inappropriate economic policy pursued after independence. As will be argued, starting with benevolent intentions, the government's strategy increasingly reflected an unholy alliance between well-minded but utopian ideologists on the one hand and blatant rent-seeking profiteers on the other. As a consequence, Tanzania manoeuvred itself into a deep crisis at the end of the 1970s and early 1980s, which was severe even in an inter-African context.

A lot has changed in the meantime. At the political level Tanzania introduced the multi-party system and free elections. On the economic front it stabilised the economy and undertook far-reaching liberalisation in markets and institutional reforms. In recent years even some problems related to corruption have been successfully addressed. The economic reform process however has been lengthy and cumbersome, and it included many setbacks. Today Tanzania's economy is still fragile. Even though compared to the crisis at the beginning of the 1980s the economic situation of the majority of the population has improved, changes in the 1980s and 1990s were very slow and disappointing. For instance in 1993, many years after the adoption of reforms, one third of Tanzanians were still unable to afford the basic needs for survival, i.e. they lived in absolute poverty (1993 World Bank Poverty Profile cited in World Bank (1994c, p. 3)). The situation is not much different today. On the social front Tanzania has lost much of what it had achieved by 1980. For instance, according to the World Bank (1994c, p. 4), secondary school enrolment in 1990 was the lowest in the world and only one fourth of the average for sub-Saharan Africa.

Taking the Human Development Index (HDI) as a guide to describe the well-being and future potential of the population, until the end of the 1990s there was only a minor change in Tanzania (an increase from 0.406 in 1990 to 0.440 in 2000) and the country has a long way to go to reach the developing country average of 0.654. The low HDI rank in 2000 (position 151 out of 173 countries) is particularly striking since Tanzania has been a main beneficiary of donor support and a peaceful country. It never suffered from severe ethnical clashes or long-lasting civil wars as did many other countries with a low HDI ranking.

b) Ujamaa, Macro-Economic Imbalances and the Crisis

'Tanzania was a guinea-pig for socialist ideas'

Former colonialist farmer, Iringa 2000

At independence in 1961 Tanzania's level of economic development was very low in comparison to other African countries, largely because the colonial power had neglected the country for many years (Hofmeier (1993, p. 183)). Tanzania was an agricultural country; it produced food for its own consumption, and sisal, coffee and cotton for export. The economic system was based on private enterprises with limited protection and minimum government regulation.

After independence Tanzania aimed, like many other countries in Africa, to develop its own distinct national identity. On the level of economics and politics it finally found this identity in the African socialism characterised by *equity* and *self-reliance*. Hardly anybody would dispute that at the onset the goals of its leadership were of a benevolent nature. To guarantee that welfare increases would benefit the largest possible share of the population, its leadership emphasised the creation of an egalitarian society. It aimed to extend social services such as schools, healthcare and water supplies to rural areas. It also strongly mistrusted the market process and intended to encourage a self-reliant industrialisation.

The *Arusha Declaration* of 1967 laid down the new development orientation. State control of important industries, collective production in ujamaa villages, satisfying the population's basic needs, egalitarian principles and the emphasis on using own abilities and resources were crucial elements of the programme. Self-reliance was supposed to be achieved by an import-substitution strategy that minimised the dependence on the outside world for basic capital and consumer goods. A system of uniform prices for the whole country, universal primary education and health services and an income policy involving a relatively small difference between minimum and maximum wages aimed to guarantee widespread equity.

During the first years the implementation of the Arusha strategy was gradual; only in the 1970s did its speed and intensity increase considerably. The development strategy comprised three major economic components with far-reaching implications for the country's future economic structure: the creation of ujamaa villages, the creation of an extended parastatal sector, and the general government control and intervention into the market process.

With the policy of *villagisation*, i.e. moving the dispersed population into ujamaa villages, the government intended to ease the delivery of social services to the rural population and to increase efficiency in agricultural production by replacing individual farming with communal and state farming. Villagisation also made it easier for socialist speechmakers to address communities and strengthened the government's control of the population. 'Ujamaa', which means 'family', reflects the strong family solidarity in traditional African societies and is, as Berg-Schlosser and Siegler (1990, p. 70) note, 'part of the ideological attempt to use elements of traditional culture for the legitimisation of political strategies and for the establishment of a national identity'.

Until 1973 villagisation was voluntary and created little disruption. At the end of 1973 only 15% of the rural population were living in villages. Because of the slow pace the leadership decided to speed up the process, no longer relying on mere incentives but making villagisation compulsorily. Additional villages were formed along the roads and the rural population was no longer allowed to live more than a certain distance from the villages. The following massive resettlement, which was largely accompanied by force, reflected a far-reaching social disruption of the rural population. Only a few years later 90% of the rural population lived in villages. Many people view villagisation as the best-organised operation ever carried out in Tanzania. However instead of increasing efficiency it led to a progressive decline in agricultural production. Most farmers did not produce as well collectively as they had individually.

The second component of Tanzania's development strategy was the development of a large *parastatal sector*. Its leadership believed that the expansion of the public sector would stimulate the overall development of the economy. At the end of the 1960s the government began to nationalise foreign companies from the production, distribution and finance sector and created new companies. A more systematic approach was taken after 1975, when the government introduced its *Basic Industry Strategy*. With the focus on import substitution, the leadership intended, among other things, to develop domestic heavy industry to replace the importation of inputs used in the production of domestic consumer goods. At the beginning of the 1980s the public sector had grown to more than 400 companies. However from the very start virtually all public enterprises suffered from mismanagement, embezzlement and widespread inefficiency.

The development of the parastatal companies was also accompanied by a strong anti-private sector drive. As Henley (1993, p. 463) notes, 'what was left of the private sector was placed at a disadvantage relative to the public sector'. The *Leadership Code* was introduced, which did not allow public employees to have a second source of income from private business or from renting property. This further reinforced an environment hostile to private sector. As many authors point out, the situation was contrast to neighbouring Kenya, where civil servants were encouraged by the president to have private sidelines.

The third characteristic component of Tanzania's development strategy was the strong *anti-market philosophy* which was reflected in far-reaching government controls and interventions. Nyerere believed that prices had little or no role to play in allocating economic resources; changes in nominal prices were a symptom of profit-making and thus of a capitalistic mentality, and allocative decisions had to be made on socialist and political grounds using the rapidly growing central bureaucracy (Hyden and Karlstrom (1993, p. 1396)). In 1973 the National Price Commission was created, one year later the Price Control Act followed. At the beginning of the 1980s the government regulated prices of more than 2000 different goods. The departure from the market price mechanism, in particular the long-lasting maintenance of an overvalued exchange rate, caused major economic distortions followed by severe imbalances at the beginning of the 1980s.

In spite of its original benevolent intentions, Ujamaa socialism—which meanwhile had even advanced to a '*model for the third world*' (Hofmeier (1993, p. 183))—was not able to bring about the intended transformation. On the contrary, it became the major hindrance to Tanzania's development. Starting with an average growth rate of 6% per annum after independence, GDP growth averaged at 4.3% per annum during 1967-73, slowed down to 2.5% in 1973-79 and finally settled at 1.4% per year between 1979 and 1985 (World Bank (1990a)). At the same time the population grew at a rate of 3% annually, which implied that GDP growth per capita turned negative after 1973, leaving the population at a lower income level in 1985 than when the socialist development strategy began almost twenty years earlier.

Obviously the drop in growth after 1973 partly reflected external shocks, but Tanzania also experienced positive shocks, such as the coffee boom in 1974/75 and the doubling of donor support in per capita terms during the 1970s. These positive shocks only reinforced Tanzania's biased development strategy and therefore exacerbated the country's later economic problems. For a monetary calculation of the burden of the external shock, see for instance Wagao (1992, p. 98).

The data in Table 6-3 show the steady increase of *external and internal imbalances*. Imbalances were to a large extent attributable to failures in

Tanzania's active development strategy and mostly resulted from adverse incentives and disruptions the strategy included. Tanzania's public sector-led approach, which was undertaken in an environment of excessive protection and the complete absence of performance indicators, resulted in the creation of a large and extremely inefficient parastatal sector. Studies done by donors as early as 1971 raised the issue of excessive protection (World Bank (1990a, p. 5)).

Table 6-3: Selected Economic Indicators

GDP Indicators (average annual changes)	1967-73	1974-78	1979-81	1982-84
GDP per capita	2.5	-0.9	-1.1	-2.9
Consumer Price Index (Δ=Inflation)	8.5	15.1	23.2	30.6
Exports	3.6	-6.8	7.1	-16.7
Imports	3.6	2.8	14.3	-8.4
Ratio of net exports to GDP	-2.6	-9.6	-11.4	-7.1
Debt and Support (average level)	**1967-73**	**1974-78**	**1979-81**	**1982-84**
Ratio of debt to exports	120.6	187.1	261.1	513
Per capita donor support (1983 prices)	18.1[a]	29.0	43.2	30.7

a: 1973 only

Source: Hyden and Karlstrom (1993, p. 1397, p. 1398)

There were also critical comments in the 1970s which did not fundamentally question Tanzania's development strategy but pointed to areas of improvement that were necessary to make the development strategy successful:

> 'Central control does not eliminate the need to measure enterprise performance and calibrate investment and output decisions accordingly. On the contrary, it places greater demands for the creation of systematic performance criteria. Despite this clear need, performance indicators consistent with the control system are still lacking.' (World Bank (1977, p. 28))

Unfortunately, suggestions of this type were never implemented, as will be discussed below, mainly because the originally benevolent socialist intentions were thwarted by rent-seeking.

The lack of efficiency in the parastatal sector coupled with the inherent soft budget constraint meant an ever-increasing drain on government resources for parastatal support. Inefficiency therefore not only contributed to a slowdown in growth, it was also responsible for the creation of an unsustainable fiscal imbalance, making the government increasingly less able to finance its core duties such as social services or the maintenance of an adequate infrastructure. The support to implement the Basic Industry Strategy, which turned out to be import-intensive, coincided with a neglect of the agricultural export sector and thereby also led to a deterioration of the external balance. In particular the disruption introduced with forced villagisation, and the inefficiency of the state marketing boards and crop authorities, led to a decline in agricultural output and export earnings. Most critical were the low producer prices marketing boards paid to farmers. In addition lower agriculture output for food crops also made Tanzania more vulnerable to droughts and hence more dependent on costly food imports.

A major cause of the adverse development of the economy and the structural problems that emerged at the end of the 1970s was the government's pricing policy, which affected all sectors and markets. Pricing followed equity targets (for social reasons this was often below equilibrium prices) and aimed to ease the financing of development priorities. The pricing policy however did not take sufficient regard of economic essentials and implications. The leadership did not appear to believe in the social benefits of profit-seeking incentives or the possible negative consequences of disequilibria between supply and demand; it treated prices as external to any market process.

The price-setting procedures and the environment of excess demand in which monopolised parastatals operated (competition through imports was largely banned) enabled cost increases to be passed on. Income tax rates ranged between 25% and 95% and destroyed incentives for profit-seeking endeavours already at moderate income levels. Real public wages were increasingly depressed and affected public sector employees' motivation and productivity. In 1985 average real wages were less than one fifth of their value in 1969. Most crucial for the unsustainable economic structure was the government's exchange rate policy. The policy-determined rate did not reflect economic fundamentals, became increasingly overvalued and made a very restrictive foreign exchange allocation necessary. In the two decades following the Arusha Declaration the parallel market exchange rate rose more than three times as rapidly as the official exchange rate (Kaufmann and O'Connell (1999, p. 1)). In 1985, in the days of the worst disequilibrium of the official exchange rate, it temporarily peaked at nearly ten times the official rate.

Adverse price incentives led to the creation of an economic structure which was highly inefficient, vulnerable to external shocks, macro-economically unbalanced and—in contradiction to the originally stated development goal of self-reliance—increasingly dependent on external support to bridge the external and fiscal gap. The large degree of direct and indirect price interventions, which distorted decisions from what maximises value added at world market prices, implied an extensive use of capital relative to labour, a neglect of rural land, the favouring of import-intensive production methods and large disincentives to produce exportables. For instance, although in the 1970s prices of primary exports almost doubled, exports drastically decreased in real terms, reflecting the shift in the emphasis of the development strategy from agriculture to industry. The drop was mostly a result of the very low producer prices marketing boards paid to farmers. Not sufficiently taking advantage of profitable opportunities in the export sector, the country gave away windfall gains which could have supported social and development goals.

Donors also contributed to the adverse economic development of Tanzania's economy in the 1970s. Feeling pressured to disburse aid, many of them uncritically supplied an ever-increasing amount of loans and grants. This view is also shared in a World Bank evaluation of the past Bank-Country relation:

> 'The bank's support to Tanzania in the early 1970s also very probably reflects strong pressures to lend. The targets for lending to Africa had increased several-fold between 1968 and 1977, but many of the countries of the region were not good candidates for Bank lending because of political instability or clearly unacceptable policies. By contrast, Tanzania with its stable government and commitment to growth and equity was a prime candidate for loans. Although there were indications that Tanzania's absorptive capacity for lending was limited, it was assumed that this capacity could be increased through technical assistance.' (World Bank (1990a, p. 3))

The same study also notes (p. 10) that 'in most sectors the highest failure for project was in the mid-1970s, and coincided with the rapid build-up in lending'.

The weaknesses of the Tanzanian economy became obvious at the end of the 1970s and early 1980s when several negative external shocks hit the country (the fall in coffee prices, the second oil-price shock, a sharp increase in interest rates, war with Uganda and the reduction in aid flows). Nyerere's vision of developing an egalitarian and self-reliant society that would enjoy a steady increase in welfare had largely failed. It failed because it underestimated the exorbitant monitoring and information requirements a command economy demands to be efficient. It failed in particular because it relied too heavily on the assumption of benevolent politicians and bureaucrats, thereby neglecting a more realistic view of opportunistic behaviour and greed.

The distribution of scarce goods, inputs and services, subsidies, Treasury investments and other funds, and the government decisions on pricing, licences and a wide range of other permits of considerable value required an ever-increasing bureaucracy. Given the not always benevolent nature of humans, the difficulties in the 1970s and 1980s and the weak monitoring capacity of the state, a corruption-prone and rent-seeking motivated bureaucracy developed. It created a dangerous self-sustaining dynamic, increasingly misusing social ideology as a pretext for blatant rent appropriation. Together with the few ideologues who naively continued to believe in the original development strategy, they formed a coalition of resistance against urgently needed economic reforms.

c) Early Reform Efforts—An Unholy Coalition of Rent-Seekers and Ideologues

'When did the IMF become an International Ministry of Finance? When did nations agree to surrender to it their power of decision taking?'

President Nyerere, 1980 [125]

At the end of the 1970s the structural problems and macroeconomic imbalances had become obvious. Some donors including the World Bank and IMF were convinced that the increasingly poor performance of the economy was, in contrast to Tanzania's official view, mainly the result of *inappropriate economic policies* and therefore to a much lesser extent a temporary problem of exogenous shocks that could be solved by additional finance. The Breton Woods institutions suggested reform measures that would unmistakably mean a departure from the original Tanzanian development strategy (e.g. World Bank (1990a, p. 3) or Stein (1992, p. 66)). These suggestions included the common *austerity policies to achieve a stabilisation of the economy*, i.e. restraining aggregate demand, reducing the budget deficit, increasing interest rates to positive levels in real terms and devaluing the Tanzanian Shilling. Suggestions also addressed important *structural changes* such as eliminating the heavy burden of inefficiencies, which was a result of the centrally planned and public sector-led approach, and reinstating agriculture as the leading sector.

The government was unwilling to accept this diagnosis of Tanzania's economic situation and the policy recommendations it implied, in particular as it would have meant breaking with long-standing principles and it would have been a clear confession that the development strategy pursued since independence had failed. Probably more consequential was the complete absence of effective opposition within the country against the government's policies. Discontent did not result in protest and opposition against the government as it would have in Kenya; it was simply manifested in a quiet retreat from the formal economy. In addition the ruling elite enjoyed the full support of the party and state bourgeoisie (including the parastatal employees)—the major profiteers in the ailing economy (not through salaries but through other rent-seeking opportunities such as collecting surcharges, extra fees, and stealing company property).

Critical voices within the country complained that the system of controlled distribution did not favour the poor and powerless. Most of the public institutions, such as the foreign exchange-allocating Bank of Tanzania, the grain-distributing national Milling Corporation or, for instance at the village level, cooperative village shops, did little or nothing to reduce poverty and to ease shortages, except for the members of the party, parastatals and government bureaucracy (e.g. Booth, et al. (1993, p. 59)). However, any of the policies could always be justified on the grounds of its original social and developmental

[125] Quoted from Loxley (1989, p. 15)

intentions, even though it simply reflected a transfer from a set of 'losers' to privileged 'winners'.

In spite of the dramatic reversal of economic fortunes, the government did not react with appropriate policy measures affecting the rents of privileged groups. The leadership, having meanwhile become a coalition of true and false ideologues, argued that problems could be solved with measures in line with the development strategy. Party and state bureaucracy were very keen to support this view, as it promised the greatest chance for them to maintain their benefits and rent-seeking income. In subsequent years Tanzania became the only sub-Saharan country to withstand the pressures of the IMF (Wagao (1992, p. 111)).

In September 1980 Tanzania managed to come to a very soft three-year standby agreement with the IMF, which excluded, among other things, a devaluation of the Tanzanian Shilling. Not being able to comply with even the soft conditions (the government failed to contain the spending and deficits of the parastatal sector), the agreement was suspended after only one tranche was drawn and Tanzania lost its structural adjustment loan from the World Bank, which was contingent on an IMF agreement. Relations between Tanzania and the multilateral institutions became very frosted.

In direct response to the failure of negotiations with the IMF, the Planning Commission submitted in May 1981 the *National Economic Survival Plan (NESP)*. The NESP intended to re-establish a macroeconomic balance with supply incentives in the export sector, however without devaluing the national currency. It did not address the control of aggregate demand and it included extremely overoptimistic export targets, for instance quoting the most extreme case, an anticipated expansion of cement exports as high as sixteen times the 1979 levels (Stein (1992, p. 66f)). How useless the programme was is also supported by the following comment:

> 'NESP was formulated in a hurry, its targets were not realistic and it did not articulate ways of mobilising the people and resources in order to achieve the targets. There was little discussion of NESP even among policy-makers themselves. At the end of the period most targets of NESP were not achieved. If anything, most variables (e.g. exports, industrial output) moved in the opposite direction to the ones projected.' (Wangue (1987) quoted in Wagao (1992, p. 102))

In less than a year the ill-formulated and rent-protecting NESP was abandoned. In the meantime a team of independent experts financed by the World Bank and acceptable to Tanzania's leadership had prepared an analysis of reform requirements. The main goal of this *Tanzania Advisory Group (TAG)* was to mediate between the hardening positions of the IMF and the government. The conclusions were partly in line with the IMF, i.e. the TAG suggested tightening control of state expenditures and emphasised that some exchange rate depreciation would be necessary. On the basis of the TAG recommendations the Ministry of Planning formulated a new *Structural Adjustment Programme (SAC)*, however omitting any reference to exchange rate depreciations. The programme was contradictory. On the one hand, it included some liberal elements such as the Own Fund Scheme, which allowed using own foreign exchange for imports (explained later on page 343). On the other hand it included a continuation and further tightening of directive rent-distributing policies.

Because of the ideology-based interpretation of the problems and the rent-seekers' involvement, adjustments between 1979 and 1985 were hesitant and from the perspective of economic development unnecessarily costly, i.e. they caused higher costs to society than a swift and encompassing adjustment would have. In particular the dramatic compression of imports through the licensing system had disastrous effects on domestic production. By 1986 manufacturing GDP was only 30% of its 1979 level, agricultural export revenue fell from a peak of US$426 million in 1977 to US$184 million in 1985 (Mans (1994, p. 393, 399)). The infrastructure was run down, inflation accelerated to 30% in 1984 and remained at this level, real wages declined and minimum real wages in 1984 were less than half of what was paid in 1980. In rural areas virtually all basic household goods had become scarce or unavailable. The World Bank (1994b, p. 111) even remarked that 'cash was so useless in rural areas that the peasant farmer responds to an increase in the price of a cash crop was to limit production'.

The most overt resistance to necessary adjustment reached its peak in March/April 1983 when the government passed the *Economic Sabotage Act*, declaring war against 'smugglers, saboteurs, hoarders and racketeers' (Maliyamkono and Bagachwa (1990, p. ix-xix)). This period, which became known as the *economic crackdown*, demonstrated Tanzania's hopeless struggle with symptoms, without addressing underlying economic fundamentals. Summarising from Maliyamkono and Bagachwa, in April 1983 the Tanzanian Daily News reported that 1057 people had been 'netted', most of them businessmen, but also civil servants, parastatal employees, party employees and one member of parliament (MP). They were found guilty of 'frustrating the nation's efforts to distribute scarce commodities throughout the country' and were seen as 'evil elements' prospering at the expense of others. Startling stories of hoarded goods confiscated by the police were published by the national media. Having more than two soaps in a bag was an offence. Maliyamkono puts it laconically, arguing that the 'basic problem was not punishment, but to ensure that what was confiscated got to the people'.

The ever-increasing crisis and the hunting of saboteurs led to a qualitative change in the type of opposition to market reforms. The crackdown did not just attack the few markets that still worked smoothly—i.e. the black markets where goods were available although at high prices—it also threatened the rents of the members of the bureaucratic class and the employees of the privileged parastatals, both heavily involved in parallel market dealings. Rents which originally increased when the economy slipped into crisis, i.e. rents related to scarcities, inflation (nominally fixed prices for goods or interest rates) and donor support (appropriation of aid), now began to decline. In particular aid had fallen since 1982 as bilateral donors made their support contingent on an agreement with the multilateral institutions.

The economic basis of the rent-seeking patronage network was vanishing (Rösch (1995, p. 139)) and distributional conflicts among rent-seekers intensified. Demands for reforms increasingly came from the group of rent-seeking losers, e.g. employees within bureaucracy and some parastatal companies, and less from a more realistic understanding of socialist ideologues. Some liberalisation measures introduced from 1984 onwards, such as the own funds import ('no questions asked'), legalised the very economic 'offences' that the crackdown aimed to eradicate.

Towards the mid-1980s the balance of those who still opposed the reforms suggested by the international donor community and those who supported them began to turn. Already the budget of 1984/85 reflected a tightrope walk between reform supporters and opponents. In 1985 President Nyerere deliberately resigned and Mwinyi took office. The new government started negotiations with the IMF, however in secret. Even members of the cabinet and the Central Committee of the National Executive of the party were unaware of the specific conditions under discussion (Campbell and Stein (1992, p. 14)). By August 1986 an agreement with the IMF was signed and the *Economic Recovery Programme (ERP) was formally adopted.* The ERP defined a detailed agenda of market-oriented reform steps to be undertaken in the subsequent three years.

With the design of the ERP Tanzania had largely accepted the package of conditions it had vehemently rejected five years earlier. Many authors, however, point out that the adjustments up to the mid-1980s helped the government to legitimate its accord with the IMF without losing face. Mwinyi even interpreted the conditions agreed as a 'victory for Tanzania' (Rösch (1995, p. 143)). The ERP document itself states that the programme 'represents a continuation of the structural adjustment effort' (GoT (1986b, p. 14)).

In spite of the agreement with the IMF in 1986, which marked the beginning of a new policy orientation, it cannot be ignored that there was a *deep conflict* between reform supporters (new government and academic intellectuals) and opponents (people within the bureaucracy and higher ranks of the party). The 1987-2002 Party Programme, for instance, essentially reiterated the Basic Industry Strategy of 1975-78 (Henley (1993, p. 470)). And the Budget Speech held in June 1986 by the Minister for Finance, Economic Affairs and Planning, C.D. Msuya, praised both sides. In particular the glorification of Nyerere's development strategy appears to be rather cynical, considering the poor performance of Tanzania's economy:

> 'Honourable Members will recall that the past 25 years have witnessed the creation of a good economic base made possible by the excellent Leadership of the Father of the Nation and Chairman of the Party. Our country has managed to create a united and democratic nation under one party system founded under the policy of socialism and self-reliance which focuses more on bringing about development for all with special emphasis on the less privileged group of society. In those 25 years we have succeeded in establishing viable institutions and services which will greatly assist us in our endeavours towards improving our economic

well-being in years to come. Indeed, we have achieved a great deal and it is opportune for us to again thank Mwalimu for his outstanding contribution to the nation.' (Budget Speech, GoT (1986a, p. 2))

Obviously, from a more realistic and critical perspective neither equity nor self-reliance had been achieved. Even though president Nyerere had a benevolent goal, he was guided by an unrealistic vision of human nature. He left behind an economy that was highly dependent on donor support and a society which was still very poor, stifled by a privileged and unproductive rent-seeking class. Looking back at the policies in the 1970s and early 1980s, it was the initial development strategy that created rent-seekers, but rent-seekers also influenced and shaped the subsequent policy direction and implementation. Their success can be explained by the ease with which the socialist ideology was misused as a pretext for rent appropriation and the automatic rent-increasing mechanisms inherent in a command economy that gets out of balance.

d) Deficiencies of the 1986-2000 Reform Period and the Rent-Seeking Focus

Table 6-4 summarises important aspects of Tanzania's political and economic path since independence.

Table 6-4: Selected Political and Economic Events 1961-2000

1961	Independence from British Colony
1962	Tanganyika becomes Republic, President Julius Nyerere
1964	Union with Zanzibar: United Republic of Tanzania
1967	Arusha Declaration
1969-77	Villagisation
1975	Start Basic Industry Strategy
1978-79	War with Uganda
1980	Soft Agreement with IMF, cancellation shortly afterwards
1981	National Economic Survival Plan (NESP)
1982	Structural Adjustment Programme (SAC)
1985	Julius Nyerere resigns (remains Party Chairman until 1990)
1985-90	President Ali Hassan Mwinyi (first term)
1986-88	Economic Recovery Programme (ERP)
1989-91	Economic and Social Action Programme (ESAP or ERP II)
1990-95	President Ali Hassan Mwinyi (second term)
1992	Abolition of one-party system
1994	Tanzania reform programme 'off-track' due to major macroeconomic slippages
1995-2000	President Benjamin Mkapa (first term)

The Economic Recovery Programme (ERP) introduced in 1986 was followed three years later by the Economic and Social Action Programme (ESAP or ERP II). On paper the two reform packages reflected a timid, but for Tanzania progressive approximation to the common measures of stabilisation and structural adjustment. They included market-oriented economic reforms, such as trade liberalisation, devaluation, a reduction of government interventions and the closure of some unviable parastatal companies. However, in spite of the stated intentions responsive to donor ideas, the reform process up to 2000 was characterised by many *delays and setbacks*. Macroeconomic stability was only attained after 1995; there was no effective liberalisation in the most relevant traditional export crops until 1993/94 and budget management remained non-transparent and fragile throughout the 1990s.

This study focuses on rent-seeking as a major cause of the main problems Tanzania faced in the 1980s and 1990s. From the late 1980s onwards, virtually every year donors expressed strong concerns about the slow pace of reforms, in particular the widening gap between Tanzania's intentions and the actual delivery of reforms. In 1994 donors even suspended the balance of payments support due to major problems related to tax evasion. Tanzania's reform programme went 'off-track', the World Bank IDA Credit was frozen and the IMF Enhanced Structural Adjustment Facility cancelled. The slow pace of reform progress continued. The following remark of a donor on the 1996 Structural Adjustment Credit is symptomatic of this situation:

> 'The structural issues addressed are critical and form a continuum with previous adjustment operations (so much so that I recognize some of the conditions of the 1986 multi-sector rehabilitation credit…).'

Besides the poor delivery of reforms, Tanzania also became one of the most corrupt countries in the 1990s and was still ranked 76 (out of 90) in the Transparency International Index of 2000. Most of the delays and setbacks can be directly attributed to the attitudes of the entrenched *rent-seeking society* engendered during the socialist intervenistic period and subsequent crises.

Weaknesses were particularly pronounced during President Mwinyi's terms. His second term (1990-95) was characterised by a lack of real commitment among top leaders to combat corruption and other rent-seeking opportunities. When President Benjamin Mkapa took office in 1996 the track record began to improve. Among other things, he formed a new government without reappointing many of veteran CCM members from the previous government to his cabinet, a measure which did away with some of the core rent-seekers. Yet Mkapa and a few committed leaders, civil servants and active individuals from the civil society are still struggling to transform the state and the economy from an emergency case driven by rent-seeking to a more efficient, social market economy.

All in all, the main argument put forward in this study is that the results of reform cannot be understood without a detailed assessment of the rent-seeking environment. Rent-seekers are crucial stakeholders in Tanzania's ailing economy. As explained earlier, at the beginning of the 1980s when the economy virtually collapsed and donor support declined, more and more rent-seekers began to opt for reforms. The crucial point is that rent-seekers changed their position not because they believed that the socialist ideology failed (or because they favoured a liberal market economy), but because they could no longer make a living from the rents. The crisis had developed beyond a critical level. It was during this time in the mid-1980s when pro-reform groups gained sufficient momentum.

It is important to understand that the interest group environment at the onset of reforms consisted of reform advocates with true reform-minded individuals *and* an increasing number of rent-seeking losers. The latter have great potential to change their pro-reform orientation once their rent-seeking profits are restored, for instance by renewed but insufficiently monitored and evaluated donor support. At the other end are the inveterate ideologues who collude with remaining rent-seeking groups who continue to benefit. Both have a strong incentive to undermine the reform process. It is against this mixed background of reform support and opposition and the splitting of rent-seekers into two groups that the analysis of the reform efforts of 1986 to 2000 will proceed.

As explained in Chapter 5, some reforms may only be adopted as a by-product of a more complex struggle for power, status and even self-enrichment. Furthermore, rent-seekers' stakes are diverse and include interests to speed up, slow down, alter or prevent certain reform measures. The discussion in the remaining chapters will outline in detail how important reform measures have been delayed or undermined by countervailing rent-protecting actions. Many of the problems can be explained by the eagerness of the state bureaucracy and the parastatal managers and employees to appropriate resources. In particular highly inefficient loss-making parastatals, including marketing boards and cooperatives, succeeded in capturing a large share of the country's own resources and donor aid many years after the initiation of the ERP.

Chapters 7 and 8 are structured as follows. Chapter 7 describes the different *reform measures* initiated after 1986, including the major delays, setbacks and related costs. The first part illustrates how Tanzania's poor macroeconomic policy in the 1980s and early 1990s had its origin in the profitable tax evasion business, in rent-seekers' virtually unlimited access to bank credits and in the rent-seeking allocation of subsidised foreign exchange. Chapter 7.2 then focuses on the various price, tariff and quantitative restrictions in markets and examines these from a rent-seeking perspective, illustrating among other things, the extremely costly protection in the petroleum refining industry, resistance of rent-seekers to liberalisation of export crop marketing (and processing) and the poor rehabilitation and restructuring of parastatal companies in general. Chapter 7.3 analyses public service delivery from the two perspectives of the private sector and civil service. It looks at the conditions hostile to business in Tanzania and the failures in the civil service to implement a speedy reform of public employment, to enforce budget priorities and to prevent and sanction the large-scale embezzlement of public funds. The last section concludes with a general assessment of corruption and the lack of government commitment.

Whereas Chapter 7 presents many examples of how different stakeholders in Tanzania's society undermined the reform process officially adopted with the Economic Recovery Programme (ERP) and the subsequent reform programmes,

Chapter 8 focuses entirely on *the parastatal sector*. It analyses indicators of rent-seeking support and embezzlement within the parastatal companies, referring to their profit and loss statements, the quality and timeliness of their accounting and the amount of support they obtained. This *support* is defined in a *broad sense*, i.e. it not only includes access to direct subsidies or donor aid but extends to any type of legal and illegal support (access and defaults on loans and overdrafts from the banking system and the Treasury, access to direct support from the Treasury in the form of Treasury investments or loan guarantees, benefits from access to cheap foreign exchange, and forced benefits from arrears and defaults on income taxes, dividends and inter-parastatal liabilities (outstanding liabilities on pension fund contributions, electricity, water, and telephone service)).

7 Stabilisation and Structural Adjustment in Tanzania: A Rent-Seeking Approach to Explain Reform Records

The question of *who opposes reforms* is to a large extent rhetorical. Every interest group will say they are in favour of reforms, but when it comes down to it, a group will only support certain types of reforms, basically those which do not negatively affect their income. Chapter 5.2 described different rent-seeking strategies that may interfere in the reform process and categorised them into two broad groups: direct and indirect resistance of rent-seekers to reform measures, and rent-seeking activities which take advantage of reform steps and the transition. In the latter case individuals and groups motivated by rent-seeking may also support partial reforms: a temporary rent-seeking opportunity may exist provided that other reform steps have not yet been initiated.

Ideally, to account for different rent-seeking strategies, interactions and shifts between strategies, an analysis has to take a broad approach which looks at different sectors and actors simultaneously and which covers a broad range of reform steps and measures. As explained in Chapters 3 and 4, there are many parameters which co-determine rent-seeking activities, rent-seeking outlays and the size of rents.

Even though this chapter has aimed at a broad approach, structuring it into sub-units and sections proved to be challenging. Looking at *rent-seekers*, it would be appropriate to differentiate among interest groups with regard to policymakers, bureaucracy, private and public enterprises, with further differentiations as necessary according to the sub-sectors interest groups operate in (agriculture, industry and trade). From the *reform perspective*, in contrast, a grouping should be according to instruments such as devaluation, price liberalisation, tax reforms and privatisation. Finally, a narrow *rent perspective* must address an entire set of instruments, as only together may they determine the size of a rent (when several policy measures overlap altering only one of them may have no impact).

The division of Chapter 7 is based on a compromise. It addresses rent-seeking by explaining *policy goals, policy implementation and actual performance*. The main structure of the chapter follows the dichotomy between stabilisation (eliminating macro imbalances) and structural reforms (reducing state interventions and addressing institutional reforms). Table 7-1 gives a framework for analysing rent-seeking impacts on reform outcomes. Depending on the topic and information available, the discussion will be more or less closely organised according to this set of questions.[126]

---

[126] It would have involved squaring the circle to eliminate any overlap in the discussion of rents, rent-seekers and reform policies. For instance, the late reform of parastatal companies (addressed in Section c) of Chapter 7.2) was largely financed by bank lending (taken up in Chapter 7.1 as the

Table 7-1: A Framework for a Rent-Seeking Analysis of Reform Outcomes			
Goals and perfor-mance	General goals (What should have been planned)? Tanzanian government goals (What has been planned)?	⇔	Performance in different sub-periods (What was implemented, what worked?)
Inter-pretation	**Rent aspects** (of a given policy) What are the rents? Who profits, who loses? What are the characteristics of the rent-seeking 'game'. What determines access to rents? **Rent-seeking strategies** (to defend or create rents) Why do rents exist? Analysis of policy failure, chain of cause and effect (direct/indirect strategies: deferred liberalisation, institutional friction, countervailing measures, bad sequencing, etc.) **Arguments** Arguments of benefiting groups, arguments in favour of a rent-abating policy change **Explaining outcome** Power of stakeholder, importance of rents, key aspects that helped maintain policy, key aspects that finally led to reforms (how did the power equation change? who tipped the balance?) **Conclusion**: Implication of the costs to society		

financing was a major cause of macro imbalance). Also the division between stabilisation and structural adjustment sometimes requested looking at the same instruments from different angles. This is the case with tax reforms and foreign exchange policies, which aim to eliminate macro imbalances (mostly in the short run), but which are also an important part of structural reforms since the policies determine the level of protection of public enterprises against foreign competition or private sector competitors (assuming the former enjoy preferential access). Finally it was necessary to find an adequate balance between describing reform outcomes and closely focusing on rent-seeking aspects. For the cases where the description of the reform background appears not to be sufficiently detailed, the reader is referred to the literature cited.

7.1 Repeated Failures in Eliminating Macro Imbalances

a) Introduction: Overall Goals and Records

'The Government intends to take measures for increasing revenue by adjusting tax levels, expanding the tax base and improving efficiency in revenue collection. Moreover, the programme also aims at inculcating a high degree of discipline and efficiency in Government resource utilization, the reduction or complete elimination of misuse of Government funds, reduction of unnecessary and non-essential expenditures and instituting cost-reduction and control measures. This will also entail strict adherence to Budget ceilings as approved by Parliament. Government, Parastatals, District Councils, and Co-operative Societies are expected to institute measures aimed at generating revenues and controlling expenditures and reduce dependence on bank credit.'

Budget Speech of the Minister for Finance, Economic Affairs and Planning, 19 June 1986

At the beginning of the 1980s many countries in Africa faced substantial external and internal imbalances, which reflected an unsustainable gap between income and spending. In Tanzania, the unwillingness of the leadership to depreciate the currency and the inability to reduce the budget deficit severely deepened the macroeconomic crisis. The standard macroeconomic package recommended in such a situation is a tightening of fiscal and credit policies and a depreciation of the real exchange rate.[127] This was also understood by the Tanzanian leadership at the onset of reforms in 1986.

Ideally, a tight fiscal and credit policy cuts overall spending in the economy, while depreciation expands production in the tradeable sector, both improving external and internal balance. What makes the policy controversial is that depending on the general demand and supply responses and the price adjustments in the non-tradeable sector, expenditure-reducing and expenditure-switching policies may also lead to a severe recession accompanied by a high level of inflation, in particular if the timing, fine-tuning and sequencing had been inadequate. In the case of Tanzania however the economy had already deteriorated to a very bad level and many prices were determined in parallel markets (at higher levels than administered prices), i.e. markets which already reflected equilibrium market prices. Under such conditions immediate negative side effects of stabilisation are unlikely, even if the speed of stabilisation is fast. On the contrary, additional donor financing, which was contingent on an agreement with the IMF, reduced the severe scarcity of foreign exchange in the economy—the major constraint of the import-dependent manufacturing sector.

[127] For a discussion of adjustment policies see for instance chapters of Krugman, Fischer or Bruno in Dornbusch and Helmers (1991). A brief survey (in German) on the short and long-term impacts of adjustment policies is provided by Fischer (1994).

During the economic recovery programme (FY87-92), Tanzania received almost US$6 billion net foreign aid to support the adjustment programme, which was an increase of 60% over assistance during the crisis years, and US$1 billion debt relief (Mans (1994, p. 391)).

Tanzania's Economic Recovery Programme and the subsequent policy announcements in budget speeches or policy framework papers clearly stated the objective of restoring internal and external balance. Initial targets included a unification of the exchange rate and positive real interest rates by 1 July 1988, a reduction in inflation to below 10% in 1989/90 and the restoration of a sustainable balance of payments position in the early 1990s (GoT (1987, p. 12f)). The actual development is summarised in Figure 7-1. As the diagrams show, none of these goals was met at the beginning of the 1990s. The major reason, as will be argued, was entrenched rent-seeking forces. Deliberately or not, the decision-makers and technocrats in charge of designing and implementing reform policies apparently did not sufficiently anticipate the weight of these forces.

The *balance of payments position* remained weak throughout the 1990s, though it improved slightly after 1994. The first diagram in Figure 7-1 shows the relation of exports to imports. Between 1985 and 1994, on average, exports financed only one third of imports.[128] The second diagram shows the relation between the official and parallel market exchange rate and indicates that they were unified only in 1994.[129] According to the third diagram, the imbalance between government revenue and expenditure had already substantially declined when the ERP was launched. The decline in the *budget deficit* partly reflects the removal of direct subsidies to crop parastatals, the closure of some public entities and changes on the revenue side such as the introduction of development levies and secondary school fees (GoT (1986b, p. 9f)). The deficits continued to decrease until 1992, when government savings after grants turned positive for the first time since independence. Major slippages however occurred in the subsequent two years.

Although the reduction of the budget deficit reflected in some years a progress in controlling expenditure over revenues, it does not sufficiently describe the interaction between central government spending and public sector spending, nor does it account for efficiency considerations in the public sector in general. In budget speeches the government usually stressed the importance of adhering to budget ceilings and improving efficiency in revenue collection and

---

[128] Because the Tanzanian Shilling was substantially devalued between 1985 and 1993, it would not make sense to express the current account deficit or the value of exports as a percentage of GDP since the increase of the ratio is mainly a result of the exchange rate adjustments and less a result of changes in real flows.

[129] The difference between official and parallel rates is only an approximation for overvaluation. In the short run expectations may influence the parallel market rate (in 1985, for instance, the rate temporarily peaked at 10 times the official rate) and in the long run a bias may prevail, for instance when the parallel market rate includes a premium reflecting the risks of transactions. However, the data shown here indicate annual averages, and transactions in the parallel market were implicitly legalised with the Export Retention Scheme and the Own Fund Facility (explained later).

Figure 7-1: Macro Data Indicating External and Internal Imbalances

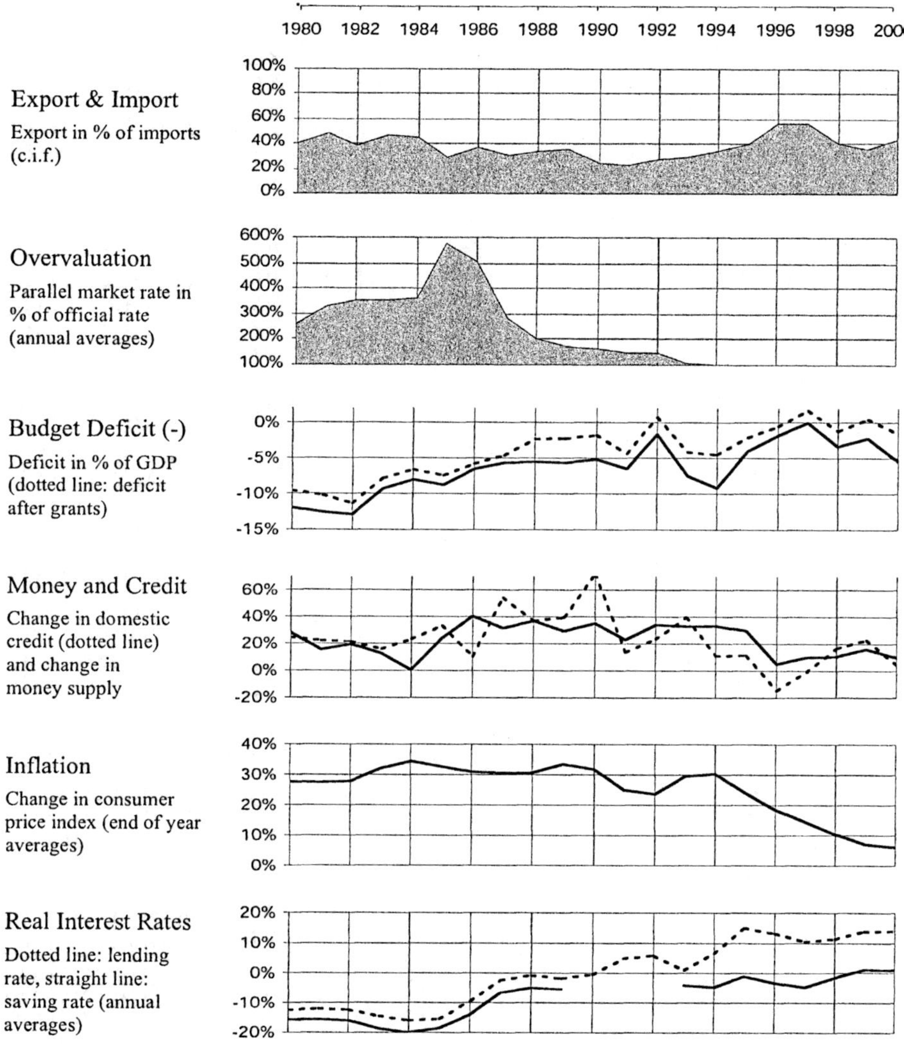

Source: Data according to IMF International Financial Statistics; parallel market rates from BoT, Dar es Salaam

spending. The extract of the 1986 Budget Speech quoted in the lead to this section summarises the government's goals to balance the budget and to improve public administration. The quote also serves as a good summary of what finally did *not* work! This is particularly evident if the entire public sector is considered and not just central government activity.

The target to reduce *bank borrowing* was initially met by the government but largely undermined by the parastatal sector. In the financial year 1987/88, for instance, credit expansion was three times the set target.[130] As a consequence Tanzania became ineligible for the final IMF tranche. Also in 1992/93 the government contradicted its own stated goals and ignored its commitment to the agreement with the IMF, when it borrowed from local banks more than TSh 30 billion (i.e. more than US$90 million) to meet its expenditures. Owing to continued fiscal slippages in the subsequent months Tanzania's reform programme even went 'off-track' and the balance of payments support was suspended.

As a result of government slippages, unbound parastatal lending and because commercial banks enjoyed almost unlimited access to refinancing at the Bank of Tanzania (BoT), Tanzania failed to reach all its *monetary targets* in the 1980s and early 1990s. Money supply was virtually endogenous, with an average growth rate of close to 40% up to 1992. Given the monetary expansion, Tanzania also failed to reduce inflation. In addition, due to a lack of adequate adjustment of nominal interest rates, real saving rates remained negative for a long time. It is true that Tanzania's macro stance improved in the second half of the 1980s compared with the first half, but the improvement largely reflects the poor initial conditions as opposed to serious efforts of the government.

Tanzania often blamed external factors, including the late disbursements of donor funds, for the macro instability and saw itself as only marginally at fault. This contrasts with the analysis in this study. The Deputy Principal Secretary of the Planning Commission went even so far as to note a direct link between macro instability and the size of donor support (quoted from Doriye (1995, p. 9f)):

> 'The magnitude of credit to government varied with the external financial inflows...Considering that nearly ten years into the programme this situation has not changed, one is inclined to conclude that there is little commitment to macroeconomic stability on the art of the policy makers: there seems to be an unstated principle that the onus is on the donors to pay for macro economic stability; hence the recourse to bank borrowing every time there is a shortfall in external financial support.'

Sections b) to d) will look at the problems of raising tax revenues, restraining credit expansion and postponing devaluation in detail, and explain the outcome from the rent-seeker's perspective. Other related aspects, such as the embezzlement of state resources, which remained a major problem throughout the 1980s and 1990s, will be discussed in subsequent chapters.

---

130 See for instance the 1990 Budget Speech (printed in GoT (1990a)) or the ERP II document (GoT (1989)).

b) Persistent Problems in Raising Tax Revenues

> *'Tanzania is not a duty free zone. Duty gets paid on every shipment brought into the country, the only problem is that the Government gets very little or none of it.'*
>
> *Businessman, Dar es Salaam, November 1996*

Mobilising sufficient tax revenues would have been important for Tanzania, not only to gain macro stability but also to be able to reduce the severe underfunding of core state activities like social services or the maintenance of a basic infrastructure. The inability to raise tax revenues undermined these goals; in addition, it made Tanzania more dependent on donor support. As will be argued in this chapter, low revenue collection was to a large extent a result of *rent-seeking* forces and not so much an *institutional capacity* problem.[131] It was also indirectly encouraged by the generous budget and balance of payments support from donors.

Tanzania has several sources of tax revenues: import duties and sales and excise taxes levied at the border, domestic sales and excise duties, VAT that replaced sales tax in 1998, income taxes and a large number of other levies and fees, which are not so relevant for the central government budget but are important to local government finance. An equally important source of budget financing is donor support, which in 1993/94 for instance represented 80% of Tanzania's development budget and nearly 30% of its recurrent expenditures (World Bank (1994c, p. x)).

Tax revenues were low for several, partly related reasons. First, like many other developing countries, Tanzania has a large and mostly untaxed *informal sector*. The ESRF (1996b, p. viii) estimates the parallel economy to be at 60-70% of official GDP and actual revenue collection to be about 30-40% of potential collection. Second, in the 1980s and early 1990s, many transactions were *exempted* from taxes, or an agreement was reached to *pay in instalments*, which is often equivalent to an exemption as the taxes due are not paid later on or are renegotiated. And third, colluding with businesspeople, tax collectors deliberately reduced taxable amounts by *misreporting* and cheating, of course in exchange of an adequate 'side payment'. To prepare and develop the rent-seeking argument, the types and magnitudes of tax evasion are briefly explained below.

Types and Magnitudes of Tax Evasion

Consistent information on early *tax exemptions* in Tanzania does not exist. Different sources usually indicate different data. Part of the problem is that in

[131] There is clearly a link between the two aspects, i.e. the inability to implement checks and balances to restrain tax leakages and to increase revenue collection is in fact an institutional capacity problem. Yet what matters is commitment, and this was lacking among the top leadership and middle-ranking bureaucrats.

the 1980s exemptions were not computerised; in addition, data were not stored in a central place but were scattered among the Treasury, numerous customs offices and other institutions, e.g. the Investment Promotion Centre. The measurement problem is further exacerbated as many exemptions are of an illegal nature. If records are deleted and files are destroyed to hide transactions, the information will obviously not be part of the official data collection.

Table 7-2 gives data on *import tax exemptions* granted either discretionary or on a statutory basis. The Minister of Finance decides on discretionary exemptions or, if there is proof that an imported item is damaged, the Commissioner for Customs; the latter may also agree to defer the tax payment (Eriksson (1993, p. 29)). As Table 7-2 reveals, exemptions were often as high as tax collections and sometimes even surpassed this level.

Table 7-2: Indicative Data for Import Tax Exemptions (TSh m)

	Customs & Excise Duty:			Sales Tax:		
	Exempted (1)	Collected (2)	(1) in % (1+2)	Exempted (3)	Collected (4)	(1) in % (3+4)
1982/83	1,015	840	55%			
1983/84	910	870	51%			
1984/85	1,200	1,650	42%			
1985/86	1,394	1,468	49%			
1986/87	2,844	4,020	41%			
1987/88	7,534	5,586	57%			
1989/90	12,289	25,987	32%	12,693	28,571	31%
1990/91	27,185	56,320	33%	25,575	20,172	56%
1991/92	40,214	51,639	44%	14,544	44,862	24%
1992/93	(14,505) [a]	36,706	(28%) [a]	10,267	41,048	20%
1993/94	76,709	57,363	57%	(15,820) [b]	63,254	(20%) [b]
1994/95	68,129	91,248	43%	30,270	72,643	29%
1995/96	83,500	131,397	39%	77,813	84,558	48%
1996/97	54,903	168,548	25%	48,740	123,503	28%

Source: (2), (4) from Bank of Tanzania (2001); exemptions 1982/83-1990/91 from Eriksson (1993, p. 75) (value for 1988/89 is missing), exemptions 1991/92-1996/97 from Tanzania Revenue Authority, Customs Department, Dar es Salaam. The latter information was retrieved from old PC data files.

The data may be incomplete and include errors. In particular the figures indicated with the superscript *a* or *b* cannot be interpreted (due to an apparent error in the file, some items had to be omitted):

a: Government projects and religious organisations excluded. If included, the value of exemptions becomes 842,064, which is more than twenty times the previous year's value, or 96% of the total.

b: Religious organisations excluded. If included, the value of exemptions becomes 117,540, which is more than ten times the previous year's value, or 65% of the total.

Probably not included in the TRA data are exemptions related to diplomatic missions, duty-free shops, bonded goods, transit cargo and investment promotion (the disaggregated data indicated zero for these sub-items).

As noted earlier, another means of avoiding taxes was to defer payment. Table 7-3 presents selected information for the years 1993 and 1994. Between July and September 1993 more than two thirds of the value of import taxes that should have been paid was not settled. Other sources indicate that between July and

December 1993 the ratio of import taxes paid to taxes payable (net of exemptions) was as low as 15%! (IMF (1996a, p. 23)). The majority of the people who did not pay taxes were civil servants (60%), allegedly including the country's vice president (personal communication at the University in Dar es Salaam, November 1996).

Table 7-3: Assessment and Collection of Import Taxes (TSh m)

	July-Sept. 93	Jan-March 94	April-June 94	July-Sept. 94
I. Duties and taxes assessed	25,626	29,752	31,480	48,988
II. Exemptions	5,435	8,550	10,971	19,364
III. Taxes payable (I-II)	20,191	21,202	20,509	29,624
IV. Taxes paid	4,072	6,241	8,692	9,962
V. Taxes legitimately deferred (bonded warehousing)	6,060	3,228	3,026	8,908
VI. *Unpaid taxes / unreconciled* (VI in % of taxes which had to be paid (IV+VI))	*10,059* (71%)	*11,733* (65%)	*8,791* (50%)	*10,754* (52%)
VII. *Revenue loss (II+VI)* (VII in % of taxes paid or legitimately deferred (IV+V))	*15,494* (153%)	*20,283* (214%)	*19,762* (169%)	*30,118* (160%)

Source: Internal donor document, November 1994 (percentage values added by the author). The data was originally provided by the preshipment companies SGS and Cotechna.

Many of the exemptions were granted illegally. According to discussions held in Dar es Salaam, many people used civil servants to buy exempted goods as they enjoyed tax-free status for selected items. The Warioba Report (a comprehensive report on the state of corruption in Tanzania in the 1990s) also found that individuals could easily claim to be acting on behalf of a religious organisation, the party (CCM) or the government, or they could easily get a waiver by claiming that imported raw materials would be used for goods destined for export (see also Warioba Report (1996, p. 294)).

Another source of information on tax evasion is the reports of the Controller and Auditor General. Every year the Office of the Controller and Auditor General (OCAG) produces an independent audit review of public accounts, reporting to parliament whether government revenues have been properly collected and utilised. According to their mandate their goal is to encourage 'public accountability in government financial operations, with the overriding concern to promote efficient and effective use of the taxpayers' money' and 'instilling a culture of financial discipline within the Government machinery' (OCAG (1997b, p. 1)). This chapter and the following chapters will refer frequently to these reports. Among other things, the reports document numerous incidences of doubtful exemptions. Although impressive, the information obtained probably only reveals the tip of the iceberg.

An area particularly prone to abuse has been tax exemption related to *investment promotion*. The Investment Promotion Centre (IPC)—a government body established in July 1991—was quickly transformed into a major rent-capturing institution. Although IPC exemptions also promoted a number of efficient investments, the misuse of IPC exemptions largely contributed to the severe macro imbalances between 1993 and 1995. Because of the magnitude of the problem, donors urged the government to investigate the exemptions. The confidential report, which finally came out in August 1997 (Coopers&Lybrand (1997a)), revealed major irregularities:

- 'From a sample of 228 files reviewed at IPC's offices, only 42% of them contained certificates of incorporation. We were unable to confirm whether the remainder ever existed.'
- '15 of the letters sent to project addresses by registered mail were returned to us unopened. This implies that several organisations had either failed to provide IPC with correct addresses or did not exist.'
- '31 organisations (of 228) no longer existed (investors were either unknown to locals in the areas, have been under receivership, left the country, never started, closed down or refused inspections).'

Furthermore the team complained that the documentation needed, such as approval letters, exemption lists from the Treasury, customs import entries and various registers, were delayed, missing or incomplete and contained inconsistent information.

The IPC scandal is in fact a good example to demonstrate what happens if a new policy (investment promotion) is introduced in a rent-seeking environment. The measure did not reach its stated objectives. On the contrary, it became an instrument used by blatant rent-seeking interests.

Also characteristic of a rent-seeking tax administration is that the dividing line between legal and illegal exemptions is blurred. The following comment (personal communication at the University in Dar es Salaam, November 1996) is a case in point:

> 'There was once an order to waive beer tax. It lasted six days and was then declared a mistake. During this time, masses of beer had been imported. Of course the importers were unknown.'

Besides the legal and illegal tax exemptions, Tanzania suffered from widespread *tax evasion* through *misreporting* and *smuggling*. Both activities were largely undertaken in collaboration with government officials. The correctness of an import assessment depends on many factors such as tariff classification, tariff rate, exchange rate for conversion, the quantity of the imports assessed and the declared value of the imported good. Each year the Controller and Auditor General (CAG) discovered many 'mistakes' in all these respects.

Another area of tax evasion was *bonded warehousing and transit trade*. Bonded warehouses are special compounds for the storage of 'uncustomed' goods. They are usually situated on the premises of importers and should be under control by the Customs Department. Goods however often find their way out of these installations without taxes being paid. Given the low control of bonded warehouses, donors several times urged the government to close them. The situation has been equally bad with transit trade, which was partly channelled through bonded warehouses. Goods simply disappeared between Tanzanian's entry and exit ports, as for instance criticised in an internal paper presented at a donor SPA/JEM-meeting in 1995:[132]

> 'In many cases, the importer is able to acquire a certificate evidencing entry into a bordering country, although there is no corresponding exit certificate showing that the goods have passed thorough a Tanzanian border post. Also, the signature of the exit port official is apparently quite often forged. In any event this is the major source of tax evasion and is very difficult to control.' (SPA/JEM (1995))

The Controller and Auditor General openly complaint about similar problems. The comments in Table 7-4 show that the problem was well known already in the early 1990s.

Table 7-4: CAG Complaints on Bonded Warehouse and Transit Trade

1990: (43/57 -43/59)	The *warehouse register is not kept up to date*... with the result that the balances at the warehouses at any given time are not known... In these circumstances *the Department cannot be said to have any effective control* over the warehouse goods. *Constructive warehousing* of imports is a procedure followed by which some importers are allowed to clear imported goods without payment of duties and taxes without fulfilling any of the conditions attached to normal warehousing... *The procedure has no legal authority*, but a large number of imports has been allowed to be cleared... In view of the *alarming results of the sample survey*, a complete verification of all imports which were constructively warehoused is required.
1991: (56/51)	In paragraph of my last report I had made adverse comments on the procedure of allowing 'constructive' warehousing... *It is imperative that this irregular procedure is discontinued.*
1992: (50/61)	A test audit of *transit goods* records...revealed that security bonds filed for transit goods...was not sufficient..., 241 transit entries were not recorded in the bond register..., 1799... have not been recorded in the waiver register... In the absence of such records, *I do not know how the Department can control goods in transit* for which there is no security cover. I am still awaiting evidence showing that these goods were actually exported.

Source: Controller and Auditor General Reports of Financial Years 1990 to 1992 (in parentheses indication of paragraph and page in respective volume)

Finally, the *Zanzibar route* has been another important, if not the most important channel of tax evasion. Zanzibar, which is part of the United Republic of Tanzania, had lower tax rates, particularly for basic commodities such as rice, sugar, wheat, flour, cooking oil, kangas, soap, etc. The Zanzibar government

[132] Part of the Special Programme of Assistance to Africa (SPA) initiated by the World Bank is Joint Evaluation Missions (JEMs). Most donors participate in these missions, which aim to coordinate and evaluate donor programmes and evaluate the country's progress.

maintains that its people are poorer and can therefore not afford to pay high taxes. Whatever the reason, the fact is that it is a lucrative smuggling business. Goods are imported through Zanzibar to be finally sold on the mainland. Sometimes the goods do not even enter Zanzibar, but only the documents make the journey for certification purposes (SPA/JEM (1995)). Critics have even said that if the port facilities of Zanzibar were in better shape or would be expanded, smuggling through Zanzibar would increase further.

All in all, opportunities for tax exemptions and evasion have been numerous. Import tax evasion at customs, diversion of transit trade including the Zanzibar route, abuses of bonded warehouses, payment in instalments, and discretionary exemptions happened in an environment of a weak but rent-seeking tax administration, low risks of detection and an almost total absence of punishment. The rent-seeking situation appears to have been of a strong non-rival type with little rent-seeking investments of involved parties but a large negative impact on government revenues.

Given this rent-seeking environment, it is not a surprise that the government found it difficult to balance the state budget. Between 1989/90 and 1996/97, in many years tax exemptions were even larger than the government's budget for health and education combined. In 1993/94, for instance, duty and excise exemptions alone amounted to TSh 76.709 billion and practically equalled the sum of budgeted expenditures on health and education (TSh 77.445 billion, calculated from PER, World Bank (1997d, p. 47, 53)). Put differently, the World Bank (1996a, p. 51) finds that the import revenue losses in 1994 could have covered the budget for the agricultural sector for three years.

Government Position Versus Rent-Seeking Explanation

The government usually downplayed all these problems, and suggested other than internal reasons for the failure in raising tax income. In a special donor meeting organised in response to the tax crisis the Tanzanian delegation argued that the substantial deviations between projections and actual collections in domestic revenue were mainly associated with insufficient external inflows. They even warned donors not to withdraw their support:

> 'It may be important to add here that the curtailment of disbursement of the Balance of payments resources has had four main consequences: firstly it denied the budget of counterpart funds; secondly, it denied the Government of customs revenue; thirdly, it reduced imports and subsequently production levels; and fourthly, it also reduced sales taxes due to lower production. All these consequences were experienced in 1992/93 and could happen again in 1993/94, if normal disbursements are not resumed.' (GoT (1994b, p. 5))

In other cases, the government simply pretended to be ignorant and astonished about adverse developments:

> 'Treasury had offered importers, in good faith, the so called staggered payment facility, allowing them to pay in stipulated monthly instalments due taxes on imports. Unfortunately, this privilege has been grossly abused…' (OCAG (1995, p. 8))

Even at a cursory glance it is obvious that the problems were not primarily of an institutional or external nature but reflected the pervasive rent-seeking interests so well embedded in Tanzania's society. Four aspects support this view: First, the government's continuous announcements with no follow up; second, the involvement of high-level bureaucrats, ministers and parliamentarians in tax evasion and exemptions; third, early, long-lasting and largely ignored complaints from the Office of the Controller and Auditor General (OCAG); and fourth, increasing and ignored concerns from donors about the slow progress of reform.

Announcements without subsequent action were frequent throughout the 1980s and 1990s. Improving the tax system appears to have been a never-ending topic. Even constraint-relieving reform measures, such as the introduction of a simplified (and therefore less corruption-prone) tax system or the elimination of discretionary exemptions took many years to be implemented. Already at the Consultative Group meeting in 1988, which discussed the first results of the Economic Recovery Programme (ERP I), the Tanzanian delegation emphasised the need to achieve a quick progress in improving the tax administration and to avoid new exemptions (see GoT (1988b, p. 12)). Among other things, Tanzania's Policy Framework Paper from 1992 aimed at a review of all discretionary exemptions with the final goal of eliminating them (GoT (1992b, p. 6)). If anything, the contrary has happened. Another example of lack of follow-up is the comment on taxation in the June 1993 Budget Speech. The speech was held only a few months before the real tax crisis broke out:

> 'In order to enhance our self reliance, especially in view of the current decline in foreign assistance, all Tanzanians must cultivate the habit and accept the responsibility for paying tax…In recent years, there has emerged a negative trend of tax evasion…We have to take strong exception over such habits.' Prof. K.A. Malima, Minister for Finance (GoT (1993a, p. 52)).

The very same minister was forced to resign later on because hc approved blank exemptions for the import of sugar, rice and wheat in September 1994!

This last statement points to the second aspect, which is the involvement of *high level bureaucrats and politicians* in the tax cheating. The Minister of Finance's disregard of an agreed policy on progressively phasing out tax exemptions caused donors to doubt the commitment of the Ministry to tackle issues of corruption and aid dependency. Tax evasion in Tanzania is, as Mufuruki and Rugemalira (1996, p. 1) note, a multi-billion dollar enterprise and has its most ardent supporters and beneficiaries within the highest ranks of both business and government. Besides Kighoma Malima, another Minister of Finance (Simon Mbilinyi) also had to resign two years later on account of a scandal over tax exemptions. This was particularly embarrassing as the investigating committee's report came out while the accused Minister was negotiating with the IMF to lift the freeze on funding which was imposed in 1994 because of Tanzania's chronic failures in collecting tax revenues (Financial Times, 30 September 1996).

The most striking example of total ignorance however comes from the *Controller and Auditor General's reports*, particularly if one follows up the problems mentioned there each year. Two examples are summarised in Tables 7-5 and 7-6, another even more striking case (poor customs record keeping) is summarised in Table 7-24 on page 414.

Table 7-5: CAG Complaints on Discretionary Tax Exemptions

1990: (41/54)	I am not certain whether the Treasury letters granting exemptions have any legal basis or are followed up by proper Government Notices issued by the Minister. It is therefore *necessary to discontinue the practice...*
1991: (54/49)	Cases of exemptions...continued to be noticed... *I would therefore once again urge, as I did in my last report, to discontinue the unsalutary practice* of granting exemption of taxes through Treasury letters.
1992: (48/59)	Letters issued by the Treasury *continued* to be used as authority for exemption of import duty and sales tax during 1991/92 *in spite of pointing out in my previous reports* that these have no legal basis.
1993: (40/48)	It was noticed during a test audit of import entries that import duty and sales tax amounting to TSh 2,345,763,480 was exempted on the authority of Treasury letters although these letters have no legal basis.
1994: (48/58)	Letters issued by the Treasury were *still used* as authority for exemptions of import duty, sales tax and excise duty, as shown below, during the year under review *in spite of pointing out in my previous reports* that these letters have no legal basis.
1995: (44/56)	Letters issued by the Treasury *continued* to be used as authority for exemptions... *in spite of pointing out in my previous reports* that these have no legal basis.

Source: Controller and Auditor General Reports of Financial Years 1990 to 1995 (in parentheses the paragraph and page in the respective volume)

As the tables reveal, discretionary exemptions and the practice of payment in instalments (as well as poor record keeping, addressed in Table 7-24) were criticised already at an early stage and mentioned thereafter in all subsequent years. In spite of these warnings, the government did not act. Looking at the 1992 and 1993 statements in Table 7-6 the CAG even predicted the tax crisis of 1993/94!

Donors also complained about the inaction of the Tanzanian government and the slow pace of reform. 'Nothing has been done so far', 'no progress has been made...', 'the issue has not been addressed', 'despite requests and promises from the Ministry of Finance, the report has not been submitted', etc. were common complaints between 1995 and 1997. Already at an early stage, donors were suggesting highly efficient ways to address the problem of misreporting and cheating on taxes, for instance suggesting that data on imports collected

Table 7-6: CAG Complaints on Payments of Duty and Taxes in Instalments

1988: (43/45)	*I am very much concerned* that a large amount of Government revenue may be lost if the Treasury will continue deferring collection of duties without vigorous follow up of recoveries thereof.
1989: (41/44)	In my last report I raised my concern over a possible loss of large amount of Government revenue that may occur as a result of deferring collection of duties... After a period of nearly one year *only a small fraction*...has been *recovered*... In spite of the problem already in hand *new cases* amounting to TSh 1,190,470,533.25 *continued to be recorded*... It is now high time for the Treasury to look at this practise from a different angle for the good of Government revenue.
1990: (42/55)	...*the need* to defer payment of duty and taxes on import is *not very clear.* Evidently the concession allowed to importers to pay duties in instalments has been *detrimental to the realisation of Customs revenue* on imports...
1991: (57/52)	There has *not been any significant progress* in the recovery of outstanding instalments... In spite of the difficulties...import duty in a further of 203 cases...was sanctioned to be paid in instalments... In all these cases the sanction to pay the duties in instalments was given through Treasury letters instead of Government Notices...[they] have therefore no legal authority.
1992: (49/61)	It appears that the Department is facing difficulties in effecting recoveries, and if Treasury is not going to tackle this problem seriously *a big amount of revenue might not be recovered.*
1993: (42/49)	*It is of great concern* to note that *no effective follow-up* action is being taken *to recover the large amount* due to the Government.
1994: (51/60)	*It is of great concern to me* that such huge and most needed government revenues *remains outstanding for collection for many years* now and due to doubtful existence of a number of the debtors, it is possible that a substantial amount of this revenue *may prove unrecoverable.*
1995: (46/59)	A sum of TSh 1,127,307,491 only was settled as at 30th May, 1996, leaving a balance of TSh 3,708,680,634... It appears that *little effort is being made to recover* the big amount of outstanding revenues.

Source: Controller and Auditor General Reports of Financial Years 1988 to 1995 (in parentheses indication of paragraph and page in respective volume)

by the preshipment inspection companies be reconciled with the effective declaration of taxes at customs departments. SGS, the preshipment inspection company in Tanzania, collected all data on imports and could therefore easily compare this data with customs data on import duty actually paid. SGS in fact offered this service repeatedly, at no charge, but the Tanzanian authorities were not interested (personal communication with donor, April 1998).

Table 7-7 summarises Tanzania's progress in revenue collection. All the problems were discovered already at the beginning of the 1990s; many of them took almost a decade to be solved in a satisfactory way, while others were still an issue in 2000. During the entire period Tanzania continuously lost considerable amounts of revenues—revenues, which ideally could have been allocated to finance urgently needed infrastructure projects, basic healthcare or education.

Table 7-7: Progress Report on Revenue Collection

	Horgan Report 1995	ESRF Report 1998	Situation in 2000
Enforcement of tax laws	4	3	3
Control/leakages through bonded warehouses	4	2	1
Tax evasion: transit trade	4	3	3
Zanzibar leakage	4	2	3
Losses through exemptions (no recovery)	3	3	3
CIS/OGL counterpart fund collections (discussion follows in Section d)	3	3	2

4: no progress, 3: unsatisfactory, 2: satisfactory, 1: task accomplished

Source: 1995 and 1998: ESRF (1998, p. 30-33); 2000: Personal communication in Dar es Salaam, April 2001

Shifts in Rent-Seeking Strategies and the Difficulty of Addressing Rent-Seeking

The enforcement of tax laws and the fight against tax evasion was still poor at the end of the 1990s. When the scandal of exemptions granted by the Investment Promotion Centre was finally settled, smuggling and tax evasion became rampant in the petroleum sector, again threatening government revenues. Legal tax exemptions also remained sizeable (in 1999 they were estimated to be at 42% of total imports (WTO (2000))). In addition the Zanzibar route has proven to be a well-protected rent-seeking channel, escaping effective rent-abating reform measures for a long time.

In 1997 the long-debated tax harmonisation of the four major commodities was finally accomplished. According to owners of ferry companies, the measure had such a great impact that traffic between the island of Zanzibar and Dar es Salaam had decreased, reducing the profitability of the ferry companies (personal communication in Dar es Salaam, April 2000)! Yet, in spite of this partial success, tax evasion and exemptions remained a serious problem in Zanzibar:

> 'The situation is far from satisfactory. For instance, there are wide differences in income tax thresholds as well as in practices on tax exemptions. While on the mainland, the GoT has closed the loophole (only the TRA can approve exemptions), in Zanzibar, Ministers can use their discretion to grant exemption. No figures were available on the extent of the use of this discretionary power, but it is believed to be quite significant. Moreover, while pre-shipment inspections are required on the mainland for the imports of all goods above US$5000, the same hold true in Zanzibar only, weirdly enough, for Government imports.' (Internal Donor Report, September, 1997).

The problem in Zanzibar then took a different form. Importers did pay higher tariff rates, but they colluded with Zanzibar officials, making sure that they only paid taxes for a portion of goods they import (the rest were not assessed, or were exempted or simply smuggled).

In the subsequent years as well the Zanzibar route remained a lucrative channel for tax evasion. The Zanzibar government provided new opportunities to evade taxes on the mainland, for instance by exempting sugar from taxation in Zanzibar as a gift during the month of Ramadan. It simply meant that during Ramadan sugar was imported to cover the demand for the entire year—not just in Zanzibar, but also to some extent in the mainland through the Zanzibar route. Even in April 2000, after many reforms have been implemented, a manager of a shipping company estimated that 20-30% of the imports he handled reached the mainland through Zanzibar. He claimed that customers wanted their containers to be shipped there but in examining their content it was evident that these goods (foodstuffs, electronic equipment, refrigerators, etc.) were going to be smuggled back to the mainland (personal communication in Dar es Salaam, March 2000).

The picture presented so far clearly shows that Tanzania's tax system was driven by rent-seeking; it was characterised by different tax rates, weak enforcement, tax evasion and a large number of statutory and discretionary exemptions. This system was not designed to secure sufficient funds to finance government activities but to feed a privileged elite. In this context, having higher tax rates for cooking oil than for unrefined oil, for instance, simply implies that whatever oil is imported will most likely be categorised as unrefined (see for example the scandals reported in GoT (1996)). Or official statistics may show that no textiles and only inexpensive second-hand cars have been imported, but the shops will be full of clothes and kangas from abroad and the streets of Dar es Salaam will have an ever-increasing number of brand-new 4WD cars.

There is wide agreement among Tanzanian's businesspeople that bureaucrats, including high-ranking officials, are eager to cooperate, assist and even offer guidance on how to beat the system, for a fee of course (Mufuruki and Rugemalira (1996, p. 4) or Simpkins (1996, p. 104)). Together with tax-evading businesspeople tax enforcers have benefited from the rent-seeking tax system and therefore directly and indirectly resisted changes that threatened their rent income.

Rent-seekers are patient and, as the case of tax evasion shows, strategies to beat the system are numerous. It took quite some time before the mainland allowed preshipment inspections, and a much longer time for Zanzibar to do so. Preparing speeches, ordering investigations and describing problems that are already known will not affect rents. What matters is that effective rent-abating actions are implemented. In particular mid-level civil servants from the Customs Department and the Attorney General's Office have been slow and reluctant or even counterproductive in the reform process (Korsgren (1996, p. 4)). There were also rumours that 'important' people tried to manipulate the CAG's work, and in 1995 the chairman of a committee on tax evasion (Thomas Kama) resigned because he was not able to do his job in a correct manner (personal communication in Dar es Salaam, April 2000). Furthermore the government suspended the abolition of a number of exemptions because of pressures from various interest groups. Comments on this matter were for instance made in the 1994 Budget Speech (GoT (1994a, p. 45)).

Obviously tax evaders would not have succeeded so well without the collaboration of government officials who created and maintained the parallel tax system. How profitable this system was is well described in Mufuruki and Rugemalira (1996, p. 5):

> 'High tax rates, bureaucratic red tape, arbitrary fixing of tariffs and other trade barriers encountered in the government tax administration have helped to create a *parallel tax department* which operates side by side with the government, the difference being that it (the parallel dept) is more efficient, more service oriented, has absolutely no bureaucrats and collects more money than its government counterpart...
>
> Tanzania is therefore not a duty free zone, but a country with bad tax laws that have made corruption and tax evasion not only inevitable but also the *most profitable forms of business* in Tanzania.'

Looking at the development after the mid-1980s, there are many factors that contributed to the increase of tax evasion and exemptions. The development can be seen as a rent-seeking response to the changed institutional setting initiated with the reform process. With liberalisation economic conditions and activities changed, the share of the private sector increased and Nyerere's charismatic influence steadily diminished. In addition devaluation was counteracting the decrease in tax rates as it increased the taxable amount of imports in TSh and therefore maintained the incentive to cheat the system. That the tax crisis only broke out in the 1990s is, according to discussions at a donor embassy in April 1998, a reflection of an old system breaking down. In the past the system was based on loyalties; there was a network and people had to bribe their way through. In the 1990s, the government started to introduce more and more formal criteria but with the same rent-seeking bureaucrats. There was hardly a mechanism to enforce this new system.

Major institutional changes related to taxation occurred after 1995. Because of the persistent weaknesses and problems in the tax administration and the related increasing discontent and pressures from the donors' side, Tanzania created a new autonomous body in 1996, the *Tanzania Revenue Authority (TRA).* In fact, already in 1991 the Presidential Commission of Enquiry into Public Revenues had suggested establishing an independent Revenue Authority as a measure to improve government revenue collection, but it took half a decade for this suggestion to materialise.

TRA became responsible for the assessing, collecting and accounting of revenue on behalf of the government. Several measures to improve performance and to reduce incentives for cheating were introduced at the onset or in subsequent years. These include the dismissal of 1100 staff members of the old tax department (i.e. not all staff members were reemployed at TRA), substantial increases in salaries (salaries paid at TRA were much higher than in other government departments), adaptation of revenue targets (defined according to collections in previous years), as well as measures to make cheating more difficult, such as the introduction of asset declaration, telephone hotlines for complaints and technical measures (computerisation, the Taxpayers Identification Number TIN, etc.).

In the first fiscal year in which the institution was operating (June 1996/97), revenue collection increased by 26%, and in the subsequent year it increased another 12% (World Bank (1999a, p. 13)). In spite of this favourable development, the rent-seeking problem related to revenue collection was not really solved, as many people still openly talk about corruption in TRA, for instance:

> 'True payable tax may be 4 million, 2 million may be settled. With discussion, TRA will settle 1 million, however, write a receipt of 700,000 and get 300,000 into the pocket' (personal communication in Iringa, April 2000).

Examples from Dar es Salaam show similar patterns (e.g. an assessment of 80 million, settlement at 18 million, and 6 million goes 'under the table') (personal communication in Dar es Salaam, April 2000). What has changed apparently is the division of rent-seeking benefits, which shifted with the creation of the TRA to the disadvantage of businesspeople. This development is understandable when looking at the corruption formula described in Table 4-1 (page 153). For the tax collector, these costs of engaging in corrupt activities have increased, but they are in many cases still smaller than the maximum bribe businesspeople are willing to pay.

In addition many changes have *empowered remaining corrupt tax enforcers* and thereby made them more 'efficient' in what they were previously doing, i.e. being corrupt and extracting rents for private enrichment. Having additional means to catch tax evaders (vehicles to patrol the borders, telephone lines between border points, tax identification numbers, etc.) also makes it easier to extort dishonest businesspeople. An increasing number of people have been complaining about harassment from TRA, in particular between 1998 and 2000. The changed environment also negatively affected honest people. With the new incentive system, TRA officials began to assess arbitrarily high taxes and then extorted side payments from businesspeople to reduce the level of taxes. Income tax collectors for instance may come on the busiest day of the year, count the revenues of that day and simply multiply the figure by 365 to calculate the basis for the annual taxation. Other people complain that they have been paying taxes which they legally were not supposed to. But it was still cheaper and much less cumbersome to pay these than to go to court.

Conclusion: Major Changes in the Rent-Seeking Setting

The rent-seeking game has changed. Donors are pleased because TRA collects more official revenue after a decade of poor performance. The parallel tax system however has not disappeared. The increase in tax revenues is not so much effected at the expense of the parallel tax system, but to a considerable extent at the expense of honest taxpayers and some petty tax-evaders. At least in the year 2000 paying taxes has still predominantly been a matter of negotiation.

Productive income earning opportunities were not high in Tanzania in the 1990s. The benefits of cheating, in contrast, were initially very high and the cost of capturing rents was small. This constellation implies that a very large increase in costs would have been necessary to reduce the profitability of rent-seeking versus productive income earning activities.

Although progress has been considerable if measured in terms of inputs in the tax system (establishing and equipping the TRA, implementing new procedures, etc.), the critical break-even point has apparently not yet been achieved. The rent-seeking setting has become more competitive, implying higher direct rent-seeking costs. Tax evasion however still remains profitable. In fact, even in 2003, it was explicitly noted that a major constraint in Tanzania was the high level of tax evasion and tax fraud, explaining the very low level of government revenue collection, which has been at 12.5% of GDP (Internationales Afrikaforum (2003)).

The country's performance in this decade will show whether these are only intermediate costs on the way to setting up a highly efficient tax administration or whether rent-seekers will again attain a new strong position in a changed institutional framework. What matters critically is the commitment of the leadership and high-level civil servants. At least in the 1990s donors took a far too optimistic view and thereby even strengthened a corrupt tax administration.

c) Failure in Restraining Parastatal Credit Expansion

> *'Officials at all levels interfered in the day to day business—encouraging lending here, directing that resources be used there, influencing decisions directly and indirectly—almost always without recognizing and accepting responsibility for their final consequences.'*
>
> *Presidential Commission of Enquiry into the Monetary and Banking System, July 1990.*[133]

The macro imbalance that persisted after the initiation of the Economic Recovery Programme in 1986 had several rent-seeking origins. One cause is the parallel tax administration described before, which was also responsible for the high credit expansion in 1992/93, when the government could no longer finance its activities with regular revenue collection. Another important cause of macro instability is the rent-seeking allocation of credits to the parastatal sector.

In Tanzania most of the credits have been allocated to poorly performing parastatals. This undermined macro stability in two ways: directly by the credit expansion, and indirectly by the allocation of the credits to loss-makers. Well-protected and not threatened with bankruptcy, many inefficient parastatals contributed to inflation in passing on their high costs of production. In addition, as loss-makers they failed to pay taxes and dividends to the government, making it more difficult for the government to finance its budget.

---

[133] GoT (1990b, p. 2), quoted from Eriksson (1993, p. 46).

The discussion below provides a brief overview of bank lending and poor performance. Failures in the banking system are often a symptom of more fundamental weaknesses in the economy. Many rent-seeking aspects which finally led to high bank lending in Tanzania will be discussed in later sections. Above all Chapter 8.2, which examines the efficiency of different types of support allocated to the parastatal sector, will include a detailed evaluation on bank loans and overdrafts.

Magnitudes and Performance of Bank Lending

In the late 1980s Tanzania had one of the least developed financial sectors in Africa, with no capital or money markets (IMF (1996a, p. 2)). The financial system was state-owned; banks operated in a closed and protected environment, each one with its own sphere and with little overlap (World Bank (1989c, p. 94)). Large shares of credits were allocated on the basis of government directives and the interest rate was determined administratively. Before the liberalisation of the banking system in 1991, the following banks (all state-owned) lent to individuals and parastatal companies: National Bank of Commerce (NBC) with a market share of roughly 90%, the Cooperative and Rural Development Bank (CRDB), Tanzanian Investment Bank (TIB), Tanzania Housing Bank (THB) and the Peoples Bank of Zanzibar (PBZ).

Unfortunately it was not possible to obtain a detailed and complete overview of the magnitude and changes of annual bank lending. Nearly all data provided by the banks are of poor quality and include major errors. Errors and inconsistencies become particularly apparent if there is information on individual loan statements (and not just sector aggregates) and if the data allow following up individual statements over several years.

Before 1991 banks largely failed to consolidate their data. The problem is well known. Regarding NBC, Eriksson (1993, p. 42) for instance notes that it was impossible to obtain information from the bank itself as it had severe problems related to internal data collection and compilation. These data were complied branchwise and only consolidated at the head office after computerisation started in 1990. Similar compilation problems exist with other banks.

After the 1990s changes of aggregates became difficult to interpret and demanded additional information since many loans were taken out of the balance (written off, assumed by the government or transferred to the liquidating and privatising institutions LART and PSRC). It is therefore not surprising that different sources of information may deviate considerably, as they may not include the same sample of loans and overdrafts.

Table 7-8 gives some information on bank lending to marketing boards, cooperatives and other parastatals, as well as lending to individuals and private companies. Cooperatives are important stakeholders in the Tanzanian economy. Formally not state-owned, they are close to the ruling party and play a major role in resource allocation and the mobilisation of votes for parliamentary elections. Not included in the table are the Peoples Bank of Zanzibar and the Tanzania Housing Bank, because it was not possible to obtain annual data. The banks are relatively small; PBZ had an outstanding balance in June 1992 of only TSh 6.48 billion (US$22 million) (World Bank (1997a, p. 37)).

Table 7-8: Indication of Bank Lending 1985-92, in TSh bn

	Outstanding balance, end of June values								Percentage change						
	85	86	87	88	89	90	91	92	86	87	88	89	90	91	92
NBC	13.2	16.6	28.3	55.8	84.7[a]	106.5	134.0	(124)[b]	26	70	97	52[a]	26	26	
Marketing boards	7.8	7.0	10.8	24.0	19.3[a]	22.4	22.5[c]	(3.7)[b]	-10	53	123	-20[a]	16	0	
Cooperatives	0.5	2.5	6.2	11.0	15.8	21.7	23.5	(33)[b,d]	429	149	79	44	37	8	
Other parastatal	2.7	4.0	7.0	12.7	32.3	38.1	52.5	(41)[b]	49	74	83	154	18	38	
Private	2.3	3.2	4.4	8.1	17.3	24.2	35.5	(46)[b]	39	40	83	114	40	47	
CRDB (sample)[e]		*1.3*	*1.7*	*1.7*	*2.0*	*3.5*	*6.8*	*11.6*		*38*	*-3*	*19*	*71*	*98*	*69*
Cooperatives		*0.1*	*0.2*	*0.2*	*0.4*	*0.7*	*0.9*	*1.2*[d]		*102*	*16*	*61*	*96*	*25*	*36*
Other parastatal		*0.3*	*0.2*	*0.3*	*0.3*	*0.6*	*0.7*	*0.9*		*-3*	*5*	*10*	*117*	*12*	*29*
Village		*0.6*	*0.7*	*0.3*	*0.4*	*0.4*	*0.6*	*0.8*		*18*	*-49*	*6*	*12*	*33*	*40*
Private		*0.3*	*0.6*	*0.9*	*1.0*	*1.7*	*4.7*	*8.7*		*85*	*39*	*17*	*70*	*174*	*85*
TIB[f]			5.0[g]	7.4[g]	11.6	17.6	24.8	37.4			48	57	51	41	51
Parastatal			3.5[g]	5.5[g]	8.3	12.7	18.2	29.0			57	50	54	44	59
Private			1.5[g]	1.9[g]	3.4	4.9	6.5	8.5			27	78	46	33	30
Total	13.2	17.9	35.0	64.9	98.4[a]	127.6	165.6	(173)[b]		68[h]	85	52[a]	30	30	
Marketing boards	7.8	7.0	10.8	24.0	19.3[a]	22.4	22.5	(3.7)[b]		53[h]	123	-20[a]	16	0	
Cooperatives	0.5	2.6	6.3	11.2	16.2	22.4	24.3	(34)[d]		148[h]	77	44	39	9	
Other parastatal	2.7	4.3	10.7	18.5	40.9	51.4	71.4	(71)[b]		70[h]	72	121	26	39	
Private & village	2.3	4.1	7.2	11.2	22.1	31.3	47.3	(64)[b]		40[h]	55	97	42	51	
Rate of Inflation (June-June):									32	30	31	26	36	29	22

a: According to the 1989 Public Expenditure Review, during 1988 the government took over 40% of the liabilities of crop marketing parastatals (World Bank (1989b)).
b: NBC balance after some non-performing loans have been excluded. In Dec. 1991, the NBC Loan portfolio was at TSh 180 billion (see Figure 7-2 on page 337).
c: 19.021 billion alone belong to National Milling Corporation, which went bankrupt in 1991.
d: According to the World Bank (1994b, p. 70) the debt position of the Cooperative System was almost TSh 60 billion in June 1992 (CRDB TSh 13.0 billion, NBC TSh 45.8 billion).
e: E.g., according to the World Bank (1997a, p. 35) CRDB loans and bills were at TSh 37.2 billion in June 1992 (and TSh 65.2 billion in June 1993).
f: Except for 1987, June values calculated from average of previous and subsequent December value.
g: Loan statements of 1987 and 1988 did not include loans with arrears of less than 3 month but only the name of the recipients. Based on an estimated average size of similar loans in 1989, these loans have been added. (previous values: parastatal 2.8 and 5.0, private 1.0 and 1.1).
h: Change of NBC and CRDB only, as there is no value for TIB in 1986.

Source: NBC data from Eriksson (1993, p. 85) who refers to BoT; data of CRDB and TIB based on annual loan statements collected at the respective banks in Dar es Salaam; inflation calculated from the change in the Consumer Price Index published by BoT

Already in the Budget Speech of June 1986, the government emphasised that parastatals and cooperative societies were expected to reduce their dependence on bank credit (recall quotation in the lead on page 317). And at the Consultative Group meeting in Paris in July 1988, the government formulated the goal to reform agricultural marketing as a measure to avoid deficits of marketing boards (GoT (1988b, p. 13f)). The goals proved to be illusory and all monetary targets were missed by wide margins in the 1980s and early 1990s.

Table 7-8 shows that bank lending increased dramatically after the initiation of the ERP in 1986. The table however underestimates this development since several loans were assumed by the government, in particular in 1988 and after 1991. Even the 1991 data of NBC exclude considerable amounts (as indicated in note 'b' only six months later, an alternative source shows a balance of TSh 180 billion, which is nearly TSh 50 billon higher).

Data on CRDB loans are highly incomplete; they were collected directly at the bank's headquarters in Dar es Salaam.[134] Some of the increases in Table 7-8 also reflect the capitalisation of interests. For the TIB loans, where detailed information was available, the share of interests due in the balance outstanding increased between 1987 and 1992 from 1/4 to 2/3 for parastatals and from 1/5 to 2/5 for private companies.

The high growth rates of bank lending undermined macro stability in the 1980s and early 1990s. However, more consequential for the economy than the high level of bank lending was the *poor status of the bank's loan portfolio.* Even though arrears had already been common before 1987, the share increased substantially thereafter. The state of the loan portfolio in 1992 is documented in Figures 7-2 and 7-3.

Figure 7-2: National Bank of Commerce Portfolio Status, 31 December 1991

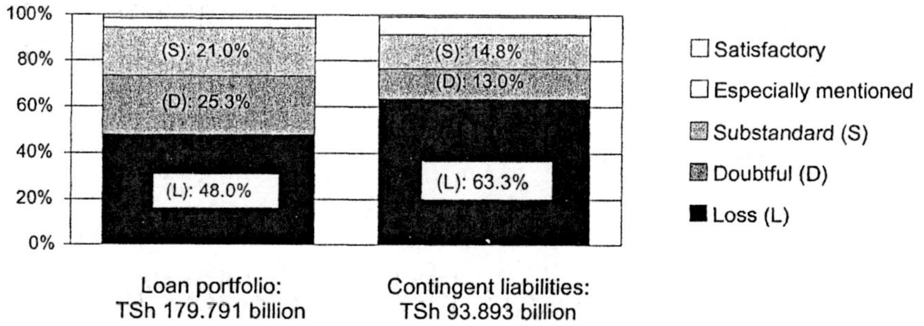

Source: Data according to Eriksson (1993, p. 86), who refers to a confidential report

[134] In the 1991 Economic Survey—a statistical book which used to be produced annually by the Bureau of Statistics and the Planning Commission—alternative data for the years 1989 to 1991 are available. According to this source of information outstanding balances were TSh 3.2, 5.4 and 4.3 billion for the financial years 1989, 1990 and 1991, the largest share being cooperatives with TSh 2.7, 1.5 and 1.0 billion respectively (Planning Commission (1992, p. 71)). However, it is not clear how reliable this information is, as official data used to be equally poor and politically manipulated (personal communication in Dar es Salaam at the Bureau of Statistics in March/April 2000).

Figure 7-2 shows the NBC portfolio status of loans and contingent liabilities. As described in Eriksson (1993, p. 47), contingent liabilities are commitments made by the bank in terms of guarantees or securities. An unused overdraft limit is an example. Once a guarantee becomes effective or an overdraft limit is drawn upon, the bank pays and the loan balance increases. It is striking to see that in 1991 almost 95% of the NBC portfolios had been adversely classified (substandard, doubtful and loss). Only 1.6% of the loans and 1.0% of the contingent liabilities have been rated as satisfactory.

Equally poor is the performance of outstanding balances of TIB loans at the end of 1991, as indicated in Figure 7-3. The number of non-defaulting loans, which include loans with arrears of less than three months, decreased from a share of 35% in 1987 to 9% in 1991. In value terms, the share decreased from 24% to 2%.

Figure 7-3: Tanzania Investment Bank (TIB) Loan Classification 1987-91

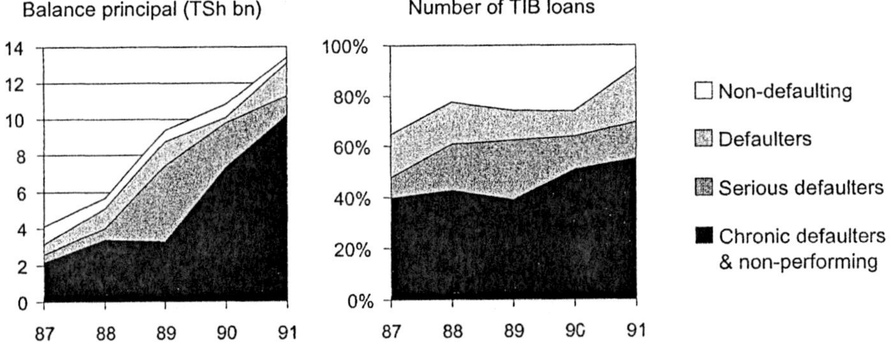

Until 1991, Tanzanian Investment Bank categorised its loans in non-defaulting loans (arrears less than 3 months), defaulters (arrears 3-12 months), serious defaulters (arrears 1-2 years) and chronic defaulters (arrears larger than two years).

Source: Annual loan statements (end of December values) from Tanzania Investment Bank, Dar es Salaam

With all other banks, it was not possible to receive detailed information on the classification of loans. Arrears however have been high. Nearly two thirds of the CRDB balance had been considered as irrecoverable in 1990 (World Bank (1994b, p. 92)) and roughly 70% of the PBZ portfolio in 1994 was rated substandard, doubtful or loss (World Bank (1995, P. 2)).

The poor loan portfolios of the Tanzanian banks suggest that also after the initiation of the Economic Recovery Programme in 1986 loans were not allocated according to efficiency criteria. A major cause of high bank lending was the system of crop marketing, which obliged the banks, often at government order, to lend to undercapitalised and inefficient companies (World Bank (1994b, p. 92)). The World Bank notes that in spite of government takeovers of loans in the 1980s, accumulated arrears of crop marketing overdrafts in 1991 equalled almost 20% of agricultural GDP. The largest debtor was the National

Milling Corporation (NMC), which stopped most of its activities in 1991. As with other marketing boards, the debt reflected a mixture of political interference (government pricing policy) and parastatal inefficiency. In the financial year 1987/88, the company's unsecured overdrafts amounted to four times the Ministry of Agriculture's budget (World Bank (1989c, p. 124)).

Other non-agriculture companies also accumulated high debts and debts did not only increase within the banking system but also within the government or parastatal organisations, such as the Parastatal Pensions Fund and utility parastatals. The unmet debt servicing of Tanzania Electric Supply (TANESCO) to the government in 1989, for instance, was larger than the entire recurrent funding of the Ministry of Health (World Bank (1989b, p. 35)).

At the end of June 1992 total public enterprise debt to the banking system, to private companies and to the government was estimated to be as high as TSh 1000 billion (Due (1993, p. 1982)), equivalent to US$3.3 and 2.3 billion at the then-prevailing official and parallel market rate. The indebtedness of the public sector had been increasing steadily, despite early complaints from the donor side and vague government goals in policy framework papers (e.g. World Bank (1988, p. 13f) and GoT (1987, p. 6-8, 13)). This increase in debt reflected the continued success of rent-seeking forces to withstand reform measures thus far undertaken.

With the Banking Act of 1991, banks were no longer required to lend to parastatal companies. However in subsequent years banks still accumulated non-performing loans. Accumulated losses in the 1993/94 financial year alone accounted for 3% of GDP and the NBC portfolio at the end of 1994 equalled TSh 214 billion (almost 10% of GDP), 77% still classified as non-performing despite previous reschedulings (IMF (1995, p. 6)).

Postponing Reforms, Countervailing Actions and Personal Enrichment

There are different explanations for the high level of bank lending to dubious debtors. On the non-rent-seeking side, some of the increases in indebtedness may be justified with external factors and problems related to the speed of reforms. Arguments include unfavourable export market prices, high production and marketing costs due to the poor transport and communication infrastructure or the general difficulty in implementing capacity-intensive reforms in the financial sector.

Much more obvious, however, are rent-seeking arguments. In short, bank lending has been high as urgent reforms of loss-making parastatals have been postponed and because privileged individuals and groups enjoyed easy access to bank credits as members of a well-established patronage system. These two aspects are briefly considered below.

In developing countries bank loans to parastatal companies were only rarely evaluated on a commercial basis, as the companies enjoyed explicit or implicit backing by the government (World Bank (1994a, p. 113)). Tanzania was not an exception and the reforms from the mid-1980s onwards did not change this pattern of support. On the contrary, continued access to loans and overdrafts or government-guaranteed loans allowed policymakers to delay certain reforms and permitted parastatals, marketing boards and cooperative unions to *postpone urgently needed adjustments* within the company or organisation. Earlier liberalisation in traditional export crops, for instance (it only started in 1993), would most likely have avoided the huge accumulation of bad debts in the agriculture sector. Even though the inefficiency had been obvious and much criticised throughout the reform process, it took years for effective actions.

Bank lending was not only responsible for the postponement of necessary reforms; it also explains why other *reform measures* already undertaken *failed to have the desired impact*. The reduction of the fiscal deficit is a case in point. Before the mid-1980s the fiscal deficit has been very high and it was a major cause of monetary expansion and inflation. To improve the situation the government decided, among other things, to abolish many subsidies to parastatal companies. If evaluated on its own, this measure was fairly successful. From the mid-1980s onwards, the budget deficit declined and with it the need of the government to finance the gap with bank borrowing.

However, apparently as a reaction to the abolition of subsidies, parastatals increased their own borrowing from the banking sector. The expansion of credits to the parastatal sector replaced government borrowing and had the same negative effect on monetary expansion and inflation as had the government deficit before. With the abolition of government subsidies, not the amount of parastatal support changed but essentially the type of support. Flows of funds simply shifted from 'indirect' bank lending (the government pays the parastatals but has to finance its budget deficit with bank lending) to direct parastatal financing from the banking sector.

That the stake of the government had not much changed is also obvious from the performance in the subsequent years when bank credits became budget-effective again. Between 1986 and 1996 the government stepped in several times taking over bad debt of marketing boards and other parastatal companies; in 1994 the government also assumed a share of the cooperative unions' debt.

Clearly, many parastatals were hit very hard by the devaluation, price liberalisation and the reduction of import barriers. With economic liberalisation, most of the parastatal companies consequently defaulted on their outstanding loans and they had to borrow additional funds to cover their operational costs. It is not the purpose of reforms to provoke a total collapse of the parastatal sector. Companies need time and resources to adjust. The crucial point is however that they should not get resources to postpone adjustment. In Tanzania, parastatal companies enjoyed long-lasting support despite being technically bankrupt.

The second obvious and anecdotally widely-documented rent-seeking explanation is *blatant personal enrichment*. The Indian Ocean Newsletter (No. 767, 31 May 1997) comments on NBC losses that occurred in 1991/92 and 1993/94:

> 'These included "loans" made, with no hope of their ever being repaid, to cooperatives, semi-public bodies, and groups linked to the government party, to ministries or even to VIPs. The loan decisions were often made outside of NBC board meetings on direct orders from the finance ministry, the prime minister's office, or the president's office.'

Given the extensive patronage network in Tanzania, it is not surprising that the economic wing of CCM, i.e. Sukita, was a main debtor of NBC. The company accumulated a total debt of more than TSh 12 billion (Africa Intelligence (1998)). Bank officials were also major profiteers of the lending deals, as intermediaries and as recipients of loans. For instance, according to personal communication (Dar es Salaam, November 1997) an NBC chairman was dismissed because his company was one of the largest debtors to NBC, and a businessman who applied for a TSh 40 million NBC loan was asked to take on another 10 million to be able to pay off the NBC official for the favour. (When worried about the high cost of the loan, the NBC official simply replied, 'Who told you to pay the loan back?')

Since rent-seeking recipients of loans collaborated with rent-seeking bank officials, and the government frequently stepped in to take over non-performing loans, key stakeholders did not have an interest to change the system. Not surprisingly, the informal rent-seeking network of credit allocation continued to function after the 1991 Banking Act, which gave the banks more freedom in their decision (banks were no longer required to lend to non-commercial entities, including the heavily indebted cooperatives (e.g. GoT (1991, p. A-3))).

This argument points to the last, most obvious 'rent-protecting' strategy, i.e. the *deliberate delay of bank reforms*. The rehabilitation programme for NBC, which started in 1991, took more than half a decade to be nearly accomplished. Although the bank closed several branches and retrenched 20% of its employees by early 1993, the most important elements of the original restructuring plan such as effective changes in the bank's credit policies and internal monitoring mechanisms were hardly implemented (IMF (1995, p. 6f)), with the effect that lending to parastatal and cooperatives in default continued and became a major cause of the monetary expansion. In 1994 the NBC restructuring programme had virtually come to a standstill. As already argued in the previous section on taxation, the involvement of high-level civil servants in the rent-seeking business largely explains inaction with financial sector reforms.

The government frequently justified the lack of progress with the argument that bank reforms are capacity intensive and therefore need time to be implemented and to become effective. What is striking, however, is that also the easiest constraint-relieving reform measures, such as the abolition of state interference in credit allocation, had not been undertaken for a long time. And when these interventions were formally abolished they continued to be effective in informal relations, also making the rent-seeking involvement of high government officials apparent.

Delayed bank reforms also had a negative impact on the expansion of private bank activities, and because bank competition remained limited, a negative impact on the effectiveness of the Bank of Tanzania's new instruments of monetary management. As noted in IMF (1995, p. 6) 'loan interest rates were negative in real terms and well below the yield paid on Treasury bills, and the bank fees were well below cost and lower than the fees charged by other commercial banks'. Even after the mid-1990s, NBC was so inefficient that it needed a spread of 15% to break even. In addition, NBC's weak financial position also hampered the development of an interbank credit market since private banks hesitated to engage in lending to the state-owned banks (IMF (1996a, p. 1)).

All in all, the continued accumulation of non-performing bank loans after the initiation of the Economic Recovery Programme provides additional evidence that many rent-seekers managed to secure their rent income for years. For a long period of time, reforms largely addressed non-binding constraints, which only marginally affected the size of the rents available through the banking system. The easy access to bank credits has been particularly costly as it delayed or undermined the pace and success of other reform steps, i.e. attaining macro stability and introducing efficiency-increasing incentives through price reforms and trade liberalisation.

d) Poor Foreign Exchange Administration and Hesitant Devaluation

> *'In the best case, the money was used to subsidise ailing parastatals. In the worst case, the money went directly into the pockets of the managers of the recipient companies. The truth may be found somewhere in between.'*
>
> *Internal paper on Commodity Import Support, Donor Embassy, Dar es Salaam, Nov. 1996*

Since the late 1970s Tanzania's official exchange rate had been substantially overvalued. The long-lasting departure from the equilibrium rate caused major distortions and made an increasingly restrictive foreign exchange allocation necessary, which opened doors for all kind of manipulation and fraud. The negative impact of sustained overvaluation is well known. As for instance argued in Mistry (1994, p. 117), there are a number of cases where developing countries benefited from prolonged undervaluation, in particular in East Asia, however, no country ever benefited from sustained overvaluation. It is thus not surprising that he finds that in the cases of 'successful' adjustments effective devaluations have been an integral component of the policy mix.

Tanzania's officially stated goal at the initiation of the ERP in fact included a rapid devaluation of the Tanzanian Shilling, with the objective of unifying the official rate with the parallel market rate by 1 July 1988 (GoT (1987, p. 12)). Since foreign exchange allocation was one of the most, if not the most profitable area of rent-seeking in the mid-1980s, such an early exchange rate unification would have unmistakably demonstrated the government's seriousness in moving ahead with economic reforms and breaking with vested rent-seeking interests.

Tanzania's record tells another story. Instead of a speedy devaluation the government maintained a complex, non-transparent and *corruption-prone system of foreign exchange allocation*. Even more consequential was the *non-payment of the TSh equivalent* in exchange transactions, i.e. beneficiaries either did not pay TSh for the foreign exchange they received or they paid by drawing on a bank credit on which they later defaulted. This strategy reflects the most blatant reaction of rent-seekers to any devaluation achieved in the reform process.

Tanzania's Complex Foreign Exchange System

Already in the early 1980s the government began to create an increasingly complex system of foreign exchange allocation. As a reaction to the severe balance of payments problems and an unwillingness to devalue the Tanzanian Shilling, the government introduced the *Export Retention Scheme* in 1982. Depending on the goods traded, the Export Retention Scheme allowed exporters to retain a certain percentage of their foreign exchange earnings, which could be used to finance imports or which could be 'illegally' converted at the parallel market rate. A high retention rate implied a much more favourable effective exchange rate and was therefore meant to stimulate exports. This measure can be interpreted as the first implicit compromise between the government and the IMF on the long-debated issue of currency devaluation.

Traditional exports initially had an export retention rate of 10%; the rate for non-traditional exports, in contrast, depended on the commodity and was finally harmonised in 1987 to 50%. Two years later export retention rates were temporarily abolished for traditional export goods and they were reduced for non-traditional goods to 35%.

Because of the severe shortages of goods in 1983/84, the government additionally introduced the *Own Fund Import Facility* in 1984. The scheme was highly efficient in bringing, within a very short time, essential goods into the country and, as emphasised in Booth, et al. (1993, p. 57), the goods did not just reach the shops of Dar es Salaam and Arusha but also many of the remote villages. Individuals with assets abroad could repatriate their wealth by purchasing own-funded imports. On the one hand, the scheme represented the reversal of capital flight; on the other hand, it offered an excellent opportunity to use illegal export earnings from smuggling or earnings from overinvoicing of officially-financed imports. Kaufmann and O'Connell (1999, p. 7) assume that after 1988 repatriation had largely been completed, and the Own Fund Facility reflects foreign exchange earnings from illegal activities. The use of illegal earnings is well known and not questioned by the Tanzanian authorities.

Table 7-9 summarises official figures on imports based on import licences issued. They indicate that in the mid-1980s more than one third of imports were financed with own funds and the share was even larger than the 'normal' ('free') allocation, which was financed by Tanzania's own official export earnings. The magnitudes demonstrate how lucrative smuggling has been. Yet the data still underestimate the true level of own funds. To avoid taxes many own-funded imports were underinvoiced or not registered at all. In contrast, officially financed imports tended to be overinvoiced, as the additional benefits obtained from a higher official foreign exchange allocation were larger than the additional costs from higher taxation (personal communication at the University in Dar es Salaam, November 1997).

Table 7-9: Import Licences Issued Under Different Sources of Funds

		1986	1987	1988	1989	1990	1991
General windows		71.7%	72.4%	58.4%	58.4%	49.8%	50.5%
Normal / Free allocation	o	24.6%	32.5%	18.6%	29.1%	22.0%	20.5%
Supplier's credit		11.3%	4.3%	3.7%	1.6%	0.7%	0.5%
Barter trade		0.8%	0.9%	0.6%	0.3%	0.2%	0.3%
Export retention (since 1982)	p	0.1%	0.2%	0.4%	1.1%	1.1%	0.3%
Own funds imports (since 1984)	p	35.0%	34.6%	35.0%	26.4%	25.8%	29.0%
Donor funded windows		28.3%	27.6%	41.6%	41.6%	50.2%	49.5%
Loans, grants & credit (project funds)	o	14.7%	19.3%	29.7%	21.3%	23.3%	18.4%
Commodity Import Support programme	o/x	13.6%	8.2%	9.2%	11.1%	9.0%	3.7%
Open General Licence (since 1988)	o/x			2.7%	9.1%	17.8%	27.3%
Total (in US$ billion)		1.360	1.489	1.825	1.835	1.739	1.705

o: Imports at official exchange rate
p: Imports at parallel market rate
x: Foreign exchange acquired for less than official rate or even for free as payment of counterpart TSh value was either delayed or never made.

Source: Data obtained from the Bank of Tanzania, Import Data & Analysis Department, Dar es Salaam 1998

The second part of Table 7-9 shows donor-financed imports. Besides the direct funds spent on projects, Tanzania received traditional *Commodity Import Support (CIS)* and funds related to the *Open General Licence (OGL) facility*. The CIS programme already existed in the 1970s. Under this scheme the donor supplied the foreign exchange, which was allocated through an administrative approval procedure to the recipient. The recipient was supposed to pay the counterpart in local currency to the Treasury. In contrast, the OGL—a facility, which started in 1988 under the management of the Bank of Tanzania—was more market based and was mainly introduced as a measure to eliminate non-tariff barriers. Licences for OGL imports are automatically issued once the trader submits an application to import goods that are specified in the OGL list. The TSh counterpart, which has to be paid up front at the bank, is channelled to the Treasury and used as budget support. Both CIS and OGL funds were converted at the official exchange rate. When donors discovered in the early 1990s that CIS counterpart funds had to a large extent not been paid, they increasingly shifted their balance of payments support to OGL.

The Rent-Seeking Allocation of Foreign-Exchange Related Benefits

The access to imports at a favourable cheap exchange rate was not equal for all, but largely in favour of a privileged rent-seeking elite. For some transactions the effective exchange rate paid by the beneficiary was even cheaper than the official rate. Errors in the application of exchange rates, as well as the non-payment of counterpart funds implied an extremely low-cost, if not free, source of foreign exchange.

To investigate the *incidence of errors*, it was necessary to obtain information on individual foreign-exchange allocations, for instance channelled through the 'normal' ('free') window. Although in the 1980s there was a complex administrative procedure of approval for individuals and companies to obtain foreign exchange, neither the Bank of Tanzania (BoT) nor the National Bank of Commerce (NBC) have been able to provide disaggregated information, which indicate the beneficiary, the amount received, the date of transaction and the exchange rate applied. The only information of this type could be traced from a databank of outstanding commercial foreign debt; however, due to difficulties in conversion, only from one NBC branch.[135]

Figure 7-4 displays the results of a comparison of the applied exchange rate in the data set with the official exchange rate prevailing in the month of transaction. In 6.5% of the cases deviations of more than 10% have been noticed. The data obviously include typing errors or computing errors since deviations run both ways. However deviations where foreign exchange recipients benefited have been more frequent. The data may therefore indicate rent-seeking manipulations in which some foreign exchange had been allocated at a rate even cheaper than the already underpriced official rate. Following up one example in Dar es Salaam at the NBC Foreign Branch in April 2000 in fact confirmed that the file involved a wrong exchange rate. As it took the staff quite some time to retrieve the original documents, it cannot be expected that they will ever follow up the other 636 cases identified in the data set, which again only represent a fraction of the foreign exchange transaction undertaken in the 1980s.

In contrast to the above issue, the *non-payment of counterpart funds* on Commodity Import Support, which was discovered in the early 1990s, and later the non-payment of funds related to the OGL attracted much more attention and was widely discussed in the local press. In January 1993, under strong pressure from donors, the Ministry of Finance set up a special task force to investigate the non-payment of overdue CIS counterpart funds. The study was co-financed by the Canadian and Belgian Resident Missions and the final report (Ministry of Finance (1993)) was submitted in July 1993. The study covers CIS allocations between June 1987 and December 1992.

---

[135] The data set only includes transactions where the Bank of Tanzania failed to transmit the foreign exchange to the recipient abroad (e.g. payment for imports). In addition, some of the items are no longer included in the list as they have been externalised by debt buy-back schemes (personal communication at NBC foreign branch in Dar es Salaam, April 2000).

Figure 7-4: Errors in Applied Exchange Rate of Foreign Exchange Transactions

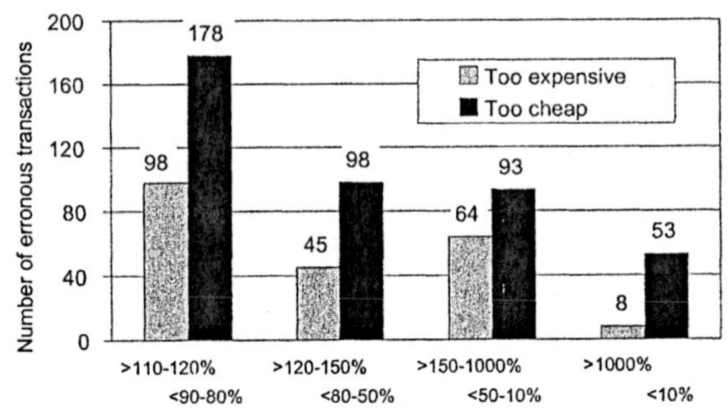

The figure is based on an analysis of 9847 foreign exchange transactions, which were part of the still outstanding commercial foreign debt of NBC Foreign Branch in April 1999. The transactions originate from the period 1979 to 1993 (81.1% from 1980-82, 17.3% from 1983-88).

A comparison with monthly official exchange rates reveals that in 637 cases (6.5% of total) the actual exchange rate applied deviated by more than 10% from the official rate. In 2/3 of these cases (422) foreign exchange was obtained too cheaply.

a: Applied exchange rate in per cent of corrected exchange rate

Source: Data set of 9847 foreign exchange transactions obtained at NBC Foreign Branch, Dar es Salaam, 1999

The Task Force discovered major weaknesses in the monitoring system and complained that the process of data collection has been very difficult. According to their findings (p. 11-26), beneficiary records were incomplete, mixed up or missing, the allocation criteria had been increasingly subjective and beneficiaries continued to get foreign exchange allocations in spite of previous failures in paying cash cover.[136] The outcome is surprising since the letter of allocation, which was signed by the beneficiary, explicitly stated that in case of failure the Treasury would refrain from making available any import support in future and it would take legal action against the firm (letter of allocation shown in Appendix 1 in Ministry of Finance (1993)). The team also found that there was no verification on the imports brought into the country. Any cheating by over-invoicing or by the misapplication of funds could therefore not be discovered.

Given the widespread rent-seeking motivation of the state bureaucracy discussed so far it is not surprising that the CIS scandal happened. Korsgren (1996, p. 8) puts it rather timidly, noting, 'it is probable that part of the deficiencies, as missing documents and poor record keeping, were intentionally created by Treasury officials involved in the scandalous administration and allocation of funds'. As a party to the dubious deals, the administration largely failed to enforce counterpart payments. The report of the task force concludes (p. 25), 'it appears as if the cash cover repayment was left to the beneficiary's initiative'. The lack of seriousness is also evident from the beneficiaries' excuses documented in the report (p. 20):

> '...her partner and business operator had *passed away.* She was therefore not aware of the debt...'

[136] A detailed analysis of the last aspect follows in Chapter 8 (Table 8-26 and Figure 8-8 on page 506).

'The company was aware that they owed *some* money to the Government...'

Table 7-10 summarises the amounts of CIS cash cover outstanding and the subsequent records of cash cover recovery. Despite shortcomings in the data collection, the table presents a fairly good picture of the magnitude of the problem. Initial cash cover collection from the Treasury had been on average less than 40% of the import support provided between 1987-92, the major defaulters being government institutions and parastatal companies. The amount outstanding is larger than the entire government budget on health during the same period, which was approximately TSh 60 billion. The government decided to charge an additional 17% interest on the period of default. However, since inflation was running at an average of 30% between 1987 and 1994 and only declined to less than 17% after 1996, the real interest rate was negative, making any further delay of payments profitable. This incentive may have aggravated the poor debt collection records after 1992. At the end of October 1997 only 9.3% of the outstanding debt had been collected. In addition, a large share of the remaining balance outstanding is disputed by parastatals and private debtors—another facet of the rent-seeking strategy.

Table 7-10: Commodity Import Support, in TSh bn

	Gov.	%	Parastatal	%	Private	%	Total
Balance outstanding 31.12.1992	8.189		70.851		31.546		110.587
Balance including 17% interest [a]	12.563	8%	105.549	65%	43.522	27%	161.635
Cash Cover (CC) paid	1.010		42.320		27.550		70.880
CC in % of total excluding interests	11%		37%		47%		39%
Balance outstanding 30.10.1997 [b]	12.615		81.963		37.884		132.462
Percentage disputed	0%		82%		75%		72%

a: After minor adjustments, which were undertaken later, the total including interest increased to 163.364 (government 12.633, parastatals 106.064 and private 44.667).

b: Only TSh 15.1 billion, which is 9.3% of the 163.364 billion due in Dec. 1992, had been recovered by October 1997! The remaining balance indicated above includes a downward adjustment of TSh 72.3 billion because of write-offs, bankruptcy proceedings under LART, conversions of outstanding balances into government shares, etc. The figures also include a total of TSh 41.4 billion interests charged.

Source: Ministry of Finance (1993, Appendix 3) and TRA (1997, p. 3f)

Obviously, the poor debt collection after 1992 was partly a result of the poor record keeping on CIS allocations. Debt collection was also poor because of the absence of effective legal institutions to enforce CIS cash cover liabilities. The two problems are mentioned in the CIS Progress Report of 1997 (TRA (1997, p. 4f)):

'Some of the beneficiaries gave false information to the Treasury at the time of obtaining the funds. It has thus proved difficult to trace them...'

'As soon as the liabilities have been clearly ascertained with sufficient documentation for prosecution, defaulters are taken to court but as is well known, in the absence of a Commercial Court, such cases suffer

> from the same abuse as the other tax cases that are pending in ordinary courts.'

The aspect of the weak legal system, which is systemic in a rent-seeking society, will be taken up in Chapter 7.3.

The non-payment of cash cover is a good example that confirms the hypothesis that rent-seekers adjusted their behaviour to a changing policy environment in the 1980s. The government agreed to gradually increase competition, to eliminate subsidies and to devalue the Tanzanian Shilling. In so doing, it progressively undermined the rents of the privileged elites, above all parastatal managers and bureaucrats. To ensure continued access to support other strategies needed to be pursued. These included the simple non-payment of cash cover. Eriksson (1994) provides an excellent and detailed analysis on Swedish, Norwegian and Dutch import support in Tanzania and confirms this hypothesis of countervailing actions:

> 'Non-enforcement of cash-cover payment was a means by which the government could continue its discretionary subsidisation of the parastatals, when other, more explicit, forms of subsidies had to be reduced.' (Eriksson (1994, p. 87))

She also points to the shift in the relative values of the two subsidy components that resulted from devaluation and non-payment, i.e. with devaluation the value of getting access to foreign exchange at the official rate declined, whereas the value of not paying counterpart funds increased (p. 12).

An analysis of the 356 parastatal CIS records obtained from the report of the Task Force in fact revealed a close correlation between the shrinking size of the parallel market premium and the non-payment of cash cover (Figure 7-5). The less overvalued the official exchange rate (the smaller the parallel market premium, the more expensive official foreign exchange), the less cash cover had been paid to avoid this increase in cost.

Unfortunately there was no information available on cash cover payments prior to 1987. Eriksson (1994, p. 68) notes 'non-payment of cash cover is generally considered to have become a problem since 1986, when the Tanzanian Shilling was substantially devalued'. Hence the value of cash cover payment is likely to have been at nearly 100% in 1986; it dropped impressively with devaluation to almost 40%, recovered slightly after the first shock and then steadily decreased with further devaluation.

The non-payment of cash cover had not only been a problem in CIS but also with the *OGL Facility*. One of the arguments to provide funds through the OGL system was to replace the inefficient and discretionary allocation mechanism of the CIS system (Eriksson (1994, p. 18)). This goal partly proved to be illusory. In 1991/92 the donors discovered that TSh 18.7 billion counterpart funds (US$70 million) owed by the commercial banks had not been transmitted to the Bank of Tanzania and the standards of accounting, monitoring and reporting had been far from acceptable.

Figure 7-5: Decreasing Rents and Countervailing Non-Payment of Cash Cover

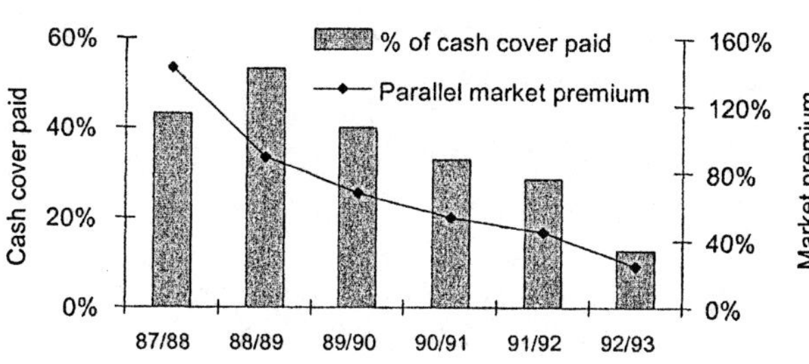

The figure displays the rent-seeker's reaction in Tanzania to devaluation. The larger the devaluation, the smaller implicit rents in official foreign exchange allocations. Rent-seekers compensated part of this loss by simply reducing cash cover payments.

1) The cash cover value has been calculated according to the average of cash cover paid in each statement.

2) Alternatively one may compare the share of CIS allocations in each year that include full cash cover payments with the parallel market premium. With this specification, the same relation holds, only the difference between the first two values becomes smaller.

3) If the percentage of cash cover paid is weighted according to the size of the CIS allocation, a second but smaller peak results in the financial year 1990/91 (1988/89: 53.2%, 1989/90: 37.3%, 1990/91: 43.5%, 1991/92: 14.8%, 1992/93: 2.8%).

Source: Data of 356 CIS records of parastatal companies from Ministry of Finance (1993, Appendix 3b)

Several hints point to the involvement of high-level civil servants in the OGL scandal—a feature, which has already been found for the problem of tax evasion and poor credit allocation. According to personal communication (November 1996) with Augustine Mrema, a former presidential candidate and leader of the opposition party, the missing OGL counterpart funds had not been paid back from beneficiaries, and nobody had been taken to court. According to Mrema, beneficiaries did not spend the money themselves but shared it with the government, which explains the lack of action. Related comments, such as 'there is a lot of "dirt" sticking to the OGL facility' or 'you won't get information, it is politically too sensitive' came from personal interviews at the University. Another indication of high-level involvement is the Warioba Report (1996, p. 297), which emphasises that the procedure for the use of OGL funds was clear, but it was the NBC leadership itself which introduced the loopholes.

Summing up, instead of a swift devaluation of the Tanzanian Shilling, which would have unified the parallel and official rates, Tanzania opted for a gradual process, introducing a complex system of multiple exchange rates, where different groups and individuals enjoyed different access and conditions. Given the weaknesses in the Tanzanian foreign exchange allocation, the system was, intentionally or unintentionally, basically designed to *protect the interests and opportunities of well-entrenched rent-seeking profiteers*. Applying different exchange rates, denying equal access to foreign exchange, tolerating the non-payment of counterpart funds while simultaneously opening the Own Fund window that permits 'illegally' acquired funds to be cleaned, made the business of foreign exchange allocation an extremely profitable area of rent-seeking. This system most likely also included opportunities to gain from arbitrage profits between the foreign exchange handled in the different import windows.

Devaluations, which reduced the spread between the official and the parallel market rate, largely failed to translate into efficiency-improving economic signals for many years. Many rent-seekers continued to benefit from the access to foreign exchange at virtually zero costs, either because they did not pay for foreign exchange or they enjoyed preferential access to credits on which they later defaulted.

Even with the OGL, as noted in Eriksson (1994, p. 17f), discretionary elements remained important; the intended equal access to foreign exchange was undermined by the preferential access to credit. Increasing credit allocation was in fact an openly suggested policy of the government, as the following government statement at the 1988 Consultative Group meeting indicates:

> 'As exchange rate adjustment has increased the shilling price of foreign exchange, some potential foreign exchange users find it increasingly difficult to utilize foreign exchange allocations because of shortage of shilling "cash cover". From the point of view of macroeconomic management, it will be necessary to strike a balance between the need to restrain monetary expansion in order to check inflationary pressure while providing sufficient credit to ensure that available foreign exchange can be utilized to expand real productive activity.' (GoT (1988b, p. 3))

However, as the records in the subsequent years proved, the balance was not maintained. The system of foreign exchange allocation was jointly responsible for the poor macroeconomic condition of Tanzania. The non-payment of CIS undermined the government budget, and the OGL scandal increased monetary expansion since the Bank of Tanzania had already paid the Treasury the equivalent of those outstanding funds.

Economically, Tanzania would have benefited from a faster effective devaluation. Kaufmann and O'Connell (1999) analysed this aspect, constructing a counterfactual simulation of fiscal and balance of payments flows under alternative exchange rate assumptions. Their main conclusions are straightforward:

> 'A more aggressive move toward exchange-rate unification in Tanzania would have delivered a fiscal bonus by the mid-1980s—and unification of the exchange rate would have reduced monetary growth and inflation pressures. From a fiscal viewpoint there was no economic rational for gradualism in exchange-rate unification and delay of a move toward convertibility.' (Kaufmann and O'Connell (1999, p. i))

—clearly it was the rent-seeking elite that provided the rationale.

Seen from the rent-seekers' perspective, costs to obtain cheap foreign exchange did not significantly change in the late 1980s and early 1990s. The size of the rents remained high, although the origin of the rent shifted from cheap foreign exchange in the form of official allocations to the non-payment of counterpart funds. As argued in Chapter 5.2, if rent-seeking opposition against the adoption of a specific policy measure (here devaluation) is no longer feasible, resistance shifts to countervailing actions.

The system worked because donors made available large amount of funds, without scrutinising whether recipients paid counterpart funds. Once again an important reform measure failed to have an immediate efficiency-increasing impact, as expectations relied on incorrect assumptions about rent-seekers' reactions, above all their power to undertake countermeasures. What is striking is that the problems with the CIS scandal did not lead to a more careful implementation of the OGL facility. Apparently very little had been learnt from previous experience.

7.2 Systematic Delays in Reducing Protectionism and Other State Interventions in Markets

'Lint consumption by domestic mills has drastically gone down ... This situation is really pathetic and calls for immediate government assistance.'

1993/94 Industry Review of Cotton, Ministry of Agriculture, Dar es Salaam, December 1994

Tanzania's poor macroeconomic policy stance in the 1980s and early 1990s had its origin in the profitable tax evasion business, in the rent-seekers' easy and virtually unlimited access to bank credits, and in the rent-seeking allocation of subsidised foreign exchange. A large part of this outcome is also directly related to long-lasting protectionism and other state interventions in production and trade, apparently reflecting strong rent-seeking interests. The slow pace in 'unleashing' markets and introducing a 'level playing field' for private actors is the topic of Chapter 7.2. Well into the reform process, it was the thinking of policymakers that markets had to be protected and that parastatal companies needed assistance whenever there was a problem. Chapter 7.2 focuses on the various price, tariff and quantitative restrictions in markets, and considers the logic underlying rent-seeking.

Tanzania has come a long way in liberalising its economy. In the years 1999 and 2000, the IMF trade restrictiveness index—a 10-point scale for classifying trade regimes from open (1) to most restrictive (10)—rated the country as moderate (6), in contrast to the very poor score of (10) in the 1980s (see for instance Kanaan (2000, p. 32)). However this process of unleashing markets from excessive state controls had been slow and unbalanced. In addition neighbouring countries like Uganda, Mozambique or Zambia performed better with a stable open rating of (2) since 1998. Only Kenya's trade regime was rated as slightly more restrictive than Tanzania's.

Section a) starts with a discussion of price liberalisation and tariff reforms in Tanzania. The reader will notice that rent-seeking influence may have determined a specific design of a policy or a specific sequencing of reform measures. Yet the discussion mainly points to possible areas of rent-seeking influence or resistance without providing clear-cut evidence, as there was frequently not sufficient information available. The situation is different with Sections b) and c), which point more directly to areas of major rent-seeking activities. These includc maintaining quantitative and other non-tariff restrictions, or postponing reforms of parastatal companies. Section b) outlines two examples, rent-seeking in the petroleum sector and rent-seeking resistance against liberalisation of export crop marketing and processing. Section c) addresses the late reform of public enterprises including the soft budget relation to the government and the late and slow privatisation or closure of companies that were to be divested.

The discussion in Sections b) and c) will need to consider several institutional, political and other arguments which are not directly related to rent-seeking. As already argued in Chapter 5.2, even though there are many aspects which point to rent-seeking activities and resistance there is in most cases also a non-rent-seeking explanation or excuse for a specific outcome. This makes an analysis of rent-seeking particularly difficult. For instance there is no homogenous agricultural sector and therefore no general recommendation for content, sequence and speed of reforms. Every crop has its own particularities and institutional requirements. Some crops are traded and used in the country, others are exported, some are harvested several times a year, others need considerable prefinancing, some are only smallholder crops, others are mostly grown in large plantations, some crops can be stored, others need to be processed immediately, and finally with some crops the quality is only visible after processing or the seeds from the crops have to be brought back to the original farmer, without mixing seeds from others. These particularities may demand a sophisticated institutional framework before the cooperative and marketing board monopoly is abolished and private trading is allowed. As will be argued, liberalisation has often been opposed on these grounds, even though hidden rent-seeking motives may have mattered much more.

Given the limited space in this study and the specific focus on rent-seeking, it is not possible to discuss each agricultural aspect in detail and to sufficiently consider all the problems related to parastatal reforms and privatisation. The discussion may therefore appear in some cases to be incomplete, though it will point out the rent-seeking aspects. For more background information on institutional and technical problems the reader is referred to the specific literature.

a) Mixed Records of Price Liberalisation and Tariff Reforms

After the Arusha Declaration, and in particular after 1973 when the National Price Commission (NPC) was established, the government increasingly fixed prices of 'essential' producer and consumer goods. It thereby replaced the pricing mechanism of the market, which used to signal shortages and surpluses, as well as costs of inputs, production, marketing or transportation.

In the early 1980s wholesale trade in over 50 major commodities, staple foods and export crops was restricted to parastatals, over 400 goods were subject to price controls, and producer prices for traditional agriculture crops were fixed at an average rate of 65% of world prices (Mans (1994, p. 417)). Since the official pricing system was neither 'anchored' to international prices, nor dependent on internal shortages and surpluses, many goods including basic staple foods had been simultaneously traded in illegal parallel markets. The parallel market price of sembe (maize) or rice, for instance, was at more than twice the official price in 1983/84 (see Van der Geest and Köttering (1994, p. 82)).

Tanzania's pricing policy included major *subsidies and artificially low prices*, which had been an immense burden for some parastatal companies and the government. As noted in Chapter 7.1, the government had to take over the National Milling Corporation's unsecured overdrafts, which reflected a multiple of the Ministry of Agriculture's budget. Because in many cases subsidies were not affordable or had to be paid by the producers (i.e. the government directed artificially low prices), the policy also disrupted the supply of these goods. Subsidised fertiliser, for instance, had been constrained in the early 1980s by the availability of foreign exchange, and in the late 1980s and early 1990s by the lack of government budget funds (World Bank (1994b, p. 79)). Underpriced fertiliser also had negative environmental effects in areas where people enjoyed preferential access. The Southern Highlands received over 70% of the total fertiliser supplied in the country. According to personal communication in Iringa (April 2000) in some areas the land has been completely destroyed by the overuse of the highly subsidised fertiliser.

Two methods characterised Tanzania's pricing system. *Pan-territorial pricing* aimed to avoid any price discrimination between regions, as well as between urban and rural consumers. It implied that goods had to be sold for the same price throughout the country, thus ignoring any differences in transportation costs. In addition pan-territorial pricing often failed to account for variations in quality. In the agricultural sector, depending on the crop, the pan-territorial pricing system included payments to producers with up to three instalments, i.e. an advance, interim and a final payment.

The *cost-plus pricing* system in contrast was a method to determine the final or maximum price or, in the case of export products, the distribution of revenues between production and marketing. Companies presented cost calculations for their imports or products to the National Price Commission, which scrutinised the figures and added a mark up to fix the maximum price (Eriksson (1993, p. 52)). With traditional export crops the pricing method ran in the opposite direction. The marketing boards deducted their marketing costs from the export revenue and paid the rest to the cooperative unions. The unions then again deducted their costs and paid whatever was left to farmers (e.g. World Bank (1994b, p. 120)).

Although the government intended to implement development goals and social aspects when defining the pricing system, the cost-plus pricing mechanism destroyed any incentives for companies to be efficient and it opened avenues for large-scale embezzlement, as corruption-related costs could be easily concealed and passed on. The inefficiency and rent-seeking opportunities are well described in Eriksson (1993, p. 53f). She notes, referring to various authors, that companies could report non-existent costs, which were difficult to trace by the limited staff of the National Price Commission, or they could even corrupt price-fixing NPC officials. She also finds evidence from personal communication with staff members of parastatal companies, who confirm that 'both inflated costs and lobbying have been used within the price setting process' (p. 54). The abolition of this non-market based pricing system therefore reflects an important step towards an elimination of rent-seeking opportunities.

The Economic Recovery Programme in 1986 emphasised the important role of price signals. The greater reliance on correct prices in fact became an explicitly stated medium-term objective in Tanzania's 1987 Policy Framework Paper (see GoT (1987, p. 3)). Tanzania has gone a long way in liberalising prices since. There is a huge difference if one compares the situation of early 1980s with the situation in 1989 or the mid-1990s. At their peak with more than 400 goods in the early 1980s, price controls included 22 categories in 1988, were reduced to 10 categories in 1989 and consisted of only 3 categories (petroleum products, sugar and fertiliser) in 1991. In spite of this apparent progress in the removal of price controls the overall record is nevertheless mixed, in particular if one takes the speed and sequence into account and considers other key prices such as exchange rates, interest rates and utility tariffs, which are not included in the above listing.

Rent-Seeking Resistance and Transitional Rent-Seeking Opposition with Price Liberalisation

Five possible areas of rent-seeking activities can be identified from the records of price liberalisation. First, rent-seeking resistance may be found in the *sequence of price liberalisation*. Products such as cement, beer, electrical cables, tyres and tubes, as well as some steel products were only liberalised after the early 1990s. Together with sugar, fertiliser, and petroleum they are likely to comprise a large share in domestic value added of tradeable items (see World Bank (1994a, p. 73)). Unfortunately it was not possible to obtain sufficient data to prove a sequencing that protected rent-seeking interests. Depending on the item and free-market equilibrium, government-mandated prices either benefit or tax producers, consumers and companies that use the goods as intermediate inputs. In addition price interventions and other interventions overlap and affect inputs and outputs differently. An analysis would therefore need to calculate the sequence in the protection of value added—a calculation that requires substantial amount of data, which was not available.

There are however at least some indications of possible rent-seeking lobbying. For instance, in the mid-1990s protection increased for some selected goods, among others for tyres, as mentioned above. Korsgren (1996, p. 18) comments, 'it should be noted that the local industry uses an outdated technology and cannot provide the type of tyres transport companies demand'. Tyre licensing requirements were finally introduced in early 2001. Given this development, it is not far-fetched to suppose that the increase in protectionism may be a result of rent-seeking activities as a response to earlier steps to liberalisation.

Second, an area where price fixing has been removed very late is the *traditional export sector*. Even though the government abolished the pan-territorial pricing system in 1989, it continued to fix the advance payment. In the

1991/92 season, the government set this payment far too high and caused the opposite effect to the years before, i.e. an excessive remuneration to farmers and major losses to cooperative unions, in particular within the coffee and cotton sector (e.g. World Bank (1994b, p. 109)).[137]

Detrimental for agricultural development in turn was the cost-plus pricing mechanism, which was effective until the 1990/91 season and undermined the success of other reform steps already undertaken. Because of the inefficiency of the marketing boards and cooperative unions and their tactic to avoid any effective own reforms, the higher TSh export prices from gradual devaluations were not passed on to farmers. The development contradicts the government's originally stated goal in the Economic Recovery Programme:

> 'Given the central role of agriculture in the recovery programme, priority will be given to raising producer incentives... The Government intends to set producer prices at a level equivalent to 60 to 70% of FOB prices or increase them by 5% per annum in real terms, whichever is the higher.' (GoT (1986b, p. 15))

In spite of this explicit goal, there is surprisingly little information on the share of prices paid to farmers shown in donor and government documents. Being a political issue it appears that the government avoided a transparent documentation and monitoring of these indicators or simply did not collect the data because it was not interested. Figure 7-6 displays some calculations based on available data on producer prices and export prices.

Figure 7-6: Producer Price Relative to Export Price for Selected Cash Crops [a, b]

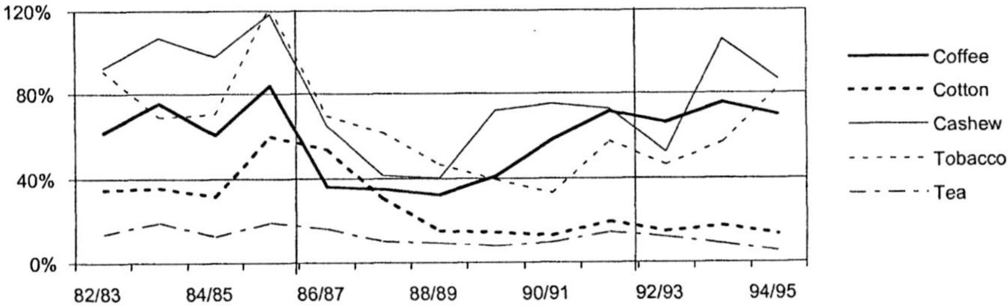

The figure shows the sharp decline in the share of prices paid to farmers after the initiation of the ERP (percentage shares calculated according to the formula: TSh producer price / $ export price • TSh/$)

a: Producer prices refer to averages of financial years starting on 1 July, export prices and exchange rates are based on annual January to December averages. Since payments to farmers have usually been late, the producer price is related to the earlier export price (e.g. 1986/87 producer prices relate to 1986 export price).

b: Depending on the source (World Bank (1996a, p. 19), IMF (1996a, p. 66) or Bank of Tanzania (1997, p. 65)), export prices in dollars of the years 1993-95 vary. For instance, for the year 1994 average coffee prices are indicated to be 1.60, 2.62 and 2.75, respectively and for cashew prices 0.58, 0.79 and 0.50.

Source: Producer prices (in TSh) and export prices (in US$) for the years FY83-90 from World Bank (1996a, p. 19, 50) and the years FY91-95 from IMF (1996a, p. 47, 66)

[137] 'When the farmer share (at official exchange rates) swings above 80 percent, the cooperatives lose money' (World Bank (1994b, p. 109)).

Unfortunately, for some crops the two prices do not appear to represent the same stage of processing; unit prices in the two categories may therefore relate to different aspects. For instance, sisal producer prices (not included in the diagram) fluctuated around 75-250% of indicated export prices, which does not make sense if the data refer to exactly the same product. Despite possible 'level' and 'scale' effects that result from different stages of processing, the diagram can still indicate the change in the share paid to farmers. In fact, the diagram reveals a sharp drop in the share of world market prices paid to farmers after the initiation of the ERP. In the period 1987/88 to 1989/90, the average share was only half of the average share obtained between 1982/83 and 1985/86. Since the cost-plus pricing system had still been in place when reforms started it appears that increasing costs of marketing boards and cooperatives as a result of the reform process were simply passed on to farmers.

Other sources, which seem not to have the above-mentioned shortcomings, reveal that the target to pay a share of 60-70% of world market prices to farmers has not been met. For instance, for cotton the share of export prices paid to producers fell from an average of 86% between 1981/82 and 1984/85 to an average of 40% in the period 1989/90 to 1991/92 (Putterman (1995, p. 316)). In the tea sector the government only set producer prices for smallholder tea, as the crop has not been fully controlled by parastatal marketing and processing.[138] The government administered prices well into the mid-1990s (liberalisation started in 1997). Table 7-11 displays producer prices for green tea leaf and also indicates that they have not been reflecting movements in export markets. The inefficiency of the tea authority, in particular the repeated non-payment of farmers and the failure to collect tea from estates which are remote, caused farmers to increasingly abandon tea production (e.g. The Guardian, No. 965, 9 January 1998).

Table 7-11: Tea Prices (Green Leaf) Paid to Producer Relative to Export Prices

Year	Producer Price (1)	Export Price (2)	(1) in % of (2)	Year	Producer Price (1)	Export Price (2)	(1) in % of (2)
1991/92	40	66	61%	1994/95	50	155	32%
1992/93	40	131	31%	1995/96	55	132	42%
1993/94	45	152	30%	1996/97	55	146	38%

Source: Cargill Technical Services (1997, table 2.3, p. 7)

Third, another area where the government has been reluctant to adjust prices is *utility tariffs*. The 1989 Public Expenditure Review, for instance, criticises that the average electricity tariff yield had been about one third the average incremental cost of supplying electricity (World Bank (1989b, p. 34)). In particular Zanzibar resisted any changes in tariffs for a long time, selling

[138] Besides smallholder tea, there are large estates owned by Tanzania Tea Authority and private companies. Out of 22 tea-processing factories, 16 are under private ownership (Cargill Technical Services (1997, p. 4)).

electricity at highly subsidised rates (see also discussion on page 207 in Chapter 4.3).

According to personal communication with staff of the State Fuel Corporation (SFC) in Zanzibar, January 1998, the company had no money left for maintenance. Only emergency repairs were carried out and the few cars which were still working in the company were mainly used to drive around officials from management and not for the much more needed operations. The tariff had not been adjusted for more than four years, despite inflation running at an average of 20% during this period (see Zanzibar consumer price index in Bank of Tanzania (2001, Table 1.22)). Given the tariff structure of March 1998 only a 100% increase in tariffs could cover all costs, including production and delivery of electricity, pay and maintenance of infrastructure and provisions to replace existing fixed assets in the future. If the same amount of electricity had to be supplied by using diesel-powered generation—this could happen if the main electricity company TANESCO cancelled the cheap supply of hydropower—tariffs would even need to increase by 350%. This mark-up would also be necessary for any additional supply in power, as it would have to be generated with diesel. In spite of these hard economic facts, prices for electricity have only been adjusted moderately.

Fourth, as already outlined in Chapter 7.1, progress in the devaluation of the *exchange rate* or the increase of the *real interest rate* to positive levels had been slow, despite the government's goal to reach these targets in 1988. The complex system of directed preferential interest rates was only replaced in 1991 (IMF (1996a, p. 4)) and the exchange rate was unified as late as August 1993. However, given rent-seekers' access to credits, it has to be admitted that at least on the lending side an increase in interest rates would not have affected the incentive system of major borrowers since they had already defaulted on the small nominal interest rates applied in the 1980s without losing access to credits.

Fifth, besides the resistance of rent-seekers to price liberalisation, such a move may also create *transitional rent-seeking opportunities* as the following example of the Treasury bill market may suggest. Treasury bill auctions were introduced in 1993 as part of the financial market reforms. Because of slippages in tax revenue collection in the same year, the government sharply increased its borrowing. During the first two-year period the interest rates of Treasury bills fluctuated between 21% and 71% (Bank of Tanzania (1995, p. 7)), allowing participants in the Treasury bill market to earn exorbitant profits.

The Bank of Tanzania (1995, p. 7) explains the high yields partly with the 'lack of a large enough group of regular wholesale bidders' in the auctions. From personal communication in Dar es Salaam at the Bank of Tanzania and the NBC it was not possible to find out whether the Treasury bill market at that time constituted a real insider market where a limited group enjoyed privileged information and access. Given that the favourable interest rates lasted until late 1995, without the general public effectively participating (their interest rates for saving at commercial banks were at 24%), it cannot be excluded that bidders colluded or were able to prevent others from participating.

If this was the case then it can be argued that deliberately undermining or delaying the efficient functioning of the Treasury bill auctions as a measure to sustain insider benefits is plain rent-seeking. A more open market would then have significantly reduced the high 'equilibrium' interest rates—interests which had been another burden in the government budget. Yet with the little information available, the rent-seeking explanation remains speculative. High interest rates can also reflect a high risk of default and even with a more open market it is not clear whether participation increases immediately, taking into account that some markets indeed take a long time to develop.

Apparent Rent-Seeking Patterns on the Taxation Side

Besides direct price interventions, prices had also been affected by the *tax structure*. In 1988, the World Bank characterised Tanzania's tax system as follows:

> 'Revenue have become overly dependent on high rates of taxation of the formal sector, while at the same time there is widespread evasion and under-collection' (World Bank (1988, p. 11)).

The statement clearly points to the rent-seeking nature of Tanzania's tax system, i.e. the apparent implicit compromise of the ruling elite to mobilise sufficient government revenues on the one hand (high tax rates) and to allow for benefits of a rent-seeking constituency on the other (exemptions and evasion).

From a technical point of view making the tax system more efficient is not a major task. Implementing and sustaining a simplified tax system with more uniform tariff rates, a reduction in the level of tariffs and an elimination of discretionary and statutory exemptions are all constraint-relieving reform measures (see for instance World Bank (1991, p. xvi)). They can therefore be implemented within a short period of time. Obviously Tanzania's record was different; this has already been explained in Section b) of Chapter 7.1.

Similar to price liberalisation, Tanzania has gone through comprehensive tax reforms since the mid-1980s. For an overview see Morrissey (1995) and IMF (1996a, p. 17-29). In the early 1980s sales tax and tariff rates were as high as 500% and 1100%, respectively (Osoro (1997, p. 59)) and in 1986 there were 50 different tariff rates, ranging between zero and 750% (Morrissey (1995, p. 644)). Major revisions were implemented thereafter, in particular in 1988/89, when tariff and sales tax were both simplified to six rates, ranging between zero and 60%.

However, in spite of this positive development, effective progress has been ambiguous, most likely reflecting the resistance of rent-seeking traders and bureaucrats. Besides the problems of tax evasion and exemptions, which particularly overshadowed the period from the late 1980s to the mid-1990s, rent-seekers succeeded in maintaining protectionism. In the 1993 and 1994 Budget Speeches, for instance, the government openly justified the increase of maximum customs tariff rates as a measure to protect local industries from foreign imported goods (see, GoT (1993a, p. 46) and GoT (1994a, p. 41f)). Korsgren (1996, p. 18) comments that what is needed is not increased tariff rates but simply the enforcement of legislation already in place. It therefore appears that a major element of Tanzania's rent-seeking tax system, i.e. the non-enforcement or unequal enforcement of tax laws, has been effective for a long time.

The need to harmonise, simplify and streamline taxes did not disappear from the agenda in the 1990s. As businesspeople from Dar es Salaam note, newspapers are full of complaints from the business community (e.g. The Guardian, 1 January 1997). A comprehensive study of the business environment undertaken by Coopers&Lybrand (1997b) for USAID reports that in Tanzania 'taxes are so numerous and complex that businesses are forced to resort to illegal actions' (p. vi). The study also quotes from a business organisation which estimates that 80% of all businesses have to cheat to be able to survive (p. vi). Similar problems were identified in subsequent years. A SPA/JEM progress report emphasises the need to 'urgently synchronise, categorise and uniformly operate all exemption legislations to enhance transparency and simplify TRA's monitoring role by reducing revenue losses' (ESRF (1998, p. 29)). And the WTO's Trade Policy Review for Tanzania mentions for the year 1999 that there are a large number of exemptions, amounting to 42% of all imports (WTO (2000)). Finally, the need to rationalise the tax system, in particular to remove nuisance taxes at local government level, is mentioned as a measure to improve the business environment in the World Bank's Programmatic Structural Adjustment Credit of 2000. It is difficult to understand that these aspects are still such a big issue after more than ten years of tax reforms. It clearly suggests resistance and manoeuvres on the part of tax-creating and tax-enforcing bureaucrats with rent-seeking interests.

b) Strong Resistance to Eliminating Quantitative and Other Non-Tariff Restrictions

> *'BP knows how to operate in Africa, but the situation in Tanzania is really challenging.'*
>
> *Roger Ivens, Managing Director of British Petroleum Tanzania, Dar es Salaam, April 2000*

It is well known that non-tariff barriers are a particularly prevalent form of protection since they are not transparent in the rent transfers and distortions they create. In the early 1990s the World Bank criticised in a report on the economic situation of the adjustment programme that 'the processing of important agricultural exports is dominated by inefficient monopolies, regulations continue to impose substantial costs on private sector operations, and inefficient (and often bankrupt) parastatals continue to play a major role in the industrial sector' (World Bank (1993b, p. 1)). Many key industries such as cement, sugar, fertiliser, petroleum, telecommunications and insurance, and in part banking and export crop marketing were still subject to effective parastatal monopolies in 1992. Also the speed of the transition of the OGL had been slow compared with other countries. In Zambia for instance the scheme began in 1989 with only 10% of imports eligible; three years later it already covered 95% of the products, while in Tanzania, in contrast, it took four years to move to a negative list, and Tanzania still had a fifth of non-oil items not eligible for import in April 1992 (World Bank (1994a, p. 72)). The slow speed has to be interpreted against the background that the removal of trade restrictions is a constraint-relieving and capacity-saving reform measure and could therefore, at least technically, be undertaken quickly.

Ineffective deregulation also characterised the situation in labour and land markets. In particular land market regulations have been favouring incumbent parastatal companies. Although the 1992 Policy Framework Paper specified the objective to simplify access to land, in 1997 investors still complained that the biggest problem was obtaining land:

> 'No legislation has addressed the usual year required to acquire land, nor the additional year required to develop land. It really doesn't matter that licenses can be issued in 14 days, if a business is still 2 years away from operation.' (Coopers&Lybrand (1997c, p. 15))

Below two examples of rent-seeking resistance against effective liberalisation are considered. The description of the petroleum sector is based mainly on personal communication with staff from petrol retailing companies, donors, and studies obtained at the Ministry of Energy in Dar es Salaam during March and April 2000. The discussion on the slow pace of reforms related to traditional export crop marketing draws from personal communication with agriculture specialists at the University, marketing boards and donor embassies (Dar es Salaam, March/April 1998 and April 2000), as well as general and crop-specific reports obtained from these institutions.

Rent-Seeking and Petroleum Market Liberalisation

In spite of Tanzania's decision in the mid-1980s to transform its economy to a liberal-market based system, the petroleum sector has proved to be a bastion of rent-seeking resistance for more than a decade. By the time some pseudo-liberalisation had been finally introduced, smugglers in close collaboration with high government officials took over the stage and began to appropriate additional extraordinary rents.

Until January 1997 Tanzania Petroleum Development Corporation TPDC had a monopoly on imports of crude oil and finished petroleum products. Crude oil was imported to be refined at TIPER (Tanzania and Italian Petroleum Refining Company)—another parastatal jointly owned by TPDC and AGIP Tanzania. The extremely poor operation of TIPER, together with the government's control over prices and imports, resulted in substantial inefficiencies and rents in the petroleum sector, which finally had to be paid by consumers.

The Nordic Consulting Group (1999) has undertaken a study evaluating the efficiency of TIPER. According to their findings, TIPER is one of the smallest operational refineries in the world and cannot meet international specifications.

The extremely low product quality is even low within the already poor standard of developing countries. Some 80% of the refinery's instrumentation is out of service, off-stream time is very high, and cash operating costs are almost double the normal benchmark. In addition there is no information and hardly any monitoring on environmental and safety issues. The study concludes that Tanzania's economy loses each year between US$10 and 20 million only to maintain operation of the refinery, compared to directly importing refined products on a free market basis. Dividing the amount by the number of people employed in TIPER gives a loss of US$25,000 to 50,000 per employee each year! The loss is particularly striking if compared with Tanzanians' low average annual income of little more than US$200.[139]

Evidently, from an economic point of view it makes absolutely no sense to keep the refinery going. And a strategic supply argument does also not hold since it would be sufficient to maintain tanks of imported refined petroleum. The major problem is, as some interviewees note, that there are well-entrenched rent-seeking interests which go back to Nyerere's time, with a few people allegedly earning substantial extra profits. Different indications support this view. According to interviewees, TPDC has constantly bought oil at higher than world market prices (and the last ten years from the same supplier). The business is absolutely not cost driven and it appears that benefits are shared under the table. The TRA has also frozen accounts of TPDC since billions of TSh were missing; however the managing director of TPDC did not have to resign and became a member of the newly transformed ADAC. The Controller and Auditor General also reports severe irregularities in the petroleum sector. Some comments to the years 1987 and 1991 are shown in Table 7-12, yet they only reflect a random example (the reports have not been systematically analysed with regard to petroleum related issues).

In 1997 the government started to licence private traders (about 40) who were allowed to bring in fuel for own consumption. On paper, any savings made by importers from the difference to the regulated purchase price was supposed to be taxed at 100% to ensure that petroleum was not imported in preference to purchasing from TIPER. International companies such as BP and Agip were not allowed to import their own petrol but were forced to buy through TIPER and TPDC. After the partial liberalisation had started, within 12 months official import volumes decreased by 30%. Petrol apparently became the most lucrative smuggling business. A highly competitive but uneven playing field had developed. Besides the obvious conclusion that petrol consumption in a country cannot just drop by 30% without specific reasons, there are several other indications which point to major rent-seeking activities and a well-connected rent-seeking elite.

---

[139] Losses calculated in 'per employee' terms are even higher if one takes into account that TIPER is overstaffed and could reduce its personnel by 25-50%. Although total losses will fall slightly with less employment (the company's costs for wages decrease), the change will be small, so that the effect of dividing the loss by a smaller number of employees dominates, implying higher costs per employee.

Table 7-12: CAG Complaints Related to Petroleum

1987: (45/42)	Sales tax of TSh 11,330,741.00 on losses arising from difference between quantities of petroleum products pumped from Tiper Refinery and those received by oil companies after allowing normal transit losses for the years 1980-87 has not been collected.
1991: (55/50)	Test audit of customs revenues on petroleum products revealed that the import duty imposed in 1983 was never levied and collected in the Department.
1991: (55/51)	[A test audit reveals] there are substantial differences between the quantities delivered to the oil companies and the quantities accounted for by the Department during the three years from 1989 to 1991. The Department's control over deliveries of petroleum products, assessment of duties and taxes, and collection of tax revenues, is grossly inadequate.

Source: Controller and Auditor General Reports of Financial Years 1987 and 1991 (in parentheses indication of paragraph and page in respective volume)

First, investigations on petroleum in transit indeed revealed huge differences between documents in the country and the papers presented abroad; many operations were also mere portfolio transactions. Second, for a long time it was not possible to address this smuggling problem. In 2000 smugglers still controlled 25% of the market. Information gained from personal interviews indicate that the problem was not the inability to control imports but the involvement of high-level bureaucrats, parliamentarians and other stakeholders in the lucrative rent-seeking business and therefore an enormous lethargy to change the situation.

> 'Smuggling is not unique, but the difference in this country is that smugglers get away with it' (personal communication in Dar es Salaam, April 2000).

Interviewees emphasised that well-connected people with relations to the establishment obtained import licences disregarding formal application criteria. Some of them even failed to produce accounts. The army and the CCM had their own oil companies, and senior members of government including ministers had crucial stakes in the oil business. Finally, even though licences had been taken away from some smugglers, they often got them back very soon. A regional executive council from CCM for instance was said to have been arrested twice on the same matter and then released.

Summing up, this brief account of the petroleum sector has pointed to an area of major rent-seeking activities in production as well as smuggling. In spite of the apparent extremely high costs of running an own petrol refinery, the leadership hesitated to close down the company, thereby causing very high annual losses, which for example equalled a fifth of the central government's budget on health. Or to put it the other way round, if these resources had been available for primary education, they could have funded between 666,000 and 1.333 million additional pupils each year (according to World Bank (1994c, p. viii) government spending on primary education comes to US$15 per pupil).

From a policymaking point of view, the example shows that if there is effective enduring resistance to the liberalisation of a specific sector, very strong rent-seeking opposition and countervailing actions can be expected in the transition to a market-based regime. The 'liberalisation' of imports did not affect the inefficiency of TIPER, but simply opened up additional rent-seeking opportunities for some well-connected people. Unfortunately it was not possible to find out whether some of these people were part of the old rent-seeking elite in the petroleum sector, but anticipating the behaviour of rent-seekers would suggest this.

Traditional Export Crops: Between Institutional Concerns and Rent-Seeking Resistance.

Another major area of resistance to liberalisation has been in Tanzania's main source of foreign exchange, i.e. the traditional export sector. Several problems, in particular the indebtedness of the cooperative system, the inefficiency of marketing boards and the late liberalisation of prices have been addressed in previous sections. The discussion below aims to review arguments which have been put forward for or against reforms and thereby identify rent-seeking resistance. It is not however intended as a detailed overview of the performance of agriculture crop production during the reform period. The interested reader is referred to the literature cited. For a general overview see World Bank (1994b).

In contrast to the situation in the petroleum sector it is easier to conceal rent-seeking intentions in agriculture markets and argue against liberalisation by referring to institutional concerns. Nevertheless, many aspects support the hypothesis that Tanzania's record of agricultural reform was shaped by rent-seeking resistance and to a much lesser extent by true institutional constraints.

The most relevant export crops in foreign exchange terms are coffee and cotton. Together with tea, cashew, sisal, tobacco, and pyrethrum they constitute the country's traditional agriculture exports. The total of non-traditional agriculture exports is approximately the size of either coffee or cotton, and includes pulses and starches, cereals, sugar products and oilseeds.

As outlined in World Bank (1994b, p. 6f)), export crop production steadily declined from the mid-1970s to the mid-1980s because of the disincentive created by the domestic agriculture policies. The negative trend was aggravated by the decline in international prices for traditional agriculture products and finally led to the sustained trade imbalance between Tanzania's export and import earnings (recall the first diagram in Figure 7-1).

Especially dramatic has been the decline in sisal and cashew nut production. In 1970 Tanzania was the world's largest producer of sisal and had one of the largest cashew industries. The production of sisal declined from a level of 202,000 tones in 1970 to 30,000 tonnes in 1986 (Ministry of Agriculture (1994a, p. 20)). And the production of cashew fell from 145,000 tonnes in the early 1970s to 17,000 in the late 1980s, in spite of a buoyant international market (World Bank (1994a, p. 82)). In the mid-1980s none of the cashew nut factories were working any longer. Construction of the factories had been financed by long-term loans (World Bank (1994b, p. 128)) and some of the factories actually never operated. These investments aggravated Tanzania's large unmet external debt. Six factories had remained closed since 1982, four other resumed operation in late 1988 and were closed again in 1992. TSh 20 million is required each year simply for the maintenance of closed factories (Ministry of Agriculture (1994c, p. 22)). Other crops also suffered from low yields and poor marketing and processing output.

Despite the poor performance of the traditional export sector, the government was not prepared to initiate a rapid transition to a more efficient competitive market that included private sector participation. As will be argued later, only when problems had become unbearable was private participation in trade allowed. Tanzania's overall agricultural reforms represented a very gradual approach. Starting with the liberalisation of non-traditional export crops and food crops after the early 1980s, the country slowly moved to liberalise cashew in 1991, coffee and cotton in 1994 and tobacco and smallholder tea in 1997. The liberalisation of food crops was nearly completed in 1989, when all grains at the village level (primary society level) were liberalised (see, for instance World Bank (1994b, p. 138f)). Prior to the 1994/95 season, marketing of the most important export crops, coffee and cotton, was still monopolised. The government first guaranteed the monopoly of the marketing boards and after 1989, when marketing boards became an agent of the unions, it guaranteed the monopoly of the cooperative unions. Until 1989 cooperative unions succeeded in covering all costs; from the 1989/90 season onwards they ran their own accounts; the government however still set prices at farmgate level, which programmed future problems (personal communication at donor embassy in Dar es Salaam, April 1998).

What were the arguments for preventing or postponing liberalisation? There were several, partly justified *institutional concerns* which could account for slowing down the process of liberalisation. Marketing boards and cooperatives had a function that went beyond the simple marketing of exports. Their role included the supply of seasonal credits, the consideration of remote, less profitable areas and the control and efficient distribution of inputs and adequate processing of outputs.

The function of cooperatives and marketing boards to act as a rural *credit institution* was largely implicit. Farmers obtained fertiliser, seeds and other farm inputs at highly subsidised prices or even for free. The cost of this subsidy, however, was finally deducted from the prices the marketing boards and cooperatives were paying farmers for the harvest. If liberalisation included a collapse of the seasonal credit system, the development could severely disrupt agricultural production. Some people in fact argued that many farmers stopped buying fertiliser when they did not get subsidised inputs any more. This was said to have led to a reduction in quality and therefore reduced the positive impact of reforms.

How important the credit problem in Tanzania was is not clear from the discussions held in Dar es Salaam. According to a specialist at a donor embassy part of the reason why the use of inputs dropped was not the lack of credits but the failure of some farmers to realise that in earlier days they did not get inputs for free. With private traders farmers received much higher prices. Considering the large portion of export revenue absorbed by the previous marketing system, inputs in fact used to be much more expensive. And even if the credit problem was a real constraint, it did not justify maintaining an inefficient marketing system. What is effectively needed in such a situation are alternative solutions to provide sufficient working capital.

The second institutional concern relates to the problem that many farmers live in *remote areas*, where the supply of inputs or the collection of the harvest cannot be done economically. The problem partly reflects distorted production incentives caused by the pan-territorial pricing system, which did not allow a differentiation of prices according to transportation costs. It is also a reflection of the poor maintenance of the road infrastructure. According to information gained from personal interviews, cooperatives were afraid that with liberalisation private traders would simply rush into areas around centres and leave the less profitable areas to cooperatives.

The argument certainly has some relevance. It should however not be misused to prevent liberalisation, as there are much more efficient ways to address the problem, such as improving infrastructure or paying cooperatives and private traders for collecting crops in remote locations. In addition the latter policy would make the costs of supporting remote areas much more transparent than the previously applied system of cross-subsidies. Finally, according to personal communication, there have also been many instances where cooperatives themselves failed to collect the crop in remote places, for instance in the case of tea.

The third institutional argument refers to the control and efficient *distribution of inputs and processing of crops*. Seeds of coffee and cotton for instance, it is argued, should only be used in the regions where they originate since regions differ in terms of climate, chemicals needed, and the quality of the crop they produce. Allowing for regional trade can mix seeds of different origin. If seeds are no longer used in the areas from where they originate, productivity may decrease, diseases can spread more easily and the quality in terms of variety may suffer. What is therefore needed are efficient controlling institutions, which take time to set up.

The argument is legitimate, but it does not justify the lack of action for an entire decade, nor the poor performance of the current cooperative system. For instance, before cotton liberalisation started, low purity of seeds and low-yielding varieties had already been mentioned as a major constraint in the sector, as the following quote from the Ministry of Agriculture shows:

> 'The failure to closely observe the set by-laws and regulations governing the production of cotton and purity of seeds distributed to farmers has resulted into spread of diseases…Limited research resources

and poor management have delayed the spread of high yielding varieties to production areas.' (Ministry of Agriculture (1994b, p. 27))

According to personal communication in Dar es Salaam, other crops had similar problems. Since the cooperative system has failed to supply these services efficiently, the argument does not call for a delay or even abolition of liberalisation, but for moving ahead and addressing the above-mentioned concerns in a more efficient, competitive framework. Among other things, it may be decided to run a government-financed research centre and inform farmers about the findings. They could then choose the best-yielding crops themselves.

Closely related to institutional concerns are *quality arguments*. Cooperative and marketing board officials often try to justify their existence by arguing that private traders do not care about quality. This is seen to be the result of either competition or simple ignorance and avarice. Table 7-13 summarises some of this criticism, but also indicates that the arguments have a weak standing. With cashew liberalisation, for instance, the contrary happened. According to the Ministry of Agriculture (1994c, p. 3) procurement of raw nuts started especially in areas which produce the best quality.

Table 7-13: Questionable Quality Arguments Against Liberalisation

Criticism	Counter Argument
'Some unfaithful farmers take the advantage and mix sand, water and stones in the cotton they sell. The result is dirty cotton which is sold to the world market, thereby fetching low prices.' 'Before liberalisation, there was a grading system. Farmers no longer separate the two types. This affects the quality of the cotton hence fetching lower prices.'	People had already poured water or put stones in cotton before liberalisation and the deterioration of the grading system started in the late 1970s. With liberalisation, traders are even in a better position to ensure that they get the best cotton.
'Private coffee producers buy wet coffee.' 'Private coffee buyers do not offer quality incentives to farmers and so depress quality.' 'By establishing their own mills private coffee buyers can circumvent quality controls.'	'This ignores the fact that the previous system presided over a gradual but constant decline of coffee quality. It is unrealistic to expect the private sector to reverse the damage of years in a few seasons.' 'Growers have not been paid 'according to quality' for years.' 'It is in buyer's interest to extract maximum value from their purchases' which often implies quality.
With liberalisation, ginneries desperately needed cotton. Competition forced them to disregard quality.	This is transitional. There is a positive correlation between quality and quantity. The main concern should therefore be to increase production.

Source: Cotton: Maro (1997, p. 37f), Coffee: Agrisystems (1996, p. 31); as well as comments not indicated with quotation marks from personal communication at the University, Dar es Salaam, March 2000

The quality argument is in particular not credible if contended by cooperatives, as cooperatives themselves are directly responsible for poor quality. As noted in

Agrisystems (1996, p. 32) improved quality requires investment in both production and processing. Many of the cooperatives however refused to let private companies participate in the crop processing business, while letting their own processing facilities deteriorate (see also The Guardian, No. 963, 7 January 1998). Private companies have proved to be more efficient and have usually sufficient means to invest in the business, which would also improve quality. Examples of better private-sector performance are numerous in Tanzania, also where private and public companies operated side by side (e.g. tea processing factories owned by private companies and the Tanzania Tea Authority or private versus public spinning mills).

Besides institutional and quality concerns, there are warnings on corruption. Many cooperative and marketing board officials believe that *private traders are inherently corrupt*. They think private traders do not care about the rules of the game and only want to win; they are said to operate without licences, evade paying levies, engage in smuggling, use transfer-pricing methods, and, as asserted below, even steal the farmers' crop:

> 'Liberalised market has created a loophole for fraud in selling cotton. The cotton can be stolen from one place and be sold to another place … without notice. If this happens then it is definite that some farmers may lose a years income which could have bad consequences on food security, especially for the poor' (Maro (1997, p. 39f), quoting views of cooperative officials).

Clearly, during the twenty years of Ujamaa socialism there was not much room for private companies to make profits officially. According to personal communication at the Chamber of Commerce (Dar es Salaam, November 1996), those private companies who still survived at Nyerere's time depended on 'using' the socialist system, also in a dishonest way. This particularity may explain the thinking of some civil servants that people in the private sector are not to be trusted. Nevertheless, the situation has changed in the meantime. The argument that private traders are inherently corrupt is more likely an excuse, and meant to distract from own fraudulent behaviour. Officials from cooperatives and marketing boards have themselves proved to be corrupt and misuse funds. Given the numerous reports on such issues and the poor performance of many cooperatives and marketing boards, it even appears that embezzlement has been on a much larger scale than could ever be expected with private trading. Some references to corruption and embezzlement are summarised in Table 7-14.

So far different arguments have been considered for and against liberalisation, emphasising however that arguments for delaying or even preventing reforms are based on weak grounds. The possibility that Tanzania had been capacity-constrained and therefore delayed reforms does not appear to hold since many of the reform measures not undertaken would not have absorbed a lot of the government's capacity. There remains at least one important aspect which provides some explanation for Tanzania's gradual, 'unbundled' approach. Given that the pre-reform system was inherently inefficient and any delay implied further costs, one reason (other than rent-

Table 7-14: Corruption and Embezzlement in Cooperative Unions

Cotton	'Theft and misconduct: [In the period 1985-90] there have been numerous reports on dubious deals by some corrupt cooperative employees which resulted in huge financial losses. The practice which is locally branded as "ghost purchases or ununuzi hewa" extends widely from primary societies to regional cooperatives.' 'Misuse of funds: There have been some reports that the overdrafts meant for purchases of seedcotton from farmers were being used for personal use... [or] to lend money to employees at friendly terms.'
Coffee	'The slide of the Unions continued unabated in subsequent years [i.e. after 1991] in virtually all coffee areas of the country. This was coupled with major losses of coffee Union funds in certain cases, apparently caused through corruption.' 'The continued political interference by Government in the running of the Unions resulting in incompetent organisation and management which ran the Unions poorly and often dishonestly. ... This led to large losses for the Unions often not from coffee but from other activities and from defalcations.
Cashew	'Prior to 1991/92, export of raw nuts, kernels and by-products were the exclusive domain of TCMB...Because of the lack of transparency, the method drew considerable criticism for under-invoicing, inefficiency, and delays in payments to farmers.'

Source: Cotton: Ministry of Agriculture (1994b, p. 24), Coffee: Agrisystems (1996, p. 19, Appendix B, p. 18 and 57), Cashew: World Bank (1994b, p. 129)

seeking resistance) to implement a gradual and unbundled approach would be *uncertainty* and thus the need to learn from previous reform experience. Dewatripont and Roland, for instance, argued that in the case of uncertainty unbundling and gradualism might have lower experimentation and learning costs than a 'big bang' approach (Tommasi and Velasco (1996, p. 206)). However in the case of Tanzania most agriculture reforms, which abolished distorted incentives and trade restrictions and allowed private businesspeople to participate, had a positive impact. Learning from the experience of earlier liberalisation would have therefore suggested speeding up reforms. Most evident and widely perceived are the *early positive experiences* from food crops and non-traditional agricultural exports:

> 'The volume of food sales increased by 100 percent between 1983, when marketing reforms began, and 1988. Increased food availability essentially restored Tanzania's ability to feed itself and by 1990 virtually eliminated the need for food imports.' (Mans (1994, p. 399))
>
> '...the value of non-traditional agricultural exports increased fivefold since 1985, with strong growth recorded for each of the non-traditional crop groups.' (Mans (1994, p. 400))

Evidently non-traditional exports could have performed even better if exporters had faced a more appropriate exchange rate in the 1980s. This view is for instance explicitly stated in the Tanzania Economic Report (World Bank (1991, p. viii)). This favourable development contrasts with the poor performance of the traditional export sector. As emphasised in World Bank (1991, p. iv), the dollar-export value of traditional export crops continued to fall even after 1986; in 1990 it was 22% below the 1981 level. Also conditions for farmers were poor. They did not get cash for their crops, payments were often greatly delayed and in many cases they did not even receive the promised payments. This induced several farmers to change to alternative crops, in particular food crops like for instance tea or cotton (Cargill Technical Services (1997, p. 10) and Maro (1997, p. 36)).

Ex post reforms in the traditional export sector were *positive* and in sharp contrast to the poor performance of the previous monopolistic system. For all crops marketing costs significantly decreased, and the speed of marketing, a critical factor for some crops, improved. Farmers were paid earlier and received higher prices. A dramatic change was also apparent in the cashew sector. The World Bank (1994b, p. 129) notes:

> '...although there was a breakthrough on producer price incentives starting 1985, production did not respond until recently because of the collection and payment difficulties created by the cooperative unions and the monopolistic Tanzania Cashew Marketing Board... Starting 91/92 farmers were allowed to sell directly to traders as well as coops. Traders were allowed to export directly, without recourse to the marketing boards. Farmgate terms of payment have improved and production and exports of raw nuts have increased dramatically.'

The better service of private traders is equally reflected in their rapid gain of market share they obtained with liberalisation. In the cashew sector it increased from 3% in 1990/91 to 75% in the season 1992/93 (Ministry of Agriculture (1994c, p. ii)). With coffee, still affected by many implicit restrictions, the share of private traders increased between the seasons 1994/95 and 1996/97 from 30% to 90% for Mild Arabicas and from 20% to 40% for Robustas and Hard Arabica (Agrisystems (1996, Appendix B, p. 61)).

Evidence of Rent-Seeking Connected with Liberalising Traditional Export Crops

The previous discussion emphasised that Tanzania's record of reform could have been better. The slow pace of liberalisation was only marginally an institutional problem but apparently reflected resistance by rent-seekers. Several more direct indications of rent-seeking further support the hypothesis. They are the subject of the remaining section and include the sequence of reforms, the disregard of donor concerns, poor implementation records, continued lobbying for protection, as well as strategies against private sector participation after liberalisation.

Already the *sequence of liberalisation* indicates rent-seeking patterns rather than a logical approach to reforms. It appears that Tanzania reformed selected parts of its agriculture sector either when rents had 'evaporated' or when pressures from inside the sector became sufficiently high.

Given the balance of payments problems in the 1980s, it would have made sense to first reform and liberalise the most relevant foreign-exchange earning sectors, i.e. the traditional export sector with coffee and cotton. What actually happened was the contrary. Tanzania began by liberalising non-traditional exports—not surprisingly, as they were never included in the monopsonic marketing channels (Mans (1994, p. 400))—and within the traditional export sector, it started with the not-relevant sisal production. Coffee and cotton were only liberalised at a time when the government no longer depended on cheap foreign exchange to subsidise selected importing beneficiaries. With the unification of the exchange rate in 1993 rents from the allocation of foreign exchange disappeared, and almost simultaneously the strong resistance of policymakers against private-sector participation vanished (participation was finally allowed in the season 1994/95).

The sequence of reforms also indicates the relevance of pressure from inside the market. Three examples support this argument. First, limited liberalisation of cashew nuts happened only in the season 1991/92, when the industry was, as the World Bank (1994a, p. 82) puts it, 'at the brink of collapse'. Second, items which already had been liberalised in the early 1980s were perishable goods, such as fruits and vegetables (World Bank (1994b, p. 165)). This is not surprising since perishable goods demand a more efficient and faster distribution. Embezzlement and other modes of rent appropriation that undermine efficiency would have implied much higher costs. Third, liberalisation was faster in some areas where farmers had ample alternative opportunities of production. According to personal communication at the Tanzania Cotton Board approximately 95% of cotton is grown around Lake Victoria; hardly anything else can grow there. With sisal production, in contrast, much of the land has an alternative use. If rent extraction by the government becomes unbearable, sisal producers can therefore more easily protest by shifting to alternative crops than can cotton producers. Sisal was liberalised in 1984, cotton only ten years later. In the case of sisal, also the profitability of exports was marginal at best (World Bank (1994b, p. 134)); this again limited the government's abilities to extract rents.

However rent-seeking arguments on the sequence of reform steps have to be understood in the right context. There are obviously many other non-rent-seeking aspects which also influenced the sequence of reforms. Which of the overlapping forces finally tipped the balance to initiate early or late reforms would demand a more detailed analysis, which is beyond the scope of this study.

Besides the arguments on the sequence, *long-lasting and largely ignored donor concerns and advice* can be interpreted as another indication of rent-seeking resistance, even though ideology certainly mattered a lot in the early days. Direct criticism on the inefficiency of the marketing system goes back as far as 1973, when the World Bank first mentioned in a review report 'serious defects of the supply and marketing system' (World Bank (1994b, p. 163)). In the early 1980s, when many donors strongly recommended liberalising agricultural marketing and processing, the government ignored the warnings and continued to maintain the monopolistic state-controlled system. Donor concerns did not diminish in subsequent years. The 1989 Public Expenditure Review for instance mentions, among other things, the need for 'aggressive action to increase competition at all levels of the agricultural marketing system' (World Bank (1989b, p. 27)). In particular in the late 1980s and early 1990s there was still strong dissatisfaction with the inefficiency of agricultural marketing and the delay and slow pace of liberalisation with traditional export crops (e.g. spelled out in Consultative Group meetings).

When the government was finally pressured into liberalisation, *implementation of necessary measures tended to be slow.* For instance in the case of cashew liberalisation, policymakers only issued vague guidelines in the media and sent no official instructions to the local authorities in charge of the policy changes (World Bank (1994a, p. 82)). In addition, as the World Bank notes, to protect cooperatives, private traders were only given access to certain buying areas and were restricted to official buying prices. Liberalisation did not even include processing.

Also at the ministry level initial progress on restructuring was slow. A report on the coffee sector (Agrisystems (1996, p. 35f)), for instance, notes on the organisational aspects of the Agricultural Sector Management Project that progress was slow, several aspects on rationalisation had not advanced at anything like the pace that was expected and there had been little or no redeployment of staff to move them into the new Ministry structure. On the last point the report concludes that there had therefore been no improvements in the direction of quality and quantity of output.

Part of the problem was that many people in the state bureaucracy did not effectively understand what liberalisation and market forces meant. They were therefore still willing to assist ailing parastatal companies and industries. The quote at the beginning of Chapter 7.2—that a decline in lint processing calls for immediate government assistance—is symptomatic of this line of thinking. Another example from the Ministry of Agriculture, which indicates rent-seeking interests and an obvious lack of understanding what liberalisation means, is given in Table 7-15. Suggestions i and ii call for total liberalisation, iii-v and viii for increased protection.

The suggestions did have some effects later. In 2000 suddenly cashew-traders were no longer allowed to use jute bags for exports, but had to buy the homemade sisal bags, produced by a single company, that were three times more expensive. In most of the world cashew is traded in jute-bags. When the minister banned these bags, there were already jute bags worth US$3 million in the country (personal communication with cashew trader in Dar es Salaam, April 2001).

Rent-seeking forces have been most apparent in the strong *resistance against private sector participation.* As noted earlier, in particular cooperatives have been reluctant to work together with private sector investors. Resistance among public officials also led to the collapse of an entire Dutch aid programme for reviving the cotton industry. According to the 1993/94 Cotton Review of the Ministry of Agriculture (Ministry of Agriculture (1994b, p. 12)), the programme intended, among other things, to establish new cotton ginneries run by an independent private sector management. When Tanzania reneged on its earlier

Table 7-15: Suggestion of the Ministry of Agriculture on the Sisal Industry

The Tanzanian Government is strongly advised to take various measures to assist the sisal industry to restructure. The recommended areas of concentration include:

(i) *Complete deregulation* of the industry.
(ii) *Privatisation* of the existing TSA estates and assets.
(iii) *Reintroducing the exemption* of import duty and sales tax for inputs and parts while impose a *high tariff on imported jute products* which threaten sisal products in the domestic market.
(iv) *Abolition of any* foreign exchange retention schemes on export earnings *which have adverse effect* on the sisal industry while *welcoming those in favour* of it.
(v) Limited term *tax-free status* to sisal product industries (this may be alternative to iii above).
(vi) Regulating charges set by monopoly institutions such as THA, TANESCO, and TRC whose negative [economic effects] on the sisal industry are far reaching.
(vii) Reestablishment of the Mlingano research institution with a firm financial foundation for the sisal industry.
(viii) Allowing active sisal bag factories to *import duty-free* jute bags as profit centre activity to support more costly production facilities.

Source: Ministry of Agriculture (1994a, p. vi)

agreement to allow a private management, the project collapsed. The Dutch felt that 'Tanzania was not seriously interested in the development of the Cotton Sector'. Evidently, what mattered were rent-seeking considerations.

Once private sector participation was finally tolerated, countervailing rent-seeking actions from cooperatives, marketing boards and the Ministry of Agriculture again hampered the creation of a 'level playing field'. The case of African Gourmet Coffee in Malawi discussed in Chapter 5.2 (Table 5-4 on page 272) provided a glimpse of the many possibilities. In Tanzania, liberalisation was not easy either. The coffee sector has largely remained in the hands of the government and cooperatives, which marginalised private traders and thereby limited success in the coffee sector (The Guardian, No. 963, 7 January 1998). Three examples of rent-seeker resistance against private traders are described below.

First, cooperatives' resisted letting private traders *use established buying posts*. Coffee traders were prohibited from buying coffee at the farmgate level but had to use permanent buying posts in villages and market centres. At the lowest level, farmers are organised in primary societies. In Tanzania there are about 5000 primary societies nationwide, of which 560 are involved in coffee (Agrisystems (1996, Appendix B, p. 58)). Ideally, farmers should have the choice between selling their coffee to private buyers or cooperative unions. Several cooperative unions, in particular in the north, however, refused to let private traders use primary societies as buying posts. Private traders therefore had to set up their own locations, which did not make sense economically and was very costly. (Ministry of Agriculture (1996, p. 24))

Second, with liberalisation the Tanzania Coffee Board introduced an extremely complicated, lengthy and costly *procedure of licensing*, as documented in Agrisystems (1996, Appendix E, p. 3). Besides the application for a business licence, the procedure included going through villages, districts, regions and the Coffee Board. According to the study, a large private coffee exporter typically collects coffee from about 600 buying posts. For each buying post the trader needed the approval of the village committee. Attendance can reach 25 participants, all requiring sitting allowances. The trader then had to go on to the district level, regional level and national level. As noted in the report, 'this process can take up to three months to complete and because all recommendations, inspections, and licences are valid for one year only, has to be repeated annually'. Evidently, particularly in smaller regions the costs have been prohibitive for private traders and actually explain why private traders had to ignore marginal areas (an argument used by cooperatives against liberalisation). In addition there are even allegations that some cooperative unions themselves did not have the required licences and the Tanzania Coffee Board was unwilling to enforce the licensing regulation against them (Agrisystems (1996, p. 18)).

Third, cooperatives successfully resisted the abolition of the prescribed *pseudo-'auctioning' of private coffee*. The Coffee Sector Study argues against this auction system as follows:

> 'The prescribed auction is a real constraint because it has continued as though no change has taken place. There are no valid marketing reasons why coffee already bought by an exporter should pass through an "auction" where that same exporter "repossesses" it. This has an impact on export marketing because the present forced auctioning of "private" coffee (which have already been sold) causes delays of between 30 and 50 days in chain to FOB.' (Agrisystems (1996, p. 34))

The procedure is even less understandable if one considers that Tanzania has a time advantage in coffee. The bulk of its harvest occurs before that of its major competitors. According to personal communication with a donor (Dar es Salaam, April 2000), the auction system had remained in place simply because the political costs were too high to remove it. Cooperatives do not want private traders to benefit again from a further reduction in costs. The situation appears to be the last battle cooperatives are fighting after having lost many privileges. Since the costs are not prohibitive, and cooperatives are even threatening to stop private traders again, the latter are not pushing it any further.

Summing up, this section demonstrated that rent-seeking and rent-protecting activities have crucially co-determined the pace and content of Tanzania's agriculture reforms. Certainly, total liberalisation is not the answer to all problems and there are many justified institutional concerns. Agriculture liberalisation in Tanzania has also been accompanied by some transitional problems. In some cases the use of inputs had declined. Some farmers even experienced worsening marketing conditions in areas were competition remained limited in spite of private traders. This was reported for instance by a small number of coffee producers, even though the majority of coffee growers see an unambiguous improvement (Agrisystems (1996, p. 13)).

However, given the on average better performance of liberalised markets even in the transition period, the question is not whether or not to liberalise but how to create an efficient institutional setting which takes account of possible problems and concerns. Liberalising markets has brought about many benefits, which outweigh, at least for the vast majority of non-rent-seeking stakeholders, any possible transitional costs. Without resistance from rent-seekers, performance could have been much better.

The challenge to limit rent-seekers remains an ongoing task, also within a liberalised setting. On the one hand, it is relatively easy to fall back and reintroduce restrictive and competition-limiting measures. In the Kagera region, for instance, all of a sudden private traders were no longer allowed to buy coffee. According to personal communication in Dar es Salaam (April 2001), the authorities temporarily assured the monopoly to the cooperative union to avoid its liquidation since the union was highly indebted to a bank. The market intervention implied, among other things that the price paid to farmers declined.

On the other hand, there is also a danger that new institutions will be captured and misused by the old rent-seeking elite. For instance, with liberalisation the role of marketing boards has changed to become one in which authorities regulate and promote the quality, marketing and export of crops. The Cashew Board however has meanwhile degenerated to a bunch of entrenched rent-seekers. The Cashew Development Fund was thoroughly misused thanks to corruption—with the leaders of cooperative unions in the foreground.

c) Late Reform and Divestiture of Parastatal Companies

> *'The situation had to become a real disaster, to get out of hand. Only when parastatal companies were being chased by evrybody did privatisation become feasible.'*
>
> *First Secretary of a Donor Embassy, Dar es Salaam, April 2000*

That parastatal companies have contributed much to the stagnation and decline in growth in Africa is not disputed. Opinions however deviate as to the relative importance of underlying reasons, i.e. whether poor parastatal performance is more attributable to inappropriate government investments and interference, to a lack of knowledge of parastatal managers or to external factors, or whether it is essentially the result of rent-seeking enrichment from management, employees or middle and top-level civil servants. The fact that Tanzania for a long time has not effectively implemented recommendations to improve the efficiency of parastatal companies suggests that rent-seeking resistance played a key role.

To better understand the need for reforms and the role of rent-seekers' resistance, it is helpful to recall the *history and performance* of the parastatal sector. At independence the public sector was still very small and included only a few parastatal companies. In 1966 a total of 43 companies were fully owned by the government (PSRC (1993, p. 3)); the number however quickly increased following the policy change initiated with the Arusha Declaration in 1967. The use of public resources—to a considerable extent funded by donors—became a principal tool to transform the economy in the desired direction. In the 1970s the number of public companies increased at a greatly accelerated pace. To control the mushrooming parastatal sector the government even had to set stringent conditions on the creation of new companies (TAC (1991, p. 11)). The number reached 380 in 1979 and further increased to 425 in 1990 (PSRC (1993, p. 3)). With over 400 companies, Tanzania ended up with the largest parastatal sector in sub-Saharan Africa; three quarters of formal wage employment was either within central and local government or the parastatal sector (World Bank (1989c, p. 89f)).

However, distorted prices, production and marketing, as well as the lack of mechanisms to guarantee a minimum level of efficiency finally led to the creation of a highly unproductive, overstaffed and corruption-prone parastatal sector. Instead of supporting the government budget, parastatals became a major financial burden on the budget. As the World Bank (1989c, p. 91)) notes, only three companies paid dividends on a worthwhile basis and only few (i.e. those concerned with petroleum products, beer and soft drinks, cigarettes and textiles) provided significant amounts of excise and sales tax revenue—not because they were efficient, but simply because of the taxable properties of their products.

Inappropriate initial decisions on the location and size of the companies, the use of import-dependent technologies, as well as an inadequate product mix characterised many of the enterprises. Following Campbell (1992, p. 96), the Morogoro Shoe Company, for instance, was designed to be the largest shoe factory in the world. Planned to export over 80% of its production, the company intended to import the major portion of its inputs. However, as Campbell notes, 'the factory never operated above 7% of the installed capacity, which was achieved when the World Bank chief visited Tanzania'. On average it only maintained a 4% capacity utilisation and it never exported. He provocatively states that 'there has been a conspiracy of silence concerning those who got rich out of this project both inside and outside Tanzania'. Other examples of 'white elephants' offer donor co-financed cashew factories. As noted in the previous section, some of these never operated at all. According to personal communication (University in Dar es Salaam, April 2000), they were planned at a time when cashew output was already declining. Finally, the textile sector is another case in point. National Textile Corporation (TEXCO) was established in 1973 by presidential order to 'clothe the nation' (Henley (1993, P. 648)). The entire textile industry in Tanzania was never viable and depended on very high protection. The companies belong to the largest loss-makers in the parastatal portfolio.

Problems and deficiencies have also been substantial with other parastatal companies. According to World Bank (1996a, p. 9) manufacturing output losses from technical inefficiencies alone were estimated at about 50% on average between 1968 and 1988. And in the mid-1980s, partly a result of severe macro imbalances, most parastatals in the industry sector operated below one third of their capacity, one third of the companies generated negative value added at world market prices (GoT (1986b, p. 7), Mans (1994, p. 394)). Although problems had dramatically increased in the 1980s, immediate corrective action to improve the efficiency of the parastatal sector was already urgent in the 1970s.

The largest problem was that the companies increasingly depended on government support. Irrespective of whether uncovered costs had been caused by technical inefficiencies or a lack of flexibility to adjust to changed market conditions, or if losses originated from obvious embezzlement and stealing of assets, the government (and in many cases donors) took over the 'bill'. A pronounced soft budget relation between parastatals on the one hand and the government and donors on the other had developed with highly negative consequences. Chapter 8 will describe the soft budget relation in detail.[140]

Besides the immediate exit solution of closing down unviable companies, there are two approaches to address parastatal inefficiency. *A change to private ownership,* i.e. privatisation, accompanied by no further market distortions and protection, would immediately implement a hard budget constraint and make efficiency a condition for survival. Also staff would be accountable to the shareholders and would be dismissed if it did not perform. For political, technical and marked-based reasons privatisation is often not an option in the short or even long run. Alternatively, the government may decide to apply *a 'partial' approach*, i.e. to keep the company in the public portfolio, to rehabilitate and restructure it and to try to enforce a hard budget constraint.

Applying a hard budget constraint to parastatal companies is important for the development of private-sector participation. If soft budget constraints prevail in a market for some companies, a level playing field and fair competition is not guaranteed. For instance, marketing boards can 'squeeze out private agents by setting unprofitable low price margins and relying on the Government or state banks to subsidise their losses' (World Bank (1994a, p. 82)). This type of 'crowding out' of private agents occurred in the banking sector in Tanzania. When the National Bank of Commerce (NBC) set unrealistically low interest rate margins and fees, it effectively hampered the expansion of private banks (IMF (1996a, p. 1)). Hard budget constraints on parastatal companies also reduce the possibility of staff appropriating rents by misallocating and embezzling funds.

Experiences from parastatal reforms in developing countries in the 1980s and early 1990s suggest that reform efforts which left the parastatals in the state portfolio have largely failed (see, for instance, World Bank (1994a, p. 108f)). As Adam (1994, p. 142) emphasises, 'only with the "trauma" of privatisation are attitudes and incentives sufficiently altered for them to be realized'. And an early study on privatisation in Tanzania (Augustin (1997))—based on interviews

[140] Note that loss-making is not necessarily bad if the company produces a socially desired good and corrects for other market failures. However, it does not justify the company operating inefficiently. In Tanzania most of the losses have been caused by inefficiencies.

with managers of 36 public companies, 18 privatised companies and 19 private companies in 1995/96—finds that private companies performed much better.

From the point of view of economic efficiency, privatisation is therefore usually the preferred strategy. From the rent-seekers' perspective, in contrast, the answer depends on whether the process of privatisation itself offers major rent-capturing opportunities (to parastatal managers and other stakeholders who so far benefited from the parastatal system). In general, as long as companies remain in public hands and as long as they are not thoroughly reformed, access to rents can be maintained.

Tanzania's record of reform in the parastatal sector in the 1980s and 1990s can be summarised as follows. First, despite government goals there was hardly any effective rehabilitation of parastatal companies in the 1980s and early 1990s. Second, well into the 1990s a hard budget constraint had not been enforced. Third, privatisation started very late. And fourth, the process of privatisation has been very slow. Again, similar to earlier findings, there are many other reasons than rent-seeking to justify this development. The four arguments and some explanations that do not involve rent-seeking are the subject of the discussion below.

Evidence of Poor Reform Record in the Parastatal Sector

In the 1980s privatisation was never a real option for the government. Instead, it opted to reform parastatal companies and to reduce their burden on the government budget. In the 1986 Budget Speech (GoT (1986a, p. 21)), the Minister of Finance emphasised that the time had come for parastatal companies 'to run their operations without frequent recourse to Government for financial assistance'. At the initiation of the ERP II in 1989, the government promised to minimise transfers through the promotion of joint ventures, the closure or selling of persistently loss-making parastatals and by making sure that commercial parastatals were managed commercially and did not depend on budgetary support (GoT (1989, p. 12f)). In spite of these announcements many of the goals either were not implemented or were implemented late.

Strong resistance goes back to early 1980. Already at that time the government was well aware of inefficiencies but unwilling to implement suggested measures. As a result inefficient firms survived, and in many cases even expanded their activities despite being persistent loss-makers. The lack of government action finally lasted an entire decade, as documented with the quote from Mans and complaints from donors (Table 7-16):

> 'In 1983 a government commission identified gross inefficiencies in the sector, yet little action was taken to implement the recommended remedies. In 1987 another high-level commission reported on the persistently poor performance of the parastatal sector and the need to reform. However, with the exception of a substantial reduction in direct treasury subsidies, little was done.' (Mans (1994, p. 381))

Table 7-16: Donor Comments in Selected Consultative Group Meetings

1989 and earlier	'Regarding the parastatals, a number of donors expressed disappointment with lack of progress since this issue was discussed in the last two CG meetings. They stressed that what was needed was not further reviews but an action-oriented timetable.'
1992	'All donors welcomed the initial steps...However, all of them expressed strong concern about the very slow progress noting that overall, the picture remained largely that of intentions and preliminary steps. They emphasised to the delegation that they had heard enough words and that henceforth, they expect to see action. They urged the Government to develop a specific timetable for action.'
1993	'Most donors expressed strong dissatisfaction with the very slow pace of the parastatal reforms. They noted that no significant progress was made since the last CG and that the picture remains largely that of intentions. The Government had not made any convincing effort to liquidate even those public enterprises which clearly, would never be viable.'

Source: Protocols distributed among donors and government (World Bank (1989a, p. 6), World Bank (1992a, p. 9), World Bank (1993a, p. 8))

Long after the initiation of the Economic Recovery Programme parastatal companies continued to suffer from overstaffing and severe management problems, as well as a massive backlog of neglected maintenance and catch-up expenditures. Utility and infrastructure parastatals also constrained the development of the private sector. The comments in Table 7-17 suggest that the situation had not much improved in the 1990s.

Table 7-17: Comments on Parastatal Performance

Tele-communi-cations (1980s, 1996)	'Telephone service in Tanzania is incapable of supporting a modern economy. The current unmet subscriber demand is estimated at three times existing capacity, and call completion rates have fallen to 20-30% of calls placed. While international tariffs in Tanzania are close to the highest in the world, the sector operated at a loss from 1985-89 due to excessively low domestic tariffs, inefficient operation, and extremely poor collection performance of accounts receivable.' (World Bank (1993b, p. 11)) 'There is currently a backlog of approximately 50,000 applicants within Dar es Salaam metropolitan area and 117,200 nationally. The number of applicants on the waitlist is 130 percent of the existing customer base...Call completion rate is reportedly 45 percent in Dar es Salaam City Centre, this rate, however, was perceived as overly optimistic by most workers in the area.' (Coopers&Lybrand (1997b, 96f))
Electricity (2000)	TANESCO has a grossly inefficient bureaucracy and there are many losses and inefficiencies related to the generation and distribution of power. Even though the company produces enough power, it cannot get the power to the customer. Even people who live in Dar es Salaam have to have their own generator! This is frustrating. (Manager of petrol retailing company)

Water (1990s)	NUWA was extremely inefficient; there is complete chaos. You don't get the bill, but then they suddenly cut off the water. (Government employee) '47 per cent of the water tapped from the source is lost through leakage.' (The EastAfrican, No. 178, Mar-Apr 5, 1998)
Shipping (1997)	National Shipping Agencies Company (NASACO): 'Monopoly on shipping agent services to all ships calling at Tanzanian ports. Poor service, high prices, unwarranted diversification and financial mismanagement.' Tanzania Central Freight Bureau (TCFB): 'Monopoly. Complaints from the entire sea trade market: TCFB as an unnecessary burden and a high cost bureaucracy rather than an organization facilitating free trade and transport. Fee charged is essentially an export tax.' (World Bank (1997b, p. 12f))
Ports (2000)	Tanzania Harbours Authority (THA): Monopoly. There is a lot of corruption in THA. If THA brings a bill of US$10,000, they offer a 50% reduction if they get between 10% and 20%. Hence, although THA is a profit-maker, the company is not collecting all the money, their monopoly profits should be much higher. Everybody is involved in corruption, including the top management. Deals are made just everywhere; a lot of the goods also get stolen. THA has to compete with Mombassa in Kenya, which is also a mess. Whichever harbour will be privatised first will win a lot of customers. (General manager, shipping company)
Railways (2000)	Have you ever seen the final terminal of the TAZARA in Zambia? You would expect hundreds of containers to be handled. There is no activity going on there. I could see only a crane and a few containers. No way can they make profits like this. And in Tanzania Railways Corporation (TRC) they don't even know how many locomotives they possessed! (General manager, shipping company)

Source: Personal communication in Dar es Salaam, April 2000 as well as above quoted reports and studies

The inefficiency of the parastatals has been very costly, not only for the economy in general but also for the government. A conservative estimate indicates that in the years 1989 to 1992 subsidies to parastatals have still averaged 3-5% of GDP (World Bank (1993b, p. 6)). The report emphasises that this figure does not include bank loans, nor does it account for the losses due to inefficiency as compared with providing the same volume of resources to the private sector. Even more striking results on the support to parastatals will be presented in Chapter 8.

Because the soft budget problem persisted well into the 1990s, in 1996 the government of Tanzania, together with the World Bank, commissioned a detailed study on the direct and indirect subsidies provided to 22 selected parastatal companies covering the sectors utility and infrastructure, agricultural marketing, natural resource and industry. The study carried out by Coopers&Lybrand (1996) found that during the period 1993-96, in spite of the official hard budget policy, the 22 companies received a total of TSh 78 billion (TSh 120 billion at mid-1996 prices or US$190 million) in the form of direct and indirect subsidies. The largest components comprised grants, overdrafts from state banks, utility arrears and tax arrears and exemptions. Ten out of the 22 parastatal companies were rated unviable even if the subsidy would be at the same level in the future. This group included all marketing boards, as well as companies in the sectors textile, paper, coal, water and transport. At the other end are four companies which would have been viable even without the subsidy (TANESCO, TPDC, THA and SUDECO). The companies are however either monopolies or protected in other ways and well known for their inefficiency.

Evidently, the soft budget relation was kept intact long after reforms started in the mid-1980s. That major rent-seeking forces explain this picture is apparent, among others as the closure and liquidation of non-viable enterprises, as well as many hard-budget enforcing activities are capacity-saving and constraint-relieving reform measures for the government and could therefore have been undertaken at an early stage.

After the mid-1990s transfers to parastatal companies declined. This outcome is a result of a more stringent enforcement of a hard budget policy. To a large extent it is a direct result of the privatisation process that began in 1993, which eliminated most opportunities for large-scale embezzlement in the company (or at least made the company bear the consequences without government support).

The goal to systematically *privatise* most parastatal companies was first mentioned in 1992 and documented in the Master Plan of August 1993 (PSRC (1993)). Parastatals were categorised into three groups: social service institutions (non-commercial parastatals), public utilities and commercial enterprises. According to the government announcement in the Consultative Group meeting of that year, the divestiture of parastatal companies was intended to be implemented within a relatively short time:

> 'Government would complete its disengagement within the next 3-7 years. Meanwhile, those enterprises which remain in the public sector would be subject to a Hard Budget Constraint policy.' (World Bank (1993a, p. 3))

However, strategic firms, i.e. public utilities such as ports, railways, electricity and telecommunications were excluded from this decision, based on vague political arguments, including their economic importance. Since the economic costs of the public utilities had been enormous, it would have made sense to privatise these companies first. Only in 1996 did the Cabinet change its position and decide that these companies should also be privatised. Finally, the third group, i.e. social service institutions, were to be absorbed by the government.

In 1992, the government created the Parastatal Sector Reform Commission (PSRC) to coordinate, prepare and implement the privatisation programme. The Loans and Advances Realisation Trust (LART)—an agency set up to recover non-performing assets from state banks—complemented the reform process. Non-viable parastatal companies, which were not planned to be privatised or to be restructured, were transferred to LART for liquidation.

It is difficult to get a clear picture of the course of privatisation of commercial parastatals including public utilities, even though the PSRC produces an action plan each year and an annual review on the companies divested. The PSRC reports, however, are surprisingly mute on the total of parastatal companies which still have to be divested. The major problem is that nobody appears to know, even at the Treasury, how many parastatals were in the portfolio of the government.[141] Furthermore, in the process of privatisation many of the companies are split into several units and divested separately. In addition, some companies are sold to other parastatals, and others have been divested several times, apparently because original deals fell through at the last minute and the company returned to the state portfolio.

A government evaluation made in 2001 reports that 333 companies, i.e. 84% of a total of 395, had been divested and restructured by June 2000 (TISCO (2001, p. 2)). This conclusion is wrong. The December 2000 report from PSRC indeed mentions 333 divestiture transactions (PSRC (2000, p. 5)); the number however includes several sub-units and double counting. If these are excluded the number is only 160.[142]

The situation gets even more confusing if information in all previous PSRC reports is taken into account. The reports show at least 19 other companies to have been divested.[143] Depending on whether the divestiture of these companies was successful and depending on the initial total (Footnote 141), between 41% and 57% of commercial parastatals appear to have been divested by 2000. The figure contrasts with the above-mentioned 84% and the announcement in the 1993 CG meeting to complete privatisation within three to seven years. It also does not consider that the large and more difficult divestitures were still in the pipeline (public utilities).

---

[141] The Masterplan gives a list of 315 commercial parastatals (PSRC (1993, Appendix 3)). Not included in the list are, among others, non-commercial parastatals and cooperative unions. Another list obtained at the Treasury (apparently the draft of Appendix 3), shows 355 commercial parastatal (including 29 cooperative unions). Both lists include public utilities. PSRC (1997a, p. 1) mentions a total of 385 earmarked for divestiture through the parastatal reform programme and a recent evaluation (TISCO (2001, p. 2)) refers to 395 parastatal enterprises (the notation 'parastatal enterprises' indicates commercial parastatal in contrast to 'parastatal organisations' which refer to non-commercial entities).

[142] The Annex of the 2000 PSRC report (p. 15-20) gives the divestitures completed by 30 June 2000, grouped according to ministries. The total number of entries is 243, including 18 companies under receivership by LART. If individual units within a company are not counted separately and double counting of same companies is avoided, the list effectively shrinks to 160 companies.

In particular agricultural marketing boards appear in the list as many sub-units. NMC, for instance, includes at least 13 units explicitly shown in the table such as 'NMC Morogoro Rice Mill (asset sale 1996), NMC Mikumi Godown (asset sale 1997), NMC Head office (asset sale 1999), etc. In addition, some of the companies are mentioned several times. For instance, Tanzania Hides & Skins Limited and Tanzania Leather Board are shown on page 15 as well as on page 19, and Capital Construction Co. is mentioned twice on the same page (p. 18) as 'lease under review in 1993' and liquidation in Feb. 1998.

[143] Apparently not included in PSRC (2000), but mentioned as divested in earlier reports are Afina Pencils Co Ltd (receivership 1993), Aluminium Africa Ltd (share sale 1997), Arusha Metal Industries Ltd (sold to employees 1993), Bima Motors Ltd (closed 1995), Friendship Textile Mill Ltd (joint venture 1996), Mbozi Coffee Farms Ltd (outright sale 1995), Moshi Hand Tools Ltd (sold to employees 1993), Mwanza Brewery Ltd (share sale 1993), National Poultry Co Ltd (liquidation 1996), Tanzania Automobile Manufacturing Co Ltd (closure 1995), Tanzania Clay Products Ltd (closed receivership) 1993), Tanzania Crown Corks Ltd (liquidation 1993), Tanzania Diamond Cutting Co Ltd (liquidation 1997), Tanzania Electrical Goods Manufacturing Co Ltd (share sale 1994), Tanzania Maltings Co Ltd (share sale 1993), Tanzania Publishing House Ltd (MEBO 1994), Tanzania Seed Co Ltd (share sale 1995), TBL Farms Ltd (share sale 1993), Ubungo Garments Ltd (outright sale 1996).

The visibly slow process of privatisation is criticised in the World Bank's follow-up privatisation project from November 1999 (World Bank (1999b, p. 4)):

> 'The process of Government approval has tended to be long, and subject to multiple reviews and revisions...'
>
> 'PSRC procedures for divestiture transactions have entailed the use of multiple—and at times subjective—criteria in the evaluation of bidders and the awarding of sales...The process has been time-consuming and less than full transparent to all participants.'

Arguments to Delay Privatisation Versus Rent-Seeking Motivation

An obvious answer to the slow pace of privatisation and the far too cumbersome privatisation procedures is found in *rent-seeking.* Many managers, parastatal employees and high government officials did not have an interest in speedy divestiture. As noted earlier, as long as parastatals remained in the state portfolio, many opportunities for enrichment remained intact. And once the policy announcement to privatise all companies had been made, opportunities shifted to asset stripping and grew more the longer the delay was. Finally, even officials in privatisation agencies may have had a stake in delaying the process if doing so offered them some additional bribing income.

Before addressing these rent-seeking claims it is helpful to recall a few arguments against privatisation in general and against a rapid privatisation. These arguments are of institutional, technical, as well as political nature. Privatising a company is often complex and the preparation may require considerable time, resources and technical capacity. As frequently emphasised (e.g. Bienen and Waterbury (1989, p. 622f)), preconditions in sub-Saharan Africa are largely unfavourable. Often financial markets are not sufficiently developed, parastatal companies are in poor shape and therefore difficult to divest, and the workers' reemployment prospects are frustrating, requiring expensive exit solutions.

In Tanzania, the *'lack of adequate buyer' argument* has been frequently advanced as the major reason for the slow process of privatisation. The argument applies to three aspects (personal communication at the University and with staff of PSRC and LART in Dar es Salaam, April 1998 and 2000): First, politicians see privatisation as 'gifts under a Christmas tree' and 'selling the family silver'. It is argued that the government invested a lot of money in parastatal companies and therefore wants to make sure that the companies are sold for a good price. Second, the government wants to be sure that the company is not just closed down after privatisation, which demands that bidders have to show a real interest in maintaining the company. And third, companies should be preferably sold to Tanzanians, and among Tanzanians a balance should be kept between people of indigenous African origin and the more prosperous Indian community.

In particular the last aspect could not be achieved in a satisfactory way. Indigenous Tanzanian politicians argue that because of the Leadership Code in the socialist past, which did not allow leaders to earn income from side businesses, many indigenous Tanzanians did not have the opportunity to accumulate wealth. Tanzanians of Indian origin and foreigners, in contrast, were not among the leaders and they therefore have sufficient resources to buy the companies. The lack of 'politically' acceptable buyers also applied to other countries. In Kenya, for instance, there was a deep concern that 'commercial, financial and managerial capital is concentrated in the hands of foreigners, Kenyan Asians and, to a lesser extent, the Kikuyu' (Adam (1994, p. 146)).

Ultimately, any delays in privatisation can be explained with concerns that a government does not have the capacity to carry out rapid privatisation, that it lacks the funds to pay for all retrenchment costs or that it may not be able to find adequate buyers. However, a more realistic evaluation suggests that the hidden agenda in Tanzania included major rent-seeking motives. On the one hand, as will be argued below, privatisation started late because a strong coalition of interest groups benefited from the rents of public companies; on the other hand, there are many indications that the process of privatisation had been deliberately delayed.

Until the early 1990s *direct resistance against privatisation* was very strong, above all among the main stakeholders. Already Nyerere warned that in the event of privatisation leading managers would only be junior executives and would be marginalised (personal communication at the Department of Politics, University of Dar es Salaam, April 2000). Not only managers but also politicians had an obvious interest in maintaining parastatal companies. As Board Members they benefited from fringe benefits, status and the power of making decisions on employment and funds. And within the party it was opportune to be against privatisation. It is therefore no surprise that resistance in Tanzania came less from workers but much more from the management, as well as from larger organisations such as SCOPO (Standing Committee on Parastatal Organisation) or the party.

A critical factor with any privatisation of inefficient and overstaffed companies is the people working in the companies. Many of the managers in Tanzania came to their positions without proper qualifications. Privatisation not only meant losing a job, it also meant not being able to find another position with similar status and benefits. The situation for civil servants is just as bad, if not worse. Bienen and Waterbury (1989, p. 626), which comment on developing countries in general, describe the problem as follows:

> 'Even when the top executives of the Ministries of Finance or the central banks urge privatisation, we should not forget that there are sprawling middle echelons of civil servants in ministries and agencies whose primary function is to control and monitor the PSEs. Privatisation would cut directly into their functional raison d'être. Top-level civil servants may not have the same exit options as the managers of public enterprises.'

Resistance among middle and high-level bureaucrats as well as the party appears to have been crucial in delaying the main decision to divest the entire parastatal portfolio. As late as 1997 President Mkapa complained at the Consultative Group meeting that he had a troubled time preparing to argue the case for privatisation of certain large public enterprises and utilities before his own party (GoT (1997, p. 5)). To accelerate matters, Mkapa put the privatisation portfolio under his own office (President's Office, the State House).

The strongest force that broke the resistance to privatisation was the *rents* themselves, which dwindled as a result of the combination of several ongoing reform measures such as the unification of the exchange rate, the reduction in access to credits and trade liberalisation. There has been resistance related to these policies, too. But resistance could only be sustained for a few years, and could only slow but not reverse the general trend to removing rents.

At the beginning of the 1990s an increasing number of companies were running losses but no longer receiving compensation. This weakened their position. At the onset, the low cash flow parastatals generated (mostly from non-payment of tax liabilities, utility liabilities and other creditor liabilities) was still sufficient to pay wages and to finance dubious deals. As noted by a donor (recall the lead quote on page 375), the situation had to become a real disaster, 'to get out of hand'. Only when the companies were being pursued by everybody, did rents disappear and privatisation become politically feasible. In fact, those companies which still could benefit, i.e. basically strong monopolies and the National Bank of Commerce (which enjoyed a factual monopoly outside Dar es Salaam) were also those who resisted most and longest.

As soon as the main decision to privatise most parastatals had been taken, rent-seeking incentives changed to *delay privatisation*. Delays were already built into the procedures of privatisation. Even though the PSRC was charged with coordinating and implementing privatisation, it had no power to decide on the divesture; it only functioned as a principal advisor to the government (PSRC (1993, p. 15)). The subsequent government approval process turned out to be long and subject to multiple reviews and revisions.

In Tanzania, the privatisation process included many of the people who were the major profiteers of the public companies, such as members from the management, holding companies, Treasury and parent ministries, as well many key politicians within the parliament or party. Augustin (1997, p. 71f) notes that some holding companies were still run by the same members who initially set up the parastatal. Since their position depended on the existence of the parastatal, they had no interest in a speedy transition. In many instances, ministries and holding companies suddenly changed their opinion despite earlier agreements and thereby blocked the divestiture at a late stage.

An obvious example of delay is that of Tanganyika Packers, which had almost been divested in 1997 when another group suddenly became interested. Even though the winner of the tender had already been selected and had paid the required deposit of 10%, the sale was stopped and the responsibility of divesting the company transferred from LART to PSRC. Three years later, the company was still not sold (personal communication in Dar es Salaam at LART, March 2000).

A far too close involvement of the board of directors in the decision-making process became obvious in the privatisation of Tanzania Harbours Authority (THA). This parastatal operated the harbours in Dar es Salaam and Tanga. Despite THA's high inefficiency, the government decided to privatise the container terminal only and not the entire company. According to personal communication with a manager of a shipping company (Dar es Salaam, April 2000), five interested buyers had been shortlisted. Surprisingly, the board of directors of THA were doing the tenders themselves. Since it was not in their interest to privatise the terminal (obviously they would lose a lot of income from bribes), they simply did not agree on the price. THA asked an unrealistic US$8 million, having been offered US$3 million. There was no chance to solve this dispute unless THA drastically changed its position. Negotiations were bound to crash and privatisation was delayed again.

There are many other incidences which indicate that the companies themselves resisted privatisation. Particularly strong resistance came from financial institutions, which even employed lawyers. Or in the agriculture sector, The Guardian (No. 963, 7 January 1998) wrote regarding coffee, 'cooperatives which own most of the farms in the northern regions are reluctant to let the farms be run privately'. In some cases other stakeholders influenced the process. An interviewee openly admitted to having delayed privatisation of a company simply by calling the Principal Secretary of a ministry, asking him not to forward the paper to the Cabinet (personal communication, Dar es Salaam, April 2000).

While privatisation was delayed *asset stripping and vandalism* took place on a large scale (personal communication with staff members of PSRC and LART, March 2000). In 1998 the Criminal Investigation Department (CID) presented an annual report on corruption, listing for the first time corruption in public institutions as a crime. The report finds that misappropriating assets in state-owned companies increased by over 70% from TSh 996 million in 1996 to TSh 1.7 billion in 1997 (The Indian Ocean Newsletter, No. 801, 28 February 1998). During that year thefts were particularly high at NBC, which was in the process of being privatised and which was split into two separate companies in October 1997. The newspaper clip notes, 'as NBC now faces early privatisation, this clearly encouraged many to plunge hands into the financial jampot while it was still there'. The CID report cites as the underlying cause for the increase in crime economic hardships, insecurity among employees in the face of retrenchment and the sale of public firms, and emphasises that the presented figures 'are only the tip of the iceberg, as many more cases go unreported' (The EastAfrican, No. 167, 12-18 January 1998).

All in all, this section has shown that there was hardly any effective rehabilitation and restructuring of parastatal companies prior to privatisation and also no enforcement of a hard budget constraint. A large number of public enterprises survived that should have gone bankrupt in the new environment after the Economic Recovery Programme began. Furthermore, for a long time privatisation was not an option. Although there are several non-rent-seeking arguments to explain this development and Tanzania had come a long way since the mid-1980s, the country's pattern of parastatal reforms suggests a strong influence of rent-seeking. The continued access to rent-seeking income since 1986 did not just contribute to the macro instability, as outlined in Chapter 7.1, it also undermined private sector participation and development, either because competing parastatal enjoyed preferential status or because the poor performance of utility and infrastructure parastatals made many private sector activities unprofitable.

Once the main decision to privatise most parastatal companies had been taken, rent-seeking incentives changed to delay privatisation. This situation contrasts with the situation in eastern Europe and the former Soviet Union, where rent-seekers rushed into privatisation, as they anticipated major opportunities from insider sales. In Tanzania, it appears that insider sales have been a minor issue, although some probably occurred.[144] People in Tanzania usually comment that insiders who know their way will succeed. There is however no hard evidence for such transactions.

Much clearer is the issue of asset stripping, which contributed, together with the poor management, to a deterioration of assets in parastatal companies. As many interviewees emphasised, companies were often left an empty shell. The mere announcement of privatisation had changed the rent-seeking game into an intermediate, even more costly rent-seeking contest, characterised by asset stripping and continued embezzlement, while privatisation was not yet finalised. The rent-seekers' stake obviously explains why records of privatisation did not meet the government's publicly proclaimed targets.

[144] A possible explanation is that many parastatals were of so little value that buying at prices far below market was more difficult.

7.3 Slow Progress in Institutional Reforms: Poor Public Service Delivery

'Mr. Speaker, in 1985, His Excellency Ndugu Ali Hassan Mwinyi, the President of the United Republic of Tanzania, charged your National Assembly with the responsibility of fostering economic recovery. In this regard, a lot has been done. However, we should not be complacent about our achievements because a lot more is yet to be done. No stone should therefore be left unturned in our efforts to increase productivity and efficiency as well as restoring accountability in the management and supervision of our public and private enterprises... we should not hesitate to take disciplinary action against anyone who proves to be irresponsible in the execution of his duties.'

Budget Speech of the Minister for Finance, Hon. Steven A. Kibona, 7 June 1990

This chapter focuses on the basic functions of the state to guarantee the supply of various public goods, such as secure property rights, an enabling and supportive market environment, the build-up of an efficient infrastructure or the provision of social services (health and education). As will be argued, rent-seeking activities of civil servants (partly in cooperation with private actors) have crucially undermined the implementation of these objectives, which were important components of Tanzania's reform package in the 1980s and 1990s. Civil servants captured rents either by extracting them from individuals and companies through extortion or by misallocating and embezzling public funds. The actual development in the 1990s stands in sharp contrast with many officially stated intentions by the government, for instance, the above quote from the 1990 Budget Speech (see GoT (1990a, p. 15f)).

The Chapter analyses poor public service delivery from two perspectives: private sector and civil service. Section a) looks at the general environment hostile to the private sector, highlighting cumbersome and largely inefficient bureaucratic procedures. Section b) focuses on the civil service and outlines the slow progress in improving the overall budget process. It emphasises the failures in the 1990s to implement a speedy reform of civil service employment, to enforce budget priorities and to prevent and sanction the large-scale embezzlement of public funds. Section c) finally concludes with a general assessment on corruption and commitment.

a) The Private-Sector Perspective: Struggling with a Hostile Environment

'I feel like having committed a crime when asking for an A-permit.'

Businessman in Iringa, April 2000

The previous chapters have already pointed out several aspects of conditions hostile to business in Tanzania. The preferential treatment of parastatal companies, the inefficiency of public utilities and the macro imbalances constrained private sector activities. The creation of an enabling and supportive environment to private sector initiatives is indisputably an important component of a pro-market and welfare-oriented reform strategy. This goal however has been largely undermined by the state bureaucracy, in particular by its poor public service delivery.

Deliberately introducing bureaucratic barriers and other hindrances as a means to extract rents is a phenomenon that has been widely described in the literature on rent-seeking and corruption. Besides bureaucrats in the narrow sense, police forces, military units and parastatal employees are known to abuse their power to enrich themselves. Then methods are numerous and are usually based on cost-enhancing and benefit-reducing corruption. They follow a simple pattern, i.e. the artificial creation of a problem for a private person or company and a suggestion how to be rid of it, of course at a fee. The other source of illegal income where both parties benefit is cost-reducing and benefit-enhancing corruption (recall the typology presented in Table 2-3 on page 50). It may involve embezzlement of funds and is likely to undermine a level playing field, putting those companies at a disadvantage which cannot benefit from similar 'favours'. In addition, cost-reducing and benefit-enhancing corruption may equally undermine important regulations and standards. Figure 7-7 shows an example of a questionable form obtained at the Malindi Police Station in Zanzibar, which was meant to replace the driving licence for one day (the writer never claimed to have a driving licence, and in fact did not).

Characteristic for a bureaucracy driven by rent-seeking is that problems originate in different institutions, making victims culprits as well. The following example of a Japanese passport holder who was not able to obtain an extension of his visa within a reasonable time is a case in point. He left the country 12 days after the visa expired, without having the requested extension. The immigration officer threatened a fine of US$400 and opened up negotiations. A side payment of US$40 to the immigration officer and another TSh 20,000 (US$22) to the policeman who had been called by the officer solved the problem (personal observation and communication with 'victim' at the airport in Dar es Salaam, 20 March, 2001). Obviously, the foreign passport holder was violating a law, but so were the Tanzanian bureaucrats indirectly, by depriving the 'client' from getting a service (visa extension) on time. Bribery would have speeded up the process of issuing a visa; alternatively, as in the above case, it solved the problem at the airport.

Figure 7-7: Temporary Driving Licence

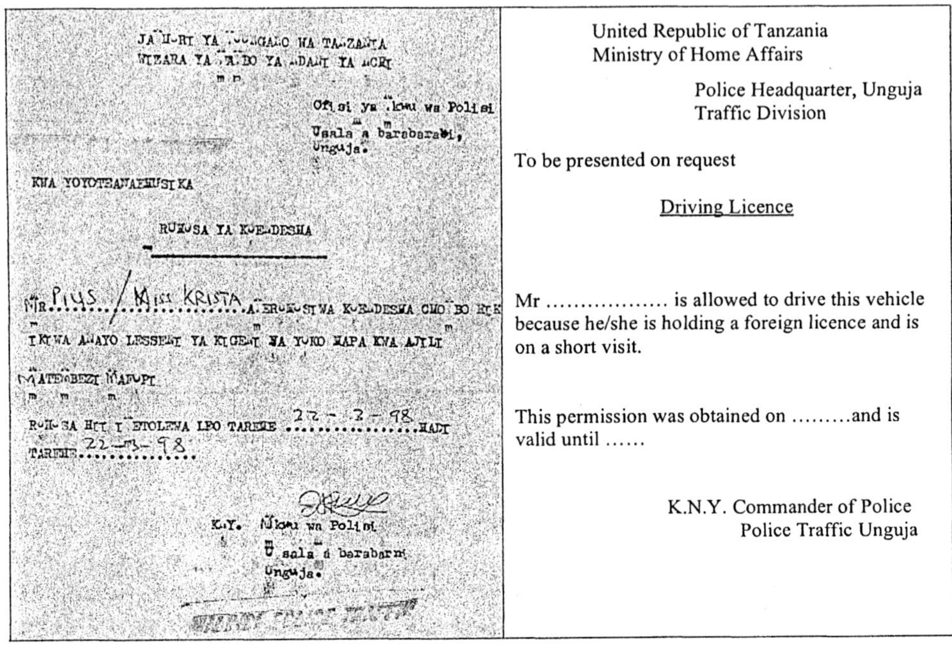

United Republic of Tanzania
Ministry of Home Affairs

Police Headquarter, Unguja
Traffic Division

To be presented on request

Driving Licence

Mr .... is allowed to drive this vehicle because he/she is holding a foreign licence and is on a short visit.

This permission was obtained on ....and is valid until ......

K.N.Y. Commander of Police
Police Traffic Unguja

Source: Form organised by the moped-renting agency for US$5 or $10

These introductory examples of the driving licence and visa extension are not salient; but they point out the characteristic rent-seeking nature of Tanzania's civil service, which may sometimes be in favour of the client or against the client, depending on the situation and depending on what offers higher side payments. As will be argued below, since side payments and other rents were an important part of civil service income and since they were easily accessible (implying a low rate of dissipation), rent-abolishing measures either had been ineffective or were implemented very late.

The Economic Recovery Programme (ERP) in 1986 did not include explicit goals to improve the private sector environment, but it included many *implicit measures* such as gaining macro stability, improving trade regimes and strengthening other services such as transportation, communication, water and energy. Macro stability was achieved in the mid-1990s; however, the business environment and the quality of public services remained extremely poor. In the early 1990s, the delivery of most public services including education, health, water, agricultural extension, etc., was below the standards achieved by the early 1970s (e.g. World Bank (2000b, p. 5)).

A major constraint of growth in Tanzania was the lack of private investments, which is obviously a direct reflection of the poor business environment. At the CG meeting in 1989, several donor delegations emphasised the importance of encouraging the private sector (World Bank (1989a, p. 8)).

These aspects were explicitly taken up in subsequent policy framework papers (e.g. the 1992 PFP, which included the goals of reviewing the Investment Act, limiting the scope of industrial licensing and rationalising registration and business licensing (GoT (1992a, p. 22))). In spite of these intentions, several studies, as well as proceedings of seminars and workshops, have documented that not much happened. As with other aspects of the Tanzanian reform process, improving the business environment remained a never-ending topic well into the next millennium.

Six years after the initiation of the ERP participants at a *workshop on import handling systems* in Tanzania (Bank of Tanzania (1991)) thoroughly complained about the bureaucratic procedures involved in importing goods. These included (p. 17f) long delays in establishing letters of credit (a result of red tape, laxity, typing errors and voluminous paperwork), cumbersome and costly procedures of documentation (in particular because of uncoordinated and unharmonised activities by the institutions involved in import handing) and major delays in processing shipping documents (too many and unharmonised forms, short validity of licences, reluctance and sluggishness in adopting new technological advances, lack of accountability and seriousness, etc.).

Six years later similar complaints were again mentioned in the *Investor Road Map*. The report was prepared by Coopers&Lybrand for USAID and represents the most comprehensive study of the business environment in Tanzania undertaken in the 1990s (see Coopers&Lybrand (1997b) and Coopers&Lybrand (1997c)). It meticulously documents the procedural and administrative barriers to investment in Tanzania, outlining and analysing the steps required for each agency involved in the business start-up (including import handling). Figure 7-8 depicts the investment process, which comprises general approvals, permits and licences, specialised approvals (required only for certain types of investments), site development (construction and utilities) and operational requirements (foreign exchange, labour and import/export processes).

The report emphasises that bureaucratic hazards and delays are tremendous in Tanzania. It is against this background that Figure 7-8 should be interpreted. Although the figure includes several necessary steps in the start-up of a company, the main problem is that the steps are not settled in one go. The report sardonically states that the figure 'should have 3-4 times more steps to more accurately reflect the delays faced by investors' (Coopers&Lybrand (1997b, p. ii)).

Quoting from the main findings (Coopers&Lybrand (1997b, p. i-viii)), the biggest problem faced by investors in Tanzania was obtaining land. Several investors had to wait two to six years. Delays in obtaining utility hook-ups correlated with willingness to pay bribes, and obtaining work permits involved very long delays even for well-known international companies. The import handling process was equally frustrating. In spite of the problems mentioned in the workshop on import handling in 1991, the situation had not changed much six years later. The report found that the import clearance process in Tanzania

Figure 7-8: Overall Flowchart for a Foreign Manufacturing Firm

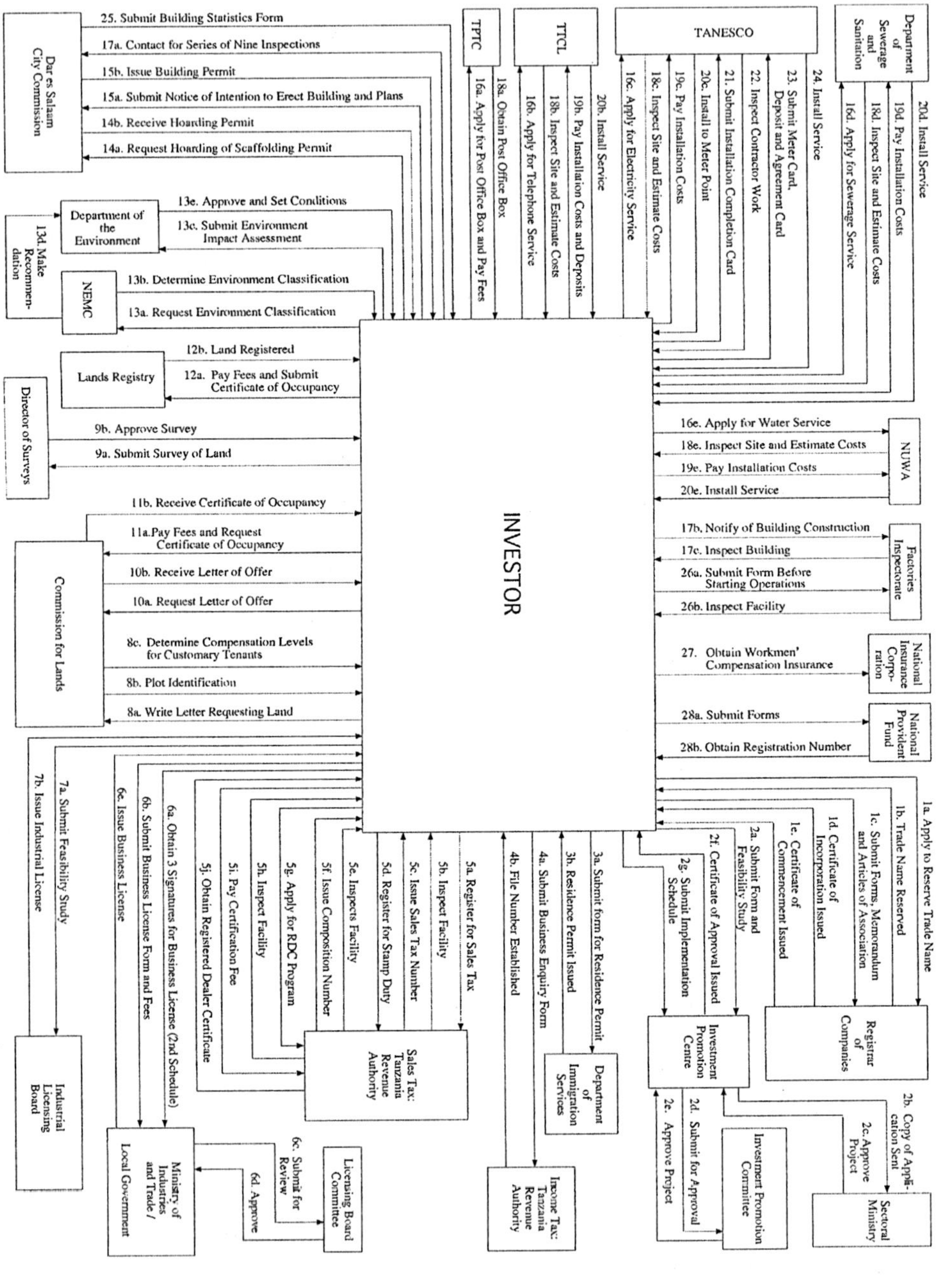

Source: Redrawn according to Figure X-1 in Coopers&Lybrand (1997b, p. ix)

was still one of the most complicated in Africa, including more than 20 steps and eight organisations.

Finally, extensive bureaucratic operational requirements did not end once the firm was legally established. According to the report (p. iii) a firm in Dar es Salaam had to submit at least 89 separate filings per year, excluding any import/export documentation, repatriation of funds and sectoral forms (a bank needed 285 filings a year, a hotel 454 separate filings a year).

The findings are striking, also when they are compared with the three other countries Namibia, Ghana and Uganda, where the Roadmap exercise had been undertaken. The report concludes (Coopers&Lybrand (1997b, p. vi)):

> 'Of the four countries...Tanzania is the most difficult in which to establish business. We estimate that the average delay to commence operations in Tanzania is 18 to 36 months. This compares to the 6 to 12 months in Namibia and the 12 to 24 month delay in Ghana and Uganda.'

> 'The start-up process is more ambiguous and less transparent in Tanzania. An investor comes into contact with more agencies and more steps—each of which represents another individual "fiefdom" or "toll booth". Virtually everything appears to be negotiable.'

> 'Given the complexity of the procedures, the number of agencies, the costs, and the concentration of approvals obtainable only in Dar es Salaam, it is virtually impossible for small businesses—particularly outside Dar es Salaam—to operate legally.'

Anecdotal evidence from personal communication in Tanzania in April 2000 indicated that problems had not much improved. A managing director of the Tanzanian branch of a large international company, for instance, still commented in 2000 as regards import handling: it takes longer to clear goods in Tanzania than at any place in the world—'they basically delay till you ask'. In the mid-1990s, beer was even left in the harbour until it past its sell-by date and had to be thrown away. In that specific case, rumours said it was cheaper for the businessman to abandon the beer than to pay a bribe! (personal communication at Chamber of Commerce in Dar es Salaam, November 1996). Starting a small company legally was also still a major undertaking and in many cases virtually impossible to do in a reasonably short time. A businessman in Iringa, for instance, complained:

> 'I feel like having committed a crime when asking for an A-permit. At the immigration office you have to get through a 6-level approval. On each level, some documents are missing and the lot is sent back to the customer. Once you have gone through all levels in Dar es Salaam, they may ask for the same forms in Iringa again. Even if Dar es Salaam would become more efficient, I can assure you, Iringa is *not* Dar es Salaam!' (personal communication in Iringa, April 2000).

Given the Tanzanian laws and procedures and the inefficient and rent-seeking behaviour of bureaucrats, operating a small business legally can only be approached step by step. Quoting again from the same businessman:

> 'In the last two years I haven't been able to be fully legal in business due to the cumbersome procedures. This furthermore caused the problem that I could not rent an office for my business. To settle the problem I was asked to pay TSh 100,000. At the evening the amount was increased to 200,000. This "kitu kidogo" ["something small"] was necessary to make my business *"a little more" official...*'

Also other businesspeople, donors and government officials admit that there are still many key impediments to private sector development, such as tariff barriers, nuisance taxes, bureaucratic red tape, non-transparent policies and laws governing property ownership as well as major weaknesses in the legal framework (e.g. World Bank (2000a, p. 8f)). Interviews from 2000 on still revealed that many people were complaining about the attitudes of bureaucrats, although the situation had improved compared with the late 1980s or early 1990s. For comments, see for instance quotes of businesspeople in World Bank (2001b) or an evaluation of 500 complaints on the performance of the Tanzania Revenue Authority (study undertaken by the Bank of Tanzania in spring 2001).

Rent-Seeking Strategies

Clearly, the slow pace of improving the business environment is not so much a reflection of capacity constraints in implementing reforms, but reflects to a large extent well-targeted rent-protecting activities. Many of the officials have been working for the government for a decade and more, enjoying privileged rent-capturing positions. Partial improvements, such as streamlining bureaucratic procedures, were often compensated by new cumbersome procedures. Because of the easy access to bribes and embezzling funds, in many settings effective rent-seeking costs would have to be increased substantially before the rent-seeking activity would lose its profitability. It is not surprising that the issue of improving the business environment had already been raised in the 1980s but very little had happened thereafter.

Two closely-related rent-seeking aspects are worth emphasising: first, *no success in abolishing binding constraints*, above all resistance against the creation of a well-functioning legal and judicial system; second, the implementation of *ineffective measures* which even extended rent-seeking opportunities. Other aspects which also explain the hostile business environment and rent-seeking strategies of the bureaucrats are discussed in the subsequent Sections b) and c).

Tanzania has a very *poor legal and judicial system*. The problem is systemic and affects all parts of civil life. Few people have access to legal services and one basically needs an informal network to be protected. Even advocates betray their own clients by receiving bribes from the opposite side (The Guardian, No. 944, 16 December 1997), and many court cases are dropped or left pending for years without a specific reason. The 1993 Report of the Controller and Auditor General, for instance, notes that sales tax was demanded through the court; these civil cases, however, had been pending since 1983 'for reasons apparently not clear' (OCAG (1994, p. 52)). A local businessman in Dar es Salaam commented on tax evasion: 'In many instances, there are no court cases, even though the names are known—being caught for tax evasion is a joke!' (personal communication in Dar es Salaam, November 1996).

The second rent-seeking strategy, i.e. the adoption of ineffective measures, becomes evident when looking at the poor and counterproductive performance of the *Investment Promotion Centre (IPC)*. To improve the business environment, in February 1990 the government issued the National Investment Promotion Policy. It was designed to 'create an environment which will attract and promote both local and foreign investments of both public and private ownership' (GoT (1991, p. 3)). Following the Act, the *Investment Promotion Centre (IPC)* was set up in June 1990.

As noted in the section on taxation (p. 324), IPC was quickly transformed into a major rent-seeking instrument. The problem finally cumulated in the severe tax crisis in 1993/94. Instead of doing away with complex procedures, the government had simply established another corruption-prone institution. The Investment Promotion Centre did not play a useful role in coordinating and facilitating private businesses; it administered a non-transparent and arbitrary system of tax exemptions. In other countries similar bodies have been created with similar problems.[145]

The policy of introducing exemptions in 1991 was equally questionable. As several authors emphasise, investment sweeteners such as tax holidays and tax exemptions are not effective if other conditions like adequate government policies and attitudes do not hold; they are like 'icing without a cake' (Doriye (1995, p. 17)) and they include serious trade-offs, in particular, as the case of Tanzania demonstrates, high macro costs (Ndulu and Wangwe (1997, p. 35)). Nevertheless, seen from the rent-seeker's perspective the measure was perfect and sustained rent-seeking income.

In 1997 the government finally passed a new investment law which unified all investment incentives in the country. In response to persistent complaints from the business environment, it converted IPC into a new body, the 'one-stop' Tanzania Investment Centre (TIC), with the goal of making the agency much more client-oriented and of making it an effective private investment promotion agency (World Bank (2000a, p. 14)).

There it is still a long way to go to further improve the business environment however, and resistance can be expected from different sources guided by different motives, as was for instance the case with liberalisation of the coffee market, where cooperative unions resisted private sector participation (Chapter 7.2). More recent donor projects such as the Privatisation & Private Sector Development Project (World Bank (1999b)) or the Accountability, Transparency

---

[145] An early example is the Agence de Promotion des Investissements (API) in Tunesia, which was established in the 1970s but later charged with corruption and favouritism (Nugent (1989, p. 312)).

and Integrity Project (World Bank (2000b)) give some hope that Tanzania will continue (albeit slowly) to move ahead. Substantial risks of a relapse nevertheless remain. This is also emphasised in the Private Sector Development project:

> 'Equally, the risk must be viewed as high that inadequate government commitment to necessary reforms (aimed at freeing up markets, increasing competition and removing bureaucratic controls), combined with inadequate governance and corrupt practices, may continue to constrain the business environment for private and foreign investment.' (World Bank (1999b, p. 26))

What matters is to differentiate more closely between 'stated' and 'true' commitment. As will be argued in the following sections, many of the signs which questioned true commitment were largely ignored in the 1980s and 1990s.

b) Civil Service: Persisting Resistance to Reforms on All Fronts

> *'Significant outstanding items on the bank reconciliation statements..., lack of control over the issue and accounting of advances and imprests, continued violation and disregard of financial regulations..., abject failure to rectify serious matters raised during audit. Consequently I have excluded all the accounts from my general certificate of correctness.'*
>
> *Controller and Auditor General, June 1991 on the accounts of the Ministry of Works (OCAG (1992, p. 130))*

To be able to carry out the most crucial functions of a state, any government has to make sure that sufficient revenues are collected and that expenditures are undertaken in a reasonably efficient way. The civil service, which is charged with making operative decisions and handling resources according to the specified purposes critically determines the success of government goals. However, in Tanzania during the 1980s and 1990s the government and the civil service were not able to carry out most of the stated goals in a satisfactory way. In particular the inadequate funding of critical expenditures resulted in high costs for society and the poor.

Three problems were identified in the 1980s: the inability to collect sufficient revenues, the over-extended base of activities the government wanted to finance and the failure to allocate scarce resources according to set priorities. The Public Expenditure Reviews (PERs), which have been regularly undertaken since 1989, documented these problems in detail (World Bank (1989b,1994c, 1997d, 1998b)).

The difficulty in raising sufficient revenues has been extensively discussed in Chapter 7.1. As argued there, individuals and companies are paying taxes, but a large share of the payments are captured by the 'parallel tax department', i.e. a lot of the money is either stolen or simply paid in the form of bribes to corrupt officials.

Having to operate with limited revenues, the situation is further aggravated by the *inadequate composition of public expenditures*—a problem observed in most sub-Saharan countries. The World Bank, for instance, emphasises that out of twenty-one African countries surveyed, only two had a reasonable degree of efficiency in spending in 1991 (World Bank (1994a, p. 126)). Common problems include 'underspending in the sectors most vital for development, funding of investment projects without allocation of sufficient resources to meet future recurrent charges, poor maintenance of existing capital stock, overspending on wages, and high levels of military spending' (p. 126). All these aspects have also been major constraints in Tanzania.

Finally, expenditures are also under pressure from *high demands to service the government's internal and external debt*. The internal debt is partly a result of the takeover of bad debts from the banking system, and the external debt is largely a reflection of the general economic and lending policy of the past twenty-five years. At the CG meeting in December 1997 President Mkapa emphasised that the country was spending five times more money to service only part of the external debt than it could afford for health and education combined (GoT (1997, p. 10)). Such a comparison is striking but it does not reflect Tanzania's ready available alternatives to improve its revenue collection and budget allocation, if only the leadership and a sufficiently large share of civil servants were committed to do so.

Government Goals and the Rent-Seeking Diagnosis

Already the 1987 Policy Framework Paper set the goal of improving the productivity of public expenditures by restructuring them to more fully fund high priority programmes and projects (GoT (1987, p. 12)). In the subsequent decade, the government made many more announcements to improve the budgeting process and to redefine the role of the government with a view to reducing its size and to confining itself to traditional functions which it could reasonably sustain (e.g., the June 1992 Budget Speech).

Parallel to such statements, donor complaints, in particular from CG meetings, document that there has been no or very little improvement over the years on many reform fronts. Comments such as 'many fundamental issues remain unresolved...most activities are badly underfunded' (World Bank (1988, p. 11)), 'most donors expressed concern about the slow progress in addressing the social sector issues' (World Bank (1992a, p. 10)), 'the budget process has not been taken seriously and expenditure controls remain weak... at the same time, all programmes are grossly underfunded' (Helleiner, et al. (1995, p. 30)) or 'sufficient funding has not been available in recent years even for the approximate 125 super core projects' (World Bank (1997d, p. 15)) are not exceptions but are typical representations of the situation.

As will be argued below, the problem of the government budget, characterised by the poor budgeting process, inadequate expenditure controls and the failure to enforce core budget priorities, is not just a reflection of Tanzania's limited means and skills to implement capacity-intensive reforms. It is to a considerable extent the result of well-entrenched rent-seeking forces and reflects a rent-seeking and patronage-related allocation of resources on all government levels and in all institutions. The method is based on two pillars. One, which is partly legitimate, partly less official (i.e. due to weak regulations) and in many instances illegal, is that of *budget allocation based on rent-seeking interests*. This is characterised by non-transparency, off-budget accounts and unrealistic planning. The second is the *clear absence of measures to curb the systematic and well-documented embezzlement of public funds*.

In 1989 major shortcomings in the budgeting process were raised. These included the unpredictability, irrelevance and non-transparency of the budget. The Public Expenditure Review (PER) of that year comments:

> 'Four fifths of the Ministry of Finance, Economic Affairs and Planning's recurrent budget is transferred from the Ministry as subventions or contingency amounts. The Ministry's vote thus constitutes a budget within the budget, an accommodation point for unforeseen requirements, parastatal rescue operations, and the general shortcomings of departmental expenditure estimation.' (World Bank (1989b, p. 42))

Almost ten years later, the budgeting process was still poor. The 1998 draft PER noted that symptoms such as the high levels of budget deviation, the fragmentation of the budget and the poor predictability of resource flows 'are very evident to any observer of the Tanzanian system' (World Bank (1998b, p. 8)). According to the report (p. 1) average deviations between budget and outturn had exceeded 25% and senior managers in line ministers perceived the budget, given the large variations in Other Charges, as 'essentially irrelevant with respect to anything but the wage bill'.

The deviations between budget and effective outcome were to some extent a result of a major underfunding of various key activities, which inevitable led to pressures for additional expenditures (e.g. IMF (1995, p. 12)), and they were a result of over-optimistic budget projections on the revenue side. The problems were documented in the 1997 PER:

> 'Budget projections were over-optimistic, thus evading the problem of attaining a realistic initial budget. The Government's political commitment to the budget figures it announced was weak: thus, there were frequently large reallocations early in the budget year. General expenditure discipline was poor, and budgets were also thrown off by expenditure arrears carried forward. Weaknesses in estimating, monitoring and accounting were another source of uncertainties.' (World Bank (1997d, p. viii))

Under-funding key activities in the budget, over-optimistic budget projections and large off-budget accounts provide an ideal ground for ex-post reallocations of the budget according to rent-seeking pressures and priorities. The general lack of transparency and missing checks and balances have been widely criticised by, among others, the Ambassador of the European Union at the CG meeting in Dar es Salaam in December 1997:

> 'I almost daily hear about different projects on which the decision making has been neither transparent nor clear. I realise, that the Tanzanian society is still missing the necessary democratic checks and balances. I must plead incredulity, when I hear that major investment projects and subsequent major commercial and even multilateral loan commitments can be approved by the executive without reference to Parliament. A Parliament which is otherwise charged with the scrutiny of Government's plans and its spending of public resources.' (European Union (1997, p. 2))

From a rent-seeking perspective, it is not surprising that the Country Assistance Evaluation of the World Bank finds the civil service reform to have been 'very much a donor driven process with little or no backing at the political level' (World Bank (2000c, p. 15)). Effective civil service reforms, including institutional reforms related to improving the budgeting process, aim to abolish rents and therefore provoke rent-seeking resistance. These reforms are not going to be supported by rent-seekers, let alone to be suggested by them. The main problem, however, is that many of the profiteers from the inefficient, rent-seeking system are also the ones charged implementing the rent-abating measures.

Below, three related aspects of rent-seeking patterns and resistance are outlined in more detail. First, the late reforms of civil service staffing; second, the failure to stick to budget priorities; and third, and most important, the apparent total indifference to address large-scale embezzlement of public funds.

Late Reforms of Civil Service Staffing: Stepping on a Patronage Network

Since independence the growth rate of *civil service staff* had been on average 50% above the growth rate of the population (World Bank (1994c, p. 20)). According to the World Bank (1989b, p. 41) the fastest manpower growth in the late 1970s and 1980s occurred in defence, foreign affairs and home affairs. Because the increase in revenue collection could not keep pace and because there were other demands, such as covering ever-increasing deficits from the parastatal sector, the rapid growth of the civil service reinforced the erosion of their pay and the neglect of other essential activities.

In the mid-1980s, the government was well aware of the problem. In the 1986 Budget Speech it announced a freeze on employment in all sectors of the civil service, except for teachers and medical personnel (GoT (1986a, p. 19)). This policy was again emphasised at the 1988 CG meeting (GoT (1988b, p. 12)), with the exception that the employment freeze did not include the revenue department. Also the 1989 Public Expenditure Review concluded that staffing levels should be critically reviewed (World Bank (1989b, p. 41)).

In 1987/88 employment in the civil service was around 300,000 and constituted half of total public sector employment in Tanzania, the rest being parastatal employees (GoT (1989, p. 12)). Despite the unaffordable size already recognised in the mid-1980s, in 1992 the civil service had grown to more than 350,000 employees (World Bank (1994c, p. 20)), which implied an increase of almost 20% since 1987/88.

Under pressure from donors the government finally initiated a comprehensive programme of civil service reform in 1992. It included three major elements: personnel control and management, reducing the size of the civil service and introducing pay reforms (World Bank (1994c, p. 21)). Progress however remained slow and reflected a stop and go policy. At the informal CG meeting held in Paris in July 1995, for instance, donors complained about the lack of progress in civil service reforms and noted that the dismissal of 50,000 civil servants, which also included the 'dismissal' of many ghost workers, was by far not enough (SDC (1995, p. 3)). Part of the problem was that the reform exercise excluded retrenchment from certain areas, such as the army.

By 1997, 20,000 ghost workers had been identified and removed from the payroll (World Bank (1997d, p. 28)), however without effectively addressing all remaining weaknesses. As noted in the draft of the subsequent Public Expenditure Review (World Bank (1998b, p. 46)), 'there is no means of ensuring that employees who resign or abscond are taken off the payroll and it has been estimated that 3% of salaries are "uncollected" and retained at pay stations...If this estimate is accurate, there could be as many as 8000 "ghost" workers on the payroll'.

Hardly anyone would dispute that a large amount of employment in Tanzania was based on patronage relations. Also the Warioba Report (1996, p. 28) criticises that the 'recruitment of junior staff has not followed established procedures; favouritism of relatives, friends and corruption have ruled the day'. To maintain an effective patronage network, the civil service system had to offer opportunities to appropriate income and to distribute benefits selectively. Besides direct embezzlement, which also included the 'employment' of ghost workers, the *structure of the pay* offered such opportunities. It was based on fine-tuning close to forty different *allowances*. As many of them reflected contingencies, they contributed to the poor predictability of public expenditures.

The problematic nature of Tanzania's system of allowances is well documented, for instance in the 1994 Public Expenditure Review (World Bank (1994c, p. 23f)) or in World Bank (1996a, p. 36f)). According to the PER, payroll-based allowances in the 1990s were more than 50% of the basic salary in most salary grades, in some grades they even constituted four times the basic pay. The difference appears to be even more pronounced in the parastatal sector, where senior employees received allowances that represent eight times their basic salary (ESRF (1996a, p. 30)).

On the one hand, excessive allowances result in a total lack of transparency in the remuneration structure, in particular a lack of horizontal equity. As noted in the 1994 PER 'within the same salary grade, it is possible for some civil servants to receive allowances that amount to as much as twenty times what others receive' (p. 24). On the other hand, excessive allowances offer easy opportunities to embezzle funds. For instance, receiving thirty days subsistence allowance for oneself, one's wife, ten children and dependants on being transferred from one place to another (OCAG (1990, p. 39)) is not in itself suspect. But as the OCAG report goes on to say that 'whilst the existence of the children and legality of the dependants could not be established, there was no evidence of the transfer having been effected', the rent-seeking nature of such allowances becomes obvious.

Seen from the patronage perspective, the system of allowances is ideal for assuring discretion and rewarding loyal subordinates. And since Tanzania used to have a rather extreme tax progression on income (to ensure, at least on paper, social equity), the non-transparent allowances were simply exempt from taxation. They contributed to an erosion of the tax base and given their unpredictability they weakened the budgetary control on the wage bill. According to personal communication (Dar es Salaam, April 1998), senior officials received travel allowances which were as high as US$260 per day. The amount is approximately the average annual income in Tanzania! It is not far-fetched to assume that this kind of reward system does not just encourage ghost trips, but evidently also a large number of unnecessary journeys motivated by rent-seeking.

Only at the end of the 1990s, after a lot of pressure from donors, were allowances rationalised and monetised with the salary—something which could have been accomplished much earlier.

Continued Failures in Adhering to Budget Priorities

More consequential for Tanzania's society than the non-transparent and rent-seeking driven system of civil service employment and remuneration was the country's inability to channel funds according to stated budget priorities. Despite explicit goals in virtually all official government statements on sectoral programmes since the mid-1980s, high priority programmes and projects were not funded in a satisfactory way until 1999. There seems to be lack of lobbying power, not only for the poor but also for the vast majority of the population.

The 1989 PER explicitly warned that earlier achievements from Nyerere's term of office were in danger of being lost (p. vi). The Economic and Social Action Programme of the same year (ERP II) further promised that in coming budgets the government would allocate additional resources to the social sectors, among others, to address the deteriorating quality in education 'as evidenced by the extremely poor performance...in both primary and secondary schools' (GoT (1989, p. 23)). Additionally, the Minister of Finance in the June 1993 Budget Speech said that due to the importance of the health sector, 'the Government will continue raising the budgetary allocation to pay for health services' (GoT (1993a, p. 23)). These statements sharply contrast with the assessment in the 1994 PER:

> 'Despite the pressing needs of these sectors for additional resources, the share of the social sectors in total public resources has been declining in recent years. To make matters worse, a large proportion of the limited resources that are available to these sectors is wasted on non-priority expenditures.' (World Bank (1994c, p. vi))

At the beginning of the 1970s Tanzania spent 14% of government funds on education and 7% for the army; in contrast, in 1986/87 it spent less than 7% on education and more than twice as much on the army (Campbell (1992, p. 155)). Even though a reduction of the army had been initiated in 1987, its size was still considered unaffordable in the 1990s, given the pressing and unmet needs in the social sector. For instance, the 1997 PER compared Tanzania's expenditure on defence with the expenditures on defence in Ghana and found that Tanzania spent four times more, if measured as a percentage of GDP (World Bank (1997d, p. 62)). The PER also noted that the Presidential Cost Cutting Commission from 1993 came up with many recommendations to reduce expenditures on administration and defence, but in subsequent years hardly any of them were implemented (p. iv, 63). On the contrary, in the financial year 1997/98, for instance, the army even managed to buy 750 new cars on credit! The deal was part of a package of TSh 17 billion, which had bypassed the official budget and had therefore not been scrutinised by the parliament (personal communication in Dar es Salaam, April 1998).

Given the lack of lobbying power other than donor pressure, it is not surprising that the 1997 PER found that the moderate increases achieved in social sector spending between 1990 and 1996 were just sufficient to preserve the low level of real per capita expenditure on education, but not for health (p. 42).

Clearly, insufficient social sector expenditures constrain the development of human capital in Tanzania. The 1994 PER found that the country spent only 50 cents per capita for preventive healthcare (which is according to the World Bank the most cost-effective use of public resources) instead of the recommend US$4.20 for Low Income Countries (World Bank (1994c, p. viii-ix, 36f)). As for education, Tanzania's secondary school enrolment rate was the lowest in the world and only one fourth of the average for sub-Saharan Africa and one tenth of the average for the group of Low Income Countries (p. 4).

As noted earlier, the problem is not just a reflection of a general underfunding of priority sectors, but also the result of a misallocation of resources within these sectors. For instance, all PERs emphasised that actual expenditure patterns showed gross underfunding of non-wage expenditures (in particular 'other charges', which include critical inputs such as textbooks and medicines) relative to personal emoluments (e.g. World Bank (1997d, p. 20), World Bank (1998b, p. 1)). Furthermore, as argued in the PERs, secondary and tertiary education include the financing of many non-essential expenditures such as student boarding and welfare expenditures. This results in a rather inequitable use of public funds since mostly children from wealthier families enjoy higher education. According the 1994 PER (p. viii), 'the costs of sending one student to university in Tanzania is not sending 238 students to primary school' (or 21 to secondary school). The trade-off is particularly striking as the greatest externalities of education are estimated to come from primary and lower secondary levels (World Bank (1997d, p. 45)). Problems are similar in the health sector, where the emphasis is still on curative activities and not on the much more cost-effective preventive healthcare.

Finally, the scope to improve the quality of social services remains large. According to personal communication at a donor agency (Dar es Salaam, December 1997), the University in Dar es Salaam had a student-to-teacher ratio of only three to one and the Muhimbili hospital had three employees for each bed! The World Bank (1994c, p. viii) notes that 'within the existing resource envelope for secondary education, the enrolment rate could be quadrupled from the current 4% to 16% (the average for sub-Saharan Africa) if student welfare expenses were eliminated and if teachers in public schools were required to work additional hours'.

Problems are similar in other priority sectors, such as *road infrastructure.* The availability of good roads critically determines transaction costs and thereby the profitability of economic activities. However, maintaining roads in Tanzania was severely neglected in the 1980s and 1990s. Because of the importance of roads and the high costs they actually caused in Tanzania, the example will be outlined below in more detail.

In 1990 more than half of trunk roads (national and international roads which link several regions) and regional roads were rated as poor and only 15% of trunk and 10% of regional roads were in good condition (Lyatuu (1998, p. 46)). It is well known, also among officials in developing countries, that it costs much more to let a road entirely deteriorate and subsequently rebuild it, than to keep it maintained in a fairly good condition over the entire period. Some time after a new road is constructed, the first cracks and potholes will appear. As long as these are relatively small and not too old, little expense is needed to repair the road. However, the longer repairs are delayed, the more cars will pass over the damaged sections and the larger the damage will become. Water will get into the holes and cracks and start to soften and wash away the foundation. At this stage major and expensive repairs are necessary. If repairs are still postponed, the damage will increase further and additional holes will appear. The road becomes impassable, particularly during the rainy seasons, and would have to be reconstructed from scratch for ordinary cars to be able to use it again.

This relation between timing and costs of maintenance holds for virtually any infrastructure object. Once the roof of a building leaks, little time will pass before major damages occur; or if holes in the insulation of electricity cables are not sealed, the metal will oxidise and the cables will have to be replaced entirely. Figure 7-9 shows this relationship in a stylised and simplified way.

Figure 7-9: Costs of Maintenance Versus Costs of Reconstruction

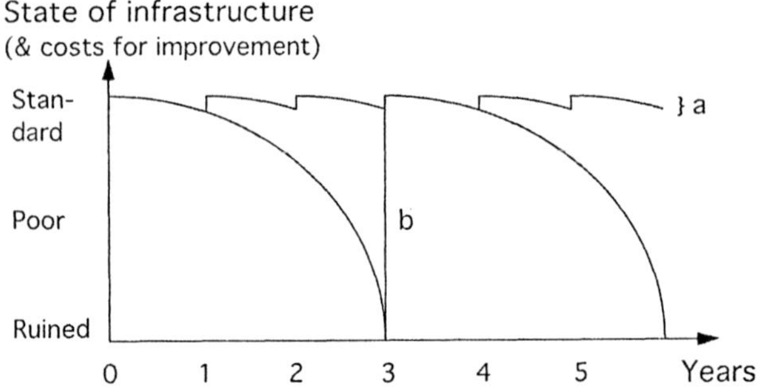

The diagram indicates the relation between the frequency of maintenance and the costs of maintenance. In most instances, doing maintenance on a regular basis turns out to be far cheaper than waiting till the infrastructure has deteriorated badly. In the diagram spending 'a' on an annual basis is clearly cheaper than spending 'b' every third year.

Source: Drawn according to personal communication at the Regional Engineers Office, Arusha, April 1988

Much infrastructure in developing countries, including infrastructure funded by donors, has suffered from the deplorable and highly inefficient cycle of neglect and reconstruction. Given the importance of roads in Tanzania and the experience of poor maintenance in the past, the government established in 1991 and 1992 a Road Fund designated for funding maintenance of trunk roads, regional roads and district roads. However, despite readily available funds financed by a fuel levy, in the mid-1990s the country was only undertaking little more than 10% of the required maintenance. The unfavourable outcome reflected a combination of legal and illegal rent-seeking activities, severe budget constraints and a poor process of resource allocation.

Figure 7-10 shows the allocation of Road Fund Collections from the Treasury to the Ministry of Works (MoW) and the Prime Minister's Office (PMO), the former being responsible for trunk and regional roads, the latter for district roads. Until the financial year 1994/95 allocations from the new Road Fund were close to collections; they dropped, however, sharply thereafter. The missing funds were used for other purposes such as debt service or paying meal allowances to soldiers (personal communication in Dar es Salaam, April 1998). Only after a lot of pressure from the donor community did allocations increase again at the end of the 1990s.

Matters are in fact even worse than presented in Figure 7-10 since the diagram only shows a small part of the problem. According to personal communication at the Ministry of Works and the European Embassy in Dar es Salaam, as well as at the Regional Engineer's Office in Arusha (April 1998), very little of the funds finally made it to the road to be used for maintenance. Given the severe budget constraints of the Ministry of Works, between one third and one half of the Road Fund released by the Treasury was 'misused' for contracts and allowances. Of the little which was finally channelled to the regions, again a sizeable share was spent on other purposes than road maintenance.

Figure 7-10: Road Fund Collection and Actual Release (TSh bn)

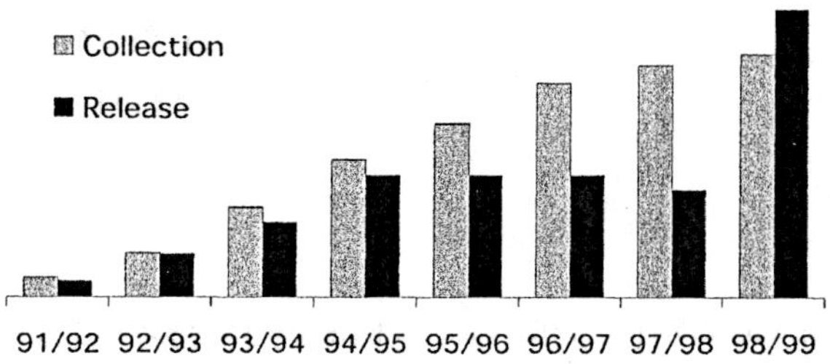

Collection
Release

91/92 92/93 93/94 94/95 95/96 96/97 97/98 98/99

Year	Collection (1)	Release (2)	(2) in % (1)
91/92	3.1	2.6	82%
92/93	7.0	6.9	98%
93/94	14.2	11.9	84%
94/95	21.7	19.5	90%
95/96	27.4	19.4	71%
96/97	33.9	19.5	57%
97/98	36.7	17.1	47%
98/99	38.4	45.4	118%

Source: Data on collection and release for financial years 1991/92 to 1995/96 from World Bank (1998b, p. 101, US$ values converted into TSh) and for 1996/97 to 1998/99 from Berger (2000, Table 0)

Regional offices were responsible for many different activities, for which there was no money set aside. If they had to undertake renovations on a house or remove cars from an accident scene, they often took the money out of the Road Fund. All these payments were treated as overheads but are in fact operational expenses. Overheads consumed about 50 to 60% of the Road Fund money at the regional level. Half of this amount took the form of 'legal' and illegal corruption. Deliberately creating situations to capture allowances, even though there are easy ways to avoid such expenses, is an example of the former. Working on holidays doubles wages and driving to the construction site although there is no need guarantees extra income. Direct theft is also rampant. A two-year audit report on the Road Funds, for instance, noted that the Regional Engineer's Office in Arusha had written off 194,503 litres of fuel as 'loss through evaporation' (OCAG (1997a, p. 16)).

All in all, out of the original amount collected with the Road Fund, after having passed through several layers of bureaucracy (Treasury, Ministry of Works and Regional Offices), in the period 1995/96 to 1997/98 only 10-25% of the Road Fund was effectively spent for road maintenance.[146] This sharply contrasts with the amount needed, which is approximately US$90 million (or more than TSh 50 billion) per year (e.g. Marmo, Kimambo and Andreski (1998, p. 16) or World Bank (1998b, p. 100)). Arusha, for instance, would require TSh 215 million a month to maintain its 1800 kilometres of roads. Monthly allocations at the beginning of 1998, however, were only at TSh 30 million.

With so few funds, it is clearly not possible to carry out effective maintenance. Even worse, given the severe budget constraints at the ministries and regional offices, the country has been continuously forced into rehabilitation rather than maintenance. If a road is no longer passable, it is difficult to argue that funds should not be spent there but on the roads which are still in a fairly

[146] The Road Fund Collection is 100%. In 1997/98 47% was released by the Treasury; 50% thereof was released by the Ministry of Works (low-end estimate); 40% thereof (deducting overhead expenditures) was released in the Regions. This is $0.47 \cdot 0.5 \cdot 0.4 = 9.4\%$. Alternatively, using high-end estimates and figures on collections in 1995/96: $0.71 \cdot 0.66 \cdot 0.5 = 24.9\%$.

good condition. A road has to deteriorate severely before pressures are sufficiently high to release funds. This is exactly the high-cost strategy outlined in Figure 7-9, i.e. the quality of the road has to drop beyond the level of 'poor' before action is taken.

Adverse pressures are similar in other priority sectors, such as health, where the shift from curative to preventive healthcare had not taken place by 1998, although donors had repeatedly been urging the government since the late 1980s. Also here it is evidently difficult to argue that health funds should not be spent on a sick or injured patient but rather on healthy people.

It appears that the country is trapped in a Prisoner's Dilemma situation. Marmo, Kimambo and Andreski (1998, p. 15) estimated that the lack of effective road maintenance in Tanzania costs the country more than four times the maintenance costs, i.e. US$365 million annually or US$1 million per day—the major part as vehicle operating costs and loss of assets of the existing (reconstructed) roads. They conclude (p. 17):

> 'This confirms the famous World Bank dictum that "a country pays for a good network whether it has one or not".'

It is against this background that donors have pushed for increased lobbying power by strengthening the Road Fund and making it independent of the pressures of the remaining public budget. It appears meanwhile that the strategy has succeeded at least at the first and second level (allocation to Ministry of Work and regional offices). However, where a lot of work still remains to be done with legal and illegal embezzlement. The next section looks at the latter aspect in more detail.

Failure to Sanction and Prevent Embezzling of Public Funds

The costs to Tanzania's society of the large-scale embezzlement of public funds are probably as high as those stemming from problems in adhering to budget priorities. As mentioned earlier, every year the Office of the Controller and Auditor General (OCAG) produces an independent audit review of public accounts, reporting to the parliament whether government revenues have been properly collected and utilised. Even though the OCAG does not audit all accounts in detail, the documentation of embezzlement is impressive. Particularly if one takes into consideration that, given the prevalence of corruption, part of their work is most likely also affected by side payments from audited 'clients'. Comments such as 'wrong computation resulted in non-collection', 'names had been erroneously deleted', 'wrong application of exchange rates', 'salaries wrongly paid to retired employees', 'no competitive quotations', 'cost has been very high, the quality very low', 'the whereabouts were unknown', 'goods paid for but not received', 'government vehicles sent to private garages for repairs over three years not returned', 'payment postponed for one month, ...could not confirm collection two years later', etc. give an idea of the modes of embezzlement. In particular the Ministry of Works, which every year approves huge contracts worth millions of dollars, has constantly received major complaints. The lead quote on page 396 is just an example of an arbitrary year; the same statements are repeated in previous and subsequent reports, apparently without any consequences.

The many methods for stealing and embezzling funds occur with public expenditures as well as in collecting public revenues. Table 7-18 surveys different categories of anomalies described at the introduction of the annual OCAG reports, which will be discussed below.

Table 7-18: Selected 'Anomalies' in Public Accounts Identified in OCAG Reports

Standard of Accounting (1)	Despite my adverse comments in previous years' reports, *little or no action* seems to have been taken by Accounting Officers *to rectify the recurring weakness* in accounting control. The implication of this situation is that in many cases the *proper utilisation of public money cannot be demonstrated.*
Unvouched / Improperly Vouched Expenditures (2)	In all cases of inadequate vouching the authenticity of the expenditure incurred and the purpose for which the payments were made *cannot be ascertained* and *fraud or misappropriation* of the sums involved *cannot be ruled out.*
Outstanding Advances and Imprests (3)	In several cases Accounting Officers do not have adequate records of the sums advanced and repayments made, and are *unable to exercise effective control*, in other cases although records exist *no attempt appears to be made to enforce the appropriate regulation*, including surcharge of 10% penalty.
Poor Control over Purchase and Accounting of Stores (4)	The control...continues to be a cause for concern...*contrary to financial regulations*, payments had been made for goods which were not delivered...; purchases were made *without proper authority* ...
Losses of Cash and Stores (5)	Annexures...depict a *serious trend and widespread incidences of embezzlement* of cash and stores....In addition, I am aware of many cases where Accounting Officers *fail to report losses* of cash and stores. *Urgent action* to eliminate losses of cash and stores *is needed.*
Projects Appraisal and Performance (6)	As I commented...in my previous report...*concern* is mounting especially during Public Accounts Committee hearings, *whether Full value for money is being derived from large amounts spent* on many government projects/works carried out in the country.
Payroll Integrity (7)	For quite some time, the Government has been facing *serious problems regarding its payroll integrity.* Basically, it is not certain whether expenditure on personal emoluments (item 1100) goes to the intended recipients. Evidence abounds indicating that salary payments *continue* to be made to ghost workers, retrenchees, deceased, absconded and retired workers.
Payments made on Proforma Invoices (8)	In each year's audit report I refer to the increasing number of payments made on the strength of proforma invoices and the difficulty encountered in verifying the property of much of these expenditure in the absence of adequate subsequent supporting information. *Little action to rectify this anomaly has been evidenced.*
Bank Reconciliation Statements (9)	I have *repeatedly* referred to the extent to which non-production of bank reconciliation statements has affected the audit certification of the accounts. In addition there is real danger that *non-completion of reconciliation statements could be deliberately effected to conceal misappropriation of public funds.*

Response to Audit Reports (10)	Generally, *response to audit' reports and queries has been particularly poor. Accounting Officers pay scant regard* to matters reported upon, suggesting indifference to matters that demand financial accountability over funds...

Source: Introduction of Controller and Auditor General Report of Financial Year 1996, p. 6-9

The first item, very poor *accounting standards (1),* has always been a characteristic feature of bookkeeping in Tanzania, at least in government organisations. Major delays in reconciling and submitting accounts, as well as subsequent 'qualified' or 'adverse' ratings, have been widespread in the ministerial and regional votes audited by the OCAG and, as will be discussed in Chapter 8.2, are equally prevalent in parastatal accounts. Table 7-19 surveys the certificates issued by the OCAG in recent years. On average 60% of accounts audited had been adversely classified.

Table 7-19: Summary of Audit Certificates Issued

	Total	Clean			In % of	Qualified			In % of	Adverse			In % of
		Min.	Reg.	All	Total	Min.	Reg.	All	Total	Min.	Reg.	All	Total
FY94	220	46	28	74	34%	8	4	12	5%	91	43	134	61%
FY95	197	40	24	64	32%	24	4	28	14%	53	52	105	53%
FY96	214	69	31	100	47%	10	8	18	8%	55	41	96	45%
FY97	210	48	20	68	32%	4	10	14	7%	82	46	128	61%
FY98	154	31	9	40	26%	11	0	11	7%	43	60	103	67%
FY99	192	25	5	30	16%	36	3	39	20%	51	72	123	64%

Min.: Accounts of Ministries/Departments, Reg.: Accounts of regions

Source: Appendix in Controller and Auditor General Reports of Financial Years 1994 to 1999 (data for FY99 directly collected at the OCAG in Dar es Salaam since the pages were missing in the report)

Ignorance of proper accounting is one explanation for the problem. However, much more obvious is the rent-seeking hypothesis, i.e. poor accounting standards do not reflect civil servants' *real* inability but their *strategic* inability. Late submission and poor standards are the backbone of large-scale embezzlement. Rent-seekers have to obscure their activities; they have to disguise information that may expose suspicious transactions.

The OCAG reports are full of complaints on bad procedures that make it impossible for audited institutions to control the proper collection and utilisation of revenues. 'Poor supervision over payments procedures, resulting in overpricing, wrong calculations, double payments', 'there is no system in use to correlate the late payment of the levy and the imposition of addition levy', 'the Department is not keeping any records to follow up disposal', 'there is no procedure in use to ensure that the value of benefits is actually taxed', 'the report disclosed numerous irregularities and weaknesses in the accounting system of the Ministry', are just a sample of what was mentioned in OCAG reports.

Unvouched expenditures (2) arise when there is 'a complete absence of payment voucher and other documentary evidence to substantiate the authenticity of the expenditure'; *improperly vouched expenditure*, in contrast, occurs if there is a payment voucher which is not supported by other documentation such as local purchase order or invoice (OCAG (1997b, p. 7)). Obviously, particularly in the latter case, there is suspicion of forgery.

Most of the *outstanding advances and imprests (3)* are personal advances and 'safari' imprests (i.e. advances for official journeys). The former have to be paid back in specified instalments within a certain period, the latter need to be cashed up within two weeks after returning to the office. Table 7-20 provides an example from the Ministry of Works (MoW). Even though comments related to the MoW after 1991 are not as extreme, the problem has not entirely vanished.

Table 7-20: Comments on Outstanding Advances and Imprests, Ministry of Works

1987: (159/97)	In view of the above, it is evident that there is *total lack of control over advances and imprests* and I do not hesitate to say that the *Government stands to lose substantial sum of money unless immediate remedial measures are taken* to bring the situation under control.
1988: (173/116)	This Ministry has exerted *little effort, if any* to clear other advances appearing in the accounts, some of which date back to 1980. The account was not being analysed/reconciled... Lack of control over safari imprests in the regions has assumed *alarming proportions and a loss of considerable magnitude cannot be ruled out.*
1991: (227/132)	Despite my comments and recommendations...of my previous report...the Ministry *still lacks proper control* over the issue and accounting for advances and imprests. The worsening trend is shown below...Urgent corrective measures are required to rectify this trend, *which is fraud with misuse of public funds.*

Source: Controller and Auditor General Reports of Financial Years 1987, 1988 and 1991 (in parentheses indication of paragraph and page in respective volume)

Poor control over purchase and accounting of stores (4) is mentioned in all OCAG reports to 'continue to be a cause for concern' and *losses of cash and stores (5)* highlight in each report 'a serious trend and widespread incidences of embezzlement'. Finally, with increasing computerisation computer fraud appeared as a new way of embezzling cash and stores.

Item (6) of Table 7-18, *project appraisal and performance,* is relatively new and reflects the first step to complement financial audits by performance audits. The latter are much more powerful for detecting fraud related to delivering lower than agreed quality—a common method of rent appropriation which is often part of an informal kickback agreement and a way of illegitimately winning a tender. In fact, the procurement of goods and services, which includes procurement through tendering processes, is a major area of embezzlement in Tanzania (see for instance complaints in the Warioba Report (1996, p. 36f and 209f)). Many donor projects are also directly affected. According to personal communication with donors in (Dar es Salaam, March 1998), in particular the World Bank has had problems with their tendering procedures, losing approximately 5-10% of project money through corruption (with other donors, losses are estimated to be in the order of 1%).

In an environment motivated by rent-seeking it is not uncommon to find local bidders competing in tendering processes even though they do not own a company. They aim at capturing advance payments for personal use, and outsource the work if they win, mostly at the cost of major delays so that they can maximally exploit the implicit credit (personal communication with building contractor, Dar es Salaam, April 1998).

Tanzania does not lack professional advisers to evaluate bidders and to guarantee an efficient outcome of the tender process. Professional advice, however, becomes irrelevant whenever corruption enters a deal. A striking example is the case of the New Bagamoyo Road, which has been described in detail in the Warioba Report (1996, p. 253-61). Despite much professional advice and many reports, the Principal Secretary of the Ministry of Works in collusion with the Minister, the Director of Roads and the Chief Engineer of Rural Roads awarded the contract to a totally inexperienced and unprofessional bidder. Even after several noncompliances, major delays and vehement protests, the Ministry continued to refuse to cancel the contract. By the time the contract period had expired, only 4% of the work had been done.

The Warioba Report actually intended to give a clear example of high-level involvement in apparently corrupt practices. But the case was never published in full since the more embarrassing pages (257, 259 and 261) 'surprisingly' went missing when the Warioba Report was printed. These pages include the president's advice to cancel the contract, the renewed deferment of a deadline, the strong protest of project consultants to the Ministry and the final reference to the high costs incurred to the nation. Appendix A shows the full text, which was obtained at the World Bank in Dar es Salaam in 1997 from an unpublished pre-print version (missing pages highlighted).

The cost overruns of the New Bagamoyo Road finally mounted to 152%. Such overruns are not an exception in Tanzania. Once a company has won a tender, extra money is often stolen with large variations in price and substandard work. As documented in the Warioba Report and summarised in Table 7-21, throughout the 1990s the government in Tanzania tolerated large cost escalations in their road projects.[147]

The Warioba Report (1996, p. 249) additionally finds 'enormous variations in unit costs...of roads whose contracts were concluded during the same period', 'abnormally big variations in the scope of work from that originally agreed', 'the repetitive nature of the reasons which caused the escalations in...costs', as well as 'overextended delays' and 'surface failures...shortly after they were completed'. Even though these shortcomings are not direct proof of corruption, they are a very strong indication thereof. At least the Warioba Report makes a very clear assessment in its executive summary (p. 35):

---

[147] Note this is only part of the costs, as the table does not quantify the costs of lower quality.

Table 7-21: Cost Escalation in Road Projects

Road	Time of execution	Increase in cost	Road	Time of execution	Increase in cost
Igawa-Igurusi	1992-96	6%	Kongowe-Mji-Mwema	1992-93	101%
Bukombe-Isaka	1991-92	20%	Himo-Moshi-Arusha	1993-	117%
Songea-Mbinga	1991-94	41%	Igawa-Mbeya Songwe	1988-93	136%
Tunduma-Sumbawanga	n.a.	43%	Dar-Chalinze	1990-	150%
Ibanda-Uyole	1991-94	65%	New Bagamoyo Road	1991-95	152%
Kobero-Nyakasanza	1992-96	66%	Sam Nujoma Road	1992-96	154%
Usagara-Lusahunga	1991-95	69%	Kilwa Road	1992-	165%
Kibiti-Ikwiriri	1991-92	70%	Shekilango Road	1992-	176%
Melela-Mikumi	1988-91	87%	Old Bagamoyo Road	1991-94	183%
Himo-Tarakea Tanga-Horohoro	1993-96	96%	Pugu-Chanika-Mbagala	1992-	353%

Source: Warioba Report (1996, p. 250-51)

> 'The Commission is convinced that these increases in cost have been used to defraud government and justify acts of "grand corruption". Indeed there are no administrative or legal steps which have been taken against those who were associated with these projects even if it is only to know whether the reasons behind the increases were due to negligence, professional ineptitude or corruption.'

Evidently Tanzania's society does not get full value for money in many of its projects. The outcome is particularly regrettable considering that the road sector has not received sufficient resources in the past and is trapped in a highly inefficient cycle of neglect and reconstruction (recall Figure 7-9). Given the high level of corruption, there is no easy way out. Real commitment from senior officials to address these problems cannot be expected if they are themselves deeply involved in corrupt deals. And without commitment additional rules and regulations will do very little to improve the situation, as they will remain unenforced. The Warioba Report also emphasised the total disregard of existing regulations in construction contracts, which were, according to the Commission 'quite good and the product of long proven experience' (p. 34). All in all, the problem of missing value for money, which is meant to be detected by quality audits, is likely to persist well into the present millennium.

Taking up the thread of the overview in Table 7-18, item (7), *payroll integrity*, indicates embezzlement concerned with wages. This issue has already been discussed earlier (p. 399f). *Payments made on proforma invoices (8)* and the non-production of *bank reconciliation statements (9)* are to a large extent a reflection of the rent-seeking strategy to hide information and to obscure transactions. The Warioba Report (1996, p. 37) also explicitly pointed out that 'the procurement of imaginary goods through the use of Proforma Invoices is widespread because of this procedure'. In general, the non-delivery of data (vouchers, records, reconciliation statements, etc.) was complained about very frequently in the OCAG reports. Table 7-22 displays a few arbitrarily selected comments from the years 1987 to 1993.

Table 7-22: Examples of Non-Production and Non-Delivery of Records

1987: (161/97)	*No physical or documentary evidence had been made available* to audit to confirm receipt of services/goods paid for and *my 45 queries raised on this matter have not been replied to.*
1988: (55/50)	Loss of cash: It appears that bank reconciliation statements in respect of that particular Deposit account are *not being compiled*, thus the *theft would have remained undetected* if it had not been revealed by a businessman.
1989: (52/47)	Unsatisfactory keeping of records: The Regional Customs and Sales tax office, Mara (Musoma) was visited twice in January, 1987 and November 1989, but *in both occasions audit of records...could not be carried out effectively* because these records were not filed properly, thus they could not be produced for audit.
1990: (48/63)	[Sales tax records] were not produced for audit, showing that the *department is not taking effective measures* to keep assessment records in an orderly manner ready for audit. Two queries had been issued in this matter and are still outstanding to date.
1991: (50/47)	*[No] reconciliation has been done* by the Customs headquarters for any month...In the above circumstances I am not able to confirm that all Customs revenue collections by the Customs and Sales Tax Department have actually reached the Commissioner's revenue account...*This is a matter of grave concern and needs to be remedied forthwith.*
1992: (68/67)	Bank reconciliation Statements which are required to be prepared monthly by each region and the Headquarters were not prepared and submitted for audit examination. *This is a very serious omission* on the part of the management, as such neglect *could be the cause for not discovering frauds* in time and to prevent its re-occurrence.
1993: (262/201)	Doubtful payments: ...documents to authenticate these payments were *not furnished to me.* I am concerned at this anomaly, a *repetition* of paragraph 219.3 *of my last year's report.*

Source: Controller and Auditor General Reports of Financial Years 1987 to 1993 (in parentheses indication of paragraph and page in respective volume)

Finally, the last item displayed in Table 7-18, the poor *response to audit reports (10)* provides the most evident support of the rent-seeking hypothesis for embezzlement. The disregard of OCAG complaints has already been mentioned several times (see, in particular, Tables 7-4 to 7-6 in Chapter 7.1), and many of the comments listed above further document this aspect. Resistance by rent-seekers becomes manifest on two levels: first, by *not-responding to audit queries*, and second, by *disregarding recommendations and complaints* once improper collection or utilisation of revenues has been identified.

Table 7-23 surveys an example of queries resulting from test audits of customs records published in the ten OCAG reports between 1988 and 1997 before the Customs and Tax Department was removed from the Ministry and the Tanzania Revenue Authority was created. For each report, the table indicates the number of outstanding enquiries and shows a brief analysis of the queries that have been settled during the year. Looking at the entire ten-year period, on average more than half (i.e. 1508 or 55%) out of 2728 settled queries were pending two years and longer; with an average delay of five years; more than a third (i.e. 985 or 36%) were pending at least three years (average delay 6.6 years).

Table 7-23: Audit Queries on Assessments and Collections of Customs Revenue

Queries issued in year:	No. of queries	Still outstanding audit queries in OCAG report published in 1988	1989	1990	1991	1992	1993	1994	1995	1996	1997
FY77/78	300	30	29	20	20	1	1	1	1	1	
FY78/79	278	30	25	18	18						
FY79/80	279	31	26	7	7	1					
FY80/81	334	49	47	24	22	17	12	12	12	11	1
FY81/82	152	37	36	30	29	25	25	*25*[a]	25	13	1
FY82/83	133	33	31	28	26	20	*20*[b]	*20*[c]	20	11	1
FY83/84	308	60	48	37	28	28	27	22	17	9	4
FY84/85	258	100	89	79	71	62	43	37	30	21	7
FY85/86	260	143	79	51	44	36	22	22	13	3	1
FY86/87	245	217	96	69	59	52	48	46	28	22	14
FY87/88	406		369	202	153	111	106	95	89	86	23
FY88/89	520			499	318	195	176	153	137	127	52
FY89/90	342				342	196	131	112	96	89	66
FY90/91	421					406	255	206	171	165	96
FY91/92	312						310	215	159	150	129
FY92/93	311							294	169	130	112
FY93/94	213								197	133	82
FY94/95	152									135	90
FY95/96	120										120
Total outstanding:		730	875	1064	1137	1150	1176	1260	1164	1106	799
Queries settled in previous year[d]			261	331	269	408	286	227	309	210	427
of which delayed[f] ≥2 years[e]			103	143	88	247	133	115	168	129	382
(average delay)			(3.2)	(5.7)	(3.3)	(4.7)	(3.8)	(3.5)	(4.2)	(6.5)	(6.6)
of which delayed[f] ≥3 years[e]			39	116	39	124	68	66	112	90	331
(average delay)			(5.3)	(6.6)	(4.9)	(7.3)	(5.7)	(4.7)	(5.3)	(8.5)	(7.3)

a, b, c: The OCAG report indicates 23, 19 and 18, however in the subsequent year the number increased again.
d: Outstanding queries in previous year + new queries – outstanding in current year, e.g. 261 = 730+406-875.
e: Excluding settled queries issued in the two (resp. three) previous years, e.g. 103 = 261-(406-369)-(217-96).
f: Weighted average of settled queries, e.g. 3.2 = (1·10+5·9+5·8+2·7+1·6+2·5+12·4+11·3+64·2) / 103.

Source: Controller and Auditor General Reports of Financial Years 1987 to 1996 (Section Customs and Sales Tax Department, Ministry of Finance)

Apparently hardly any effort has been made to clear these large arrears of outstanding audit queries. The problems are similar in other departments and ministries. For instance, outstanding queries at the Ministry of Communication, Transport and Works averaged more than 1300 from 1987 to 1990. After the split of the Ministry, outstanding queries at the Ministry of Works continued to average more than 700 in the period 1991-96. Looking at the entire period from 1987-96, 80% of the settled queries were pending at least two years, 60% at least three years.

What remains unanswered in the OCAG reports is the specific outcome of queries that were completed. Given the large delays, it can be assumed that some of them were not truly settled but simply closed and the funds 'written off'. On the other hand, one could equally assume that unofficial side payments may have influenced the outcome of the settled queries (though this is unlikely if there are no consequences anyway).

Besides the non-response to audit queries, another obvious indication of embezzlement is the *apparent disregard of recommendations and complaints.* The OCAG reports are full of comments on this matter: 'the Chief Accountant is apparently not interested in replying to audit observations', 'During the year under review no improvement was made since not a single loss was finalised', 'Most of the issues raised in this report are a repetition of similar matters made in my previous years' reports', 'I am perturbed at the persistent laxity on the part of the Customs Administration in the levying and collection of government revenue', 'Despite my repeated adverse comments in the previous years, unvouched and improperly vouched expenditure in the Ministry has assumed alarming proportions', 'It is now over three years since the suspension order was effected but no decision has been taken...Meanwhile, procedures are avoiding tax using the declared price loophole', etc.

Following up a single example makes the absence of effective action even more evident and transparent. The extreme case shown in Table 7-24 is self-explanatory. After 1996, the Customs and Tax Department was removed from the Treasury and transformed into the semi-independent Tanzania Revenue Authority. Its annual audit reports are no longer included in the main volume of the OCAG and they have a different structure. Whether the problem of missing customs documents was solved after 1996 could not be assessed; the matter has simply disappeared in the newly-structured audit reports.

Table 7-24: CAG Complaints on the Non-Production of Customs Records

1987: (40/40)	*Missing Customs documents* has remained a big problem and it appears that the situation is *getting out of control*...I am very much concerned that an average of 200 entries are missing each month...
1988: (38/42)	The position regarding missing entries has *not improved*... The issue had *repeatedly been mentioned* in my previous reports and despite *promises* by the Department that action is being taken to improve the situation, *the problem is persisting.*
1989: (39/42)	The Dar es Salaam longroom alone accounts for 5,427 of the missing entries showing that the *measures* which are being taken by the Department to rectify the situation *are not effective.*
1990: (37/50)	Apparently *no serious effort is being made* by the Department to rectify the situation *in spite of my comments* on this issue in my previous reports.
1991: (49/46)	The Department does *not seem to have taken any serious efforts* to improve the situation *in spite of my comments* on this issue in my previous reports.
1992: (43/57)	*Despite mention having been made* in my previous reports of non-production of Customs documents for audit *the situation has still remained unsatisfactory.*
1993: (37/47)	The issue of missing customs documents has repeatedly featured in my previous reports but *no positive signs* are seen on the part of the Department in rectifying the situation.
1994: (41/54)	Despite mention having been made in my previous reports of non-production of Customs documents for audit, *the situation has not improved.*

1995: (39/55)	Despite mention having been made in my previous reports of non-production of Customs documents for audit, *the situation has still remained unsatisfactory.*
1996: (41/57)	Despite mention having been made in my previous reports of non-production of Customs documents for audit, the *situation has not improved.*

Source: Controller and Auditor General Reports of Financial Years 1987 to 1996 (in parentheses indication of paragraph and page in respective volume)

All in all, the reference to the annual audit reports of the Controller and Auditor General and the comments in the Warioba Report unmistakably demonstrated that Tanzania's society suffered from large-scale embezzlement of public funds. To be sure, some of the disorder and irregularities identified in the reports do not necessarily indicate embezzlement. Some people lack the capacity for proper accounting, and poorly organised offices and sloppy work attitudes are likely to explain part of the picture.

Still, the reports do not show the entire scale of embezzlement. Many of the complaints, like the queries mentioned in Table 7-23 are based on test audits and not on an evaluation of all records. More importantly, if Tanzania has an incentive system that makes it one of the most corrupt countries in the world there is no reason to assume that auditors in Tanzania should be exempt from that temptation. They face similar incentives and constraints as other bureaucrats and therefore most likely do not report all incidences (unless nobody really cares what they write). For these reasons, this section did not quantify the level of embezzlement; it only intended to show that it exists and to demonstrate that embezzlement is widespread and most likely substantial.

That the same complaints constantly recurred in the OCAG reports between 1986 and 1996 suggests that the rent-seeking situation of bureaucrats did not change much during this period. Embezzlement appears still to have been an important source of income in 1996 and it obviously did not require major rent-seeking efforts. The irrelevance of the comments of the OCAG reports can be interpreted as an additional example of the government's attitude in predominantly addressing non-binding constraints, i.e. measures which do not affect the size and distribution of rents. From the rent-seekers' perspective the activity of the OCAG was not a threat, as there were hardly any subsequent measures to control or rectify the problems.

c) Fighting Corruption: A Matter of Commitment

> *'It has become evident that the greatest source of corruption in the country is not the poor economy and low salaries; although these too have played some part. The greatest source is the laxity of leadership in overseeing the implementation of established norms.'*
>
> *Report of the Commission on Corruption (i.e. Warioba Report (1996, p. 9))*

The previous discussion showed that pressure groups and individuals in Tanzania have institutionalised a rent-seeking distribution of budget funds away from the effective needs in the society. The problem goes back at least to the late 1970s or early 1980s and has not changed much since. In addition, in spite of the pro-market philosophy increasingly adopted since the mid-1980s, individuals and entrepreneurs in Tanzania faced major bureaucratic impediments, which were often not the result of a lack of capacity or knowledge, but which reflected intrinsic rent-seeking interests of state officials to make extra money by extorting bribes. Both aspects have much contributed to the poor public service delivery in Tanzania.

The lack of effective action against corruption, in particular the long history of systematic and unsanctioned misuse of public funds, has not just been an issue in the previous sections. Already Chapters 7.1 and 7.2 pointed out situations where severe shortcomings remained untouched over long periods of time, despite ongoing criticism and the evident high costs to society. These shortcomings referred to both activities of 'legal' rent-seeking and plain corruption. This section will take up the issue of corruption in general terms and attribute it to the lack of government commitment.

According to the *Corruption Perception Index* of Transparency International (TI) Tanzania was one of the most corrupt nations in the world (see Transparency International (2003)). It figured in 1998 (the first year the index was calculated for Tanzania) at position 81 out of 85 countries surveyed and in the subsequent year at the position 96 out of 99 (scores 1.9 out of 10.0 in both years, 10 indicates highly clean). Only from 2000 onwards did the rating improve slightly.[148]

The long record of no effective action raises the legitimate question whether the government ever intended to address corruption and whether it had the power to do so successfully. At least until the mid-1990s, i.e. ten years into the reform process, the answer is straightforward: There was no intention to address corruption, and any action undertaken simply reflected ineffective measures apparently set up to please the donors. Two related arguments demonstrate the lack of commitment.

First, as noted in the lead quote to this section, Tanzania does not appear to lack appropriate policies, regulations and procedures. The problem is the *deliberate disregard of established norms and rules*; it reflects to a large extent a lack

---

[148] Scores 2.5, 2.2, 2.7 and 2.5 and positions 76 of 90, 82 of 91, 71 of 102 and 92 out of 133.

of commitment among high-ranking officials and top leaders to apply and enforce what has already been instituted (see also Warioba Report (1996, p. 28)).

The second argument is the *lack of punishment*, i.e. the lack of a well-functioning legal and judicial system that ensures conviction and punishment. Considering the logic of rent-seeking, this outcome is not surprising since effective institutions which enforce laws and regulations are *binding constraints* on corruption (once corruption is detected). They are therefore the last to be addressed in an environment motivated by rent-seeking. As the 1980s and 1990s proved, comments from the Office of the Controller and Auditor General were useless unless they were followed up. Even the Warioba Report will not change anything without an effective follow-up.

Political statements about fighting corruption are typically full of praise for the efforts that have been made—ignoring that the country figures among the most corrupt in the world, and ignoring in particular that earlier efforts had been totally ineffective in preventing, or even reducing the high level of corruption. The extract of the brochure on Tanzania's achievements and challenges to fight corruption, produced by the President's Office, provides such an example:

> 'The political will and commitment to fight corruption is evident in the First [1961-86], Second [1986-95] and Third Phase of Governments' administrations...The First Phase Government... immediately saw the need to adopt appropriate policy and legal framework to address corruption...In the First and Second Phase Government a good deal of anti-corruption measures were instituted. Among many other actions taken, are the review of anti-corruption laws and establishment of agencies...[In the 1990s] the policy and strategy changed from tapping corrupt people to focusing on prevention of corruption measures.' (GoT (1999, p. 1-3)).

Such assessments are symptomatic of a government that focuses on the input side, and perfectly fits the strategy of implementing symbolic and non-binding constraints. Table 7-25 summarises the laws and institutions implemented during Nyerere's and Mwinyi's terms. After the enacting of the Prevention of Corruption Act in 1971, the Anticorruption Squad was established in 1975, and finally became the Prevention of Corruption Bureau (PCB) in the 1990s.

Anti-corruption bodies without a real commitment from the top leadership usually aim to effectuate the contrary, i.e. they are an important element in *sustaining* a corrupt system. They are created to produce legitimacy, i.e. to please the international community (donors and trade partners) by giving the impression that the country is doing something. From time to time, even members of the anti-corruption institutions are fired for alleged corruption, as for instance happened in 1998 with the PCB's director (The Indian Ocean Newsletter, No. 815, 16 June 1998). An earlier newspaper article on Kenya nicely describes the often dubious and futile nature of such anti-corruption bodies:

Table 7-25: Anti-Corruption Laws, Institutions and Manifests 1958-95

Year	Law, institution or manifesto
1958	Prevention of Corruption Ordinance Chapter 400 (Colonial law)
1966	Permanent Commission of Inquiry (Office of the Ombudsman in 1966)
1971	Prevention of Corruption Act
1973	Leadership Code
1975	Anti-Corruption Squad
1983	The Economic Sabotage Act
1984	The Economic and Organised Crimes Control Act
1990	Presidential Circular No. 1 on Guidelines for Deterrence of Corruption
	Renaming the Anti-Corruption Squad as the Prevention of Corruption Bureau
1995	Public Leadership Code of Ethics, Creation of Ethics Secretariat
1995	Election Manifesto of CCM

Source: GoT (1999, p. 1-3), Warioba Report (1996, p. 8)

> 'The government has formed an anti-corruption squad to look into the conduct of the anti-corruption commission which has been overseeing the anticorruption task force which has been investigating matters concerning corruption.' (The EastAfrican, No. 171, 9-15 Feb. 1998)

Looking at the recent work of the PCB in Tanzania also supports the above contention that anti-corruption institutions are not effective. They are often created to catch a few small fish, but they do not have the power, means or incentives to address the problem more systematically. In particular large-scale corruption is left untouched. The Warioba Report (1996, p. 21) also notes that the spread of corruption is sufficient testimony to the failure of the Anti-Corruption Bureau, the Police Force and the Department of National Security.

According to personal communication at the PCB (Dar es Salaam, April 2001, as reported in World Bank (2001b, p. 29)) in the period 1995-2000 PCB received almost 2500 complaints. The complaints were usually of a poor quality, (i.e. unreliable or sketchy), or they referred to other issues than corruption so that fewer than 50 per cent were worth investigating. Of the 1037 preliminary investigations, 161 lead to court cases of which 99 were still ongoing, 21 were withdrawn and 27 acquitted. In the five-year period, PCB ended up with only 14 convictions, i.e. an average of 2.3 convictions per year. As noted in the World Bank document, 'assuming the ongoing cases will have the same result as previous decisions and assuming all the results would have occurred in 2000 (to completely remove the backlog), PCB would still only be producing 6.1 convictions/year'. There is no need to emphasise that the figure is petty, but this is understandable, considering that Tanzania's legal and judicial system is not exempt from corruption.

The strategy of imposing no punishment is particularly evident from the lack of clean-ups in the higher ranks of government institutions. Too many senior officials in the 1990s were not held accountable and benefited from corrupt practices and non-transparent policies. For instance, even though corruption is known to be rampant in the police force (an institution also meant to fight corruption) the Warioba Report (1996, p. 18) notes that between 1991 and 1996 'not a single Senior Officer was terminated from service because of corruption' and concludes that the 'same situation holds for the Judiciary, Government Departments and Parastatal'.

In the 'Third Phase' of government, i.e. the period from when President Mkapa took office in 1995, the situation started to improve. Mkapa did not reappoint many of long-standing CCM members to his Cabinet and he initiated the Warioba Commission to assess the level of corruption in government institutions. Yet in spite of these promising steps major rent-seeking constraints remained. Even though some of the leaders, such as Mkapa himself, appear to be dedicated in addressing corruption, there are still too many who are not. The President is squeezed between powerful rent-seekers and true reformers. This tightrope walk was also apparent in his speech at the December 1997 CG meeting, where he reacted to donor complaints on the lack of action:

> 'Anyone mentioned in the Warioba Report, or anyone else against whom sufficient evidence that can stand in court is established, will be sent to court – and that is official. I have no intention or reason to protect one. Corruption must and will be made a high-risk, low-profit endeavour.
>
> But I also make it plain that I did not establish the Warioba Commission as an investigative agency to collect evidence of corruption for purposes of prosecuting suspects from previous Government administrations. My priority was to determine and deal with the loopholes and deficiencies in law and governance procedure...Actions reflect a desire to learn from the past, so as to avoid a repetition of its errors in the future. *I do not ignore the past, even as I do not want to be tied to it.*' (GoT (1997, p. 6))

In spite of Mkapa's good intentions, in subsequent years punishment has largely been absent. More worrying is the fact that hardly any of the loopholes and deficiencies mentioned in the report have been addressed successfully. Three years after Mkapa's speech at the CG meeting, the World Bank (2000b, p. 7), for instance, concluded 'while there have been some public procurement reform initiatives since mid-1990s, little, if any, real progress has been attained'. At least in the 1990s, the Warioba Report has largely remained a piece of paper—another decorative example in the history of addressing non-binding constraints.

Mkapa faced the major challenge of finding a sufficiently high number of committed people, at the top as well as in higher-middle ranks. Given the prevalence of corruption in Tanzania, this task is indeed difficult. The government may evaluate the option of a broad-based amnesty. The far-reaching infiltration and dissemination of corruption makes most people who work for the public sector (or come in contact with public officials) victims and culprits, and therefore exposed to extortion if they intend to incriminate others.

With political liberalisation, corruption also affected elections. Leaders who gain or remain in power by manipulating votes or paying off voters are certainly less inclined to fight corruption. The top-down pressure of corruption obviously also destroys any incentives at lower levels. The Warioba Report (1996, p. 7), for instance, noted that many people are afraid to talk about corruption because they are worried 'if they mention names of corrupt elements, they will become victims of persecution by State Organs in collaboration with the people they accuse...' A police officer will not forgo a bribe by taking all culprits to the station, because he knows the bribe will then be simply accepted by his superior.

Obviously, corruption also spread from the business side, in particular from the old guard of rent-seeking entrepreneurs. They survived years of socialism and thereby grew symbiotically with a system of protection, favouritism and 'knowing who and how'. Because of this history, it is not surprising that members of the Chamber of Commerce have admitted that some of their own people were accused of perpetuating the system. The situation is likely to improve as more international investors set up their businesses in Tanzania (though some of them may also have 'contingencies' in their project budgets).

On the donor side there are at least some promising projects such as the Tanzania Accountability, Transparency and Integrity Project (World Bank (2000b)) or the support of the reorganisation of the Office of the Controller and Auditor General. However, given the past history of regular setbacks in addressing binding constraints, these actions are still far too young to be evaluated. The lower corruption rating in the most recent years is encouraging but needs to be evaluated critically to make an appropriate assessment and to understand the rent-seekers' reaction in full.

All in all, corruption has resulted in very high costs to society. Corruption is still seen as a major business cost in Tanzania, at least for honest people (e.g. World Bank (2000a, p. 9)). Together with 'legal' rent-seeking activities, corruption has negatively affected the quality of public service delivery. High expenditures in non-priority sectors, poor investment decisions, major underfunding of critical expenditures in health, education and infrastructure, and the many comments on embezzlement from the Office of the Controller and Auditor General make the rent-seeking patterns and costs apparent.

Given the tight budget constraint, which was further tightened by introducing a cash-budget system in the mid-1990s, Mkapa noted at the 1997 CG meeting that the government was not able to employ hundreds of graduate and certified teachers, and many thousands of qualified primary school teachers (GoT (1997, p. 4)). In addition, not being able to pay the stipulated 15% of local counterpart funding, the country even had to forgo project-related donor funds (p. 11). At the same time Tanzania has been losing US$10 to 20 million annually in the petroleum sector alone (page 361f). And it is going to lose even more each year because of an extremely corrupt and overpriced twenty-year power purchasing agreement between TANESCO and IPTL, known as the Malaysian Power Deal (for a brief description, see World Bank (2001b, p. 16f)).

The poor appear to suffer most, and not only through reduced development prospects. As noted in the Warioba Report (1996, p. 19), the biggest receiver of bribes is not the poor, but people 'who are well paid', people 'who own residential and rented houses and vehicles for leisure and for business'; people 'who eat and dress well and who educate their children in expensive private schools outside and within the country'.

Clearly, the problem Tanzania faces is not a real budget constraint. The country does not primarily need more funds; what it needs is to be liberated from the forces that promote rent-seeking. This is not just a matter of appropriate institutions, but also a matter of effective commitment in the government, i.e. finding a sufficiently large number of truly committed leaders in middle and top ranks. Only then will actions announced (such as the quote from the 1990 Budget Speech on page 388), become more than lip service.

8 Where Rent-Seekers Seek Rents: Parastatals—Hardliners in a Rent-Seeking Economy

'These are not parastatals—we used to call them "nobody's companies"; our company collapsed because of that.'

Former employee of Tanzania Elimu Supplies

Chapter 7 described many examples of how different stakeholders in Tanzania's society undermined the reform process officially adopted with the Economic Recovery Programme (ERP) and the subsequent Economic and Social Action Programme (ESAP or ERP II). Besides civil servants, parastatal companies played an especially crucial role in the rent-seeking economy. As referred to in the opening quote, many of these companies have been real strongholds of inefficiency and embezzlement. This chapter presents additional evidence of the rent-seeking behaviour of parastatals, but from a new perspective. In contrast to Chapter 7, which was organised according to different reform measures, Chapter 8 analyses indicators of rent-seeking support and embezzlement within the parastatal sector, referring to their profit and loss statements, the quality and timeliness of their accounting and the amount of support they obtained.

Parastatal support is defined in this study in a broad sense, i.e. it not only includes access to direct subsidies or donor aid but comprises any type of legal and illegal support. This support includes access and defaults on loans and overdrafts from the banking system and the Treasury, access to direct support from the Treasury in the form of Treasury investments in the parastatal or Treasury guarantees on national and foreign loans, direct subsidies and benefits from the access to cheap foreign exchange. It also includes different types of arrears and defaults on income taxes, dividends and inter-parastatal liabilities (outstanding liabilities on pension fund contributions, electricity, water, and telephone service).

Hard data on the level of support and the scale of embezzlement makes it possible to draw conclusions on the costs of rent-seeking, especially as there is also a trade-off between the resources channelled to the parastatal sector and the resources available for other purposes such as social services and the development of an efficient infrastructure that supports the private sector.

Any rent-seeking economy depends on resources that can be appropriated, and in the case of Tanzania (as well as in many other LDCs) the donor community supplied a large share of these funds. However, since a rent-seeking distribution of resources is unlikely to reflect the preferences of a vast majority within a country as well as the intentions of donors, these activities and related transfers are typically concealed. In this respect Tanzania is not an exception. Obtaining more detailed information on the distribution and use of resources in the parastatal sector—sometimes the goal was to find data on vague indicators only—has therefore been difficult and has demanded considerable endurance and persistence.

Clearly, the more efficient concealment strategies are, the more difficult it is to obtain reliable data and the more constrained is the subsequent analysis. However, as emphasised in the preliminary comments of Chapter 6, the process of collecting and preparing information in the context of rent-seeking is not just an inevitable task related to the empirical investigation. Collecting information on the characteristics of parastatals and their support provides at the same time valuable information on the very aspect of rent-seeking under focus, i.e. information on the strategy to *obscure* rent-seeking transactions. Struggling with missing data and finding contradictions is therefore not necessarily frustrating; both types of examinations, data *collection* and data *evaluation,* enhance the understanding of rent-seeking. The rent-seeking explanations in this chapter are based on this duality. To document how severely information may be distorted, for instance how important it is also to focus on the most disaggregated level, this chapter also devotes considerable space to describing the process of finding adequate data for the characteristics and performance of parastatals.

Chapter 8.1 begins with a brief methodological discussion of measuring rent transfers and enterprise performance, addressing Kornai's concept of soft budget constraints. The section also defines the parastatal sample—an aspect which turned out to be less trivial than assumed at first glance. Following this introduction, Section b) provides initial indicative evidence on rent-seekers' concealment strategies. It illustrates why comparing information can be crucial in a rent-seeking economy and how a rent-seeking evaluation can gain a lot if researchers have access to aggregated *and* disaggregated data. The grouping and characterisation of the parastatal sample is the subject of Section c) and to some extent Section d). The group definitions constitute the basis for the subsequent evaluations. To get a clearer idea of the value of parastatal data and to understand rent-seekers' concealment strategies, Section d) provides a detailed discussion of the two accounting features 'quality' and 'arrears' of parastatal accounts. Understanding the way parastatals report to the government gives an idea of patterns of accountability and also adds another important element to the picture of rent-seeking elaborated in this chapter.

Whereas Chapter 8.1 addresses definitions, methodology and problems, Chapter 8.2 examines the soft budget. It is organised in three parts: Section a) describes and quantifies the different channels of support and emphasises inconsistencies and problems of missing data. Section b) presents a qualitative analysis of support. It develops and substantiates the rent-seeking and soft budget hypothesis. After essential preliminary comments it identifies the main beneficiaries, purpose and conditions of support and thereby demonstrates the role of soft budgets. Particularly strong evidence is presented in the final part, which examines the profit and loss characteristics of recipients of support. Section c) concludes the chapter with a general assessment of the role of soft budget and a striking comparison of aggregate support channelled to parastatal companies with government expenditures in the sectors of health and education.

Readers who are primarily interested in the rent-seeking evaluation of the data may omit Section 8.1c (and part of Section 8.2a) but should not disregard Sections 8.1d, 8.2b and 8.2c (except the technical paragraphs dealing with data compilation and statistical methods).

8.1 Methodology, Problems and Indicative Rent-Seeking Evidence

'Perhaps the major problem of any researcher in Tanzania is the lack of data, the most complete unreliability of what data is available and the absence of any recent data.'

Lane (1984, p. 2), cited from Rösch (1995, p. 10)

a) Soft Budget Constraints and Parastatal Sample

Rent-Seeking and the Concept of Soft Budget Constraints

Rent-seeking is often not easy to measure and quantify, either because information is concealed or because information is too decentralised to be collected efficiently. Consequently, empirical analyses typically depend on evaluating second-best indicators. This is also the case in this chapter, which mainly focuses on the link between the support provided to parastatals and their effective performance. The underlying rent-seeking hypothesis behind this approach is the assumption that if regular support does not improve performance resources have most likely been used for rent-seeking purposes. The approach largely rests on János Kornai's concept of *soft budget constraints*. As noted in Chapter 2.1, soft budget constraints describe the bailing out of predominantly public companies which receive transfers from the government when revenues do not cover costs.

The possibility to loosen an enterprise's budget constraint questions the most fundamental neo-classical assumption that enterprises maximise profits subject to limits of technology and resources. Soft budget constraints closely relate to the rent-seeking concept; they basically reflect a way that rents occur in an economy. How soft budget constraints weaken (or even entirely remove) incentives to use resources economically and thereby undermine the efficient allocation and use of resources has been well documented. Jalan, for instance, notes:

> 'Losses do not matter, and the efficient use of resources is of no consequence, for nothing depends on it. The survival and expansion of

> the enterprise depends on external assistance and decisions, and not on its own capabilities and performance. This has several economic consequences. The price responsiveness of the enterprise declines, and the capacity to adjust to relative prices, interest rates and exchange rates diminishes. The unit also becomes unresponsive to technological changes and to unfavourable external conditions.' (Jalan (1991, p. 198), cited in Majumdar (1998, p. 379f))

In an environment where companies are persistently bailed out by state agencies whenever revenues do not cover costs, highly inefficient companies are not threatened with bankruptcy from competition but can survive for decades. Most detrimental for economic development is the fact that government support is not only provided ex-post but also anticipated ex-ante. This situation can occur if the company realises that it is ex-post more optimal for the government to bail out the company rather than liquidating it (see, for instance, Berglof and Roland (1998, p. 20) or Majumdar (1998, p. 379)). More frequently in developing countries, however, support is anticipated as managers are embedded in a patronage network.

Soft budget constraints are often responsible for large imbalances in an economy and the successful outcome of reform measures then depends on whether soft budget constraints have been effectively eliminated. As noted in Chapter 7 macroeconomic stabilisation or trade reforms do not work or fail to have the expected impact if parastatal companies are not forced to cover costs of production out of their own revenues (see also Raiser (1994, p. 1851f)). In fact, as Eriksson (1993, p. 2) emphasises in the case of Tanzania, it appears that hardening budget constraints are an important condition for effective stabilisation, structural adjustment and sustainable economic recovery.

Ideally, a rent-seeking analysis will present some evidence as to whether resources were obtained or used so as to imply rent-seeking. The formulation of the problem in terms of soft budget constraints is not an all-encompassing approach to identify rent-seeking, but needs to be accompanied by further investigation to satisfy the broader concept of rent-seeking. Focusing on the support or survival of loss-makers will provide indicators on the prevalence of soft budget constraints and rent-seeking; it fails however to describe rent-seeking behaviour of other more efficient companies (or companies with substantial monopoly protection) which may make profits but still receive sizeable rents.

There are different ways to identify and trace soft budget constraints in an economy. As a first approach one can simply check whether persistent loss-makers have survived over longer periods of time. This approach is based on the assumption that there are no other reasons to explain or justify the survival of loss-makers (discussed below). Empirically more demanding than simply identifying persistent loss-makers is relating the performance of companies to the level of support they obtained. If the hypothesis of bailing out inefficient companies holds, government and donor support will be channelled predominantly to loss-making companies.

Unfortunately, an analysis of soft budget constraints is more difficult than it first appears. Several problems need to be addressed. A major problem is to find *adequate data on performance and support*. Given the limited availability of reliable information in Tanzania, the analysis in this chapter will be largely confined to relating gross profits of parastatal companies (profits excluding corporate taxes and dividends) to the level of financial support the companies obtained. The approach however reflects a simplification and results will have to be interpreted accordingly.

Using only statements on *gross profits* as an indicator of enterprise performance has in particular two shortcomings. On the one hand, the data can be easily manipulated. Losses, for instance, can be deferred from one period to another if the company does not make sufficient provisions for bad debts or if it applies inadequate depreciation methods. This aspect has been also evident from the erratic development of profits indicated by the time series data of parastatal companies in Tanzania (see also discussion following in Section d). On the other hand, gross profits are only a very rough indicator of enterprise performance; they cannot adequately differentiate between different types and degrees of financial and economic distress. Arrears on dividend payment, for instance, have been common in Tanzania among profit-making companies.

Schaffer (1998, p. 86) suggests using the two alternative profit categories *gross profits* and *operating profits*. Both exclude taxes on profits; the latter also exclude interest payments, depreciations, as well as extraordinary and exceptional charges. As Schaffer notes, operating profit is a measure which is independent of the capital structure of the firm. It basically shows the company's generated income to pay creditors, tax authorities and owners. Furthermore, negative operating profits indicate severe economic distress, 'in the sense that the firm is unable to cover the basic costs associated with its activity, i.e. labour and materials costs and associated taxes such as payroll taxes and VAT' (p. 86). To describe the severity of economic distress in more detail, Claessens and Peters (1997, p. 315) even define a group where *value added* is negative, i.e. the company cannot even cover its material expenses.

Besides the problem of finding adequate data on enterprise performance, it is also difficult to collect and quantify sufficient information on *parastatal support*. On the one hand, there are usually many different channels of financial support, such as loans from banks, the Treasury and donors, investment finance, subsidies, foreign exchange at below market prices and inter-enterprise arrears—information which is often stored in a decentralised manner. On the other hand, government interventions in markets also affect the profitability of companies, in both ways. A company may obtain support in the form of monopoly power or protection from foreign competitors, and it may be negatively affected by price interventions or government directives to supply to insolvent customers.

Especially if there is not sufficient data on each channel of positive and negative government interference, the results of an evaluation may be biased in one direction, for instance if some government support has been provided to offset other negative interventions that are not included in the analysis. In Tanzania both, the direct subsidies channelled to the National Milling Corporation (NMC) as well as the government's takeover of cooperatives debts partly reflected compensation for negative price interventions.

In addition to the compensation argument, there are also other *reasons not related to rent-seeking*, which may explain the support provided to loss-makers. First of all, losses are not a problem (even over a longer period of time) if large profits can be expected in the future (e.g. Schaffer (1998, p. 86)). Second, as also noted in Schaffer, from a perspective of sunk costs, it can be less costly to provide extra financing to keep a company operating than to let it close down immediately. Third, government support may be justified if the company exerts positive externalities despite making losses. And fourth, transfers may be the result of an income redistribution which reflects preferences of the society. Nevertheless, the crucial point is that any support related to these arguments does not justify letting the company operate inefficiently and deliver poor services.

Finally, in particular from a *short-term and medium-term dynamic perspective*, problems of measuring parastatal performance according to the size of profits are exacerbated by the fact that changes in performance over time are also determined by factors which are not directly related to the managers' efforts. These factors include changes in general government policy and changes in world market conditions. Furthermore, as noted earlier, frequently not all support information is available. Some of the changes in performance may then reflect the outcome of tightening rent-seeking competition that has not been accounted for. For instance, a few companies may be profitable (or remain so) because they are successful rent-seekers and keep their 'hidden' monopoly protection. Others, however, may quickly drop out of the increasingly competitive battle among rent-seekers, resulting from selected rent-abating reform measures or an intensifying crisis where all types of rents (budget-related, scarcity-related and inflation-related) shrink. Although it is important to identify and consider all these additional aspects, it is often difficult to do so.

The approach adopted in this chapter will take into account the limited scope and different problems related to an analysis of soft budget constraints and the difficulty of obtaining relevant and reliable data. The goal is not to prove a soft budget relationship, but to provide some indicative evidence while considering the above reservations when collecting and compiling data or interpreting the results of the analysis. With the rent-seeking perspective in mind, the emphasis will be on finding additional indicators for rent-seeking strategies and embezzlement, partly relying on anecdotal evidence based on personal communication.

Defining the Parastatal Sample

If the parastatal sector is not to be treated as a diffuse conglomerate decisions must be made as to which commercial companies and parastatal organisations to focus on. This was more challenging than first expected. Besides deciding which type of parastatals to focus on and choosing between a full census versus a limited sample, identifying parastatals and demarcating companies from mere sub-units or projects proved to be difficult and to some extent a matter of choice.

As noted in earlier chapters, in the 1980s the parastatal sector in Tanzania comprised more than 400 *commercial and non-commercial* parastatals. The former were companies from all sectors of the economy, i.e. agriculture (crops, livestock, fishery), mining, manufacturing (food and beverage, textile and leather, wood and paper, chemicals, construction, machinery and other industries), as well as services (such as power, water, postal and telecommunication services, transport, storage, wholesale and retail trade, tourism, banking, insurance and others).

The non-commercial parastatals in Tanzania comprise social service institutions, research parastatals, district development corporations and other non-commercial bodies. Since these organisations were not created to produce and distribute goods and services at a profit but to meet certain social goals (TAC (1991, p. 11)), to include non-commercial parastatals in a rent-seeking analysis which applies 'profits' as a major performance indicator would be incorrect. Nevertheless many non-commercial parastatals also undertook commercial activities. District corporations for instance were running hotels, restaurants and bakeries, and owned farms or provided transport services. The problem however is that without obtaining detailed information on the institution it is impossible to untangle commercial from non-commercial undertakings. The following analysis will therefore focus on commercial parastatals only, even though non-commercial parastatals have also been involved in large-scale embezzlement and other rent-seeking activities.

The decision whether to collect information on all commercial parastatals or whether to confine the study to a representative sample was also a matter of consequence. Although there are more than 300 commercial parastatals, the following considerations led to a decision to consider them all.

First of all, given the nature of rent-seeking, some of the information obtained will be distorted. As noted earlier, information related to rent-seeking activities is typically concealed. Reducing the sample to a few companies and generalising thereafter would have created additional uncertainty. Second, collecting information on all parastatal companies permits making crosscheck to be made with aggregated data from other sources. It therefore helps to examine the validity of the data. Third, parastatals in Tanzania are embedded in a complex structure of holding and affiliated companies. For the cases where support is provided to a holding company, it may not be clear whether the company itself is the final recipient or whether the support is channelled to an affiliated company. However, collecting all information at least allows additional general statements to be made on the distribution of support to the entire holding complex. Fourth, the handling and interpretation of outliers or missing data is easier in larger samples. More fundamentally, a full sample is both representative and relevant, i.e. it does not run the risk of excluding important parastatals. Finally, there is a simple argument of data collection, which favours the full-sample approach. Instead of asking for information on a specific subset it is often easier to obtain information in a more general way. For instance, an institution or company may keep a complete list of arrears of private and public clients. Having obtained this list, it makes sense to use all the parastatal data, rather than selecting some of it and generalising afterwards.

To be able to collect information on all commercial parastatals requires knowing the *identity* of the companies. Creating a full list of commercial parastatals, however, was more difficult than expected. It appears that not even the Treasury, the owner of all parastatal companies, knew exactly how many companies there were and how they were related to one another. The most comprehensive list of commercial parastatals, with 316 companies, was prepared by the Parastatal Sector Reform Commission and published in the Appendix of the Masterplan (PSRC (1993, p. i-ix)).

However, in the process of collecting information on commercial parastatals it soon became evident that the distinction between commercial and non-commercial parastatals, as well as the distinction between a parastatal, a private company or a mere project (in the last two cases the government may have a minority share), was not clear-cut and was handled differently. Furthermore, since parastatals have been embedded in a complex structure of holding and affiliated companies, it was often not clear whether a specific entity reflected a sub-unit of another company or whether it should be treated as an individual parastatal.

To be on the safe side, already at an early stage of the research project a broad list of 392 commercial parastatals was compiled. Table B-1 in the Appendix lists the companies. Most of them are given in the above-mentioned Masterplan of the PSRC. The list, however, has been extended according to an earlier version of the Masterplan obtained at the Treasury, which included the major stakeholders in the agricultural sector, i.e. the cooperative unions. Some additional parastatals have been identified, as they appeared as commercial parastatals in other sources.

Besides the names of the parastatals, Table B-1 also shows the holding relations, location and sector coding of the companies, permitting a more differentiated aggregation of data and testing of rent-seeking hypotheses. The coding according to sectors and location is based on an own assessment (for a detailed description see Tables B-2 and B-3 in the Appendix).

After data collection was concluded, 56 ‘companies’ were removed (names in the Appendix marked in italics). Based on personal communication and the evaluation of the information obtained, they were identified as private companies, non-commercial parastatals or projects in a planning stage, companies which were mentioned twice under different names, those which ceased production prior to 1987, and those, which lacked separate accountings (reflecting a mere sub-unit of a parastatal).

b) Initial Results of Data Collection: What Official Statistics May and May Not Show

> *'In earlier days, we used to keep two types of data, one which gave the correct picture and one which showed the political acceptable picture. This double standard was part of our work as a society.'*
>
> *Senior official, Bureau of Statistics, March 2000*

Reliable statistical information is important in any country. Data on the state of the economy and the demographic and social characteristics of the population serve as a basis for making efficient decisions on economic and social policy. Statistical data are often a crucial component of different controlling and feedback mechanisms; or, to put it differently, in most cases *good governance* is closely related to having access to reliable information. Furthermore, reliable economic data are not only of great value for actors within the public or government sphere, such as ruling elites, senior bureaucrats or parliamentarians; they are also important for other stakeholders in the society, such as voters, academic institutions, and managers of local and foreign companies. Any benevolent government therefore has an interest in producing reliable and up-to-date statistical information to run the state efficiently, to create an environment supportive of private and public sector activities and to allow democratic forces to work efficiently.

In a rent-seeking economy things are different. As emphasised in this book, concealing or distorting information is part of a rent-seeking strategy. To the extent that rent-seeking-related decision-making is well entrenched in the public sector, up to the highest government level, the collection and production of statistical information will most likely be affected, as well. Besides the manipulation of data, the government typically devotes too little resources to producing useful statistics.

As in many other rent-seeking economies, concealing, distorting or not producing information used to be common practice in Tanzania. Problems were particularly severe in the 1980s and early 1990s. LDC governments usually justify such situations by referring to their *limited capacity* for producing complete, reliable and publicly available data. At a closer look, however, it becomes obvious that a great deal of the problem is of a systemic, rent-seeking nature. The above statement of the official from the Bureau of Statistics (personal communication in Dar es Salaam, March 2000) confirms the rent-seeking hypothesis. He had been confronted with substantial irregularities and contradictions in the data obtained at the Bureau (discussed below).

Since publishing certain information is not always in rent-seekers' interest and a rent-seeking budget allocation does not allow spending too much on data collection and evaluation, it is not surprising that problems, once identified, are not addressed effectively in a timely way. Even in the mid-1990s, the IMF for instance emphasised that Tanzania had received considerable technical assistance to alleviate statistical difficulties, but insufficient efforts had been devoted by the authorities to implementing the recommendations (IMF (1995, p. 37)). This assessment was repeated in subsequent years (e.g. IMF (1996b, p. 77)).

Obviously, in a rent-seeking economy data requested to conduct an analysis of *parastatal companies* is not easy to obtain and will, depending on the source, most likely be *distorted, as well.* This section, which describes the process of collecting information on parastatal profits, documents how severe individual and 'aggregated' data may be distorted.

Collecting Information

In Tanzania there are basically three sources where information on the individual performance of parastatal companies may be obtained: the companies themselves, the Bureau of Statistics and the Tanzania Audit Corporation (the last is a parastatal; it audits the accounts of most other parastatal companies). At least in theory, the Treasury should also keep detailed information, as it owns the parastatal companies. But it was not possible to get this kind of information from the Treasury Registrar.

The most direct source for obtaining specific data is the *company* itself. However, in the case of Tanzania, such an approach implies prohibitive costs for several reasons. A major problem is the large number of parastatal companies. As noted above, in the 1980s Tanzania had more than 400 parastatals. Besides the problem that many of them were located far away from Dar es Salaam and several companies had been closed, quick inquiries by telephone are generally not possible. Connections often do not work and demanding information typically requires a personal introduction, including presentation of a letter of recommendation. Furthermore the procedure of collecting information often requires between four and ten personal visits, as managers, employees and bureaucrats tend to send the 'visitor' to other members of staff, many of them requiring further appointments (for instance, because they are attending meetings, are 'on safari', i.e. travelling, or because they could not come to work as their children were ill or the rains had washed away the road). In addition appointments are often cancelled on short notice for such reasons and the promised information will not be available on the date agreed.

Confining the study to a representative sample of companies would have reduced the number of visits and time-consuming inquiries but this was not the approach of this study and costs would nevertheless have been high. The only promising strategy was therefore to look where information was stored centrally.

The *Bureau of Statistics (BoS)* in Dar es Salaam collects and compiles, among other things, individual accounting data for a large number of parastatals. This institution looked promising since access to balance sheet data also makes it possible to differentiate among indicators of economic and financial distress.

In 1998 when information was requested on parastatal performance for the period 1986 to 1996, the BoS could only provide disaggregated data for the years 1987, 1988, 1990 and 1993 (1993 data computerised in an Excel sheet, all other years written by hand). The tables, which showed detailed accounting information (balance sheets, in particular profit and loss statements), included individual statements of approximately one half to two thirds of all parastatal companies (depending on how one defines the total parastatal sample).

The BoS also stored *individual files* of companies for specific years. These files, however, were in total disorder and were piled in a dark unfurnished storeroom with no windows; they were covered in black dust and barely accessible. Finally, together with the Planning Commission, BoS produced various *publications* with aggregated information, which could be used for a quick crosscheck or overall evaluation.

Another source where disaggregated information is collected in a centralised way is the *Tanzania Audit Corporation (TAC)*. TAC keeps individual files of each company it audits in one of the four branches Dar es Salaam, Arusha, Moshi and Mwanza. Unfortunately this information is not publicly available. However, TAC used to publish a report each year which included information on the performance of parastatal companies according to the accounts audited. Until 1991 the report included a listing of individual profit and loss statements of all parastatal companies whose profits or losses exceeded the threshold of TSh 5 million. As inflation steadily reduced the real value of the threshold, the minimum level was increased to TSh 20 million for the years 1992 and 1993. From 1994 onwards TAC did not publish any more individual data, as the privatisation process had gained momentum and data became too sensitive.

A major problem with parastatal data was that most companies had been in arrears for several years in scrutinising and submitting their accounting information to TAC. This aspect will be discussed in detail in Section d). Annual TAC reports therefore only published profit and loss statements of the accounts audited during the respective year, i.e. a profit and loss statement of a parastatal for the year 1988 would appear in the 1993 report if the audit had been done between July 1992 and June 1993. Together with the fact that there was no individual information on profits and losses under TSh 5 million (and later on less than TSh 20 million), evaluating reports for the years 1987 to 1994 only would have left a major gap in data. However, upon request in April 1998, TAC kindly provided additional information on some of the missing profit and loss statements by sending questionnaires to its different branches.

Comparing Data

The strategy of collecting information from both BoS and TAC had two advantages. Neither institution was able to provide all the data requested but they had slightly different samples. Also any overlap between the two sources could be used to check the consistency or validity of the data.

The crosschecks turned out to be disillusioning. Out of the 116 profit and loss statements for 1987 where information was available from both sources, only 22 figures matched. In 35 cases discrepancies exceeded a factor of 2, i.e. profits (or losses) of one source were more than twice as large as indicated by the other source.[149] Twenty-one records even showed profits instead of losses and vice versa. The computerised 1993 data, which had 14 matches out of 76, showed a similarly devastating picture. In fact, it was discovered only later that the BoS data belonged to the year 1993 whereas it was originally provided as information for the year 1991 (which still would have implied two matches!).[150] Table 8-1 summarises the results of the analysis and Table B-4 of the Appendix displays the data of the two sources for the year 1987.

Table 8-1: Comparison of Parastatal Profit/Loss Statements Obtained from the Bureau of Statistics and the Tanzania Audit Corporation

BoS (records of year)	TAC (records of year)	Number of over-lapping records	Match [a] Number	Match [a] in %	Large deviation [b] Number	Large deviation [b] in %	Correlation coefficient
1987	1987	116	22	19%	56	48%	0.50
1993 [c]	1993	76	14	18%	42	45%	0.19
"	*1992*	*76*	*2*	*3%*	*54*	*71%*	*0.45*
"	*1991*	*75*	*2*	*3%*	*42*	*56%*	*0.10*
"	*1990*	*81*	*2*	*2%*	*57*	*70%*	*0.14*

a: If both sources show the data of the same year a 100% match would be required. Since the probability that a company has exactly the same profit or loss in different years is very low, matches between different years (e.g. BoS 1993 and TAC 1992) most likely indicate that the same profit/loss statement has been cited (implying that at least one source uses a wrong year).

b: TAC statement has different sign or is smaller than half or larger than double of BoS figure.

c: The 1993 BoS data had also been compared with other years. There was no match with TAC data referring to the years 1987 and 1994-96, and one match in the years 1988 and 1989.

Source: Own calculation, based on annual profit/loss statements of parastatal companies obtained at the Bureau of Statistics (BoS) and the Tanzania Audit Corporation (TAC). Individual data for 1987 is displayed in Table B-4 in the Appendix.

Clearly, either the BoS data or the TAC data showed a different type of profits or at least one of the two sources was totally unreliable. Discussions with a senior official at the Bureau of Statistics in March 2000 quickly revealed that the problem was with the BoS records:

> 'Our data collection is based on questionnaires. We used what the parastatals sent back. For those who did not respond we sometimes repeated last years figures or made another estimate. If a company consisted of 10 sub-units and only 6 responded, we took the average and extrapolated to 10. Sometimes we even used the newspaper as a source of information. And we tried to retrieve the figures by working backward; i.e. if you know profits and revenues of a year, you can calculate expenses. The major problem, however, was that the auditing lagged years behind. Hence we could not compare the figures with information from the Tanzania Audit Corporation (in fact, we would not

[149] The profits and losses are displayed in Table B-4 in the Appendix. Ideally, discrepancies would be defined in per cent of the companies' turnaround or assets; however this information was not available for both sources.

[150] Murjanda wheat company and Gidagamowd wheat company, which indicate a profit of TSh 20.4 million and TSh 60.9 million in both sources.

have had the time for it). Preparing data was also a political issue. Sometimes the figures did not suit the Planning Commission. They were then sent back to the Bureau of Statistics to work over the files again…'

The Bureau of Statistics has been constrained in producing reliable statistics for the country. It appears however that none of the high-level civil servants had been interested in changing the situation. How severe the problem of missing data was and what working backwards at the BoS in earlier days implied was revealed by a brief glance at the Excel sheet obtained from the BoS, which included the 1993 profit and loss statements. The sheet lists balance sheet information for 106 parastatals. Under normal conditions stated revenue minus stated expenses equals stated profits or losses. In Tanzania however data are scarce. To fill the information gap, the balance sheet included an additional column for 'other expenses'. On average this column covered 62% of all expenses, and with 42% of the sample unexplained expenses accounted for more than 80% of total expenses. Although this does not mean that the amount necessarily reflects embezzlement—most of the data have simply not been collected—it points to an important feature of recording information in Tanzania, i.e. a great deal of data are usually produced and presented in a form where it is impossible to check the consistency and to find errors. This is systemic.

The extreme unreliability and political manipulation of data produced by the Bureau of Statistics and other institutions such as the Planning Commission becomes even more apparent when comparing *aggregated data*. Table 8-2 displays overall profits of commercial parastatals from official statistics obtained at BoS and contrasts this with the data shown in the annual reports of the Tanzania Audit Corporation. In the table TAC (5) represents the closest approximation to reality; all other figures are entirely misleading (as will be explained below, they do not use audited figures, give wrong years, omit important parastatals or add non-commercial units). For instance, according to official statistics, in 1989 commercial parastatals made net profits of nearly TSh 30 billion, while the hardly-noticed TAC figure (5) indicates an overall net loss of over TSh 20 billion! In fact, the comparison of the individual profit and loss statements presented earlier also revealed the same discrepancies, i.e. a systematically much more favourable picture presented by the Bureau of Statistics.

However, even aggregated data from the more reliable TAC used to be misleading if not carefully interpreted. A glance at the data set underlying the aggregated TAC result revealed at least three major flaws: wrong aggregation prior to 1990, a questionable composition of companies included in the total and poor primary data quality of highly relevant companies.

Until 1990 the TAC overview consisted of an aggregation of all profits from the accounts audited during the indicated period. Since many of the parastatals, in particular loss-making companies, had been in arrears during several years in submitting their reports, the figure represented an *aggregation of profits from different financial years* and therefore had no economic meaning. This

Table 8-2: Accumulated Profits of Commercial Parastatals (TSh m)

	Net operating profits [b]		Net profits [b]		
Year [a]	BoS (1)	BoS (2)	BoS (3)	TAC (4)	TAC (5)
1986	n/a	-1,239	415	3,540	-8,772
1987	n/a	9,325	17,301	654	-11,445
1988	20,641	2,213	17,712	-7,454	-14,356
1989	24,093	20,394	27,149	-11,177	-23,357
1990	58,737	46,009	52,264	-4,199	16,223
1991	n/a	42,033	50,125	-4,616	7,766
Accumulated net profits/losses 1986-91:			164,966	-23,252	-33,941

BoS data: Official statistics from 'The Economic Survey 1991' and 'Analysis of Accounts of Parastatal Enterprises 1982-91'. *TAC data* from annual report of auditing company. TAC (4) shows aggregate profits and losses of all accounts audited during the indicated period, TAC (5) groups profit/loss statements according to the financial year the data refer to.

a: Calendar years, except for TAC (4), which indicates financial years, i.e. 1 July to 30 June values.

b: BoS defines *Net Operating Profits* as receipts (the sum of sales, subsidies, other operating income, increase in stocks) minus expenditures (the sum of wages and salaries, interest paid, rent paid, depreciation and miscellaneous purchases). *Net Profits* equal the sum of Net Operating Profits, interest & dividends received and rent received. Or to put it differently, they reflect the profit before tax and dividend payments.

Source: (1): Planning Commission (1992, p. 84); (2), (3): Bureau of Statistics (1993, p. 15); (4): TAC (1988, p. 15), TAC (1989, p. 9), TAC (1990, p. 9), TAC (1991, p. 10f); (5): TAC (1992, p. 12), TAC (1993, p. 14), TAC (1994, p. 11), TAC (1995, p. 11)

encouraged misinterpretations, as for instance happened at TAC (1988, p. 14f). In the 1980s the skewed aggregation also suggested a more favourable picture of the parastatal sector since inflation was running at 30 per cent and losses were coming on average from earlier years than profits (a loss of TSh 10 million in 1985 has the same real value with the opposite sign as a profit of TSh 40 million in 1989; however, adding the two figures gives a net profit of TSh 30 million). Only from the 1990 report onwards did TAC produce overviews that grouped profit and loss statements according to the financial years they refer to. TAC (4) and TAC (5) display the different aggregates.

The second flaw relates to the *identity of companies*. The TAC total of commercial parastatals includes the profits of the Bank of Tanzania (Tanzania's Central Bank). It is debatable to define an institution which is primarily concerned with supplying a public good (conducting monetary policy, in particular securing macro stability) as a commercial parastatal. However, what distorts the aggregated data set most is that the Bank of Tanzania is also the parastatal with the largest reported profits! Excluding the Central Bank from the TAC (5) sample would have more than doubled accumulated losses during the six-year period and would have therefore given a much less favourable picture.[151]

[151] According to the figures presented in the annual TAC report, profits of the Bank of Tanzania are (in TSh million): 545 (1986), 2,106 (1987), 5,514 (1988), 9,162 (1989), 13,842 (1990) and 12,402 (1991). If excluded from the TAC (5) sample, overall net losses would increase by 43,571, indicating and accumulated loss of –77,508 (instead of –33,941).

Finally, the last qualification refers to the *questionable value of primary data*. In most aggregated overviews there are companies which distort the overall picture in one way or the other. As long as their influence is not too large this is not a serious problem. Looking at the data set that underlies the aggregated TAC result, however, shows that the largest profit-makers are all highly inefficient monopolies (National Bank of Commerce, Tanzania Harbours Authority and Tanzania Petroleum Development Corporation). Both the inefficiency of the petroleum sector as well as the poor performance of NBC have been discussed in Chapter 7. According to the TAC data NBC profits averaged nearly TSh 5 billion during the period 1986 to 1991, even though the bank had to be declared insolvent shortly thereafter (indicating a loss of TSh 37 billion in 1992!).[152] The issue points to an important question, i.e. how reliable accounting data can be. In Tanzania there are certainly major shortcomings. Section d) will look at this aspect in more detail.

All in all, the distortion of information on parastatal companies in Tanzania relates to both levels, the primary data level, where the information is created, and the 'statistical' level, where information is collected and compiled to produce official statistics. Knowing the data set that underlies an aggregated result is crucial. Policymakers, donors and scientists often do not have sufficient time to look into the details on how information is produced. They therefore run a higher risk of interpreting misleading data. In particular aggregated data are prone to include unexplained biases and manipulations, and the data are often presented in a way where it is not possible to prove inconsistencies.

It is not far-fetched to conclude that the contradictions between the different sources of information presented in this section, in particular the general shortcomings at the Bureau of Statistics, do not just represent a mixture of incompetence and lack of resources, but also an apparent disinterest in an efficient allocation of resources (meaningful statistics are a necessary tool for efficient management decisions), and systematic rent-seeking interests. Even though not every deficiency relates to rent-seeking, the chaos additionally helps to hide and protect rent-seeking activities.

c) Characterising Parastatals According to Profits and Losses

This section (and part of Section d) defines the grouping of parastatal companies and describes the distribution of parastatal characteristics according to sectors and location. The group definitions constitute the bases for the subsequent evaluation of rent-seeking.

---

[152] This figure corresponds to US$120 million or 4% of monetary GDP in Tanzania.

Information on Profits and Employment

In Section a) it was argued that profits and losses are not an optimal indicator of enterprise performance for various reasons. More appropriate is the measurement of operating profits or value added as a share of revenues. However, the balance sheet information received from the Bureau of Statistics, which would have allowed a more detailed and more adequate approach, was of such poor quality that using this data was highly questionable. The remaining analysis therefore is based on measuring performance according to the less optimal but more reliable profit and loss statements obtained from the Tanzania Audit Corporation (and other sources). Since macroeconomic and microeconomic distortions were particularly high prior to the agreement with the IMF and the World Bank in 1986, parastatals are primarily characterised according to their profit and loss statements from 1987 onwards. Only if there is too little information, for instance if the company closed in the late 1980s, is additional information for the period 1984 to 1986 taken into account.

Table 8-3 surveys the type of annual profit and loss information collected from different sources for the period 1987 to 1996, i.e. TAC reports, complementary TAC questionnaires and several other reports. The number of profit and loss statements obtained for a specific year ranged between 199 and 222 prior to 1992 and declined thereafter to 91, as more and more parastatals either closed or were privatised. More decisive, however, was the problem that companies also had been in arrears in submitting their accounts for audit. Since the publication practice of TAC changed after 1991 and 1993, most information on accounts not audited by then had to be obtained through questionnaires, filled in by TAC staff members. Given their time constraints in looking through company files, only part of this information was retrieved.

Detailed information on parastatal profits is given in Table B-6 in the Appendix. The table includes the number of profit and loss statements obtained for each company for the period 1987-96, average profits of the company calculated at constant prices (1994 prices), the trends in profits derived from the data and further information on the categorisation of the companies (discussed below).[153]

To get an idea of the relative size of the parastatals, employment figures for individual companies have been collected, whenever possible on an annual basis. Ideally, such information should be complemented by data on capital-intensities, sales and other company features; however, as noted earlier, in Tanzania there was no useful information stored in a centralised way.

Several branches of the Bureau of Statistics provided employment figures. Additional information on employment could be obtained from personal interviews and various publications (in particular PSRC (1993, Appendix 3)). Since the data collected was very incomplete and partly contradictory, and the

---

[153] Because of the high rates of inflation, most TSh values presented in this study have been converted into constant prices (1994 prices). The monthly price indices are explained and given in Table B-5 in the Appendix.

Table 8-3: Information on Profits 1987-96

	87	88	89	90	91	92	93	94	95	96
Profit/loss statements [a]	199	206	221	217	222	192	175	142	118	91
Interval information [b]	70	56	34	24	12	9	-	-	-	-
No information [c]	15	22	29	43	50	83	109	142	166	193
Subtotal	284	284	284	284	284	284	284	284	284	284
Comp. (no stat. at all) [d]	52	52	52	52	52	52	52	52	52	52
Total	336	336	336	336	336	336	336	336	336	336

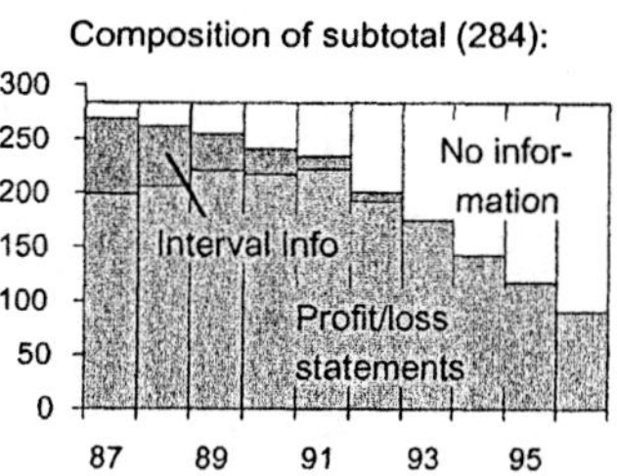

a: 55% of the statements according to TAC reports 1988-93, 40% from questionnaires filled by TAC. The remaining 5% from various sources (Treasury: 65 statements, Coopers&Lybrand (1996): 13 statements, PSRC (1997b): 22 statements and Ministry of Agriculture (1994a): 1 statement).

b: Audit mentioned in the TAC report; the profit or loss figure however was not published, as it did not exceed the threshold of TSh 5 million (audits mentioned in reports 1987-91) or TSh 20 million (audits mentioned in reports 1992-93). The exact figure could also not be retrieved from other sources.
Interval information has been taken into account to evaluate the grouping of companies with only a few profit/loss statements (i.e. a company with few statements would be still categorised if the grouping does not change after missing values (intervals) are replaced by maximum profits (+5, +20) for a loss-maker or maximum losses (-5, -20) for a profit-maker.

c: Company either not operating any more, privatised, audit for specific year not undertaken or information for the specific year not obtained.

d: Companies where no profit/loss information could be obtained at all. Most of these are parastatals from the agriculture and mining sector not audited by TAC; this group includes all regional cooperative unions (27).

quality of information was unknown (some sources explicitly indicated data to be poor), it was not possible to prepare reliable time series. However, to get an idea of the size of a company (to evaluate the magnitude of stated profits and losses), an average was taken from whatever employment information had been obtained. The individual averages of 323 companies are shown in Table B-6 in the Appendix; they represent a total of 183,500 employees.[154]

As noted earlier, to be able to undertake a more specific economic interpretation of parastatal characteristics and support, parastatals were categorised according to their sector affiliation (five-digit sector coding) and regional distribution (four-digit location coding). Being close to the centre can matter when it comes to lobbying for government support. In contrast, greater distance from the centre is likely to increase parastatal autonomy and thereby also opportunities to embezzle funds.

Figure 8-1 shows the distribution of parastatal employment according to sectors and location. Based on the collected data, only 14% of employment was in the agriculture sector. Although Tanzania's economy was still predominantly agrarian, this outcome is not surprising as a great deal of farming is done by

[154] According to personal communication at the Bureau of Statistics (Dar es Salaam, March 2000), in some cases not all units of a company reported their employment figures in each year. To the extent that this distortion prevails, using *maximum values* of the time series data collected (and not *averages)* is more appropriate. This alternative approach would inflate employment by 25% and indicate a total of 229,000. However, information has also been distorted in other ways. It was partly based on guesses and older figures; in addition, for some companies, employment indeed decreased in the 1990s. Using 'averages' therefore seemed to be a better approximation.

private smallholders (farmers only sell their harvest to state-owned cooperatives and marketing boards).

Figure 8-1: Distribution of Parastatal Employment

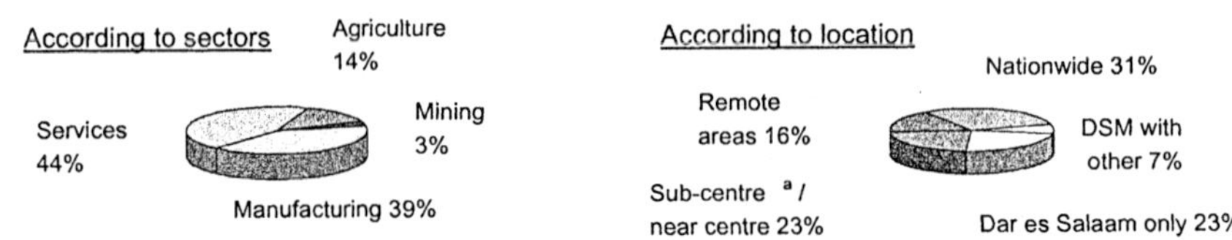

a: Including Dodoma

Source: Table B-7 in the Appendix, which gives more detailed category data at the 1-3 digit level

Nearly 40% of parastatal employment belonged to the manufacturing group, above all food processing, beverages and tobacco (14%), as well as textile and leather (10%). And 44% was in the service sector, of which two thirds were in public utilities, transport and storage.

Looking at the regional distribution of parastatal employment, more than 80% of employees worked for companies which have all or part of their employment in or near major urban centres.[155]

Table 8-4 shows a grouping of profit and loss data according to sectors and location. Of the 266 companies where profit and loss information for at least one year was available for the period 1987 to 1996, 105 companies made on average profits (representing 74,000 employees) and 161 losses (representing 97,000 employees).[156]

Looking at the sector-wide distribution, all categories except mining indicate both types of companies, i.e. average profit-makers and average loss-makers. This assessment also holds if the groups 'agriculture', 'all other manufacturing' and 'all other services' are further disaggregated, as shown in the Appendix (only the small residual group 'other plants' consists of two profit-makers only). The fact that both categories, average profit-makers and average loss-makers, are represented in most sub-sectors makes looking at soft budget constraints particularly interesting, as company performance is not just a matter of sector affiliation.

[155] As explained in Table B-2 in the Appendix, nationwide companies are represented in the entire country and have their main branch in Dar es Salaam. They comprise among others banking, postal services and telecommunications, electricity and food crop marketing boards. Other companies are located in Dar es Salaam or have their main branch there and include one or a few branches in other cities. Sub-centres comprise Arusha and Moshi, and towns near Dar es Salaam are Morogoro, Tanga and Zanzibar. Dodoma, which is the capital, takes a special role.

[156] The average is defined as the sum of profits and losses divided by the number of observations (henceforth called *'average rule'*). Employment data were available for 103 average profit-makers and 157 average loss-makers. As noted earlier, the data have to be interpreted with caution, in particular as some highly inefficient companies also figure as profit-makers, above all THA, NBC and CRDB.

Columns (3) to (5) of Table 8-4 indicate different ways of calculating sector-wide and location-based profit and loss averages. Depending on the problem of missing data and the economic interpretation, it is more appropriate to weight average profits and losses according to the number of companies, the number of profit and loss statements or the number of employees within a sector/location category. Each of the average methods is briefly discussed below.

Table 8-4: Distribution of Profits and Losses (1987-96, TSh m, 1994 prices)

		Number of 'average'		Average profits/losses per company		per 1000	Annual sector totals: (accumulated averages)		
Grouping by sector	Comp. in group	Profit-makers (1)	Loss-makers (2)	no weights (3)	weighted[a] (4)	employees (5)	Profit-makers (6)	Loss-makers (7)	All averages (8)
Agriculture & mining	90	16	32	-69	-59	-147	2,954	-6,282	-3,328
Agriculture	78	16	24	-3	14	-6	2,954	-3,079	-125
Mining	12	0	8	-400	-518	-1,477		-3,203	-3,203
Manufacturing	137	38	79	-482	-494	-818	28,147	-84,529	-56,381
Textile & leather	29	1	24	-2,332	-2,838	-3,102	22	-58,320	-58,298
All other	108	37	55	21	22	40	28,126	-26,209	1,917
Services	109	51	50	-10	-48	-14	28,634	-29,625	-991
Public utilities	5	1	3	-5,204	-6,322	-1,110	179	-20,994	-20,814
Finance	14	9	4	808	755	745	12,430	-1,926	10,505
All other	90	41	43	111	161	197	16,024	-6,706	9,319
Total	336	105	161	-228	-238	-354	59,735	-120,436	-60,700
Grouping by location									
Centre	157	67	75	42	59	53	52,086	-46,163	5,923
Nationwide	18	7	10	-873	-1,594	-264	12,947	-27,786	-14,839
Dar es Salaam	130	60	59	178	291	393	39,139	-17,954	21,185
- DSM only	(115)	(53)	(54)	(121)	(206)	(315)	(29,914)	(-16,999)	(12,915)
- DSM & other towns	(6)	(5)	(1)	(1,272)	(1,535)	(621)	(8,361)	(-726)	(7,635)
- DSM suburb	(9)	(2)	(4)	(106)	(193)	(842)	(864)	(-229)	(636)
Dodoma	9	0	6	-71	-58	-602		-423	-423
Sub-centre/near centre	81	20	40	-391	-508	-627	5,352	-28,830	-23,478
Remote areas	98	18	46	-674	-653	-1,849	2,298	-45,443	-43,145
Total	336	105	161	-228	-238	-354	59,735	-120,436	-60,700

a: Company averages weighted according to the number of annual statements available to calculate the company average.

In the Appendix, Table B-7 also shows column (5) weighted. Table B-8 further shows column (5) separated according to the two sub-categories 'average profit-makers' and 'average loss-makers' and it indicates the above columns (6) to (8) as weighted sector totals.

Source: Columns (1) to (5): see Table B-7 in the Appendix, columns (6) to (8): see Table B-8

Column (3) shows for each category simple annual averages per company, column (4) takes the average of all profit and loss statements obtained from companies within a specific category, i.e. a company has more weight if profit and loss information has been available for ten years rather than two years only. Column (5) indicates the average annual profit and loss per employee within a category and time period. In a similar manner, columns (6) to (8) (and the additional data in Table B-8) indicate annual sector totals (accumulated averages of companies), based on a simple aggregation (each company has the same weight) or, as additionally shown in Table B-8 in the Appendix, a weighted aggregation (company averages weighted according to the number of profit/loss statements available from the ten year period).

Evaluations using unweighted (or employment-weighted) company averages are more useful when significant data are missing; and accordingly averages weighted according to the number of profit and loss statements become less meaningful. By contrast, the calculation of weighted averages is more appropriate if the missing data is primarily attributable to the fact that the parastatal closed or was excluded from the sample because it became privatised. Unfortunately it was not possible to get sufficient information on this differentiation. This study therefore shows both averaging methods to demonstrate that the main findings do not depend on the method applied.

Adding up all annual profit and loss averages gives the profit-making group a total of TSh 59.7 billion per year, and the loss-making group a total of TSh 120.4 billion (US$114 million and US$230 million). Looking at the sector-wide distribution, average profits and losses as well as sector totals (accumulated averages) are negative for all three main categories.[157] The parastatal losses in the economy may appear small if compared with the losses of companies in industrialised countries. However, Tanzania is a poor country and has a small economy. The average GDP between 1987 and 1996, for instance, was only TSh 2300 billion (1994 prices). The parastatal losses are particularly striking if compared with Tanzania's annual recurrent expenditures on health and education, which have been TSh 96 billion combined (average of FY90-96, 1994 prices, calculated from World Bank (1997e, p. 47, 53)).

An interesting aspect is the apparent relation of the profits and the distance to the centre. As Table 8-4 indicates, in Dar es Salaam the number of profit-makers and loss-makers are balanced and accumulated averages of the profit-making group more than compensate the loss-making group. In the sub-centres and areas close to Dar es Salaam, there are only half as many profit-makers as loss-makers and accumulated averages indicate a relation of 1 to 5, meaning that profit-makers only cover 20% of the losses suffered by the loss-making companies. Finally in remote areas figures are even more pronounced (more than twice as many loss-makers, and accumulated averages of the loss-making group are almost twenty times as high as those of the profit-making group).[158]

---

[157] At a lower sector aggregation (indicated in the Appendix B), the categories food & beverage and tobacco, chemicals, metal & machinery, transport, finance as well as tourism reveal positive values regardless of the averaging method used. The same holds for the two groups cash-crops and wholesale/retail trade, repair and maintenance; the two categories, however, contain more average loss-making companies than average profit-making companies. Finally, the categories other plants, live animals, mining, wood, paper & printing, construction and public utilities always indicate negative values and more loss-makers with any averaging method used.

[158] Also statistically it can be shown that differences, in particular between Dar es Salaam, moderately-far and remote areas, are highly significant (e.g. comparing means by a Kruskal-Wallis test procedure).

There are in particular two reasons which explain this outcome. First, to the extent that part of this difference in performance is a result of embezzlement, the finding may support the rent-seeking hypothesis that embezzlement and inefficiency increase with a greater distance to the centre. Second, as will be explained later, part of the answer is also that companies in Dar es Salaam had much easier access to support, which partly reduced their annual losses.

Detailed Grouping of Parastatals and Addressing the Problem of Missing Data

For the subsequent evaluation, above all to describe patterns of support channelled to commercial parastatals, companies were grouped according to several criteria. Besides a more refined distinction of average profit-makers from average loss-makers, companies were categorised according to the *size* of profits and losses, the *regular or random* appearance of profits and losses, as well as the *trend* over time. The explicit identification of large loss-makers, for instance, helps to assess sector-specific rent-seeking costs. Information on the share of *regular* loss-makers is useful in evaluating the role of soft budget constraints, and the parastatal categorisation according to trends in profits and losses provides second-best indicators to describe managers' efforts or the impact of policy changes. The groupings, which are indicated for each company in Table B-6 in the Appendix, are briefly described below and summarised in Table 8-6 on page 450.

In general, classifying companies into profit-makers and loss-makers is not difficult. The previous section also used a simple 'average rule', i.e. companies which made profits on average during the period 1987 to 1996 have been defined as profit-makers, and those, which made losses on average have been defined as loss-makers (see Footnote 156). However, at least when it comes to testing hypotheses on the distribution of parastatal support to profit-making and loss-making companies, a more sophisticated categorisation is desirable.

The major caveat is the *problem of missing data*. As noted earlier, information on profits is lacking for several reasons. Some profits and losses were not published since they did not exceed the threshold of TSh +/-5 million (or TSh 20 million for the TAC reports 1992 and 1993)[159] or because accounts in arrears were only audited after June 1993, when TAC no longer published the data and the information could not be obtained otherwise. In addition, it was often not known whether information was missing for other reasons, i.e. because the company was dormant during a certain period, or because it ceased production, waiting to be liquidated or privatised.

One possible approach to deal with the problem of missing data is to treat observations as random values and to test for each company whether calculated

[159] In real terms, this threshold varied considerably, depending on the time of audit and the year and month audited accounts referred to. Calculated at constant prices (1994 prices), the threshold ranged between TSh 12.6 million (threshold TSh 5 million, 'end of December 1990 accounts' audited by June 1991) and TSh 134.8 (threshold TSh 20 million, 'end of June 1987 accounts' audited by June 1993). The figures correspond to US$24,000 and US$258,000.

averages are significantly larger (if profit) or smaller (if loss) than zero. Such a procedure, however, would not be appropriate for several reasons. On the one hand, in many cases there are no missing values in the sense of 'unknown but existing' profits and losses. As noted above, the company may no longer have been operating so that the data originally obtained was in fact complete (implying that the simple average method would exactly determine whether the company was a profit-maker or loss-maker during the specified period). On the other hand, company profits and losses often developed erratically, as necessary adjustments and corrections had been omitted and postponed for years. The combination of relatively large standard deviations and small numbers of observations (some companies collapsed during the first one to five years of the period under investigation) would have implied large confidence intervals, many of them including parameter values of zero as a possible outcome.

Scientists are primarily concerned with minimising statistical errors of the type I (accepting a hypothesis, although the hypothesis is wrong). In doing so, they accept large errors of type II, i.e. they much more frequently reject a hypothesis although the hypothesis describes a true situation. However, if above-mentioned tests are applied to group companies into profit-makers and loss-makers, a biased treatment of statistical errors is in fact misleading. To understand the patterns of profit-makers and loss-makers in Tanzania, it makes much more sense to focus on a large sample rather than excluding the majority of the companies from the analysis, just because there is no statistical 'proof' available that they are significant profit-makers or significant loss-makers (and the test is even inappropriate as some values are not unknown but rather do not exist).

To undertake an economically meaningful grouping and to make use of all reliable information and indicators obtained, a more differentiated approach was taken. Companies were grouped into significant and not-significant profit or loss-makers based on the following criteria (for a more detailed description see comments to Table B-6 in the Appendix):

First, as done earlier, the broad distinction between profit-makers and loss-makers is defined according to average profits and losses from the period 1987-96. Not included are statements severely qualified by the audit company, i.e. statements which obtained the worst rating from TAC (adverse opinion). These accounts do not represent the true situation of the company. But for the 1987-92 data, where information on the quality of accounts was available for most companies, adverse statements were not a major problem and only affected ten cases. Second, to qualify as a 'significant' profit or loss-maker, average profits/losses have to exceed a minimum threshold (at 1994 prices TSh 5000 per employee and TSh 5 million per company). This criterion reflects the view that companies whose average profits and losses are close to zero are neither typical profit-makers nor typical loss-makers. Third, a company is only assigned to one of the two 'significant' categories if there is information for at least four arbitrary years. The number of statements may include interval information or information from the period 1984 to 1986, but only if these additional indicators do not change the categorisation but rather confirm it. Selectively using data from the period 1984 to 1986 avoids an a priori exclusion of companies which collapsed in the late 1980s.

All companies with five and more statements and indicators (based on the above rules) were defined to be significant profit or loss-makers. Companies with four statements were still defined as significant profit or loss-makers if all statements belonged to the same category, i.e. they were either profits or losses exclusively. In contrast, companies with three and fewer statements were assigned to a non-significant group.

All in all, the grouping resulted in 89 companies categorised as significant profit-makers (16 'not significant') and 133 companies as significant loss-makers (28 'not significant'). In value terms, this grouping includes 96% (TSh 57.3 billion) of the accumulated averages of the profit-making group and 99% of the accumulated averages of the loss-making group.

Besides the principal categorisation as profit-makers and loss-makers, companies were further categorised according to the size of profits and losses and how regularly either profits or losses occurred. For the latter grouping, the entire period 1984-96 was taken into account. To qualify as a *regular profit-maker* or *regular loss-maker*, between 80% and 100% of the profit and loss statements needed to be within the same category (i.e. zero deviations were tolerated for companies with four statements only, one deviation for companies with five to nine statements, and two for companies with 10-13 statements). Furthermore, the company had to be rated as significant (which was not the case for one company only). Despite the rather restrictive definitions, there are nevertheless 70 regular loss-makers and 51 regular profit-makers (comprising 964 profit and loss statements of which 7.8% (75) deviate from the group category). The survival of a large number of persistent loss-makers is a strong indication of the prevalence of soft budget constraints.

Evaluating the relative distribution in the economy, regular loss-makers are over-represented in textiles (17 out of 24 average loss-maker), food and beverage (6 out of 8), public utilities (2 out of 3) and mining (5 out of 8). The share of regular profit-makers is particularly high with food crops (5 out of 6), sugar, breweries and cigarette (8 of 8) and chemicals (6 of 8).[160]

Companies were also assigned the attribute *'large'* profit or loss-maker if their average profits and losses exceeded TSh 500 million (US$1 million) per company or TSh 1.5 million (US$3000) per employee. Roughly 20% of the companies for which profit and loss statements were obtained belong to one of these categories. With the exception of two companies all are rated as significant and most of them (74-88%) are regular profit or loss-makers. The fact that many of the large loss-makers survived into the 1990s again corroborates, or at least does not contradict, the assumption that soft budget constraints were relevant.

According to the data, profits and losses in Tanzania have been highly concentrated. The 20 largest loss-makers represent more than 80% of losses

[160] The data at the two-digit level are given in Table B-9 in the Appendix.

(however only 37% of total employment in the loss-making group and 12% of loss-making companies). And the 20 largest profit-makers comprise 82% of the profits (60% of total employment in the profit-making group and 19% of profit-making companies). Figure 8-2 presents graphs for the overall data set.

Figure 8-2: Concentration of Average Profits and Losses (1987-96)

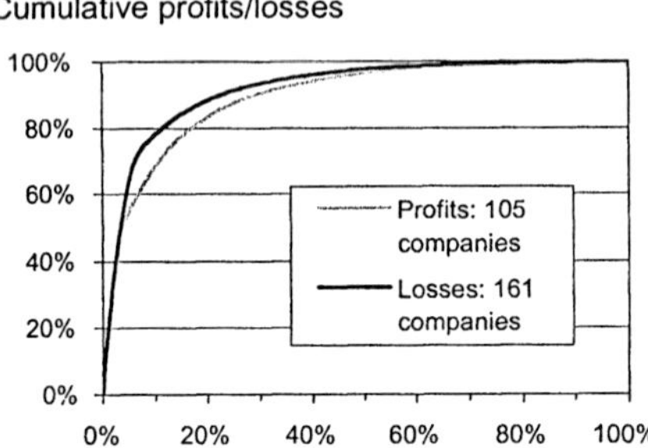

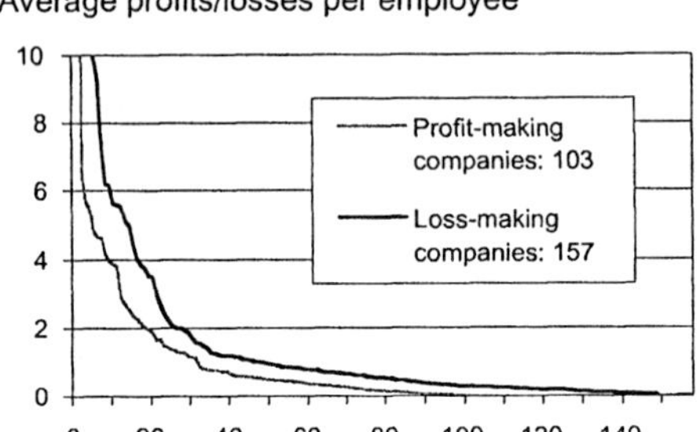

a: TSh million, average of 1987-96, 1994 prices. Values of four loss-makers and one profit-maker exceeded TSh 10 million (losses per employee TSh 22.9, 16.1, 11.5 and 11.4 m, profit per employee TSh 38.4 m).

Tables B-10 and B-11 in the Appendix additionally list the 20 largest profit-makers and loss-makers, sorted according to their average profits/losses per company and average profits/losses per employee.

Note: The profit-making group includes the banking sector with NBC as the largest profit-maker (16% of cumulative total), which is, using internationally accepted accounting standards, a large loss-maker (other financial institutions with large profits: National Provident Fund 2.8%, National Insurance Corporation 1%, all other <1%). In terms of averages per employee, NBC holds position 29.

Source: Data calculated according to columns b) and d) of Table B-6 in the Appendix

Among the top loss-makers are in particular textile and shoe companies, as well as utility parastatals (electricity, telephone and water); top profit-makers, by contrast, include NBC (a totally misleading assessment), companies from the petroleum sector, as well as parastatals related to transport infrastructure.[161]

Finally, companies have been assigned the attribute *'improving'* or *'deteriorating'*, if their annual profits and losses 'significantly' increased or decreased over time. Even though this categorisation is appealing and to some extent powerful for characterising parastatal companies, it needs to be interpreted with caution. As noted earlier in Section a), an indicator which measures changes in performance according to changes in profits and losses is problematic if calculated for a period where market prices change considerably or where the country undertakes thorough economic reforms which affect profitability in specific markets. Accordingly, in the short and medium term, trends do not just reflect a company's efforts but also changing market conditions and the impact of trade reforms or devaluations of the national currency. TAC (1991, p. 16) in fact emphasises that the devaluation of the

[161] For detailed information on the sector-wide and location-based distribution of large profit/loss-makers see Table B-9 in the Appendix.

Tanzanian Shilling from 1986 onwards contributed significantly to the worsening situation of parastatal companies in Tanzania.

Despite these reservations, changes in profits and losses are still a useful indicator to measure parastatal efforts and performance, if interpreted carefully and if other indicators are taken into consideration. On the one hand, reforms are typically initiated to change economic incentives so that companies operate within an institutional framework where all prices reflect true economic costs, i.e. the companies are expected to *change* their behaviour and to make profits, at least in the medium and longer run. On the other hand, in the case of parastatals in Tanzania, although devaluation mattered, many of the parastatals still managed to access foreign exchange at below market prices, for instance, by not paying the TSh equivalent (counterpart funds) or by defaulting on loans, which were drawn to access foreign exchange (see Chapter 7.1). Last but not least, having data on average changes in performance enables possible differences within sectors and sub-sectors to be identified. Such differences would suggest that changes in the performance of parastatals are more likely a reflection of management efforts rather than policy changes.

Defining and measuring the change in performance of parastatals turned out to be difficult. Most parastatal profits and losses in Tanzania do not change uniformly—more commonly, they fluctuate, and they rise, fall or remain constant during certain sub-periods. If the emphasis is on individual statements instead of period averages, the common approach is to check whether the time series data show a significant positive or negative trend. If averages matter one can simply split the data into two equal sub-periods and test whether the average of the first period is significantly larger (or smaller) than the average of the second period. Both methods are legitimate, but they explain different things.

For the subsequent data analysis, the trend approach was chosen, calculated for the entire period 1987(84)-96, as well as for the sub-periods 1987-93 (period of major devaluations) and 1993-96. The *overall trend*, which is used to characterise the company, is in most cases calculated for the period 1987-96. (Additional data from the period 1984 to 1986 are selectively taken into account for companies with three and fewer profit and loss statements during the period 1987-96.) Trends for the two sub-periods are supposed to answer the question whether negative values only reflect the impact of devaluation, which would prevail if profits of companies within a sector were affected uniformly.

Once more it was necessary to compromise between an economically meaningful categorisation and one which was based on the commonly-applied confidence intervals. Because of the erratic fluctuation of many profits and losses standard deviations are generally high. This implies that several trends are not significant at the 95% confidence level. To deal with the problem, two different significance levels 95% (sharp) and 75% (fuzzy) were applied.

The unusually low confidence level of 75% is justified since the major goal is not to test significant trends but to differentiate between companies, whose situation was more likely to have improved from others, whose situation was more likely to have worsened (with a large number of companies in between which drop out). As noted earlier, profits and losses of parastatal companies fluctuated considerably because of the generally poor quality of accounting (which still can be poor when accounts are rated 'clean' by the Tanzanian Audit Corporation). Many of the companies therefore have large standard deviations and may not show an improving or deteriorating trend significant at the 95% level. Partly as a reflection of this, but also for other reasons, companies may show opposite trends within smaller sub-periods. On average, however, it still makes sense to categorise some of them as generally improving or deteriorating, even though the trends are not significant at a level of 95%. Similar to the argument used when defining profit-makers and loss-makers, broadening the sample and reducing statistical errors of type II can permit a more accurate description of company characteristics.

Information on individual companies is presented in Table B-6 in the Appendix. In all, 126 companies indicate a significant trend for the period 1987(84)-96 (six by including data prior to 1987). To qualify as an 'improving' or 'deteriorating' profit or loss-maker, trends also had to reach a minimum annual change per employee, which was arbitrarily set at TSh 50,000 (US$100). Based on these definitions, only 40 companies are rated as improving, 70 are deteriorating and 16 do not reach the minimum threshold.[162]

Table 8-5 shows the sector-wide distribution of companies with significant positive and negative trends for all three periods (Table B-12 in the Appendix provides additional information on the overall trend, including a location-based differentiation as well as information on parameter values).

The fairly even distribution of improving and deteriorating companies between and within sectors, as well as the distribution of positive and negative trends between the two sub-periods indicated in Table 8-5 suggests that trends are not determined by devaluation and other policy changes only. A similar result has already been noted when differentiating between average profit-makers and average loss-makers. The findings are relevant for the interpretation of the results in Chapter 8.2.

To get an idea of the magnitude of negative and positive trends from 1987(84)-96, Table B-12 in the Appendix shows various specifications of average changes in performance (average changes per company, per employee—both unweighted or weighted according to the period the trends of the companies refer to). Interestingly, none of the group averages changes its sign (i.e. the rating as improving or deteriorating) with an alternative averaging method. With the exception of the category 'textile and leather' the same holds when contrasting averages of trends significant at 75% (F) with trends significant at 95% only (S).

162

Average annual change per employee	Improving (profit-maker + loss-maker)			Deteriorating (profit-maker + loss-maker)		
	All	at 95%	at 75% only	All	at 95%	at 75% only
≥ TSh 50,000	40 (7+33)	17 (5+12)	23 (2+21)	70 (38+32)	31 (17+14)	39 (21+18)
< TSh 50,000	7 (0+7)	2 (0+2)	5 (0+5)	9 (4+5)	0 (0+0)	9 (4+5)

Table 8-5: Number of Companies with Improving or Deteriorating Trends

	Comp in group	Comp. with P/L	Trend 1987(84)-96 [a]				Trend 1987-93 [a]				Trend 1993-96 [a]			
			No. (pos) F	No. (pos) S	No. (neg) F	No. (neg) S	No. (pos) F	No. (pos) S	No. (neg) F	No. (neg) S	No. (pos) F	No. (pos) S	No. (neg) F	No. (neg) S
Agriculture	78	40	5	4	10	3	7	4	4	1	2	1	6	4
Cash crops	26	20	3	3	4	1	2	2	2	1	2	1	3	3
Food crops	13	12	1	1	6	2	3	1	2				3	1
All other	39	8	1				2	1						
Mining	12	8	3				3		1		2	1		
Manufacturing	137	117	16	5	26	10	18	8	28	9	6	3	10	2
Food, beverage, tobacco	19	17	4	2	3	1	5	3	4	1	2	1	1	1
Textile & leather	29	25	3		5	3	3		6	3	1	1		
Wood, paper, printing	26	22			6	3			6	4			1	
Chemicals	14	12	1	1	5	2	2	1	4				3	
Construction	23	18	5	1	1		5	2	3		2		3	1
Metal & machinery	26	23	3	1	6	1	3	2	5	1	1	1	2	
Services	109	101	16	8	34	18	20	6	24	11	7	2	12	6
Public utilities	5	4	1	1			1							
Trade, repair & maintenance	39	36	7	3	12	9	7	3	11	7	1		3	
Transport & storage	24	22	4	1	12	6	6	2	4	2	1	1	4	4
Tourism	20	19	1		7	2	1		7	2	1		2	2
Finance	14	13	2	2	3	1	2		1		2		2	
Other services	7	7	1	1			3	1	1		2	1	1	
Total	336	266	40	17	70	31	48	18	57	21	17	7	28	12

a: Number of companies where annual profits/losses per employee indicate a significant positive or negative trend larger than TSh +/- 50,000 per year and employee (data shown for significance levels 75% (F: fuzzy) and 95% (S: Sharp)). The unusually low confidence level of 75% has been applied since the major goal was not to test significant trends but to differentiate between companies which had more likely improved their situation from others which had more likely worsened (see explanation in the text).

Source: Data calculated according to annual profit/loss statements and employment data (for more information see Table 8-3 and Tables B-6 and B-12 in the Appendix)

At the highest aggregation level, 'agriculture' shows on average a deteriorating profit and loss situation, 'mining', 'manufacturing' and 'services', in contrast, an improving trend. The trends within manufacturing and services are mixed however, i.e. they are on average negative for the categories 'wood, paper & printing', 'metal & machinery' as well as 'wholesale/retail trade, repair & maintenance' and 'tourism'. The grouping according to location indicates a heterogeneous picture. On average, however, it is positive for the categories 'centre' and 'sub-centre/near centre' and negative for remote areas.

All in all, this section categorised parastatals based on their annual profit and loss statements in different sub-groups, as regular or large loss-makers or companies with an improving or deteriorating trend. Despite several reservations, at least for the majority of companies, profits and losses are a sufficiently good second-best indicator on their performance. Table 8-6 displays a summary of the grouping criteria.

Table 8-6: Summary of Criteria for Grouping Profit or Loss-Makers

Criterion	Description
Profit or loss-maker	Grouping according to average rule, i.e. sum of profits and losses divided by number of observation.
Significant profit or loss-maker	Average profit/loss exceeds TSh 5000 per employee and TSh 5 million per company (1994 prices) and one of the following criteria holds: • 5 and more profit/loss statements (either from 1987-96, if not, with intervals that do not change the result, if not available with additional data from 1984-86) • 4 statements: Each single statement points to same category (either data from 1987-96, if not four statements available, with additional data from 1984-86).
Not significant profit or loss-maker	• Either 1-3 statements only • or 4 statements, but not all of them belong to same category • or 5 and more statements, but minimum size not reached.
Regular profit or loss-maker	• Significant profit/loss-maker and • between 80% and 100% of the profit and loss statements of the company (1984-96) indicate the same category, i.e. either profits only or losses only.
Large profit or loss-maker	• Per company: Average profits/losses exceeds TSh 500 million. • Per employee: Average profits/losses exceeds TSh 1.5 million.
Improving / deteriorating company	Trend from 1987-96 unless there are less than 4 statements and trend with 3 statements is not significant, additional data from 1984-86. • Fuzzy: Annual change ≥ TSh 50,000 and trend significant at 75%. • Sharp: Annual change ≥ TSh 50,000 and trend significant at 95%.

In the following analyses, those companies which would be most obviously badly categorised will be treated separately. As explained earlier, some of the regular profit-makers were highly inefficient and only made profits thanks to monopoly protection or inappropriate accounting (e.g. NBC's definition of non-performing loans). The five companies Tanzania Harbours Authority (THA), Tanzania Petroleum Development Corporation (TPDC), TIPER (Tanzania and Italian Petroleum Refining Company), the National Bank of Commerce (NBC) and the Cooperative and Rural Development Bank (CRDB) belonged to this group.

All the banks virtually collapsed in the early 1990s because of inefficiency and the government had to take over large amounts of non-performing assets. Stated profits of NBC and CRDB actually reflected an inappropriate assessment of the banks' lending portfolio. Moreover Tanzania's petroleum refining sector has been one of the most inefficient in the world. Tanzania's economy lost between US$10 and 20 million each year just in keeping the refinery in operation; this corresponded to a loss of US$25,000-50,000 per employee. Finally THA, which was operating the harbours in Dar es Salaam and Tanga, could only compete, because the nearest foreign harbour, i.e. in Mombassa, was also highly inefficient; and transporting goods thousands of kilometres by rail or road was not a real option, given the poor transport infrastructure in sub-Saharan Africa.

There are also many other profit-makers and loss-makers in Tanzania that benefited from monopoly protection. It has been assumed however that monopoly protection for these companies was fairly evenly distributed, i.e. profits and losses still indicate the relative performance of the companies (the ranking of the company relative to others).

d) The Reliability of Accounting Information: Between Real and Strategic Inability

> *'While the public enterprises may be state owned, in reality they are run on as avenues for personal enrichment,*
> *and fraud and embezzlement are nicknamed "lack of management skills".'*
>
> *Seith L. Chachage (1994, p. 12), University of Dar es Salaam*

So far the emphasis has largely been on discussing the magnitude of stated profits and losses of parastatal companies. With the exception of the reference to the Bureau of Statistics, not so much has been said about the quality of accounting information from which profit and loss statements are derived. A rent-seeking economy, which is characterised by a high degree of corruption and embezzlement, is likely to distort information at different levels. Looking at the parastatal sector, this distortion does not just apply to the generally non-transparent soft budget relation with the state (discussed in Chapter 8.2). It also affects the question of how parastatal staff are accountable for the funds, stocks and assets they handle. This second level, i.e. the 'relation' between the staff and the publicly-owned enterprise, is an important area where rent-seeking takes place, or to put it differently, it constitutes an important element in the rent-seeking chain. Rent-seeking at this level becomes observable through the non-production and distortion of accounting information.

Having the opportunity to evaluate data on the quality of accounting information is beneficial for several reasons. On the one hand, it provides some ideas on *how to treat and evaluate profit and loss data.* Adversely qualified profit and loss statements can be excluded from an analysis and poor accounting practices caution the researcher not to place too much emphasis on annual profit and loss statements but rather to look at averages over time.

On the other hand, information on the quality of accounting constitutes an additional interesting *indicator of rent-seeking.* As noted earlier, efforts of management may run counter to the development of profit-relevant constraints dictated by general government policy changes and the development of prices in world markets. Furthermore the development of profits and losses may also reflect success or failure in rent-seeking contests not accounted for. An indicator of rent-seeking which is based on the quality of accounts does not have these disadvantages, even though there will be other distorting effects. However, selectively combining different indicators may tell more about the management's efforts to run a company efficiently than an indicator which is solely based on profit and loss statements. With this motivation in mind, the study includes a detailed reference to accounting practices of parastatal companies.

The Poor Quality and Large Arrears of Parastatal Accounts

Prior to 1994 the annual reports of Tanzania Audit Corporation included general and individual information on parastatal and other accounts TAC audited during the year, indicating that accounting performance of commercial and non-commercial parastatals has been poor in the 1980s and only improved slowly over time. The inadequate process of recording and classifying transactions in accordance with the most basic accounting principles and standards implied a generally *poor quality* of parastatal accounts on the one hand, and intolerably *large arrears* in finalising annual financial statements on the other. These shortcomings mainly occurred in the public sector, where poor performance was of no direct consequence for the survival of the enterprise (or non-commercial parastatal). The systematic difference is also emphasised in the 1989 TAC report:

> 'In the private sector, a qualification to the accounts is a rare exception. For the pubic sector, however, qualifications to the accounts have tended to be the norm.' (TAC (1989, p. 12))

Besides clean audit reports, TAC assigns different degrees of 'poor quality' or qualification in their audits. Audited accounts may obtain a *'qualified'* audit report, a *'disclaimer of opinion'* report or even an *'adverse opinion'* report. The reasons for these qualifications are numerous. According to TAC (1990, p. 15), they mostly hinge on violation of the following standards: maintaining proper books, having available documentary evidence to support transactions, complying with disclosure requirements, and adhering to fundamental accounting principles and policies. As will be outlined below, it can be assumed that a great deal of these failures and the absence of disciplinary actions are closely related to rent-seeking activities.

Poor record keeping implied, among other things, that it was not possible to control the movement of fixed assets, inventories, and even cash. TAC (1989, p. 12f) describes the desolate situations as follows:

> 'Cases are abound where fixed assets have never been physically verified...Where attempts have been made...the results of the counts are not agreed with the fixed assets records...'
>
> 'It is commonly accepted business practice to physically verify stocks and stores at each year end and reconcile the results... In the case of parastatals, the year-end physical stock count is rarely properly planned and executed...Slow moving, damaged and obsolete stocks are rarely ascertained...'

The accounting company further complains that contradictions between entries in the bank statements and cash books are not regularly investigated and appropriate corrective measures are not taken; copies of cash receipts, original payment vouchers and cash books are not made available, and the poor record keeping also affects records of debtors, staff debtors and creditors—some public enterprises do not even have accounting policies on how to make provisions for bad and doubtful debts (TAC (1989, p. 13f)).

As noted earlier, it was decided not to use any profit and loss information that obtained the worst rating ('adversely' qualified accounts) to measure enterprise performance. Profit and loss statements of such accounts are evidently wrong. Although the other two poor-quality categories may also imply distorted profit and loss information, there are good reasons to include them. On the one hand, accounts may be qualified because the enterprise does not supply documentary evidence on specific transactions upon request. This problem often reflects different degrees of carelessness and embezzlement. But it will not distort the profits and losses of the company (with embezzlement losses are simply higher but these are the true losses the company incurs). On the other hand, accounts may be qualified and receive a qualified or disclaimer opinion because important procedures were not adhered to. If a company does not physically verify its assets and stocks for several years, large losses are likely to occur when it finally takes a thorough inventory. The losses then largely reflect the neglect and embezzlement of previous years. Even though annual profit and loss information are distorted if taken alone, evaluating parastatals according to their average profits and losses over an extended period largely reduces this distortion (excluding all qualified accounts from the calculation of averages would actually distort averages more).

Finally, a major area of failure in complying with statutes, which becomes obvious when looking at any of the TAC reports produced since the early 1980s, is the *large arrears in finalising annual accounts*. Tanzania has a well-specified Act from 1981 which requires parastatal accounts to be finalised, audited and presented to the parliament within six to eight months. This Act has been completely ignored by both companies and enforcing institutions.

Similar to the collection of profit and loss information, the original goal was to obtain annual information on the quality and arrears of all the 336 companies defined as commercial parastatals for the period 1987-96. However, besides the problem that not all companies were audited by Tanzania Audit Corporation, TAC only published individual information on parastatal accounts up to the June-1993 report. It was impossible to get access to the missing data, apparently as the TAC management realised the topic was too sensitive.[163] The subsequent analysis is therefore based on a restricted sample.

[163] Requesting information in March 2000, the first answer was a 'maybe'. However, despite my promises to handle unpublished information confidentially (not revealing any parastatal names), TAC finally argued that they could not afford to lose any clients and auditing of parastatal accounts had become competitive. Furthermore, they emphasised that the company was acting like a private company and would have to be paid a certain fee if they agreed to collecting the information internally (twice the average annual income in Tanzania for a few hours' job). I interpreted this as a polite refusal (I was neither allowed to do the data collection myself nor allowed to observe data

The restrictions implied a bias in the data, because information on large arrears of accounts from the late 1980s and early 1990s was not included in the reports prior to 1994 and accounts in arrears tended to be of lower quality. Table 8-7 shows the extent of missing information for each year, as well as the information obtained (number of audits finalised by June 1993 referring to the commercial parastatal sample).

Table 8-7: State of Accounts of Commercial Parastatals (1986-92) as at 30 June 1993

	86	87	88	89	90	91	92
Accounts not audited by June 1993	1	3	9	17	33	61	141
Accounts in progress [a]	0	0	3	8	11	20	47
Accounts in arrears [b]	0	2	3	3	13	16	4
Subsequent accounts in arrears [c]	1	1	3	6	9	22	38
Other accounts not mentioned [d]						3	28
Dec. 1992 accounts [e]							24
Accounts audited by June 1993	267	267	259	252	234	203	122
Total of the sample under TAC	268	270	268	269	267	264	263

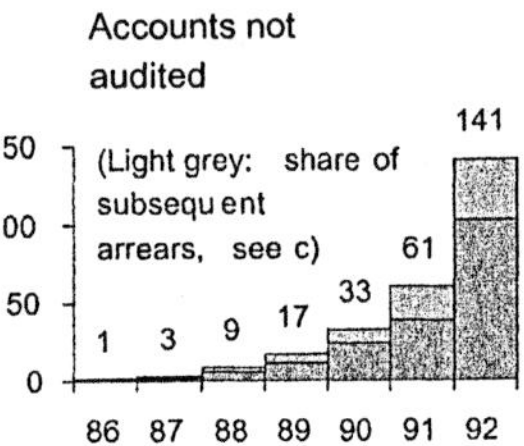

a: Audits mentioned in TAC (1993, p. 29-34) to be in progress.
b: Accounts explicitly mentioned in TAC (1993, p. 35-39) to be in arrears. However, TAC reports only indicate 'since when' accounts are in arrears, i.e. above row does not include accounts of subsequent years.
c: Accounts of subsequent years after an account has been mentioned to be in arrears (see b), assuming the company did not close but still owes financial statements to be audited each year.
d: Accounts of parastatal companies apparently mistakenly not mentioned in TAC (1993). TAC provided profit/loss information on these accounts later on, so they must have been in progress or arrears by June 1993.
e: These accounts are in arrears from 1 July 1993 onwards and are therefore not explicitly mentioned in the 1993 TAC report (which evaluates the period from 1 July 1992 to 30 June 1993).

Source: Calculated according to information shown in TAC (1993) and information obtained from TAC through questionnaires (see also Table 8-3)

The period to analyse information on quality and arrears was set as 1986-91 (instead of 1987-92), since it was possible to retrieve nearly all information for the year 1986, but for the year 1992 information on audits was only available for 46% of the commercial parastatals under TAC (122 audits out of 263 done within a year). To minimise remaining distortions from missing data and to allow for a meaningful interpretation of the development of quality and arrears over time, two different data sets are considered: a set with quality and arrears information of *audited accounts only,* and an extended data set which additionally includes *assumptions on the quality and arrears of missing data* referring to the years 1986-91.[164]

Missing values on quality are replaced with the quality the company obtained in the last report audited. Because there is an improving trend over time, this procedure may effectively over-estimate poor quality. However, as will be shown in detail later, accounts finalised and audited with large arrears

collection if somebody else was assigned). There is no need to emphasise that the other excuses were also flawed. Obviously, all parastatals should be accountable to the general public.

164 The company averages are shown in the Appendix (columns i and j of Table B-6).

also tended to be accounts of lower quality—which again counteracts the improving trend.

More problematical is the replacement of missing 'time until audit' values of the accounts of 1986-91 not audited by June 1993. Several problems arise. First of all, it is necessary to guess when the audit after June 1993 was actually made. The approach taken here was a best-case scenario, which is not the likely outcome but allows accounts in arrears to be included. All accounts not audited by June 1993 are assumed to have been audited by June 1994. Another problem arises because it may not be evident whether a company continued to produce or whether it was waiting to be privatised or liquidated. For instance, if a company had been mentioned to be in arrears since the 1988 accounts, it is not clear whether to include values for the years 1989 to 1993. To apply a conservative estimate, the latter accounts are only included if there is some indication that the company was still operating in the 1990s (e.g. profit and loss statements later obtained through TAC questionnaires and other sources).

Finally, if a company ceases production, nobody may bother about finalising the last accounts or the management may just wait for the final decisions on what is going to happen with the company. In the meantime, with each year that passes arrears simply accumulate. Treating these companies the same as operating companies may distort the picture. Hence if there is an indication that the company stopped operating, it can even be argued to exclude remaining accounts in arrears. However, besides the problem that the identity of dormant companies is not known (and the figure is not large), companies which lack an orderly closure or 'transition' are most likely also the companies prone to asset stripping and other malpractices. Since the ultimate goal is to obtain an indicator of rent-seeking, above all corruption and embezzlement, it makes sense to include these accounts.

All in all, the assumptions applied to replace missing values on quality and arrears are not optimal and they remain open to criticism. However, not including missing data at all may show an even more distorted picture, in particular with the data on arrears. Given the uncertainty, it has been decided to keep both figures in view (though most results are only presented for audited accounts with the indicator for quality, and for extended values with the indicator for arrears).

Tables 8-8 and 8-9 present the development of quality and time until audit of the two different data sets, i.e. commercial parastatal accounts whose audits were finalised between 1986 and 1992 and published in the TAC reports 1987-93 and averages calculated from the adjusted data set (henceforth called 'extended' values).[165]

---

[165] Strictly speaking, it is not possible to calculate averages from ordinal values. The assigned quality categories (1-4) are ordinal values, i.e. even though the relation 1 < 2 < 3 < 4 holds, distances between the values are not defined (a clean report (1) is not twice as good as a qualified report (2) or four times as good as an 'adversely-qualified' (4) report). However, since the target is to reach (1) and the table equally indicated a percentage distribution, the average-like indicator still allows a meaningful interpretation of the development of quality over time.

Table 8-8: Quality of Accounts Audited (Relative Distribution and 'Averages')

Type of report: [a]	1986	1987	1988	1989	1990	1991	*1992*
Clean (1)	46%	52%	59%	65%	68%	72%	*83%*
Qualified (2)	40%	37%	31%	31%	29%	27%	*17%*
Disclaimer (3)	10%	10%	8%	4%	2%	0%	*0%*
Adverse (4)	4%	1%	1%	1%	1%	0%	*0%*
'Average' quality [a, c]	1.72	1.61	1.51	1.40	1.35	1.29	*1.17*
'Av.' quality ext.[b, c]	1.72	1.60	1.52	1.43	1.43	1.40	*1.34*

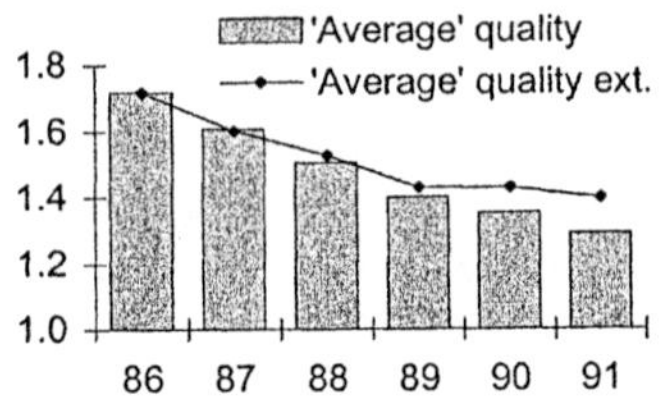

a: Qualification according to Tanzania Audit Corporation.

b: Missing values replaced with the value of the quality in the last report available, if indicators had been available that the parastatal was still operating.

c: The data only indicate an approximation of average, as figures are ordinal (see Footnote 165). Maximum quality =1.00.

Source: See Table 8-7

Not shown in the tables is the development of the nature of accounting for non-commercial parastatals. In particular the accounts of *District Development Corporations (DDC)* and *Sports Associations* were much worse. TAC for instance noted in 1990 that 75% of active DDC were in arrears, some for more than a decade, and some of the Sports Associations had been in arrears for as many as fifteen years (TAC (1990, p. 11f)).[166]

Even though there is a clear positive trend in the change of the quality of accounts and the reduction in arrears of commercial parastatals shown in the tables, it is evident that accounting performance in Tanzania has been poor all along. Deviation from a clean report cannot be accepted by any standards, and delays in finalising annual accounts hinder the management from using accounting information as a controlling and feedback instrument. As noted earlier, the annual TAC reports repeatedly complained about the poor quality and large arrears. The question emerges why this situation did not improve more quickly. To adequately answer this, it is helpful to first get an idea about the relation between the different company characteristics.

Statistics on Poor Quality and Large Arrears

This section describes the relation between the company-features 'poor quality', 'large arrears', 'profits and losses' as well as the 'size of the company'. The distinct properties of the variables examined (interval data for arrears and ordinal values for qualities, lack of normal distribution, etc.) suggest an analysis based on cross-tabulations and non-parametric test procedures. Figure 8-3 (p. 458) visualises average quality, average time until audit and average profits for

[166] Looking at the 1993-TAC report (the last report where data were available), 47 Public District Development Corporations are still mentioned as in arrears (10 for ten years and more!), 24 DDC have accounts in progress (one third of these accounts are older than 1986!) and accounts of only 3 companies were audited between June 1992 and June 1993 (Pare DDC received a 'clean report' for its 1991 accounts, Hanang and Karagwe DDC obtained a 'disclaimer opinion report' for their accounts of 1983-89 and 1986-89).

Table 8-9: Time Until Accounts Are Audited (Distribution and Averages)

Periods (months) [a]		1986	1987	1988	1989	1990	1991	*1992*
No. of accounts in each group [b]	1 (1-17)	87	106	100	116	124	113	*122*
	2 (18-24)	122	120	138	116	96	90	*n.a.*
	3 (25-36)	43	32	14	16	14	n.a.	*n.a.*
	4+ (37-)	15	9	7	4	n.a.	n.a.	*n.a.*
Relative distri-bution [b]	(1)	33%	40%	39%	46%	53%	56%	-
	(2)	46%	45%	53%	46%	41%	44%	*n.a*
	(3)	16%	12%	5%	6%	6%	n.a	*n.a*
	(4+)	6%	3%	3%	2%	n.a	n.a	*n.a*
Average period [b]		1.97	1.81	1.72	1.63	1.53	1.44	*1.00*
Average period ext. [c]		1.97	1.84	1.82	1.78	1.76	1.72	*1.48*

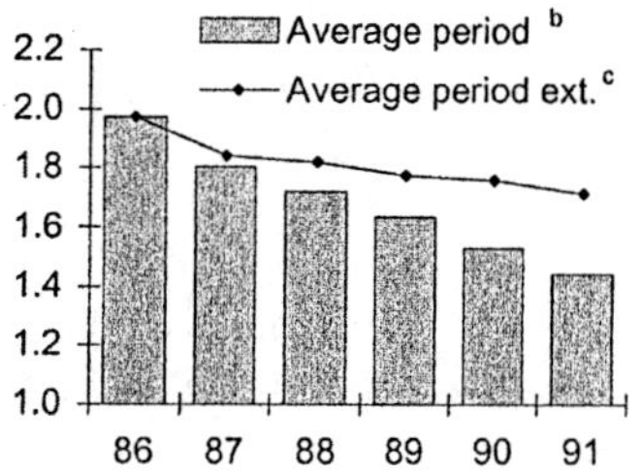

Information on arrears is only available in terms of intervals since annual TAC reports only indicate accounts audited during the preceding twelve months (1 July to 30 June), but not the exact date when submitted accounts were audited within this period. Taking into account a grace period of six months until accounts have to be audited, accounts can only be identified to be in arrears if they do not appear in the following year's TAC report (assigned the value 1). This is of course a conservative treatment, as for instance a company which closes its annual accounts in March may already be nine months in arrears. This is the case if the audit is done in June of the following year (for accounts closing in March arrears start to accumulate from September onwards).

a: Periods: Number of annual TAC reports until accounts are mentioned to be audited, however including a grace period of six months. In parentheses indication of maximum months till audit, which depends on the month a company closes its annual accounts (for additional information see comments to column (i) of Table B-6 in the Appendix).

b: Arrears of audited accounts only. This implies a bias, as any account audited after June 1993 is not included.

c: The data include accounts which had not yet been audited by June 1993. Accounts explicitly mentioned to be in progress or in arrears in the 1993 TAC report are assumed to have been audited by June 1994. All subsequent accounts in arrears are treated the same (i.e. assumed to have been audited in June 1994), if indicators were available that the parastatal was still operating.

Source: See Table 8-7

different combinations of the variables, and Table 8-10 additionally displays the statistics of the cross-classifications, which allow a description of the extent of the relation and the statistical significance.

Calculations have been made either with annual accounts (I) or company averages for the period 1986-91 (II). Among other things, the differentiation helps to assess whether a relation is more strongly tied to the character of a company or to the outcome in a specific year.

The *Spearman correlation* shown in Table 8-10 measures correlations according to ranks (and not actual values). *Gamma* values and the *Kendall's Tau* are two measures of monotonicity, which compare the number of concordant and discordant pairs.[167] The three indicators reflect versions of the widely-used

[167] The concept of concordant and discordant pairs and the meaning of the coefficients are best explained with an example. If the values (1, 12), (3, 18), (3, 24) and (2, 36) represent the extent of poor quality and the number of months until accounts are finalised and audited, the pairs (1, 12)&(3, 18), (1, 12)&(3, 24), as well as (1, 12)&(2, 36) are concordant. They join the property that a worse quality (e.g. 2 instead of 1) is associated with a longer time until audit (36 months instead of 12 months). Discordance is given with the opposite relation (in the example, discordant cases are the combinations (3, 24)&(2, 36), as well as (3, 18)&(2, 36)). Having evaluated all possible combinations of pairs in a data set, a domination of either concordant or discordant cases indicates

Figure 8-3: Grouping According to Quality of Accounts, Arrears in Audit and Average Profits and Losses (TSh m, 1986-91)

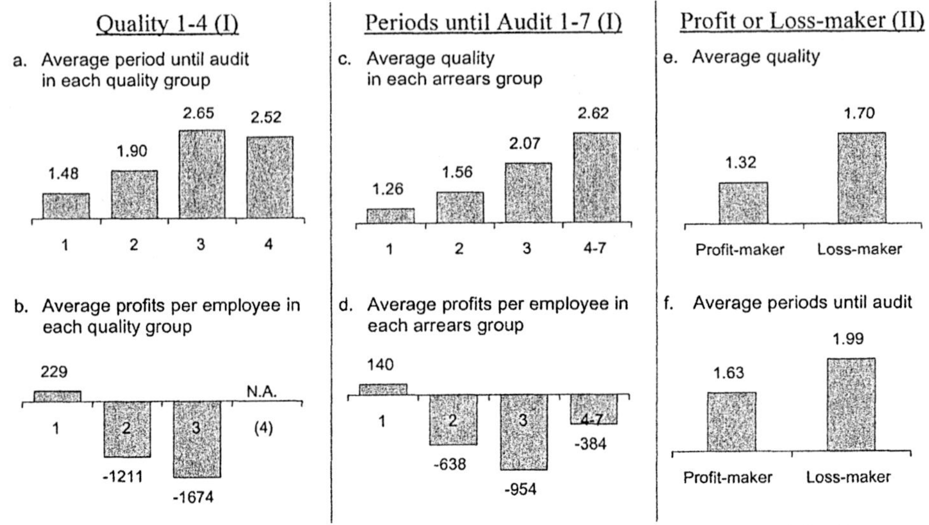

The diagrams are either calculated from annual statements (I) or company averages (II). There are no profit and loss data for the quality group 'adverse' (4), as these profit/loss statements are per definition wrong and have been excluded from the data set. The groups 'profit-maker' and 'loss-maker' are defined according to average profits per employee (excluding the badly-categorised profit-makers) and they refer to the years 1986 to 1991 (to match the years with the accounting data). 'Periods until audit' represent extended values. The intersection of the vertical axes in the diagrams a, c, e and f is 1, reflecting the benchmark 'no delay' (period 1) and 'clean' report (quality 1).

Results are similar with alternative specifications: extended/not-extended accounting data, average profits of 1987-96. Except for diagram d, the same relations between categories hold if profits and losses are defined 'per company'.

Source: See Table 8-7

Pearson correlation coefficient and are appropriate for ordinal data or for interval data that do not satisfy the normality assumption.[168] Under statistical independence all values will be zero. The approximate t-values shown in parentheses in the table indicate that the calculated coefficients are highly significant (confidence level well above 99%) and different from zero.

As can be expected, there is a positive relation between *the poor quality of data and the arrears in audit*, i.e. accounts in arrears tend to be of lower quality. It is obviously more difficult to finalise annual financial statements if they refer to several years back. A missing inventory cannot be taken ex-post and important documents may have gone lost or have not been produced at the time.

that there is a monotonic relation (negative, if discordant cases dominate). In contrast to Kendall's Tau, which is a measure for strict monotonicity, Gamma ignores tied values, i.e. values where only one variable changes (for instance comparing (3, 18) with (3, 24)).

168 Similar to the Pearson correlation coefficient, values range from -1 to +1; the sign indicates the direction of the relationship and its absolute value indicates the strength.

Table 8-10: Relation Between Poor Quality of Accounting, Arrears in Audits, and Profits and Losses

	Poor Quality and Arrears		Poor Quality and Profits		Arrears and Profits	
	I. annual statements	II. company averages	I. annual statements	II. company averages	I. annual statements	II. company averages
Spearman correlation	0.372 *0.023* (15.411)	0.507 *0.050* (9.851)	-0.291 *0.027* (-10.298)	-0.354 *0.055* (-6.404)	-0.184 *0.028* (-6.435)	-0.284 *0.054* (-4.711)
Gamma	0.581 *0.031* (15.104)	0.444 *0.044* (9.590)	-0.337 *0.031* (-10.679)	-0.270 *0.043* (-6.404)	-0.194 *0.029* (-6.614)	-0.207 *0.039* (-5.307)
Kendall's Tau-c	0.261 *0.017* (15.104)	0.359 *0.037* (9.590)	-0.246 *0.023* (-10.679)	-0.239 *0.037* (-6.404)	-0.132 *0.020* (-6.614)	-0.195 *0.037* (-5.307)
No. of valid cases	1482	283	1148	255	1179	255

For data specification see Figure 8-3. Values in italics are *asymptotic standard errors* (not assuming the null hypothesis) and values in parentheses indicate *approximate t-values* (since absolute values are larger than 1.96, coefficients are all highly significant). For a brief explanation of Gamma and Tau see Footnote 167. All relations hold and remain highly significant with the alternative specifications mentioned in the comments to Figure 8-3.

People who know important details may have left the company, others do not remember specific matters, and so forth.

The fact that Table 8-10 does not show a very strong statistical relation between quality of data and arrears in audit (parameter values close to 1 or -1) does not undermine the result. As will be argued below, there are several reasons which explain why on-time accounts may also be of poor quality or accounts audited very late may obtain clean reports. In particular the considerable difference between the Gamma value (0.581) and the Kendall's Tau (0.261) (when comparing annual statements and not company averages) indicates that there are many tied values, i.e. statements with similar quality but different arrears and vice versa.

Also the finding on the relation between the nature of the accounting and the companies' *profits and losses* is in line with what can be expected and corresponds to what has been indicated in Figure 8-3. As shown in Table 8-10, the coefficients are not very large, but they are still highly significant and reveal the expected negative sign.

Hardly anybody will dispute that the size of profits and losses of a company does not just depend on the quality and timeliness of accounting. Nevertheless, the estimated coefficients still indicate that companies with poor accounting quality and late audits are more likely companies with smaller profits and higher losses. Without proper accounting tools and without timely and reliable financial data it is more difficult, if not impossible, to run a company efficiently, above all to exercise meaningful and effective financial management and control. Even though the relation is only weak, this is a very strong finding.

As discussed earlier, accounting performance improved over time. Having the generally positive trend in mind, another interesting question is to examine which of the two groups (profit-maker or loss-maker) has been the better improver. For this purpose, indicators on the *change in arrears* and *change in quality* have been defined, taking the difference between the two means of the years 1989-91 and 1986-88. Alternatively, as with profits and losses, one could have estimated a trend in the annual observations. However, the 'average' approach was favoured, as the specific shape of the trend and its significance is not relevant for the purpose here; what is of interest is the change in average performance between the two sub-periods (and not the exact distribution therein).

The indicator includes an unpleasant bias in the specification, as both underlying variables have a lower limit, meaning that the better accounting performance of a company is in the first period, the less the company is able to improve in the second period. In the extreme, a company may have clean and on-time accounts in both periods and may therefore indicate no change, while another company is rated as a good improver as it reduces its average arrears or improves its average quality. Due to this effect, it can be expected that the loss-making group, which has on average a worse quality and higher arrears, turns out to be the better improver than the profit-making counterpart.

Table 8-11 shows the Mann-Whitney test statistics from the comparison of the two groups profit-maker (P) and loss-maker (L), taking up the earlier analysis on average quality and arrears as well as the new question regarding changes in accounting.[169] The test procedure assigns ranks to each value in the data set in an ascending order from best to worst (without regard to the profit/loss group membership) and compares the mean rank between the groups. If the groups do not differ, the mean ranks will be similar.

The first two tests (a. and b.) provide the statistics for what has been suggested with the diagrams e) and f) in Figure 8-3. Profit-makers have a significantly better average quality and smaller average arrears than loss-makers. Particularly interesting are the results of the four tests relating to the change in accounting performance. The results are shown for audited accounts (c. and e.), as well as extended values, which include accounts of 1986-91 that were not audited by 1993 (d. and f.). The latter specification is important when focusing on changes in arrears, since excluding all accounts not audited by 1993 would considerably distort the indicator (most of the accounts of the second sub-period audited late would not be included). The situation is different with the quality category, as missing values can only be replaced with the value of the last audited account.

[169] The Mann-Whitney test—a nonparametric equivalent to the t-test—is a robust method to answer the question whether two groups differ from one another. The generalised form, which allows more than two groups to be compared, is the Kruskal-Wallis test (nonparametric equivalent to the one-way ANOVA). In contrast to a t-test or the analysis of variance, the tests do not demand a normal distribution and constant variance but only require that the underlying variables have an ordinal ranking and a continuous distribution.

Table 8-11: Differences in Accounting Between Profit and Loss Groups

Mann-Whitney test	a. Average Quality		b. Average Arrears ext.		c. ø Change Quality		d. ø Change Quality ext.		e. ø Change Arrears		f. ø Change Arrears ext.	
	(P)	(L)	(P)	(L)	(P)	(L)	(P)	(L)	(P)	(L)	(P)	(L)
No. of cases in group	114	141	114	141	108	126	108	133	108	126	108	133
Mean rank	99.9	150.7	105.8	145.8	110.2	123.8	112.5	127.9	115.8	119.0	114.0	126.7
Asymptotic significance	0.000		0.000		0.106		0.070		0.707		0.152	

Test statistics are based on company averages of 1986-91 accounts that were audited by June 1993 (a, b, c, e), as well as extended values (d, f) (see Table 8-7). Profit-makers (P) and Loss-makers (L) are defined according to the years 1986-1991. Mean ranks are higher for the group with a worse quality, larger arrears and smaller improvements. Significance levels below 0.050 indicate that the groups differ at the 95% confidence level.

Despite concerns of bias in the indicator, profit-makers are still better improvers than loss-makers, though the differences are not significant at the 95% confidence level. However, as will be shown below, applying a more appropriate indicator on the 'change in performance', which corrects for the different ability to improve, will reveal highly significant differences between profit-makers and loss-makers for any specification.

To correctly assess changes in quality and arrears, the companies are assigned codes, reflecting one of nine performance categories. The coding takes into account the overall positive trend in accounting performance and corrects for the distorting effect of different starting points. A smaller code value indicates a better accounting performance (ordinal relation). Table 8-12 presents the definition of the codes and the corresponding new test statistics.[170] To document the intensity of the relation, Table 8-12 also shows the Gamma values calculated from the cross-tabulation of the 'change in performance' codes with the two groups (profit-makers / loss-makers).

As expected, with the new specifications differences between the profit-making and loss-making groups are now much more pronounced and all significant. The Gamma values are also significant and indicate the expected relation. The better results prove that the above-mentioned concerns regarding the bias in the 'change in performance' indicator were justified, i.e. profit-makers are at a disadvantage if performance is only measured according to differences between the two sub-period averages.[171]

The links of poor quality, large arrears and profits and losses have been discussed above. Another interesting question is whether accounting features are related to the *size of the company*. There are two opposing effects which determine this relation. On the one hand, larger companies are more likely to

[170] For additional information see descriptions to columns (k) and (l) of Table B-6 in the Appendix.

[171] Results further improve if only significant profit-makers and loss-makers, as defined in Chapter 8.1, are included in the analysis (asymptotic significance 0.000, 0.001 and 0.000 in the Mann-Whitney test and Gamma values of 0.600, 0.278 and 0.373, all highly significant (0.000)).

Table 8-12: Differences in Accounting Between Profit/Loss Groups with Recoded Change in Performance (1986-91)

Change in Performance [a]	Code	Underlying change Δ [b]	Mann-Whitney test	ø Change Quality	ø Change Arrears	ø Change Arrears ext.
Maximum always achieved	11	$\Delta = 0$		(P) (L)	(P) (L)	(P) (L)
Improving (from fairly good)	21	$\Delta < 0$	No. of cases	108 126	108 126	108 133
Strong improving (from bad)	22	$\Delta \leq -1$	Mean rank	88.8 142.1	87.0 115.1	106.6 126.9
Weak improving (from bad)	23	$0 > \Delta > -1$	Asymp. signific.	0.000	0.021	0.002
No change (from fairly good)	31	$\Delta = 0$				
No change (from fairly bad)	33	$\Delta = 0$	Gamma	0.530	0.199	0.261
Weak worsening (from fairly good)	41	$0 < \Delta \leq 0.5$	Asymp. stand. error	*0.071*	*0.084*	*0.080*
Strong worsening (" fairly good)	42	$\Delta > 0.5$	Approx. T-value	(6.954)	(2.365)	(3.217)
Worsening (from bad)	43	$\Delta > 0$	Approx. signific.	0.000	0.018	0.001

Grouping: Profit-maker (P) and Loss-maker (L), as defined in Table 8-11. Mean ranks in the Mann-Whitney statistics are higher for the group with a smaller improvement. For the calculation of Gamma profit-makers are assigned the code (1) and loss-makers code (2).

a: In parentheses rating of mean in first period (1986-88): Fairly good, if average < 2.0; bad, if average ≥ 2.0.
b: Negative values for change (Δ) indicate improvements (i.e. a reduction in poor quality or arrears).

employ better-qualified staff and to use more automated accounting procedures. This suggests that larger companies have an advantage in producing reliable and on-time accounts. On the other hand, accounts of large companies are more complex. They may therefore be of lower quality and more time-consuming to finalise.

Similar to the approach taken in Table 8-10, a cross-tabulation of employment data (indicator for the size of the company) with average qualities and average arrears has been calculated. However, all the estimated coefficients turned out to be highly insignificant and were close to zero (ranging from 0.01 to -0.06), which suggests that there is no difference in accounting performance between smaller and larger companies. A possible explanation of this result, with no reference to rent-seeking, is that the opposing effects mentioned above simply cancel each other out.

How to Explain Poor Quality and Large Arrears: Hypotheses on Poor Performance

When confronted with the problem of poor accounting performance in the public sector, Tanzanian officials often refer to lack of training and other technical shortcomings. This was also emphasised by the Deputy General Director of Tanzania Audit Corporation (personal communication in Dar es Salaam, March 2000). Similarly, several donors followed this line of reasoning, in particular when justifying new projects which aimed to improve financial management in Tanzania (e.g. World Bank (1992b)).

There is no doubt that this argument is relevant. Even though Tanzania has more than a dozen training institutes for accountants, and accounting and auditing standards and ethics were established long ago, there is a huge gap between the demand and supply of qualified accountants and auditors. This is to some extent a result of wrong priorities. As emphasised in World Bank (1992b, p. 1), in the 1970s and 1980s, the expansion of the public administration and parastatal sector was not matched by a corresponding expansion in the supply of professional accountants and auditors.

According to an assessment by Tanzania Audit Corporation in 1988 (TAC (1988, p. 11)) parastatals 'require about 624 fully qualified accounting/auditing personnel of whom only 314 are estimated to be employed'. And the above-mentioned Word Bank document (proposal for a credit to upgrade financial management in Tanzania) even points to an unquoted study of 1989 which identifies a national shortage of presumably 2000 certified public accountants, 5600 semi-qualified accountants and over 15,000 accounting technicians (World Bank (1992b, p. 2f)). These figures, however, may indicate an upper estimate, considering that the World Bank was justifying its engagement in this report.

Besides the lack of training, another reason for poor accounting performance is partly attributable to the low *wages* set by the government or the general *lack of funds* of parastatal companies. A parastatal may not be allowed to pay higher wages or it may not have the means to hire well-paid accountants. Given the socialist background and poor performance of parastatals, it is not surprising that TAC (1988, p. 13) finds the share of good accountants to be much higher in the private sector; the private sector also pays much better wages, which can be six times as high. Audit fees, in contrast, are not a real financial constraint for parastatals, as auditing by Tanzania Audit Corporation is inexpensive. Whatever the reasons for this situation, having accounts audited and employing good accountants, even if they are relatively expensive, is indispensable because parastatal companies must fulfil minimum criteria of efficiency and accountability.

Finally, a third frequent argument is the *lack of parastatal supervision.* Weak boards of directors and uncoordinated regulatory agencies, where duties and responsibilities are not clearly defined or demarcated (e.g. TAC (1991, p. 14f)) may not encourage parastatal managers to comply with all guidelines, including accounting principles and policies.

All these arguments are not related to rent-seeking and have in common that problems can be addressed with inputs from outside, i.e. training, a better regulation, improved supervision and donor support in the form of expertise and financial assistance. The diagnosis is mainly a 'lack of ability' combined with unfavourable regulations and the indifference of the parastatal management and supervisory agencies.

Although these aspects are highly relevant, the diagnosis presented so far fails to include the most important driving force behind poor accounting standards in Tanzania, which is often simply the *avarice of rent-seeking* at all levels of parastatal employment and supervision. Evidence for the rent-seeking hypothesis is abundant and easy to discern. Even TAC reports have been open and critical on this matter.

In essence, there are many reasons to believe that the *'lack of education'* argument has been overemphasised. As the introductory quote to Section d) states, it is easy to attribute (and obscure) fraud and embezzlement to 'lack of management skills'. Many of the managers and board members of Tanzania's public enterprises and bureaucracy are probably more capable than they pretend to be. This is the consensus of the Tanzanian public and is also emphasised in the literature, albeit often in a more diplomatic way. Henley, for instance, comments on the World Bank's diagnosis of weak management (assessed in the 1989 Public Expenditure Review):

> 'Alternatively, the management cadre may be more competent than the World Bank gives it credit for. Present behaviour could be a consequence of the prevailing system of incentives and level of managerial rewards.' (Henley (1993, p. 468))

This incentive structure, which is of an obvious rent-seeking nature, guides behaviour in many companies and institutions in the public sector. Rent-seeking manifests itself in the lack of seriousness of the parastatal management. It has its roots in the way parastatals are imbedded in the system, above all in the way the management and members of supervising boards are recruited. And it translates into a lack of commitment, demonstrated by promises without action and pseudo-control structures.

The *lack of seriousness of the management and accounting staff* has been repeatedly cited in the annual TAC reports. Already the earliest TAC report available for this study (June 1984) is unambiguous (in 1983/84, less than 40% of the accounts audited received a clean report):

> 'Most of the accounting weaknesses responsible for the qualification of the accounts are capable of being rectified without the deployment of extra resources... We believe that if the concerned parastatals made concerted and serious efforts to rectify the accounting weaknesses reported, a much higher percentage of audited accounts would get CLEAN audit reports.' (TAC (1984, p. 11))

Virtually identical assessments follow in later reports, e.g. TAC (1990, p. 12), TAC (1992, p. 21) or (TAC (1989, p. 15)):

> 'Many of the accounting weaknesses discussed could be rectified without the deployment of extra resources and personnel. What is lacking is commitment on the part of the concerned parties and appropriate supervision by the relevant regulatory bodies.'

That accounting systems are not necessarily overly complex (and therefore difficult to understand) is another important aspect which corroborates the rent-seeking hypothesis. Tanzania Audit Corporation, for instance, explicitly notes that accounting systems are often simple and only require basic knowledge of double entry bookkeeping, which is not in short supply in the country. There is no lack of people with these basic skills, but a lack of seriousness and commitment among management (TAC (1990, p. 12)).

A similar opinion came from discussions with a member of the NBAA (National Board of Accountants and Auditors). The interviewee even noted that some accountants had a real conflict of interest, i.e. to follow accounting policies or to hide information. He said that managers and accountants often spend considerable time trying to square things up and balance illegal transactions; their task is 'to get something close to a clean report' (personal communication in Dar es Salaam, April 2000).

There is no need to point out that additional training and education for managers will not change this unsatisfactory situation, as long as they have no incentive to use their acquired knowledge to improve their company's performance. This explains a great deal of what was noted in TAC (1991, p. 17):

> 'Several measures have been taken by the Government to upgrade the quality of management of public enterprises, but such measures have, for various reasons, not produced the desired results. Public complaints about mismanagement of public enterprises is the order of the day.'

In a rent-seeking state, companies and non-commercial entities are not accountable to the general public but are accountable, if at all, to the rent-seeking elite. The relationship becomes apparent upon examining how parastatals are embedded in the system. Such *'structurally-rooted' rent-seeking patterns* are evident in Tanzania. TAC (1987, p. 13f) finds that the objectives of parastatals are often 'too general and broad to enable monitoring of performance in relation to the set objectives' and it emphasises that duties and responsibilities of parastatals and boards of directors have not been clearly defined. Chachage (1994, p. 12) explicitly says of Tanzanian public companies:

> 'In a nutshell, here we are dealing with a situation whereby people who are in positions are accountable only to the appointing authorities (i.e. the top) but not to the people they serve (i.e. the bottom)...It is for this reason that corruption, embezzlement and fraud is almost institutional.'

The example basically demonstrates that the accountability relationship between the parastatal and policymakers works; it outlines a rent-seeking distribution of resources. What does not work however is the accountability that should exist between policymakers and the citizens.

Another central feature of a regime driven by rent-seeking is *political employment and nepotism*. It affects all levels of parastatal decision-making and is characterised by the situation that individuals qualify for specific tasks, positions or jobs on grounds of political (and other) loyalties. Economic efficiency considerations, in contrast, play at most a minor and subsidiary role.

In Tanzania political employment is not a secret but very visible. TAC reports include both indirect references (criticism of the incapability of parastatal management and supervisory agencies) as well as more direct references, where political employment is almost spelled out:

> 'Appointment to some Boards are sometimes not made on the basis of qualification and experience...' (TAC (1988, p. 16))

> 'Only persons with the right qualifications and experience should be considered for appointment.' (TAC (1989, p. 19))

> 'The Boards of Directors should be composed of persons with the right qualifications and experience...The selection and appointment of Chief Executives and heads of department should be based on qualifications, experience and competence.' (TAC (1991, p. 18))

In a system where rent-seeking is systemic and political employment has an important stake, announcements and directives are usually of a solely rhetorical nature and specific control structures which aim to improve and guarantee efficiency are rarely effective. This was clearly demonstrated in Chapter 7. With reference to the persistent problem of poor accounting performance, similar problems have been identified here, i.e. *pronouncements without follow-up action* and the establishment of *additional layers of ineffective control.*

In response to the persistently poor accounting situation, President Mwinyi passed a directive in November 1985, requiring parastatals with accounts in arrears to be up to date by 1987. In 1988 Tanzania Audit Corporation counted 129 clients in arrears for one year or more as compared to 141 at 30 June 1987 and concluded: 'This is a positive and encouraging response to the directive given in November 1985' (TAC (1988, p. 11)). Clearly this was not an 'encouraging response' to the President's directive but a glaring example of non-fulfilment! The deadline was later on extended to 1989, without any change. (The situation continued to improve only gradually, with 94 commercial and non-commercial parastatals still in arrears in December 1989). Although not so critical of Mwinyi's directive, TAC places at least the problem of poor quality in the appropriate context:

> 'We still have too many accounts being qualified and some of them very heavily. We believe we do not need another Presidential directive in this regard. All the concerned supervisory organs should direct their respective institutions to take appropriate measures to improve the standard of accounting and record keeping.' (TAC (1990, p. 13))

It is interesting to contrast this comment with the laudable policy announcements on the public sector made in the same year's Budget Speech (also quoted at the beginning of Chapter 7.3):

> 'No stone should ... be left unturned in our efforts to increase productivity and efficiency as well as restoring accountability in the management and supervision of our public and private enterprises... we should not hesitate to take disciplinary action against anyone who proves to be irresponsible in the execution of his duties...' (GoT (1990a, p. 16))

As an instrument to monitor and enforce public accountability, Tanzania's government instituted in 1978 the *Parastatal Organisation Committee (POC)*—a standing parliamentary committee which each year selects between 60 and 140 parastatals to scrutinise their accounts. In 1981 the scope of the POC investigation was further enhanced to include operational aspects of parastatal activities. As emphasised in each TAC report, the POC is the highest authority in monitoring public accountability of parastatals in Tanzania (all annual TAC reports include a short reference to the activities of POC). Given the importance of POC, it is not surprising that the Committee's activities are also praised in political speeches and strategic documents (like the above-mentioned 1990 Budget Speech which praises POC for 'an extremely good job' (p. 47)).

In general, the work of POC certainly helped to bring many accounts up to date. However, considering that POC has been operating since the late 1970s and the accounting performance of many parastatals remained poor throughout the 1980s, this also gives the impression that the institution could have been far more effective. The most obvious evidence for this allegation is the weird fact that every year a large number of selected parastatals manage to escape the inspection of POC on rather dubious grounds.

According to the TAC reports and personal communication with members of the POC committee (Dar es Salaam, April 2000), cases were not discussed if for instance a parastatal official did not show up. As an excuse some officials simply argued that they could not afford the transport fare to appear before the Committee! Other POC investigations were dropped or postponed because the submitted papers did not conform to POC requirements. Finally, in many cases, accounts were too old to serve any useful purpose or accounts had not been audited, which again was an argument to drop or postpone a case. According to the director of parliamentary committees, officials sometimes felt too embarrassed to appear without audited books and managers claimed not to have the money to pay for audit fees. Whatever the reasons given, it appears to have been quite easy for a parastatal to avoid, or at least to postpone, the inquiries of POC.[172]

Table 8-13 shows the number of parastatals selected in each year and the share of companies which managed to evade examination (i.e. the share of selected companies, which were not reviewed during the year). The table also displays the frequencies with which companies were selected between 1991 and 1996. These latter figures were compiled from a comprehensive list obtained at the Office of the Standing Committees in Dar es Salaam in June 2000. According to the data obtained, 50% of the companies were selected between one and three times during the six-year period, and 13% even more frequently.[173]

---

[172] There are also reported cases where parastatals tried to evade scrutiny and POC still insisted on examining the company. This was for instance the case with Sabuni Industries in 1989. Visiting the company, POC found many anomalies in their accounts (personal communication with member of POC in Dar es Salaam, April 2001).

[173] Unfortunately the information obtained has been of much less use than expected. Having requested information on the parastatal names selected between 1986 and 1996, only information from the year 1991 onwards was provided. This was unfavourable, as data on earlier years would have allowed a systematic comparison with the companies' quality and arrears of accounting. (An analysis of the 1991 data did not reveal any specific patterns.) Furthermore, despite promises, the list did not indicate which of the selected companies had not been discussed. It appears that this matter was too sensitive. Finally, the general reliability of the information obtained also had to be

Table 8-13: Parastatals Selected and Examined by POC (FY87-96)

TAC info	Number selected	Number not examined	% not examined
1987	80	38	48%
1988	114	39	34%
1989	105	30[a]	29%
1990	90	12	13%
1991	113	15	13%
1992	122	24	20%
1993	139	27	19%
1994	109	31	28%
1995	89	22	25%
1996	68	9	13%

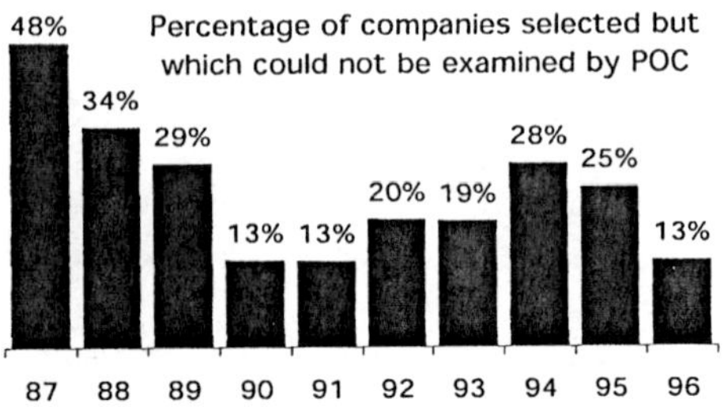

Percentage of companies selected but which could not be examined by POC

48% 34% 29% 13% 13% 20% 19% 28% 25% 13%

87 88 89 90 91 92 93 94 95 96

a: Eight companies have not been discussed because of time constraints (TAC (1989, p. 20)).

Frequency of selection between FY91 and FY96:

In parentheses number of companies and percentage distribution between the groups. The data refer to the 336 commercial parastatals only.

0 (125, 37%) 1 (72, 21%) 2 (53, 16%) 3 (43, 13%) 4 (31, 9%) 5 (10, 3%) 6 (2, 1%)

Source: TAC information from TAC reports 1987-96; information on the frequency of selection compiled from a list obtained at the Parliamentary Committee's Office

All in all, the discussion of parastatal accounts showed that good and timely accounts were not a major concern in Tanzania, despite the rhetoric surrounding this matter. In addition different layers of control do not appear to have been sufficiently effective. The poor performance cannot be justified on economic grounds, nor is it in line with the intentions of the Arusha Declaration, which laid down the foundation of Tanzania's earlier socialist approach.

Clearly, many non-rent-seeking arguments can explain why accounting performance has been poor and why the situation improved only gradually during the 1980s and early 1990s. There is no doubt that the 'lack of education' explanation has been relevant. However, what matters for donors and reform-minded policymakers within the country is to differentiate between *'real'* inabilities and *'strategic'* inabilities.

It is obvious that better knowledge of accounting procedures and other financial tools, such as management information systems, budgetary control systems, cost control and working capital management, is important and desirable. But as long as managers are employed for reasons other than economic qualifications and as long as embezzlement remains largely unrestrained, the situation will not improve. As noted earlier, real inabilities, i.e. real gaps and incompetence can be addressed by additional training, accounting manuals and related financing—strategic inabilities, however, cannot. It appears that for a long time donors have been blind to this.

This section intended to demonstrate that poor accounting quality and large arrears reflect to a considerable extent rent-seeking activities. Indications of

questioned, as the number of companies in each year did not correspond to the totals shown in the TAC reports (e.g. in 1991 TAC mentions a total of 113 companies, whereas the alternative source only lists 89 companies).

evidence which support the rent-seeking hypothesis are abundant, and many of them are explicitly mentioned in the annual TAC reports. The fact that there is no direct 'proof' of embezzlement (each problem typically has an additional non-rent-seeking explanation) does not undermine the findings. What makes the rent-seeking hypothesis highly plausible is the systematic occurrence of indicators that all point in the same direction.

The figures and tables showed that elements of poor accounting (poor quality and late audits) are not just related to one another; they are also more prevalent among loss-makers than profit-makers. And although loss-makers had greater potential to improve their accounting standards, they still turned out to be 'worse improvers'. An interesting finding is that accounting performance is not related to the size of the company. Although there are different opposing forces that can explain this, it is still surprising that they exactly cancel out for both indicators 'quality' and 'arrears'. The result may suggest that accounting problems are not primarily determined by real problems and difficulties (real inabilities) but strategic inabilities.

The anecdotal evidence quoted from TAC reports, above all the apparent inactivity and incapability of the responsible authority to address urgent problems, is in line with the rent-seeking patterns presented in earlier chapters. As is typical for Tanzania, identifying severe accounting shortcomings does not imply that these will be addressed within a reasonable time.

All in all, the data on average qualities and arrears of parastatal accounts, as well as the change of quality and arrears over time, provide an interesting *alternative or subsidiary rent-seeking indicator* to the profit and loss information of the companies. The ability of a company to adjust its behaviour in the reform process and its seriousness in shifting to productive activities depend on the quality of its management. In the short and medium term, however, the behaviour of the management may only partly translate into higher profits; it may however be visible in the company's change in accounting performance. Under circumstances where changes in profits and losses are largely affected by external factors, poor accounting quality and large arrears may even constitute a more adequate indicator on rent-seeking.

Nevertheless, distortions of a rent-seeking indicator based on the quality and arrears of accounting are likely to be considerable as well. First of all, real inabilities are not irrelevant but matter to some extent. Second, even *audited accounts* which obtain clean reports have frequently been found to be *unreliable*. Part of this problem has been associated with political interventions in the 1980s and early 1990s, for instance in the banking sector. Probably more important is the problem that accountants can easily collude with corrupt parastatal officials and give clean reports despite unexplained irregularities. This possibility is supported in many discussions with donors, private sector businesspeople and even members of POC and OCAG. Furthermore, some people also argue that especially the most corrupt people know how to keep their books clean.

Third, it has to be kept in mind that rent-seeking has many facets and is not a uniform phenomenon. Rent-seeking activities may be associated with accounting features in different ways. For example, timely audits may be relevant to secure specific types of government support or donor funds, or they may be important for obtaining approvals related to rent-seeking. This aspect may explain the slightly less good fit of the arrears indicator in contrast to the quality indicator, for instance when relating accounting features to the profit-making and loss-making group. At least for parastatal budgets this aspect is relevant, as the following quote from the 89-TAC report suggests:

> 'Some [parastatals] are known for preparing budgets for such purposes as securing Government subventions, approval of prices by the Price Commissioner, and a formal satisfaction of Government Agencies and Board of Directors. However, these budgets are not used as management tools for control purposes. The budgets are rarely realistic. Actual performances are never compared with budgets and variances investigated for appropriate corrective measures.' (TAC (1989, p. 17))

The three lines of argument imply that even though poor accounting standards are associated with rent-seeking activities, clean and timely accounts may also be attended by large-scale embezzlement and other rent-seeking activities. These reservations should be kept in mind when interpreting the results.

8.2 Soft Budget Constraints: Parastatal Support and Overt Inefficiency

Chapter 7 gave many examples of how parastatal companies in Tanzania have enjoyed government support despite being extremely inefficient. The persistence of poor performance combined with ongoing support of various forms critically undermined the success of the reform process, in particular the goals of obtaining macro stability and regaining growth. Whereas Chapter 8.1 discussed different means of measuring parastatal performance, this chapter quantifies the financial support provided to the parastatal sector. It presents an analysis of disaggregated, company-based information and makes a strong case for the influence of rent-seeking.

The first section surveys the type and total amounts of support and addresses difficulties in identifying, collecting and preparing information. The discussion again shows the limitations and deficiencies inherent in some of the data, which had become particularly apparent as information had been collected in a disaggregated form. The actual evaluation of the influence of rent-seeking follows in Section b) and c).

a) Identifying and Measuring Parastatal Support

'You can go on collecting information. But I can assure you that at the end of the day you cannot make a logical conclusion. Every data collection had its own purpose.'

Senior official from a Tanzanian bank, April 2000

In Tanzania there is a lot of general, aggregated information available on parastatal performance and even on support provided to parastatal companies. The reduction of government resources allocated to parastatals was a major goal in the reform process in the 1980s and 1990s and was therefore more closely monitored. In particular documents produced by the government for the donor community, as well as the many reports, reviews and studies written or financed by donors, contain a lot of information. However, to know more about the distribution of support to individual beneficiaries, to uncover irregularities and contradictions, to explain discrepancies and to examine the question of whether in particular inefficient companies obtained support it is necessary to look at the disaggregated, company level, where it is harder to obtain information.

As will be demonstrated, collecting and preparing information on support to individual parastatal companies has been challenging. At the outset, the goal was to obtain information on an annual basis on each of the parastatal companies for the period 1986 to 1996. After countless hours spent computerising, structuring and analysing information, far more questions arose than answers were found. In particular the attempts to follow up individual records on loans and overdrafts turned out to be time-consuming and frustrating. Yet, as will be shown in this chapter, both the process of collecting and preparing information as well as the subsequent evaluation of soft budget constraints provide crucial insights on rent-seeking patterns in Tanzania.

Table 8-14 lists four major channels of support addressed in the primary data collection. As explained in Chapter 7 macro stability has been largely undermined by *bank borrowing* of parastatal companies (A). Even after the Banking Act of 1991, lending to parastatals and cooperatives in default continued. Besides the commercial banks the government has also been heavily involved in lending activities, either in the form of *Treasury loans* or *guarantees* of commercial bank loans, or in the form of *Treasury investments* (B). In value terms, most of the Treasury loans reflected loans from bilateral and multilateral donors, channelled through the government of Tanzania. Guarantees have been issued in particular when banks were forced to lend to non-performing parastatals, above all marketing boards and cooperatives. As a result of this policy, the government had to take over a large amount of non-performing bank assets in the 1990s.

Table 8-14: Indicators of Direct and Indirect Support Provided to Parastatal Companies in Tanzania

A. Commercial bank loans and overdrafts
- National Bank of Commerce (NBC)
- Cooperative and Rural Development Bank (CRDB)
- Tanzania Investment Bank (TIB)
- Tanzania Housing Bank (THB) [a]
- Peoples Bank of Zanzibar (PBZ) [a]

B. Treasury loans and investments
- Treasury loans
- Treasury guarantees
- Treasury investments

C. Other state & donor support
- Subsidies and subventions
- FOREX allocation (BoT) [a]
- Commodity Import Support (CIS)
- Tax exemptions [a]
- Income tax arrears
- Dividend payment arrears

D. Inter-parastatal arrears other than banking
- Arrears to TANESCO (power)
- Arrears to TTCL (phone)
- Arrears to NUWA (water) [a]
- Arrears to PPF (pension)

a: No or only limited company-based information obtained for the period 1986/87 to 1995/96.

Parastatal companies also enjoyed financial support from government and donors through different modes of *subsidies and subventions* (a particularly non-transparent area)[174], preferential access to cheap *foreign exchange*, statutory and

[174] As noted in Eriksson (1993, p. 23f), subsidies are usually given to commercial enterprises, whereas subventions are provided to non-commercial parastatals and other semi-government bodies as well as local governments. In Tanzania however different concepts have been applied inconsistently.

discretionary *tax exemptions*, as well as the not-agreed but apparently tolerated non-payment of *income taxes* and *dividend claims* (C). Finally, the non-payment of debts also affected *inter-parastatal relations*, i.e. companies benefited from access to goods and services of other parastatal companies, even though they had not been able to pay the bills (D).

However, although Table 8-14 is comprehensive it only indicates channels of *financial* support provided to parastatal companies. Not included in the listing but equally decisive for the companies' financial standing are government interventions into markets, which took the form of *administered pricing, trade protection* and granting *monopoly* rights. As extensively discussed in Chapter 7.2, interventions in Tanzania have been complex and have affected companies differently. Nevertheless it appears that the majority of parastatal companies have been net beneficiaries of this type of government interference. Besides the fact that most companies enjoyed monopoly protection, the cost-plus pricing method (a method whereby prices were set based on the companies' effective costs plus a margin) effectively reflected an institutionalised soft budget constraint. Also the suppression of agricultural prices in most years did not negatively affect agro-processing and marketing, but was a major disincentive for farmers.

Bank Information

Until the end of the 1980s, the banking sector in Tanzania was government owned and each bank operated in a closed and protected environment. As already mentioned in Chapter 7.1, most banks failed to consolidate their accounts before 1991. PSRC (1997b, p. A9), for instance, complained that NBC could not even provide annual data in an aggregated form on opening balance, new disbursements, repayments, accrued interest and closing balance for the period 1984-91. It is therefore not surprising that it was difficult and usually impossible to obtain disaggregated information for each parastatal on an annual basis. Information has been partly stored in 'godowns', although in a way that only allowed access to piles of paper and not data. Furthermore, according to personal communication at the NBC and CRDB (Dar es Salaam, March 1998), some of the storerooms had burned down and others sold, apparently together with their contents.

To find information on arrears and non-performing bank loans and overdrafts one needs to know which institutions store what 'piece' of information on parastatal accounts. In general there was no information left at the banks as to whether loans had been written off in earlier days or if accounts had been transferred to other institutions (like the liquidating agency LART, the privatisation agency PSRC or the government). In the case of the Tanzania Housing Bank, it was necessary to consult the official liquidator as the bank had been closed.

This obviously decreased transparency and made an evaluation of data particularly difficult. The issue will be discussed in more detail on page 483f.

By the end of the data collection period nearly a hundred appointments had been made with staff members of NBC, CRDB, TIB, PBZ, the Treasury and the privatising and liquidating agencies. Personnel typically claimed there was no information, or that other people, units or institutions should have copies of some records.

After having gone through the maze of different institutions, the useful information collected was rather poor. Instead of including annual balances on principal, interests, disbursements, possible foreign exchange adjustments, repayments and arrears for the period 1986 to 1996, in most cases the data referred to outstanding debts of one or two specific years in the 1990s. Tanzania Investment Bank was the only bank that provided annual loan statements on outstanding balances and arrears of principal and interests for all years.

A main problem with the other data was the frequent lack of information on interest rates or information on cut-off dates, i.e. dates after which no interest is charged. Because inflation was still high in the 1990s (on average more than 25% between 1990 and 1996), the real value of debts steadily declined if there was no adjustment to inflation. Interest due on the outstanding debt of cooperative unions, for instance, suddenly disappeared from the outstanding amount indicated in the LART files. It meant that the real value of the remaining unpaid debt shrank to less than a fourth of the value in 1991, even though not a single Shilling had been repaid. Finally, most reports did not specify to what extent they were complete and whether records had already been deleted, for instance because cases had been finalised.

This lack of information constrained the analysis and made it necessary to operate with different sets of assumptions. Table C-1 in the Appendix shows an overview of the type of information and number of parastatal records obtained. The table lists 16 different sources with more than 6000 records of which nearly 1200 were identified as belonging to parastatal companies. In value terms the share of parastatals is above 80%. The sources comprise lists on non-performing accounts, management information reports, divestiture progress reports and status reports on debt positions and recoveries. Table C-2 in the Appendix additionally lists the assumptions made when aggregating the data.

Besides the general *incompleteness* of banking information, the *consistency* of the data was also poor. Whenever it was possible to follow up individual records, for instance from opening to closing balance or from one year to another, unexplained changes and contradictions were frequent. Balances of principal, interests and corresponding arrears often increased or decreased without explanation. Differences mainly arose from typing errors, unexplained and arbitrary adjustments and write-offs, as well as late or missing consolidations.

Inconsistencies were also found when comparing records with aggregated totals of other sources. For instance, according to the Agricultural Memorandum of the World Bank (World Bank (1994b, p. 70)), outstanding CRDB balances of cooperative unions for the year 1992 indicated a total of TSh 13.034 billion, while the management information reports of CRDB showed as little as TSh 1.104 billion. Or TIB totals (end of December 1990 to 1992) are TSh 20.3, 29.3

and 45.6 billion, while an OED performance audit report (World Bank (1997a, p. 39)) indicates TSh 6.9, 7.7 and 11.1 billion only.[175]

Table 8-15 summarises the totals of the banking data calculated for the commercial parastatal data set. It shows a minimum and maximum specification of various non-performing loans and two indicators of parastatal portfolio and parastatal support (the latter defined as balance excluding amounts recovered). The figures are converted into constant prices (1994 prices) as the data are compiled from different years.

Table 8-15: Non-Performing Bank Loans 1987-96 (TSh m, 1994 prices)

	Total		Division according to Bank				Division according to Institution[b]				*Recovered*[c]	
	No.	Amount	NBC	CRDB	TIB	THB	NPA	LART	PSRC	Treasury	*No.*	*Amount*
Min.[a]	137	219,549	158,727	13,099	46,906	818	50,472	19,606	20,816	101,171	*60*	*15,498*
Max.[a]	148	249,998	180,678	21,596	46,906	818	68,588	50,263	30,104	104,743	*42*	*11,399*
in%	108%	114%	114%	165%	100%	100%	136%	256%	145%	104%		

	NBC	CRDB	TIB	THB
Indicative portfolio[d]	174,278	13,446	32,463	818
Indicative support[d]	165,118	13,350	28,732	818

a: Minimum and maximum interpretations. For detailed specifications see Table C-2 in the Appendix.

b: Non-performing assets (NPA) which are mentioned in the bank accounts and loans and overdrafts that have been transferred to other institutions for recovery or write-offs. The total does not coincide with the overall total shown in the table, as the sources of information deviate somewhat.

c: Collections by LART, PSRC, Treasury and data on expected amounts of TIB balances.

d: Average of Min. and Max. The indicator for support equals the portfolio excluding repayments and recoveries (where information was available). Furthermore all CRDB data exclude accounts shown in the management information reports, as these loans appear to have been disbursed prior to 1986. TIB Support: Sum of annual changes (converted in 1994 prices) of principal, excluding companies with a better rating than 'loss' in 1996. TIB: Portfolio: Sum of positive annual changes (converted in 1994 prices).

Source: Non-performing NBC loans and overdrafts recommended for LART or to be claimed from Treasury (Dec. 1991 and June 1992), Non-performing NBC accounts (Dec. 1996), NBC loans issued to parastatals (1996 and 1997), Database for classification of loans and overdrafts (NMB and NBC(1997)ltd.), NBC loans under PSRC (Status Report Dec. 1999), PSRC Divesture Progress Report of CRDB loans (Dec. 1999), CRDB management information reports (Dec. 1991 and Sept. 1994), TIB loan approvals net of cancellations 1970-96, TIB annual schedules of unclassified loans and loans of defaulting companies (1987-97), Status of TIB companies under PSRC Divestiture (Feb. 2000), Balance of commercial THB loans (April 96), List of non-performing THB borrowers (status June 1999), LART Status 1999 of debt and recoveries from non-performing accounts. Data provided by the indicated institutions.

The minimum and maximum versions shown in Table 8-15 result from the different sets of assumptions applied when compiling the data, such as the treatment of loans which disappear without being explicitly recovered, assumptions related to missing dates on outstanding balances and repayments, and adjustments due to inconsistencies between overlapping sources of information. 'Maximum', however, does not imply that these are high-end

[175] Note the TIB figures in Table 7-8 on page 336 are smaller since they are end of June values. With the OED data it has been assumed that the source included a misprint (figures are not TSh thousands but millions).

estimates.[176] The NBC share is most likely underreported, while CRDB data and THB data are incomplete. TIB figures, which indicate the balance of arrears in 1992, actually appear to be high. It is not clear whether these loans have been shielded against real losses caused by inflation.

Similar to the findings in earlier chapters, there is no doubt that the widely recognised 'major problems' in record keeping and reconciling data and the many contradictions did not just reflect constraints on resources or capacity but was a crucial element of a well-entrenched rent-seeking society. When the banking staff of NBC, CRDB or TIB was confronted with observed differences, their explanations would typically be either technical or related to rent-seeking:

> 'We have a severe problem of missing data', 'Many differences appear because of poor updating of records', 'Within the Bank, there are several wings; you may only have one of these sources', 'Data from branches may not match data from head office', 'I don't know what source of information the World Bank used', ... 'Data have been used for different purposes; this explains, why they may deviate', 'Everything was Government; nobody cared where the money went in or out', 'Differences may occur from air purchases, fake transactions', etc.

The most extreme statement is the comment that opens this section (p. 471). If every data collection has its own purpose in the sense that results depend on whether the official wants to show a large or small amount, interpreting data becomes meaningless. Fortunately, however, problems are not always as bad as that, and depending on the question and the type of distortion even poor data can allow several meaningful analyses and interpretations.

Information on Treasury Loans, Investments and Guarantees

As noted earlier, the Ministry of Finance has also been involved in lending to parastatals, among other reasons because it has channelled substantial amounts of foreign aid to companies. Besides Treasury loans, which were meant to be repaid, the Ministry also provided funds in the form of investments. Treasury investments implied that the recipient had to pay dividends on future profits. Treasury guarantees are contingent liabilities. They become effective once a parastatal defaults on its outstanding debt, for which the Treasury has issued the guarantee. A lot of bank lending has been covered by Treasury guarantees.

Annual *Treasury loan statements* for the financial years 1986/87 to 1996/97 provided the most comprehensive information obtained on a specific type of parastatal support. Besides opening and closing balances, most of the loan records included information on disbursements, repayments, arrears of principal and interests, as well as explicit information on changes due to foreign exchange

[176] On the one hand, it was not always possible to assign each account to a specific parastatal, in particular if loans had been issued for unknown subsidiaries, e.g. ranches or estates. On the other hand, several balances refer to the years 1999 or 2000, which do not include information on non-performing accounts written off earlier. Finally, some of the data were incomplete for other reasons which could not be explained (for instance, the data of the CRDB management reports).

fluctuations of loans which had been fixed in a foreign currency (information on the last point however was only available from the 1990/91 Treasury loan statement onwards). In addition, most statements specified the origin and purpose of a loan, interest rates and the terms of repayment.

Nevertheless, in spite of this detailed information a great deal of effort was necessary to get the data in a form which allowed a satisfactory interpretation, i.e. one that made it possible to understand anomalies and get a non-distorted picture of disbursements, repayments and other adjustments. Even though figures reflected simple accounting identities, the examination of the nearly 400 loans was challenging.

Problems were numerous, in particular as a large number of balances increased or decreased without explanation. Even the closing balances for a specific year did not necessarily coincide with the opening balances of the subsequent year. Sometimes adjustments were delayed for several years; specific entries have been revoked or the terms of a loan renegotiated so that earlier increases or decreases would be cancelled again. In many cases foreign exchange adjustments could only be identified as unexplained changes in outstanding balances, which followed a pattern similar to the development of one of the 26 'bilateral' exchange rates found in the Treasury statements (TSh/$, TSh/Ecu, etc). Intermediate repayments or disbursements made an identification of adjustments related to foreign exchange fluctuations even more complex. Information was often missing on several aspects at once and coincided with misprints of available information. Solving all these problems required meticulously following up all hints and indicators, above all analysing the comments on the loans in each annual statement.

Table 8-16 shows the total of the loan balances identified for the commercial parastatal data set, after correcting errors and replacing missing information on foreign exchange adjustments. The table additionally shows the total of the increases and decreases, calculated at constant prices (II) and a specification of support that excludes all loans already mentioned in June 1986 (III). The latter makes it possible to show the group of new loans during the reform period starting in June 1986. Finally, the table indicates arrears (sum of principal and interests) as a percentage of stated closing balances. The figures however underestimate true values since arrears also decrease due to write-offs or are hidden through 'evergreening' (e.g. an overdraft that has no repayment date).

Even though much of the missing information could be reconstructed, the amount of unexplained changes nevertheless remained considerable. Looking at the totals in terms of constant prices (total II), 26% of total increases remained unidentified, i.e. the balance of a loan simply increased (5%) or a loan appeared the first time in the opening balance without being issued earlier (21%). The data also show that only 9% of decreases were due to explicit repayments; more than half are write-offs and almost 40% remain unexplained, i.e. the value of a loan decreases or the loan just disappears.

Table 8-16: Treasury Loans to Commercial Parastatals FY87-97 (TSh m)

	Balance according to accounting identities:						Unexplained				Arrears[b]
	Opening balance (1)	Amount issued (2)	FOREX changes (3)	Amount repaid (4)	Written off[a] (5)	Closing balance (6)	In-crease (7)	De-crease (8)	,New, loans (9)	Lost loans (10)	Princip. & int. (11)
86/87	25,246	2,879	4,237	49	0	34,231	2,152	236	11,613	1,157	15%
87/88	44,787	648	23,271	174	505	67,815	265	377	7,747	563	22%
88/89	74,998	2,188	27,881	776	3,957	95,606	281	5,011	7,154	0	35%
89/90	102,760	6,983	33,755	477	1,315	141,704	25	26	0	4,358	49%
90/91	137,347	14,954	21,336	1,331	15	180,141	8,957	1,107	25,842	1,868	50%
91/92	204,115	12	60,636	1,239	3,330	258,290	118	2,023	0	17	61%
92/93	258,273	225	66,117	1,644	1,077	321,203	332	1,023	52,977	89	65%
93/94	374,084	117,839	97,559	3,015	70,298	523,544	14,971	7,596	0	0	49%
94/95	523,544	4,005	100,540	2,009	24,924	576,909	2,308	26,556	0	0	58%
95/96	576,909	137	-17,145	2,363	0	554,775	17,309	20,072	0	0	61%
96/97[c]	*554,775*	*0*	*-1,249*	*13,904*	*52,236*	*461,887*	*0*	*25,499*	*0*	*0*	*112%*
I. Total FY87-97		149,871	416,960	26,981	157,657		46,720	89,526	105,252	8,052	
II. Total FY87-97[d]		250,302	*897,646*	31,831	181,264		77,495	102,959	317,976	31,573	
% of total I increase		21%	58%				6%		15%		
% of total I decrease				10%	56%			32%		3%	
% of total II increase		16%	58%				5%		21%		
% of total II decrease				9%	52%			30%		9%	
III. Defining Support FY87-96:[d, e]		249,200	409,795	8,988	77,610		54,026	55,634	314,119	16,523	Support 608,357

There are four sources of inconsistencies. For each loan the closing balance (column 6) should equal columns (1)+(2)+(3)-(4)-(5). If the closing balance was higher than this, it was recorded as an increase in column (7); if it was lower it was recorded as a decrease in column (8). In addition to this, the closing balance of each loan on 30 June was not necessarily the same as the opening balance on 1 July in the subsequent Treasury loan statement (there is a separate book for each financial year, i.e. FY86/87, FY87/88, etc.); this difference is reflected in columns (9) and (10).

The totals I+II indicate accumulation over the period 1986-97 (I at current prices, II at constant prices) and III defines Treasury Support used in the subsequent analyses.

a: 40% effectively written off, 41% loans converted into equity, 19% are cancelled FOREX adjustments (at constant prices, the shares are 27%, 46% and 27%).

b: Arrears of principal and interests in % of stated closing balance (6). Values decline mostly due to write-offs.

c: Incomplete Treasury loan statement, probably still in preparation when the data were collected in April 1998.

d: Annual values of 1986/87-1995/96 first converted into constant prices (1994 prices). Note because FOREX changes partly compensate the country's inflation there is no sensible interpretation of the total at constant prices (897,646) other than calculating the percentage shares.

e: The specification only includes new loans, i.e. loans not mentioned prior to July 1986 and it covers the period June 1986 to June 1996 only. Parastatals with no write-offs and arrears are excluded, as it is assumed that these amounts are recovered later on in full (5862). Total support is defined as (2)+(7)+(9)-(4), assuming that unexplained decreases and lost loans have not been repaid (further explanations follow on page 495).

Source: Treasury loan statements 1986/87 to 1996/97

The poor quality of the data and the magnitudes of the remaining unexplained balances and changes are striking. As noted above, the figures are simple accounting identities. That many of them did not balance is certainly not just a capacity constraint of the government, but most likely again a reflection of the intrinsic rent-seeking environment within which government and donor support occur. The Controller and Auditor General also regularly complained about the poor quality of the Treasury loan statements. Many of the shortcomings identified above, such as the differences between opening and closing balances within and between annual statements, missing entries on payment and drawn amounts, etc, have been mentioned regularly in the annual OCAG reports.[177]

Even though the above-mentioned problems on record keeping are serious, they are nothing compared with the inadequacies found in the Treasury Registrar's Statements on *Government Investments*. Similar to Treasury loans, the Registrar compiles a list each year which shows for commercial and non-commercial parastatals the 'total of shareholder funds', divided into 'paid up share capital' and 'other investments'. However, unlike the loan statements the statements on investments do not group information on a specific year but reflect an arbitrary collection of parastatal data. The reason behind this odd situation is, as the OCAG report complaints, that the Treasury does not maintain independent records but compiles the data from the accounts of parastatals, most of which are in arrears (OCAG (1989, p. 41)). Analysing the data collected however suggests that it is pure coincidence whether or not a company is included in a statement, as also information on audited accounts may not be included.

The poor quality of the Treasury investment records is not a secret but has been commented on and criticised for a long time. Drawing on the above reference, the Controller and Auditor General criticises among other things that there is no monitoring system for funds channelled from parent ministries to parastatals; information flows between subsidiary companies, holding corporation and Treasury are inadequate; and for some companies the capital structure is unknown and therefore also the Treasury's investments in it (OCAG (1989, P. p. 41)). Given these shortcomings it is not surprising that the OCAG cannot ascertain the correctness of the Treasury statements, even though the Treasury is required by law to control and monitor all government investments made to parastatal organisations (see also (OCAG (1990, p. 36)).

For the analysis here data for 1987-96 were collected in 1998; the problems, however, have remained the same since then. To quantify the balances and to determine the support to commercial parastatals between 1987 and 1996 from Treasury investments, Treasury data first needed to be reorganised according to the date the balances belonged to. Tracing individual records over the years again helped to correct misprints. Sometimes more than one statement on a parastatal referred to the same year, of course with different values.

Obviously, it would not have made sense to evaluate overall totals without first filling gaps (most companies only included information on a few arbitrary years). Table 8-17 shows how they were reconstructed for the commercial parastatal sample. Column (1) indicates the information (number of companies) originally extracted from the Treasury statements. Columns (2) to (4) show the total of information when gaps are replaced by averages of preceding and

---

[177] E.g. OCAG (1989, p. 36f, 1992, p. 48f, 1995, p. 73f).

subsequent values or other sources of information. The total data steadily increases. In column (4), for values missing after the last available figure the last figure was reiterated (to make a conservative estimate, it was simply assumed that the balance did not change).

Having reorganised balances and replaced missing values, annual Treasury investments were determined from the change in the balances. The indicated figures are nonetheless low-end estimates since the Treasury database was thin in the 1990s and the replacement of missing values with last available figures (33% of data) implied zero additional investments. In addition, for 223 parastatals there was no information on Treasury investments.

Table 8-17: Treasury Investments to Commercial Parastatals FY87-96 (TSh m)

	Information (No. of companies) [a]				Balances (Extended III data set) of			Increases (Ext. III data set) [b] in		
	Treasury statements (1)	Extended I (2)	Extended II (3)	Extended III (4)	Paid up share capital (5)	Other investments (6)	Total shareholders funds (7)	Paid up share capital (8)	Other investments (9)	Shareholders funds (10)
Prior 86	80	80	80	80	11,833	13,682	25,515			
86/87	53	72	96	97	20,047	19,598	39,645	3,051	2,141	5,192
87/88	17	52	91	97	26,349	25,189	51,537	6,403	5,590	11,993
88/89	22	59	96	102	37,882	22,106	59,988	6,142	-1,825	4,316
89/90	75	90	98	107	40,499	28,610	69,109	4,089	5,948	10,038
90/91	31	61	77	107	64,769	81,586	146,355	26,245	52,976	79,221
91/92	13	45	65	107	72,535	122,750	195,285	13,864	41,164	55,028
92/93	21	46	57	107	83,874	148,477	232,351	16,785	25,727	42,512
93/94	20	35	44	108	91,737	231,259	322,997	7,958	82,290	90,248
94/95	26	39	41	113	100,191	259,350	359,540	6,183	28,090	34,274
95/96	10	14	14	113	103,437	290,054	393,491	3,271	30,705	33,976
Total:	368	593	759	1138				93,991	272,807	366,797
Averages and totals at 1994 prices: [c]					ø 120,288	ø 174,852	ø 295,140	242,478	476,145	718,623

a: Column (1) shows the number of companies for which information on Treasury investments was obtained at the Treasury Registrar. Columns (2) to (4) also include data extracted from balance sheets of parastatal companies contained in Coopers&Lybrand (1996), however only if Treasury information on the company was available for an earlier year. More decisively, columns (2) to (4) fill missing values, referring to increasingly less restrictive assumptions.

In the specification (2) all gaps have been replaced if there was information on the balance of an earlier and later year and the balance had not changed. In (3) the gaps have also been replaced if the balances varied. In this case missing values were interpolated from previous and subsequent values. Specification (4) additionally fills all gaps after the latest information, assuming that the value did not change.

b: Increases do not correspond to the differences in balances for two reasons. On the one hand, columns (5) to (7) include companies which are mentioned for the first time after 1986. One possible interpretation is to assume that this is an increase from zero. However, more likely is that most of these investments are not new; there is just no information on the values of earlier balances. The problem is more severe in older statements (in real value terms, 73% of the 'increases from zero' occurring in 1986/87). On the other hand, negative changes of 'paid up share' capital have been eliminated as these more likely reflect write-offs and sale of government shares.

c: Annual values first converted into constant prices. Balances indicate averages (ø), increases are totals.

Source: Treasury Registrar's Statements of Government Investments (June 1987, 88, 91, 94, 95, 96) collected in April 1998. Other statements were not available at the Treasury, probably as they have never been compiled.

From a confidential report (Coopers&Lybrand (1996)) two to four balance sheets of 22 companies were available referring to the years between 1991 and

1996. The balance sheets permitted crosschecks with the Treasury statements (and missing information to be added for the more recent accounts not included in the Treasury reports). Two aspects were of particular interest: first, as earlier OCAG complaints also suggested, assessing the possibility that companies with no Treasury information nonetheless included Treasury share capital; second, to be able to interpret the Treasury data, information on the effective contents of 'paid up share capital' and 'other investments' was needed.

As expected, there are companies which have never been mentioned in the Treasury statements but which include explicit share capital in their balance sheets. Since the companies are parastatals it is unlikely that the share capital does not belong to the government. This proves again that estimated figures in Table 8-17 are most likely highly incomplete, above all as there is no information on 223 parastatals.

Crosschecking further reveals that the contents of Treasury investments, in particular the category 'other investments', is not clear. *'Paid up share capital'* could be found in the balance sheets as 'capital fund', 'share capital', 'advance towards equity' or 'capital grants'. *'Other investments'* included a large variety of different items, among others long-term liabilities, general grants and development grants, various funds (technical assistance funds, pension funds and provisions, price stabilisation funds, development levy funds, etc.), as well as accumulated profits and losses and reserves (investment revaluation reserves, capital reserves). In other cases, Treasury investments were mentioned but they did not include reserves, capital funds or accumulated surplus/deficits.

The inconsistent treatment of items and the mixture of effective support and carried-over profits and losses constrain an evaluation of Treasury assistance. Such distortion of information is however typical in a rent-seeking economy. Support does not just flow through well-declared channels but is also embodied in other items, which makes an assessment and interpretation difficult.

In contrast to the data on Treasury investments, where at least statements for six years were available, very little information could be traced on *Treasury guarantees*. Table 8-18 summarises the data of Treasury guarantees for commercial parastatals, based on three different sources (statements of June 1995, October 1996 and December 1996). According to the statements, guarantees were issued, among other reasons, for overdrafts, to finance the foreign cost part of loans and to support construction projects. Guarantees also took the form of counter-guarantees, e.g. for NBC loans transferred to LART.

Besides total balances, Table 8-18 shows the share of outstanding guarantees issued between 1986 and 1995, however only for the guarantees which are still mentioned in the 1995 and 1996 Treasury statements. Information from other sources suggests that the 1995 and 1996 balances are not complete. According to the 1997 Public Expenditure Review (PER), for instance, contractual and contingent liabilities for the enterprises incurred before 1993 are estimated to exceed TSh 550 billion, of which 75% relates to external debt guaranteed by the Treasury (World Bank (1997d. p. 19)). To what extent part of this amount refers to defaulting bank loans that have been taken out of the Treasury guarantee statements could not be assessed. Table 8-15 on page 475 indicated NBC loans worth TSh 100 billion (US$190 million), which had been transferred to the Treasury in 1991/92 since the payment was guaranteed by the Ministry of Finance. If the total is added to either total shown in Table 8-18 the magnitude of guarantees is still roughly half of the value mentioned in the in the PER.

Table 8-18: Treasury Guarantees to Commercial Parastatals (TSh m)

Treasury statement	Number of guarantees	Number of companies	Total balance at current prices	Total balance at 1994 prices	Share [a] local	Share [a] foreign
30 June 1995	48	13	171,914	148,458	8.3%	91.7%
31 Oct. 1996	62	18	318,026	215,465	4.1%	95.9%
31 Dec. 1996	44	14	240,143	158,667	0.6%	99.4%

New guarantees [b]	86-95	86/87	87/88	88/89	89/90	90/91	91/92	92/93	93/94	94/95
I. (Current)	26,578	1,655	1,798	128	3,405	4,129	1,020	11,199	663	2,583
I. (1994 prices)	68,979	12,391	9,738	568	12,333	10,467	2,079	18,372	801	2,230
II. (1994 prices)	62,564	12,323	10,167	83	9,771	8,828	1,252	16,042	1,868	2,230

a: The Treasury issues guarantees on local and foreign loans.

b: Only guarantees which are still mentioned in the Treasury statements of 1995 and 1996. Most records include information on the date and original amount of the loan guaranteed. This information is used in (I). Version (II) is based on the values of the balances shown in 1995 and 1996 (converted into 1994 prices and using the maximum value if statements deviate).

Source: Treasury Statements of Guarantees issued for liabilities of various institutions as at 30 June 1995, 31 October 1996 and 31 December 1996)

Also the difference between the number of guarantees outstanding in the years 1995 and 1996 indicates that the Treasury statements are not complete but more likely show the status of intermediate work (the 1996 Treasury statements include several additional guarantees issued in the 1980s). Again it is not a secret that the Treasury had considerable difficulties keeping track of all its contingent liabilities. The problem has been criticised frequently in OCAG reports and is also documented in Treasury letters written to parastatals.

For instance, in order to verify the correctness of the government's contingent liabilities, the Ministry wrote in 1996 to several parastatals to crosscheck Treasury guarantees identified by the Ministry, i.e. to identify the loans which had been fully repaid, and not to hesitate to include other government-guaranteed loans, which were missing in the Treasury records (statement in a letter of the Treasury to parastatal companies).

All in all, the tables on Treasury loans, investments and guarantees, even though incomplete, show that large amounts of funds have been transferred to parastatal companies (Treasury loans, paid up share capital and the few guarantees that belong to the period 1987-96 alone accounted for more than TSh 900 billion or nearly US$1.8 billion). Collecting information on individual parastatals and linking annual statements was useful to understand records, identify contradictions, correct misprints and calculate and add important missing information. As noted earlier, the problems related to record keeping are symptomatic of a rent-seeking environment. Even though the Controller and

Auditor General discovered and criticised many of the shortcomings long ago, hardly anybody within the administration seemed to have been worried or felt responsible. Donors were also silent on this matter, which is surprising since large amounts of the Treasury support constituted on-lent donor funds.

Information on Other Support from Government and Donors

Besides the direct support from the banking sector and the Treasury through loans, investments and guarantees, parastatals benefited in various other ways from cheap (or free) funds and payment relief from government and donors. Support included access to subsidies, underpriced foreign exchange, tax exemptions, as well as apparently tolerated arrears on both income taxes and dividend payments.

Subsidies in Tanzania represent an extremely opaque area of parastatal support. On the one hand, information is often only available in an aggregated form; on the other hand, subsidies typically appear under different headings, mixed with different aspects. The problem has been well described in Eriksson (1993, p. 23f). As she notes, data on subsidies vary depending on the source. However the different sources overlap, and a simple aggregation would produce double counting. Besides the term subsidy, the support may be denoted as subvention, grant, transfer, allocation, negotiated compensation, overdraft, financial assistance, foreign exchange equalisation, rehabilitation; or it may be more generally summarised under the heading of 'contractual and contingent liability' or 'miscellaneous subventions, grants and subsidies'.

Having said this, it is not surprising that collection of individual, company-based data has been difficult. Table 8-19 shows the total of data obtained where information on individual parastatals was available. Whenever possible, overlaps are eliminated. Nevertheless, the table is likely to be incomplete since substantial amounts of subsidy-related funds could not be included because there was no information on the specific purpose or the final recipient.

Table 8-19: Subsidies to Commercial Parastatals FY87-96 (TSh m)

	86/87	87/88	88/89	89/90	90/91	91/92	92/93	93/94	94/95	95/96	Total
Agri. & mining	311	295	664	1,768	837	1,032	1,144	103	252	601	
Manufacturing	338	345	475	1,867	1,855	5,854	7,594	4,356	2,330	866	
Services		64	76	134	228	171	1,361	8,564	2,313	1,712	
Total	648	705	1,214	3,768	2,920	7,057	10,099	13,022	4,895	3,178	
Total at 1994 prices	4,940	4,109	5,417	12,591	7,401	14,321	16,568	16,487	4,753	2,484	89,071

The table includes only data where information on individual parastatals was available.

Source: Data compiled from budget figures (GoT (1990c), GoT (1993b), GoT (1994-98)), Studies on parastatal subsidies (Coopers&Lybrand (1996, Volume 2 and 3), Eriksson (1993, p. 72)) and various documents obtained at the Ministry of Finance

In addition to information-related problems, interpreting the data can also be problematic since some of the subsidies are disbursed to compensate parastatals for negative government interventions, in particular maximum price regulations. As for instance noted in Eriksson (1993, p. 25), in such cases the subsidy effectively becomes a consumer subsidy.

Unfortunately, detailed and complete information on the allocation of *underpriced foreign exchange* has not been available. Because of the large parallel market premium in the 1980s, the allocation of scarce but underpriced foreign exchange constituted a lucrative source of support. In spite of the complex administrative procedure of approvals to obtain foreign exchange in the 1980s, neither the Bank of Tanzania (BoT) nor the National Bank of Commerce (NBC) have been able to provide disaggregated information on beneficiaries of foreign exchange. As discussed in Chapter 7.1, it was however possible to retrieve some information from a databank of *Tanzania's outstanding commercial foreign debt* and from a comprehensive report on the non-payment of counterpart funds of the donor-financed *Commodity Import Support (CIS) programme.*

The information obtained on Tanzania's outstanding foreign debt turned out to be of little use for various reasons.[178] Much more promising was the information obtained from the report on the non-payment of CIS counterpart funds (Ministry of Finance (1993)). As described in Chapter 7.1, the CIS programme, which is a specific kind of balance of payments support, was one of several channels through which parastatals and other clients could obtain foreign exchange at the cheap official exchange rate. Since recipients were required to pay the TSh equivalent into a counterpart fund which could be used by the government, the CIS scheme also constitutes, at least in theory, an important source of government revenue.

The reality in Tanzania however looked different. Foreign exchange was drawn, but a large amount of counterpart funds were never paid. For many recipients the CIS constituted a source of free funds and was therefore no different from a grant or a subsidy. In response to donor pressures, in early 1993 the Ministry of Finance set up a task force to review the non-payment of overdue counterpart funds. The Appendix of their final report includes a comprehensive list of all beneficiaries of the CIS allocation between June 1987 and December 1992 and detailed information on the non-payment of cash cover.

---

[178] Because of difficulties in converting old files, the data only showed records of one NBC branch where the Bank of Tanzania had failed to transmit the foreign exchange to the recipients abroad. In addition more than 80% of the data referred to the period 1980 to 1982 and the data included only records which had not yet been removed through debt-buy back schemes. Even though the file was large and still contained information on nearly 10,000 transactions from 1979 to 1993 (a third relating to parastatals), only 429 records on parastatals belonged to the period after June 1986 (26 parastatals, 76% of the records referring to four companies only).

Considering that a large import-dependent parastatal can easily have several hundred import-related bills a year, it would not make sense to interpret the small amount of data on the years 1986 to 1993. Even the interpretation of earlier records is problematic since it was not possible to assess whether the data were representative. There was no information on the relevance of the NBC branch, i.e. the question to what extent parastatals accessed foreign exchange through this branch. Furthermore, information was not available on the BoT's policy of not transmitting foreign exchange abroad. Data are distorted if, depending on the 'importance' of the client, the administration treated payments differently. Finally, the data only show records which have not yet been removed by earlier debt-buy back schemes and related write-offs.

This information provided a unique opportunity to evaluate the effectiveness of a specific type of donor support to parastatal companies.

The support can be divided into two components. The first component is the benefit from the access to cheap foreign exchange. In 1987, for instance, the average official TSh/$ rate was TSh 64, while the average parallel market rate was three times as high, implying that access to foreign exchange at the official rate saved two thirds of the costs. The second component constitutes the non-payment or late payment of the TSh equivalent, which can be treated as a cheap loan with a negative real interest rate (the 17% interest rate charged on outstanding cash cover was significantly less than the country's rate of inflation). Yet most of the outstanding CIS cash cover was never paid later.

Table 8-20 summarises the data compiled for the commercial parastatals. In December 1992 the balance of outstanding cash cover (including interests due) exceeded TSh 100 billion.[179] If the government had charged a zero real interest rate, i.e. a nominal interest rate sufficiently high to compensate the annual rate of inflation, the value would have been even TSh 184 billion (or TSh 302 billion in 1994 prices, which corresponds to nearly US$600 million). Yet this adjustment still represents a conservative method. To fully account for alternative costs, it would have been even more appropriate to apply a positive real interest rate (e.g. using LIBOR, and adding a mark-up for the risk premium).

Table 8-20: Commodity Import Support: Subsidy Component and Unpaid Cash Cover of Commercial Parastatals FY88-Dec. 92 (TSh m)

Benefit from cheap FOREX	87/88	88/89	89/90	90/91	91/92	1992	Total 87-92	at 1994 prices
TSh overvaluation [a]	2.42	1.89	1.68	1.54	1.45	1.25		
Support at current prices [b]	21,756	13,568	18,807	7,394	7,812	3,375	72,712	
Support at 1994 prices	126,858	60,521	62,842	18,744	15,855	5,537		290,356
Outstanding cash cover							**Total 12.92**	**at 1994 prices**
Principal [c]	14,370	23,063	41,027	46,122	58,907	70,401	70,401	115,496
Interests 87-92 (18%)							34,514	56,622
Total balance 31.12.92							104,915	172,118
Balance (value conserving) [d]	*18,852*	*35,722*	*72,425*	*99,340*	*136,290*	*184,007*	*184,007*	*301,874*

a: June to June average of parallel market rate divided by the official exchange rate.

b: Difference of parallel market rate and official exchange rate, times the foreign exchange obtained.

c: Principal net of repayments. Although the CIS report does not indicate the date of the cash cover payment, it shows the total amount of interest charged by December 1992. Knowing the interest rate, this information allows the missing dates to be calculated (assuming that partial repayment was made in one instalment).

d: Same as c, however assuming a fictive interest rate that equals the annual rate of inflation.

Source: Figures compiled and calculated from Ministry of Finance (1993); parallel market rates from BoT, Dar es Salaam

[179] The earlier data shown in Table 7-10, which is slightly higher, includes 3 companies not defined as commercial parastatals (Tanzania Bureau of Standards, Tanzania Fishnet and Tanzania Match Assemblies).

Another area of indirect support from the government is the non-payment of taxes, realised either through tax exemptions or tax arrears. Even though exemptions have been sizeable and had to be granted by the Minister of Finance, it was not possible to obtain any information on parastatal beneficiaries in the 1980s and early 1990s. One reason was that this matter was far too sensitive. A lot of information has never been collected; some records have also been deleted and files destroyed.

The only information which could be obtained on an individual company-based level was information on *income tax arrears*. Table 8-21 shows the totals. The Tanzania Revenue Authority has been very generous in providing this information since most of the data were not available at the headquarters in Dar es Salaam, but had to be collected from a large number of regional income tax departments. Of the many documents, faxes, telexes and telegrams sent to Dar es Salaam, it was however not always possible to identify whether indicated income tax arrears showed balances or flows (in most cases the former was assumed). In addition not all regional offices responded, and some offices also missed a few relevant parastatals. The Zanzibar Revenue Authority, for instance, reported that Zanzibar did not have any parastatals, which was false. The figures, which include 162 parastatals, therefore only indicate a conservative estimate of the balances of income tax arrears.

Table 8-21: Income Taxes Arrears of Commercial Parastatals FY87-96 (TSh m)

	86/87	87/88	88/89	89/90	90/91	91/92	92/93	93/94	94/95	95/96	Support
I. Total	1,218	2,251	2,404	4,736	5,077	6,929	6,358	21,645	19,755	19,525	
II. at 1994 prices	8,212	11,566	9,475	13,734	11,436	12,798	9,381	23,997	17,060	13,937	
III. Change		1,033	153	2,332	341	1,852	-572	15,288	-1,890	-230	
IV. at 1994 prices [a]		5,307	602	6,763	769	3,420	-843	16,948	-1,632	-164	40,050 [b]

a: Since IV equals III converted into constant prices, it does not correspond to the change in II. The chosen specification compensates reductions in the real value of outstanding balances caused by inflation.

b: Balance 1986/87 (II) plus changes of balances between 1986/87 and 1995/96 (IV), however excluding negative company totals. Negative values occur when a company overpays taxes due to an initially wrong assessment of profits. (There are only three companies with a negative overall total; if included, the total becomes 39,381.)

Source: Data obtained from regional offices of Tanzania Revenue Authority in March/April 1998

Particularly problematic is the interpretation of changes in balances since some of the income tax arrears have also been written off. According to personal communication with the Commissioner of Income Tax (Dar es Salaam, March 2000) only two of the ten largest defaulters paid back their arrears. Apparently penalties and interest was also charged on outstanding arrears. With the data obtained, however, several outstanding balances remained the same over several years, indicating that penalties and interests were not included.

A related area of indirect parastatal support is *dividend payment arrears*. Similar to income taxes, dividend liabilities arise if a company makes profits. In most cases arrears accumulate, as companies are liquidity constrained. Again it was difficult to obtain individual company-based information. In response to a request in April 1998, the Treasury Registrar only provided data on four selected years. It has nevertheless been possible to trace additional, partly overlapping information from alternative sources, i.e. from a study on the parastatal fiscal impact (PSRC (1997b)) and a document produced for a POC seminar on the financing of public enterprises (Ministry of Finance (1997)).

Surprisingly, although all three sources quote information from the Treasury Registrar, not a single figure corresponded. The data obtained directly from the Treasury Registrar included weaknesses identified in earlier Treasury statements, i.e. a closing balance for a specific year did not necessarily coincide with an opening balance of the subsequent year. Table 8-22 summarises the information collected and the discrepancies found.

It has not been possible to find out which of the sources gave reliable data. In addition, the small number of companies mentioned in the Treasury statements may suggest that none of the statements are complete. Although the Treasury invested large amounts of funds in commercial parastatals and although there have been more than 100 average profit-makers, the Treasury statements include on average less than eight companies which declare dividends (25 in 1987/88, very few in the 1990s). Perhaps the Treasury is not assessing dividends for all the companies it could consider.

Table 8-22 also shows that a considerable amount of declared dividends were in arrears. It is not clear whether the companies finally paid their duties. According to the data, more than 90% of effective dividend payments are from the Central Bank (BoT), which is not a commercial parastatal but an institution primarily concerned with conducting monetary policy and making profits from its privileged position of earning seignorage. Paying dividends is obviously not a characteristic of commercial parastatals.

Inter-Parastatal Arrears Other Than Banking

A final area of parastatal support extends to defaults outside the banking sector or government institutions. A parastatal may not settle its accounts due for the goods and services it obtained; it may delay contributions to the pension fund or may even defer monthly wage payments. Particularly if penalties on arrears are moderate or absent (during the 1980s, for instance, none of the penalties compensated the rate of inflation and the costs of short-term bank credits) delays are lucrative and efficiently reduce the real value of the outstanding debt.

Arrears and defaults on wage bills have not been common, as they can generate immediate unrest among workers. In contrast, *arrears on pension fund contributions*, which sooner or later also affect workers, have been much more frequent. Defaults on payments are not immediately felt but if not corrected finally cause workers to lose the retirement pay due to them. *Utility services* like water, power or telecommunications are another area where defaults regularly occur, though prices have generally been low. This poor payment record is

Table 8-22: Treasury Statements on Dividend Liabilities FY87-96 (TSh m)

A. Overall totals of different sources (data include Bank of Tanzania):

(source in parentheses)	86/87	87/88	88/89	89/90	90/91	91/92	92/93	93/94	94/95	95/96
Div. payable (1)		2,591						9,800	14,159	14,982
Dividends paid (1)		2,194						6,400	12,364	13,991
Dividends (2a) [a]	35.4	490	6,308	9,171	8,834	8,056	3,584	7,473	818	173
Dividends (2b) [a]	490	6,308	9,171	8,834	8,056	3,584	7,473	818	173	
Div. payments (3)						10,519	9,435	9,089	13,755	

B. Examples of differences of individual statements:

Source	National Insurance Corporation.			Tanzania Cigarette Company			Tanzania Petroleum Development Corp.			Bank of Tanzania (BoT)		
	87/88	93/94	94/95	87/88	93/94	94/95	87/88	93/94	94/95	87/88	93/94	94/95
(1)	9.6	0.0	265.0	150	0	1,500	40	1,850	0	2,000	6,200	12,289
(2a) [a]	20.8	41.0	60.0	100	300	0	250	800	700	0	6,284	0
(2b) [a]	10.0	60.0	0	120	0	0	221	700	0	5,738	0	0
(3)	n.a.	9.2	185.5	n.a.	400	200	n.a.	0	3,433	n.a.	8,658	8,971

C. Breakdown source (1) in commercial parastatals and Bank of Tanzania:

Source (1)	Opening balance of div. in arrears	Dividends declared for last FY	Dividends paid	Closing balance of div. in arrears	Unexplained change	Balance at 1994 prices	*Div. paid by BoT*	*In % of total paid*
87/88	n.a.	591	194	397	n.a.	2,040	*2,194*	*91%*
93/94	3,392	3,600	200	6,792	4,755	7,530	*6,400*	*97%*
94/95	2,037	1,870	75	3,832	1,980	3,309	*12,289*	*99%*
95/96	1,852	1,607	616	2,842	n.a.	2,029	*13,991*	*96%*

D. Indicator of support:

Source (1)	Balance 87/88	ΔBalance 93	ΔBalance 94	ΔBalance 95	ΔBalance 96	Support [b]
In current prices	397	2,995	3,400	-2,960	-990	2,842
At 1994 prices [c]	2,040	4,419	3,769	-2,556	-706	6,966

a: The Treasury compiles information according to Financial Years (FY); source (2), however, only indicates years (1986, 1987, ...), which may either denote the beginning (2a) or the end (2b) of the FY.
b: Unpaid dividends of 1987/88 (closing balance of FY88) plus differences with later closing balances.
c: Real values calculated from changes at current prices to compensate decreases caused by inflation.

Source: (1) Treasury Registrar Statements of Arrears of Dividend (1988, 1994, 1995, 1996) collected in April 1998 at the Treasury in Dar es Salaam, (2a, 2b) PSRC (1997b, p. 24), (3) Ministry of Finance (1997, Table 2)

mainly a result of the inefficiency of parastatals in looking after their debtors. The problem is further exacerbated by the behaviour of the government, which frequently directed utility parastatals to continue to supply services to defaulting companies.

One might think that it would be fairly easy to get detailed information on outstanding payments of clients to a company. In Tanzania in the 1990s this was not the case. Neither the Parastatal Pensions Fund (PPF) nor the utility companies TANESCO, TTCL and NUWA had a sufficiently sophisticated debtor management system, to make it possible to quickly trace the performance of their clients over the years and to immediately cut services to defaulters. In most cases data on the years prior to 1990 were non-existent and information on more recent years was not available for all parastatals. Figure 8-4 summarises the data collected. The difficult and time-consuming process of retrieving information on outstanding TTCL debt is briefly described below.

Figure 8-4: Inter-Parastatal Arrears of Commercial Parastatals (TSh m)

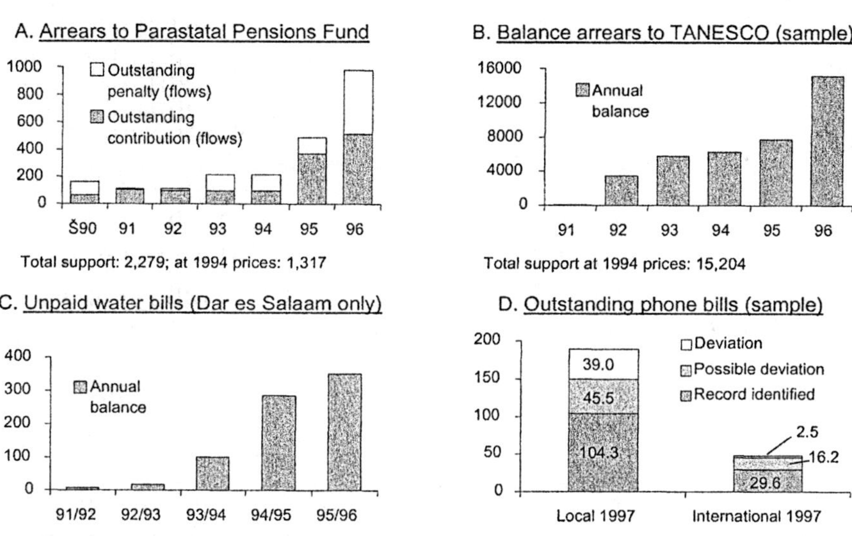

Parastatal Pensions Fund (PPF): Breakdown of outstanding balances of contributions 2186 and penalties 1284 of Dec. 1997 (of which 843 and 347 belong to the year 1997). Outstanding contributions of 1992-94 and penalties of 1993-95 calculated from an even distribution of the difference in balances of earlier and later years.

Tanzania Electric Supply Company (TANESCO): Due to the difficulty and time constraints of TANESCO in retrieving information, balances only indicate data on 125 companies and even for this group data are not complete.

National Urban Water Authority (NUWA): The data show 29 companies from Dar es Salaam (DAWASA).

Tanzania Telecommunications Company (TTCL): Data compiled from a print-out of defaults of local and international calls sorted according to phone numbers. Since information on parastatal phone numbers was obtained from the national telephone directory, the names shown in the TTCL list did not always correspond to the parastatal name identified with the phone number. Data are compiled as 'deviation' if the list indicates a different company or institution, 'possible deviation' if the list shows the name of a person (the line and the outstanding phone bill may still belong to the company).

Source: Data obtained from PPF, TANESCO, TTCL and NUWA (DAWASA) in March and April 1998

In particular TTCL had poor debtor management. The telecom company did not store information on outstanding phone bills according to clients but according to phone numbers. It was therefore not possible to find direct information on how much a parastatal owed to TTCL. A company will never be able to control its debtors if it only has access to totals based on phone numbers. In earlier days, defaulting on a bill therefore appeared to have been relatively simple.

The company provided a computer print-out (a pile of paper 40cm high, A3 format) showing more than 10,000 defaulting phone numbers and corresponding unpaid balances. However, to be able to identify the 336 parastatals it was first necessary to know their phone numbers (the print out did not always indicate the name of the parastatal, although the connection belonged to the company). This information could be obtained from the national telephone directory. Not only did many parastatals, such as the NBC, TANESCO or Tanzania Railways Corporation, have several hundred phone numbers, the data needed to be retrieved from an old phone book (1991/92 edition), as many companies had collapsed in the mean time. Using old numbers, however, necessitated getting additional information on area codes since some had changed, and this implied that there would be no information on new phone numbers, i.e. numbers allocated after 1991 (simultaneously evaluating several phone books was not an option at the time, among other reasons because the TTCL data could only be accessed after several unsuccessful requests one week before leaving Dar es Salaam).

Because of time constraints, ten companies with the largest number of phone connections had to be excluded from the data collection (they represented more than thirty pages in the telephone directory). Furthermore for 68 companies there was no information on a telephone connection. For all the remaining parastatals, 2628 phone numbers were identified and crosschecked with the list on outstanding balances obtained from TTCL.

Despite the considerable efforts needed to compile this information, the TTCL data were still poor. Many records could not be identified, partly because not all phone numbers were known. In addition, many phone numbers found in the national phone book did not correspond to the names mentioned in the print-out, which added to the insecurities related to the data. Equally constraining for the evaluation was information missing for the time when outstanding balances had been accumulated. It was therefore not possible to assess the extent to which inflation had reduced the real value of the outstanding debt. The major benefit from the entire exercise was therefore that of understanding the chaos in the TTCL customer records.

As noted above, other data on inter-parastatal arrears shown in Figure 8-4 correspond to samples only. The PPF data show the breakdown of the outstanding debt still mentioned in 1998. They do not include information on earlier write-offs or delayed contributions finalised prior to 1998. In addition, two arbitrary crosschecks with affected companies did not reveal the same figures. As a manager notes, PPF is probably not always aware of the number of people companies employ (personal communication in Dar es Salaam, March 2000). Similarly, outstanding electricity bills did not correspond to the data shown with alternative sources of information (e.g. Coopers&Lybrand (1996)). The findings again support the provocative statement of the bank manager cited earlier, i.e. every data collection had its own purpose.

All in all, research on the channels of support showed that reliable information was difficult to access in Tanzania, as in some cases it simply did not exist. Although many of the problems reflect a lack of competence, inabilities and true bottlenecks, many others are the result of sheer rent-seeking, i.e. the embezzlement of funds and the creation of a largely impervious veil to conceal many of the flows and transactions connected with rent-seeking activities.

The extent of missing information, the frequent contradictions and errors found, the odd situation that closing balances for one year do not necessarily correspond to opening balances of the next provide a clear message. Also situations in which totals in Excel sheets are not entered as a formula but are written out (apparently to avoid discrepancies with other sources) raise another red flag. Many of these shortcomings do not need sophisticated skills and capacities to be eliminated. Tanzania is not just an inefficient country struggling with inadequate capacities and a lack of know-how, as many policymakers and donors may see it. If rent-seeking was the benchmark, the country would be rated as highly efficient and flexible, quickly adapting to new circumstances.

The legitimate question emerges whether it makes any sense to put so much effort into collecting information if most of the available data are of poor quality. The answer is yes. Besides the fact that the activities involved in data collection help to answer questions on rent-seeking behaviour and strategies, most of the data still included a lot of information on parastatal support and embezzlement. In particular if data are not just collected on one type of support but include as many aspects as possible, many of the relevant patterns become clearly visible.

b) Distribution and Conditions of Parastatal Support

This section links the data on parastatal support with the detailed company characteristics discussed earlier in Chapter 8.1. The specific type of information collected and the poor quality of some of the data demanded a careful evaluation. Six important aspects guided the analyses and helped to substantiate the validity and scope of the results.

First of all, properties regarding the type of information influenced the *choice of indicators and statistical procedures*. The data on support are characterised by many outliers and an original distribution of support which does not look like a statistical normal distribution. Another aspect is that the support data are mutually interdependent with the companies' profits and losses. And finally, in spite of the missing data problem with some channels of support, the data reflect actual support to parastatal companies and not just a representative sample. These features required a differentiated perspective.

In most analyses it does not make sense to exclude outliers since the data show amounts effectively allocated to the companies. However, it makes sense to discuss properties of support in terms of both 'total amounts allocated' as well as 'number of benefiting companies'. The former helps in understanding economic costs, the latter characterisccs beneficiaries and is neither distorted by outliers nor distorted by errors in the size of identified support.

Cross-sectional analyses and time series would have been interesting, but the nature of the data made this approach potentially unreliable. For instance, to solve the problem of mutual interdependency it would have been necessary to find instrumental variables, which was not possible. Missing data and distortions were particularly high with annual values (as compared to ten-year averages), which again constrained the analysis. The analyses taken in this chapter therefore mainly use descriptive statistics and some non-parametric test procedures, and evaluate company properties in terms of averages (and not time series). Only the final evaluation (p. 519f) will present a Tobit model which links parastatal support with the profit and loss characteristics, employment, location and sector affiliation.

Second, it is necessary to assure that results are not just the outcome of an *arbitrarily chosen specification* of either the grouping data, the support data or both. As shown in Chapter 8.1, even apparently simple questions such as defining profit-makers and loss-makers do not have straightforward solutions. Moreover the support data presented so far suggest that there are many ways of dealing with missing data, unexplained changes and contradictory values. However, a large number of possible specifications for each aspect implies an even greater number of theoretical permutations in an analysis that combines grouping features and support data. The major challenge has been to reduce the number of combinations to manageable levels and to make them robust (without overlooking any relevant specification that might indicate that the results do not necessarily always hold).

Third, most analyses which differentiate between profits and losses or profit-makers and loss-makers exclude (or treat separately) the *badly-categorised profit-makers* NBC, CRDB, THA, TPDC and TIPER. As noted earlier, despite declared profits the companies have been highly inefficient and have benefited from strong monopoly protection (in terms of internationally-accepted accounting standards, the banks were actually loss-makers). If anything, the companies should therefore be treated as large loss-makers. Because information on support provided to the banking sector is also suspicious in the sense that the support is often a compensation of government directives to lend to uncreditworthy parastatals, in most analyses the core banks NBC, CRDB and TIB are either excluded or treated separately (in contrast to NBC and CRDB, TIB effectively shows average losses).

Fourth, some of the data obtained refer to *holding companies* which occasionally only function as intermediate institutions. If there is no information on the distribution to final recipients, including these data could distort the conclusions regarding patterns of support. For instance, in focusing on the distribution between profit-makers and loss-makers results are distorted if the holding company does not keep the funds but is rated as a profit-maker while final (unknown) beneficiaries are all loss-makers. To avoid misinterpretations and to substantiate the validity of the results this has been taken into consideration.

The analysis therefore also identifies holding companies, and it mentions the companies which received substantial amounts but have different characteristics than affiliated companies. To validate general findings most results are crosschecked against the assumption that funds allocated to holding companies are evenly distributed to the holding complex. This 'benchmark' assumption does not make sense with all channels of support however. Arrears on income taxes and dividend payments, as well as unpaid liabilities to PPF, TANESCO, TTCL and NUWA most likely always belong to the specified companies.

Although only some of the holding funds are effectively redistributed to other commercial parastatals and the reallocation is unlikely to be equal, different distribution scenarios offer additional ideas as to the robustness of obtained results. As will be argued however, the results only change marginally if at all, and all the principal conclusions remain valid. (The holding companies are listed in Table C-3 in the Appendix.)

Fifth, a sensible interpretation of the support data needs to differentiate between the two sub-groups *'core infrastructure parastatals'* and *'all other companies'*. Tanzania's infrastructure was very poor in the 1980s and 1990s. The development of a fairly good infrastructure is capital-intensive and usually (at least on paper) a top priority in any third world country, as it has high positive externalities for private sector activities. In Tanzania there are private companies charged with road construction; however, the supply of electricity, water and telecommunication services as well as the development and maintenance of airports, harbours and railways have been the domain of eight commercial parastatals. Given that most of them are monopolies, highly inefficient and recipients of substantial amounts of government and donor funds (in particular Treasury support), it makes sense to discuss them separately and, depending on the question, to formulate a specification that excludes them. Eight companies have been defined as 'core infrastructure parastatals' (they are listed in Table C-3 in the Appendix).

Finally, depending on the specific questions, it is important to make a distinction between *different aggregates of support*. The main purpose of this chapter is to quantify and describe support allocated to parastatal companies in the form of 'rents' or 'free money'. With this in mind, support is defined as 'net of repayments or recoveries'. However, in evaluating the lending behaviour of an institution such as the Treasury or a commercial bank, an analysis should also be made of the entire portfolio (i.e. not excluding companies that repaid the loans), as this will provide information on the allocation of scarce resources. Unfortunately, in particular for NBC and CRDB, it was not possible to obtain information on a complete portfolio and conclusions concerning their lending behaviour depended on alternative sources of information.

Top Beneficiaries and Sector Distribution of Parastatal Support

To get an idea of the largest beneficiaries of support an appealing approach would be to calculate for each parastatal an overall total of the various channels of support identified in Section a). The only problem is to adequately *combine information which is of different types and quality*. As noted earlier, some of the data refer to balances of funds obtained as subsidies, loans or share capital (investment); other data only indicate liabilities in default (or what is left after several unknown write-offs and reschedulings), and some of the support takes the form of contingent liabilities.

Furthermore there are different *definitions of support* and it is not always clear-cut or possible to identify the period support relates to. A loan is a good example of this. A loan may have to be repaid in ten annual instalments after a grace period of five years. The support is received on the day of disbursement but the loan may be used to finance investments over the next three to five years. If the recipient of the loan finally defaults, arrears on principal only start to accumulate after the grace period has expired. Hence different definitions of the size and timing of support may apply, i.e. cash support on the day of disbursement; effective support, which relates to the period in which the funds have been spent; and support that takes the form of tolerating arrears, i.e. support, which prevents an outflow of funds after the grace period has elapsed. Looking at the data discussed in Section a), information effectively relates to different types of support, and even for a particular type of support it was not always possible to discriminate between different periods of time.

Therefore with the data available any calculation of an overall total includes an implicit or explicit weighting of the different indicators of support, depending on what information is used and what assumptions are made. The only satisfactory solution is not to put too much emphasis on the overall total but also to consider the values and specifications of each channel of support.

For the evaluation below, the aim was to identify support that takes the form of *cash support* (non-performing loans and overdrafts, free money in the from of Treasury investments and subsidies) and support in the form of *preventing cash outflows* (non-payment of taxes, dividends and inter-parastatal services). Furthermore any support relating to the period prior to 1986 or after 1996 had to be eliminated.

Unfortunately, except for Tanzania Investment Bank, there was no useful information on annual support provided by the banking system. The only information available from NBC, CRDB and THB was outstanding balances of non-performing assets and loans transferred to the Treasury, PSRC and LART. This was not optimal. On the one hand, some of the amounts transferred to the privatising and liquidating institutions probably included loans issued prior to June 1986, even though persisting negative real interest rates would have reduced the share of these loans and overdrafts substantially. On the other hand, in particular for the PSRC data where only information on the balance in 1999 was available, data on loans already written off was missing.

Support from Tanzania Investment Bank was defined according to the annual changes of outstanding principals, applying a value-conserving approach (changes at current prices converted into constant prices to compensate decreases caused by inflation). For the last year it was assumed that companies with a better rating than 'loss' did not default on the loan and paid back the outstanding amount. The TIB data were nevertheless suspect and could not be understood in full. In each year only a few balances (principal) did not change, while on average one third decreased and two thirds increased. This contrasts with information given in the TIB annual report, which states that there were only a few loan approvals after June 1986 (Tanzania Investment Bank (1996, p. 29-37)). It appears that new loan approvals and additional disbursements (which could be from open credit lines approved earlier) are not treated the same.

Support from Treasury loans is defined as disbursements plus unexplained increases minus repayments, but excluding any loans that existed prior to 1986, even though some of these still increased afterwards. This solution reflects a compromise between ignoring all unexplained increases (assuming that they simply indicate an updating of old records) and treating unexplained increases as effective disbursements in the year when the discrepancy occurs. For the last year it was assumed that companies with no arrears in June 1996 and no later loss qualification (information obtained at the Treasury in March 2000) had paid back their loans.[180]

Funds allocated by way of Treasury investments do not have to be repaid. For the definition of support only increases in 'paid up share capital' are considered since the category 'other investments' has been too distorted by the inclusion of accumulated profits and losses. Finally, Treasury guarantees have been added in full, after separating guarantees issued prior to June 1986. It can be argued that beneficiaries of Treasury guarantees would not have obtained support without the guarantee. Furthermore crosschecks reveal that there is no overlap with banking data shown above (more than 90% of the guarantees relate to foreign loans and defaults prior to June 1996 have already been excluded).

Detailed information on annual disbursements could be used for subsidies and Commodity Import Support. There was however no disaggregated information on CIS loan recoveries, which would have amounted to roughly 10%. Information on recoveries after 1996 was also missing on the remaining data on arrears, but again these recoveries are likely to be insignificant. With arrears on income taxes, dividend payments, bills on electricity and water (TANESCO and NUWA), annual changes were first converted into constant prices and then added. This procedure compensates any decreases in the real value of outstanding balances caused by inflation.[181] With the PPF data the share of the 1997 balance belonging to the years prior to 1997 was identified, while TTCL data, which comprise only 0.01% of the overall total, were added as a total, as disaggregated information indicating different years was not available.

The Tables 8-23 and 8-24 (p. 498f) display the results of the aggregation. Table 8-23 lists the names and overall totals for the thirty largest beneficiaries, comprising almost 80% of total support, and Table 8-24 shows the distribution of support according to sectors for both the overall total and the values of each channel of support used in the calculation.

---

[180] This rule was not applied for Tanzania Harbours Authority and State Fuel Corporation. With THA there had been earlier write-offs and the highly inefficient company continued to benefit from its strong monopoly position. For SFC information on write-offs was not available, but the company had severe problems.

[181] As noted earlier, this is in fact a conservative approach. To fully account for alternative costs, an argument can be made for using a positive real interest rate (e.g. using LIBOR, and adding a mark-up for the risk premium).

Table 8-23: The 30 Largest Beneficiaries of Support FY87-96 (TSh m, 1994 prices)

Pos.	Name	Indicative Total	Cu-mul.	Pos.	Name	Indicative Total	Cu-mul.
1	Tanzania Harbours Authority	191,693	10%	16	Tanzania Petroleum Develop. Cor.	27,750	67%
2	Tanzania Electric Supply Co Ltd	170,230	19%	17	General Tyre East Africa Ltd	23,085	68%
3	Tanzania Railways Corporation	155,765	28%	18	State Fuel Corporation	21,860	70%
4	Tanzania Telecommunications Co	140,327	35%	19	TAZARA (Railways)	20,468	71%
5	Tanzania Coffee Marketing Board	113,378	41%	20	Tanz. Automobile Manufact. Co	19,063	72%
6	Tanzania Fertilizer Co Ltd	86,546	46%	21	National Bank of Commerce	18,355	73%
7	National Textile Corporation	78,407	50%	22	National Urban Water Authority	18,070	74%
8	Cooperative and Rural Dev. Bank	42,202	52%	23	Agip (Tanzania) Ltd	17,880	75%
9	National Milling Corporation	41,771	54%	24	Tanzania Investment Bank	16,791	75%
10	National Agricultural and Food Co	38,633	57%	25	Tanzania Cotton Marketing Board	16,160	76%
11	National Transport Corporation	35,760	58%	26	Air Tanzania Corporation	14,018	77%
12	Southern Paper Mills Co Ltd	35,560	60%	27	National Chemical Industries	13,921	78%
13	Aluminium Africa Ltd	34,347	62%	28	Tanz. Cashewnut Marketing Board	13,727	79%
14	Tanzania Saruji Corporation	33,868	64%	29	Small Industries Dev. Org.	12,851	79%
15	Tanzania Oxygen Ltd	31,052	66%	30	Tanzania Tobacco Processing MB	12,607	80%

Source: See Table 8-24

According to the data shown, in the ten-year period commercial parastatals obtained on average TSh 187 billion annually (US$360 million), which corresponds to more than 8% of GDP in Tanzania (all prices are 1994 prices). The figures should also be compared with total government expenditures (recurrent and development expenditures), which were at TSh 500 billion per annum, i.e. parastatals support equalled almost 40% of government expenditures. Since not all information on parastatal support had been obtained, this is a low-end estimate.

As emphasised earlier, the totals and the specific ranking of the companies need to be interpreted with caution. Figures on Treasury loans and Commodity Import Support are nearly complete in the sense that there was sufficient information available to include all records and to compensate real losses incurred by inflation. Not surprisingly, these channels of support are the largest in size and correspond to 64% of the overall total. In contrast, data on NBC balances have not been adjusted to inflation in earlier years, i.e. items given as outstanding balances in the 1990s had already been diminished by real negative interest rates in earlier years. Furthermore some balances only serve as an indicator to determine patterns of support; they are however not relevant in quantitative terms, either because the values are small or data are incomplete (balances of CRDB and THB, arrears on dividend payments and all data on 'other inter-parastatal arrears'). Finally, the table does not include a quantification of monopoly rents and price interventions.

Table 8-23 nevertheless gives a good picture of the main beneficiaries of parastatal support. An alternative ranking was made which excluded Treasury loans and CIS support. The top 30 companies in this new ranking include only nine enterprises that are not in the top 30 list above, the most relevant being

Tanzania Sisal Authority, which has position 18 instead of 32; all other beneficiaries occupy positions 23 to 30.

As expected, top beneficiaries listed in Table 8-23 include all the core infrastructure parastatals (rankings 1 to 4, 18, 19, 22, 26), a large number of holding companies and the three largest banks (NBC, CRDB and TIB). Eleven of the 30 companies (rankings 5, 7, 9-11, 14, 16, 25, 27-29) belong to the holding companies specified in Table C-3.[182] Obviously, holdings received large amounts of funds because they were considered strategic and because they partly reallocated funds to other parastatals and beneficiaries. Five holding companies are crop marketing boards and four belong to the manufacturing sector.

Since outstanding balances from the banking sector are underrepresented in the overall total of support to parastatals (due to the poor data), it makes sense to take a closer look at the largest NBC defaulters. Among the top ten NBC defaulters there are four companies not included in the ranking of Table 8-23 (in parentheses NBC position and position of overall total): Mbeya Cooperative Union (6/56), Tabora Region Cooperative Union (7/49), Kagera Cooperative Union (8/67), and Tabora Textile Mills (9/61). As discussed in Chapter 7, cooperative unions had a crucial stake in the economy and they have been jointly responsible for the macro imbalance caused by non-performing loans. It is therefore not surprising that ten cooperative unions figure among the top 30 NBC defaulters and the three largest defaulters of CRDB loans are also cooperative unions (Singida, Tanga and Tabora Cooperative Union).

Table 8-24 shows that support tended to favour certain sectors, and major beneficiaries varied between different channels of support. Since in most cases holding and affiliated companies belong to the same sector, the distribution between sectors only changes marginally if all holding funds are reallocated evenly among affiliated companies (some minor changes also cancel out). The high share of holding funds with NBC is partly explained by the two largest defaulters (National Textile Corporation and National Milling Corporation, which both are holding companies and account for 47% of NBC defaults).

The table confirms that substantial amounts of support have been allocated to core infrastructure parastatals. Even though the companies represent only 2.4% of the total number of commercial parastatals, their support is 39% of the total and clearly reflects the country's and donors' priorities. The Treasury supported the companies with loans, investments and guarantees (loans predominantly benefited public utilities and transport, and large investments went into harbours and railways; and TANESCO has been the major recipient of guarantees). Other main beneficiaries of Treasury support are the finance sector (loans, probably on-lent or a compensation for directed bank credits to unviable commercial parastatals), construction and chemicals (above all Tanzania Saruji Corporation and National Chemical Industries, which received large Treasury investments) and National Textile Corporation (the second largest recipient of Treasury guarantees).

---

[182] The companies with the ranking 3, 21, 24, 26 are also holding companies; they are however treated differently in the analysis (see comments to Table C-3 in the Appendix).

Table 8-24: Indicators of Support According to Sectors (TSh m, 1994 prices)

PART (A)	Comp in group	Total (incl. PART B) Amount	%	Banking (defaults) NBC	CRDB	TIB	THB	Treasury Loans	Invest-ment	Guaran-tees
Agriculture	78	265,970	14%	47,777	9,929	154	3	41,087	19,659	150
Cash crops	26	176,243	9%	12,448	693	154		14,042	17,994	150
Food crops (& other pl.)	16	40,086	2%	10,037				25,531	995	
Live animals	8	6,227	0%	61	57		3	201	670	
Cooperative unions	28	43,413	2%	25,230	9,180			1,313		
Mining	12	16,290	1%	293		98		7,652		4,395
Manufacturing	137	661,393	35%	108,748	1,456	25,978	814	50,061	65,561	30,185
Food, beverage, tobacco	19	76,306	4%	25,796	9	2,531		4,866	2,223	
Textile & leather	26	120,735	6%	62,851	909	14,947		8,607	1,830	22,639
Wood, paper, printing	26	67,251	4%	3,181	404	6,059	51	23,080		3,954
Chemicals	14	203,611	11%	1,256	123	352		1,276	19,250	
Construction	23	69,307	4%	961	10	2,089	353	9,174	34,949	3,592
Metal & machinery	26	124,184	7%	14,703			410	3,058	7,309	
Services	109	929,540	50%	8,300	1,965	2,502	1	509,557	157,258	34,248
Public utilities	5	350,487	19%					243,880	16,545	28,867
Trade, repair & maint.	39	45,581	2%	6,142	1,034				1,150	1,624
Transport & storage	24	424,056	23%	2,151	931			206,488	124,690	3,531
Tourism	20	8,434	0%	8		2,431	1	509	3,711	
Finance	14	85,442	5%					54,725	9,722	
Other services	7	15,539	1%			71		3,954	1,439	227
Total	336	1,873,193	100%	165,118	13,350	28,732	818	608,357	242,478	68,979
Of which infrastructure	8	732,432	39%	1%				73%	58%	47%
Of which holding	28	497,030	27%	60%	5%	0%	50%	11%	33%	30%
No. of benefiting comp.	336	320		115	30	26	9	77	53	12
Average per company		5,854	100%	1,436	445	1,105	91	7,901	4,575	5,748
ø excluding infrastructure		3,656	62%	100%	100%	100%	100%	29%	47%	64%
Average per 1000 employees		10,267	100%	3,090	919	2,135	328	5,860	3,469	4,221
ø excluding infrastructure		8,513	83%	101%	100%	100%	100%	47%	105%	102%

Specifications PART (A): Total: Part A+B; Banking: indicator of support; Treasury Loans: support 1987-96; Treasury Investments: sum of increases in 'Paid up share capital'; Treasury guarantees: only guarantees mentioned in the 1995 and 1996 statements which were issued after June 1986.

PART (B)	Comp in group	Other state & donor support Subsi-dies	CIS CC	CIS Subsidy	Income Tax	Divi-dend	Other inter-parastatal arrears Pension PPF	TA-NESCO	Water NUWA	Phone TTCL
Agriculture	78	18,893	67,493	52,495	7,775		161	365	3	27
Cash crops	26	18,240	59,648	46,091	6,389		79	292	3	20
Food crops (& other pl.)	16	634	739	850	1,253		34	9		4
Live animals	8	19	3,197	1,968	2		48			1
Cooperative unions	28		3,908	3,586	131		0	64		3
Mining	12	998	935	653	252		15	995		3
Manufacturing	137	50,438	150,695	156,171	8,862	4,492	616	6,953	291	70
Food, beverage, tobacco	19	12,702	10,689	9,991	1,976	3,525	55	1,904	22	18
Textile & leather	26	455	1,950	2,513	2,367		116	1,516	17	18
Wood, paper, printing	26	5,653	10,729	10,095	857	90	254	2,824	11	8
Chemicals	14	28,467	81,479	68,673	1,853	792	31	44	8	5

(PART (B) continued)	Comp in group	Other state & donor support					Other inter-parastatal arrears			
		Subsi-dies	CIS CC	CIS Subsidy	Income Tax	Divi-dend	Pension PPF	TA-NESCO	Water NUWA	Phone TTCL
Construction	23	3,161	6,898	7,376	287	26	81	154	182	15
Metal & machinery	26		38,950	57,523	1,523	59	79	512	51	6
Services	109	18,742	82,751	81,036	23,161	2,474	525	6,890	35	96
Public utilities	5	8,007	18,706	20,799	7,623		49	6,007		5
Trade, repair & maint.	39	2,401	13,982	16,831	1,138	1,097	96	31	13	42
Transport & storage	24	5,190	41,308	35,126	2,976	1,071	132	429	20	14
Tourism	20	99			1,375		177	101		22
Finance	14	554	4,768	5,004	10,017	306	28	311		6
Other services	7	2,491	3,987	3,276	32		43	12	1	7
Total	336	89,071	301,874	290,356	40,050	6,966	1,317	15,204	328	196
Of which infrastructure	8	15%	15%	13%	25%	10%	8%	42%	0%	4%
Of which holding	26	39%	31%	30%	18%	15%	18%	15%	5%	25%
No. of benefiting comp.	336	29	74	80	137	31	263	119	20	155
Average per company		3,071	4,079	3,629	292	225	5	128	16	1
ø excluding infrastructure		91%	94%	95%	78%	93%	94%	60%	100%	98%
Average per 1000 employees		4,087	3,036	2,800	389	259	8	141	38	3
ø excluding infrastructure		98%	158%	151%	139%	126%	91%	100%	103%	103%

Specifications PART (B): Subsidies: sum of annual values; CIS-CC (unpaid CIS cash cover): value-conserving balance 1992, CIS Subsidy: sum of annual values 1987 to 1992; Income Tax Arrears 1986-96, Dividend Arrears 1988, 1993-96, Arrears to TANESCO 1990/92-1996 and NUWA 1991-96: balance of first year plus changes of subsequent years; PPF: share of balance 1997 that refers to earlier years; TTCL: identified records and records with possible deviations (no adjustment to constant prices).

For an evaluation of the size and relative importance of support, Tables C-4 and C-5 in the Appendix additionally display sector totals in terms of percentage shares and sector data on the number of benefiting companies, averages per company and averages per 1000 employees.

Source: See Tables 8-15 to 8-22 and Figure 8-4

In the banking sector a disproportionately large share of support has been allocated to cooperative unions, National Milling Corporation and the textile and leather industry. Furthermore, as expected, CRDB predominantly invested in agriculture while TIB mostly supported manufacturing.

The high subsidies allocated to cash crops, food and chemicals again reflect large allocations to individual companies, i.e. Tanzania Cotton Marketing Board, National Milling Corporation and Tanzania Fertilizer Company. The last is also the second-largest beneficiary of Commodity Import Support (top position: Tanzania Coffee Marketing Board). The largest defaulter on income taxes is NBC, which accounted for more than 20% of the annual changes. Dividend payments have been due only for a few parastatals; Tanzania Cigarette Company accounts for almost half of the total dividend 'support'. Finally, while PPF and TTCL data indicate a rather smooth distribution of accumulated changes in arrears, the highest sector shares of unpaid TANESCO and NUWA bills are determined by outliers (the NUWA data, however, cannot be meaningfully interpreted, as figures include only a few companies located in Dar es Salaam).

All in all, at a brief glance the sector distribution reflects the typical priorities of a developing country, i.e. to build up and maintain its infrastructure and to selectively promote a few sectors, such as textile or chemicals, as part of a basic industry strategy. However supporting an economy is not just a matter of sector priorities. Equally crucial is to guarantee an efficient use of resources. As the remaining analysis will demonstrate, this has not been the case. Support in Tanzania has been allocated according to criteria other than efficiency and many of the priority sectors include large loss-making companies. There are many reasons to conclude that rent-seekers have been successful in capturing large shares of the generously allocated funds.

Purpose and Conditions of Parastatal Support

The main objective in the preceding section was to find an indicator of free support, i.e. support net of repayments and recoveries between 1987 and 1996. As has been argued above, support allocated to commercial parastatals has been substantial and equalled roughly 40% of total government expenditures. This section, which provides additional insights on the purpose and conditions of support, contributes greatly towards developing and substantiating the rent-seeking hypothesis, above all toward an understanding of patterns of allocation between profit-makers and loss-makers.

With a great deal of support allocated to parastatal companies, rent-seeking is obvious from the *type of support* under consideration. The non-payment of CIS cash cover, defaults on income taxes, dividends and pension fund liabilities, as well as arrears on the payment of inter-parastatal services (electricity, phone and water) violate contracts and therefore indicate rent-seeking and soft budget constraints. With other types of support, such as bank loans and overdrafts, Treasury loans, Treasury investments and Treasury guarantees, as well as direct subsidies, additional considerations are necessary to identify the rent-seeking component, in particular if there are no arrears involved.

Detailed information on the *purpose of support* could be obtained for Treasury loans. Nearly 60% of the Treasury loans issued after June 1986 are on-lent donor funds. In value terms the funds amount to 97% of the total and are for the most part investment related (financing new projects, rehabilitation, or financing part of an investment, such as the foreign exchange costs). The pattern is different for the 75 Tanzanian government loans. Even though in value terms they only represent a small share of all Treasury loans, most of them were allocated for reasons other than financing investments. Of the 75 loans, only 24 relate to investment (and rehabilitation); 51 loans were issued to finance current expenditures.

Figure 8-5 shows the detailed grouping of the Treasury loan portfolio. Some 18% of TSh 19,878 million in 'direct' Tanzanian government loans have been issued to settle obligations on behalf of defaulting parastatals, i.e. to convert the companies' unpaid liabilities into Treasury loans; 5% of the amount issued was used to pay duties and taxes, 17% to buy inputs and 34% was related to other bridging finance (such as 'financing urgent commitments', 'meeting prudential regulations' or financing working capital in general).

Figure 8-5: Purpose of Treasury Loans Issued Between FY87 and FY96

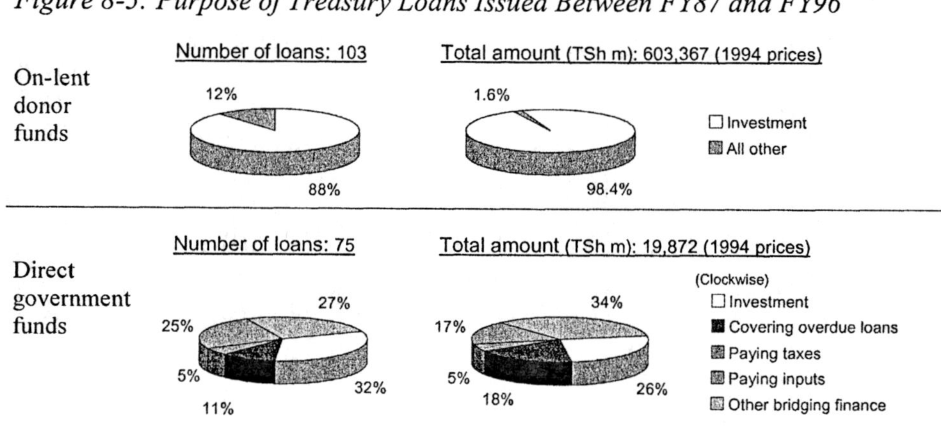

Source: Categorisation according to information obtained in the Treasury loan statements 1986/87 to 1996/97. For an analysis of the entire loan portfolio see Figure C-1 in the Appendix.

Further examination focused on the subset of commercial parastatals (data excluding core infrastructure parastatals and banking) and the entire Treasury loan portfolio. The findings are the same for all specifications, i.e. it seems that direct Tanzanian government loans have been primarily issued for rescue operations, apparently to protect an inadequate management, to compensate cost overruns and to fill gaps not paid by donors.[183] Although investment-related funds may also be associated with rent-seeking (above all large-scale embezzlement), the point emphasised in Figure 8-5 is that in the case of direct Tanzanian government funds the purpose of support seems to be more obviously linked to rent-seeking. In fact, as will be argued later, most companies did not just have liquidity problems but were insolvent.

An important aspect in determining support is the softness of loans. A differentiation can be made between *ex-ante loan conditions* and *actual (ex-post) loan costs*. Ex-ante conditions comprise interest rates, currency denomination and the terms of repayment. Actual costs critically depend on whether arrears on principal and interests occurred and were tolerated, and whether any defaults finally led to write-offs. Obviously a high interest rate is irrelevant if the company never pays the interest rate or entirely defaults on the principal.

In Tanzania real interest rates have been negative for a long time. Whether a loan was expensive or not entirely depended on the link to a foreign currency. From the mid-1980s onwards the government strongly devalued the Tanzanian Shilling, which implied that the TSh value of outstanding loans denominated in a foreign currency increased substantially—or to put it differently, the earlier preferential access to cheap foreign exchange at the official rate was cancelled in

[183] Donors do not usually pay for recurrent costs (also because they want to sell their export goods). The government then typically appears as a lender of last resort, for instance for salary payments.

retrospect. This may be seen as an unfair treatment of old loans. However from the mid-1980s onwards the policy of unifying the exchange rate with the parallel market rate was a matter of public knowledge, i.e. companies which were still obtaining new loans linked to a foreign currency should have been aware of the upcoming increase in the TSh value of their debts. Apparently the implicit assurance of government bailouts of troubled companies created moral hazard and companies therefore did not factor in foreign exchange rates.

Most loans in the banking system were not denominated in a foreign currency and their real values decreased over time without a single Shilling being repaid. For instance the average interest rate of the CRDB loans mentioned in the 1991 loan statement was 10%, while inflation was running at 30%.

The nominal interest rate for Treasury loans was also far lower than the rate of inflation. Yet, unlike bank loans, many Treasury loans were linked to a foreign currency, which implied high costs when the Tanzanian Shilling was devalued. The costs for the loans issued after June 1986, i.e. loans where future foreign exchange adjustments could be anticipated, are summarised in Table 8-25 (to control for the impact of outliers, data are displayed as averages per loan and as the usual weighted averages according to the size of the loan).

Table 8-25: Average Costs of Treasury Loans to Commercial Parastatals FY87-96

	86/87	87/88	88/89	89/90	90/91	91/92	92/93	93/94	94/95	95/96
Number of loans [a]	31	56	70	80	119	117	122	134	136	133
excl. bank & infra	*21*	*39*	*51*	*57*	*88*	*86*	*88*	*89*	*93*	*93*
Average costs per loan										
Nominal interest rate	4.7%	6.0%	5.9%	5.3%	7.5%	7.4%	7.7%	8.2%	7.6%	7.7%
Real loan costs [b]	n.a.	-9.3%	-13.1%	-21.4%	-18.5%	-4.1%	-10.2%	-16.0%	-13.7%	-14.2%
excl. bank & infra	*n.a.*	*-14.8%*	*-14.6%*	*-23.4%*	*-19.5%*	*-7.8%*	*-12.2%*	*-18.5%*	*-17.4%*	*-12.9%*
Weighted average [c]										
Nominal interest rate	3.5%	4.4%	5.3%	6.2%	7.1%	7.8%	7.9%	8.0%	7.5%	7.4%
Real loan costs [b]	n.a.	12.9%	5.7%	-1.0%	-10.4%	14.9%	4.5%	-0.2%	-1.0%	-16.9%
excl. bank & infra	*n.a.*	*-6.3%*	*7.5%*	*-8.3%*	*-13.4%*	*6.9%*	*2.8%*	*-1.0%*	*-13.2%*	*-10.6%*
Rate of inflation	30.0%	31.2%	30.4%	35.9%	28.8%	21.9%	25.2%	33.1%	28.4%	21.0%

a: Loans issued after June 1986 with closing balance larger than zero in specified year. Table C-6 in the Appendix shows the same data for the entire loan portfolio (i.e. including loans issued prior to July 1986).

b: Real loan costs equal interest rate plus foreign exchange adjustment minus inflation.

c: Interest rates weighted according to the size of the loans.

Source: Data on commercial parastatals compiled from annual Treasury loan statements

The table documents that both real interest rates and real loan costs were negative if averages are calculated according to the number of loans issued. For many companies, access to Treasury loans was therefore equal to obtaining a subsidy. Only if averages are weighted according to the size of the loans are average real loan costs positive in four out of nine years. This outcome reflects the situation that most large loans included foreign exchange adjustments. The majority of the Treasury loans on-lent from donors belonged to this category (in value terms 81% of the multilateral loans and 68% of bilateral loans), while Tanzanian government loans did not include such an anchor. Subsidy components are even higher for the loans issued to the sub-group of companies which excludes the core infrastructure parastatals and banking, basically because there were fewer loans with foreign exchange adjustments.

What about the more relevant question whether loans have been effectively repaid? Figure 8-6 shows a conservative estimate of the share of Treasury loans in arrears. Besides the characteristic that new loans do not tend to be in arrears during the first few years, above all as they may include long grace periods, the figure underestimates the true proportions since several loans were written off or disappeared without explanation during the ten-year period.

Figure 8-6: Share of Treasury Loans in Arrears FY87-96

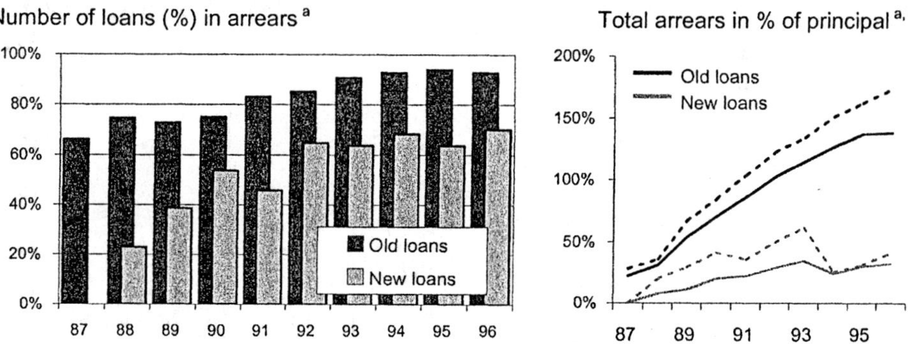

a: 'Old loans': loans issued prior July 1986, 'New loans': loans issued after June 1986.
b: Arrears include arrears on principal and interests. Dotted lines indicate the values for the subset of parastatals excluding core infrastructure and banking.

Source: Data compiled from Treasury loan statements 1986/87 to 1995/96. A detailed breakdown of figures is presented in Table C-7 in the Appendix.

There are in fact many reasons to assume that unexplained decreases and 'lost' loans represent write-offs, as a large share belongs to loss-makers (93% of unexplained decreases and 98% of 'lost' loans). The pattern is similar to the amounts explicitly written off or converted into equity (100% and 97% belong to loss-makers) and differs notably from the amounts mentioned as repaid (only 40% of all loan repayments come from loss-makers). Most decreases in the overall balance of arrears shown in the figure are the result of explicit and implicit write-offs.

In spite of these improvements in the books, Treasury loans still indicate a very poor repayment performance. The dramatic development of arrears, even for new loans, suggests that many of the parastatals never intended to pay back Treasury loans and the costs of the loans in terms of interest rates and foreign exchange adjustments are irrelevant. It even appears that parastatals responded to higher loan costs in the course of ongoing reforms by simply defaulting on the loans.

A particularly interesting aspect in evaluating the role of rent-seeking and soft budget constraints is the question whether companies obtained *additional support despite previous unsettled arrears.* Clearly, if companies are not punished for earlier defaults but, on the contrary, can rely on additional allocations, budget constraints become soft and changes in relative prices are to a large extent irrelevant in guiding economic behaviour. More decisively, the continued allocation of support in spite of earlier defaults opens the door for large-scale embezzlement.

Below, this relation of support and arrears is investigated for Treasury loans and Commodity Import Support, however using a narrow definition, i.e. the two channels of support are addressed separately (ignoring any cross relations). Between June 1986 and June 1996 a total of 81 companies benefited from explicit disbursements or increases in Treasury loans. Information on CIS allocations are available for the period June 1987 to December 1992, during which 80 commercial parastatals obtained at least one CIS allocation, 66 companies received more than one and nine companies even benefited from more than 10 allocations.

To enhance the validity of results, above all to demonstrate that the results do not depend on assumptions on missing information, two different specifications have been analysed with Treasury loans. A partial set only includes amounts explicitly denominated as 'disbursements' in the loan statements, while the full data set additionally includes unexplained increases, as well as loans which appear for the first time in the subsequent year's opening balance.[184]

Figures 8-7 and 8-8 and Table 8-26 summarise the results and show a very clear picture. Neither in the case of Treasury loans nor in the case of Commodity Import Support did arrears and defaults prevent additional disbursements. On the contrary, given the high share of support provided to companies with arrears, it is not far-fetched to assume that the opposite relation holds, i.e. particularly defaulters were rewarded with additional support. This pattern of allocation thoroughly corresponds to a picture of soft budget constraints; arrears obviously indicate companies in distress which need additional funds—and they obtain them.

Figure 8-7 shows the three groups core infrastructure, banking and all other parastatals separately since only 15% of the funds were allocated to the last group, and core infrastructure parastatals as well as the core banks (which partly on-lent funds) hold a strategic position. The high share of loans allocated despite earlier defaults is striking. The overall averages (not shown in the figure) are 61% and 94% for the partial data set and 63% and 90% for the full data set. Although companies excluding banking and core infrastructure indicate a slightly better performance, the share is still far from acceptable in terms of economic

---

[184] As noted earlier when defining Treasury support, unexplained increases have been treated as disbursements in the year they occurred, and loans which appear without being issued are assumed to represent disbursements of the preceding year (recall definition in Table 8-16). However, unlike in the definition of overall support, assumptions on unknown dates of issue may critically influence the outcome here. The analysis is therefore done with two data sets.

efficiency. Furthermore allocating support to strategic companies regardless of their past records does not create incentives for strategic companies to operate more efficiently. This can obviously not be in the interest of the country.

Figure 8-7: Treasury Loans Issued to Parastatals (FY88-96) Despite Unsettled Arrears

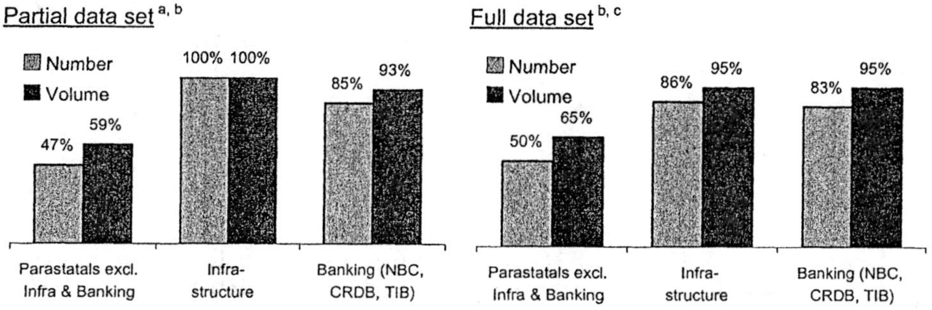

Definition of Arrears: Recipient is in arrears with other Treasury loans in the current *as well as* the previous Treasury loan statement. Considering two subsequent years rules out the possibility that the new loan was granted before the company was in arrears (there is only information on the financial year and not on the exact date within the year).

a: Loans explicitly issued according to the annual Treasury loan statements.

b: Only disbursements between July 1987 and June 1996 are considered, since there was no information on arrears for the financial year 1985/86.

c: Partial data set (a) plus unexplained increases plus loans which appear the first time in the following year's opening balance.

Source: Data compiled from Treasury loan statements 1986/87 to 1995/96. A detailed breakdown of figures is displayed in Table C-8 in the Appendix.

The negative impact of adverse signals on future performance is also suggested with the CIS data shown in Table 8-26 and Figure 8-8. According to the calculations presented in Table 8-26, the probability that a company would default on the cash cover of a new allocation was 54% if the company had not been in arrears. This probability increased to 74% if the company had already obtained CIS allocations in the previous year without paying cash cover in full, and it reached 100% for companies which had already started to default five years earlier.

Figure 8-8 additionally shows the share of defaults with new CIS allocations as a function of the number of previous defaults. Results are similar to the distribution shown in Table 8-26, i.e. the longer the period the company is in default (Table 8-26) or the larger the number of earlier defaults (Figure 8-8) the more likely will the company also default on the renewed CIS allocation.

All in all, the analysis of the purpose and conditions of support clearly strengthens the view that commercial parastatals obtained large amounts of free support either ex-ante through concessionary loans, free investments, cheap foreign exchange or ex-post by simply defaulting on liabilities. Most important, adhering

Table 8-26: Commodity Import Support Allocations and Defaults FY88-92

Number of CIS allocations between July 1987 and December 1992			TSh paid with new allocation: [a] yes	no	in %
A. CIS allocations in the 'first year' [b]		124	30	94	76%
B. Renewed CIS allocations					
B1. Number of renewed CIS allocations where company paid Cash Cover (CC) on previous allocations		24	11	13	54%
B2. Number of renewed CIS allocations despite previous defaults		202	33	169	84%
Allocations despite company in default since	one year	77	20	57	74%
	two years	58	8	50	86%
	three years	42	4	38	90%
	four years	18	1	17	94%
	five years	7	0	7	100%
A + B: Total number of CIS allocations		350	74	276	79%

a: Recipients of CIS allocations had to pay the TSh counterpart (TSh equivalent at the official exchange rate).
b: 'First year' denotes first year between 1987/88 to 1992/93 when company obtained one or more CIS allocations. The group is treated separately as there is no information on the state of preceding CIS allocations (i.e. the parastatal may have obtained earlier allocations and it may have defaulted on these).

Source: Data compiled from Ministry of Finance (1993)

Figure 8-8: Probability of Default with New CIS Allocations (1989-92)

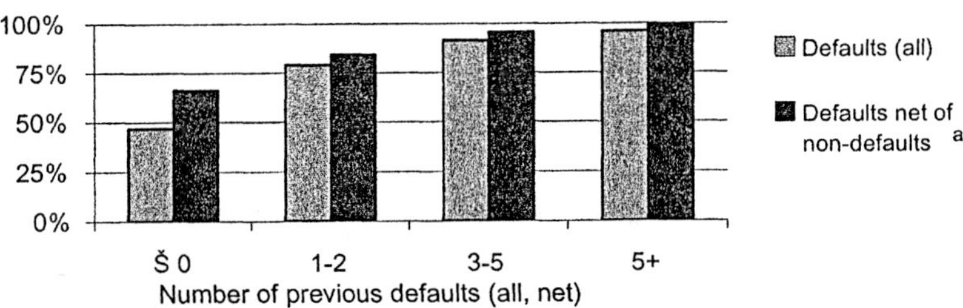

a: Number of defaults minus number of non-defaults, i.e. a company with 4 defaults and 3 non-defaults is assigned to group 1-2.

Source: Data compiled from Ministry of Finance (1993)

to agreed conditions has not been a criterion in the allocation of support. On the contrary, it appears that in particular defaulting parastatals benefited from additional generous support. This finding has been corroborated by other authors and contrasts with official statements from the Tanzanian government. Eriksson (1994, p. 55), for instance, who undertook a detailed investigation among donors on the allocation of Commodity Import Support, notes:

> 'Renewing CIS allocations despite previous default would seem to have been the rule rather than the exception, and shows that cash cover

payments have not been enforced by the Tanzanian government. These findings contrast sharply with a statement of a senior Treasury official involved that "if the recipients do not pay the counterpart funds, the Treasury refuses them future allocation," and that "the Treasury is always firm in this respect".'

The remaining part of this section focuses on the economic performance of the parastatal companies that obtained support. The discussion is highly relevant for substantiating the hypothesis regarding the role of rent-seeking and soft budget constraints.

Distribution of Support According to Economic Performance

Finding a high share of loss-makers among benefiting companies is a strong indicator for the prevalence of soft budget constraints and supports the hypothesis that rent-seeking was involved in the allocation of resources. The question of the extent loss-makers benefited from support is not only relevant for policymakers within a country but also for bilateral and multilateral donors, which have invested considerable funds in the parastatal sector in Tanzania.

Table 8-27 (and Table C-9 in the Appendix) reiterate a full version of the data presented earlier and group support according to the companies' profit and loss characteristics. Since the focus is on the efficiency of support-allocating institutions, the analysis uses the data set that does not exclude amounts repaid or recovered (the data would underreport the share of profit-makers if support was defined 'net of repayments and recoveries' as there are obviously more profit-makers which pay back loans).[185] However, as noted earlier, it was not always possible to obtain complete information on repayments and recoveries. The problem is not so severe since distortions from missing data partly offset each other, i.e. in some cases information is missing on funds that were repaid by good performers as well as funds for worst performers, which have already been written off.

Ideally, the definition of profit-makers and loss-makers should be adjusted for the size of support the company obtained. Support which takes the form of direct subsidies, preferential interest rates or access to foreign exchange at underpriced official exchange rates, reduces the costs of a company and may therefore explain why a loss-maker can become a profit-maker. However these corrections are not indisputable. It can be argued that some companies may not have taken a loan or may not have bought foreign exchange if they had to pay the full market price. The main analysis below is therefore undertaken with the conservative definition of loss-makers, not taking into account the impact of support. Obviously, if the hypothesis of allocating support to loss-makers holds

[185] According to the information available, the inclusion of funds that have been repaid leads to the following increases: the NBC total increases from 165,118 to 174,287, CRDB from 13,350 to 13,446, TIB from 28,732 to 32,463 and Treasury loans support from 608,357 to 623,239. This implies a total increase of TSh 27,878 million (increase of overall total shown in Table 8-24 from 1,873,193 to 1,901,071).

with this conservative approach, it will also hold with an alternative, more restrictive definition of profit-makers.

Table 8-27: Distribution of Support FY87-96 According to Profit and Loss Categories (TSh m, 1994 prices)

	No. in Group	Overall Total		Holding redis.[a]		Bank NBC		Bank CRDB		Bank TIB		Bank THB	
		No.	*Sum*	*No.*	*Sum*	No.	Sum	No.	Sum	No.	Sum	No.	Sum
Profit-makers	84	*83*	*425,672*	*84*	*340,114*	16	19,286	1	5	5	2,627	2	253
Loss-makers	132	*128*	*1,012,018*	*128*	*1,030,002*	65	114,837	19	4,187	21	24,437	3	410
of which regular[b]	53%	*53%*	*41%*	*53%*	*41%*	52%	80%	53%	79%	71%	81%	67%	40%
Not categorised[c]	120	*109*	*463,380*	*113*	*530,954*	37	40,164	12	9,255	8	5,399	4	155
Total	336	*320*	*1,901,071*	*325*	*1,901,071*	118	174,287	32	13,446	34	32,463	9	818
I. Share loss-makers[d]	61%	*61%*	*70%*	*60%*	*75%*	80%	86%	95%	100%	81%	90%	60%	62%
II. + badly-categor.	62%	*62%*	*76%*	*61%*	*80%*	80%	86%	95%	100%	81%	90%	60%	62%
III. excl. core infra	60%	*60%*	*55%*	*59%*	*61%*	80%	85%	95%	100%	81%	90%	60%	62%

(continued)	No. in Group	TR Loans		TR Investments		TR Guarant.		Subsidies		CIS CC		CIS Subsidy	
		No.	Sum	No.	Sum	No.	Sum	No.	Sum	No.	Sum	No.	Sum
Profit-makers	84	20	20,701	21	39,615	0	0	3	12,253	23	154,061	25	156,040
Loss-makers	132	45	417,284	21	117,685	12	68,979	18	66,950	29	88,979	31	81,865
of which regular[b]	53%	62%	37%	33%	21%	67%	49%	56%	45%	38%	19%	42%	27%
Not categorised[c]	120	16	185,254	11	85,178	0	0	8	9,868	22	58,833	24	54,450
Total	336	81	623,239	53	242,478	12	68,979	29	89,071	74	301,874	80	290,356
I. Share loss-makers[d]	61%	69%	95%	50%	75%	100%	100%	86%	85%	56%	37%	55%	34%
II. + badly-categor.	62%	71%	97%	54%	82%	100%	100%	87%	85%	60%	43%	59%	41%
III. excl. core infra	60%	67%	82%	45%	57%	100%	100%	84%	81%	51%	29%	51%	27%

(continued)	No. in Group	Income Tax		Dividends		Pension PPF		TANESCO		NUWA		TTCL	
		No.	Sum	No.	Sum	No.	Sum	No.	Sum	No.	Sum	No.	Sum
Profit-makers	84	57	13,626	14	4,393	78	308	25	2,157	9	258	52	89
Loss-makers	132	56	13,167	9	200	119	788	56	12,104	10	63	67	82
of which regular[b]	53%	41%	54%	22%	48%	50%	52%	57%	83%	70%	92%	51%	53%
Not categorised[c]	120	24	13,257	8	2,373	66	222	38	942	1	7	36	24
Total	336	137	40,050	31	6,966	263	1,317	119	15,204	20	328	155	196
I. Share loss-makers[d]	61%	50%	49%	39%	4%	60%	72%	69%	85%	53%	20%	56%	48%
II. + badly-categor.	62%	51%	64%	48%	28%	61%	73%	70%	85%	53%	20%	57%	48%
III. excl. core infra	60%	48%	29%	39%	4%	59%	70%	68%	73%	53%	20%	56%	46%

a: Same as overall total, however, redistributing funds of holding companies to affiliated companies.

b: At least four out of five annual profit/loss statements indicate losses.

c: Includes the core banks (NBC; CRDB and TIB) and THA, TPDC and TIPER. For a detailed breakdown of data see Table C-9 in the Appendix.

d: Loss-making group in per cent of total profit-making and loss-making group. Specification (I) shows the default specification, i.e. the shares according to the categorised data shown in the table. Specification (II) includes all the banks and treats the five badly-categorised profit-makers as loss-makers; specification (III) excludes core infrastructure parastatals.

Source: Data as defined in Table 8-24, however not excluding data on repayments and recoveries (see Footnote 185). Further information and additional specifications are shown in Table C-9 in the Appendix.

Besides the number of benefiting parastatals and total amounts allocated to profit-making and loss-making companies, the tables present several specifications on the *share of loss-makers*. Except for specification (VII) in

Appendix C, all exclude or treat differently the core banks NBC, CRDB and TIB and the badly-categorised profit-makers THA, TPDC and TIPER.[186]

In Table 8-27, the default specification, which categorises 216 parastatals as profit-makers and loss-makers, is indicated with (I). Specification (II) additionally includes the core banks and adds NBC, CRDB, THA, TPDC and TIPER to the group of loss-makers, even though their accounts indicate on average profits. (These companies have been highly inefficient and only showed profits because of monopoly rents or wrong valuations of their assets.) With this approach more than 90% (instead of 76%) of the support data is categorised.[187]

As explained earlier, extending and improving the country's infrastructure is a top priority in any developing country. Core infrastructure parastatals therefore obtained a high share of support whether they were profit-makers or loss-makers. They may thus dominate the overall picture. In order to show whether there are different support patterns, specification (III) additionally presents the distribution between profit-makers and loss-makers of companies excluding the core infrastructure parastatals. This partial approach categorises 50% of the support data according to profit-makers and loss-makers. Ignoring core infrastructure parastatals however does not suggest that core infrastructure parastatals are better tolerated as loss-makers. The economic costs of inefficient infrastructure parastatals have been extremely high. A lot of support provided to these companies simply vanished into thin air.

Table C-9 in the Appendix additionally displays the results of some extra, and at times extreme categorisations to demonstrate the robustness of the results. In specification (IV) holding funds are evenly redistributed among the holding complex. (Table 8-27 also provides this information, but for the overall total only.) Specification (V) displays the share of loss-makers if all companies are evaluated, i.e. also companies rated as not significant (yet still excluding badly-categorised profit-makers). This increases the sample of parastatals with profit and loss information from 216 to 260. Specification (VI), in contrast, takes the opposite approach and only includes companies based on highly restrictive assumptions on the properties of their profits and losses. Only 90 companies with 31% of the support data are assigned to the profit and loss categories.[188]

Specification (VII) does not correct any of the badly-categorised profit-makers but strictly groups all parastatals according to their profit and loss statements (i.e. treating NBC, CRDB, THA, TPDC and TIPER as profit-makers). Obviously this specification grossly overstates profit-makers. Finally, specifi-

---

[186] Treating differently means adding these companies to the group of loss-makers.

[187] Note Tanzania Harbours Authority (THA), according to the data collected, was the largest recipient of parastatal support between FY87 and FY96.

[188] The specification treats annual information on profits and losses as random data and only categorises a company if the average profit or average loss from the ten-year period is significantly different from zero at the 5% confidence level. As explained in Chapter 8.1 (p. 443f), such a categorisation is too restrictive and includes important reservations. Among others profits and losses fluctuated considerably because of omitted adjustments, which implied high standard deviations. Furthermore some companies closed down early and showed few profit-loss statements because others did not exist.

cation (VIII) considers part of the earlier qualification, i.e. profits and losses are defined net of selected support items. The parastatals are grouped according to the average profits and losses that would prevail if companies had not obtained any direct subsidies and foreign exchange at underpriced official exchange rates. With this specification, 13 parastatals change from profit-makers to loss-makers and the overall share of support allocated to loss-makers becomes 90% in value terms and 67% according to the number of benefiting parastatals.

The results of the various specifications shown in the two tables are striking and corroborate the rent-seeking hypothesis. Support predominantly benefited highly inefficient and large loss-making companies. This finding does not depend on the chosen specification; the relative shares vary only slightly so that the main conclusion continues to hold. Ideally support should only benefit companies which can make profits (on average), at least in the medium or longer term. Support for a loss-making company is justified if it helps the company to reach this target and to become viable without further continued support. But in Tanzania this has not been the case. Besides the fact that the majority of beneficiaries are loss-makers, on average more than half of the loss-making recipients of support have been *regular* loss-makers (53%, 68 companies). In the period from 1984 to 1996, the group of regular loss-making beneficiaries showed 496 loss statements and only 36 for profits, which is on average less than one profit statement in 13 years.

Even though loss-making might be justified for companies that supply public goods, the resulting macro imbalances would have suggested that not making losses would have been less damaging for society, especially considering that the services were extremely poor anyway. In Tanzania, as noted in TAC (1991, p. 11f), public companies have been basically classified into two broad categories, commercial parastatals (i.e. the companies analysed here), which were established to produce and distribute goods and services at a profit, and social service and research parastatals, which were created to meet certain social goals. Yet, as argued in TAC, for commercial parastatals 'the realisation of profits was not given the emphasis it deserved' and some members in the party and government at times treated 'profits' as synonymous with 'capitalism'.

Figure 8-9 demonstrates the high proportion of loss-making companies among the recipients of parastatal support. The diagrams show the default specification (I) and specification (II). The predominance of loss-makers is most remarkable with Treasury guarantees. According to the data obtained, 100% of the guarantees were issued for loss-making companies. Obviously these companies depend on guarantees if they wanted to obtain loans and overdrafts, in particular loans from banks abroad. It is still surprising not to find any profit-makers since profit-makers can also not be creditworthy.[189] It appears that

[189] The database may have been too small (it only includes guarantees mentioned in the 1995 and 1996 statements). Of the guarantees issued prior to 1986 there are two profit-making beneficiaries. In value terms the two companies account for less than 5%—nearly all relating to a guarantee for the highly inefficient Tanzania Harbours Authority! Furthermore 14% of the non-performing NBC loans and overdrafts transferred to the Treasury in 1991 (see column 'Treasury' in Table 8-15 on page 475) are from companies rated as profit-makers. These NBC transfers most likely reflect

Treasury guarantees have primarily been an instrument to help hopelessly insolvent companies to obtain additional credits abroad and within the country.

Treasury loans and Treasury investments have also gone to profit-makers though the funds channelled to this group are relatively small.[190] However the data on Treasury investments appear to be biased. Since the Treasury compiled Treasury investment statements from audited accounts only, companies with late accounts are likely to be underrepresented. As demonstrated in Chapter 8.1, these are also the companies with higher losses. In fact, the group of companies with average arrears of more than two years represents a share of 30% in the parastatal sector, while the Treasury investment data only show a relative share of 8% (or 4% in value terms).

The banking data was expected to reveal a relatively high share of loss-makers benefiting from bank loans, since some of the bank information was compiled from statements on non-performing loans and overdrafts. Only for TIB loans was it possible to get annual information on all outstanding bank liabilities. Surprisingly, also here the share of loss-makers is considerable. (Alternatively evaluating TIB closing balances instead of the sum of total increases indicates for the years 1986 to 1996 on average a share of 86% loss-makers in terms of number of benefiting companies and 97% in terms of total amounts.) Another opportunity to evaluate a full sample, albeit not within the banking sector, was offered by Treasury loans. As shown in Figure 8-9, again a large share of the benefits was allocated to loss-makers. The Treasury and TIB data therefore clearly suggest that a high share of loss-makers reflect general patterns of support and not simply the type of information collected.

Relatively high shares of profit-makers are found with arrears on income *taxes and dividend payments*. It would, however, be misleading to conclude that the government had allocated support more efficiently. On the one hand, unlike Treasury loans and Treasury investments, the data do not show support that was agreed upon ex-ante but rather indicate arrears, which are bad per definition. On the other hand, a high share of profit-making companies can be expected as income taxes and dividends are paid on profits and not on losses. The share of loss-makers is only greater than zero since loss-making companies may still make profits in some years. It would have been much more interesting to obtain company-based information on tax exemptions of import taxes or sales taxes. However, as explained in Chapter 7, this information has not been available in a disaggregated form, partly because it was too sensitive or because it was not collected (or purposely deleted to hide the preferential treatment).

---

older Treasury guarantees. However, since the definition of profit and loss-makers is mainly based on averages from 1986 to 1996, some of the guarantees in contrast may be older, the figure has to be treated with reservations.

[190] Note the highly inefficient monopoly THA, which was the second largest recipient of Treasury loans and the largest recipient of Treasury investments has not been treated as a profit-maker in both specifications (I and II), which decisively influenced the result for the relative share of profit-makers. As shown in Appendix C, the share of support to loss-makers would decline to 72% (Treasury loans) and 49% (Treasury investments), if badly-categorised profit-makers were included in the profit-making group.

Figure 8-9: Support to Loss-Making and Highly Inefficient Parastatals FY87-96

Share of Loss-Making Beneficiaries (number of companies)

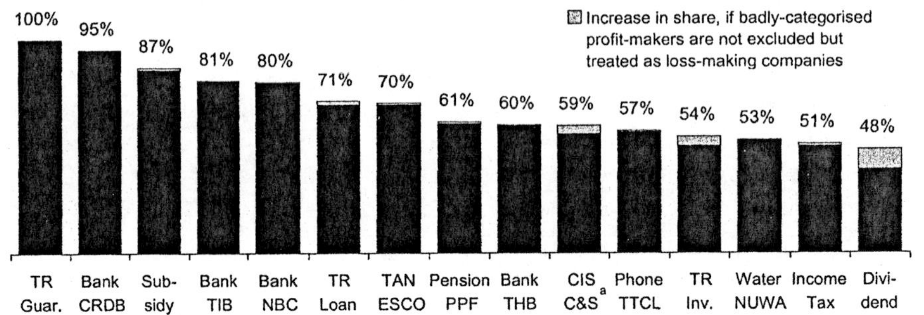

Share of Support provided to Loss-Making Beneficiaries

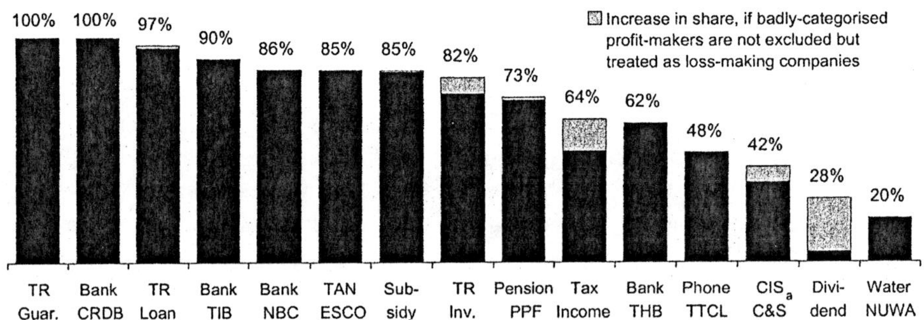

a: CIS loan component (unpaid cash cover) and CIS subsidy component (cheap foreign exchange) have been combined.

Source: Default specification and specification II (additional grey areas and % values) as defined in Table 8-27

The allocation of foreign exchange from the *Commodity Import Support programme* shows a relatively good performance, even though the non-payment of agreed cash cover is not acceptable by any means. In particular if core infrastructure companies are excluded, more than two thirds of the cheap foreign exchange was allocated to profit-making companies (specification III in Table 8-27). The result suggests an interesting conclusion. Governments of recipient countries and donors typically have different preferences regarding how funds should be spent. These differences are probably considerable in a rent-seeking economy. The outcome that CIS support, which has been closely monitored by donors, predominantly benefited profit-makers, while support from the Treasury and the domestic banking system helped loss-making companies, corroborates the assumption that aid is fungible, with the government simply helping out companies that were left out.

Aid fungibility implies that a certain share of donor support ultimately does not reach its target. The more donors focus on priority areas (in the context above on efficient companies), the less the government will do so. Seen from this perspective, aid ultimately allows the government to withdraw resources from non-rent-seeking areas. Or to put it differently, the more donors support efficient companies, the more the government concentrates on allocating funds to loss-makers. In the extreme, the net impact of aid then goes toward supporting a rent-seeking economy, i.e. additional support for loss-making companies. Therefore, unless donors closely monitor not only the use of their aid money but also the use of government funds, the efficient use of aid will remain elusive.

However, at a closer look, large amounts of donor funds have also been allocated to loss-makers, although indirectly. As noted earlier, the majority of Treasury loans are on-lent donor funds. Of the 185 loans issued after 1986, 108 are of bilateral or multilateral origin; in value terms the funds even amount to 97% of the total (the largest lenders are IDA 31%, ADF 13%, Sweden 9%, IBRD 7%, Kuwait 5% and ADB 5%). Furthermore, if profits and losses are defined net of support, the share of CIS funds allocated to loss-making beneficiaries would also increase substantially, reaching almost 90% (see specification (VIII) in Table C-9 in the Appendix). The reason is that the 13 companies which changed from the profit-maker classification to the loss-maker group are all recipients of CIS support.

Another interesting conclusion arises from comparing the data of *PPF, TANESCO, TTCL and NUWA*. Since all figures denote arrears, one would expect a large share of loss-makers. A high share of profit-makers would be interpreted as an indicator of the company's inefficiency in collecting debts. According to this interpretation TTCL and NUWA would show rather poor debtor management.[191] In fact, as noted earlier, TTCL used to store customer information according to phone numbers rather than clients, i.e. the company did not necessarily know which of the defaulting phone numbers belonged to the same client. Poor debtor management obviously encourages both loss-makers and profit-makers not to bother about unpaid bills.

The data presented so far has revealed that in a large number of cases support predominantly benefited loss-making companies. Equally remarkable are the results from the opposite perspective. For most channels of support beneficiaries show on average a considerably less favourable profit and loss position than the non-benefiting group. The differences are summarised in Figure 8-10 and are striking since the analysis includes a distorting bias in the grouping, i.e. for each type of support the remaining non-benefiting counterparts include companies that obtained support from other sources.[192]

---

[191] Clearly it is also poor debt management to continue to provide services to clients with arrears, whether or not they are loss-makers, but not collecting debt from profit-makers is even more suspicious.

[192] Since most support is allocated to loss-makers, the distortion implies that the differences are less pronounced. Alternatively one may aggregate the different types of support and focus on the total. However, since most companies received some kind of support the comparison becomes meaningless. Of the 266 companies with profit and loss information, there are 258 companies with support and only eight companies without support.

Figure 8-10: Average Loss of Support Beneficiaries FY87-96 (TSh m, 1994 prices)

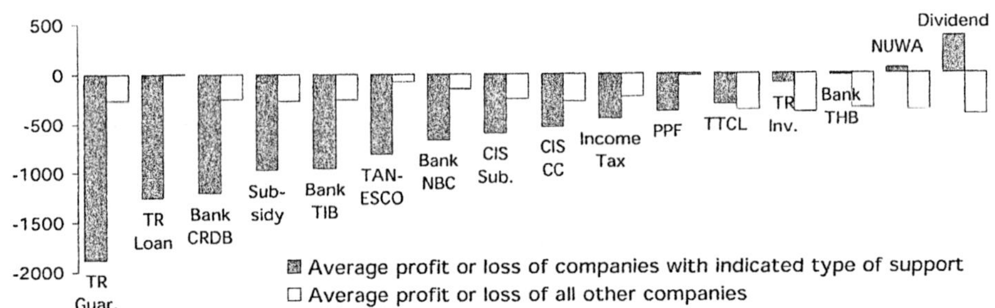

Source: Categorisation according to the support data (default specification) in Table 8-27. Results are similar with alternative specifications.

Only Treasury investments and the quantitatively irrelevant data on dividend payments, THB, TTCL and NUWA suggest a reverse pattern of support. The results are similar with other specifications (redistributing holding funds or including badly-categorised profit-makers) and also hold (except for CIS support) for the subset of data excluding core infrastructure parastatals.

Yet, the figure needs to be interpreted appropriately. THB data for instance only include eight benefiting companies, while the non-benefiting counterpart represents almost the entire parastatal economy. Averages of the grouping related with income taxes and dividends demand a special interpretation since the grouping is closely linked to the parameter under focus (profits and losses). Obviously, companies which never made profits cannot be in arrears with income taxes or dividend payments (company income taxes and dividends are paid on profits). Most regular loss-makers are therefore automatically added to the group 'no support'. With this qualification in mind, it is still surprising that the average loss of income-tax defaulters is higher than the average of the remaining parastatals. The result suggests that defaulters include companies with particularly high losses in other years. Finally, the large difference with Treasury guarantees may be surprising since the benefiting group includes only twelve companies. This reflects the situation that the companies have particularly high losses; many of the companies also received support from other sources.

The Mann-Whitney test provides an analysis independent of outliers and it offers additional insights into the characteristics of group differences. As noted earlier (p. 460), the test procedure assigns ranks to each value in the data (without regard to group membership) and compares the mean rank between the two groups. Table 8-28 displays the results of the profit and loss ranking. Even though the grouping includes the same distorting bias as Figure 8-10, with NBC, CRDB or TIB loans and overdrafts, Treasury loans, Treasury guarantees, subsidies and unpaid TANESCO bills, the average ranking of the benefiting group is still significantly lower, implying that beneficiaries have on average smaller profits and higher losses (with CIS support and THB loans the difference is not significant). All significant differences also hold with alternative specifications, such as including all companies, redistributing holding funds or excluding core infrastructure parastatals.

Table 8-28: Mann-Whitney Test on Differences in Profit/Loss Characteristics Between the Groups 'Beneficiary' and 'Non-Beneficiary' of Support FY87-96

Type of support	Bank NBC		Bank CRDB		Bank TIB		Bank THB		Treasury Loan		Treasury Inv.		Treasury Guar.		Treasury Subsidy	
Support obtained:	yes	no	yes	no	yes	no	yes	no	yes	no	yes	no	yes	no	yes	no
No. of cases in group	93	167	23	237	29	231	8	252	70	190	49	211	12	248	25	235
Mean rank	100	147	80	135	82	137	130	133	99	142	148	127	30	135	88	135
Asymp. significance	0.00		0.00		0.00		(0.94)		0.00		(0.08)		0.00		0.00	
Type of support	**CIS Cash Cover**		**CIS Subsidy**		**Income Tax**		**Dividend**		**Pension PPF**		**Power TANESCO**		**Water NUWA**		**Phone TTCL**	
Support obtained:	yes	no	yes	no	yes	no	yes	no	yes	no	yes	no	yes	no	yes	no
No. of cases in group	58	202	62	198	124	136	26	234	231	29	91	169	20	240	139	121
Mean rank	127	131	126	132	147	116	168	126	131	129	114	139	143	129	135	125
Asymp. significance	(0.71)		(0.61)		0.00		0.01		(0.91)		0.01		(0.43)		(0.27)	

Source: Categorisation according to the support data (default specification) in Table 8-27. Results are similar with alternative specifications.

This time the group of income tax defaulters reveals the expected results, i.e. in contrast to the conclusion suggested from Figure 8-10, they have on average higher profits or smaller losses. This seemingly implies that support was given more to profit-makers than to loss-makers. However, as noted above, the favourable pattern reflects the link of income taxes to profits. For instance, addressing part of the distortion by excluding companies which always made losses (they therefore cannot have income tax arrears) reduces the number of non-defaulters from 136 down to 89. The mean rank becomes 110 for the group with support and 103 for the group without support. The difference is small and no longer significant (asymptotic significance 0.47).

Finally, another aspect which corroborates the rent-seeking hypothesis is the finding that support not only benefited loss-makers—even worse, it predominantly benefited the companies with *large* losses. Figure 8-11 displays the share of large loss-makers among loss-making beneficiaries (large defined in 'per company' terms) and demonstrates that these companies are over-represented. Results are similar if holding funds are redistributed among the holding complex. However, if the companies are grouped according to large losses 'per employee' (recall definition on page 445), results are less pronounced and the values for Treasury loans, Treasury investments and income taxes drop below average. What apparently matters more is the size of overall losses in a company and less the number of employees, i.e. large losses are compensated with support, irrespective of whether the company employs many or few workers; small losses, in contrast, need less compensation. The outcome again substantiates the assumption of soft budget constraints.

Figure 8-11: Share of Large Loss-Makers Among Loss-Making Beneficiaries FY87-96

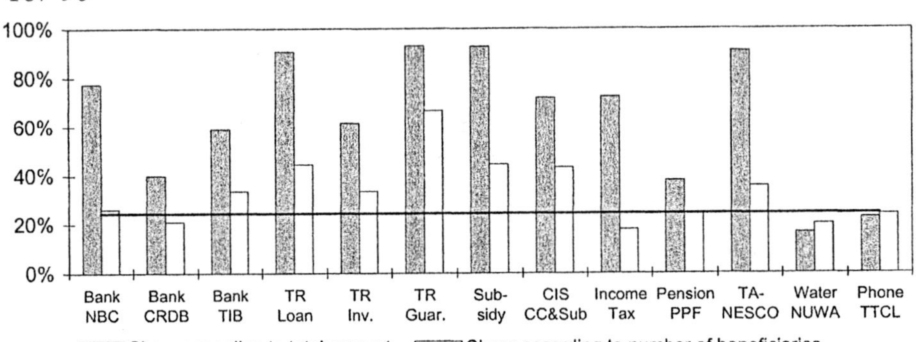

Companies whose average losses exceeded TSh 500 million p.a. (US$1 million) have been rated as 'large loss-makers'. Although only 24% of all loss-makers belong to this category, large loss-makers have been the main beneficiaries of support. The horizontal line in the diagram indicates the 24% share of large loss-makers which would prevail if all loss-makers had the same chance of obtaining support. The values for dividend arrears and THB arrears are zero.

Source: Default specification (Table 8-27); data on large loss-makers shown in Table C-9 in the Appendix

With several channels of support, there is even a significant negative correlation between the size of support and the size of profits, i.e. on average, higher support for a company is associated with higher losses (or smaller profits). The statistics are shown in Table C-10 in the Appendix. Because there are several outliers, and the grouping between beneficiaries and non-beneficiaries overlaps, it does not make sense to assume a linear correlation. Table C-10 therefore only shows the Gamma values (measure of monotonicity) and Spearman coefficients (rank correlation). For each channel of support the table includes two versions of the default specification (I) defined in Table 8-27. The first estimates the parameters for all companies where profit and loss information was available; the second version exclusively focuses on the companies that obtained support.

Depending on the version and the channels of support significant negative Gamma values range between –0.178 and –0.799 (Spearman correlation coefficients between –0.114 and –0.503). Values are always negative and significant at the 95% confidence level for NBC, CRDB and TIB loans and overdrafts, as well as Treasury loans and subsidies. With Treasury guarantees and TANESCO arrears the significance of the negative coefficient depends on the chosen version. The data linked to profits (tax arrears and dividend payments), in contrast, show a positive relation with the ranking of profits (tax arrears not always significant). Most results in the table are similar if holding funds are redistributed or if the analyses are made with a subset of companies that excludes the core infrastructure parastatals.

Finally, equally interesting is the grouping of companies according to dynamic considerations, i.e. to differentiate between the group of companies which improved their performance in the ten-year period and companies which worsened their performance. A high share of the former would indicate support to have been allocated efficiently, while a high share of deteriorating companies would suggest soft budget constraints. However, using only averages and not having information on all companies for the entire period (some companies collapsed in the late 1980s or early 1990s) implies that this analysis is at the most indicative. As explained in Chapter 8.1, profits and losses fluctuated for various reasons; there are therefore only a few companies with a significant trend in profits and losses (48 at the 95% confidence level, 110 at the 75% confidence level).[193]

Table C-11 in the Appendix summarises the results for three specifications (default specification, a specification excluding core infrastructure and a specification with redistributed holding funds) for trends significant at the 75% level ('fuzzy') and 95% level ('sharp'). One example is shown in Figure 8-12 (default specification in terms of number of beneficiaries). The results from the analyses indicate that for most channels of support the share of deteriorating companies has been considerable, which corroborates the hypothesis that rent-seeking and soft budget constraints are present. Obviously, if continued support does not improve performance resources have most likely been used in a way that reflects rent-seeking.

Figure 8-12: Support and Performance Over Time FY87-96

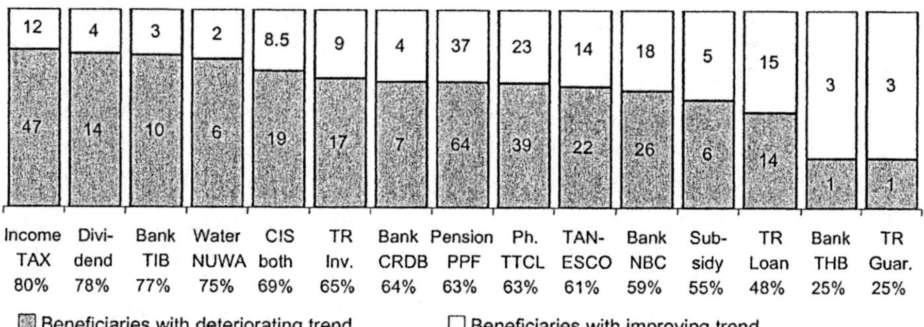

Relative distribution of beneficiaries of support with an improving or deteriorating trend of their profits and losses (trends significant at 75% confidence level, as defined in Chapter 8.1). Percentages indicate the share of companies with deteriorating trends.

Source: Categorisation according to the support data (default specification) in Table 8-27 and the definition of improving and deteriorating companies in Table 8-5. For additional specifications see Table C-11 in the Appendix.

[193] The unusually low confidence level of 75% has been applied since the major goal was not to test significant trends but to differentiate between companies which more likely improved their situation from others which more likely worsened their situation (for more information see the discussion in Chapter 8.1 on page 447).

So far not much has been said about the *relation of the quality and timeliness of accounting* introduced in Chapter 8.1 *and parastatal support.* Although the results of analyses have not been striking, a few aspects are briefly mentioned below. There are two opposing hypotheses, which makes an empirical investigation of the relation difficult.

On the one hand, it can be argued that for several types of support fairly good accounts (clean reports and on-time audits) have been a necessary condition to receive support. This view would suggest a positive correlation between the quality of accounts and support. The relation does not have to be linear or strictly monotone however. With some channels of support it may be sufficient to have fairly good accounts and further differentiation will not matter; with other types of support the chances of obtaining support may increase the better parastatal accounts are.

On the other hand, poor accounting practices can also be an indicator of embezzlement and may therefore suggest an opposite relation. To the extent that large-scale embezzlement is associated with large-scale support, one may find a negative relation between the quality of accounts and the scale of support, i.e. major beneficiaries of support may use less favourable accounting practices. Several problems explain why this relation may be weak at best.

First of all, some accounts have been qualified or were in arrears for other reasons than embezzlement. Second, in Tanzania accounting standards have also been poor for companies that obtained clean reports. A company's ability to successfully lobby for support may even correlate with an ability to influence auditors to provide clean reports. Third, the link between poor accounting practices and embezzlement may hold, but not the link between embezzlement and the identified level of support, i.e. the company may embezzle funds earned through monopoly rents or minimum price regulations not included in the support data analysed here.

The major problem however is that both hypotheses may hold to some degree and overlap, making an empirical 'verification' with the limited data available impossible. Calculating monotonic relations or rank correlations between accounting features and the various types of support in fact shows the expected diverse picture. Most coefficients are relatively small and not significant. That patterns are not uniform is also indicated in Table C-12 in the Appendix, which groups the support data (number of benefiting companies, amount of support allocated) according to the quality and timeliness of accounting of the beneficiaries. Obviously, it is highly speculative to draw conclusions from this table since the allocation of support depends on many other factors, above all, as shown in Section d) of Chapter 8.1, on profits and losses.[194]

---

[194] Some general patterns may be described as follows. In value terms, non-performing accounts of NBC, CRDB and TIB are underrepresented with the group of companies that always obtained clean reports (6%, 4%, and 20%, instead of 30%). The shares for Treasury loans, Treasury investments and guarantees, in contrast, are much higher (46%, 40% and 47%). Also direct donor support (CIS) indicates relative high amounts allocated to beneficiaries with clean reports. Clean reports may thus have been more relevant in many situations where donors were involved.

In short, accounting features are probably best used as an additional tool to evaluate data on parastatal support, although their usefulness is limited. An interesting approach is to define a group of core rent-seekers which combines the three properties of large losses, large arrears and poor accounting performance. Alternatively one could show support allocated to loss-makers plus the share of profit-makers with poor accounting practices.

The analyses presented in this section have been based on descriptive statistics and non-parametric test procedures; they did not however combine several company features. This aspect will be considered below. The main challenge was to overcome the problem of biased estimates. The support data do not appear to be normally distributed nor are the explanatory variables independent of the dependent variable (interdependence between company profits and support).

As a first approach, *ordinary least squares (OLS) regressions* have been estimated in the attempt to examine overall support with several explanatory variables. The explanatory variables comprised profits and losses, employment, location, sector affiliation and accounting characteristics. Even though in almost all specifications and combinations of explanatory variables the parameter for profits and employment had the expected sign, and the distance to the centre was frequently negatively related to the size of support, the analysis of the residual term clearly indicated that none of the preconditions for unbiased estimates (constant variance and normal distribution) was remotely satisfied.

The data therefore needed to be transformed first. Rescaling support with the companies' employment figures and taking the logarithm in fact provided a relatively good distribution of support that satisfied the requirement of a statistical normal distribution and constant variance.[195] The equation has then been specified as follows:

$$\log\left(\frac{\text{Support}}{\text{Employee}}\right)=\alpha+\beta_1\frac{\text{Profit}}{\text{Employee}}+\beta_2\log(\text{Employee})+\beta_3(\text{Location})+\beta_4(\text{Sector})$$

For profits per employee it was not possible to take the logarithm since profits can also be negative. The parameter β_2 has been introduced to test for a possible non-proportional relation between support and employment. It can be assumed that employment provided a strong argument in lobbying for support. 'Location' is a dummy variable and takes the values 1 if the company is in Dar es Salaam (or has its main representation there), and 0 otherwise. Finding a significant positive effect for Dar es Salaam corroborates the rent-seeking hypothesis that the link to the centre is important to get access to support. Finally, the variable 'sector' tests for possible level effects arising from sector affiliation. The impact

As another example, relatively high shares of funds have been allocated to companies with very late accounts in the case of CRDB (58%) and little to the group 'not very late' (6%). This contrasts with the NBC data (share of funds in the group 'not very late' 58%, 'very late' 11%). The data might suggest the conclusion that at least for large credits NBC demanded audited accounts.

[195] Both eliminate heteroscedasticity; taking the logarithm further eliminates the skewness of the distribution.

has been controlled on the first digit level (agriculture, mining, manufacturing and services).

Another problem with using the ordinary least squares regressions mentioned above was that support defines a variable which is truncated at the lower end, i.e. parastatals did not just receive more or less support, many of the companies received no support at all. For the companies with zero support there was no further information indicating whether the company was just below the benchmark of receiving support or whether it was far beyond. This property suggests that ordinary least squares regressions are not appropriate. Using a censored regression model (known as the Tobit model) solved this difficulty.[196]

The results of the estimates for two definitions of total support are displayed in Table 8-29. Total I shows the total of support as defined in Table 8-27 (total including data on all the 16 channels of support). This specification is however distorted (explained below). More appropriate is an aggregate that excludes inter-parastatal arrears, as well as unpaid income taxes and dividend liabilities. Total II represents this specification. Both version Total I and Total II are portfolio versions, i.e. the data do not exclude repayments.

Table 8-29: Estimates of a Tobit Model for Explaining Support

Dependent variable:		Total I (distorted) Log of support per employee				Total II (adjusted) Log of support per employee			
		Coeffi-cient Estimate	Stan-dard Error	Wald Chi-Square	Signi-ficance Pr	Coeffi-cient Estimate	Stan-dard Error	Wald Chi-Square	Signi-ficance Pr
Intersection	α	-1.0370	0.3450	9.03	0.003	-1.8946	0.4284	19.56	0.000
Profit per employee	β_1	-0.0387	0.0270	2.05	0.151	-0.0767	0.0315	5.94	0.015
Log employment	β_2	0.2905	0.1401	4.30	0.038	0.4357	0.1677	6.75	0.009
Location [a]	β_3	*0.2932*	*0.1521*	3.71	0.054	*0.4879*	*0.1829*	7.12	0.008
Sector [a]	β_4	.	.	11.85	0.008	.	.	15.36	0.002
		Number of Observations = 261 Censored = 45, Missing = 75 Log of Likelihood = -382.81				Number of Observations = 261 Censored = 110, Missing = 75 Log of Likelihood = -334.58			

a: Location and Sector are factors, they therefore do not have single parameter estimates. Since location only includes two values (indicating companies with and without representation in Dar es Salaam) the level effect for Dar es Salaam (as compared to companies outside Dar es Salaam) is shown in the table.

Total I: All information on support, Total II: Aggregate of banking (NBC, CRDB, TIB, THB), Treasury (loans, investments, guarantees), subsidies and Commodity Import Support (CIS cash cover and CIS subsidy component).

Source: Default specification as defined in Table 8-27

As explained in Section a), data on inter-parastatal arrears were incomplete. Since some of these data mainly show a sample from Dar es Salaam, this would

[196] The model has been first analysed in the econometrics literature by Tobin (1958).

distort the estimate of the parameter location. Furthermore most inter-parastatal arrears occurred because the company providing the service (i.e. TANESCO, PPF, NUWA and TTCL) was inefficient in its debtor management. Including these data could therefore distort the picture. Equally relevant for an unbiased estimate was the exclusion of income tax arrears and dividend payment arrears, as these two channels of support are directly related to a company making profits (a company making only losses cannot be in arrears as there are no income taxes and dividends to be paid). Total II therefore only includes bank data, Treasury support, direct subsidies and donor Commodity Import Support (CIS).

The results presented in Table 8-29 are striking. All estimates reveal the expected outcome, i.e. sector affiliation matters and support has been predominately allocated to loss-making companies and companies located in Dar es Salaam. All results are highly significant for the non-distorted specification (Total II). Especially the finding on the negative impact of profits on support is remarkable, as profits are significant even when factors of sector affiliation and location are included. The link to the centre was clearly important to get access to support. The estimates also reveal a significant and positive parameter for employment (β_2), which implies that support has been allocated over-proportionally with respect to company size (employment).

The same analysis has also been made with the subset of data 'excluding all core infrastructure parastatals.' The findings continued to hold even though the companies taken out were major beneficiaries of support; they all had a representation in Dar es Salaam, were almost all loss-makers and had very high employment levels.[197]

However, as emphasised earlier, the results have to be interpreted with caution. The data used for the estimate and the specification of the equation in the Tobit model are still open to critique. As noted earlier, the problem of interdependence between support and the explanatory variables could not be solved, as there were no useful instruments available and the model does not specify time series data. The results therefore mainly describe the relation, and not necessarily the causality which most likely runs both ways.

[197] By contrast, an interpretation of the Tobit regression for the benchmark specification 'redistributing holding funds' would include important reservations, as the modification of the data set implies a reallocation of funds to smaller subsidiaries within the same sector and away from Dar es Salaam, as well as a redistribution of funds to so far non-benefiting profit-makers. These modifications therefore directly affect the parameters to be estimated. The parameters for employment and location did indeed become negative (the latter, however, no longer significant). Furthermore, although profits still revealed the expected sign, the parameter was no longer significant at the 5% confidence level (Pr value 0.146).

c) Conclusion: Rent-Seeking Evidence and Social Costs

'All the officials who would otherwise resist the adoption of private enterprise could perhaps be compensated and put into comfortable retirement with plenty of social gain left over.'

Winiecki (1991, p. 76) quoting Steven Cheung

Chapter 8 has studied the behaviour of parastatal companies, which in addition to civil servants have been the main rent-seekers in the Tanzanian economy. It devoted considerable space to describing the difficult and time-consuming process of finding and interpreting data. As noted earlier, although it was frequently frustrating, a great deal of the chaos encountered represented an additional opportunity to further develop and corroborate the rent-seeking hypothesis.

It is characteristic of a rent-seeking economy that both real flows of resources and the identity of recipients are not obvious but are concealed. The situation makes it difficult to pin down rent-seekers and it leaves rent-seekers in the comfortable position that most unfavourable outcomes can be justified or explained by other arguments than rent-seeking, above all explanations which cannot be verified as decisive information is not available.

The approach taken in this chapter, however, represented an attempt to challenge the rent-seekers' 'argumental' advantage by exploring the maze of endless, mostly disaggregated information, and by tracing as many indications of suspected rent-seeking as possible. The difficulty of obtaining reliable information and the related uncertainties made it necessary to analyse various specifications simultaneously—an approach that paid off since the results of the numerous specifications gave a surprisingly similar picture as regards rent-seeking.

The main focus of the analysis was on *soft budget constraints*. However, these alone cannot account for all rent-seeking activities as profit-making companies can also benefit from sizeable rents. It was therefore necessary to take a broader perspective and to address several additional indicators to corroborate the rent-seeking hypothesis. Before summarising the principal findings, attention will be given to some constraints of the analyses as well as extensions that could have been made if additional and more precise information had been available.

General Limitations and Suggestions for a More Sophisticated Analysis

A large part of the evaluation focused on companies' *profits and losses*. As noted earlier, annual profits are only a rough indicator of performance; they provide no detailed differentiation of types and degrees of financial and economic distress, and the size of profits is partly dependent on the company's capital structure. Furthermore, since profits are a residual it is relatively easy to manipulate annual data, for instance by neglected or late adjustments on inventories. Moreover short-term or even medium-term fluctuations may more closely reflect changes in economic policies, as well as cyclical movements in prices or general economic activity.

Because of these constraints most analyses evaluated ten-year averages instead of annual values, and attention has been given to identifying and excluding (or treating separately) the most obvious badly-categorised 'profit-makers'. With these adjustments it can be argued that at least on average, the analyses of companies based on profit and loss characteristics were no longer distorted. Because regular loss-makers were pervasive and the scope of losses considerable, any remaining distortions are unlikely to have affected the main findings.

Ideally it would have been interesting to explain parastatal support in a longitudinal analysis with several parameters simultaneously. However the type and quality of the data available, above all the missing values and the erratic distribution of annual support allocated to parastatal companies, prevented such an approach. Certainly more appropriate information on support and company features would have allowed expanding the analysis in several ways. Two aspects should be mentioned in this regard.

First, trying to determine the *impact of support on economic performance* by evaluating annual data and not period averages was not helpful. Several approaches to defining changes in economic performance as a function of overall support were evaluated. All results however only indicated R-squares near zero. Besides the main problem of a distorted overall total, annual values included much higher fluctuations than ten-year averages. In addition, for several types of support annual values were missing.[198] Hence the only feasible approximation to document the relation between the change in parastatal performance and support was the approach documented with Figure 8-12, i.e. to rely on averages and show the allocation of support according to improving and deteriorating companies.

Second, it would have been interesting to identify and describe successful rent-seekers, i.e. companies which managed to compensate a reduction in one type of support with an increase of support from other sources. As noted in earlier chapters, *countervailing actions* characterised rent-seeking strategies in the reform process. For instance losses from adjustment of the official exchange rate and increases in the costs of loans were partly offset with additional finance from the banking system. Unfortunately, at the disaggregated company level crucial information to test this hypothesis was not available, above all information on annual values on NBC loans or FOREX allocation other than CIS. Furthermore, besides the general problem concerning the distortion of annual values, an identification of successful rent-seekers would not have been straightforward since not only the change in support matters but also the overall level.

---

[198] Attempts to split up outstanding balances which were only available for one year over several years proved not to be helpful and mainly implied introducing additional insecurities (this approach was initially pursued to reallocate NBC and CRDB balances according to the pattern of annual sector totals shown in Table 7-8).

The Five Main Arguments for Evidence of Rent-Seeking

Although the above considerations constrained the analysis to some extent, there are several conclusions which are obvious and make the rent-seeking hypothesis the most plausible explanation for the performance of parastatal companies in Tanzania. Eriksson (1993, 1994), who undertook an initial excellent analysis of parastatal support in Tanzania, emphasised the following criteria for support to become budget softening: the discretionary character of support, the negotiability of support, the adjustment of support to costs or more generally, the adjustment of support to cover losses. The discussion in this and earlier chapters demonstrated that all these criteria hold and it provided additional arguments which corroborate the broader rent-seeking hypothesis. The main findings and conclusions are summarised below.

First, already the *type of support* described in this chapter confirms the impact of rent-seeking in the allocation of resources. From the rent-seekers' perspective, it is irrelevant whether arrears on Treasury loans or defaults on CIS counterpart payments come from profit-makers or loss-makers—the mere persistence of such arrears documents the prevalence of rent-seeking activities. These arrears have indeed been substantial.

Second, the distinct *conditions for support* are one of the most obvious indications of a soft budget constraint in the parastatal sector. The argument holds for bank loans, Treasury support and Commodity Import Support. On paper, parastatal banks in Tanzania have been supposed to adhere to commercial principles, especially in to evaluating potential clients according to their creditworthiness. In reality however, as already explained in Chapter 7, bank lending did not use commercial criteria. According to personal communication with banking staff (Dar es Salaam, April 1998 and March 2000), although many of the loans were not recommended by the credit office the management nevertheless decided to grant them. In many cases the Treasury also directed banks to lend to the cooperative unions, marketing boards or other parastatals. A comprehensive study of the cooperatives' debt to NBC and CRDB even concludes that the 'departure from a number of the formal lending criteria was not only observed, but was found to be the rule rather than the exception' (cited from Eriksson (1993, p. 45)). In effect many of the parastatals were still getting loans in spite of their low repayment levels.

That formal rules were considered irrelevant is also demonstrated in the case of Treasury loans and Commodity Import Support, where parastatals continuously obtained new allocations despite previous defaults. The irrelevance of formal rules suggests that support has been negotiable. The findings are in line with conclusions from earlier studies. Eriksson (1994, p. 46), quoting from Bhanduri, Rutayisire and Skarstein (1993), for instance, notes for CIS allocations that 'some firms would pay full cash cover, other would pay some, and a large number which were given "high priority" by the GOT (almost without exception parastatals), would pay nothing'.

Finally, additional indications of a probable soft budget constraint in connection with support were found when analysing the purpose of direct Tanzanian government loans. As emphasised, these loans have been primarily issued for rescue operations, apparently to protect an inadequate management, to compensate cost overruns, and to postpone politically unpopular decisions such as necessary reduction of personnel. Unfortunately similar information on the purpose of commercial bank loans was not available. Given the large defaults and the virtual collapse of the banking system in the early 1990s, it would however not be surprising if an analysis of the purpose of bank support revealed a similar pattern.

Third, finding *a large share of loss-makers* among benefiting companies is a strong indicator of a soft budget constraint. The results are particularly striking since the grouping of companies was based on a conservative definition of profits and losses. Obviously, the share of loss-makers and the size of losses would further increase without monopoly protection and if profits and losses were defined excluding support of the profit-increasing type (preferential access to cheap loans, foreign exchange or subsidies).[199]

Besides the high share of loss-makers, the most obvious patterns that corroborate the hypothesis of a soft budget constraint are the survival of loss-makers and the conclusion that support was predominantly allocated to companies with regular and large losses or companies with a deteriorating trend. As demonstrated, although more than half of the loss-making recipients were regular loss-makers (on average they had no more than one profit statement in 13 years) virtually all of them survived into the 1990s. Finally, the pattern of allocating support to loss-making companies is further corroborated by the results of the Tobit regressions presented in Table 8-29, which also tested for the impact of company size, sector affiliation and location (lobbying).

Fourth, *anecdotal and qualitative evidence* on rent-seeking further suggests that rent-seeking is the most plausible explanation for the behaviour of parastatals and the allocation of support. Chapters 7 and 8 included many references to wasteful use of resources, large-scale embezzlement and the poor management of parastatal companies. Rent-seeking explanations for poor performance are widely accepted among Tanzanians.

For instance, a senior official believed (personal communication in Dar es Salaam, April 2000) that National Milling Corporation (one of the largest loss-makers in Tanzania and the main distributor of maize and rice) was not business-minded because it obtained subsidies on a large scale. Moreover the substantial losses of textile companies were not only a result of inefficient production; there was also a lot of cheating when purchasing raw materials. Other people remarked that the telecom department at TTCL incurred large losses because employees were known to arrange free international calls, of course, for a side payment to top up their salaries. Also the quote on parastatals cited in the introduction to Chapter 8 '...we used to call them "nobody's

[199] Specification VIII in Table C-9 in the Appendix give an idea of the potentially higher share of loss-makers.

companies"; our company collapsed because of that' perfectly describes rent-seeking attitudes and explains the considerable 'support' found to have been 'consumed' by parastatal companies. Finally, Moshi (1998) sums up the attitudes of parastatal managers as 'life is very easy'; 'don't worry about costs'; 'some one else should be accountable for the performance, not myself' and 'political patronage does matter more than business acumen as a strategy for survival'.

Last but not least, the discussion on the *large arrears and poor quality of parastatal accounts* in Chapter 8.1 added a fifth telling element to the rent-seeking picture. Understanding the way parastatals report to the government gives an idea of the seriousness of management and patterns of accountability. It would be wrong to assert that parastatals have not been accountable. The point is that they have not been accountable to the Tanzanian population but to a privileged rent-seeking elite, where parastatal efficiency, clean reports and on-time accounts did not matter.

Who to Blame: Why Donors Bear a Considerably Share of Responsibility

The indictors and evidence for rent-seeking presented in this study show that although initially ideology-driven, ruling elites and their cronies managed to capture sizeable rents from the Tanzanian economy. The soft budget constraints, above all the patterns of accountability, undoubtedly suggest that 'privatising' benefits mattered more than achieving a minimum level of public accountability and economic efficiency. Support was not reduced because of losses or arrears and defaults; on the contrary, losses and defaults explained the disbursement of additional support. Economic activity as well as reforms were guided by the logic of a market of mutual favours by rent-seekers at all ends. Apparently rents have not been an unwanted side product of the government-led development strategy but a decisive, if not the most important, component.

By ensuring that the survival of a company does not depend on economic performance, the Tanzanian government bears the greatest responsibility for the poor performance of parastatal companies. Yet there is much evidence that the government did not institutionalised the soft budget constraint on its own. An equally important stake is held by the donor community. As argued earlier, 97% of the amount of Treasury loans allocated to commercial parastatals are of on-lent donor funds. Furthermore CIS allocations, which have been regularly renewed despite the parastatals' previous defaults, are also resources from donors. The two types of parastatal support constitute a considerable share of the overall support allocated to commercial parastatals. Also Eriksson (1994, p. 80) suggests that donors have been jointly responsible for the poor reform records of parastatal companies after the initiation of the Economic Recovery Programme (ERP):

> 'Although some soft assistance from the government had been reduced, other forms grew instead and, perhaps most importantly, the amounts of budget softening import support increased substantially as the donors

poured aid into the country in support of the ERP. The donors hence came to rescue many inefficient parastatals, although this was contrary to the intention of the ERP, which aimed at making resource allocation more efficient through e.g. devaluations and liberalisation.'

Considering on-lent Treasury loans, which were also allocated to previous defaulters, further strengthens this argument. Obviously it is not only the parastatals that face a soft budget constraint but also the government itself, which benefited from generous funds from donors in spite of its poor performance.

Assessing the Trade-off: Parastatal Support Versus Social Sector Expenditures

Looking at Tanzania's social indicators and the low level of average income (recall Tables 6-1 and 6-2 on page 298f), Tanzania still figures among the poorest countries in the world. In a country like Tanzania with a large potential for improvement, any allocation of resources inevitably includes high alternative costs of not using the resources for other purposes. This is also true for the support channelled to the parastatal sector, which could have been used differently, for instance to increase the financing of social services or to put more emphasis on the development of an efficient infrastructure supportive of the private sector. The extremely high level of support allocated to parastatal companies as opposed to the moderate funds spent on health and education is shown in Figure 8-13.

According to the data available and the value-conserving approach taken when defining parastatal support, the average annual support allocated to parastatals has been almost double the average recurrent expenditures in the sectors health and education combined.[200] Furthermore, more than two thirds of parastatal support benefited highly inefficient parastatals. This rent-seeking-related allocation of funds is especially regrettable and costly considering that the social sector in Tanzania has been severely underfunded, i.e. even a moderate increase in social sector spending, if allocated efficiently, would have had a high positive impact on the country's development prospects (recall the discussion in Chapter 7.3). Clearly some of the funds allocated to parastatals also included important investments in the country's infrastructure. One could therefore argue that the figures presented are not so dramatic. Yet there are several reasons why this position is untenable.

First of all, only a small portion of the funds allocated to core infrastructure parastatals has been used efficiently. It can be assumed that the companies would have absorbed much less support to achieve the same level of output if they had been operating at least reasonably efficiently, i.e. restraining the worst cases of embezzlement and undertaking effective and regular maintenance.

[200] As noted earlier, applying a value-conserving approach to outstanding balances of unpaid parastatal liabilities (i.e. compensating real losses incurred by inflation only) provides a conservative estimate of parastatal support. To fully account for alternative costs, positive real interest rates could have been applied, e.g. using LIBOR and adding a mark-up for the risk premium.

Figure 8-13: Average Annual Support FY87-96 (TSh bn, 1994 prices)

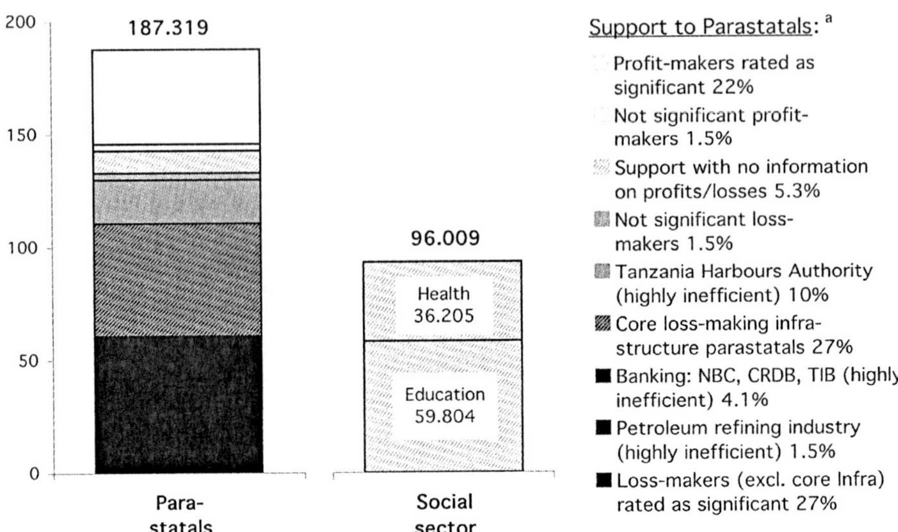

a: The categories significant profit-maker/loss-maker are defined on page 444f; the special treatment of other companies is explained on page 450f. (For additional information see comments in Table B-6 and Table C-3 in the Appendix.)

Source: Support to commercial parastatals as defined in Table 8-24; annual averages on recurrent expenditures on education and health calculated from World Bank (1997e, p. 47, 53)

Second, reallocating the support given to the group of loss-makers that excludes core infrastructure parastatals would in itself have made it possible to double expenditures on either health or education. Third, the above figures also include defaults of profit-makers, which created moral hazard and high costs for the banking system (and ultimately macroeconomic instability). Fourth, the figure even underestimates the size of support to parastatals. On the one hand, consumers also had to pay for the inefficiency of parastatals in terms of higher prices and lower quality, not quantified here. On the other hand, as noted earlier, it was not possible to identify all support; much information on bank loans, Treasury investments and Treasury guarantees, illegal tax exemptions, the allocation of foreign exchange at preferential rates other than CIS allocations, etc. was either not accessible or only available in the form of a total aggregate, without detailed information on the identity of individual recipients (parastatals, private companies, administration, individuals or the party and other organisations).

The question arises whether the distribution of resources shown in Figure 8-13 somehow reflects the preferences of Tanzania's socialist society. A fairly good indicator of these preferences is the official announcements of the Tanzanian government (e.g. Budget Speeches on page 317 and 388) and the claims of the donor community. These announcements and claims are obviously not in line with the effective outcome, which closely reflects preferences according to the distribution of power, above all the preferences of the privileged rent-seekers. If Tanzania's democracy worked better, pressure would have mounted against the low spending in health and education and against poor services (telephone, electricity, etc), and decision-makers would have been held responsible.

The reduction of the flow of government resources to parastatals was indeed a major goal of the reform process in the 1980s and 1990s. Already in the 1970s the problem was recognised by donors, and a more efficient allocation of support was demanded. The World Bank, for instance, emphasised in 1977 that 'it would be desirable to consider devices for transferring income to those parastatals which have demonstrated a capacity to generate large surpluses'; it even suggested a 'complete banning of subsidies from the Treasury for loss-making parastatals and to use greater performance indicators for investment decisions' (World Bank (1977, p. 34, 36)). What happened was the contrary. Support has been continuously increased to loss-making parastatals. Even after the launch of the Economic Recovery Programme in 1986, this pattern of support did not change.

Obviously the poor performance of parastatal companies and the far too low allocation of funds to the core priority sectors health and education cannot be justified on economic grounds, nor are they in line with the intentions of the Arusha Declaration, which laid the foundation for Tanzania's earlier socialist approach.

In an ideal economy a government may support specific companies or sectors based on the infant industry argument or the externality argument. As explained in Chapter 2, developing an industry takes time and a new industry is unlikely to compete successfully against well-established competitors abroad. Protectionism based on the infant industry argument would be reduced however, and eliminated after a few years. Furthermore support can be justified if an activity of a company exerts large uncompensated positive externalities or if support contributes to achieving the society's vision of a just income distribution. All these arguments were relevant when Tanzania's Basic Industry Strategy was designed and implemented in the mid-1970s. However, no government will ever argue that its goal is to create an unviable, inefficient economy, and no society will ever support the large-scale embezzlement of funds as found in Tanzania.

Where Are Tanzania's Millionaires, or Have Rents Vanished into Thin Air?

The lead quote on privatisation at the introduction to this section ironically suggests that rent-seekers could 'be compensated and put into comfortable retirement with plenty of social gain left over'. Matters are not different in Tanzania. In retrospect it can be assumed that there would have been plenty of 'social gain left over' if rent-seekers had been compensated in the 1980s and 1990s, but resources had been invested efficiently in the first place. The reason for this outcome is that costs do not just represent transfers to rent-seekers but a large share of the costs are the result of allocative inefficiencies, i.e. dead-weight losses (or Harberger triangles), which could have been avoided if rents had been paid directly.

As explained in Chapter 3, rent-seeking activities include two main cost components. On the one hand, there are 'pecuniary' transfers, which represent the difference between distorted factor payments and the payments valued at competitive factor prices. These transfers also include topping-up the salaries of civil servants, parastatal managers and other parastatal employees by stealing cash and assets or by extorting bribes. On the other hand, rent-seeking activities include pure waste, i.e. technical or allocative inefficiencies, which imply that fewer resources would have been needed to produce an output that guarantees the same level of utility.

Besides the relatively large number of rent-seeking beneficiaries in Tanzania, inefficiencies explain why Tanzania is not a country with plenty of millionaires. A large share of the transfers to parastatals mentioned in Figure 8-13 has not been captured by the rent-seekers in cash, but was simply dissipated by the companies' inefficiency. In fact the cash and other benefits diverted by the rent-seeking elites are most likely negligible if compared with the costs engendered by the rent-seeking allocation of resources.

Costs of allocative inefficiencies are particularly high from a dynamic perspective. As emphasised earlier, soft budget constraints undermine the most fundamental neo-classical assumption that enterprises maximise profits subject to technology and resource limits. Since the survival and expansion of the enterprise does not depend on the company's own capabilities but on external assistance from the government and donors, the companies are less responsive to changes in prices, technologies and unfavourable external conditions and may therefore become highly inefficient and wasteful. In particular the mere anticipation of support can exert a thoroughly negative impact on the companies' present and future performance.

The large number of inefficient companies among beneficiaries of support in Tanzania and the large scale of embezzlement clearly question the success of Tanzania's development strategy. The results even suggest for the ten-year period after the initiation of the Economic Recovery Programme that distributing enterprise support randomly would have brought much better results!

9 Conclusions and Policy Recommendations

'The success of formal reform proposals varies considerably depending on the prevailing informal constraints—most decisive for the success, however, is the type of the rent-seeking environment.'

Adapted from Douglass North

It is both evident and a matter of general consensus that the adoption of sound government policies is a precondition for a country's success in achieving sustainable growth and development. Though differences may exist as to what exactly constitutes appropriate policies, there is broad agreement among economists, policymakers and bilateral and multilateral donors that a number of government activities are highly relevant for a country to achieve sustainable growth and welfare. These include the development of an enabling and supportive market environment by guaranteeing secure property rights (building up effective legal and judicial institutions), conducting sound macroeconomic policies, avoiding severe price distortions and ensuring that the country has an efficient but affordable infrastructure. This is a rough description of what is known as the Washington consensus (Williamson (1990)).[201] Furthermore, a state should enable citizens to access core social services, which include primary and secondary education and healthcare, and most important, it should institutionalise checks and balances, above all accountability and transparency within government institutions in general and public service delivery in particular.

However, everyone knows that the reality looks quite different. Political markets are often inefficient and accountability is not implemented. Government officials charged with public duties and decision-making have their own priorities. Together with powerful interest groups, key stakeholders can influence policy outcomes to their own advantage, at high costs in terms of welfare to the society in developing and industrialised countries alike. The reality of inefficient political markets and powerful interest groups capable of disrupting reform policies explains why in many cases policymaking is not about achieving first-best solutions but is rather about designing solutions that are appropriate, implementable and politically sustainable.

The case study on Tanzania demonstrated how large the gap can be between economically and socially desirable policies and the actual public service delivery. Although Tanzania has been a main beneficiary of donor support and is a peaceful country (it never suffered from severe ethnical clashes or protracted civil war), its achievements since independence have been modest. As noted earlier, the World Bank even concluded in 2000 that the 'best available

---

[201] For an augmented version see Rodrik (2003).

estimates suggest that per capita income today is certainly no higher than it was four decades ago' (World Bank (2000c, p. i)). What are the reasons for this poor development? Why did the economy in Tanzania (and many others in sub-Saharan Africa) not grow like those of better-performing countries? A more provocative question: Has sub-Saharan Africa not been ready or capable of implementing well-designed policy prescriptions?

This book described the problems and failures in achieving sustainable growth and development from a rent-seeking perspective, using a broad definition of rent-seeking which includes not only rents tied to production but also any kind of socially undesirable transfers, above all the embezzlement of public funds (recall the definition in Chapter 2-1 on page 33).

Rent-seeking is a general and abstract economic concept; simply put, it describes the opportunity to earn *non-productive* income and stands in sharp contrast to profit-seeking activities. The more the rules in a society reflect the situation that income can be earned without making a productive contribution, the more will a society fail to capture gains from the division of labour and trade and the less will it achieve sustainable growth and development. From an economic point of view it is irrelevant whether this non-productive income has been obtained legally or illegally (e.g. by means of corruption)—the costs to society are similar.

Chapters 2 to 5 described and elaborated the rent-seeking phenomenon in general and in the African context. Starting with a definition and systematic overview of what constitutes rents and rent-seeking activities, Chapter 2 emphasised the crucial role of the government in creating rent-seeking opportunities. Chapter 3 focused on the neo-classical approach of rent-seeking, explaining what determines the size of rent-seeking investments and rent-seeking costs. In particular non-rivalry has been identified as an important feature of many rent-seeking settings in LDCs.

Yet to thoroughly understand rent-seeking behaviour it is necessary to go one step further and broaden the perspective. This was the main message of Chapter 4, which extended the discussion on rent-seeking beyond the narrow neo-classical approach by examining three different perspectives. The first elaborated on the individual decision-making situation. Borrowing from New Institutional Economics, the discussion addressed the role of limited rationality and transaction costs as well as the role of values, culture and traditions. The second extension focused on the rent-seeking power of interest groups, which in accordance with the theory of collective action, depends on the ability of interest groups to organise themselves and to provoke conflict. The third extension addressed the typology of states in which individuals and interest groups are embedded, discussing the role of rents for governments to maintain power and the ability of predatory rulers to appropriate rents.

Finally, Chapter 5, which was the most direct theoretical counterpart to the case study on Tanzania, put the rent-seeking perspective into the context of reform. The main conclusion is that rent-seekers (whether responsible for the initial rent-creating policy or whether created by it) are in most cases an integral part of an ailing economy. When it comes to designing and implementing adequate reforms, they resist and develop strategies to safeguard their easier but unproductive income earning opportunities. Reform measures which ignore this aspect run a great risk of failure.

Since rents and rent-seekers are not irrelevant but have a crucial stake in the reform context, it is essential to understand rent-seeking mechanisms and structures, i.e. to know details concerning the character of rents, rent-seeking actors, dependencies and rent-seeking costs. This implies examining how a specific rent-seeking situation was originally created, how it developed over time and how it changes when reform measures are implemented.

In pointing out the importance of informal constraints, Douglass North noted that the 'same formal rules and/or constitutions imposed on different societies produce different outcomes' (North (1990, p. 36)). Similarly, it can be argued that the same formal policy measures imposed to address an apparently similar reform problem (opening up highly inefficient but protected markets, balancing the state budget, achieving macro stability, removing soft budget constraints, strengthening the rule of law, etc.) can produce very different outcomes in different societies or countries. It can make a big difference whether reforms are implemented in an environment with or without deep-rooted rent-seeking forces, and the outcome can vary considerably depending on the specific character of the rents and the alternatives to the rent-seeking situation.

There is no doubt that reforms can work if they are designed in a consistent way and vigorously implemented. This is also the conclusion of the well-known study *'Assessing Aid: What Works, What Doesn't, and Why'* (World Bank (1998a)). However reforms demand commitment and the implementation of adequate reforms requires a great deal of information and is often not politically feasible. The World Bank study identified a poor policy environment and weak institutions as the reasons that a great deal of aid, above all financial support, had not produce the expected results. These factors however are largely an outcome of and precondition for rent-seeking forces. An analysis of rent-seeking can therefore significantly contribute to understanding resistance to the adoption of sound economic policies and it can support reform-minded policymakers in designing policies which are not only appropriate but also feasible and sustainable.

This chapter summarises the main policy conclusions for designing and implementing appropriate reforms derived from rent-seeking theory and the Tanzanian case study. Chapter 9.1 explains why understanding rents and rent-seeking resistance offers valuable insights for reform-minded policymakers and Chapter 9.2 specifically addresses the role of the donor community. The reader will note that several findings and conclusions are not new if taken alone, and some of the findings corroborate insights which have been adopted with reforms. Yet what is important here is understanding the constellation of aspects and conclusions presented as a whole and being able to relate these to a specific reform context.

Most relevant for reform-minded policymakers is the need to take a broader perspective beyond isolated elements of reforms. Above all this implies expanding the analysis of important relations between (official and unofficial) policy players and anticipating possible complications. The complexity of rent-seeking also explains why this chapter alone, though valuable, cannot provide all the insights to be gained by reading the Tanzanian case study in full. Even though policymakers prefer concise briefings (they aim for quick solutions) Chapters 6 to 8 give a detailed picture of the numerous and persistent rent-seeking opportunities and strategies in Tanzania. As noted earlier, Tanzania is not just an inefficient country struggling with inadequate capacities and a lack of know-how, as many policymakers and donors may see it: if rent-seeking was the benchmark, the country would be rated as highly efficient and flexible, quickly adapting to new circumstances. Chapters 6 to 8 discuss the different features and facets of rent-seeking and explain why meticulous work is often requited to pin down rent-seekers. These chapters can help make policymakers more aware of situations that are characterised and motivated by rent-seeking. These considerations should be kept in mind when reading the following findings and policy conclusions.

9.1 Understanding Rents and Rent-Seeking Resistance

a) Why Insights into the Origin and Relevance of the Rent are Important

> *'You would expect that it is frustrating for the driver if the bus had a problem and broke down. Here in Tanzania, it was the contrary. It meant more income—another opportunity to buy spare parts and artificially inflate the price. If UDA would still be running the buses in Dar es Salaam, everybody would be walking.'*
>
> *Citizen of Dar es Salaam and former parastatal employee*

The extent and success of rent-seeking resistance can be much better understood if policymakers have an idea of what exactly engenders the rent, what the costs are for rent-seekers to access it, what alternatives look like and what the magnitude and nature of rent dissipation are like. The range of costs associated with rent-seeking are known to vary considerably; in some cases rent-seeking produces mere transfers and relatively few distortions, in other cases, as in the above quote, it completely perverts incentives for productive activity and can cause major costs to society.

Removal of the same amount of rents can provoke resistance to a very different degree, depending on the specific source of the rent, the degree of dissipation and the nature and extent of non-monetary values attached to a rent-creating situation. Obviously, removing rents that are related to the creation of jobs is much more difficult to communicate than removing rents that directly relate to the embezzlement of public resources. A detailed understanding of what creates rents and what determines rent-seeking incentives is therefore essential to formulate appropriate policies, set priorities and decide on the preconditions, sequence and fine-tuning of reforms.

Rents are often the result of several overlapping policies and constraints

The size of a rent will remain unaffected or change only marginally if policymakers fail to address all relevant binding constraints. Improved reporting on incidences of corruption, for instance, may not affect the level of corruption if there is no conviction or effective punishment. Allowing private participants to enter and to operate in previously monopolised markets may not lead to private sector development if other privileges of incumbent parastatals are not removed simultaneously. What makes policy design and policy implementation challenging is that in many cases critical rent-protecting constraints are not apparent. Often policymakers put too much emphasis on or devoted too much rhetoric to addressing one type of policy measure or constraint, without assessing whether rents are eliminated. The case study on Tanzania described numerous situations where ongoing reforms did not reduce the size of rents.

An economic crisis affects the size of rents and access to rents

The size of a rent may increase or decrease with the magnitude of a crisis. As explained in Chapter 5.1, *budget-related* rents, i.e. support financed through the government budget, usually decline as a crisis worsens; *scarcity-related* and *inflation-related* rents, by contrast, may increase substantially. This happens because government revenues typically decline, while the differences between officially-fixed prices (of scarce goods, services, loans or foreign exchange) increase relative to the parallel-market and black-market prices. High rates of inflation also make access to loans and overdrafts particularly lucrative and reduce the real value of outstanding debt substantially if nominal interest rates are fixed and not adjusted correspondingly.

A crisis also affects the distribution of rents. As a crisis intensifies, powerful rent-seekers often increase the relative share of the rents they obtain (relative to the benefits or support allocated to other groups). The group of successful rent-seekers, however, becomes smaller as many of the rents, though sizeable and even increasing in size, are less available and less powerful rent-seekers drop out. Depending on the intensity of the crises and the distributional consequences, a crisis strengthens or weakens the position of specific rent-seeking groups within the society. In extreme cases an economy can be driven to total collapse before rent-seeking rulers decide on urgently needed remedial measures.

As described in Chapter 6, the Tanzanian situation from the mid-1970s to the mid-1980s comes close to a scenario where many powerful rent-seekers, who colluded with inveterate ideologues, initially benefited from the crisis and finally also began to lose. Many of the rent-seekers changed their position not because they believed that the socialist ideology failed (or because they favoured a liberal market economy), but simply because they could no longer make a living from the rents. The crisis had developed beyond a critical level. It was during this time in the mid-1980s that pro-reform groups gained sufficient momentum.

Yet between the two positions of implementing thorough reforms and doing 'nothing' there exists a broad range of intermediate alternatives, and a country typically adopts selected reforms only. In some cases the inefficiency of a certain organisation or rent-creating policy 'overshoots' and explains an early adoption of reforms. In Tanzania, for instance, the National Milling Corporation (NMC) became the only marketing board that stopped most of its activities by 1991, while effective reforms of other marketing boards were delayed much longer. As explained in Putterman (1995, p. 314f), NMC was already a major drain on the government budget in the late 1970s and early 1980s, and the company accounted for 88% of the subsidies allocated to agricultural parastatals:

> 'The grain monopoly had become a financial black hole, an operation encouraging high-cost producers to produce a climatically risky crop for a guaranteed buyer whose internal accounts were unaudited over long periods, inviting massive waste and fraud...

> In the context of Tanzania's overall economic crisis, the enormity of the NMC losses was simply too great to permit the managers of that body, who were the main beneficiaries of the monopoly, to stave off pressures for reform. By contrast, the inefficiency of export parastatals came at the expense of cash crop producers and of potential foreign exchange earnings, but the direct drain on the treasury was small compared with that associated with NMC.'

Understanding the source of rents, changes in the access to rents and the changes in the size of the rents provides valuable insights into the incentives and power of interest groups to oppose (or support) the adoption of reforms. A close monitoring of this aspect is also relevant because entrenched rent-seekers are likely to change a pro-reform orientation once their rent-seeking profits are restored, for instance by renewed but insufficiently monitored and evaluated donor support. Continuously monitoring all rents in the economy during the reform process therefore helps to anticipate which interest groups have an interest in delaying or speeding up reforms.

Insights from rent-seeking models are valuable if interpreted appropriately

The profitability of a rent-seeking situation not only depends on the size of the rents but also on the valuation and the costs for rent-seekers to capture the rent. If rent-seeking investments are relatively small, rent-seekers are more likely to oppose rent-abolishing policies. Chapter 3.2 discussed a large number of formal rent-seeking models and parameter specifications which predict the magnitude of individual rent-seeking investments and the level of *dissipation*, i.e. the relation between rent-seeking investments (or alternatively rent-seeking costs) and the rents transferred. The models include parameters which determine the objective and subjective value attributed to a rent and the costs to obtain the rent, and suggest how rent-seeking or dissipation can be reduced (see overview in Table 3-2, p. 75, and the results summarised in Table 3-4, p. 118).

Policymakers should be aware that there are many factors which ultimately determine the profitability of rent-seeking. However insights offered by a single rent-seeking model cannot be applied uncritically to a real situation since the impact of a parameter depends on the specific rent-seeking setting. What matters is to get a clear picture on which parameters are relevant and to assess how the parameters interact.

Changes in policies that increase the costs of rent-seeking, for instance, may immediately reduce rent-seeking activities in a competitive setting but may have no impact if part of the rent-seeking setting is of a non-rival nature, as it may be necessary to increase costs beyond a critical minimum level.

For instance, if public officials are threatened with higher penalties for being caught receiving bribes, their primary reaction is to compensate higher risk by demanding higher bribes for the same illegal favours.[202] As long as the

[202] In Tanzania in the road sector, the more or less standardised bribe to win a tender may increase from 2% of the project money to 4% and civil servants, who are in a position to speed up the

maximum bribe offered by the corrupt counterpart still exceeds the bribe demanded (see conditions displayed in Table 4-1, p. 153), corrupt deals continue and the number of corrupt transactions may only change marginally. Even worse, in the above example the higher bribes paid to the public officials may imply that there is less money left to carry out the project properly. Cheating during implementation is therefore likely to increase and results in a much poorer quality of the project.

It is therefore more than desirable that reform-minded policymakers on the strategic level as well as on the operative level systematically try to identify the character of a rent-seeking situation by explicitly specifying all the relevant parameters and assessing how policy changes can affect these parameters and how the change of parameters finally affects the rent-seeking outcome. Operating with different scenarios and continuously monitoring results helps in handling uncertainties.

The value attributed to a rent critically depends on alternative income earning opportunities

A specific rent-seeking situation should not be evaluated in isolation since the value attributed to a rent depends on all alternatives available. This insight has policy implications on both sides—rent-seeking and profit-seeking. On the one hand, reducing a rent-seeking opportunity does not necessarily mean a switch to profit-seeking. The importance of obtaining unproductive income from one source declines if other sources of income become available, including alternative rent-seeking opportunities. On the other hand, the value of sustaining any type of rent-seeking income is particularly high if *profit-seeking alternatives* are not available.

In most developing countries, prospects and returns for profit-seeking alternatives have been poor, above all if corruption was rampant and the country had not yet developed an enabling and supportive market environment with secure property rights, sound macroeconomic policies and a reliable basic infrastructure. Civil servants or parastatal employees who are threatened to lose their jobs or income if rent-abolishing policies are implemented will therefore resist much more forcefully. They do not see alternative employment opportunities and for many of them opening up an own 'honest' business is not an option, as adequate resources and skills are lacking.

Knowing that rent-seeking behaviour is embedded in a broader context of different income earning opportunities implies that a rent-seeking problem can be addressed on different fronts, i.e. not only by combating rent-seeking directly but to some extent also by increasing profit-seeking opportunities. Though there are often direct links between the two, some policies may predominantly address one aspect only. For instance, privatisation packages may include an agreement on the training of employees so that the new owners take over a considerable share of the original staff. And the package may include government-supported

tendering process and usually demand fixed amounts (irrespective of the value of the favour), may demand a bribe of TSh 100,000 instead of the previous TSh 50,000.

training programmes for those who lose their jobs. If this type of reform package is announced in advance, the value attributed to the original rent-protecting policy (protecting inefficient parastatals) will decline and with it resistance.

Foreign investors play a particularly important role in the creation of new job opportunities. Foreign direct investment typically increases when a country manages to eliminate cumbersome bureaucratic procedures, but also if a country can offer a fairly good transport infrastructure and reliable utility services. Improving transport and utility services may therefore contribute to address rent-seeking resistance, indirectly by improving profit-seeking opportunities. In addition to job opportunities, new foreign investors are also more likely to bring in anti-corruption ethics than incumbent corrupt companies, which have grown symbiotically with the rent-seeking system (they have their established connections and are therefore less likely to change their behaviour).

A single rent-abating measure may create unwanted rent-seeking opportunities

Insights on policy changes that are derived from basic rent-seeking models may not be appropriate if the same policy affects different rent-seeking and non-rent-seeking income earning opportunities simultaneously. This aspect can be demonstrated with the above example of improving infrastructure and utility services. Making regional and trunk roads passable or setting up a telephone network that allows using cellular mobile phones in remote areas not only contributes to create an enabling business environment and thereby attracts foreign investors. These changes may at the same time improve opportunities to smuggle goods.

A similar example is the OGL facility, which has been implemented in many developing countries to gradually liberalise imports. The facility removes rents in the domestic industry by allowing import competition for an increasing number of goods. It thereby contributes to create a profit-seeking environment, among other things, attracting investors as they can freely decide to buy inputs from domestic producers or from abroad. But in Tanzania OGL also increased rent-seeking opportunities. The weak and corrupt customs administration could not cope (or did not want to cope) with the influx of imports. As a consequence, many of the imports entered the Tanzanian economy untaxed and thereby created the opposite problem, putting part of the tax-paying domestic industry at a severe disadvantage against imported goods (see for instance Mans (1994, p. 367)).

The argumentation again demonstrates why taking a broader perspective is important. Knowing that a single reform measure can affect opportunities for rent-seeking and profit-seeking activities simultaneously and understanding interactions between the two types of income earning opportunities therefore contributes to adequately designing, sequencing and complementing reform measures.

Situations where rents have become existential demand special attention

This aspect builds on the argument of missing alternative income opportunities. Rents may have a particularly high subjective value if the rent income constitutes an important part of the income of a community or clan. The rent income of civil servants or parastatal employees may be the basis to feed large extended families. If this pattern of income allocation has grown over many years and is well established, an immediate removal of the rent might cause major social unrest.

For instance, until the mid-1990s the Ministry of Works in Arusha existed on paper only. The budget was basically used to pay salaries to the 160 people employed, feeding 3000 people behind them. Suggesting to the Tanzanian government that it should immediately close the local ministry or substantially reduce employment would not just remove the income of the public employees, but simultaneously threaten the basis of existence of a large community (personal communication in Arusha, April 1998). Similarly, a privileged community may be threatened with losing rent income from different sources simultaneously.

Unlike in industrialised countries, where the state provides some social protection, policy changes in developing countries that affect the basis of existence of a community as a whole (and not just the income of a few members within this community who could be supported by other members), need to be carefully designed. It may be necessary to complement the removal of rent income by an intermediate social safety net, preferably providing income tied to productive activities only, for instance community work (e.g. cleaning roads, marketplaces, coasts and other public places to reduce the spread of disease; or undertaking basic maintenance and repairs of public infrastructure and buildings during the rainy seasons). The scheme may not only include the people who lost their employment (or high rent income) but offer income earning opportunities to other members of the community who used to benefit indirectly from the earlier rent income indirectly.

Insights on the difference of what constitutes the size of a rent and the value attributed to a rent-seeking situation can be decisive

The value of keeping a rent-creating policy is not necessarily directly related to the size of the rent. On the one hand, direct benefits to rent-seekers can be small relative to the rent if rents are to a large degree dissipated by inefficiencies. On the other hand, keeping a rent-creating policy alive can include large non-monetary values in the form of power, prestige, reputation, responsibility or ideological perception—for the recipient of the rent *as well as* for other stakeholders. Understanding who benefits from a rent-creating policy and what exactly constitutes the benefit makes it possible to design more appropriate reform steps, above all, to identify essential preliminary and complementary measures.

The access to rents may support a hopelessly inefficient company or government organisation but only include small transfers, if any at all, in the form of higher income to managers and employees. Situations where implicit rents are substantial but where there are no, or only few, people becoming rich from the rent-creating policy are frequent. Yet often such situations provide little scope for rent-abating policy actions.

The main drawback is that inefficiencies created by the access to artificial rents do not simply disappear once support or protection has been removed. Inefficiencies may be deep-rooted and systemic; in the extreme, a parastatal has no chance to become viable and removing rents is synonymous to closing down the company or organisation. For the people affected reforms are then not a matter of trying to be more efficient and foregoing excess profits but a matter of losing the job. Even though from an economic point of view all unviable companies and organisations should be closed down and, at least in theory, there is sufficient social gain left over to compensate those who lose their jobs, this situation can be the cause of strong resistance, above all if high non-monetary values are associated with the original job position.

It is widely acknowledged that emotions and non-monetary values can influence decision-making. Reducing a salary may not affect these components but removing a job position entirely will certainly do so. Overcoming reform resistance may therefore demand compensations higher than what would be appropriate according to the lost salaries. In particular if high compensations are not an alternative for reform-minded policymakers, as they are unwanted or politically unfeasible, addressing non-monetary values associated with a rent-creating policy may become an option. As noted above, this requires understanding who benefits from a rent-creating policy and what exactly constitutes the benefit.

Making available alternative income earning opportunities may to some extent prevent or reduce the loss in prestige, reputation or responsibility of direct beneficiaries (assuming these benefits are communicated correspondingly). However, often a rent-creating situation also benefits policymakers indirectly.

In Tanzania, for a long time, it has not been opportune within the party or government to argue for the devaluation of the Shilling or the privatisation of parastatals. Taking this position would have implied losing prestige, spoiling opportunities for career advancements and even losing votes in one's own constituency. Politicians may therefore have voted for high rent transfers, not because they directly benefited from the rent (financially) but because the intellectual position offered them benefits in the form of reputation or votes. Strategically investing efforts in making the costs of a policy more transparent within the parliament and critical constituencies can reduce or even remove this type of 'ideological' opposition.

All in all, understanding which of the rents are important (for instances because they are essential to keep a company or organisation operating or because they include benefits not directly related to the size of the rent) makes it easier to assess resistance and to formulate well-targeted policies to weaken it.

Understanding mechanisms how rent-seekers externalise costs provides ideas on how to reduce the profitably of rent-seeking

Successful rent-seeking activities always include some externalisation of costs, i.e. rent-seekers benefit at the expense of other individuals. These benefits are generally considerably smaller than the costs incurred to those who lose from a rent-seeking situation, above all as rent-seeking is often a highly inefficient way of transferring income. Understanding the costs of rent-seeking helps in setting priorities in the sequence of abolishing rents; it shows where checks and balances are most urgently needed, and having an idea on the mechanisms of externalising costs helps in directly addressing the problem at its source.

As explained in this book, rent-seeking not only describes a situation of earning income without making a corresponding productive contribution; rent-seeking is also associated with additional costs as the resources invested to obtain this unproductive income are not available for other purposes and the creation of rents distorts the allocation of resources away from what maximises output and social welfare. Both components, rent-seeking *investments* as well as *inefficiencies* associated with the creation of rents, can be very high.

It is widely recognised that in many developing countries rent-seeking has led to a large misallocation of resources, in particular with public investments. Either urgent investments have been undertaken inefficiently or inappropriate investments projects ('white elephants') were selected in the first place. A bribe of a thousand dollars may be sufficient to motivate a senior civil servant to allow a highly-inefficient company to win a tender on a road project, which finally incurs social costs of several million dollars, as the road is completed very late and deteriorates quickly due to its poor quality (becoming a major cause of car damage, accidents and general delays in transportation). And the easier ability to appropriate funds with specific types of investments explains why investment projects are over-dimensioned and unnecessarily capital-intensive and why important activities, such as maintaining infrastructure or teaching at primary and secondary schools, are not allocated sufficient funds, basically because these activities offer fewer opportunities for embezzlement and appropriating bribes.

The case study on Tanzania offered many examples of how public funds have been misallocated or poorly invested. Between 1986 and 1996 commercial parastatals obtained on average TSh 187 billion annually, which corresponds to more than 8% of Tanzania's GDP (prices of November 1994). The large share of loss-making and highly inefficient companies among beneficiaries of parastatal support (Figure 8-9, p. 512) or the extremely unfavourable distribution of support between parastatal companies and social sector activities (Figure 8-13, p. 528) do not need further explanation. Furthermore, cost overruns with public projects such as road construction have been extremely high and most likely involved large-scale corruption (see, for instance, Table 7-21, p. 411, and 'erroneously' deleted pages in the Warioba report printed in Appendix A, p. 575f).

Unlike private individuals and companies, which at least have to invest *their own* resources to access a rent, civil servants and parastatal employees can often use *public funds* to appropriate a benefit for themselves. Rent-seeking then becomes a low risk and particularly profitable endeavour. This circumstance implies that the most fundamental constraint elaborated in rent-seeking theory, i.e. rent-seekers are not prepared to invest more than the rents at stake, is not given any more. Using public funds, a rent-seeker does not care if he spends a thousand dollars as long as he can personally appropriate a fraction of it.

A senior civil servant may arrange an official journey to Europe for the mere sake of appropriating the US$200 travel allowance, while incurring costs to the government of several thousand dollars as the government additionally has to pay flight expenses. Or a parastatal manager may deliberately avoid any maintenance so that the buildings and equipment need to be replaced early, allowing the manager to appropriate a share of the reconstruction funds (e.g. paid with additional Treasury allocations or direct donor support) in the form of corrupt side payments. As already outlined in the lead quote on page 535, this type of rent-seeking is based on the perverse incentive that 'bads' become 'goods' or costs become benefits, as costs offer additional opportunities to appropriate income. It explains why the extremely inefficient situation of *overdissipation* (i.e. rent-seeking expenditures and costs are larger than the rents at stake) becomes possible and is most likely frequent in the public sector.

Similar rent-seeking mechanisms hold for politicians. They can make decisions on the allocation of funds which impose extremely high costs on the country, although the politicians themselves benefit relatively little. The most prominent example in Tanzania is the Malaysian Power Deal in the mid-1990s, where the Mwinyi administration agreed to buy electricity for twenty years at a rate two and a half times more expensive as power from alternative sources, implying unnecessarily cost for the country of hundreds of million dollars (e.g. Transparency International (1998a, 1998b)).

A detailed understanding of rent-seeking processes and cost implications allows reform-minded politicians to identify critical areas and to choose appropriate measures. The worst cases of rent-seeking are situations which include high shares of externalising costs. They occur when rent-seekers do not have to gamble with own resources and where rent-seeking decisions impede or undermine urgently needed public investments. Ultimately it all boils down to implementing the rule of law and accountability. Strengthening selected institutions which allow close monitoring of high-risk situations identified by the rent-seeking analysis, and making politicians and bureaucrats involved in the decision process personally and publicly accountable, are the most promising steps.

b) The Power of Rent-Seekers

> *'We haven't yet transformed the way of political thinking. Only in rhetoric we agreed to pro-market policies.'*
>
> *Businessman, Dar es Salaam, Nov. 1996*

As explained in Chapter 5 and demonstrated with the case study on Tanzania the adoption of reforms hardly ever rests on the unanimous agreement of all affected parties. On the contrary, the political environment may have just changed slightly and tipped the balance in favour of reform support. Moreover, some reform steps are the result of pressure from donors, for instance in the form of conditionalities. Governments are then not primarily interested in the reform itself but in obtaining promised resources in exchange for reforms.

Having said this, reforms are typically carried out in a more or less intense environment of opposition. Since reforms usually intend to remove rents, direct or indirect rent-seeking resistance is likely to occur, either from the government itself or from groups which have been overruled by the government's decision. In addition, the reform process also offers additional rent-seeking opportunities which are not directly linked to reform opposition but which depend on single reform measures and which can be explained by weaknesses in the transition phase.

A realistic assessment of the *identity, power* and *strategies* of rent-seekers is therefore decisive for reform-minded policymakers and donors to formulate and implement appropriate policies. Information on the origin and characteristics of rents is valuable, as the removal of the same amount of rent may provoke resistance to a different degree. Many of the reasons have been explained in Section a). This section further elaborates on this aspect and summarises the arguments why insights into the specific power and strategies of rent-seekers are indispensable for successful reforms. Though examples and conclusions are mainly derived from the case study, the conclusions are general and applicable to other rent-seeking settings.

As explained in Chapter 6 the interest group environment in Tanzania at the onset of reforms in 1986 consisted of reform advocates with true reform-minded individuals and an increasing number of rent-seeking losers. At the other end were inveterate ideologues who colluded with remaining, still benefiting rent-seeking groups. Both had a strong incentive to undermine the reform process. Even rent-seeking losers who opted for reforms constituted a critical interest group since many of them were most likely prepared to change their pro-reform orientation if rent-seeking profits were somehow restored. The mere circumstance that reforms were initiated by the ruling party itself had to be rated as risky. Obviously not giving away the agenda allowed keeping control over reform steps in a way that could ultimately ensure the continued flow of already established rent distribution to privileged party members and associated cronies.

The rent-seeking analysis of the case study on Tanzania rested on a comparison of actual and desirable policies, whenever possible including a reference to the stated objectives of the Tanzanian government as well as a detailed assessment of the effective outcome (the general framework is summarised in Table 7-1 on page 316). Although some of the announcements of the Tanzanian government (as well as praise and criticism of donors) were of a strategic nature and may therefore not always have to be taken too literally, the case study demonstrated that the deviations between actual and intended reforms have been enormous. The main findings and conclusions can be summarised as follows:

Rent-seeking strategies are numerous and diverse and they can be complex

The case study confirmed many of the rent-seeking strategies outlined in Chapter 5.2. The macro imbalances in the 1980s and 1990s are almost entirely attributable to rent-seeking behaviour, and the insight that at least capacity-relieving measures can be implemented quickly did not hold for the Tanzanian case. Looking at what was implemented up to the mid-1990s gives the impression that there was, if anything, *a rent-seeking logic of reform sequencing*, which allowed rent-related income to be protected as long as possible. Constraint-relieving and relatively less capacity-intensive reforms, such as trade or price liberalisation, exchange rate devaluation, the closing of non-viable public enterprises or tax and tariff rationalisations had been delayed for years. In addition, many important institutional reforms, such as strengthening the rule of law, privatisation or the restructuring of financial institutions, were addressed far too late and therefore continued to be a major burden for the Tanzanian society.

As outlined in Tables 5-2, 5-3 and 5-7 (p. 266, 268 and 283f), rent-seeking resistance manifests itself on different levels, i.e. policy formulation, policy implementation and policy outcome, and it takes direct and indirect forms. Obvious direct resistance, which already occurred on the level of policy formulation, included in Tanzania the liberalisation of export crops and markets within which public utilities operate, the abolition of marketing boards, the restructuring and privatisation of the largest commercial bank (NBC), as well as any reforms of public enterprises prior to the creation of the privatising organisations PSRC and LART. Delayed reforms all referred to areas where the loss of substantial rents had been at stake. Indirect resistance was found in situations where only partial reforms or initial steps of a reform had been implemented because these measures did not yet affect the rents in critical areas. This resistance affected all areas, above all the problem of raising tax revenues, civil service reforms (reduction in staffing, adhering to budget priorities, condemning and preventing embezzlement of public funds) and creating a business-friendly environment (recall, for instance, the flowchart in Figure 7-8, p. 392). In many cases indirect resistance also took the form of effective countermeasures against implemented reforms.

Understanding where rent-seekers agree and where they severely oppose directly points to the relevant rent-creating constraints

This aspect takes up the earlier conclusion that rents are often a result of several overlapping policies and constraints. To sustain a high level of donor support rent-seekers usually demonstrate an interest in reforms. However, a closer look reveals that only those measures are successfully implemented that do not threaten the rents of powerful interest groups. The case study on Tanzania offers many examples where rent-seekers continued to benefit from sizeable rents despite ongoing reforms.

Prior to the mid-1990s beneficiaries of bank loans, for instance, did not have to worry about increases in real interest rates seeing that creditworthiness was not evaluated anyway and default remained an option. For the same reason the increase in interest rates did not reduce the demand for credits. The reorganisation and reforming of the Prevention of Corruption Bureau (PCB) was never directly opposed, as it did not really increase the risk of corrupt transactions, but rather helped to demonstrate donors that the country was doing something. (As explained in Chapter 7.3 though Tanzania has been rated as one of the most corrupt countries in the world, the activity of PCB finally led to fewer than 2.5 convictions a year.) Furthermore, some of the trade liberalisation in the 1990s did not provoke opposition as other relevant discriminatory regulations against private sector participation remained intact or could be easily implemented.

A particularly efficient way of sustaining rents is the strategy of implementing *initial reform steps* only. In the 1980s and 1990s Tanzania developed a pronounced attitude of writing reports, commissioning donor-financed studies, undertaking meetings and workshops, but with no follow-up. Similarly, institutions that were supposed to establish accountability did not threaten rent-seeking income. The continuous reiteration of the same complaints in the annual reports of the Controller and Auditor General (recall for instance the case of customs record keeping summarised in Table 7-24, p. 414f) makes the absence of effective follow-up actions evident. As explained in Chapter 7.3 the irrelevance of the comments of the OCAG reports clearly showed the government's attitude in predominantly addressing *non-binding* constraints, i.e. measures which do not affect the size and distribution of rents. From the rent-seekers' perspective the OCAG was not a threat as there was virtually no action taken to rectify the problems.

Anticipate rent-seekers' countervailing actions to reforms

If an unwanted reform cannot be prevented, rent-seekers often maintain their unproductive income by *countervailing actions*, partly also by taking advantage of intermediate weaknesses.

Devaluation, for instance, which should have removed rents associated with foreign exchange allocations, initially did not translate into efficiency-improving economic signals, as many importers, above all parastatal companies, either did not reimburse the Tanzanian Shillings or they paid by drawing on bank credits which they later defaulted on. On the export front devaluation was not accompanied by liberalising agricultural marketing. This implied that there was little positive impact for farmers left, as intermediaries (inefficient monopolised marketing boards) reaped most of the benefits from devaluation.

Most consequential has been the countervailing action of increasing bank lending to compensate both reform-induced losses in revenue and increases in costs (losses in revenue resulting from the removal of direct subsidies or the introduction of private sector competition; increases in costs due to higher prices of foreign exchange, public services or capital in general). As demonstrated in Chapter 8, parastatal companies and cooperatives obtained considerable support throughout the 1980s and early 1990s, despite the announcements of the government to apply a hard budget constraint. Aggregated support between 1986 and 1996 was even much larger than government spending in the high priority sectors health and education combined, and support predominantly benefited highly inefficient and loss-making companies. The failure to implement a hard budget constraint was not only costly in terms of revenue foregone for other purposes, persisting soft budget constraints also undermined for almost a decade the goal of introducing more realistic efficiency-enhancing price signals and ultimately strong and sustained economic growth.

Anticipate rent-seekers' reaction to reform announcements and possible intermediate weaknesses in the transition phase

Several measures in Tanzania did not function properly as they were implemented in a strong rent-seeking environment that had not been sufficiently taken into consideration. The non-payment of counterpart funds in the Commodity Import Support programme (CIS), similar problems related to the Open General Licence facility (OGL), initial failures to establish the Tanzanian Road Fund, the fiasco of the Investment Promotion Centre (IPC), as well as large-scale asset-stripping of parastatals (directly stealing cash, materials, goods and equipment or undertaking corrupt transactions with 'friends', i.e. selling goods too cheaply and buying inputs too expensively) demonstrate the numerous and divese rent-seeking opportunities mostly associated with the transition phase.

As explained in Chapter 7.3, because of the lack of funds to finance maintenance of roads in Tanzania, in 1991 the government established a Road Fund financed by a fuel levy. Yet in the mid-1990s the country was undertaking little more than 10% of the required maintenance. The unfavourable outcome reflected a combination of legal and illegal rent-seeking activities, a poor process of allocating Road Fund resources and pressures from other areas due to the cash-budget system adopted in the mid-1990s.

Another example to demonstrate what happens if a new policy is introduced in a rent-seeking environment is the IPC scandal. In Tanzania the Investment Promotion Centre did not function to reach its stated objectives. On the contrary, IPC was quickly transformed into a major rent-seeking instrument. The problem finally cumulated in the severe tax crisis in 1993/94. Instead of doing away with complex procedures and providing a 'one-stop' investment centre, the government had established a corruption-prone 'one-stop more' body.

Sometimes, already the *announcements* of a reform or specific actions may increase rent-seeking behaviour. This problem has been widely noticed with parastatal reforms (privatisation, closure). Most critical is financial asset-stripping in the banking sector, which may immediately follow the announcement of a planned removal of the management and within a few hours cause costs of several million dollars. Though this is an extreme case, a more systematic anticipation of any negative rent-seeking reactions to reform measures or reactions to the announcements of reforms has to be an integral component in the design of reform programmes and operative reform steps.

Understanding rent-seekers' concealment strategies

Rent-seeking strategies are closely connected with a lack of transparency. This aspect has been extensively elaborated in Chapter 8. Since a rent-seeking distribution of resources is unlikely to reflect the preferences of a vast majority within a country, as well as the intentions of donors, rent-seeking activities and related transfers are typically concealed. Concealment strategies occur on different levels.

Information is often severely distorted at the *primary data level* (e.g. data on parastatal accounts and parastatal support or data on civil service activities). Rent-seeking at this level becomes observable through the non-production and distortion of accounting information and manifests itself in the widely admitted 'major problems' in record keeping and reconciling data, as was for instance the case with parastatal data on Treasury investments or bank support. Problems at this level usually do not just reflect constraints in resources and capacity but are a crucial element of the rent-seeking strategies.

The need to hide real flows also explains why rent-seekers may have no incentives to change a situation where several positive and negative interventions overlap, as this situation helps to reduce the degree of transparency. Soft budget constraints, for instance, are usually not explicitly planned and they may not be directly visible, but they finally 'materialise'. In particular the insecurity on the net impact of government interference in the parastatal sector puts the companies in a strong position to lobby for compensation that exceeds the original government interference. In addition, being already a loss-maker (and facing soft budget constraints) reduces scruples to embezzle and misappropriate funds. This line of reasoning may for instance explain the lack of resistance of cooperative unions against the price-setting procedure of the government. When the cost-plus pricing system was abolished, the government still interfered in fixing farm-gate prices—a policy, which in the 1991/92 season resulted in major losses to cooperative unions (and simultaneous large-scale embezzlement).

To the extent that rent-seeking decision-making is well entrenched in the public sector, running up to the highest government level, reform-minded policymakers and donors should be careful in selecting and interpreting *statistical data*. The collection and production of statistical information is most likely distorted, too. Besides the manipulation of data, there are typically too little resources devoted from the government budget to produce useful statistics—not because the funds are not available but because there is no interest of policymakers in accurate data.

Counteracting rent-seeking strategies requires a broad focus

As rents often depend on several overlapping polices and rent-seekers can adjust their strategies to new conditions and take countervailing actions, efficient policymaking depends on taking a broad focus. Often only a combination of several measures can finally eliminate a rent-seeking situation. Reform-minded policymakers and donors should therefore draw their attention away from single measures and focus more directly on the *entire policy mix* and relevant *output and outcome indicators*. Although there are usually several necessary conditions to be accomplished, effective progress which translates into higher welfare finally depends on sealing the ring, i.e. closing all loopholes and removing all binding rent-creating constraints. This is the final benchmark against which to evaluate the government's performance.

Taking a broad focus also necessitates applying a *broad definition* of rents and rent-seeking. The general phenomenon that corruption increased during reforms is to some extent attributable to a mere substitution of rent income from legal sources to illegal sources. For instance, in the case of Commodity Import Support, the access to rents changed the form from obtaining official underpriced foreign exchange (legally) to not paying counterpart funds (illegally). Focusing on corrupt transactions alone would have missed the former aspect and the interrelation between the two types of rent income.

Taking a broad focus obviously requires *anticipating* potential complications and countervailing actions and *monitoring* a rent-seeking situation as other reform measures are successively implemented. Reforms are an ongoing task, above all as new rent-seeking interest are likely to emerge and countervailing actions can always dislodge earlier success.

The distribution of rents is in most cases an image of the structure and relations of power in the country

Successful rent-seekers usually have one thing in common: they are powerful. They may enjoy favourable conditions to organise themselves and provoke conflict, they may belong to the ruling elites or they may be well embedded in patronage relations. Whether rent-abating policies have a real chance of implementation and whether the reforms can have the expected impact critically depends on a realistic assessment of the power of rent-seekers and the structures that explain power. Though the situation varies from country to country, the case study on Tanzania clearly demonstrates how important this information is.

Shortly after independence Julius Nyerere had transformed the Tanzanian Republic into a one-party system and eliminated and co-opted all forms of competition. Trade unions, cooperatives, NGOs and parastatal companies had been fully integrated into the one-party structure. Nyerere's original vision to develop an egalitarian and self-reliant society that enjoyed a steady increase in welfare, however, relied too heavily on the assumption of benevolent politicians and bureaucrats. This assumption proved to be wrong. Instead of creating an efficient public sector charged with carrying out the crucial functions of a state and implementing the development policy, the bureaucracy and parastatal sector degenerated to a complex administrative rent-seeking apparatus.

The system basically worked on loyalties and patronage relations—CCM (the party) being the *parent*, using parastatals, cooperatives, military and the bureaucracy as its *instruments*. This was also the situation at the onset of reforms in 1986, when the Economic Recovery Programme was initiated. The main rent-seeking problem was therefore closely related to the patronage relations that had evolved over two decades and were held together by the party leadership.

Until the early 1990s secretary generals of cooperatives and trade unions, the chairman and managing director of NBC, as well as senior members of the army or the SCOPO (Standing Committee on Parastatal Organisations) were all part of the party's *National Executive Committee (NEC)*. NEC was the centre of political decision-making in Tanzania and usually debated behind closed doors (the cabinet only carried out the decisions, while the parliament basically had an acclamatory function).

Cooperatives, which were dissolved in the 1970s and re-established after 1982 from 'above', were no longer accountable to their members but to the party, especially as the leaders had been appointed by the ruling elites before cooperatives recruited their members. In effect, cooperatives functioned like branches of the party. On the one hand, they constituted the main campaigning institutions to win parliamentary elections; on the other hand, they formed an important patronage instrument. Since agriculture was the backbone of the economy, the leaders of cooperatives could easily argue for considerable support. Obviously, this constellation explains strong resistance against any attempts to reorganise cooperatives within the marketing system (farmers–cooperatives–marketing boards) in a way that results in a loss of power or rents for the party.

Political employment has been equally rampant in the remaining *parastatal sector* and it became most apparent, as extensively discussed in Chapter 8, with the poor management and high losses of parastatal companies. Parastatals also had political commissioners, who observed the implementation of the party's policy. Furthermore, there were close relations between the different patronage instruments and 'important' people shifted from one place to the other.

People in high ranks in the army, for instance, were members of parliament, they were in the central committee or held posts as regional or district commissioners. When parastatal mangers retired or lost their jobs, as the company closed down or was privatised, they often came back to CCM. The rent-seeking network is also apparent when looking at cases of corruption. For instance, when cooperatives were accused for large-scale embezzlement, members of parliament were involved. Causes of corruption also referred to people who held several senior posts in the army, the government administration and parastatals.[203]

Knowing the importance of cooperatives or bearing in mind that many of the senior posts in the banking system had still been occupied by people with close relations to the party elites, explains why cooperatives put up the strongest resistance to the liberalisation process and why bank lending to uncreditworthy parastatals, cooperatives or members of the party continued long after formal reforms had been adopted. Instead of trying to reduce economic support, it might have been easier to first replace managers in the banking sector and reorganise the structure of cooperatives to make them accountable to their members. Being aware of critical relations equally helps to assess the consequences of changes in the reform transition. For instance, the success of reforms may be negatively affected the more parastatal managers return to the parliament and take up senior posts in the bureaucracy. Understanding rent-seeking structures and shifts therefore provides crucial insights to anticipate possible complications and to design and sequence specific reform measures. Some aspects will be taken up below.

Understanding what explains the political power and importance of rents and how reforms affect this importance

Chapter 4.3 explained in detail the distinct role rents may hold in different typologies of states. Critical aspects that have to be addressed when designing reforms include the following questions: Are there rents which are indispensable for a government to hold power? Are there economic constraints or dependencies which explain why rents cannot be removed? Which of the rents mainly function to help consolidate the government's position? How does political liberalisation (introducing multi-party systems and free elections) affect the role of rents?

In the case of Zanzibar, which had its own government, rents played an important *role in maintaining power*, in particular when political liberalisation started in the early 1990s and CCM was struggling to retain a majority. Removing rents implicit in excessively low electricity prices, for instance, would have reduced the chances of staying in power. The delicate power constellation probably also explains why Zanzibar so severely resisted removing the 'Zanzibar route'—one of the main channels for tax evasion. The introduction of the multi-party system and free elections obviously increased the dependency on distributing rents.[204]

---

[203] For instance, General Muhidin Kimario was a member of parliament in Moshi, defence minister in 1983 and interior minister between 1985 and 1990. In March 1990 he was removed from government as a result of an anti-corruption campaign. He then became regional commissioner for the Dar es Salaam and Kilimanjaro district and was appointed as director general of the CDA (Capital Development Authority). In 1996 he was suspended again for several charges of corruption committed between 1993 and 1996. (The Indian Ocean Newsletter, No. 719, 18 May 1996)

[204] According to personal communication at the Department of Politics (University Dar es Salaam, April 2000), in the 1990s 90% of the people in Zanzibar voted strictly according to party lines

Other examples of politically important rents are extra benefits to parliamentarians (e.g. bank credits to buy cars) or the maintenance of a different salary structure in the army (salaries were much higher than in the remaining civil service); in addition, the army benefited from new uniforms and 750 new Land Rovers at a time when Tanzania was severely budget-constrained and could not even employ all the teachers who applied for work. Even Road Fund collections were misused to pay meal allowances for members of the army. Interestingly, in some cases pressures for support did not so much come from the parliamentarians and the military themselves, but it was the government who apparently tried to buy them off.

Rents can also take an important role if deep-rooted *economic dependencies* have been created. Several of the monopolised companies in Tanzania, above all utility parastatals, have been in a powerful position since the government depended on their functioning and could not risk their collapse by reducing support. This aspect is also emphasised in Eriksson (1994, p. 41), who mentions for instance the government's dependence on Tanzania Fertilizer Company, the sole distributor of fertiliser in the country (TFC was highly inefficient and only survived because of continued high support). Mutual dependencies are therefore not just characteristic of patronage-related rent-seeking systems; they are also reinforced by inappropriate economic policies.

Frequently, the supply of strategic rents takes *indirect forms*. The Mwinyi administration was certainly aware of the major problems which caused the main slippages in the 1980s and 1990s, i.e. the non-payment of CIS counterpart funds, corruption in the OGL facility, the abuse of the Investment Promotion Centre for tax evasion or the continued accumulation of non-performing loans in the banking sector after the Banking Act in 1991. The government obviously tolerated these slippages. (Most people would in fact argue that the government was directly involved.) Seen from this perspective, the rents simply constituted a calculated measure of the ruling elites to nourish and maintain their patronage-based system.

Being aware of hybrid systems and self-sustaining rent-seeking structures

The Tanzanian case study demonstrates that a rent-seeking system with entrenched patronage relations changes only slowly. The poor performance points to Douglass North's emphasis on *'path dependency'*, i.e. once a country has taken a specific track of development, it is difficult to divert it from this path. Even when new formal rules are nominally implemented, informal rules (old habits, traditional relations, etc.) can continue to be relevant for a long time.

This overlap of new rules with traditional loyalties characterised the situation in Tanzania during the entire reform process in the 1980s and 1990s (recall the lead quote at the beginning of this section on page 544). Civil servants and parastatal employees faced the conflicting objectives of adopting

(45% always voted CCM, 45% always voted for the opposition party CUF). Only the remaining 10% changed their position. The ruling party was therefore not prepared to do anything that made it lose votes. (In fact, in 1995 CCM only remained in office by election fraud.)

new rules or following traditional party loyalties. Most reforms in Tanzania therefore initially created *hybrid systems*. Even in the early 1990s the party still opposed fundamental reforms suggested by reform technocrats. Since many of the senior civil servants, parastatal managers, leaders of cooperatives and parliamentarians were loyal to the party and the old system, it could be anticipated that nominal reforms would not have the expected results.

The main problem with established hybrid systems is that they may affect policy outcomes along all *hierarchical lines*. Furthermore entrenched corrupt systems are often *self-sustaining*, i.e. being honest and following new rules is not necessarily rewarded. The simple example of discouraging traffic policemen from accepting bribes may demonstrate this problem. Obviously, traffic policemen have no incentives (other than benefiting their colleagues) to insist on a traffic fine or to send offenders to the police station, knowing that at the station offenders will be offered the opportunity to bribe their way out.

The removal of hybrid systems demands encompassing reforms and a commitment from the top leadership that results in sufficiently high pressure down the hierarchical lines. The reality, however, is that powerful rent-seekers usually remain in strategic positions. There are several measures (explained below) which can help to address the problem indirectly. These include strengthening the political opposition, elaborating second-best solutions and finding ways to strategically sequence reform steps.

Strengthening the anti-rent-seeking coalition

As widely argued, a way to break opposition to reform is to develop strategies that mobilise rent-seeking losers and strengthen the anti-rent-seeking coalition (reform-minded policymakers, donors and the civil society in general). This strategy is particularly important in deadlock situations, as described above, where rent-seekers remain in strategic positions and reforms mainly create a hybrid system.

Suggestions to *empower rent-seeking losers* (i.e. those who lose because others were rent-seekers) involve directly strengthening specific economic interest groups, including consumers' organisations and the poor, for instance by organising seminars between affected groups (citizens' participation) or by directly strengthening the capacity of these organisations. Suggestions furthermore include the *strengthening of the civil society* in general by independent media, the adoption of multi-party systems and free elections and the strengthening of the role of the parliament and parliamentary committees, the judiciary or specific controlling institutions such as the Controller and Auditor General. Suggestions may also include specific measures such as creating or supporting watchdog institutions (e.g. Transparency International), installing telephone hotlines or appointing ombudspeople.

A particularly relevant precondition and key to success is increasing basic knowledge on the costs of rent-seeking, not only for technocrats but also for the civil society in general. However, as emphasised in Chapter 4, rent-seeking is a concept of economic theory and a specific way of looking at the behaviour of a society. It cannot simply be assumed that people in strategic positions will analyse problems in the same way. One of the most important goals is therefore to *raise public awareness* and make the costs of rent-seeking as *transparent* as possible.

If people know how economics works and what the trade-offs of adopting certain policies are, their decision-making may be less guided by populist propaganda or short-term personal benefits. Though it is widely acknowledged that people have to understand reforms, much more emphasis should be placed on this aspect. For instance, if political liberalisation in Zanzibar had been accompanied by a broad-based strategy to communicate and explain urgently needed reforms, the link of maintaining power and distributing rents could have been significantly weakened.

As often argued, a promising strategy to strengthen the civil society is to bring politics closer to the population by desentralisation (restructuring and strengthening local government). Communicating responsibilities and making local civil servants and politicians personally accountable for benefits and failures (e.g. by publishing lists of good performers and failures in the local media—a task, which could be accomplished by a local watchdog organisation) adds significant non-monetary value to adopting sound policies and delivering high-quality public services.

Frequently there is no first-best solution available

Though specific watchdog institutions can be set up relatively quickly (technically), experience shows that many take a long time to become effective and rent-seeking remains a major impediment. This problem requires taking a *longer-term perspective* and *balancing different goals*. In some cases it is appropriate to take high intermediate costs into account when trying to limit rent-seekers. In other cases, a distribution of rents will have to be tolerated and policies focus on reducing the costs.

The cash budget system applied in Tanzania in the 1990s is an example of the former aspect. It constituted a radical measure to discipline the government to balance revenues and expenditures on a monthly basis and thereby restrained rent-seeking pressures. Yet, the system also included high costs. Besides the general problem of imposing short-term planning horizons on budget managers, powerful rent-seekers can still capture sizeable shares of the remaining funds. In Tanzania, due to a lack of finances, donor funds were not disbursed as they were tied to a minimum share of government contributions, and Road Fund collections were misused for debt service payments. Furthermore, as noted earlier, Road Fund collections were used to pay food allowances and the government could not employ all the teachers who applied for work.

What makes the cash budget system beneficial are, among other things, dynamic considerations. Benefits are highest if the negative consequences of a cash budget system are openly communicated and directly linked to the rent-seeking problem of not allocating scarce resources to core priority sectors. An open debate on the costs accelerates a rethinking and thereby contributes to a strengthening of anti-rent-seeking forces and institutions. Furthermore, since rents are less available for rent-seekers (in absolute terms), the cash-budget system can remove rent-seeking structures, for instance by 'breaking the neck' of highly inefficient parastatals, which so far resisted privatisation but are currently not receiving any more support.

In other situations, reform-minded policymakers and donors will have to accept that a certain removal of rent-seeking income is not feasible for the time being. The distribution of extra benefits to the army and parliamentarians may be unavoidable, given the country-specific interest group constellation. The same may hold for the abolition of costly rent-creating regulations, which may not be possible unless losers are generously compensated. Or it can be argued that a zero corruption outcome is not realistic, at least not in the short term, but overreacting and not undertaking any projects would be even worse. (People who are suffering are not guilty and it would not make sense to subordinate the objectives to the rules.)

Obviously, this line of reasoning is delicate as it can be misused to justify any legal or illegal rent transfers. It only holds in the overall context of balancing realistic measures and strategies and assessing all inter-temporal trade-offs, for instance, the short-term and medium-term costs of withdrawing all support and closing down all projects, with the expected long-term benefit of enabling a change in the political equilibrium against rent-seeking forces.

If the distribution of rents *cannot be prevented*, policymakers may try to reduce the costs associated with the rent transfers and/or make the support transparent. In the case of rent-creating regulations, the most obvious suggestion from economic theory is transforming any policy-induced rents (price distortions and protectionism) into direct transfers. For instance, to be able to close an inefficient parastatal it may be necessary to promise managers and staff a 'golden handshake'. Though not optimal, this is justified if compensation is the only feasible strategy to stop the parastatal from operating. Or if it is not possible to have public projects without corrupt side payments, more emphasis can be put on quality controls in project implementation, so that at least minimum quality standards are achieved.

Strategic sequencing may surmount apparently insurmountable opposition

This aspect summarises earlier suggestions and considerations and builds on the argument of second-best strategies, i.e. situations where swift and comprehensive reforms are not attainable. A rent-seeking situation is typically characterised by two main aspects: the *political and institutional structure*, which explains the power of rent-seekers, and the *size of the rent*, which codetermines the value of a rent-seeking situation. If a rent-seeking situation cannot be removed directly, a strategic sequencing of reform steps entails initially focusing on limited aspects only, i.e. taking advantage of the problem of addressing non-binding constraints in a strategic way. Initial measures will, as argued below, not remove rents but open the way for future effective rent-abolishing policies.

Strategically sequencing reforms demands a detailed understanding of the rent-seeking situation and an assessment of where it would be easiest to implement reforms (for instance, removing rent-supporting structures or removing rent-creating constraints and policies). The strategy may require taking many small steps (measures which do not provoke immediate opposition) and deciding which steps are a precondition for the successful implementation of subsequent measures.

As demonstrated by corrupt transactions of bureaucrats or soft budget constraints of parastatal companies, rent-creating situations often depend on several policies and constraints, and the rent can only be successfully removed if these aspects are addressed simultaneously. If reforms to remove a rent are made sequentially, resistance tends to be strongest when addressing the last binding constraint. Strategically sequencing reforms would then imply first removing the difficult constraints and making sure that the last binding constraints are constraints that can be easily communicated and are technically easier to implement.

The strategy may be applied to the implementation of a single reform measure (i.e. the sequential steps of improving public service delivery within a department) or the sequencing of a bundle of reform measures. For the case of Tanzania, such a strategy might have started with bank reforms first and removed the direct subsidies to parastatals last. But the strategy has its limitations. On the one hand, there may be important crossover effects, i.e. although five constraints have to be addressed to remove a certain rent, addressing one constraint may already have a beneficial impact in another area. On the other hand, some measures may take a relatively long time to be implemented so that it would not be possible to withhold other measures for political reasons.

Strategic sequencing also relates to the question whether it makes sense to start with reforming rent-supporting structures or addressing rent-creating constraints and policies. Rent-supporting structures may be so powerful that a change first demands that certain rents should become less relevant or meaningless. In Tanzania severe resistance against privatisation only disappeared when the benefits of parastatals were significantly reduced as hard budget constraints increasingly began to be implemented. Or system changes that made the profits of marketing boards residual effectively removed the stakes in the marketing boards and therefore the resistance. In other situations it is easier to first address rent-seeking structures. For instance, it may be argued that an early but continuous and thorough restructuring of the cooperative system would have greatly reduced direct opposition to the liberalisation of agricultural marketing. Finally, a combination of the two strategies (reducing rents and breaking rent-seeking structures) may also help to overcome resistance. For instance, removing subsidies to parastatals entirely may not be politically feasible. However, limiting subsidies and letting parastatals decide how to share these remaining benefits could break the resistance and would set powerful rent-seekers against each other. In the end some of them would drop out of the rent-seeking contest and there would be fewer left to deal with in the future.

What is the right policy for which country?

The last aspect to be treated in this section has been formulated provocatively. The question concerning the right economic policy raises a fundamental issue, i.e. the role and appropriate size and type of the state in society. As noted in Chapter 1, although the government should provide public goods, offset externalities and other market failures, it is also the government that provides most of the rent-seeking opportunities. Given this duality, what answer can this discussion offer? Two conclusions emerge as regards general policymaking. On the one hand, government interventions should be designed to approximate a *market situation* as close as possible; on the other, policymakers have to assess *what a government can do* and *what it cannot do*.

Obviously, markets are not always perfect; they may include sizeable frictions and externalities. Furthermore, international markets may be severely distorted by unpredictable and short-term rent-seeking related export policies in other countries. Under these conditions, government interventions into market outcomes are necessary and economically justified. The critical task is however to design these interventions to be as compatible as possible with an efficient market situation, where prices reflect true opportunity costs and are not distorted by uncompensated externalities.

But rent-seeking insights from institutional economics and public choice also demonstrate that what is needed is a critical assessment of the *government's abilities* to rectify a specific unfavourable situation. In the real world transaction and information costs matter, political markets are not perfect and principal-agent conflicts occur, for instance between the leadership, the government bureaucracy and the citizens of a country. These problems explain why policies and regulations often fail to maximise social welfare, either because interventions and regulations are poorly specified or poorly implemented. The case study on Tanzania clearly demonstrates that rent-seekers within and outside the government successfully lobbied for poor policies or misused originally well-intended policies and regulation for their personal benefit, at the expense of the society's welfare.

In a state with weak institutions and where checks and balances are not sufficiently implemented, it is crucial to balance the benefits from an intervention with possible negative rent-seeking consequences that may result, for instance, from a poor implementation of the policy. Needless to say, once interventions and regulations are implemented, they have to be continuously reassessed and evaluated, to see whether they achieve their stated goals.

A committed leadership that cannot sufficiently control its bureaucratic apparatus would have to opt for more simple and minimal regulations and interventions. The optimal level of government activity then depends on the extent of the 'rent-seeking environment' and the government's capacity and commitment. This is also one of the main conclusions of a forthcoming World

Bank study on regulations (World Bank (2004)), which emphasises that 'one size often fits all' or to put it differently, 'less' is 'more'. The report argues, for instance, that in poor countries sophisticated bankruptcy regulations often result in inefficiency and even corruption and concludes that it might be wise to simply rely on 'existing contract-enforcement mechanisms or negotiations between private parties' (p. xvi).

Most important for weak governments, however, is the understanding that social policy often does not demand distribution of benefits. Many policymakers still equate social policy with distributing rents and other favours, without being aware that much of social policy simply consists in making welfare-enhancing profit-seeking activities profitable.

In evaluating appropriate policies, an interesting question is whether general conditions exist that make a country susceptible to rent-seeking policies. Three aspects may be identified: First, a *socialist or planned economy*; second, the availability of large quantities of *natural resources;* and third, access to *substantial aid.* These factors, if combined with a weak capacity of state institutions or a poor design and implementation of policies, can considerably increase opportunities to appropriate income in a non-productive way and therefore explain why a country may have a higher risk of becoming a rent-seeking economy.

As a rule socialist and planned economies experience more frequent and large-scale interventions that generate outcomes which do not approximate a market situation. These systems are therefore much more prone to abuse. Countries with abundant natural resources benefit from natural rents. (In particular mineral resources usually have a market value which exceeds the costs of extraction by a considerable extent.) Elites within the country typically control these resources and are less dependent on creating a productive economy. Furthermore, large stocks of resources are often the cause of major violent conflicts and military coups of rival groups to capture the state apparatus—an extremely costly means of rent appropriation. Finally, sizeable amounts of insufficiently monitored and evaluated aid obviously allow governments to sustain inappropriate and poor policies, and rent-seekers can appropriate a share of the aid in the form of non-productive income. As the World Bank (1998a, p. 16) has shown in the past, aid was not allocated according to performance criteria but predominantly benefited former colonies and political allies. In Tanzania socialist policies coincided with a high level of donor support.

9.2 Rent-Seeking and the Role of Donors

a) The Duality Between Preventing and Supporting Rents and Rent-Seeking

'Financial assistance leads to faster growth, poverty reduction, and gains in social indicators in developing countries with sound economic management. And the effect is large...'

World Bank (1998a, p. 2)

'... foreign aid has become the fuel that drives the engine of adverse political culture in Africa... The closure of the African Division of the World Bank and the cessation of all international aid to Africa must be viewed as a first priority for the concerned international community if the peoples of that region are ever to take realistic steps towards reforming their institutions and their organisations.'

Charles K. Rowley (2000, p. 155)

The discussion of rent-seeking and the case study on Tanzania demonstrated that donors play a twofold role in the context of rent-seeking. On the one hand donors *directly promote rent-abating policies* and are a main force in building up accountability. Ideally, they are a powerful interest group and try to represent the interests of the poor and civil society in general.[205] Providing conditional aid in the form of direct project support (expertise and financial resources), as well as balance of payments support and budget support, donors aim to assist the recipient country in improving core infrastructure, strengthening the state and implementing good governance policies, with the final goal of reducing poverty and promoting sustainable development, growth and welfare.

On the other hand, donors are also *a main target of rent-seeking activities*, directly and indirectly. Because of inadequate policies, weak institutions, and above all the lack of accountability and checks and balances in recipient countries, rent-seekers have managed to reap a large share of donor support as individuals, interest groups, government bodies and NGOs. Even worse, the continuous and high support poured into many LDCs over the last forty years even promoted, sustained and strengthened rent-seeking skills and structures. Many parastatal managers, civil servants and politicians learned much more about the willingness of donors to provide help than about the requirements and rules for running a company, organisation, government or country efficiently. Aid therefore also became jointly responsible for the creation of unviable institutions and the implementation of inadequate policies, which in many cases could not have been sustained so long without generous donor support. In

[205] Clearly they also pursue other compatible or incompatible objectives, as discussed later.

Tanzania many of the inefficient parastatals supported by donor credits and loans were initially created because donor financing was available.

Part of the problem or explanation of why aid has been appropriated by rent-seekers derives from the simple logic of aid: Aid is predominantly allocated to poor countries; many poor countries, however, are poor because by one way or another, they have become rent-seeking economies. The more donors operate in rent-seeking environments, i.e. countries with corrupt and institutionally weak governments and strong rent-seeking interest groups, the more it is indispensable to understand rent-seeking forces and take them into consideration when designing policies and deciding on the type and size of donor engagement.

The thin line between supporting and preventing good governance policies has been widely discussed in the context of *aid fungibility*. Many people concerned with development cooperation have argued that aid allocated to priority sectors may induce recipient governments to withdraw their own resources from these sectors and use them for other purposes, or it may allow governments to lower their own revenue mobilisation.[206] For predatory type governments in particular, the problem of aid fungibility is largely a reflection of the power and persistence of rent-seeking forces. In the extreme, the net impact of aid simply becomes that of feeding a rent-seeking economy.

Considering the possible negative side effects of aid, especially that aid can help rent-appropriating regimes hold on to power and ignore the needs of society, it is not surprising that there have been calls to withdraw all aid. But would it make sense to cease all international aid to Africa, as Rowley suggests in the opening quote to this section? Certainly not to such an extreme.

Besides the fact that it would be far too simplistic to treat all African countries the same, 'pulling out' would not necessarily guarantee that a situation in a country would improve, even in the long run. Particularly in countries where large rents can be extracted from mineral resources, predatory-type regimes can endure for decades without donor support. Aid could however still be helpful in other forms, for instance as activities which encourage political change or prepare a foundation which would become effective once the political environment changed.

What is therefore needed is a foreign aid policy which is tailored to the specifics of the recipient's type of regime and level of commitment and to the specific modes of appropriating and sustaining rents. The duality between abolishing and promoting rent-seeking policies implies that donors have to be extremely careful in designing their policies or evaluating and justifying their support. Obviously, warnings and recommendations summarised in Chapter 9.1 not only hold for reform-minded policymakers in the recipient country, but even to a larger degree for the donor community, in particular if they intend to support the poor in a corrupt and rent-seeking environment. A differentiated

206 See for instance World Bank (1998a, p. 60f) on an overview of papers or Gupta, et al. (2003). The latter study presents empirical evidence for the period 1970-2000 and shows that in countries plagued by high levels of corruption, any increase in grants was fully offset by reduced revenue efforts (e.g. reduced efforts to ensure tax compliance).

analysis can offer ways of addressing rent-seeking problems. Based on the insights of Chapter 9.1, the following section summarises additional donor-specific conclusions and recommendations that arise from the previous discussion and the Tanzanian case study.

b) Successfully Addressing Rent-Seeking Problems Demands a New Emphasis, Sequencing and Design of Aid

Since aid has not always been beneficial but has also been responsible for severe crises and poor development in recipient countries, much more emphasis has to be put on de-linking support from the ability to earn non-productive income. Depending on the specific setting, rent-seeking therefore demands a new design and sequencing of aid and related reform measures.

This main conclusion largely corresponds to the findings from the 'Assessing Aid' study (World Bank (1998a)), which demonstrates that aid works if it is designed appropriately and if it finds the right balance between providing ideas and financing projects or general budgets. The study shows that financial aid increases growth and can lift many people out of poverty, if it is allocated to countries with sound economic management, i.e. countries with a good policy environment and good institutions (rule of law, efficient public service, stable macroeconomic environment, open trade regimes and protected property rights). Countries with poor management, by contrast, should only be given ideas and donors should focus on reform-minded elements in the community and government.

Insights from the rent-seeking analyses of this book can demonstrate in more detail which preconditions and aspects are significant. It argues that the policy environment and quality of institutions have been poor largely because of rent-seeking forces. Understanding these forces therefore helps to provide ideas for effective reforms to countries without sound economic management and to assess the type of aid that can be beneficial under given rent-seeking conditions.

Critically differentiate what development cooperation can contribute to and what has to be accomplished by the recipient country

The discussion on rent-seeking demonstrated that the removal of rents usually necessitates addressing several conditions simultaneously; furthermore, rent-protecting strategies, which include the poor implementation of specific measures and countervailing actions, are numerous and diverse. Donors face the problem that in most cases they can only influence, control or evaluate *some of the relevant constraints*; all other aspects depend on the activities (and abilities) of the recipient country. The problem applies to different types of support, i.e. project support, the financing of sector-wide strategies or general budget support.

As a first step donors need to be much more aware of the *consequences of failures* related with aid, which can vary considerably depending on the type of support. In some cases non-existent preconditions and countervailing rent-seeking strategies will have a deferring impact only, while in other situations they will effectively subvert donor-supported reforms or even make the reform counterproductive. For example, closing four out of five smuggling loopholes will have no immediate impact but will become beneficial once the last loophole has been addressed. By contrast, donor support that directly or indirectly pours aid into unviable companies or projects where most of the funds 'disappear' will never have a positive impact. The same holds for the worst-case situation, where donors support strengthens a corrupt body or government, making these institutions more efficient in what they have been doing previously, i.e. appropriating rents.

Donors have to critically assess, what type of *commitment* from the recipient country (commitment on the strategic management level, on the operative level, commitment to undertake specific complementary reforms, etc.) is required in which areas and for which reform steps. Ideally commitment becomes redundant if a country undertakes important complementary measures in advance. Frequently this option is not available.

Sequencing that takes rent-seeking into account implies providing support at any time (or in a strategic sequence) where commitment is not critical, and withholding support where the necessary commitment is lacking or where it is not clear. It requires developing strategies to reduce the risk that support can be lost or become counterproductive. And it must balance trade-offs between short-term benefits and higher risks in sustainability on the one hand, and high short-term costs and longer-term benefits on the other.

Make all assumptions underlying support highly transparent and monitor them

Since aid can be easily undermined by rent-seeking strategies and a lack of government commitment and capacity, it is important to specify and monitor in detail how donor-supported measures are assumed to work. This entails listing explicitly the *chain of assumptions* which have to hold to justify support and the assumptions which need to hold so that a measure finally leads to the intended outcome (for an example see the case of strengthening the tax administration in Table 5-8, p. 287).[207] This evaluation is not only relevant for project support, but should also be undertaken when deciding on financing a government's development strategy with general budget support.

Assessing assumptions requires, among other things, differentiating between the recipient country's *real inabilities* (lack of skill) and *strategic inabilities* (pretending a lack in skill or having no interest in acquiring better skills). In Tanzania, for instance, at least until the mid-1990s the customs administration was poor because customs officers (and senior officials) did not want to do a better job (customs posts were a principal vehicle for rent appropriation). The same holds for the inability of many parastatals to improve accounting practices since these were instrumental in hiding the embezzlement of funds. Aid which

[207] This approach for instance adopted by the Operations Evaluation Department (OED) of the World Bank is also referred to as *'theory-based' evaluation* or developing a *'logic model'*.

aims to rectify real inabilities would obviously have to be designed differently than aid which intends to address strategic inabilities. The lack of differentiation between the two aspects actually explains a great deal of reform failures in the 1980s and 1990s.

Taking a broad perspective, which includes the entire range of assumption (as outlined in the tax administration case in Table 5-8), helps to identify rent-seeking strategies and other possible complications. It thereby provides crucial information on the design, sequencing, fine-tuning and bundling of reforms and it helps donors to find an appropriate mix between ex-ante and ex-post conditionalities (i.e. floating tranches and supporting a new project only if the previous was successful) or to define the preconditions to engage in general budget support.

Choose the right modes of support: know-how and ideas versus financial aid

Prospects to misappropriate aid (directly and indirectly) vary between different modes of support, which range from supplying ideas and technical assistance (employing foreign experts, providing educational programmes, etc.) to financing projects or specific services (e.g. preshipment inspections), to providing general balance of payments and budget support. Depending on the severity of the rent-seeking environment, support has to be confined to communicate the costs of the current government policy and to build up and strengthen watchdog institutions within the civil society, assuming that any other type of support would either be directly appropriated by rent-seekers or even strengthen their position. The need for a differentiated approach in aid has been clearly articulated in the 'Assessing Aid' study, which emphasised 'if commitment, money—if not, ideas' (World Bank (1998a, p. 58)).

Where policies are poor and institutions weak, support is most effective if it mainly provides *ideas*, above all making the costs of inefficient (mostly rent-seeking) policies more transparent within the government and civil society and explaining how a change in policy can improve the situation. This approach can strengthen reform-minded elements within the society and the government.

As explained in Chapter 4.1, rent-seeking is a *concept of economic theory*. It describes a mode how economists analyse the consequences of economic policies in a society. Although highly effective in demonstrating the costs and benefits of a specific policy, economic concepts are not an accurate picture of how humans think and act, i.e. other people cannot be expected to decipher problems in the same way. A main goal of development cooperation should therefore be to make the costs of rent-seeking policies as transparent and understandable as possible and to promote projects that contribute to increasing a general knowledge of economics. In most countries there is still much scope for disseminating ideas on sound economic policies.

Even if ruling elites try to 'justify' rent-seeking policies by references to aspects of culture, there is a strong economic link to 'cultural' values; i.e. social norms and values are not without opportunity costs. To the extent that values become too expensive, they are likely to lose their binding impact. However there is probably no traditional African culture that explains the extreme extent of rent-seeking in many African countries. What has happened is that traditional cultural values have been used selectively and opportunistically as a pretext for personal enrichment.

Besides providing general ideas and explanations on the costs of economic policies, in many cases *technical assistance* is crucial and needs to start at an early stage (though the empowerment of corrupt officials has to be ruled out). Donors may tie technical assistance in a way that increases their own abilities to monitor the performance of the country. For instance, poor countries often have weak statistics departments. Donor support to strengthen the statistics department could be linked to obtaining direct access to the collected and analysed data (not only evaluations and aggregates, but especially also information on handling and compiling raw data). This type of support would help both government and donors to have reliable data and it would provide donors with a powerful tool to monitor the performance and impact of aid, for instance when it finally comes to evaluating their engagement in general budget support. Another example is computerisation, above all the implementation of computerised networks which link different systems and help to reduce discretion (the official's freedom of choicc) and to dctcct discrepancies. Again support may be tied to having direct access to sensitive information that allows assessing the countries performance in greater detail, above all possible rent-seeking strategies. If the government's commitment is real, access to the data should not be a problem.

Requirements to evaluate and monitor direct *project support* or a specific *change in policy* are often similar to evaluating general budget support, not only because of aid fungibility as a result of different preferences, but also because rent-seeking strategies are numerous and diverse and include countervailing actions not necessarily directly related to a specific project or policy. In many cases a rent-seeking problem can only be successfully addressed by taking a broad perspective and evaluating the entire government budget cycle. As demonstrated in Chapter 8, this is most obvious in the case of parastatal companies, which received substantial support in various forms.

Since the mid-1990s donors have increasingly shifted their emphasis from direct project support to financing an *overall sector strategy* of a government or even to providing *general budget support*. This shift in emphasis is limited to countries with sound economic management and has the advantage of simultaneously addressing the problems of ownership, donor coordination and fungibility. From the rent-seeking perspective, the shift is helpful as rent-seeking strategies explain a great deal of fungibility, i.e. though foreign aid may be used for specified purposes, rent-seekers appropriate the benefits directly and indirectly (e.g. aid strengthens a corrupt administration, bribes paid to tax enforcers increase and additional official government revenues are appropriated by a rent-seeking elite).

Yet the rent-seeking problem also requires a rethinking of government ownership and conditionality in situations without sound economic management where general budget support is not feasible.

Understand ownership and conditionality in the rent-seeking context

Rent-seeking puts the issue of ownership in a different perspective. The case study on Tanzania demonstrates that ownership has to be understood in the right context, in particular if rent-seeking forces drive government decision-making. This problem directly points to the fundamental question of *'ownership for whom?'*. If ruling elites in a country have no other goals than personally enriching themselves and keeping their rent income intact, then full ownership of a 'reform programme' by the ruling authorities would hardly be beneficial for the poor. In this case, well-designed support from donors can by definition not be owned by the government. Furthermore, a government is not homogenous, i.e. specific measures may be owned by a considerable number of politicians and civil servants.

More useful than the question of ownership—a notion that is often emotionally loaded—in explaining the effectiveness of aid is an analysis from a rent-seeking perspective. Rather than 'ownership', effective aid requires that reforms can be designed in a way that reduces the ability to appropriate rents. For instance in the Tanzanian case study presented here, many of the failures were indeed related to an inappropriate anticipation of rent-seeking strategies.

Obviously a government which is urged to implement an unwanted measure will try to apply strategies to undermine its implementation and will even take countervailing measures. Advocates of an 'uncompromising' need for government ownership therefore conclude that the reforms will not work—and this may well be so. The discussion on rent-seeking in fact demonstrated that there are many strategies that can easily undermine unwanted reforms. The point is however not to wait until recipient governments accept the initially unwanted reforms and gain 'ownership' (or to impose reforms at the expense of the government's ownership). Rather the solution lies in finding areas within the non-homogenous government where reforms are feasible and *understanding and anticipating* rent-seeking strategies when designing and sequencing reforms. These reforms will automatically be 'owned' by winners (which may be the unorganised poor with little political clout), but not by the losers (the previously successful rent-seekers and often the current rulers of the country).

Only in the situation where major anticipated problems cannot be removed by an appropriate design of a reform does aid become ineffective and 'ownership' of the rent-seekers (who ought to be the losers from reforms) becomes indispensable. In extreme cases, after rent-seekers have manoeuvred themselves into a severe crisis and eroded virtually all rents for distribution, the 'losers' of reforms may actually seek reforms themselves and thus acquire 'ownership' because the rents they still have to lose are insignificant compared with the increase in wealth that renewed (substantial) aid can bring. Rent-seekers would probably still try to get a (badly-designed) reform package that enabled them to acquire new rents. Thus the most difficult challenge for donors remains supplying aid in a form that makes the support sustainable and less prone to rent-seeking.

In conclusion, in a severe rent-seeking environment, as was the case in Tanzania in the 1980s and 1990s, donors need to be much more restrictive in designing support by making support contingent only on relevant conditions that (i) help removing anticipated problems (and thus conditionality works with limited or no 'ownership') and (ii) are monitorable in detail in order to effectively check compliance of planned reforms. It demands a much more detailed specification and elaboration of a monitoring system and an anticipation of expected countervailing rent-seeking strategies—measures, which partly replace the problem of insufficient commitment and ownership. Obviously if recipient governments want to demonstrate commitment and credibility they can hardly argue against donors closely monitoring the outcome of reforms (besides the donor's own requirement to be accountable vis-à-vis their taxpayers).

To ensure accountability donors may link conditionalities to the promises and statements governments make vis-à-vis the donor community, i.e. statements, where governments emphasise the importance of undertaking specific reforms. The statements usually include the removal of severe (and apparent) inefficiencies, which no government can argue against. Donors should be much more persistent in linking such statements with the effective outcome of reforms.

However, such an approach also requires that donors invest much more in the policy dialogue. A government may be committed to undertaking specific measures but it may not be able to do so. It is in fact one of the most difficult aspects for donors to differentiate between the lack of government commitment and the lack of government power and to ensure that any statement by the government vis-à-vis donors is realistic.[208]

If donors support specific reforms, the projects have to clearly define the responsibilities and competence within government institutions, most preferably making sure that responsibility and competence is held by the same position. This could additionally include not only making transparent responsibilities for positions but also specifying that responsibilities have to be passed on in a transparent and unambiguous way to other staff when personnel changes occur, without creating a break in the chain of responsibilities. Most preferably, the project and responsibilities should be openly discussed in the media in advance when planning the reform, and in retrospect when evaluating it.

As noted earlier, where the rent-seeking environment is severe and involves government leaders, anticipated problems may not be rectified. In this case, aid

---

[208] Accountability of governments for promises made to donors may of course be at odds with populist unaffordable promises the government makes to its voters (e.g. delivery of free healthcare, new subsidies, etc.), which have to be avoided in the first place (again by pressing governments to have a more coherent discourse). If populist announcements nevertheless occur, donors have to take a clear position of not providing support if such unaffordable polices are adopted. As argued later, this again helps the standing of a weak government and reform-minded forces. Ultimately much of the rhetoric and discourse is a political game.

would be ineffective and wasteful and donors would thus have to put more emphasis on explaining the inefficiencies and costs of the prevailing system and making clear how donor-supported reforms work, *assuming that* suggestions will be understood by *reform-minded forces* within the government and civil society. Reform-minded forces within the government would thus be 'empowered' to argue for difficult reforms, i.e. reform-minded politicians can explain why reforms are necessary and that the country does not have other options since donors are no longer willing to support the inefficient system. Under these circumstances, not providing financial aid may ultimately better help the country to develop and reduce poverty.

Identify rent-seeking supporting structures within donor organisations

The incentives for donors to disburse funds and support large projects are often cited as behind the continued provision of insufficiently evaluated large-scale support to poorly-performing countries. These incentives obviously do not help to address severe problems of rent-seeking but may instead strengthen the rent-seekers' position. Donors need to be much more aware of the necessity to rethink and reorganise incentive structures in their organisation. The most relevant adverse incentives can be summarised as follows.

First of all, it has often been argued disbursing funds is an important rationale and critical output measure for donor agencies (including institutions such as the World Bank) and the incentives of staff are basically *approval-focused* (and not result-focused). Furthermore, project and programme failures are not in the interest of donors once the engagement is under way, i.e. donors are *less critical when it comes to their own projects* and may therefore have a strong incentive to throw good money after bad. This problem has been particularly apparent with projects that supported companies in the parastatal sector. In Tanzania mutual dependencies were obvious. As also emphasised by Eriksson (1994, p. 33f, 72f), while the parastatals depended on support for their continued survival the donors depended on the survival of their projects for their own legitimacy (ensuring continued operation of their parastatal projects and covering their past mistakes). Unless criteria to freeze funds or abandon support entirely are clearly defined, incentives may not be much different once donors have moved on to balance of payments support or budget support.

Second, donors did not always have a sufficiently large number of good performers to choose from. They may therefore have been less critical in allocating aid to countries like Tanzania, which was one of the few stable countries in Africa and did not experience military coups or protracted wars. However this argument is flawed. As the 'Assessing Aid' study demonstrates, aid has been predominantly allocated to former colonies and political allies, whether or not they were good performers (World Bank (1998a, p 16)). Donors should therefore investigate and rethink their constraints in disbursing aid to 'partnered' countries.

Third, a large amount of project support also served as *export promotion* in the donor country. A more restrictive policy of disbursing aid would have negatively affected strong economic interests in the donor country and was therefore not adopted.

Last but not least, donors in charge of designing and surveying support may have an *incentive to inflate projects*. On the one hand, individual projects and lending operations include a high share of communication and monitoring costs independent of the size of disbursement. Donors can reduce their work by focusing on a few large projects rather than many small ones. On the other hand, being responsible for large projects tends to create higher fringe benefits in the form of responsibility and reputation than a donor could obtain with smaller projects (e.g. donors with large projects are more likely to have important appointments with senior civil servants and the project and the donor's name are more likely to be prominently featured in the press). Sometimes donors even 'compete' for the largest project within a sector to ensure that they can take the lead among the donors.

Obviously, if aid is disbursed in a rent-seeking environment, such adverse incentives entirely coincide with the interests of rent-seekers. Incentives are most negative if donors are pressured to spend a certain amount of resources within a fiscal year (for fear of reduced allocations in subsequent years).

There are several ways to weaken adverse incentives. Besides a more careful ex-ante evaluation of support, any engagement of donors should include well-specified exit strategies, as well as regular internal and external evaluations. Helpful, though sometimes difficult to implement, are automatic and explicit mechanisms to freeze funds, not only for a short period of time but if necessary for many years. These benchmarks have to be clearly specified and communicated in advance and also give the recipient country reasonable time to react to an unwanted slippage. Furthermore, officials in the donor's administration should be more explicitly honoured for their engagement in continuously reassessing and monitoring a recipient country's performance, i.e. the cancellation of a project or even an entire aid portfolio should not necessarily be treated as a failure. In a difficult environment, the burden of 'proof' may even be reversed so that support would automatically expire after a relatively short period unless officials could ascertain that the government was making a good effort, that the financial aid was having a positive impact and that it was still needed. Finally, donor agencies should be allowed to temporarily allocate undisbursed financial aid to escrow accounts without being penalised with a reduced budget allocation for development aid in the subsequent fiscal year.

Strengthen representatives and offices in recipient countries

An important conclusion that directly follows from the discussion in Chapter 9.1 is that assessing and anticipating all relevant rent-seeking strategies is complex and requires a great deal of information and local knowledge. Successfully understanding and anticipating rent-seeking therefore demands that donors have strong local representation, i.e. an adequate level of staff in the recipient country who are embedded in the informal network, take the time to analyse problems that go beyond the narrow project focus and are not subject to too much turnover. These conditions are often not met, though the need for 'generalists' has been increasingly acknowledged since donors have started shifting their emphasis from project support to general budget support.

Because of the need to take a broad perspective, it is indispensable that local offices strengthen their *general knowledge of economics*, for instance by having economists or political scientists on their team to oversee the reform process, interpret outcomes based on their informal local knowledge and communicate problems with project-related staff.[209] In this respect, institutions such as the IMF or World Bank provide important discussion forums. However their scope is limited to specific areas (and like bilateral donors to some extent politically constrained) and could therefore be usefully complemented by efforts of the donor community, academia and NGOs. Furthermore, economic papers and reports are not of much use to bilateral donors for formulating strategies or deciding to finance a comprehensive government development framework, if the staff cannot read and understand them in full.

An increased emphasis on economic analysis in general and rent-seeking in particular would also provide local offices with a capacity to evaluate or investigate more specific problems. As the case study on Tanzania demonstrates, donors have been blind to many aspects for a long time because they relied too much on general information and aggregated data without taking the time to explore the details, or simply because they operated under the assumption that islands of effective aid and accountable institutions could be created in a corrupt system and could gradually be extended to cover the entire system.[210] This strategy has proven to be highly wasteful as the case of Tanzania shows.

The crucial point is that many rent-seeking problems and proof of commitment become manifest on the operative level and show up in numerous and diverse 'small' incidences (and not necessarily in aggregates and general overviews).

The staff responsible for overseeing the general reform process may for instance hire students from the local university to undertake specific inquiries and to monitor critical aspects. Studies similar to the analysis of soft budget constraints presented in Chapter 8, or the evaluation in the present study of the (ignored) comments of the Controller and Auditor General (see in particular Chapter 7.3) would have provided valuable information to assess commitment and to improve the design and sequencing of aid, if they had been undertaken earlier on.

---

[209] The interests of donors obviously depend on the structure of the staff in the office. In the second half of the 1990s, when the case study on Tanzania was undertaken, the staff of the Swiss Coordination Office in Dar es Salaam was mainly concerned with project-related work. Though they provided logistical support, their interest in the results of the rent-seeking study was limited. The situation was different with the Dutch and Swedish donor agency, which had motivated economists in their team and even suggested organising a workshop on this matter.

[210] For example many problems such as repetitive complaints on some issues in the OCAG reports were apparent but donors simply did not consider them relevant enough—year after year.

Another difficulty for donor agencies is the *high fluctuation of expatriate staff and/or the lack of institutional memory.* Though job rotation brings in new ideas, it may impede the accumulation of important local knowledge and experience. For instance, when finalising the case study on Tanzania in 2001, it was amazing to see how little new members of staff at various local donor offices knew about the major problems that occurred only few years before they arrived. The answer 'I don't know anything about your request, it refers to the time I wasn't here yet' is typical not only of the attitude of donors in local offices but also staff in head offices in donor countries. Since rent-seeking patterns tend to be repetitive and persist after the departure of donor staff, it is not surprising that donors are criticised for not learning from past errors. The fact that there was again a high level of embezzlement with the OGL facility in Tanzania after the CIS scandal had been discovered is evidence of a weak institutional memory.

If it is not possible to reduce the staff turnover, great emphasis should at least be given to strengthen institutional memory in monitoring and periodic evaluations. In addition new personnel should be extensively briefed, making sure that they are much more familiar with the details of the country's past performance, above all with the problems that undermined the expected positive impact of aid.

Further improve coordination among donors

This claim directly follows from the suggestion that greater efforts should be devoted to keeping a detailed overview of the reform process and investing more time and resources in reform-related research and monitoring. Bilateral donors could provide part-time staff to form a standing unit or committee to monitor the country's general performance in close collaboration with multilateral donors, academic institutions, reform-minded government officials and other stakeholders in the civil society. This approach would pool resources and achieve economies of scale. As staff would still work part-time in their donor agencies, there would be a closer integration of findings and conclusions with the project-related team.

On the other hand, the need for coordination among donors is a consequence of the *nature of the rent-seeking problem*. The need to take a broad perspective that goes beyond the narrow focus of a specific project is obvious, given the numerous indirect rent-seeking strategies that could undermine a specific project. However rent-seekers can also play off donors against each other. A broad-based anti-rent-seeking strategy therefore not only requires a broad focus but also will need to coordinate donors, i.e. to include as many donors as possible in the strategic planning of reform design and sequencing. The same holds for the situation where donors decide on a benchmark to support a government's development framework.

This again suggests strengthening local representatives and offices in recipient countries. Notably, Joint Evaluation Missions (JEMs) initiated by the World Bank have been important to coordinate and assess donor programmes and to evaluate the country's progress; nevertheless, this type of work would have to be intensified and complemented.

Improving donor coordination means donors have to be flexible and cooperative, which is only possible if decisions are not sidetracked by hidden agendas. It also requires strengthening the position of donors in their countries, so that individual contributions and strategies are predictable and not hampered by sudden political changes in the donor country (e.g. sizeable cuts in aid budgets).

To ensure effective use of donor funds improved coordination among donors is not only desirable within a recipient country but also between different recipient countries. The World Bank's 'Assessing Aid' study confirmed that until the early 1990s countries were able to benefit from ODA funds irrespective of their performance. It emphasised that reallocating financial aid to countries with sound economic management, i.e. countries with a good policy environment and good quality of institutions, would have provided much better records.

The discussion on rent-seeking corroborates this insight. As noted earlier, depending on the rent-seeking structures and strategies, it is important to choose the right modes of support. What should determine the level of aid allocated to a recipient country is not primarily *need* but the *impact* aid can provide. An appropriate sequencing and design of reforms is therefore important (assessing under which preconditions which type and level of aid is appropriate) not only in one country but also between recipient countries, as resources are limited and would have a different marginal impact in different countries.

Strategically sequencing aid between recipient countries requires good coordination among donors, but it would improve the effectiveness of aid. Furthermore openly communicating the type and level of support allocated to one country rather than another can strengthen anti-rent-seeking forces in both countries that have been good or poor performers.

Promote and do homework in donor countries

This last aspect departs from the main subject of this book, but deserves to be mentioned here. It points to the high level of rent-seeking activities in donor countries, which regardless of aid effectiveness negatively affect third world economies. It is hard to make a case against rent-creating policies in developing countries if policies in rich donor countries are driven by rent-seeking considerations.

The problem already starts with basic aid, above all procurement contracts, which are in many countries still limited to the donor country (sometimes, including other countries). The World Development Report 'Attacking Poverty', for instance, emphasises that 'driven by domestic political interests, this practice goes against the very free market principles that most donors are trying to encourage in developing countries and results in inefficient use of aid' (World Bank (2000d, p. 200)). One way to solve this problem on a broad front is to subject aid to WTO rules.

However, much more consequential for developing countries are the trade policies in rich countries for agricultural products and manufactured goods, which still discriminate heavily against developing country exports. A recent study from the International Food Policy Research Institute (Diao, Diaz-Bonilla and Robinson (2003)) estimates that the combination of domestic support, market protection and export subsidies in industrialised countries (above all in the EU and the United States) costs developing countries more than US$30 billion annually in lost agricultural and agro-industrial income. The study concludes that eliminating protectionism would triple developing countries' net agricultural trade. The recent Human Development Report notes for OECD countries that average tariffs on manufactured goods from developing countries are more than four times those on manufactured goods from other countries and the size of agricultural subsidies in rich countries is nearly six times (US$300 billion a year) that of official development assistance (UNDP (2003, p. 12)).

If donors were to address their own rent-seeking policies more forcefully, prospects for development in the third world could be increased considerably. The necessity is obviously greatest for those countries of sub-Saharan Africa which are poorest and more dependent on agricultural income. Though externalities, above all environmental considerations, are significant and should always be included in the design of national and international policies, they do not explain the high degree of protectionism in rich countries. Unfortunately the Cancun negotiations in September 2003 sadly demonstrated how little industrialised countries are prepared to open their markets for agriculture products. Even worse, because of the enduring success of relatively small pressure groups with excellent political lobbying, highly subsidised products will continue to be sold in African markets and displace locally produced goods with much lower production costs. As ambassadors of the poor in developing countries, donor agencies should make it their task to campaign against agricultural protectionism in their own countries.

9.3 Outlook

Development and aid can work, but the right modes, concepts and approaches are needed. Development not only demands great efforts in developing countries but also a rethink in industrialised countries. Central to this is the problem of understanding and communicating the causes and consequences of poor policies in both LDCs and industrialised countries.

This book has identified rent-seeking behaviour as a principal cause of poor economic performance. The challenge that politicians and civil servants face is to limit rent-seeking and to channel or force an ever larger part of the society, business community and civil service into productive activities. To combat rent-seeking, there must be a greater awareness of the consequences of poor policies. If more people both within and outside government understand the mechanisms, costs and dynamics of rent-seeking, reform-minded forces will have a better chance to gain sufficient power to restrain or even prevent such activities. This book aims to contribute to this goal by examining and discussing numerous *aspects related to rent-seeking*, and by *exposing the costs* of rent-seeking in Tanzania during the 1980s and 1990s.

Tanzania is moving forward and the government has meanwhile achieved some success. But rent-seeking forces are strong and are likely to endure. This book intends to remind policymakers that reforms are an ongoing task and that maintaining sound economic policies and good institutions is a constant challenge and largely depends on the attitudes of those who are in power. In this sense, the book is particularly devoted to the people (from the rural poor to the urban entrepreneur) who suffer most from ill-conceived and badly implemented polices and weak government institutions, in the hope that they will press for transparent policies and hold ruling elites more accountable.

Appendix A: Extract of Warioba Report

Unpublished pre-print version including missing pages (highlighted at the left border) as explained in Chapter 7.3 on page 410f. Text corresponds to pages 253-262 of the Warioba Report (1996).

Detailed Analysis of Individual Contracts

504. **New Bagamoyo Road:**

(a) **Length**: 13.4 Kilometers beginning from the junction with Sam Nujoma to the turn off to Wazo Hill cement factory.

(b) **Analysis**:

(i) The contract was awarded to K.V. Construction out of five competitive bids. The contract was signed on 14th March, 1992 at a price of Tshs. 737,956,406/30 or an average of Tshs. 55,071,374/= per kilometer.

(ii) On 20th September, 1991 a meeting was held under the then Chief Engineer Construction to discuss the Tender Evaluation Report on the contract. All the participants at the meeting were Engineers of the Ministry of Works. Although K.V. Construction Limited was the lowest evaluated Tenderer, the Meeting did not recommend them for the award of the contract for the following reasons:

- That K.V. Construction Ltd did not appear to own any Road Construction Equipment. The Meeting was stunned by the fact that K.V. Construction had to resort to the production of a High Court Certificate to authenticate their ownership of equipment which was stored at Masanga Camp in Mwanza. In the opinion of the Meeting, the involvement of the High Court in justifying the award of the contract was an ominous beginning in the implementation of the project.

- That K.V. Construction Ltd had failed to act on the Ministry's directive which required them to provide a list of the equipment they had purchased from MJs G.S.E. S/A. Moreover, the company had failed to indicate how much money they had spent on the purchase and their plans of obtaining the equipment.

Instead, the Meeting had advised that the contract be awarded to M/s ZAKHEM International Construction Ltd. which was the second lowest bidder.

(iii) In the various correspondences which eventually ensued between the Evaluation Team and other experts and the higher officials of the Ministry of Works, there are several reports which were against the award of tender to M/s K.V. Construction Ltd. because of its low capacity. Thus the experts were worried that the award would result in losses and a embarrassment to the Government.

Despite the negative opinion of the Ministerial Expert Team which had been assigned the responsibility to guard the interests of Government, the Principal Secretary of the Ministry of

Works opposed this recommendation and on 4/10/91 wrote the following 'Minute" to the Minister of Works:

'......I do not agree with the views of the Committee on K.V. Construction. What is required here is whether K.V. Construction has the equipment or not. Despite the doubts expressed by earlier reports which testify of having seen the equipment but were not sure whether it belonged to K.V.. I advise that we give him the 'benefit of doubt' and award this 'CONTRACT'. But I advise that we give him one month within which to move the equipment to the site. If he fails. then we should cancel the Contract.'

The Minister agreed with the advice of his Principal Secretary with the variant that he be given three months in which to move the equipment to the site instead of one month.

On 16th October, 1991 the decision to award the contract to M/s K.V. Construction Ltd. was formally taken at a meeting chaired by the Principal Secretary, Ministry of Works as follows:-

'Since the bidder has cleared the problem associated with ownership of equipment/plant, the meeting recommends award of contract for package No. 2 to M/s K.V. Construction, the lowest bidder.'

The decision taken on 16th October, 1991 at the Meeting chaired by the Principal Secretary contrary to the negative recommendations of the Expert Committee on the Package on New Bagamoyo Road, was conveyed to the Minister by the Principal Secretary Ministry of Works by a 'Minute' of even date. The Minister approved the award of contract to M/s K.V. Construction Ltd. instead of ZAKHEM International Construction Ltd.

Other problems associated with M/s K.V. Construction Ltd. concerned his ownership of the list of equipment he had provided. The ownership saga and other problems continued for a long time; causing the Project Consultants to caution the Ministry to be more circumspect in reaching a decision on the matter. In their letter Ref. No. DCMK/MOWlPkg.2/03 of 25th February, 1992, the Project Consultants cautioned the Ministry of Works in the last page of their letter as follows:-

'K.V. Construction Limited is a brand new company with no experience in building roads; has acquired all their equipment by a round-about method and has shown reluctance to submit detailed verification of clear ownership and has made what appears to be a serious error in their tendered price for a major construction item which could mean a Tshs. 50 million loss of revenue which amounts to 10 percent of the net contract amount and a majority of their potential profit. We have also failed to locate their office. At each of the locations which they have designated, our messengers have drawn a blank - none has heard of K.V. Construction Limited. Their designated site agent is inexperienced in road construction management.

We have recently written to them, Ref. DCMK/Pkg.2/Gen/02 21 February, 1992 (copy attached) instructing them to submit:

1. documentation verifying the multiple transfer of equipment
2. certified financial statement for K.V. Construction Limited
3. particulars of key personnel.

We recommend caution in signing a contract with K.V. Construction Limited, particularly for the New Bagamoyo Road which is the highest visibility package. K.V. Construction Limited should be required to submit full performance securities and bank guarantees for advance payments before the contract is signed.'

Cautious remarks similar to those made by the project consultants were forwarded to the principal secretary by the Tender Negotiations Committee on 10th March 1992.

Without considering all the negative observations; on 13th March, 1992 by letter Ref. No. MOW/M.30/384/A/9 signed by Mr. H.G. Urio on behalf of the principal secretary, M/s K.V. Construction Ltd. were officially notified by the ministry that their tender had been approved.

On 16th May, 1992, the president of the United Republic of Tanzania wrote letter Ref. No. SHC/R.270/2 to the Hon. N.L. Kiula, Minister for works expressing the following among others:-

'Construction should have started on 8th April, 1992. It did not start. Afterwards, the project manager came to yourselves to apologise for this shortcoming and promised that work would begin on 20th April 1992. Up to this 6th day of May 1992, work has not started. The importance of this road includes rendering service to tourism for the hotels in Kunduchi area from which already some clients are moving out because of the inconvenience caused by bad roads. This is tantamount to sabotaging the economy.'

In another paragraph of the same correspondence, the president made the following remarks:

'It is also alleged that this tender has been awarded through favouritism and loss to the Nation. Under these circumstances, it would be wise to cancel the Contract and award it to other people who have equipment and organisation ability.'

On 13th May, 1992, the Project Consultants wrote to the Ministry of Works a letter Ref. No. DCMK/MOW/Pkg. 2/Cont/48 which recommended the issuance of a Notification to the Contractor that the contract would be cancelled for the reasons that were given in the said letter.

In a minute to the Director of Roads and Aerodromes of 28th May, 1992, the principal secretary, Ministry of Works directed that the notification for the cancellation of the Contract with K.V. Construction Limited should be delayed for ten more days because: 'We had written the Contractor through the Consultants that we are giving them 14 days to complete their arrangements and that the plant and equipment must reach the site by *22/5/92*. Information available to me from Mwanza indicates that many pieces of equipment have already been loaded in railway wagons and have left Mwanza, some are still in Mwanza South waiting to be transported by TRC. Moreover, almost all pieces of equipment have been moved out of Masanza Camp. With that information it is not good to remove the contractor from 'site'. The Minister of Works has already informed the president that mobilisation deadline is 8th June, 1992 - due to the fact that the commencement letter was issued on 8th April, 1992. With due respect to all this, it is better to direct the consultant to extend the 14 days notice by another ten days.'

On 9th June, 1992, the project consultants wrote letter Ref. No. DCMK/MOW/Pkg.2/Gen/52 to the ministry to inform of the implications of delaying the date of cancellation of the contract as follows:

'On 8 June 1992, at approximately 1800 hrs, I inspected the equipment mobilised by K.V. Construction for the above Contract.
There was one grader and one tipper truck with water tank on board.......

The above is all the evidence there is of the Contractor's mobilisation as of the extended date for complete mobilisation.

It is your consultant's opinion that K.V. Construction Ltd. has, by its inaction, defaulted under Clause 63 of the General Conditions of Contract. We recommend that the Ministry act in accordance with Clause 63 to terminate the employment of K.V. Construction as of this date, having given the required 14 days notice on 15 May, 1992 and an extension on 5 June 1992'.

In another letter written on 9th June 1992 with Ref. No. DCMK/MOW/Pkg.2/Gen/53 to the Ministry of Works, the project consultants have emphasised:

'Terminate K.V. Construction without prejudice, cancel their performance bonds, pay them for the small amount of advance maintenance they carried out, and allow them to tender for smaller projects, where they can gain the experience they now lack.'

The ministry's reply to the project consultants was by letter Ref. No. MOW/M.30384/A/25 of 10th June, 1992 signed by Dr. P.F. Komba in which they were informed among other things that: 'The Ministry has taken note of the recommendations mentioned in the above referred letter and found that physical evidence to support the recommendations is lacking.'

On 26th June, 1992, Mr. H.G. Urio wrote, on behalf of the principal secretary, letter Ref. No. MOW/M.30/A/28 to the project consultants indicating the ministry's refusal to cancel the contract, thus:

'In light of efforts which the contractor M/s K.V. Construction has shown so far and due to the fact that some equipment has already arrived on site from Mwanza we would like to revisit your recommendation. May we request you to appraise the employer on the current status of the project and whether there is any intent on the part of the contractor to start the road works.'

After about five months, the project consultants wrote letter No. DCMK/MOW/Pkg.2/01 of 8th December, 1992 in which they vehemently protested to the ministry for the lack of action in the whole matter regarding the incompetence of M/s K.V. Construction Ltd in implementing the project. Among other things, they wrote as follows:-

'As of 25 November, 1992 approximately 63 percent of the Contract Period had elapsed with about 2 percent of the works completed.

'We have twice recommended that this contractor be terminated for lack of progress and gross inexperience. Both times the process dragged out to where the ministry said to drop the recommendation.

'Our credibility has been badly eroded and has reached the point where the contractor simply ignores instructions. This attitude has visibly expanded to other contractors.

'We would like to meet with the principal secretary and yourself to decide what the ministry is prepared to do and how to proceed'.

The performance of K.V. Construction Limited continued at a snails space and the idea of cancelling the Contract continued to be avoided till the Minister for Works finally admitted openly in a minute to the principal secretary of 13th January, 1993 that 'Beyond Lugalo, this road is beginning to be monstrous. This job is too much for K.V. Enough is enough'.

On 20th January, 1993, Dr. P.F.C. Komba, Chief Engineer for rural roads in the ministry wrote a minute to the Director of Roads admitting that the progress of work was truly frustrating; but at the same time, he refused to accept the recommendation of the project consultants to cancel the contract. Instead he apparently advised that K.V. should be left with a section of the road while another contractor is sub-contracted to handle the rest of the contract. Most surprisingly, that advice was accepted by the Director of Roads and subsequently by the principal secretary.

That, notwithstanding, on 21st April, 1993, the project consultants M/s De Leuw Cather International, wrote another letter to the Ministry of Works Ref. No. DCMK/MOW/Pkg. No. 2/240 advising them to cancel the contract with K.V. Construction Limited - thus:-

'K.V. Construction Ltd's contract was signed on 14 March 1992 with a 300 day contract Period. This period has now expired with only 4 percent of the work certified.

Despite numerous instructions and warnings the contractor has failed to perform. We hereby recommend that you, as the engineer, declare the Contractor, K.V. Construction Ltd., to be in default....'

Ultimately, after the lengthy process of directives. recommendations and advice, wisdom dawned on the experts and the top leadership of the Ministry of Works; and on 22nd April, 1993, the principal secretary of the Ministry of Works Dr. George Mlingwa wrote a letter Ref. No. MMC/R.30/10/97 to M/s K.V. Construction Limited cancelling the contract.

(iii) The process of cancelling the contract was finalised on 8th September, 1993 and the works handed over to MECCO on 20th August, 1993. In the original contract agreement with K.V. Construction Limited the cost had been estimated at Tshs 737,956,406/30 or an average of Tshs. 55,071,374 per kilometre. The final cost of the project was Tshs. 1,861,120,832/44 or an average of Tshs. 138,889,614.00 per kilometre. Work was formerly completed on 31st January 1995. The 152 percent increase in cost was the result of among other problems, the inordinate delay in the completion of the project because of poor selection of the contractor coupled with the failure by some experts and the top leadership of the Ministry of Works to heed the advice given by their juniors as well as by the project consultants.

(c) Views of the Commission

After careful analysis of the flow of events surrounding the appointment of K.V. Construction Limited for this contract, the Commission is satisfied that the company had deliberately been given unwarranted favour which was totally against tender procedures and without any consideration at all of the national interest. That the minister and the principal secretary of the Ministry of Works deliberately planned to defeat all attempts to prevent the contract being concluded with K.V. Construction Ltd; and afterwards, against recommendations to have the contract terminated early. Moreover, the senior officers of the Ministry especially the Director of Roads Mr. H.G. Urio and the Chief
Engineer rural roads Dr. P.F. Komba failed in their primary responsibilities of protecting the interests of the nation as well as professional ethics by not acting on time on the negative advice and recommendations of their juniors and the project consultants. By their inaction, the nation has incurred heavy losses financially and lost respect resulting in great inconvenience to the public which resulted in the people losing faith in their government.

505. **The Pugu - Chanika - Mbagala Road:**

(a) Length: 46.7 kilometres.

(b) Analysis of project:

(i) The contract for the construction of this rural road was signed by the Ministry of Works and M/s ADUCO. B.V. of Holland on 3rd February, 1992 at a price of Tshs 606,841,760.00 or Tshs 12, 994,470.00 per kilometre. According to the contract, it was to construct a murram road measuring 46.7 kilometres.

(ii) The contract was amended by a 'Contract Addendum' which varied the cost to Tshs 962,152,460.00 or an average of Tshs 20,602,836.40 per kilometre.

(iii) According to information received by the Commission from the principal secretary of the Ministry of Works, the road was faced by poor soils for the construction of embankment leading to an increased scope of work. The construction of the earth road was completed on 31st December, 1993.

(iv) The report by the principal secretary has added that the government sent a request to the Dutch government for the upgrading of the road to bitumen or murram standard and that the Dutch government had agreed in October 1995 to provide the necessary assistance on condition that the job be undertaken by the original contractor i.e. M/s ADUCO INT. B.V. and under the original contract. The second 'Contract Addendum' was signed on 18th October, 1995.

Thus the contract for the construction of this road had been varied twice. The first variation order raised the price from Tshs

606,841,760/= to Tshs 962,152,460/=; and the second Variation Order raised the cost further to Tshs 2,750,321,582.00 which is equal to an average of Tshs 58,893,396/= per kilometer.

(v) The sequence of events which led to the construction of an earth road instead of a gravel one and eventually forcing the citizens of this country and the government to incur heavy losses is as follows:

Bids had been received from the following four companies:

Appendix B: Data on Parastatal Characteristics

This Appendix indicates the parastatal sample and shows the data which has been used to group and characterise the companies according to their performance and other features.

Table B-1: The Parastatal Sample

Table B-1 lists the total of commercial parastatals *identified* in Tanzania, based on several sources (indicated in column e). Each parastatal has been assigned a unique code ranging from 1 to 392. The names marked in italics are 'companies' which were *excluded* after the data collection. These companies were either identified to be private companies, non-commercial parastatals and projects, companies which had been mentioned twice under different names, companies which ceased production prior to 1987 and companies which reflected sub-units of other parastatals (financially, they appear not to have been treated as individual entities). For 16 of the 56 companies information was entirely missing on both profits and losses and support (which again indicates that they may represent sub-units without separate accounting or that they are private companies).[211]

Since parastatals in Tanzania are embedded in a hierarchical structure of holding and affiliated companies, column (b) shows the holding relations (in parentheses the code of the holding company). Additional codes which define the location of a parastatal and the sector affiliation are mentioned in column (c) and (d). These codes are described in Tables B-2 and B-3. Location and sector codes allow aggregations at distinct levels of differentiation (1 to 5 digits), e.g. grouping companies according to the first digit only (1, 2, 3) or differentiating among the groups by including the second digit (11, 12, 13, 21, 22, 23, 31, 32).

Parastatal (Code, name, and in parentheses: abbreviation) (a)	Group (b)	Location (c)	Sector (d)	Source (e)
1. Afina Pencils Co Ltd	TKAI (326)	1210	33230	T93
2. African Marble Co Ltd		*9000*	*90000*	*M*
3. Agip (Tanzania) Ltd	TPDC (340)	1210	42220	M
4. Agricultural & Industrial Supplies Co Ltd (AISCO)	BIT (23)	1100	42130	M
5. Air Communications Technologies Co Ltd		9000	90000	M
6. Air Tanzania Corporation (ATC)	ATC	1210	43310	M
7. Aluminium Africa Ltd (ALAF)	NDC (186)	1210	36112	M
8. Arusha Burnt Bricks Ltd		9000	90000	M
9. Arusha Cooperative Union Ltd		2110	15000	Mx
10. Arusha International Conference Centre (AICC)	—	2110	44220	M
11. Arusha Metal Industries Ltd		9000	90000	M
12. Arusha Regional Trading Co Ltd ((RTC))	BIT (23)	2110	42120	M
13. Bagamoyo Farmers Ltd	NAFCO (181)	1233	14100	M
14. Bagamoyo Fishing Co Ltd (BAFICO)	—	1233	14200	M
15. Bahari Hotel Ltd		9000	90000	Mx
16. Basotu Plantations Ltd	NAFCO (181)	3211	12140	M

[211] No information: 8. Arusha Burnt Bricks Ltd, 11. Arusha Metal Industries Ltd, 20. BIT Export Co Ltd, 75. Kahama Gold Mines Ltd, 120. Lube Oil Co Ltd, 121. Lupa Gold Mines Co Ltd, 166. Mtua Saw Mills Ltd, 204. Natron Soda Co Ltd, 220. Plant and Equipment Hire Co Ltd, 285. TANSORT, 286. Tanzamex Cordage, 331. Tanzania Magnesite Co Ltd, 333. Tanzania Mexico Factory, 336. Tanzania Natural Development Co Ltd, 376. TTC Gift Shops Ltd, 382. Uvuvi Kigoma Ltd.

Also with 3 of the 28 cooperative unions (Karagwe, Biharamulo and Dar es Salaam Multipurpose) there was no information obtained. Cooperative unions are however all kept in the sample.

Parastatal (Code, name, and in parentheses: abbreviation) (a)	Group (b)	Location (c)	Sector (d)	Source (e)
17. Biashara Consumer Service Co Ltd (BCS)	BIT (23)	1210	42130	M
18. Biharamulo Cooperative Union Ltd		3232	15000	Mx
19. Bima Motors Ltd	NIC (191)	1210	42210	M
20. BIT Export Co Ltd		9000	90000	M
21. Blankets Manufactures Ltd (BML)	TEXCO (201)	1210	32213	M
22. Board of External Trade (BET)	BET	1210	42310	M
23. Board of Internal Trade (BIT)	BIT	1210	42110	M
24. BP (Tanzania) Ltd (BP[T])	TPDC (340)	1210	42220	M
25. Buck Reef Gold Mining Co Ltd	STAMICO (256)	3232	21410	M
26. Buha Cooperative Union Ltd		3129	15000	Mx
27. Building Hardware & Electrical Supplies Co Ltd (BHESCO)	BIT (23)	1210	42130	M
28. BUKOP Ltd		3122	11122	M
29. Burns and Blane (Tanzania) Ltd	SMC (257)	1210	36220	M
30. Capital Ceramics Co Ltd (CIL)	CDA (32)	1300	35220	M
31. Capital Construction Equipment Co Ltd (CAPCECO)	CDA (32)	1300	35240	M
32. Capital Development Authority (CDA)	CDA	1300	35210	M
33. Capital Supplies Co Ltd (CASCO)	CDA (32)	1300	35240	M
34. Central Maintenance Service Centre Ltd	NAFCO (181)	3211	42210	M
35. Central Region Cooperative Union Ltd		1300	15000	Mx
36. CMB Packaging Ltd (Metal Box)	NDC (186)	1210	36112	M
37. Coast Region Cooperative Union Ltd		1232	15000	Mx
38. Coast Regional Trading Co Ltd ((RTC))	BIT (23)	1232	42120	M
39. Coastal Salt Works Ltd	STAMICO (256)	1233	21300	M
40. Cooperative and Rural Development Bank (CRDB)	—	1100	45120	M
41. Cooperative Audit and Supervision Cor. (COASCO)	—	1210	46120	M
42. Cooperative Union of Tanzania		1210	15000	Mx
43. Dairy Farming Co -> see 307		9000	90000	M
44. Dakawa Rice Farm Ltd	NAFCO (181)	2321	12130	M
45. Dar es Salaam Airport Handling Co Ltd (DAHACO)	ATC (6)	1210	43310	M
46. Dar es Salaam Multipurpose Coop Union Ltd		1210	15000	Mx
47. Dar es Salaam Regional Trading Co Ltd ((RTC))	BIT (23)	1210	42120	M
48. Dar es Salaam Textile Co Ltd (DARTEX)	BIT (23)	1210	42130	T92
49. Darbrew Ltd	—	1220	31420	M
50. Dindira Tea Estate Ltd	TTA (359)	2221	11312	M
51. Dodoma Brick & Tile Works Ltd	CDA (32)	9000	90000	M
52. Dodoma Regional Trading Co Ltd ((RTC))	BIT (23)	1300	42120	M
53. Dodoma Wine Co Ltd (DOWICO)	NMC (193)	1300	31500	M
54. East Africa Publication Ltd (EAPL)	TKAI (326)	2110	33240	M
55. East Usambara Tea Co		9000	90000	Mx
56. Enterprise (Tanzania) Ltd - Embassy Hotel	—	1210	44210	M
57. Express Tanzania Ltd	SMC (257)	1210	36220	M
58. Fibreboards Africa Ltd (FAL)	TWICO (369)	2110	33130	M
59. Friendship Textile Mill Ltd (URAFIKI)	TEXCO (201)	1210	32212	M
60. Gawal Wheat Co Ltd	NAFCO (181)	3211	12140	M
61. General Agricultural Products Export Corporation (GAPEX)		9000	90000	E93
62. General Tyre East Africa Ltd	NCI (185)	2110	34220	M
63. Gidagamowd Wheat Co Ltd	NAFCO (181)	3211	12140	M
64. Giraffe Extract Co Ltd	TWICO (369)	2221	33130	M
65. Hotel Seventy Seven Ltd	TTCorp (364)	2110	44121	M
66. Household Supplies Co Ltd (HOSCO)	BIT (23)	1210	42130	M
67. Imara Wood Products Ltd	TWICO (369)	2120	33130	M
68. Integrated Concrete Industries Ltd (ICIL)	CDA (32)	1300	35230	M
69. Iringa Maintenance Co Ltd (IMCO)		3111	42210	M
70. Iringa Regional Trading Co Ltd ((RTC))	BIT (23)	3111	42120	M
71. Iringa/Mufundi Cooperative Union Ltd		3111	15000	Mx
72. Kagera Cooperative Union Ltd		3122	15000	Mx

Parastatal (Code, name, and in parentheses: abbreviation) (a)	Group (b)	Location (c)	Sector (d)	Source (e)
73. Kagera Regional Trading Co ((RTC))	BIT (23)	3122	42120	M
74. Kagera Sugar Co Ltd	SUDECO (263)	3232	31330	M
75. Kahama Gold Mines Ltd	STAMICO (256)	9000	90000	Mx
76. Kahe Estates Co Ltd	NAFCO (181)	3212	11320	M
77. Kampuni ya Uchukuzi Dodoma (KAUDO)	NTC (202)	1300	43120	M
78. Kampuni ya Uchukuzi Iringa (KAURI)	NTC (202)	3111	43120	M
79. Kampuni ya Uchukuzi Kagera	NTC (202)	3122	43120	M
80. Kampuni ya Uchukuzi Mbeya	NTC (202)	3127	43120	M
81. Kampuni ya Uchukuzi Mkoa wa Lindi (KAULI)	NTC (202)	3113	43120	M
82. Kampuni ya Uchukuzi Mtwara (KAUMU)	NTC (202)	3125	43120	M
83. Kampuni ya Uchukuzi Mwanza (KAUMA)	NTC (202)	3121	43120	M
84. Kampuni ya Uchukuzi Ruvuma (KAURU)	NTC (202)	3126	43120	M
85. Kampuni ya Uchukuzi Tabora (KAUTA)	NTC (202)	3128	43120	M
86. Karadha Co Ltd	NBC (182)	1210	45110	M
87. Karagwe Cooperative Union		3232	15000	Mx
88. Kariakoo Market Corporation	—	1210	42320	M
89. Keko Pharmaceutical Industries Ltd (KPI)	NCI (185)	1210	34240	M
90. Kibo Match Corporation		2120	33330	E95
91. Kibo Paper Industries Ltd	TKAI (326)	1210	33220	M
92. Kigamboni Poultry Farm Ltd	NAFCO (181)	2310	14100	M
93. Kigoma Regional Trading Co Ltd ((RTC))	BIT (23)	3129	42120	M
94. Kilimanjaro Hotels Ltd	TTCorp (364)	1210	44121	M
95. Kilimanjaro Machine Tools Manufacturing Co Ltd (KMT)	NDC (186)	3212	36113	M
96. Kilimanjaro Native Cooperative Union Ltd (KNCU)		2120	15000	Mx
97. Kilimanjaro Regional Trading Co Ltd ((RTC))	BIT (23)	2120	42120	M
98. Kilimanjaro Textile Corporation Ltd (KILTEX)	TEXCO (201)	1220	32213	M
99. Kilimanjaro Timber Utilisation Co Ltd (KILTIMBER)	TWICO (369)	2120	33130	M
100. Kilombero Sugar Co Ltd	SUDECO (263)	2321	31330	M
101. Kilombero Sugar Institute -> see 100		9000	90000	M
102. Kilosa Carpet Co Ltd -> see 295		9000	90000	Mx
103. Kilwa Ammonia Co Ltd (KILAMCO)	TPDC (340)	3113	34112	M
104. Kimamba Sisal Estates Co Ltd	TSA (354)	2210	11512	M
105. Kisarawe Brick Factory	NHC (190)	1210	35330	M
106. Kiwanda cha Zana za Kilimo Ubungo Ltd (UFI)	NDC (186)	1210	36113	M
107. Kiwira Coal Mines Co Ltd	STAMICO (256)	3127	21200	M
108. Korea Tanzania Agricultural Joint Co Ltd		9000	90000	M
109. Kunduchi Beach Hotel Ltd	TTCorp (364)	1210	44121	M
110. Kwamkono TEA Estates Ltd		9000	90000	T88
111. Kwamtili Estate Ltd		2221	11512	M
112. Kyela/Rungwe Cooperative Union Ltd		3231	15000	Mx
113. Landrover Tanzania Ltd (LRT)	SMC (257)	1210	36230	M
114. Lehmans (EA) Ltd		9000	90000	Mx
115. Lewa Estates Ltd		3127	11512	M
116. Light Source Manufacturers Ltd (LSM)	NDC (186)	1210	36114	M
117. Lindi Regional Cooperative Union Ltd		3113	15000	Mx
118. Lindi Regional Trading Co Ltd ((RTC))	BIT (23)	3113	42120	M
119. Longido Gemstone Mining Co Ltd	STAMICO (256)	2120	21430	Mx
120. Lube Oil Co Ltd		9000	90000	M
121. Lupa Gold Mines Co Ltd	STAMICO (256)	9000	90000	M
122. Mafia Coconuts		9000	90000	Mx
123. Mafia Island Lodge	TTCorp (364)	2232	44122	M
124. Mafuta ya Ilulu Ltd	—	3222	31700	M
125. Mang'ula Mechanical and Machine Tools Co Ltd (MMMT)	NDC (186)	2321	36113	M
126. Mara Cooperative Union Ltd		3124	15000	Mx
127. Mara Regional Trading Co Ltd ((RTC))	BIT (23)	3124	42120	M
128. Mbarali Rice Farms Ltd	NAFCO (181)	3231	12130	M

Parastatal (Code, name, and in parentheses: abbreviation) (a)	Group (b)	Location (c)	Sector (d)	Source (e)
129. Mbeya Cement Co Ltd	TSjC (349)	3127	35131	M
130. Mbeya Ceramics Ltd	SIDO (252)	3127	35420	M
131. Mbeya Cooperative Union Ltd (Mbecu)		3127	15000	Mx
132. Mbeya Regional Trading Co Ltd ((RTC))	BIT (23)	3127	42120	M
133. Mbeya Textile Mills Ltd (MBEYATEX)	TEXCO (201)	3127	32212	M
134. Mbinga Coffee Curing Co Ltd	TCofMB (301)	3231	11113	M
135. Mbinga Cooperative Union Ltd		3231	15000	Mx
136. Mbozi Coffee Curing Co Ltd	TCofMB (301)	3127	11113	M
137. Mbozi Coffee Farms Ltd	NAFCO (181)	3127	11122	M
138. Mbozi Maize Farms Ltd	NAFCO (181)	3127	12120	M
139. Mikumi Hotels Co Ltd	TTCorp (364)	2321	44121	M
140. Mingoyo Sawmill Co Ltd (MISACO)	TWICO (369)	3113	33120	M
141. Minjingu Phosphate Co Ltd (MIPCO)	STAMICO (256)	2110	21300	M
142. Mkate Sawmills Ltd	TWICO (369)	1233	33120	M
143. Mkonge Hotels Ltd		9000	90000	Mx
144. Mkonge Livestock Co Ltd (MLICO)	TSA (354)	2322	14100	M
145. Mombo Sisal Estates Co Ltd (MOSECO)	TSA (354)	2322	11512	M
146. Monact Seed Co Ltd		2110	13100	M
147. MOPROCO-> see 173		9000	90000	M
148. Morogoro Bag Factory		9000	90000	Mx
149. Morogoro Canvas Mill Ltd	TLAI (327)	2210	32312	M
150. Morogoro Ceramic Wares Ltd (MOCERA)	TSjC (349)	2210	35120	M
151. Morogoro Hotel Ltd		2210	44210	M
152. Morogoro Leather Board	TLAI (327)	2210	32312	M
153. Morogoro Leather Goods Co Ltd	TLAI (327)	2210	32313	M
154. Morogoro Polyester Textiles Ltd (POLYTEX)	TEXCO (201)	2210	32212	M
155. Morogoro Region Cooperative Union Ltd		2210	15000	Mx
156. Morogoro Regional Trading Co Ltd ((RTC))	BIT (23)	2210	42120	M
157. Morogoro Regional Transport Co Ltd (MORETCO)	NTC (202)	2210	43120	M
158. Morogoro Shoe Co Ltd (MOROSHOE)	TLAI (327)	2210	32313	M
159. Morogoro Sisal Estates Ltd	TSA (354)	2321	11512	M
160. Morogoro Tanneries Ltd (MOROTAN)	TLAI (327)	2210	32312	M
161. Moshi Hand Tools Ltd		2120	36123	M
162. Moshi Hotels Ltd	TTCorp (364)	2120	44121	M
163. Motor Mart (Tanzania) Ltd	NDC (186)	1210	36113	M
164. Mount Meru Hotels Ltd	TTCorp (364)	2110	44121	M
165. Mtibwa Sugar Estates Ltd	SUDECO (263)	2321	31320	M
166. Mtua Saw Mills Ltd	TWICO (369)	9000	90000	M
167. Mtwara Cashew Co Ltd	TCashMB (296)	3125	11412	M
168. Mtwara Region Cooperative Union Ltd		3125	15000	Mx
169. Mtwara Regional Trading Co Ltd ((RTC))	BIT (23)	3125	42120	M
170. Mufindi Tea Co		9000	90000	Mx
171. Muheza Sisal Estates Co Ltd	TSA (354)	2322	11512	M
172. Mulbadaw Wheat Farms Ltd	NAFCO (181)	3211	12140	M
173. Multipurpose Oilseed Processing Co Ltd (MOPROCO)	TCotMB (304)	2210	31700	T93
174. Murjanda Wheat Co Ltd	NAFCO (181)	3211	12140	M
175. Musoma Textile Ltd (MUTEX)	TEXCO (201)	3124	32213	M
176. Mwananchi Engineering & Contracting Corp. (MECCO)	—	1210	35440	M
177. Mwanza Brewery Ltd	TBL (292)	3121	31413	M
178. Mwanza Regional Trading Co Ltd ((RTC))	BIT (23)	3121	42120	M
179. Mwanza Tanneries Ltd	TLAI (327)	3121	32312	M
180. Mwanza Textiles Ltd (MWATEX)	TEXCO (201)	3121	32213	M
181. National Agricultural and Food Corporation (NAFCO)	NAFCO	1100	12110	M
182. National Bank of Commerce (NBC)	NBC	1100	45110	M
183. National Bicycles Co Ltd (NABICO)	NDC (186)	1210	36115	M
184. National Bus Services Ltd (KAMATA)	NTC (202)	1210	43130	T93

Parastatal (Code, name, and in parentheses: abbreviation) (a)	Group (b)	Location (c)	Sector (d)	Source (e)
185. National Chemical Industries (NCI)	NCI	1210	34210	M
186. National Development Corporation (NDC)	NDC	1210	36111	M
187. National Distributors Co Ltd (NDL)	NMC (193)	1210	42320	M
188. National Engineering Co Ltd (NECO)	NDC (186)	1210	35440	M
189. National Estates and Designing Corporation (NEDCO)	—	1210	35440	M
190. National Housing Corporation (NHC)	NHC	1100	35310	M
191. National Insurance Corp of Tanzania (NIC)	NIC	1100	45320	M
192. National Lotteries	—	1210	45400	M
193. National Milling Corporation (NMC)	NMC	1100	31200	M
194. National Pharmaceutical Co Ltd (NAPCO)	BIT (23)	1210	42130	M
195. National Poultry Co Ltd (NAPOCO)	NAPOCO	1210	14100	M
196. National Printing Co Ltd (NPC)	TKAI (326)	1210	33240	M
197. National Provident Fund (NPF)	—	1210	45310	M
198. National Ranching Co Ltd (NARCO)	NARCO	1100	14100	M
199. National Shipping Agencies Co Ltd (NASACO)	BIT (23)	1220	43400	M
200. National Steel Corporation (NSC)	NDC (186)	1210	36112	M
201. National Textile Corporation (TEXCO)	TEXCO	1210	32211	M
202. National Transport Corporation (NTC)	NTC	1210	43110	M
203. National Urban Water Authority (NUWA)	—	1210	41200	M
204. Natron Soda Co Ltd	STAMICO (256)	9000	90000	M
205. New Africa Hotels Ltd	TTCorp (364)	1210	44121	M
206. New Almasi (1967) Ltd -> see 387	STAMICO (256)	9000	90000	M
207. New Mwanza Hotels Ltd	TTCorp (364)	3121	44121	M
208. New Safari Hotel (1967) Ltd	TTCorp (364)	2110	44121	M
209. New Sugar Co Ltd		9000	90000	Mx
210. Ngombezi Bag Project		9000	90000	Mx
211. Ngombezi Sisal Estate Co Ltd	TSA (354)	2322	11512	M
212. Ngorongoro Conservation Area Authority	—	3211	44300	T92
213. Njombe/Ludewa/Makete Cooperative Union Ltd		3221	15000	Mx
214. Nyanza Cooperative Union Ltd		3121	15000	Mx
215. Nyanza Engineering & Foundry Co Ltd (NEFCO)	SIDO (252)	3121	36122	M
216. Nyanza Glass Works	TSjC (349)	3121	35120	M
217. Nyanza Salt Mines (Tanganyika) Ltd	STAMICO (256)	3231	21300	M
218. Pamba Engineering Co Ltd	TCotMB (304)	3121	36123	M
219. Peoples Bank of Zanzibar Ltd (PBZ)		9000	90000	Z
220. Plant and Equipment Hire Co Ltd (PEHCOL)		9000	90000	Mx
221. Polysacks Co Ltd	NCI (185)	1210	34230	M
222. Printpak (Tanzania) Ltd	TKAI (326)	1210	33240	M
223. Pugu Kaolin Mines Co Ltd	STAMICO (256)	1231	21300	M
224. Ralli Estates	TSA (354)	2221	11512	Mx
225. Rasilimali Ltd	TIB (325)	1210	45130	M
226. Riddoch Motors Ltd		9000	90000	T84
227. Rift Valley Cooperative Union Ltd		3211	15000	Mx
228. Rift Valley Seed Co Ltd (RVSL)	NAFCO (181)	3211	12150	M
229. Rotian Seed		9000	90000	Mx
230. Rubber Industries Ltd	NCI (185)	1210	34220	M
231. Rukwa Region Cooperative Union Ltd		3231	15000	Mx
232. Rukwa Regional Trading Co Ltd ((RTC))	BIT (23)	3231	42120	M
233. Rukwa Regional Transport Co Ltd	NTC (202)	3231	43120	M
234. Ruvu Rice Farms Ltd	NAFCO (181)	2310	12130	M
235. Ruvuma Cooperative Union (1989) Ltd -> see 236		9000	90000	Mx
236. Ruvuma Cooperative Union Ltd		3126	15000	Mx
237. Ruvuma Regional Trading Co Ltd ((RTC))	BIT (23)	3126	42120	M
238. Sabuni Industries Ltd	NCI (185)	2221	34250	M
239. Sao Hill Sawmill Ltd	TWICO (369)	3221	33120	M
240. Saruji Trucking Co Ltd	TSjC (349)	1210	35140	M

Parastatal (Code, name, and in parentheses: abbreviation) (a)	Group (b)	Location (c)	Sector (d)	Source (e)
241. Savoy Hotel Ltd	TTCorp (364)	2210	44121	M
242. Serengeti Safari Lodges (T) Ltd (SSL)	TTCorp (364)	3232	44122	M
243. Setchet Wheat Co Ltd	NAFCO (181)	2110	12140	M
244. Shinyanga Region Cooperative Union Ltd		3123	15000	Mx
245. Shinyanga Regional Trading Co Ltd ((RTC))	BIT (23)	3123	42120	M
246. Shirika la Usafiri Dar es Salaam Ltd (UDA)	NTC (202)	1210	43130	M
247. Sikh Saw Mills Ltd	TWICO (369)	2221	33120	M
248. Singida Region Cooperative Union Ltd		3112	15000	Mx
249. Singida Regional Trading Co Ltd ((RTC))	BIT (23)	3112	42120	M
250. Sisal Kamba Spinning Co Ltd	TSA (354)	2221	32111	M
251. Sisalana/Hycogenin Products Ltd		9000	90000	Mx
252. Small Industries Development Organisation (SIDO)	SIDO	1100	46130	M
253. Southern Paper Mills Co Ltd (SPM)	NDC (186)	3221	33320	M
254. State Fuel Corporation (SFC)		2231	41100	Z
255. State Insurance Brokers (SIB)	NIC (191)	1210	45320	M
256. State Mining Corporation (STAMICO)	STAMICO	1210	21100	M
257. State Motor Corporation (SMC)	SMC	1210	36210	M
258. State Trading Co		9000	90000	E93
259. State Travel Service Ltd (STS)	TTCorp (364)	1220	44130	M
260. Stationary and Office Supplies (T) Ltd (S&O)	BIT (23)	1210	42130	M
261. Steel Rolling Mills Ltd (SRM)	NDC (186)	2221	36112	M
262. Stone Valley Tea Co Ltd		9000	90000	Mx
263. Sugar Development Corporation (SUDECO)	SUDECO	1210	31310	M
264. Tabora Msitu Products Ltd	TWICO (369)	3128	33130	M
265. Tabora Region Cooperative Union Ltd (Tarecu)		3128	15000	Mx
266. Tabora Regional Trading Co Ltd ((RTC))	BIT (23)	3128	42120	M
267. Tabora Textile Mills Co Ltd (TABOTEX)	TEXCO (201)	3128	32212	M
268. Tanga Cement Co Ltd	TSjC (349)	2221	35131	M
269. Tanga Cooperative Union Ltd		2221	15000	Mx
270. Tanga Regional Trading Co Ltd ((RTC))	BIT (23)	2221	42120	M
271. Tanganyika Coffee Curing Co Ltd	TCofMB (301)	2120	11113	M
272. Tanganyika Dyeing and Weaving Co Ltd (SUNGURATEX)	TEXCO (201)	1210	32212	M
273. Tanganyika Farmers' Association		9000	90000	Mx
274. Tanganyika Industrial Organisation		9000	90000	Mx
275. Tanganyika Instant Coffee Co Ltd (TANICA)	TCofMB (301)	3122	11113	M
276. Tanganyika Meerschaum Corporation	STAMICO (256)	2110	21500	M
277. Tanganyika Packers Ltd (TPL)	—	1210	43500	M
278. Tanganyika Planting Co Ltd (TPC)	SUDECO (263)	3212	31320	M
279. Tanganyika Post Office Savings Bank	TPTC (344)	1100	45150	M
280. Tanganyika Pyrethrum Board (TPB)	—	3111	11610	M
281. Tanganyika Tegry (Plastics) Ltd	NCI (185)	1210	34230	M
282. Tangold Products Co Ltd	NMC (193)	1210	13100	M
283. Tanita Company Ltd	TCashMB (296)	1210	11412	M
284. Tanscan Timber Co Ltd	TWICO (369)	9000	90000	Mx
285. TANSORT		9000	90000	M
286. Tanzamex Cordage	TSA (354)	9000	90000	Mx
287. Tanzania and Italian Petroleum Refining Co Ltd (TIPER)	TPDC (340)	1210	34112	M
288. Tanzania Animal Feeds Co Ltd (TAFCO)	NMC (193)	1210	31200	M
289. Tanzania Audit Corporation (TAC)	—	1220	46120	M
290. Tanzania Automobile Manufacturing Co Ltd (TAMCO)	SMC (257)	1232	36230	M
291. Tanzania Bag Corporation Ltd	TEXCO (201)	2120	32213	M
292. Tanzania Breweries Ltd (TBL)	TBL	1210	31411	M
293. Tanzania Building Society (TBS?)		9000	90000	M
294. Tanzania Cables Ltd	NDC (186)	1210	36114	M
295. Tanzania Carpet Co Ltd	TSA (354)	3212	32112	M
296. Tanzania Cashewnut Marketing Board (TCashMB)	TCashMB	3125	11411	M

Parastatal (Code, name, and in parentheses: abbreviation) (a)	Group (b)	Location (c)	Sector (d)	Source (e)
297. Tanzania Central Freight Bureau (TCFB)	—	1210	43500	M
298. Tanzania Cigarette Co Ltd (TCC)	—	1210	31600	M
299. Tanzania Clay Products Ltd	TSjC (349)	2110	35132	M
300. Tanzania Coastal Shipping Line Ltd (TACOSHILI)	NTC (202)	1210	43130	M
301. Tanzania Coffee Marketing Board (TCofMB)	TCofMB	2120	11111	M
302. Tanzania Concrete Articles Ltd (TACONA)	NHC (190)	1210	35330	M
303. Tanzania Cordage Ltd (TANCORD)	TSA (354)	2221	32112	M
304. Tanzania Cotton Marketing Board (TCotMB)	TCotMB	1210	11210	M
305. Tanzania Crown Corks Ltd		1210	33330	M
306. Tanzania Dairies Ltd (TDL)	TDL	1210	31120	M
307. Tanzania Dairy Farming Co Ltd (DAFCO)	TDL (306)	1100	31110	M
308. Tanzania Diamond Cutting Co Ltd (TANCUT)	STAMICO (256)	3111	21420	M
309. Tanzania Distilleries Ltd		1210	31500	M
310. Tanzania Electric Supply Co Ltd (TANESCO)	—	1100	41100	M
311. Tanz. Electrical Goods Manufacturing Co Ltd (TANELEC)	NDC (186)	2110	36114	M
312. Tanzania Elimu Supplies (TES)	TES	1210	33330	M
313. Tanz. Engineering & Manufacturing Design Org. (TEMDO)	—	2110	35440	M
314. Tanzania Fertilizer Co Ltd (TAFECO)	NCI (185)	2221	34250	M
315. Tanzania Film Co Ltd (TFC)	—	1210	46200	M
316. Tanzania Fisheries Corporation (TAFICO)	—	1210	14200	M
317. Tanzania Gemstone Industries Ltd	STAMICO (256)	2120	21430	M
318. Tanzania Gypsum Co Ltd		3212	35430	M
319. Tanz. Handicrafts Marketing Corporation Ltd (HANDICO)	SIDO (252)	1210	42320	M
320. Tanzania Harbours Authority (THA)	—	1220	43400	M
321. Tanzania Hides and Skins Ltd (TANHIDE)	—	1100	32320	M
322. Tanzania Hotels Investment Ltd (TAHI)		1210	45220	M
323. Tanzania Housing Bank (THB)	THB	1210	45210	M
324. Tanzania Industrial Studies and Consulting Org. (TISCO)	—	1210	46130	M
325. Tanzania Investment Bank (TIB)	TIB	1210	45130	M
326. Tanzania Karatasi Associated Industries (TKAI)	TKAI	1210	33210	M
327. Tanzania Leather Associated Industries (TLAI)	TLAI	1210	32311	M
328. Tanzania Legal Corporation (TLC)	—	1210	46110	M
329. Tanzania Liquids Storage Co Ltd		9000	90000	M
330. Tanzania Livestock Marketing Co Ltd		1100	42320	T87
331. Tanzania Magnesite Co Ltd	STAMICO (256)	9000	90000	M
332. Tanzania Maltings Co Ltd (TAMACO)	TBL (292)	2120	31413	M
333. Tanzania Mexico Factory (TANZAMEX)		9000	90000	M
334. Tanzania Motor Services Co Ltd (TMSC)	SMC (257)	1210	36220	M
335. Tanzania National Parks (TANAPA)	—	2110	44300	M
336. Tanzania Natural Development Co Ltd (TANADE)		9000	90000	M
337. Tanzania News Agency (SHIHATA)	—	1210	46200	M
338. Tanzania Oxygen Ltd (TOL)	NDC (186)	1210	34300	M
339. Tanzania Packages Manufacturers Ltd	TEXCO (201)	2210	32213	M
340. Tanzania Petroleum Development Corporation (TPDC)	TPDC	1210	34111	M
341. Tanzania Pharmaceutical Industries Ltd (TPI)	NCI (185)	2110	34240	M
342. Tanzania Portland Cement Co Ltd (TPCC)	TSjC (349)	1210	35131	M
343. Tanzania Postal Bank		1210	45150	T93
344. Tanzania Posts & Telecom. Cor. (TPTC) -> under 362)[212]	TPTC	9000	90000	M
345. Tanzania Posts Corporation		1100	41320	T-i
346. Tanzania Publishing House Ltd (TPH)	TKAI (326)	1210	33240	M
347. Tanzania Railways Corporation (TRC)	TRC	1100	43210	M

212 After 1993 Tanzania Posts & Telecommunications Corporation (344) appears as two companies: Tanzania Posts Corporation (345) and Tanzania Telecommunications Co Ltd (362). Since the latter is considerably larger, TPTC (344) has been taken out and the data was assigned to TTCL (362).

Parastatal (Code, name, and in parentheses: abbreviation) (a)	Group (b)	Location (c)	Sector (d)	Source (e)
348. Tanzania Railways Hotels-> 347	TRC (347)	9000	90000	Mx
349. Tanzania Saruji Corporation (TSjC)	TSjC	1210	35110	M
350. Tanzania Seed Co Ltd (TANSEED)	—	3211	13100	M
351. Tanzania Sewing Thread Manufacturers Co Ltd	TEXCO (201)	1210	32212	M
352. Tanzania Sheet Glass Ltd	TSjC (349)	1210	35120	M
353. Tanzania Shoe Co Ltd (BORA)	TLAI (327)	1210	32313	M
354. Tanzania Sisal Authority (TSA)	TSA	2221	11511	M
355. Tanzania Standard Newspapers Ltd	—	1210	33340	M
356. Tanzania Starch Manufacturers Co Ltd (TSMC)	NCI (185)	3232	34250	M
357. Tanzania Stationery Manufacturers Co Ltd (TSMC)	TES (312)	1210	33330	M
358. Tanzania Tanneries Co Ltd	TLAI (327)	2120	32312	M
359. Tanzania Tea Authority (TTA)	TTA	1210	11311	M
360. Tanzania Tea Blenders Ltd (TTB)	TTA (359)	1210	11313	M
361. Tanzania Telecommunication Commission		9000	90000	T-i
362. Tanzania Telecommunications Company Ltd (TTCL)		1100	41330	T-i
363. Tanzania Tobacco Processing & Marketing Board (TTMB)		2210	11710	M
364. Tanzania Tourist Board (TTCorp)	TTCorp	1210	44110	M
365. Tanzania Tractors Manufacturing Co Ltd (TRAMA)	SMC (257)	1232	36230	M
366. Tanzania Twine & Rope Works Ltd		9000	90000	E93
367. Tanzania Watch Assembling Co Ltd (TWACO)	NDC (186)	1210	36115	M
368. Tanzania Wildlife Corporation (TAWICO)	—	2110	44300	M
369. Tanzania Wood Industry Corporation (TWICO)	TWICO	1210	33110	M
370. Tanzania Zambia Railway Authority (TAZARA)	—	1100	43210	M
371. TBL Farms Ltd	TBL (292)	3211	31412	M
372. TDFL		9000	90000	Mx
373. Tembo Chipboards Ltd	TWICO (369)	2222	33130	M
374. THB Estates Ltd (TECO)	THB (323)	1210	45210	M
375. Trailers & Lowloaders Manufacturing Co Ltd (TRALLCO)	SMC (257)	1210	36230	M
376. TTC Gift Shops Ltd	TTC (364)	9000	90000	M
377. Twiga Plantation		9000	90000	Mx
378. Typesetting Services Ltd	TKAI (326)	1210	33240	T93
379. Ubungo Garments Ltd (UGL)	TEXCO (201)	1210	32213	M
380. Ubungo Spinning Mill Ltd (USM)	TEXCO (201)	1210	32212	M
381. Ushirikiano Wood Products Co Ltd (UWP)	TWICO (369)	1210	33130	M
382. Uvuvi Kigoma Ltd	TWICO (369)	9000	90000	M
383. Uyole Agricultural College (UAC)	—	9000	90000	M
384. Vuasu Cooperative Union Ltd		3212	15000	Mx
385. Warret Wheat Farms Ltd	NAFCO (181)	3211	12140	M
386. West Kilimanjaro Livestock Breeding Farm		3212	14100	M
387. Williamson Diamonds Ltd	STAMICO (256)	3232	21420	M
388. Zana Za Kilimo Ltd (ZZK)	NDC (186)	3127	36113	M
389. Zanzibar Insurance Corporation		9000	90000	Z
390. Zanzibar Shipping Corporation		2231	43400	Z
391. Zanzibar State Trading		2231	42320	Z
392. ZZ COTEX Zanzibar		2231	32220	Z

Sources: Parastatals identified according to the Masterplan (M: PSRC (1993)), a preliminary version of the Masterplan obtained at the Treasury (Mx); annual reports from Tanzania Audit Corporation (T84, T87, T88, T92, T93: TAC (1984-93)), TAC interviews (T-i), 4 companies (E93, E94) mentioned in Eriksson (1993) and Eriksson (1994) and 6 parastatals from Zanzibar (Z) added during data collection. Information on holding relations (column b) is based on these reports and interviews, as well as on various 'Reviews and Action Plans' from PSRC and a 'Parastatal Organisation Directory' provided by the Treasury (GoT (1988a)). Not explicitly specified are the holding companies 22, 195, 198, 347, as there was no information on subsidiaries (subsidiaries are probably not treated as individual parastatals but integrated).

Table B-2: Coding According to Location

Being close to the centre may matter when it comes to lobbying for government support. In contrast, being further away from the centre is likely to increase parastatal autonomy and thereby opportunities to embezzle funds. To be able to test these hypotheses and to describe the distribution, parastatals were assigned a four-digit code reflecting the distance and connections to the centre. The coding divides the sample into three major groups: parastatals which have a stake in the *centre*, parastatals located in *sub-centres and near the centre* and parastatals in *remote areas*. The figures in parentheses indicate the total number of parastatals in a group or sub-group.

Since Dodoma is the official capital of Tanzania and is the seat of the parliament (which may also be relevant for lobbying) it is listed within the group *centre*. There are, however, equally acceptable arguments which would justify another assignment (Dodoma could be considered a sub-centre or a remote place as it is far away from both the capital and tourist centres).

The sub-group *'Dar es Salaam & other'* specifies companies which are located in two or more cities, including Dar es Salaam. *Nationwide* companies, finally, have their main branch in the centre Dar es Salaam (and other towns) and a large number of subsidiaries in remote areas.

Digits 1-2	Digit 3	Digit 4
1. Centre (157)		
1.1 Nationwide (18)		
1.2 DSM (130)	1.2.1 Dar es Salaam only (115)	
	1.2.2 Dar es Salaam & other (6)	
	1.2.3 Dar es Salaam suburb (9)	.1 Kisarawe, .2 Kibaha, .3 Bagamoyo
1.3 Dodoma (9)		
2. Sub-centre / near-centre (81)		
2.1 Arusha & Moshi (33)	2.1.1 Arusha (19)	
	2.1.2 Moshi (14)	
2.2 Towns near DSM (36)	2.2.1 Morogoro (16)	
	2.2.2 Tanga/Korogwe (15)	.1 Tanga, .2 Korogwe
	2.2.3 Zanzibar & Mafia (5)	.1 Zanzibar, .2 Mafia Island
2.3 Rural near DSM (12)	2.3.1 DSM rural (2)	
	2.3.2 Morogoro & Tanga rural (10)	.1 Morogoro, .2 Tanga
3. Remote areas (98)		
3.1 Towns (60)	3.1.1 Towns moderate far (13)	.1 Iringa, .2 Singida, .3 Lindi/Kilwa
	3.1.2 Towns far (47)	.1 Mwanza, .2 Bukoba, .3 Shinyanga, .4 Musoma, .5 Mtwara, .6 Songea, .7 Mbeya, .8 Tabora, .9 Kigoma
3.2 Rural (38)	3.2.1 Arusha & Moshi rural (19)	.1 Arusha, .2 Moshi & Kilimanjaro
	3.2.2 Rural moderate far (4)	.1 Iringa, .2 Lindi
	3.2.3 Rural far (15)	.1 South/West: Mtwara, Ruvuma, Mbeya, Rukwa, Kigoma, .2 North/West: Mara, Mwanza, Shinyanga, Kagera

PS/ Code 9000: Companies excluded (56)

Table B-3: Sector Coding

To be able to undertake a more specific economic interpretation of parastatal characteristics and support, parastatals have been additionally grouped according to the sector affiliation. The table shows the definitions applied for the 5-digit sector coding. Again, figures in parentheses indicate the total of parastatals assigned to a group or sub-group.

The grouping is defined to mirror the institutional and economic structure in Tanzania. It reflects a compromise between a standardised *ISIC-classification* (International Standard Industrial Classification), a classification according to *product lines* (e.g. coffee plantation, coffee processing, and coffee trading) and a classification according to *parastatal holding relations*. Given the horizontal and vertical diversification of holding companies, it has, however, not always been possible to unify all affiliated companies in one group.[213]

Digits 1-3	Digit 4	Digit 5	Code	No.
1. Agriculture (78)				
1.1 Cash crops (26)				
1.1.1 Coffee (7)	.1 Coffee marketing board	.1 Marketing board	11111	(1)
		.3 Coffee curing / other	11113	(4)
	.2 Other	.2 Plantation	11122	(2)
1.1.2 Cotton (1)	.1 Cotton marketing board		11210	(1)
1.1.3 Tea (4)	.1 Tanzania Tea Authority	.1 Marketing board	11311	(1)
		.2 Plantation	11312	(1)
		.3 Blenders	11313	(1)
	.2 Other		11320	(1)
1.1.4 Cashew (3)	.1 Cashew marketing board	.1 Marketing board	11411	(1)
		.2 Companies	11412	(2)
1.1.5 Sisal (9)	.1 Tanzania Sisal Authority	.1 Marketing board	11511	(1)
		.2 Estates	11512	(8)
1.1.6 Pyrethrum (1)	.1 Tanganyika Pyrethrum Board		11610	(1)
1.1.7 Tobacco (1)	.1 Tanz. Tobacco Processing & Marketing Board		11710	(1)
1.2 Food crops (13)				
1.2.1 NAFCO (13)	.1 Marketing board		12110	(1)
	.2 Maize		12120	(1)
	.3 Paddy / rice		12130	(3)
	.4 Wheat		12140	(7)
	.5 Seed / not identified		12150	(1)
1.3 Other plants (3)				
1.3.1 Seed & spices (3)			13100	(3)
1.4 Live animals (8)				
1.4.1 Livestock (6)			14100	(6)
1.4.2 Fishery (2)			14200	(2)
1.5 Cooperative unions (28)			15000	(28)
2. Mining (12)				
2.1 STAMICO (12)				
2.1.1 Holding (1)			21100	(1)

213 Companies not in same group or sub-group as holding: 3, 19, 24, 34, 53, 92, 130, 137, 144, 173, 187, 199, 215, 218, 250, 253, 279, 286, 295, 303, 319, 338, 348.

Note, the coding in sub-groups does not necessarily start with 1 or may leave out numbers. This is of no consequence but has been applied to describe congruencies between close sub-groups (e.g. using for marketing board (.x.x.x.x.1), for plantation (x.x.x.x.2), etc.).

Digits 1-3	Digit 4	Digit 5	Code	No.
2.1.2 Coal (1)			21200	(1)
2.1.3 Salt & other (4)			21300	(4)
2.1.4 Gold, diamond, gemstone (5)	.1 Gold mines		21410	(1)
	.2 Diamond		21420	(2)
	.3 Gemstone		21430	(2)
2.1.5 Meerschaum (1)			21500	(1)

3. Manufacturing (137)

Digits 1-3	Digit 4	Digit 5	Code	No.
3.1 Food & beverage, tobacco (19)				
3.1.1Dairy products (2)	.1 Farming		31110	(1)
	.2 Production		31120	(1)
3.1.2 Grain & animal feed (NMC 2)			31200	(2)
3.1.3 Sugar (SUDECO 5)	.1 Holding		31310	(1)
	.2 Plantation		31320	(2)
	.3 Production		31330	(2)
3.1.4 Breweries (5)	.1 TBL	.1 Holding	31411	(1)
		.2 Plantation	31412	(1)
		.3 Production	31413	(2)
	.2 Other		31420	(1)
3.1.5 Wine & distilleries (2)			31500	(2)
3.1.6 Cigarette (1)			31600	(1)
3.1.7 Other (2)			31700	(2)
3.2 Textile & leather (28)				
3.2.1 Rope & carpet (3)	.1 Tanzania Sisal Authority	.1 Spinning	32111	(1)
		.2 Finished goods	32112	(2)
3.2.2 Textile (15)	.1 TEXCO	.1 Holding	32211	(1)
		.2 Spinning & weaving	32212	(7)
		.3 Finished goods	32213	(7)
	.2 Other		32220	(1)
3.2.3 Leather (10)	.1 TLAI	.1 Holding	32311	(1)
		.2 Tanneries	32312	(5)
		.3 Products	32313	(3)
	.2 Other		32320	(1)
3.3 Wood, paper & printing (26)				
3.3.1 TWICO (12)	.1 Holding		33110	(1)
	.2 Sawmills		33120	(4)
	.3 Products		33130	(7)
3.3.2 TKAI (8)	.1 Holding		33210	(1)
	.2 Paper		33220	(1)
	.3 Products (stationery)		33230	(1)
	.4 Printing		33240	(5)
3.3.3 Other (6)	.2 Paper		33320	(1)
	.3 Products		33330	(4)
	.4 Printing		33340	(1)
3.4 Chemicals (14)				
3.4 1 Petro (3)	.1 TPDC	.1 Holding	34111	(1)
		.2 Refining	34112	(2)
3.4.2 NCI (10)	.1 Holding		34210	(1)
	.2 Rubber		34220	(2)
	.3 Plastic		34230	(2)
	.4 Pharmaceutical		34240	(2)
	.5 Other NCI (soap, fertiliser, starch)		34250	(3)
3.4.3 Other (oxygen 1)			34300	(1)

Digits 1-3	Digit 4	Digit 5	Code	No.
3.5 Construction (24)				
3.5.1 TSjC (9)	.1 Holding		35110	(1)
	.2 Glass & ceramic		35120	(3)
	.3 Cement & clay	.1 Cement	35131	(3)
		.2 Clay	35132	(1)
	.4 Other (trucking)		35140	(1)
3.5.2 CDA (5)	.1 Holding		35210	(1)
	.2 Ceramic		35220	(1)
	.3 Concrete & brick		35230	(1)
	.4 Other (equipment & supplies)		35240	(2)
3.5.3 NHC (3)	.1 Holding		35310	(1)
	.3 Concrete & brick		35330	(2)
3.5.4 Other companies (6)	.2 Ceramics		35420	(1)
	.3 Gypsum & brick		35430	(1)
	.4 Architecture & other		35440	(4)
3.6 Metal & machinery (26)				
3.6.1 Non-automobile (18)	.1 NDC	.1 Holding	36111	(1)
		.2 Metal	36112	(4)
		.3 Machine & tool	36113	(5)
		.4 Electrical machinery	36114	(3)
		.5 Other (bicycle, watch)	36115	(2)
	.2 Other	.2 Metal	36122	(1)
		.3 Machine & tool	36123	(2)
3.6.2 Automobile (SMC 8)	.1 Holding		36210	(1)
	.2 Motor		36220	(3)
	.3 Motor vehicles		36230	(4)
4. Services (109)				
4.1 Public utilities (5)				
4.1.1 Power (2)			41100	(2)
4.1.2 Water (1)			41200	(1)
4.1.3 Post & Tel (2)	.2 Post		41320	(1)
	.3 Telecom		41330	(1)
4.2 Wholesale / retail trade, repair and maintenance (39)				
4.2.1 BIT (28)	.1 Holding		42110	(1)
	.2 Regional trading companies		42120	(20)
	.3 Other supplies & services		42130	(7)
4.2.2 Vehicle (5)	.1 Repair and maintenance		42210	(3)
	.2 Automotive fuel		42220	(2)
4.2.3 Other (6)	.1 Export		42310	(1)
	.2 Other		42320	(5)
4.3 Transport & storage (24)				
4.3.1 NTC (15)	.1 Holding		43110	(1)
	.2 Regional transport corporation		43120	(11)
	.3 Other (bus, shipping)		43130	(3)
4.3.2 Railways (2)	.1 TRC & TAZARA		43210	(2)
4.3.3 Air (2)	.1 ATC		43310	(2)
4.3.4 Shipping (3)			43400	(3)
4.3.5 Freight and storage (2)			43500	(2)

Digits 1-3	Digit 4	Digit 5	Code	No.
4.4 Tourism (20)				
4.4.1 TTCorp (14)	.1 Holding		44110	(1)
	.2 Hotel & lodges	.1 Hotel	44121	(10)
		.2 Lodges	44122	(2)
	.3 Other		44130	(1)
4.4.2 Other hotels (3)	.1 Hotel		44210	(2)
	.2 Conference centre		44220	(1)
4.4.3 National parks (3)			44300	(3)
4.5 Finance (14)				
4.5.1 Bank (7)	.1 NBC		45110	(2)
	.2 CRDB		45120	(1)
	.3 TIB		45130	(2)
	.5 Post office		45150	(2)
4.5.2 Building related (3)	.1 THB		45210	(2)
	.2 Other (hotel investments, national estates)		45220	(1)
4.5.3 Insurance (3)	.1 Pension (NPF)		45310	(1)
	.2 Other insurance		45320	(2)
4.5.4 National lotteries (1)			45400	(1)
4.6 Other Services (7)				
4.6.1 Business related (5)	.1 Law		46110	(1)
	.2 Audit		46120	(2)
	.3 Consulting		46130	(2)
4.6.2 News and film (2)			46200	(2)

PS/ Code 90000: Companies excluded (56)

Table B-4: Profits of Parastatals from 1987 (TSh m) According to Tanzania Audit Corporation (TAC) and Bureau of Statistics (BoS)

Same information obtained from different sources may deviate considerably. In countries like Tanzania, where statistical data in the 1980s and early 1990s had been very poor and partly manipulated, it is crucial to be aware of both, the quality of primary data, as well as the way how data has been selected and complied. The profit and loss statements below (current prices, in TSh million) show a striking example of deviating figures (aggregated values are displayed in Table 8-1).[214]

Name of parastatal	BoS 1987 (1)	TAC 1987 (2)	Difference BoS vs. TAC	(1) in % of (2)	(2) in % of (1)
187. National Distributors Co Ltd	0.1	-52.6	*Change in Sign*	0%	-64938%
195. National Poultry Co Ltd	0.0	-13.6	*Change in Sign*	0%	-30222%
344. Tanz. Posts & Telecommunications Cor.	384.5	-4,260.7	*Change in Sign*	-9%	-1108%
230. Rubber Industries Ltd	0.8	-7.4	*Change in Sign*	-11%	-902%
353. Tanzania Shoe Co Ltd	28.7	-173.0	*Change in Sign*	-17%	-603%
48. Dar es Salaam Textile Co Ltd	4.1	-24.9	*Change in Sign*	-17%	-600%
145. Mombo Sisal Estates Co Ltd	-3.7	13.3	*Change in Sign*	-28%	-355%
312. Tanzania Elimu Supplies	-8.5	22.6	*Change in Sign*	-37%	-267%

[214] Percentage values shown have to be interpreted adequately, as very high or small values mainly result from one figure being close to zero. Ideally, discrepancies would be defined in per cent of the companies' turn around or assets; however, this information was not available for both sources.

Name of parastatal	BoS 1987 (1)	TAC 1987 (2)	Difference BoS vs. TAC	(1) in % of (2)	(2) in % of (1)
23. Board of Internal Trade	2.4	-6.1	*Change in Sign*	-40%	-253%
238. Sabuni Industries Ltd	8.0	-19.2	*Change in Sign*	-42%	-240%
167. Mtwara Cashew Co Ltd	3.7	-8.2	*Change in Sign*	-45%	-222%
224. Ralli Estates	-4.2	8.5	*Change in Sign*	-50%	-201%
149. Morogoro Canvas Mill Ltd	56.3	-87.2	*Change in Sign*	-65%	-155%
347. Tanzania Railways Corporation	1,681.2	-2,152.0	*Change in Sign*	-78%	-128%
222. Printpak (Tanzania) Ltd	14.0	-14.0	*Change in Sign*	-100%	-100%
65. Hotel Seventy Seven Ltd	-15.7	11.7	*Change in Sign*	-135%	-74%
157. Morogoro Regional Transport Co Ltd	-1.5	0.7	*Change in Sign*	-211%	-47%
257. State Motor Corporation	895.6	-255.7	*Change in Sign*	-350%	-29%
189. National Estates and Designing Cor.	4.9	-1.3	*Change in Sign*	-377%	-27%
310. Tanzania Electric Supply Co Ltd	1,305.4	-290.6	*Change in Sign*	-449%	-22%
203. National Urban Water Authority	984.3	-152.0	*Change in Sign*	-648%	-15%
194. National Pharmaceutical Co Ltd	5.3	0.1	> Factor 5	5279%	2%
291. Tanzania Bag Corporation Ltd	234.6	14.9	> Factor 5	1574%	6%
165. Mtibwa Sugar Estates Ltd	54.5	6.7	> Factor 5	814%	12%
192. National Lotteries	3.9	0.5	> Factor 5	771%	13%
255. State Insurance Brokers	71.8	10.4	> Factor 5	690%	14%
323. Tanzania Housing Bank	176.2	30.4	> Factor 5	580%	17%
40. Cooperative and Rural Development Bank	211.8	39.9	> Factor 5	531%	19%
200. National Steel Corporation	407.0	89.6	> Factor 2	454%	22%
186. National Development Corporation	53.2	12.1	> Factor 2	439%	23%
280. Tanganyika Pyrethrum Board	-73.3	-20.9	> Factor 2	351%	29%
292. Tanzania Breweries Ltd	332.7	101.9	> Factor 2	326%	31%
296. Tanzania Cashewnut Marketing Board	1,256.1	438.8	> Factor 2	286%	35%
106. Kiwanda cha Zana za Kilimo Ubungo Ltd	147.3	51.7	> Factor 2	285%	35%
264. Tabora Msitu Products Ltd	3.0	1.1	> Factor 2	273%	37%
129. Mbeya Cement Co Ltd	-391.2	-151.0	> Factor 2	259%	39%
363. Tanz. Tobacco Processing & Mark. Board	-366.7	-147.1	> Factor 2	249%	40%
44. Dakawa Rice Farm Ltd	-28.9	-12.4	> Factor 2	233%	43%
328. Tanzania Legal Corporation	0.9	0.4	> Factor 2	218%	46%
82. Kampuni ya Uchukuzi Mtwara	20.1	9.4	> Factor 2	213%	47%
199. National Shipping Agencies Co Ltd	237.9	113.9	> Factor 2	209%	48%
190. National Housing Corporation	-40.6	-20.6		197%	51%
4. Agricultural & Industrial Supplies Co	18.0	9.2		196%	51%
355. Tanzania Standard Newspapers Ltd	-20.9	-10.9		192%	52%
179. Mwanza Tanneries Ltd	-93.6	-54.9		170%	59%
98. Kilimanjaro Textile Corporation Ltd	-201.2	-120.0		168%	60%
84. Kampuni ya Uchukuzi Ruvuma	14.2	9.3		152%	66%
342. Tanzania Portland Cement Co Ltd	253.9	169.0		150%	67%
198. National Ranching Co Ltd	14.4	10.1		143%	70%
185. National Chemical Industries	52.2	40.2		130%	77%
340. Tanz. Petroleum Development Cor.	2,483.2	1,939.7		128%	78%
191. National Insurance Corp of Tanzania	128.1	103.9		123%	81%
368. Tanzania Wildlife Corporation	145.7	130.3		112%	89%
184. National Bus Services Ltd	-15.9	-14.7		108%	93%
303. Tanzania Cordage Ltd	12.9	12.2		106%	95%
300. Tanzania Coastal Shipping Line Ltd	39.4	37.5		105%	95%
298. Tanzania Cigarette Co Ltd	787.9	750.3		105%	95%
27. Building Hardware & Electrical Supplies	46.0	43.8		105%	95%
6. Air Tanzania Corporation	-620.8	-591.9		105%	95%
62. General Tyre East Africa Ltd	97.9	93.9		104%	96%
193. National Milling Corporation	-1,876.2	-1,808.2		104%	96%
197. National Provident Fund	36.3	35.8		101%	99%
160. Morogoro Tanneries Ltd	-35.8	-35.5	correct	101%	99%
58. Fibreboards Africa Ltd	11.0	11.0	correct	100%	100%
315. Tanzania Film Co Ltd	-19.2	-19.2	correct	100%	100%
294. Tanzania Cables Ltd	65.2	65.2	correct	100%	100%
359. Tanzania Tea Authority	18.9	18.9	correct	100%	100%
272. Tanganyika Dyeing and Weaving Co Ltd	-94.6	-94.6	correct	100%	100%
360. Tanzania Tea Blenders Ltd	45.8	45.8	correct	100%	100%

Name of parastatal	BoS 1987 (1)	TAC 1987 (2)	Difference BoS vs. TAC	(1) in % of (2)	(2) in % of (1)
7. Aluminium Africa Ltd	59.6	59.6	correct	100%	100%
182. National Bank of Commerce	3,013.7	3,013.7	correct	100%	100%
3. Agip (Tanzania) Ltd	239.2	239.2	correct	100%	100%
180. Mwanza Textiles Ltd	-1,344.8	-1,344.8	correct	100%	100%
83. Kampuni ya Uchukuzi Mwanza	15.3	15.3	correct	100%	100%
324. Tanz. Industrial Studies and Consult. Org	27.3	27.3	correct	100%	100%
77. Kampuni ya Uchukuzi Dodoma	12.8	12.8	correct	100%	100%
36. CMB Packaging Ltd (Metal Box)	57.3	57.3	correct	100%	100%
59. Friendship Textile Mill Ltd	37.7	37.7	correct	100%	100%
297. Tanzania Central Freight Bureau	25.8	25.8	correct	100%	100%
289. Tanzania Audit Corporation	19.3	19.4	correct	100%	100%
202. National Transport Corporation	-10.9	-10.9	correct	100%	100%
373. Tembo Chipboards Ltd	11.7	11.7	correct	100%	100%
196. National Printing Co Ltd	-33.8	-34.0	correct	100%	100%
88. Kariakoo Market Corporation	21.3	21.6	correct	98%	102%
74. Kagera Sugar Co Ltd	-240.8	-245.2		98%	102%
281. Tanganyika Tegry (Plastics) Ltd	80.3	82.7		97%	103%
320. Tanzania Harbours Authority	1,639.0	1,762.9		93%	108%
85. Kampuni ya Uchukuzi Tabora	10.2	11.0		93%	108%
28. BUKOP Ltd	-6.3	-6.9		91%	110%
16. Basotu Plantations Ltd	44.8	49.3		91%	110%
243. Setchet Wheat Co Ltd	33.1	38.3		86%	116%
263. Sugar Development Corporation	8.9	10.4		85%	117%
25. Buck Reef Gold Mining Co Ltd	-30.5	-36.3		84%	119%
176. Mwananchi Engineering & Contract. Corp.	-40.9	-48.9		84%	120%
316. Tanzania Fisheries Corporation	10.4	13.9		75%	133%
261. Steel Rolling Mills Ltd	-17.8	-26.2		68%	148%
358. Tanzania Tanneries Co Ltd	-18.1	-26.9		67%	148%
21. Blankets Manufactures Ltd	9.9	15.7		63%	159%
256. State Mining Corporation	10.9	17.5		63%	160%
173. Multipurpose Oilseed Processing Co Ltd	-13.2	-22.8		58%	173%
201. National Textile Corporation	-103.8	-184.8		56%	178%
271. Tanganyika Coffee Curing Co Ltd	-3.8	-7.6	< Factor 2	50%	201%
89. Keko Pharmaceutical Industries Ltd	26.8	57.0	< Factor 2	47%	212%
217. Nyanza Salt Mines (Tanganyika) Ltd	-13.4	-33.1	< Factor 2	41%	247%
164. Mount Meru Hotels Ltd	17.9	64.3	< Factor 2	28%	359%
275. Tanganyika Instant Coffee Co Ltd	4.6	16.9	< Factor 2	27%	367%
307. Tanzania Dairy Farming Co Ltd	2.5	9.1	< Factor 2	27%	368%
154. Morogoro Polyester Textiles Ltd	-1,108.3	-4,202.6	< Factor 2	26%	379%
268. Tanga Cement Co Ltd	16.8	107.1	< Factor 5	16%	637%
66. Household Supplies Co Ltd	52.1	356.0	< Factor 5	15%	683%
354. Tanzania Sisal Authority	-8.2	-59.4	< Factor 5	14%	722%
141. Minjingu Phosphate Co Ltd	-38.7	-353.0	< Factor 5	11%	912%
311. Tanz. Electrical Goods Manufacturing Co	4.5	48.4	< Factor 5	9%	1067%
247. Sikh Saw Mills Ltd	5.0	98.8	< Factor 5	5%	1961%
304. Tanzania Cotton Marketing Board	-17.1	-943.3	< Factor 5	2%	5525%
158. Morogoro Shoe Co Ltd	-7.0	-1,438.0	< Factor 5	0%	20412%
Sum of all profits	18,379.8	10,805.4			
Sum of all losses	-6,969.7	-19,645.1			
Overall net profits	11,410.1	-8,839.7			

Table B-5: Price Indices (End of Month-Values)

The table displays the deflation factors used to calculate constant prices. End of June values are identical with the *Consumer Price Index* (annual average) obtained from the Tanzanian authorities (reliable GDP-deflators have not been available). All other monthly rates are a linear calculation of the change between these annual June averages. This approach has been chosen to eliminate seasonal changes and other effects, such as the increase in prices during the month of Ramadan. Whenever the study uses 'constant prices' or '1994 prices' prices refer to the Consumer Price Index 100.

In general, depending of the data set, end of June or end of December values are used to calculate constant prices. Annual profit and loss statements, however, are deflated according to the year and month the financial statement refers to (see notes to Table B-6).

Year	Jan.	Feb.	Mar.	Apr.	May	June	July	Aug.	Sept.	Oct.	Nov.	Dec.
1980	2.1	2.1	2.2	2.2	2.3	2.3	2.4	2.4	2.5	2.5	2.6	2.6
1981	2.7	2.7	2.8	2.8	2.9	2.9	3.0	3.0	3.1	3.2	3.2	3.3
1982	3.4	3.5	3.5	3.6	3.7	3.7	3.8	3.9	4.0	4.1	4.2	4.2
1983	4.3	4.4	4.5	4.6	4.7	4.8	4.9	5.0	5.2	5.3	5.5	5.6
1984	5.8	5.9	6.0	6.2	6.3	6.5	6.6	6.8	7.0	7.2	7.4	7.5
1985	7.7	7.9	8.1	8.3	8.4	8.6	8.9	9.1	9.3	9.6	9.8	10.0
1986	10.3	10.5	10.7	11.0	11.2	11.4	11.7	12.0	12.3	12.6	12.8	13.1
1987	13.4	13.7	14.0	14.3	14.6	14.8	15.2	15.6	16.0	16.4	16.8	17.2
1988	17.5	17.9	18.3	18.7	19.1	19.5	20.0	20.4	20.9	21.4	21.9	22.4
1989	22.9	23.4	23.9	24.4	24.9	25.4	26.1	26.9	27.7	28.4	29.2	29.9
1990	30.7	31.4	32.2	33.0	33.7	34.5	35.3	36.1	37.0	37.8	38.6	39.4
1991	40.3	41.1	41.9	42.8	43.6	44.4	45.2	46.0	46.8	47.7	48.5	49.3
1992	50.1	50.9	51.7	52.5	53.3	54.1	55.3	56.4	57.5	58.7	59.8	61.0
1993	62.1	63.2	64.4	65.5	66.6	67.8	69.6	71.5	73.4	75.2	77.1	79.0
1994	80.9	82.7	84.6	86.5	88.3	90.2	92.3	94.5	96.6	98.7	100.9	103.0
1995	105.1	107.3	109.4	111.5	113.7	115.8	117.8	119.9	121.9	123.9	125.9	128.0
1996	130.0	132.0	134.0	136.1	138.1	140.1	142.0	143.9	145.7	147.6	149.5	151.4
1997	153.2	155.1	157.0	158.9	160.7	162.6	164.3	166.1	167.8	169.6	171.3	173.0
1998	174.8	176.5	178.2	180.0	181.7	183.5	184.7	185.9	187.1	188.3	189.5	191.9

Source: Table 3.12 in Bank of Tanzania (1994) and Bank of Tanzania (1997); data for the years 1997 and 1998 from Bank of Tanzania (2001)

Table B-6: Parastatal Employment, Performance and Support (1987-96)

The table shows the data set used to characterise parastatals according to performance and support. Detailed explanations, in particular explanations on the definitions of the grouping variables, are described below (p. 603-607).

Columns (c) to (f) indicate *profit/loss information*, i.e. the number of profit and loss statements obtained for the years 1987 to 1996 (c), the average profit/loss calculated from the data (d), the categorisation of the company according to the profits/losses (e), as well as the trend over time (f).

Accounting features display the month at which the company closes its annual financial statements (g), the number of statements obtained for the years 1986 to 1991 (h), the average time it took until accounts have been audited and reported in the annual TAC reports (i), the average quality of the accounts (j), as well as the codes on average changes in accounting performance (arrears (k), quality (l)).

Column (m) shows for each of the categories '*Banking*', '*Treasury*', '*Other state & donor*' and '*Inter-parastatal arrears*' the number of support information obtained. And column (n) indicates privatisation or lease prior to 1997.

Code & name	Employ-ment	Profits/losses				Accounting features						Support info	Pr.
		No.	ø	type	Δ	M	No.	P'	Q	ΔP'	ΔQ		
(a)	(b)	(c)	(d)	(e)	(f)	(g)	(h)	(i)	(j)	(k)	(l)	(m)	(n)
1. Afina Pencils Co Ltd	*120*	1	-31			12	2	4.3'	3.0	53	53	0-0-0-0	
3. Agip (Tanzania) Ltd	359	10	1,723	*/r/B	n.s.	12	6	1.0	1.0	11	11	1-0-2-2	96
4. Agricultural & Industrial Supplies Co	248	4	-290	*	-	6	6	1.7	2.2	23	43	2-1-2-2	
6. Air Tanzania Corporation (ATC)	1,299	9	-1,173	*/C	+	12x	5	2.0	3.2	32	23	1-3-2-3	
7. Aluminium Africa Ltd (ALAF)	1,028	9	1,329	*/C	n.s.	12	6	1.7	1.3	42	21	1-0-2-3	
9. Arusha Cooperative Union Ltd	*200*											1-0-1-1	
10. Arusha International Conference Centre	*300*	10	47	*	-	6	6	1.5	2.0	41	32	0-1-1-2	
12. Arusha Regional Trading Co Ltd (RTC)	230	7	-18	*	n.s.	6	6	1.2	1.0	21	11	0-1-0-2	
13. Bagamoyo Farmers Ltd	38	3	-10		n.s.	9	4	3.0'	2.0	32'	32	0-0-0-1	
14. Bagamoyo Fishing Co Ltd (BAFICO)	*60*											0-0-0-0	
16. Basotu Plantations Ltd	54	10	122	*/E	-	9	6	1.7	1.3	23	21	1-0-1-1	
17. Biashara Consumer Service Co Ltd	299	9	36	*	++	6	6	1.8	2.0	23	23	0-0-1-2	
18. Biharamulo Cooperative Union Ltd	*80*											0-0-0-0	
19. Bima Motors Ltd	*60*	5	9	*/r	--	12	6	1.5	1.2	41	21	0-0-0-2	
21. Blankets Manufactures Ltd (BML)	629	8	22	*	--	12	6	1.0	1.0	11	11	1-0-1-2	95
22. Board of External Trade (BET)	108	6	-11	*	--	6	6	1.0	1.0	11	11	0-1-2-2	
23. Board of Internal Trade (BIT)	157	7	-19	*/r	(+)	6	6	1.0	1.2	11	41	0-0-1-2	
24. BP (Tanzania) Ltd (BP[T])	324											0-0-2-2	96
25. Buck Reef Gold Mining Co Ltd	339	5	-203	*/r	+	12	6	2.3	2.0	32	32	0-1-0-1	93
26. Buha Cooperative Union Ltd	*60*											2-0-0-0	
27. Building Hardware & Elect. Supplies	152	6	68	*	-	6	6	1.8	1.7	23	31	0-1-2-2	
28. BUKOP Ltd	277	9	-16	*	n.s.	4x	6	1.7	1.8	22	23	0-0-0-2	
29. Burns and Blane (Tanzania) Ltd	100	2	-3			12	6	1.7	1.2	23	21	0-0-0-1	
30. Capital Ceramics Co Ltd (CIL)	*60*											0-0-0-1	
31. Capital Construction Equipment	110	4	-36	*	n.s.	6	4	2.2'	1.3'	42	42	1-0-0-3	
32. Capital Development Authority (CDA)	769					6	6	1.7	1.3	23	21	2-1-3-3	
33. Capital Supplies Co Ltd (CASCO)	120	4	-223	*/r/E	+	6	4	1.3	1.3	22	22	0-1-1-3	
34. Central Maintenance Service Centre		6	-16	*/r	n.s.	9	6	1.7	1.2	23	41	0-0-0-1	
35. Central Region Cooperative Union Ltd	*130*											2-0-1-1	
36. CMB Packaging Ltd (Metal Box)	*287*	7	209	*/r	n.s.	12	6	1.2	1.0	41	11	1-1-1-3	93
37. Coast Region Cooperative Union Ltd	*160*											0-0-0-0	
38. Coast Regional Trading Co Ltd (RTC)	100	3	-43		-	6	5	2.3'	2.0	23'	32	1-0-0-2	
39. Coastal Salt Works Ltd	*220*	2	-148	*		12	6	1.0	1.0	11	11	0-0-0-1	
40. Cooperative and Rural Dev. Bank	1,196	7	466	*	n.s.	6	6	1.0	1.3	11	31	0-2-1-2	
41. Cooperative Audit and Supervision	*30*	7	50	*/E	n.s.	6	6	1.2	1.3	21	21	0-1-0-1	
42. Cooperative Union of Tanzania	*100*					6	3	6.0	3.0	53	53	0-0-1-1	
44. Dakawa Rice Farm Ltd	357	5	-164	*/r	n.s.	9	6	1.7	1.0	42	11	1-0-0-2	
45. Dar es Salaam Airport Handling Co	*200*	10	771	*/r/B	+	12	6	1.5	1.0	21	11	0-0-1-1	
46. Dar es Salaam Multipur. Coop Union	*80*											0-0-0-0	
47. Dar es Salaam Regional Trading Co	*120*	9	52	*/r	++	6	6	1.3	1.0	31	11	0-0-2-2	
48. Dar es Salaam Textile Co Lt	145	5	-39	*/r	n.s.	6x	6	1.8	2.0	41	32	1-0-1-2	
49. Darbrew Ltd	199	9	62	*/r	(-)	12	5	2.3'	1.0	32'	11	0-0-1-3	
50. Dindira Tea Estate Ltd	286					12	3	3.3	3.0	53	53	0-0-0-0	
52. Dodoma Regional Trading Co (RTC)	*120*	7	-28	*	n.s.	6	6	1.0	1.0	11	11	0-1-1-3	
53. Dodoma Wine Co Ltd (DOWICO)	*119*	3	-112	*/r	n.s.	12	4	2.7'	2.0	43'	32	1-1-2-3	
54. East Africa Publication Ltd (EAPL)	21	3	1		n.s.	12	6	1.5	1.7	21	22	0-0-0-1	
56. Enterprise (Tanzania) - Embassy Hotel	*160*	9	-562	*/r/B	n.s.	12	6	1.8	1.3	42	42	0-0-0-2	
57. Express Tanzania Ltd	105	8	26	*	-	12	6	1.7	1.0	42	11	0-0-0-2	
58. Fibreboards Africa Ltd (FAL)	805	8	-23	*	n.s.	12	6	1.8	1.2	41	21	1-1-2-2	
59. Friendship Textile Mill Ltd (URAFIKI)	3,440	8	-484	*	(-)	12	6	1.5	1.7	42	31	2-1-0-3	96
60. Gawal Wheat Co Ltd	56	10	-64	*	--	9	6	1.7	1.3	22	21	0-0-1-1	96

Code & name	Employment	Profits/losses No.	ø	type	Δ	Accounting features M	No.	P'	Q	ΔP'	ΔQ	Support info	Pr.
(a)	(b)	(c)	(d)	(e)	(f)	(g)	(h)	(i)	(j)	(k)	(l)	(m)	(n)
62. General Tyre East Africa Ltd	632	10	471	*/r	n.s.	12	6	1.2	1.5	21	41	0-0-2-2	96
63. Gidagamowd Wheat Co Ltd	71	10	138	*/r/E	n.s.	9	6	1.7	1.3	22	21	0-0-1-1	
64. Giraffe Extract Co Ltd	*75*	3	44		n.s.	12	4	2.4'	1.0	43'	11	0-0-1-1	
65. Hotel Seventy Seven Ltd	250	10	-30	*	n.s.	12	6	2.0	1.3	32	21	0-0-1-2	
66. Household Supplies Co Ltd (HOSCO)	155	10	177	*	--	6	6	1.5	1.0	22	11	0-0-2-2	
67. Imara Wood Products Ltd	*60*	1	-40			12	1	2.0	1.0			0-0-0-1	95
68. Integrated Concrete Industries Ltd	50	1	-20			6	5	2.5'	2.0	22	32	1-0-1-2	93
69. Iringa Maintenance Co Ltd (IMCO)	52	5	-138	*/r/E	n.s.	6	6	1.8	2.0	22	32	0-0-1-1	93
70. Iringa Regional Trading Co Ltd (RTC)	167	3	-20		+	6	6	1.0	1.3	11	21	1-1-2-3	
71. Iringa/Mufundi Cooperative Union Ltd	*70*											0-0-0-1	
72. Kagera Cooperative Union Ltd	*80*											1-0-0-3	
73. Kagera Regional Trading Co (RTC)	191	7	-20	*	n.s.	6	6	1.0	1.7	11	23	1-0-1-2	
74. Kagera Sugar Co Ltd	2,612	10	-1,177	*/r/C	n.s.	6	6	1.2	2.0	21	32	0-0-0-2	
76. Kahe Estates Co Ltd	50	6	-50	*/r	++	9	6	1.7	1.2	23	41	1-0-0-1	
77. Kampuni ya Uchukuzi Dodoma	184	9	-4		-	6	6	1.0	1.0	11	11	0-0-1-2	
78. Kampuni ya Uchukuzi Iringa (KAURI)	*100*	4	30	*/r	--							0-0-1-1	
79. Kampuni ya Uchukuzi Kagera	145	7	40	*	-	6	6	1.0	1.3	11	21	0-1-1-2	
80. Kampuni ya Uchukuzi Mbeya	*100*	4	7		--	6	4	1.3	1.8	21	23	0-0-1-2	
81. Kampuni ya Uchukuzi Mkoa wa Lindi	28											0-0-1-0	
82. Kampuni ya Uchukuzi Mtwara	176	7	102	*/r	n.s.	6	6	1.0	1.0	11	11	0-0-1-2	
83. Kampuni ya Uchukuzi Mwanza	191	9	83	*/r	--	6	6	1.0	1.0	11	11	0-0-1-2	
84. Kampuni ya Uchukuzi Ruvuma	132	9	54	*	-	6	6	1.0	1.0	11	11	0-0-1-2	
85. Kampuni ya Uchukuzi Tabora	124	9	55	*/r	n.s.	6	6	1.0	1.0	11	11	0-1-1-1	
86. Karadha Co Ltd	*135*	9	67	*	--	6	6	1.3	1.0	21	11	0-0-1-2	
87. Karagwe Cooperative Union	48											0-0-0-0	
88. Kariakoo Market Corporation	246	9	13	*	--	6	6	1.0	1.0	11	11	0-0-2-2	
89. Keko Pharmaceutical Industries Ltd	154	5	219	*/r	-	12	6	1.8	1.3	41	21	1-1-1-3	95
90. Kibo Match Corporation	723											2-0-0-1	
91. Kibo Paper Industries Ltd	407	6	-128	*	--	12	6	2.0	1.2	32	41	2-1-2-2	
92. Kigamboni Poultry Farm Ltd	21											1-0-0-1	
93. Kigoma Regional Trading Co Ltd	134	6	-47	*	+	6	6	1.0	2.2	11	23	0-0-1-1	
94. Kilimanjaro Hotels Ltd	508	4	57		--	12	6	2.2	2.8	23	22	0-0-1-2	
95. Kilimanjaro Machine Tools Manufact.	144	9	-503	*/r/B	+	12x	6	2.2	2.2	23	42	1-0-0-2	
96. Kilimanjaro Native Cooperative Union	*300*											0-1-0-0	
97. Kilimanjaro Regional Trading Co Ltd	*120*	3	-65		n.s.	6	6	1.8	1.8	23	42	0-0-1-2	
98. Kilimanjaro Textile Corporation Ltd	1,052	5	-726	*/r/C	n.s.	12	6	1.8	1.0	41	11	1-0-0-2	
99. Kilimanjaro Timber Utilisation	562	5	-109	*/r	(-)	12	6	2.2	1.7	23	23	2-1-1-1	
100. Kilombero Sugar Co Ltd	7,779	10	1,658	*/r/C	n.s.	6	6	1.5	1.0	22	11	0-1-2-2	
103. Kilwa Ammonia Co Ltd (KILAMCO)	*100*					12	1	5.0'	1.0	53	51	0-0-0-0	
104. Kimamba Sisal Estates Co Ltd	*170*	3	-59	*/r	++	12	3	4.0	2.7	53	53	0-0-0-2	
105. Kisarawe Brick Factory	183	4	-216	*/r	+	6	5	2.0'	1.8'	23'	22	0-0-1-1	94
106. Kiwanda cha Zana za Kilimo Ubungo	685	8	-100	*	-	12	6	2.0	1.0	32	11	1-0-2-3	
107. Kiwira Coal Mines Co Ltd	*200*	7	-1,019	*/r/B	n.s.	12	1	3.0'	3.0			0-0-1-1	
109. Kunduchi Beach Hotel Ltd	*100*	5	-47	*/r	--	12	5	2.5'	2.8'	43	22	1-0-0-2	94
111. Kwamtili Estate Ltd	*50*					9	2	1.0	1.0	11	11	2-0-0-0	
112. Kyela/Rungwe Cooperative Union Ltd	*80*											0-0-0-1	
113. Landrover Tanzania Ltd (LRT)	*90*											0-0-1-1	
115. Lewa Estates Ltd	*80*											1-0-0-0	
116. Light Source Manufacturers Ltd	170	8	-217	*/r	++	12	5	1.8'	1.6'	41'	42	2-1-1-1	94
117. Lindi Regional Cooperative Union Ltd	*100*											1-0-1-1	
118. Lindi Regional Trading Co Ltd (RTC)	*120*	4	-13		++	6	6	1.5	1.8	21	23	1-0-0-3	
119. Longido Gemstone Mining Co Ltd	*60*	2	-55			9	1	3.0'	3.0			0-0-0-0	93
123. Mafia Island Lodge	*40*	3	-10		+	12	3	3.5'	3.0	43'	53	0-0-0-1	94
124. Mafuta ya Ilulu Ltd	*90*					6	3	3.0'	2.0	43'	53	1-0-1-2	
125. Mang'ula Mech. and Machine Tools	461	7	-45	*	(-)	12	5	2.2'	1.0	43'	11	1-0-2-2	
126. Mara Cooperative Union Ltd	*120*											0-0-1-1	

Code & name	Employ-ment	Profits/losses No.	ø	type	Δ	Accounting features M	No.	P'	Q	ΔP'	ΔQ	Support info	Pr.
(a)	(b)	(c)	(d)	(e)	(f)	(g)	(h)	(i)	(j)	(k)	(l)	(m)	(n)
127. Mara Regional Trading Co Ltd (RTC)	151	7	13	*/r	n.s.	6	6	1.0	1.3	11	21	2-1-1-3	
128. Mbarali Rice Farms Ltd	*130*	6	-141	*	n.s.	9	5	2.7'	3.4'	23'	22	0-0-1-1	
129. Mbeya Cement Co Ltd	479	10	-993	*/r/B	+	6	6	1.0	1.2	11	21	2-2-1-2	96
130. Mbeya Ceramics Ltd	*60*					6	4	2.6'	2.0	43	32	0-0-0-1	94
131. Mbeya Cooperative Union Ltd	*100*											1-0-1-1	
132. Mbeya Regional Trading Co Ltd	245	6	33	*	--	6	6	1.0	1.3	11	21	1-1-2-3	
133. Mbeya Textile Mills Ltd	358					12	6	1.7	1.3	31	31	1-0-0-2	
134. Mbinga Coffee Curing Co Ltd	*285*	6	-76	*	n.s.	9	2	2.5	1.0			0-0-1-1	95
135. Mbinga Cooperative Union Ltd	*150*											1-0-0-0	
136. Mbozi Coffee Curing Co Ltd	*228*	7	-67	*	++	9	3	2.0	1.0			0-0-1-2	95
137. Mbozi Coffee Farms Ltd	117											0-0-0-1	95
138. Mbozi Maize Farms Ltd	67	8	-49	*	--	9	6	1.3	1.7	21	31	1-0-1-1	
139. Mikumi Hotels Co Ltd	*70*	1	-48			12	6	2.7	2.7	43	22	0-1-0-0	96
140. Mingoyo Sawmill Co Ltd (MISACO)	*60*	2	-11			12	6	2.7	2.2	43	23	0-0-1-1	
141. Minjingu Phosphate Co Ltd (MIPCO)	75	6	-420	*/r/E	+	12	6	2.0	1.5	32	22	0-0-0-1	
142. Mkate Sawmills Ltd	140					12	2	3.7'	2.0	43'	52	1-0-2-1	95
144. Mkonge Livestock Co Ltd (MLICO)	*40*	3	-33		n.s.	12	6	2.7	2.0	23	32	0-0-0-1	
145. Mombo Sisal Estates Co Ltd	1,726	2	51			12	3	2.0	2.3	53	53	0-0-0-1	
146. Monact Seed Co Ltd	6	5	-30	*/r/E	n.s.	12	4	2.7'	2.0'	43'	22	0-0-0-0	
149. Morogoro Canvas Mill Ltd	1,054	8	-281	*	n.s.	12	6	1.3	1.8	31	22	2-1-1-3	94
150. Morogoro Ceramic Wares Ltd	415	6	-587	*/r/C	n.s.	6	6	1.8	1.8	23	23	2-1-1-3	
151. Morogoro Hotel Ltd	*80*	1	27			12	4	1.8'	1.5'	41'	31	1-0-0-2	
152. Morogoro Leather Board	*30*											0-0-1-1	
153. Morogoro Leather Goods Co Ltd	146	3	-29	*	n.s.	12	6	1.8	1.2	41	21	1-1-1-3	
154. Morogoro Polyester Textiles Ltd	1,585	10	-14,705	*/r/B	n.s.	12	6	1.2	1.5	41	42	2-1-1-3	
155. Morogoro Region Cooperative Union	*120*											1-0-1-2	
156. Morogoro Regional Trading Co Ltd	90	5	-16	*	n.s.	6	6	1.0	1.0	11	11	2-0-1-3	
157. Morogoro Regional Transport Co	155	10	-1		n.s.	6	6	1.7	1.2	23	41	0-0-0-2	
158. Morogoro Shoe Co Ltd	242	5	-5,543	*/r/B	+	12	6	2.3	2.0	32	32	1-1-0-3	94
159. Morogoro Sisal Estates Ltd	*100*					12	2	3.5	2.0	53	52	0-0-0-2	
160. Morogoro Tanneries Ltd	188	4	-363	*/r/E	n.s.	12	5	2.7'	2.0	43	32	2-1-0-2	93
161. Moshi Hand Tools Ltd	*135*					6	3	2.0	1.0	51	51	0-0-0-1	93
162. Moshi Hotels Ltd	107	6	1		n.s.	12	5	2.2'	1.8	43'	41	0-0-1-1	95
163. Motor Mart (Tanzania) Ltd	36	1	-2			12	6	1.3	1.0	42	11	1-0-0-1	
164. Mount Meru Hotels Ltd	280	6	61	*	-	12	6	1.8	1.3	41	31	0-0-1-2	93
165. Mtibwa Sugar Estates Ltd	3,782	10	644	*/r/C	n.s.	6	6	1.0	1.0	11	11	0-1-2-2	
167. Mtwara Cashew Co Ltd	32	3	-2		n.s.	9	6	2.0	2.3	23	23	0-0-0-2	
168. Mtwara Region Cooperative Union	*110*											1-0-0-1	
169. Mtwara Regional Trading Co Ltd	*120*	7	-44	*	+	6	6	1.0	1.3	11	42	2-0-1-3	
171. Muheza Sisal Estates Co Ltd	935					12	2	5.5	3.0	53	53	1-0-0-1	
172. Mulbadaw Wheat Farms Ltd	44	9	127	*/r/E	-	9	6	2.0	1.0	23	11	0-0-1-1	
173. Multipurpose Oilseed Processing	203	8	-243	*/r	--	6	2	1.0	2.0	11	22	1-0-1-2	95
174. Murjanda Wheat Co Ltd	123	10	100	*/r	-	9	6	1.8	1.3	22	21	0-0-1-1	
175. Musoma Textile Ltd (MUTEX)	1,467	5	-14,669	*/r/B	n.s.	12	6	1.7	2.0	31	32	1-1-1-2	
176. Mwananchi Engineer.&Contracting	2,165	9	-40	*	(+)	12	6	2.2	1.8	43	23	0-0-1-3	
177. Mwanza Brewery Ltd	*200*					12	6	1.7	1.8	23	22	0-0-0-1	
178. Mwanza Regional Trading Co Ltd	*120*	6	-103	*/r	n.s.	6	5	1.2	1.6	21	42	1-1-1-3	
179. Mwanza Tanneries Ltd	176	2	-297	*/r/E	-	12	3	3.4'	2.0	43'	53	2-1-0-3	93
180. Mwanza Textiles Ltd (MWATEX)	2,095	6	-9,199	*/r/B	n.s.	12	6	1.5	1.7	42	42	2-1-0-3	
181. National Agricultural and Food Cor.	1,752	7	-421	*	-	9	6	2.3	1.7	32	42	1-2-2-2	
182. National Bank of Commerce (NBC)	8,000	7	9,357	*/r/C	n.s.	6	6	1.0	1.0	11	11	0-1-3-2	96
183. National Bicycles Co Ltd (NABICO)	*163*	8	11	*	n.s.	12	6	1.8	1.3	22	21	1-1-1-2	
184. National Bus Services Ltd	273	5	-48	*/r	+	6x	6	1.2	1.2	41	21	0-0-0-2	
185. National Chemical Industries (NCI)	39	10	104	*/r/E	--	12	6	1.3	1.0	42	11	0-1-2-1	
186. National Development Corporation	151	8	48	*	n.s.	12	6	1.3	1.0	21	11	0-2-1-1	
187. National Distributors Co Ltd (NDL)	488	4	-250	*/r	n.s.	12	5	2.5'	2.4'	43	23	1-0-0-2	

Code & name	Employ-ment	Profits/losses No.	ø	type	Δ	Accounting features M	No.	P'	Q	ΔP'	ΔQ	Support info	Pr.
(a)	(b)	(c)	(d)	(e)	(f)	(g)	(h)	(i)	(j)	(k)	(l)	(m)	(n)
188. National Engineering Co Ltd (NECO)	349	9	57	*/r	n.s.	12	6	1.0	1.0	11	11	0-1-1-3	96
189. National Estates and Designing Cor.	183	10	1		n.s.	12	6	1.2	1.0	41	11	0-0-1-2	
190. National Housing Corporation (NHC)	722	10	400	*	++	6x	6	2.2	1.3	23	21	1-2-0-2	
191. National Insurance Corp of Tanzania	2,046	10	569	*/r/C	n.s.	12	6	2.0	1.0	32	11	0-1-3-2	
192. National Lotteries	43	10	21	*	n.s.	6	6	2.7	1.7	32	42	0-1-0-2	
193. National Milling Corporation (NMC)	1,197	10	-6,626	*/r/B	+	12x	6	1.2	2.0	21	32	1-1-3-3	
194. National Pharmaceutical Co Ltd	290	9	-161	*	n.s.	6	6	1.5	1.0	21	11	2-1-2-2	
195. National Poultry Co Ltd (NAPOCO)	154	3	-29		+	12	4	2.8'	2.3'	43'	43	3-2-1-2	
196. National Printing Co Ltd (NPC)	410	9	-984	*/r/B	-	12	6	2.2	1.5	43	42	2-0-2-1	
197. National Provident Fund (NPF)	1,257	9	1,714	*/r/C	++	6	6	1.5	2.3	22	23	0-1-1-2	
198. National Ranching Co Ltd (NARCO)	1,487	2	50			6	4	2.2'	1.0	43'	11	2-0-2-2	
199. National Shipping Agencies Co Ltd	892	10	1,470	*/r/B	-	6	6	1.0	1.2	11	21	0-0-1-3	
200. National Steel Corporation (NSC)	100	10	187	*/r/E	--	12	6	1.2	1.2	21	21	1-0-2-1	
201. National Textile Corporation	83	6	-939	*/r/B	n.s.	12	6	1.3	1.2	31	21	2-3-1-3	
202. National Transport Corporation (NTC)	89	10	350	*/E	n.s.	6	6	1.2	1.0	41	11	0-2-1-2	
203. National Urban Water Authority	1,548	10	-3,423	*/r/B	n.s.	6	6	2.0	2.2	22	22	0-1-3-3	
205. New Africa Hotels Ltd	281	7	-65	*	n.s.	12	5	2.3'	2.8'	32'	22	1-0-1-2	93
207. New Mwanza Hotels Ltd	*70*	6	-5		n.s.	12	5	2.2	2.0	23	32	0-1-1-2	
208. New Safari Hotel (1967) Ltd	118	5	-28	*/r	-	12	5	2.0'	1.0	42'	11	1-1-0-2	96
211. Ngombezi Sisal Estate Co Ltd	2,006	4	48	*/r	n.s.	12	3	2.0	2.0	53	53	0-0-0-1	
212. Ngorongoro Cons. Area Authority	*210*	6	447	*/r/E	n.s.	6	6	1.5	1.7	22	23	0-0-1-2	
213. Njombe/Ludewa/Makete Coop. Union	*120*											1-0-0-0	
214. Nyanza Cooperative Union Ltd	*130*											0-0-0-2	
215. Nyanza Engineering & Foundry Co	80	4	-23	*/r	n.s.	12	5	3.8'	3.0	22	32	0-0-0-1	
216. Nyanza Glass Works	20	10	-322	*/r/E	n.s.	6	5	1.6	1.2	22	41	0-0-1-2	
217. Nyanza Salt Mines (Tanganyika) Ltd	739	7	-739	*/r/C	n.s.	12	6	2.5	3.0	22	22	0-2-0-1	
218. Pamba Engineering Co Ltd	213											0-0-2-2	
221. Polysacks Co Ltd	174	5	92	*	n.s.	12	6	2.0	1.3	32	21	0-0-2-3	
222. Printpak (Tanzania) Ltd	396	7	-20	*	n.s.	12	6	2.0	1.0	32	11	1-0-1-3	
223. Pugu Kaolin Mines Co Ltd	*160*	4	-27	*/r	+	12	5	2.5'	2.6'	43	43	0-0-0-1	
224. Ralli Estates	538	1	50			12	3	2.7	2.3	53	53	0-0-0-1	
225. Rasilimali Ltd						6	2	2.3'	1.0	42'	51	0-0-0-0	
227. Rift Valley Cooperative Union Ltd	*180*											1-0-0-0	
228. Rift Valley Seed Co Ltd (RVSL)	*120*					12	4	3.3	2.8	43	43	0-0-0-1	93
230. Rubber Industries Ltd	104	3	-55	*	n.s.	12	4	2.3'	1.5'	42'	42	1-0-0-2	
231. Rukwa Region Cooperative Union Ltd	*130*											2-0-0-1	
232. Rukwa Regional Trading Co Ltd	152	6	-128	*/r	--	6	6	1.3	2.2	31	23	0-0-1-2	
233. Rukwa Regional Transport Co Ltd	78	7	-14	*	--	6	3	1.0	1.0			0-1-1-2	
234. Ruvu Rice Farms Ltd	90	6	-69	*/r	++	9	4	2.7'	1.8	43'	41	0-1-1-1	
236. Ruvuma Cooperative Union Ltd	*160*											0-0-0-1	
237. Ruvuma Regional Trading Co Ltd	*90*	6	-71	*	+	6	6	1.0	1.8	11	23	2-1-1-2	
238. Sabuni Industries Ltd	290	6	-425	*/r	-	12	6	1.8	1.2	41	41	3-0-2-1	
239. Sao Hill Sawmill Ltd	468	9	-133	*	--	12	5	2.2'	1.0	43'	11	2-0-2-2	96
240. Saruji Trucking Co Ltd	*200*	7	-43	*	-	6	6	1.2	1.2	21	41	0-0-1-2	
241. Savoy Hotel Ltd						12	1	3.0	4.0	53	53	0-0-0-2	95
242. Serengeti Safari Lodges (T) Ltd (SSL)	313	7	244	*	-	12	6	1.8	1.0	23	11	0-1-0-2	94
243. Setchet Wheat Co Ltd	203	10	156	*/r	n.s.	9	6	1.8	1.5	23	21	0-0-1-1	
244. Shinyanga Region Cooperative Union	*140*											0-0-0-1	
245. Shinyanga Regional Trading Co Ltd	*120*	6	-57	*	n.s.	6	6	1.0	1.3	11	31	0-0-0-2	
246. Shirika la Usafiri Dar es Salaam Ltd	*1,000*	9	-172	*/r	(-)	6	6	1.2	1.0	41	11	1-1-1-3	
247. Sikh Saw Mills Ltd	460	7	303	*/r	n.s.	12	6	2.0	1.0	32	11	0-0-2-2	
248. Singida Region Cooperative Union	*110*											1-0-0-1	
249. Singida Regional Trading Co Ltd	148	5	-58	*/r	n.s.	6	5	1.3'	2.0	42'	32	1-1-0-2	
250. Sisal Kamba Spinning Co Ltd												2-0-0-1	
252. Small Industries Development Org.	*400*	10	-1,190	*/r/B	++	6	6	1.7	1.5	42	22	0-2-2-2	
253. Southern Paper Mills Co Ltd (SPM)	2,209	10	-8,463	*/r/B	n.s.	12x	6	2.0	1.3	32	21	1-2-3-3	

Code & name	Employ-ment	Profits/losses No.	ø	type	Δ	Accounting features M	No.	P'	Q	ΔP'	ΔQ	Support info	Pr.
(a)	(b)	(c)	(d)	(e)	(f)	(g)	(h)	(i)	(j)	(k)	(l)	(m)	(n)
254. State Fuel Corporation (SFC)	*40*											0-1-1-0	
255. State Insurance Brokers (SIB)	48	10	71	*/r	-	12	6	1.5	1.0	21	11	0-0-0-2	
256. State Mining Corporation	376	10	-593	*/B	n.s.	12	6	1.7	1.5	31	22	0-1-1-2	
257. State Motor Corporation (SMC)	80	7	-451	*/E	n.s.	12	6	1.8	1.3	23	42	1-1-2-2	
259. State Travel Service Ltd (STS)	253	8	47	*/r	(-)	12	6	1.8	1.0	41	11	0-1-1-2	
260. Stationary and Office Supplies (T) Ltd	90	8	37	*	--	6	6	1.5	1.3	21	21	0-1-2-2	
261. Steel Rolling Mills Ltd (SRM)	371	6	-225	*	n.s.	12	6	2.0	1.0	32	11	2-1-2-2	
263. Sugar Development Corporation	141	10	910	*/r/B	n.s.	6	6	1.2	1.3	21	21	0-0-3-3	
264. Tabora Msitu Products Ltd	85	6	-16	*	-	12	3	3.5'	3.0	43'	53	2-0-1-1	
265. Tabora Region Cooperative Union Ltd	*150*											2-0-0-0	
266. Tabora Regional Trading Co Ltd	*90*	7	-23	*	--	6	6	1.2	1.2	41	41	2-1-2-1	
267. Tabora Textile Mills Co Ltd	428	5	-4,907	*/r/B	n.s.	12	5	2.0'	2.0	32'	32	2-0-0-1	
268. Tanga Cement Co Ltd	745	9	235	*	+	6	6	1.0	1.2	11	41	2-1-0-2	95
269. Tanga Cooperative Union Ltd	*160*											2-0-0-0	
270. Tanga Regional Trading Co Ltd	*100*	6	-14	*	--	6	6	1.0	1.0	11	11	1-1-1-2	
271. Tanganyika Coffee Curing Co Ltd	637	7	-6	*	(++)	9x	6	1.5	1.0	21	11	1-0-1-2	94
272. Tangan. Dyeing & Weaving	1,379	6	-1,160	*/r/C	n.s.	12	6	2.0	1.3	32	42	0-2-0-2	
275. Tanganyika Instant Coffee Co Ltd	104	10	55	*	n.s.	9x	6	2.0	1.8	22	23	0-0-0-3	
276. Tanganyika Meerschaum Corporation	147					12	2	3.6'	2.0	43'	52	0-1-0-2	
277. Tanganyika Packers Ltd (TPL)	324	1	-645	*/r/B	-	6x	2	2.7'	1.0	42'	51	2-1-0-3	
278. Tanganyika Planting Co Ltd (TPC)	4,630	9	542	*/r/C	n.s.	6	5	1.0	1.8	11	23	0-1-2-2	
279. Tanganyika Post Office Savings Bank	*400*	6	-620	*/r/B	n.s.	12	6	1.5	1.7	22	31	0-0-0-0	
280. Tanganyika Pyrethrum Board (TPB)	279	9	-179	*	-	6	6	1.0	1.0	11	11	1-2-2-3	
281. Tanganyika Tegry (Plastics) Ltd	192	7	99	*	-	12	6	1.7	1.0	31	11	1-0-2-2	
282. Tangold Products Co Ltd												0-0-0-1	92
283. Tanita Company Ltd	914	6	-310	*/r	n.s.	9	6	2.5	2.0	22	32	1-0-0-2	92
287. Tanz. and Italian Petroleum Refining	528	10	1,240	*/r/B	n.s.	12	6	1.0	1.3	11	21	0-0-2-1	
288. Tanzania Animal Feeds Co Ltd	208	3	-200	*/r	+	7	4	2.3'	2.0	43'	32	1-0-0-2	
289. Tanzania Audit Corporation (TAC)	404	10	57	*/r	(-)	6						0-1-1-3	
290. Tanz. Automobile Manufacturing	128	6	725	*/r/B	n.s.	12	6	1.7	1.0	31	11	1-0-2-1	
291. Tanzania Bag Corporation Ltd	571	10	-177	*	n.s.	12	6	1.5	1.0	21	11	1-0-2-2	
292. Tanzania Breweries Ltd (TBL)	2,579	7	1,228	*/r/C	n.s.	12	6	2.0	1.2	32	21	0-2-2-3	93
294. Tanzania Cables Ltd	96	10	527	*/r/B	n.s.	12	6	1.0	1.0	11	11	0-0-0-3	96
295. Tanzania Carpet Co Ltd	*125*	4	-104	*/r	-	12	2	4.2'	3.0	23'	53	0-0-0-3	
296. Tanz. Cashewnut Marketing Board	763	10	-806	*/C	--	9	6	1.7	1.5	31	22	0-2-2-2	
297. Tanzania Central Freight Bureau	45	10	210	*/r/E	-	6	6	1.0	1.0	11	11	0-0-2-1	
298. Tanzania Cigarette Co Ltd (TCC)	1,430	8	5,457	*/r/B	++	12	6	1.0	1.0	11	11	0-1-1-3	95
299. Tanzania Clay Products Ltd	*120*					6	6	2.5	1.0	22	11	0-0-0-2	
300. Tanzania Coastal Shipping Line	218	6	104	*	--	6	6	1.3	1.0	42	11	0-1-2-2	
301. Tanzania Coffee Marketing Board	764	8	159	*	-	9	6	1.7	2.7	23	22	1-1-2-2	
302. Tanzania Concrete Articles Ltd	*300*	6	-18	*/r	n.s.	6	6	2.2	2.0	43	32	0-1-0-2	
303. Tanzania Cordage Ltd (TANCORD)	315	8	-219	*	--	12	6	1.8	1.2	41	41	2-1-0-1	
304. Tanzania Cotton Marketing Board	299	10	1,383	*/B	n.s.	6	6	1.7	2.0	22	22	1-2-1-3	
305. Tanzania Crown Corks Ltd	*80*											0-0-0-1	
306. Tanzania Dairies Ltd (TDL)	240	6	-67	*	-	12	6	2.0	1.3	32	31	0-0-2-2	
307. Tanzania Dairy Farming Co Ltd	540	4	-51	*/r	-	12	6	2.7	1.7	23	23	1-0-1-1	
308. Tanzania Diamond Cutting Co Ltd	553											1-0-1-2	93
309. Tanzania Distilleries Ltd	127	2	525	*/B		12	5	1.2	1.0	21	11	0-0-1-2	
310. Tanzania Electric Supply Co Ltd	6,563	9	-7,086	*/C	n.s.	12	5	2.5'	1.0	43	11	0-2-2-1	
311. Tanz. Electrical Goods Manufact.	197	8	253	*/r	-	12	6	1.3	1.2	21	21	1-0-2-2	94
312. Tanzania Elimu Supplies (TES)	561	8	-115	*/r	n.s.	6	5	2.0'	2.2	42'	23	0-0-2-3	
313. Tanz. Engin. & Manufact. Design Co.		7	-2		(+)	6	6	1.0	1.0	11	11	0-1-1-1	
314. Tanzania Fertilizer Co Ltd (TAFECO)	500	10	-1,872	*/B	++	12	6	2.0	1.7	32	31	0-0-2-2	
315. Tanzania Film Co Ltd (TFC)	363	9	-25	*	(+)	12	6	1.7	1.3	23	21	1-0-1-3	
316. Tanzania Fisheries Corporation	246	8	4		n.s.	6	5	1.7'	1.4'	42'	21	1-1-0-2	96
317. Tanzania Gemstone Industries Ltd	74					12	4	2.8'	2.0'	43'	42	1-1-1-2	

Code & name	Employ-ment	Profits/losses No.	ø	type	Δ	Accounting features M	No.	P'	Q	ΔP'	ΔQ	Support info	Pr.
(a)	(b)	(c)	(d)	(e)	(f)	(g)	(h)	(i)	(j)	(k)	(l)	(m)	(n)
318. Tanzania Gypsum Co Ltd	40					6	1	2.0	3.0	52	53	0-0-0-1	
319. Tanz. Handicrafts Marketing Cor.	*85*	7	3		n.s.	12x	6	1.7	1.2	42	21	1-0-0-2	
320. Tanzania Harbours Authority (THA)	9,503	10	6,725	*/C	--	6	6	1.7	1.0	22	11	0-2-3-2	
321. Tanzania Hides and Skins Ltd	159	1	-66	*	(++)	12	4	2.6'	1.8	43'	41	1-1-0-1	
322. Tanzania Hotels Investment Ltd		8	2		n.s.	12	5	2.7'	2.0	23'	32	0-0-0-0	
323. Tanzania Housing Bank (THB)	671	7	-541	*/C	-	6	6	1.7	1.5	31	41	0-1-1-2	
324. Tanz. Indust. Studies and Consulting	114	9	7	*/r	(-)	6	6	1.0	1.0	11	11	0-0-1-2	
325. Tanzania Investment Bank (TIB)	119	10	-737	*/B	n.s.	6	6	1.0	1.0	11	11	0-2-2-2	
326. Tanz. Karatasi Associated Industries	41	3	-32		n.s.	12	6	1.5	1.0	41	11	1-0-1-2	
327. Tanz. Leather Associated Industries	27	5	-167	*/r/E	n.s.	12	6	2.0	1.0	42	11	0-2-1-2	
328. Tanzania Legal Corporation (TLC)	84	10	24	*/r	n.s.	6	5	2.7'	1.2	23'	21	0-0-0-2	
330. Tanzania Livestock Marketing Co Ltd	*170*					5	1	1.0	3.0	51	53	0-0-0-2	
332. Tanzania Maltings Co Ltd	167	6	333	*/r/E	n.s.	12	6	1.5	1.3	22	31	0-0-0-0	93
334. Tanzania Motor Services Co Ltd	443	7	59	*	-	12	5	2.0	1.0	32	11	1-0-1-1	
335. Tanzania National Parks (TANAPA)	663	10	742	*/r/C	n.s.	6	6	2.0	1.5	23	41	0-1-0-2	
337. Tanzania News Agency (SHIHATA)	171	5	1		n.s.	6	6	1.0	1.5	11	22	0-1-1-1	
338. Tanzania Oxygen Ltd (TOL)	130	9	326	*/r/E	--	12	3	1.7	1.0			0-0-2-0	
339. Tanzania Packages Manufacturers Ltd	557	8	-2,233	*/r/B	n.s.	12	5	1.0	1.2	11	41	2-1-0-3	
340. Tanz. Petroleum Development Corp.	229	10	8,784	*/r/B	n.s.	12	6	1.0	1.0	11	11	0-1-3-1	
341. Tanzania Pharmaceutical Industries	172	5	-215	*	n.s.	12	6	1.5	1.0	41	11	1-1-2-2	95
342. Tanzania Portland Cement Co Ltd	1,013	10	865	*/C	n.s.	6x	6	1.5	1.0	42	11	1-0-2-2	
343. Tanzania Postal Bank		5	-27	*	++							0-0-0-0	
345. Tanzania Posts Corporation	*2,000*	3	179		n.s.							0-0-0-1	
346. Tanzania Publishing House Ltd (TPH)	38					12x	2	3.3'	2.0	53'	52	0-0-0-2	
347. Tanzania Railways Corporation (TRC)	18,364	9	-950	*/C	++	12	6	1.7	2.0	23	22	1-2-1-2	
349. Tanzania Saruji Corporation (TSjC)	*70*	9	-7	*	n.s.	6	5	1.0	1.4	11	22	0-1-0-2	
350. Tanzania Seed Co Ltd (TANSEED)	*80*	5	-94	*	n.s.							0-0-0-2	
351. Tanzania Sewing Thread Manufact.	71	4	-520	*/r/B	--	12	6	1.8	1.0	23	11	2-0-0-1	
352. Tanzania Sheet Glass Ltd	*230*	1	-227	*		6	6	1.2	1.7	41	42	0-0-0-1	
353. Tanzania Shoe Co Ltd (BORA)	1,962	1	-1,009	C		12	2	4.0'	2.0	53	52	2-1-1-2	94
354. Tanzania Sisal Authority (TSA)	2,468	9	-319	*/r	n.s.	12	6	2.3	1.8	23	22	2-3-2-2	
355. Tanzania Standard Newspapers Ltd	175	10	-51	*	n.s.	12	6	2.0	1.5	32	21	0-0-0-0	
356. Tanzania Starch Manufacturers Co	10					12	1	4.0'	1.0	53'	51	1-0-0-1	
357. Tanz. Stationery Manufacturers Co	*180*	3	-42		-	6	5	2.2'	2.2	42	23	0-0-0-3	
358. Tanzania Tanneries Co Ltd	258	3	-97	*/r	+	12	4	2.2'	1.0	42'	11	2-1-0-2	93
359. Tanzania Tea Authority (TTA)	737	10	181	*/r	-	6	6	1.0	1.0	11	11	1-2-3-2	
360. Tanzania Tea Blenders Ltd (TTB)	621	9	225	*/r	n.s.	6	5	1.0	1.0	11	11	0-0-1-2	
362. Tanzania Telecommunications Co.	*8,635*	10	-10,484	*/r/C	++	12	6	2.0	1.5	32	21	0-2-2-2	
363. Tanz. Tobacco Processing & MB	2,270	10	-9		n.s.	3	6	1.7	2.5	22	22	1-1-3-3	
364. Tanzania Tourist Board (TTCorp)	*90*	3	54	*	n.s.	12	6	2.2	1.8	23	22	1-1-0-2	
365. Tanzania Tractors Manufacturing	110	6	139	*	-	12	5	1.6	1.0	23	11	0-0-1-2	
367. Tanzania Watch Assembling Co Ltd	23	4	-13		+	12	6	1.8	1.0	41	11	1-0-0-2	
368. Tanzania Wildlife Corporation	178	10	65	*	-	12	5	1.7'	1.0	42'	11	0-1-0-2	
369. Tanzania Wood Industry Corporation	194	6	12	*	--	12	5	2.3'	1.4'	43	21	1-0-2-3	
370. Tanz. Zambia Railway Authority	*2,500*	3	1,926	C	n.s.							0-1-0-1	
371. TBL Farms Ltd	234	7	-130	*	++	12	6	2.0	1.8	32	23	0-0-0-1	93
373. Tembo Chipboards Ltd	615	7	-4		(-)	12	6	1.7	1.3	31	42	2-1-2-1	
374. THB Estates Ltd (TECO)		4	164	*/r	n.s.	6	5	1.0	1.0	11	11	0-0-0-2	
375. Trailers & Lowloaders Manufact.	105	6	-209	*/r/E	n.s.	12	6	1.5	1.0	41	11	1-0-2-1	
378. Typesetting Services Ltd		1	-81			12	3	4.2'	2.0	43'	53	1-0-0-0	
379. Ubungo Garments Ltd (UGL)	289	4	-37	*/r	(+)	12	6	1.0	1.3	11	42	1-0-0-3	
380. Ubungo Spinning Mill Ltd (USM)	498	5	-390	*/r	+	12	5	1.6	1.2	23	41	2-0-0-3	
381. Ushirikiano Wood Products Co Ltd	94	1	-62	*		12	3	3.0'	2.0	43'	53	0-0-0-1	
384. Vuasu Cooperative Union Ltd												1-1-0-0	
385. Warret Wheat Farms Ltd	182	8	103	*/r	n.s.	9	6	2.2	1.3	23	21	0-0-1-1	
386. West Kilimanjaro Livestock Breeding	*115*	4	-72	*/r	n.s.	9	5	2.5'	2.0	22	32	0-0-1-0	

Code & name	Employ-ment	Profits/losses				Accounting features						Support info	Pr.
		No.	ø	type	Δ	M	No.	P'	Q	ΔP'	ΔQ		
(a)	(b)	(c)	(d)	(e)	(f)	(g)	(h)	(i)	(j)	(k)	(l)	(m)	(n)
387. Williamson Diamonds Ltd	2,114											2-1-0-2	94
388. Zana Za Kilimo Ltd (ZZK)	259	6	-160	*/r	n.s.	12	6	2.0	1.8	32	23	2-0-1-1	
390. Zanzibar Shipping Corporation												0-0-1-0	
391. Zanzibar State Trading												0-0-1-0	
392. ZZ COTEX Zanzibar												0-0-1-0	

Explanations to Table B-6

(a): Parastatal code and name

Companies that have been excluded from the data set are no longer shown (see comments in Table B-1).

(b): Employment figures

Figures represent averages of information published in PSRC (1993, Appendix 3) and data obtained from various sources at the Bureau of Statistics in Dar es Salaam. The database has been rather poor and incomplete. Some of the information refers to a specific year; other information reflects an average of several years. Figures in italics are (or include) guesses of a senior official at the Bureau of Statistics, as there was no other information available (see also comments in Section c) of Chapter 8.1). For the analysis in Chapter 8.2, parastatals with no information on employment (Codes 34, 225, 241, 250, 282, 313, 322, 343, 374, 378, 384, 390, 391, 392) have been assigned the arbitrary value 80, so that the companies do not drop out of the analysis (in the above table the value is left blank). Results do not however depend on this adjustment.

(c): Number of profit and loss statements

Number of profit and loss statements between 1987 and 1996 (maximum 10, if the company was not privatised prior to 1997). Not counted in this figure are profit and loss statements prior to 1987, interval information and profit and loss statements that obtained the worst rating 'adverse'. Interval information occurs if the accounts of a company are mentioned to be audited but the value of the profit and loss is not shown, as it does not exceed the minimum threshold of TSh 5 million (TSh 20 million in 1993) to be published in the TAC report.

(d): Average profits and losses for 1987-96

Averages of all profits and losses for the period 1987-96 (where information was available), in TSh million and at 1994 prices. Profits and losses are deflated according to the years and months (column g) the financial statement refers to. Not included in the calculation are the years after the privatisation or lease of a company, interval information and all profit and loss statements from accounting figures which have been rated 'adverse' (see discussion in Section d) of Chapter 8.1).

Source: 95% of data from TAC (1987-93) and questionnaires filled by TAC, remaining information from Treasury, Coopers&Lybrand (1996), PSRC (1997b) and Ministry of Agriculture (1994a).

(e): Profit and loss categories

This column defines additional attributes assigned to the companies: 'Significant Profit/loss-maker' (*), 'Regular Profit/loss-maker' (r) and 'Large Profit/loss-maker' (C, E or B, depending on whether large 'per company', 'per employee' or both).

Companies are grouped into *significant (*) and not significant profit/loss-makers*, according to their annual accounting data. Excluded from any evaluation are profits and losses of accounts which have been rated as 'adverse' by Tanzania Audit Corporation. As a precondition to qualify for a significant group average profits and losses have to exceed TSh 5000 per employee and TSh 5 million per company (1994 prices), which is approximately US$10 per employee and US$10,000 per company. In addition, at least 4 useful statements and indicators are required (however, as will be shown below, more restrictive criteria will be applied in cases where only few information is available).

192 companies have been rated as significant profit/loss-makers and grouped according to the simple average rule, as there were 5 and more explicit profit and loss statements for the period 1987-96. With 16 companies profits and losses were too small and they were therefore rated as not significant.

An additional 26 companies reached 5 profit and loss statements only if interval information was counted. Knowing that an unknown profit or loss is within a certain range makes it possible to test whether the overall profit/loss category of the company can change at all, once unknown values are replaced by upper or lower limits of the intervals. With 14 of the 26 companies, the sign of the average did not change and they were therefore defined as significant. 12 were not significant.

For companies where less than 5 useful profit and loss statements were obtained, even when including interval information, additional profit/loss information from the period 1984-86 was taken into account. This data has not been collected systematically but was only known for accounts which had been audited after June 1987. For 9 companies, the inclusion of the period 1984-86 allowed the target of at least 5 statements to be reached. Similar to the above procedure, 8 companies were finally defined to be significant, as the profit/loss category did not change when including data prior to 1987.

With the remaining companies, it was not possible to have at least 5 statements. Companies with 4 profit and loss statements for the period 1987-96 were nevertheless rated as significant if each individual statement indicated the same category, i.e. either profit or loss. The same rule was applied for companies which reached 4 statements if data prior to 1987 was included. This procedure allowed grouping another 4, respectively 6 companies as significant (6 + 1 were not significant).

Finally, 15 companies were rated as not significant as fewer than 4 profit and loss statements had been obtained and 61 companies could not be grouped at all as there was no explicit profit and loss information (9 contained only interval information).

The attribute *regular (r)* is based on an evaluation of all profit and loss statements between 1984 and 1996. To qualify as a *regular profit-maker or regular loss-maker* between 80% and 100% of the profit and loss statements needed to be within the same category (i.e. zero deviations were tolerated for companies with 4 statements only, one deviation for companies with 5 to 9 statements, and two for companies with 10 to 13 statements). In addition, a company needed to be rated as significant, which was not the case for one company (144). 10 companies (10, 59, 138, 181, 202, 261, 281, 320, 341, 342) were not rated as regular, as they only met the criteria for the sub-period 1987 to 1996 but not 1984 to 1996.

To qualify as a *large profit/loss-maker*, average profits/losses have to exceed TSh 500 million (US$1 million) per company (C) or TSh 1.5 million (US$3000) per employee (E). If both criteria hold, the company is marked as (B).

(f): Trend of annual profits and losses

The signs indicate the trend of the annual profits and losses mostly from the period 1987 to 1996. Only if there were fewer than 4 profit and loss statements and the company did not show a significant trend, were additional data from the period 1984 to 1986 taken into account. Trends have been estimated according to the specification y=mx+b (y: vector of the company's profits and losses, x: corresponding years). Because annual profits and losses are unlikely to be independent, the time series data was equally tested for autocorrelation (to justify the use of an alternative model). However, given the small number of observations per company, autocorrelation needed to be very high to become significant (0.6 with 10 observations or 0.8 with 5 observations), which was not the case for most companies. For the few companies where autocorrelation was significant, estimated trends of the alternative model were not much different.

An improving or deteriorating trend is marked as ++, -- or +, -, depending on whether the trend were significant at the confidence level 95% or 75% only (explained below).[215] If the trend is in parentheses, annual changes are small, i.e. less than TSh 50,000 per employee. Companies with no significant trend at the confidence level 75% are marked 'n.s'.

The unusually low confidence level of 75% has been applied since the major goal was not to test significant trends but to differentiate between companies which more likely improved their situation from others which more likely worsened their situation. Since profits and losses of parastatal companies fluctuated considerably because of the generally poor quality of accounting (which still can be poor although accounts are rated 'clean' by the Tanzanian Audit Corporation), many of the companies have large standard deviations and may therefore not show an improving or deteriorating trend significant at the 95% level. Partly a reflection of this, but also for other reasons, companies may indicate opposite trends within smaller sub-periods. On average, however, it still makes sense to categorise some of them as generally improving or deteriorating companies, even though the trends are not significant at a level of 95%. Visualising each trend rated as significant also confirmed that this approach was useful, i.e. the graphs clearly showed either improving or deteriorating trends.

(g): Months at which the company closes its annual financial statements

Most of the companies close their accounts either in December or June (of the 1783 annual statements evaluated, 49.2% refer to December, 39.3% to June, 9.9% to September, 0.6% to March, 0.5% to April, 0.4% to July and 0.1% to February). Figures with 'x' indicate 'majority only', i.e. the month of closing accounts has changed during the ten-year period.

(h): Number of years with accounting information (1986-91)

The figure indicates the number of statements according to which averages in the columns (i) to (l) have been calculated.

(i): Average periods until audit (extended data set)

The data shows the average time (periods) until financial statements were submitted and audited. It includes all accounts which were mentioned in the TAC reports between 1987 and 1993 and which refer to the years 1986 to 1991. (From 1994 onwards, TAC no longer published individual information on parastatals and the 1992 accounts were excluded as less than half of the accounts were audited by June 1993.)

Information on arrears has been available in terms of intervals. Each parastatal has a specific month when it closes its annual financial statements (see column g). Annual TAC reports only indicate the identity of accounts audited during the preceding twelve months (1 July to 30 June), but not the exact date when submitted accounts were audited within this period. Taking into account a grace period of six months before accounts have to be audited, accounts can only be identified to be in arrears if they do not appear in the following year's TAC report. This is, of course, a conservative treatment, as June accounts may already be six months in arrears, March accounts even nine months (a June account has to be audited by December, a March account by September).

Audits of accounts mentioned in the TAC report of the following year are assigned the value 1. If the audit is only mentioned in a later report, the value will be 2, 3, 4, etc.,

[215] The rating of the companies 38, 70, 179, 277, 288 and 321 includes data prior to 1987.

depending on the year. For instance, to be on-time, a June or December 1988 account would have to be mentioned to be audited in the June 1989 TAC report. If the account appears in the 1991 TAC report, the assigned value will be 3. A value of 3 implies for a June account that an audit was only done after 25 to 36 months and for a December account after 19 to 30 months (depending on whether the account was audited just before or after a TAC closing date).

For the calculation of company averages, a best-case scenario was assumed, i.e. accounts of 1986-91 still in progress or in arrears in June 1993 are assumed to have been audited by June 1994. Accounts not explicitly mentioned in arrears are only replaced if there is some information that the company was still operating after the last accounts in arrears.[216] If the replacement of missing values changes the value of the average, the figure is marked with an apostrophe ('), indicating that the average includes estimated values.

(j): Indicator on average quality of audited accounts

Indicator on average quality of accounts audited. The raw data is based on the following nominal values: 1 (clean report), 2 (qualified report), 3 (disclaimer opinion report) and 4 (adverse opinion report). For the extended data set (not shown here), accounts not audited by June 1993 but mentioned to be in arrears are assigned the quality the company obtained in its last audited report. If the replacement of missing values would change the value of the average, the figure is marked with an apostrophe (').

(k) and (l): Codes on 'Change in average periods' and 'Change in average quality'

The codes indicate the change in accounting performance over time, based on a comparison of the two sub-periods 1986-88 and 1989-91 (the quality category only includes values of audited accounts). If the replacement of missing values changes the code, the code is marked with an apostrophe ('). Except for the separate group with the codes 51 to 53, a smaller code value indicates a better accounting performance (ordinal relation). The codes are defined according to the following sub-period means and average changes in performance (Δ):

	Change (Δ)
(11) Maximum always achieved	$\Delta = 0$
(21) Improving from fairly good position (average first period < 2.0)	$\Delta < 0$
(22) Strong improving from bad position (average first period ≥ 2.0)	$\Delta \leq -1$
(23) Weak improving from bad position (average first period ≥ 2.0)	$0 > \Delta > -1$
(31) No change (average first period < 2.0)	$\Delta = 0$
(32) No change (average first period ≥ 2.0)	$\Delta = 0$
(41) Weak worsening from fairly good position (average first period < 2.0)	$0 < \Delta \leq 0.5$
(42) Strong worsening from fairly good position (average first period < 2.0)	$\Delta > 0.5$
(43) Worsening from bad position (average first period ≥ 2.0)	$\Delta > 0$

[216] Of the companies with accounts in arrears earlier than 1991, this was only the case for Bagamoyo Farmers, Monact Seed, Ruvu Rice Farms and Tabora Msitu products.

No subsequent information (in bracket last explicitly mentioned accounts in arrears) has been obtained from the following companies: 1. Afina Pencils Co Ltd (account 88), 64. Giraffe Extract Co Ltd (account 90), 92. Kigamboni Poultry Farm Ltd (account 85), 103. Kilwa Ammonia Co Ltd (account 86), 124. Mafuta ya Ilulu Ltd (account 89), 130. Mbeya Ceramics Ltd (account 90), 179. Mwanza Tanneries Ltd (account 90), 198. National Ranching Co Ltd (account 90), 225. Rasilimali Ltd (account 89), 276. Tanganyika Meerschaum Corporation (account 90), 277. Tanganyika Packers Ltd (account 89), 317. Tanzania Gemstone Industries Ltd (account 90), 321. Tanzania Hides and Skins Ltd (account 90), 346. Tanzania Publishing House Ltd (account 88), 353. Tanzania Shoe Co Ltd (account 88), 356. Tanzania Starch Manufacturers Co Ltd (account 86), 358. Tanzania Tanneries Co Ltd (account 90), 378. Typesetting Services Ltd (account 90).

(continued)	Change (Δ)
(51) Maximum always achieved (only first period data available)	n.a.
(52) Average first period ≤ 2.0 (only first period data available)	n.a.
(53) Average first period > 2.0 (only first period data available)	n.a.

The range of the attributes weak/strong is not defined symmetrically as there is an overall improving trend. The differentiation within the improving group (21-23) is not symmetric since the underlying variable has a lower limit, i.e. average quality and average periods until audit cannot be less than 1 (which implies that an improvement from a fairly good position (21) cannot reach -1). Partly for similar reasons and also because there is an overall improving trend, the category 43 is not divided into 'weak' and 'strong' worsening.

(m): Parastatal support

The four digits indicate the categories of 'support-information' obtained, grouped according to the four channels of support *Banking* (loans and overdrafts in arrears or in default from NBC, CRDB, TIB and THB), *Treasury* (loans, investments and guarantees), *Other state and donor support* (subsidies, Commodity Import Support programme, income tax arrears, dividend payment arrears) and *Inter-parastatal arrears* (pension, power, water, phone). E.g. '2' in the first digit means that the parastatal received some support from two banks (this support may comprise one or several loans and overdrafts from each bank) or '3' in the second digit shows that the parastatal benefited from all the three sources of Treasury support, i.e. Treasury loans, Treasury investments and Treasury guarantees (again, with each source, the company may have obtained one or several loans, investments or guarantees). More detailed information on support could not be displayed for reasons of confidentiality.

(n): Year of privatisation (or lease) prior to 1997

Most of the information is obtained from the annual reports of the Parastatal Sector Reform Commission (PSRC).

Table B-7: Employment and Profit and Loss Data (TSh m, 1994 prices) According to Sectors and Location 1987-96 (I)

Grouping by sector	Comp. in group	Employment (ø 1987-96) Comp. with info	Accumu-lated	% of total	ø per comp.	Average profits/losses 1987-96 (TSh m) No. of profit-makers	No. of loss-makers	ø per company no weights	ø per company weights (years)[a]	ø per 1000 empl. no weights	ø per 1000 empl. weights (years)[a]
Agriculture & mining	90	88	30,659	17%	348	16	32	-69	-59	-147	-123
Agriculture	78	76	25,602	14%	337	16	24	-3	14	-6	28
Cash crops	26	26	16,738	9%	644	8	12	13	27	17	35
Food crops	13	13	3,248	2%	250	6	6	-13	11	-52	47
Other plants	3	2	86	0%	43	0	2	-62	-62	-1,443	-1,443
Live animals	8	8	2,161	1%	270	2	4	-15	-16	-44	-62
Cooperative unions	28	27	3,368	2%	125	0	0				
Mining	12	12	5,057	3%	421	0	8	-400	-518	-1,477	-1,629
Manufacturing	137	133	72,047	39%	542	38	79	-482	-494	-818	-677
Textile & leather	29	27	19,183	10%	710	1	24	-2,332	-2,838	-3,102	-3,284
All other	108	106	52,864	29%	499	37	55	21	22	40	31
Food, beverage, tobacco	19	19	26,474	14%	1,393	9	8	162	86	105	44
Wood, paper, printing	26	25	8,979	5%	359	4	18	-454	-828	-1,238	-1,566
Chemicals	14	14	3,251	2%	232	8	4	731	985	2,791	3,367
Construction	23	22	8,403	5%	382	5	13	-66	-35	-160	-71
Metal & machinery	26	26	5,757	3%	221	11	12	68	94	294	369
Services	109	101	80,608	44%	798	51	50	-10	-48	-14	-51
Public utilities	5	5	18,786	10%	3,757	1	3	-5,204	-6,322	-1,110	-1,212
Finance	14	10	13,914	8%	1,391	9	4	808	755	745	718
All other	90	86	47,908	26%	557	41	43	111	161	197	233
Trade, repair & maint.	39	37	6,155	3%	166	11	25	13	53	87	327
Transport & storage	24	23	36,119	20%	1,570	14	8	406	496	247	263
Tourism	20	19	4,069	2%	214	11	8	53	67	245	267
Other services	7	7	1,565	1%	224	5	2	-154	-182	-688	-766
Total	336	322	183,314	100%	569	105	161	-228	-238	-354	-308
Grouping by location											
Centre	157	151	112,931	62%	748	67	75	42	59	53	63
Nationwide	18	18	56,378	31%	3,132	7	10	-873	-1,594	-264	-394
Dar es Salaam	130	124	54,890	30%	443	60	59	178	291	393	561
Dar es Salaam only	115	109	41,472	23%	380	53	54	121	206	315	503
DSM & other towns	6	6	12,302	7%	2,050	5	1	1,272	1,535	621	682
Dar es Salaam suburb	9	9	1,115	1%	124	2	4	106	193	842	1,584
Dodoma	9	9	1,663	1%	185	0	6	-71	-58	-602	-424
Sub- / near centre	81	75	40,856	22%	545	20	40	-391	-508	-627	-634
Arusha & Moshi	33	32	9,133	5%	285	11	15	38	76	132	226
Arusha	19	18	4,595	3%	255	8	8	64	106	250	358
Moshi	14	14	4,539	2%	324	3	7	-6	6	-17	13
Towns near Dar es Salaam	36	31	14,356	8%	463	5	20	-1,060	-1,443	-1,938	-2,048
Morogoro	16	15	7,305	4%	487	1	12	-1,849	-2,496	-3,360	-3,340
Tanga & Korogwe	15	14	6,971	4%	498	4	7	-222	-319	-378	-465
Zanzibar & Mafia	5	2	80	0%	40	0	1	-10	-10	-240	-240

(continued)	Comp. in group	Comp. with info	Employment (ø 1987-96) Accumu-lated	% of total	ø per comp.	Average profits/losses 1987-96 (TSh m) No. of profit-makers	No. of loss-makers	ø per company no weights	ø per company weights (years)[a]	ø per 1000 empl. no weights	ø per 1000 empl. weights (years)[a]
Rural near Dar es Salaam	12	12	17,366	9%	1,447	4	5	227	450	125	163
DSM rural	2	2	111	0%	56	0	1	-69	-69	-768	-768
Morogoro & Tanga rural	10	10	17,255	9%	1,726	4	4	264	525	130	167
Remote areas	98	96	29,528	16%	308	18	46	-674	-653	-1,849	-1,556
Towns remote	60	60	12,923	7%	215	10	29	-843	-745	-3,324	-2,863
Towns moderate far	13	13	1,887	1%	145	1	6	-56	-82	-420	-520
Towns far	47	47	11,036	6%	235	9	23	-1,015	-843	-3,625	-3,060
Rural remote	38	36	16,605	9%	461	8	17	-411	-531	-764	-837
Arusha & Moshi rural	19	17	6,458	4%	380	7	8	36	49	92	106
Rural moderate far	4	4	2,887	2%	722	0	2	-4,298	-4,517	-3,211	-3,263
Rural far	15	15	7,260	4%	484	1	7	-279	-341	-481	-471
Total	336	322	183,314	100%	569	105	161	-228	-238	-354	-308

a: Company averages weighted according to the number of annual statements available to calculate the company average.

Source: See Table B-6

Table B-8: Profit and Loss Data (TSh m, 1994 prices) According to Sectors and Location 1987-96 (II)

Grouping by sector	Comp. in group	No. of P/L makers	Annual Sector Totals: Accumulated average profits/losses of companies — No weights: All	Profit-makers	Loss-makers	Weighted[a]: All	Profit-makers	Loss-makers	Average profits/losses per 1000 empl.: All	Profit-makers	Loss-makers
Agriculture & mining	90	48	-3,328	2,954	-6,282	-1,846	2,711	-4,557	-147	321	-468
Agriculture	78	40	-125	2,954	-3,079	381	2,711	-2,329	-6	321	-273
Cash crops	26	20	252	2,153	-1,901	373	1,984	-1,610	17	317	-227
Food crops	13	12	-162	747	-909	108	714	-606	-52	1,104	-371
Other plants	3	2	-124		-124	-62		-62	-1,443		-1,443
Live animals	8	6	-91	54	-145	-38	13	-51	-44	31	-418
Cooperative unions	28	0									
Mining	12	8	-3,203		-3,203	-2,228		-2,228	-1,477		-1,477
Manufacturing	137	117	-56,381	28,147	-84,529	-36,703	25,069	-61,771	-818	935	-2,183
Textile & leather	29	25	-58,298	22	-58,320	-38,031	17	-38,049	-3,102	35	-3,210
All other	108	92	1,917	28,126	-26,209	1,329	25,051	-23,722	40	954	-1,273
Food, beverage, tobacco	19	17	2,753	11,360	-8,607	1,044	9,287	-8,243	105	545	-1,608
Wood, paper, printing	26	22	-9,985	361	-10,346	-9,601	233	-9,834	-1,238	481	-1,416
Chemicals	14	12	8,766	11,334	-2,568	8,865	11,116	-2,251	2,791	5,459	-2,412
Construction	23	18	-1,179	1,557	-2,736	-440	1,528	-1,968	-160	517	-630
Metal & machinery	26	23	1,562	3,514	-1,952	1,461	2,887	-1,426	294	1,252	-777
Services	109	101	-991	28,634	-29,625	-3,355	23,344	-26,700	-14	816	-655
Public utilities	5	4	-20,814	179	-20,994	-20,231	54	-20,285	-1,110	90	-1,254
Finance	14	13	10,505	12,430	-1,926	7,705	9,206	-1,502	745	964	-1,596

(continued)	Comp. in group	No. of P/L makers	Annual Sector Totals: Accumulated average profits/losses of companies — No weights: All	Profit-makers	Loss-makers	Weighted [a]: All	Profit-makers	Loss-makers	Average profits/losses per 1000 empl.: All	Profit-makers	Loss-makers
All other	90	84	9,319	16,024	-6,706	9,171	14,084	-4,913	197	795	-246
Trade, repair & maint.	39	36	476	2,165	-1,690	1,195	2,098	-903	87	1,104	-452
Transport & storage	24	22	8,921	11,928	-3,007	8,286	10,454	-2,168	247	828	-139
Tourism	20	19	998	1,792	-794	780	1,409	-629	245	601	-729
Other services	7	7	-1,077	139	-1,215	-1,090	123	-1,213	-688	173	-1,593
Total	336	266	-60,700	59,735	-120,436	-41,904	51,123	-93,028	-354	803	-1,237
Grouping by location											
Centre	157	142	5,923	52,086	-46,163	5,577	44,441	-38,864	53	1,119	-716
Nationwide	18	17	-14,839	12,947	-27,786	-17,857	8,486	-26,343	-264	721	-726
Dar es Salaam	130	119	21,185	39,139	-17,954	23,596	35,955	-12,359	393	1,370	-703
Dar es Salaam only	115	107	12,915	29,914	-16,999	15,152	27,091	-11,939	315	1,754	-710
DSM & other towns	6	6	7,635	8,361	-726	7,982	8,345	-363	621	743	-690
Dar es Salaam suburb	9	6	636	864	-229	462	519	-56	842	3,639	-442
Dodoma	9	6	-423		-423	-162		-162	-602		-602
Sub- / near centre	81	60	-23,478	5,352	-28,830	-19,056	4,825	-23,882	-627	259	-1,725
Arusha & Moshi	33	26	976	2,290	-1,314	1,299	2,049	-750	132	652	-334
Arusha	19	16	1,032	1,797	-765	1,271	1,721	-450	250	727	-461
Moshi	14	10	-55	493	-548	28	328	-299	-17	475	-242
Towns near Dar es Salaam	36	25	-26,497	659	-27,156	-22,517	445	-22,962	-1,938	348	-2,307
Morogoro	16	13	-24,041	27	-24,068	-20,221	3	-20,224	-3,360	342	-3,402
Tanga & Korogwe	15	11	-2,446	632	-3,078	-2,294	442	-2,736	-378	348	-661
Zanzibar & Mafia	5	1	-10		-10	-3		-3	-240		-240
Rural near Dar es Salaam	12	9	2,042	2,402	-360	2,162	2,332	-170	125	157	-354
DSM rural	2	1	-69		-69	-41		-41	-768		-768
Morogoro & Tanga rural	10	8	2,112	2,402	-291	2,204	2,332	-129	130	157	-314
Remote areas	98	64	-43,145	2,298	-45,443	-28,425	1,857	-30,282	-1,849	324	-2,798
Towns remote	60	39	-32,861	474	-33,334	-18,549	372	-18,921	-3,324	323	-3,960
Towns moderate far	13	7	-389	30	-419	-261	12	-273	-420	301	-508
Towns far	47	32	-32,471	443	-32,915	-18,288	360	-18,648	-3,625	324	-4,336
Rural remote	38	25	-10,284	1,824	-12,109	-9,876	1,485	-11,361	-764	324	-1,547
Arusha & Moshi rural	19	15	546	1,580	-1,034	549	1,314	-765	92	297	-1,267
Rural moderate far	4	2	-8,596		-8,596	-8,583		-8,583	-3,211		-3,211
Rural far	15	8	-2,234	244	-2,478	-1,842	171	-2,013	-481	780	-572
Total	336	266	-60,700	59,735	-120,436	-41,904	51,123	-93,028	-354	803	-1,237

a: Company averages weighted according to the number of annual statements available to calculate the company average.

Source: See Table B-6

Table B-9: Regular and Large Profit/Loss-Makers According to Sectors and Location

Grouping by sector	Comp. in group	Profit-makers (average 1987-96, 1994 prices)					Loss-makers (average 1987-96, 1994 prices)				
		All	Regular		Large, per		All	Regular		Large, per	
		No.	No.	Rel. dist. [a]	comp.	empl.	No.	No.	Rel. dist. [b]	comp.	empl.
Agriculture & mining	90	16	8	103%	1	4	32	13	93%	4	4
Agriculture	78	16	8	103%	1	4	24	8	77%	1	1
Cash crops	26	8	3	77%	1	1	12	4	77%	1	
Food crops	13	6	5	172%		3	6	2	77%		
Other plants	3	0					2	1	115%		1
Live animals	8	2					4	1	58%		
Cooperative unions	28	0					0				
Mining	12	0					8	5	144%	3	3
Manufacturing	137	38	21	114%	13	11	79	39	114%	19	21
Textile & leather	29	1					24	17	163%	11	11
All other	108	37	21	117%	13	11	55	22	92%	8	10
Food, beverage, tobacco	19	9	8	183%	7	4	8	6	173%	2	1
Wood, paper, printing	26	4	1	51%			18	4	51%	2	2
Chemicals	14	8	6	154%	2	4	4	1	58%	1	1
Construction	23	5	1	41%	1		13	6	106%	2	3
Metal & machinery	26	11	5	94%	3	3	12	5	96%	1	3
Services	109	51	22	89%	9	7	50	18	83%	11	7
Public utilities	5	1					3	2	153%	3	1
Finance	14	9	5	114%	3		4	1	58%	3	2
All other	90	41	17	85%	6	7	43	15	80%	5	4
Trade, repair & maint.	39	11	4	75%	1	1	25	8	74%		1
Transport & storage	24	14	7	103%	4	4	8	3	86%	3	1
Tourism	20	11	3	56%	1	1	8	3	86%	1	1
Other services	7	5	3	124%		1	2	1	115%	1	1
Total	336	105	51	100%	23	22	161	70	100%	34	32
Grouping by location											
Centre	157	67	31	95%	19	17	75	32	98%	19	15
Nationwide	18	7	2	59%	3		10	5	115%	6	3
Dar es Salaam	130	60	29	100%	16	17	59	25	97%	13	11
Dar es Salaam only	115	53	24	93%	13	15	54	23	98%	12	11
DSM & other towns	6	5	4	165%	2	1	1	1	230%	1	
Dar es Salaam suburb	9	2	1	103%	1	1	4	1	58%		
Dodoma	9	0					6	2	77%		1
Sub- / near centre	81	20	9	93%	3	1	40	16	92%	5	7
Arusha & Moshi	33	11	5	94%	1	1	15	5	77%		2
Arusha	19	8	4	103%	1		8	3	86%		2
Moshi	14	3	1	69%		1	7	2	66%		
Towns near Dar es Salaam	36	5	1	41%			20	9	104%	5	5
Morogoro	16	1					12	7	134%	4	4
Tanga & Korogwe	15	4	1	51%			7	2	66%	1	1
Zanzibar & Mafia	5	0					1				

(continued)	Comp. in group	Profit-makers (average 1987-96, 1994 prices)					Loss-makers (average 1987-96, 1994 prices)				
		All	Regular		Large, per		All	Regular		Large, per	
		No.	No.	Rel. dist. [a]	comp.	empl.	No.	No.	Rel. dist. [b]	comp.	empl.
Rural near Dar es Salaam	12	4	3	154%	2		5	2	92%		
DSM rural	2	0					1	1	230%		
Morogoro & Tanga rural	10	4	3	154%	2		4	1	58%		
Remote areas	98	18	11	126%	1	4	46	22	110%	10	10
Towns remote	60	10	5	103%			29	12	95%	6	8
Towns moderate far	13	1	1	206%			6	2	77%		1
Towns far	47	9	4	92%			23	10	100%	6	7
Rural remote	38	8	6	154%	1	4	17	10	135%	4	2
Arusha & Moshi rural	19	7	6	176%	1	4	8	5	144%	1	1
Rural moderate far	4	0					2	1	115%	1	1
Rural far	15	1					7	4	131%	2	
Total	336	105	51	100%	23	22	161	70	100%	34	32

a: Compared to average distribution of regular profit-makers in economy, i.e. 51/105 = 100%. Values indicate over-representation or under-representation of regular profit-makers in specified sector or location.

b: Compared to average distribution of regular loss-makers in economy, i.e. 70/161 = 100%. Values indicate over-representation or under-representation of regular loss-makers in specified sector or location.

Source: See Table B-6

Table B-10: The Largest Profit/Loss-Makers According to Average Profits and Losses (TSh m, 1994 prices)

Pos	Parastatal name (in parentheses code)	No. of stat.	Profits	Cumulative in % [a]	Employment	Cumulative in % [a]	Pos. in Table B-11
1	National Bank of Commerce (182)	7	9,357	16%	8000	11%	29
2	Tanzania Petroleum Development Corporation (340)	10	8,784	30%	229	11%	1
3	Tanzania Harbours Authority (320)	10	6,725	42%	9503	24%	39
4	Tanzania Cigarette Co Ltd (298)	8	5,457	51%	1430	26%	11
5	Tanzania Zambia Railway Authority (370) [b]	3	1,926	54%	2500	29%	36
6	Agip (Tanzania) Ltd (3)	10	1,723	57%	359	30%	5
7	National Provident Fund (197)	9	1,714	60%	1257	31%	25
8	Kilombero Sugar Co Ltd (100)	10	1,658	63%	7779	42%	73
9	National Shipping Agencies Co Ltd (199)	10	1,470	65%	892	43%	22
10	Tanzania Cotton Marketing Board (304)	10	1,383	67%	299	43%	7
11	Aluminium Africa Ltd (7)	9	1,329	70%	1028	45%	26
12	Tanzania and Italian Petroleum Refining Co (287)	10	1,240	72%	528	46%	15
13	Tanzania Breweries Ltd (292)	7	1,228	74%	2579	49%	52
14	Sugar Development Corporation (263)	10	910	75%	141	49%	2
15	Tanzania Portland Cement Co Ltd (342)	10	865	77%	1013	51%	32
16	Dar es Salaam Airport Handling Co Ltd (45)	10	771	78%	200	51%	10
17	Tanzania National Parks (335)	10	742	79%	663	52%	31
18	Tanzania Automobile Manufacturing Co Ltd (290)	6	725	80%	128	52%	3
19	Mtibwa Sugar Estates Ltd (165)	10	644	81%	3782	57%	76
20	National Insurance Corp of Tanzania (191)	10	569	82%	2046	60%	69
1	Morogoro Polyester Textiles Ltd (154)	10	-14,705	12%	1585	2%	6
2	Musoma Textile Ltd (175)	5	-14,669	24%	1467	3%	5
3	Tanzania Telecommunications Company Ltd (362)	10	-10,484	33%	8635	12%	37
4	Mwanza Textiles Ltd (180)	6	-9,199	41%	2095	14%	15
5	Southern Paper Mills Co Ltd (253)	10	-8,463	48%	2209	16%	17
6	Tanzania Electric Supply Co Ltd (310)	9	-7,086	54%	6563	23%	44
7	National Milling Corporation (193)	10	-6,626	59%	1197	24%	12
8	Morogoro Shoe Co Ltd (158)	5	-5,543	64%	242	25%	1
9	Tabora Textile Mills Co Ltd (267)	5	-4,907	68%	428	25%	3
10	National Urban Water Authority (203)	10	-3,423	71%	1548	27%	24
11	Tanzania Packages Manufacturers Ltd (339)	8	-2,233	73%	557	27%	16
12	Tanzania Fertilizer Co Ltd (314)	10	-1,872	74%	500	28%	18
13	Small Industries Development Organisation (252)	10	-1,190	75%	400	28%	21
14	Kagera Sugar Co Ltd (74)	10	-1,177	76%	2612	31%	85
15	Air Tanzania Corporation (6)	9	-1,173	77%	1299	32%	52
16	Tanganyika Dyeing and Weaving Co Ltd (272)	6	-1,160	78%	1379	34%	55
17	Kiwira Coal Mines Co Ltd (107)	7	-1,019	79%	200	34%	13
18	Tanzania Shoe Co Ltd (353) [b]	1	-1,009	80%	1962	36%	80
19	Mbeya Cement Co Ltd (129)	10	-993	80%	479	36%	25
20	National Printing Co Ltd (196)	9	-984	81%	410	37%	23

a: 100% equals total in group. For instance, the 10 largest profit-makers account for 67% of profits in the economy and employ 43% of the people working in profit-making companies.

b: Profit/loss-maker (353, 370) not rated as significant, as there were too few statements and indicators.

Source: Based on the data displayed in columns (b) and (d) in Table B-6

Table B-11: The Largest Profit/Loss-Makers According to Average Profits and Losses per Employee (TSh m, 1994 prices)

Pos	Parastatal name (in parentheses code)	No. of stat.	ø Profit per employee	Average Profit 87-96	ø Employment 87-96	Pos. in Table 8-10
1	Tanzania Petroleum Development Corporation (340)	10	38.4	8,784	229	2
2	Sugar Development Corporation (263)	10	6.5	910	141	14
3	Tanzania Automobile Manufacturing Co Ltd (290)	6	5.7	725	128	18
4	Tanzania Cables Ltd (294)	10	5.5	527	96	22
5	Agip (Tanzania) Ltd (3)	10	4.8	1723	359	6
6	Tanzania Central Freight Bureau (297)	10	4.6	210	45	37
7	Tanzania Cotton Marketing Board (304)	10	4.6	1,383	299	10
8	Tanzania Distilleries Ltd (309)	2	4.1	525	127	23
9	National Transport Corporation (202)	10	3.9	350	89	28
10	Dar es Salaam Airport Handling Co Ltd (45)	10	3.9	771	200	16
11	Tanzania Cigarette Co Ltd (298)	8	3.8	5,457	1430	4
12	Mulbadaw Wheat Farms Ltd (172)	9	2.9	127	44	48
13	National Chemical Industries (185)	10	2.7	104	39	51
14	Tanzania Oxygen Ltd (338)	9	2.5	326	130	30
15	Tanzania and Italian Petroleum Refining Co (287)	10	2.3	1,240	528	12
16	Basotu Plantations Ltd (16)	10	2.3	122	54	49
17	Ngorongoro Conservation Area Authority (212)	6	2.1	447	210	26
18	Tanzania Maltings Co Ltd (332)	6	2.0	333	167	29
19	Gidagamowd Wheat Co Ltd (63)	10	1.9	138	71	47
20	National Steel Corporation (200)	10	1.9	187	100	39
1	Morogoro Shoe Co Ltd (158)	5	-22.9	-5,543	242	8
2	Nyanza Glass Works (216)	10	-16.1	-322	20	42
3	Tabora Textile Mills Co Ltd (267)	5	-11.5	-4,907	428	9
4	National Textile Corporation (201)	6	-11.4	-939	83	22
5	Musoma Textile Ltd (175)	5	-10.0	-14,669	1467	2
6	Morogoro Polyester Textiles Ltd (154)	10	-9.3	-14,705	1585	1
7	Tanzania Sewing Thread Manufacturers Co (351)	4	-7.3	-520	71	33
8	Tanzania Investment Bank (325)	10	-6.2	-737	119	25
9	Tanzania Leather Associated Industries (327)	5	-6.2	-167	27	63
10	State Motor Corporation (257)	7	-5.6	-451	80	36
11	Minjingu Phosphate Co Ltd (141)	6	-5.6	-420	75	39
12	National Milling Corporation (193)	10	-5.5	-6,626	1197	7
13	Kiwira Coal Mines Co Ltd (107)	7	-5.1	-1,019	200	17
14	Monact Seed Co Ltd (146)	5	-5.0	-30	6	121
15	Mwanza Textiles Ltd (180)	6	-4.4	-9,199	2095	4
16	Tanzania Packages Manufacturers Ltd (339)	8	-4.0	-2,233	557	11
17	Southern Paper Mills Co Ltd (253)	10	-3.8	-8,463	2209	5
18	Tanzania Fertilizer Co Ltd (314)	10	-3.7	-1,872	500	12
19	Enterprise (Tanzania) Ltd - Embassy Hotel (56)	9	-3.5	-562	160	31
20	Kilimanjaro Machine Tools Manufacturing Co (95)	9	-3.5	-503	144	34

Source: Based on the data displayed in columns (b) and (d) in Table B-6

Table B-12: Change in Performance According to Sectors and Location

Average Annual Change 1987(84)-1996 (TSh m, trends significant at 75% or 95% only)[a]

Grouping by sector	Comp. in group	No. of pos. trends		No. of neg. trends		Average change per company				Average change per 1000 employees			
						unweighted		weighted[b]		unweighted		weighted[b]	
		75%	95%	75%	95%	75%	95%	75%	95%	75%	95%	75%	95%
Agriculture	78	5	4	10	3	-70	-65	-84	-90	-196	-321	-236	-390
Cash crops	26	3	3	4	1	-122	-100	-141	-141	-287	-330	-300	-393
Food crops	13	1	1	6	2	-36	-19	-36	-25	-115	-268	-140	-369
All other	39	1				62		62		403		403	
Mining	12	3				93		119		488		676	
Manufacturing	137	16	5	26	10	132	70	156	89	400	186	429	233
Food beverage, tob.	19	4	2	3	1	435	198	615	192	751	318	941	310
Textile & leather	29	3		5	3	218	-89	177	-81	755	-264	550	-205
Wood, paper, print.	26			6	3	-72	-88	-81	-89	-249	-246	-254	-244
Chemicals	14	1	1	5	2	126	302	177	316	581	1,357	798	1,394
Construction	23	5	1	1		104	123	115	123	254	171	232	171
Metal & machinery	26	3	1	6	1	-22	-24	-22	-31	-98	-182	-94	-240
Services	109	16	8	34	18	38	92	64	134	40	58	51	63
Public utilities	5	1	1			2,914	2,914	2,914	2,914	337	337	337	337
Trade, rep.& maint.	39	7	3	12	9	-21	-24	-24	-28	-140	-159	-157	-183
Transport & storage	24	4	1	12	6	-25	-108	-25	-144	-13	-27	-10	-24
Tourism	20	1		7	2	-81	-179	-72	-147	-352	-589	-305	-560
Finance	14	2	2	3	1	45	230	49	218	108	497	104	369
Other services	7	1	1			198	198	198	198	495	495	495	495
Total	336	40	17	70	31	61	62	76	86	99	62	98	68
Grouping by location													
Centre	157	21	10	39	17	86	105	120	136	90	64	99	68
Nationwide	18	5	4	3		802	1,065	996	1,065	201	152	212	152
Dar es Salaam	130	15	6	35	17	-28	-63	-39	-76	-56	-90	-65	-92
-Dar es Salaam only	(115)	(14)	6	(31)	(16)	(11)	(8)	(15)	(17)	(36)	(28)	(45)	(55)
-DSM & other towns	(6)			(2)	(1)	(-885)	(-1,618)	(-885)	(-1,618)	(-170)	(-170)	(-170)	(-170)
-DSM suburb	(9)	(1)		(2)		(-41)		(-54)		(-336)		(-462)	
Dodoma	9	1		1		54		23		358		136	
Sub- / near centre	81	8	3	10	3	128	135	115	174	475	586	385	686
Arusha & Moshi	33	2		6		-31		-44		-112		-157	
Towns near DSM	36	5	2	4	3	283	159	265	195	977	619	801	710
Rural near DSM	12	1	1			11	11	11	11	118	118	118	118
Remote areas	98	11	4	21	11	-24	-43	-31	-64	-132	-218	-156	-283
Towns remote	60	7	2	12	7	-26	-57	-36	-91	-134	-269	-159	-350
Rural remote	38	4	2	9	4	-21	-21	-24	-30	-128	-123	-151	-163
Total	336	40	17	70	31	61	62	76	86	99	62	98	68

a: Constant prices (1994 prices), trend parameters estimated according to the specification y=mx+b. The unusually low confidence level of 75% has been applied since the major goal was not to test significant trends but to differentiate between companies which more likely improved from others which more likely deteriorated. For more information see comments to column (f) in Table B-6.

b: Individual trends weighted according to the number of annual statements available to calculate the trend.

Source: See Table B-6

Appendix C: Data on Parastatal Support

This Appendix provides additional information on the composition of support data and the analyses of parastatal support presented in Chapter 8.2.

Table C-1: Information on Bank Loans and Overdrafts to Parastatals

Type of bank information	Share Parastatals Number	Values (TSh billion)[a]	Comment
Non-performing NBC loans and overdrafts Dec. 1991 and June 1992, approximately 25% transferred to LART, 75% to be claimed from Treasury	Of 367 records 171 identified as belonging to 84 parastatals	Dec. 1991: 87.3, June 1992: 79.4 *(79% and 81% of total)*	Some columns do not correspond to one another, several misprints
Dec. 1996: Non-performing NBC accounts (substandard 12%, doubtful 21%, loss 67%)	Of 2067 records 37 identified as belonging to 29 parastatals	Balance 18.9 *(34% of total)*	55% referring to one parastatal
NBC loans issued to parastatals (1996 and 1997)	Of 86 and 48 records, 75 and 40 identified as belonging to 64 and 33 parastatals	Balance 23.8 and 18.9; unpaid interest 4.2 and 3.6 *(>98% of total)*	Balances only, date of disbursement not indicated
Database for classification of loans and overdrafts (NMB and NBC(1997) limited)	Of 1966 records, 42 identified as belonging to 33 parastatals	Balance 14.7; unpaid interest 3.2	
NBC loans under PSRC, Status Report Dec. 1999	36 parastatal companies	Original balance 31.8, in 1999: 9.6; repaid 11.4	Only remaining companies; date of original balance not shown
PSRC Divesture Progress Report of CRDB loans from Dec. 1999	Of 23 records, 21 identified as belonging to 19 parastatals	Original balance 2.8 *(99.5% of total)*, repaid 0.2	Only remaining companies
CRDB management information reports on disbursements, balances and arrears referring to 1991 and 1994	57 records identified as belonging to 18 parastatals	Closing balances: 0.6 and 1.0; arrears 0.2 and 0.4	Full of contradictions, total chaos, apparently incomplete information
CRDB management information reports, aggregated values for years 1986-93	Indicating total of cooperatives, parastatal companies, villages and individuals		Full of contradictions, total chaos, apparently incomplete information
TIB loan approvals net of cancellations 1970-96	33 approvals refer to FY87-93, 20 identified as parastatal	Less than 1 billion per year	Small amounts, no approvals after FY93
Balances of principal, interests and arrears of TIB beneficiaries for the years 1987-97	Of 759 records, 456 identified to refer to 64 parastatals	E.g. arrears 1992: principal 6.6, interest 22.2	Changes not clear when following up records over the years
Status of TIB companies under PSRC Divestiture as of February 2000	13 companies, 9 with data	Total outstanding 20.7 (whereof still expected 1.1)	Only remaining companies and remaining balance

Type of bank information (continued)	Share Parastatals Number	Values (TSh billion) [a]	Comment
Commercial loans at THB, balance April 1996	Of 179 records 81 identified as belonging to 14 parastatals	Loan balance 1.3	
Commercial loans at THB, balance June 1997	264 records, 79 identified as belonging to 6 parastatals	Balance 0.8 *(28% of total 3.1)*	62 records refer to National Housing Corporation
List of non-performing THB borrowers, status June 1999	412 records, no parastatals	*(zero of total 0.7)*	
PBZ loans and overdrafts to Parastatals in Zanzibar 1986-97	9 records referring to 6 parastatals	Outstanding unpaid balance 0.5	No serious information obtained
LART Status 1999 of debt and recoveries from nonperforming accounts (NBC, CRDB and other?)	Of 32 records, 29 identified as belonging to 29 parastatals	Principal 1991 22.3 *(90% of total)*, interest accrued by 1999: 93.1 *(97% of total)*	Cooperatives 39% of principal, 69% of interest; all interest to cooperatives suddenly removed

a: Reference in italics: Proportion of total for parastatals (as defined in Chapter 8.1).

Source: Data received from National Bank of Commerce (NBC), Cooperative and Rural Development Bank (CRDB), Tanzania Investment Bank (TIB), liquidators of Tanzania Housing Bank (THB), Peoples Bank of Zanzibar (PBZ), as well as LART and PSRC. In most cases, data received in the form of paper copies.

Table C-2: Specifications of Non-Performing Loans (TSh m, 1994 prices)

	'Minimum' specification	Total [a]	'Maximum' specification	Total [a]
NBC	Balance June 1992 of NBC loans transferred to LART	45,188	Same as minimum	45,188
	Balance Dec. 1999 of NBC loans transferred to PSRC (net of repayments)	9,957	Balance reflects value at unknown cut-off date assumed to be the same as the parastatal's CRDB loans transferred to PSRC (or June 1996 if no CRDB transfer)	17,447
	Balance June 1992 of NBC loans transferred to Treasury, minus repayments (assumption: repayment in June 1992)	101,171	Balance June 1992 of NBC loans transferred to Treasury (ignoring repayments as date and write-offs are not known)	104,743
	All NPA of Dec. 1996, which are rated as loss	2,411	All NPA of Dec. 1996 which are rated as substandard, doubtful and loss	13,301
CRDB	Balance June 1992 of CRDB loans transferred to LART	11,475	Same as minimum	11,475
	Balance Dec. 1999 of CRDB loans transferred to PSRC, minus repayments	1,287	Balance assumed to belong to the cut-off date shown in the file	2,558
	NPA: Arrears of Dec. 1991 according to the management information reports	337	Arrears corrected for earlier real losses due to inflation	7,563
TIB	Arrears of NPA shown in Dec. 1992	46,906	Same as minimum	46,906
THB	Remaining balance of April 1996	818	Same as minimum	818
NPA	NBC min., CRDB min., TIB, THB	50,472	NBC max., CRDB max., TIB, THB	68,588
LART	Remaining balance according to LART-Status 1999 (no differentiation between different bank sources)	19,606	Loans transferred to LART in 1991 (ignoring repayments (3%) as date and write-offs are not known)	50,263
PSRC	Loans (min.) transferred from NBC and CRDB plus Dec. 1999 PSRC balance of TIB loans, minus expected TIB amount	20,816	Loans (max.) transferred from NBC and CRDB plus Dec. 1999 PSRC balance of TIB loans	30,104
Treasury	NBC min.	101,171	NBC max.	104,743
Data on recovery [b]	NBC loans transferred to PSRC (value 12.99: 11,460)			5,598
	CRDB loans transferred to PSRC (value 12.99: 200)			98
	TIB loans expected from PSRC (value 12.99: 1,081)			528
	Loans transferred to LART (value 12.99: 11,676): No differentiation between banks			5,703
	NBC loans transferred to Treasury (amount collected after 6.92: 1,934)			3,571

a: Factors used to convert balances into constant prices critically depend on assumptions on the date of outstanding amounts. Knowing cut-off dates matters as no interest is charged afterwards and the value of an outstanding balance denoted in constant prices (1994 prices) would decrease with each passing year.

b: High recovery: 15,498; low recovery 11,399 (excluding Treasury collection and expected TIB amount). Values in parentheses are current prices (and not constant prices).

Source: See Table C-1

Table C-3: List of 'Core' Companies (Infrastructure, Banking and Holding)

To adequately analyse and interpret data on parastatal support, the three groups *core infrastructure parastatals, core banks* and *holding companies* are also considered separately. Core infrastructure parastatals are capital intensive and typically received large amounts of support. The largest banks obtained funds partly as a compensation for directed credits. Finally, knowing the identity of holding companies makes it possible to see whether results would still be valid if funds allocated to holding companies were evenly redistributed throughout the holding complex.

Core Infrastructure Parastatals					
320	Tanzania Harbours Authority (THA)		254	State Fuel Corporation (SFC)	
310	Tanzania Electric Supply Co Ltd (TANESCO)		370	Tanzania Zambia Railway Authority (TAZARA)	
347	Tanzania Railways Corporation (TRC)		203	National Urban Water Authority (NUWA)	
362	Tanzania Telecommunications Co. (TTCL)		6	Air Tanzania Corporation (ATC)	
Core Banks					
182	National Bank of Commerce (NBC)		325	Tanzania Investment Bank (TIB)	
40	Cooperative and Rural Dev. Bank (CRDB)		*219*	*Peoples Bank of Zanzibar (PBZ)* [a]	
Holding Companies [b]		No. [c]			No. [c]
23	Board of Internal Trade	29	32	Capital Development Authority	5
181	National Agricultural and Food Cor.	18	193	National Milling Corporation	5
186	National Development Corporation	18	263	Sugar Development Corporation	5
201	National Textile Corporation	15	301	Tanzania Coffee Marketing Board	5
202	National Transport Corporation	15	340	Tanzania Petroleum Development Cor.	5 [d]
364	Tanzania Tourist Board	14	252	Small Industries Development Org.	4
256	State Mining Corporation	12	292	Tanzania Breweries Ltd	4
369	Tanzania Wood Industry Corporation	12	190	National Housing Corporation	3
354	Tanzania Sisal Authority	11	191	National Insurance Corp of Tanzania	3
185	National Chemical Industries	10	296	Tanzania Cashewnut Marketing Board	3
327	Tanzania Leather Associated Industries	9	304	Tanzania Cotton Marketing Board	3
349	Tanzania Saruji Corporation	9	359	Tanzania Tea Authority	3
257	State Motor Corporation	8	306	Tanzania Dairies Ltd	2
326	Tanzania Karatasi Associated Ind.	8	312	Tanzania Elimu Supplies	2

a: PBZ excluded from the data set (no useful information obtained).

b: Only holding companies for which a redistribution has been calculated. The list does not include companies with no information on subsidiaries (22, 195, 198, 347), as well as Air Tanzania and the banks NBC, TIB and THB (these last four companies include one affiliated parastatal only). Calculating a redistribution does not make sense because funds either remain within the holding or the subsidiary parastatal is not the main recipient.

c: Number of companies belonging to the holding complex (including holding company).

d: Holding funds only redistributed to the petroleum refining part (and not the retail companies BP and AGIP).

Source: See Table B-1

Table C-4: Indicators of Support FY87-96 According to Sectors (I)

Total amount as % shares	%No. in Group	TOT [a]	Bank NBC	Bank CRDB	Bank TIB	TR Loan	TR Inv.	TR Guar.	Sub-sidy	CIS Sub.	Inc. Tax
Agriculture	23%	14%	29%	74%	1%	7%	8%	0%	21%	18%	19%
Cash crops	8%	9%	8%	5%	1%	2%	7%	0%	20%	16%	16%
Food crops and other	7%	2%	6%			4%	1%		1%	1%	3%
Cooperative unions	8%	2%	15%	69%		0%				1%	0%
Mining	4%	1%	0%		0%	1%		6%	1%	0%	1%
Manufacturing	41%	35%	66%	11%	90%	8%	27%	44%	57%	54%	22%
Food & beverage, tobacco	6%	4%	16%	0%	9%	1%	1%		14%	3%	5%
Textile & leather	9%	6%	38%	7%	52%	1%	1%	33%	1%	1%	6%
Wood, paper & printing	8%	4%	2%	3%	21%	4%		6%	6%	3%	2%
Chemicals	4%	11%	1%	1%	1%	0%	8%		32%	24%	5%
Construction	7%	4%	1%	0%	7%	2%	14%	5%	4%	3%	1%
Metal & machinery	8%	7%	9%			1%	3%			20%	4%
Services	32%	50%	5%	15%	9%	84%	65%	50%	21%	28%	58%
Public utilities	1%	19%				40%	7%	42%	9%	7%	19%
Trade, repair & maintenance	12%	2%	4%	8%			0%	2%	3%	6%	3%
Transport & storage	7%	23%	1%	7%		34%	51%	5%	6%	12%	7%
Tourism	6%	0%	0%		8%	0%	2%		0%		3%
Finance	4%	5%				9%	4%		1%	2%	25%
Other services	2%	1%			0%	1%	1%	0%	3%	1%	0%
Total	100%	100%	100%	100%	100%	100%	100%	100%	100%	100%	100%
of which infrastructure	2%	39%	1%	0%	0%	73%	58%	47%	15%	13%	25%
of which holding	8%	27%	60%	5%	0%	11%	33%	30%	39%	30%	18%

Number of beneficiaries	No. in Group	TOT [a]	Bank NBC	Bank CRDB	Bank TIB	TR Loan	TR Inv.	TR Guar.	Sub-sidy	CIS Sub.	Inc. Tax
Agriculture	78	71	32	10	1	9	10	1	8	10	24
Cash crops	26	25	10	2	1	5	7	1	6	3	10
Food crops and other	24	22	7	2		2	3		2	3	11
Cooperative unions	28	24	15	6		2				4	3
Mining	12	11	2		1	6		1	1	1	2
Manufacturing	137	133	59	12	22	39	11	6	12	49	60
Food & beverage, tobacco	19	18	3	1	2	4	3		2	7	13
Textile & leather	29	29	21	6	9	16	2	3	2	4	6
Wood, paper & printing	26	24	11	3	6	4		2	1	10	15
Chemicals	14	13	5	1	2	2	2		2	9	8
Construction	23	23	5	1	3	7	3	1	5	5	5
Metal & machinery	26	26	14			6	1			14	13
Services	109	105	22	8	2	23	32	4	8	20	51
Public utilities	5	5				3	2	1	1	4	3
Trade, repair & maintenance	39	39	18	7			14	1	1	5	21
Transport & storage	24	24	3	1		7	7	1	1	6	12
Tourism	20	20	1		1	7	2		1		8
Finance	14	10				4	5		2	3	5
Other services	7	7			1	2	2	1	2	2	2
Total	336	320	115	30	26	77	53	12	29	80	137
of which infrastructure	8	8	1			6	6	2	2	7	4
of which holding	28	28	10	1	1	16	16	4	11	16	15

a: Total includes other support not explicitly shown (Bank THB, CIS cash cover, Dividend, PPF, TANESCO, NUWA, TTCL).

Source: See Table 8-24

Table C-5: Indicators of Support According to Sectors (II), TSh m, 1994 prices

Average per company	No. in Group	TOT [a]	Bank NBC	Bank CRDB	Bank TIB	TR Loan	TR Inv.	TR Guar.	Sub-sidy	CIS Sub.	Inc. Tax
Agriculture	78	3,746	1,493	993	154	4,565	1,966	150	2,362	5,250	324
Cash crops	26	7,050	1,245	346	154	2,808	2,571	150	3,040	15,364	639
Food crops & other	24	2,386	1,443	28		12,866	555		326	939	114
Cooperative unions	28	1,809	1,682	1,530		656				897	44
Mining	12	1,481	147		98	1,275		4,395	998	653	126
Manufacturing	137	4,973	1,843	121	1,181	1,284	5,960	5,031	4,203	3,187	148
Food & beverage, tob.	19	4,239	8,599	9	1,266	1,216	741		6,351	1,427	152
Textile & leather	29	4,163	2,993	152	1,661	538	915	7,546	227	628	394
Wood, paper & printing	26	2,802	289	135	1,010	5,770		1,977	5,653	1,009	57
Chemicals	14	15,662	251	123	176	638	9,625		14,234	7,630	232
Construction	23	3,013	192	10	696	1,311	11,650	3,592	632	1,475	57
Metal & machinery	26	4,776	1,050			510	7,309			4,109	117
Services	109	8,853	377	246	1,251	22,155	4,914	8,562	2,343	4,052	454
Public utilities	5	70,097				81,293	8,272	28,867	8,007	5,200	2,541
Trade repair & maint.	39	1,169	341	148			82	1,624	2,401	3,366	54
Transport & storage	24	17,669	717	931		29,498	17,813	3,531	5,190	5,854	248
Tourism	20	422	8		2,431	73	1,856		99		172
Finance	14	8,544				13,681	1,944		277	1,668	2,003
Other Services	7	2,220			71	1,977	719	227	1,245	1,638	16
Total	336	5,854	1,436	445	1,105	7,901	4,575	5,748	3,071	3,629	292
Infrastructure only	8	91,554	2,022			74,013	23,431	16,199	6,598	5,382	2,465
Holding only	28	17,751	9,840	693	110	4,239	5,063	5,191	3,183	5,518	473

Average per 1000 empl.	No. in Group	TOT [a]	Bank NBC	Bank CRDB	Bank TIB	TR Loan	TR Inv.	TR Guar.	Sub-sidy	CIS Sub.	Inc. Tax
Agriculture	78	10,621	3,293	2,083	168	6,014	2,020	61	1,879	6,831	738
Cash crops	26	10,712	1,461	275	168	3,089	2,374	61	2,676	12,219	706
Food crops (& other)	24	8,767	2,453	38		13,501	774		202	831	1,106
Cooperative unions	28	14,095	13,492	12,405		3,454				6,897	375
Mining	12	3,260	110		1,322	2,019		5,947	4,992	1,739	402
Manufacturing	137	9,211	3,547	182	2,197	1,379	7,133	6,585	9,066	4,074	197
Food & beverage, tob.	19	2,901	16,931	17	8,639	417	285		9,655	491	91
Textile & leather	29	6,242	4,095	165	2,087	570	16,685	15,204	7,974	932	434
Wood, paper & printing	26	7,674	493	320	2,286	5,507		1,512	2,559	1,756	115
Chemicals	14	64,622	1,639	425	794	3,926	71,896		39,050	27,802	860
Construction	23	8,170	382	24	1,640	2,428	40,068	7,495	2,524	2,438	70
Metal & machinery	26	21,570	3,630			2,505	48,405			14,207	356
Services	109	11,532	1,482	1,130	3,885	8,956	3,085	4,005	3,138	1,415	496
Public utilities	5	18,657				16,005	1,625	4,398	5,173	1,239	455
Trade repair & maint.	39	7,218	2,149	730			559	5,604	22,183	15,045	354
Transport & storage	24	11,715	820	2,873		6,735	3,894	2,719	3,995	1,189	251
Tourism	20	2,033	69		8,652	420	4,417		352		696
Finance	14	6,285				5,848	1,838		256	537	827
Other services	7	9,927			195	9,196	2,504	566	4,362	6,378	42
Total	336	10,267	3,090	919	2,135	5,860	3,469	4,221	4,087	2,800	389
Infrastructure only	8	15,117	1,557			10,001	3,359	4,121	4,636	820	376
Holding only	28	29,128	11,795	281	1,327	5,403	6,320	6,974	3,276	9,129	554

a: Total includes other support not explicitly shown (THB, CIS CC, Div., PPF, TANESCO, NUWA, TTCL).

Source: See Table 8-24

Figure C-1: Purpose of Treasury Loans in Portfolio FY87-96 (All)

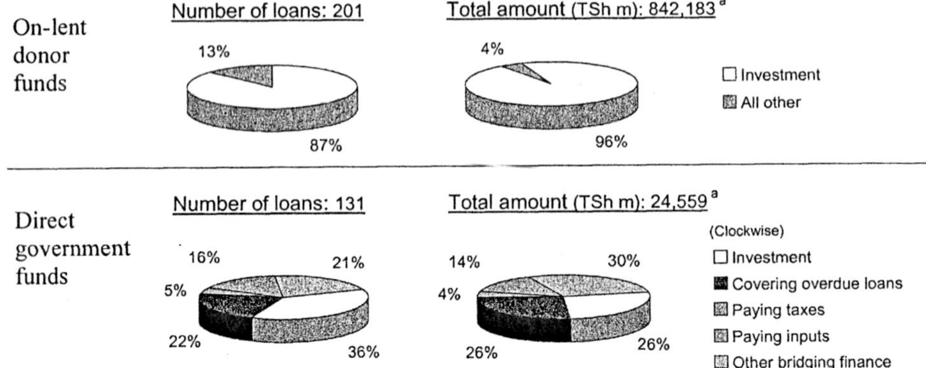

a: Balance June 1986 plus disbursements and unexplained increases from June 1986 to June 1996 (1994 prices), see also partial analysis in Figure 8-5.

Source: Categorisation according to information obtained in the Treasury loan statements 1986/87 to 1996/97

Table C-6: Average Costs of Treasury Loans to Commercial Parastatals FY87-96 (All)

	86/87	87/88	88/89	89/90	90/91	91/92	92/93	93/94	94/95	95/96
Number of loans [a]	179	174	188	197	227	225	228	216	217	215
excl. bank & infra	*113*	*129*	*140*	*143*	*167*	*166*	*166*	*159*	*162*	*163*
Average costs per loan										
Nominal interest rate	5.2%	5.7%	5.7%	5.4%	6.6%	6.6%	6.8%	7.4%	7.0%	7.0%
Real loan costs [b]	*-16.4%*	-2.8%	-8.8%	-17.3%	-17.4%	-3.7%	-9.4%	-15.4%	-14.4%	-14.6%
excl. bank & infra	*-14.7%*	-4.0%	-9.1%	-18.1%	-17.8%	-5.9%	-10.0%	-17.2%	-17.0%	-14.0%
Weighted averages [c]										
Nominal interest rate	6.7%	6.4%	6.8%	7.3%	7.6%	8.1%	8.1%	8.1%	7.7%	7.6%
Real loan costs [b]	*-5.2%*	25.9%	13.3%	5.7%	-7.4%	17.5%	7.3%	2.2%	-0.6%	-16.2%
excl. bank & infra	*3.0%*	23.5%	15.1%	5.5%	-8.2%	14.0%	9.1%	3.4%	-5.9%	-12.7%
Rate of inflation	30.0%	31.2%	30.4%	35.9%	28.8%	21.9%	25.2%	33.1%	28.4%	21.0%

a: Number of loans to commercial parastatals in Treasury loan portfolio with closing balance larger than zero in specified year (see also partial analysis in Table 8-25).

b: Real loan costs equal interest rate plus foreign exchange adjustment minus inflation. Data on foreign exchange adjustments incomplete for the year 1986/87.

c: Interest rates weighted according to the size of the loans.

Source: Data on commercial parastatals compiled from annual Treasury loan statements

Table C-7: The State of Arrears in Treasury Loans FY87-96

Specification A: All Treasury loans

No. of loans		86/87	87/88	88/89	89/90	90/91	91/92	92/93	93/94	94/95	95/96
Loans in arrears	Old (≤ June 86)	102	98	86	88	94	93	97	78	77	77
	New	0	13	27	43	55	76	78	92	89	95
Loans not in arrears	Old (≤ June 86)	52	33	32	29	19	16	10	6	5	6
	New	31	44	43	37	65	41	44	42	50	40
Arrears as % of total in group	Old (≤ June 86)	66%	75%	73%	75%	83%	85%	91%	93%	94%	93%
	New	0%	23%	39%	54%	46%	65%	64%	69%	64%	70%
	All	55%	59%	60%	66%	64%	75%	76%	78%	75%	79%
Total amount (TSh bn)		86/87	87/88	88/89	89/90	90/91	91/92	92/93	93/94	94/95	95/96
Loans in arrears	Old (≤ June 86)	6.6	14.0	30.5	55.1	76.3	115.6	163.2	162.2	208.0	210.4
	New		2.3	5.1	11.8	25.5	41.9	79.8	95.3	126.8	128.7
Total balance (principal)	Old (≤ June 86)	30.4	45.5	56.6	77.9	88.2	112.9	142.0	127.8	151.5	152.3
	New	14.3	29.5	46.1	59.4	115.9	145.3	232.1	395.8	425.4	402.5
Arrears as % of total balance	Old (≤ June 86)	22%	31%	54%	71%	86%	102%	115%	127%	137%	138%
	New	0%	8%	11%	20%	22%	29%	34%	24%	30%	32%
	All	15%	22%	35%	49%	50%	61%	65%	49%	58%	61%

Specification B: Treasury loans, excluding loans to core infrastructure and banking

No. of loans		86/87	87/88	88/89	89/90	90/91	91/92	92/93	93/94	94/95	95/96
Loans in arrears	Old (≤ June 86)	64	66	68	68	71	71	74	66	66	67
	New	0	9	21	32	41	52	56	68	72	77
Loans not in arrears	Old (≤ June 86)	31	25	23	22	17	13	8	6	5	5
	New	21	30	28	21	43	30	28	20	22	16
Arrears as % of total in group	Old (≤ June 86)	67%	73%	75%	76%	81%	85%	90%	92%	93%	93%
	New	0%	23%	43%	60%	49%	63%	67%	77%	77%	83%
	All	55%	58%	64%	70%	65%	74%	78%	84%	84%	87%
Total amount (TSh bn)		86/87	87/88	88/89	89/90	90/91	91/92	92/93	93/94	94/95	95/96
Loans in arrears	Old (≤ June 86)	6.0	11.8	26.1	45.0	62.9	94.4	129.7	108.8	137.5	144.2
	New		2.3	4.7	7.9	11.8	18.9	28.8	15.0	18.5	25.2
Total balance (principal)	Old (≤ June 86)	21.6	32.9	38.8	53.1	60.5	76.8	96.6	71.9	84.9	83.2
	New	5.5	11.7	16.2	19.0	32.9	38.3	46.7	59.3	59.9	61.1
Arrears as % of total balance	Old (≤ June 86)	28%	36%	67%	85%	104%	123%	134%	151%	162%	173%
	New	0%	20%	29%	41%	36%	49%	62%	25%	31%	41%
	All	22%	32%	56%	73%	80%	98%	111%	94%	108%	117%

Figure 8-6 in Chapter 8.2 shows a diagram of the data. Loans issued after June 1986 are defined as new. (Minor deviations from the number of loans included in the analyses of average loan costs occur as the former analyses only include loans with a positive closing balance.)

Source: Data compiled from Treasury loan statements 1986/87 to 1995/96

Table C-8: Share of Treasury Loans Issued Despite Unsettled Arrears FY88-96

	Disbursements (Partial data set)[a]						Disbursements (Full data set)[b]					
	Recipients in arrears for more than one year[c]						Recipients in arrears for more than one year[c]					
	no		yes		in % total		no		yes		in % total	
	No.[d]	Amount	No.[d]	Amount	No.[d]	Amount	No.[d]	Amount	No.[d]	Amount	No.[d]	Amount
All Parastatals	35	13,719	55	214,645	61%	94%	58	50,345	97	462,523	63%	90%
Parastatal excl. I&B	33	11,418	29	16,700	47%	59%	50	27,149	51	50,167	50%	65%
Infrastructure (I)	0		15	168,465	100%	100%	3	20,351	31	361,828	86%	95%
Banking (B)	2	2,301	11	29,479	85%	93%	3	2,845	15	52,285	83%	95%

a: Disbursements explicitly shown in annual Treasury loan statement between July 1987 and June 1996.

b: Disbursements (July 1987-June 1996) including unexplained increases as well as 'new' loans which appear the first time in the following year's opening balance. Unexplained increases and new loans are most likely additional disbursements.

c: At least two Treasury loan statements (i.e. current and preceding statement) indicate arrears. Considering two subsequent years rules out the possibility that the new loan was granted before the company was in arrears (there is only information on the financial year and not on the exact date within the year).

d: Number of loans with one or several disbursements. Four loans included both types of disbursements (disbursements with arrears and without arrears) and therefore appear in both groups.

Source: Data compiled from Treasury loan statements 1986/87 to 1995/96. Disbursements of the year 1986/87 are not included since there was no information on the arrears of 1985/86.

Table C-9: Detailed Distribution of Support (FY87-96) According to Profit and Loss Categories (1994 prices)

	No. in Group	*Overall Total*		*Holding redis.*		Bank NBC		Bank CRDB		Bank TIB		Bank THB	
		No.	*Sum*	*No.*	*Sum*	No.	Sum	No.	Sum	No.	Sum	No.	Sum
1 Profit-makers	84	*83*	*425,672*	*84*	*340,114*	16	19,286	1	5	5	2,627	2	253
1a of which regular	48	*47*	*185,000*	*48*	*196,974*	5	2,780	1	5	3	664	0	0
1b " " large p. c.	18	*18*	*141,474*	*18*	*132,671*	4	13,070	0	0	1	1,887	0	0
1c " " large p. e.	20	*19*	*151,522*	*20*	*100,851*	5	4,896	0	0	0	0	0	0
2 Loss-makers	132	*128*	*1,012,018*	*128*	*1,030,002*	65	114,837	19	4,187	21	24,437	3	410
2a of which regular	70	*68*	*416,960*	*68*	*418,237*	34	91,708	10	3,294	15	19,885	2	164
2b " " large p. c.	32	*31*	*825,933*	*31*	*746,959*	17	88,985	4	1,674	7	14,437	0	0
2c " " large p. e.	31	*29*	*334,156*	*29*	*245,749*	17	88,685	3	1,664	9	16,449	0	0
3 Not categorised	120	*109*	*463,380*	*113*	*530,954*	37	40,164	12	9,255	8	5,399	4	155
3a Too few info	114	*103*	*162,219*	*107*	*239,042*	37	40,164	12	9,255	8	5,399	4	155
3b Core bank	3	*3*	*78,580*	*3*	*78,580*	0	0	0	0	0	0	0	0
3c THA & petro	3	*3*	*222,581*	*3*	*213,331*	0	0	0	0	0	0	0	0
Total	336	*320*	*1,901,071*	*325*	*1,901,071*	118	174,287	32	13,446	34	32,463	9	818
I. Share loss	61%	*61%*	*70%*	*60%*	*75%*	80%	86%	95%	100%	81%	90%	60%	62%
II. I + 3bc as loss	62%	*62%*	*76%*	*61%*	*80%*	80%	86%	95%	100%	81%	90%	60%	62%
III. No. core infra	60%	*60%*	*55%*	*59%*	*61%*	80%	85%	95%	100%	81%	90%	60%	62%
IV. Holding redis.	60%	*60%*	*75%*	*60%*	*75%*	75%	81%	91%	98%	82%	90%	72%	88%
V. P/L All	62%	*61%*	*70%*	*61%*	*74%*	80%	87%	91%	99%	83%	91%	63%	65%
VI. P/L 5%	56%	*56%*	*66%*	*55%*	*64%*	90%	97%	83%	100%	80%	97%	50%	39%
VII. P/L no correction	61%	*60%*	*59%*	*60%*	*63%*	80%	87%	91%	99%	83%	91%	63%	65%
VIII. P/L net of sub.	67%	*67%*	*90%*	*67%*	*87%*	89%	96%	95%	100%	85%	91%	60%	62%

(continued)	No. in Group	TR Loans		TR Investments		TR Guarant.		Subsidies		CIS CC		CIS Subsidy	
		No.	Sum	No.	Sum	No.	Sum	No.	Sum	No.	Sum	No.	Sum
1 Profit-makers	84	20	20,701	21	39,615	0	0	3	12,253	23	154,061	25	156,040
1a of which regular	48	8	10,082	11	26,826	0	0	2	274	14	65,092	16	65,078
1b " " large p. c.	18	4	4,332	7	11,630	0	0	2	12,080	8	36,324	9	51,721
1c " " large p. e.	20	3	7,951	4	16,731	0	0	1	11,978	6	54,257	6	48,271
2 Loss-makers	132	45	417,284	21	117,685	12	68,979	18	66,950	29	88,979	31	81,865
2a of which regular	70	28	155,527	7	25,204	8	33,904	10	30,401	11	17,341	13	21,770
2b " " large p. c.	32	20	378,419	7	72,385	8	64,135	8	62,118	12	66,229	14	56,713
2c " " large p. e.	31	16	44,912	3	1,830	5	27,108	8	55,612	9	46,691	11	38,429
3 Not categorised	120	16	185,254	11	85,178	0	0	8	9,868	22	58,833	24	52,450
3a Too few info	114	12	18,649	7	21,704	0	0	6	6,981	17	30,239	19	25,522
3b Core bank	3	3	55,915	2	3,805	0	0	1	453	3	4,768	3	5,004
3c THA & petro	3	1	110,690	2	59,668	0	0	1	2,434	2	23,826	2	21,924
Total	336	81	623,239	53	242,478	12	68,979	29	89,071	74	301,874	80	290,356
I. Share Loss	61%	69%	95%	50%	75%	100%	100%	86%	85%	56%	37%	55%	34%
II. I + 3bc as loss	62%	71%	97%	54%	82%	100%	100%	87%	85%	60%	43%	59%	41%
III. No. core infra	60%	67%	82%	45%	57%	100%	100%	84%	81%	51%	29%	51%	27%
IV. Holding redis.	60%	63%	95%	59%	76%	94%	98%	76%	94%	59%	52%	63%	48%
V. P/L All	62%	71%	95%	51%	66%	100%	100%	80%	84%	59%	38%	58%	36%
VI. P/L 5%	56%	73%	95%	38%	40%	100%	100%	88%	99%	52%	20%	54%	24%
VII. P/L no correction	61%	69%	72%	49%	49%	100%	100%	78%	82%	56%	34%	55%	32%
VIII. P/L net of sub.	67%	75%	97%	55%	77%	100%	100%	86%	85%	81%	89%	79%	88%

(continued)	No. in Group	Income Tax No.	Income Tax Sum	Dividends No.	Dividends Sum	Pension PPF No.	Pension PPF Sum	TANESCO No.	TANESCO Sum	NUWA No.	NUWA Sum	TTCL No.	TTCL Sum
1 Profit-makers	84	57	13,626	14	4,393	78	308	25	2,157	9	258	52	89
1a of which regular	48	33	7,784	9	4,299	45	165	15	1,725	3	175	27	51
1b " " large p. c.	18	12	3,921	5	4,214	17	103	10	2,074	4	74	10	46
1c " " large p. e.	20	12	2,312	6	4,043	17	49	5	980	3	27	7	27
2 Loss-makers	132	56	13,167	9	200	119	788	56	12,104	10	63	67	82
2a of which regular	70	23	7,132	2	96	60	413	32	10,018	7	58	34	44
2b " " large p. c.	32	10	9,492	0	0	29	299	20	11,018	2	10	16	19
2c " " large p. e.	31	9	1,988	1	59	27	275	17	10,427	2	10	16	18
3 Not categorised	120	24	13,257	8	2,373	66	222	38	942	1	7	36	24
3a Too few info	114	21	2,569	4	829	61	171	35	551	1	7	34	23
3b Core bank	3	1	8,358	1	64	3	4	2	209	0	0	1	0
3c THA & petro	3	2	2,330	3	1,479	2	46	1	182	0	0	1	1
Total	336	137	40,050	31	6,966	263	1,317	119	15,204	20	328	155	196
I. Share Loss	61%	50%	49%	39%	4%	60%	72%	69%	85%	53%	20%	56%	48%
II. I + 3bc as loss	62%	51%	64%	48%	28%	61%	73%	70%	85%	53%	20%	57%	48%
III. No. core infra	60%	48%	29%	39%	4%	59%	70%	68%	73%	53%	20%	56%	46%
IV. Holding redis.	60%	54%	60%	36%	3%	61%	73%	69%	86%	71%	20%	59%	50%
V. P/L All	62%	51%	52%	42%	4%	61%	66%	70%	85%	55%	21%	57%	49%
VI. P/L 5%	56%	43%	53%	0%	0%	53%	72%	67%	94%	60%	16%	49%	44%
VII. P/L no correction	61%	50%	38%	37%	3%	60%	63%	68%	83%	55%	21%	57%	49%
VIII. P/L net of sub.	67%	58%	71%	39%	4%	66%	75%	74%	88%	74%	89%	62%	53%

1-3: Grouping (significant, regular and large profit/loss-makers—large per company and per employee) according to definition in Table B-6, however excluding the core banks NBC ('profit-maker'), CRDB ('profit-maker') and TIB (loss-maker), which have been added to group (3), as some of the funds may reflect a compensation for directed credits and defining NBC and CRDB as profit-makers does not make sense. Group (3) also includes the badly-categorised 'profit-makers' Tanzania Harbours Authority and two companies from the petroleum refining industry (TPDC and TIPER). All the companies listed under 3b and 3c are highly inefficient and are only profit-makers due to their monopoly protection (and inappropriate assessment of the banks' lending portfolio).

I-VIII: Percentages of profit-makers and loss-makers only, i.e. excluding not-categorised data. (I) represents the default specification, i.e. the shares calculated from the data displayed in 1 and 2. (II) adds the companies listed under 3b and 3c to the group of loss-makers. (III) shows the share of loss-makers, excluding all the core infrastructure parastatals.

Specifications (IV) to (VIII) are benchmark specifications. Specification (IV) and the columns 'Holding redis.' show the results if holding funds are evenly redistributed within the holding complex. In (V) the profit and loss grouping includes all profit/loss-makers, i.e. also companies rated as not significant. Specification (VI) in contrast treats annual information on profits and losses as random data and only categorises a company if the average profit or average loss from the ten-year period is significantly different from zero at the 5% confidence level. (VII) shows the results if badly-categorised profit-makers are left in the group of profit-makers and (VIII) groups the companies according to the profits and losses that would prevail if the companies had not obtained direct subsidies from the Treasury and if the companies had to buy foreign exchange from the Commodity Import Support programme (CIS) at the equilibrium parallel market rate (other support data are ignored).

Source: See Table 8-27

Table C-10: Monotonic Relation Between Average Profits and Support (FY87-96)

Version A: Companies with information on profits/losses except THA, NBC and CRDB

	NBC	CRDB	TIB	THB	TR Loan	TR Inv.	TR Guar.	Subsidy
Gamma	-0.331	-0.421	-0.408	0.011	-0.308	0.150	-0.799	-0.363
	0.062	*0.087*	*0.109*	*0.176*	*0.079*	*0.093*	*0.049*	*0.124*
	0.000	0.000	0.001	(0.951)	0.000	(0.112)	0.000	0.010
Spearman correlation	-0.321	-0.114	-0.233	0.004	-0.271	0.107	-0.296	-0.190
	0.062	*0.049*	*0.065*	*0.053*	*0.070*	*0.069*	*0.044*	*0.067*
	0.000	0.000	0.000	(0.947)	0.000	(0.086)	0.000	0.002
No. of valid cases	260	260	260	260	260	260	260	260

	CIS CC	CIS Sub.	Tax	Dividend	PPF	TANESCO	NUWA	TTCL
Gamma	-0.008	-0.011	0.198	0.327	-0.057	-0.178	0.108	0.060
	0.096	*0.093*	*0.058*	*0.105*	*0.046*	*0.070*	*0.133*	*0.054*
	(0.935)	(0.909)	0.001	0.007	(0.208)	0.012	(0.424)	(0.270)
Spearman correlation	-0.002	-0.002	0.223	0.175	-0.088	-0.176	0.053	0.073
	0.077	*0.077*	*0.065*	*0.058*	*0.065*	*0.069*	*0.064*	*0.066*
	(0.975)	(0.971)	0.000	0.005	(0.159)	0.004	(0.398)	(0.243)
No. of valid cases	260	260	260	260	260	260	260	260

Version B: Like A, however excluding companies with no support data

	NBC	CRDB	TIB	THB	TR Loan	TR Inv.	TR Guar.	Subsidy
Gamma / Kendall's Tau	-0.215	-0.252	-0.281	-0.357	-0.187	0.056	-0.273	-0.387
	0.076	*0.140*	*0.128*	*0.388*	*0.081*	*0.116*	*0.206*	*0.148*
	0.005	0.012	0.028	(0.357)	0.020	(0.628)	(0.185)	0.009
Spearman correlation	-0.291	-0.503	-0.368	-0.262	-0.262	0.053	-0.406	-0.487
	0.111	*0.174*	*0.176*	*0.515*	*0.117*	*0.163*	*0.258*	*0.203*
	0.005	0.014	0.049	(0.531)	0.029	(0.719)	(0.191)	0.014
No. of valid cases	93	23	29	8	70	49	12	25

	CIS CC	CIS Sub.	Tax	Dividend	PPF	TANESCO	NUWA	TTCL
Gamma / Kendall's Tau	0.162	0.193	0.113	0.432	-0.075	-0.120	0.147	0.025
	0.106	*0.097*	*0.067*	*0.156*	*0.048*	*0.083*	*0.151*	*0.059*
	0.127	0.046	(0.090)	0.005	(0.119)	(0.148)	(0.329)	(0.676)
Spearman correlation	0.224	0.281	0.166	0.543	-0.114	-0.186	0.235	0.034
	0.149	*0.135*	*0.096*	*0.194*	*0.070*	*0.117*	*0.215*	*0.088*
	(0.091)	0.027	(0.065)	0.004	(0.084)	(0.077)	(0.319)	(0.688)
No. of valid cases	58	62	124	26	231	91	20	139

Values in italics are *asymptotic standard errors*; the values beneath indicate *approximative significance* (in parentheses if the parameter is not significant at the 95% confidence level). Results are similar if support for holding companies is first redistributed or if the calculation excludes core utility parastatals.

In Version B values for Gamma and Kendall's Tau are equal (implying the absence of tied values). Version A, in contrast, includes many tied values (all companies with no support, but different average profits), and the measurement of Kendall's Tau does not make sense. (Tau is a measure of *strict* monotonicity; the values would be closer to zero simply because companies without support do not have identical average profits.)

Source: Data on support as defined in the default specification in Table C-9 (and Table 8-27)

Table C-11: Percentage Shares of Beneficiaries with Deteriorating Trends 1987-96 [a]

Specification A: All parastatals with significant trends (75% or 95% only)

	TOT	Bank NBC	Bank CRDB	Bank TIB	Bank THB	TR Loan	TR Inv.	TR Guar.	Sub-sidy	CIS CC	CIS Sub.	Inc. Tax	Divi-dend	Pens. PPF	TAN ESCO	NU-WA	Phone TTCL
T75 [b]	109	44	11	13	4	29	26	4	11	27	28	59	18	101	36	8	62
No.	64%	59%	64%	77%	25%	48%	65%	25%	55%	70%	68%	80%	78%	63%	61%	75%	63%
Val.	50%	40%	76%	80%	0%	42%	53%	13%	11%	67%	65%	63%	26%	74%	36%	86%	55%
T95 [b]	47	14	2	5	3	11	13	2	4	13	13	30	11	42	17	4	21
No.	66%	71%	100%	100%	33%	45%	62%	50%	50%	62%	62%	80%	82%	64%	65%	75%	62%
Val.	40%	76%	100%	100%	0%	37%	51%	82%	14%	45%	36%	42%	19%	67%	36%	93%	53%

Specification B: Subset of A excluding core infrastructure parastatals

	TOT	Bank NBC	Bank CRDB	Bank TIB	Bank THB	TR Loan	TR Inv.	TR Guar.	Sub-sidy	CIS CC	CIS Sub.	Inc. Tax	Divi-dend	Pens. PPF	TAN ESCO	NU-WA	Phone TTCL
T75 [b]	105	42	11	13	4	25	22	3	10	23	24	57	17	97	32	8	61
No.	66%	62%	64%	77%	25%	52%	73%	33%	60%	78%	75%	81%	76%	65%	66%	75%	64%
Val.	63%	41%	76%	80%	0%	74%	77%	22%	12%	72%	71%	86%	12%	76%	52%	86%	58%
T95 [b]	44	13	2	5	3	8	10	2	4	10	10	28	10	39	14	4	21
No.	68%	77%	100%	100%	33%	50%	70%	50%	50%	70%	70%	82%	80%	67%	71%	75%	62%
Val.	43%	81%	100%	100%	0%	49%	72%	82%	14%	43%	33%	65%	3%	69%	80%	93%	53%

Specification C: Same as A, however redistributing holding funds

	TOT	Bank NBC	Bank CRDB	Bank TIB	Bank THB	TR Loan	TR Inv.	TR Guar.	Sub-sidy	CIS CC	CIS Sub.	Inc. Tax	Divi-dend	Pens. PPF	TAN ESCO	NU-WA	Phone TTCL
T75 [b]	109	56	13	15	13	66	70	13	29	52	58	78	28	108	43	13	94
No.	64%	61%	62%	73%	54%	59%	64%	46%	59%	69%	66%	73%	82%	64%	56%	85%	65%
Val.	44%	47%	75%	80%	4%	38%	46%	30%	17%	54%	52%	51%	29%	76%	34%	87%	53%
T95 [b]	47	20	3	6	5	26	34	6	12	22	25	38	13	46	19	8	39
No.	66%	65%	67%	100%	60%	65%	65%	67%	58%	64%	64%	71%	77%	65%	63%	88%	67%
Val.	40%	80%	77%	100%	3%	37%	45%	98%	21%	44%	37%	39%	20%	74%	37%	98%	51%

No.: Share of beneficiaries with a deteriorating trend.
Val.: Share of support allocated to beneficiaries with a deteriorating trend.

a: For 5 companies trend includes data prior to 1987 (see comments to column (f) in Table B-6).

b: T75/T95: Total number of beneficiaries with significant positive or negative trends of profits and losses (trends significant at the confidence levels 75% or 95% only, as defined and explained in Chapter 8.1 (p. 447)).

Source: Categorisation according to the support data (default specification) in Table C-9 (and Table 8-27) and the definition of improving and deteriorating companies in Table B-6

Table C-12: Distribution of Support (FY87-96) According to the Quality and Timeliness of Accounting

Type of support	all[a]	NBC No.	NBC Val.	CRDB No.	CRDB Val.	TIB No.	TIB Val.	THB No.	THB Val.	TR Loan No.	TR Loan Val.	TR Inv. No.	TR Inv. Val.	TR Guar. No.	TR Guar. Val.	Subsidy No.	Subsidy Val.
Quality						/b										/b	
Clean	30%	29%	6%	17%	4%	19%	20%	22%	36%	24%	46%	37%	40%	25%	47%	30%	7%
Mostly clean	31%	37%	51%	33%	38%	38%	36%	44%	63%	34%	29%	35%	29%	50%	41%	26%	15%
Mixed	26%	27%	32%	33%	46%	41%	36%	11%	0%	36%	25%	14%	26%	8%	0%	26%	59%
Poor	14%	8%	11%	17%	12%	3%	8%	22%	0%	5%	0%	14%	5%	17%	11%	19%	20%
Arrears (ext.)										/b		/b					
On time	17%	16%	3%	20%	10%	16%	35%	0%	0%	11%	1%	35%	20%	8%	5%	22%	7%
Not very late	20%	20%	58%	20%	6%	19%	13%	11%	6%	22%	4%	20%	12%	17%	29%	11%	15%
Late	33%	38%	28%	24%	25%	25%	19%	44%	62%	35%	66%	37%	63%	50%	17%	44%	75%
Very late	30%	26%	11%	36%	58%	41%	33%	44%	31%	32%	29%	8%	4%	25%	48%	22%	3%
Number of cases		98		31		34		9		74		49		12		27	

Type of support	all[a]	CIS CC No.	CIS CC Val.	CIS Sub. No.	CIS Sub. Val.	Tax No.	Tax Val.	Dividend No.	Dividend Val.	PPF No.	PPF Val.	TANESCO No.	TANESCO Val.	NUWA No.	NUWA Val.	TTCL No.	TTCL Val.
Quality																	
Clean	30%	40%	42%	39%	40%	38%	34%	55%	87%	30%	40%	26%	7%	35%	65%	34%	29%
Mostly clean	31%	37%	15%	37%	25%	32%	31%	28%	11%	33%	32%	34%	41%	40%	26%	31%	36%
Mixed	26%	13%	19%	13%	15%	22%	13%	7%	1%	25%	21%	29%	12%	15%	6%	23%	20%
Poor	14%	11%	24%	10%	19%	%	21%	10%	2%	13%	7%	12%	40%	10%	3%	11%	14%
Arrears (ext.)												/b					
On time	17%	13%	8%	13%	10%	18%	5%	48%	78%	18%	17%	23%	3%	20%	53%	20%	22%
Not very late	20%	19%	14%	21%	21%	27%	24%	28%	3%	21%	10%	18%	18%	30%	19%	26%	28%
Late	33%	51%	71%	49%	63%	34%	56%	24%	18%	34%	44%	35%	76%	30%	19%	32%	37%
Very late	30%	17%	7%	17%	6%	20%	15%	0%	0%	27%	29%	23%	3%	20%	9%	22%	12%
Number of cases		58		60		128		29		246		98		20		143	

a: Distribution of companies in the economy (270 companies with information on accounting quality and delays of audit).

b: Gamma, Kendall's Tau and Spearman correlation significant at the 95% confidence level.

The data shows the relative distribution of support according to the quality of reports as well as the length of delays with which reports were audited. The relative distribution is made both in terms of number of beneficiaries (No.) and the value of benefits provided (Val.). Deviations from the average in the economy by more than a third are underlined (and additionally highlighted in italics if share is too high).

Group specifications: Average quality of accounts 1986-91: clean (1.0), mostly clean (1.1-1.6), mixed (1.7-2.0), poor (2.1-4.0). Average delays (periods, extended values): on time (1.0), not very late (1.1-1.6), late (1.7-2.0), very late (2.1-6.0).

Data set: Companies with information on accounting and support, excluding core banks.

Source: Data on support as defined in the default specification in Table C-9 (and Table 8-27); data on accounting are given in Table B-6

References

Adam, Christopher; Bigsten, Arne; Collier, Paul; Julin, Eva and O'Connell, Steve (1994). Evaluation of Swedish Development Cooperation with Tanzania. Ministry of Foreign Affairs. Stockholm, August 1994.

Adam, Christopher (1994). Privatisation & Structural Adjustment in Africa. In Willem Van der Geest (ed.): Negotiating Structural Adjustment in Africa. Utpapers presented at a seminar held in March 91 in Oxford; pp. 137-60, 1994.

Africa Intelligence (1998). Sukita Debts with NBC. Internet: http://www.africaintelligence.com/ps/AN/Arch/ION/ION_793.asp (access date: Nov. 2003).

Agrisystems (1996). Coffee Sector Strategy Study — Phase 2. A Study prepared for the Government of Tanzania.

Ake, Claude (1996). Democracy and Development in Africa. The Brookings Institution, Washington 1996.

Alchian, Armen A. (1987). Rent. In John Eatwell, Murray Milgate and Peter Newman (eds.): The New Palgrave: A Dictionary of Economics; Vol. 4, pp. 141-3, Macmillan Press, London 1987.

Alexeev, Michael (1999). The Effect of Privatization on Wealth Distribution in Russia. In: Economics of Transition; Vol. 7, No. 2, pp. 449-65, 1999.

Allard, Richard J. (1988). Rent-Seeking with Non-Identical Players. In: Public Choice; Vol. 57, pp. 3-14, April 1988.

Allard, Richard J. (1995). The Measurability of Budget Related Rent-Seeking. In: Public Choice; Vol. 85, Iss. 3-4, pp. 389-94, December 1995.

Allen, Chris (1995). Understanding African Politics. In: Review of African Political Economy; Vol. 22, No. 65, pp. 301-20, 1995.

Amegashie, Atsu J. (1999a). The Design of Rent-Seeking Competitions: Committees, Preliminary and Final Contests. In: Public Choice; Vol. 99, No. 1-2, pp. 63-76, April 1999.

Amegashie, Atsu J. (1999b). The Number of Rent-Seekers and Aggregate Rent-Seeking Expenditures: An Unpleasant Result. In: Public Choice; Vol. 99, No. 1-2, pp. 57-62, April 1999.

Ampofu-Tuffuor, Emmanuel; DeLorme, Charles D. and Kamerschen, David R. (1991). The Nature, Significance, and Cost of Rent Seeking in Ghana. In: Kyklos; Vol. 44, Iss. 4, pp. 537-59, 1991.

Anam, Mahmudul (1989). Rural-Urban Wage Differential, Rent Seeking, and a Justification for Free Trade. In: Journal of Urban Economics; Vol. 26, Iss. 3, pp. 328-34, November 1989.

Anam, Mahmudul and Katz, Eliakim (1988). Rent-Seeking and Second Best Economics. In: Public Choice; Vol. 59, No. 3, pp. 215-24, December 1988.

Anderson, Garry M.; Rowley, Charles K. and Tollison, Robert D. (1988). Rent-Seeking and the Restriction of Human Exchange. In: Journal of Legal Studies; Vol. 27, pp. 83-100, January 1988.

Applebaum, Elie and Katz, Eliakim (1987). Seeking Rents by Setting Rents: The Political Economy of Rent-Seeking. In: Economic Journal; Vol. 97, No. 387, pp. 685-99, September 1987.

Åslund, Anders (1994). Lessons of the First Four Years of Systematic Change in Eastern Europe. In: Journal of Comparative Economics; Vol. 19, No. 1, pp. 22-38, August 1994.

Augustin, Ulrike (1997). Privatisierung in Tansania. Dissertation (draft). Universität Bayreuth, Bayreuth 1997.

Aumann, Robert J. (1987). Game Theory. In John Eatwell, Murray Milgate and Peter Newman (eds.): The New Palgrave: A Dictionary of Economics; Vol. 2, pp. 460-82, Macmillan Press, London 1987.

Ayittey, George B. N. (1991). Indigenous African Institutions. Transnational Publisher, New York 1991.

Ayittey, George B. N. (1992). Africa Betrayed. St. Martin's Press, New York 1992.

Baik, Kyung H. (1993). Effort Levels in Contests: The Public-Good Prize Case. In: Economics Letters; Vol. 41, No. 4, pp. 363-7, 1993.

Baik, Kyung H. (1994). Effort Levels in Contests with Two Asymmetric Players. In: Southern Economic Journal; Vol. 61, No. 2, pp. 367-78, October 1994.

Baik, Kyung H. (1998). Difference-Form Contest Success Functions and Effort Levels in Contests. In: European Journal of Political Economy; Vol. 14, No. 4, pp. 685-701, November 1998.

Baik, Kyung H. (1999). Rent-Seeking Firms, Consumer Groups, and the Social Costs of Monopoly. In: Economic Inquiry; Vol. 37, No. 3, pp. 541-53, July 1999.

Baik, Kyung H. and Lee, Sanghack (1997). Collective Rent Seeking with Endogenous Group Sizes. In: European Journal of Political Economy; Vol. 13, No. 1, pp. 121-30, February 1997.

Baik, Kyung H. and Shogren, Jason F. (1995). Contests with Spying. In: European Journal of Political Economy; Vol. 11, No. 3, pp. 441-51, September 1995.

Baird, Douglas G. (1998). Game Theory and the Law. In Peter Newman (ed.): The New Palgrave. Dictionary of Economics and The Law; Vol. 2, pp. 192-8, Macmillan Reference Limited, London 1998.

Bank of Tanzania (1991). Report on the 'Workshop on Import Handling Information System in Tanzania (IHIS)' held in Arusha from 21st January - 1st February 1991. Directorate of Import Licensing. Dar es Salaam 1991.

Bank of Tanzania (1994). Economic Bulletin. Vol. 13, No. 4, December 1994.

Bank of Tanzania (1995). Development of Money Markets in Tanzania. Dar es Salaam, September 1995.

Bank of Tanzania (1997). Economic Bulletin. Vol. 27, No. 3. September 1997.

Bank of Tanzania (2001). Quarterly Economic Statistical Tables. Dar es Salaam 2001. Internet: http://www.bot-tz.org (access date: July 2001).

Barro, Robert J. (1991). Economic Growth in a Cross-Section of Countries. In: Quarterly Journal of Economics; Vol. 106, Iss. 2, pp. 407-43, May 1991.

Bartsch, Elga and Thomas, Ingo (1993). Spieltheoretische Ansätze in der Rent-Seeking-Theorie, ein Literaturüberblick. Kiel Working Paper Nr. 564, Kiel 1993.

Bartsch, Elga and Thomas, Ingo P. (1995). Rent-Seeking, Umverteilung und soziale Kosten: das Tullock-Modell und seine spieltheoretischen Erweiterungen. In: Wirtschaftswissenschaftliches Studium; Vol. 24, Iss. 4, pp. 174-9, April 1995.

Barut, Yasar and Kovenock, Dan (1998). The Symmetric Multiple Prize All-Pay Auction with Complete Information. In: European Journal of Political Economy; Vol. 14, No. 4, pp. 627-44, November 1998.

Barzel, Yoram (1985). Transaction Costs: Are They Just Costs? In: Journal of Institutional and Theoretical Economics; Vol. 141, Iss. 1, pp. 4-16, March 1985.

Bates, Robert H. (1988). Toward a Political Economy of Development: A Rational Choice Perspective. University of California Press, Berkley 1988.

Bates, Robert H. and Krueger, Anne O., eds. **(1993)**. Political and Economic Interactions in Economic Policy Reform: Evidence from Eight Countries. Blackwell, Oxford 1993.

Baumgartner, Ruedi; Aurora, Gurdip S.; Karanth, Gopal K. and Ramaswamy, V. (2002). Researchers in Dialogue with Local Knowledge Systems—Reflections on Mutual Learning and Empowerment. In Manuel Flury and Urs Geiser (eds.): Local Environmental Management in a North-South Perspective; v/d/f, Zurich 2002.

Baumol, William J. (1990). Entrepreneurship: Productive, Unproductive, and Destructive. In: Journal of Institutional and Theoretical Economics; Vol. 146, No. 3, pp. 893-921, September 1990.

Baye, Michael R.; Kovenock, Dan and De Vries, Caspar G. (1993). Rigging the Lobbying Process: An Application of the All-Pay Auction. In: American Economic Review; Vol. 83, No. 1, pp. 289-94, March 1993.

Baye, Michael R.; Kovenock, Dan and De Vries, Caspar G. (1994). The Solution to the Tullock Rent-Seeking Game When R Is Greater Than 2: Mixed-Strategy Equilibria and Mean Dissipation Rates. In: Public Choice; Vol. 81, No. 8-4, pp. 363-80, December 1994.

Baye, Michael R.; Kovenock, Dan and De Vries, Caspar G. (1999). The Incidence of Overdissipation in Rent-Seeking Contests. In: Public Choice; Vol. 99, No. 3-4, pp. 439-54, June 1999.

Baysinger, Barry and Tollison, Robert D. (1980). Evaluating the Social Costs of Monopoly and Regulation. In: Atlantic Economic Journal; Vol. 8, No. 4, pp. 22-6, December 1980.

Becheri, Mohamad Z. (1989). The Political Economy of Interest Rate Determination in Tunisia. In Mustapha K. Nabli and Jeffrey B. Nugent (eds.): The New Institutional Economics and Development: Theory and Applications to Tunisia; Vol. 183, pp. 375-403, Elsevier Science Publishers B.V., Amsterdam 1989.

Beck, Roger; Hoskins, Colin and Connolly, Martin J. (1992). Rent Extraction through Political Extortion: An Empirical Examination. In: Journal of Legal Studies; Vol. 21, No. 1, pp. 217-24, January 1992.

Beez, Peter and Mäder, Niklaus (1997). Wie kommt es zu erfolgreichen volkswirtschaftlichen Reformen? Vorschlag eines ökonomischen Rasters. Seminar für Wirtschafts- und Sozialpolitik der Universität Freiburg / Schweiz 1997.

Bellin, Eva (1994). The Politics of Profit in Tunisia: Utility of the Rentier Paradigm? In: World Development; Vol. 22, No. 3, pp. 427-36, March 1994.

Berg-Schlosser, Dirk and Siegler, Rainer (1990). Political Stability and Development. A Comparative Analysis of Kenya, Tanzania, and Uganda. Lynne Rienner Publishers, London 1990.

Berger, Louis S. A. (2000). Study of Tracking of the Roads Fund. Interim Report prepared for the Ministry of Finance. Paris, March 2000.

Berglof, Erik and Roland, Gérard (1998). Soft Budget Constraints and Banking in Transition Economies. In: Journal of Comparative Economics; Vol. 26, No. 1, pp. 18-40, March 1998.

Betz, Joachim, ed. **(1995)**. Politische Restriktionen der Strukturanpassung in Entwicklungsländern. Deutsches Übersee-Institut, Hamburg 1995.

Bhagwati, Jadish N. (1980). Lobbying and Welfare. In: Journal of Public Economics; Vol. 14, pp. 355-63, December 1980.

Bhagwati, Jadish N. (1982). Directly Unproductive, Profit-seeking (DUP) Activities. In: Journal of Political Economy; Vol. 90, No. 90, pp. 988-1002, October 1982.

Bhagwati, Jadish N. (1994). Directly Unproductive Profit-Seeking (DUP) Activities. In John Eatwell, Murray Milgate and Peter Newman (eds.): The New Palgrave: A Dictionary of Economics; Vol. 1, pp. 845-6, Macmillan Press, London 1994.

Bhagwati, Jadish N. and Srinivasan, T. N. (1980). Revenue Seeking: A Generalisation of the Theory of Tariffs. In: Journal of Political Economy; Vol. 88, pp. 1069-87, December 1980.

Bhanduri, Amit; Rutayisire, Laurean and Skarstein, Rune (1993). Evaluation of Macroeconomic Impacts of Import Support to Tanzania. University of Trondheim. August 30, 1993.

Bienen, Henry (1993). Leaders, Violence, and the Absence of Change in Africa. In: Political Science Quarterly; Vol. 108, pp. 271-82, 1993.

Bienen, Henry and Waterbury, John (1989). The Political Economy of Privatization in Developing Countries. In: World Development; Vol. 17, No. 5, pp. 617-32, May 1989.

Bigsten, Arne and Moene, Karl Ove (1996). Growth and Rent Dissipation: the Case of Kenya. In: Journal of African Economies; Vol. 5, No. 2, pp. 177-98, 1996.

Bjorvatn, Kjetil (1995). Leviathan in a Dual Economy. In: Public Choice; Vol. 84, No. 1-2, pp. 137-51, July 1995.

Block, Steven A. (2002). Political Business Cycles, Democratisation, and Economic Reform: The Case of Africa. In: Journal of Development Economics; Vol. 67, Iss. 1, pp. 205-28, February 2002.

Blomqvist, Åke and Mohammad, Sharif (1986). Controls, Corruption, and Competitive Rent-Seeking in LDCs. In: Journal of Development Economics; Vol. 21, No. 1, pp. 161-80, April 1986.

Bonus, Holger and Maselli, Anke (1997). Transaktionskostenökonomik. In: Gabler Wirtschaftslexikon; pp. 3804-7, Gabler, Wiesbaden 1997.

Boone, Catherine (1994). Trade, Taxes, and Tribute: Market Liberalizations and the New Importers in West Africa. In: World Development; Vol. 22, No. 3, pp. 453-67, March 1994.

Booth, David; Lugangira, Flora; Masanja, Patrick; Mvungi, Abu; Mwaipopo, Rosemarie; Mwami, Joaquim and Redmayne, Alison (1993). Social, Cultural and Economic Change in Contemporary Tanzania. A People-Oriented Focus. Dar es Salaam, 1993.

Bourguignon, François and Morrisson, Christian (1992). Adjustment and Equity in Developing Countries. A New Approach. OECD, Paris 1992.

Brooks, Michael A. and Heijdra, Ben J. (1988). In Search of Rent-Seeking. In Charles K. Rowley, Robert D. Tollison and Gordon Tullock (eds.): The Political Economy of Rent-Seeking; pp. 27-49, Kluwer Academic Publishers, Amsterdam 1988.

Brooks, Michael A. and Heijdra, Ben J. (1989). An Exploration of Rent-Seeking. In: Economic Record; Vol. 65, No. 188, pp. 32-50, March 1989.

Brooks, Michael A.; Heijdra, Ben J. and Lowenberg, Anton D. (1990). Productive Versus Unproductive Labor and Rent Seeking: Lessons from History. In: Journal of Institutional and Theoretical Economics; Vol. 146, Iss. 3, pp. 419-38, September 1990.

Buccola, Steven T. and McCandlish, James E. (1999). Rent Seeking and Rent Dissipation in State Enterprises. In: Review of Agricultural Economics; Vol. 21, No. 2, pp. 358-73, 1999.

Buchanan, James M. (1993). How Can Constitutions Be Designed so That Politicians Who Seek to Serve 'Public Interest' Can Survive and Prosper? In: Constitutional Political Economy; Vol. 4, No. 1, pp. 1-6, Winter 1993.

Buchanan, James M., Tollison, Robert D. and Tullock, Gordon (1980). Toward a Theory of the Rent-Seeking Society. A & M University Press, Texas 1980.

Bujo, Bénézet (2000). Wider dem Universalanspruch westlicher Moral: Grundlagen Afrikanischer Ethik. Herder, Freiburg im Breisgau 2000.

Bureau of Statistics (1993). Analysis of Accounts of Parastatal Enterprises 1982-91. Government of Tanzania, Dar es Salaam, October 1993.

Buser, Marcos (1984). Umweltschutzgesetzgebung und Wirtschaftsverbände. In: Wirtschaft und Recht; Vol. 36, Iss. 4, March 1984.

Cairns, Robert D. and Long, Ngo V. (1991). Rent-Seeking with Uncertain Opposition. In: European Economic Review; Vol. 35, No. 6, pp. 1223-35, 1991.

Campbell, Bonnie K. and Loxley, John, eds. **(1989)**. Structural Adjustment in Africa. Macmillan Press, London 1989.

Campbell, Horace (1992). The Politics of Demobilization in Tanzania: Beyond Nationalism. In Horace Campbell and Howard Stein (eds.): Tanzania and the IMF. The Dynamics of Liberalization; Westview Press, Boulder 1992.

Campbell, Horace and Stein, Howard, eds. **(1992)**. Tanzania and the IMF. The Dynamics of Liberalization. Westview Press, Boulder 1992.

Cargill Technical Services (1997). Restructuring of Tanzania Tea Authority. A Report prepared in Association with Tanzania Industrial Studies and Consulting Organisation (TISCO) for the Government of Tanzania. Draft Final Report. Dar es Salaam, December 1997.

Chachage, Seithy L. (1994). Corruption in Tanzania. Some Issues For Consideration. University of Dar es Salaam, September 1994. Paper presented at the 'Workshop on Corruption and Drug Trafficking in Tanzania', held at the Kilimanjaro Hotel 12th October, 1994.

Chazan, Naomi; Mortimer, Robert A.; Ravenhill, John and Rothchild, Donald (1988). Politics and Society in Contemporary Africa. Lynne Rienner Publishers, Boulder 1988.

Che, Yeon-Koo and Gale, Ian (2000). Difference-Form Contests and the Robustness of All-Pay Auctions. In: Games and Economic Behavior; Vol. 30, No. 1, pp. 22-43, January 2000.

Chung, Tai-Yeong (1996). Rent-Seeking Contest When the Prize Increases with Aggregate Efforts. In: Public Choice; Vol. 87, No. 1-2, pp. 55-66, April 1996.

Claessens, Stijn and Peters, Kyle R. (1997). State Enterprise Performance and Soft Budget Constraints: The Case of Bulgaria. In: Economics of Transition; Vol. 5, No. 2, pp. 305-22, November 1997.

Clark, Derek J. (1997). Learning the Structure of a Simple Rent-Seeking Game. In: Public Choice; Vol. 93, No. 1-2, pp. 119-30, October 1997.

Clark, Derek J. and Riis, Christian (1998). Influence and the Discretionary Allocation of Several Prizes. In: European Journal of Political Economy; Vol. 14, No. 4, pp. 605-25, November 1998.

Clark, Derek J.; and Riis, Christian (1996). A Multi-Winner Nested Rent-Seeking Contest. In: Public Choice; Vol. 87, No. 1-2, pp. 177-84, April 1996.

Cohen, John M. (1993). Importance of Public Service Reform: the Case of Kenya. In: Journal of Modern African Studies; Vol. 31, No. 3, pp. 449-76, 1993.

Congleton, Roger D. (1984). Committees and Rent-Seeking Effort. In: Journal of Public Economics; Vol. 25, No. 1/2, pp. 197-209, November 1984.

Congleton, Roger D. (1991). Ideological Conviction and Persuasion in the Rent-Seeking Society. In: Journal of Public Economics; Vol. 44, Iss. 1, pp. 65-86, February 1991.

Coopers&Lybrand (1996). Review of Subsidies to Public Enterprises 1993-96. Vol. 1-3, Draft. A Study Carried out for the PER by Coopers&Lybrand with LART. December 1996.

Coopers&Lybrand (1997a). Audit of IPC Exemptions. Executive Summary. A Report Prepared for the Government of Tanzania. August 1997.

Coopers&Lybrand (1997b). The Investor Roadmap of Tanzania. Final Report. A Report Prepared for USAID Tanzania. July 1997.

Coopers&Lybrand (1997c). The Investor Roadmap of Tanzania. Phase II. A Report Prepared for USAID Tanzania. October 1997.

Corcoran, William J. (1984). Long-Run Equilibrium and Total Expenditures in Rent-Seeking. In: Public Choice; Vol. 43, No. 1, pp. 89-94, 1984.

Corcoran, William J. and Karels, Gordon V. (1985). Rent-Seeking Behaviour in the Long-Run. In: Public Choice; Vol. 46, Iss. 3, pp. 227-46, 1985.

Courbois, Jean-Pierre (1991). The Effect of Predatory Rent-Seeking on Household Saving and Portfolio Choices: A Cross Section Analysis. In: Public Choice; Vol. 70, Iss. 3, pp. 251-65, June 1991.

Cremer, Georg (2000). Korruption begrenzen. Praxisfeld Entwicklungspolitik. Lambertus, Freiburg im Breisgau 2000.

Crew, Michael A. (1987). Rent-Seeking Is Here to Stay. In Charles K. Rowley (ed.): Democracy and Public Choice: Essays in Honour of Gordon Tullock; pp. 158-62, Basil Blackwell, Oxford 1987.

Crew, Michael A. and Rowley, Charles K. (1988). Dispelling the Disinterest in Deregulation. In Charles K. Rowley, Robert D. Tollison and Gordon Tullock (eds.): The Political Economy of Rent-Seeking; pp. 163-78, Kluwer Academic Publishers, Amsterdam 1988.

Cullis, John G. and Jones, Philip R. (1992). Does It Make Sense to Double Count? Problems in Assessing Rent-Seeking Costs. In: Public Finance Quarterly; Vol. 20, Iss. 3, pp. 378-89, July 1992.

Czichowski, Frank (1990). Rent-Seeking, Stagnation und Unterentwicklung. Der Beitrag der neuen politischen Ökonomie zur Theorie der Entwicklung und Unterentwicklung. In: Konjunkturpolitik; Vol. 36, Iss. 2/3, pp. 169-92, 1990.

Davis, Douglas D. and Reilly, Robert J. (1998). Do Too Many Cooks Always Spoil the Stew? An Experimental Analysis of Rent-Seeking and the Role of a Strategic Buyer. In: Public Choice; Vol. 95, No. 1-2, pp. 89-115, April 1998.

Davis, Douglas D. and Reilly, Robert J. (1999). Rent-Seeking with Non-identical Sharing Rules: An Equilibrium Rescued. In: Public Choice; Vol. 100, No. 1-2, pp. 31-8, July 1999.

Demery, Lionel and Addison, Tony (1993). The Impact of Macroeconomic Adjustment on Poverty in the Presence of Wage Rigidities. In: Journal of Development Economics; Vol. 40, pp. 331-48, 1993.

Dessus, Sebastien; Lafay, Jean-Dominique and Morrisson, Christian (1998). A Politico-Economic Model for Stabilisation in Africa. In: Journal of African Economies; Vol. 7, No. 1, pp. 91-119, March 1998.

Dewatripont, Mathias and Roland, Gérard (1992). Economic Reform and Dynamic Political Constraints. In: Review of Economic Studies; Vol. 59, pp. 703-30, 1992.

Diao, Xinshen; Diaz-Bonilla, Eugenio and Robinson, Sherman (2003). How Much Does it Hurt? Measuring the Impact of Agricultural Trade Policies on Developing Nations. IFPRI. August 26, 2003. Internet: http://www.ifpri.org/media/trade20030826.htm (access date: Sept. 2003).

Doriye, Joshua (1995). Structural Adjustment in Tanzania: Progress and Prospects. In Lucian A. Msambichaka, Ali L. Kilindo and Godwin D. Mjema (eds.): Beyond Structural Adjustment

Programmes in Tanzania. Successes, Failures and New Perspectives; pp. 7-26, Economic Research Bureau, Dar es Salaam 1995.

Dornbusch, Rudiger; and Helmers, Leslie C. H., eds. **(1991).** The Open Economy. Tools for Policymakers in Developing Countries. Oxford University Press, New York 1991.

Dougan, William R. (1991). The Cost of Rent-Seeking: Is GNP Negative? In: Journal of Political Economy; Vol. 99, No. 3, pp. 660-4, June 1991.

Drazen, Allan (1996). The Political Economy of Delayed Reform. In: Policy Reform; Vol. 1, pp. 25-46, 1996.

Due, Jean M. (1993). Liberalization and Privatization in Tanzania and Zambia. In: World Development; Vol. 21, No. 12, pp. 1981-8, December 1993.

Duncombe, William; Miner, Jerry and Ruggiero, John (1997). Empirical Evaluation of Bureaucratic Models of Inefficiency. In: Public Choice; Vol. 93, No. 1-2, pp. 1-18, October 1997.

Durden, Garey (1990). The Effect of Rent-Seeking on Family Income Levels: Some Suggestive Empirical Evidence. In: Public Choice; Vol. 67, Iss. 3, pp. 285-91, December 1990.

Eggertsson, Thráinn (1990). Economic Behavior and Institutions. Cambridge University Press, Cambridge 1990.

Ekelund, Robert B. and Tollison, Robert D. (1981). Mercantilism as a Rent-Seeking Society: Economic Regulation in Historical Perspective. A&M University, Texas 1981.

Ellickson, Robert C. (1991). Order Without Law: How Neighbours Settle Disputes. Harward University Press, Cambridge 1991.

Ellingsen, Tore (1991). Strategic Buyers and the Social Cost of Monopoly. In: American Economic Review; Vol. 81, No. 3, pp. 648-57, June 1991.

Epstein, Gil S.; Hillman, Arye L. and Ursprung, Heinrich W. (1998). The King Never Emigrates: Political Culture and the Reluctant International Movement of People. Centre for Economic Policy Research Discussion Paper: 1815, February 1998.

Eriksson, Gun (1993). Tanzania: Incidence and Patterns of the Soft Budget Constraint in Tanzania. Part One: Suggestions from Data on Loss Makers and Budget Softening Mechanisms via the Government. Macroeconomic Studies No. 44/93. Department of International Economics and Geography, Stockholm School of Economics, November 1993.

Eriksson, Gun (1994). Tanzania: Incidence and Patterns of the Soft Budget Constraint in Tanzania. Part Two: Suggestions from Budget Softening Mechanisms via the Donors: The Case of Import Support. Macroeconomic Studies No. 60/95. Department of International Economics and Geography, Stockholm School of Economics, November 1994.

ESRF, Economic and Social Research Foundation (1996a). Budget Proposals For 1996/97. A Synthesis of Views from the Business Community. Submitted to Government by the ESRF, Dar es Salaam, May 1996.

ESRF, Economic and Social Research Foundation (1996b). The Parallel Economy in Tanzania: Magnitude, Causes and Policy Implications. Submitted to the Parliamentary Finance and Economic Affairs Committee. Dar es Salaam, April 1996.

ESRF, Economic and Social Research Foundation (1998). SPA/Jem Project: Analysis of Progress and Relevance. Dar es Salaam, July 1998.

European Union (1997). European Commission Statement at the CG Meeting 10.12.1997 in Dar es Salaam.

Fabella, Raul V. (1995). The Social Cost of Rent-Seeking Under Countervailing Opposition to Distortionary Transfers. In: Journal of Public Economics; Vol. 57, No. 2, pp. 235-47, June 1995.

Fatton, Robert Jr. (1990). Liberal Democracy in Africa. In: Political Science Quarterly; Vol. 105, No. 3, pp. 455-73, 1990.

Fernandez, Raquel and Rodrik, Dani (1991). Resistance to Reform: Status Quo Bias in the Presence of Individual-Specific Uncertainty. In: American Economic Review; Vol. 81, No. 5, pp. 1146-55, December 1991.

Fessler, Pamela (1986). Russel Long: Tax Master and Senate Mentor. In: Congressional Quarterly Weekly Report; Vol. 44, No. 3, p. 797f, 1986.

Financial Times (1996). Monday September 30, 1996. Tanzania Minister Under Threat.

Findlay, Ronald (1990). The New Political Economy: Its Explanatory Power for LDCs. In: Economics and Politics; Vol. 2, Iss. 2, pp. 193-221, July 1990.

Findlay, Ronald and Wilson, John D. (1987). The Political Economy of Leviathan. In A. Razin and E. Sadka (eds.): Economic Policy in Theory and Practice; Macmillan, 1987.

Finn, James, ed. (1994). Freedom in the World. The Annual Survey of Political Rights & Civil Liberties 1993-1994. Freedom House, New York 1994.

Fischer, Pius V. (1994). Erhöht Anpassung die Armut? Anpassungsprogramme und Einkommensverteilung in Entwicklungsländern. Universität Konstanz, Oktober 1994.

Fleming, Euan (1998). Rent-Seeking in Rural Development Projects: Its Potential Causes and Measures to Reduce Its Costs. In: Journal of International Development; Vol. 10, No. 3, pp. 277-99, May-June 1998.

Freedom House (2002). Political Rights and Civil Liberties. Internet: http://www.freedomhouse.org/ratings/index.htm (access date: April 1999 and May 2002).

Frey, Bruno S. and Eichenberger, Reiner (1994). The Political Economy of Stabilization Programmes in Developing Countries. In: European Journal of Political Economy; Vol. 10, No. 1, pp. 169-90, May 1994.

Gaillard, Laurent and Rüegg, Willy (1987). Korruption, Klientelismus und Bürokratie. Beziehungen zwischen traditionellen Wertsystemen und modernen Strukturen. Seminararbeit NADEL, January 1987.

Gallagher, Mark (1991). Rent Seeking and Economic Growth in Africa. Westview Press, Oxford 1991.

Gelb, Alan; Hillman, Arye L. and Ursprung, Heinrich W. (1995). Rents and the Transition. Draft of Background Paper, World Bank Development Report 1996.

Gibbon, Peter (1992). Authoritarianism, Democracy, and Adjustment. The Politics of Economic Reform in Africa. Nordiska Afrikainstituet, Uppsala 1992.

Glazer, Amihai and Hassin, Refael (2000). Sequential Rent-Seeking. In: Public Choice; Vol. 102, No. 3-4, pp. 219-28, March 2000.

GoT, Government of Tanzania (1986a). Budget Speech for the Financial Year 1986/87. Dar es Salaam, 1986.

GoT, Government of Tanzania (1986b). Programme for Economic Recovery. Dar es Salaam, May 1986.

GoT, Government of Tanzania (1987). Tanzania: Policy Framework Paper, 1987-90. Dar es Salaam, September 1987.

GoT, Government of Tanzania (1988a). Parastatal Organizations Directory. June, 1988 Edition. Compiled by: Presidential Standing Committee on Parastatal Organizations (SCOPO). Dar es Salaam, 1988.

GoT, Government of Tanzania (1988b). Programme for Economic Recovery. Report Prepared by the Government of Tanzania for the Meeting of the Consultative Group for Tanzania. Dar es Salaam, June 1988.

GoT, Government of Tanzania (1989). Economic Recovery Programme II (Economic and Social Action Programme) 1989/90-1991/92. Report prepared by the Government of Tanzania for the Meeting of the Consultative Group for Tanzania, Dar es Salaam, November 30, 1989.

GoT, Government of Tanzania (1990a). Budget Speech for the Financial Year 1990/91. Dar es Salaam, 1990.

GoT, Government of Tanzania (1990b). Financial Sector Restructuring in Tanzania: The Report and Recommendations of the Presidential Commission of Enquiry into the Monetary and Banking System in Tanzania. Dar es Salaam, July 19, 1990.

GoT, Government of Tanzania (1990c). Volume II Estimates of Public Expenditure Consolidated Fund Services and Supply Votes for the Year from 1st July, 1989 to 30th June, 1990.

GoT, Government of Tanzania (1991). Developments in Policy and Institutional Reforms since December 1989. Report prepared by the Government of Tanzania for the Meeting of the Consultative Group for Tanzania. Dar es Salaam, June 12, 1991.

GoT, Government of Tanzania (1992a). Policy Framework Paper, 1992/93-94/95. Implementation Matrix (July/December 1992 Report). Dar es Salaam, 1992.

GoT, Government of Tanzania (1992b). Tanzania: Economic Policy Framework Paper, 1992/93-94/95. Dar es Salaam, June 5, 1992.

GoT, Government of Tanzania (1993a). Budget Speech for the Financial Year 1993/94. Dar es Salaam, 1993.

GoT, Government of Tanzania (1993b). Volume II Estimates of Public Expenditure Consolidated Fund Services and Supply Votes for the Year from 1st July, 1992 to 30th June, 1993.

GoT, Government of Tanzania (1994a). Budget Speech for the Financial Year 1994/95. Dar es Salaam, 1994.

GoT, Government of Tanzania (1994b). Recent Economic Developments in Tanzania and Government's Response. A paper presented to the Special Donor's Meeting held in Paris on 8th March, 1994.

GoT, Government of Tanzania (1994-98). Volume II Estimates of Public Expenditure Consolidated Fund Services and Supply Votes for the Years 1993/94-1997/98. Diskette.

GoT, Government of Tanzania (1996). Preliminary Report of the Parliamentary Select Probe Committee on Allegations of Corruption by Three Top Government Officials and Two CCM Officials. Dar es Salaam, September 23, 1996.

GoT, Government of Tanzania (1997). Opening Statement by the President of the United Republic of Tanzania, His Excellency Benjamin William Mkapa, at the Consultative Group Meeting for Tanzania, Dar es Salaam, December 10, 1997.

GoT, Government of Tanzania (1999). Tanzania's Third Phase Government Fight Against Corruption: A Brief on Achievements and Challenges 1995-1999. President's Office, State House. Dar es Salaam, February 1999.

Gradstein, Mark (1993). Rent Seeking and the Provision of Public Goods. In: Economic Journal; Vol. 103, No. 420, pp. 1236-43, September 1993.

Grissa, Abdessatar (1989). Interest Group Analysis of Tunisia's State Enterprises. In Mustapha K. Nabli and Jeffrey B. Nugent (eds.): The New Institutional Economics and Development: Theory and Applications to Tunisia; Vol. 183, pp. 404-27, Elsevier Science Publishers B.V., Amsterdam 1989.

Grossman, Philip J. (1988). Government and Economic Growth: A Non-Linear Relationship. In: Public Choice; Vol. 56, No. 2, pp. 193-200, February 1988.

Gulhati, Ravi (1988). The Political Economy of Reform in Sub-Saharan Africa. Report of the 'Workshops on the Political Economy of Structural Adjustment and the Sustainability of Reform' held in Halifax, Canada in November 20-22, 1986 and Washington, D.C. in December 3-5, 1986.

Gupta, Sanjeev; Clements, Benedict; Pivovarsky, Alexander and Tiongson, Erwin R. (2003). Foreign Aid and Revenue Response: Does the Composition of Aid Matter? WP/03/176. International Monetary Fund, Washington D.C., September 2003. Internet: http://www.imf.org/external/pubs/ft/wp/2003/wp03176.pdf (access date: Oct. 2003).

Gupta, Sanjeev; Davoodi, Hamid R. and Alonso-Terme, Rosa (1998). Does Corruption Affect Income Inequality and Poverty? IMF Working Paper Series WP/98/76. International Monetary Fund, Washington, May 1998.

Gupta, Sanjeev; de Mello, Luis and Sharan, Raju (2000). Corruption and Military Spending. IMF Working Paper WP/00/23. International Monetary Fund, Washington, February 2000.

Haggard, Stephan and Webb, Steven B. (1993). What Do We Know about the Political Economy of Economic Policy Reform? In: World Bank Research Observer; Vol. 8, No. 2, pp. 143-68, July 1993.

Hardin, Russell (1982). Collective Action. Resources for the Future. Washington, D.C. 1982.

Harris, Jon R. and Todaro, Michael P. (1970). Migration, Unemployment and Development: a Two Sector Analysis. In: American Economic Review; Vol. 60, pp. 126-42, 1970.

Hazlett, Thomas W. and Michaels, Robert J. (1993). The Cost of Rent-Seeking: Evidence from Cellular Telephone License Lotteries. In: Southern Economic Journal; Vol. 59, Iss. 3, pp. 425-35, January 1993.

Helleiner, Gerald K.; Killick, Tony; Lipumba, Nguyuru; Ndulu, Benno J. and Svendsen, Knud E. (1995). Report of the Group of Independent Advisers on Development Cooperation Issues Between Tanzania and Its Aid Donors. Royal Danish Ministry of Foreign Affairs. June 1995.

Henley, John S. (1993). Privatization in Africa: Prospects for Tanzania. In Thomas Clarke and Christos Pitelis (eds.): The Political Economy of Privatization; pp. 455-74, Routledge, London 1993.

Higgins, Richard S.; Shughart, William F. and Tollison, Robert D. (1985). Free Entry and Efficient Rent-Seeking. In: Public Choice; Vol. 46, Iss. 3, pp. 247-58, 1985.

Hillman, Arye L. and Katz, Eliakim (1987). Hierarchical Structure and the Social Cost of Bribes and Transfers. In: Journal of Public Economics; Vol. 34, No. 2, pp. 129-42, November 1987.

Hillman, Arye L. and Riley, John G. (1989). Politically Contestable Rents and Transfers. In: Economics and Politics; Vol. I, No. 1, pp. 17-39, Spring 1989.

Hillman, Arye L. and Samet, Dov (1987). Dissipation of Contestable Rents by Small Numbers of Contenders. In: Public Choice; Vol. 54, No. 1, pp. 63-82, 1987.

Hillman, Arye L. and Swank, Otto (2000). Why Political Culture Should Be in the Lexicon of Economics. In: European Journal of Political Economy; Vol. 16, No. 1, pp. 1-4, March 2000.

Hillman, Arye L. and Ursprung, Heinrich W. (2000). Political Culture and Economic Decline. In: European Journal of Political Economy; Vol. 16, No. 1, pp. 189-213, March 2000.

Hines, James R. (1999). Three Sides of Harberger Triangles. In: Journal of Economic Perspectives; Vol. 13, No. 2, pp. 167-88, Spring 1999.

Hirshleifer, Jack (1989). Conflict and Rent-Seeking Success Functions: Ratio vs. Difference Models of Relative Success. In: Public Choice; Vol. 63, No. 2, pp. 101-12, November 1989.

Hofmeier, Rolf (1993). Tanzania. In Dieter Nohlen and Franz Nuscheler (eds.): Handbuch der Dritten Welt; pp. 178-200, Dietz, Bonn 1993.

Hyden, Goran and Karlstrom, Bo (1993). Structural Adjustment as a Policy Process: The Case of Tanzania. In: World Development; Vol. 21, No. 9, pp. 1395-404, September 1993.

ICRG, International Country Risk Guide (2003). IRIS-3 File of International Country Risk Guide (ISRG) Data. Internet: http://ssdc.ucsd.edu/ssdc/pdf/IRIS_doc.pdf (access date: Nov. 2003).

IMF, International Monetary Fund (1986). Fund Supported Programs, Fiscal Policy, and Income Distribution. A Study by the Fiscal Affairs Department of the International Monetary Fund. Occasional Papers 46, Washington D.C., September 1986.

IMF, International Monetary Fund (1995). Tanzania—Staff Report for the 1995 Article IV Consultation. November 8, 1995.

IMF, International Monetary Fund (1996a). Tanzania: Selected Issues and Statistical Appendix. October 25, 1996.

IMF, International Monetary Fund (1996b). Tanzania: Staff Report for the 1996 Article IV Consultation and Request for a Three-Year Arrangement Under the Enhanced Structural Adjustment Facility. October 25, 1996.

IMF, International Monetary Fund (2001). International Financial Statistics.

Internationales Afrikaforum (2003). Tanzania. In: Chronik Ostafrika, Weltforum Verlag. 39. Jg, 3. Quartal; 2003.

Jackson, Robert H. and Rosberg, Charles G. (1985). The Marginality of African States. In Carter G. and O'Meara P. (eds.): African Independence: The First Twenty-Five Years; Indiana University, 1985.

Jain, Arvind K., ed. **(1998)**. Economics of Corruption. Recent Economic Thought Series. Vol. 65. Kluwer Academic Publisher, Boston 1998.

Jalan, Bimal (1991). India's Economic Crisis: The Way Ahead. Oxford University Press, Delhi 1991.

Jesse, Eckhard (1998). Staatsformenlehre. In Dieter Nohlen and Rainer-Olaf Schultze (eds.): Lexikon der Politik; Band 1: Politische Theorien, pp. 589-92, C. H. Beck, München 1998.

Kahneman, Daniel (1994). New Challenges to the Rationality Assumption. In: Journal of Institutional and Theoretical Economics; Vol. 150, No. 1, pp. 18-36, March 1994.

Kanaan, Oussama (2000). Tanzania's Experience with Trade Liberalization. In: Finance & Development; pp. 30-3, June 2000.

Katz, Eliakim; Nitzan, Shmuel and Rosenberg, Jacob (1990). Rent Seeking for Pure Public Goods. In: Public Choice; Vol. 65, Iss. 1, pp. 49-60, April 1990.

Katz, Eliakim and Rosenberg, Jacob (1989). Rent-Seeking for Budgetary Allocation: Preliminary Results for 20 Countries. In: Public Choice; Vol. 60, No. 2, pp. 133-44, February 1989.

Katz, Eliakim and Rosenberg, Jacob (1994). More on Measuring Budget-Related Rent-Seeking: A Comment. In: Public Choice; Vol. 78, No. 2, pp. 187-91, 1994.

Katz, Eliakim and Tokatlidu, Julia (1996). Group Competition for Rents. In: European Journal of Political Economy; Vol. 12, No. 4, pp. 599-607, December 1996.

Kaufmann, Daniel (1997). Economic Corruption: Some Facts. Paper presented at the 8th International Anti-Corruption Conference. Lima, September 1997. Internet: http://www.transparency.org/iacc/8th_iacc/papers/kaufmann.html (access date: May 2002).

Kaufmann, Daniel (1998a). Corruption in Transition Economies. In Peter Newman (ed.): The New Palgrave. Dictionary of Economics and The Law; Vol. 1, pp. 522-30, Macmillan Reference Limited, London 1998.

Kaufmann, Daniel (1998b). Research on Corruption: Critical Empirical Issues. In Arvind K. Jain (ed.): Economics of Corruption (Recent Economic Thought Series); pp. 129-76, Kluwer Academic Publisher, Boston 1998.

Kaufmann, Daniel and O'Connell, Stephen A. (1999). The Macroeconomics of Delayed Exchange-Rate Unification. Theory and Evidence from Tanzania. Policy Research Working Paper 2060. World Bank, February 1999.

Khan, Mushtaq H. (1996). A Typology of Corrupt Transactions in Developing Countries. In: IDS Bulletin; Vol. 27, No. 2, pp. 12-21, April 1996.

Kimenyi, Mwangi S. (1989). Interest Groups, Transfer Seeking, and Democratization: Africa's Political Stability. In: American Journal of Economics and Sociology; Vol. 48, No. 3, pp. 339-49, July 1989.

Kimenyi, Mwangi S. and Mbaku, John M. (1993). Rent-Seeking and Institutional Stability in Developing Countries. In: Public Choice; Vol. 77, No. 2, pp. 385-405, October 1993.

Kimenyi, Mwangi S. and Mbaku, John M. (1995). Rents, Military Elites, and Political Democracy. In: European Journal of Political Economy; Vol. 11, Iss. 4, pp. 699-708, April 1995.

Klitgaard, Robert (1991). Bribes and Gifts. In Richard J. Zeckhauser (ed.): Strategy and Choice; pp. 211-39, Cambridge 1991.

Klitgaard, Robert (2000). Subverting Corruption. In: Finance & Development; Vol. 37, No. 2, pp. 2-5, June 2000.

Kornai, János (1979). Resource-Constrained Versus Demand-Constrained Systems. In: Econometrica; Vol. 47, No. 4, Iss. 4, pp. 801-19, July 1979.

Korsgren, Eric (1996). Macroeconomic Report Tanzania. Embassy of Sweden, June 1996.

Krueger, Anne O. (1974). The Political Economy of the Rent-Seeking Society. In: American Economic Review; Vol. 64, No. 3, pp. 291-303, June 1974.

Krueger, Anne O. (1989). Asymmetry in Policy Between Exportables and Import-Competing Goods. NBER Working Paper 2904, Cambridge, MA, March 1989.

Krueger, Anne O. (1993). Political Economy of Policy Reform in Developing Countries. MIT Press, Cambridge 1993.

Krueger, Anne O. (1996). Political Economy of Agricultural Policy. In: Public Choice; Vol. 87, No. 1-2, pp. 163-75, April 1996.

Laband, David N. and Sophocleus, John P. (1988). The Social Cost of Rent-Seeking: First Estimates. In: Public Choice; Vol. 58, No. 3, pp. 269-75, September 1988.

Lafay, Jean-Dominique and Lecaillon, Jacques (1993). The Political Dimension of Economic Adjustment. OECD, Paris 1993.

Laffont, Jean-Jaques (1989). A Brief Overview of the Economics of Incomplete Markets. In: Economic Record; Vol. 65, No. 188, pp. 54-65, March 1989.

Lal, Deepak (1988). The Hindu Equilibrium. Volume 1: Cultural Stability and Economic Stagnation. Clarendon Press, Oxford 1988.

Lal, Deepak and Myint, Hal (1996). The Political Economy of Poverty, Equity, and Growth. Clarendon Press, Oxford 1996.

Lane, P. A. (1984). The State of the Tanzanian Economy. E.R.B. Paper 84.1, Dar es Salaam 1984.

Lauth, Hans-Joachim (1998). Autoritäre versus totalitäre Regime. In Dieter Nohlen and Rainer-Olaf Schultze (eds.): Lexikon der Politik; Band 1: Politische Theorien, pp. 27-32, C. H. Beck, München 1998.

Lee, Dwight R. and Tollison, Robert D. (1988). Optimal Taxation in a Rent-Seeking Environment. In Charles K. Rowley, Robert D. Tollison and Gordon Tullock (eds.): The Political Economy of Rent-Seeking; pp. 339-50, Kluwer Academic Publishers, Amsterdam 1988.

Lee, Sanghack (1995). Endogenous Sharing Rules in Collective-Group Rent-Seeking. In: Public Choice; Vol. 85, No. 1-2, pp. 31-44, October 1995.

Leininger, Wolfgang (1993). More Efficient Rent Seeking — A Münchausen Solution. In: Public Choice; Vol. 75, No. 1, pp. 43-62, January 1993.

LeVine, Victor T. (1993). Administrative Corruption and Democratisation in Africa: Aspects of the Theoretic Agenda. In: Corruption and Reform; Vol. 7, pp. 271-8, 1993.

Lewis, Peter M. (1994). Role of Government in the Economy and the Role of Rent-Seeking in African Political Economies: Introduction. In: World Development; Vol. 22, No. 3, pp. 423-5, March 1994.

Lewis, Peter M. and Stein, Howard (1997). Shifting Fortunes: The Political Economy of Financial Liberalization in Nigeria. In: World Development; Vol. 25, No. 1, pp. 5-22, January 1997.

Linster, Bruce G. (1993). A Generalized Model of Rent-Seeking Behavior. In: Public Choice; Vol. 77, Iss. 2, pp. 421-35, October 1993.

Linster, Bruce G. (1994). Cooperative Rent-Seeking. In: Public Choice; Vol. 81, Iss. 2, pp. 23-34, October 1994.

Loehman, Edna; Quesnel, Fabrice N. and Babb, Emerson M. (1996). Free-Rider Effects in Rent-Seeking Groups Competing for Public Goods. In: Public Choice; Vol. 86, No. 1-2, pp. 35-61, January 1996.

Long, Ngo V. and Vousden, Neil (1987). Risk-Averse Rent Seeking with Shared Rents. In: Economic Journal; Vol. 97, No. 388, pp. 971-85, December 1987.

Loxley, John (1989). The Devaluation Debate in Tanzania. In Bonnie K. Campbell and John Loxley (eds.): Structural Adjustment in Africa; pp. 13-36, Macmillan Press, London 1989.

Lyatuu, W. A. (1998). The Integrated Roads Project (IRP). In Tanzania Roads Association (ed.): ARC 97. Annual Roads Convention on Road Transport: The Key to Development. Proceedings of the seminar held at the Karimjee Hall in Dar es Salaam, September 24-26, 1997; pp. 38-56, 1998.

Magee, Stephen P.; Brock, William A. and Young, Leslie (1989). Black Hole Tariffs and the Endogenous Policy Theory. Cambridge University Press, Cambridge 1989.

Magill, Michael J. P. and Quinzii, Martine (1996). The Theory of Incomplete Markets. MIT Press, Cambridge 1996.

Mair, Stefan (1996). Politischer Wandel in Ostafrika. Kenia, Tansania und Uganda auf dem Weg zur Demokratie? SWP- S 412. Stiftung Wissenschaft und Politik, November 1996.

Majumdar, Sumit K. (1998). Slack in the State-Owned Enterprise: An Evaluation of the Impact of Soft-Budget Constraints. In: International Journal of Industrial Organization; Vol. 16, No. 3, pp. 377-94, May 1998.

Maliyamkono, Ted L. and Bagachwa, Mboya S. D. (1990). The Second Economy in Tanzania. James Currey, London 1990.

Mans, Darius (1994). Tanzania. Resolute Action. In Ishrat Husain and Rashid Faruqee (eds.): Adjustment in Africa. Lessons from Country Case Studies (World Bank Regional and Sectoral Studies); pp. 352-426, 1994.

Marcouiller, Douglas and Young, Leslie (1995). The Black Hole of Graft: The Predatory State and the Informal Economy. In: American Economic Review; Vol. 85, Iss. 3, pp. 630-46, June 1995.

Marmo, Francis; Kimambo, Immanuel N. and Andreski, Adam (1998). Road Financing for Sustainable Development. In Tanzania Roads Association (ed.): ARC 97. Annual Roads Convention on Road Transport: The Key to Development. Proceedings of the seminar held at the Karimjee Hall in Dar es Salaam, September 24-26, 1997; pp. 15-26, 1998.

Maro, Wilbald E. (1997). Cotton Sector Study. Human Development Report for Shinyanga Region. University of Dar es Salaam, January 1997.

Massing, Peter (1987). Interessengruppen. In Dieter Nohlen and Reiner-Olaf Schultze (eds.): Pipers Wörterbuch zur Politik: Politikwissenschaft; Band 1, pp. 388-9, Piper, München 1987.

Mauro, Paolo (1995). Corruption and Growth. In: Quarterly Journal of Economics; Vol. 110, Iss. 3, pp. 681-712, August 1995.

Mauro, Paolo (1996). The Effects of Corruption on Growth, Investment, and Government Expenditure. IMF Working Paper 96/98, Washington, September 1996.

Mauro, Paolo (1997). Why Worry About Corruption? Economic Issues No. 6. International Monetary Fund, February 24, 1997.

Mauro, Paolo (1998). Corruption and the Composition of Government Expenditure. In: Journal of Public Economics; Vol. 69, Iss. 2, pp. 263-79, August 1998.

Mbaku, John M. (1992). Bureaucratic Corruption as Rent-Seeking Behavior. In: Konjunkturpolitik; Vol. 38, Iss. 4, pp. 247-65, 1992.

McChesney, Fred S. (1987). Rent Extraction and Rent Creation in the Economic Theory of Regulation. In: Journal of Legal Studies; Vol. 16, pp. 1-13, January 1987.

McChesney, Fred S. (1997). Money for Nothing. Politicians, Rent Extraction. and Political Extortion. Harvard University Press, Cambridge 1997.

McGowan, Patrick and Johnson, Thomas (1984). Military Coups d'État and Underdevelopment: A Quantitative Historical Analysis. In: Journal of Modern African Studies; Vol. 22, No. 4, pp. 633-66, 1984.

McGuire, Martin C. and Olson, Mancur JR. (1996). The Economics of Autocracy and Majority Rule: The Invisible Hand and the Use of Force. In: Journal of Economic Literature; Vol. 34, Iss. 1, pp. 72-96, March 1996.

Medema, Steven G. (1991). Another Look at the Problem of Rent Seeking. In: Journal of Economic Issues; Vol. 25, Iss. 4, pp. 1049-65, December 1991.

Millner, Edward L. and Pratt, Michael D. (1989). An Experimental Investigation of Efficient Rent Seeking. In: Public Choice; Vol. 62, No. 2, pp. 139-51, August 1989.

Millner, Edward L. and Pratt, Michael D. (1991). Risk Aversion and Rent Seeking: An Extension and Some Experimental Evidence. In: Public Choice; Vol. 69, No. 1, pp. 81-92, February 1991.

Ministry of Agriculture (1994a). 1993 Review of the Sisal Marketing. Marketing Development Bureau, Government of Tanzania, Dar es Salaam 1994.

Ministry of Agriculture (1994b). 1993/94 Industry Review of Cotton. Marketing Development Bureau, Government of Tanzania, Dar es Salaam, December 1994.

Ministry of Agriculture (1994c). 1993/94 Market Review of Cashewnuts. Marketing Development Bureau, Government of Tanzania, Dar es Salaam 1994.

Ministry of Agriculture (1996). Coffee: Production, Processing and Marketing, 1976-95. An Overview. Coffee Management Unit, Government of Tanzania, Dar es Salaam, May 1996.

Ministry of Finance (1993). Final Report of the Task Force on Collection of Overdue Import Support Counterpart Funds. Fiscal Years 87/88 to 92/93. Government of Tanzania, Dar es Salaam, July 1993.

Ministry of Finance (1997). Financing of Public Enterprises in Tanzania. Paper presented at the 'Seminar for Parliamentary Committee on Parastatal Organisations (POC)'. February 24-26, 1997.

Mistry, Percy (1994). Exchange-Rate Adjustment: A Review of Developing Country Experience. In Willem Van der Geest (ed.): Negotiating Structural Adjustment in Africa. Utpapers presented at a seminar held in March 91 in Oxford; pp. 115-36, 1994.

Mitchell, Shannon K. (1993). The Welfare Effects of Rent-Saving and Rent-Seeking. In: Canadian Journal of Economics; Vol. 26, Iss. 3, pp. 660-9, August 1993.

Mohammad, Sharif and Whalley, John (1984). Rent Seeking in India: Its Cost and Policy Significance. In: Kyklos; Vol. 37, Iss. 3, pp. 387-413, 1984.

Morrissey, Oliver (1995). Political Commitment, Institutional Capacity and Tax Policy Reform in Tanzania. In: World Development; Vol. 25, No. 4, pp. 637-49, April 1995.

Morrisson, Christian; Haggard, Stephan and Lafay, Jean-Dominique (1995). The Political Feasibility of Adjustment in Developing Countries. OECD, Paris 1995.

Moshi, Humphrey P. B. (1998). Enterprise Restructuring and Adjustment in Transition to Market Economy: The case of Tanzania. Economic Research Bureau, University of Dar es Salaam 1998.

Mosley, Paul; Harrigan, Jane and Toye, John (1991). Aid and Power, The World Bank and Policy-Based Lending in the 1980s. In two volumes. Routledge, London 1991.

Mufuruki, Ali A. and Rugemalira, J. B. (1996). Tax Evasion—Its Causes and Logical Cure. Paper presented at the workshop organised by the Economic and Social Research Foundation at 21/03/1996 at the Sheraton Hotel, Dar es Salaam, March 1996.

Murell, Peter (1994). Comment on 'The Institutions and Governance of Economic Development and Reform' by Williamson. In: Proceedings of the World Bank Annual Conference of Development Economics; pp. 201-5, 1994.

Murphy, Kevin M.; Shleifer, Andrei and Vishny, Robert W. (1991). The Allocation of Talent: Implications for Growth. In: Quarterly Journal of Economics; Vol. CVI, Iss. 2, pp. 503-30, May 1991.

Nabli, Mustapha K. and Nugent, Jeffrey B., eds. **(1989)**. The New Institutional Economics and Development: Theory and Applications to Tunisia. Contribution to Economic Analysis. Vol. 183. Elsevier Science Publishers B.V., Amsterdam 1989.

Ndulu, Benno and Wangwe, Samuel (1997). Managing the Tanzania Economy in Transition to Sustained Development. In Dirk Bol, Nathanael Luvanga and Josef Shitundu (eds.): Economic Management in Tanzania; TEMA Publishers Company Ltd, Dar es Salaam 1997.

Neary, Hugh M. (1997). A Comparison of Rent-Seeking Models and Economic Models of Conflict. In: Public Choice; Vol. 93, No. 3-4, pp. 373-88, December 1997.

Neugebauer, Gregory (1978). Grundzüge einer ökonomischen Theorie der Korruption. Eine Studie über Bestechung. Basler sozialökonomische Studien. Band 9. Schulthess, Basel 1978.

Nitzan, Shmuel (1991). Collective Rent Dissipation. In: Economic Journal; Vol. 101, No. 409, pp. 1522-34, November 1991.

Nitzan, Shmuel (1994a). Modelling Rent-Seeking Contests. In: European Journal of Political Economy; Vol. 10, Iss. 1, pp. 41-60, May 1994.

Nitzan, Shmuel (1994b). Transfers or Public Good Provision? A Political Allocation Perspective. In: Economics Letters; Vol. 45, No. 4, pp. 451-7, August 1994.

Nordic Consulting Group (1999). Petroleum Product Price Setting Mechanisms: A Survey and Analysis Prepared for the World Bank. Oslo, June 1999.

North, Douglass C. (1990). Institutions, Institutional Change and Economic Performance. Cambridge University Press, Cambridge 1990.

Nti, Kofi-O (1999). Rent-Seeking with Asymmetric Valuations. In: Public Choice; Vol. 98, No. 3-4, pp. 415-30, March 1999.

Nugent, Jeffrey B. (1989). Collective Action in Tunisia's Producer Organizations: Some Variations on the Olsonian Theme. In Mustapha K. Nabli and Jeffrey B. Nugent (eds.): The New Institutional Economics and Development: Theory and Applications to Tunisia; Vol. 183, pp. 289-322, Elsevier Science Publishers B.V., Amsterdam 1989.

OCAG, Office of the Controller and Auditor General (various). Reports of the Controller and Auditor General for the Financial Years ended 30th June. Government of Tanzania. Annual Volumes, Dar es Salaam 1987-99.

OCAG, Office of the Controller and Auditor General (1995). Final Report on Imports Tax Evasion. Government of Tanzania, February 23, Dar es Salaam 1995.

OCAG, Office of the Controller and Auditor General (1997a). Audited Accounts and Management Audit Report on the Financial Statements of the Roads Fund For the Two (2) Years Ended 30th June, 1995. Government of Tanzania, November 1997.

OCAG, Office of the Controller and Auditor General (1997b). Report of the Controller and Auditor General for the Financial Year ended 30th June, 1996. Government of Tanzania, Dar es Salaam 1997.

OECD, Organisation for Economic Co-operation and Development (1995). What Policy Responded to an Integrating World Economy. Research Programme for 1996-98. December 1995.

Olson, Mancur JR. (1965). The Logic of Collective Action: Public Goods and the Theory of Groups. Harvard University Press, Cambridge 1965.

Olson, Mancur JR. (1982). The Rise and Decline of Nations. Yale University Press, New Haven 1982.

Olson, Mancur JR. (1987). Collective Action. In John Eatwell, Murray Milgate and Peter Newman (eds.): The New Palgrave: A Dictionary of Economics; Vol. 1, pp. 474-7, Macmillan Press, London 1987.

Olson, Mancur JR. (2000). Power and Prosperity: Outgrowing Communist and Capitalist Dictatorships. New York: Basic Books, 2000.

Osoro, Nehemiah E. (1997). Fiscal Performance, Adjustment and Management: The Tanzanian Perspective. In Dirk Bol, Nathanael Luvanga and Josef Shitundu (eds.): Economic Management in Tanzania; pp. 47-70, TEMA Publishers Company Ltd, Dar es Salaam 1997.

Paul, Ellen F.; Miller, Fred D. and Paul, Jeffrey, eds. **(1994)**. Property Rights. Cambridge University Press, Cambridge 1994.

Péan, Pierre (1988). L'Argent noir. Librairie Arthème Fayard, Paris 1988.

Pedersen, Karl R. (1997). The Political Economy of Distribution in Developing Countries: A Rent-Seeking Approach. In: Public Choice; Vol. 91, No. 3-4, pp. 351-73, June 1997.

People's Daily (2001). Mkapa: Tanzania Proud of 40-Year Achievement Since Independence; People's Daily, December 9, 2001. Internet: http://english.people daily.com.cn/200112/09/eng20011209_86220.shtml (access date: Oct. 2003).

Perkins, Dwight H.; Radelet, Steven; Snodgrass, Donald R.; Gillis, Malcolm and Roemer, Michael (2001). Economics of Development. W.W. Norton & Company, New York 2001.

Picot, Arnold and Wolff, Brigitta (1997). Informationsökonomik. In: Gabler Wirtschaftslexikon; pp. 1870-8, Gabler, Wiesbaden 1997.

Pinheiro, Paulo Sergieo (1994). Corruption in Brazil. In Duc V. Trang (ed.): Corruption & Democracy. Political Institutions, Processes and Corruption in Transition States in East-Central Europe and the former Soviet Union; pp. 37-40, Budapest 1994.

Planning Commission (1992). The Economic Survey 1991. Government of Tanzania, Dar es Salaam, November 1992.

Posner, Richard A. (1975). The Social Costs of Monopoly and Regulation. In: Journal of Political Economy; Vol. 83, pp. 807-27, 1975.

Potters, Jan; De Vries, Caspar G. and Van Winden, Frans (1998). An Experimental Examination of Rational Rent-Seeking. In: European Journal of Political Economy; Vol. 14, No. 4, pp. 783-800, November 1998.

Potters, Jan and Sloof, Randolph (1996). Interest Groups: A Survey of Empirical Models That Try to Assess Their Influence. In: European Journal of Political Economy; Vol. 12, No. 3, pp. 403-42, November 1996.

Pritzl, Rupert F. J. (1997). Korruption und Rent-Seeking in Lateinamerika. Zur politischen Ökonomie autoritärer Systeme. NOMOS Verlag, Baden-Baden 1997.

PSRC, Parastatal Sector Reform Commission (1993). Parastatal Privatization and Reform. Master Plan. Dar es Salaam, August 1993.

PSRC, Parastatal Sector Reform Commission (1994). 1993 Review and 1994 and 1995 Action Plan. Dar es Salaam, March 1994.

PSRC, Parastatal Sector Reform Commission (1996). 1995/1996 Review and the Action Plan for 1996/1997. Dar es Salaam, July 1996.

PSRC, Parastatal Sector Reform Commission (1997a). 1996/1997 Review and the Action Plan for 1997/1998. Dar es Salaam, September 1997.

PSRC, Parastatal Sector Reform Commission (1997b). Study on Parastatal Sector Fiscal Impact and Adaptation to Macro-Economic Reforms. Government of Tanzania, March 1997.

PSRC, Parastatal Sector Reform Commission (2000). Privatisation In Tanzania. Annual Review 1999/2000 and Action Plan for 2000/2001. Dar es Salaam, December 2000.

Putterman, Louis (1995). Economic Reform and Smallholder Agriculture in Tanzania: A Discussion of Recent Market Liberalization, Road Rehabilitation, and Technology Dissemination Efforts. In: World Development; Vol. 23, No. 2, pp. 311-26, February 1995.

Raiser, Martin (1994). The No-Exit Economy: Soft Budget Constraints and the Fate of Economic Reforms in Developing Countries. In: World Development; Vol. 22, No. 12, pp. 1851-67, December 1994.

Raiser, Martin (1996). Soft Budget Constraints and the Fate of Economic Reforms in Transition Economies and Developing Countries. Kieler Studien. Vol. 281. Mohr (Siebeck), Tübingen 1996.

Ranis, Gustav (1989). The Role of Institutions in Transition Growth: The East Asian Newly Industrializing Countries. In: World Development; Vol. 17, No. 9, pp. 1443-53, September 1989.

Richter, Rudolf (1994). Institutionen ökonomisch analisiert. Mohr, Tübingen 1994.

Riley, John G. (1999). Asymmetric Contests: A Resolution of the Tullock Paradox. In Peter Howitt, Elisabetta De Antoni and Axel Leijonhufvud (eds.): Money, Markets and Method; pp. 190-207, Edward Elgar Publishing Limited, Cheltenham 1999.

Rodrik, Dani (1995). The Dynamics of Political Support for Reform in Economies in Transition. In: Journal of the Japanese and International Economies; Vol. 9, pp. 403-25, 1995.

Rodrik, Dani (1997). Why Is Trade Reform so Difficult in Africa? In: Journal of African Economies; Vol. 7, Supplement 1, pp. 43-70, June 1997.

Rodrik, Dani (2003). Growth Strategies. A Paper for the 'Handbook of Economic Growth', revised September 2003.

Rösch, Paul-Gerhardt (1995). Der Prozeß der Strukturanpassung in Tanzania. Dissertation. Hamburger Beiträge zur Afrika-Kunde 46; Hamburg 1995.

Rose-Ackermann, Susanne (1998). Corruption. In Peter Newman (ed.): The New Palgrave. Dictionary of Economics and The Law; Vol. 1, pp. 517-22, Macmillan Reference Limited, London 1998.

Rowley, Charles K. (1988a). Rent-Seeking in Constitutional Perspective. In Charles K. Rowley, Robert D. Tollison and Gordon Tullock (eds.): The Political Economy of Rent-Seeking; pp. 447-64, Kluwer Academic Publishers, Amsterdam 1988.

Rowley, Charles K. (1988b). Rent-Seeking Versus Directly Unproductive Profit-Seeking Activities. In Charles K. Rowley, Robert D. Tollison and Gordon Tullock (eds.): The Political Economy of Rent-Seeking; pp. 15-25, Kluwer Academic Publishers, Amsterdam 1988.

Rowley, Charles K. (2000). Political Culture and Economic Performance in Sub-Saharan Africa. In: European Journal of Political Economy; Vol. 16, No. 1, pp. 133-58, March 2000.

Rowley, Charles K. and Elgin, Robert (1988). Government and Its Bureaucracy: A Bilateral Bargaining Versus a Principal-Agent Approach. In Charles K. Rowley, Robert D. Tollison and Gordon Tullock (eds.): The Political Economy of Rent-Seeking; pp. 267-90, Kluwer Academic Publishers, Amsterdam 1988.

Rowley, Charles K. and Tollison, Robert D. (1988). Rent-Seeking and Trade Protection. In Charles K. Rowley, Robert D. Tollison and Gordon Tullock (eds.): The Political Economy of Rent-Seeking; pp. 217-37, Kluwer Academic Publishers, Amsterdam 1988.

Rowley, Charles K.; Tollison, Robert D. and Tullock, Gordon, eds. **(1988)**. The Political Economy of Rent-Seeking. Kluwer Academic Publishers, Amsterdam 1988.

Schaffer, Mark E. (1998). Do Firms in Transition Economies Have Soft Budget Constraints? A Reconsideration of Concepts and Evidence. In: Journal of Comparative Economics; Vol. 26, No. 1, pp. 80-103, March 1998.

Schlicht, Ekkehart (1990). Rationality, Bounded or Not, and Institutional Analysis. In: Journal of Institutional and Theoretical Economics; Vol. 146, No. 4, pp. 703-19, December 1990.

Schnytzer, Adi (1994). Changes in Budgetary Allocations and International Comparisons of the Social Cost of Rent-Seeking: A Critical Note. In: Public Choice; Vol. 79, Iss. 3, pp. 357-62, June 1994.

Schnytzer, Adi (1995). Why Do Rational Communist Not Obstruct the Transformation Process? In: Public Choice; Vol. 85, No. 1-2, pp. 157-72, October 1995.

Schubert, Klaus (1992). Leistungen und Grenzen politisch-ökonomischer Theorie. Eine kritische Bestandsaufnahme zu Mancur Olson. Wissenschaftliche Buchgesellschaft, Darmstadt 1992.

Scott, Kenneth E. (1994). Bounded Rationality and Social Norms: Concluding Comment. In: Journal of Institutional and Theoretical Economics; Vol. 150, No. 1, pp. 315-9, March 1994.

Scully, Gerald W. (1991). Rent-Seeking in U.S. Government Budgets, 1900-88. In: Public Choice; Vol. 70, No. 1, pp. 99-106, April 1991.

SDC, Swiss Development Cooperation (1995). Mission Report. Informal Consultative Group Meeting for Tanzania held in Paris July 25, 1995. August 3, 1995.

Selten, Reinhard (1990). Bounded Rationality. In: Journal of Institutional and Theoretical Economics; Vol. 146, No. 4, pp. 649-58, December 1990.

Shleifer, Andrei and Vishny, Robert W. (1993). Corruption. In: Quarterly Journal of Economics; Vol. 108, No. 3, pp. 598-617, August 1993.

Shogren, Jason F. and Baik, Kyung H. (1991). Reexaming Efficient Rent Seeking in Laboratory Markets. In: Public Choice; Vol. 69, No. 1, pp. 69-70, February 1991.

Shogren, Jason F. and Baik, Kyung H. (1992). Favorites and Underdogs: Strategic Behavior in an Experimental Contest. In: Public Choice; Vol. 74, No. 2, pp. 191-205, September 1992.

Simon, Herbert A. (1987a). Behavioural Economics. In John Eatwell, Murray Milgate and Peter Newman (eds.): The New Palgrave: A Dictionary of Economics; Vol. 1, pp. 221-5, Macmillan Press, London 1987.

Simon, Herbert A. (1987b). Bounded Rationality. In John Eatwell, Murray Milgate and Peter Newman (eds.): The New Palgrave: A Dictionary of Economics; Vol. 1, pp. 266-8, Macmillan Press, London 1987.

Simpkins, Fiona A. (1996). Investigative Journalism in Tanzania I. United Republic of Tanzania. Proceedings of a Workshop, Seventy-Seven Hotel, Arusha, Tanzania, 29 April-4 May 1996.

Sjöstrand, Sven-Erik (1992). On the Rationale Behind 'Irrational' Institutions. In: Journal of Economic Issues; Vol. 26, No. 4, pp. 1007-40, December 1992.

Smedley, Charles V. (1994). Anomie and Deviance. In Frank N. Magill (ed.): Survey of Social Science; Vol. 1, pp. 100-6, Salem Press, Passadena California 1994.

SPA/JEM, Special Program of Assistance/Joint Evaluation Mission (1995). Aide Memoire. Dar es Salaam, February 6-15, 1995.

Stein, Howard (1992). Economic Policy and the IMF in Tanzania: Conditionality, Conflict, and Convergence. In Horace Campbell and Howard Stein (eds.): Tanzania and the IMF. The Dynamics of Liberalization; Westview Press, Boulder 1992.

Stein, Howard (1994). Theories of Institutions and Economic Reform in Africa. In: World Development; Vol. 22, No. 12, pp. 1833-49, December 1994.

Stiglitz, Joseph E. (1992). Reflections on Economics and on Being and Becoming an Economist. Unpublished.

Szeftel, Morris (1998). Misunderstanding African Politics: Corruption & the Governance Agenda. In: Review of African Political Economy; Vol. 25, No. 76, pp. 2221-40, June 1998.

TAC, Tanzania Audit Corporation (various). Annual Report and Accounts for the Year Ended 30th June. Government of Tanzania. Annual Volumes 1984-96.

Tanzania Investment Bank (1996). The Twenty Fifth Annual Report. July 1995-June 1996. Dar es Salaam, 1997.

Tanzi, Vito and Davoodi, Hamid R. (1997). Corruption, Public Investment, and Growth. IMF Working Paper WP/97/139, October 1997.

Tanzi, Vito and Davoodi, Hamid R. (1998). Roads to Nowhere: How Corruption in Public Investment Hurts Growth. Economic Issues No. 12. International Monetary Fund, March 31, 1998.

Tanzi, Vito and Davoodi, Hamid R. (2000). Corruption, Growth, and Public Finances. IMF Working Paper WP/00/182, November 2000.

The Economist (1999). Honest Trade. A Global War Against Bribery. In: The Economist; pp. 23-5, January 16, 1999.

The EastAfrican (1996-98). Various issues.

The Guardian (1997-1998). Various issues.

The Indian Ocean Newsletter (1996-99). Various issues.

Tietz, Reinhard (1990). On Bounded Rationality. Experimental Work at the University of Frankfurt/Main. In: Journal of Institutional and Theoretical Economics; Vol. 146, No. 4, pp. 659-72, December 1990.

TISCO, Tanzania Industrial Studies and Consulting Organisation (2001). Final Evaluation of the Parastatal and Public Sector Reform Project. A Report Prepared by TISCO for the Ministry of Finance, Government of Tanzania, Dar es Salaam 2001.

Tobin, James (1958). Estimation of Relationships for Limited Dependent Variables. In: Econometrica; Vol. 26, pp. 24-36, 1958.

Tollison, Robert D. (1982). Rent Seeking: A Survey. In: Kyklos; Vol. 35, Iss. 4, pp. 575-602, 1982.

Tollison, Robert D. (1987). Is The Theory of Rent-Seeking Here to Stay? In Charles K. Rowley (ed.): Democracy and Public Choice: Essays in Honour of Gordon Tullock; pp. 143-57, Basil Blackwell, Oxford 1987.

Tommasi, Mariano and Velasco, Andrés (1996). Where Are We in the Political Economy of Reform? In: Policy Reform; Vol. 1, Iss. 2, pp. 187-238, 1996.

Toye, John (1992). Interest Group Politics and the Implementation of Adjustment Policies in Sub-Saharan Africa. In: Journal of International Development; Vol. 4, No. 2, pp. 183-97, 1992.

TRA, Tanzania Revenue Authority (1997). Report of the Commodity Import Support Fund. Government of Tanzania, Dar es Salaam, November 1997.

Transparency International (1998a). Default of IPTL Deal Victory for the Tanzanian People. June 12, 1998. Internet: http://www.transparency.org/pressreleases_archive/1998/06.12.tanzania-iptl.html (access date: Sept. 2003).

Transparency International (1998b). Tanzania Cancels Controversial Malaysian Power Deal. In: TI Newsletter, June 1998 (Original source: Financial Times, 20 April 1998). Internet: http://www.transparency.org/newsletters/98.2/reports.html#Tanzania (access date: Sept. 2003).

Transparency International (2003). The Transparency International (TI) 1998-2002 Corruption Perceptions Index. Internet: http://www.gwdg.de/~uwvw/ (access date: Aug. 2003).

Tullock, Gordon (1967). The Welfare Costs of Tariffs, Monopolies, and Theft. In: Western Economic Journal; Vol. 5, Iss. 3, pp. 224-32, June 1967.

Tullock, Gordon (1975). On the Efficient Organization of Trials. In: Kyklos; Vol. 28, Iss. 4, pp. 745-62, 1975.

Tullock, Gordon (1980). Efficient Rent-Seeking. In James M. Buchanan (ed.): Toward a Theory of the Rent-Seeking Society; A & M University Press, Texas 1980.

Tullock, Gordon (1988a). Efficient Rent-Seeking Revised. In Charles K. Rowley, Robert D. Tollison and Gordon Tullock (eds.): The Political Economy of Rent-Seeking; pp. 91-4, Kluwer Academic Publishers, Amsterdam 1988.

Tullock, Gordon (1988b). Future Directions for Rent-Seeking Research. In Charles K. Rowley, Robert D. Tollison and Gordon Tullock (eds.): The Political Economy of Rent-Seeking; pp. 465-80, Kluwer Academic Publishers, Amsterdam 1988.

Tullock, Gordon (1988c). Rents and Rent-Seeking. In Charles K. Rowley, Robert D. Tollison and Gordon Tullock (eds.): The Political Economy of Rent-Seeking; pp. 51-62, Kluwer Academic Publishers, Amsterdam 1988.

Tullock, Gordon (1988d). Why Did the Industrial Revolution Occur in England? In Charles K. Rowley, Robert D. Tollison and Gordon Tullock (eds.): The Political Economy of Rent-Seeking; pp. 409-19, Kluwer Academic Publishers, Amsterdam 1988.

Tullock, Gordon (1989). The Economics of Special Privilege and Rent Seeking. Kluwer Academic Publishers, London 1989.

Tullock, Gordon (1994). Rent Seeking. In John Eatwell, Murray Milgate and Peter Newman (eds.): The New Palgrave: A Dictionary of Economics; Vol. 4, pp. 147-9, Macmillan Press, London 1994.

UNDP, United Nations Development Program (1997). Human Development Report 1997. Oxford University Press, New York 1997.

UNDP, United Nations Development Program (2000). Human Development Report 2000. Oxford University Press, New York 2000.

UNDP, United Nations Development Program (2002). Human Development Report 2002. Oxford University Press, New York 2002.

UNDP, United Nations Development Program (2003). Human Development Report 2003. Oxford University Press, New York 2003.

Ursprung, Heinrich W. (1990). Public Goods, Rent Dissipation, and Candidate Competition. In: Economics and Politics; Vol. 2, No. 2, pp. 115-32, July 1990.

Van Arkadie, Brian (1989). The Role of Institutions in Development. In: Proceedings of the World Bank. Annual Conference of Development Economics; pp. 153-75, 1989.

Van de Walle, Nicolas (1994). Political Liberation and Economic Policy Reform in Africa. In: World Development; Vol. 22, No. 4, pp. 483-500, April 1994.

Van der Geest, Willem and Köttering, Andreas (1994). Structural Adjustment in Tanzania. Objectives and Achievements. In Willem Van der Geest (ed.): Negotiating Structural Adjustment in Africa. Utpapers presented at a seminar held in March 91 in Oxford; 1994.

Wagao, Jumanne H. (1992). Adjustment Policies in Tanzania, 1981-89: The Impact on Growth, Structure and Human Welfare. In Giovanni A. Cornia, Rolph Van der Hoeven and Thandika Mkandawire (eds.): Africa's Recovery in the 1990s: From Stagnation and Adjustment to Human Development; pp. 93-115, Macmillan Press, London 1992.

Warioba Report (1996). Presidential Commission of Inquiry Against Corruption. Commission Report on the State of Corruption in the Country. November 1996.

Wei, Shang-Jin (1997a). Gradualism Versus Big Bang: Speed and Sustainability of Reforms. In: Canadian Journal of Economics; Vol. 30, No. 4, pp. 1234-47, November 1997.

Wei, Shang-Jin (1997b). How Taxing Is Corruption on International Investors? NBER Working Paper No. 2048. National Bureau of Economic Research, Cambridge 1997.

Weimann, Joachim; Yang, Chun-Lei and Vogt, Carsten (2000). An Experiment on Sequential Rent-Seeking. In: Journal of Economic Behavior and Organization; Vol. 41, No. 4, pp. 405-26, April 2000.

Weiss, Carol H. (1995). Nothing as Practical as Good Theory: Exploring Theory-Based Evaluation for Comprehensive Community Initiatives for Children and Families. In: New Approaches to Evaluating Community Initiatives. Volume 1: Concepts, Methods, and Contexts. The Aspen Institute, 1995. Internet: http://www.aspenroundtable.org/vol1/index.htm (access date: July 2002).

Wenders, John T. (1987). On Perfect Rent Dissipation. In: American Economic Review; Vol. 77, No. 3, pp. 456-9, June 1987.

Williamson, John (1990). What Washington Means by Policy Reform. In John Williamson (ed.): Latin American Adjustment: How Much Has Happened?; Institute for International Economics, Washington 1990.

Williamson, Oliver E. (1994). The Institutions and Governance of Economic Development and Reform. In: Proceedings of the World Bank. Annual Conference of Development Economics; pp. 171-97, 1994.

Winiecki, Jan (1991). Resistance to Change in the Soviet Economic System: A Property Rights Approach. Routledge Press, London 1991.

Wise, Sherry J. and Sandler, Todd (1994). Rent-Seeking and Pesticide Legislation. In: Public Choice; Vol. 78, Iss. 3, pp. 329-50, March 1994.

World Bank (1977). Economic Memorandum on Tanzania. Prepared for the May 1977 Meeting of the East Africa Consultative Group—Tanzania. Washington, April 12, 1977.

World Bank (1988). Report to the Consultative Group for Tanzania on the Government's Economic Recovery Program. June 16, 1988.

World Bank (1989a). Chairman's Report of Proceedings of the Meeting of the Consultative Group for Tanzania held in Paris December 18-20, 1989.

World Bank (1989b). Tanzania. Public Expenditure Review. Volume I: Executive Report. Report No. 7559-TA. May 22, 1989.

World Bank (1989c). Tanzania. Public Expenditure Review. Volume II: Technical Report. Report No. 7559-TA. May 22, 1989.

World Bank (1990a). Country Assistance Review. World Bank Tanzania Relations, 1961-1987. Operations Evaluation Department. Washington, January 1990.

World Bank (1990b). Making Adjustment Work for the Poor—A Framework for Policy Reform in Africa. Washington, 1990.

World Bank (1991). Tanzania Economic Report. Towards Sustainable Development in the 1990s. In two Volumes. Washington, 1991.

World Bank (1992a). Chairman's Report of Proceedings of the Meeting of the Consultative Group for Tanzania held in Paris June 29-30, 1992.

World Bank (1992b). Memorandum of the President of the International Development Association to the Executive Directors on a proposed credit in the amount equivalent to SDR 14.6 Million to the United Republic of Tanzania for a Financial and Legal Management Upgrading (FILMUP) Project. June 1, 1992.

World Bank (1993a). Chairman's Report of Proceedings of the Meeting of the Consultative Group for Tanzania held in Paris July 12-13, 1993.

World Bank (1993b). Economic Situation and Status of the Adjustment Program. Dar es Salaam, June 1993.

World Bank (1994a). Adjustment in Africa. Reforms, Results, and the Road Ahead. A World Bank Policy Research Report. Oxford University Press, Oxford 1994.

World Bank (1994b). Tanzania. Agriculture Sector Memorandum. In Three Volumes. Report No. 12294-TA. July 29, 1994.

World Bank (1994c). Tanzania. Role of Government. Public Expenditure Review. Report No. 12601-TA, Vol. I: Main Report. June 17, 1994.

World Bank (1995). Memorandum of the President of the International Development Association to the Executive Directors on a Proposed Credit in the Amount Equivalent to SDR 7.5 Million to the United Republic of Tanzania for a Financial Institutions Development Project. May 23, 1995.

World Bank (1996a). Tanzania. The Challenge of Reforms: Growth, Incomes and Welfare. Vol. I-III. Report No. 14982-TA. May 31, 1996.

World Bank (1996b). World Development Report 1996. From Plan to Market. Oxford University Press, 1996.

World Bank (1997a). Performance Audit Report. Financial Sector Adjustment Credit. June 23, 1997.

World Bank (1997b). Report and Recommendation of the President of the International Development Association to the Executive Directors on a Proposed Credit of SDR 93.2 Million of Which SDR 2.8 Million Have Been Allocated from IDA Reflows to the United Republic of Tanzania for a Structural Adjustment Credit Project. May 7, 1997.

World Bank (1997c). The State in a Changing World. Oxford University Press, 1997.

World Bank (1997d). Tanzania. Public Expenditure Review (in Two Volumes). Volume 1: Main Report. Report No. 16578-TA. August 11, 1997.

World Bank (1997e). Tanzania. Public Expenditure Review (in Two Volumes). Volume II: Statistical Appendix. Report No. 16578-TA. August 11, 1997.

World Bank (1998a). Assessing Aid. What Works, What Doesn't, and Why. Oxford University Press, Washington 1998.

World Bank (1998b). The United Republic of Tanzania. Public Expenditure Review. Volume 1: Main Report.

World Bank (1998c). World Development Report 1998/99. Knowledge for Development. Oxford University Press, Washington 1998.

World Bank (1999a). Project Appraisal Document on a Proposed Credit in the Amount of SDR 28.6 Million to the United Republic of Tanzania for a Tax Administration Project. Africa Regional Office. March 11, 1999.

World Bank (1999b). Project Appraisal Document on a Proposed Credit in the Amount of SDR 33.3 Million to the United Republic of Tanzania for a Privatization & Private Sector Development Project. Africa Regional Office. November 15, 1999.

World Bank (2000a). Report and Recommendation of the President of the International Development Association to the Executive Directors on a Proposed Credit of SDR 141.8 Million (US$190 Million Equivalent) to the United Republic of Tanzania for the First Phase of a Programmatic Structural Adjustment Credit. Africa Regional Office. June 8, 2000.

World Bank (2000b). Tanzania Accountability, Transparency and Integrity Project. Africa Regional Office. November 1, 2000.

World Bank (2000c). Tanzania. Country Assistance Evaluation. Operations Evaluation Department. Washington, September 13, 2000.

World Bank (2000d). World Development Report 2000/2001. Attacking Poverty. Oxford University Press, Washington 2000.

World Bank (2001a). African Development Indicators 2001. Washington D.C. 2001.

World Bank (2001b). Tanzania: An Impact Evaluation of World Bank–Country Partnership in Curtailing Corruption. Operations Evaluation Department. November 2001.

World Bank (2004). Doing Business in 2004: Understanding Regulation. A copublication of the World Bank and Oxford University Press, 2004. Internet: http://rru.worldbank.org/business/doingbusiness2004.aspx (access date: Oct. 2003).

WTO, World Trade Organisation (2000). Tanzania: February 2000. Trade Policy Reviews: The Secretariat's Report: Summary. Internet: http://www.wto.org/english/tratop_e/tpr_e/tp128_e.htm (access date: Nov. 2001).

Yang, Chun-Lei (1999). A Complete Resolution of the Efficient Rent-Seeking Paradox. In: Taiwan Economic Review; Vol. 27, No. 4, pp. 431-59, December 1999.

Yeldan, Erinc A. and Roe, Terry L. (1991). Political Economy of Rent-Seeking Under Alternative Trade Regimes. In: Weltwirtschaftliches Archiv; Vol. 127, Iss. 3, pp. 563-83, 1991.

Zeigler, Harmon (1992). Interest Groups. In Mary Hawkesworth and Maurice Kogan (eds.): Encyclopaedia of Government and Politics; Vol. 1, pp. 377-92, Routledge, London 1992.

Zouari, Abderrazak (1989). Collective Action and Governance Structures in Tunisia's Labor Organisation. In Mustapha K. Nabli and Jeffrey B. Nugent (eds.): The New Institutional Economics and Development: Theory and Applications to Tunisia; Vol. 183, pp. 323-51, Elsevier Science Publishers B.V., Amsterdam 1989.

Author Index

Subject Index

D

E

F

J

K

N

O

P

S

U